Praise for *Trampling O*

D1066580

"The best workplace study of labour in North Am
history of California, no history of Mexican-Americ... ... and no history of agricultural
production can be written again without the insights contained in these pages."

Paul Buhle, *New Left Review*

"Bardacke is a talented writer, burning with rage against injustice, and his subject is one of
the most attractive and charismatic figures U.S. politics has produced."

Francis Beckett, *Guardian*

"The first comprehensive history of the rise and fall of the UFW, written from the viewpoint of the farmworkers who vitalized the movement known as 'La Causa.'"

San Francisco Chronicle

"Superb."

Mother Jones

"In the era of so many book-a-year authors, *Trampling Out the Vintage* has a lifetime-
achievement feel. It skillfully tells the dramatic story of the rise and fall of the UFW, but
what makes this a landmark book is its emphasis on the rank-and-file leaders, who are too
often obscured by the long shadow cast by Chavez. It is these workers who are the heroes
of Bardacke's book—workers whose leadership was essential to the union's success, and
whose betrayal contributed to its eventual demise."

Nation

"There's so much marvelous stuff in Frank Bardacke's book that's simply not been done
before. At the book's core are the men and women who pick the crops in California's fields
and orchards, their skill and endurance, the world they built among themselves, the ways
they shaped the history of the UFW. It is their story—refreshingly, sympathetically, and
beautifully told—that makes this book stand apart and will make it stand forever."

Alexander Cockburn, coauthor of *Whiteout: The CIA, Drugs and the Press*

"Magnificent and tragic history . . . Bardacke's enormously insightful and nuanced book
thus radically reconfigures the social, political, and moral narrative with which most
Americans have understood the history of the farm worker movement and its leadership."

Nelson Lichtenstein, *Dissent*

"You can take little sections out of the book and they're the best thing ever written on the
subject."

Harold Meyerson, Editor-at-Large at the *American Prospect* and Hillman Prize judge

"Frank Bardacke's long-awaited masterpiece is the kind of book that comes along only once
in a generation, if we're lucky. Not only is the research spectacular and his analysis of the
United Farm Workers as a social movement nuanced and compelling, but he finally places
rank-and-file farm workers at the center of the story as savvy and opinionated activists. Best
of all, he's a superb writer who's constructed a gripping tale."

Dana Frank, Professor of History at the University of California, Santa Cruz

"It is the human beings that come alive here—union officials, organizers and workers—with
their foibles, rivalries, and triumphs. Cesar Chavez emerges as a hugely complex individual
with a full range of all too human traits. An extraordinary book about an extraordinary
movement and man, and a story as inspiring as it is tragic."

Douglas Monroy, author of *The Borders Within: Encounters between Mexico and the US*

"An expansive, readable study of one of the more meaningful struggles of the twentieth
century and an instruction book for anyone interested in organizing workers to regain the
wealth that they create."

International Socialist Review

"The best history ever written of the United Farm Workers and Cesar Chavez. Cert*
become a classic of U.S. working-class history."

Upside Down

A celery crew at work, Pajaro Valley, 1982. Photo by Fred Chamberlain.

Trampling Out the Vintage

CESAR CHAVEZ AND THE TWO SOULS OF THE UNITED FARM WORKERS

Frank Bardacke

VERSO

London • New York

The publishers gratefully acknowledge the assistance of the Political Economy Research Institute, University of Massachusetts, Amherst

This paperback edition first published by Verso 2012
First published by Verso 2011
© Frank Bardacke 2011
The Revolt of the Cockroach People © Oscar Zeta Acosta 1989. Used by permission of Alfred A. Knopf, a division of Random House, Inc

The moral rights of the author have been asserted
1 3 5 7 9 10 8 6 4 2

Verso
UK: 6 Meard Street, London W1F 0EG
U.S.: 20 Jay Street, Suite 1010, Brooklyn, NY 11201

www.versobooks.com

Verso is the imprint of New Left Books
ISBN-13: 978-1-78168-066-7

British Library Cataloguing in Publication Data
A catalogue record for this book is available from the British Library

Library of Congress Cataloging-in-Publication Data
A catalog record for this book is available from the Library of Congress

Typeset in Bembo by Hewer Text UK Ltd, Edinburgh
Printed in the U.S. by Maple Vail

For Cleofas Guzman,
and with love and thanks to
Julie Miller

"O what a fall was there, my countrymen! Then I, and you, and all of us fell down . . ."

Julius Cesar, Act III, scene II

Contents

The Car Pool

Most California farm workers do not ride to work alone. They travel in company buses and vans, or squeeze together in private cars with other workers, who often are also their relatives or lifelong friends. For three-quarters of a century, people have been driving their cars up and down and across the Golden State looking for work. Caravans of cars—perhaps the most essential agricultural implements in California—loved and hated by mechanically skilled Joads of all nationalities, who intimately knew the carburetors and fuel pumps and transmissions of the Studebakers, Fords, and Chevys, and now struggle with the injection systems of the popular Toyotas that may also be their homes, death beds, and birth beds. Cars are so vital to the internal relations of farm workers that the Farm Placement Service, faithful servant of California agribusiness, had as one of its policies in the 1950s and '60s to break up car pools and disperse their members to separate farms, as the bosses knew from bitter experience that the bonds of solidarity built from traveling and living together often spilled over onto the job.

Pablo Camacho remembers every car. In his first car pool, from 1961 to 1967, "we started with my '49 Ford; next we got a '55 Ford, but after that it was all Chevys." In 1977 and 1978, Camacho drove two identical 1969 Impalas, and I was in his car pool. We were part of a crew that cut and packed celery for InterHarvest in the Salinas Valley, a region made famous by the travails of some of Steinbeck's protagonists, and still one of the most productive agricultural areas in the world. Those were the high days—among the last high days, as it turned out—of the United Farm Workers. Just a little more than ten years earlier the union had been born, improbably, in a grape strike in a dusty town in California's Central Valley, and, decisively, amid a mass movement in America that, for a very brief time, made everything seem possible. By 1968, Cesar Chavez[1] was being hailed as a hero in a country quickly running out of them, and the union was making its name outside the fields with the most powerful boycott in U.S. history. In Salinas, where the union was most successful in the fields for the longest time, and where farm workers' wages were the highest, piece-rate vegetable workers such as Camacho formed the core strength of the United Farm Workers union (UFW).

We worked on one of the several dozen piece-rate vegetable crews in the valley. Piece-rate crews are paid collectively. Each member gets an equal share of the price the company pays for each box or bin of lettuce or celery or broccoli. Those were the three main crops harvested by piece-rate crews when I worked in the fields; other crops were harvested by the hour, by individual piece rate, or by machines. At InterHarvest we were paid about $1.40 for each box of celery we cut and packed, which we split thirty-eight ways. It worked out to about $12 an hour, more than $48 dollars in today's money. The four loaders were paid separately, and they made even more. Positions on these crews were greatly prized in farm worker communities, and the workers were highly skilled, tightly organized, and deeply loyal to the UFW. They were hard to replace during strikes except with similarly skilled workers, and in nonstrike periods they wielded their power through slowdowns, work stoppages, and mild forms of sabotage.

For anyone who was not there, it may be hard to imagine that celery workers in the 1970s made what would be about $50 an hour in today's economy. Piece-rate lettuce cutters and melon pickers made even more. People who tied rubber bands around cauliflower leaves to protect the flowers from the sun made quite a bit more. These people, working seasonally, earned annual incomes comparable to those of other well-paid unionized U.S. workers. Although piece-rate vegetable workers were a minority of farm laborers, they were not a tiny one. In the 1970s they constituted about 10 percent of all California farm workers who worked at least six months a year.

Such crews earned substantially more than other farm workers, but even the lowest-paid fieldworkers in the late 1970s made more than one and a half times the minimum wage. There is no better measure of the UFW's success than the formidable ranks of those well-paid vegetable workers who once dominated their industries, and no better measure of its defeat than a list of current wages. Union membership, mostly vegetable workers, had hit 50,000 by the end of the 1970s. By 1985 it had collapsed to around 6,000, where it has hovered ever since.[2] Today, entry-level farm workers make just above the $8.00 California minimum hourly wage; celery workers make about the same per box that they made thirty years ago, meaning their real wages are about one-third of what they once were; and most lettuce workers—once the princes of their communities—no longer work by the piece and are lucky if they make $9.00 an hour.

The full history of the UFW, then, is not just a tale of how Cesar Chavez came out of obscurity to lead his new farm worker union to victory, although it is authentically that. It is also the story of the farm workers who were at the center of the union's strength in the fields, and of how, once Chavez lost their support, the UFW was doomed.

When I found him again in 1994, Pablo Camacho, at sixty-one, was a short, plump man five feet two inches tall and 180 pounds. He had a full head of dark hair and an unlined face, and he was still packing celery. I walked onto his crew early one morning, cutting across the harvested rows where the loaders were just beginning to throw the first celery-filled boxes onto a large pallet being driven through the field on a tractor. Camacho was at one of the "burros," the three-wheeled carts on which the men pack celery into cardboard boxes. Three people work on each burro, picking up, sorting, and packing the celery that has just been cut by three men working ahead of them. This is a regular-size crew: six burros, thirty-six cutters and packers, two closers, four loaders, a couple of tractor drivers, two foreman, and a few other men hanging around.

Camacho introduced me without interrupting the work. I explained to the handful of men nearby that Camacho had taught me how to pack some twenty years earlier, and I began to pick up some celery in his row, trying to remember how it went in the various boxes. We continued to chat: reporting on kids, wives, mutual friends. I was doing less than half of one job. It was a cool December morning on California's Central Coast, yet within ten minutes I was in a heavy sweat.

I worked along for an hour, eventually telling Camacho that I was going to write a book and I wanted to start by interviewing him and the three other men from our car pool.

"What's so special about us?" he asked.

"Nothing. That's almost the point."

"Well, what's the book about?"

"Farm workers and what happened to the UFW."

When I mentioned the union, Ismael, one of the other packers, looked around to see where the foreman was. So far, the field foreman had not been bothered by my presence. People often come by a crew to visit and give a hand; the only thing unusual about me was that I am not Mexican. But mentioning the UFW was something else. I had made a mistake—I had figured that because the union had been so thoroughly defeated in the California fields nearly ten years before, it would be okay to mention it on the job now. Ismael didn't think so. Camacho, too proud to show any fear of a foreman, refused to acknowledge that I had said something wrong, but quickly arranged to come by my house and talk to me later.

At the time, Camacho was living in the house he had bought in 1973 with a $3,000 down payment; a three-bedroom home in what passes for the industrial section of Watsonville, next to the city's recycling center. His wife had worked at Green Giant for more than twenty years before it moved to Mexico. She then went to work at Del Mar Frozen Foods. They were family-proud, with reason. Of their five children, the three oldest had graduated from college and were working, one in Watsonville, and two others a hundred miles away in San Francisco. Their two youngest children were still in school.

Camacho is a responsible man. The three seasons we packed celery together, he never missed a day of work. His reliability, combined with his outspoken, militant support for the union, made him among the first people nominated for crew shop steward, a post he held on various occasions.

When Pablo came to my house to be interviewed, it was the first time I had put a tape recorder in front of him. It was not the first time I had heard his stories, whose major theme was how bad it was before the UFW arrived. The Bracero Program was one of his favorite targets. Under this friendly arrangement between the U.S. and Mexican governments, which lasted from 1942 to 1964, a total of five million Mexican men were contracted to work in the United States—mostly in the Texas and California fields— under strict conditions that limited their freedom of movement and kept farm workers' wages artificially low. Camacho had been a bracero, and the bad old days seemed to get worse as he told the stories over and over. At my kitchen table, Camacho recounted one of my favorites:

> My first job was in the desert in Borrego Springs, picking grapes. We used to wake up at three in the morning, eat breakfast, and start working in the warehouse at four. We worked there until it was light enough to see outside. In the morning light we started picking grapes, and we worked until about two in the afternoon, stopping only to eat lunch. Then we had a two-hour break, when most people returned to the bunkhouse to rest. At around four it was back to the warehouse, where we worked until ten at night, with a break for dinner. In bed by eleven, for four hours' sleep. Six days a week, seventy-five cents an hour. It wasn't bad—except for the rattlesnakes.[3]

Pablo was born on a little ranch near Novolato, a town of maybe 25,000 people in Sinaloa, Mexico. His father was a campesino, a small farmer who grew and harvested sugar cane to send to the Novolato sugar refinery, built and owned by the local hacienda owners. Soon after Pablo was born, in 1933, the local campesinos organized themselves into an *ejido*—the system of communal land tenure that was a main achievement of the Mexican Revolution—and took the land away from the *hacendados*.

President Lázaro Cárdenas had already proclaimed that every campesino should have his own piece of land to work. My father became president of the *ejido*. He grew sugar cane for the refinery. But you know how it is, after a few years the refinery owners didn't pay the *ejiditarios* a good price for the sugar cane, and there were seasons when the campesinos couldn't make it. People continued to grow corn, garbanzos, chilies, but it wasn't enough, and the bank wouldn't give them credit unless they agreed to grow cane. So even though they had their own land, they fell into debt and remained poor and under the power of the bankers and the old landlords, who still owned the refinery.

Camacho had a rude introduction to politics. His father was assassinated by local political rivals when Pablo was ten, and the boy had to leave school and work full-time. He started as a human scarecrow. Armed with a sling-shot, he guarded the newly sown fields from the birds. He graduated to a helper in the cane fields and finally became a regular cane cutter. When he was fifteen, he got a job in a sugar factory.

Refinery work is seasonal, so in May of 1954 Camacho traveled to the United States as a bracero. Only the hardest and most efficient workers, about a third of those who signed on to the program, made it. After three months battling the rattlesnakes Camacho was sent to Chula Vista, near San Diego, to work in the tomato fields. There, the workforce was thinned out some more. Camacho and a few others were made "specials," braceros who carried a plastic card (called a *mica* by the workers) that allowed them to work for the same employer year after year without going through the formal contracting procedures. Being a special was a privilege, reserved for model workers. Camacho described his first several months in the United States:

I was a young man and I have always liked adventures. I had heard about the U.S., but I never dreamed I would be able to go. The work was not as hard as the work I had done in Mexico. I cut sugar cane in Mexico. No work I have ever done has been as hard as that. And ever since I was a kid I have liked to work. I like the companionship. I like the activity. When I was young I didn't like games where you sat down. I liked soccer and boxing. When I worked in Chula Vista thinning celery, I would grab the short-handled hoe out of pure pleasure and race the other young men. We raced for the fun of it.

In Chula Vista, Pablo raced through tomatoes, celery, squash, and cucumbers. He bought his 1949 Ford, rented a room in a Tijuana hotel, paid board at a local restaurant, and using his *mica*, commuted across the border every day but Sunday. He worked for the same Japanese boss—all the bosses in Chula Vista were Japanese back then, he said—for six years, from 1954 to 1960, returning regularly to Mexico in December to work a few months at the sugar refinery. In 1960 his boss in Chula Vista gave him the documentation he needed for a visa. He never went back to the refinery.

In 1964, Pablo married Bertaliza Lopez, a woman from Culiacán, Sinaloa. After having two children, the family dropped out of their car pool and made the apple, strawberry, and lettuce town of Watsonville their permanent home. Bertaliza went to work with Pablo in the strawberries while Pablo's sister took care of their kids. "Bertaliza had never worked outside the house before. In Mexico in the old days we didn't have the custom of the women working. The man worked and the woman stayed home and took care of the household. But Bertaliza wanted to work. She was stubborn about it."

It is tough to begin farmwork in the strawberries, not only because the plants are so low to the ground but because of the way people are paid—by how many flats of berries they pick individually. Bertaliza, with no agricultural experience, ignorant of the tricks of strawberry picking, and unaccustomed to bending over or squatting all day long, worked harder than she ever had, without making much money. Farm workers say that people who work for an individual piece rate "die alone." A friend of mine from Vera Cruz, a city boy who also tried to begin life as a farm worker in the strawberries, quit after three days. "That's not work," he said. "It's a punishment from God."

The Japanese owner of the strawberry farm paid half the Camachos' rent even after Pablo moved on to a celery crew. It was 1965, the braceros were gone, labor was scarce, and the strawberry farmer wanted to make sure that Pablo would return the next spring, after the celery was finished. But it was still the bad old days in the celery:

> There were two foremen, one was a Filipino and the other was a Mexican. They would put names of people on the work list who were not working. We called them *muertos*, dead men. Since the whole crew was being paid by the number of boxes we cut and packed, the *muertos* were getting part of our money. It was a perfect scam. The rancher was still paying the same amount, so he wasn't upset, but the foremen were taking part of our earnings.
>
> And we had to work hard. There were times we worked so long that they had to turn on the lights of the trucks so that we could see the celery. We worked ten, eleven, twelve hours a day. The Filipino used to tell us at the end of the day that we had done a good job and probably made thirty or forty dollars. But when we got our checks all we had made was a hundred or a hundred twenty for a six-day week. People were angry, but we never went beyond complaining.
>
> In 1970, Chavez arrived. I got a dispatch for a job in the celery that

very first year and began working with a union contract. The difference was tremendous. They paid well, but the main thing was they couldn't rob us anymore. They had to give us a piece of paper for every truckload of celery that left the field. We now had proof of how many boxes we had cut and how many people were working. And so the *muertos*—the dead men—were dead forever.

"The union was the best thing that ever happened to California farm workers," Camacho maintained. Most farm workers old enough to remember agree, as do the people who study them. Phillip Martin, an agricultural economist at the University of California at Davis, calls the high years of the UFW, 1965 to 1985, the Golden Age for California farm workers. But some farm workers give the union mixed reviews. After all, the union rose and fell twice: in the early 1970s, when membership fell from about 50,000 to 6,000; and ten years later, after it had been rebuilt in Salinas, when its power finally collapsed. Nevertheless, the worst thing that most farm workers say about the UFW now is that it eventually got beat, and that wages and working conditions quickly deteriorated once it did.

How it got beat, and to what extent it was responsible for its own demise, are the biggest questions posed in this book. I asked Camacho what happened. He had his answer ready:

> The main thing that went wrong was that the Republicans won the governorship in 1982. And the governor put the friends of the growers on the Agricultural Relations Board. And they wouldn't pay any attention to our grievances. Also, the peso collapsed, and more people had to come here to work. We were swamped with workers from Mexico.

I didn't argue with Camacho's answer, not on that occasion, as we sat in my kitchen drinking coffee, sixteen years after we had last worked together. His was the answer of a good *chavista*, and it has some truth to it. And I agree that the UFW was "the best thing that ever happened to California farm workers." But did the union happen to California farm workers, or did California farm workers make the union happen? It is not just a question of the Spanish language's proclivity for the passive voice. What led to the demise of the UFW is not the kind of question that has a straightforward answer. Rather, if this were a detective story, it would be a question for the reader to ponder. Think about it long enough and hard enough, and perhaps the fog will clear.

But if this is a detective story, it is a modern Mexican one, in which, as Paco Ignacio Taibo II, the master of the form, says, the main issue is not "who did it" but the context in which "it" was done. The mystery of the UFW's rise and fall cannot be solved without understanding the fighting tradition of California farm workers, the character of farmwork itself, the history and opinions of some of the people who do that work, the nature of the UFW staff and the internal life of the union, the political weight of the union's friends and supporters measured against the weight of its enemies and how that relationship changed over time, and, finally, the character, background, and ideas of the UFW's leader, Cesar Chavez. Learn that context, and perhaps the mystery will dissolve. At least the story will have been told.

No one has told it yet, despite the appearance of a fair number of books about the union. The early ones were mostly hagiography, tales of how the wise and saintly Cesar Chavez miraculously built the UFW. More recent works blame Chavez for the union's fall, citing his "personal demons" and his periodic purges of the UFW staff, especially the dismissal of his highly skilled top aides. In almost all accounts, the history of the union is essentially a story of Cesar Chavez and his staff, in which farm workers provide little more than background color as either the beneficiaries of his genius or the victims of his faults.

Pablo Camacho, who considers himself one of the beneficiaries agrees that it was Chavez who built the UFW and made history, and that farm workers only helped out. Pablo is proud to have been one of Chavez's soldiers, and what a soldier he was! Once, during a 1979 strike, we were on a picket line together on the edge of a struck lettuce field. We had homemade slings, the kind that Camacho had used as a boy in Mexico to scare away the birds. They require some skill. You spin the piece of leather around your head and then let one end go; if you do it correctly, you can send a good-sized rock hurtling toward your target at a respectable speed. We were mostly fooling around, trying to see how close we could get our rocks to a helicopter spraying the middle of the struck field, some hundred yards away. Not very close—that was part of the joke. Suddenly, Camacho ran into the field, directly toward the helicopter, screaming a warrior's roar and twirling a rock the size of a baseball in the sling above his head. The rest of us were astounded. Who knows what the pilot thought as he yanked the helicopter straight up and away from our little David's attack.

Pablo Camacho did his job on the picket lines, went to the membership meetings, argued forcefully with his fellow workers about the importance of the union. Even the official historians of the UFW acknowledge that without people like Pablo Camacho there would have been no union. The union just didn't happen to them. That much is clear.

But there was another level of farm workers' involvement in the union, almost exclusively in the Salinas Valley, that was deeper than Camacho's. Scores of farm workers, many of whom had been active in farm worker struggles before the UFW arrived in 1970, some of whom came from backgrounds in Mexico more radical than Camacho's, and almost all of whom worked on piece-rate vegetable crews, became the leaders of the UFW in the Salinas Valley. Some of them, not all, called themselves *chavistas*, and throughout the 1970s they worked in alliance with Chavez and some of his staff. But they never became an official part of that staff until 1980, and when they did, differences between them and Chavez quickly arose. Chavez united most of the staff against them, trampled them, and pushed them out of the union. One might say that for ten years they made the UFW happen in the Salinas Valley, and then the UFW happened to them. Once they were gone, the union lost its authority in the fields, and the growers discarded their UFW contracts without serious opposition. The golden age was over.

I talked to another of my old car pool mates to see what he thought had happened to the UFW. In 1994, Raúl Medina, universally called Maniz, lived with his wife, son, and brother in one of Watsonville's more solid working-class neighborhoods. They had no phone. It was not worth the money, he said; if you wanted to see him, you could drop by his house. Each time I did, Maniz and his brother, Samuel, were entertaining. They prepared and served food: hot tea with brandy, honey, and lemon one morning; freshly cut salsa with beans and corn tortillas one afternoon; and the next day, pork blood sausages served on a plate with more tortillas and salsa. Each dish was delivered with an elaborate explanation of how and why it was good for you, and although no one said grace before the meals, the food was prepared and eaten slowly, joyfully, with reverence.

The TV was always on, but the only time anybody paid any attention to it was during Telemundo's live coverage of opening statements in O. J. Simpson's murder trial. Maniz, suspicious of the official version of everything, thought O. J. was being framed and argued his position so forcefully that we all said nothing in response. Most often, the talk was about work: where to find it, how much the rains would delay it, the overall prospects for the coming season.

Maniz, although very much a Mexican, spoke English well and was the only person I met while working in the Salinas fields who could have been mistaken for a second-generation Mexican American farm worker. He followed U.S. sports more closely than the others and was a big Jackson Browne fan. Without being as deeply involved in the UFW as Pablo Camacho, he was an even more devoted follower of Chavez, joking in the car at the time of the Jonestown massacre in Guyana in 1978 that he was with Chavez "right up to the Kool-Aid." He was of unfailing good humor, and performed the greatest single feat of farmwork I ever heard about: one day he dropped acid and cut celery.

"Maniz, what was it like?" I asked him.

"Green, Frankie, green, green, green."

Maniz came to the United States from Jacona, Michoacán, in November 1963, when he was fifteen years old. "The very damn day I arrived was the day they killed Kennedy. We were at the house of one of my aunts in the Imperial Valley, and we saw it on television. Kabluey. Bang. Bang. On my very first day."[4]

Maniz settled in Hollister, California, and enrolled in high school. What he remembered is:

> fights, all the fights, that was the worst thing about the United States. There were more fights at Hollister High than I had ever seen in Mexico. Hey, there was every kind of person you could name at Hollister High. Tejanos, Michoacanos, people from other Mexican states, Chicanos, blacks, Chinese, Japanese, Filipinos. Son-of-a-bitch, if there were any Martians around, you could find them at Hollister High. Nobody would leave you alone. It was war, all against all. Every race had to prove who was the toughest. Back in Jacona there were fights but only now and then because we all knew each other. Everybody was somebody's cousin; everybody spoke the same language. But at Hollister High there were fights every day. I couldn't stand it, so I went to work.

Maniz's father had been a fieldworker in Jacona, a small city in Michoacán. He worked on other people's land for wages, or sometimes he was paid just with food. He claimed that he paid fifty centavos (about twenty-five cents) to cross the border to the U.S. in 1944. He worked his way up the coast: Oxnard, Santa Barbara, Salinas. In 1950, he went to work for an Italian named Joe Felice in Hollister, who let him live rent-free in a house next to one of his orchards. Felice had apricots, plums, and walnuts. Maniz's dad pruned, irrigated, sprayed, thinned, and harvested. Soon Joe Felice fixed Maniz's father's papers. He was working for Felice on the day he died.

Maniz joined his dad on Felice's farm in the late 1960s. The bracero program was over, and there was no shortage of work:

> The growers grabbed everybody: drunks, cripples, drug addicts. If you were a Mexican and you could stand on your own two feet, they tried to put you to work. There wasn't any trouble with the *migra* [immigration authorities] back then. I went to work with my dad and some of my other brothers in 1967 in the apricot orchards. We all picked together and a few of us pruned together. We all thinned. When picking time came, the women worked in the sheds while we picked in the fields. And when we finished on Joe Felice's farm, we would go work on the ranches owned by Felice's friends. All those Italians passed us around.

They didn't pay much. They started at a dollar and change an hour. But you could buy a pair of Levis for six or seven dollars. Gasoline was twenty-five cents a gallon. At that price you could drive forever.

Drive they did. Maniz and his brothers followed the harvests into the Central Valley for a few years, but then Maniz settled down in Watsonville and got a job in a frozen-food plant, stacking boxes at Green Giant. He didn't like it. The machines were so loud he couldn't talk to anyone. He missed the fellowship of the fields. In 1974, one of his brothers invited him to learn the celery and brought him to the UFW union hall in Oxnard.

Celery was the hardest job I had ever done. When you entered the celery with a union dispatch they gave you three days to learn. They couldn't fire you in the first three days for not being able to keep up with the crew. But, really, if you didn't have anybody helping you it was impossible to make it. People just walked off the job, sometimes in the first hours. Lots of times they would just not show up the second day. But you know, at that time, they needed celery cutters, so the foremen themselves would cut in your row for you. The foremen wanted you to make it. And the people would encourage you. "Go to it, Maniz, don't give up, you can make it. Here is where you can make the money." Or some people would scream, "Oh, you will never make it," as a way of encouraging you. Most people who come out to learn the celery don't make it. The best thing is to have relatives or friends on the crews helping you. Afterward, you are even closer to your friends. You drink beers together, you become compadres, you look out for each other the rest of your lives.

Once Maniz learned to cut, he worked year round for a while, on the circuit from Salinas to Oxnard and back to Salinas. The men who did that made as much as $25,000 a year. The good times lasted from the mid-1970s to the early '80s. *Apieros*, celery workers (from the Spanish word for "celery," *apio*), bought homes and established small businesses in Mexico. A few rented land in the U.S. and tried their hand at farming, usually in the strawberries. Maniz wasn't really careful with his money, did not buy a house, and had no desire to become a small businessman. Then, in 1981, he got hurt.

He was packing. There was a ditch in the middle of the field. It was a muddy day, and he and two fellow packers had to get the burro, or packing cart, over the trench. They took the partially filled boxes off the burro, and lifted it over the ditch. Then Maniz picked up one of the boxes and jumped over the trench with it in his arms. When he hit the other side he couldn't move. He had injured his back.

I was like a dried-out mummy. I knew it was bad. Ever since then it has been one doctor after another. I damaged a disc is what they tell me. They wanted to operate, put me under the knife. But I have seen a lot of people come out of those back operations worse than before they went in. So I said forget it. Then they wanted to send me back to work, but I refused. Eventually I got a thirteen-thousand-dollar settlement and the promise of a free doctor for my back.

In 1994, Maniz was getting $660 a month from Social Security for his disability. That barely paid the rent. His wife, Beatrice, who worked as a bilingual aid in the local school district, covered the rest of the bills. Their son, Carlos, went to nearby Cabrillo Community College, and Maniz's brother Samuel lived with the three of them. Samuel still worked in the fields, making about $7 an hour, less than he had made twenty years earlier.

I asked Maniz what happened to the union. How did it fall so far so fast? He did not hesitate:

We got sold out. Some *gabacho** working for the union, he was supposed to be representing us. He and a woman they called the Golden Parrot, they both sold us out and then disappeared. They left us for the grave. They had a whole lot of secret meetings with the company, and signed a short-term contract that let it go out of business. They told us about it at the union office. By the time Cesar found out what happened, all the papers had been signed and there wasn't anything the union could do. The *gabacho* pretended to be our friend, and then he left with the money. They divided up the sweets among themselves, that *gabacho*—I can't remember his name—and the Golden Parrot.

So we not only lost our high wages but also our benefits, our vacations, our seniority, our pensions. We lost everything. They had their whole scene together: the contractors, the scabs, the new companies, the police. And what did we have? Traitors in our midst.

I argued with Maniz for a while, but it was no use. Nothing I could say would dissuade him. This story, which he had been told in the union office, is a wild fabrication, but it's interesting because it was part of a concerted UFW campaign to blame the union's demise on what Cesar Chavez would call "malignant forces" inside his organization, forces that Dolores Huerta, a cofounder of the UFW, still claims were led by Marshall Ganz, the union's lead organizer from 1970 to 1980.

---

* Originally a derogatory Mexican word for a Frenchman, *gabacho* has replaced gringo as a favored farm worker term for an Anglo from the United States.

What to make of such charges is one of the concerns of this book, as are the various internal purges and debates that preceded the attacks on Ganz. Who were the traitors and who were the loyalists, and what was being betrayed? Where did farm workers fit in these internal troubles? How important were these battles in the crushing defeat suffered by the UFW, and all California farm workers, in the 1980s?

There are not too many peasants in my family tree. The closest I can come is my paternal grandfather. A nonreligious Odessa Jew, he became a devoted Tolstoyan, believing that Russia's redemption lay in a prosperous peasantry and a return to the cultural values of the countryside. Depending on which family story you believe, he either borrowed and never paid back or stole a large sum of money from some distant in-laws in Manchuria, and then, in 1910, he, his wife, mother, and four younger brothers left Vladivostok for Alberta, Canada. There they tried to put their ideals into practice, homesteading a farm, but the Bardackes were city folk who knew nothing about farming. They lost the farm and most of the money.

Unlike my grandfather, I didn't go into the fields for political reasons. I was a New Leftist, but not one of those who consciously set out to "proletarianize" myself as a way of reaching out to the working class. I just needed a job. It was 1971; I was in my thirtieth year and was living in Seaside, California, renting a house right next to the fence that separated the Fort Ord army base from the local community. I had been working at the GI Coffee House in Seaside, one of a string of coffee houses around the world where antiwar activists tried to talk with U.S. soldiers about Vietnam. I made my money as a physical education teacher at an elementary school, but was fired after the school learned I had been arrested six times in Berkeley and Oakland during various demonstrations. I was out of work and down to my last dollars when I picked up a hitchhiker who told me he had gone to the UFW hall in nearby Salinas, where he joined the union and was dispatched to work on a lettuce-thinning crew.

I decided to give it a try, and convinced a friend, who also worked at the coffee house and was in a small Maoist group, to go along with me. Nineteen seventy-one was quite a time to enter the Salinas fields. The previous year farm workers there had fought one of the biggest strikes in California agricultural history, and the UFW had come out of that strike with a few contracts, including one at the transnational giant United Fruit, which had recently changed its name to United Brands, and called its Salinas subsidiary, InterHarvest. On the thinning crew at InterHarvest, where we were dispatched, the workers were still celebrating their victory, as well as testing its limits. It wasn't as dramatic as stumbling into a Detroit automobile factory in 1937, one year after the victorious sit-down strike. But it had some of the same flavor.

We worked with short-handled hoes and were paid by the hour. The crew was about half men and half women, old and young, all Mexican, except for my friend and me and a Puerto Rican. "Puerto," as he was called, was the elected shop steward and seemed to have more power than the two company foremen. Every day after lunch, the crew slowed down together, talking and visiting as we worked, as if to say to the foremen, "We have already done a day's labor; now it is time to rest." In that first summer the crew twice refused to enter fields that smelled of pesticides. Once, the foreman tried to give a warning ticket to someone who he claimed was leaving two small lettuce plants where he should have left one. The foreman beckoned the shop steward, who by contract rule had to co-sign the ticket; three warning tickets, and a worker could be fired. Puerto listened to both sides and then tore up the ticket in the foreman's face. Nothing happened to Puerto or the accused worker. The foreman was fired several weeks later because "he couldn't control the crew."

I was astounded. I had been part of the wing of the New Left that considered the working class hopelessly reformist, bought off by post–World War II prosperity. Part of what made us New Leftists, and not old ones, was our disagreement about the role of the traditional working class as the main enemy of capitalism. The working-class jobs I had had before— as a janitor, an usher at a race track, a beer vender at Raiders games—had given me some appreciation for the resiliency and militancy of black culture but had not shaken my view that the Old Left had put too much hope in the working class. But here I was now, witnessing, almost by accident, a level of sustained militancy among workers that I had never known in twelve years of New Left politics.

It gave me pause. I had left Berkeley despairing of the future of youth culture politics, thinking I might restore my political faith by getting deeper into antiwar work. But the coffee house was also pretty much a disaster, as we dedicated white antiwar activists didn't have too much to say to the black soldiers who had just returned from Vietnam and were awaiting their discharges. We lived through a series of bad misunderstandings over drugs, sex, and politics. By the time I got to the fields, I was politically washed out.

It was the people in the fields who revived my political zeal. But did I want to be a farm worker? I went back and forth on that question. The work was hard, and the pay was low. And as a farm worker I would always be different, a stranger, a sport, almost, for among the 15,000 farm workers in the Salinas Valley less than a dozen were Anglos. But there was an upside: I liked the physical challenge of the work. It was hard but not impossible. Also, the political life of the crew was almost always interesting, and some-times exhilarating. And then there was the UFW. As a student at Berkeley I had gone on one of the union's marches, but I knew little about its struggles. Now, working in the fields, I became interested in the union, thrilled by the possibility that the militancy on the crew was reflected in the politics of the union. Finally, there was Spanish. I had never been able to learn a foreign language. In the fields, swimming every day in a sea of Spanish, I slowly began to learn. So slowly that I exasperated my farm-worker teachers, who had to spend a couple of days teaching me my first words: *Mucho trabajo y poco dinero*—a lot of work and a little money.

I wanted to stay in the fields, and when the thinning crew's work ended and we were laid off, I tried to deal with the *poco dinero* by making the *mucho trabajo* into a whole lot more work. I figured if I could make it onto a piece-rate crew, I could earn a reasonable amount of money. I worked out in preparation, lifting weights and running.

Trying to make that first piece-rate crew in the celery, after only six months' experience as a farm worker, was one of the more ridiculous things I have ever done. When I got to the field the first day and gave the foreman my dispatch, he asked me if I had any experience cutting or packing celery. I said no, but I was willing to give it a try. He gave me a funny look, handed me a celery knife, and put me in a row. I watched the person next to me cut for a short while before trying it myself. Five minutes later he took the knife away, saying he was worried I was going to cut myself. Making me a packer, he explained, was out of the question as it requires very quick sizing of the celery, and it appeared that maybe I had never even seen a piece of celery let alone tried to size one. He decided to give me a chance as a *cajero*, one of two people who make and distribute the empty celery boxes to the fifteen packers.

Although it was by far the least skilled job on the crew, there were various tricks to unfolding, fastening, and carrying the wood and wire boxes. The other *cajero*, an experienced worker, was eager to teach me, but I was too slow; we could not keep up with the packers, who shouted for more and more boxes. Many had to run up to us and carry their own boxes back to their rows. As we fell further behind, some packers had to unfold and fasten the boxes themselves. I could have been fired after three days. The workers graciously granted me a couple more, but after a week I was out.

Over the next eight years I worked short stints in the Spreckles sugar factory near Salinas, as a laborer on a large housing project and in road construction, as a lumper (truck loader) at Watsonville's frozen food plants, and as an adjunct lecturer at the University of California at Santa Cruz. But I never found anything like the ambience of the fields. Like Maniz, I particularly hated the factory work; it was noisy, hot, dirty, lonely, oppressive. So I found myself during those same years back in the fields again and again. In the spring and summer of 1972 I returned to thinning lettuce. In 1975 I thinned some more and harvested cauliflower, broccoli, and lettuce. In 1976 I finally made it onto a piece-rate crew at West Coast Farms in Watsonville, where I met Pablo Camacho. The car pool years, when I worked in the celery at InterHarvest, were 1977 and 1978. When you count them up, it is six seasons in the fields between 1971 and 1979.

By the time I was part of the car pool, I felt very much like a farm worker, a rather bizarre Anglo one but a farm worker all the same. It was hard on my body—I had already had two back incidents—but it was an okay job. I felt like I was part of a poorly paid athletic team, absent the cheers of the crowd. The work was seasonal: at InterHarvest we began work on the summer solstice, June 21, and ended on the winter solstice, December 21, and we collected top unemployment for the other six months. My wife, Julie Miller, managed to get jobs in the fields, apple sheds, and frozen food plants around Watsonville and Salinas for stretches of time that did not overlap with mine, and we took turns working and being at home taking care of our young children.

Although politics did not bring me into the fields, politics drove me out. In the early 1970s I had worked closely with a handful of would-be Maoists (including my friend from the coffee house) who were working in the fields. But I didn't last long as a card-carrying Maoist revolutionary—less than a year. I was a strong supporter of the union, went to the meetings, participated in the life of the crew, but was not deeply involved in the internal life of the UFW. Then the 1979 strike came, and it was impossible not to be caught up in union politics. During the strike, some UFW staffers moved against the people in my old collective, roughing up my friend and prohibiting the distribution of their newspaper on the picket line. Those people were all UFW members, and although I disagreed with much of what their newspaper said, I thought they had the right to pass it out at union events. That was too subtle a distinction in the middle of a strike, and as far as the staff was concerned, I was an unwelcome member of the union.

I wasn't excluded from the strike, but when it ended in a victory I was among those who were not called back to work. The company and the union had agreed to cross some people off the seniority lists. I didn't fight it. I figured in the long run it was going to be hard to be an Anglo farm worker and at the same time be free to express differences with the union leadership. That was too tight a jacket, so I left the fields.

I went back to loading trucks at the frozen-food plants. I did that for a couple of years, and helped form a Watsonville branch of Teamsters for a Democratic Union, which got me blacklisted from loading trucks. I got a job on an assembly line at Hansen's Bottling Plant for another year as a way of staying in the Teamsters local, but I hated it and eventually managed to get laid off. By 1983, my sojourn in the traditional working class was over, and I got a job teaching English as a second language at Watsonville Adult School, where I worked for the next twenty-five years.

Most of the people who came to my classes were farm workers or children of farm workers. Watsonville is a small town, and I still see farm workers I used to know in the fields. Sometimes I run into Pablo Camacho as I walk my dog on the levee. Every once in a while I get together with Maniz. I am often asked if I miss the fields. I have a standard answer: *Todavía siento el dolor en mi espalda, pero extraño el ambiente del fil*—"I can still feel the pain in my back, but I miss the life of the fields."

People know what I am talking about.

I have my own bag of fieldwork memories, but this book is not a memoir. It is my explantion of what happened to the UFW, my account of its rise and fall. It differs from what Camacho and Maniz have said, but it puts people like them into the story. Not as noble victims nor as adjuncts to the grand work of one great man, but as political actors who helped make their own history.

The Founding

I

The Territory

UFW history cascades over much of California's famously diverse topography. A striker was shot dead in an irrigated patch of its immense Southeastern Desert. Petitioning pilgrims walked three hundred miles through the state's great Central Valley. Boycotters raised money in the living rooms of its populous port cities. Farm workers controlled the pace and quality of their work in two of California's narrow coastal valleys. The embattled union set up its headquarters in the foothills of the mountain pass that used to be the main gateway to the Golden State. Only the mighty Sierras lie outside the UFW saga—although it is their melted snows that, through marvels of engineering, make much of California agribusiness possible.*

But topography, like everything else under the California sun, is no fixed mark. It is a field of battle, a clash of contending forces. Grinding, jerking subterranean plates pushed the California coast up out of the sea, shaped its two massive mountain ranges, and still alter the contours of the state. Water rushed through hills, robbing them of their topsoil and depositing it in long valleys, boggy deltas, and an enormous bay. Fire raged through the prairies, destroying the old and making way for the new. Wind tore away soil, taking from one place and giving to another. Later on, people transformed a barren prairie into productive farmland; converted swamps and sloughs, once diverse in flora and fauna, into a homogeneous dry basin; rerouted, dammed, and nearly tamed the great rivers; and made one enormous lake disappear while creating several others.

Topography buckled before capital. The federal government funded the four dams along the Colorado River that transformed a large section of the Colorado Desert into the Imperial Valley. State and federal money financed the twenty-five dams in the Sierras that channeled water to the men who owned the grapes, cotton, tomatoes, and rice in the Central Valley. By the mid-twentieth century California was the most highly capitalized agricultural region in the history of humanity. People who threatened its returns could expect to be treated as harshly as any river, lake, or desert that stood in the way.

---

* Readers may want to refer periodically to the maps on pp. 837–40.

Three valleys figure most prominently on the UFW map: the Salinas Valley, west of the central coast range; the Central Valley, between the coast range and the Sierras; and the Imperial Valley, southeast of Los Angeles. The Imperial and the Central were constructed as intentionally as any theatrical set. Only in the Salinas Valley did agriculture come easily to the land. But even there, human labor shaped the stage on which the UFW actors played their parts, made their exits and their entrances. Typically that first entrance happened in a dark spot in the desert, at the Mexican border, about a hundred miles directly east of San Diego.

Farm workers didn't talk much as they lined up at the Mexicali border crossing. They started arriving at about 2 am, and some stood with their eyes closed, as if to convince themselves that they could sleep standing up. Between November and March, thousands waited in darkness to show their papers to the uniformed men guarding the entry gates to California. They came to cut and pack lettuce and a few other crops in what was once the Colorado Desert, called the Valley of the Dead by Mexicans, and rebranded as the Imperial Valley by Anglos in an early-twentieth-century real estate scheme.

Mexicali has no twin city on the other side of the border, unlike Tijuana and Juarez, which are matched by San Diego and El Paso in size and heft. In the 1970s, midway through the golden age for California farm workers, more than half a million people crowded Mexicali's streets, while all of Imperial County claimed a population of less than 75,000. The California town of Calexico, named as if it were a twin, had just a few thousand residents and was little more than a privileged Mexicali barrio with a U.S. postmark.[1]

People only come to the Imperial Valley to make money. It is not a valley— no river runs through it—and with no potable water of its own, only irrigation canals keep it alive. Only at its edges are foothills in sight, and they are less impressive than the twenty miles of sand dunes along Highway 8 on the Imperial's eastern side, mountains of sand so desolate that in the nineteenth century the U.S. Army used camels to cross them.

Local postcards feature pictures of the border entry, as no natural sight is worth reproducing. The native plants are armed with thorns and the animals with fangs, claws, and poison. In the summer, the Imperial Valley is one of the hottest places in the United States, the July temperature averaging 107 degrees. An old joke has it that when people from Mexicali die and go to hell, they come back for their blankets.

Cheap labor and cheap water made the Imperial Valley into America's winter garden, supplying most of the lettuce and cantaloupe consumed in the U.S. from December to March. Converting the desert for agriculture was not easy. It could not be done without tapping the wild Colorado River, nicknamed the Red Bull, which in most years bypassed the area and fed into the Gulf of California. The first men who attempted this feat—a small group of irrigation visionaries, Protestant teetotalers, land speculators, financiers, Indian killers, and engineers—failed. So did two of America's richest men: E. H. Harriman, whose Southern Pacific Railroad built a series of inadequate floodgates and irrigation ditches in the early 1900s, and A. P. Giannini, whose Bank of America in the 1920s bailed out the Imperial Irrigation District, which had fallen into bankruptcy trying to keep up with the costs of irrigating the desert.[2]

Finally the federal government stepped in. In 1931, it contracted seven private companies to build what would be Hoover Dam, which, along with three other publicly financed dams farther down river, finally tamed the Red Bull. Starting in 1940, Colorado River water arrived on a regular, predictable basis to the Imperial Valley. Two years later the first braceros arrived.

All of the braceros were brought across the border from Mexicali, fumigated, and then sent to a holding station in El Centro, where growers' agents checked their hands for calluses, sized up their ability to work, and took them away for their first contracted try-outs in the fields. Mexicans who were not part of the bracero program but still wanted to work the California harvests also came to Mexicali and, legally or not, made their way across the border, where labor contractors and farm foremen waited. Wives, children, and older men often remained on the Mexican side, where rent and food were cheaper, so Mexicali became not only a port of entry but a home base, the place where many farm workers returned after the seasonal harvests were over.

At the same time, Hoover Dam was changing the American West. Three of the construction companies that built it—Kaiser, Bechtel, and Utah Construction—used the money and contacts they made to launch themselves into the highest ranks of the coming military-industrial establishment. Water from the dam made some of the suburbs of semi-arid Southern California possible and allowed people to settle in fully arid Arizona. The dam's electrical power fueled the development of Southern California's industrial base just in time to make the state a major platform for military production during World War II and a center of military research and spending in the Cold War.

But those who simply wanted water for the old Colorado Desert—the dam's first proponents—were among its main beneficiaries. They received the bulk of the dammed water, now 80 percent of the allotment, at highly subsidized prices. The All-American Canal, eighty miles of concave concrete laid through the sand dunes on the U.S. side of the border, allowed big growers and absentee landholders to solidify their control over the old Valley of the Dead, as Imperial County became the first place where the federal government allowed Bureau of Reclamation irrigation water to be used on farms over 160 acres. The project also freed the men who ruled Imperial County from the compromises that had been required when sections of an earlier canal ran through Mexico, and turned the once-fertile lower Colorado Valley, on the Mexican side of the border, into a salty desert.[3]

Farm workers making their way through Mexicali after the bracero program ended came upon one more residue of irrigation history. Its Chinese-owned bars, whorehouses, restaurants, and small shops were a reminder of one of the earliest water schemes, one engineered in 1901 by General Harrison Gray Otis and Harry Chandler, the powerful owners of the *Los Angeles Times*. The first cut along the western bank of the Colorado River had diverted water to the desert through Baja California, allowing the Mexican dictator, Porfirio Díaz—advised and probably bribed by the two newspaper moguls—to demand that half the flow be assigned to Mexico. Otis, Chandler, and other officials of the *Times* then bought 860,000 acres of Baja California land, at 60 cents an acre; they planned to hire Mexican peons to farm it.[4]

But few Mexicans were around. Mexicali is far from the interior of Mexico and there was no settlement on the southern side of the border. Agents for Otis and Chandler recruited some Mexican tenant farmers from among the railroad workers who had been laying Southern Pacific tracks in the U.S. Southwest, but there were not enough of them. New Japanese immigrants were also recruited, but Japanese workers had better opportunities in the San Joaquin, Sacramento, and Salinas valleys. The Chinese became the perfect choice. Run out of California cities in the 1870s, out of the fields in the 1880s, first banned from immigrating in 1882, and permanently banned in 1902, many Chinese laborers had already moved south to Mexico. A fair number had settled in Tijuana. Mexico was both a refuge and a convenient base from which to smuggle newly arrived immigrants into California. Accordingly, the U.S. Border Patrol was set up, not to stop Mexicans but to keep out Chinese.[5]

Mexicali became a classic sin city: a fortuitous combination of border town and Chinatown serving the recreational needs of a male frontier settlement built only to extract wealth. The town was the moral complement of what was happening across the border. The earliest water imperialists were also semi-utopian dreamers and moral reformers. In each of Imperial County's little towns they passed antiliquor, antigambling, and antiprostitution laws. Subsequently the Women's Christian Temperance Union became one of the most important organizations in the county, doing what it could to see that those laws were observed. The laws could be enforced on the U.S. side only because liquor, gambling, and prostitution, all in wide variety, were available on the Mexican and Chinese side. Even when the Chinese were pushed out and the city became mostly Mexican, after railroad tracks linked the Imperial Valley to the Mexican interior in 1926, Mexicali never lost its Chinatown feel. Chinese vice lords, swindlers, and smugglers were simply replaced by Mexican ones, who developed smooth working relationships with corrupt Mexican politicians and police. Those relationships would play a surprising role in UFW history.

From 1965 to 1985, Imperial County typically ranked no better than fourth among all California counties in gross agricultural sales. The $750 million generated from farming in the county in 1982 was still less than 10 percent of California's agricultural production.[6] Most farmwork occurred elsewhere, performed by workers based in Mexicali but traveling around the state alongside migrants from deeper in Mexico and from Texas, and by local residents, primarily Mexicans and Filipinos, who had settled in the areas that offered more abundant work.

Farm workers favored different routes out of the Imperial Valley, depending on the crops they intended to pick. Grape workers traveled north on Highway 86 to the desert vineyards of Coachella. On the way, they passed the Salton Sea, formed in 1905 when the Colorado River first refused to be dammed. Just forty miles from Palm Springs, it was once promoted as a place for working-class recreation; now it is contaminated by pesticides from the Imperial Valley and has become a death trap for migratory birds.

After the six-week Coachella harvest, grape pickers moved on to their main destination: the Central Valley. Most favored a back road that led into the small towns around Bakersfield. They drove to the eastern foothills of the Tehachiapi Mountains through the high desert, which was untouched by irrigation or major human settlements, apart from the sprawling Edwards Air Force Base. Although just as hot as the Imperial Valley, its multicolored canyons, Joshua trees, various kinds of yucca, and seasonal desert wildflowers are a more attractive sight. Then winding through the Tehachapis and passing the UFW headquarters at La Paz, they could catch fleeting glimpses of the enormous plain that awaited them below: miles of fields, brown and gray, with occasional patches of irrigated green, stretching out endlessly without a landmark to measure the vast emptiness in between.

Once they were on Highway 99, competing with produce trucks and tractors on the two-lane, undivided road, they got a closer view of the valley, only to find each town on the 275-mile stretch between Bakersfield and Sacramento—McFarland, Delano, Tulare, Madera, Chowchilla—barely distinguishable from the next. The monotony was achieved honestly: meant to be collection depots for wheat, the valley's first bonanza crop, most of these towns had been designed in the 1870s according to a standard pattern. Almost a hundred years later they were still company farm towns, with Anglos living on the east side of the tracks and Mexicans, Filipinos, and a few blacks crowded into the older, more rundown houses on the

west. Their flat, often treeless main streets featured a Fosters Freeze, a few
diners, gas stations, a Giant Orange drive-in, tractor retailers and always a
branch of the Bank of America, which held much of the town's money and
where many of the most important decisions were made.

The poverty of the towns stood in contrast to the wealth generated by
the Central Valley's unique combination of a long growing season, alluvial
soil, extensive irrigation, and farm worker labor. The lower part of the
valley alone, the 112-mile stretch between Fresno and Bakersfield, was the
most productive agricultural area in the world. Its grains, fruits, vegetables,
meat, and dairy products were worth more than $1 billion in 1970, about a
quarter of California agribusiness's total gross receipts.[7] But the money did
not spread around. It remained under the control of large growers and their
bankers, who owned vast amounts of land along with the necessary processing and shipping facilities, and who were loyal to their dynastic families and
not to the towns nor to the people who worked the valley's soil.

This area has little to do with the California that looms large in the
national imagination. The whole region, from Mt. Shasta in the north to
the Tehachapis in the south, is home to less than 15 percent of California's
population. Delano, which the UFW put on the map in 1965, had fewer
than 15,000 residents then, and has about 50,000 now. Although it produced
most of the crops that made agriculture California's number one industry,
the Central Valley was relatively unknown even to most Californians, until
the UFW came along to point an accusing finger at it.

Its name hides its history. As recently as a hundred years ago, what is
now called the Central Valley was made up of four different regions. In the
north were thick riverside forests. In the Sacramento Delta, marshes,
swamps, and sloughs meandered west, rose and fell with the seasons and
flowed into the sea. In the wider midsection the San Joaquin River made
its way to the sea from the Sierras through a much smaller riparian forest
and a broad expanse of grassy plain. In the south, three seasonal lakes in the
Tulare Basin produced tropical springs and genuine autumns, unlike the
incessant ten-month summer the current residents endure.

The diverse flora once supported an impressive array of fauna: perch,
beavers, turtles, and otters inhabited the region's lakes, and salmon, trout,
and sturgeon swam in its rivers. Badgers, raccoons, minks, and foxes lived
not far from the water, while antelope, deer, and elk roamed its plains.
Bears and wolves ate the smaller critters; coyotes were everywhere, and
hundreds of different birds crowded its skies.

Most of that is gone. One estimate has it that 4 percent of the original
landscape remains. The lakes of the Tulare Basin vanished, victims of
successive irrigation systems. Even the idea of the Tulare Basin as a separate
region has been largely forgotten, as the area has been merged into the San
Joaquin to its north or the Central Valley as a whole. No comparable area

in the world was transformed so quickly, for the valley was settled by Europeans while they were perfecting their electrical and petroleum-driven technologies of destruction. They hunted the animals and fished out the rivers and lakes. They cut down the trees, diverted the rivers and streams, pumped out the aquifers, and loaded the land with insecticides, fungicides, herbicides, biocides, and chemical fertilizers. And they built the monumental system of dams and canals that remade the valley into a farm factory floor.[8]

What drove those settlers was profit, not farming. The people who directed the transformation of the valley sought quick fortunes as surely as the miners who preceded them. New names had to be coined for what they were up to: wheat mining, vandal agriculture, bonanza farming, shopkeepers with crops, and, finally, the one that stuck, agribusiness. Although they were in competition with one another, these agribusinessmen knew how to cooperate when necessary. They worked together in irrigation districts to capture the water and distribute it among themselves. They formed marketing associations to restrict production and publicize their products. They funded lobbying associations to protect their interests. They formed labor associations in attempts to fix the price of the men and women they employed to maintain their property and to tend and harvest their crops.

By the early 1960s, these men had already beaten back many attempts to organize the workers on whom their agricultural empire depended. It had not been an easy victory. People were more resourceful than rivers, lakes, and animals. The sixties brought new opportunities that allowed the farm workers to deliver a series of astounding, unprecedented defeats to these virtually undefeated men. It took awhile for them to recover—but only awhile.

Agribusiness is not a single industry, like the auto or steel industries. It is more like the garment industry, a series of separate but related businesses that specialize in different products. The men who grow grapes differ from those who grow lettuce, each possessing particular, specialized knowledge about how to produce and distribute the commodity. The industry as a whole shares a common infrastructure that is largely subsidized by federal, state, and local governments. Various irrigation districts deliver water at scandalously low prices: growers in Kern County, in the San Joaquin Valley, have paid as little as $10 per acre foot while Northern California households were paying $1,000 for the same amount of water.[9] The state and national highway systems, improved and expanded with large amounts of public money in the 1950s, freed growers from their dependency on railroad oligopolies. The University of California does much of the industry's research at public expense. Nevertheless, the men running the whole operation do not sit on a single board of directors, or even a group of inter-locking boards. They have their capital invested in particular crops and separate regions, and do not often mix in one other's businesses.

The farm workers who made UFW history also specialized in particular crops. Typically they were either grape pickers or vegetable workers, people who spent most of their time in either the Central Valley or in Salinas. Some of them lived side-by-side in Mexicali or worked together in the Imperial Valley, but once the desert harvest season ended in March, they went their separate ways. Some people who worked the winter lettuce followed the harvest through the desert towns of Yuma and Blythe and then to the Central Valley town of Huron, before cutting through the Coast Range at Pacheco Pass on Highway 152 and dropping down into the lush San Benito Valley, to enter the Salinas Valley from the north. But many skipped the small intermediate harvests, took time off, and traveled from Mexicali to Salinas by taking Highway 10 to the edge of Los Angeles, and then 101 up the California Coast. There, along the edge of the conti-nent where the vast majority of Californians live, the traveling workers passed some of California's picture postcard sights: missions, surfers, citrus orchards near the sea, gentle hillsides, the affluence of Santa Barbara, and the weekend party town of Pismo Beach.

Some eight hours after leaving Mexicali, they entered the Salinas Valley. On this western side of the Coast Range, rain-bearing winter storms arrived irregularly from the Pacific Ocean, and so water did not have to be trans-ported long distances for agriculture to thrive. The temperature is mild and the feeling is rural, even bucolic, with oaks shading the nearby foothills and red barns scattered through the countryside.

Only the long rows of crops signal that this, too, is an altered landscape. Its black earth, once hidden below the Pacific, was grassland, swamp, and river bottom for thousands of years. Small groups of Indians lived off the land, fishing its waters and gathering its acorns, and the Spanish and Mexicans pastured their cattle wherever it was dry enough. Not until Chinese workers in the 1870s dug out the tules, cattails, and sedges, uprooted the willows, cottonwoods, elders, and sycamores, and used shov-els, spades, and steel forks to dig the ditches that drained the water away could this rich land be ravaged by commercial agriculture.[10]

The Salinas Valley was, throughout the UFW years, the leading producer of fresh vegetables (other than tomatoes) in the United States. It carried most of the marks of agribusiness: much of the land was in the hands of absentee owners, and a small number of big growers made most of the money and almost all of the basic decisions about what to grow and how. Farm managers lived in ranch-style homes, not farmhouses, and bought their food at the supermarket. And even in this valley rich with water, so many wells were pumping the aquifer that the ocean itself was being sucked underground, seeping inland, and driving coastal acreage out of production.

Although the Salina Valley is a tiny piece of real estate compared with the vast acreage of the Central Valley, Salinas's combination of soil, water, and a Mediterranean climate provided as much as ten months of work for local farm laborers, and throughout the UFW years many of them settled in, traveling to Mexicali less and less and making parts of Salinas into outposts of Mexico, more than four hundred miles north of the border. Here, the UFW's support among farm workers was strongest and most long-lasting. That was not unrelated to topography. Salinas's particular place on the map was a key to its long harvest season, a partial explanation of why so many farm workers could make it their permanent home, a base from which they were comfortable enough to fight. But the militancy of the Salinas workers, their undeniable power, was not encoded in any map. It had to do with the particular way so many of them did their jobs, with the nature of the work itself.

The Work Itself

Behind every fruit and vegetable for sale in the supermarket lies an unknown world of toil and skill. Broccoli is one of the easiest vegetables to harvest because it grows on plants that are about waist-high, so workers don't have to bend over completely to cut the unopened, densely compacted flower buds that people eat. The plants grow two rows to a bed in lush fields that extend for hundreds of acres. From a distance, workers, organized into crews of a few dozen, clad in bright yellow rain slickers to ward off the morning dew, seem to be plodding through the plants, hunched over, tiny specks of gold too few to make an impact on so much green. Up close, any illusion of sluggishness dissolves before the athletic spectacle of the broccoli cut.

The heads of green compacted buds, three to six inches in diameter, shoot off the main stalk of the plant, sheltered by the broad leaves at the top and hidden among the long leaves that surround the buds before they flower. Not all the heads mature at the same time, and only through keenness of sight can the harvesters—most of them are men—quickly find the ones that are ready to cut. The harvester grabs the head with one hand while with the other he thrusts the short, broad knife downward, cutting the leaves away from the stalk. Then with a sideways stroke of the knife he cuts the head off the plant, leaving just the right length of stalk below the wide unopened flower. He stretches his fingers to grab another head with the first still in his grip and cuts a second stalk. Depending on his quick judgment of the size of the heads and the proximity of the next one ready to cut, he may even grab and cut a third head while holding the other two in his extended hand. Finally he throws the heads onto a conveyer belt moving through the fields, or onto a small platform pulled by a tractor, or into a metal-framed basket on his back, as he looks ahead for the next bud mature enough to be harvested. Each cut takes about three seconds; in an average eight-hour day he might cut 11,000 heads of broccoli.

In the UFW years harvesters often used the baskets, especially when it was too wet to pull the awkward conveyer belt through the fields. They are not so popular now, but they are still used, and when they are full of broccoli they weigh about thirty pounds. The workers carry them across the rows of plants to dump the broccoli into larger bins, which are being towed through the fields by a tractor. Those bins, four feet high, sit on flatbed trucks, which are already a few feet off the ground. So the harvesters must transfer the baskets to the loaders (usually two per crew) who are standing on a makeshift platform that extends out from the bed of the truck.

The exchange between the harvester and the loader is done with the precision of a handoff in football, or the flip of a baseball between two middle infielders at the beginning of a double play. The cutter backs up to the loader who is hovering above him, and at the exact moment that he feels a hand take hold of the top of the metal frame, he thrusts his shoulders up, giving the basket a boost so that the loader can more easily lift it up and over the top of the bin. If the loader lifts the basket just a little bit late, he does not get the full effect of the boost—more important, though, the weight of the basket may come back down heavy on the harvester's shoulders. It is not exactly Melville's monkey rope, where the life of the sailor cutting blubber alongside the ship depends on the care and sense of responsibility of his comrade above him, but when a loader is late he puts his fellow worker at risk of serious injury. Word travels fast among the pickers, and loaders who don't get it right don't last long on the crews.

Not all farm jobs require equal skill. Different techniques are required for thinning, weeding, or harvesting, for working on the ground or climbing on ladders, for working by the hour or doing piece work, and each crop has its own craft secrets and know-how. It is one thing to cut and pack lettuce, another to girdle table grapes, another yet to pick lemons. Not all the physical skill of farmwork depends on the coordination of accomplished hands and sharp, experienced eyes. The work also requires physical endurance. Farmwork is hard not only in the sense of being skilled but also in the sense of requiring toil, exertion, and extended physical effort. When arriving in the early morning to begin work, Pablo Camacho would often say, *"Ya llegamos al campo de la batalla"* —"Now we arrive at the field of battle." Although intending to provoke a smile, Camacho was not being ironic. Most people who have worked in the fields say that it is the hardest work they have ever done. It is hard to put up with the inevitable pain and physical exhaustion, to last until the end of the row, the end of the day, the week, the season. "To last" is not quite the right word. The right word is a Spanish one, *aguantar:* to endure, to bear, to put up with.

Pablo Camacho was proud of his ability to *aguantar,* even arrogant about it, often claiming that he never felt pain while he was working. That is a pose that a lot of farm workers assume, even among themselves. At work, no one complains about pain. Camacho believed that the ability to put up with pain was part of the Mexican national character, especially evident in sports. Like many farm workers, he was an avid boxing fan. He could name all the boxing champions in the lighter divisions from the 1930s to the 1970s, as well as recount the ways Mexican fighters had been denied championship opportunities. Mexicans were the best boxers in the world, he argued, especially in their ability to withstand punishment. They were also good marathon runners and long-distance bicycle racers, he said, sports in which endurance and patience are the essential virtues.

But Mexicans do not have an exclusive franchise on the ability to tolerate hard work. Endurance is a trait of slaves and the oppressed in general, and also characteristic of peasants and other agricultural people—whether free or unfree. Agriculture by its very nature requires patience. Farm workers have to wait for nature to do her work. They must plant, water, and wait. Weed and wait. And finally, after enduring the wait, they may harvest.

Physical labor has received bad reviews since people began to write. It is Adam's curse in the Old Testament. Aristotle contended that "occupations are . . . the most servile in which there is greatest use of the body." The dynamic relationship between the brain and the hand was ripped asunder by early philosophers, leaving two separate activities: valued intellectual labor (suitable for free men) and devalued manual labor (suitable for women and slaves). This philosophical predisposition against the work of the body had its greatest worldly triumph in the development of capitalism and the factory system. As Marx so passionately chronicled, English factories destroyed English handicrafts. What he called "modern industry"— machines built by other machines strung together in a continuous process of production where laborers are "mere appendages" to the machinery— replaced the earlier system of production that "owed its existence to personal strength and personal skill, and depended on the muscular development, the keenness of sight, and the cunning of the hand."[1]

The cunning of the hand, what farm workers call *maña*, remains the basis of California farmwork as surely as it is the basis of a major league pitcher's job, or a skilled craftsman's. Many farm worker jobs are not only hard to do but hard to learn, often requiring years to master, and skills typically are passed from one generation to the next. Farm workers use hand tools: knives, hoes, clippers, pruners. They do not tend machines or have to keep up with an assembly line.

This plain fact has been obscured by all the current references to factory agriculture and industrial farming. The confusion began with the title of the first popular book about California agriculture, Carey McWilliams's *Factories in the Field*. What McWilliams meant by that wonderful, albeit misleading, title was that California agriculture was not made up of small family farms but rather was dominated by large-scale farm businesses, tied to international markets, which employed a landless agricultural proletariat to do the actual work. Those workers, the book's title implied, should be protected by the same laws as factory workers. But McWilliams never argued, nor is it true, that the actual labor process, the work itself, is like a factory assembly line.

That is not likely to change. Agriculture remains dependent on natural cycles and rhythms. Agribusiness cannot escape the seasons, unpredictable changes in the climate, and the natural tempo of individual plants, which do not mature at the same rate. It cannot escape mysterious differences in seed performance, or the interactions between water, sun, and soil, all of which make it relatively hard to mechanize agriculture, and virtually impossible to convert it into a kind of deskilled manufacturing process.

This is not equally true for all farmwork. The planting and harvesting of so-called field crops—grains, sugar beets, and dry beans—have been successfully mechanized and deskilled. But field crops take up a rapidly diminishing percentage of California farm acreage, and the UFW never tried to organize the few people who operate field-crop machinery. Where the UFW did organize, among fresh fruit, vegetable, and nursery workers, mechanization has been mostly an unattainable goal, and the workforce remains skilled: people working with tools in their hands.

Broccoli cutting has never been mechanized. Workers pass through a broccoli field several times, selecting the heads ready to harvest and leaving the immature ones for a later pass-through. Agricultural engineers have never been able to build a machine that can do that. This is the typical technical problem in trying to mechanize fresh fruit and vegetable production. Because plants mature unevenly, they can't be treated as identical inanimate objects moving along an assembly line.

Biologists have tried to redesign the plants genetically so they mature all at once, but nature has proved to be too stubborn. In the early sixties, when growers realized that the bracero program, thus their guaranteed cheap labor supply, was coming to an end, they and their collaborators at the University of California began to build machines and remake seeds that they predicted would mechanize farm workers out of existence.[2] That project has been a colossal failure. Eighteen years of research and millions of dollars were thrown away on the lettuce machine alone. Early schemes involved gamma rays or mechanical fingers that would give each head a little squeeze before cutting, but gamma rays couldn't beat the eye, and the metal fingers damaged the lettuce. A USDA engineer, Paul Adrian, finally announced that he had solved the main technical problem: his machine would X-ray every head of lettuce to decide which ones were mature enough to harvest. It, too, was useless; Adrian couldn't figure out how to get the harvested lettuce into a box without the help of human hands and eyes.[3]

Each failed attempt has its own story. The strawberry machine bruised the berries. The asparagus machine couldn't cut the shoots without destroying the ability of the bulb to generate more shoots for a later harvest. The celery machine couldn't cut the stalks cleanly enough to be suitable for the fresh market. The lemon tree shaker produced three to seven times as much unmarketable fruit as did hand picking. Most other tree shakers do too much damage to the tree roots, although many nut trees can withstand the shaking. The one great mechanical success is the contraption that picks canning tomatoes, which, combined with a reengineered tomato, did replace thousands of workers. Otherwise, fresh tomatoes, like most other fruits and vegetables, are harvested by proficient workers making judgments and wielding tools. As the anthropologist Juan Vincent Palerm quipped about the growers' dream of mechanization, "What we have witnessed over the past years is not the mechanization but rather the 'Mexicanization' of California agriculture."[4]

Farm workers evoke comparisons to athletes—football players and middle infielders, long-distance runners, bicycle racers, boxers—because the centuries-long destruction of craft work is almost complete, and the only context in which people still believe in the skill of physical activity is sports. At work, Marx's world of modern industry is triumphant and the wisdom of the idle philosophers whose leisure depended on slaves is completely vindicated: mental labor is skilled, physical labor is not. Only in play and in certain kinds of physical art such as dance do we continue to recognize and admire the skills of the body.

The most striking athletic comparison, however, does not involve the graceful agility of the individual worker but rather the collective abilities and internal solidarity of the harvest piece-rate crews. These crews are like athletic teams: they closely coordinate difficult physical maneuvers in a contest that lasts an entire season. And they are professional teams in which everyone is paid at the same rate. If a baseball team worked the way a piece-rate vegetable crew does, there would be a set rate for each completed game, and the players on the field would divide the take evenly among themselves. Crews take great care to make the individual jobs equally difficult and to organize the work so that it can be done quickly. They stay together for years and are often made up of groups of relatives—fathers and sons, brothers and cousins—or people from the same rural Mexican town. The crews lose a few members every season to retirement or injury, drink or other forms of dissipation, while recruiting new members to replace them, on the basis of extended family connections and ability. The new recruits often work for a couple of years on hourly crews, the equivalent of minor leagues.

While working on the hourly crews, new men hone their skills, continuing to get better and faster, and learn to put up with the physical pain. This is a much different experience from that of production line workers in a factory. (Factory maintenance workers, whose jobs are skilled and often interesting, are a different case.) On the line a person either learns the job in a few hours or is not going to learn it at all; the biggest problems are adjusting one's rhythms to the pace of the machinery and fighting the boredom and isolation imposed by the task. Working hourly in the fields, a worker has to master the tool in his hands rather than accommodate himself to a machine, and although a person may choose to work alone, he can also work alongside other people—joking, talking, arguing, singing, bitching, philosophizing.

Not all vegetables have extensive "minor leagues." In the celery there are few hourly crews. Most *apieros* learn the job as Maniz did. They go to an already established crew where friends or relatives help them get by until they learn the job. Some people trying to make it in the celery will go to a regular crew and join in the work without sharing in the pay, thereby both learning the job and helping others get through the day. This is fine with the bosses, because they get the free labor of those trying to learn. There are two rows of celery to a bed and each *apiero* cuts his own bed, so it is easy for a new man (they are all men) to help the veteran by cutting in his bed, ten or twenty yards in front of him. This is also called giving another worker "a ride." When the *apiero* assigned to the bed gets to the place where the *raitero* (the person giving the ride) began working, the celery is already there on the ground, and he can simply walk ahead to the spot where the other man is cutting. Both stand up, stretch their backs, and exchange a few words. Usually the *raitero* will then cut in someone else's row, so that the cutters advance evenly.

However new celery workers start out, the first thing they must understand is the knife. It has a short wooden handle, not much longer than the palm of an average adult hand and about an inch wide. Embedded in the handle is a steel blade, one-eighth of an inch thick, eight to ten inches long, and three-quarters of an inch wide. The inside of the blade has a sharp edge. At the end of the blade, the knife widens and makes an abrupt thirty-degree angle upward. The outside edge of the fanned blade is also sharp. Knives differ quite a bit as workers fashion them to their own liking, changing the angle of the bend through their own smithing skills or by getting a friend to make the desired variations.

The celery knife has its own folk history. Up until the early 1960s, it was completely flat, without the bend at the end. An Oxnard celery worker who had been a blacksmith in Mexico was the first to bend the last two inches of the knife, so that when he thrust it into the root of the celery it made a better cut at the bottom of the stalk. His improvisation was so successful that he started to buy the standard knives, convert them, and sell them to other *apieros* or to foremen, who distributed them to the men. He supposedly made so much money refashioning the knives that he retired

Celery Crew, Pajaro Valley, 1982. Photo by Fred Chamberlain.

from the fields. The knife company didn't get around to manufacturing the knives with a bent, upturned end until years later. *Apieros* still reinforce the bend with a homemade weld, and dismiss a knife unmodified from the store as *el bruto*—unfinished.

"The only knives that are any good are called Ontario," Maniz said many years after leaving the fields:

> I think the steel is better. They come from Canada. They are famous, those knives. But even those knives the people adapt, reinforcing the bend with a weld. Any knife without the reinforced weld is worthless. With a good knife you can work all day without getting tired. With a bad knife you are wasted in a couple of hours. A person who does not know celery, and who has a new knife in his hand—I swear to you, he could not cut a single piece of celery. . . .
>
> And, you know, the knives are passed around quite a bit. Some sell for thirty dollars, some for twenty. Among friends they are given away. Of course, nobody is going to sell his favorite knife. No. You can't buy somebody's favorite knife. He might give it to you. But you couldn't buy it.[5]

Apieros talk a lot about their knives. They discuss the differing qualities of the steel, the feel of the handle, and the correct angle of the lift at the end of the knife. When a new man is learning how to cut, people come over to

help him out, to teach him how to do it right. After some instruction, they might take his knife and demonstrate, just as a tennis instructor can only talk so long before taking the racket out of the student's hands and telling her to watch. With the knife in their hands, the teachers finally understand the problem. The knife is dull, they say, or it is made of the wrong kind of steel, or the balance between the handle and the blade is wrong, or the fan at the end is too broad or too narrow, or the angle at the end is too steep or too flat. New men might buy more than a few different celery knives (some from the very pros who are giving them instructions), trying to get the perfect one that will make them good cutters. "*Es el cuchillo*," those trying to learn jokingly tell each other. "It is all in the knife."

Celery is planted only inches apart, and unlike lettuce, broccoli, cauliflower, and many other vegetables, the worker cuts every piece. Usually the celery is cut with three strokes. For the first cut the *apiero* grabs the celery with his non-knife hand at about midstalk. He bends the plant back slightly and, with a short thrust of the knife, cuts the piece of celery at the root, using the angled, fan end of the knife. Just where to cut it, and the exact angle of the first thrust, is part of the skill. Every piece of celery is a little different, so where the first cut lands varies. Cut it too high, and all the individual stalks will separate; it will no longer be a whole piece of celery. Cut it too low, and the next stroke will be more difficult. Cut it at the wrong angle, and some of the outside stalks will be lost.

If the first cut is made correctly, the worker lifts the celery to a horizontal position parallel to the ground and makes the second cut, a sharp downward thrust with the straight edge of the knife, squaring off the first cut at the root. As he finishes this cut he loosens his hold on the knife to make a circular motion with his hand at the just squared-off root, trimming away the remaining loose strands and tendrils. While trimming these "suckers" he turns the piece of celery over with his other hand and then makes the third cut, which trims the top edge of the piece of celery and leaves it about fourteen inches long. Then he drops the celery on top of all the trimmed stalks that protect it from the dirt. When a worker is learning, he masters the strokes, develops his own style, and takes his time. An experienced *apiero* does the whole operation in one fluid motion, at a rate of about one piece of celery every three to five seconds.

People who can do it well are a sight to behold. The fastest cutter at West Coast Farms in the mid-1970s was nicknamed Tremendo. He was not tall; he had earned his name with his massive chest and arms. He had Indian features, came from a small town in Michoacán, and was particularly robust, on a job where everyone is vigorous. He was one of the younger men, in his early twenties. Piece-rate crews do not generally have teenagers on them; most people are between their mid-twenties and their mid-thirties, with a sprinkling of veterans in their forties and fifties, and sometimes even sixties. Very young men don't have enough endurance to do this work, some *apieros* say, pointing out that long-distance runners (unlike sprinters) reach their peak when they are middle-aged. Others say that the young are too easily distracted to get through a season, or that the only way to make yourself do this work is if you face deep necessity and obligation, and the young have not lived long enough for that. Quite simply, they say, it is a job for family men, not bachelors. Tremendo, young and with neither wife nor children, was an exception on the crew.

His cutting technique was nothing to marvel at. What made him special was the energy with which he went about his task. He rarely straightened up or paused at the end of a row, and he seemed to get stronger as the day went on, like the NBA great Moses Malone, who at the height of his career came on strongest in the fourth quarter, earning himself the nickname Train, as in "this train just keeps on comin'." Tremendo didn't start quickly, but usually by midmorning he was ahead of the other cutters, and he always extended his lead in the afternoon. He worked alongside his compadre, Jose Olivarez, who was not as fast, so during the day Tremendo would move over to Jose's row and give him a little ride, enabling the two men to remain close together as they worked. That in itself was not unusual; sometimes even three people would help one another out in this way. What was remarkable was that Tremendo could do it and still lead the crew.

One Thursday, Tremendo was challenged to a race. It wasn't a formal challenge, not begun with a bet or a dare or even a word, as far as anyone could tell, and most of the workers didn't even realize the race was happening until it was well under way. There was a man on the crew who usually worked as a closer, stapling shut the filled boxes of celery. He was called Manguera ("hose"), because his body was so flexible. He was also called *el Joker*, because he could do any job on the crew well—cut, pack, close, or make and distribute boxes. On Monday he had traded positions with a cutter and spent the whole day cutting, which was odd because the position of closing the boxes belonged to him by seniority, and closing is easier than cutting. He kept quiet about what he was doing, telling those who asked only that he wanted to "loosen up my back," which, as Pablo Camacho later remarked, was like a scorpion saying he wanted to sharpen up his sting.

Manguera's stroke was beautiful. Long and narrow, his movements fluid, he made the job appear effortless, as if the celery were gliding through his hands and floating to the ground below. He often made his first thrust of the knife so accurately and cleanly that he didn't have to make the second cut. He just had to clean the end of the celery with the short circular motion of the side of his knife hand and then cut the top end off and drop it to the ground. By sparing himself the middle cut, he saved a lot of time. He worked Monday, Tuesday, and Wednesday this way, staying in the middle of the pack, loosening up his back. On Thursday, at some point before the morning break, Manguera, several rows away from Tremendo, was working ahead of him. This was not happenstance. It had to be a race.

It turned out to be a long race: about six hours, with a half hour for lunch and two ten-minute breaks. A marathon takes about three hours, and the competitors aren't stooped over, with dangerous knives in their hands. The two cutters were soon working far ahead of the rest of the workers, who stood up for long periods to watch, thereby holding up the general progress of the day's work. There was no clear finish line, as foremen hardly ever tell the crews how long they are going to work. How much *apieros* cut and pack depends on how many boxes the brokers will sell that day, and foremen say that if they were to tell the workers one thing in the morning it might change by the afternoon, so it is best not to tell them anything at all.

But if the foremen at West Coast Farms that day didn't help the race by establishing a finish line, neither did they hurt it by hassling the two racers about the quality of their cuts or by telling the other workers to stop watching and hurry up. The race was the event of the day. Even the supervisor, who usually didn't spend much time in the fields, spent a good part of the day watching the two men work.

Nothing dramatic happened. Neither man dropped dead of a heart attack. Nobody keeled over with a back spasm. No fingers were cut. Manguera now works as a high-in-demand handy man in Watsonville, a

true joker, and suffers no particular aches and pains that he could trace to
his years as an *apiero* and strawberry picker. Tremendo has not been so
lucky. His chronic back pain earns him a small disability check but prevents
him from doing physical labor. That is hard on him, but he and his wife
have managed: they run licensed daycare out of their home that supports
their family of five. Although that one-day race did not do him in,
Tremendo's bad back is certainly a legacy of his time in the fields.

Manguera built up a big lead. At lunchtime it looked insurmountable.
But after lunch he began to fade, and on came the big train. As he gained
on his challenger, Tremendo began to bellow out screams of joy. It was a
slow process; Tremendo was gaining but Manguera did not collapse, and
when the crew stopped for the afternoon break, the foreman marked the
place where the cutting would stop for the day. The mark seemed to clinch
victory for Manguera, as there didn't seem to be enough time for Tremendo
to catch him. And that is the way it happened, but with a twist. Twenty
yards before Manguera got to the finish line, he straightened up and stopped
cutting in his row. Then he walked over to Tremendo's row and, starting
at the finishing point, cut back toward Tremendo, giving him a ride. In no
more than five minutes Tremendo's row was done. Then the two of them
walked back to Manguera's row and finished the last twenty yards, talking,
comparing strokes, standing up while they were trimming the celery,
enjoying the end of the day together.

"It is back breaking work," people say, and although backs don't exactly break,
back pain is nearly universal in the fields, and back injuries are common. The
work stresses the muscles and the frame. From bending over much of the day,
the muscles in the back get overstretched and strained. The long up and down
muscles in the front of the torso get overcontracted, which is why it is hard to
stand up at the end of a row. The overworked muscles sometimes spasm, and
cause farm workers to spend days in bed on their backs or crawling around
their homes on their knees. Also, while a worker is bent over, the front of the
vertebrae get compressed, which over time causes arthritis. All of these conditions taken together—overstretched back muscles, overcontracted stomach
muscles, overworked vertebrae—are dangerous to the discs between the vertebrae, and in the worst cases can cause those discs to bulge, slip, or rupture.

Agriculture ranks third (behind construction and transportation and
public utilities) in nonfatal job-related injuries and illnesses in California.
Nationally, "overexertion" is listed as the most prevalent cause of injuries
on the job. Such statistics are incomplete and certainly underestimate
damage to the back. The workers' refusal to complain while working does
not alter the grim reality. Cesar Chavez's bad back was emblematic. Most
people who spend a significant number of years working in the fields have
chronic back problems.[6]

Only infrequently do *apieros* cut themselves. Usually the cut is bandaged in the fields, and the cutter goes back to work. During the UFW years, if the cut was bad, the worker was given another job not as demanding on the hand—making and carrying boxes, or packing, or even closing the boxes— and somebody else took the person's place cutting. This slowed the crew down a bit, which meant everyone had to work longer to make that day's quota of boxes, but it was done in good cheer. It was a decision made among the crew, not by the foreman.

On piece-rate crews the workers drive themselves hard. Celery crews in the 1970s raced through the day, starting slowly as they warmed up in the morning, hitting their fastest pace in the two hours between the ten-minute morning break and the half-hour lunch, and then slowing down in the afternoon. The faster they got the work done, the sooner the workday was over, and the higher the hourly wage. On many days crews worked six hours or less, which was the way the workers liked it. Foremen still gave workers a lot of grief. But, generally, they watched out for the quality of the pack, and tried to slow down the crews so that they would do a better job. Foremen also wanted workers to specialize as much as possible, as they thought this resulted in a higher-quality pack. But because rotating the tasks of cutting, packing, closing, and making and distributing the empty boxes is easier on the body, workers would often trade positions for a while among themselves.

The pain is why most *apieros* prefer to pack celery rather than cut it. Packing requires constant up-and-down motion, as the packer picks up pieces of celery off the ground and then straightens up and puts them in boxes that ride about waist-high on the large, wheel-barrow-like burro. Up and down all day long is not easy on the back, either, but it is easier than the near-constant bent-over position that cutting requires.

Celery is packed in five different sizes, as many as four sizes at a time. The biggest celery goes into boxes containing eighteen pieces, the next biggest into boxes of twenty-four pieces, then thirty, thirty-six, and forty-eight as the celery decreases in size. The boxes all have their special places on the burro, and particular ways that they are filled, so that the packers know where and in what direction (root end left or right) to put the celery, and can count in multiples of six, rather than one piece at a time. The basic problem is that lying on the ground, all the different sizes of celery are mixed together. The packer has to pick up the same size celery and place it in the right box as quickly as possible, keeping track of what goes where and when a box is full. Some cutters, unable quickly to master the intense concentration and careful counting, decide to stick with the job they already know, despite the pain. Others prefer cutting for what they consider the privilege of working alone.

Packers work three men to a burro, packing behind three cutters. The three have a highly coordinated routine. Two of them work less than an arm's distance from each other, and the third not much farther away. If one man is slow, the others can help out, "carrying" him for a while, but the responsibilities of the three men are clearly defined and conscientiously executed, unless there are special circumstances—somebody is learning the job, or not feeling well for a few days, or hung over in the morning, or distracted by a problem at home. These trios often stay together for years, and sometimes are made up of close relatives. All sorts of informal adjustments and accommodations are made among them, as is required by the surprises of life and work. But bad trios do not last as long as bad marriages, as bickering packers damage the whole crew, and the squabblers return to cutting or trade places with other packers sooner rather than later.

During the UFW years, some piece-rate crews formed soccer teams and played in recreational leagues, at night or on weekends. Well paid, skilled, proud of their jobs and their abilities, they were greatly admired in farmworker communities. The cooperative nature of so much of their work prepared them for various kinds of collective action. The dominant ethos of the crews, that combination of solidarity and competition that is essential to a successful sports team, had always been useful in coordinating harvest-time job actions, like slow-downs and short work stoppages. It was also useful in building a union. The piece-rate crews of Salinas were not the only workers who built the organization that ultimately became the UFW, nor even the first. In fact, in the beginning none of the people who founded the union were thinking much about the ways the jobs in the fields had already organized workers, and what that might mean for a union. Only later would it be clear that the character of the work itself was as pivotal in the story of the union as the workers who did it and as telling as the character and deep background of the founders.

3

Childhood as Destiny

'27 to '39

The tenant sat in his doorway, and the driver thundered his engine and started off, tracks falling and curving, harrows combing, and the phalli of the seeder slipping into the ground. Across the dooryard the tractor cut, and the hard, footbeaten ground was seeded field, and the tractor cut through again; the uncut space was ten feet wide. And back he came. The iron guard bit into the house-corner, crumbled the wall, and wrenched the little house from its foundation so that it fell sideways, crushed like a bug. And the driver was goggled and a rubber mask covered his nose and mouth. The tractor cut a straight line, and the air and the ground vibrated with its thunder. The tenant man stared after it, his rifle in his hand. His wife was beside him, and the quiet children behind. And all of them stared after the tractor.

—The destruction of the Joads' house, John Steinbeck,
The Grapes of Wrath

I remember the tractor heading for the corral. I shudder now to think of it. It was there that Richard and I had fun together riding the horses and the young calves bareback . . . Now the tractor was at the corral, and the old sturdy fence posts gave way as easily as stalks of corn. It was a monstrous thing. Richard and I were watching on higher ground. We kept cussing the driver, but he didn't hear us, our words were lost in the sound of tearing timbers and growling motor. We didn't blame the grower, we blamed the poor tractor driver. We just thought he was mean. I wanted to go stop him but I couldn't. I felt helpless.

—Cesar Chavez remembering the destruction of the family
homestead in Arizona, Jacques Levy, *Cesar Chavez,
Autobiography of La Causa*

Cesar Chavez was twelve years old in 1939 when he and his brother Richard watched the tractor destroy their childhood. It was the same year *The Grapes of Wrath* was published; a year later, moviegoers in theaters across America watched as a tractor smashed the Joad homestead on celluloid, and Tom Joad (played by Henry Fonda) told enthralled audiences that wherever people were fighting against injustice that is where you would find him. By that time the Chavez family was on the migrant trail, sleeping in a leaky tent in Oxnard, trying to squeeze a living out of the California fields. Cesar and his younger brother, Richard, got jobs sweeping out an Oxnard movie theater every day after school. They earned a nickel each, which they gave to their mother, and a free movie pass. The young migrants soon became movie fans: Cesar told his main biographer, Jacques Levy, that he went to the movies so often that he saw almost every Lone Ranger serial.[1] But he never said anything about seeing the popular movie version of his own family's tragedy, even as he told Levy about an incident in his life that seemed to come right off the screen. Maybe he missed the movie. What he didn't miss, what he knew in his soul, was the shocking difference between his Arizona homestead and the California fields: a family surrounded by a community of friends and relatives, working on their own plot of land; that same family uprooted, traveling among hostile strangers, working on large corporate-owned farms for other people's profits.

The Chavez family's doomed corral was part of their hundred-acre ranch outside Yuma, in Quechan Indian country. It had been homesteaded by the boys' grandfather Cesario, a muleskinner from Chihuahua. Cesario laid claim to the land thirty years before the family lost it, and he was lucky not to live long enough to witness the disaster. Cesario's son, Librado, had been unable to pay all the taxes on the farm. An Anglo absentee landowner who held title to the adjoining property had paid the taxes and wrenched the family homestead away from the Chavez family.

Losing his father's land was just the latest in Librado's long series of losses. When the Depression first hit, another Anglo, a lawyer, had swindled him out of the title to his own forty-acre ranch. As the bad times got worse, Librado lost the grocery store, pool hall, and garage that he had bought in the prosperous twenties. Broke, he moved the family back to his father's original homestead, where he tried to make a go of it growing corn, squash, chilies, and watermelon. But the Gila River, which irrigated the farm, was unreliable. Twenty years of overgrazing had destroyed the native grasses along its banks. Often it was dry, but in wet years it flooded.[2] Librado's first harvests were hampered by drought. Then, in the midst of his troubles, the rampaging river broke through the irrigation ditches his father had built. Librado couldn't sell the crops he managed to salvage. By the time the boys saw the tractor crush the corral, the family had spent one last year on the homestead after a wasted season working in the California fields in hopes of raising money to pay the taxes. Now they would have to go back to California.

Until the family hit the road, Librado Chavez's problems had barely registered on his oldest son, Cesar. It had been mostly good times in the North Gila Valley: playing in the grocery store that had doubled as the family's first home; learning about horses from his father and charity from his mother; catching gophers, feeding them to the cats, and selling their tails for a penny a piece to the local irrigation district; playing pool with Richard on the table that sometimes doubled as their bed; gathering chicken eggs and bartering them for bread or flour with neighbors and relatives; listening to the old people's stories at summer barbecues at night; playfully teasing his nearly blind grandmother, who was almost one hundred and who taught him prayers in Latin and instructed him in the lives of the saints.

For the young Cesar Chavez, the California fields were a disaster. He saw his father, a master horseman, tricked and humiliated. He went hungry for the first time and joined the family to search for wild mustard greens to have something to eat. Alongside his father, he walked out of the fields in informal strikes, losing every time. His world of play, interrupted only by chores on the family farm, was replaced by a world of unrelieved work on other people's land. "Unlike the ranch, the work was drudgery," he told Levy. It was hard, unbearably hard. He remembered working with the short-handled hoe as a kind of crucifixion. He had lost the corral, the horses, the dogs and cats; the pool table had been left behind. He had lost the community of the North Gila Valley, peopled by relatives, friends, other Mexicans. Now home, or what passed for it, was the family's 1927 Studebaker. He slept in a series of tents, shacks, hovels. He traveled among strangers in unknown places, victim of a new set of rules. When he went to the store, he was cheated. He was beaten by older boys. When he left his toys outside, they were stolen.

This is a familiar story: a family hits the road to California when the old homestead is lost to unpaid taxes, lawyers, and the Depression. But it is more familiar as an Okie story, and the Chavez family—Librado, his wife, Juana, the children, Rita, Cesar, Richard, Vicky, and Lenny—were clearly not Okies. They called themselves Mexicans; sociologists today probably would classify them as Mexican Americans. Cesar and his siblings had all been born in Arizona. Librado had been brought across the border when he was only two; Juana, when she was six months old. Cesario had voted in Texas elections before the turn of the century and had carved the homestead out of the Colorado desert three years before Arizona became a state. But despite the three generations in the United States, the family did not "hyphenate" itself. People didn't start doing that until after World War II. Speaking Spanish, living in close contact with new immigrants who had firsthand news from home, settling in a territory they knew had been taken from Mexico in a war of conquest, they remained Mexicans and were proud of it.

Only in school did Cesar feel that there was anything suspect about being Mexican; teachers in the North Gila Valley punished him for speaking Spanish, but what had been occasional in the valley was normal in California.* There, Cesar first saw a sign stating "White Trade Only." There, he was denied service at a restaurant, was stopped by the *migra*, and for the first time felt somehow diminished because his skin was dark and he was Mexican.

The California fields robbed the young Cesar of almost everything that was good in his life except the love and comfort of his family. "I was like a wild duck with its wings clipped," he said.[3] Farmwork for wages was an affliction. It took his youth. It hurt his back. It humbled his proud father. Everything about it was wrong. He could know it was wrong because he had lived right: "Some had been born into the migrant stream. But we had been on the land, and I knew a different life."[4]

The Chavez family hit the migrant circuit in what arguably were the hardest times in California agricultural history. It wasn't just that wages were low. What made matters worse was that the sweeping farm worker upsurge of the early 1930s had passed. As the Studebaker carried the sometimes-hungry Chavez family from job to job, the strikes that had raised both wages and spirits in the fields in 1933 were long gone, replaced by losing battles directed by disheartened union organizers who would soon leave the fields to focus their attention on cannery workers rather than farm workers.

No sophisticated economic analysis is required to understand the melancholy that dominated the California fields at the exact moment that the young Cesar Chavez picked up a short-handled hoe. Too many workers were chasing too few jobs. In cotton, where most farm workers were employed, acreage had climbed steadily, from 130,000 acres in 1924 to 670,000 in 1937. In the next two years, though, under the provisions of Roosevelt's Agricultural Adjustment Act, California cotton acreage was cut nearly in half, to 340,000 acres, just as displaced people from Oklahoma, southern Missouri, Arkansas, and Texas were pouring into the state.[5] Some 400,000 of these Okies came to California between 1935 and 1939, and many of them headed directly for the fields, where they competed for disappearing jobs with the 200,000 mostly Mexican farm workers who were already there. It was a competition that only the large growers won.

For those entering the fields in 1939 it would have been easy to regard the natural condition of farm workers exactly as it was depicted in the

---

* Victor Villaseñor, born in 1940 in Carlsbad, California, about fifty miles from the Mexican border, writes in *Rain of Gold* (New York: Delta, 1991) that not until he first went to school did he learn that he didn't live in Mexico.

documentary art and literature of the period. In that one remarkable year, three books of photographs of farm workers and dispossessed small farmers evoked a wave of sympathy among large swaths of the American public: *You Have Seen Their Faces*, with photographs by Margaret Bourke and text by Erskine Caldwell; *An American Exodus*, with the photos of Dorothea Lange and a text written by her husband, Paul Taylor; and *Let Us Now Praise Famous Men*, by James Agee and the photographer Walker Evans. These books were stared at, studied, worried over, looked at again and again by millions of people, most of them far from the California fields. Steinbeck's magnificent *Grapes of Wrath* became an immediate best-seller that year. Carey McWilliams's *Factories in the Field* also was published in 1939, and became popular at the same time that hundreds of witnesses in a sensational few weeks of testimony were telling the U.S. Senate Labor Committee and its chair, Senator Robert M. La Follette Jr., about the systematic, well-organized, usually brutal, and often legal repression of California farm workers.

This was more than a coincidence or an inexplicable agreement among diverse artists and journalists about what was important and how to present it. It was a campaign with an agenda. As Arthur Rothstein, the first photographer to work for the Farm Security Administration and Lange's colleague, put it: "It was our job to document the problems of the Depression so that we could justify the New Deal legislation that was designed to alleviate them."[6] McWilliams's book was a straightforward call for farm workers to be covered by the protections of the 1935 National Labor Relations Act and to be granted the same rights as factory workers. Steinbeck, whose purpose and art were more complicated than the others', nonetheless fully affirmed the overall agenda, and made it clear directly in his pamphlets and indirectly in his novel, that the migrants deserved government help because they were true American whites. La Follette, the professional politician, could be most direct. His introduction to the transcript of the hearings called for farm workers to receive the full range of federal protections and benefits.

The campaign failed to achieve its immediate aim, as concern for farm workers was pushed aside by the approaching world war, and as the white migrants who were featured in the photos and the prose moved out of the fields and into California's expanding war and food-processing industries. But those early images of suffering, kept alive by reprints and museum revivals and by the continuing popularity of Steinbeck's masterpiece, remained seared in the national psyche. They came to stand for the entire farm worker experience and engendered a latent nationwide sympathy for farm workers that Cesar Chavez would later use as a powerful lever with which he moved the world. He could do it so convincingly because the images of 1939 documented his own childhood tragedy and thereby enabled him, in good faith, to draw on the deposits of empathy that Steinbeck, Lange, and the others had made a generation before.

But the collective portrait created by Popular Front artists and their colleagues was incomplete: at best it related only to a particular time and place; at worst, it was an insult to farm workers' genuine tradition and history. Workers acting on their own behalf never win in these representations. They can't, because winning, or even fighting effectively, would muddy the moral waters. This cultural agenda was so fixed that in Steinbeck's morality tale of an apple strike, *In Dubious Battle*, farm workers suffer a grand defeat, although farm workers won in the actual 1933 peach strike on which his story was based.[7] In Lange's photographs, noble migrants suffer and endure. Rarely in the photos do we see images of farm workers throwing back tear gas canisters, or angrily confronting scabs, or giving a rousing speech at a mass meeting. All of that happened on a regular basis in the early 1930s, and even amid the general defeat of the late 1930s. The farm workers' combative tradition and their recurring power during harvest seasons and in times of labor scarcity have been trumped by the images of 1939, where, as the cultural historian William Stott put it, farm workers come to us "only in images meant to break our hearts."*

A more complete portrait of California farm workers requires quite different images. In the early Depression, farm workers were united in a movement that had blown hot and cold since 1928 and became a mighty storm by 1933. Of the several winds that have blustered through the California fields, that was the biggest. Never before had so many farm workers gone on strike. At the height of their struggle in 1933, led by the Communist-sponsored Cannery and Agriculture Workers Union (C&A), ten thousand people were striking in the peaches, four thousand in the grapes, and fifteen thousand in the cotton—three of the most important harvests in the state at the time. Five days into the cotton strike the battle's first chroniclers, Paul Taylor and Clark Kerr, called it an

---

* They are allowed but a single emotional register. Lange's famous "Migrant Mother,' holding a swaddled babe in her lap and framed by two distracted young children, leans forward with a hand to her face, looking past the photographer with an inexplicable combination of worry and grace. "She has all the suffering of mankind in her, but all the perseverance too," Lange's boss at the Farm Security Administration, Roy Stryker, said. The actual woman, Florence Thompson, was a full-blooded Cherokee, but she comes into history as an Okie, an honorary white. Lange took seven shots of Thompson. The ones that showed the two young children smiling for the camera and her teenage daughter with a dreamy, flirtatious look were never published until after Lange died. See Levine, "Photography and the History of the American People in the 1930s and 1940s" in Fleischhauer and Brannan, 1988, p. 16; and Geoffrey Dunn, "Photographic License," *Metro* [Santa Cruz], January 19–25, 1995.

earthquake and the *New York Times* called it a war; the *San Francisco Chronicle* compared it to a volcano. No cataclysmic metaphor was too excessive. For the almost exclusively Mexican strikers the first days were a determined, joyful demonstration of their unity and strength. Trucks and cars overflowing with strikers went from field to field, the caravans getting larger as other pickers joined them. The growers and police were overwhelmed. Twenty-five strikers stopped a rancher's car and broke all the windows before allowing the two frightened growers to escape. In the midst of a small confrontation, a woman striker took a cop's gun and car keys. Some strikers ran into the fields to chase off scabs. Others set fires. Thousands of pounds of picked cotton went up in smoke. Everywhere the deepest mark of the workers' power was on display: deserted fields helplessly guarded by frustrated farmers who had no one to pick their crops. When three strikers were shot and killed, their *compañeros* held mass funerals, which even former strikebreakers attended. In a large caravan after the murders, strikers openly displayed their guns, and the Mexican consul reported that workers had told him they "were prepared to die fighting for their rights."[8]

Official government sources reported that nearly 50,000 people struck in the California fields in 1933, about 25 percent of farm workers then in the state. By way of comparison, in 1937, at the apex of strike activity among industrial workers, only 8 percent of the workforce went on strike. The big industrial strikes were more successful than the farm workers', for industrial workers not only won higher wages but also secured union contracts in major industries, while most—but not all—of the farm worker strikes were settled without workers winning recognition of their unions. But farm workers did not strike in vain. More than 80 percent of the twenty-five strikes officially recorded in 1933, including the peach and cotton wars, won the strikers higher wages, increasing farm worker pay by about 40 percent.[9]

The great upheaval of the early Depression was not a unique event. Periodically throughout their history, California farm workers have fought vigorously, sometimes in small, local battles unknown to anyone but the immediate participants, and at other times in large campaigns—directed by radical or even openly revolutionary leaders—that have lasted for several seasons. The nature of these fights is rooted in the special character of agricultural production and in the real opportunities that farm workers have encountered in the fields for nearly a hundred years.

Commercial farmers of whatever size have two special vulnerabilities. Although they must work the land much of the year—preparing the soil, planting, thinning, weeding, irrigating, fertilizing—only during the harvest do they produce a commodity. If the harvest is delayed or interrupted by a

strike, they cannot warehouse their fields or shut down production temporarily and then work people overtime once the strike is over. If the strike is
effective, growers can lose their entire investment in a few weeks or even
less, as some fruits and vegetables must be harvested within days of becoming harvest-ready. Also, because the growers' demand for labor varies
greatly during the year, there is not enough work in any particular area to
sustain an extensive settlement of agricultural workers. That is why farm
towns are small, and growers depend on migrants. But migratory trails are
not always reliable, and occasionally enough farm workers don't arrive in
time to work the precious, short-lived harvest.

Time is often on the workers' side, and they have not hesitated to seize
it. Brief harvest walkouts, sit-downs, slow-downs, and stay-at-homes are
part of farm worker tradition, weapons used much more regularly by agricultural workers than by industrial workers. When conditions have been
favorable, these short strikes and quasi-strikes have been transformed into
large, extensive campaigns, like the coordinated shutdowns of the early
thirties, or the later battles out of which the UFW emerged.

The pattern of militant farm worker action, significant wage gains, and
an ultimate failure to build a lasting union was set nearly a generation before
the Depression-era upheaval. Between 1914 and 1917, in a period of overall labor scarcity, the Industrial Workers of the World (IWW), at times
working in tandem with the Partido Liberal Mexicano (PLM), led a series
of walkouts in the California fields, orchards, and vineyards that pushed up
wages, forced labor-camp managers to provide better food, and prompted
the state of California to build an extensive series of new labor camps,
which improved the lives of many migrants. A harvest-time strike in the
hops in 1914 doubled piece-rate wages, and by 1917, the average wage of
California farm workers had risen to nearly 90 percent of the average wage
of California's city workers.[10]

Although the major strikes received the most publicity, the Wobblies,
or Wobs, as IWW members were called, applied much of the pressure on
the growers through smaller on-the-job actions. Using tactics as old as
agricultural slave labor, they skipped over fruits and vegetables ready to
harvest, worked sloppily enough to ruin some of what they picked, and
often labored at so slow a pace that they enraged their overseers and foremen. In 1915, the Wobblies proposed a regular slow-down of fifteen
minutes per hour, during which farm workers would neglect their jobs
and turn their "full attention" to the cases of two IWW leaders, Richard
(Blackie) Ford and Herman Suhr, who had been framed for murder, and
for whom the union was demanding pardons. The Wobs also threatened
to sabotage the entire 1915 harvest if Ford and Suhr were not freed. In
March 1915, E. Clemens Horst, a major California hop grower, and
W. H. Carlin, one of the prosecutors who had helped frame Ford and Suhr,

both testified in support of a pardon for the two hated agitators—a clear indicator of Wobbly power.

The Wobblies openly advocated acts of sabotage such as burning barns, sheds, and haystacks. Nineteen fifteen and 1916 were bad years for fires in rural California, but none of the blazes was ever pinned on a Wob. One act of sabotage easily traced to the IWW was the popular poster affixed to thousands of California fruit trees with copper nails; the poster warned people not to drive copper nails into fruit trees because it would damage them.

According to the Wobblies, their actions in the fields cost the growers about $10 million a year in lost crops between 1914 and 1917. The U.S. Justice Department, which had its own reasons for exaggerating IWW power, figured the growers' total loss at a smaller but still significant $15 million to $20 million for the entire period.

As powerful as the movement was, it did not establish a stable union that might have consolidated farm worker victories. That was partly a result of ideological disposition. The Wobblies were anarchists, trying to build an anticapitalist culture among workers rather than a formal union, and even at the conclusion of successful strikes they refused to sign contracts, as they opposed any agreements with the boss class. But the failure to build a regular union was not only a product of IWW ideology. Just as conditions in the fields made growers vulnerable, they also made building a regular union extremely difficult—so much so that it wasn't even an important goal of most striking workers. Moving from one part of the state to another, working for several employers in any given year, farm workers did not build up a commitment to any particular place or job. Why fight for a contract with an individual boss when you might work for that boss for only a few days, weeks, or months? Workers were willing to fight for an immediate upgrade in wages or working conditions but were less willing to engage in an extended battle for union contracts. For their part growers might grant short-term raises to get the harvest in, but they did not want their periodic vulnerability to be converted into long-term gains for the workers. So the workers fought hard and often, sometimes winning and sometimes not, but they were unable to make their victories stick.

Federal and State power abruptly ended IWW farm worker organizing in 1917, as the United States entered the Great War. The attack on the Wobblies was only partly prompted by the Wobbly opposition to the war; in California it was mostly motivated by IWW's strength in the fields, where they had about five thousand card-carrying members and many thousands of sympathizers. Raids began at the IWW's two most powerful farm worker locals, in Stockton and Fresno. They continued until about half the California IWW membership was in jail, with more than a hundred doing hard time in San Quentin.[11]

Among contemporary farm workers the IWW is forgotten, but what the Wobblies called sabotage—quick harvest strikes, slow-downs, purposely damaging the crop while picking it, burning barns and sheds—reoccurs regularly whenever farm workers do battle. The tactics are linked to the character of agricultural production, and each generation of farm workers is fully capable of figuring out where its leverage lies. Nevertheless, the tactics do have a lineage, and among militant Mexican workers they have long been associated with the name Ricardo Flores Magón.

Flores Magón was the leader of the PLM, a sort of half-sister to the IWW in California. His interest was not primarily California farm workers. Flores Magón was an early opponent of the Mexican dictator Porfirio Díaz, and published a weekly newspaper, *Regeneración*, for which he wrote political and social commentary. He and a small band of comrades fled Mexico in 1904. They resumed publishing their newspaper in the United States and smuggled it back into Mexico, often hidden between the pages of Sears, Roebuck catalogues. As the crisis in Mexico intensified, *Regeneración* became the main tribunal of the Mexican Revolution, distributed clandestinely throughout the country, and, famously, read out loud by campfire light to the troops of Emilaiano Zapata.

Flores Magón, who is celebrated in Mexican secondary school textbooks as a "precursor" of the revolution, remained in exile in the United States for the last eighteen years of his life. Although Ricardo Flores Magón, his brother Enrique, and a substantial number of displaced Mexican revolutionaries focused primarily on political developments in Mexico, they also set up a series of PLM clubs in the Southwest and California. Those clubs attracted Mexican migrant workers, some of whom began to call themselves *Magonistas*. The clubs were linked through *Regeneración* and several other local, less regular PLM newspapers. Club leaders read the newspapers out loud to assembled groups of workers, who then discussed the situation in Mexico and their own troubles in the United States.

The hub of PLM power was Los Angeles, which was still an agricultural town in 1907 when the Flores Magón brothers settled there, and already was the center of the Mexican community in the United States. The PLM's LA clubhouse became a center of multilingual, multiethnic activity where socialists and Wobblies famous and obscure mixed with *Magonistas*. *Regeneración*, its back page printed in English, built up an LA circulation of 10,000, making it both the first bilingual paper in California and the largest Spanish-language newspaper in town. The PLM club, which was also considered a Spanish-speaking IWW local, had 400 active members, most of whom were farm workers.[12]

Elsewhere in California, Spanish-speaking IWW locals were filled with people who were also *Magonistas*. San Diego had a joint IWW–PLM local, and the highly active Fresno Wobbly local had a large number of Mexican workers. Given the loose attitude of the two anarchist groups toward questions of formal membership, among the rank-and-file the primary differences between Wobblies and *Magonistas* were language and nationality rather than ideology or practice.[13]

The PLM clubs and IWW locals were not just debating societies and places to hang out. In San Diego in 1910, a joint IWW-PLM local organized a strike at the local gas and electric company that won equal pay for equal work. That same year a fight for free speech that ultimately did so much to popularize the IWW among California farm workers, began in Fresno in the midst of a battle to organize Mexican workers who were being contracted to build a dam on the outskirts of town. In hop fields, vineyards, sugar refineries, and citrus orchards, many farm worker walkouts were joint Wobbly-*Magonista* efforts.

The PLM and the IWW went down together. In 1918, Ricardo Flores Magón, along with other PLM and IWW leaders, was convicted of violating the Espionage Act in 1918 for "obstructing the war effort." At Leavenworth Penitentiary, in Kansas, he had a cell next to Ralph Chaplin, a prominent Wobbly poet, cartoonist, and songwriter. They did their time translating the poetry of a slain *Magonista* soldier, Práxedis Guerrero. For Ricardo, it was the last time of his life. The new Mexican government offered its help, but he declined because he deplored the government's conduct following the revolution. He died in jail, in 1922.[14]

The IWW and PLM, along with most other anarchist groups, did not survive as effective organizations after World War I. The Bolshevik victory in Russia seemed to confirm that Communist parties, not anarchist ones, were the best vehicle for fighting capitalism. But *Magonismo* never totally disappeared from the California fields. Remaining underground in unfavorable times such as 1939, *Magonismo* has reappeared whenever farm workers have had an opportunity to fight. It is there when they slow down on the job, sabotage the crops, or strike at the beginning of a harvest. *Magonistas* played a part in Imperial Valley melon and lettuce strikes in the late 1920s. They worked together with other militants when California farm workers shook the state in the early 1930s. A generation later a few *Magonistas* would play a small role as the movement that produced the UFW was getting under way. And in 1979, the ghost of Ricardo Flores Magón would make a cameo appearance at one of the most dramatic moments in UFW history.

For the young Cesar Chavez, in 1939, that was not only an unknown future, it was an unknown past. The Chavez family was unconnected to any political tendency. More than that, families like the Chavezes were, in a sense, at an angle to history. Displaced Mexican homesteaders were only a tiny part of the great migration made famous by Steinbeck. In fact, across the 1930s, Mexicans who hit the road with all their worldly possessions were overwhelmingly headed not west, but south, to Mexico, driven by a combination of necessity, nativist attacks, and Mexican government inducements. Unacquainted with established farm worker traditions and communal networks in California, the Chavez family might easily have regarded isolation and loss as the steady state of people who work for wages in the fields.

More typical of the Mexican experience in California is the story of one of the other founders of the UFW, Gilbert Padilla.* Padilla was born the same year as Chavez, 1927, but unlike the latter he was "born into the migrant stream," in the Hamburg labor camp in Los Banos, Merced County, located in central California, where his family was picking cotton. Gilbert's parents, his paternal grandmother, and three uncles had come to the United States from Mexico in 1917, traveling on a troop train carrying revolutionary soldiers to Juárez. After crossing the border at El Paso, the Padilla clan went to Needles, California, worked on the railroad, and lived in railroad camps. In 1920 the family moved to Azusa, a town in East Los Angeles County. Gilbert's father built a house, and most of the family worked in the nearby fields and orchards. They started migrating north to Los Banos in the Central Valley in 1926, leaving in June and returning in December or January.[15]

Padilla cannot recall when he first started working in the fields, as it was always so. Often he worked with his dad and his eight brothers and sisters on the same crew. Padilla remembers his first miniature cotton sack tied around his waist. It wasn't cute; he hated it. Unlike Chavez, he didn't associate the work with the loss of home or childhood. Working in the California fields was his childhood. Later that would seem an injustice, but at the time it was just hard work.

Padilla says he learned about work from his dad and about justice from his mom. Juana Cabrera Padilla had little children to care for and food to prepare, and Gilbert listened to her stories at home in the kitchen. She and the rest of the Padillas had paid two centavos each to cross the border, where U.S. agents had sprayed her and the others with DDT, a synthetic pesticide. She called it the most degrading moment of her life. She talked about how hard life had been back in Mexico and about the early hopes for the revolution. She had strong opinions and delivered a running commentary on contemporary politics: on Herbert Hoover (she hated him), FDR (she

---

*   When Padilla's parents went to Merced to register his birth, a county clerk listed his name as Gilbert rather than Gilberto (another clerk had listed his brother Carlos's name as Charles). His family always called him Gil or Flaco—meaning Skinny. When he went to school, people started calling him Gilbert. Monolingual Mexicans know him as Padilla. Among the UFW staff he was usually called Gilbert.

liked him), and war (it was the most hateful of all). She had learned English listening to the radio but refused to speak it. She was the first person Gilbert Padilla heard talk about equality.

The Padillas had been part of the migration of more than a million Mexicans who came to the United States between the outbreak of the Mexican Revolution in 1910 and the beginning of the Depression in 1930. Pushed out by economic disaster in the Mexican countryside and the violence of the revolution and attracted by the growing demand for labor and the relatively high wages in the U.S., most of the migrants settled in the Southwest and California. Many worked in the fields, and as early as 1920 California farm journals were running stories about the "Mexican Harvest." In the decade that followed, the Mexican population of California more than doubled, and by 1930 Mexicans were the vast majority, perhaps 80 percent, of the state's 200,000 farm workers. When the Depression hit, most of them had been doing farmwork for a good many years and were familiar with the California scene. Like the Padillas, they traveled a regular migratory route; they knew the crops, the contractors, the small towns of the Central Valley, the labor camps, the limits and opportunities of any potential fight.[16]

This community of people, connected to one another through networks of extended families and self-help organizations called *mutualistas*, was badly battered by the Depression. Blamed for the unemployment of white "American" workers, among the first to be fired as the economy spiraled downward, kicked off public and private welfare rolls, shoved back to Mexico in a series of highly publicized Border Patrol raids, hundreds of thousands of Mexicans left the U.S. and returned to Mexico.[17] It was so bad that by 1933, one-third of the Mexican population of Los Angeles, including many U.S.-born children, had gone.[18]

The Padillas were among those who stayed and fought, not as militants but as rank-and-file participants in the great upheaval in the fields in the early 1930s. Gilbert Padilla's father, Longino, and his oldest brother, Cesario, walked out of the cotton fields along with thousands of others in 1933. They returned home to Los Banos after walking the picket line for several days. They talked excitedly about the collective dashes into the fields to confront the scabs and heard reports about the strikers who were shot down in response. Family friends told them of the enormous funeral marches and of the encampments that became living quarters for the embattled strikers. They got news of the 3,000-strong Corcoran camp, with tents in long rows along dusty paths named for Mexican towns and heroes of the revolution. They learned how the authorities tried to starve the workers into submission and then bribe them with food; how, at Corcoran, with everyone hungry and at least two children dead of starvation, the strike committee called a general meeting, and people debated, took a vote, and decided not to accept the food as long as it was conditioned on their return to work; how at another meeting workers shouted, "We are all leaders"; and how after all that, the strikers won higher wages but failed again to win recognition for their union.

Gilbert Padilla was only six years old during the great cotton strike of 1933, but he heard the stories as the years passed, and he absorbed the essential lesson: his father, his brother, the ordinary laborers who peopled his world, were hard workers and proud fighters. When he was a boy, it was not work in the California fields that struck him as wrong and degrading, but inequality, segregation, and discrimination. On the Hamburg ranch in Los Banos, the Mexicans lived in one camp and the whites in another, though they often picked cotton together in the same crews. School was worse. Azusa had one elementary school for Mexicans and two for whites. At Lee Intermediate School, Mexicans stayed on one side of the school and whites on the other. They had separate recesses, and at lunchtime whites ate in the cafeteria while Mexicans ate outside. That and the segregated movie theaters in town had a deep impact on Gilbert. But his most lacerating memory was of the Azusa public swimming pool. The white kids could swim all week; the Mexicans and African Americans, only on Fridays. Friday nights the water was drained and the pool was filled again so that the whites wouldn't have to swim in the supposedly contaminated water.

Work in the California fields didn't feel wrong until Padilla came back from the U.S. Army, in 1947. He had been a squad leader in basic training and had been sent to Japan, where he worked as a crane operator. The Army "opened my eyes," he says. He became a noncommissioned officer. He made friends with whites. He operated complicated equipment. When he and two of his brothers were discharged and returned to chop cotton at the Hamburg ranch, they were making less than the braceros. Once when he and his brothers stopped at the end of a row to have a cigarette, the foreman came by and bawled them out. The three brothers walked out of the field together, and then walked six miles home.

"My brother had been a prisoner of war, another brother was wounded and a hero, and David had just come back from the Philippines. There were six of us in the Army, and to come back and be treated that way! So we left. We weren't going to chop cotton anymore."

Gilbert went to work for a dry cleaner, but he didn't like it much. Then it was back to the fields. He listened to the old-timers talk about earlier strikes. He saw some melon workers sit down on the job until they got the wages they wanted. He remembered his mother's stories. He got interested in politics. When more braceros came during the Korean War and drove wages down further, he went back to the job at the dry cleaner, but he still didn't like it. He joined an old *mutualista* and tried to revive its burial insurance plan. He was looking for a fight, looking to learn how to do it, listening to everybody with a plan. In 1955 he met Cesar Chavez. Chavez had a plan.

4

The Lay Catholic Activist

Cesar Chavez left the North Gila Valley with two other treasures besides his memories. Although he had not liked school, he had become a good, quick learner out of the classroom. One uncle taught him to read Spanish; another read him the Mexican newspapers. A classic autodidact, throughout his life he would suck up one subject after another, move from one enthusiasm to the next: the art of shooting pool, Catholic Social Action, the theory and practice of Saul Alinsky, the life of Gandhi, the history of unionism in the fields, the varieties of religious experience, the intricacies of labor law, printing, faith healing, the Synanon Game, theories of scientific management. His biographer Jacques Levy, who was also a dog trainer and helped Chavez train his two dogs, told me that Cesar was the most absorbed, committed student of dog training he had ever met. Chavez read, he questioned, he listened, he learned.

Just as Cesar did not learn to read in school, he did not learn religion in church. There was no church in the North Gila Valley; his mother taught him his first prayers, as well as the power of charity and nonviolence. The spiritual leader of the family, she transformed a folk Catholicism filled with Mexican *dichos* (popular aphorisms) into a rough moral sensibility that helped the Chavezes through their tough times. Her improvised ethical code was backed up by the formal Catholicism of Cesar's grandmother, who had spent time in a convent; she taught the children Latin prayers and Bible stories. Chavez's religious faith would not be shaken by the loss of his childhood or by his family's trials. In Brawley, a regular stop on the migrant circuit, he was a *crucero*, an altar boy, who helped the priest celebrate Mass. Nor did his mild adolescent rebellion—it didn't amount to much more than *pachuco*-style clothes and a taste for jazz—ever interfere with his devotion to the Church. Many years later he said, "I don't think that I could base my will to struggle on cold economics or on some political doctrine. I don't think there would be enough to sustain me. For me the base must be faith."[1]

So it is not at all odd that a Roman Catholic priest was the one who introduced Chavez to politics in 1950. At twenty-three years old, Cesar was a World War II vet trying to make his way in the world. He had joined the Navy when he was seventeen, "mostly to get away from farm labor," he told Levy. Two years later, in 1946, after serving as a deck hand in the Pacific and a painter in Guam, he was discharged. Like Gilbert Padilla, he was uncomfortable in the fields after the war. He worked in cantaloupes, grapes, cotton, and apricots. He tried his hand at celery, where he could have earned higher wages, but he didn't have a buddy on the crew to help him, and he couldn't learn it fast enough. "Oh my God it was awful," he said. "I couldn't keep up with the crew . . . I was soft. I quit about ten-thirty . . . It was animal like."[2]

In 1948 he married Helen Fabela, a girl from a farm worker family in Delano. On their honeymoon they toured the California Missions, from Sonoma to San Diego. They set up house in Delano but soon moved to San Jose, where Chavez's brother Richard had a steady job on an apricot farm and could get Cesar part-time work in the orchards. Chavez walked the streets looking for some job away from the fields but found nothing. Trying to escape low wages, he, his father, and Richard share-cropped strawberries for two seasons, but they could have earned more picking someone else's berries. Soon two babies, one son and one daughter, arrived. Cesar was now a family man, unsure of how he was going to make a living and what he wanted to do with his life.[3]

When Father Donald McDonnell knocked on his door, wearing a Roman collar and speaking a scholar's Spanish, Cesar was inclined to listen. When Father McDonnell explained that he was trying to set up a church in San Jose's Mexican barrio, Chavez, who attended Mass at a Portuguese parish across town, was enthusiastic. Teacher and student had met.[4]

McDonnell quickly understood that his new student did not need to be brought into the bosom of the Church. What was lacking, and what McDonnell was particularly able to provide, was the connection between Catholic faith and politics. The injustice of the world had been seared into Cesar's heart when his childhood toys were replaced by a short-handled hoe, but the great disjunction between the world of the North Gila Valley and the world of California seemed impossible to remedy. What Chavez had seen of politics had not impressed him. He had been on the periphery of union struggles in the late 1930s that had ended in defeat. Strikes seemed to be all symbolic show; union leaders were remote, union politics filled with debilitating internal disputes. His father's willingness to walk off the job when slighted or in defense of others who had been mistreated was fine and dignified, but it changed nothing. One could hope to get out of the fields, but Chavez saw no basis for any hope in the fields, and without hope there could be no politics.

Father McDonnell was a professional of political hope. He was only five years older than Cesar, not yet thirty, but he spoke with the authority of a priest and the confidence of an intellectual who had worked on his ideas and was not just repeating a memorized doctrine. He had learned those ideas the conventional way, in school, from a favorite teacher and in the company of fellow, similarly inspired, students. At St. Patrick's Seminary in Menlo Park, Father Joseph Munier taught the basic course in Catholic Social Action, which included careful readings of Pope Leo XIII's 1891 encyclical, Rerum Novarum ("Of New Things"), and Pius XI's 1931 encyclical, Quadragesimo Anno ("In the Fortieth Year"). McDonnell considered, discussed, debated, and worried over the encyclicals. He prayed for understanding. He and a few others formed a study group, "a seminary within the seminary," to consider Munier's teachings. They studied Spanish.

When he was ordained in 1947 and sent to San Jose, McDonnell tried to put those ideas into practice. He kept in close touch with Father Thomas McCullough, a childhood friend and seminary mate and who was trying to do the same in Stockton. Their pastoral duties were mainly in the Mexican barrios. McCullough got involved in a tomato strike, while McDonnell spent a lot of time at bracero camps. Their early experiences were encouraging. In 1948, the two went to Archbishop John J. Mitty of the San Francisco diocese and asked to be released from their territorially based parishes so that they could work exclusively with Mexican farm laborers in central and northern California. Mitty granted their request, and four members of St. Patrick's "seminary within the seminary" became the Spanish-speaking Mission Band. Their ministry continued for twelve years, until 1962.[5]

When Chavez first met McDonnell, the priest "sat with me past midnight telling me about social justice and the Church's stand on farm labor and reading from the encyclicals of Pope Leo XIII in which he upheld labor unions. I would do anything to get the Father to tell me more about labor history. I began going to the bracero camps with him to help with Mass, to the city jail with him to talk to prisoners, anything to be with him so that he could tell me more about the farm labor movement." The lessons went on for months, and their relationship went on for years. Father McDonnell, Chavez said, "radically changed my life."[6]

If there is a geometry of the soul, and if we could look at Chavez's soul in 1950 before he met Father McDonnell, we would see two strong parallel lines, one marked "Catholic faith" and the other "anger at injustice." Most of Cesar Chavez was bracketed by those two lines: Catholic faith up above, close to the surface, and easy to see; anger at injustice down below, hidden from sight. The lines were parallel; they were not contradictory, but they could never meet. Chavez was not torn between the two, stretched apart as if upon a medieval rack. It was not a tortured man who met Father McDonnell at the door. It was just that Catholic faith and social justice had little to do with one another. His mother's religious charity resonated between the lines, but Chavez knew that charity was not nearly strong enough to right the wrong that his family had suffered in the fields. Father McDonnell rearranged the lines. Catholic faith, Father McDonnell argued, had everything to do with social justice. Traveling the streets of the San Jose barrio, Sal Si Puedes, in his collar and black suit, he carried four pictures with him to make his point: a worker's shack and a grower's mansion; a grower's labor camp and the high-priced San Francisco apartment building owned by that same grower. Catholics had the power and duty to right this wrong, McDonnell argued, and he had the encyclicals to back him up.

Rerum Novarum and Leo XIII's four encyclicals that lead up to it, although not without antecedents in the thought of Aquinas, were a significant departure in Catholic doctrine. Since the fifteenth century the official church had unstintingly condemned the contemporary world, and Catholic doctrine was mostly about protecting the power, claims, and prerogatives of the heavenly city in the face of the growing secular one. This trend had been neatly summed up by Leo's immediate predecessor, Pius IX, who detailed his condemnation of all things modern in his Syllabus of Errors. Leo, however, without surrendering the Church's jurisdiction over matters of the soul, called on Catholics to participate in solving the world's social, economic, and political problems. By the time he issued Rerum Novarum, in 1891, those problems, especially the problems of the European proletariat, were plain to see.[7]

Rerum Novarum begins with an acknowledgment of the raging class war between the "rich" and the "proletariat." It moves quickly to a defense of private property, an attack on socialism, a call for charity from the rich, and an appeal to the proletariat to form worker associations, preferably Catholic ones. This last point was a direct intervention in a contemporary debate about whether European Catholic workers should join unions, and if they should, whether they should join existing unions or form their own Christian ones. Leo's words on the subject of unions (he always called them "associations") continued to be cited more than a hundred years later by Catholics engaged in union struggles, although his most significant contributions were his emphasis on "social justice" and his assertion that Catholics, both clergy and laity, had not only a legitimate right but a positive duty to struggle for it. His entire argument was logically presented, and the encyclical, although virtually ignored by secular intellectuals, became an influential popular manifesto, combining an argument against socialism with a call for proletarian political action.

Leo's argument is that production and trade have been brought under the power of a "very few exceedingly rich men," who have "laid a yoke almost of slavery on the unnumbered masses of non-owning workers." Socialists take advantage of the situation by proposing commonly owned property, administered by the state in the interests of the workers. This is wrong because property is a natural right inherent in the natural differences among men. Justice, however, requires that each man earn a high enough wage to provide "a life without hardship" for his wife and family. Justice can be achieved only when the rich, the state, the employers, the workers, and the Church properly understand and carry out their duties and obligations. The rich have the duty of charity; the state has the duty to establish regulations about working hours, rest times, child labor, and housing; the employers have the duty to pay a decent family wage; the workers have the duty to join together in associations for their mutual benefit and to behave themselves properly; and the Church has the duty to teach everyone else their duties, and thus to guide society away from the debilitating war between the classes, and to the natural harmony of all.

The encyclical closes with a description of the essential character of the new worker associations. It is the culmination of Leo's argument, his answer to Lenin's question of a decade later, "What is to be done?". The associations are of "first importance," Leo writes, and are the instrument through which the workers "will rise from their most wretched state and enjoy better conditions." But securing these better conditions, necessary to social justice, is not the primary purpose of the new associations. Within them, Catholic clergy and laity must guide workers to the conduct necessary for eternal salvation. Leo is unbending on that issue: "It is clear . . . that moral and religious perfection ought to be regarded as [the associations'] principal goal . . . [for] what would it profit a worker to secure through an association an abundance of goods, if his soul through lack of its proper food should run the risk of perishing?" Thus, workers must refrain from "violence and rioting." They must not injure the property of others. They must not associate with socialists, "vicious men who craftily hold out exaggerated hopes and make huge promises . . . usually ending in vain regrets and the destruction of wealth." Finally, Leo pragmatically observes that the workers' righteous behavior is not only good for the soul, it is also good strategy. It will move the conscience of the rich and mobilize the resources of the state. Leo cites the early Christians as models: "Yet destitute of wealth and power, they succeeded in winning the good will of the rich and the protection of the mighty."

Rerum Novarum provided papal authority for what came to be called Catholic Social Action, and for the next seventy-five years, up until Vatican II, the encyclical served as the basis for Catholic social doctrine. But Leo's absolute opposition to socialism and his call for the reform of capitalism provided a large space for serious disagreement over theory, strategy, and tactics. In Europe, Catholic liberals and worker priests, citing Leo XIII, helped build Christian unions and worked to reform capitalism. Catholic conservatives, also citing Leo, developed the idea of harmony into a full-fledged corporatism, and flirted (or worse) with fascism, especially in Spain,

Portugal, and Italy. In the midst of worldwide Depression, Pius XI's Quadragesimo Anno, in 1931, built on Leo's thought while stretching the space for disagreement to the left with its emphasis on the "social character of ownership," its warning against individualism, and its assertion that "the right ordering of economic life cannot be left to a free competition of forces."[8]

In the United States, the Church received special dispensation to participate in "neutral" unions rather than to build separate Christian ones, and Catholic activists both helped build the labor movement and later joined the attack against Communists that so debilitated the CIO after World War II. The Reverend Joseph Ryan, a principal architect of the 1919 Bishops' Program of Social Reconstruction, which called for a minimum wage, subsidized housing, labor participation in industrial management, child labor laws, and social insurance thirteen years before "New Deal" was even a slogan, later used Leo XIII as a papal shield against conservative Catholic opposition to Franklin Roosevelt's program. Reverend Charles Coughlin— the popular radio priest who deserted FDR in 1934, defended the Nazis, and blamed the Depression on Jewish bankers—also was a great proponent of Rerum Novarum. The warring radio appeals of Ryan and Coughlin in the mid-1930s set the outer limits of clergy-approved left and right Catholic opinion during the Depression, but Coughlin's trajectory alone maps the territory: in the name of opposition to Bolshevism and in support of the reform of capitalism, he moved easily from early Roosevelt champion to Roosevelt enemy without ever deserting the ideas of Leo XIII.[9]

Cesar Chavez would come to use Rerum Novarum in the same general way as other lay Catholic activists of the left: as doctrinal justification for building a workers' organization. But for Chavez, Leo provided more than just papal support for his organizing work. When Chavez formed the Farm Workers Association in 1962, the precursor of the UFW, he called it an "association," not a "Union." Its potential members, California farm workers, were almost all Catholics, and Cesar Chavez's piety was used as a way to attract and recruit them. Catholic symbols and ideology dominated the association's, and then later the UFW's, presentation of itself, to both farm workers and potential supporters. Membership in the organizations was not meant to be just about earning better wages and improved benefits; it was supposed to be good for the soul. Cesar Chavez insisted on this last point. In the struggle, farm workers would learn the virtues of sacrifice, and through sacrifice would become better people, closer to God. Even UFW strategy was leonine: the exemplary conduct of the farm workers in struggle was meant to mobilize the good will of the more fortunate and win over the protection of the state.

The hand of Leo was not only manifest in the organization, it also shaped the internal life of the UFW leader. Rerum Novarum, as taught by Father McDonnell, not only connected the two central claims on Cesar's soul—loyalty to his mother's religion and anger about his childhood disaster—but also was a basis for his famous will and intensity of purpose, a certainty that if not God (and maybe even He) then at least the Pope was on his side.

One other religious influence was formative for Chavez in this period before the founding of the union: *cursillismo*. The cursillo movement was begun on the island of Mallorca in 1932 by the young men's branch of Acción Católica and was firmly entrenched within the right wing of organizations inspired by Leo XIII. The *Cursillos de Christiandad* were developed by the young laymen to inspire adolescent men in preparation for a pilgrimage to Santiago de Compostela, the Church of St. James in Compostela in northwestern Spain. The actual pilgrimage was delayed first by the Spanish Civil War, then by World War II, and didn't take place until 1948, by which time the *cursillos*, formalized during the period of waiting, had taken on a life of their own as instruments of religious renewal, and Acción Católica had become a major supporter of the Franco counterrevolution. In the 1950s the *cursillos* jumped to the old Spanish colonies of Latin America and the Philippines. They hit the United States in 1957, brought over by a pair of Spanish air cadets being trained by the U.S. Air Force in Waco, Texas.[10]

In the United States *cursillismo* affirmed a specifically Spanish-rooted Catholicism for Latinos, especially Puerto Ricans and Mexicans, who until then had not found a comfortable home within the institutional Church, dominated as it was by Irish Catholic clergy. *Cursillo* activists, both priests and laymen, brought Spanish liturgy, Latino folk music, and popular cultural traditions into regular church services. A form of Catholic Pentecostalism, it nevertheless always enjoyed a relationship of mutual support with church authorities. Like the Catholic Mass and other rituals, the *cursillo* itself is a highly structured experience where, according to one of the movement's two most important leaders, Juan Hervas, "nothing is trusted to improvisation." Similarly, the Cursillo Movement (the name has now been trademarked) is directed by a tightly structured organization, where absolute authority resides in a spiritual director appointed by the head of the local diocese. He in turn works through a local secretariat made up predominantly of laypeople.[11]

Cesar Chavez did his *cursillo* in the late 1950s or early '60s, according to his brother Richard.[12] Richard's uncertainty about the date comes from the air of secrecy that surrounded the early *cursillos*, and from Chavez's own subsequent reluctance to talk about his commitment to the movement. The *cursillo* is a four-day experience, which a person goes through only once. The initiate has to be invited by a veteran who has remained active in post-*cursillo* activities. Each potential participant also has to be approved by the regional secretariat. He must have been baptized, should be a stable adult between the ages of twenty-five and fifty-five, not be going through any emotional crisis, and be either an actual or a potential leader in the community. Although women can make a *cursillo* separate from men—but wives cannot go through the experience unless their husbands have done so first—the movement's emphasis has always been on making Christianity a "manly" activity.

The four days are heavily rehearsed events. A leadership group of ten people, a mixture of clergy and laity, takes a few months to prepare for a *cursillo* that will intiate forty new members. On the first day, the initiates, thinking they are on a semiconventional Catholic retreat, are asked to meditate on their own sinfulness. They are prohibited from talking to one another, and all efforts are directed toward making them feel helpless and lonely. The first meditation is introduced like this: "Would you like to have the true story of your life filmed? Would you be able to view all your actions, your ambitions, your pretenses, your conversations on the screen without blushing? Would you want your friends to be present at the showing: Would you want your children, your mother, your wife, your sweetheart to know it?" The following three days are meant to resurrect the sinners, through singing, gifts, relaxed conversation, joyful witness in small groups, and a final meeting with family and friends, who welcome the revived initiates into the company of *cursillo*. It is all meant to produce an atmosphere of intimate spirituality, and characteristically the new *cursillistas* express feeling "joy," "euphoria," and "a new enthusiasm for life."[13]

The new recruits then join the "army of militant Christians" who will combat the enemy of "lifeless Christianity." The military language is quite pronounced in *cursillista* manuals. According to Hervas the *cursillista* mission is "(a) to look for militants; (b) to choose them; (c) to welcome them; (d) to train them; (e) to use them."[14] How to use them is not as clear as the injunction to use them. *Cursillistas* learn that in a good Christian life, "piety and study are the inhale, and action is the exhale." A committed *cursillista* is expected to participate in follow-up weekly events with his fellow initiates and in monthly events with a wider group; to take responsibility for leading new retreats; and to participate in regular church activities with a new spiritual intensity. But what to do in the world, beyond becoming a better Christian and a *cursillo* leader, is left undefined.

Chavez participated in follow-up *cursillo* events after his initiation and ultimately used *cursillismo*'s silence on what the new initiates should do to his own organizational advantage. UFW organizers recruited farm workers from *cursillo* groups, sometimes even waiting for them as they left the last meeting of the four-day course, so that, in the words of Brother Keith Warner, they could "pluck fish from the river as they flowed out of the *cursillo*."[15] *Cursillo* leaders, both clergy and laymen, came to the aid of the early UFW while the more conservative Catholic bishops remained uncommitted. For a while, support for the UFW became the "exhale" of action for many *cursillistas*. The *cursillista* theme song, "De Colores," became the UFW anthem.

Both *cursillismo* and Catholic Social Action assumed the existence of hierarchies within both the Church and society. The *cursillista* rhetoric of forming an "army" for Christ had its analogue among the legions of clergy who answered the call expressed in Rerum Novarum to work for social justice. Armies, like the Catholic Church, are not characteristically egalitarian. They depend on the willing submission of the lesser to the higher orders—as did Leo XIII. The word "democracy" does not appear in Rerum Novarum. To leave no doubt about his intentions, Leo followed that encyclical with another, Graves de Communi Re ("On Christian Democracy"), in which he warned that all Catholic initiatives in the secular world should be "formed under Episcopal authority," and instructed Catholic clergy to be vigilant "lest any under the pretext of good should cause the vigor of sacred discipline to be relaxed." In the United States, clerical advocates of Rerum Novarum on the left and the right fully accepted hierarchical prerogative.[16]

Chavez did not see anything contradictory in his commitment to both social justice and institutional hierarchy. His mixture of Mexican folk Catholicism, *cursillismo*, and the progressive tradition of Leo XIII was not shaken by Pope John XXIII's sweeping move for democratic reform in the church by means of Vatican II. Although Chavez's commitment to farm workers and the poor came before John's 1961 encyclical, Mater et Magistra, and the subsequent articulations of liberation theology, Chavez never got interested in the work of low-level Catholic priests and Catholic laity in the slums of Brazil and the rural areas of Mexico and Central America. His autodidacticism led him to an idiosyncratic study of widely diverse political leaders and their theories of society and social change: St. Paul, Gandhi, John L. Lewis, Eugene Debs, Machiavelli, Charles Dietrich, Peter Drucker. None of the Latin American Catholic revolutionaries of the post–Vatican II era—Gustavo Gutierrez, the Peruvian priest who was the main theoretician of liberation theology; Camilo Torres, the Mexican revolutionary priest of the late 1960s; Ernesto Cardenal and other Central American Catholics who were so important in the Nicaraguan revolution—made their way onto Chavez's reading list.[17]

To a certain extent this was a matter of political convenience. After the brief spring of Catholic liberation theology, the low-level clergy who challenged church hierarchy often got themselves in serious trouble with their religious superiors. Chavez could not afford to be a religious rebel, as he was in the process of building a coalition that included the American Catholic hierarchy. But it was more than convenience. Chavez's Catholic politics did not wander into the uncharted shores of post–Vatican II thought but instead remained where they had been formed, in Leo XIII's combination of commitment to social justice, opposition to socialism, and acceptance of hierarchy.

Two years after they met, Father McDonnell passed Chavez on to the second man whom Chavez would later say "radically changed my life," the community organizer Fred Ross. By then Cesar and his brother Richard had changed their own lives. Anxious to get out of the fields, they had gone with their cousin Manuel to Crescent City, near the California-Oregon border, where they found work as lumberjacks. No one liked the cold weather, so soon they and their families were all back in San Jose. Richard went to work as an apprentice carpenter and Cesar got a job in a lumberyard. They were no longer farm workers.

The sojourn in Crescent City did not diminish Cesar's interest in Father McDonnell. Back in San Jose, Chavez continued to visit McDonnell and help him with his work. When Fred Ross came to town to set up a voter registration campaign among Mexican Americans under the auspices of the American Friends Service Committee, Ross asked McDonnell, the local Spanish-speaking priest, if he knew anyone who might be interested in working on such a project. McDonnell suggested Chavez. Ross had to be persistent, as Chavez was suspicious of the white organizer and tried to duck him. But Ross finally worked his way into the Chavez household, and Cesar's confidence.

For the next ten years, Ross would be Chavez's immediate supervisor,the man who would train him to be a professional organizer and who would be the principal architect of the Community Service Organization (CSO)for which they both worked. Some of those who met Cesar Chavez after his apprenticeship with Ross never appreciated the extent to which Chavez remained a lay Catholic leader. They admired his shrewd, plainspoken, yet sophisticated understanding of political power and his single-minded drive to achieve it. They could see the political purpose of all the religious imagery he would employ but not the religious conviction behind it. They figured that Chavez's Catholicism was little more than another tool in building the union.

That was a large misunderstanding. In the tradition of Catholic Social Action there is little contradiction between a full engagement in the game of politics and a deep sense of religious faith. The good Christian can be, in the ancient counsel of St. Matthew that was Chavez's favorite biblical citation, "as wise as the serpent and as gentle as the dove." Chavez was precisely that, serpent and dove. Ultimately he worked out the contradictions that do exist between piety and politics in his own unique, dramatic way, but only after a long series of secular political battles. He was taught how to wage those battles by Fred Ross and by Ross's boss in the CSO years, a man who was a master at bringing religious people into the world of power politics, the political wizard, Saul Alinsky.

The Alchemist

Saul Alinsky started doing politics in the late 1930s amid the enthusiasm of the Popular Front and CIO organizing. His ability to thrive despite a series of attacks from Chicago's political bosses during World War II, plus the eventual antifascist victory in Europe and Japan, deepened his optimism and patriotism. Strike victories by his close allies in the United Packing House Workers of America at most of Chicago's slaughterhouses right after the war confirmed the value of the work he had been doing in the city's white ethnic Back of the Yards district. His 1946 best seller, *Reveille for Radicals*, propelled him to national prominence. When the Popular Front collapsed in the early years of the cold war, Alinsky refused to cooperate with government repression of the Communist Party or the persecution of individual reds, but promoted his own political ideas as the best way to combat Communism, once even traveling to the Vatican to advise the Catholic hierarchy on how to defeat Communist Party trade unions in Italy.

By the early fifties, Alinsky had found an idiosyncratic non-Communist niche, and he continued to be the chief theoretician and sometimes active protagonist of several community organizing projects. The early New Left was attracted by his non-Communist stance and emphasis on democratic values. Later, however, as the student and black movements of the 1960s shifted away from community organizing, Alinskyism positioned itself as an alternative to New Left politics. Eventually, in the late 1970s and '80s, Alinsky's followers and his left (both old and new) antagonists would all wonder whether the Alinskyite community organizations that continued to flourish after his death, in 1972, were even a part of the left tradition.

That debate has not weakened Alinsky's influence on American politics, which remains strong. More than 150 community organizations throughout the country were originally sponsored, promoted, and organized by openly Alinskyite organizing centers. Alinsky's fingerprints are also all over the progressive movements within the Protestant and Catholic churches. His voice still echoes in the strategy sessions of activist officials in contemporary organized labor. Finally, famously, the first African American president had his first taste of big-city politics while working for an Alinsky-inspired organization.

For any set of ideas, eighty years of political relevance is quite an achievement and cannot be dismissed as merely a reflection of the particular pragmatic adaptability of Alinskyism. And there is an "Alinskyism." With Saul as the fountainhead, community organizing has become a codified discipline, with core theoretical propositions, recognized heresies, disciples, fallen neophytes, and splits. It is a political theory, with the emphasis on the political, and Alinsky is the grand theorist.

Heather Booth, founder of the Midwest Academy, one of the many Alinskyite centers where organizers are trained, calls Alinsky "our Sigmund Freud." What Booth means is that both Freud and Alinsky founded schools of thought, but there is another, deeper link: the role of training and lineage. Just as psychoanalysts trace their pedigree back to the grand master (they were either analyzed by Freud or by someone who was analyzed by Freud, or by someone who was analyzed by someone who . . .), so Alinskyite and neo-Alinskyite organizers trace their training back to Alinsky himself. And just as the psychoanalyst in training gains knowledge of the discipline through an examination of his or her own personal experience, guided by the skillful questioning of the analyst and a consideration of case histories, the ideal Alinskyite training places a would-be organizer out in the field, systematically analyzing his or her own political experience, with the help of the more experienced, theoretically advanced trainer, who teaches through a combination of stories and questions. Although there are some schools of neo-Alinskyism that attempt to train novice organizers in six weeks, arming them with neat, codified summations of Alinskyite technique, traditionalists, such as Mike Miller of San Francisco, continue to insist that it takes at least three years to train a professional organizer.

Cesar Chavez was trained for ten years. His chief teacher, Fred Ross, although not exactly an Alinsky trainee, was one of the first people on Alinsky's payroll and an early practitioner of Alinsky-style community organizing. Chavez watched Ross work and was watched by him; he filed weekly and sometimes daily reports to Ross and to Alinsky's Industrial Areas Foundation (IAF). He studied *Reveille for Radicals*. He read and reread Alinsky's 1949 biography of John L. Lewis.[1] The group Chavez worked for, the Community Service Organization, was Alinsky's most successful early project outside Chicago. During Alinsky's regular visits to California, which often lasted several weeks, Chavez worked alongside the master in formal trainings, conferences, and fundraising events.

There was no training manual, but the training was systematic and included written critiques of the obligatory work reports. These were serious people doing serious work, making their living doing politics. Not a fabulous living, but after 1953, a respectable one. Alinsky signed both Fred

Ross's and Cesar Chavez's checks. Not everything that Alinsky and Ross taught Chavez in the years between his twenty-fifth and thirty-fifth birthdays stuck, but understanding Alinskyism is one way of making sense of Cesar Chavez and the foundational architecture of the United Farm Workers.

Alinsky could sign the checks for Ross and Chavez because Alinskyism was funded—no small matter for promoting a political discipline. The money came from liquor. Alinsky's first major benefactor was the Emil Schwarzhaupt Foundation, especially its executive director, Carl Tjerandsen. Schwarzhaupt was a German-Jewish immigrant who had made his fortune in Chicago. He had worked as a clerk in the liquor industry, and made some money buying and selling warehouse inventories. Anticipating Prohibition, he stockpiled those inventories before 1919 and then sold them through some "partners" for "medicinal purposes" during the 1920s. He came out of Prohibition with enough capital to set up the National Distillers Corporation, which he eventually sold to the Schenley Corporation. When setting up his foundation, Schwarzhaupt stipulated that his money be given away within twenty-five years of his death, as it was incumbent upon each generation to solve its own political problems, including its funding challenges.[2]

Schwarzhaupt died in 1950, and Tjerandsen, the executive secretary of the foundation, gave most of the old man's money away so fast that almost all of the $3.5 million was gone before 1962. Tjerandsen gave fairly large chunks to just a few groups, relatively unknown at the time, among them the Highlander Folk School, the Southern Christian Leadership Conference, and the Migrant Ministry; but the main recipient was Alinsky's Industrial Areas Foundation. Starting in April 1953, the IAF received a direct grant of $150,000, which in the next ten years expanded to $608,486. More money went to other organizations and groups that had ties to Alinsky but were not directly funded by the IAF. Add it all up, and over a twelve-year period of intense giving nearly $3 million of Schwarzhaupt's fortune went to fund Alinskyism.[3]

Fortuna also played her part. Carl Tjerandsen was a graduate student at the University of Chicago when he was appointed to the Committee on Education for American Citizenship, which had been created to decide, in the most general terms, how to spend Schwarzhaupt's money. The sociologist Louis Wirth headed the committee. Alinsky and Wirth played poker together. Tjerandsen was a friend of both. Without both Wirth and Tjerandsen, Alinsky might not have made his way to the money. He had already been turned down by a dozen potential funders, including the Rockefeller and Ford foundations. He was neither a social worker nor an academic, and in the early fifties, liberal, corporate foundation money primarily went to institutional intellectuals or charity operations.

After Tjerandsen had given away most of the money, he remained a part-time director of the foundation and moved on to the University of California at Santa Cruz, where he kept up his interest in questions of democratic political participation, sponsoring conferences and retreats where the people who had received Schwarzhaupt Foundation funds were encouraged to discuss their work. Alinsky came to most of those events, established a second residence in the nearby Carmel Highlands, and made California one of his regular stops. Chavez had plenty of direct contact with him, much of it sponsored by Tjerandsen. Those connections made others possible, between Chavez and the young Protestant clergy who made up the Migrant Ministry, Chavez and the New York Union Theological Seminary, Chavez and the United Packing House Workers, Chavez and the National Council of Churches. All of them would be important to him for the rest of his life. But it wasn't just, or even mainly, the infrastructure of Alinskyism that secured for Saul Alinsky a place in Chavez's small pantheon of heroes; it was Alinsky's ideas.

Born to immigrant, working-class Russian Orthodox Jews in 1909, Saul Alinsky begins *Reveille for Radicals* with a hymn to multiracial, multicultural, multiethnic working-class America. Written between the summers of 1944 and '45, the first pages have the feel of triumphant World War II movies, where the heroic Army platoon includes representatives of various ethnicities: GIs and full-fledged Americans all. Alinsky adds to that mix Negroes, whom the army had segregated and the Hollywood movies had left out. Among this nation of beautiful cultural complexity are a few radicals who belong, according to the Jeffersonian typology that Alinsky affectionately quotes, to one of the two opposing parties that have existed throughout world history: the democrats, who trust the people and want to spread political power among them, and the aristocrats, who fear and distrust the people and want power to remain in the hands of the upper classes.[4]

Although Alinsky often merges the radical and the democrat, for him they are theoretically distinct: radicals are the politically active democrats, who historically have led the struggles—sometimes revolutionary, sometimes not—for democratic power. The essential Alinsky argument is that in the postwar period the radical must become a new kind of leader, a community organizer, who creates but does not exactly lead a new kind of organization. What happens between the organizer and the community is an art, which cannot be reduced to method, but when it works it produces a successful organization, and an organization is the key to power. Without organization there is no power. Without the organizer, there is no organization.

Who is this contemporary radical and what does he believe? In the first pages of *Reveille for Radicals*, Alinsky describes the principles of the radical democrat, a hodge-podge of Popular Front and Enlightenment ideas, with an emphasis on "trusting" or even "loving" real people in all their complexities, plus the insistence that democracy comes from "the bottom up." The list of the radical's convictions begins with the belief that all people should have high standards of "food, housing, and health," that "human rights" are more important than "property rights," and goes on to mention "full employment," "real equality of opportunity," "local rights" (so long as they don't become a cover for "Tory reaction"), "social planning" (so long as it is not "top down"), and various New Deal slogans of the left variety. Early in the book he lists as a radical democratic belief the "hope for a future where the means of economic production will be owned by all of the people instead of just a comparative handful," yet in the book's last pages he calls for a new American democracy based on a rejuvenated "organized labor, organized business, and organized religion." The contradiction between "owned by all the people" and a central role for organized business doesn't count for much. What the radical believes is just an incantation; there is no real attempt to analyze the connections, or possible contradictions, between its various goals and principles. And even if it is possible to characterize the early Alinsky as some kind of social democrat, the "social" part of the formulation was always secondary, always the adjective. Democrat was the noun, the central idea.

Of more consequence to him is the line separating the radical from the liberal. Although he doesn't argue the point explicitly, he identifies liberalism with an effete middle-class approach to politics, while radicalism is real, rough, plain-talking, unadorned working-class democracy. Nevertheless the difference is not primarily an issue of class or belief but the fact that the radical, unlike the liberal, is a political fighter and that liberals are afraid of power, while radicals know that ordinary people wielding power is what democracy is all about.

After this cursory attempt to establish a philosophical basis to his politics, Alinsky gets down to what he does best: strategy. American radicals, he argues, have joined the rest of the world's radicals in throwing their main energy into organizing the labor movement. That is sensible, he argues, because the constituency of the American labor movement is not just another "interest" but the overwhelming majority of the American people. Nonetheless, there is a problem: "As labor unions have become strong, wealthy, fat, and respectable, they have behaved more like organized business," and are in danger of losing their original democratic purpose.[5]

This formulation, unlike Alinsky's earlier list of radical beliefs, was in 1946 an important departure within Popular Front thinking. *Reveille for Radicals* was published before *New Men of Power*, C. Wright Mills's critique of top union leaders, and although Alinsky's ideas share some similarities to earlier Communist critiques of the American Federation of Labor (AFL), this was not the way most of his left contemporaries talked and wrote about the CIO. During World War II Alinsky had worked with the War Manpower Commission in what his principal biographer, Stanford Horwitt, calls "efforts to maintain worker morale and harmony in key industries, such as in defense plants."[6] In the course of that work, Alinsky got a first-hand view of the new collaboration between industry managers, union leaders, and government officials, who often fought a united battle against rank-and-file initiative and shop-floor control of production, at the same time as they were imposing union contracts in some industries and helping unions become thoroughly institutionalized in others.[7] This collaboration was a first step in the remaking of much of the top CIO leadership into "new men of power," who by the time the war ended had lost what little contact they once had with the rank and file. Alinsky was astute enough to see this as it was happening, and to raise a warning cry.

What to do about a labor movement that is becoming corrupt and anti-democratic? Abandon it? Alinsky answers that suggestion with a quip: "The fault with the American radical is not that he chose to make his bed in the labor movement but that he fell asleep in it."[8] The radical's job is to reawaken the democratic promise of unionism by building community organizations, made up of labor unions and other community groups, whose own struggles for power in the neighborhood will renew union (and American) democracy. How to do this is what *Reveille for Radicals* is all about. Another obvious alternative—for workers to fight within their unions for democratic union-ism—is not even mentioned. Instead, the solution to union corruption is to build a new kind of community organization, what Alinsky dubbed, using capital letters, a People's Organization.*

Unions, Alinsky argues, are languishing precisely because they have insti-tutional power. Through ritualized contract negotiations they can win higher wages without the active participation of their members. The People's Organization, or PO—an organization of pre-existing organizations, includ-ing local unions—is designed to resolve that. To fight for the community's agenda, it must propel people into action because, unlike the unions, the PO does not have established, formal power. It can win new parks or youth recreation programs or rent control or some other demand only if people are willing to become politically active. Since the unions are a part of the PO, the community battles involve union members, too. Political activity in the community then carries over into the unions, restores internal democracy, and saves them from corruption. Argument complete.

---

* In the sixty-three years since Alinsky wrote *Reveille for Radicals*, unions have lost much of what strength they had as well as much of their attraction for would-be radi-cals; most contemporary Alinskyites no longer place them at the center of their concerns. They still build People's Organizations, but most often the core groups of a PO are religious congregations rather than unions.

Despite Alinsky's rhetorical accent on democracy, this approach left Cesar Chavez ill-equipped to think about the actual dynamics of union democracy. In making his case, Alinsky does not go beyond the idea that civic participation in the PO will spill over into nearby unions. Just as Alinsky never considered the idea that union members would wage a direct battle for union democracy, he is uninterested in the kinds of internal union structures that might make democratic unionism more likely. That was a road Alinsky chose not to take in either his book or his political practice, perhaps because it would have upset the few union chiefs who were among his early supporters. Alinsky has no discussion of the potential power of independent union locals; nothing about encouraging rank-and-file debate, political education, and contested elections; no comment on how union conventions might take up issues of real concern to their members. None of that was in Cesar Chavez's intellectual arsenal; all of it was missing from the UFW.

In his biography of John L. Lewis, the book he wrote right after he finished *Reveille for Radicals*, Alinsky was even worse on the question of internal union democracy. Here, in a book that Chavez read and reread and gave as a gift, Alinsky championed Lewis's destruction of independent locals in the United Mine Workers of America, arguing that eliminating their power was essential to all that Lewis accomplished on the national scene.

Part II of *Reveille for Radicals* is mostly a string of Alinsky stories, highly fictionalized tales of how he organized the Back of the Yards Neighborhood Council and a few other partly real, mostly imaginary People's Organizations. The stories make good reading, but they are not as delectable as the story-teller seems to believe. Most of Alinsky's friends would agree with Fred Ross's assessment: "Saul could tell a better story than he could write it. He gave it certain inflections and body language, and he was great with a deadpan delivery." Also, harsher standards apply to the written word. Alinsky's publisher insisted that he leave out most of the real names, thus denying the reader part of what made the spoken stories so enjoyable: the inside dope on some famous people, and how the wily community organizer outwitted them.

Alinsky's stories were not merely enjoyable, however. They were the essential vehicle through which he conveyed his political knowledge. Alinsky insisted on a few general principles of organizing, but beyond those principles and guidelines about the structure of a PO, there are just his stories and whatever lessons they might suggest. Alinsky is a political actor more than a grand theorist; he is immersed in particular, specific problems, and his knowledge of the complexity of those problems seems to over-whelm his capacity to make big theories about what he is doing. He would rather just tell us a few aphorisms and describe some of his tricks.

Not that Alinsky is unable to theorize; rather, he is unwilling.

Overtheorizing, coming into a community with a full set of abstract notions about what the people should do, is both a violation of his democratic principles and monumentally impractical. It won't work. The people have to set their own agenda; they will not fight for someone else's. The Alinsky organizer in a working-class community, like the Leninist organizer, is there to combat "straight trade unionism." (Alinsky no doubt borrowed the term from his CP friends.) But the community organizer, unlike the Leninist, is not the bearer of scientific socialism or any other complete set of ideas that the workers must learn. Alinsky's organizer has a ton of techniques, but he has only two main ideas to teach: popular participation, and a specific form of organization. And his brief is not to teach those ideas—it is to get people to try them out. As they do, and win power as a result, they can almost teach the ideas to themselves.

According to Alinskyite theory, stories do just fine for teaching democratic politics. Alinsky, Ross, and Chavez were all storytellers, masters of the art of conversation. They knew how to talk, and they knew how to listen. This is no accident of personality. It is a consciously acknowledged element of the theory. All of the various Alinskyite training centers teach conversation, which requires, first, listening, and among the Alinskyites, Chavez is the most famous listener. His ability to give his full attention to the person with whom he was talking is the stuff of legend, and in this case the legend is firmly grounded.

But Chavez and Ross and Alinsky didn't just listen—they told stories that made points, specific ones. "You want higher wages, better working conditions, rent control, an end to police brutality? Let me tell you what happened over in Los Angeles, where the people got together and won some of those things." And a story would follow. Probably an exaggeration, as most good stories are. But that was okay, because the story was intended to inspire and instruct, not be an accurate historical account. What did the stories teach? If you build an organization and get active in it, you can improve your world. And if you want to do that, the organizer can show you how. It is that simple.

The emphasis on small, intimate conversation as the essential political discourse starts with Alinsky, builds with Ross, and becomes perhaps Chavez's supreme contribution to organizational theory and practice. "One-on-one" organizing, like the feminist consciousness-raising groups to which it is related, was promoted not just as another way of talking politics but as the way of doing it. Its enemy, its opposite, is political oratory: the great transforming speech delivered to a gathering of listeners, which inspires, instructs, and gives historical meaning to that which the audience has just done or is about to do. This is an enormous departure in democratic theory. So much for the great speeches and speechmakers who helped define democracy: the big boys like Pericles, Danton, Lincoln, Debs, and

King; and adios to all the soap-boxers whose ability to hold and inspire a crowd has for so long been a touchstone of popular politics. In this new view, such speeches, and the people who make them, are suspect, perhaps even essentially antidemocratic, because they are so often full of bombast and rhetoric, and are talking at the people instead of listening to them.

It would be wrong to give full credit (or blame) to Alinsky for this departure. It is part of his idea of how the community organizer operates, but it is not his primary emphasis. It is Chavez, the shy, ineffective public speaker, who mastered small-scale conversation, who ultimately developed it into a full-blown theory. Throughout his telling of the story of the UFW—the story of the founding, the grape boycott, the union contracts— the tale that was then retold by most of Chavez's chroniclers, the success of the union depended on overcoming the error of grand speeches and radical rhetoric. Beware the inspiring speech, Chavez learned and taught. Trust only direct, personal contact.

Part II of *Reveille for Radicals* does contain a few general principles about how to form a People's Organization, basically how to weave the essential elements of the neighborhood together to make a community. These essential elements are what the organizer tries to identify as he listens to people talk. He listens in order to help them find their own agendas, to identify the "native leadership," to familiarize himself with preexisting community organizations (and the divisions within those organizations), and to understand and appreciate community traditions. Sometimes Alinsky—and Ross and Chavez, too—compare the organizer to a juggler, a performer who already has six plates in the air and must add a seventh. Organizers do their work through the proper juggling of local leaders, preexisting organizations, and community traditions. They must keep all of the elements coordinated, happily in the air at once, without dropping a single one. But jugglers don't change the character of what they toss. The plates remain plates. Here Alinsky underestimates the organizer's powers, because the organizer can change the character of the plates. When the juggled elements become an organization of elements, they are transformed. They are no longer just local leaders, preexisting community groups, and community traditions. Through the magic of organization they become political power. The juggler analogy does not do the organizer justice. A better image—and one that Alinsky also used—is the wizard, the alchemist. Through the philosopher's stone of organization, the alchemist transmutes an apathetic, powerless, divided neighborhood into a powerful community, fighting for its own agenda.

In *Reveille for Radicals*, as well as in most Alinskyite and neo-Alinskyite organizations, the community organizer must be an outsider. Generally this is an uncontested and unsupported assumption. Alinsky makes but a single partial argument in *Reveille* about the necessity of the organizer's otherness.

In three brief paragraphs toward the end of the book, Alinsky asserts "one simple maxim: in order to be part of all, you must be part of none." The organizer must stand above all the "innumerable rivalries, fears, jealousies, and suspicions within a community." It is hard to do that if one is already part of the community. Here, characteristically, Alinsky tells a story (one he probably made up for the purpose), which concludes with the crucial lesson:

> In one Western community an organizer who held an official position within the CIO was Protestant by religion and a leader in his church club, and his wife was the president of a local women's club. Shortly after beginning his organizational drive this organizer discovered that he had to resign from his church in order to remove certain barriers between himself and representatives of other Protestant churches in the community. He had to resign from the CIO because of suspicion on the part of the American Federation of Labor and the Railroad Brotherhood. His wife had to resign from her women's club because of the rivalry of another women's society. Very shortly this organizer found that he could not be an official member of any of the community agencies. These circumstances do not apply in the same severe fashion to an organizer who comes into the community from the outside.

Coming from the outside is so essential to the organizer that if by chance he were originally an insider, he would have to replicate the condition of outsider by cutting off all of his (and his wife's!) organizational connections to fellow workers, worshipers, friends, and neighbors. "In a sense" the organizer "is selfless," Alinsky says elsewhere in *Reveille for Radicals*, standing above all the victories and defeats, the ordinary hopes and fears of the local community leaders. Here Alinsky quotes Schiller: "Know this, a mind sublime puts greatness into life, yet seeks it not therein."[9] Organizers are not, and must not be, caught up in the ordinary life of the community. They are outside it, above it.

That is a rather peculiar view of democratic leadership—yet the outside organizer is both leader and not leader. Like a movie cowboy he rides into a troubled town alone, reconstructs legitimate authority, and then rides out again; he never stays to become sheriff or mayor. This is a view of politics that has attracted any number of talented, ambitious, would-be American political heroes, including many of the founding fathers of the New Left who were so audacious in their conception of themselves as "new" that they could not acknowledge their debt to Alinsky. Not just New Leftists but all sorts of young people—especially men, and often religious ones—fell victim to this particular siren's call. The future journalist Nicholas von Hoffman captured the essence of Alinsky's challenge and romantic allure:

You drive up in a car, and you know nobody, and you've got to organize it into something that it's never been before. You know, you're not a Democrat or Republican. You don't have much going for you. You don't have prestige, you don't have muscle, you've got no money to give away. All you have are your wits. You've just got your wits, charm, and whatever you can put together. So you [had] better form a very accurate picture of what's going on, and you had better not bring in too many a priori maps [because] if you do, you're just not going to get anywhere.[10]

No fast six gun, no maps, just your wits and charm. So how is it done? By what magic does the organizer transform people who are divided among themselves by ethnic and other rivalries, as well as by their own self-interested scheming designs on power, into the united leadership of the People's Organization? Alinsky's particular kind of political knowledge is the answer to this question, and he delivers it through a series of stories that illustrate his hard-headed, practical political art. Hard-headed because it accepts self-interest as the basic human motivator and does not wish it away into what Alinsky considers the mushy-headed idea that people will do good because they believe in the good. Practical because, although it might do violence to some too-easy ethical standards of action, it actually works.

The hero-organizer is also a trickster. Alinsky gives the reader a series of small deceptions, little lies through which the organizer uses his knowledge of human psychology and his understanding of society to maneuver the local leadership into the newly formed PO. He tells two rival leaders that the other one has joined the PO, and thereby tricks them both into joining; he gives one leader a letter to deliver knowing that he will open it and read the contents; he and a few other people spend a whole day with a crucial but recalcitrant leader, acting out a complicated charade about their supposed important but secret business, which forces the confused victim to join the PO so he will know what's going on. Pretty mild stuff, and used almost exclusively at the beginning of the organizer's work within a neighborhood.

Later, tricks become less necessary because the divided neighborhood changes after a few early political victories. These victories, no matter how small, teach the local leaders and their followers that they all need each other, and that united political action is in the self-interest of all. That precept helps explain why Alinsky, a self-described "revolutionary," would attract support from some distinctly nonrevolutionary figures and institutions: Alinsky didn't just promise a non-Communist radicalism during the fifties and an "orderly" revolution during the disorderly sixties. In addition, in his plain-talking and deceptively simple theorizing, competing interests are manipulated in such a way that they create community, and thus the "radical democrat" solves a main paradox of interest-based liberal pluralism.

But not without some sleight of hand. Alinsky recognizes that he is in the middle of a dilemma of ends and means, and he faces it straight on. He has little patience with moral compunction about his tricks. The People's Organization is in a permanent war, and must operate in a world of "smashing forces, clashing struggles, sweeping cross-currents, ripping passions, conflict, confusion, seeming chaos."[11] Go into such a world without your bag of tricks and you are sure to lose. And early defeats will doom the organization. This was so obvious to Alinsky that he spent little time arguing the point in *Reveille for Radicals*. But twenty-six years later it became the dominant theme of Alinsky's second political handbook, *Rules for Radicals*, which was directed toward what he considered the overly moralistic New Left.

Alinsky's disdain for "moral quibbling" is perhaps responsible for his failure to consider in either work one of the most elementary problems of the ends-versus-means debate: Is there any difference between the tactics that can be used among friends and the tactics that can be used against enemies? After Alinsky demonstrates how the organizer uses questionable techniques among friends to put the PO together, he then shows how to use a whole arsenal of dirty tricks against the community's external enemies. Do both set of techniques come out of the same bag? Alinsky ignored this question, as did Chavez, who would eventually dissolve all doubts about ends and means into rituals of religious faith, while allowing his lieutenants to use all manner of dirty tricks both inside and outside the UFW.

But one of the corollaries of the ends and means debate did interest both Alinsky and Chavez. They knew that political knowledge was dangerous stuff. What was to prevent a person from using Alinskyite tactics to pursue "undemocratic objectives"? Since the successful organizer must use an arsenal of dirty tricks to achieve the good, why wouldn't such a person (one who can trick, cheat, and steal) use those techniques for some ultimately dirty end?

Alinsky's answer is based on the hero's democratic faith. Behind the petty, dirty tactics of the organizer is a bigger, nobler one: "The fundamental tactic is the organizer's own complete faith in people and his complete devotion to that faith."[12] The organizer cannot fake it, Alinsky says. If he has the faith, the people will know it; if he doesn't, the people will know that, too. Therefore, Alinsky's tactics cannot be used by an undemocratic politician, as people cannot be tricked into doing things by someone who they know doesn't believe in them.

Chavez was not so sure. In his early political career, in the midst of being trained by Ross and Alinsky, he worried that people could be organized for anything, even the worst of causes. He also believed that some very bad people had been very good organizers. He read Goebbels, and told colleagues on several occasions that the Nazi propagandist was, after all, a good organizer.[13] In this case, as in many others, Chavez seems to have looked a little deeper into the face of evil than did his mentors, and his answer would have to be tougher, harder.

Alinsky has been accused of lacking a coherent ideology, but this charge misses the point. Alinsky's ideas may not explain everything that happens in the world; he does not have a total system such as Catholicism or some closed versions of Marxism, yet Alinskyism certainly meets the first requirement of a political ideology: it provides a guide to action. Moreover, the main reason that Alinsky appears nonideological is because so many of his ideas are taken straight from the almost invisible ideology that we live and breathe: the ideology of American democracy. The dilemmas of Alinskyism, then, are similar to the problems of the whole American political tradition, where the core confusion resides in the various vague, often conflicting ideas of what democracy is.

This is not just a popular misunderstanding, a confusion among the folk. It goes as far back as the founding of the country and is as deep as our political roots. We are originally a mixture of two contradictory Old World impulses: the political optimism of the European Enlightenment, which culminated in the French Revolution, and the political pessimism of English liberalism as it defined itself against the radical implications of the English revolution. Theoretical revolutionaries and counterrevolutionaries mixed together in the New World. It was a true blend in which each tradition was changed by the encounter, and then reformulated over the course of American history. By now the jumble is difficult to separate back into its original ingredients, even as an intellectual exercise. Perhaps the two traditions were clearest at the founding in the difference between the Declaration of Independence and the Constitution: the first written in an open spirit of equality and rebellion as a call to arms; the second composed in secret session by men who explicitly set out to construct a republic that would minimize the threat of popular power.

Where does Alinsky fit in those conflicting traditions? He wants it both ways. Tom Paine is an Alinsky hero because of his call to patriotic sacrifice and his attack on the privileges of the aristocracy. But James Madison is also a hero because he was hard-headed, like Alinsky himself, and started with the proposition that people act only out of self-interest. Alinsky often described himself as a Jeffersonian, but in *Reveille for Radicals* he cites only Jefferson's division of the world into aristocrats and democrats, and joins Jefferson on the side of the democrats. Trying to find Alinsky's exact place within the American democratic tradition, we come up against the philosophical poverty of the first pages of *Reveille for Radicals*, a list of contradictory propositions in which the contradictions are ignored.

Alinsky's conflation of conflicting ideas of democracy was partly an expression of the times. For him, and for many of Popular Fronters inside and outside the New Deal, democracy was a list and a magic charm. It included both the call—the reveille—to the people to shake off their apathy and participate in politics and a celebration of political institutions that were set up to blunt popular participation. That is a subtle trap, and a problem that Alinsky simply ignored. One will find no criticism anywhere in Alinsky of American political institutions as such. He never questions an institutional structure that places political power far from where people actually live and work. He has no problem with the two-party system and winner-take-all elections. He does not challenge the particular way that U.S. politics divides the public from the private; he is not worried that the elaborate system of checks and balances that were put into the Constitution as protection against popular power help protect corporate control of the U.S. government. Alinsky's hero Madison was afraid of the political participation of ordinary people. Madison and his Federalist buddies consciously built a polity that they hoped would make direct political participation both difficult and unnecessary. Alinsky has nothing to say about that—as far as he's concerned, American political institutions are just fine. Nor does he ever ask how there can be a demo-cratic society without a democratic economy—that is, how capitalism can be compatible with democracy. For Alinsky, the problem—the essen-tial problem of American democracy—is the people's lack of participation. It ends up being our own fault.

Attacking Alinsky for his lack of ideology instead of exploring his ideas about democracy obscures what is perhaps Alinsky's main addition to democratic theory: not the building of community coalitions but the particular role of the outside organizer. Alinsky has no confidence that individuals can learn, through their own leadership, to measure their inter-ests against the community interest, and to think of the good of the whole as well as of themselves. Blinded by their own ambitions, indigenous lead-ers will never find a way to unite a neighborhood, or a city, or a region. This problem, the problem Madison called factionalism, is solved by the organizer. Organizers alone do not want power for themselves. Masters of restraint, they guide without dominating. They are the ones who help the people achieve a collective understanding of themselves, the understanding that makes democratic action possible. It is the organizers, not the indige-nous leaders or the people, who are the heroes in all of the stories Alinsky loved to tell.

Consistent with Alinsky's view, Cesar Chavez remained a CSO orga-nizer—not its leader—for ten years, for as long as Alinsky signed the checks. But soon after Chavez left CSO and launched his own career, he blurred the line between organizer and leader. Within Alinskyism, that was heresy.

Merging the position of organizer and leader was dangerous because what the organizer knew, what he had learned through his special training, might be used to build power not for others but for himself. That would lead not to internal democracy but to some form of corruption or autocratic power. Chavez explained his decision to a group of SNCC organizers in 1965:

> People say, "I'm just an organizer." An organizer is an outsider in many cases—there's nothing wrong in that. But then he assumes a sort of special position in that program. First thing he says is "I'm not going to be an officer; it's a people's program." What he's saying is he's something special, not an integral part of that group. I think that's a mistake. If you organize a good group, pretty soon you find yourself hoping, "I wish I had a vote in this outfit."[14]

Talking to his SNCC supporters, Chavez did not acknowledge any danger. All he wants, he humbly argues, is a vote in his own outfit. Those who would deny him that vote, he says, make too much of the difference between the organizer and the indigenous leaders; they think that the organizer is too special, so different from the others that he cannot be a regular part of the group. Ten years an organizer, Chavez had a good sense of how artificial it can be for the organizer to remain in the background, supposedly leaving the important decisions up to others. Didn't that often become a kind of charade? Why wasn't it possible for the organizer to become a full member of the group and still maintain his capacity to guide and to lead in a respectful, democratic manner? If that was apostasy, so be it. That's what he was setting out to do.

It was a great departure. Alinsky had started with Madison and an exclusively self-interested humanity, so it was awfully hard for him to end with community and participatory democracy. The way to get there, the Alinsky way, was to introduce the idea of a superhuman who would manipulate competitors into a community—and then leave. But why is the organizer the one person who is not captive to Madisonian self-interest? If the organizer can learn to think of the whole, why can't each member of the divided neighborhood? And if they can all learn together, what makes the organizer so different? Why can't he settle down and stay? Understood this way, Chavez's decision is an act of democratic faith, a statement that he is right down here with the rest of us, like all ordinary human beings, who are not Madison's self-interest machines but a mixture of self-interest and connection to others, selfishness and idealism, regular people, capable of democratic politics.

But does this really happen? When Chavez assumed the role of leader, did he leave behind all the assumed superiority of the juggler, the catalyst, the alchemist, the essential human ingredient who could transform the factions into the united community? Or was Chavez still the only one who could truly think of the whole, the only one who could rise above the battle for personal power, the living embodiment of the community's best version of itself?

Throughout his political life Cesar Chavez, the leader–organizer, continued to believe that organizers rather than local leaders were the crucial people who made politics happen. The organizers were, he said in 1969, "the heroes of the farm worker movement." Without the guidance of skilled organizers, ultimately without his own direction and management, rank-and-file leaders would be forever trapped in a competitive individualism, incapable of building their own movement. That idea came from Saul Alinsky.

6

The Organizer in Oxnard

September '58 to June '59

John Soria, at six foot two and 220 pounds, was eight inches taller and seventy pounds heavier than his traveling companion, Cesar Chavez. Big John and Little Cesar, some people playfully dubbed them in Oxnard, California, in 1958. They both came from farm worker families, where Soria had once been Juan, and Cesar's name had been pronounced as the softer, more melodious "Sáyzar." Chavez, thirty-one, was the senior organizer who had been making a living doing Mexican American community politics for six years. Soria, twenty-three, was the apprentice who had recently left his job as a psychiatric attendant at the nearby state mental hospital in order to earn his living helping Chavez and learning to be an organizer. They both were married with children, but spent a lot of time riding around Oxnard in Chavez's 1953 Mercury, talking politics.

Soon after they met they discovered that they both had read the Alinsky biography of John L. Lewis. They both liked Lewis, but the two organizers' political enthusiasms were not the same. Soria favored secular left politics. His mother, Luz, had been one of the better-known leaders of a major Ventura County lemon workers' strike against Sunkist in 1941, and his strongest public memories growing up were of his Uncle Jesus, a socialist, talking politics in Oxnard's barrio, La Colonia; of Sunday afternoon gatherings where men would read the Mexican papers and Los Angeles' *La Opinión*; and of one 1938 fiesta in particular when the grown-ups threw their hats in the air and shouted praises to President Lázaro Cárdenas, who had just kicked the gringo oil companies out of Mexico. Like Chavez, Soria was an avid reader. The first book Chavez gave him was Saul Alinsky's *Reveille for Radicals*.[1]

Cesar and John's project was to build a Ventura County chapter of the Community Service Organization, to be based in La Colonia. Although supported by Alinsky's foundation, the CSO did not follow Alinsky's pattern as an organization of organizations. It was, instead, a direct-membership organization. In what has come to be seen as Fred Ross's contribution to organizing theory, and one of the most enduring of neo-Alinskyite variations, people joined the local chapter of the CSO, paying $12 a year, not because some leader of theirs had joined first but as a result of the outside organizer's skill at bringing individuals together, developing leaders from among them, and uniting them to address local matters while also advancing a centralized statewide agenda.

When Alinsky complained about this structural departure, Ross answered that California's Mexican American barrios had no community groups comparable to the unions and the local Catholic parishes Alinsky knew in Chicago. Some people were in unions, but they did not control them. All of the major dioceses were controlled by white conservatives, and the local Mexican American parishes were not independent enough to help form a classic People's Organization. What Mexican communities in the 1950s did have, Ross argued, was extended family groups. Thus, the house meeting, which someone in the community agreed to host and be responsible for inviting others to attend, was the standard building block of the CSO.[2]

In La Colonia, John went along to these meetings to watch how Cesar handled them. He listened as Chavez told stories in a soft, even voice about what CSO had accomplished in other areas: fighting police brutality, getting more services into the barrios, helping people become citizens so that they would be eligible for state disability and pension programs. When he finished, people asked questions, often about particular problems with welfare or immigration or their children's schools. Chavez was expert at answering them. When the questions were about community problems, he explained again how people in other areas had formed their own CSO chapters. To handle individual complaints, he made appointments. Finally he asked if anyone in the room wanted to host another meeting. By pyramiding the house meetings, helping people with their individual problems, and keeping detailed records of his activities, he got a picture of the community.

Big John took it all in. He came to admire how well Cesar listened, how he gave people his full attention, how he never showed disappointment if only a few people had turned up. Cesar seemed very sure of himself, always upbeat. Soria also noted a standard answer Chavez would give to a typical kind of hard question, a complaint that could not be solved by a visit to a local agency or pressure on a politician. Once in Santa Paula, across the river from Oxnard, at a meeting at the Limoneira company's labor camp, the local lemon pickers had complained that they had been swamped by braceros who were taking most of their work. Could CSO do anything about that? Sure, Chavez said, after we get organized, if people agree, we can make it the first item on the agenda. Then he urged people to sign up as an important step in making that happen.

On the way home, John asked Cesar how in hell were CSO and a couple of hundred local *limoneros* going to get rid of the thousands of braceros work-ing in the trees? Chavez seemed mystified by Soria's question. Soria was struck by the incongruity of it. Here they were, two guys with a limited budget, operating out of a donated office, driving through miles of lemon orchards where everything but the air was owned by the Sunkist Corporation: the trees, the bosses' gated mansions, the labor camps where the workers lived, the packing sheds and the railroad spurs that led to them, the land, and the water. Unless you looked up in the sky, whatever you saw belonged to Teague, McKevett, Hardison, or Blanchard. Yet here was Chavez, having just told a small group of local *limoneros* in company-owned housing, some of whom were scared even to be seen in the meeting lest they be fingered by a Sunkist spy, that if they got organized they could throw the braceros out of the orchards. He had said it without flinching, swallowed up by the chair he was sitting in, characteristically pushing his lank, black Indian hair off his wide brown forehead. Now in the car, with nobody to overhear, John asked Cesar to come clean. Did he really believe it was possible to take the braceros away from the Sunkist Corporation?

Chavez, his hands on the wheel, turned to him and smiled. "Why not, John? If enough people get together they can do anything."

Soria laughed. Then he took a long look at Chavez. Cesar meant it. He was not the least bit overwhelmed by the power that surrounded him. Soria thought it would be nice to feel that way, but he couldn't. He thought Cesar was a little bit crazy. Not crazy like the people John had worked with at the mental hospital. Not sad and disfigured. Chavez was beautiful crazy.

Oxnard was an atypical CSO project. Usually Chavez would spend ninety days in a town and leave behind a new chapter when he moved on. But in Oxnard he was planning to stay an entire year because the project was co-sponsored by the United Packing House Workers of America (UPWA), the same union with which Saul Alinsky had had such success in Chicago's Back of the Yards neighborhood. Alinsky and the union had subsequently initiated other projects in several Midwestern states, where they tried to duplicate their Chicago experience—with mixed results. Oxnard was their first West Coast venture. The UPWA had won union representation elections in five Sunkist packing sheds there in 1952, but the growers had so far refused to sign contracts. The union president, Ralph Helstein, and Alinsky hoped that building a CSO chapter in La Colonia, where the lemon packers lived, would help the UPWA fight for contracts where the packers worked. Helstein agreed to pay the bills: $20,000 for the year's expenses, including the salaries of Chavez and Soria.

By this time CSO had about twenty chapters across California, but Fred Ross had not built that network in conjunction with labor unions or with a particular emphasis on workers' issues. Instead, his focus was more conventionally political. It was not true, as Ross told Alinsky in 1947, when he decided to organize Mexican Americans, that the community had no groups to call its own. In fact, Mexicans had small civic organizations all over California and a few influential large ones, like La Comisión Honorifica, a surviving *mutualista*. They just did not have the kind of organization that Ross wanted to build. They didn't have a statewide organization whose goal was to win formal political power.

Ross, who was not Mexican, Catholic, nor Spanish-speaking, was in no position to lead such an organization, but he didn't care: he did not want to lead the CSO, he wanted to organize it, and he had been organizing communities he was not a part of for a long time. Born into a middle-class Methodist family in San Francisco in 1910, he graduated from the University of Southern California with a teaching credential during the Depression and worked as a welfare case manager, finally getting a New Deal job with the Farm Security Administration. Working his way up, he eventually became head of community services at the seventeen FSA camps that housed displaced farm workers (mostly Dustbowl refugees) in California and Arizona. While managing the famous Arvin camp, which was the model for the "good" camp in *The Grapes of Wrath*, he met radical farm worker organizers and also Woody Guthrie, who came by with a sleeping bag, a guitar, and his songs. Ross always said he did his first organizing there as the camp director, encouraging the dispirited workers to establish the self-governing councils that so impressed Steinbeck. Ross was a very special kind of outsider here: both organizer and highest community authority; both the "self-effacing . . . behind the scenes" player, as he was described in the *San Francisco Chronicle*, and the boss. Moving on to the War Relocation Authority, Ross managed a Japanese internment camp in Idaho and worked to resettle and find jobs for Japanese Americans. Next, at the Council on Race Relations, he began working with Mexican Americans in Southern California and developed the idea of the new kind of organization that CSO would become.[3]

Ross began by attaching himself to a group in East LA that was part of a general movement to elect Mexican Americans to local office. Great changes were happening in American politics in 1947, and before the group would accept Ross's voluntary help, its members had to assure themselves that he neither was a Communist nor had Communist sympathies. Through a daisy chain of connections beginning with Alinsky, Ross got a letter from an auxiliary bishop of Los Angeles verifying his anti-Communist status.[4] He then helped build the CSO partially as a rival to other local groups, especially those that were close to the Communist Party, then active in East LA, and to unions that had been expelled from the CIO because aledgedly they were dominated by reds.

Ross and the CSO organizers had their own particular brand of anti-Communism. Their aim was to "out-organize the Communists" but they never spearheaded the red-baiting campaign that would lead to McCarthyism, devastate the Communist Party and the entire left in the 1950s, and continue to reverberate for years, even within the UFW. But they were not beyond using the anti-Communism of the times to achieve their aims. "Ross was a heavy red baiter," said Bill Chandler, UFW volunteer, who first got to know him in a CSO registration drive and who otherwise was a great admirer of the man he considered a master organizer.[5] Bert Corona, a longtime Mexican American activist and an early member of CSO in Northern California, also criticized Ross: "One thing I didn't like . . . was that one of its stated reasons for organizing was to keep the 'reds' from establishing a base in the communities. I knew that when they referred to 'reds' they meant those Mexicans who were either working with the CP or involved with ANMA, the Asociación Nacional México-Americana."[6]

The CSO's brand of anti-Communism meshed smoothly with its own narrow definition of politics, one that took no positions on the big questions of the day—for instance, the Taft Hartley Act's rollback of labor rights—but maintained a careful focus on community action, voter registration, and voter participation.[7] On those terms, the CSO was wildly successful, more so than both more conservative and more conventionally left Mexican American organizations. By 1962 it would have thirty-two chapters from Sacramento to Calexico that had registered 400,000 new voters. Before the CSO's drives, no serious statewide attempt at voter registration had ever been made among California's Mexican Americans, and nothing like it would be seen again until the 1990s. Far more than any other organization, the CSO was responsible for the more than one hundred Mexican American politicians who won California local elections in the 1950s and early '60s.[8]

It achieved its presence on the state's conventional political stage through a remarkable series of organizing innovations. Its paid organizers—starting with Ross, adding Chavez in 1952, and eventually the other future founders of the UFW, Gilbert Padilla and Dolores Huerta—combined the idea of naturalization and registration with specific struggles for improvements in the Mexican and Mexican American barrios. They linked CSO membership to access to services at CSO Service Centers, where translation, immigration, workmen's compensation, and welfare problems were either free for CSO members or significantly cheaper than the those of the competing accountants, lawyers, and notary publics. The CSO often got initial entry into communities through either the Catholic Church or a union, and then organized those communities through the system of pyramiding house meetings. They pressured local adult schools into providing teachers for CSO-sponsored English and citizenship classes, and they took great advantage of their knowledge of the details of immigration and welfare law to teach people about the concrete benefits of becoming citizens and registering to vote.[9]

Chavez arrived in Oxnard in the midst of all this success in September of 1958, and began doing what he already knew how to do well. The UPWA might be signing the checks, but its agenda would have to wait, as a get-out-the-vote campaign for the November elections was his first order of business. He had to operate faster than he liked, but he had no choice, as a good showing in the local elections would increase CSO power with the local politicians and within all the local social agencies where Chavez would need leverage. He and Soria put the names of all of La Colonia's 1,400 registered voters on index cards, recruited a team of volunteers, and borrowed the Latin American Veterans Hall for Election Day. Days before the election, Cesar put his portable sound system on top of his car and drove through the neighborhood urging people to vote. As CSO had done in other areas to combat widespread cynicism about politicians, he and John patiently explained to people that the important thing was to show up at the polls and cast a ballot; it could be a blank ballot, if they wished. What mattered was the number of voters, because with a big enough turnout, as Ross said, "the CSO leaders . . . could approach the politicians as the official spokesmen for a powerful new constituency, which they could use as a club over the heads of those politicians."[10]

The campaign was a success. More than a thousand people from La Colonia went to the polls, more than double the turnout at the previous election, which prompted the *Oxnard Press Courier* to editorialize that CSO was starting to build a "political machine" in La Colonia.[11] Although the CSO was officially nonpartisan, no one doubted the Democratic Party identification of most of its members. These 1958 elections marked a decisive turn in California politics, as Democrats took control of the governorship, the state senate, and the state assembly for the first time in eighty years. Moreover, the victory of the liberal Edmund G. (Pat) Brown over conservative William Knowland for governor was relatively ideological, by U.S. standards. Knowland ran an anti-union campaign and endorsed a "right-to-work" proposition on the ballot. Brown opposed it, and won the active support of organized labor, whose members and their families then constituted one-third of all registered voters in the state. Labor's efforts were matched by the equally successful efforts of the Catholic Church against a proposition to end the tax-exempt status for private and church schools. Brown—Democrat, Catholic, pro-labor—was the big victor.[12]

Chavez was one of the little ones. La Colonia had voted a straight Democratic ticket, and Cesar was ebullient about the victories, both local and statewide. Here was the shape of a possible future. Here was the promise of a large coalition that might possibly be bigger than even the Sunkist Corporation.

He and Soria wasted no time celebrating. Two days after the election they held a mass meeting to formalize the establishment of CSO's Ventura County chapter. An Oxnard priest, impressed by CSO's ability to turn out the vote, gave the invocation. The speakers who followed included Tony Del Buono, of a preexisting local Mexican civic group that was now going to merge with CSO; Jimmy Flores, from the local Laborers Union; Rachel Guajardo, of the UPWA; Joe Piña, of the Latin American Veterans; Fred Brown, of the local

NAACP; the Reverends Washington and Zamora of Trinity Baptist and First Mexican Baptist churches; and Tony Rios, president of the statewide CSO. People voted unanimously to set up a CSO chapter. Cesar announced that a CSO Service Center would open, which meant that Chavez and Soria wouldn't have to handle everybody's individual problems personally. Eventually the service center would be staffed by thirty volunteers and operate eighteen hours a day, seven days a week. People came to celebrate on the day of its opening, and they kept coming. Some kind of mass movement was building in La Colonia. The *Oxnard Press Courier* reported that the Friday night following the CSO celebration, 3,500 people walked through La Colonia, candles in hand, behind a statue of the Virgin of Guadalupe, from one bracero labor camp to another. The march was a mixture of La Colonia residents and braceros. Chavez joined in.[13]

In house meetings during the voter drive Chavez had continued to listen for the "key issue" that could unite large numbers of people, just as Ross and Alinsky had taught him. In his Activity Report to Ross of October 24, 1958, he identified that issue:

> One that seems to be the most urgent at the time is the unemployment of the local workers in the area due to the Braceros. Have had reports in the house meetings where whole crews of locals have been displaced from their jobs to hire Braceros. The most recent experience was the one where a labor contractor, Eleuterio Gonzales, had a local crew of about forty men and about three weeks ago he was asked by his employer to lay off these men and go pick up Braceros at the camp the following morning. So forty locals were displaced at once because there are plenty of Braceros in the area. I happened to have talked to one of these men at one of the house meetings and believe me he was fighting mad when he was telling me about the problem. At the meeting after I got through giving them the CSO history he wanted to know what if anything could the CSO do to help them. My only answer was that we would try to do something after we were organized. And again at all, most all, the house meetings, the same question is asked of me. In discussing this with Tony Rios I was asking him for advice and also for permission to commit the organization in this line of action.[14]

The question of braceros had not come up in Chavez 's earlier CSO work, and although there were some farm workers in other chapters, braceros did not dominate the local fields as they did in Oxnard. Braceros were not evenly distributed throughout California agriculture. They were contracted by the biggest and best-organized growers and grower associations and became the primary labor force in some crops but not others. When Chavez arrived in 1958, Ventura County growers enjoyed the use of 6,140 braceros during the peak harvest period; 2,500 were concentrated in the lemon orchards, with only 150 local workers sprinkled among them.[15]

The braceros had changed the landscape of Ventura County agriculture. Before the program that brought them into the fields during World War II, the picture was simple: along the narrow Santa Clara River valley thousands of lemon trees were controlled by a few big and many medium-sized ranches. Through their ownership of the processing sheds and distribution services, a few of the biggest farmers became very big indeed, masters of the company town of Santa Paula, and some of the most important businessmen in California. On the southeast side of the river in the large Oxnard coastal plain, production was mostly sugar beets, which had replaced the first cash crop, lima beans, at the beginning of the twentieth century. The sugar beet farmers were much smaller than the big boys across the river, and most of the sugar beet profits went to the Oxnard brothers, whose antecedents had generously given the town its name. Their descendents still owned the huge sugar refinery that sat on the southeast border of La Colonia.

Both the well-organized lemon bosses and the smaller, relatively unorganized farmers of the plain were blessed by Ventura County's unique combination of deep alluvial soils, abundant ground water, mild climate, and coastal fog. When the braceros were added to the mix as something other than a temporary answer to a wartime labor shortage, the lemon baron C. C. Teague and his partners built the Sunkist Corporation into one of the most powerful agricultural associations in the world, and the farmers of the Oxnard plain expanded acreage and diversified production, moving away from sugar beets and into more profitable, labor-intensive crops such as celery, broccoli, strawberries, and cut flowers. In 1948, Ventura County's total farm receipts had been less than $40 million. In 1958, agricultural sales topped $100 million.[16]

Local workers were the big losers. In a period when agriculture was booming and agricultural employment climbing, there was less work for locals and at lower wages. A small group of local farm workers held on, finding work mostly in the vegetables from the spring to the fall. Meanwhile, real wages of braceros actually declined during this remarkable decade of growth: the nominal wage in lemons, the best paid of all local agricultural jobs, was ninety-five cents an hour in 1947, and just ninety-seven cents an hour in 1959.[17] Lots of people made money off the braceros. The men who ran the labor camps overcharged them for meals that were so bad they often went uneaten. Small businesses that catered to the bracero trade flourished, not only legal establishments such as bars and cafés, and grocery, clothing, bicycle and appliance stores but also plenty of what the Mexicans called *transa*, dirty business, including bogus public accountants, who sold counterfeit documents, and women who sold their favors to the men who had left wives and girlfriends back in Mexico.[18]

During the year he spent in Oxnard, Chavez could do nothing about getting UPWA contracts in the lemon sheds or getting the braceros out of the trees. But CSO's employment committee did contribute to the growing pressure against the entire Bracero Program. About a dozen workers, mostly middle-aged men, attended the weekly Friday night meetings. They began documenting the particular way that the local Farm Placement Service (FP, as it was called) got around Public Law 78, which contained a legal guarantee that the Bracero Program would not "adversely affect" domestic labor and decreed that braceros could not be contracted to a job if there was enough domestic labor to do it. The scam in Ventura County worked like this: in order for a local to get dispatched to a job, he first had to go to the FP for a referral card. Then he had to take that card to the Farm Labor Association, where workers were sent out every morning to the fields. The problem was that the FP office didn't open until eight in the morning, while the braceros, who did not need referral cards, were all dispatched by six. And here is the clincher: one day's referral card was not good for the next day's work, so the cards that were issued in the morning by the FP were obsolete before they were written.

Chavez and three or four members of the employment committee made the useless twenty-four-mile round trip to the FP office several times a week, making copies of all the worthless forms they were issued. Meanwhile, Chavez cashed in some of his CSO voter registration chips. After Edward Hayes, the state director of the Farm Placement Service, ignored his telephone call, Chavez sent a telegram to Governor Brown with a copy to the CSO president, Tony Rios, describing the problem and reminding him that over the previous few years CSO had registered 300,000 new voters in the state, most of them Mexican American Democrats. Brown wired back, saying that he would direct Hayes to investigate. The telegram from the governor produced high excitement in the little CSO Oxnard office, but Chavez, who had been taught by Ross and Alinsky not to be limited by what politicians were willing to give but rather to push them to deliver what he wanted to get, sent another telegram: "Hayes unacceptable." Brown wired back that he would put Hayes's immediate boss, the state's employment director, John Carr, on the case instead. Carr called the CSO office directly and urged Chavez to get as much documentation as he could.

It was quite a boost to the employment committee. More people made the trek to the FP office to document the fraud, and the committee took a census of unemployed farm workers in Oxnard. By then it was fully winter, and the list of the unemployed had grown to nearly one thousand. Chavez followed up his calls to the state officials by making contacts with federal bureaucrats, developing relationships with people in the Labor Department and in the Bureau of Employment Services. His relationship with Carr became increasingly close.

Nor were Little Cesar and Big John content just to establish a paper trail. They organized increasing numbers of unemployed workers to go out to the fields to claim the jobs where braceros were working. They pressured local, state, and federal officials into coming to large meetings where farm workers told their stories. They organized a march in front of television cameras where the angry workers burned their useless referral cards.[19]

Nothing on this scale had ever been done before to combat the Bracero Program, although everywhere that the program operated the fiction had to be maintained that there were not enough locals to do the work. That was not the only fraud essential to the game. By law braceros had to be paid the "prevailing wage" in the crops and area where they worked. In a giant sham, grower associations throughout California announced the "prevailing wage" at the beginning of the season and then, with that wage fixed at a level below the minimum wage, the various state farm employment services certified farm labor shortages. It was a fixed wage, fixed at a level that would not attract significant numbers of domestic workers.

Even at the fixed wage, however, there were locals who wanted the jobs. Since the late 1940s farm workers had made various attempts to get them and to expose Bracero Program fraud. Just the year before, in 1957, the remarkable Ernesto Galarza—farm worker, novelist, pamphleteer, the first Mexican American to earn a doctorate in political science, U.S. diplomat, and defeated organizer of California farm workers—had waged a documentation campaign superficially similar to the Oxnard effort. Outside of Marysville, he had gotten hundreds of domestic farm workers to sign affidavits saying that they were willing and able to work in the peach orchards and that braceros were working in their stead, and then submitted the documents to the Republican governor, Goodwin Knight, who ignored them.[20] The CSO strategy of constant mobilization to pressure the new administration in Sacramento was more visible, more insistent, more dependent on the active participation of displaced farm workers. Nor did it hurt that the CSO had helped put the new Democratic governor into office.

By the spring, the CSO campaign had pressured some of the embattled growers to pick up their workers in front of the CSO office in La Colonia. Other local workers had their own arrangements with individual employers and were hired directly. This example of what was called "gate hiring" had been forced on the employers by a group of people who earlier had been refused work by those same bosses. It was a remarkable organizing achievement of more than just local significance.

Even as the employment committee was successfully exposing bracero fraud in the spring of 1959, things were getting sticky between Chavez and two UPWA organizers, Rachel Guajardo and Eddie Perez. The UPWA also had an office in La Colonia, around the block from CSO headquarters. Guajardo and Perez occasionally came to CSO employment committee meetings, and attended most of its demonstrations, marches, and big public events. Chavez was the lead organizer, but the understanding between Alinsky and the UPWA president, Helstein, back in Chicago was that after a year, Chavez would turn the employment committee over to the UPWA. Guajardo, who had come from the main UPWA office in Chicago, was well versed in the history of the epic slaughterhouse battles between workers and their bosses. Perez, a World War II vet from industrial Vernon, in East LA, was a veteran of CIO organizing drives. They both felt that Chavez consistently missed opportunities to educate people on the benefits of union contracts. Guajardo also argued that Chavez treated workers like children and did not engage them in open, adult political conversation.[21]

Chavez insisted that his criticisms of unions were only a reflection of the workers' own suspicions, and that they had good reason to be cautious, because unions had never done much for farm workers. He also believed that Guajardo and Perez were strike-happy, overanxious to throw up a picket line in the middle of any dispute. He told Soria that they were lazy, always looking for shortcuts, unwilling to put in the time to be effective organizers.[22]

Soria, who Chavez eventually concluded was also too lazy to be a good organizer, felt that the relationship between Cesar and Rachel had got nasty. Chavez made fun of her big-city clothes, and Guajardo complained about Chavez's "holier than thou act." She took to calling him "the little priest" behind his back, and complained to Soria that working with Chavez could only mean working for him.

"Rachel and Eddie were willing to argue with workers, to try to convince them that the union way made sense," Soria reported years later. "Chavez was more for engaging the workers in do-gooder projects, like health committees, welfare committees, and fundraising drives. CSO was more like a church organization than a labor union . . . and Chavez never argued with the workers. He just listened to them. He didn't make enemies that way, like Rachel and Eddie did, but he never set anybody straight, either. He didn't convince people of some idea. He won people over to him, Chavez."[23]

Rather than being a joint venture, the bracero fraud project became a tug of war between the two groups. Chavez also began to have differences with Clive Knowles, who was above Guajardo and Perez in the UPWA hierarchy. Knowles, noting that Public Law 78 made it illegal for braceros to work at places where strikes were in process, believed that when domestic workers were on mixed crews with braceros, the locals should declare a strike as a way to force the Labor Department or the Mexican government to remove the braceros. If the braceros were removed, production would stop, and the locals' leverage would increase.[24]

Chavez strongly disagreed. Premature strikes had a long history of failure in the California fields, he said, and would only demoralize the workers. At various points in the employment committee's extended campaign, UPWA organizers wanted to set up picket lines and declare a strike. Chavez opposed those plans, and looked for ways to put pressure on growers and government officials without calling a strike. He had more influence with the workers and won the local debate.

But he didn't win in the discussions back in Chicago. In the spring of 1959, Helstein and Alinsky agreed that it was time for the employment committee to be turned over to the Oxnard UPWA chapter. Chavez would return to helping people with their individual problems, the CSO's English and citizenship classes, and another voter registration drive. On May 23, 1959, a month after the dramatic public burning of the referral cards, Chavez dryly noted in his daily Activity Report to Ross: "The employment committee has been turned over to the UPWA lock, stock, and barrel."[25]

That June, Governor Brown announced a ten-point program to "strengthen controls over the state's Farm Placement Service." The program included longer hours for the FP offices, and no more issuing of out-of-date referral cards; a prevailing wage high enough to "attract and keep domestic workers"; "gate hire" and "day haul" arrangements for local workers "whenever practical"; consulting with and soliciting cooperation with unions and other public groups [like the CSO] who have a "legitimate interest in the program"; and all "complaints documented and followed up by necessary action."[26] The program, devised by John Carr, and U.S. Labor Department officials at the very time that they were intervening in the Oxnard fracas, was never implemented. Governor Brown was turned around in the middle of his term by the power of agribusiness, politically expressed by the rural, pro-grower Democrats who dominated the California State Senate. He went on to defend the Bracero Program up until its last days, even arguing for a special extension for California after the national program had been ended.

Nevertheless, the announcement of the regulatory plan was directly followed by the dismissal, forced retirement, or dishonorable resignation of several officials of the state's Farm Placement Service, including the director, Edward Hayes. California agribusiness was on notice. Their beloved Bracero Program, which for twenty years had checked union organizing and stifled farm workers' wages, might not be around much longer. It would be abandoned only later, when the contracted Mexican workers themselves became increasingly unruly, a flashpoint of labor trouble rather than an instrument to suppress it. Seven years after Chavez's show of apparently wild optimism, there would be no more braceros anywhere in the United States. Enough people had gotten together and done it.

Climbing the Fence

November '60 to March '62

The red sky in the east gave way to the full light of early morning, making visible a drama that had begun several hours earlier in total darkness. It was the second day of February, 1961, at the Dannenberg Ranch labor camp in the Imperial Valley. About a thousand men walked a picket line along a fence surrounding the camp in a strike called by the United Packinghouse Workers of America.[1] Hundreds of braceros stood on the other side of the fence, watching the picket line. It was a flimsy wire fence, ten feet high, topped off by another three feet of barbed wire, which jutted out at an angle above the picketing men. The fence was meant to keep the braceros from running away, which they were wont to do, escaping into California to become undocumented but relatively free workers. On this morning, the picketing men also wanted to keep the braceros in the camp, away from the struck lettuce fields. The signs leaning on the demonstrators' shoulders proclaimed the popular demand of the strike: "*uno veinte cinco,*" which stood for $1.25 an hour. Some men carried flags, mostly the red and black standards that the official Mexican labor movement had inherited from international anarchism; but there were a few red flags, too, homemade ones, scarlet fabric fastened to tomato stakes.

The demonstrators had arrived by car in the dark, after gathering a few hours after midnight at *el hoyo*, the hole, where a huge shape-up took place, a few feet this side of the Mexican border. As light arrived, some braceros and picketing men began to talk across the wire, in Spanish. Although the locals were either U.S. citizens or legal residents, they also called themselves Mexicans, and many lived across the border in Mexicali.

The men had a lot to talk about. The strike was in the interest of the braceros, too, the locals argued. Instead of the ninety cents an hour offered by the growers (up from eighty cents an hour the year before) the UPWA was demanding $1.25 for all hourly workers, locals and braceros alike. The strikers even passed union cards through the fence. The men were not unknown to one another, but there were differences to hash out. In the mixed crews they had worked on together for years, the braceros always worked by the hour, while the locals often worked at a piece rate that could earn a good lettuce cutter on a good day as much as $4 an hour, $1.70 more than the average factory worker made in 1961.[2] The braceros knew that the growers' unilateral decision to end piece-rate work had made the locals strike, and that while "*uno veinte cinco*" may have been the slogan of the strike, the restoration of piecework was the demand most important to the locals. Yes, the braceros agreed, they would benefit from the hourly raise, but when could they, too, start earning the piece rate? And did the union want them all sent back to Mexico? And what was the Mexican consul going to do to protect their interests? The strike was six weeks old on that February morning, so there were already a lot of stories to tell, a lot of rumors to consider and evaluate. Soon, most of the demonstrators stopped circling the camp. It was hard to walk around and also talk to the braceros. The picket line ceased to exist in the ordinary sense; it had been transformed into scores of conversations, carried on across the wires of a now mostly pointless fence.

Not until 8 a.m. did Sheriff Slim Lyons drive up, bringing two deputies and a machine gun. The lawmen had been unprepared for the demonstration, thinking the trouble that morning would be across town, where two hundred California ranch foremen and their friends had scheduled their first public rally of the strike. But the union had not wanted to engage in a scripted confrontation. The cops were late getting the news. When Lyons finally arrived at the camp, he tried to enter, but the demonstrators had blocked both gates. "Get more men out here; they won't let me in the damn gate," he shouted over his radio as he drove off. More than a hundred deputies, many of them recently deputized local foremen as well as police, Highway Patrolmen, and federal agents answered the call and swarmed to the camp. They carried shotguns, billy clubs, tear-gas canisters, and gas masks.

A man on horseback holding a huge flag emblazoned with the union demand rode back and forth in front of the cops, raising cheers from the strikers. Inside the camp, some foremen herded a couple dozen braceros onto two flatbed trucks and drove them up to the front gate as if to break through the blockade. Over bullhorns, Lyons and another sheriff ordered the demonstrators to clear the way. The demonstrators sat down and began calling out to the braceros to get off the trucks. Soon the flatbeds were nearly empty. As the demonstrators chanted, a bracero began to climb the fence. Ten feet up, he still had three feet of barbed wire to clear. The great mass of men sitting in front of the gates urged him on. He made it over the top, jumped to the ground, and joined the sit-in. Others followed. All along the fence, braceros were climbing up and over. Sitting among the striking workers, John Soria remembered that more than a hundred braceros braved the barbed wire and made it to the other side.[3]

Sheriff Lyons was in a difficult position. He was under instructions to avoid any incident that would alarm the Mexican government about the braceros' safety and give it reason to pull them out of the valley. If the eight thousand bracero lettuce harvesters were ordered back to Mexico, the strike would be a sure winner, as the overwhelming majority of the three thousand locals were refusing to work. What could he do? There were too many people to arrest everybody, and besides, it didn't look as though they would come quietly. Tear gas would cause just the kind of incident that he had to avoid, and the demonstrators knew it. When he took the bullhorn to declare the demonstration an unlawful assembly, the UPWA's Clive Knowles shouted, "Stay put. Sit down. They'll probably use tear gas. If they do they will lose every bracero in Imperial County." The sheriff responded by calling out the names of the strike committee and a few of the paid union staff, asking them to come forward peacefully to be arrested for illegal assembly. Only one person stepped forward, a confused striker who happened to have the same name as one of the union organizers. The sheriff knew whom he was looking for and refused to arrest the man. Finally, some deputies bullied their way into the crowd and pulled out fourteen union leaders. Before he was arrested, John Soria turned to one of the men sitting next to him and gave him his red flag. It was just before noon; the day's work had been lost.

The Imperial Valley lettuce "deal" (as the growers call the seasonal harvests), which starts in mid-November and ends in early March, expanded rapidly during the 1950s, and grossed nearly $20 million by 1959. But costs also rose. By 1959 only 10 percent of the Imperial Valley farmland was owned by people living in the valley, and fifty years of speculation by absentee landlords had made land rent high. "Making the desert bloom" also had required extraordinary expenditures on chronic drainage problems and periodic pest infestations. The growers with the deepest pockets, and especially those who had become grower-shippers—handling the wholesale distribution of lettuce as well as managing its production—were the winners. The smaller growers, who couldn't survive one bad season, were the losers. As bracero labor enabled the growers to expand production, the industry became more concentrated: by 1959, eighteen grower-shippers produced half of Imperial Valley's lettuce, and distributed 80 percent of it. And yet size was no guarantee of profits. The Imperial Valley Lettuce Association complained that since 1956 its members had had only one profitable lettuce season.[4]

In the fall of 1960, months before the Dannenberg Ranch sit-in, there had been no union plan to strike in the Imperial Valley. But when the season started, the growers, in an attempt to end their string of losses, refused to pay the piece rates. Quickly, momentum for a strike started to build among the lettuce piece-rate workers. These *lechugueros* (from "lechuga," Spanish for lettuce) were the precursors of the proficient workers who later would feature so prominently in the UFW. But in 1960 they were not yet organized in crews of thirty; rather, they worked and were paid in groups of three, and these "trios" moved independently from job to job, field to field, harvest to harvest.[5] Although they were highly skilled and invaluable to the growers when fields had to be picked quickly, they were not essential to production because the braceros did the bulk of the work. Mario Bustamante, who started working in the lettuce with his dad in 1963 and was still a *lechuguero* twenty years later, remembers the difference between the early and later workers:

> They were all tough guys back then, or at least most of them. They were very skilled, but they fought among themselves, and there was a lot of drinking and some drug addicts. But they could cut and pack lettuce so they weren't ordinary winos, and they didn't live on Skid Row. They were from all over—Arizona, Texas, Mexico—true wanderers. Oh, they could get together and fight the bosses for a few days, but they didn't have the same staying power we had later.[6]

In late November 1960, a group of *lechugueros* had gone to the UPWA office seeking help. They were led by Francisco Olivares, known as El Machete, a self-proclaimed *Magonista* who lived in Mexicali and was a veteran of many earlier farm worker strikes. Some of the men had walked off the job already. Others hadn't gone to work in the first place after they heard about the wage cut. The rest were working but damn angry about their pay. They knew about the union because the year before, Neil Busby, a local UPWA official, had led several large marches to the El Centro Farm Placement Office protesting the hiring of braceros in place of domestic workers. They figured the union was looking for a fight.[7]

At the office they found Jerry Breshears, whose family had come to California from Arkansas in 1943. As a child, Breshears had followed the crops: tying carrots and picking cotton, peaches, and grapes. When he was fifteen he got a job in a lettuce shed, but when most lettuce packing was moved to the fields, he went to work for the union. His main job was organizing Anglo fruit tramps, but he had learned a pretty good Spanish over the years. Well versed in Clive Knowles's strategy of encouraging strikes by locals so that the Labor Department would be pressured to remove braceros from the struck fields, he asked the men if they were willing to strike. That's what they had come there for, they said, so Breshears and the *lechugueros* wrote up a leaflet asking people to come to a meeting about the pay cuts. Eight hundred lettuce cutters showed up and voted to strike. Breshears had to urge them to wait until Knowles returned from an out-of-town trip.[8]

Knowles was enthusiastic. The thunder in the distance was getting louder. A few months before, in the summer and fall of 1960, Anglo fruit tramps working in the orchards of the Sacramento and San Joaquin valleys had resumed their infamous practice of stopping work at harvest time to force growers to raise the picking rates. Ninety-two of their strikes had been officially certified by the state of California, but countless others were not.[9] The pickers had come down off their ladders and walked out of the fields because they knew the AFL-CIO-financed Agricultural Workers Organizing Committee (AWOC) was nearby, and the tramps figured that support from the AWOC would magnify the power they had always had during harvests.[10]

Knowles also knew that the growing militancy in the fields was matched by increased opposition to the Bracero Program in the rest of the country. The National Advisory Committee on Farm Labor, the first organizational expression of that opposition, had been founded in 1958, co-chaired by A. Philip Randolph, the social democratic vice president of the AFL-CIO, and Frank Graham, a liberal southern Democrat. Public hearings sponsored by the committee in 1959 had convincingly demonstrated the adverse effect of the Bracero Program on farm worker wages. As the deepening African American civil rights movement, in which Randolph was prominent, began to transform American politics, ending the Bracero Program was becoming a regular item on the new liberal agenda, alongside legislative support for the end of segregation, federal aid to depressed areas, increased health care for the elderly, and a higher minimum wage.

Singularly important in mobilizing public opinion in favor of farm worker organizing and against contracted labor was Edward R. Murrow's "Harvest of Shame," which was televised on November 25, 1960, the day after Thanksgiving, soon after the delegation of workers led by Francisco Olivares had had its first conversation with Jerry Breshears. The program, a portent of the power of TV news, featured impoverished farm workers from Florida and California and concluded with the anguished confession of Eisenhower's secretary of labor, James Mitchell, a liberal Catholic Republican:

> I feel sad. I feel sad because I think that it's a blot on my conscience as well as the conscience of all of us whom society has treated a little more favorably than these people. They have no voice in the legislative halls. They certainly have no voice in Congress, and their employers do have a voice . . . As a citizen, in or out of this office, I propose to continue to raise my voice until the country recognizes that it has an obligation to do something for farm workers."[11]

He was true to his word. In more than half of the 1960 farm worker strikes called when braceros were in the fields, Mitchell prevented the continued use of the contracted workers after the strikes were declared.[12]

The November victory of John F. Kennedy made the UPWA organizers even more optimistic, as the 1960 Democratic Party platform had explicitly denounced the Bracero Program. Surely, they thought, Kennedy's new secretary of labor, AFL-CIO Special Counsel Arthur Goldberg, would be even more willing to intervene on the side of the strikers.[13] The UPWA called all of its organizers to the Imperial Valley in preparation for a strike throughout the lettuce fields, and successfully petitioned its union rival, the AFL-CIO's AWOC, active in the the ladder strikes, to co-sponsor it. The *lechugueros* elected their own ten-member strike committee and prepared for what they believed would be a defining battle.

The strike began on Friday, January 13, 1961, when eighty-three of the ninety-eight *lechugueros* working in grower-shipper Bruce Church's lettuce fields walked out and set up a picket line. Company supervisors immediately sent braceros to continue the cutting and packing. UPWA and AWOC representatives brought Labor Department officials to the fields to see the braceros working behind a picket line, and sent telegrams of complaint to Washington. On Monday, James Mitchell's Labor Department (Kennedy had not yet been inaugurated) rescinded Church's authorization to use braceros and ordered the removal of six hundred braceros from the company's camps. The unions sent roving picket lines to other large ranches, and over the next two weeks, they struck all eighteen major grower-shippers.[14]

It was now the middle of the harvest season, and the strikers were racing the clock. Would the Labor Department remove braceros from all the struck fields before the season slowed down and ended? And if it did, would the growers negotiate with the unions, something they had sworn they would never do? The sit-down in front of the Dannenberg Ranch labor camp had aimed to bring those questions to a head. It was also intended to force the hand of Kennedy's new secretary of labor, Arthur Goldberg. That hand turned out to hold a big surprise.

Instead of removing braceros from the Dannenberg camp, Goldberg set up a meeting in Los Angeles to "resolve the strike." At that two-day affair, Under Secretary of Labor Willard Wirtz was obliged to travel back and forth between the two parties, because the growers' representatives refused to meet in the same room with the union men. Clive Knowles, the primary union leader of the strike, was not invited. At the conclusion of the meeting, Goldberg and Wirtz announced that the braceros would be prohibited from working only on fields that were being picketed. Moreover, no braceros would be sent back to Mexico; rather, they could be transferred to other growers, whose fields were free of pickets. It was a disastrous ruling for the strikers. They couldn't picket all 40,000 acres at once, and so the struck growers could continue to use bracero labor. In addition, some growers had lured local trios back to work by unofficially restoring piece-rate wages. Knowles was furious at Goldberg. The *Imperial Valley News* reported, bluntly, "Growers are now said to feel that Secretary Goldberg is more sympathetic to their cause than was his predecessor James Mitchell."[15]

The only hope that remained for the strikers was the Mexican government, which had ordered the removal of all braceros from the struck ranches after the Dannenberg sit-in. That order had been ignored in the Goldberg settlement, an insult to Mexican officials. They were further annoyed when a federal judge in San Diego issued an unprecedented order restraining the Labor Department from interfering in any way with the struck growers' use of braceros.

In response, the unions planned a second, more aggressive, labor camp demonstration, playing to the oft-stated Mexican fears for the safety of braceros during strikes. This time some strikers ran through a labor camp, brandishing broomsticks and attacking the camp manager, a labor contractor, and even a few braceros. Next, the Mexican ambassador in Washington sent an official, public letter to Secretary Goldberg calling the judge's ruling and the Labor Department's settlement "an affront and a challenge to the sovereignty of Mexico . . . which has all the undertones of holding Mexican citizens in peonage."[16] When its complaints went unheeded, the Mexican government announced that no more braceros would be sent to California until the Imperial Valley strike was over and it was safe for them to work. In response, on March 5, Goldberg finally ordered the complete removal of all braceros from all the fields of the eighteen struck ranches.[17]

It was much too late. The lettuce harvest was just finishing up. Braceros and a few scab trios had cut enough lettuce to maintain sufficient levels of production. Sheriffs had raided the union office and arrested more than fifty strikers, some of whom were charged with multiple felonies. In court, one judge even ruled that all local picketing was illegal because its intent was to subvert Public Law 78, which authorized the Bracero Program. Even the Mexican government's threat eventually fizzled. Goldberg reauthorized the use of braceros in time for the upcoming cantaloupe harvest, and plenty of workers arrived from Mexico to do the job.

In the immediate aftermath of the strike, Fathers Donald McDonnell and Thomas McCullough, active among farm workers and leaders of the Spanish-language Mission Band ministry since 1950, saw their organizing careers ended because of their support for the strikers. Under pressure from the growers and their allies in the San Diego diocese, their bishop disbanded the Mission Band and transferred McCullough and McDonnell away from farm worker parishes. Back in Chicago, Ralph Helstein, the head of the UPWA, decided to pull his union out of farm worker organizing and focus on the shed workers whom the union already had under contract. Clive Knowles left the union and returned to Oxnard, where he and John Soria formed the Emergency Committee to Aid Farm Workers, an effort that didn't last long. In June, George Meany, the head of the AFL-CIO, disbanded the Agricultural Workers Organizing Committee.

Knowles blamed Goldberg—and behind him, Kennedy—for the loss of the strike and the dismantling of AWOC: "Later I found out that Kennedy had said to Goldberg, 'Get rid of that thing, get it out of our hair, we don't have time for it.'" Knowles's story, though undocumented, is easy to believe.[18] In those early days of the administration, Kennedy would not have had much patience with some Imperial Valley farm worker strike that threatened to foment diplomatic trouble with Mexico. He was considering what he hoped would be his twin policy for Latin America: the stick of the Cuban invasion and the carrot of the Alliance for Progress. Kennedy needed acceptance, if not complete support, for this dual policy from other Latin American countries, especially the diplomatically important ones such as Mexico, Argentina, and Brazil. The feelings of Mexican officials had rarely been high on the list of priorities of those in the United States who administered the Bracero Program, but this time the U.S. could not ignore Mexican complaints entirely. Although Goldberg's final order to remove all the braceros from the struck ranches did not affect the strike, it did mollify the Mexicans and was a harbinger of the administration's subsequent reforms of the program.

Once the strike was over, the best way for Kennedy and Goldberg to ensure that such a difficult situation did not recur was to muscle the AFL-CIO into abandoning its organization of farm workers. Goldberg was Meany's man in the White House, and Meany would not have been hard to convince. He had not been enthusiastic about setting up AWOC two years earlier and had done so simply to blunt criticism that organized labor was doing nothing about farm labor conditions and to head off efforts in the fields by his rival, Walter Reuther of the United Automobile Workers, who had been funding various small farm worker projects. Meany closed down AWOC because, he said, the group had spent a lot of money and had not recruited any workers, and because of internal bickering among the various unions. No doubt those factors played a role, but neither had been unexpected two years earlier. If Goldberg did indeed ask Meany to shut down AWOC, neither would have said so publicly, and the request would have carried far more weight than Meany's other explanations.

Goldberg would have been a willing executor of Kennedy's order. One of the chief architects of the CIO's expulsion of the Communists in 1947, he was no friend of rank-and-file militancy. In a speech to the National Association of Manufacturers on December 7, 1960, just before he was named secretary of labor, he argued that ensuring that "our military establishment and our industrial way of life remain superior in all respects to that of the Russians requires the wholehearted cooperation of all elements of our society, including, as a first priority, that of management and labor." A failure to cooperate would be "disastrous," as it would "lead to an eventual militant class consciousness, the absence of which has been one of the strengths of democratic America." Goldberg advocated the establishment of a tripartite Advisory Board to the president, modeled on the War Labor Board of World War II, which would bring together high-level labor, management, and government officials to "help settle great disputes by mediation, fact-finding, and recommendations which, though not binding, will help the conflicting parties find satisfactory common solutions to their problems."[19]

Goldberg never got the Advisory Board, but his intervention in the Imperial Valley strike and his subsequent reforms of the Bracero Program are excellent examples of his cold war labor theories in action. The first priority was to get rid of the strike and any agitation that might threaten U.S. foreign policy objectives. Then, through administrative reforms, Goldberg proposed to look out for the interests of the workers whose strike he had helped to break, and whose prospective union he had helped destroy.

In October of 1961, when President Kennedy signed the new extension of Public Law 78, reauthorizing the Bracero Program, he publicly acknowledged that braceros had adversely affected farm worker wages: "Therefore, I sign this bill with the assurance that the Secretary of Labor will, by every means at his disposal, use the authority vested in him under the law to prescribe the standards and to make the determinations essential for the protection of the wages and working conditions of domestic workers."[20] And so Goldberg did. In 1962, he established a federally mandated minimum wage for California braceros of $1 an hour (the national minimum wage was $1.15), placed fifty-seven new Labor Department officials in the fields to monitor the growers, restricted the amount of time that braceros could be used, and, finally, ordered the restoration of piece rates in the Imperial Valley lettuce deal. In other words, the government had officially mandated the wage concession the workers had unofficially won during the strike the year before. Union leaders were properly thankful. Bud Simonson, director of West Coast operations for the UPWA, put it simply: "It looks like we won the Imperial Valley strike of 1961 after all."[21]

As it happened, neither Arthur Goldberg nor George Meany could shut down the incipient farm worker movement. The AWOC's chief, Norman Smith, a veteran of the 1930s CIO wars, had held some money in reserve.

He had put the union dues that organizers were collecting into a separate trust fund, which he did not turn over to Meany. With that money he maintained some of the old union offices, which were staffed by some AWOC veterans and a new set of volunteers, including students and farm workers. These independent "area councils" carried on their own organizing campaigns, primarily in the Sacramento and upper San Joaquin valleys, but also as far south as Delano, where Larry Itliong, who had a long history in farm worker unions, led efforts among Filipino grape workers.

Many of the area councils began to work with the Mexican American families who lived in the small *barrios* and *colonias*. Others focused on the braceros. Smith continued to focus on the mostly white ladder workers. Some councils collected dues; most of them concentrated on educational and agitational activities. They did not encourage strikes, but the strike movement among the workers, once begun, was not so easy to turn off. In 1961 there were forty-seven other state-certified strikes, most of them without any outside support from labor organizers.[22] The ladder workers continued to be active, but they were no longer alone. Row crop workers—in the peas, cauliflower, asparagus, and Brussels sprouts—also struck. The majority were in Imperial County, but others hit Salinas, Oxnard, and San Diego County fields. After Meany's shutdown order, moreover, the ratio of informal walkouts to certified strikes increased.

AWOC's volunteer period died, or rather was murdered, in its infancy. In 1962 AWOC sent a delegation of workers to the AFL-CIO national convention to ask that body to resume support for its organizing efforts. After hearing an inspiring speech from Maria Moreno, a farm worker, the delegates voted to resume funding. But Meany was determined not to let things get out of hand. His appointee to head up this new version of AWOC, a conservative AFL career official named Al Green, immediately ordered all the area councils to disband and told the farm worker and student volunteers that they were no longer needed. One of the first people he fired was Maria Moreno. "You can't fire us, we are the union," one farm worker volunteer objected, to which Green replied, "You may be the union, but I'm the boss."[23]

Green put all of AWOC's efforts into getting out the 1962 vote for Governor Pat Brown, who by then had become one of the country's most ardent advocates of the bracero program. Next, Green signed agreements with labor contractors, who simply took union dues out of farm workers' checks without giving them any benefits. But Green could not corral all farm worker organizing. Itliong continued to organize among Filipino grape workers; nominally part of AWOC, Itliong was collecting his own dues and running his own operation. Many of the dispersed volunteers simply regrouped, in organizations such as Citizens for Farm Labor (headed by the old AWOC's former publicist, Henry Anderson), the American

Friends Service Committee, and Cesar Chavez's National Farm Workers Association. Although the wave of farm worker strikes ebbed in 1963 and 1964, they started up again even more powerfully after the bracero program was formally ended in 1965.

Historians and academics have taken the victory over the bracero program out of the hands of farm workers. The classic argument, summed up by Linda and Theo Majka, sociologists and early chroniclers of the United Farm Workers, attributes the defeat of Public Law 78 to the victorious liberalism of the "civil rights Congress," the eighty-eighth, which passed the Civil Rights Act and also voted to end the program in 1964. That Congress, so the argument goes, acted in response to several years of educational work by farm worker supporters, especially members of the AFL-CIO and liberal religious groups, who had been thrust into a more powerful position in national politics by the civil rights movement. The scholar David Runsten points out, too, that the introduction of the cotton-harvesting machine undercut grower support of the bracero program nationally. In Texas, where braceros had primarily harvested cotton, the new machines rumbled through the fields, reducing the portion of the crop harvested by hand in 1964 to only 22 percent. Thus, by the time the bracero program was vulnerable, the Texas growers didn't need it anymore. It was left to California's politicians to defend the program, and they were not powerful enough alone to defeat their adversaries in one of the most liberal Congresses in U.S. history. Finally, as Kitty Calavita argues in *Inside the State*, the reforms initiated by Goldberg's Labor Department in 1962 made braceros less useful to the growers; hence the growers were not so desperate to keep them.[24]

These arguments have some merit, but they all ignore the role that farm workers—both braceros and domestics—played in putting an end to Public Law 78. Goldberg's reforms were not just a response to the educational activity of farm worker supporters, nor just a reflection of the strength of AFL-CIO and liberals in Congress and the Kennedy administration. They were also a direct concession to the farm worker movement, especially the wave of strikes in the California fields from 1959 to 1962. Most ominous for the future of Public Law 78 was the role that the braceros themselves were beginning to play in that resurgence. Braceros, it turned out, were not that different from other immigrant groups who had been brought to California to work in the fields. Like the others, the braceros initially were relatively inactive politically. It took some time for them to get acquainted with the territory, to feel comfortable enough to fight. Thus, in the mid-fifties they made only short, ineffective attempts to defend themselves and to unite with striking domestic workers. But by the late 1950s and early '60s, they had begun to exercise what power they had. In Stockton, a bracero crew refused to get on a bus taking them to the fields when they figured out that they had been shorted on their checks; in Salinas braceros and locals struck together in the strawberry fields. Increasing numbers were running away from the camps and joining the ranks of undocumented workers outside any government control. As braceros began to take part in the emerging fight in the fields, especially in crops like Imperial Valley lettuce where they dominated production, growers started to have second thoughts about the program that had brought them here, and looked for ways to replace them.[25]

The increased rebelliousness of the braceros was bad enough, but the growing protests that the presence of the contracted workers provoked among the local farm workers was even worse. Ernesto Galarza and Chavez had begun to organize domestic workers around the demand that they be given their legal right to be hired before braceros. Clive Knowles was provoking walkouts on mixed crews in hopes that the strikes would be officially certified and the braceros removed from the fields. Even on the few occasions when braceros were brought in to break AWOC strikes, the use of bracero scabs tended to increase the commotion rather than end it. The locals sitting in front of the Dannenberg Ranch labor camp were just the latest and most impressive example of how braceros had intensified the battles of local workers. The Bracero Program, whose main purpose was to maximize control of the labor force, had now become a major focus of farm worker revolt.

That first unnamed bracero who climbed that fence, wiggled over the barbed wire, and jumped to the ground to join a strike of local farm workers was the beginning of the end of the bracero program. He deserves a place in U.S. history alongside Rosa Parks and the Montgomery bus boycotters of 1955, beside the four black college students who kicked off the student civil rights movement by sitting-in at a lunch counter in North Carolina in 1960, and beside the white students who ended the fifties by humiliating HUAC in San Francisco in 1959. The rousing cheers from his new comrades must have been matched by a collective shudder among the cops, the foremen in charge of the braceros, and any growers who happened to be present. Who could ignore this singular act of courage and political will? Braceros would not automatically remain forever the passive instruments of grower interests. If they saw an opportunity to fight, they might snatch it.

One lettuce grower who had been watching the farm worker movement closely and read it correctly was Bud Antle, a maverick in the Salinas and Imperial valleys. Right after the Imperial Valley strike, he concluded that Public Law 78 was doomed and therefore farm worker unionization was inevitable. He figured that a union he could work with was better than the kind of unionism that was sure to come, and when braceros and locals struck at a strawberry company in Salinas soon after the Imperial strike ended, Antle signed a contract with the Teamsters. His prescience earned him the hatred of the rest of the Salinas Valley and Imperial Valley lettuce growers, who were still determined to stop farm worker unionism entirely, independent of what happened to Public Law 78. Antle, who had also been the first to replace his relatively well-paid domestic shed workers with the low-paid braceros in the fields in the early fifties, once again proved to be way ahead of his competitors. They would turn to the Teamsters eight years later, after the UFW had won the first grape contracts, but by then it was too late.

Certainly, the strike wave of 1959–62, of which the Imperial Valley lettuce strike was the most significant single event, did not end Public Law 78 immediately, but given the slow pace at which legislation usually responds to social reality, it didn't take long for the workers' movement to have its effect. Senators Eugene McCarthy and George McGovern first introduced legislation to end the program in 1960. California's Senator Claire Engle, visiting Mexico during the Imperial Valley strike in 1961, told Mexican legislators that largely because of the strike he did not expect the Bracero Program to be renewed again by the U.S. Congress.[26] In 1963 the program barely got enough votes to continue. In 1964, it passed only after its proponents promised that this would be its last year. Even *Time* magazine in 1961 got the story better than the historians who now claim that "farm labor activity during the early 1960s was comparatively weak and ineffective." At the end of its six-paragraph article on the Imperial Valley strike *Time* concluded, "With a foot in the ranchers' gate, the unions are now hoping to kick the gate down."[27]

Cesar Chavez was a minor player in the 1960–61 Imperial Valley strike. He had come to the valley as the executive director of Community Service Organization, the job he had taken after he left Oxnard. John Soria remembers seeing him at some of the picket lines and at the big rallies, quietly taking them in. But Chavez did more than that. He helped organize local Mexican Americans into what he called the Committee to Advance the Valley Economy. The group circulated a petition supporting the workers' right to organize and issued leaflets detailing how much money the Imperial Valley was losing because braceros sent their wages back to Mexico. It also picketed the grower-sponsored Citizens to Save the Harvest when mostly wives and children of the growers made some widely publicized but ineffectual attempts to pack lettuce in the struck fields. Less than a year later, as strikes continued to batter California growers and formal labor organizing was in disarray, Chavez returned to the Imperial Valley for the CSO's annual convention. He tried to convince the delegates, many of whom he had brought into politics, to commit CSO resources to organizing farm workers. When the delegates refused, he resigned, abruptly leaving the organization that he had been building for ten years. Bud Antle was not the only man in California to guess the shape of the future.

A Family Affair

April '62 to March '65

Once in Delano, the first thing I did was draw a map by hand of all the towns between Arvin and Stockton, eighty-six of them, including farming camps. I decided to hit them all. I wanted to see the San Joaquin Valley as I'd never seen it before, all put together. Of course, I knew the area, but I never had seen it with the idea of organizing it.

—Cesar Chavez, 1975

If, as John Soria believed, Cesar Chavez was a little crazy to think that he could organize Ventura County, then trying to organize the entire Central Valley would have to be judged absolute madness. In Ventura a few families seemed to own everything in sight—but everything was in sight; the place was small, it had edges. But 250 miles separate Arvin from Stockton, in a valley sixty miles wide at its midsection—an area so vast that John Muir did not call it a valley at all but named it the Great Central Plain. Hundreds of thousands of people worked the fields of the Central Valley, but just how many hundreds of thousands nobody knew for sure.[1] And although power there was shared among many more farm corporations and farm families than in Ventura, those corporations and families, taken together, had nearly complete control over the provincial politics of the small agricultural towns. Oil was agriculture's only economic rival in the Great Central Plain, and it was a measure of the awesome power of Chavez's chosen adversary that the extensive oil fields around Bakersfield were but a minor money-maker compared with the the cotton, tomatoes, grapes, and orchards of the Central Valley.

If enough people get together they can do anything, Chavez had told Soria driving down the road in Ventura. In the Central Valley in the spring of 1962, he had another driving companion: Jim Drake, whose Renault and gasoline credit card had been made available to Chavez by Chris Hartmire of the California Migrant Ministry. Developed nationally out of liberal Protestant charity work during the Depression and later coordinated by the National Council of Churches as part of its nascent civil rights mission, the CMM had, since the mid-1950s, become increasingly frustrated with what it viewed as the limits of Christian charity. Rather than continue to alleviate the symptoms of poverty, its small paid staff in California wanted to change the social structures that made people poor. They were not sure how to do that, but decided to start by trying to organize farm workers. Drake had just been hired, at $500 a month, by the CMM to set up a community organization in the small town of Goshen, less than fifty miles up Highway 99 from Delano. Hartmire, whom Chavez had helped train a few years earlier, knew that Chavez would put the car, the driver, and the credit card to good use.

Jim Drake was one of many Christian activists educated at New York's Union Theological Seminary. His father, also a UTS graduate, worked in a public school in the oil-field country outside of Tulsa, Oklahoma, where he taught the children of migrant families, who followed the wells. In 1947, when Jim was ten, the family moved to Thermal, California, in the Coachella Valley, where his father taught in the local junior high school. All of the growers' kids were in one class, and the Mexicans, Negroes, and Okies were together in the remedial class. Drake's dad taught the remedials. Like his father, Drake did not want to be a minister—"I didn't want to be separated from the people," he said—and soon after he earned his degree he and his wife, Susan, moved back to California to organize farm workers.[2]

"I really thought Cesar was crazy," he told Jacques Levy. "Everybody did except Helen [Chavez 's wife]. They had so many children and so little to eat, and that old 1953 Mercury station wagon gobbled up gas and oil. Everything he wanted to do seemed impossible."[3]

"Crazy" back then was a measure of the Chavez will—and his will was part of the reason so many men and women circled around him. People, poor people especially, are not going to throw in their lot with one who is easily deterred. To lead one must be steadfast, even when unyielding determination may seem somewhat ridiculous. And Chavez's will was no less powerful, seemed no less outrageous to his compatriots, than did the will of his famous contemporary in the Caribbean, Fidel Castro. Castro's wild boast that "the days of the dictatorship are numbered" to a dozen would-be guerrilla fighters in the foothills of the Sierra Maestra after sixty-eight of their comrades had just been gunned down was nearly matched by Chavez's quiet plans to change the face of California agribusiness as he rode around the Central Valley with hardly enough money to buy his own dinner.

Whence this confidence and will? Gandhi was born into the prosperous merchant caste. Martin Luther King, Jr. was the son of a preacher with his own established church. Che Guevara was from the solid middle class with a medical degree in his pocket. Fidel Castro, perhaps the most willful and confident of them all, was from a wealthy, land-owning family, a light-skinned man in a world where whiteness mattered, a successful lawyer, and an excellent athlete. But Chavez? Chavez was a victim of the migrant trail, a small dark-skinned man, a failure in school who lacked the athletic prowess that could have impressed his childhood peers. He did have his faith, however, his sure belief in the righteousness of his cause, and by the age of thirty-five, when he decided to "organize the San Joaquin," he had a long string of adult successes to sustain him. He had worked himself out of the fields. He had been the director of the most powerful Mexican American organization in the United States. He had earned enough money, $150 a week, so that Helen did not have to work outside the house. He was no longer a worker; he was a professional organizer.

And was his project really so mad? A new wind was blowing. Chavez and his cohorts could feel it at their back. The whole country was alive with possibility, led by the young African American demonstrators who were battering down the walls of segregation in the South. Chavez was not the only man thinking big. And those thinking about farm workers were particularly optimistic. Paul Taylor and Varden Fuller, at the time the two most respected scholars of agriculture in California, believed that the growers were now on the defensive, that farm worker unions were on the way.[4] And Chavez had a plan. He would organize the home guard, farm workers who had been ignored by AWOC: the Mexican American families who worked the fields and made their homes in the Central Valley. And rather than organize them primarily at the point of production, around the issues they faced at work, he would organize them in their communities, around the issues they confronted off the job. Sustained by his religious convictions, using the techniques of community organizing that he had perfected over the previous ten years in the CSO, he set out to build something new, part union, part *mutualista*—a Central Valley Farm Workers Association.

"We always thought it would be different from a union," said Jim Drake. "If somebody died, the family was going to be helped. If somebody needed tires, the association could help. If they were having trouble with immigration or welfare, the association would help. We would have a radio program. *El Malcriado* would be a community paper, not a union paper . . . 'Union' was not a popular word. We wanted to be much broader than that. We wanted the whole family to be part of the union."[5]

The organizers of this new Farm Workers Association were quite conscious of the role the *mutualistas* had played in Mexican American history, particularly in the 1920s and early '30s. Chavez had read about them in the few books he could find about farm worker history, but he and the other founders didn't need books to know about *mutualistas*, as some were still around. Gilbert Padilla was even a member of one of the oldest groups, Sociedad Progresista, which had started in nineteenth-century Mexico but by the 1960s was little more than a burial society. "We had groups in Selma, Hanford, Tulare and Visalia," Padilla recalled, "and when a member died the Progresistas would give the family one hundred dollars and send over a uniformed honor guard to stand watch at the funeral. It was the same sort of thing we were trying to do with the FWA life insurance plan."[6] The one other early FWA program, the credit union, was also a more up-to-date version of the loan policy maintained by many *mutualistas* in the 1920s, and the entire approach of the new association was based on the old *mutualista* idea of building community and power through mutual self-help.

But Chavez was nothing if not eclectic and pragmatic, and the association was not merely a new *mutualista*, or a new version of the CSO. This was three years after the Oxnard effort. Chavez was no longer supervised by Fred Ross or paid by Saul Alinsky. The FWA was a community organization, but it did not fit the Alinsky mold. Starting a major organizing drive without outside funding was one clear departure from the Alinsky protocal; so was Chavez's early emphasis on avoiding conflict and publicity, and so, especially, was the role of principal organizer.

Soon after setting up house in Delano in the spring of 1962, Chavez started driving up and down the Central Valley, visiting old contacts and making new ones. He urged some of the old CSO activists to join this new effort. He surveyed workers on what wages they wanted to earn. He collected relatively high dues of $3.50 a month ($1 of which would pay for members' life insurance premiums as soon as he could sign up three hundred people), and he helped the new members with the various problems they had with government agencies. Chavez was an organizer, in the most direct sense of that word: he was trying to put together an organization. At the first FWA convention, held in Fresno in September 1962, about six months after the organizing effort began, the group had fewer than fifty voting members. Chavez, running unopposed, received sixteen votes for the position of head of staff, or general director.[7] Jesus Martinez, like a typical bombastic leader in Chavez's menagerie of political types, gave a dynamic, charismatic speech, and was elected president. But when he failed to show up at the next two executive board meetings, the board, acknowledging that Chavez was not only the organizer but also the leader of this barely surviving outfit, abolished the position of general director and named Chavez president. Three months later a second, even smaller, National Farm Workers Association convention approved the change.[8]

It seemed reasonable. As Gilbert Padilla later explained, "We weren't going to do that CSO thing again where we were the organizers, we did all the work, but we weren't the leaders of the organization."[9] Less than a year had passed since Chavez had left the CSO, disappointed in the people who had refused to follow his direction. Often taking jobs a few steps up from the fields—as railroad workers, small shop owners, low-level government employees—the CSO leaders, Chavez felt, had turned their backs on the bulk of the people in their communities. Some had even taken jobs in the new Pat Brown administration. Now, cut off from all the resources of the CSO, he was starting a new, still fragile organization, and he was not about to turn over the leadership to some slacker just because he had given a good speech at a meeting.

Nevertheless, Chavez was defensive about merging the positions of general director and president. He always left out that detail when he recounted the history of the UFW, claiming he had been elected at the first convention. He wasn't so worried about the lack of a formal vote; what bothered him was the problem of developing leadership in his new organization. Identifying and developing new leaders had been his most important job in the CSO. But now, so early in the FWA game, could he both lead and stand back enough to allow new leaders to emerge? For the previous ten years he had been schooled by Alinsky and Ross to believe that that would be very hard to do.

Such questions were much in the air in 1962. Similar discussions were going on within the Student Non-Violent Coordinating Committee, and activist church organizations. Henry Anderson, who had worked with Norman Smith to keep AWOC going after the AFL-CIO cut its funding, wrote a long paper, "To Build a Union: Comments on the Organization of Farm Workers," mimeographed copies of which were circulated among the various groups trying to organize in the fields at the time. Anderson, a democratic socialist, insisted that any successful farm worker union had to be democratically structured, with independent locals and in control of its own destiny. The organizers could legitimately come from outside the farm worker community, he argued, but the leadership of the new union must come from the farm workers themselves. Anderson had not read Alinsky, but nevertheless he argued in classic Alinsky style that the organizers must find and develop the leaders and then move on: "What is needed is someone to alter conditions in such a way that the natural leadership of the farm labor force is liberated. This someone must be keenly sensitive to the danger of his overstaying his visit. He must be as nearly without personal ambition as one can be and still be human."[10]

Thus, Anderson, too, based his democratic theory—the hope that common people can collectively run their own lives—on the existence of a most uncommon organizer, one who was without ambition, almost a saint. Soon enough, however, Anderson, enthusiastic about Chavez's leadership of the new farm worker movement, abandoned some of his earlier formulation. With Joan London he wrote a book in 1970, *So Shall Ye Reap,* celebrating the new leader's arrival. The farm worker organization was democratic, they argued, because Chavez and other leaders had been farm workers, and because they were independent and not beholden to other union officials. Chavez was fully in control and indispensable, Anderson reported, but still looked forward to a time when he could "go to the mountains or some place where it's quiet, and read all the classics in Spanish and English." Not wanting to stay around (even as he did) was a good indication that Chavez sought power not for himself but for farm workers. And, besides, how could such a man be power-hungry:

> He enters a public meeting so unobtrusively that one is hardly aware of his presence until he is introduced to speak. He never raises his voice in public utterances, any more than private. He brushes a persistent shock of hair from his forehead, and talks conversationally whether the gathering is large or small, broadcast, televised, or unrecorded. He makes little jokes as he goes along, but unless one is familiar with the farm workers' universe of discourse, one may not realize they are jokes, they are invariably understated.[11]

Chavez was precisely the kind of leader who could build a space where other leaders could thrive, because "in the course of becoming a man himself, Cesar Chavez has been a maker of men."[12]

In retrospect it is not surprising that Chavez and the FWA would wander off the established organizational charts when it came to the relationship between leaders and organizers, as the whole nature of the new association was unmapped and somewhat vague. No one thought of the FWA as an organizational stepping stone—a transitional form—on the road to becoming a regular American union. Such a union was understood as something to be avoided. Chavez shared the Alinskyite critique of postwar unionism, and he had not been happy with what he had seen of the United Packinghouse Workers Association in Oxnard or of the 1960–61 lettuce strike in the Imperial Valley. Dolores Huerta had spent a short time working in Norman Smith's early AWOC, and had left in disgust over his organizing methods and lack of interest in Stockton's Mexican American community. Unions, they agreed, were too bureaucratic, too focused on the workers' experience on the job while ignoring other problems, and too caught up in a culture of strikes and confrontation. Besides, unions had a mixed legacy in the fields. They had a long history of either ignoring the struggles of farm workers or of getting involved only intermittently, of being here today and gone tomorrow. Worse, contemporary union efforts in the fields were being led by Anglos, most of whom didn't speak Spanish and some of whom were out and out racists. Early on, the FWA leaders came to consider the revived AWOC, under the leadership of Al Green, to be a primary adversary. A conventional union was not the goal, it was, as currently constituted, a rival form of organization.

The FWA had a stamp, used on many of its leaflets: "The Farm Workers Association is not a Union." Other leaflets began with the admonition: *"Este movimiento se hace enteramente por los trabajadores y no es afiliado a ninguna unión, sindicato, or partido político*: "This movement is made entirely by workers and is affiliated with no union or political party."[13] Certainly Chavez wanted the FWA eventually to sign collective bargaining agreements—in a letter to Dolores Huerta before the first FWA convention, he called such agreements his "main purpose." Yet labor contracts did not represent the essence of what he was building. The emphasis was on self-help and mutual assistance; the FWA's first program, the group life insurance policy, was exemplary of the kind of programs the FWA had in mind.[14]

Likewise, the FWA's founders did not casually choose the term "association." If they had wanted a new *mutualista*, they would have called the group a *sociedad*. The closest model for what they were trying to build was probably the Agricultural Workers Association of Father MacDonnell and Father McCullough, which enjoyed a brief life from the fall of 1958 to the spring of 1959. The FWA was not run by priests, but it was led by an ex-altar boy, and its goal of combining mutual self-help programs with collective bargaining agreements was a central feature of Pope Leo XIII's concept of Catholic unionism. The religious character of the FWA was written into its official Statement of Purpose, which begins: "As Christians and workers we wish to realize the ideals of the Church in our lives and in the world in which we live." Most of what follows are quotes from Pope John XXIII: "Economic progress must be accompanied by a corresponding social progress"; "Workers must be paid a wage which allows them to live a truly human life and to fulfill their family obligations in a worthy manner." The Statement of Purpose emphasized that John "explicitly expressed his approval of labor unions." The executive board even asserted for the FWA a retroactive endorsement from the departed pope: "Pope John reserved a special place in his thoughts . . . for Christian associations of workers who endure great difficulties in their endeavor to promote the material and moral interests of the working people. As members of the Farm Workers Association, we draw strength from his blessing." The board members concluded with a one-paragraph summary of their program:

> The Farm Workers Association has had experience in developing cooperative efforts among farm workers. It operates a credit union, an insurance plan, and a small consumer co-op for its members. In addition, the officers and staff have been authorized by the members to act as their representatives in negotiations with employers, although, unfortunately, employers have not responded to requests to negotiate.[15]

Most people joined the FWA as families. Jessie de la Cruz, daughter, wife, and mother of farm workers, who worked in the grapes and the cotton herself, was, along with her family, one of the first women members of the new association. She later became director of the Parlier field office and hiring hall, and her memory of how she was recruited to the FWA is typical.

> We were living in Parlier at the time . . . There was a group of men who came to our house and one of them I later learned was Cesar Chavez. He started talking about the union, getting other members to join. I was in the kitchen making coffee to offer them, and he told my husband, "Your wife has to be here. She works out in the fields, too, so she needs to hear what we're talking about." So I got the coffee and then I sat down and I listened. And I liked what I heard. So after that I did join.

The experience could not have been more different from the way an AWOC organizer had treated her just a few years before. AWOC was also trying to recruit her husband, and only men were invited to the meetings, held in a bar in Fresno. One time Jessie drove to the meeting with her husband and had to wait in the car until the discussions were over.[16]

From the beginning, the FWA set out to organize the "home guard," the Mexican American families whose roots went back to what is called "the first wave" of Mexican immigration to the United States, at the onset of the Mexican Revolution. These farm worker families of the Central Valley, who generally called themselves Mexicanos or Mexicans, had not been too active in the strikes of 1960–61. That upsurge had featured others: Anglo fruit tramps, both single men and families; Mexican and Filipino male workers, mostly migrant and either single or separated from home; and, on a few significant occasions, braceros, all males and all, by definition, away from home and family. The settled Mexican families who peopled the *colonias* and barrios of the Central Valley had held back. They had more to lose in strikes. Many of them didn't migrate at all; some migrated short distances only during the summers, usually working for the same employer or the same group of employers year after year. If they struck and lost, they could more easily be blacklisted than their less-settled fellow workers because they were well known to their employers, foremen, and contractors. If blacklisted, they would have to uproot themselves and move to other areas, and moving around, following the crops, was precisely what this particular group of people had stopped doing. Moreover, many of these families had participated in strikes in the early 1950s, and still felt the effects of those defeats. Perhaps most important of all, in these families the mother and wife had enormous authority and influence, and as their first commitment was to the well-being of their families, these women often restrained their men. It is not that the women were less militant than the men; once they committed to a struggle, they were likely to be dogged in pursuing it. But the farm worker women tended to be more cautious, as did the men whose families were working alongside them in the fields, or whose families were close by. Chavez's decision to focus on the families meant that he would have to take these mothers and wives seriously, and that success or failure would depend, among other things, on his ability to recruit significant numbers of women.

It is symbolically perfect that two out of four on Cesar's original team— Helen Chavez and Dolores Huerta—were women. They were not mere feminist window dressing. True, Huerta would later become an important part of the UFW's appeal to its middle-class feminist supporters, but in 1962 there was no women's movement to consider. And Helen Chavez hardly ever allowed herself to be put forward to dress up anything; she preferred to take a back seat. These two women presented two contrasting modes of female participation in the FWA and were its authentic cofounders. Without them there would have been no initial attempt to organize the association, just as without the support of women farm workers the FWA might have died in its infancy.[17]

Leaving the CSO, like many of Chavez's other sacrifices for the good of the cause, was harder on his wife than it was on him. Although he gave up considerable status and resources, Cesar continued to do what he had done before: organize, travel from one community to another, talk to people. More was required of Helen. When the family moved to Delano, she went back to work in the fields. She was thirty-four years old, and twelve years had passed since she had picked her last string bean in a field outside of San Jose. In the intervening years she had had eight children. Although Chavez's CSO salary allowed her to remain at home to manage the household, her husband was often away and was not much help. And "home" kept shifting. In the CSO years, the Chavez family lived in six different cities: San Jose, Madera, Bakersfield, Hanford, Oxnard, and Los Angeles. In each new place it was left to Helen, with several young children in tow, to establish a home. With the loss of the CSO salary, and only their meager savings and Chavez's unemployment checks to sustain them, the family needed money, so it was back to the fields for Helen, back to the life of a farm worker mom: getting up at 4 a.m. to lay out breakfast and lunch for the kids; carrying Birdy, the youngest, still asleep, over to his aunt Teresa's; arriving in the fields by six for a full day of physical labor; going back to Teresa's to pick up Birdy; returning home to make dinner; cleaning up the kitchen; getting everyone ready for bed.

The only way she could do it was by moving to Delano, where her two sisters and two brothers still lived. Helen, not Cesar, was the one who chose Delano.[18] Chavez's brother, Richard, lived there, and that was part of the reason for the move, but Delano had been just another stop on the road for Chavez's parents, who had finally established a permanent residence in San Jose, while Helen's family, the Fabelas, had made Delano their home. As young adults they had come from Mexico in the mass immigration of the 1920s, and had settled there in the early thirties, after stops in Brawley and McFarland. Helen, the second of their five children, started working in the Delano fields with her mother when she was seven years old and remembers walking to local ranches to pick cotton and grapes. When she was twelve her father died, and she and her older sister, Teresa, had to take on more responsibilities. A few years later they both quit school and became full-time field workers. When there was no work in the fields, Helen clerked in Delano stores. When she returned home in 1962 with her husband and eight children, Teresa was still in the vineyards working as a crew pusher (a low-level supervisory job that allowed her to watch Birdy while she worked), while their younger sister, Petra, labored regularly in the table grapes.

Through the years, most of Chavez's family had gotten out of the fields, but Helen's had not. Even though her return to the fields did not last long—a year later she was working full-time as the FWA bookkeeper for $50 a week—she always remained much more a part of Delano farm worker life and culture than her husband. Cesar's class position had shifted throughout his life, first down, and then up. Helen's family had never risen high enough to own land, and never fallen low enough to be true migrants. They were settled Delano farm workers, and although Helen was carried along by the changing status of her husband, she also lived in the world of her two sisters until the family moved to La Paz in 1971. Virginia Hirsch, a volunteer who arrived in 1966 to set up the association's legal office, called Helen and her sisters and their women farm worker friends "the chewing-gum chorus . . . They would always come to the meetings and sit together on the side, chewing their gum, talking about their kids. Helen was very down to earth and pure working class. Chavez was out there, operating in wider and wider circles, on his way to becoming an important man, but Helen remained very much at home among farm workers."[19]

Even into the late sixties, male UFW organizers still joked (or half joked) that the first people they had to organize were their wives. What they meant was that organizing took up so much time and energy that they couldn't be around home much, and the wife had to be so convinced of the righteousness of the cause that she would gladly accept the absences, or at least put up with them. Such an attitude led to some strained marriages, and, quite often, to separation and divorce. Later in her marriage, Helen moved out for a while, but before then she doesn't seem to have made much fuss. She often complained directly to Cesar about his deserting the family and "putting on airs," according to Virginia Hirsch, but the complaints rarely escalated into serious trouble. Helen was raised to work hard and to take care of her family, and that is what she did. In the CSO years, she addressed envelopes and postcards, and sometimes wrote letters or the daily work reports, which Chavez dictated. She always helped out with the financial records, which led to the bookkeeping job. Later she took on the task of credit union manager, and then, as the union won some contracts, she became a primary administrator of some of its social service projects, and the center of the union's financial operations. Always she had the primary, almost exclusive, responsibility of raising the eight children. She suffered without public complaint through Cesar's absence for all but two of her children's births, his early exit from their daughter's wedding, the forgotten anniversaries, his not being able to find the time to take a sick child to the hospital. Reports of such incidents come not from Helen but from the kids or from Chavez himself, who had the audacity, on occasion, to cite his neglect of family obligations as examples of his sacrifice, his willingness to give up regular family life for the sake of the cause. Their marriage arrangement was no doubt more a matter of traditional patterns of Mexican family life than it was a result of Cesar's "organizing" Helen. But whatever the marriage's private secrets, publicly Helen was Chavez's great enabler, an organizer's wife made in heaven.

While Helen broke no cultural mold and offended no 1950s sensibilities, offending sensibilities was the specialty of the other female member of the original founding four, Dolores Huerta. Ms. Huerta, a true Ms. before the term came into use, turned the cultural norm of supportive wife and nurturing mother inside out, though less out of rebellion than as an extension of her upbringing by a mother who, like so many others, lived outside the supposedly standard female roles of her time. Alicia, Dolores' mother, a second-generation New Mexican Hispanic who was twice divorced and thrice married, was often the breadwinner of her family, while her relatives, especially Dolores's grandfather, became her children's primary caretakers.

The fortunes of mother and children fluctuated widely. Alicia grew up comfortably as the daughter of a coal miner turned store owner in the booming coal town of Dawson, New Mexico, and graduated from high school, which was unusual for a Hispanic woman in the 1920s. Against her father's wishes, she moved down in class and status by marrying a first-generation Mexican coal miner, Juan Fernández, who fathered her first three children (Dolores was the second). The marriage broke up in the early thirties when Alicia was in her third pregnancy, and like many others she left the slumping boom town of Dawson and took off for California. She and her three children settled in Stockton, where her father, no longer well off, soon joined them. The Depression years were tough on the family.

Alicia worked as a waitress during the day and sometimes did a double shift at night in the canneries. During World War II, her class trajectory pitched upward again with her marriage to James Richards, the new owner of a skid row hotel bought at a bargain price after its original owners, Japanese Americans, had been interned. Alicia managed the hotel, had a child by Richards, and then divorced him, but kept the hotel and soon leased another. By her third marriage, to Juan Silva, she had become a successful Stockton businesswoman, living in an integrated, relatively well-off neighborhood. Dolores, thoroughly bilingual and bicultural, enjoyed some of the accoutrements of American middle-class life—dancing, piano, and violin lessons—and a spot in the Stockton High School orchestra, with the prized position of majorette.

Dolores's high school graduation was followed by two years at Stockton Junior College, marriage to an Anglo high school classmate, two children, clerical work, separation, divorce, and return to her mother's home. Mother and daughter remained close. They participated in various Mexican American social service projects and belonged to the women's division of El Comité Honorifico, helping to plan community celebrations of Mexican holidays. With her mother's support, Dolores returned to college for a teaching credential. She met her second husband, Ventura Huerta, a veteran of the U.S. Marine Corps, while doing community work. They were married in 1955 and had five children—the last arrived just as they were getting divorced. Both continued to be active in community affairs, but the extent of Dolores's activity disturbed her husband. He disapproved of her haphazard child-care arrangements but was unwilling to do extensive child care himself. Despite his harsh reproaches, Dolores found more things to do outside the family, and her public commitments shifted away from conventional female community work. She joined the Stockton chapter of CSO and threw herself into its two main activities: citizenship classes and voter registration drives. She then worked with the Mission Band's Agricultural Workers Association, but she never was completely comfortable there, because Father McCullough focused his efforts on male farm workers and didn't think that farm worker organizing was a proper role for a woman. When the AWA shut down in favor of AWOC, she joined the latter's paid staff, but didn't last long there, either.

As she moved from one organization to another, her knowledge of politics and joy in public life deepened. In 1959, after she left AWOC, Fred Ross, who had brought her into the Stockton CSO four years earlier, added her to the short list of paid CSO staff. In a brilliant move, he hired her to be the CSO lobbyist in Sacramento. She was a pioneer in the state capital, for there were no other Mexican American women lobbyists. By the age of thirty, Huerta had found her vocation. She mastered the intricacies of the legislative process. As she testified at hearings and committee meetings for extending old-age benefits to noncitizens, disability insurance to farm workers, and against the abuses of the Bracero Program, she sharpened her sense of social injustice while maintaining her basic middle-class optimism about the possibilities of social change. She remembered, and reconsidered, the poverty of her early youth and the systematic discrimination against Mexican Americans and African Americans at Stockton High School. She also remembered the example of her mother and the relative lack of gender discrimination in her upbringing. When asked to tell her own story later, she rarely failed to mention that her mother never made her cook for or take care of her brothers, and that from a young age she was taught to assume that women were just as capable and valuable as men. When looking back at childhood for examples of injustice, she typically told a story about high school that combined both anger at the racist and sexist assumptions of her teachers and pride in her own abilities and powers: a teacher had said that her essays were so good that he did not believe she could have written them by herself.

She had not been cheating then, and she was not cheating now as she talked before the state legislators. She was just being herself, and it was exciting and worthwhile. Her only problem was she had all those children, didn't have a wife like Helen, and her husband was unwilling to become one. Soon, she and her husband were together only off and on. Dolores made child-care arrangements with relatives and friends, hired babysitters, and managed the best she could. Even though she had the help and example of her mother, she was still torn by the conflicting obligations of family and public life. "My biggest problem was not to feel guilty about it," she said in 1974. "I don't any more, but then everybody used to lay these guilt trips on me, about what a bad mother I was, neglecting my children."[20] One person who didn't guilt-trip her was Cesar Chavez, who became national director of CSO while Huerta was working in Sacramento. Chavez respected her dedication and accepted her unusual choices. Here was a will to match his own. "When it comes to organizing all the farm workers, I'm a fanatic," he told Jacques Levy, "and I look for other fanatics, the ones who really want to get the job done. The desire to win has got to be very strong, or else you can't do it."[21]

Those were the words, that was the idea, that Huerta needed. Here was a way not only to make sense of her internal struggles but to resolve them. Rather than urging her to cut back on her public life, Chavez asked her to give more. When Chavez left the CSO and moved to Delano, Huerta continued to collect her CSO paycheck but spent much of her time talking to farm workers about the FWA. Combining the two activities soon proved impossible, but rather than stick with the substantial employment possibilities provided by her class background, college degrees, speaking skills, political experience, and teaching credential, she quit her job with the CSO and moved deeper into poverty, working as a unpaid volunteer for the barely surviving FWA. Living on child-support payments from the fathers of her children and unemployment insurance, she worked at organizing the Farm Workers Association in the area around Stockton and in the northern Central Valley. It was a terribly difficult time, with neither a reliable car nor regular child care, but with Chavez's encouragement and support (they exchanged frequent letters and work reports), she continued. Finally in 1964 she left Stockton and moved to Delano, joining the small, relatively isolated FWA family. Although she earned only $5 a week there, her child-care problems would become a collective responsibility. Helen's sister Petra virtually adopted Peanuts, Dolores's youngest child. Laurie Head, Dolores's eldest child, took major responsibility for her younger siblings with significant help from Virginia Hirsch, Doug Adair, and other FWA volunteers. With the association helping to raise her kids, and with Chavez's ideas about sacrifice easing her mind, her decision to bet everything on Chavez and the FWA eventually led her to a series of monumental accomplishments, and justified every painful sacrifice. As she told a newspaper reporter in 1974, "You have to make a decision, when working with people, the people have the priority, and the family must understand."[22]

Helen Chavez and Dolores Huerta were not the only women in the early FWA. Those who rounded out the chewing-gum chorus included Helen's sister Petra, Rachael Orendain, Gloria Terronez, Esther Uranday, and Josefina Hernandez. All but Petra were married to men who were FWA organizers or activists, and the women's style of participation was much closer to Helen's than to Dolores's. They managed their families, freeing up their husbands' time; they organized and ran the community barbecues, which were a major source of funds for the FWA and an important organizing tool; they talked up the association among other farm worker women. The participation of so many mothers and wives gave the FWA moral weight, signifying that the association was not just another hit-and-run organizing attempt. Although the FWA demanded a sacrifice—there were dues to pay and meetings to attend—joining up became the right thing to do.

It helped that men of God also came to the FWA's aid—not primarily from the Catholic Church, whose Central Valley parishes were almost completely dominated by growers and their families, but rather from the small outpost of Protestantism, the Californian Migrant Ministry, which itself was supported by, among others, the Alinsky-linked Emil Schwarzhaupt Foundation. The CMM director in 1961, Chris Hartmire, was chiefly responsible for the long-lasting, intimate relationship between the ministry and Chavez, with whom Hartmire was closely associated until 1988. Five years younger than Chavez, Hartmire was a product of the affluent Philadelphia suburbs. His dad made a good living working for DuPont while his mother stayed home raising the children. Although Hartmire regularly attended Sunday school, actively participated in church youth groups, and went to Presbyterian summer camps, he never felt any particular religious calling. He got a scholarship to Princeton, where he majored in engineering, but it was while working at a summer camp for poor kids from New York City, Trenton and Newark, that he "got hooked on working with people."[23]

After three years in the Navy, he enrolled in Union Theological Seminary and worked in the East Harlem Protestant Parish, which by the late 1950s had become a laboratory for Protestants who were trying to rethink their mission to the poor. Always a good student, he did well in biblical studies ("he came to know the Bible like a Baptist," said one admirer), but his most important intellectual sustenance came from the prison diary of Dietrich Bonhoeffer, the upper-class Lutheran minister who in World War II Germany had attempted to help Jews escape the Holocaust and joined a conspiracy to assassinate Hitler.[24] Thrown in jail in 1944 when the plot was uncovered, Bonhoeffer based his resistance—so atypical of the mild German Protestant response to fascism—on his belief that Christians had to learn to live in reality, and respond to the evil conditions of the world. He knew that political action was fraught with moral difficulties: even helping Jews escape required killing other Germans. Contemporary Christianity did not provide much moral guidance in such decisions, so Bonhoeffer resurrected an idea he found in the sermons of the first politically inclined Lutheran, Martin himself, who spoke in defense of "bravely sinning." To fight evil in the world, one might have to sin, and one had to be brave enough to accept that, Luther argued.

Even though the intensity of the contradiction between a strict religious morality, which sees human action only in terms of its own immediate intrinsic meaning, and the political world, which requires some calculation of ends and means, diminished greatly between the sixteenth and twentieth centuries as religious sensibility weakened, it was still alive for Bonhoeffer as he sat in Hitler's jail. And it was still intense for the young Chris Hartmire, who as a seminary student sought to mesh his intimate devotion to the New Testament's other-worldly ethics with his own overwhelming impulse toward action in the world. Bonhoeffer, who was executed shortly before the Allies liberated Germany, became Hartmire's chief hero and intellectual inspiration. Over the next twenty-eight years, as Hartmire threw himself into the difficult choices involved in giving full support to a union involved in a necessarily messy struggle to establish itself in the California fields, his respect for Bonhoeffer grew, and he came to rely on the idea of "bravely sinning."

In 1961, however, when at the age of twenty-nine he was about to start on the main journey of his life, the choices did not seem so fraught with moral danger—although they were difficult and tricky enough. After he got his feet on the ground, Hartmire could see that the Migrant Ministry's change from "cookies for poor farm worker kids to community organizing" had led the organization into a new fix. How could people like him—well-meaning middle-class white clergymen—organize poor communities? Hartmire didn't share Alinsky's optimism, and even arrogance, about the role of the outside organizer. The Migrant Ministers wanted to change the nature of power in the Central Valley, but they didn't think they were the people for the job.

> We were there in the fields, and we saw all these horrible things happening. And nothing changed. Vacation Bible schools didn't change it. Movies for braceros in English didn't change it. Our churches and our community organizations didn't change it, not substantially. And then Chavez came along and offered this practical way to bring about this change that we all in our hearts wanted but we didn't know how to do. And we would have mucked it up if we had tried. It was almost like a relief, like thank God we can support this guy and his efforts and contribute to the change we all know has to come about.[25]

The support started slowly. In the early 1960s, the CMM had a budget of about $100,000 a year. It bought the FWA its first mimeograph machine and Cesar some meals and gas. When Migrant Ministers were assigned to be trained by Chavez, they worked as his assistants. Although Chavez pointedly never took money from the CMM for his own salary, the Migrant Ministry would sometimes pay the salary of other FWA organizers. This began in late 1964, when Chavez went directly to Hartmire and asked him to hire Gilbert Padilla. Next, Jim Drake and another CMM staffer, David Havens, began to function as FWA staff working under Chavez's direction, an arrangement later formalized into a system of "worker priests." At one time in the mid-sixties there were twenty-six of these worker priests, most of them with little religious background at all, working under the UFW's direction.

Meanwhile, the CMM's own organizers began to work "the other side of the street," raising money and awareness in the affluent Anglo churches. The Migrant Ministry, Hartmire asserted, had two tasks, "to help low income people deal with their own problems in organizations of their own; and to provide continuous interpretation of the needs and actions of the low income people to established citizens (churchmen and others) so they may understand and respond humanely."[26]

Part of what made Hartmire so happy about this formula was the particular presence of Chavez. Religious folks could trust him. He was a trained
community organizer, and he was also an authentically religious person.
The progressive middle-class church would have little trouble understanding and appreciating his organizing efforts. Church activists put up with
Alinsky's vulgar style because he seemed to have an organizing theory that
worked, and they suspected that their own Christian ethics were not
completely adequate for dealing with the political world. But Alinsky was
not an appealing figure. Hartmire called him a "loudmouth bitcher and
complainer."[27] How different was Chavez's style: just as calculating and
skilled as Alinsky, but also deeply spiritual. Telling the world about Cesar
Chavez, explaining his efforts at organizing farm workers to "established
citizens," would be an easy, welcome task. For Hartmire, Cesar Chavez was
the answer to a prayer, and he gave Chavez nearly unconditional support,
rarely questioning his judgment and never meddling in internal FWA affairs.
"The Church is the one group that isn't expecting anything from us,"
Chavez later told the writer John Gregory Dunne. "They're not doing any
politicking among us. All the other groups, the unions, the civil-rights
groups, they all want something in return for their support. Not the
Church."[28]

Although the FWA was a family affair, there was always a first family:
Chavez, Helen, Richard, Manuel . . . and Dolores Huerta. Dolores would
seem to be out of place in the early years, as she was a Chavez by neither
blood nor marriage. Close to Cesar, she nonetheless held a position similar
to that of Gilbert Padilla: a cherished associate with whom Chavez had
worked for ten years before he founded the FWA. But even at the beginning, Dolores got closer to the Chavez family than Gilbert. Padilla was
married, and his first wife was dubious about all the time he put into politics; she was certainly not part of the organizing team, and she kept her
husband away from the Chavez family. Huerta was mostly estranged from
her two husbands in the CSO years, and she divorced the second one as she
joined the FWA in Delano in 1964. Then, in 1972, she married Richard
Chavez, after what had been, to insiders, a scandalous affair begun while
Richard was still married. Sally, Richard's wife was a friend of Helen's, and
she complained to Cesar, who could do nothing to stop the virtually open
liaison. Besides, it made perfect political sense. Dolores was part of the
inner core but the only nonfamily member; Richard was married to a
woman who resented all the time he spent working for the union. Both
problems were solved simultaneously by shuffling the marital deck.[29]

Richard, two years younger than Cesar, was his true lifetime companion. As children they had planted and cultivated their first garden, trapped
gophers, worked at their father's gas station, gotten in and out of trouble on

the homestead, watched as it was destroyed, experienced the migrant trail, shined shoes, collected tin foil, worked in the movie house, shelled walnuts, picked raisins, and done all manner of farmwork. After World War II they got married within two months of each other, moved their new families into the same house, tried sharecropping together, moved to Crescent City together, and eventually settled across the street from each other in San Jose. In all their lives, it was only in the CSO years, from 1952 to 1962, that Cesar and Richard Chavez voluntarily spent any significant amount of time away from each other. Even then, Richard became a local leader of the CSO in Delano, where he worked as a journeyman carpenter. And although Cesar's regular explanation for his decision to start the association in Delano—that he knew Richard wouldn't let him starve there—was mostly a fiction, the core truth of it was that moving there meant Cesar and Richard would be reunited.

It also meant the return of cousin Manuel, who was two years older than Cesar. Manuel Chavez had been a late-comer to the childhood union of Richard and his brother. Manuel's family lived near Cesar and Richard's in Arizona, but the three boys didn't become close until Manuel's mother died when he was twelve. He was the youngest child, much younger than his brothers and sisters, who were already married, and at first he was passed around among some of his elder siblings. That didn't work out— Manuel was troublesome even then—and soon he was living with Richard and Cesar. Their household was already in crisis when Manuel arrived, and he became a guide for the boys to life's harsh realities—not a big brother, for Cesar was already that, but a wild, more worldly-wise junior partner. The three stayed together through the migrant years, with Manuel often getting into trouble and even spending time in jail for fighting. He went into the Navy before Cesar, came out as Cesar went in, and then joined the two brothers for the move to Crescent City. After that he went to the Mexican border and became a petty thief and con man, doing time in county jails for assault, disturbing the peace, public drunkenness, auto theft, and nearly two years in federal prison for selling marijuana. He left his most legitimate job, selling used cars, which he did off and on, to become an organizer for the FWA.[30]

The three of them made a handsome picture, their faces revealing nearly the full racial heritage of the Mexican American people. Manuel was a *güero*, white, taller than the other two, with the looks of the European conquerors. Cesar was an Indio, with dark skin, high cheekbones, straight black hair, and a short, thick body. Richard was taller than his older brother, and his face suggested an even earlier heritage: his eyes became a horizontal line when he smiled, and for many years he sported a stringy, Fu Manchu mustache and beard. But their physical differences only hinted at the moral and political drama embedded in the way these three companions had learned, over time, to get along and to not get along. Cesar in the lead: practical and imaginative, moral and cunning. Richard only practical, so deep into the way things are that he couldn't imagine a different way that they might be. Manuel was only cunning. Together, though, they lacked few political skills or sensibilities.

Richard was a careful, likable man—"sweet, sweet Richard," as one staff member called him. So sweet that he couldn't say no to Cesar, who could say no to just about anyone. While Cesar was organizing the CSO, Richard learned to build houses and built one for himself, which Cesar later used as collateral on a loan to start the credit union. Richard was reluctant but went along. It wasn't that he was worried about losing his house (he could build another); he just didn't take to all the commotion, preferring a quieter life and never asking too much of himself or of others. It was his great weakness as an organizer. Richard always thought that Cesar expected too much of ordinary human beings, that Cesar tried to get more out of people through moral persuasion than people were willing to give. Cesar often said that he couldn't understand how a man would choose to spend his free time cutting the lawn when there were so many more important things to do. Richard liked to cut the lawn himself, and he even took up golf. Richard counseled Cesar to be more conservative about his hopes, and he always pushed for what he called "realism," for keeping the association's, and then the union's, goals practical, sensible, down to earth.

Nobody ever called Manuel "sweet, sweet Manuel." Chris Hartmire called him a "charming scoundrel." Virginia Hirsch dubbed him "one of the great bullshitters of all time." And even some who never took to him— such as Gilbert Padilla, who finally concluded that he was "just a petty crook," or Marshall Ganz, who eventually called him the "evil twin in a Shakespearean drama"—spent a good deal of time sitting right beside him, scheming, listening, joking, plotting. No one was ever sure which of his stories to believe, and everyone knew that most of his tales involved wild exaggerations. Typical was his oft-stated boast that he had been dishonorably discharged from the Navy for punching an officer, although his Navy record states that he was discharged honorably.[31]

Manuel got in more than enough trouble with the law to back up his expertly crafted, humorously malevolent self-portrait. Typical was the scrape that sent him to jail in the spring of 1964, while he was a part-time organizer for the FWA. Working for a Bakersfield company, he delivered produce to local markets in Taft, and instead of turning in all the checks he received, he forged the endorsements on some of them and cashed them at a local bar and low-ball club. Records delivered to the court showed that he had forged at least twenty-one checks, amounting to more than $1,200, over about a month and a half. Since he was already on probation—the court report states, "His rather lengthy criminal record . . . occupies two and one-half pages of the standard forms used by the Sheriff's office"—he was denied further probation and the judge sentenced him to 180 days in jail.[32]

Ultimately in the UFW, Manuel survived only because he was Cesar's beloved cousin, his *primo hermano* in farm worker Spanish. And Cesar did not merely tolerate Manuel's peculiar skills; he used them and even at times enjoyed them. "Sounds like a job for Manuel" was a common phrase among top FWA officials whenever the organization found itself in a fix that was best handled by means of some sort of undercover action. Those assignments always came directly from Cesar, however, and only a few other people were privy to exactly what Manuel had been assigned to do.

Cesar loved Manuel and not just because he often depended on him in times of crisis. Marshall Ganz has a theory about why that was so: Cesar admired Manuel's shrewdness, his cunning, his ability to make a calculated assessment of exactly what it would take to get someone to do something. Ganz remembers sitting with the two of them for hours, listening to Cesar question Manuel on exactly how he got people to buy used cars. What was it that turned the trick, that convinced the prospective buyer that this was the car for him? Manuel would tell the stories, and Cesar would try to convert the stories into a method, a science of persuasion. But not all Manuel's cunning involved persuasion. Some of it was outright fraud and violence. Ganz was amazed at how deftly Cesar seemed to pick and choose among Manuel's questionable methods without becoming morally tainted himself.[33] He was convinced that Cesar would not allow Manuel to cross the line into pure malevolence. The problem was what would happen when Manuel was too far away to be held accountable? When weeks or months would go by without his having to report to Cesar? Manuel operating on his own was not a pretty picture. If Cesar was both the serpent and the dove, Manuel was all serpent.

It is not entirely clear how much of a role Manuel or even Richard played in the early years of the FWA. Fundamentally both made their mark as companions to Cesar. They helped him maintain his balance and surrounded him at work with the confidence and security of family love. He could trust them as no others. Certainly, neither man was as skilled at organizing as Gilbert Padilla. Nor as enmeshed in the local farm worker community as Julio and Josefina Hernandez, a CSO couple who became stalwarts of the new association. Nor as politically savvy as Dolores Huerta. Nor as able to provide money and political support as Chris Hartmire. Perhaps the best indication of Manuel's importance to the organization is the assignment Chavez gave him after Manuel returned to Delano from prison in the fall of 1964: helping to sell ads for the FWA's newspaper, *El Malcriado*. Manuel did the job. He got the biggest, most lucrative ad that the paper ever had: a furniture store ad that filled the entire back page for several months. Bill Esher, the paper's editor, had talked to the store owner but never gotten anything out of him. He was convinced that Manuel had made him an offer he couldn't refuse.[34]

Building an association of farm workers, Chavez was convinced, meant simultaneously building the farm worker community. Not community in the abstract, not creating just some kind of good feeling among people, but lasting social structures in which farm workers would exercise institutional power. Chavez told all who would listen that farm workers, collectively, needed not just a credit union nor even just a trade union, but land of their own, medical clinics, recreational halls, radio stations, and newspapers. He decided it was time to establish the newspaper in the fall of 1964. He had read about the Los Angeles newspaper of the *Magonistas*, *Regeneración*, and the influence it had had on the first generation of Mexican immigrants. He knew how important newspapers were in the Mexican Revolution, appearing one month, shut down by the Porfirista government the next, and then reappearing under related, often amusing, names. Chavez had stored away the name of one of those revolutionary papers that particularly delighted him and was determined to use it when it came time to set up his own newspaper, *El Malcriado*. It means, literally "the ill-bred one"—colloquially, "the brat," "the bad boy."

The name was a peculiar choice for the ex-altar boy. Cesar was not openly a *malcriado*—that would be Manuel. Cesar did everything he could to make his organization respectable and keep his own image clean. One of Chavez's early enthusiastic Catholic supporters, the Jesuit director of the National Catholic Rural Life Conference, James Vizzard, tried to correct what he considered this unfortunate choice of a title for the FWA newspaper. In a favorable article in the July 1966 *Progressive*, titled "The Extraordinary Cesar Chavez," Vizzard translated *malcriado* as "the disadvantaged." The translation, totally in error, fit the proper Catholic view of this new leader of the poor, a view that Chavez usually promoted himself. And yet *El Malcriado* was Chavez's choice, and his alone. It is probably best understood as another warning to those who would understand him too quickly. His project was nothing if not serious and moral, and yet it was leavened by humor—a sense of humor, however, that was usually purposeful, used to embarrass and skewer enemies, and rarely self-deprecating.

Chavez's first recruit to the newspaper was a cartoonist, Andy Zermeño. Chavez needed Zermeño because the culture in which he was going to start a newspaper was primarily oral and visual, rather than literate. Great storytellers enchanted small farm worker gatherings; some farm workers played musical instruments, and a few earned extra bucks playing in the bars at night. Traveling working-class theater, *carpa* (tent shows), and Mexican circuses still occasionally came through the small valley towns and were always well attended. Mexican music on the radio provided daily entertainment, and going to the movies was the special treat. Certainly there were some farm worker intellectuals, who kept up with various Mexican newspapers and magazines, but most people who read at all were devotees of illustrated pocket-book romances, adult comic books, and the sensational Mexican newspaper *Alarma*, which featured horrid photos of automobile accidents. If Cesar's paper was to have an impact, it needed a good cartoonist.

The characters who dominated the early issues of *El Malcriado*—Don Sotaco, Don Coyote, and Patroncito—were conceived in a series of extended conversations between Zermeño and Chavez, and then brought to life by the power of Zermeño's pen. Don Sotaco, in a simple line drawing, stands alone on the cover of the first issue. Pictured from above, he appears short; under a slightly oversized hat pulled down upon his large, ridiculous ears, are a pair of sad, woeful eyes looking up in an attitude of defeat. Miserable compliance is exactly the mood, reflected in his despairing frown, sloping shoulders, and arms gently folded behind his back. Don Sotaco is the victim perennial, taken advantage of by all. His chief antagonist, Don Coyote, the labor contractor or smuggler, who appeared alone on the cover of the second issue, this time viewed from below, is tall, sharp-featured, and angular, with square shoulders and a menacing look above his hatchet chin. All that's missing is the tail of a cartoon devil. Patroncito, the fat, jolly, smirking boss, appeared later. He is often shown surrounded by beautiful women, smoking a cigar, his pockets stuffed with money. Sometimes he is hoodwinking the government, other times he is outwitted by Don Coyote, but only on small matters. Despite his firm hold on power, Patroncito never merited a full-page cover.

Chavez "came up with Don Sotaco, a farm worker who didn't know anything," Zermeño explains. "We wanted [farm workers] to identify with this character and show that if you didn't know your rights, you would get into a lot of trouble."[35] Decades after the fact, Chavez said of the original characters, "We could say difficult things to people without offending them. We could talk about people being cowards, for example. Instead of being offensive, it would be funny."[36]

Portraying the farm worker (or any worker) as a loser is not unprecedented among those who have tried to organize them. Don Sotaco is an updated Mexican American version of the famous Wobbly cartoon character Mr. Block. That misguided worker, whose head was a block of wood, was constantly being fooled by the boss's false promises, losing every time. The Wobblies' intention was not that different from Zermeño and Chavez's: they, too, were trying to offer a critique of a certain kind of foolish worker without directly insulting people. But Mr. Block is not the only worker in the Wobbly cartoon portfolio. Even more prevalent is the large, muscular, proud worker, much taller than the bosses or the police, whose inherent but as yet unleashed power promises to sweep away all oppressors. Mr. Block and the powerful Wobbly worker are on the stage together; the audience is offered a choice of how to view themselves.

In Zermeño's cartoons there is just one kind of worker, Don Sotaco, and he doesn't stand up to the boss until issue 49, in November 1966, almost two years after his appearance on the first *El Malcriado* cover. For much of that period, many of the farm workers who were reading the paper had been on strike, waging an intense battle with their bosses. Counter examples to Don Sotaco were everywhere, but the cartoon character continued to take it on the chin. Although farm workers were neither uniformly Don Sotacos nor uniformly in struggle, Chavez saw himself as working with the Don Sotacos of the world. His job was to pull the veil from Don Sotaco's eyes, help him see the importance of self-organization, show him how to unite with others, and inspire him to take the world stage. Chavez did play that role for many people, and although most were not as down and out as Don Sotaco, they could still recognize themselves in the humorous caricature. But those farm workers with a sense of their own power before Chavez ever arrived did not see themselves in the cartoon figure, and did not need Chavez to lift their veils. They were willing to struggle alongside or in alliance with Chavez, willing even to do so under his leadership, but they owed him no deep debt. Such workers were not as loyal to Chavez and his organization as those whom Chavez had enlightened, and Chavez was never completely comfortable with them.

Yet Cesar Chavez should be understood as more than just the man who liberates and redeems Don Sotaco. The man who conceived Don Sotaco was also the man who named his newspaper *El Malcriado*. Rarely are those who bring sight to the blind also *malcriados*, whether secretly or openly. But here, Chavez seems to be one, as his invention Don Sotaco does not stand alone in representing farm workers. There is his newspaper too: the farm worker not as submissive victim but as mischievous boy.

Chavez never intended to be the editor of the paper. He was sure that any antigrower farm worker newspaper would eventually be sued (he turned out to be right), and he didn't want those suits to be filed against the FWA. He also didn't think his organization needed a paper so much as the whole farm worker community did. Unlike Lenin, he did not want a newspaper that developed a political line but one that could indirectly teach a point of view, and if enough people were influenced by this alternative way of understanding the news, those readers would form a community. And a community of readers was one step closer to a community itself. Chavez wanted *El Malcriado* to be closely linked to the FWA but separate. He looked around for an editor who would be loyal enough to trust, but would also have the spirit of a mildly mischievous son. His search led him out of the farm worker community to a man he would affectionately call "our first gringo."

Bill Esher's romantic idealism included a strong streak of independence, not an unusual combination. He had been a maverick editor of his high school paper, attended journalism school at Syracuse University on scholarship, and simultaneously worked at the daily *Syracuse Post-Standard* at night. By 1959, after two years in college, he had had enough. A fan of beat poetry, Jack Kerouac, and West Coast jazz, he bought a 1951 Ford "woody," fixed it up so that he could sleep comfortably in the back, and took off for California. On the way he passed through the South and wrote some stories for the *Post-Standard* about "the still-quiet-but-about-to-explode civil rights movement," and then spent a few months in the Mexican desert sleeping under the stars. He knocked around in California and elsewhere for a while before encountering Citizens for Farm Labor in San Francisco. There he met Wendy Goepel, who was working for Governor Brown's Farm Worker Health Service, pretty much fell in love, and started to do what he could to help farm workers.[37]

Bill Esher, like most everyone else who would become a member of the FWA family, did not do things halfway. His first independent project was remarkable enough: organizing the West Oakland Farm Workers Association. Using an old bus that had been donated to Oakland's Catholic Worker collective, the association attempted to circumvent the unscrupulous labor contractors who skimmed off money from farm workers' checks. The association contracted with the growers directly, passed along the full wages to the workers (outside donations paid for the gas and maintainence of the bus), and provided nutritious lunches to its members for twenty-five cents. Esher drove the bus and made the lunches at the Catholic Worker center—he was quite proud of what he could produce for a quarter. For a while he tried to work alongside the others in the bean and onion fields below Fremont, but he gave it up. It was all individual piece rate, and he was surprised to discover that although he was used to hard physical labor, having moved furniture for a living, he couldn't come close to keeping up with what he had assumed were the unskilled rejects among West Oakland's poorest people. So he took to sleeping on the bus while the experienced farm workers earned their money.

His West Oakland Farm Workers Association did not last long. The members made the mistake of striking for a higher wage. They lost, were fired, were blacklisted by most of the growers, and were harassed by the Fremont Police. The end came when Esher was out in the fields visiting the crew, and someone snuck up and broke all the windows on the bus.

The next project was even more ambitious: documenting the ways in which braceros were being cheated by the growers. To do that Esher and a friend sought jobs on a bracero crew in the cantaloupe fields outside a small

Central Valley town called Pumpkin Center. The amused straw bosses let them have a try at harvesting on the otherwise all-bracero crew. Bill's friend quit in the first couple of hours, but Bill hung on. The semi-enslaved Mexicans were working by the hour and doing the job, as slaves usually do, as slowly as they possibly could. Still, the two weeks that Esher picked cantaloupes were the hardest workweeks of his life. And when he got his paycheck, he had the documentation he wanted: the pay was about 25 percent short, and the charge for room and board was inflated to the point of fraud. Over the life of the workers' two-month contract, the growers association was cheating them out of many thousands of dollars. Citizens for Farm Labor took this to the state government and the U.S. Labor Department, but no cantaloupe-picking bracero ever saw any of the money that was coming to him. Instead, only Bill Esher received his back wages.

In the fall of 1964, Goepel told Esher, "I have a friend who is trying to start a newspaper. He has a sort of self-help co-op of a few hundred farm workers. He needs some help. I'll take you to meet him."[38] The interview went well. Esher was impressed by Chavez and was immediately attracted to Helen and the kids, many of whom still carried their affectionate baby-names: Polly, Tota, Birdy, Babo, Titibet. Chavez quickly decided that Esher might be the one for the job. Three months later Esher moved to Delano. By then Chavez had produced the first issue by himself, figuring out how to do it as he went along. Esher lived with Helen and the kids for a short time, and continued to eat most of his meals with the family even after he'd moved into a rundown motel, the Delano Plunge, and from there into a trailer. He earned extra money working in the grape fields with Chavez on occasional weekends—pruning and stacking wood—and he spent a lot more time with Cesar driving around the Central Valley, convincing small grocery store owners to carry copies of *El Malcriado* on consignment. It sold for a dime, and the store could keep a nickel.

The two men had a lot of opportunity to talk. What made Chavez so attractive to Esher was his combination of hard, day-to-day work with a large vision of eventual farm worker power. At the beginning, when the association was so small, maybe "vision" was the wrong word. "Fantasy" might be more appropriate, Esher thought. "Chavez had two fantasies of me," said Esher.

> He did that with people. He saw things in big terms. One was that I was St. Francis. Which was totally off the wall. The other was that I was Joseph Goebbels, Hitler's propagandist. I was going to be Cesar's propagandist. He would actually talk about that quite a lot. He was half joking, of course. But he had these fantasies for me, and I was not at all surprised when later it developed that he had all these big fantasies for himself.[39]

In keeping with his grand plans, Chavez renamed the FWA when it merged with a Porterville farm worker group soon after Esher arrived in Delano. Now that there were three small centers of FWA activity—Porterville, Corcoran, and Delano—and perhaps as many as two hundred dues-paying members, the new organization would henceforth be known as the National Farm Workers Association.

Once Esher came on the job, Chavez insisted that *El Malcriado* officially separate from the NFWA. Chavez had already found a moonlighting jobber who would print a thousand copies for $43.80, and he had sold enough ads to cover the print run. The nickel Esher collected from the grocery stores might pay for the gas needed to distribute the papers. Chavez talked Esher into trying to sell tires, motor oil, and soda for some extra bucks (as was the NFWA style), but Bill quickly gave that up. Wendy Goepel was always there to make sure that they didn't close down for lack of funds, and when Manuel arrived and sold the entire back page to the furniture store, the paper was able to avert immediate financial crisis.

El Malcriado was, quite naturally, both independent of the NFWA and not. Esher's Spanish was not good enough to produce a Spanish-language paper, so Chavez translated the entire newspaper for the first few months, as well as writing many of the editorials. And although Esher eventually moved the paper into its own building down the street from the NFWA offices, he continued to be a member of the NFWA family. Although Chavez did not give orders about what should be in the paper, *El Malcriado* reflected the general orientation of the NFWA's leaders, as interpreted and elaborated by Bill Esher. That elaboration was significant. Esher featured an extensive letters section (it sometimes made up a quarter of the paper), farm workers' own articles, and humorous contests (readers were challenged to "name this town" from a photo of a nondescript street in a particularly dreary valley town). Esher changed the slogan on the masthead from Chavez's choice, "Dedicated to Farm Workers," to his own, "The Voice of Farm Workers."

The resultant diversity of opinions ran somewhat counter to Chavez's editorials, which often called for unity above all else. At first the differences were not paramount. Esher promoted the legacy of the Mexican Revolution (using Cesar's extensive collection of Mexican revolutionary graphics), emphasized the benefits of joining the NFWA, and publicized the achievements of the organization and its leaders. All the while the energetic heart of the paper remained Zermeño's cartoons. Only in the fall of 1965, when farm worker strikes were in the process of transforming the association into a union, did differences between the newspaper and Chavez became significant. That's when Esher noted that Chavez wanted the paper to be both independent and under his control. For a while, Chavez had to put up with what he had consciously chosen to create: a genuine *malcriado*. But not for long.

New Wings

April to August '65

There's no other person who could give better speeches, not Dolores, not Chavez. . . . Camacho was the best and he really had an impact on people. . . . He used to give you a lot of history, and I remember he used to get the bullhorn and he could go for forty minutes to an hour on the bullhorn, and everybody was just observing, just listening. So I learned a lot from that guy.
                    —Pablo Espinoza, grape worker and NFWA volunteer, 1995

Epifanio Camacho caused a little stir in the NFWA office in the spring of 1965. "A dark-skinned, jovial, high-spirited man whose remarkable body and movements suggest the grace and strength of a panther" is how an early chronicler of the UFW described him. Bill Esher, too, noticed him right away. Camacho had walked into the Delano office looking for help, but he was not helpless himself. He approached Cesar Chavez as an equal, not a supplicant. Chavez was both intrigued and wary. Esher watched them, listened to some of their conversation, and saw Camacho's "power and emotion" matched by Chavez's "presence and cunning." Esher marveled at the skill with which "Chavez cooled him down without losing his respect." It was, he thought, another measure of Chavez's organizing genius. Gilbert Padilla saw the encounter somewhat differently. Camacho, a rose grafter in the nearby town of McFarland, had come with a plan for a strike, and Chavez didn't want to have anything to do with it, but he was happy to sign up a new recruit to the National Farm Workers Association. "Chavez was just playing around," keeping Camacho on board, without taking what he said seriously. But Camacho kept coming, kept insisting, talking up his plan to everybody in the office. And it sounded like a good plan to Gilbert Padilla. The rose workers were highly skilled; it would be hard to replace them. Padilla told Camacho that if they could get it well organized, they should go ahead and strike.[1]

There was nothing of Don Sotaco in Epifanio Camacho. A few years older than Chavez, he had been born into poverty on a small ranch in Tamaulipas in rural Mexico.[2] At eighteen, both of his parents dead, he had joined the Mexican army as a way of getting off his brother-in-law's *ejido* and out of small-town life. He had had only a couple of years of schooling, but he had learned to read, and he remained *picado*—hungry for more. He liked army discipline, but for reasons he didn't understand back then, he could barely bring himself to salute his superiors or the Mexican flag. He stayed in the army no longer than he had to, worked for a while as a carpenter, and then, motivated by the cheap detective novels he favored, joined the police force in Ciudad Victoria, the capital of Tamaulipas. He liked the tough-guy, macho ethos of police work, and as he believed what he had been reading in the paperback novels, he also saw it as a way of serving the Mexican people. He was not prepared for the petty corruption of the Victoria cops, and when the opportunity came, he moved on to the Tamaulipas State Police, hoping to find there the desired combination of public service and heroic action. What he found instead was more corruption and utter contempt for poor people. Most disturbing was the routine torture of prisoners, through which the police extorted confessions and bribes. His complaints only brought suspicion down on his own head, and soon he felt completely isolated at work. He quit and ran for the border.

In Matamoros, just shy of the Texas border, he scrounged for work and food. A couple of times, arrested as an indigent, he saw the inside of the city jail. Once he spent three days in solitary after he refused the two other choices: pay a small bribe to the guards or clean the jail toilet. In the early 1950s he regularly crossed the border for work, was picked up a couple of times by the *migra*, and taken back to Matamoros. Once the Border Patrol picked him up in Corpus Christi, where he was digging graves in a Catholic cemetery. His boss, a priest, was so upset at his being hauled away that when Epifanio returned, the priest went back with him to Matamoros and signed the papers that made Camacho a legal immigrant. On June 6, 1955, Epifanio crossed the border legally for the first time.

For three years he dug graves and picked cotton in Texas and more cotton in Arizona. Loaded lettuce in the Imperial Valley. Picked peaches, apricots, and plums—the ladder crops—in the northern Central Valley, raisins outside of Fresno, wine grapes near Delano. Finally, he worked in the roses in what would become his home town, McFarland. Never partnered up with anyone, as most farm workers do, he remained a bit of a loner. His old pickup truck, with its hand-painted Spanish slogans—"To Wander Is My Destiny"; "Don't Take Me Lightly"; "I Was Once a Virgin, Too"—were *puro Mexicano*, as was his conviction that his wife should not work outside the home, as well as his romantic, revolutionary rhetoric.[3] He was also anticlerical, a viewpoint he shared with many other farm workers—but his complaints against the papacy and the Catholic Church were somewhat more developed than most. His opinions, which had been shaped by that significant strand of Mexican revolutionary ideology that sees the Catholic Church as a central reactionary institution, were reinforced by the strong anti-Catholicism of his wife, Salome, who was a Jehovah's Witness. Together, the two were different from most of their neighbors: very Mexican and in some ways more culturally conservative. And while Salome was aggressively Protestant, Epifanio was just plain aggressive.

Always willing to fight for what he felt was right, or to defend his acute sense of honor, he frequently found himself in disputes with his bosses. That had started way back in Mexico, when he was barely an adolescent and had hired himself out to a neighboring farmer. The wages were supposed to be one peso a day, but he received only fifty centavos because, according to the foreman, he was only a child. Camacho had been doing as much work as the men beside him, so he went directly to the farmer to ask for the full wage. The boss said nothing. Instead, he reached into the belt behind him, pulled out a pistol, and fired it into the air. Epifanio the boy turned and ran. Camacho the man would never again be naive about the power of his employers. But the gun blast had worked only temporarily, as Camacho's fear passed, and he continued to petition his bosses for the wages he thought he had coming to him.

That is how the problem started in the roses, and that is what led Epifanio Camacho to Cesar Chavez and the NFWA. Camacho had become a champion rose grafter, paid by the number of stalks that he and a fellow worker could cut and and then graft with the desired variety of rose. Since the stalks were less than a foot above the ground, the work had to be done while squatting, or on your knees, or completely bent over. The graft had to be inserted carefully or it would not take. Since it was piece work, it had to be done as quickly as possible in order to make decent pay. Only a few people managed to become good at it, but for those who did, the wages were relatively high. An accomplished rose grafter such as Camacho could make $30 or $40 a day, which in the early 1960s was three or four times the minimum wage. Officially the pay was $10 for every thousand plants to the man who cut the stalk, and $8.50 for the man who went behind him and tied in the new rose, but there was a catch: $2 of that piece rate for every man was held back, not to be paid until the following year on the condition that 90 percent of the grafts took. In practice, that $2 was almost never paid, and so the real wage for even the most skilled and efficient workers was effectively 20 to 24 percent below the official wage. Like that Mexican farmer's pistol shot in the air, the withheld $2 was a naked expression of the bosses' power, as everyone knew that it had nothing to do with the success or failure of the grafts. Some workers went back to the fields the next year and checked the plants to see how they were doing. Not too many people did that, though, because once they saw that the plants were thriving, there was nothing they could do with the information; it was just bitter proof of how badly they had been cheated.

Camacho decided he would no longer put up with the yearly insult. After a series of unsuccessful attempts to get his fellow grafters to go with him, he went directly to his boss at Montebello Rose and demanded to be paid his full wage. Camacho had to threaten to change companies before the boss eventually relented. He would mail the money directly to Camacho's house, on condition that he not tell his fellow workers. The boss lived up to his end of the bargain, but not Camacho. He told the others, and even showed them the first year's check, but the following years he stopped, because the others still weren't ready to demand their own back wages.

What ultimately led him to the NFWA began with a couple of weeks' work at Konklyn Nursery in 1964, after the season was over at Montebello. The next year, after checking that the grafts had taken, Camacho got ten other grafters together, and they went to see Mr. Konklyn about their back pay. Konklyn said that they hadn't hit the 90 percent mark and refused. Epifanio called him a liar. The dispute wound up at a hearing before a state labor commissioner in Bakersfield, which only Camacho and Konklyn attended. The workers who didn't show up were regular Konklyn grafters, and they thought it likely that if they won their back pay, they would lose their jobs.

At the hearing, Konklyn argued that there never was any agreement to pay $2 per thousand for a 90 percent success rate. Rather, he occasionally tipped workers whose previous year's grafting had turned out to be particularly successful, and he had come to Bakersfield that very day with a check of $30 for Mr. Camacho, who was, indeed, an excellent and careful worker. Camacho, who was owed $62 for the two weeks' work, threw the check to the ground, exclaiming that he had never taken an unearned penny in his life, and he wanted no tips, only what was owed him. The commissioner reproached him for ungratefulness and declared the hearing closed. Camacho refused to leave; the commissioner called the cops who carried Epifanio out of the office and released him. He did not feel defeated. It had been a matter of principle. But when he returned to Montebello, the foreman refused to let him start work. He had been fired. No other rose company nor any other agricultural outfit in the area would hire him. He couldn't even get a job in the sugar beets, the absolute worst-paid job around, paying as little as $3 a day on bad days. He was on the *bola negra*, the blacklist. In the spring of 1965, he had to steal food from the fields at night so that he and his wife and their two daughters could eat.

Meanwhile, he kept talking to other rose grafters about the back pay. His story got around. Someone told him to look up Cesar Chavez and the National Farm Workers Association. He had never heard of either one, but he had no trouble finding the association's storefront office in Delano. Cesar was courteous enough, interested in Camacho's life and his work (they even went out to the roses together, so that Chavez could see how the grafting was done), but Chavez insisted up-front that the NFWA wasn't set up to organize strikes. Camacho pressed Chavez: Just what was the strategy of his group? Chavez explained that eventually they might get involved in strikes, but now they had to focus on building the organization, making it so big and strong that the members could truly help one another, and so powerful that they could force the politicians to pass laws that would give farm workers the same benefits that other workers already had: a minimum wage, unemployment insurance, workers' compensation, good pensions. Camacho was not convinced, but neither was he easily deterred. He paid his $3.50 and joined the association, in hopes that he could change Chavez's mind. In turn, Chavez suggested that Camacho set up a meeting of workers at his house, and promised to come and listen to their stories, and see what he could do to help.

Only four workers came to Epifanio's house for that first meeting, but Camacho was still eager and Chavez always liked to pyramid house meetings, so together they scheduled another one. This time, Camacho focused his efforts on a single company, Mt. Arbor, and almost all the grafters, about thirty men, showed up. After a long discussion, they decided they wanted to strike. Chavez did not oppose their decision. A third meeting was scheduled, both to see if the men's resolve would hold and to decide the details and demands of the strike. Camacho had won Chavez over. The NFWA dropped everything else and prepared for its first strike.

One last pre-strike meeting was held at Guadalupe Church. All of Mt. Arbor's rose grafters came. The NFWA contingent included Chavez, Dolores Huerta, Gilbert Padilla, and Jim Drake. Cesar chaired the meeting. The workers set their wage demands, agreed to hold out for a contract, and decided that the NFWA would represent them in negotiations with the company. They also agreed that a picket line was unnecessary, as there weren't enough skilled grafters to scab effectively. By not picketing, they would also be less exposed to potential blacklisting if it turned out that they lost the strike. They would simply not go to work, an old farm worker tactic used by the Wobbly-Magonistas, who had given it various names: walk-away, fade-out, stay-at-home.[4] At the end of the meeting, Huerta handed Chavez a ten-inch wooden crucifix with a broken cross piece. Cesar held it in the air before the small assembly. He wanted the workers to swear on the cross that they would honor the strike and not go back to work until there was a contract. He passed it back to Huerta, who handed it to one of the men. He swore fidelity and passed the crucifix to the next man. Camacho was shocked. He believed in God, but didn't believe that politics and religion should be mixed like this. He wondered what Jim Drake, the Protestant minister, thought. Camacho didn't want to complicate the proceedings with a public refusal, so when the crucifix reached him, he also swore that he would be loyal to the strike and the other men. But he was angry at Chavez for not checking with him on this particular tactic before the meeting. And he believed that it was only a tactic, meant to extract the deepest possible commitment from the grafters, as Chavez had not talked to him about religion in the thirty days that they had been working together.[5]

The strike lasted three days. The workers had been right about the incompetence of scab workers: when the Mt. Arbor management brought in a small crew of Filipino strikebreakers, they couldn't do the work. And the other grafters in town—about two hundred men, almost all known to one another—were not interested in breaking their compatriots' strike. The company's only hope was to get the strikers to return to work. For all three days of the strike, the NFWA leaders were up before dawn, scouting the workers' homes, knocking on the door of any house where the lights were on to make sure that the grafter who lived there was not preparing to go to work. Once, when Dolores Huerta doubted the word of one of the strikers, she blocked his driveway with her truck, locked it, took her key and left. Dolores's bold act, prefiguring many to come, was much celebrated inside the NFWA, and later became one of the main stories told about the rose strike—the heroine organizer preventing a reluctant worker from scabbing. The story, however, inverted the actual trajectory of the struggle, because it had been a bold worker, Camacho, who had activated the reluctant NFWA organizers.

The day the strike started, the NFWA tried to begin negotiations with the company. Huerta went to the local Mt. Arbor office, where a company official called her a Communist and briskly escorted her out of the building. The parent company, Jackson & Perkins, was more polite to Chris Hartmire, but it also refused to negotiate. Its representatives were curious about the nature of the NFWA, though. They pressed Hartmire on whether it was a union.

On Wednesday, day three of the strike, company foremen visited many of the striking grafters. Their message was both an offer and a threat. They would accept all the wage demands, including dropping the 90 percent scam, but they would not sign a contract. Anybody who did not show up for work on Thursday would never work for the company again. That night Chavez, Jim Drake, Gil Padilla, Bill Esher, and Wendy Goepel were in a little trailer behind the office talking about the strike; they were divided on how to respond to the company's offer. When a small group of grafters knocked on the door and asked Chavez to come outside, Padilla, who advocated holding out for a contract, suspected that these workers wanted to go back to work. He urged Cesar not to talk to them, to tell them to wait until the next day when all the strikers could have a formal meeting to discuss what to do. But Chavez, who favored accepting the wage concessions without a contract, went outside and gave the workers his permission to return to work without a general meeting. Padilla was furious. He knew the strike was over. After the group of night visitors went back to work on Thursday, everybody returned on Friday. The company backed down on its threat, accepted all the men back, and kept its promise on the wages. And within a couple of weeks, all the other companies had been forced to raise their wages, as they did not want to lose their best grafters to Mt. Arbor.[6]

El Malcriado hailed the victory, and the NFWA organizers assessed its meaning. Jim Drake thought that they might possibly have won a contract and was disappointed when the strikers went back to work, but ultimately he agreed with Chavez: "It was premature, we didn't have enough people, we didn't have the masses of farm workers. It was a very special situation; Epifanio was a very special person. It was better to get the raise and get out."[7] Padilla saw the incident as a lost opportunity, and an example of the NFWA's confusion over its own goals. If the association had been a union, if Hartmire could have said to the parent company, yes, we are a union, then the company might have negotiated with them. Camacho, he argued, had been exactly right about the situation in the fields: nobody who was capable of doing the work was going to scab. If the men had held out, and if the NFWA had been unequivocal, the strike might have been a total victory. But Camacho was not at all discouraged. The workers had won the full raise they demanded. He wasn't even that disappointed that the blacklist against him in the roses remained in effect. He was energized by the strike. Soon he got a job in the grape vineyards. He told his friends to be prepared, because strikes were contagious.

For the California growers, the end of the Bracero Program had become the worst kind of concession: the growers' defeat, rather than dampening farm workers' enthusiasm and channeling their battles into more acceptable venues, as concessions often do, only encouraged workers to fight, and with a more threatening set of demands. Rarely has the age-old fear of appeasement turned out to be more prophetic: the growers gave an inch, and farm workers took a mile.

The rose strike was part of a general rebellion that broke out in the fields in 1965. The California Department of Employment officially acknowledged that there were sixty-three agricultural "labor disputes" that year.[8] It is certainly a low estimate. The on-the-ground battles between farm workers and their employers in 1965 have become part of farm worker lore—and one of the reasons workers remember that time so well is that they won many of those fights. Officially, wages rose from an average of $1.33 an hour in 1964 to $1.50 an hour in 1966, but again, the official figures seem to have underestimated the change. All the farm workers I talked to who were in California in 1965 remembered the general upheaval after the termination of the Bracero Program, and many reported that wages rose sharply. Pablo Camacho, for example, remembers that in 1965 his boss not only raised his wages but also began to pay his rent and give him gas money so that he would not move to another job.

The strikes and accelerating wages were largely a consequence of the labor shortage that followed the shutdown of the Bracero Program. The growers and the INS had anticipated the problem and had done what they could to head it off. Starting in 1961 the Immigration and Naturalization Service began a massive distribution of green cards to Mexican farm workers. The agency kept no record of how many cards they gave out, but estimates go as high as 100,000; by 1969 the INS figured that there were 750,000 Mexican with green cards in the United States. In addition, between 1960 and 1969 the INS issued more than 2.2 million "white cards," designed as temporary permits but used by farm workers to immigrate illegally to the U.S.[9]

But green cards and white cards weren't enough in 1965. California growers, especially those far from the border, still had to scramble for workers. They tried to use Los Angeles County welfare recipients, members of the Lakota Sioux tribe from North Dakota, Navajos from New Mexico, high school football players, and housewives, but they still couldn't find enough experienced workers to get the job done.[10] Knowing they had the whip hand, farm workers once again moved onto the offensive. The galloping farm worker movement interfered with the plans of the NFWA, which was concentrating on self-help programs and was not prepared for mass activity. But the NFWA was flexible enough to change course, and it began to endorse the strike activity. Chavez—suffering from a bad case of pneumonia—did not have too much to do with this new direction, although he gave it a critical, lukewarm endorsement. (He had to go to the hospital in Bakersfield soon after the rose strike ended, and then spent a few weeks home in bed.) It was mostly the Migrant Ministry—sponsored staff, supported by enthusiastic articles in El Malcriado, who aligned the NFWA with the quickly ascending farm worker movement. Nobody voted on the policy change; it just seemed to happen, as if the organizers had stumbled into a small stream, liked the feel of the water, and got swept into the rapids.

The NFWA's next battle was a rent strike over bad conditions in a labor camp that Migrant Ministry organizers learned about while going door-to-door passing out contraceptive foam to farm worker women. The Woodville and Linnell camps, built by the Farm Security Administration in 1938, contained 400 structures, the majority of which were small one-room shacks, made completely out of heavy tin, or wood siding with tin roofs. For ten years the FSA had provided these "houses" to farm workers free of charge. In 1950, the FSA gave the camps to the Tulare County Housing

Authority, which charged rents—$18 to $38 a month by 1964. In 1965, the authority wanted to raise the rent by as much as 47 percent. The increase was especially steep for farm worker families that had to rent several structures so that all of their children would have a place to sleep. As an added insult, the rent was being raised for shacks that had already been condemned by the Tulare County Health Department. To keep the inside temperatures bearable during the summer months, tenants had to find heavy carpets or old mattresses, throw them over the roofs of the hovels, and keep them soaking wet day and night. After hearing the residents' complaints, Gilbert Padilla, David Havens of the Migrant Ministry, and Jim Drake decided to try to organize some kind of rent strike.[11]

One of the main complainants was Pablo Espinoza, who was occasionally employed by the housing authority to do some work in the camps, and was a member of a large extended family that rented several shacks in the Woodville camp. Espinoza, who later became a farm worker leader in the UFW, was the fourth of twelve children in a family that in the 1940s and '50s had followed the sugar beets from the Rio Grande Valley to Mississippi, Arkansas, Oklahoma, and Ohio, moving from one labor camp to another. Everywhere they went, blacks, whites, and Mexicans lived in different areas but usually shared the same toilet and shower facilities, when they existed. In Mississippi the family stayed in former slave quarters. Pablo was born in one camp, learned to read Spanish in another, fell in love in a third, and lost his mother in yet another temporary home, to severe hemorrhaging that followed the birth of her last child.[12]

As Pablo came into early manhood, the family's migratory route shifted from south–north to east–west: three generations traveling together began to follow the cotton from the lower Rio Grande Valley to West Texas, Arizona, and California. In 1960 the entire family came to Tulare County, where most of them settled, working in the wine grapes, tomatoes, and sugar beets. Only Espinoza's father continued his yearly travels, by this time almost a pilgrimage, back to the lower Rio Grande Valley.

Pablo was quick to pick up on Gilbert's way of thinking, as he was quick to pick up on everything. Having no more than a fourth-grade education, he had learned mathematics and English while working in a cotton gin, and now he learned politics from Padilla, whom he called "our first professor." He became a primary spokesman for the rent-strikers. Their strategy was simple. The tenants, organized into formal camp committees, refused to pay the rent hikes. Instead, they paid the old rates into a special escrow account. Next, they organized a seven-mile march from Linnell to Visalia; a couple of hundred people walked in mid-summer heat: residents of the camp were joined by various supporters, including representatives of the American Friends Service Committee (John Soria was one), Citizens for Farm Labor, and Students for Farm Labor, one Sister Immaculada, clad in an all-white habit, and Brother Gilbert, a member of the Christian Brothers order who taught at Garces High School in Bakersfield. A farm worker march of that size, and with that kind of broad support, stirred some liberal California politicians to sponsor an investigation into the Tulare County Housing Authority. Before the summer was over, the rent increases were formally rescinded, and promises were made (and eventually kept) to rebuild the camps.

That summer of 1965, El Malcriado began to promote strikes openly. In its first six months, it had championed the self-organization and self-respect of farm workers, and had encouraged workers to unite and fight for a better life, but its primary focus was on the benefits of NFWA membership. The overwhelming weight of cascading events, however, shifted the paper's focus. First the rose strike, then a victorious strike of grape pickers, represented by the Agricultural Workers Organizing Committee, in the Coachella Valley, next the rent strike and march, and finally another (unsuccessful) walkout of grape workers. El Malcriado enthusiastically featured them all—and called for more. "How to Strike" read a bold headline in early August, with the following suggestions:

1. Talk to your crew: make sure everyone is with you.
2. Make a strike committee.
3. Come to the association for advice and help.

This method of linking up with rank-and-file militants had been used by AWOC in the strike happy years between 1959 and 1961, but had been explicitly opposed by the NFWA at its founding convention and throughout its first three years of existence. The next issue of El Malcriado made an even greater departure, promoting strikes as the main way of gaining power, and even resurrecting the old Wobbly idea of "one big strike" that would transform the whole relationship between the workers and their bosses. The article is a lovely mixture of the old NFWA approach and El Malcriado's new attitude toward the more traditional methods and ideology of farm worker struggle.

What Can One Man Do?

Q. Is there any fast way to make wages and working conditions improve?

A. No. For people to learn their own value and to learn not to be afraid takes a long time.

Q. What is the way it can be done?

A. Through many small strikes and a final grand strike, the people will become strong enough to tell the growers how much they are worth and to get it.

Q.   But what can one man do?

A.   Everything! The roots of this country, and the roots of the Mexican Revolution, were established by a very few men. It is always a very few men who are responsible for the great social changes in the world. It was one man, for example, Gandhi, who led the huge country of India out of slavery. You, also, are one man.

Q.   Exactly how can one man do what needs to be done?

A.   One can first learn how to fight and then find ways to struggle against the system that keeps the farm worker poor. For example it was one man that started the action in the Rose Strike this year that led to big wage increases for all the workers in an entire crop.

Q.   Where can one man start?

A.   By joining together with his fellow workers in the association, which is working toward the big strike.[13]

"We were the *malcriados*, the bad boys," Bill Esher said years later, "and we were thrilled by the strike wave. But Chavez went back and forth. Some days he was the very spirit of the Mexican Revolution, but other days he was a conservative man running a small business, worried about its survival. His Mexican Revolution side welcomed the strikes; his conservative side was worried about them." Esher acknowledged that Cesar's concerns were legitimate, but he himself wasn't much worried by the growing farm worker rebellion:

> By the summer of 1965, there was no uniform strategy. Things were out of control, completely. I didn't worry about that. I was excited by the growth of the movement. I knew the history, that the growers had crushed big farm worker movements in the past, and that the same thing could happen to this one. But at the same time I loved all the action, all the rebellion, and I wanted to encourage it. Cesar was tremendously excited too, but he was also afraid. He was working on two levels: he wanted people to move, to be willing to take on the growers, to strengthen their own self-respect by taking things into their own hands, but at the same time he didn't want people to do things that would lead to defeats.[14]

A few months before *El Malcriado*'s declaration of neo-Wobblyism, the newspaper had moved a few houses down the street, and was no longer being written and laid out in the NFWA office. Chavez was not writing many of the articles and was no longer the translator. Esher still talked over the coming articles with Cesar before he wrote them up; he almost always followed Chavez's suggestions, and never defied any of his clear directives. But by mid-summer of 1965, Esher was clearly the person most responsible for the content, and Chavez and the executive board didn't really know what was going to be in the paper until it came out. Sometimes Chavez would criticize an article after he read it, but Esher doesn't remember any particular criticism of the two neo-Wobbly calls to action. Esher thinks those two articles were possibly influenced by the presence of Eugene Nelson in Delano. Nelson, an old friend of Dolores Huerta's, stopped by Delano with his daughter that summer on his way to Mexico, and stayed for the next couple of years. Esher and Nelson got along well:

> I was familiar with the Wobblies from my old Catholic Worker days, but Gene was the first card-carrying Wobbly I had ever met, although he was a revolutionary artist rather than a worker. He was really enthusiastic about the strikes, as they fit perfectly with his ideas about change. I was talking to him a lot, and those articles sound a lot like him. Of course, you can see Cesar's influence, too, with the mention of Gandhi. At the time, Cesar and I were both reading the same book about Gandhi, passing our one copy back and forth, and talking it over whenever we got a chance.[15]

Chavez's mixed reaction to the growing strike movement would soon not matter at all. Farm workers were not waiting to see on which side of the fence he finally landed. Their strikes increased, in number and intensity. In September they tumbled into Cesar's own backyard, less than two miles from the NFWA's office door. Chavez faced a stark choice: would he seize the opportunities created by the growing movement or seek a safe haven where he could wait out what he feared would be that movement's ultimate ebb and probable defeat? Although Chavez chose hope, his fears were well founded. For the NFWA, as conceived by its founder, could not survive the crucible of the strike. The association was transformed—nay, doomed. A union was in the birth canal. And Chavez, despite all the years of struggle and effort he would give to nurturing this new creation, was never entirely satisfied with what became of the new child.

The Grape Strike

August to November '65

It takes a lot of people, working much of the year, to grow table grapes. Grape vines left to themselves do not produce uniform bunches of grapes suitable for shipping, unlike, for example, lettuce seedlings, which grow into heads of lettuce with a minimum of weeding and thinning. Vines have to be pruned, tied, and girdled. The developing grapes must be thinned and tipped. Finally, just before the harvest, some of the leaves must be pulled off so that the grapes will be exposed to the sun and become sweeter. People with tools in their hands do all of that work. None of it has ever been successfully mechanized. Without this extensive pre-harvest demand for labor, large numbers of farm workers would not have been able to establish permanent residency in the area around Delano, and the two large communities of nonmigrant, professional farm workers—the Mexican Americans of the barrios and the Filipinos in labor camps, which the NFWA and AWOC were trying to organize—would not have existed.

Table grapes require not only a large number of workers but, at various points in the growing cycle, a significant supply of relatively skilled ones. In the Delano area, pruning extends from December to March and involves 2,000 people at its peak, usually in January. Before 1970 all of this work was done by men; now some women prune. How a vine is pruned goes a long way toward determining the quantity and quality of the grapes it will bear, as well as what the viticulturists call the "vigor" (rate of growth) of the plant. Nothing can be done to make a poorly pruned vine produce enough good fruit in the upcoming season, while an especially bad job of pruning can ruin a vine for years. One grower estimates that a pruner makes 200 difficult decisions in any eight-hour workday; learning to prune "comes best and most easily from years of pruning along with older workers, in the comforting shade of their years of experience."[1]

Pruning is followed by spraying (sulfur, herbicides, pesticides, and fertilizers) and careful irrigating, neither of which is labor-intensive. A large amount of labor is then needed to tie the spurs to the trellises. This work is done by men and women and requires stamina and patience but not any specialized knowledge. Girdling and thinning come next, in the spring.

Girdling is particularly difficult. Workers cut through the hard bark of the vine, completely encircling the stalk, usually down low at the trunk. This cut, when done correctly, forces the sap of the plant to remain in the upper part of the vine and increases the amount of sugar that the vine stores in the grapes, as well as the actual number of grapes. The cut is a delicate one: if too shallow, the sap won't rise; if too deep, the vine will die. And the surgical use of the special knife has to be done while bent over, by men who are working as fast as they can, because girdling is always done by individual piece-rate workers. Thus, the girdlers are the most skilled of the grape workers, and when they learn the job well enough to do it quickly, they are the best paid. At the same time that the girdlers are working, many men and women thin and tip the grapes. Left to themselves, grapes come in odd-shaped bunches, with the berries so densely packed that they impede on one another's growth and remain small. Thinning and tipping produces the characteristic shape and size of the bunches that end up at supermarkets. About 3,000 people are needed for thinning and tipping, which continues into the early summer. Large numbers are also employed in the last pre-harvest job, "pulling leaves," exposing the bunches to the sun in midsummer, and 5,000 are needed for the harvest, which in Delano usually lasts from August to November.[2]

The Delano grape growers, dependent on all of this labor, were particularly anxious about the possibility of any significant jump in workers' wages. Perhaps more worrying was the long-term decline in U.S. per capita table grape consumption, from an average high of 6.8 pounds per year from 1934 to 1938 to a low of 3.7 pounds in 1965.[3] Unable to agree on a marketing order that would keep some vineyards out of production, the growers faced an extremely unwelcome conclusion: they had planted too many vines, and unless consumption patterns changed, they stood to lose plenty of money. They could partially cover their losses by selling their grapes for wine-crush—many varieties can go both ways, although high-quality wine grapes make poor table grapes—but the crush price is far below the fresh price. A grower who paid for all the pre-harvest work necessary to produce a table grape and then, because of an oversupplied market, decided to sell for crush would not even make the average return of a straight wine grape grower. If, on the other hand, a grower decided to avoid the pre-harvest costs of fresh grapes and produce just for the wine market, he would have to write off whatever capital investment he had made in packing sheds and cooling facilities, as well as missing whatever chance he might have to take advantage of a quick upturn in the table grape market, where large profits might make up for the long years of soft markets.

None of the choices were good, and in 1965, men whose wealth was based on the production of table grapes faced an uncertain future. Would the long slump in grape consumption ever be reversed? It was hard to tell; until the 1920s, table grapes had never been an important product of the vine. Although vineyards are nearly as old as agriculture, first mentioned in Egyptian hieroglyphics around 2400 BC, the ancients were not much interested in eating grapes. Noah used his vineyard to make wine, as did the Greeks in Homeric times. The French, who received grape cuttings from the Phoenicians and started planting vineyards in 600 BC, were wine drinkers, not grape eaters. Franciscans and Jesuits, who carefully carried cuttings to California and other far reaches of the New World, drank the grapes they grew. Only during the Gold Rush did people eat enough grapes to create a small local market, and local it had to remain because fresh grapes could not travel far before they spoiled. Grapes started being put on refrigerated rail cars and moved around the country in large quantities only because Prohibition legislation allowed individuals to make up to 200 gallons of wine for their own consumption. Strong spirits and beer received no similar legal dispensation, and with most U.S. wineries closed down, the field was clear for the household winemakers. Prior to prohibition, average U.S. wine production was about forty-five to fifty million gallons. By 1930, makeshift vintners were brewing, even by the low official count, 145 million gallons of wine. The price of grapes, which had topped out at $75 a ton before 1919, had doubled by 1920, with some selling for $300 a ton within two years.[4]

California growers planted more than 128 million new vines between 1919 and 1925, an increase of more than 50 percent. Vines producing the more hardy table grape varieties that could also be used to make wine (like Thompson seedless grapes) were especially popular and increased by 250 percent.[5] Most of this new acreage was planted on the eastern outskirts of the old Tulare Basin, by relatively poor Italian and Croatian immigrants who bought cheap dry land and used the relatively new centrifugal pump to tap ground water and irrigate their vineyards. Led by Joseph DiGiorgio, the more successful new growers threw up packing sheds as quickly as possible, and in cooperation with the railroads, they improved and extended the infrastructure necessary to keep the fresh grapes cool on the trip east. Bunches of fresh grapes, the vast majority grown in and around Delano, began to appear all over the country. Most were destined for wine vats, but some made their way to the dinner table, and a new national market was born.

But bust follows boom, and by the mid-twenties the table grape market crashed. The new growers had put in too many vines. Some of them went broke even before the Depression officially arrived. A few dozen survived the crisis and acquired holdings of thousands of acres. But when Prohibition was repealed in 1933, the problem of oversupply intensified. Per capita sales fell consistently. No one knew where the bottom was.

The immigrant farmers who had prospered through the various ups and downs in the market had acquired enough land and had diversified into other fruit so that their dominant class position was secure. But this was a small group of people. Although there were thousands of table grape growers in California in 1965, only thirty-eight in the Delano-Arvin area also owned the packing sheds, enormous cold storage warehouses, and shipping facilities without which a table grape was a useless commodity.[6] These grower-packer-shippers charged the smaller, dependent growers for precooling, inspecting, storing, and selling the crop. Often they also provided the smaller producers with their harvest crews, and charged them a fee for picking and packing. In bad years—and the years had not been particularly good for a long time—the vast majority of growers often lost money, but the grower-packer-shippers were somewhat insulated from the weakening market. In 1965, the small and medium-sized growers, by this time heavily mortgaged and in debt, were in a near panic about the prospect of a significant rise in wages. The grower-packer-shippers—the DiGiorgio, Giuamarra, Divizich, Merzoian, Steel, Zaninovich, Pandol, Bianco, and Caratan families, plus a handful of others—while not nearly as threatened, were still uneasy about the industry's long-range prospects. Jack Pandol had averaged only $22,500 in net income between 1961 and 1965 on a 2,000-acre ranch valued (along with all its equipment) at about $4 million, with gross annual sales of $1.35 million. As Pandol told the writer John Gregory Dunne in 1965, "A business that grosses that much and nets that little is in trouble."[7]

These grower-packer-shipper families, all of them Catholic, some of them still headed by the patriarchs who had acquired the Tulare Basin land and put in the first vineyards, had settled in the area around Delano. Of the big grape growers, only Schenley and DiGiorgio were absentee landlords, and even the local DiGiorgio operation was run by one of the old man's nephews, who lived near Arvin. These people, especially the Slavs (as the Croatian families are called around Delano), formed an insular community, where intermarriage was common, where even the second generation spoke with a slight Croatian accent, and the highlights of social life were grower luncheons, children's christenings and first communions, dances at Slav Hall, and an occasional night on the town in Bakersfield. Even after they became rich, most remained wedded to agriculture and did not branch out into the professions. (Dunne noted that there was not one Slav doctor or lawyer in Delano).[8] The fathers and sons were hands-on directors of their farm businesses, and although they didn't prune, thin, girdle, pick, and pack themselves, they knew how that work was supposed to be done. Most of them got up early in the morning and spent a lot of time going over the various tasks of the day with supervisors and foremen. Their family stories were all about dedication and hard work, and many were intensely proud of what the first-generation immigrants had accomplished. They started out poor and now they had money. They were typically neither golf players nor country club bar sitters. They had plenty of land, big air-conditioned homes, nice cars, private planes, and expensive private educations for their children. They were more than just wealthy. They were an authentic rural bourgeoisie, but they were still proud of their peasant backgrounds, and were determined to remain rural small-town people. They were even proud of their insularity and lack of sophistication. Their one venture into big city life was their significant financial and political support for the Democratic Party.

The interests of these families were directly threatened by the farm workers' demands for higher wages and union recognition. Aside from a direct calculation of cost, their whole understanding of themselves mitigated against any easy accommodation with a Mexican or Filipino union. The big growers had no doubts about their own story. They had worked hard and prospered. Their compatriots who had not worked hard, or who had made bad decisions, had failed. Wasn't that the way of the world? Why should it be different for other poor immigrants? They lived in a world of easy assumptions about inherent racial inferiority and deficient national character, which went a long way toward explaining to themselves not only why they were successful and others weren't but why it should remain ever so. In the Delano grape fields in 1965, racism and national chauvinism were not just historical and ideological baggage warping the world outlook of the major players; they were still part of the organization of production. Although different wage rates according to race were no longer the rule, on the large ranches Mexicans, Filipinos, blacks, whites, and Puerto Ricans still lived in separate camps, worked in separate crews, and often specialized in different jobs, which did have different rates of pay. Such strict divisions made it easy for most everyone to maintain the longstanding stereotypes graven into California history: Filipino gambling and excessive sexuality; Mexican thievery and dishonesty; Negro indolence; Puerto Rican hot tempers; and Okie filth. Those fictions, combined with the self-congratulatory family stories of the big growers, served to blind the Slavs and Italians to the real life histories of their workers. But was it not better to be blind? Clear vision might have produced an uneasy conscience, and any self-doubt about the justice of their cause might have interfered with the growers' defense of their own power and interest.

As the Delano grape harvest began in late August, the Filipinos who worked for Marco Zaninovich decided that they wanted their boss to pay them the $1.40 an hour and 25 cents a box that grape workers had won in Coachella earlier in the year. It didn't seem like such a big deal. Most of the Pinoys had worked for Zaninovich for more than a decade—some had even planted the first grape vines for him back in the 1920s—and over the years they had learned how to negotiate. A respected elder, who was also often a leadman or foreman, would let Zaninovich know what the men wanted. Usually, the negotiations were carried on without rancor, even when the workers backed them up with slow downs, short work stoppages, and other semi-ritualized job actions. Zaninovich was the boss, and his power was respected. But the highly skilled Filipino workers, who were almost always completely united, had their own measure of power. Even though they had suffered from discriminatory wage rates in the 1920s and '30s, by the 1960s they were, on average, the highest-paid ethnic group in California agriculture.[9]

But this time the informal negotiations did not go well. Zaninovich was in no mood to give in. Even though the Delano growers had not used braceros, they feared that the labor shortage around the state would push up wages everywhere. The successful strike in Coachella, in the midst of statewide uncertainty and labor troubles, seemed to justify their fears. And the Delano workers were asking for a significant raise. A $1.40 minimum plus a piece-rate incentive would push the wage to around $2 an hour, about a 33 percent jump over the previous year.* The growers had beaten back the workers' attempt to extend their Coachella victory into Arvin, and they had decided that they wouldn't knuckle under in Delano, either.

The workers had another option besides the limited job actions. They could stay away from the fields entirely; they could strike. They had done it several times before, sometimes winning, sometimes losing, but usually minimizing their losses by returning to work quickly if they could not win their demands. Often they would strike without picket lines, just as the rose grafters had done; though "a stay at home" for the Zaninovich Filipinos meant remaining at the company-owned labor camp in the midst of Zaninovich's fields, playing cards, eating and drinking a bit, and waiting to see what they could extract from the boss. Starting September 5, 1965, that's what they did.

The first day of the stay-at-home, Larry Itliong came by for a talk with Zaninovich. Itliong was the head of the Agricultural Workers Organizing Committee operation in the area. He had been involved in labor fights almost since the day he got off the boat from the Philippines, in 1929; he had been a Cannery and Agricultural Workers Industrial Union (C&A) organizer in the early 1930s, and then a paid organizer off and on for various Filipino unions. Since 1959 he had been in charge of AWOC's Filipino

---

* Depending on the conditions workers could usually pick two to four boxes an hour, so the twenty-five-cent incentive the workers wanted would add a minimum of fifty cents an hour. The previous year the wage was $1.25 plus ten cents a box, putting the hourly average at about $1.50. (See Dunne, *Delano.*)

membership. He knew the work and was an excellent card player (Gilbert Padilla says that often he would collect union dues by going to a camp, playing an evening of cards, and if he won, which he usually did, making a show of subtracting each man's union dues from his winnings). He was generally respected as a shrewd, knowledgeable, capable representative of the workers to their bosses.

Itliong wanted the men to give up their stay-at-home and go to the vineyards. He didn't think it could work. The victory in Coachella had been a bit of a fluke, he said. Coachella had received a hit of especially hot weather, which made the growers even more eager than usual to get the grapes picked. But in Arvin, where AWOC had first tried to extend the new pay raise, the cops had arrested twenty-four people just for being on the picket line. Now, in Delano, Zaninovich couldn't give in to the demands even if he wanted to. To do so would shut him out of Delano's tight Slav community. Better to go back to work, he said, and wait for a better time. But the workers weren't having it. The strike in Arvin had been mostly Mexican pickers who were relatively easy to replace, they said, while they were Zaninovich's best packers; he wouldn't risk losing them. And the hot weather had lasted, so the pressure was still on. They decided to keep playing cards.[10]

The stay-at-home spread. Filipino workers at other companies refused to leave their camps. Despite his doubts, Itliong had little choice but to prepare for a formal strike vote. Hundreds of men came to Filipino Hall on September 8 and voted to strike. Some went on picket duty the next morning, but others, concerned about losing their homes in what might be a relatively long strike, decided to wait it out in the camps. The growers had other ideas and employed a tactic they hadn't used since the battles of the 1930s: they turned off the gas, water, and electricity. But the strikers were not easily bullied; they continued to sleep in their beds, built outdoor toilets, and cooked their meals on campfires. The growers then busted the stay-at-home by busting up the camps, first using private security guards, who scattered the strikers' food, moved their belongings out of the bunkhouses, and barred the doors. Later, police evicted the men from company property. Hundreds of Filipinos moved to Delano's west side, walking the streets, hanging out in the bars and cafés, sleeping at Filipino Hall. The hall, a place usually used for card games, dances, and various patriotic celebrations, was about to become a bivouac in a labor war.

Entering the 1960s, Filipino workers were the main bearers of the limited tradition of conventional unionism in the California fields. In the 1920s, when the national average for production-line factory workers was under $5 a day, they had pushed their average earnings above $6, thanks to their exclusive control over who worked in the asparagus fields, their near monopoly on the difficult skill of cutting asparagus, and their unity in various Filipino-only associations.[11] Between the springs of 1932 and 1934, they were the leading ethnic group in ten separate successful strikes, one of which even secured formal recognition of the C&A as the workers' bargaining agent, one of the few times the Communist-led union forced a grower to sign a contract. Carey McWilliams reported that by 1934, the independent Filipino Labor Union (FLU) had seven locals throughout California with about 2,000 dues-paying members. Its most stable local, in Santa Maria, operated out of a labor temple built with $8,000 from union dues.[12] Propelled by a victorious strike in 1934, and working in close cooperation with independent Anglo and Mexican unions, the Santa Maria FLU local signed contracts with the local Grower-Shipper Vegetable Association. Those contracts were strengthened through a successful 1937 strike, and in 1939 they included preferential union hiring, overtime pay, provisions about working conditions, and a joint labor-management grievance board.[13]

But for all the successes of the FLU, it was not as powerful as the Filipino Agricultural Labor Association, or FALA, which scored its first great victory in a one-day stay-at-home by 5,000 Stockton asparagus cutters in 1939. No one worked that day in 40,000 acres of ready-to-harvest asparagus, and the growers immediately capitulated and signed a collective bargaining agreement. The FALA, whose membership included not only workers but professionals, small businessmen, labor contractors and foremen, followed up that victory with strikes in the Sacramento Delta's Brussels sprout, tomato, and celery fields, all of which resulted in signed contracts and union recognition. The next year, the power of the union was somewhat diminished as the growers organized a company union with a group of breakaway Filipino contractors, but FALA still had some 7,000 workers under contract in the delta region and nearly 30,000 members in other parts of the state, organized into separate, independent locals. These remarkable achievements, virtually unacknowledged in the conventional chronicles of endless farm worker defeats leading up to the supposedly singular victory of the UFW, continued in force until World War II, when the FLU and FALA memberships were depleted by the entry of so many Filipino farm workers into the U.S. Army. Bracero labor made it difficult to rebuild the two unions, but Filipino workers maintained a level of militancy and organization which made them, since AWOC's inception in 1960, the strongest contingent of farm workers in the AFL-CIO sponsored union.[14]

For the Filipino farm workers who launched the stay-at-home in the Zaninovich camp this rich union tradition was the story of their own lives. They had lived it, they had authored it, they were the men who had sometimes lost and often won. They were mostly "Manong," the first generation of Filipinos who had come to California as young men between 1923 and

1934. The union victories in the thirties were among the great adventures of their youth. Those exploits, well told and therefore well remembered, were part of the sweetness of their bittersweet lives. The internal solidarity and unity in action that had made these triumphs possible were not apart from a daily life that combined hard work and great suffering with an almost unfathomable closeness and mutual affection. The closeness had been forced upon them. The 20,000 souls who had worked together in the California fields since the mid-1920s lived thoroughly segregated lives: restricted to a small variety of jobs; cramped together in labor camps, or in the cheap hotels and rundown apartments of various "little Manilas"; cut off from family life by the fact that few women emigrated from the Philippines and that until 1948 it had been illegal in California for whites or Mexicans to marry Filipinos.* Stranded in small islands of male friends and fellow workers, they learned to take care of each other. They rented rooms together where they shared beds, food, and money. They pooled resources and bought jointly owned cars or an expensive suit of clothes which they would take turns wearing as they posed for pictures to be sent home or when they went out for a night on the town. Some were able to extend their internal solidarity out into the world. The Manong produced a high percentage of radical internationalists, labor union activists, socialists, and Communists. Many others remained quite insular, true only to their shared bachelor society, passing their time working, playing cards, and raising and fighting their beloved roosters. Some, only a few, lived off various scams and con games, often taking advantage of the naiveté of their more trusting brothers. But most of the Manong lived deeply interrelated lives, their fates woven closer and closer together as the years went by, until the 1965 grape strike gave them one last chance to walk together onto the public stage and one last story to tell.

By the time of the strike, however, the Manong did have some company. After World War II, many Filipino veterans became citizens, traveled to Hawaii and the Philippines, got married, had children, and then returned to the U.S. and farm work. When their sons grew old enough, some followed their fathers to California, and joined them in the fields. By 1965, these men were in their early twenties, ready to become the "Huks" of the strike (a reference to the Hukbalahap guerrillas who had fought the Japanese occupation in World War II)—so called for their militancy on the picket lines and their guerrilla actions in the fields.[15]

Rudy Reyes, who would become a soldier of the early UFW, was part of this minority within a minority, but his story is different from those of

---

*   Law has it limits. Some Pinoys went to Arizona or Mexico where they could get legally married and others set up households with women and children in what I suppose could be called illegal families.

his fellow Delano Huks. His dad, an early Manong, joined the Coast Guard well before World War II, met his Filipina wife in Hawaii, and after the war moved his family to Seattle, where he got a job as a draftsman. Reyes, born in 1941, grew up in a prosperous working-class family and got good grades in high school, but instead of going to college he went to the fields. "I wanted to learn, yes, I wanted to learn . . . but not in college. I wanted to learn to be a hobo. I was a reader; I had read Hemingway and Kerouac, and I wanted to hit the road. It wasn't hard to find hobo life. I went down to the Seattle waterfront and just signed up."[16]

Rudy traveled with Native Americans, whites, and blacks on the hobo circuit. They would work for a little while at a small ranch, then move on when they had enough money in their pockets. They worked only when they had to. Otherwise it was stealing fruit and vegetables from the fields, making big pots of soup, hanging out, and telling stories. There was quite a lot of drinking, but not everyone was a drunk. While working in the apples in Yakima, Washington, he linked up with a black man named Billy, who was a little bit older and taught him how to ride the trains. They ran into some of the same people everywhere, and Rudy became a somebody in his own chosen world. "There weren't many fights," said Reyes. "Hobos are actually a pretty peaceful bunch."

> But Billy was a tough, strong man, and people gave him a wide berth. One time we were together in a railroad yard in Seattle, and five or six drunk white tramps stumbled upon us. They either didn't know Billy or they were too drunk to realize who he was. They said they were going to kick the shit out of us. Billy told me to give him my knife and leave. I gave him the knife; he knew how to use it better than I, but I didn't leave. I picked up a rock instead and hurled it at the drunks. It wasn't much of a fight; the men were too juiced up to be dangerous and soon ran off. But I knocked one down and started to kick him as he lay on the ground. Billy grabbed me. "No, no, Rudy. Don't you dare kick a man when he's down. We done defended ourselves. That's all that matters. Let's get out of here." I never forgot those words. They have always been my guide when it comes to violence.

Reyes kept on reading: cowboy stories, mysteries, nonfiction. At one hobo camp, he found a copy of *The Grapes of Wrath*. For three days running the book was hardly out of his hands. He was reading about white tramps in a camp dominated by white tramps, old Okies. As he read about the Joads, he just looked up from the book and there they were. The only things missing were the cars and the strikes. Cars didn't interest him. But strikes? Hemingway and Kerouac hadn't said anything about strikes. And the people Rudy ran with thought of themselves as hobos, not farm workers, although farm work is what they did. They never got involved in a labor dispute. If they didn't like something about a job, they just left it. Sometimes everyone went at once, knowing they had left the farmer with a big problem, but they didn't call it a strike.

Reyes had heard about Delano up in Washington; people said you could make good money in the grapes. He was in Los Angeles in 1965, in Watts, when he decided to head north. The Watts Riots had broken out, and "it was a lot of fun for a while . . . like a big party. Then the cops came and started shooting into the crowd . . . [and] it turned ugly." He took a freight train out of LA and wound up in Delano's Chinatown. "I walked into the Manila Café. I didn't have to be too smart to figure out that was a good place to start." The next day he was in a Filipino labor camp owned by Vincent Zaninovich, Marco's brother. An AWOC enthusiast, Julian Balidoy, younger than the Manong, who were the majority in the camp, but older than Reyes, told him that a strike was coming soon. Rudy wanted to start right then; he was twenty-four years old.

In September 1965 there was nothing inevitable about Mexican solidarity with the Filipinos. Such solidarity was not unheard of in California's agricultural history, but it was the exception. More Filipino strikes had been broken by strike-breaking Mexicans (and vice versa) than had been helped by acts of interethnic solidarity. And this time, the Filipinos were particularly vulnerable. They were mostly an aging, shrinking part of the workforce, and if the local Mexican majority decided to scab, not only was the Filipinos' strike doomed, but the Filipinos' very presence in the vineyards might be jeopardized.

The National Farm Workers Association's decision to join the strike, unlike the act of defiance that began it, was made by the association's leadership rather than by the rank and file. The workers were confused and divided. What should they do? Some were already crossing the picket lines; most continued to pick grapes on the ranches where there were no strikes. A few of the Mexicans saw the same opportunity that the Filipinos had seen, but no Mexican work stoppage, organized from below, added its weight to the Filipino action. Instead, people came to the NFWA office to see what the association was going to do now that the struggle had arrived at its own doorstep.

Formally joining this strike would require a commitment different from anything the association had ever attempted. Potentially some 5,000 workers might be involved, and the fight would engage a group of powerful and hostile bosses directly. The NFWA leaders did not want to be dragged into such a battle against their will if, in their best judgment, they were sure to lose. The leaders had to make that judgment. They could not avoid making it, as there were no local Mexican strikes in progress, no farm worker militants pulling them along and making the decision for them. No delegation of striking Filipinos came to Cesar Chavez and asked for his support. Rather, Mexican workers came and asked him what he was going to do. It was mostly the more militant ones who wanted to know, but they would not act on their own.

Manuel and Esther Uranday, dues-paying NFWA members, remember rushing into the office and telling Chavez about the strike and catching him by surprise. Bill Esher remembers the same moment: "Damn them," Chavez said, "we will have to either break the strike or join them. We're not ready for this." Cesar swore in Spanish, sat at his desk for a while "holding his head in misery," and then went to the bathroom, the only place he could escape the excitement and tumult of the office. Esher remembers that he was in there for half an hour. When he finally came out, he was "grim, without hope or joy." But he told Esher, "We are going to join them."[17]

But joining them would not be easy. Chavez called Padilla in Porterville. "The world's coming to an end, Gilbert; the Filipinos are out on strike. Come on down." When Padilla arrived, Cesar still seemed unsure about what to do. He asked Gilbert to go over to Filipino Hall to see what was happening. Padilla walked in on an enthusiastic meeting of a few hundred people. Five languages were flying around—Tagalog, Ilocano, Viscayan, English, and Spanish. The AWOC chief, Al Green, was there, but seemed to have very little to do with the strike. Larry Itliong chaired the meeting, and although there was a lot of talk about the wage demands, Padilla heard little mention of the issue of union recognition. Padilla had a friendly conversation with a few Mexican members of AWOC, and later, when Chavez, still hesitant, asked, "Well, what do we do?" Gilbert, caught up in the excitement of the mass meeting, had no doubts: "We are going to strike."[18]

Itliong was friendly but somewhat standoffish in his first conversation with Padilla. He didn't take the NFWA seriously. If its members really wanted to help, they could all join AWOC, he said. After that, Bill Esher wrote up a leaflet calling AWOC the "union of the north" (a reference to its Stockton headquarters, which implied that NFWA was the authentic Delano-area farm worker organization) listing the demands of the strike and the growers being struck. It ended with an injunction: "The Farm Worker Association asks of all Mexicans: HONOR THIS STRIKE. DON'T BE STRIKEBREAKERS." Chavez issued a press release that said, in part, "Now is when every worker, without regard to race, color, or nationality, should support the strike and must under no circumstances work on those ranches that have been struck." A special edition of *El Malcriado* gave unconditional support to the AWOC strike.[19]

Meanwhile, dozens of Filipino pickets walked in front of the packing sheds and cold-storage facilities alongside the railroad tracks that run through the center of Delano. On the working-class west side the talk at bars and cafés was dominated by strike stories: the foreman who shot at an evicted Filipino because he wasn't leaving his camp fast enough; police cars patrolling in front of Filipino Hall; the vulnerability of the wooden packing sheds to fire; late-night actions against water pumps. The NFWA was essentially on the sidelines. Padilla, Huerta, and Esher were anxious to be at the center of the battle. Chavez was cautious. Some Mexican farm workers were crossing the picket lines, but at one ranch, a young woman led her Mexican crew out in support of the strike. Chavez called an executive board meeting for September 14 to decide what to do.[20]

The meeting saw Chavez at his strategic best. At the very least the NFWA had to continue to support the AWOC strike, he said. If not, the Filipinos would blame the Mexicans for what was surely an upcoming defeat. The inevitable mutual recrimination would destroy all possibility for Mexican-Filipino cooperation. AWOC would be more damaged than the NFWA, but both groups would have a hard time organizing after such a major loss. No one at the meeting disagreed with that. The question was whether to go beyond support for the AWOC strike, and exactly how to do it. Itliong's suggestion that the NFWA dissolve itself into AWOC was unacceptable, and yet he had offered no other way for the association to become more involved. No half measures came to mind. If the NFWA wanted to go beyond a statement of solidarity, it would have to call its own strike. Chavez acknowledged that if the question were put to a vote at a mass meeting, people would decide to extend the strike to their own ranches. But he also argued that the enthusiasm would soon pass, the growers would hold firm, and most people would go back to work. In many ways the most prudent course was not to call a mass meeting and not to commit the NFWA any further. But that meant watching AWOC lose, and suffering all the consequences.

Chavez concluded that the NFWA had to enter the strike, despite his own assessment that the workers were not powerful enough to win. Was the organization, then, walking into a disaster? Cesar answered his own question: maybe, but not necessarily. If it could effectively involve outside supporters in the strike, it might overcome the unfavorable local balance of forces. He pointed out that Padilla and the Migrant Ministry had done just that in the rent strike. A vast mobilization of outside support might even turn this more conventional battle into a winner. It was a gamble, a long shot, Chavez argued, but what other choice did they have? They should join the strike, not be discouraged by expected early setbacks, and try to make the strike last long enough so that the power of their supporters could be felt locally. They must not strike and run.

Such a notion was much in the air in the late summer of 1965. Over the previous few years, the civil rights movement had mobilized liberal supporters in the North in an effort to overcome the seemingly all-powerful local forces supporting segregation in the South. That strategy had had its ups and downs, with SNCC and the Southern Christian Leadership Council disagreeing about its ultimate effectiveness, but it had just scored a spectacular national victory with the Selma march and the subsequent passage of the 1965 Voting Rights Act. Chavez specifically cited those gains, and the strategy behind them, at the meeting, as he had been thinking about the applicability of civil rights strategy to the farm worker movement for some time. Six months earlier he had told a meeting of Mexican American leaders, according to one of the people at the meeting, Bert Corona, "that the reason the farm workers' organizing drive could win in the days ahead was because they could ally themselves with a new feature in American social and political activity—the movement for civil rights, the movement of the youth, and the movement of the poor."[21]

And who better than Chavez to see that the strategy of the civil rights movement could be used by his newly developing National Farm Workers Association? His Community Service Organization had been essentially a Mexican American civil rights group—it was no great stretch to think of the NFWA more as a continuation of the Mexican American civil rights struggle than as a conventional effort to organize a union. Not that the two conceptions of the NFWA could be easily separated, even theoretically. As the organization's leaders often argued, one of the reasons that wages and working conditions were so bad was because farm workers were not covered by the same laws as all other Americans. Legally they were second-class workers, only recently granted workers' compensation (owing primarily to the lobbying efforts of Dolores Huerta, coupled with the voter registration campaigns of the CSO and the NFWA), still lacking unemployment insurance, not covered by organizing rights under the National Labor Relations Act, with separate and unequal coverage by Social Security, child labor, and minimum-wage laws. In its first two years, the NFWA had placed considerable emphasis on political action (forging temporary alliances with liberal Democratic politicians and participating in Sacramento legislative hearings) to change this second-class status. Righting those wrongs was surely as much a civil rights battle as it was a union fight. As Chavez had been arguing for some time, this conception of the NFWA not only made good sense in the fields, it made perfect sense in terms of the overall political situation in the country. Who was more popular with the general public, civil rights leaders or union officials?

Once Chavez came to believe that joining the strike was the least worst choice, he urged the others to make that choice with full energy and enthusiasm. They were not hard to convince. Here was another mark of his political agility: he proposed to make a virtue of necessity. The Filipino strike and the enthusiasm of the workers was a great opportunity, he concluded, because the NFWA could transform this local struggle into a statewide and regional fight. Chavez was not clear on how that might be done, but he mentioned, almost as an aside, that they would have a better chance if they fought nonviolently: the strikers should not use the guns, sticks, and chains that had been taken to hand in almost all earlier farm worker battles.

A mass meeting was called for September 16, Mexican Independence Day—two days hence. People would be ready to celebrate, and speakers could evoke the radical traditions of Mexican nationalism when urging workers to join the strike. But only an experienced crew could arrange for such a meeting in two days' time, as they would have to rush through all the necessary preparations—securing the hall, printing and distributing thousands of leaflets, arranging for numerous radio announcements, and planning the agenda. By all accounts the mood at the mass meeting was upbeat and energetic. A relaxed, humorous Gilbert Padilla chaired the meeting; a *norteño* trio sang patriotic songs; NFWA treasurer Tony Orendain warmed up the crowd (attendance estimates range from 800 to 1,500) by leading various *vivas*—"Viva la Causa!" "Viva la Huelga!" "Viva Cesar Chavez!" The local hero Epifanio Camacho gave the most impressive speech, calling on the workers to become the true "sons of Zapata." A subdued, modest Chavez tried to impress upon people how hard the struggle would be, and made a plea for nonviolence. Speakers from the floor recalled earlier battles, one even alluding to the 1933 Pixley martyrs, who had been murdered in the historic cotton strike. The crowd interrupted the speakers with rhythmic clapping and various vivas of their own, and clearly endorsed the strike, which was set to start the next Monday morning.

They had a weekend to prepare. The staff called the Oakland Catholic Worker collective and the Bay Area Friends of the Student Nonviolent Coordinating Committee, and two SNCC organizers came down immediately. Certified letters were sent to the growers, asking for negotiations. Chavez approached Delano's mayor and a friend in the California State Mediation and Conciliation Service, hoping that they could convince the growers to talk, but the growers rejected all offers. Picket captains were appointed and assigned to various ranches. Huerta met with Itliong, who dropped his request that the NFWA join AWOC, and welcomed its direct participation in the strike.

All that remained was a meeting with AWOC's Al Green. Hartmire set it up, with himself as the mediator. Chavez and Drake represented the NFWA; Green came alone. Chavez, whose NFWA had little money, proposed a joint strike fund to Green, who had access to plenty. AWOC was paying as much as $40 a week to the Filipino strikers. Green said no, he wouldn't share funds. Nor would he agree to a joint strike committee or sign a mutual nonraiding pact. He did agree that the two groups should make the same strike demands and cooperate fully in what, technically, would be separate strikes. After the meeting, Green and Chavez stood together to have their pictures taken.

Green left town immediately afterward. He was still disdainful of the NFWA and "that Mexican," as he called Chavez. He was not interested in the strike; Itliong could run it. He was confident that his backing from the AFL-CIO and his close relations with West Coast Teamster leaders meant that he held all the important cards in AWOC's rivalry with the NFWA. In fact, everything had been worked out by those below him, and the meeting had done little more than fill him in on the news. His hand was far weaker than he assumed. The AFL-CIO money would do him little good. That Mexican, the little man he had just brushed off, was several jumps ahead of him, about to become a darling of history. And although history often chooses her darlings capriciously, this time she did not. Her favors were bestowed on the one who best understood her current passions and inclinations.

The first day of the strike, Monday, September 20, about a hundred people showed up at the NFWA office ready to picket. Most of the others who had voted to strike four days earlier went back to work. Were they really on strike? No official union offering even minimum benefits had called this strike, nor had there been a spontaneous walkout to set it off. The doubt was so pervasive that even Teresa Fabela, Helen Chavez's sister and some-time babysitter, went to work at the Mid-State Vineyards. This wasn't a serious familial betrayal; it was just a reflection of the general confusion.[22]

People may have gone to work not knowing whether the strike was on, but once the pickets appeared, many walked off the job. Enough people joined in the first two weeks—several hundreds for sure, perhaps thousands—so that production was seriously reduced. The NFWA leadership transformed the quickly escalating number of volunteers, both farm workers and student, church, and labor supporters, into an effective organization. They drew a tight circle with a nine-mile radius and declared it the official strike zone, where no on could work.[23] Beyond the circle, work could proceed as usual. This had always been a common, informal strike tactic among farm workers; now, the skilled, experienced organizers of the NFWA formalized it by organizing car pools to take workers to other jobs away from the strike area. The organizers also got official strike certification at some thirty ranches within the strike zone. State certification came with documentation that showed that at least one worker at the ranch had gone on strike, which prevented the state employment service from legally sending workers to those ranches and also made it more difficult for the growers to claim that no strike existed. The NFWA organized a set of "flying squadrons," which, just like the roving automobile picket lines of the cotton strike thirty-one years earlier, set out in the early morning, armed with the workers' knowledge of picking patterns and their own informal intelligence reports, to find and harass the remaining scabs.[24]

The first great triumph of the strike was the newfound warmth and solidarity between the Mexican and Filipino strikers. The AWOC was supposed to picket certain ranches and the NFWA others, but from the beginning the Filipino and Mexican picketers intermingled, stood up to the police and growers together, and jointly tried to convince the workers to leave the fields. Gilbert Padilla's experience was representative. "For the first time I began to talk to the Filipinos as brothers and friends. Before that we never talked to them, and they never talked to us."[25] Out of conversations like that among hundreds of workers came the invitation from the Filipinos to the Mexican strikers to come eat at Filipino Hall. Food was free there for AWOC strikers, paid for by the AFL-CIO. Meanwhile, the NFWA pickets had been trying to get by on baloney sandwiches from the association hall or on the small amounts of food they could afford to prepare at home. Neither sufficed, and many NFWA strikers came to the picket lines hungry, a fact not lost on the Filipino strikers. The invitation to Filipino Hall came without prior approval from either Green or Itliong and without the knowledge of the NFWA leadership. This was just the kind of cooperation that Green had denied Chavez at their meeting just before the strike. But looking at it from the bottom up, how could there be any objection? There seemed to be plenty of food. Letting the Mexicans eat at the hall did not mean that the Filipinos would have any less. And what better way to strengthen the bonds of solidarity? Two sets of strikers sitting down to eat together, the Filipinos sharing one of the most prized parts of their culture, unable to hide their pleasure as some Mexicans began to appreciate the Filipino food they had long ridiculed. Those meals made Filipino Hall into Strike Central, and the memory of that shared pleasure would endure long after most of the Filipino and Mexican strikers had gone their separate ways.

But Chavez had been right; this time his pessimism about strikes proved to be well grounded. This was no little skirmish that the growers would be inclined to settle quickly. They were reluctant to give ground on wages and even more opposed to recognizing either of the two organizations as official representatives of the workers. Through an extensive network of labor contractors, the growers recruited strikebreakers from outside the area—first from Tulare, Stockton, and Bakersfield, later from Los Angeles and San Francisco, and finally from as far away as Oregon, Texas, and Mexico. Local judges issued injunctions that set limits on the picketers' ability to gather in large numbers or get close enough to talk to the scabs. The Delano police and California Highway Patrol faithfully enforced the injunctions, and were quick to arrest aggressive strikers but slow to constrain equally aggressive foremen and supervisors. The police were particularly reluctant to take on the growers, some of whom drove their cars dangerously close to the picket lines or threatened strikers by firing shotguns in the air. Other growers quietly met the strikers' wage demands, encouraging people to come back to work and allowing those who did to argue in their own defense that the main demand of the strike had been won.

As many local Mexican strikers returned to their jobs, the Filipinos began to waver. Their biggest concern was the possible loss of their homes, as the growers began housing strikebreakers in the old Filipino camps. At what point would they lose their place in the camps indefinitely? Where else would they live? They couldn't live in the Filipino Hall forever. In the first weeks of October, when it seemed clear that the strike would not be strong enough to force the growers to capitulate, the Filipinos started to return to the camps. The foremen, who were often the authentic leaders in the Filipino bachelor community and intermediaries between the men and the bosses, led the return. Pete Velasco, who later became a member of the UFW Executive Board, was one of only two foreman who did not go back to work. Although the AWOC officially remained committed to the strike and Itliong continued as one of the important strike leaders, most of the rank-and-file AWOC activists also resumed work. The minority of younger Filipino strikers, who tended to be more mobile—working in Alaska's canneries, on the Seattle waterfront, and in the Stockton asparagus, as well as in the Delano grapes—simply moved on to another town as the strike's power diminished. When the harvest ended in November, fewer than a hundred Filipino strikers remained at Filipino Hall. For most of those men, their act of defiance in early September came to mean the end of their working lives.[26]

In the aftermath of the strike, the NFWA leadership and the growers argued over how many people actually had participated. The growers claimed that no more than 500 people walked out in the first couple of weeks and that most of them subsequently returned. The NFWA claimed that 5,000 had walked out and that the vast majority never returned but were replaced by scabs, mostly people from Mexico. Great efforts were made on both sides to establish the validity of their own figures. But the debate was beside the point. In the long run, the number of people who originally left the fields and what percentage of them returned, mattered not one whit. The figure that counted in the battles to come was the number of loyalists who in the process of the strike were recruited, body and soul, to the NFWA and Cesar Chavez. Many of them were outside supporters, not farm workers, but the majority were exactly the people whom the NFWA had been trying to organize since 1962: the Mexican American farm worker families who had settled in the small towns of the southern Central Valley.

Although the strike's first great accomplishment among farm workers was the solidarity of the Mexican and Filipino strikers, its most lasting achievement was that about a hundred original strikers, plus a few other militant farm workers who came to Delano to get in on the action, joined the farm worker families who had been fully committed to the NFWA before the strike. These people together, somewhat more than a few hundred strong, remained fully committed to the strike even as the growers managed to resume full production in October and November. They got up early in the morning and went to the picket lines, and often volunteered at the NFWA office in the afternoon and evenings. In the early days they survived on nothing more than the donations of food and clothing that poured into the Delano office, plus the once-a-day meals at Filipino Hall. Many of these people remained part of the union family over the next five years. Some of them turned their lives upside down, leaving the small towns that had been their homes and traveling to the nation's largest cities to become the crucial players in what came next the biggest, most successful boycott in U.S. history.

The Boycott

Moral Jujitsu

September '65 to January '66

Generations of California growers and police officials have done what they could to keep farm workers separated from their potential allies in the rest of the country. In the 1950s, the DiGiorgio Corporation managed to get a court order to ban and destroy all copies of a film about a farm worker strike. In the 1930s, reporters were arrested in rural California counties for filing harvest strike stories in big city newspapers. In 1934, Imperial County's Sheriff Charles Gillett prohibited a *Nation* journalist from sending a cable to New York from a local Western Union office. Despite the sheriff's efforts, news did get to Los Angeles about the 1934 strike, and about twenty people set out for the Imperial Valley on what they called a "Good Will Tour" to bring aid to the strikers. The sheriff and his deputies stopped them at the Imperial County line, where everyone in the caravan was handcuffed and arrested.[1]

Even more than geographical distance, however, race and language separated farm workers from other people. With the brief exceptions of fruit tramps in the early 1900s and Okies in the late thirties, California farm workers have been primarily Asian or Mexican immigrants who were often monolingual in languages other than English. The fictions of race were hard enough to break through, but not being able to talk to other people made it especially difficult to reach out to them for aid. The isolation of farm workers was even codified in law. In 1936, farm workers were purposefully written out of the National Labor Relations Act, and between 1941 and 1965, a large percentage of farm workers were braceros legally separated from other U.S. workers.

But space and race were very different in 1965 than they had been thirty years before. Television, radio, faster cars, better roads, and both commercial and private airplane travel had shrunk the country and brought the California fields closer to Los Angeles, San Francisco, Chicago, and New York. World War II, the Jackie Robinson–led integration of major league baseball, and the early civil rights movement had transformed many people's attitudes towards race. The fact that farm workers were mostly "nonwhite" was no longer a guarantee that other sectors of society would not support their struggles.

Interracial solidarity had blossomed in the early sixties. Many white Americans had been willing to support African Americans, opening the possibility that they would also support Mexican Americans, and even Mexican immigrants.*

When farm workers first refused to go to work in Delano in 1965, they were still isolated, largely unknown to the dominant, citified American culture. But the conditions that had produced that isolation had changed. In retrospect, it is easy to see that the stage was set for farm workers to reach out to potential white supporters in American cities—but a set stage does not a drama make. Farm workers needed a strategy to connect them to their potential supporters in the cities. They needed someone to help them find a way out of their rural, racial, linguistic, and legal isolation. They found that someone, and he found the boycott.

Cesar Chavez first heard about the possibilities of a boycott soon after the grape strike began. Jim Drake was driving him to a fundraiser on the California coast, and in the relative calm of the drive, he told Cesar the story of the Irish campaign against Captain Charles Boycott, a story Drake had stumbled upon in a book whose name he had forgotten. In the late nineteenth century, Captain Boycott's job was to collect rents from impoverished Irish peasants and turn them over to wealthy Anglo-Irish landlords. Led by a small-town priest, the peasants, some of them literally starving, decided to stop paying the rent and to ostracize the rent collector from the community in which he lived. No one would sell him anything, nor would anyone buy his goods. Laborers refused to work on Boycott's small piece of land. He and his wife were isolated, shunned. The Irish government sent a regiment of troops to defend Boycott, but he didn't need defending. No one had threatened him with violence. Useless, the troops quartered themselves on his land, chopped down his trees for firewood, and ate his livestock. The campaign became famous, not only in Ireland but in London and New York, and was promoted by the Irish Land League as a nonviolent alternative to the contemporaneous armed struggle for Irish independence. Boycott was ruined, a prisoner in his own home, and finally left town in disgrace.[2]

Drake could see that the story pleased Chavez. How could it not? The boycott required thorough organization. The peasants' poverty and Catholicism had helped unite them. At the center of the story was an organizer, a small-town priest. But Cesar did not immediately take hold of the idea. The campaign against Captain Boycott had been a local affair. Local folks had made their power felt against a local enemy. Sure, other Irish peasants used the same technique against their own tax collectors—in that sense it had spread—but what Chavez was looking for was a way of

---

* Who was white and who was not has been an issue of much confusion and some contention in California farm worker history. Sometimes Mexicans have been considered white, other times, not. Armenians had to win a lawsuit to be included in the "white race."

involving other forces in the grape strike, not of moving the strike to other areas. He agreed it was an excellent story, but he would not commit himself.

At the time, labor boycotts—strangled by law and lacking appeal because of the general disdain toward AFL-CIO officialdom—had degenerated into the largely ignored "Unfair" lists in the back of union newspapers. The 1955 Montgomery bus boycott repopularized the word, but in that case the people doing the boycotting were the actual participants in the conflict, not outside supporters. Northerners picketing Woolworth stores after the 1960–61 Greensboro sit-ins were a better example. But although those picket lines were important in linking the civil rights movement and the new student left, they were not particularly instrumental in ending the segregation of southern lunch counters. That victory was achieved closer to home, in the southern cities themselves.

Ultimately grape workers and their supporters reawakened the country to the power of the boycott. Their example spurred the Chicana-led boycott of the Farah Pants Company from 1972 to '74, which was consciously modeled on the farm workers' efforts. After Farah capitulated, the National Council of Churches launched an unprecedented worldwide boycott of the Nestlé Company for its aggressive marketing of baby formula to third world mothers. When the church action forced Nestlé to back off its attack on breastfeeding, the boycott became a standard weapon in contemporary social struggles, finally picked up by organized labor in the early 1980s as a part of its anticorporate campaigns. But in 1965, a boycott did not quickly come to mind as a way of spreading a union fight. It took NFWA leaders a full six months of experimentation and discussion before an unexpected victory made the boycott their primary strategy. Even then it wasn't so much that the leaders chose the boycott—it was more like the boycott chose them.

When Drake first floated the idea of a boycott, picket lines were still active in the grape strike, and the NFWA was asking supporters to send them money, food, clothing, and endorsements, or to come to Delano and help build the strike. In the San Francisco Bay Area, the left was thriving, filled with energy, and quick to respond. Ann Draper, a socialist official of the Amalgamated Clothing Workers Union and a member of the Executive Board of Citizens for Farm Labor, organized a food and clothing caravan to Delano in the first weeks of the strike. She also brought $6,000 in cash. Students from the Bay Area who had just lived through the victorious Free Speech Movement and were now building the antiwar movement at full bore, came to Delano with their enthusiasm and sleeping bags. Many young radicals driving between LA and San Francisco made a semi-obligatory stop at the Delano picket lines. Independent union militants stopped by. Priests, rabbis, and Protestant clergy from all over California spent time picketing and issued statements and decrees. So much used clothing arrived that the strikers could pick and choose, and finding a place to store the extras became a problem. These moral and physical contributions were important in holding the strike together in the early days, but they were not a dramatic enough extension of the scope of the battle to make a significant difference in its outcome.

The major news outlets ignored the strike: the big papers ran a few small paragraphs, but there was nothing on TV outside of the Central Valley. The only regular newspaper reports were from Ron Taylor of the *Fresno Bee* and from a few left and labor publications: *The Valley Labor Citizen*, a weekly publication of regional labor and trade councils, edited by the brilliant photographer George Ballis; *The People's World*, published by the California Communist Party; and *The Movement*, put out by the Friends of SNCC, which publicized and analyzed developments in the rapidly changing black and student movements. "How to get the story in the news" was a common topic of conversation in Delano, just as it was becoming a major consideration in the bourgeoning antiwar movement, and among all U.S. political actors. Portable video cameras, first introduced in the early 1960s, had changed the nature of TV news. Live radio reports were becoming increasingly popular. A large group of liberally inclined young newspaper reporters were out looking for stories. Those they did pick up could have a national impact many times their local weight. If the strike could be presented in a way that pricked popular interest, shutting off the news from the Central Valley would require much more than closing down the local telegraph office.

Chavez's original idea of promoting the strike as a civil rights struggle provided a basis for winning sympathy from the general population and the rank-and-file producers of the news, but it didn't automatically guarantee coverage. Farm workers were more unknown to the rest of the country than were the South's young blacks, whose consistent courage in the face of brutal repression had pushed them into the headlines. Farm workers didn't speak English, were not yet servants in other people's homes, did not have the African Americans' deep, twisted historical ties to their white neighbors. They were considered aliens and sojourners, as well as subordinates. Their labor camps were more isolated from rural communities than the typical black section of a southern town. The farm worker strikes that followed the end of the Bracero Program were big news in farm communities but hardly mattered to anyone else. The NFWA had to make them matter if they were going to win.

Originally, only two people in the NFWA leadership had any extensive experience with the media: Cesar Chavez and Dolores Huerta. In her years as a lobbyist in Sacramento, Huerta had talked to many newsmen and participated in scores of press conferences. She was smart, fiery, and beautiful. She was good copy, and she learned how to use herself to promote her causes. Chavez's style was completely different, but even in his role as the behind-the-scenes Alinsky organizer of the CSO he had built good relations with farm town reporters, so that he had a feel for what those reporters wanted and how to make as big an impact as possible.

Early in the strike, Cesar started talking to Gilbert Padilla, Jim Drake, Dolores Huerta, his cousin Manuel Chavez, and Chris Hartmire about what he called "moral jujitsu," which he offered as a tactical solution to the problem of spreading the word and getting the story into the news. Chavez attributed the idea to Gandhi: the Mahatma had used it to defeat the English in India, and the NFWA could use it to beat the growers in Delano. Several degrees more subtle than Alinsky's "dirty tricks," moral jujitsu was a tactical approach that allowed Cesar to give full rein to his strategic sensibility and avoid the difficult political calculations of ends and means, the problem of doing bad in order to achieve the good. The growers had more strength than the NFWA, but just as the jujitsu expert with subtle feints and skillful shifts of weight can take advantage of his opponent's thrusts, Cesar proposed to turn the growers' power back upon themselves. Such a strategy seemed to present no moral danger, and although it might prove difficult to execute, it was not conceptually complicated.

One of the growers' main strengths was their influence with the Delano and Kern County police, sheriffs, district attorneys, and judges, who had a legal monopoly on the use of violence and could be quite discriminatory in how they applied the law. Police harassment didn't make the difference between winning and losing, but it made life more miserable for the picketers, and it was a measure of the growers' local power—power that Chavez proposed to turn against them.

His first opportunity came in the form of the overzealous Kern County sheriff, who, seemingly on his own, decided in mid-October to interpret the court injunction that banned any disturbance of the peace on the picket lines to mean that strikers could neither use the word *huelga*—strike—nor shout at scabs over a megaphone. There was no need to shout at the strikebreakers, he explained, because they had heard it all already, and, anyway, *huelga* was not an American word.[3] Such tactics had worked before. In the 1930s, several rural judges had made the use of Spanish on picket lines illegal. But what had worked in the 1930s simply set up the police and growers for a jujitsu move in the 1960s. The day after the sheriff's announcement of the new policy, Reverend David Havens of the Migrant Ministry tested the lawman's willingness to enforce the order by standing in the back of Epifanio Camacho's pickup truck and reading Jack London's description of a scab: "a two-legged animal with a corkscrew soul, a waterlogged brain, and a combination backbone of jelly and glue."* Havens, dressed in a coat and tie, was arrested. An

---

*   "Scab," the traditional union term for strikebreakers, is a strange choice for a derogatory epithet. A scab, after all, is a good thing. It helps a wound heal. The word for "strikebreaker" in Mexican Spanish is *esquirol*, which means squirrel, and was the most common insult yelled at those working on the other side of the picket line.

excited group of picketers returned to the NFWA headquarters. The sheriffs were nibbling at the baited hook; maybe they would swallow it whole.

Chavez chaired an open strategy meeting that night at the crowded NFWA hall on Albany Street. Animated speakers assessed the situation. What about free speech? What about the Constitution? Didn't it cover us, too? As a consensus emerged to challenge the sheriff's order, Cesar asked how many would be willing to go to jail for the right to say *"huelga"* on the picket line. All hands shot up amidst a tumultuous chant of the forbidden word. People were ready to act; now it was a matter of doing it right. Chavez had already asked Wendy Goepel to schedule a Bay Area campus tour to Berkeley, Mills College, San Francisco State, and Stanford University. Why not synchronize Cesar's tour with civil rights–style civil disobedience in Delano?[4]

Chris Hartmire was assigned to recruit ministers who would also be willing to get arrested. He organized a Day of Christian Concern. On October 19, the NFWA called the Kern County sheriff's office to say that farm workers intended to defy the gag order that very morning and were about to leave from their office in search of strikebreakers. Lawmen in sheriffs' cars and a paddy wagon rushed to the NFWA office to discover that reporters from most of the large California dailies and several TV crews were waiting for them. Undeterred, the sheriffs went to the end of "one of the strangest farm labor strike caravans of all time," as the *Fresno Bee*'s Ronald Taylor put it. Rather than racing over back roads, trying to find the scabs and elude the police, as strike caravans had been doing since farm workers started driving cars, this line of vehicles moved slowly, with the picketers making sure that the big city reporters, patrol cars, and paddy wagon did not get left behind. After an hour's search the NFWA drivers finally found a working crew, stopped, waited for reporters and sheriffs to take their places, and started to shout *"huelga."* Forty-four were arrested: thirteen farm workers and thirty-one volunteers, including nine ministers.[5]

Chavez and Goepel, waiting in the Bay Area, received the news as soon as Jim Drake could get to a phone. It had all gone according to plan. Chavez knew about the arrests before his first speech, scheduled for the epicenter of the West Coast student movement, the steps of Sproul Hall at Berkeley. There, at noon, 500 students gathered to hear a strike report. As Cesar, in his quiet fashion, gave his straightforward account, Goepel dramatically interrupted him and handed him a piece of paper. Chavez read it to himself, and then to the crowd: forty-four people, including his wife, had just been arrested in Delano for shouting *"huelga."* The response was immediate. *"Huelga! Huelga! Huelga!"* the excited crowd shouted back at the farm worker leader. Later, at the other colleges, the smaller crowds had also taken up the chant, making the strike their own. As Goepel drove the VW bug back to Delano, Cesar counted the contributions: $6,700.[6]

But the money was not as important as the publicity. The *New York*

Times, the *Chicago Tribune*, the *St. Louis Post-Dispatch*, and the *Kansas City Star* ran their very first stories about the strike.[7] The arrests were featured on TV news programs throughout California. The NFWA finally made the front page of the *San Francisco Chronicle*. The *Los Angeles Times* ran a two-column picture on page three. The growers barely knew what had hit them, but the sheriffs got the drift. They never again tried to enforce the gag order. Eventually, the injunction was declared unconstitutional, and all charges were dropped. Too late. The strike had broken out of the Central Valley. Moral jujitsu had won its first victory. But the question remained: What was the best way to leverage the growing outside support to force the growers to sign a contract?

October slid into November, and rain came down hard in Delano. The strikers were relieved. The harvest was officially over. No need for picket lines now. Significant numbers of people wouldn't be required in the fields until mid-January. The growers had held on to enough veteran workers and brought in enough new ones to collect a large harvest. For the next several months, the primary work of the industry would be to distribute its bounty. As far as AWOC director, Al Green, was concerned, the rains meant the strike was over. He cut off strike benefits and, in tune with standard farm worker practice, shifted his attention to the next stop on the farm worker circuit, the citrus harvest in Porterville.

It was the NFWA that broke farm worker custom. It refused to call off the strike, although no one—not even the top leadership—could say for sure what it meant to be on strike after the harvest was over. The strike was now like the word *huelga*. It had come to mean more than just collectively withdrawing labor power; rather, it was a general call to arms, whose very utterance, thanks to the Kern County sheriff's department, was a symbolic act of defiance. *Huelga* didn't mean that to everyone yet, only to the strikers and their few thousand supporters in the student movement, labor unions, and the church. But it would soon come to mean that to millions of people. And it is one measure of the impact of Cesar Chavez and the farm worker movement that those millions came to recognize *huelga* before most of them knew what an enchilada was.

The baby steps that would lead to the grape boycott were taken by a few people, newly liberated from the picket lines, who attempted, on the fly, to make a crude map of the grape distribution system and to develop a strategy for disrupting it. They followed the grapes out of town, trying to figure out exactly where they went, and how they got to the supermarkets. Trains carried the grapes from Delano to the Roseville yard, outside Sacramento, and then traveled east. Most of the trucks leaving the warehouses went to the big wholesale produce markets, where the grapes were unloaded, and then distributed to retail stores, primarily big chains. Some of the trucks went to the docks in San Francisco, Oakland, San Pedro, Stockton, and Long Beach, where they were unloaded and then loaded onto ships for distribution around the world. What were the possibilities? The Roseville yard was a logistical disaster, eight miles long and fifty tracks wide. As the railroad cars were switched from engine to engine the farm workers couldn't identify the trains that carried the grapes. Furthermore, federal laws against interfering with train travel were strong, and the several unions with jurisdiction in the yards almost always obeyed them. The big-city produce terminals looked more promising. The strikers could easily follow the trucks, and the Teamsters who loaded and unloaded the grapes had a lot of control over what actually happened at the terminals. Thus, the downtown LA terminal, a two-hour drive from Delano, became an early focus for activists.

But the first intimations of the future strategy came on the San Francisco Bay Area docks. Work there was entirely in the hands of the International Longshore and Warehouse Union, the large left-wing union that was born in the victorious 1934 San Francisco general strike. The ILWU had a unique historical commitment to organizing farm workers and cannery workers, starting with the 1937 "march inland," which was intended to protect the gains of longshoremen by extending some measure of the 1934 victory to "inland workers." That organizing drive had been substantially defeated by the Western Conference of Teamsters, which offered the bosses the carrot of a more friendly, business-oriented union. Nonetheless, as a few striking farm workers arrived on the San Francisco docks in early December 1965, top ILWU officials were still interested in bringing farm workers under their wing, and the rank and file was still vigorous and proud of its power and traditions.[8]

Two days after the first hard rain, Gilbert Padilla, a young striker named Tony Mendez, his wife, Socorro, and Sergio Tovar of the AWOC got into a car and drove to San Francisco. Gilbert can't remember whose car they took, but it wasn't his. He had lent his to Dolores the first week of the strike and never saw it again. Cars came and went in those days. This time, his car full of spirited young people was following a truck carrying 1,250 cases of scab grapes from the Pagliarulo warehouse in Delano. The pursuit ended at Pier 50, after dark; the truck got into a long line, apparently not to be unloaded until the next day. Despite the light rain, the four from Delano, armed with homemade signs that said "Don't Eat Grapes," started to march up and down in front of the pier. Almost immediately, longshoremen on night shift and truck drivers waiting to load and unload came over and asked them what they were doing. Many dockworkers encouraged them to remain, and one even brought them a couple of raincoats. Soon, Jimmy Herman, head of the clerks' division and one of the most powerful officials in the ILWU, rushed to the dock. He took the four wet, enthusiastic people back to his office and gave them coffee. Padilla was surprised by how much Herman already knew about the strike. Then Herman got down on his knees and made up some new signs that said "Farm Workers On Strike." He told them to return just before dawn and stand in front of the dock with those signs. Herman said that the bosses would throw an injunction at them, but it would be too late; they could stop the grapes from being unloaded first. "Don't tell nobody about who gave you these," he said, gesturing to the signs. "You just stand there. Don't say a god-damn thing."[9]

Padilla later declared that the next day's surprise was "the most fascinating thing that ever happened to me." Gilbert tends to dramatic speech, but that is still quite an assessment by a child of the labor camps, war veteran, father of eight children, and close compatriot of Cesar Chavez for twenty-six years before Chavez forced him out of the union in 1980. But in some respects, Padilla has it right. On that rainy morning and afternoon, clerks, longshoremen, and a few truck drivers took a first step in reversing the historical separation between California's rural and urban workers. It was a major reversal: at the very dawn of California labor history, in the late nineteenth century, San Francisco's Irish union workers had fought the bosses and Chinese farm workers, mistakenly believing that by taking the big growers' side against the Chinese, they could get concessions from the bosses in other areas and eliminate the competition from low-wage Chinese laborers. Those Irish anti-Chinese riots set the tone for California union history. The California branch of the American Federation of Labor acted completely within the spirit and logic of those riots when it refused to give charters to nonwhite farm-worker unions, right up until World War II. As did the vast majority of unionized city workers, who from the 1920s to the 1950s, rebuffed most appeals for solidarity from farm worker representatives. But on November 17, 1965, ILWU clerks and longshoremen on the San Francisco docks, encouraged by their own officers, gave the first indication that solidarity could, and would, be extended to farm workers.

At first Gilbert was just shocked. As soon as he and his friends arrived, the clerks started leaving the docks. Without the clerks, no work could get done. Then the longshoremen walked away. Some of them came by and gave the four bewildered picketers money. One guy gave them his lunch. Others joined the picket line; at one time fifty longshoremen were picketing in the rain. The line of idled trucks seemed to stretch back for miles. Some of the truckers were mad and started to honk their horns. That stopped quickly, though, as a group of longshoremen broke the windshields of a few of the complaining drivers. Even the lunch trucks were shooed away. One little lunch wagon whose owner refused to move had all its tires punctured. The whole dock came to a halt. "I felt like I was ten feet tall," Padilla remembered. "Everybody walked out. . . . It was something that I had never seen before—the solidarity."[10]

By 1965, this kind of elementary worker solidarity, termed "secondary boycotts," had long been illegal in the United States—several times over. Late-nineteenth-century courts had been overwhelmingly hostile to unions and often ruled that ordinary strikes were unacceptable acts of coercion. Judges considered most sympathy strikes even worse, and universally declared them illegal. In 1911, the Supreme Court, in *Gompers v. Bucks Stove and Range Co.*, ruled that even the AFL's "We Don't Patronize" list was an illegal attack by outsiders against an employer. This legal tradition was reversed by the 1936 National Labor Relations Act, which not only gave unions legitimate legal status but was silent on the issue of boycotts. The 1947 Taft-Hartley Act, however, again made secondary boycotts of "neutral parties" illegal. But the ban was difficult to interpret and enforce. Workers continued to refuse to handle scab products. Teamster truckers argued that they were not boycotting a neutral party but rather an individual commodity. Similarly, some factory workers refused to work on what they called "hot cargo." The legal web tightened significantly with the 1957 Landrum Griffin Act, which added hot cargo campaigns to the prohibition against secondary boycotts, and provided for extensive fines for unions that violated the typical "no strike, no secondary boycott, no hot cargo campaigns, and no slow down" clauses that had become prevalent in union contracts. Some of the legal language was obscure, but its meaning was not: effective, open worker solidarity was against the law.

Some boxes of Pagliarulo grapes had been loaded onto the SS *President Wilson*, whose main cargo was 400 passengers, bound for Hawaii and Tokyo. But the longshoremen refused to load the rest. After a day's wait, and with no guarantee that the rest of the grapes would be loaded anytime soon, the ship's owners decided to leave the fruit behind. Gleeful workers took the boxes off the ship, and the enraged truck driver took off for San Pedro to see if the grapes could be loaded there. No luck; the alerted longshoremen refused to touch them, so the grapes had to be taken back to Delano and deposited in cold storage. The *El Malcriado* staff found a picture of an ocean liner and put it on the front page with the headline, "The grapes are rotting on the docks." They quoted Tony Mendez: "When the unions and working people help each other, we can beat even the richest growers." A triumphant editorial closed: "The huelga is a huge social movement involving the respect of a whole race of people. When outsiders—thousands of them—decide to help the farm workers in their fight for a better life, the ranchers say it is none of their business. The huelga has become everybody's business. That is why it is winning."[11]

The strikers' surprising victory was a potentially disastrous defeat for the growers. If the ILWU, which controlled the West Coast docks, refused to handle scab grapes, the bosses would lose a lot of money and might be forced to settle with the workers despite having beaten them in the strike. The DiGiorgio Corporation, rich in antiunion experience, was sure that these activities were illegal. It got a restraining order forbidding the NFWA, AWOC, and 100 John Does from engaging in a secondary boycott and interfering with six upcoming shipments of grapes, naming the ships and the ports they would be sailing from. The strikers couldn't believe their luck. They wouldn't have to follow the grapes from Delano to figure out where they were bound. They could just meet the trucks at the docks and alert all their Bay Area support networks in advance. Large spirited picket lines easily turned back the friendly longshoremen. A few of the arrested picketers were brought before the judge for violating the injunction, but he dismissed the charges. Taft-Hartley and Landrum Griffin were amendments to the original National Labor Relations Act, but farm workers had been written out of the NLRA. They were not covered by its provisions and therefore could not be enjoined from breaking its rules. It was perfectly legal for the NFWA to engage in a secondary boycott and urge workers not to handle scab grapes. It was a sweet little irony: left out of the benefits of being covered by labor law, farm workers were also free of its restrictions.[12]

But the ILWU was not. Farm workers were free to ask for solidarity from fellow workers, but those workers were not free to give it. DiGiorgio, Pagliarulo, and other offended growers immediately got a judgment that allowed them to collect financial damages equal to the value of their grapes from any union that honored an NFWA picket line. The ILWU had very little wiggle room. All it could argue was that longshoremen had a right to refuse to cross picket lines if they felt that their health and safety were endangered by doing so. In all but one case brought before the courts, the grape growers won. Individual longshoremen, acting on their own, could refuse to work on scab grapes and maybe get away with it. But the union as a whole would have to repudiate such actions and would be liable for any losses. Finally, Padilla understood why Jimmy Herman was so adamant that those first four pickets not mention his name.

The law was not the only problem. In Los Angeles, which in its antiunion tradition was more like the rest of the West than like San Francisco, the NFWA learned that worker-to-worker solidarity was not only illegal but usually hard to put into practice. At the downtown produce market, some swampers, who unloaded the trucks, immediately agreed not to touch the scab product, others simply weren't interested, and a few were openly hostile. Debates raged in the dark hours just before dawn, as the swampers and picketers, warming themselves by fires the workers had built in fifty-five-gallon drums, waited for the first trucks to arrive. Stopping those grapes would be a tough task, the picketers reported back to Chavez, so he assigned the job to a group of strike militants, including some young Filipinos who had already proved quite adept at sabotaging packing sheds, irrigation pumps, and other grower property.[13] Among the strikers they were known as "special agents," and their work was much admired. Rudy Reyes was one of them, as was his friend Ernie Delarmente, who had made a name for himself by holding his own in a short picket-line fistfight with the grower Bruno Dispoto, who was a head and a half taller and 125 pounds heavier than Delarmente. Chavez chose Dolores Huerta to head up this group, as she was, in her own way, just as fearless as the special agents.[14]

The LA swampers were members of Teamsters Local 630, whose contract allowed the membership to refuse to cross "a legitimate and bona fide picket line." On December 3 the Los Angeles Teamsters Joint Council had ruled that the NFWA-AWOC pickets were, in fact, legitimate and bona fide, and members of Local 630 had received letters saying, "Your employer will be in violation of the contract if he discharges or otherwise punishes you for exercising your right to refuse to cross these picket lines to unload the Delano grapes."[15] But the letter also left the decision whether to unload the grapes up to the individual swampers.[16] Some friendly swampers consistently refused to unload the grapes, and at first even the hostile ones would occasionally ignore a load, as long as the picketers stayed around. But a few swampers began to specialize in unloading the scab grapes, either sheepishly explaining that they needed the $80 to $100 they could make per truckload or openly defying and confronting the small band of picketers.

Rudy Reyes and company, spurred on by the majority of the men on the docks who were sympathetic to the cause, did what they could to interfere with the loading. The grapes came from Delano on pallets and were unloaded with pallet jacks, hand-operated, heavy metal forks on wheels. Rudy and a few others, picket signs in hand, would get on the docks and do what they could to get in the way of the jacks and prevent the grapes from being unloaded. The swampers were furious and tried to hit the picketers' ankles with the forks of the jacks. One time Gilbert Padilla was knocked off the loading dock, badly twisted his ankle, and spent a couple of weeks on crutches. Only the support of the other dock-workers for the pickets prevented an all-out bloody battle. Dock supervisors started to call in the police, but by the time they arrived the folks from Delano were just peacefully parading back and forth. Nevertheless, some of the picketers were arrested, and the relations with the police deteriorated. Reyes began to dread the early-morning confrontations:

One of those forks could do some damage. One time when I was trying to get out of the way, I accidentally-on-purpose leaned into the grape boxes and made the swamper spill his load. He was really mad, and tried to corner me for a fight. I was about half his size, nimble and quick, and got away. That night when we got back to the apartment we really laughed about it. But I was laughing because I was so nervous and scared. I remember my back hurt, and I thought, well, that must be why they say you have a streak of yellow down your back, it was my yellow streak that was hurting. I could even feel it. And, as usual, the cops just made things worse. They came and tried to shove us off the docks. And they arrested us, too. Usually we got bailed out pretty quick because there were so many friendly lawyers in LA. Sometimes we had to stay in jail overnight. It was not too bad to be in jail for a while. It was not as bad as having those pallet jacks come at you. I had nightmares about those metal forks.[17]

Eventually, the drama on the docks seemed not only too dangerous but a silly waste of time. It had degenerated into a kind of turf war. One morning Rudy was sitting with a few others at a table in the coffee shop across from the terminal where the pickets and the produce workers sometimes waited for the trucks to arrive. Beside him was a college student who had come to Delano during the first days of the strike and stayed. She was an attractive young woman, and she had had to endure a string of vulgar insults from the strikers' opponents on the docks. A Los Angeles policeman had called her a whore. On this particular morning one of the enemy swampers had come by the table, put his hand on her shoulder, and suggested she come service him. Rudy Reyes couldn't let that pass. He picked up one of those old fashioned sugar bowls with a heavy bottom and delivered several quick, sharp blows to the offender's head. Blood and sugar were flying everywhere. The man slunk away, and some of the other swampers came by and told Rudy he had done the right thing. Maybe so, but the attempt to stop the grapes on the docks was now clearly the wrong thing. The NFWA would have to come up with some other tactics.

After the unexpected, dramatic success on the San Francisco docks, Chavez authorized Jim Drake to try to organize some kind of formal grape boycott. Drake had no budget, no phone of his own, no office. Cesar regularly talked to him about various boycott plans, but made no great commitment to the project—he was more concerned with other matters: figuring out how to force the governor to put pressure on the growers to negotiate; maintaining the morale of the members and volunteers; trying to set up organizing projects in different farm worker areas. Drake was on his own. To concentrate on his task, he had to find a separate place to work. During the strike, the NFWA had rented an abandoned labor camp a few miles outside of Delano. In serious disrepair, mosquito-infested, the camp seemed to sink deeper into the mud after every winter rain. But this didn't dampen the energy of some volunteers, whose hopes remained high. On the wall near the entrance someone had painted three names in large letters: Zapata, Villa, Chavez. Two old toilets with indoor plumbing stood on the grounds but separated from the rest of the buildings. Chavez designated the women's toilet as the first boycott office; the men's toilet would henceforth be genderless.

Drake had found his office space. He was delighted to be set loose on his pet project, and in good humor he hung Air Wicks in his new windowless outpost. It still stank. Drake got Richard Chavez to bolt a board on top of the old toilet bowl, and to build a regular desk next to it. He had a phone line installed. From Hartmire he got a list of progressive Protestants as potential supporters of a boycott. A new NFWA volunteer, Brother Gilbert, helped him put together a list of possible Catholic supporters. He called Mike Miller of Bay Area Friends of SNCC and got the names and numbers of student and civil rights activists. The last group was the most promising. In San Francisco in early October, SNCC, CORE, and Citizens for Farm Labor had started acting on their own even before the longshore-men had refused to touch the grapes, and 100 people had picketed the San Francisco office of the Schenley Corporation, demanding that it settle with its striking grape workers. When the office workers first saw the picket line outside, they figured the people were demanding the hiring of black office workers. The picketers returned every Friday afternoon. If such picket lines could be maintained in other areas, wouldn't that be the beginning of a national boycott?[18]

Drake asked Miller to be cochair of whatever they all decided the boycott effort might turn out to be. At twenty-seven, Mike Miller was already a political veteran. As a Berkeley undergraduate in the late 1950s, he had founded Slate, a precursor of the later New Left campus organizations. In 1960 he met Saul Alinsky, and through Alinsky he met Fred Ross, who sparked his interest in the Central Valley, kept him informed of the progress of the CSO, and introduced him to Cesar Chavez. In 1961, deeply inspired by the first southern sit-ins, Miller started working with SNCC, quickly joined the staff, and helped build the Bay Area Friends of SNCC, an orga-nization designed to raise money for SNCC's southern voter registration campaigns. Eager to get closer to the battlefield, he went to work with Bob Moses in Greenwood, Mississippi in 1963, and returned home only after a serious late-night automobile accident on a deserted Mississippi road. He remained a SNCC field secretary working in the Bay Area and helped select the West Coast students who participated in Mississippi Summer. He envisioned SNCC as a group of full-time professional organizers who would work in various communities throughout the country, not just with African Americans in the South. In 1964 he helped start an organizing project to fight urban renewal in the Fillmore District, one of San Francisco's main black neighborhoods, and the initial success of that project plus his longtime honorable service in SNCC made him one of the most influential young white activists in the country. It was that influence that Drake and Chavez needed. Several other SNCC field secretaries were already active in California, and Miller, with his quiet, unassuming, but authoritative voice, offered direction and advice to all of them. Now the NFWA was asking SNCC to cosponsor a national table grape boycott and offering Mike Miller the position of co-chairman. He did not hesitate to accept.[19]

Drake, Miller, and Chavez quickly agreed on a few essentials. They would focus on Schenley and DiGiorgio. Those were the two big Delano-area corporations that produced not only table grapes but also various other brand-name products that would be easy to identify and boycott. Since the Christmas season was near, initially they would go after Schenley, as the company produced or marketed several popular wines and liquors, including Cutty Sark, Ancient Age, and I.W. Harper. They agreed that the boycott could be put into motion quickly in the nation's major cities by various Friends of SNCC groups, CORE chapters, and the rapidly multiplying New Left student organizations. Those folks had already been doing support work for black civil rights initiatives and could easily transfer some of their energy and experience into support for Mexican American farm workers. As an extra bonus, the boycott cities would be an excellent place to send many of the white volunteers who had staffed the farm worker picket lines but were now just hanging around Delano without much to do.

Many questions remained. Drake and Miller, both deeply interested in organizational matters, talked over the possibilities. In the long run, what would the various boycott organizations look like? Would they continue to be run by the already established left and civil rights groups? Would they be new coalitions put together by those groups? Who would be part of that coalition? Religious organizations certainly, but labor unions, too? What formal relationship would the boycott organizations have to the NFWA and SNCC? What about duplicating the experience in Los Angeles, where NFWA leaders—first Dolores Huerta and then Gilbert Padilla—had built an effective boycott committee? All of that was left up in the air, as priority was given to the question of what exactly the first boycott activities should be. They were confident of their legal right to call for a direct consumer boycott of Schenley products, but beyond that they were not sure. What about a secondary boycott, asking consumers not to buy in stores that handled the boycotted liquor? Drake and Miller decided to play it safe. The first formal instructions to boycotters, signed by SNCC and the NFWA, called the proposed campaign "a consumer information boycott" and told activists that "we are forbidden by law to boycott stores merely because they handle Schenley products."[20]

Drake and Miller had it wrong—the secondary boycott was legal because farm workers were not covered by the national labor law—but it didn't matter because the actual boycotters simply ignored the instructions (if they even saw them) and began to apply pressure directly against liquor stores. CORE picketers swept through Harlem and reported back to the NFWA that all of the forty-nine liquor stores they had visited had agreed to stop handling Schenley products. In one store the thirty pickets had to "visit" for quite some time, milling around inside without making any purchases, before the owner agreed that justice was on the farm workers' side. Similar militant black and white picket lines forced the removal of Schenley liquor and wine from stores in Oakland, Berkeley, and San Francisco, where fourteen of fifteen Mission District liquor stores got rid of Schenley products in one afternoon. Many store owners refused to comply, hoping to wait out the storm, but the new wind was just beginning to blow. Picket lines became more enthusiastic and more diverse. Trade unionists arrived; church activists joined. A new coalition was beginning to form.[21]

Back in Delano, Drake could hardly keep up with the new developments. Often he didn't go back to his home in Porterville at night but instead slept on the floor of his office. One night it rained especially hard, and as water seeped onto the floor, he moved to the top of his desk. But it wasn't big enough for his six-foot-one-inch frame and the only way he could keep his feet out of the water was by resting them on the board over the commode. It didn't bother him one bit. Rain was pouring in, but so were the stories. His favorite one involved a teenage boy and girl who had arrived in Delano early in the strike, holding hands. As soon as the boycott started, Drake asked them to go to New York. They didn't hesitate. They simply picked up their sleeping bags and hitchhiked east—in the middle of December. In a snowstorm outside of Denver, they were picked up by the police and arrested for vagrancy. The cops threw them in jail, where the couple told the story of the strike and the boycott to the inmates and guards. The next morning, the police took up a collection, gave them some money, and put them on the highway outside of town to resume their journey. Drake told the story around the NFWA compound, punctuating it with "*Viva la huelga!*"[22]

But the boycott was just one of many NFWA activities. Hartmire was busy arranging for religious delegations to visit Delano and "inspect" farmworker conditions. Chavez was particularly effective with the visiting priests, nuns, ministers, and rabbis, and he was also talking to people in the Democratic Party about how to take advantage of Governor Pat Brown's upcoming campaign for reelection. The NFWA renewed some small organizing projects in Fresno, Salinas, and Bakersfield. Drake and the boycott remained headquartered in the women's toilet.

"Boycott, Baby, Boycott!": The Civil Rights Coalition Regroups

August '64 to January '66

Large numbers of Americans, especially liberal Democrats, needed the grape boycott as much as the boycott needed them. The failed attempt to seat the Mississippi Freedom Democratic Party at the 1964 Democratic National Convention in Atlantic City, New Jersey, had shattered the alliance between liberals and radicals in the early civil rights movement. The 1965 Selma march and the passage of the Voting Rights Act would prove to be the capstone of that movement, rather than a prelude of victories to come. The 1964 peace candidate, Lyndon Johnson, had escalated the war in Vietnam soon after he was elected, and the liberals' support for the war soon alienated them from the vast majority of the nation's politically active young people. In the midst of massive new violence against the Vietnamese, the Watts rebellion foretold the violent possibilities of what might happen when the civil rights struggle moved out of the South. To liberal eyes the Watts riot was pure nihilism; it marked the end of the sunny optimistic days of the early 1960s and the beginning of liberalism's long dark night. Liberals had been ready to ride the civil rights movement into a new world; it was their best hope since the Popular Front victory in World War II. But by the second half of the sixties the civil rights movement was no more, and white liberals could find no home in the movement for black power. So many people who had been so hopeful now had nothing to do except watch the twin horrors of the nightly news: black rioters burning American cities, and white radicals burning draft cards and American flags.

Enter Cesar Chavez and the table grape boycott. Here was a constructive, nonviolent, political alternative to the rioters and radicals. "Boycott, Baby, Boycott," the picketers chanted to make sure that everyone got the point. The simple peaceful act of not eating grapes would actually help poor (and grateful!) farm workers win a union contract. The beautiful simplicity of the appeal attracted millions. With so many Americans committed to not eating grapes, and thousands actively working on the boycott campaign, that wonderful calculus of politics once again took hold.

As Chavez had maintained all along, if you can get enough people together, you can change the world. The contract was won, and although the boycott did not belong to liberals alone, they were major players in the new coalition, a regrouping that allowed them to relive, in a minor key, the hopes of the early civil rights years.

The civil rights organizer Marshall Ganz and the union president Walter Reuther were on opposite sides in Atlantic City in August 1964 but on the same side in Delano in December 1965. They were flesh-and-blood examples of how the farm workers' union in the boycott years became neutral territory in the ongoing battle between American liberals and radicals. People who couldn't talk to each other anywhere else worked together on boycott committees, and the farm workers union received special dispensation to sit out the conflicts that divided its supporters. Not until the war in Vietnam was almost over did the UFW take a position against it, and yet the union received support from all wings of the antiwar movement. The liberals stayed on board even though the farm workers accepted Black Panther support and welcomed the black-jacketed, black-bereted militants in their marches and on their picket lines. Each side had its reasons. Radicals could not oppose a new union of third world workers, no matter that it waffled on the war; liberals could not oppose this oasis of nonviolent social change, even though they shunned others who tolerated support from black revolutionaries. The warmth generated by working together on the boycott was not enough to thaw overall relations between radicals and liberals in the late 1960s, but it did provide much of the energy for the UFW's first significant victories.

Marshall Ganz, destined to become a major force in the UFW, arrived in Delano in September 1965, soon after the grape strike began. At twenty-one he was a veteran of Mississippi Summer, Atlantic City, and the doomed attempts after the convention to keep the old SNCC alive and functioning. He and many other white SNCC field secretaries, no longer wanted as organizers of blacks, were looking for a place to put their radical energies. Some tried to organize poor whites; some went into the liberal establishment; some went back to school; most ended up in Students for a Democratic Society or the antiwar movement. Ganz and a handful of others found Cesar Chavez.

Marshall, an only child, was born in Michigan in 1943 but moved with his mother and father to Germany when he was only three. His father was a U.S. Army rabbi, assigned to help the Jewish survivors of the Holocaust emigrate to countries willing to receive them and to recover their faith in God and humanity. Rabbi Ganz did what he could for three years, until 1949, but never completely recovered from the stories he heard. After a stint in Washington, he worked as a rabbi in Philadelphia, Fresno, Bakersfield, Los Angeles, and finally San Diego. Not quite right after his time in Germany, he had a full mental breakdown in his later years, and his son, who was then coordinating the national grape boycott, had to put him in a hospital. With as much justification as anyone might have, Dad had gone crazy.[1]

Marshall Ganz turned five in a camp for children whose parents had been killed. He got no gifts for his birthday; instead he gave presents to the other kids. But painful lessons on sacrificing for those less fortunate than himself were not all he took from Germany. He also received an early education in living in another culture and speaking multiple languages. By the time his family settled in Bakersfield in 1953, the 10-year-old Marshall was fluent in German and English and familiar with Yiddish and Polish. He also learned some Hebrew for his Bar Mitzvah. This early education took hold. The adult Ganz's ability to learn Spanish quickly, to master the linguistic and cultural subtleties of Mexicans, to be at home among farm workers, is famous among early UFW staffers. When his Spanish fluency was combined with his large Mexican-style mustache and his proud, substantial belly, Ganz's actual origin became a mystery to many farm workers. I remember one time listening to him talk to a crowd of workers, and the man next to me asked in Spanish what country Ganz came from. I said he was a gringo, like me. The other worker wouldn't believe it. I finally said that he was a Jew. "Ahhh, that explains it," he said.

At Bakersfield High School in the late 1950s, Marshall was the only white boy in an otherwise all-black jazz band. His favorite novelist was Jack Kerouac. His parents, especially his mother, were strong antiracists, but he remembers his own concerns as more cultural than political. For college, he confidently applied nowhere but Harvard, where he was admitted in 1960. It seemed that Marx and Freud were on every reading list, and classes with two popular professors, Perry Miller and Stanley Hoffman, encouraged him to expand his notion of culture to include politics. He was attracted to the Cuban Revolution and also to Jack Kennedy, who visited Harvard soon after the 1960 election. As far as Ganz can recall, the Bay of Pigs with its obvious contradiction between Kennedy's liberal imperialism and Castro's radical revolution, did not make him reconsider his dual enthusiasms.

Uneasy at Harvard, in 1962 he moved to Berkeley, which was crackling with cultural and political energy. Berkeley students and a whole community of people around the campus were engaged in battles for nuclear disarmament, educational reform, and civil rights. This emerging sensibility was nurtured and welcomed by a Bay Area political and cultural left-wing community that had managed to survive McCarthyism and the fifties. With the International Longshore and Warehouse Union providing jobs and ballast, and the North Beach poets contributing a spirit of uncompromising cultural rebellion, the West Coast version of the new student politics not only enjoyed a sense of being new but also had a healthy connection to the old. Marshall dropped right into the middle of it. He got a job in an insurance office in Oakland and an apartment in Berkeley, and started attending night classes at the university. He went to concerts by Barbara Dane and Malvina Reynolds, attended a few Dubois Club meetings, and grew increasingly interested in the civil rights movement. One event he remembers in particular was Pete Seeger singing at the ILWU hall in San Francisco. The place was packed with an impressive combination of African American longshoremen, Old Left veterans, and student radicals. Seeger brought down the house with a roaring medley of "Wasn't That a Time," in which the last line became, "Isn't this a time, isn't this a terrible time, isn't this a time to try the souls of men, isn't this a wonderful time." It was the spring of 1963.

Marshall returned to Harvard, invigorated. He wanted to study, to figure out how politics and culture fit together. He took on Brecht. He wanted to understand what had happened to artists in the Soviet Union. He had a whole agenda he intended to explore. But the study of politics took second place to politics itself. He went to the first meetings of the campus SDS chapter. He got involved with the local Friends of SNCC. During the spring break he went to a SNCC staff meeting in Atlanta, where he learned that Harvard owned stock in the Mississippi Power and Light Company. He came back, he remembers,

> . . . as a man with a mission, to try to get something going on that. A number of us got involved. We had articles in the newspaper, and we picketed. That would have been in early 1964. By that time I was a banjo player, singing civil rights songs. And I got more attracted to the whole thing. People would come to Harvard and speak. And Barney Frank, the tutor in Winthrop House, was pushing us to get involved in civil rights stuff. There were a lot of connections. So when the Mississippi Summer Project came along, it was just made to order.

Ganz was in the second group of volunteers to arrive for training at the Western College for Women in Oxford, Ohio, where he met Bob Moses, the SNCC organizer most responsible for the Summer Project. Soon after Marshall arrived, Moses announced that Andrew Goodman, one of the students from the first group that had already left for Mississippi, was missing and probably dead along with two comrades, Michael Schwerner and James Chaney. Moses carefully explained the Summer Project strategy, accepted SNCC's own measure of moral responsibility for the murders of civil rights activists, and allowed the volunteers maximum space to return home with honor if they did not agree with the strategy or did not want to take the inevitable risks. Ganz was impressed. He soon came to share the almost universal opinion among the white volunteers that Moses was an organizer of unparalleled stature.

Later, Marshall Ganz saw many similarities between Bob Moses and Cesar Chavez: both were quiet, a little mysterious, critical of extravagant demonstrations and rhetoric. But this was still the spring of 1964, a year and a half before Ganz would meet Chavez. In Mississippi, he was assigned to Holmes County to help organize the Mississippi Freedom Democratic Party (MFDP). His roommate was Mario Savio, who had been assigned to teach in a Freedom School. Whoever was making those assignments gets five stars as a casting director: Ganz went on to be a principal organizer of the United Farm Workers; Savio became the leader of the Free Speech Movement at Berkeley. Amid the thrill and danger of Mississippi nights, Ganz and Savio stayed up late talking. Through his heavy stutter, Savio agonized about how to make political sense of his Jesuit training, and about the relationship between education and liberation, while Ganz wondered about alternative political strategies and how radical change actually happened.

Marshall and Mario were willing, conscious instruments of people with large political plans. The short-term goal of Mississippi Summer was to increase pressure on the Democratic Administration to protect voter registration in the South by putting white students from affluent, influential families and prestigious colleges in harm's way. But SNCC wanted more than that. It hoped that the sacrifices of Mississippi Summer could force the national Democrats to seat the Mississippi Freedom Democratic Party in Atlantic City, and thus begin a serious realignment of the Democratic Party, with new southern African American voters replacing the old-time Dixiecrats, southern segregationist members of the Democratic Party. Once burned—the Kennedy brothers had not lived up to their backroom promise to protect southern civil rights workers—SNCC now proposed to rush into the fire through the front door, and force an open, public, televised defeat of President Lyndon Baines Johnson at the Democratic National Convention in Atlantic City. This strategy had been put together by Moses and Democrats such as Allard Lowenstein and Joseph Rauh. Lowenstein was a wild-card Democratic Party youth operative who had made a career out of keeping liberal student organizations within the limits set by the party leaders. Rauh was general counsel for Walter Reuther's United Automobile Workers, vice president of Americans for Democratic Action, and a leading practitioner of then-triumphant cold war liberalism. SNCC, a band of self-defined nonviolent revolutionaries with less than four years of political experience, now intended to push its radical vision of direct democracy into American establishment politics. Of all SNCC's wildest dreams, this was probably the most outrageous. Most everyone sensed that the times were changing. But changing enough so that SNCC could beat the regular Democrats on their own turf, at their own convention?

Ganz accompanied the 200-strong Mississippi Freedom Democratic Party delegation to Atlantic City. His job there was to try to convince members of the California delegation to support a floor debate on the question of seating the MFDP delegates. Although by the summer of 1964, most people in SNCC doubted the power of liberal conscience, they calculated that they had a good chance of winning an open floor debate, especially after the highly publicized killings and church bombings in Mississippi and Alabama. What SNCC didn't count on was the inexorable logic of presidential politics. Lyndon Johnson, facing both Dixiecrat defection in the South and the George Wallace–led beginnings of white backlash in the North, decided that the MFDP was not a useful part of his coalition. Georgia's Governor Carl Sanders made the point most clearly in a telephone call to the president at the start of the convention: "It looks like we're turning the Democratic Party over to the nigras."[2] That impression would only be reinforced by an open floor fight between pro–civil rights liberals and southern segregationists. Since Johnson already had the pro–civil rights part of his coalition in his pocket, he could sacrifice the MFDP.

Ganz saw firsthand the pressure being put on California delegates not to support the Mississippi Freedom Democrats—all the typical moves like threatening to deny judicial appointments or to withdraw administration support for locally favored legislation. He was not at the various high-level meetings where Hubert Humphrey, Walter Mondale, and Reuther tried to force an unwanted compromise on SNCC and other civil rights leaders, or at the final, phony negotiations that tied up the MFDP leadership while party operatives maneuvered an unannounced voice vote by the credentials committee on the very question supposedly being negotiated. But he heard all about it in wrenching detail afterward. SNCC leaders were sure they had been the victims of a typical backroom ruse executed by the very people who had encouraged them to come to Atlantic City in the first place.

Ganz, like most of the SNCC organizers and those sympathetic to them around the country, was furious. He stood vigil with others from SNCC across the street from the convention center on the Boardwalk, amid a replica of Goodman, Schwerner, and Chaney's burned-out car, a bell from a bombed Mississippi church, and huge photographs of the three martyrs. He was there when Johnson came out on the balcony after his nomination and received the applause of the Atlantic City crowd, many of them deep into the drunken revelry of postconvention celebration. Huddled around the destroyed car, the SNCC vigilers had a good view of the triumphant president. Marshall hated him. August 1964: emotionally and politically as well as chronologically, the early sixties were just about over.

After the convention, Ganz traveled to the West Coast to visit his family and his friend Mike Miller, whom he had met through SNCC. Miller suggested that while in Bakersfield, Ganz might try to organize a local Friends of SNCC chapter, so Ganz called Brother Gilbert, with whom he had become acquainted as a youth. Brother Gilbert—now the vice principal and dean of discipline at Bakersfield's Catholic high school, Garces Memorial—was interested in SNCC. He agreed to hold a meeting at the high school, where Ganz showed a movie about SNCC, gave a speech, and answered questions. It was quite an event. A group of Catholic grape growers in the audience denounced Brother Gilbert for holding such a radical get-together at the Catholic high school. They didn't break up the gathering, but they were rambunctious and threatened further action. Their performance had a double, almost contradictory edge: while assured of their own power to control what should happen in their church, school, and community, they felt nervous enough about the times to make a fuss about a small meeting. Their uneasiness, not their confidence, turned out to be prophetic. It was just ten months before the Delano grape strike.

Back in Mississippi a few months later, Ganz worked with E. W. Steptoe in Amite County, the most dangerous area of the state. Although publicly committed to nonviolence, Ganz, like many other civil rights activists at the time, kept a gun in his truck. He accepted what he called the "ambiguity" of the situation. SNCC did everything it could to keep the struggle nonviolent; at the same time Marshall did not intend to be murdered on a lonely Mississippi road if a gun could prevent it. Together with Steptoe, Ganz was organizing leadership groups, Freedom Schools, and community centers, but SNCC was falling apart. Overwhelmed by the enormity of the their sacrifices (scores killed since 1960, thousands badly beaten), many SNCC organizers lost their faith in the power of nonviolence. Others doubted the ultimate effectiveness of long-term community organizing. Most smoldered with contempt for the white liberals who had betrayed them at the Atlantic City convention, and many grew suspicious of the whites in their own ranks. The most respected SNCC leaders fell ill. Executive Secretary James Foreman had an abscessed arm and ulcer. A friend said of Chairman John Lewis, "He resembled a corpse . . . so great was his exhaustion." The psychiatrist Robert Coles reported that many of the young organizers were "clinically depressed." New divisions appeared: Northern and Caribbean sophisticates versus rustic southerners; organizers versus floaters; men versus women. Staff meetings were filled with recriminations and went on through the night without reaching any conclusions. Perhaps worst of all, Bob Moses became more and more quiet, skipped meetings, and eventually lapsed into complete silence.[3]

Ganz was there for most of it. He was there at the meeting when Moses announced, "You can have Bob Moses; I am now Robert Paris," and passed out bread and wine as some sort of final benediction. "Has he gone crazy?" Ganz wondered. And what should he himself do? While working with Steptoe, Marshall had received a copy of *The Movement*, which had a front-page picture of the NFWA-sponsored march in support of the Linnell rent strike. There in the front row, with his black robes, was Brother Gilbert. Ganz returned to San Francisco to talk over the situation with Mike Miller. The grape strike had just begun, and Miller encouraged him to remain in SNCC but to see if he could get a job organizing for the NFWA. By this time Brother Gilbert had quit his job at Garces Memorial and gone to work for Cesar Chavez. He was preparing to leave the priest-hood if his order didn't like it, and was already going by his given name, LeRoy Chatfield. As it happened, Chavez was scheduled to speak about the strike a couple of days after Ganz arrived in Bakersfield.

"I introduced myself and [Chavez] said, 'Oh, yeah, yeah, LeRoy's told me about you.' I was very cautious because at that point in the civil rights movement there was a lot of polarization developing between blacks and whites, and it was sort of like, there's no role for whites in the move-ment . . . and so I was very cautious and sort of like, well, you know, I said . . . 'If you want support or help or something like that' . . . but he said, 'Oh no, no. You should come, come to Delano.'"[4]

Cesar quickly arranged for Marshall to drive him to the Bay Area for another speaking tour, and they had plenty of time alone in the car to check each other out. Ganz was immediately surprised that Chavez didn't hold his whiteness against him. Although they talked about organizing, what really seemed to spark Cesar's interest were Marshall's ideas about religion. It turned out that Chavez had met Ganz's father, and wanted to hear about Jewish belief, tradition, and custom. It was the first of what would be a long series of religious conversations. Ganz always thought that the reason he got so close to Cesar so quickly was that Chavez was more comfortable with religious people than political people, and he could see a little of both in Ganz. By the time they returned to Delano, they were sold on each other. Ganz would set up a new NFWA office in Bakersfield. It would be a backup, just in case the strike turned out to be a complete defeat. And for the time being, Ganz could still receive his symbolically important $10 a week stipend as a SNCC field secretary.

On a slim budget that was carefully monitored by Chavez, and using money he raised from Bakersfield's small liberal community, Ganz rented an office with a room in the back where he could live, bought an old car, and began his work in a barrio still called Little Okie, now filled with people who had come from Mexico in the 1940s or whose parents had come in the 1920s. He did some agitation against scab herders who were operating in Little Okie, but his main task was to set up a Service Center where he helped people with welfare, disability, and income tax problems. A student from Bakersfield Junior College, Jessica Govea, started coming by to help run the office. Her parents had been CSO activists and she had known Cesar Chavez since her early childhood. Jessica had been a semi-regular on the early grape strike picket lines and a volunteer in Delano. In the Bakersfield office and back room she taught Marshall Spanish. They fell in love over flash cards.

Soon after he began his work in Bakersfield, Ganz was called to Delano. Walter Reuther, president of the powerful United Automobile Workers, was coming to town, and since Reuther was one of the first national figures to endorse the grape strike, Chavez wanted all hands in Delano to help mobilize the turnout. At the time it bothered Ganz only slightly that Reuther had been the staff sergeant most responsible for carrying out the betrayal of the Mississippi Freedom Democrats. That summer, just over a year before, Reuther had been in the middle of negotiations with General Motors when Lyndon Johnson convinced him to fly to Atlantic City to get the situation under control. Once there, Reuther took command: he threatened to fire Joe Rauh if he didn't cooperate; he told Martin Luther King that the UAW would stop giving money to SCLC if King didn't help avoid a floor fight; he told Moses that not a penny more would be sent to Mississippi from anyone if SNCC didn't back down. When all that failed, he arranged the final slap in the face: the negotiations charade.[5]

Reuther had traveled a long way to become the instrument of a maneuver that strangled the possibility of a liberal progressive realignment of the Democratic Party—a goal he had worked for much of his political life. Originally a skilled craftsman in the automobile industry and a democratic socialist organizer, he was among the thousands of leftists who helped build and lead the working-class movement that propelled the Congress of Industrial Organizations to victory in the late 1930s. An astute strategist and a master of polemical debate, Reuther survived a series of faction fights inside the UAW and took control of the union in 1947. Using rising anti-Communism as his main weapon, he then consolidated his hold over the union, and over the following two decades transformed the UAW from a lively body whose spirited conventions were a model of popular participation and debate into a one-party union machine. His midlife anti-Communism was principled rather than just tactical; he was a founding member of Americans for Democratic Action, which became the ideological vanguard of cold war liberalism. Although not a major theorist of this particular version of liberalism, he was its main organizational hope, as most ADA activists were intellectuals without any mass base. Reuther, while no slouch as a thinker and talker, was very much a man of conventional power, and as the leader of one of the biggest, tightest working-class organizations in the country, he was in a position to use it.

Beginning in the late 1940s, Reuther put that power to the service of what labor historians call "social unionism," a second cousin of democratic socialism, and an idea of unionism that was especially attractive to Cesar Chavez. It held that unions should lead a movement of progressive social change throughout society rather than just represent the immediate interests of their own members. This watered-down version of the Marxist idea that working-class liberation meant the liberation of the whole society was explicitly reformist, with its strategy and goals tailored to meet what Reuther saw as the actual political opportunities of his time. Full employment, universal health care, high wages, stable prices, and racial harmony could all be achieved, Reuther (and many others) believed, by forcing the Dixiecrats out of the Democratic Party, where they served as a brake on New Deal policies. With the two parties realigned—the Dixiecrats part of a truly conservative Republican Party and the eastern Republicans part of a thoroughly liberal Democratic Party—the new Democrats could take their progressive program to the American people.

Reuther remained committed to this goal into the early sixties. But with his power in labor officialdom diminished in the newly merged AFL-CIO (where he took a back seat to the federation president, George Meany) he began to pin his hopes on a more conventional alliance with liberals inside the actual existing Democratic Party. Initially, he wooed and was wooed by the forces represented by Hubert Humphrey, then was enchanted by the Kennedy brothers, and finally was captured by the charms of Lyndon Johnson, the master politician, who kept Reuther and most of the rest of the cold war liberals close by his side as he took them into the jungles of Vietnam and down the path to political oblivion, where Reuther landed shortly before his physical death in a plane crash in 1970.

Reuther's main problem was that in the late 1950s and early '60s, following a decade of declining militancy among American trade unionists—that had been kicked off by the anti-Communist purges, which Reuther abetted—he had become deeply ensnared in the web of the AFL-CIO bureaucracy. Reuther's chief hope for cutting through that snare was the civil rights movement. It could reinvigorate what was left of a progressive liberal-labor alliance, he thought, and provide the energy and social weight necessary to carry out his faltering agenda. But neither official labor nor the triumphant liberalism of the cold war years could quite bring itself to embrace civil rights activists on their own terms. At the same time that he called for racial justice in general, Reuther opposed efforts by blacks inside the UAW to reclassify jobs so that they could advance into more skilled positions held by Reutherites on factory floors and workplaces in Detroit and elsewhere. Meany and many other AFL-CIO bosses were worse. With their social power partially based on the exclusive right of white workers to relatively privileged working-class jobs, they were not about to risk their place in the establishment with a wholehearted endorsement of even the early civil rights movement. The liberals of the labor-liberal alliance for their part had well-worked-out suspicions of any movement that emerged from the lower levels of society, seemingly beyond institutional control. The challenge for Reuther was to find a way to support the civil rights movement while making sure it stayed within limited, acceptable bounds.

He had powerful means: money, personnel, and his particular mixture of well-articulated progressive goals and strategies tightly woven together with anti-Communist, anti-utopian rhetoric and ideology. But he couldn't turn the trick. The gulf between the needs, interests, and demands of black Americans in the 1960s and the limits of Democratic Party–AFL-CIO politics was too wide to bridge. The young SNCC organizers had adopted the Mississippi Summer–Freedom Democrat strategy despite grave internal doubts and at the cost of a few lives and much suffering. But they had been convinced, and had convinced themselves, that it would all be worth it if at the end of the day they could remake the politics of the South and with it, all of America. Instead, SNCC militants were left with nothing but a handful of apologies and a mouthful of humiliation. Eventually, many reemerged as full-blown revolutionaries who staked their hopes far from home, in the worldwide struggle against the American empire. But over the next few years, as they went down in flames, they managed to leave a legacy that would last: a push toward the idea of black pride based on black power, an uncompromising early opposition to the war in Vietnam, and the hope that an unfettered, democratic movement by ordinary people might change the world.

The liberals who had helped design the particulars of the MFDP strategy actually turned out to be the chief victims of its betrayal. Reuther, Rauh, and Lowenstein lost all influence within the most energetic element of the civil rights movement. Cut off from the southern civil rights activists, unable to deal with the coming black power struggle in the North or with the white backlash it generated, and finally becoming the apologists for an unpopular war, the liberals lost most of their connection to any actual, existing movements or political forces in American society. Nixon and Reagan would pick up the pieces. Within a generation, the word "liberal" (although hardly the basic set of ideas it stood for) would become the "L-word" of American politics.

Reuther's trip to Delano in December of 1965 symbolized white liberalism's last, best hope for relevance. And Chavez understood the liberals well. Older and much more experienced than the SNCC radicals, he was expert at preventing the divisions that had crippled the civil rights movement from damaging his own organization. Certainly, he was able to do that because the needs and demands of the people he represented—at least as formulated by him—were potentially easier for American capital to accommodate, or so it seemed for a while. But he was also sophisticated about what he asked of his allies. He did not try to realign the Democratic Party; rather, he simply joined one segment of that party and did his best not to alienate the rest. Similarly, he tried not to get involved in the many internal battles of the church groups that supported his organization, nor in the divisions within the constantly changing student groups. He was careful to stay neutral on the gut-wrenching question of the war. Finally, he was quite conscious of the possible entanglements that went along with accepting support from powerful allies, and he did his best, in the context of the boycott alliance, to maintain maximum independence for himself and the farm workers organization.

On December 16, 1965, Reuther arrived in Delano in the UAW's private plane. Two carloads of national newsmen had preceded him to report on his visit. After disembarking, in full view of the cameras, Reuther gladly grabbed the NFWA's black eagle symbol and jauntily joined a supposedly illegal march through town, defying the police to arrest him. On this short visit, Reuther's national prominence secured him meetings with both the mayor and a committee of growers, whom he admonished to begin negotiations. He publicly announced his unqualified support for the barely existent three-month-old strike, which he guaranteed would be won sooner or later. In a speech at Filipino Hall he began by saying, "This is not your strike, this is our strike," and then announced to the cheering crowd that the UAW and the AFL-CIO Industrial Union Department, which he chaired, would donate $5,000 a month to the strike, split between AWOC and the NFWA. He did not neglect to mention the boycott, which had been officially announced just one week earlier. Thus, at a stroke, the national boycott of Schenley and DiGiorgio unexpectedly won the support of one of the most important liberals in the country, at the same time that it was being organized on the ground by radical civil rights groups that Reuther and his allies opposed. Ganz was amused by the peculiar swing of political fortunes. In the audience at Filipino Hall, Marshall felt he had compromised nothing; for him, the NFWA was a logical extension of the radical work he had been doing in SNCC. In fact, he was still working with SNCC. It was Reuther who was scrambling for a connection to another social movement.[6]

After Reuther left Delano, Ganz was invited to Richard Chavez's house to celebrate with the top NFWA leaders. Amid the eating, drinking, and exuberant toasts, only Cesar was prescient enough to offer a word of caution. "Tonight we lost our independence," he said, telling his closest associates that the AFL-CIO money and support would eventually extract a price. They were no longer their own little association, doing what they thought best, responsible to no one but farm workers. In the future, he told the surprised celebrants, they would have to guard their freedom even more closely.[7] A first move in that direction quickly followed in the form of protecting themselves not from their new labor allies, but rather from their earlier supporters in the student left. When Mike Miller, accompanied by Paul Booth, a national leader of SDS, visited Delano after the Christmas holidays to discuss the structure of the boycott, Chavez adamantly insisted that the boycott would be carried out by the NFWA alone, not in association with SNCC and SDS, as Miller and Booth had hoped. The two groups were welcome to work on the boycott and consult on strategy, but major decisions would be made by the NFWA exclusively.[8]

Given the volatile situation in both SNCC and SDS—SNCC would merge with the Black Panther Party in less than two years, and SDS would fall apart in 1969—it is hard to fault Chavez's decision. But it involved one complication that the young Mike Miller was keen enough to notice. In a letter that followed the Delano visit, he pointed out to Chavez that the new boycott plan would make the NFWA "an organization of farm workers and a staff organization—all in one." Miller made the remark in passing; it was by no means the theme of his letter, and he did not attempt to spell out the possible difficulties inherent in such a two-chambered structure. That would have been far too much to expect, as the full consequences of this seemingly reasonable, apparently unimportant, and certainly innocent shift in the boycott structure would not become clear to anyone until much later. In early 1966 no note of alarm accompanied Miller's comradely observation. He assured Cesar that civil rights organizations were still committed to helping the NFWA and the boycott. But Miller could also see that unless he was willing to join the association staff, there was now no point in continuing as the cochair of the boycott. Miller quietly left, without any great sense of disappointment.[9]

As 1966 began, Chavez put his new ideas about the boycott structure into practice. An old-time NFWA board member, Tony Orendain, was sent to Chicago to run the boycott organizing there; he was accompanied by the card-carrying Wobbly, Eugene Nelson, who had just finished writing *Huelga*, a book on the strike. Jack Ybarra was sent to San Francisco; three new NFWA volunteers, Eddie Frankle, Ida Cousino, and Sal Gonzales, were sent to Detroit, Cleveland, and Boston, respectively. Gilbert Padilla was directed to continue with the work in Los Angeles, which had become a model for boycott organizations elsewhere.[10] In New York, where the boycott was also quite strong, CORE was allowed to remain in charge. By February, Jim Drake claimed that there were 100 boycott committees throughout the country, and although the vast majority had been set up without the presence of an NFWA staff member, they all were understood to be part of the NFWA structure. Drake's status, too, had changed—he was given a small staff. Donna Sue Haber, one of the most competent new volunteers, was assigned to be his secretary, and they had a new office in downtown Delano. The boycott was now out of the bathroom.[11]

Reuther's visit had one other important effect. Newsmen had become interested in the NFWA—not in its structure or strategy or social base, but in the personalities of its leaders. Newsmen started to quote Chavez regularly and began to identify him, by name and title, in articles and photographs. Their interest in writing about Cesar was matched by the NFWA's interest in promoting him. Drake remembers several conversations among the leadership about the usefulness of projecting Chavez in the press. The thinking went like this: "Well, we have their attention now, and we want them to know what is happening. Wouldn't it be good to have Cesar as the ultimate source of information, the public representative of the effort?"[12] Chavez would not only lead the NFWA internally but also would be cast as its representative to the outside world. It didn't seem to be much of a stretch: Chavez's unique strategic sensibility had helped the NFWA survive what was essentially a losing strike and had put the organization in a position where its power was continuing to grow. Since his authority within the NFWA was well established, what could be wrong with projecting it outward? The only person who seemed to have doubts was Chavez himself. Drake remembers that Cesar, though quite comfortable about having the last word on strategic matters and quite willing to exercise his authority by, for example, asking staff members to move to cities and set up boycott offices, nevertheless did not like some of the tasks of a formal leader. He especially was uneasy as a public speaker. While driving to speaking engagements, Cesar, Drake said, "would be half desperate: 'What should I say? What should I do?' he would ask. We would talk over his speech, but when we got there he would talk for just ten minutes and then answer questions. He was good at that. But he couldn't give a big charismatic speech."[13]

Chavez never did learn to give that speech. But within two years he had mastered the big charismatic act.

13

Battle Theater

Winter '65 to '66

On most winter days in the southern Central Valley, a thick fog rises from the ground, enveloping the entire countryside in an opaque gray, which deadens the sun, obscures vision, and depresses even the most cheerful. In that persistent ground cloud—"tule fog" or "valley fog," in local parlance— the National Farm Workers Association rebuilt its picket lines in January 1966. But it was as if the picketers had ventured into the void, as they stood, befogged, in the cold, drizzly, dense mist, on deserted back roads, yelling slogans that only they could hear, holding signs that no one could see. They knew that the bosses had recruited more than enough scabs to prune the vines, that the NFWA's alliance with AWOC had collapsed, and that the bosses continued to say they would never negotiate. People went to the picket lines every day because they needed the food, clothing, and beds that the association provided, or because they wanted to remain a part of the NFWA volunteer family, or because they had a rich enough imagination to continue to dream of victory, or because they were too stubborn to accept defeat.

The NFWA had little choice but to rebuild the lines. If it was launching a boycott it had to keep the strike alive, and to do that it had to put up at least token opposition to the pruning of the vines. By mid-January *El Malcriado* claimed that there were as many as 150 to 200 people picketing (compared with 2,000 pruners), but even that was overly optimistic.[1] The pickets were divided into several groups, and Chavez, in informal consultation with the picketers, chose the picket captains. Epifanio Camacho was one of them. He took the job seriously. He agreed with the idea of seeking outside support, but he believed that the strike would ultimately be won or lost in the fields. For him, the picket line was not just a symbol that the struggle continued but a way of actually stopping the pruning. Many who agreed with him joined his picketing group. They were generally peaceful, but they did not avoid occasional face-offs with the scabs. Strikers confronted scab pruners in the fields, at their homes, or in farm worker cafés and bars. When the police were not around, they rushed into the fields—sometimes to talk with small groups of workers, at other times to fight them or to take away their pruning shears, which the workers themselves had to buy. They threw rocks and dirt clods from the sides of the vineyards. Camacho even rigged a catapult on the back of his truck so that, away from the fields and hidden in the fog, he could send several rocks at once hurtling toward the scab pruners.[2]

There were a lot of good fighters among the strikers, but Camacho was different. He didn't carry a gun or a knife, as did some others, and he did not just fight in the fog, or at night, or in secret. Although he did what he could to avoid the police, he was not shy about defending his actions, and he defended them in colorful, well-reasoned fashion. The strikers were acting in self-defense, he argued. The whole strike was an act of self-defense against the daily violence of hunger, overcrowded housing, lack of education for their children, humiliations on the job. And besides, he said, not only the scabs but this whole unjust system was being protected by uniformed, armed, violent men, who were doing in the strike what they did every day anyway: using their billy clubs, guns, jails, and laws to protect the bosses. Camacho delivered those arguments in formal meetings at the NFWA hall and in casual get-togethers at homes and bars, but most frequently on the picket line with a hand-held megaphone.

His daily picket line speeches included amusing accounts of Mexican history, a fair amount of wit, and unrelenting invective: "Pigeon-brained sons of Satan! Why don't you foul spawn of demented chimpanzees understand what it is all about? Open up your ears, you groveling pigs. Would you sell the souls of your children as well as your own to these grower swine?" The bullhorn oratory was intended as much for the good cheer of his fellow strikers as it was for the pruners, and the defiant Camacho did not tone down his rhetoric when the police arrived. They had arrested him a couple of times back in September, and now they wanted to get him out of the way as soon as possible. They made their move in early January, coming by a peaceful picket line and arresting Camacho and his friend Manuel Rosas for armed robbery, charging the two with taking a scab's pruning shears at the point of a pellet gun. Bail was set at $2,000 each. While Camacho sat in jail, three cops, only one in uniform, went to his home, talked their way past his wife, Salome, and proceeded to ransack their house. The uniformed cop spoke Spanish and told Salome that they were looking for a gun and for pruning shears. Despite throwing books, papers, boxes, clothes, and bedding about the house, they never found a gun; in the garage they did find six pruning shears, which they took with them, leaving a receipt. They also shot several rolls of film. Salome noted that they seemed peculiarly interested in the headboard of the couple's bed and in the cartons of cigarettes that Camacho had been given by someone in the NFWA office to distribute to the people on his picket line.[3]

The search had been made without a warrant, and a month later the case was dropped. By then Camacho had been arrested and released several more times. Bill Esher and his main comrade at *El Malcriado*, Doug Adair, had made reports of the police attacks against Camacho a regular feature of the paper, and added that his "brilliant speeches to the scabs on the picket line will become part of history." They ignored the contradiction between Camacho's open promotion of self-defense and Chavez's promulgation of nonviolence, although both Esher and Adair—and everyone else close to the picket lines—knew about Camacho's catapult, his frequent fights, and the generally aggressive behavior of the group of picketers he captained. As far as many were concerned, Chavez's oft-stated views simply provided good cover for the more robust maneuvers of some of the strikers. And Chavez had not yet laid down the law. The fact that Cesar himself had authorized Camacho to be a picket captain after all the trouble in September and October indicated his willingness in early 1966 to accept some of Camacho's picket line antics. In any event, in January and February of 1966, Chavez was not yet in a position to insist that the NFWA's tactics on the ground must be a complete reflection of his own temperament and ideas. Although his personal authority was growing among the strikers and supporters, many of the people actually doing the winter picketing were hard-core farm worker militants, and for them Camacho's line on self-defense made good sense. Since the NFWA could not abandon the winter picket lines, Chavez had to live with the opinions and actions of the most enthusiastic picketers. Like Marshall Ganz with his gun in Mississippi, Chavez was willing "to live with the ambiguity."

The arduous winter picket lines were not without their little victories. Often scab pruners—persuaded by the moral authority of the strikers, or the eloquence of picket line speakers, or the promise of a place to eat and sleep, or the threat of a beating, or some combination of all of those— would symbolically lower their shears and walk out of the fields. In response, the triumphant strikers would rush to embrace their new comrades, show- ering them with affection and enthusiastic chants of "*Viva la huelga!*" Each little drama had its own particulars. One mini-victory kept people talking for weeks: the time that Felipe Cantú dropped his shears and joined, not so much the strikers as the recently formed El Teatro Campesino.

Cantú, a small middle-aged man, had spent a morning pruning at the edge of a vineyard while listening to the passionate speeches of the picket captain Luis Valdez and the songs of Agustín Lira (known as Augie) and half watching the comic skits about the strike that Valdez and Lira performed on the top of a green panel truck. The skits—*actos*, Valdez called them— were meant to amuse the picketers and the scabs, as well as the two performers. Suddenly, Cantú left the vineyard, walked into the enthusiastic arms of the chanting strikers, and then climbed up onto the flatbed.

Megaphone in hand, he began to dance and sing. Totally at ease, he reeled out a comic political monologue, punctuated by an outrageous wiggle of his ass, as the astounded strikers, already high with victory, were convulsed with laughter and tears. Valdez and Lira exchanged a look: they had found an actor.[4]

Felipe Cantú became more than just the Teatro Campesino's comic genius; he was its flesh-and-blood link to the tradition of Mexican working-class popular performance culture. When he was a boy in Nuevo León, Mexico, in the late 1920s and early 1930s, Felipe had been devoted to the various traveling tent shows, *carpas*, that passed through the countryside. These *carpas*, direct descendents of earlier traveling circuses, emerged during the Mexican Revolution. They featured the singers, informal orchestra, dancers, puppets, and ventriloquists seen in the earlier circuses, but they no longer featured exotic animal acts, as the circus managers could not afford to feed the animals and instead had had to slaughter them to feed their human performers. The revolution had also transformed the circus clown into the comic *pelado**, who through his own resources and satiric tongue, manages to spoof and at times get the better of the rich and powerful.[5] This new comic sensibility helped to convert the spectacle of the circus into a popular theater of social criticism. Felipe, who never learned to read but, like many illiterates, developed extraordinary powers of recall, had memorized many of these *pelado* routines as a child and practiced them at home and among his friends. He once declared to his impoverished father, as they were both grinding corn, that one day he would be a famous actor and travel to the grand cities of the world. His dad looked down at the boy and said, "Keep grinding the corn, son."[5]

And he did keep working—first in Mexico and then in California—but he also continued to dream and to refine his comic technique by following the career of Mario Moreno, better known as Cantinflas, who grew up as a *carpa* comic and then brought the *pelado* tradition to the Mexican movie screen in a series of classic comedies from the 1930s to the 1950s. So when Felipe Cantú, in his mid-forties, with a large family to support, pruning in a scab field, saw Valdez and Lira sing, dance, and joke on the picket line, his own calculus of the right and wrong of scabbing, of personal advantage and disadvantage, was colored by his impossible dream, his lifelong nurturing of his own talent in preparation for an opportunity that he doubted would ever come. And here it was, on the edge of a vineyard, a couple of amateurs playing around on the top of a truck. All he had to do was put down the shears and walk out of the fields and onto what he had been waiting for his whole life: a stage!

Cantú's comic talent shaped the Teatro Campesino as much as

---

* Literally, "the peeled one," but it is an untranslateable word, used in many different ways. Its English equivalents include "low life," "simpleton," and "dude."

the musical sensitivity of Agustín Lira and the conscious radical goals and theatrical smarts of Luis Valdez. Nearly twenty years after the scab Felipe Cantú walked out of the fields, Lira said:

> For me, the most important person of Teatro Campesino was Felipe. Not just personally, but because of his talent. Of all the comedians . . . whom I have seen, whether they are Mexican comedians like Cantinflas, or comedians from Europe or other parts of the world, I still haven't seen anyone with the comic talent of Felipe Cantú. All he needed was an idea. He would take that idea and peel away everything it was not. He took the rock and carved away everything that was not the character. We were left with the statue: a character . . . Someone wrote that Felipe played the role of Cantinflas . . . No. Cantinflas didn't even come close to Felipe. Never even came close. Cantinflas is a *pendejo* [fool] in comparison . . . Using mime, without talking, [Felipe] would show the audience everything.[6]

Augie Lira had joined the NFWA family just a couple of weeks after the strike started. Born twenty-one years earlier in Torreón, Mexico, Lira came to Delano by way of Lordsburg, New Mexico, and then the Central Valley towns of Layton, Five Points, Fresno, and Selma. First traveling alone with his mother and then, eventually, with seven half brothers and sisters, Augie spent his youth in schools where if he was caught speaking Spanish, his mouth was washed out with soap, or he was made to sit in the corner of the classroom, or he was sent to the principal's office to be spanked with a big wooden paddle. His mother worked as a laundress, waitress, house cleaner, and farm worker. Augie started going to the fields as a toddler. At the age of nine he started working alongside her. He spent his summers, many of his weekends, and quite a few schooldays in the raisins, peaches, tomatoes, and table grapes. He learned to speak and read both English and Spanish, and graduated from Selma High School in 1963. That same year his mother died, and his stepfather kicked him out of the house. That was not a surprise. The only one of his mother's partners Lira had ever cared for was Francisco Lara, the man she lived with in the labor camp in Five Points:

> He was the only man who lived in our house who was interested in me. The only one I ever loved. He was an experienced farm worker, a lead man, a good worker. One Sunday he crashed our car into a picket fence that belonged to a grower's wife. She went ballistic, called immigration, and they came to the camp looking for him. The whole thing happened in front of us. It was the worst day of my life. The *migra* allowed us to say goodbye to him. He gave his pocket knife to my brother, and we kept it for many years. But we never saw him again.[7]

The boy roamed from household to household, making a few bucks as a busboy, or washing dishes, or out in the fields. He traveled in a mixed group of young whites, African Americans, and Mexicans who were united by their passion for rock and roll. He got his first guitar in his last year of high school, but he had started singing much earlier, way back in New Mexico, learning from his mother, who sang in various church choirs, and her brothers, one of whom played harmonica as a street musician. In 1961, when his mother left the Catholic Church—disgusted, she said, with all the hypocrites—and made her way through Fresno's various black congregations, Agustín became enthralled by gospel music. Later he brought that music, as well as the rancheros and boleros he learned from his uncles, to the jam sessions he had with his rock-and-roll friends.

He and a group of friends were sitting on a Fresno porch on a hot summer day in September 1965 when a Vista volunteer told them about the grape strike. Augie and two buddies went down to Delano for a weekend, and Augie came back telling people that someone was going to get killed down there. But two weeks later he decided to join the strike. "I thought maybe I could contribute, and after all I was homeless. Besides, the weekend I was there the place was filled with volunteers from Berkeley, Los Angeles, and San Francisco. Young people, mostly Anglos, but a lot of fun. I decided to go back whether I got killed or not."[8]

Lira did his picket-line duty, helped translate *El Malcriado*, and spent many evenings swapping riffs with farm worker musicians and a few volunteers who were folk music enthusiasts. These jam sessions were held in the NFWA's compound, or in its offices at what was called the Pink House, or in various homes around town, and they usually attracted a small audience of strikers and supporters. After one of those evenings, a man wearing a beret, smoking a cigar, and dressed in a pea coat and combat boots pulled Augie aside for what he said was going to be a little chat, but turned into a long conversation. Lira didn't understand a lot of what the guy was talking about, but he did get the idea that the man wanted to start some kind of theater group in order to teach the workers something or other, and entertain them, too. This group, which would somehow be made up of farm workers, would need a lot of music, and wouldn't Agustín like to help him get such a thing started? Sure, Augie, said. And that "sure" shaped his life more certainly than his first trip to Delano, or the first time he picked up a guitar, or his mother's death, or his loving stepfather's deportation, or anything else that ever happened to him or that he alone had ever decided to do.

The man in the pea coat was Luis Valdez. Although he arrived in Delano dressed in one of the uniforms of a would-be student revolutionary and talking a rhetorical language that Augie Lira could barely understand, he was not the arch-outsider that grower propaganda would later make him out to be. A returning prodigal son would be more accurate. Valdez was a local product, and when he came to Delano in 1965 to start El Teatro Campesino, he was in the middle of an improbable life journey that had so far taken him from Delano to San Jose to Cuba to the Haight-Ashbury District of San Francisco, and then back to Delano.

Hermila Montaño, Luis's mother, had come to Delano from Arizona in the late 1920s at the age of eight. Delano's combination of cotton and grapes provided wages nearly year-round, and the family settled into a large labor camp outside of town. Already living at the camp was the Valdez family, who had arrived from the same Tucson barrio a few years before. Since no school bus came to the camp, a sixteen-year-old farm worker was commissioned by the residents to leave work and take Hermila and other children back and forth to school in a big Dodge touring car. Hermila liked the unofficial chauffer, Francisco Valdez, and took to pulling his hair from the seat behind him. It was the beginning of a relationship that would include a lifelong marriage and ten children.[9]

The Valdez and Montaño families stayed on in Delano through the difficult 1930s. Francisco made it through the sixth grade, and Hermila the eighth. They were both bilingual. The young Hermila even became close childhood friends with Nadine Kruger, the daughter of a prominent Delano grower. In the 1933 cotton strike, however, when the two girls were adolescents, Nadine's father was one of the men who fired shots into a farm worker rally in front of the union hall. Hermila's father was one of the farm workers in the crowd. Perhaps class and ethnic differences would have separated the two girls eventually anyway, but they were never to find out. One girl's father had seen three of his compatriots killed; the other girl's father was one of the accused, and the childhood friendship was over.

Three years later, Hermila and Francisco were married. Luis was their third child, born in 1940, just six months after their second child, two-year-old Manuel, died following an operation on his intestine. The family was devastated. The young Hermila blamed herself; the firstborn son, Frank, actually jumped into the grave to try to retrieve his little brother during the burial. Although Hermila and Frank hovered over the new baby, Luis, they could not prevent harm from coming his way. When Luis was two, and the family was living in a labor camp outside San Jose, the toddler was accidentally scalded by boiling water. He was taken to a hospital, where, as Luis tells the story, "They said these are migrant farm workers, here's a severely burned child, he's gonna die, why don't you just take him home and take care of him. So . . . for the next six months, as my mother tells the story, I slept on her stomach . . . She was just riveted on even my sleeping, not rolling over on my back cause I didn't have any skin. So I recovered, obviously, and I was a robust little kid after that."

Later that same year, 1942, the Valdez family got lucky off the misfortune of the California Japanese. With the help of a bank loan and a contract guaranteeing that the Army would buy his vegetables, Francisco Valdez purchased a 300-acre farm between Delano and Earlimart that had belonged to a Japanese truck farmer who was forced off the land and interned. The new farm changed the family's life. They didn't have to migrate for the summers. They bought a nice car, and the extended family spread out comfortably into the two homes on the new ranch. Luis, playing his childhood games in the dirt of the family's own land, reached the age of reason feeling loved, protected, and secure.

The end of the war also ended the Valdezes' idyllic interlude. The government contracts were terminated, Francisco Valdez couldn't keep up with the mortgage payments, the bank foreclosed, and the ranch was bought by a first-generation Italian immigrant, John Pagliarulo—the same man whose grapes would be stopped on the San Francisco docks eighteen years later. Francisco moved the two houses onto a small lot in Earlimart, and the family hit the migrant trail again. Luis, seven, was shocked by the abrupt change in his circumstances:

> I couldn't believe some of the conditions we were being asked to live in. I eventually got used to it, if you can get used to something like this . . . like living in barns and chicken coops, sometimes just out in the car, out in the middle of a field, homeless, basically, what we call homeless today. It did make me determined to do something about it . . . I said, I can't live this way, we gotta do something . . . We gotta make more money, how can we do this?

Luis started the first grade at the same little schoolhouse that his mother had attended. He remembers that he loved school from the start. Then, by chance, he spent the fourth and fifth grades at a school where, except for his brother, all the other students were Anglos, many of them growers' children. For those two years Luis spoke only English; when he returned to the officially integrated schools, where the majority of the students were Mexicans and Mexican Americans, his English skills helped make him an outstanding student—and earned him a few beatings from his fellow Mexicans.

By that time, Francisco and Hermila had moved the family to East San Jose. There seemed to be steady work in the Santa Clara Valley, the weather was pleasant, and the orchards were lush and beautiful. Luis remembers that it seemed as though they were entering paradise compared with the dry, vacant, alkaline fields of Delano. He continued to be a straight-A student, was the Northern California gymnastics champion, and won a math and science scholarship to San Jose State College.

But Luis had always had another passion. A grade-school fascination with papier-mâché masks had led to childhood puppet plays, which had led to comic performances with a ventriloquist's dummy. He had a clever routine, which he put on for workers at the labor camps. His dummy was an Anglo—Al Nelson, he called him—and the bilingual Luis made great fun out of various brown/white, Spanish/English confusions. His consciousness of his developing art deepened when he went to a movie theater in Mendota and saw a live performance by a touring Mexican ventriloquist, Paco Miller, who was entertaining a farm worker crowd with his dummy, Don Roque. "Hey, I can do that," the young Luis thought. He added another dummy to his act, a Mexican, Marcelino Pipin, and now with a Mexican on one of his thirteen-year-old knees and an Anglo on the other, Luis could humorously work out the contradictions of his own identity, as well as the conflicting identities of the young friends for whom he put on his shows. The performances got better and better, and in 1956, when he was sixteen, he was invited to do a show during the one, half-hour, Sunday Spanish-language program on the local television station, KNTV. The station got so many enthusiastic calls that Valdez played for eighteen consecutive weeks.

He was at the end of his first year in college, calculating a change in majors, when all such considerations were swept away by the roaring political flash floods of the 1960s. The first wave, in October 1961, was the Cuban missile crisis and the threat of nuclear war. As Valdez later said, "A lot of us were just kissing our asses goodbye and asking what are we still doing in school . . . The world's not going to last, so let's just drop out . . . I had a girlfriend, and we both dropped out." He started to read about Latin America and fell in with a group of political people in San Jose whose main interest was the civil rights movement and what was then an obscure war in Indochina. (After he was called for a preinduction physical he reenrolled at San Jose State to protect himself from the draft.) The Kennedy assassination, in November 1963, deepened his political interests. He also crossed paths with Ken Kesey and the Merry Pranksters, who were headquartered in La Honda just over the hill from San Jose. It was 1964, almost summer, and this child of farm workers with a flair for the theatrical was now at the center of a world that was about to explode. "We really had to choose: it was either going to be the next bus trip with Ken Kesey, or we were going to go to Mississippi Summer, or we were going to go to Cuba."

Valdez chose Cuba. A friend from San Jose State, Roberto Ruvalcalva, went with him, on a student trip organized by the Progressive Labor Party to protest the U.S.-imposed travel ban. Valdez, Ruvalcalva, and sixty-three others traveled via Paris, stayed six weeks, and came home via Prague. One of Luis's roommates was Jerry Rubin, not yet a Yippie but a serious student radical from Berkeley. Another was Jeff Lustig, also a Berkeley radical, on whom

Valdez made a strong first impression. "He immediately began to teach us some Spanish: '*El respeto al derecho ajeno es la paz*' (Respect for the rights of others is Peace) for the politicos we would meet, and '*Tú eres linda*' (You are pretty) for the young women. He was our full-service translator."[11]

At one point during the trip a few people in the delegation, including Valdez, suggested that they spend a day cutting sugar cane. The Cubans were dubious, but the students insisted, and the hosts arranged a day of harvesting.[11] Within a few hours, almost all the American cutters had given up. It was too hard, too dirty, too hot. They were ready for it intellectually, but not physically or emotionally. Humiliated, they gathered at the end of the field, talking among themselves and to their amused guides. Soon they realized that two of their number were still out in the sugar cane: Vincent Lynch, a black man from the Fillmore district who had worked in the fields of the American South as a youth, and Luis Valdez. Those two continued to cut until the crew of Cubans stopped for the day. Lustig remembers the stupefied silence in the crowd and the sight of Luis with his red bandana, swinging his machete in perfect sync with the other cane cutters, as if he had been doing it all his life.

Cuba, for Valdez, was the resolution of the crisis that he had been going through for the previous couple of years:

> It was at Varadero, a real luxury spot on a beach of white sands that had been open only to the very rich, and now it was open to the people, so we were given very plush accommodations. And I remember having to get away from all the other students, and taking this long walk out among the sugar cane . . . and all these memories started to come back to me. I remember my mother giving birth when she was working in the potatoes and having the baby stillborn. And another time we were picking prunes and she raised her pants and her knees would bleed . . . I started crying. I'm out in the middle of the cane fields, by myself, and I'm saying I got to do something; I have got to devote myself to making some change happen. That's what Cuba did for me.

When they got back to the States, Ruvalcalva and Valdez wrote a pamphlet, "Venceremos!: Mexican-American Statement on Travel to Cuba," a short account of the U.S. war of expansion against Mexico and the genocidal campaign against American Indians. Their analysis, standard forty years later but still unusual in 1964, was not overly rhetorical and provided enough detail to demonstrate that the young authors had done some research before they sat down to write. The pamphlet also included a brief attack on U.S. "Spanish-speaking leaders . . . Americanized beyond recall, [who] neither understand nor care about the basic Mexican-American population, which has an identity of its own." Before closing with a formal endorsement of Cuba's social revolution and a call on the U.S. government "to stop immediately its aggressive policy on Cuba," the two made the one personal reference in this otherwise thoroughly political manifesto:

> As sons of Mexican manual laborers in California, we have traveled to Revolutionary Cuba, in defiance of the travel ban, in order to emphasize the historical and cultural unanimity of all Latin American peoples, north or south of the border. Having no real leaders of our own, we accept Fidel Castro. We believe the example of Cuba will inevitably bring socialist revolution to the whole of Latin America.[12]

Such sentiments could be heard from others in the San Jose of the mid-1960s. The standard historical periodization of the decade from 1960 to 1970 is that the early sixties was a time of hope, when young people were trying to make America live up to its promise, and the later sixties was a time of despair, when those same young people became bitter revolutionaries. Such a breakdown completely misses the radical intentions of many young people in the early sixties and the importance of Cuba in the formation of North America's New Left. When Fidel Castro's bearded, antibourgeois revolutionaries rode into Havana on January 1, 1959, many young Americans immediately recognized them as allies. When Castro came to the United Nations in 1960, having been kicked out of an opulent New York hotel and going instead to the Hotel Theresa in Harlem where he met Malcolm X, many young people, black, brown and white, heard the ice crack. Thousands rushed to Cuba to see the revolution for themselves, had their own version of Valdez's walk in the sugar cane, and returned with various levels of commitment, to try to bring the revolutionary spirit back home.

The white middle-class demonstrators of the early sixties were not only concerned about the bomb and the exclusion of African Americans from the American way of life. Many of them were already dissatisfied with the stifling cultural blandness of that life. They had an inchoate radical critique of the nation's culture in the early sixties, before they became the explicit revolutionaries of the late sixties and early seventies. What excited them were not the particular goals of the early demonstrations but the high excitement of taking risks and making history, and the promise of some other, nonbourgeois way to live. That promise now had a full grip on the heart and soul of Luis Valdez.

Not long after he returned from Cuba, Luis moved into the Haight-Ashbury District with a group of fellow self-defined revolutionary artists and soon became a leading actor in the San Francisco Mime Troupe. The troupe was led by its founder and director, R.G. Davis, who had trained with Martha Graham in Chicago, José Limón in New York, and Étienne Decroux (the teacher of Marcel Marceau) in Paris.

Davis had come to San Francisco in 1959 to be part of the Actors Workshop, yet another oasis in the American cultural desert of the 1950s. Some 150 professional actors and directors had dropped out of the commercial theater world and come to San Francisco to develop an alternative theater that would counter the offerings of Broadway and Hollywood. The actors in the Actors Workshop were paid virtually nothing and had to live by their wits or conventional day jobs. More than a few worked on the docks, where jobs were controlled by the left-led ILWU. The company's star actor worked at the San Francisco wholesale produce market, swamping vegetables from midnight to 5 a.m. The Actors Workshop was the most progressive regional theater in the United States, the first in the country to mount productions of plays by Samuel Becket, Bertolt Brecht, and the English playwrights known as the "angry young men."

But after two years Davis and a few others dropped out of this group of 1950s dropouts. Linking up with painters who were leaving the San Francisco Art Institute to become performance artists or rock musicians, and with a group of New Leftists at the San Francisco New School, Davis formed the Mime Troupe and started performing for free in the San Francisco parks. The idea was to go to the audience, rather than wait for it to come to them, and to do so with raucous, saucy, political buffoonery. The troupe's antinaturalism quickly took it in the direction of commedia dell'arte, the popular outdoor theater that thrived in Italy's late Renaissance. Luis Valdez arrived after the Mime Troupe had been performing commedia in the parks for two years; when he left the troupe to go to Delano to start a farm workers' theater, he took with him a year's training in outdoor performances that featured the commedia's signature masks and archetypal characters.[13]

The first call to return home came via an early issue of *El Malcriado*. Luis's grandmother had sent her somewhat wayward grandson copies of the early issues, figuring he would be interested. He was interested, though not enthusiastic. But when the grape strike broke out, and the NFWA was eager to mobilize all manner of outside support, Valdez felt the tug of Delano. When Chavez came to the Bay Area in October to raise money, Valdez followed him from appearance to appearance. The two sped back and forth across the Bay Bridge in VW bugs, and Luis finally caught up with Cesar in an Oakland church.

After introducing himself with an emphasis on his Delano roots, Valdez came right to the point: "I want to use theater to educate the workers. I'll do whatever is necessary."

"There's no money; we can't pay actors," answered the practical Chavez.

He didn't need money, Luis replied, nor a regular theater, and he could put something together with whatever materials were at hand.

Cesar was still doubtful. "We can't pay you," he repeated.

Valdez was no longer concerned about making more money than was necessary for basic survival. He told Chavez again not to worry. Chavez had already seen this kind of dedication among some of the volunteers who were streaming into Delano and had no reason to doubt Valdez's sincerity. Moreover, Chavez was a trained recruiter. He had been encouraging people to join his efforts for more than a dozen years. Why not Valdez, too?

"I couldn't believe it when I heard you went back there," Luis's older brother, Frank, told him. "How could you? It took so much effort to get out of there, and you went back willingly. Why?"

There was no simple answer to this question. The answer lay in his whole life up to then: a unique combination of world historical trends, big and small decisions, plus a large dose of that most mysterious ingredient—chance.

Luck, chance, Fortuna—they were everywhere. Valdez had one last obligation in San Francisco before he could go to Delano. The Mime Troupe, buoyed by their large following, had playfully refused to apply for a permit to perform in the city parks. In response, city officials said they would arrest the first actor who appeared at the next performance. That was supposed to be Valdez. But Luis had already decided to go to Delano and did not want to be tied down by a San Francisco arrest. The director, R.G. Davis, took his place and was carried off stage, right on cue. It was front-page news. The Mime Troupe's business manager planned a benefit to raise money for bail. A few unknown San Francisco bands agreed to perform, including the Jefferson Airplane and the Warlocks. The Warlocks soon changed their name to the Grateful Dead. So many people came to that first benefit at the Mime Troupe's rehearsal space that hundreds were left outside in the street, so they held another, which ended up being even more crowded than the first. What the hell, thought Bill Graham, the Troupe business manager. He left the Mime Troupe, rented the Fillmore Auditorium, and went into business.

El Teatro Campesino combined the Mexican *carpa* tradition and Italian commedia dell'arte. From the commedia, Valdez took masks, which were not typical in the *carpa*, and made a significant addition of his own: signs hung around the necks of the actors that identified the archetypes they represented. Thus, no theatrical time had to be wasted identifying Patroncito (the Little Boss), Huelgista (the Striker), Coyote (the wily labor contractor), and Esquirol (the strike-breaker), and the actors could immediately proceed to a comic representation of the power relationships between the various characters, which was the heart of the Teatro's improvisations and *actos*.

Like everyone else, Valdez and Augie Lira were assigned picket duty, where they came to know the other workers. To start the Teatro, they put out leaflets inviting people to a first rehearsal, which was followed by

another and another. A few workers then started doing some of the informal routines on the picket lines. The picketers were a good audience: they
were desperate for entertainment, and what they saw on top of the panel
truck was all about them, a humorous version of what was happening on
those same picket lines in the battle between bosses, strikers, and scabs. The
picket line routines also sorted out the folks who liked to perform from
those who did not, and taught the actors which bits worked and which
should be discarded. It was all excellent preparation for the next big step: a
performance at one of the Friday night meetings at Filipino Hall.

The Friday meetings were mostly about maintaining the strikers' morale and
impressing visiting supporters. They featured an opening prayer, a low-key
speech from Chavez, a string of optimistic reports from the picket lines, enthusiastic speeches from supporters who had brought money and supplies to
Delano, group singing, and some questions and answers from the floor.
Attendance varied. Big meetings attracted more than a hundred people; small
meetings had a couple dozen. This was the NFWA community on display:
farm worker families (including babes in arms and young children running
about the room), some single farm workers, and volunteers from out of town.
People sat in rows of metal chairs. A couple of feet above the chairs, at the end
of the room, was a formal stage. On it, the picket line improvisations became
regular *actos*, and the novice farm worker actors had to face a seated audience
whose attention was riveted on them. The first performance was a huge success,
and afterward Chavez asked Valdez to perform regularly at the meetings. The
Teatro Campesino was no longer crawling; it had begun to walk.

Initially, the *actos* were not written down. The actors memorized them
first in improvisations critiqued by Valdez, and then in picket line performances, which received either the approbation of laughter or the criticism
of uncomfortable silence. They were mostly funny, featuring broad satiric
portraits of the strikers' enemies. Early on, however, the *actos* acquired a
distinctive feature, not essentially derived from either commedia or the
carpa: the unexpected role reversal, where the boss is tricked into becoming
a farm worker, while the farm worker becomes the boss. In the very first
acto, *Las Dos Caras del Patroncito* (The Two Faces of the Little Boss), the
pig-masked, cigar-smoking patroncito, tries to convince the compliant
esquirol that the boss's life is hard (he has to pay a lot for his house and car,
he must worry about his business, his wife spends too much money) and
that the worker's life is easy (he gets free rent and transportation to the
fields, cheap food, and no worries). In the process, the boss convinces
himself that this might be true, and the boss and the scab exchange signs,
props, and places. The farm worker alertly takes advantage of the reversal,
and calls the security guard. The guard is fooled by the theatrical convention of the mask and sign, and drags away the boss, who screams in protest,
finally even calling on Cesar Chavez for help. The triumphant farm worker

then announces that he doesn't want the boss's house, car, and wife. But he will keep the cigar.

The archetypes of the actos were initially taken from Andy Zermeño's cartoons in *El Malcriado*. But Don Sotaco, the humble victim of the cartoons, did not survive intact in the Teatro. In *Las Dos Caras del Patroncito*, as in the other early performances, the apparently compliant, foolish worker eventually triumphed. And his triumph revealed that he was actually much smarter and aware of his own interests than he made himself out to be. This is pure *carpa*, Cantinflas-style: the apparently hopeless *pelado*, quick to take advantage of a lucky break, comes out on top while remaining true to his underdog status. He is a loser who wins but does not go over to the old winner's side. His original abject compliance is only an act required by social circumstances. The *actos'* ultimate reversals reveal that Don Sotaco was a conscious worker all along, a figure who not only owed a debt to Cantinflas (as interpreted by Felipe Cantú) but to the radical political tradition that Luis Valdez had learned on his journey away from Delano and back.

This contrast between Zermeño's Don Sotaco, who needed someone to save him, and the Teatro Campesino's Don Sotaco, who needed only some different social circumstances to save himself, did not seem to bother anyone in Delano in the winter of 1965–66. But people did notice that the folks who worked with the Teatro were a little different from the rest of the NFWA family. Teatro rehearsals included Valdez's Bay Area revolutionary artist friends and other out-of-town radicals. The farm workers who gravitated to the Teatro tended to be independent single men rather than the family members who made up the bulk of NFWA activists. And when Luis rented a rehearsal hall from his aunt (an old tortilla factory down the street from the NFWA's Pink House), the Teatro became even more separate. The actors rehearsed deep into the night, tended to drink more beer and smoke more weed than the other *huelgistas*, and were often late for picket duty in the mornings. Farm worker families tended not to want their daughters hanging out with the Teatro regulars.

The physically separate Teatro also drew close to the officially independent *Malcriado* staff. Lira and Valdez spent time with Bill Esher, Doug Adair, and the roving Wobbly, Eugene Nelson. Valdez replaced Chavez as the paper's main translator. He and Lira became admirers of Epifanio Camacho. Thus, the Teatro, like Camacho's picketing team and, to a lesser extent, the newspaper staff—occupied a position to the left of and slightly apart from the rest of the NFWA family. All of this was not lost on Chavez, although he made no complaint about any of it. After all, the Teatro's performances had quickly become fabulously popular with the strikers and crucial to morale. Nonetheless, the Teatro had become a little world for people who had a slightly different understanding of the farm worker struggle and who had, almost accidentally, established themselves as an independent presence in the NFWA.

14

The Spring Pilgrimage

February to April '66

Spring, obliterated in the old Tulare Basin by the damming of the Sierra's melting snow, still makes a brief appearance in the contemporary Central Valley as quick-blooming wildflowers splash waves of color across the mountain foothills. Except for those flowers, the changing of the seasons, from the fog-enshrouded winter to the long, dry summer, is not much noted by the hard-working people of Delano. Grape workers know spring as a period of unemployment, between the end of pruning in late February and the thinning and girdling that hit full bore in the middle of May. But in 1966 the NFWA, whose members usually worked in accordance with the rhythms of this altered nature, broke the pattern and rescued spring from the oblivion of eternal recurrence. They made it a time to remember, understood by the actors themselves as a break in nature's cycles, a human event, a moment in history.

The history makers from Delano, in an act of political genius that was opposed by some of the most committed strikers and volunteers, tied their efforts to the Mexican Catholic version of the rites of spring. They marched to Sacramento—a march that Cesar Chavez had been thinking about since the mid-fifties—not just to press their demands upon state officials but also as an act of Christian penance. They cried out for justice and prayed to be forgiven for their sins. The combination was devastatingly effective, and before the pilgrimage was over, the NFWA had won its first union contract. But as important as that first contract would be, it was but a prelude. The pilgrimage became an overture to the next four years, a preview of how all the different instruments in the National Farm Workers Association's unlikely combo—farm workers, religious enthusiasts, Democratic Party politicians, artists, union officials, student leftists, and Chicanos—could play together, under the careful direction of a master conductor, and produce such compelling harmonies that the entire Delano grape industry would be forced to sign union contracts in hopes that they could turn the music off.

The religious character of the pilgrimage did not reveal itself to the pilgrims through some flash of light in the sky. The leadership of the

NFWA thought it up, sketched it out, and then fought for it in a series of meetings with the prospective marchers. The idea first surfaced in a leadership retreat at the luxurious home of a wealthy supporter in the hills above Carpenteria, near Santa Barbara, on a mid-February weekend, as the pruning was slowing down. It was a by-invitation-only meeting of about a dozen people: along with the executive board, the major players were Luis Valdez, Jim Drake, and LeRoy Chatfield; among the minor ones were Marshall Ganz, Tony Mendez, and Robert Bustos; Mendez and Bustos were bilingual high school graduates who had been working in the fields when the grape strike began and had become full-time NFWA activists.

Ganz was astounded by the creativity of the NFWA discussions, which he attributed to the relative diversity of the leadership. Only after the conversation touched on the 1950s New Mexican miners' encampment in New York, the Selma civil rights march, Mao's long march, Zapata's Plan de Ayala, the political intricacies of the upcoming governor's race between Pat Brown and Ronald Reagan, did Cesar Chavez ask, "Why should it be a march at all?" He followed that rhetorical question with a recommendation: since Lent was coming, and since it was a time for reflection and penance, perhaps the NFWA should have not a march but a pilgrimage, a *peregrinación*, starting in Delano and ending, on Easter Sunday, at the State Capital building in Sacramento.[1]

Chavez's recommendations were not often ignored. To two of the NFWA cofounders, Gilbert Padilla and Dolores Huerta, he was considered the "first among equals," but to the other executive board members, and to those who had been informally brought into leadership, Chavez was the sole leader, the public voice and face of the association. He was now beginning to feel comfortable in that role and did nothing to deflect the growing admiration. It was a subtle shift, not fully recognized even by the sharp Padilla, but an outsider could detect it immediately. One afternoon during a break in the retreat, the participants went for a walk on the beach. As they strolled on the sand in quiet conversation, a woman approached from the other direction, paused, looked them over, and then stopped George Ballis, who was walking a little behind the rest of the group. Pointing at Cesar, the shortest and darkest of the party, she asked, "Is he an Italian movie director?"[2]

Chavez's *peregrinación* idea won over the other leaders, but they had to convince the active strikers. For some, Cesar's word would be enough, but not for all. Many workers on that tough winter picket line were spiritedly independent; they would do only what they made up their own minds to do. The NFWA could not succeed in any mass action that these people didn't wholeheartedly support. That was, to some extent, what people meant when they called the NFWA a democratic organization. The leadership, after a series of conversations, would make a decision, and then take it to the membership for discussion, amendment, and formal approval. As Luis Valdez said, "Chavez was trying . . . to get as many workers as possible to participate in the decision-making process, even though the decision was often already made."[3]

The pilgrimage plan was presented at another retreat, this one open to everybody, at Pozo Heights, a YMCA camp in the foothills above Porterville. The leadership promoted the retreat as a weekend of rest from the picket lines, "a three-day vacation," *El Malcriado* called it, with "hiking, volleyball, dances and movies in the evening, [and] a big barbecue on Saturday." Nearly a hundred people came, a good indication of the actual number of Delano-area NFWA activists at the time, and they were hardly surprised to discover that politics was also on the agenda. The date of the proposed march was less than two weeks away, and the main issue facing the association was its political character. In a series of small conversations and one big meeting, Chavez, with enthusiastic backing from Dolores Huerta, carefully explained what he had in mind: a pilgrimage to Sacramento, with the Virgin of Guadalupe in front, as in the various pilgrimages that religious enthusiasts make to holy places in Mexico—but with the pilgrims spreading the word about the NFWA and the demands of the strike.

Epifanio Camacho thought back to the cross Chavez had brought to the meeting before the rose strike. That had been a surprise; this was not. This time, Camacho had a chance to speak against mixing politics and religion, and he urged the prospective marchers not to carry the standard of the Virgin or the Star of David (which Chavez had also suggested). Nor did he want the marchers to carry American, Mexican, or Philippine flags. The workers had to rely on themselves, he said, so they should carry only their own flags and banners. A few others—rank-and-file strikers and picket line stalwarts such as Margarita Muñoz, Jorge Zaragosa, and Manuel Camacho (no relation to Epifanio)—made similar remarks, but without Camacho's flair. Chavez was forced to respond. The pilgrimage, he argued, was a way of making the association attractive to the mostly Catholic farm workers. It would also generate moral and financial support. The question was put to a vote. A bemused Dolores Huerta later said: "We put the virgin to a motion, and virginity won."[4]

After the meeting, Chavez sought Camacho out. "He consoled me," Camacho said, "telling me that if the workers thought that the growers were going to take the Virgin away from them, they would make a revolution to protect her, and so I would have the revolution I wanted." Meanwhile, to student radicals who opposed the idea, Chavez defended the Virgin in the name of organizing. He explained the long tradition of Catholic Social Action and the Virgin's symbolism as protector of the poor and oppressed in Mexico, noting that her standard had been carried into battle by Zapata's troops. And, yes, he acknowledged, trade union leaders would never use the Virgin in this way, but that was only a measure of their narrowness, their focus on nickels and dimes rather than on workers as full, whole people. Besides, he said, his method of organizing was going to win, whereas trade union tactics in the fields had only lost.[5]

The white New Leftists were in no position to argue, and besides, Marshall Ganz, the highest-placed among them, was sympathetic to the idea. Nor did Camacho try to organize against the Virgin. He was no organizer. He was an orator and a fighter. He did not follow up his big, well-received speeches with the small conversations necessary to win over doubters. Thus, while Cesar was carefully explaining his position, no one contested him. Moreover, Chavez's main argument was persuasive: the majority of farm workers would, at the very least, not be offended by the religious character of the march. The leadership's decision held; the march became a pilgrimage.

In the march's early planning stages, Sacramento had been the fourth suggested destination. Washington and New York were too far; San Francisco was a possibility because both Schenley and DiGiorgio had corporate offices there. But Chavez favored the state capital because it would concentrate pressure on Governor Pat Brown. He compared his choice to a combination shot in pool: the NFWA marchers could more effectively propel Brown into the growers than hit the growers directly.

This kind of maneuvering in state Democratic politics was nothing new for the NFWA leadership. Now, via Walter Reuther, they were about to engage in national Democratic Party politics as well. While in Delano, Reuther had realized that Chavez and the NFWA could fit into his own national strategy, and when he returned to Detroit he quickly did what he could to bring Chavez into his extensive network of political contacts and influence. Working with his aide Jack Conway, he contacted a liberal Democratic senator, Harrison Williams Jr. of Pennsylvania, and urged him to schedule hearings in California of his Senate Subcommittee on Migratory Labor. Williams, a longtime advocate of extending the benefits of the National Labor Relations Act to farm workers, set hearings for mid-March, in Sacramento, Visalia, and Delano. The timing was perfect. The day after the hearings closed in Delano could be the first day of the pilgrimage.

Reuther and Conway next went after the junior senator from New York, who was also on the Migratory Labor Subcommittee but who so far had shown no particular interest in farm workers. Robert Kennedy was then in the first stages of cobbling together a coalition for what, at the time, looked like an almost impossible task: recapturing control of the Democratic Party from President Lyndon Johnson. (Friends reported that "The Impossible Dream," the theme song from The Man from La Mancha, was his current favorite song, and he played it over and over in his New York apartment.)

So far, Kennedy's focus had been on the problems of black Americans and disaffected youths, although he was beginning to have some doubts about U.S. policy in Vietnam and could see the possibilities of staking out a position on the war different from Johnson's. Despite his well-publicized meetings with outsiders such as the New Left strategist Tom Hayden, the peace and civil rights activist Staughton Lynd, the poet Allen Ginsberg, and various black militants, Kennedy knew that no strategy would work unless he also had the allegiance of some Democratic Party insiders. Perhaps his greatest liability inside the party was the near-universal antipathy that the AFL-CIO felt toward him for his work on the McClellan Committee investigating labor and organized crime in the late fifties. In his relentless interrogations during the hearings, Kennedy not only had hounded George Beck and Jimmy Hoffa of the Teamsters but had insulted many other union bosses. Reuther was the only important national labor leader whom he could consider part of his circle, perhaps the only one who didn't pointedly dislike him. After Reuther and Conway asked Kennedy to go to California with the Williams Committee, he told his aide Peter Edelman, "If Walter Reuther and Jack Conway want me to do it, I suppose I'll do it." But he was not enthusiastic. He skipped the hearings in Sacramento and Visalia, and flew straight to Delano. On the plane, he rhetorically asked Edelman, "Why am I dragging my ass all the way out to California?"[6]

Once the hearings began, however, it didn't take Bobby Kennedy long to size up the historic opportunity that Walter Reuther had dropped in his lap. Bishop Hugh Donohue of Stockton, representing California's seven Roman Catholic bishops, testified that the bishops now supported the inclusion of farm workers in the National Labor Relations Act. Their formal statement made extensive use of Catholic social doctrine and was a significant departure from the church hierarchy's neutrality on the grape strike. Before that, only a few maverick priests had supported the strike— most of the priests from Central Valley parishes supported the growers, who were major contributors to their churches. The official sanction of the bishops was a splendid introduction to the several farm workers who testi-fied about the harsh conditions of their lives. The growers' only counter was a group that claimed to be the "authentic" voice of the farm workers but that, under Kennedy's skillful cross-examination, was revealed to be nothing more than an organization of labor contractors. When Sheriff LeRoy Gallen of Kern County explained to Kennedy that to avoid violence he had arrested the peaceful NFWA strikers rather than the replacement workers who had threatened to "cut their hearts out," the incredulous Bobby suggested that the sheriff use the lunch recess to "read the Constitution of the United States." The sheriff, the same law enforcement hero of the suppression of farm worker strikes in the 1930s, was now, in the 1960s, treated to howls of derisive farm worker laughter.

During his lunch break, Bobby met Cesar in the parking lot. The two had huddled a couple of times during the Viva Kennedy campaign of 1960, in which the CSO registered Mexican American voters before Jack's election. But this meeting in Delano became raw material in the saga of the post-Jack transformation of Bobby Kennedy. Evan Thomas of *Newsweek*, relying on Peter Edelman, reported on the meeting:

"Kennedy sized up Chavez, a gentle, soft-spoken man about his own age—at once steely and beatific—who had been fighting wealthy farmers for fifteen years. 'Time stopped,' recalled Edelman. 'The chemistry was instant.' Each man immediately admired the other, saw in each other the same qualities of suffering and pride. Chavez had never seen such honest anger in a white public official."[7]

Stopped time and instant chemistry: Edelman told Thomas this parking lot story more than thirty years after the fact, but even allowing for the exaggeration of memory and the excess of metaphor, Chavez and Kennedy had good reason to take a liking to each other. For Chavez, Kennedy was a perfect friend in high places, and when Bobby left Delano, Cesar had the senator's private phone number in his pocket. For Kennedy, Chavez was a perfect vehicle through which he could soften his antilabor reputation, and do so without going through his enemies at the AFL-CIO. But they shared more than political self-interest. They shared Catholicism, not a rarified, intellectual Catholicism, but the more devotional, liturgical Catholicism of Kennedy's mother and Chavez's grandmother. They also had enemies in common: Kennedy's early career had been made fighting Communists and corrupt labor officials; Chavez's politics was consciously designed as an alternative to Communism and business unionism. Although embraced by liberal America, they both had a certain disdain for the liberal failure to acknowledge the realities of political power. Kennedy openly scorned what he considered ineffectual Stevensonian liberalism; Chavez was quieter but had a similarly unabashed willingness to seek and wield power in the name of his mild Christian ideals.[8]

If time did seem to slow down as Cesar and Bobby felt the shock of mutual recognition, it is just as likely that what they sensed in each other was a mixture of idealism and delight in power. By 1966, Bobby's dual nature was well developed and widely known: the man who would heal the country, who promised to reconcile white and black, rich and poor, old and young, was also a ruthless prosecutor who trampled over anyone who stood between the Kennedys and power. In 1966, Cesar's dual nature was less developed and hardly understood by anyone, but many of those close to him would eventually learn that the saintly farm worker leader had a darker side, too, and was capable of vindictive attacks on anyone who made his or her way onto his own list of personal and political enemies.

★   ★   ★

After the hearings, Kennedy visited the picket lines, talked to NFWA enthusiasts at a jammed Filipino Hall, and left town. The national press, in Delano to cover the hearings, stayed to cover the beginning of the pilgrimage the next day. To the newsmen's satisfaction, Chavez easily maneuvered Delano's police chief into displaying his hostility to the peaceful marchers. Rather than give in to the chief's demand that the pilgrims get a permit to march through town, Chavez had agreed that they would take another route. But on the day itself, Cesar led about a hundred marchers straight down Delano's main street. When they were stopped by a line of Delano police, some fell to their knees and prayed. It took the startled chief about an hour to realize how badly he had been snookered, which was plenty of time for the newsmen to get their photographs, and for the pilgrimage to get off to a well-publicized start.[9]

At the head of the line was the banner of the Virgin, carried by Manuel Vazquez, one of the few Mexican strikers who was a member of the Agricultural Workers Organizing Committee rather than the National Farm Workers Association. Vasquez was marching in defiance of Al Green, who had formally forbidden his members from joining the pilgrimage, complaining in private to Chavez that the strike was "a trade union dispute, not a civil rights movement or a religious crusade."[10] Nevertheless, not just Vasquez but AWOC leaders Larry Itliong and Philip Vera Cruz, as well as a few AWOC old-timers and some young Filipino militants, including Rudy Reyes and his friends, had simply ignored Green's orders. But most of the people who left Delano that first day were male Mexican and Mexican American strikers, carrying the stridently red and black thunderbird flags of the NFWA, although a few people had reluctantly agreed to carry the more sedate "Boycott Schenley" signs. One man carried a large wooden cross, another a Star of David, and one hoisted an oversized photograph of Emiliano Zapata. Once on the road, the pilgrims either walked together in small groups or spread out single file, their flags and banners making a dramatic silhouette against the blue and cloudless Central Valley sky. A small fleet of cars and trucks followed: a lunch wagon, a flatbed truck for evening rallies, various vehicles to carry supplies or give rides to the sick, injured, or exhausted, a press truck, and finally, a portable toilet nicknamed "The Mayflower."

One of the goals of the march was to make or renew contact with farm workers along the way—to urge them not to scab on the strike, inform them about the association, and secure their pledges not to buy Schenley liquors. The pilgrimage did not go straight up Highway 99 from Delano, but rather headed east for stopovers in the small farm-worker towns of Ducor, Porterville, Farmersville, Visalia, and Parlier, before returning to 99 just south of Fresno. Young academic, Jarold Brown, reported later in his Ph.D. thesis that a NFWA picket captain gave him the following explanation of how the route had been chosen:

Chavez asked two Anglos to plan the route of the march and they set it up for us to go straight up 99 so that everyone could see us. Chavez kidded them that that was no way to reach the people and he said that we had to go through all the small farm worker towns and ask the people there to give us food and a place to sleep. With just a few days left, we changed the route to go through fifty-three farm worker towns and sent organizers ahead to tell people we were coming.[11]

It is an interesting story, especially because Brown's thesis is fairly reliable on most matters, and he lists this account as one of the standard tales of the strike, "told at union meetings, repeated to supporters, and passed on as folklore to new strikers and volunteers who joined UFWOC." It is true that at the time of the pilgrimage, there were many intimations of the coming differences between Mexicans and Anglos inside the NFWA: the militants around Camacho, and many other Mexican strikers, complained that whites were given too much authority on the picket lines; some of the Mexican women were upset because their boyfriends, husbands, and sons were cavorting with young, white "free-love" volunteers; and a few Mexican rank and filers thought that Chavez was taking too much advice from the various white men who surrounded him. But serious brown/white antagonism inside the UFW wouldn't become prominent until some ten years later and wouldn't prove decisively important until four years after that. Moreover, the supposed source of the story, Chavez himself, was in 1966 especially careful to make the NFWA racially and culturally inclusive, and even if the story of how the route was chosen were true, Chavez would not be likely to repeat it—even as a joke—to a NFWA picket captain.[12]

The particular picket captain who reported the story is not named by Brown; he might well have been one of the militants who was upset about white authority on the picket lines, who simply attributed the story to Chavez to give it more weight. The two Anglos named in the story probably were the SNCC field secretaries, Marshall Ganz and Terry Cannon, as they were the two Anglos most involved in the pilgrimage. Ganz vaguely remembers talking over the route of the pilgrimage with Chavez, Cannon, and others, but doesn't remember anything about Chavez changing the plans.[13] Terry Cannon, the press secretary for the pilgrimage, has a very clear memory of how the route was decided. He had come to Delano with the wave of supporters the summer before, after working with with SNCC in Mississippi. Cannnon says that Chavez didn't change the route; the Highway patrol did.

One thing that really helped was the CHP forced us off of Highway 99. Originally we had planned to go straight up 99, from Delano to Sacramento. They said that it would be too dangerous between Delano and Fresno, where the big trucks rushed by on a two-lane road. They ordered us to take the less traveled roads to the east, and that took us through all those small towns. And the rallies in the small towns were nothing short of beautiful. They transformed the march into an epic event.[14]

Cannon doesn't know where the other story about Chavez changing the route might have come from. He was mostly oblivious to the hostility toward whites among some of the early strikers. To him, race relations in the NFWA were a welcome relief after what he had just gone through in SNCC: "At our best, we felt, isn't it nice to be welcome—at our worst, we felt, what a relief to be helping people who are grateful."[15]

Whether the result of a lucky order from the Highway Patrol or another example of Chavez's organizing genius, the pilgrimage through the small towns on the eastern side of the valley could hardly have been more successful. Typically, people greeted the marchers as they approached a new town and accompanied them into their communities. Occasionally the night rallies were preceded by spontaneous candlelit marches through farm worker barrios, as the pilgrims and their new friends urged people to come out and join them. When the festivities closed, volunteers took the pilgrims into their homes, where there was often food and drink, more talk and celebration, and a place to sleep. In the morning, after Mass, locals often walked along as the march left town, and some risked angering their bosses by carrying the lead banners. Twenty-five days of walking, twenty-five nights of celebration.

The march was not unprecedented. In December of 1931, the California Communist Party had organized a "hunger march" from San Diego to San Francisco, with caravans passing through two dozen farm worker communities and encampments, rousing people to come to the rallies that were held in town plazas or rented halls. Orators speaking in English, Spanish, Japanese, Tagalog, and Chinese read from the Communist Party program, urged people to join the unemployed councils, and demanded immediate welfare relief. The CP's *Western Worker* reported that hundreds of people attended the small-town rallies, and the *San Francisco Chronicle* reported that 2,000 marched past Governor James Rolph in San Francisco. Many of the same people who joined the rural unemployed councils also became prime movers in the strike wave that swept through the California fields a year and a half later.[16]

Separated by thirty-five years, the two marches could not be confused with each other. Although they passed through some of the same towns, little but the names was unchanged by 1966. In the early thirties, the majority of farm workers were Mexicans, but the *colonias* were only a generation old, just digging in, and were ignored by local authorities. Such communities could neither physically harbor nor politically protect the marchers, who were sometimes prevented from entering the city limits by local and state police, and were once dispersed by firemen using a high-pressure water hose. The 1931 hunger march was more a military maneuver through enemy territory than a pilgrimage through one's own land.

The NFWA pilgrims did have a battle plan: The Plan of Delano. After the Carpenteria retreat, Chavez had asked Luis Valdez to write an NFWA program that he could announce on the pilgrimage. Chavez warned Valdez not to make it too bold, to keep it simple and low-key. While Luis was at it, his friend Eleazar Risco, a radical Cuban American NFWA volunteer who often hung out with the Teatro, came by, rifled through his duffel bag, and to Valdez 's wonderment, pulled out the original Zapatista Plan de Ayala: "I'm sitting there writing the Plan of Delano and he's got the Plan de Ayala . . . So he said 'What about this?' and I said, 'This is perfect, let's redo it.' "[17]

The document they produced skillfully captured the revolutionary impulse of the original:

> Our sweat and our blood have fallen on this land to make other men rich . . . The farm worker has been abandoned to his own fate—without representation, without power—subject to the mercy and caprice of the rancher . . . We are tired of words, of betrayals, of indifference . . . We are sons of the Mexican Revolution, a revolution of the poor seeking bread and justice. Our revolution will not be armed, but we want the existing social order to dissolve; we want a new social order . . . The time has come for the liberation of the poor farm worker.[18]

But Valdez was careful to combine this revolutionary cry for "liberation" and a "new social order" with the NFWA's political program as outlined for him by Chavez. The Plan of Delano called for farm workers "to be equal with all working men in the nation" under state and federal labor law, and to receive "a just wage and better working conditions." It appealed for the "support of all political groups and the protection of the government." And it stressed the importance of suffering, penance, and the guiding hand of the Virgin of Guadalupe, while also including a signature NFWA quote from Pope Leo XIII.

Bill Esher was at the small meeting when Valdez presented the draft to Chavez. He remembers that Cesar didn't like it, that he felt it was bombastic, too full of big promises, not the simple, straightforward plan that he had asked for. "He was angry, but he didn't make any changes."[19] Rather, he proposed that Luis read the plan at rallies and then he, Chavez, would speak later in his own quiet manner. That was fine with Valdez, who took an actor's delight in the opportunity to read his manifesto. On the pilgrimage, his dramatic night-time readings—in the sanctity of a church, in a large meeting hall, or under outdoor floodlights—became the highlight of the rallies, as the assembled farm workers responded not to the details of the program but to Valdez's impassioned call for their liberation.

The first stop on the pilgrimage was Ducor, eighteen miles from Delano.

The pilgrims had been unprepared to walk that far. Valdez was worried: "It was real bad for all of us because we were working so hard right up to the day of the march, and no one had time to rest . . . and ten to twelve miles out, everybody was dragging." Nor had the advance team been able to put together much of a welcoming committee. "There was a house that this lady had offered, a little shack in the middle of this neighborhood, by some fields. And that's where Cesar went in. And so did as many of us that could get into this little house, and we sat around and tried to get off our feet. And we all took our shoes off. We had to deal with the blisters and the unbelievable thought that we still had three hundred miles to go . . . We all thought, I don't know how we are going to make this; this is ridiculous." Valdez read the Plan of Delano to a scant audience from the steps of the woman's shack. Most people slept on her lawn. The morning came too soon.[20]

The next stop was Porterville, where former residents Gilbert Padilla, Jim Drake, and David Havens had been the advance team. There the pilgrims were greeted with a large potluck dinner at Murray Park before going to the Eagles Hall for the rally. The Plan of Delano was heartily cheered. San Francisco's Archbishop Joseph McCucken sent a message that he supported the pilgrimage and was delegating various Catholic officials to join the marchers. There were enough Porterville hosts so that all of the marchers were able to sleep in beds. In the morning, on their way out of town, the marchers took lemonade from a large silver punch bowl that a supporter had placed on a table in her front yard. Feet still hurt—Chavez and several others with bad blisters or strained muscles rode part of the way in cars—but spirits rose. That night, in Lindsay, Chavez announced that one of McCucken's representatives had brought him a gift from the archbishop: a rosary that had belonged to Pope Pius XII.

The night rallies were showcases for the Teatro Campesino. Valdez and Lira had hustled to get ready. They needed a flatbed truck for the towns where Manuel Chavez and Marshall Ganz had not been able to secure a hall. They needed better lights and a better sound system. Once the actors were forced to be on stage night after night, their performances improved. Early on, one of the lead actors got into a fight with another marcher and had to be taken to the hospital. Felipe Cantú, who until then had had a minor part, took over a lead role; he was an immediate success, and the other actors got better working around him. Lira, who never underestimated the role of Luis Valdez as the director, cofounder, and author of the Teatro's *actos*, nevertheless felt that it wasn't until the march, when Cantú became the lead actor, that the Teatro finally coalesced.

The Teatro's role in the pilgrimage was magnified by the content of one of its *actos*, *Governor Brown*, which played off an issue of the march. Before the pilgrims set out, Chavez had said that they hoped to present a petition to Governor Brown on Easter Sunday in Sacramento. Initially, Brown did not respond. He was in a fix: Ronald Reagan was running against him and threatening to take away the votes of the traditionally Democratic growers; at the same time, Brown couldn't afford to alienate his liberal support, all of which was becoming rapidly pro-worker and antigrower. Brown's first statement explained that he could not meet the marchers because he would be away on Easter. As the pilgrimage gained strength, he offered to meet the pilgrims during the march. When Chavez, feeling his increasing power, turned that down, Brown offered a private meeting with a delegation of farm workers in Sacramento the day after Easter. Chavez's answer: Easter Sunday or nothing. Brown wavered but finally said no. He would spend Easter, as planned, in Palm Springs with Frank Sinatra.

Valdez played it perfectly. He opened the performance alone on stage, with cigar and dark glasses and a sign around his neck identifying him as the grower DiGiorgio. To a series of boos, whistles, and hisses he lectured and threatened the crowd. Then he announced that his old buddy Governor Brown was going to speak to them in Spanish that very night, and just as he said that a car with a siren blaring appeared at the back of the audience and forced its way to the foot of the stage. Governor Brown was pulled out of the car by his aides, who pushed him onto the flatbed truck and told him just to say, "*No huelga.*" When Brown first spoke to the crowd his Spanish was terrible, but then as he went along it got better, and finally it got so good that, in the Teatro's characteristic fashion, he turned into a Mexican farm worker, and had to be dragged off the stage shouting, "*Huelga! Huelga!*"

The audiences loved it, and shouted for more. Two more *actos* followed, one featuring Cantú as a raisin. By the time the pilgrims reached Sacramento the Teatro had played before thousands. Newsmen had seen it, and television cameras had recorded it. Some Bay Area college students who visited the march and watched the performance decided to invite the troupe to their campuses. The Teatro hired two professional agents and began touring soon after the pilgrimage was over. Marching to Sacramento, the Teatro Campesino had become a theater company.

Jorge Garcia was a senior at Fresno State College in 1966, one of only sixty-five students with a Spanish surname in that school of 14,000. He was on his way to becoming a teacher, a successful Mexican American, when the pilgrimage came through town. Both of his parents were farm workers in Dinuba, and he had spent a good part of his youth in the fields, working with his family in the orchards and vineyards. Getting to college had required hard work. To do well in school, he had focused so intently on his English (with the help and support of his parents but the disapproval of his grandparents) that he began to lose his Spanish. After high school, he went to a seminary in Fresno, then to a community college, and finally Fresno State. Once there, he could say goodbye to the fields.

Or so he thought. "I went to the rally, and it changed my life. It was like looking in the mirror and seeing the rest of myself, the part that I had left behind in my struggle to get out of the fields. I thought college was a ticket to paradise. I realized then that I couldn't be in paradise unless I could be there as a whole person. And that meant helping farm workers."[21]

Jorge Garcia and thousands of Mexican American students like him entered politics as supporters of Cesar Chavez and the farm worker movement. Luis Valdez captured their collective sentiment and foretold their trajectory in an article for *Ramparts*, published soon after the pilgrimage ended. Still high on the triumphant march, Valdez predicted the future using the past tense. "Under the name of *huelga*, we had created a Mexican American *patria*, and Cesar Chavez was our first *Presidente*."[22] Within the next two years the new Mexican American *patria* would acquire a mythical territory, Aztlan, and its inhabitants a new name, Chicanos. Cesar Chavez would become, if not the formal president, a combination hero and godfather to the new Chicano people.

The Mexican American college students who created the idea of the Chicano Nation in the late 1960s and early '70s, used the farm worker movement to make sense of their own journey. Over the next few years they would set up student organizations whose first order of business was to help the farm workers whom they had either literally or figuratively left behind. They would visit Delano, bringing money, clothes, and food; they would picket grocery stores that handled scab grapes; they would demand that their schools begin to teach farm worker history. To create a new identity, they needed to reconstruct their connection to their real or imagined past. Through acts of solidarity with struggling farm workers, they could maintain their distance from the professional world they were about to enter, and declare themselves still part of the working-class Indio-*raza* they were about to leave. They were no longer aspiring Mexican Americans with the ambivalence the double-barreled term implied. They took a derisory word, *chicano*, which meant a low-caste Mexican living north of the border, and made it a term of pride.

Never abandoning farm worker solidarity, the new Chicano movement next sought to make a place for themselves and their history in colleges and universities. Inspired by radical black students, they fought for Chicano Studies or, together with African American and Asian American students, for Third World Studies. They pressured campus administrators to admit more people like them to college and provide financial support. They tried to construct ties to various barrio groups and organizations, so that they could use their own education to serve their old communities. Many of them opposed the war in Vietnam, and through the antiwar movement came to identify with the national and international left. They fought in defense of undocumented workers and called for open borders. And some rejected the American two-party electoral system and made various attempts to set up independent political parties.

Cesar Chavez would remain a hero to these students, but he was not one of them. He was a child of the Depression and a veteran of World War II, the two great events that had shaped the previous Mexican American generation. He was a lifelong Democrat who opposed all attempts at third-party politics. He was not a Chicano nationalist: he was dubious about the celebration of Aztlan, and he opposed open borders. Certainly, his rejection of Chicano nationalism was politically convenient, even necessary. In the late 1960s, while the Chicano movement was being born, Chavez was building a wide, diverse coalition of grape boycotters, and the Chicano students were only one part of it. Chavez couldn't afford to be a separatist if he wanted to hold together a coalition that included trade unions, the Democratic Party, churches, and antipesticide consumers. But his opposition to Chicano nationalism was not just a matter of convenience. The mature Chavez—he was thirty-nine in 1966—did not need an exclusive, militant nationalism. He was not anxious about his own identity; he appreciated other cultures and ways of life. He was a serious Catholic who sometimes wore a mezuzah around his neck, a private practice he began well before liberal Jews became an important part of his coalition.

But Chavez's differences with Chicano students did not make him any less their hero. He and the farm workers remained central to the Chicano movement, as thousands of young people discovered, each in turn, what Jorge Garcia had first learned when he went to the pilgrims' rally in Fresno: they had to help farm workers in order to make themselves whole. And Luis Valdez, among the first to make this journey out of the fields and then come back to join the farm worker struggle, remarkably understood much of this as it was happening. His *Ramparts* article was clear: the farm worker *raza* could provide a model for the acculturated Mexican Americans of the cities, people he called the "ex-*raza* . . . more concerned with status, money and bad breath than with their ultimate destiny." Rather than falling into the "Great Gringo Melting Pot," the new professionals should strive for a new *patria* that would preserve the cultural and national identity of the *raza*. Reach back a helping hand to your farm-worker mothers and fathers, he argued, and you will begin to free yourself from the gringo society that has "no depth, no faith . . . no soul, no mariachi, no chili sauce, no *pulque*, no mysticism, no *chingaderas*."

Valdez had no doubts as to who would lead this new *patria*: "Here was Chavez, burning with a patient fire, poor like us, dark like us, talking quietly, moving people to talk about their problems, attacking the little problems first, and suggesting, always suggesting—never more than that— solutions that seemed attainable. We didn't know it until we met him, but he was the leader we had been waiting for."[23] Luis Valdez had found a homegrown hero. He had no more need for Fidel Castro.

As the blisters became calluses, and the farm workers made their way up the Central Valley, their pilgrimage became a political death march for the AWOC president, Al Green. His opposition to the pilgrimage became the last in a long series of mistakes. He had fired most of AWOC's experienced organizers, dismissed the energetic student volunteers, tried to bring farm workers into the AWOC by organizing labor contractors. He ignored the early overtures of the NFWA, given the Delano strike up for lost when the strikers had not been able to stop grape picking, and attacked the NFWA for turning a union fight into a civil rights crusade. The success of the pilgrimage proved him wrong; the visible disobedience of his staff and the rank-and-filers on the march exposed his weakness. Wrong and weak: a bad combination anywhere; in union politics, a death sentence.

The political execution of a union official, although sometimes swift, is often an oblique, mysterious process, reflecting ornate considerations of loyalty, territory, and ideology, set amid a constantly shifting pattern of opportunistic alliances and semipermanent rivalries. What made Al Greene's demise unusual was that he fell largely because of the intervention of actual workers. The pilgrims demonstrated that the NFWA could mobilize a couple of hundred people to take on almost any task, and those loyalists were backed by a larger community of farm workers. Those truths shattered the baroque political calculations of the labor officials who had been coming around the fields ever since the farm worker strike wave of the early sixties.

The immediate instrument of Green's demise was Bill Kircher, the new director of organizing of the AFL-CIO, whose first assignment from George Meany was to untangle the farm labor mess in California. Meany had already shut down AWOC once for being too militant and then restarted it with the conservative Green in command. But when the end of the Bracero Program proved more a spur than a bridle to the farm worker movement, he worried that his man Green might lose out to any one of a whole string of Meany rivals: his longtime adversary, Walter Reuther; his enemy at the head of the ILWU, Harry Bridges; or his aggressive opponent at the head of the Teamsters Union, Jimmy Hoffa. Meany was particularly worried about Reuther, after whose Delano visit Meany complained that "he [Reuther] was there for one day and got six years of publicity."[24]

Bill Kircher, at fifty-one a veteran of anti-Reuther intrigue, was a good choice to protect the AFL-CIO's hoped-for franchise among farm workers. He had risen from the shop floor of a General Electric defense plant to become a medium-rung UAW official, but had lost his bid to high-level office when he opposed the Reuther forces in 1946. Now, the 200-pound, tough-talking, seasoned infighter was being sent to do battle once again with Reuther's man on the West Coast, Paul Schrade, who already had spent a good deal of time helping the NFWA and was sympathetic to its civil rights concerns.[25]

Kircher, still trying to decide between Green and Chavez, was not with the pilgrims when they left Delano; he was still in Washington. But on the fifth day of the pilgrimage, he read about it in the *New York Times*. "Implicit in the strike, and in the organizational structure of the march, the *Times* reported, "is the threat of a general farm labor strike, depending on the success of a contemplated one- or two-day work stoppage in the central valley this spring or summer." Encouraged by the turnouts, Chavez announced at the rally in the town of Cutler that formal strike committees were being organized in the small towns along the route of the march. When the pilgrimage swung back onto Highway 99 and hit Fresno (along with Bakersfield, one of the two queen cities of California agriculture) more than 1,000 people came to the Aztec Theater to greet the astounded pilgrims. As the Plan of Delano had predicted, the "movement was spreading like flames across a dry plain." Bill Kircher could feel the heat in Washington. He quickly put together a team, packed some old clothes, and flew to California.[26]

A march takes longer than a car ride, and Chavez had plenty of opportunity to "organize" the AFL-CIO director of organizing. It wasn't that hard. Kircher, carefully outfitted in his old clothes, marched along during the day and attended the rallies at night. He watched with the eyes of a veteran union official; seeing the march as an "organizing tool," its religious character did not upset him in the least. He was a Catholic who went "to Mass on a daily basis" when he could, he proudly told the *Fresno Bee* reporter Ronald Taylor, adding that "the strong, cultural, religious thing . . . was organizing people." Soon Kircher was a regular part of the rally agenda, assuring people that all the power of the AFL-CIO stood behind them.[27]

As the pilgrims walked and sang, back-room union machinations intensified: Meany versus Reuther; Kircher versus Schrade; Teamsters versus the AFL-CIO; ILWU versus the Teamsters; ILWU versus the AFL-CIO. To follow the details of the intrigues one would have to know who had done what to whom some twenty-five years ago in the back room of a union convention or in an obscure jurisdictional fight. These experienced infighters, whose maneuvers would make the College of Cardinals or members of some Politburo proud, did what they could to position themselves to catch the prize that Green was clumsily letting fall from his grasp. Some of the competing unionists were on the march. Paul Schrade and a small delegation of rank-and-file auto workers had been with the pilgrims since Delano. Schrade warned Chavez about the conservative George Meany, and reminded him that Meany was Kircher's boss. He urged Chavez to keep the NFWA independent and promised even more political and financial support from the United Automobile Workers. The International Longshore and Warehouse Union was represented on the pilgrimage by a group of rank-and-filers who had started a Five Dollars a Month Club, and presented the NFWA with a check at the rally in Manteca, pledging other checks until the strike was won. This rank-and-file committee reported back directly to Harry Bridges, the Australian American ILWU leader, who was uneasy about Chavez's religious views but still interested in the possibility that the NFWA could become a farm worker division of the ILWU. Top Teamsters officials stayed away from the pilgrimage until the final rally in Sacramento, but various locals were intermittently refusing to handle scab grapes and hoping either that they could eventually win farm worker contracts through their power in trucking and food processing or that Chavez might join the Teamsters. All of these players were mutually suspicious, trying to make contact with informers in one another's camps so that they could keep track of what everybody else was doing.[28]

Kircher came on strong. He offered the blister-tormented, sore-muscled Chavez a good night's sleep at a motel, and was surprised when Chavez accepted. In the comfort of a couple of motel nights, Kircher pleaded the case for NFWA affiliation with the AFL-CIO. Kircher's pleading was more proof of how much the pilgrimage had already increased the NFWA's power, and Chavez didn't have to mince words. Before they could even talk about affiliation, he asked Kircher, what about Green? How could the director of organizing of the AFL-CIO claim to be a friend of the NFWA while he did nothing about the hostile actions of his subordinate Green? But Green was no great concern to Kircher; he had already decided to sacrifice him and was just awaiting the opportunity.

Green stumbled blindly before his executioner. He had tried to make up for his misstep on the march by publicly changing his position on its second day, promising to send a pickup truck, station wagon, and something he called a "church wagon" to accompany the marchers. But inside labor officialdom, he continued attacking the NFWA for its reliance on ministers and students. When that semisecret lobbying was exposed by a local newspaper in Turlock (which Manuel Chavez, following Cesar Chavez's instructions, passed along to Kircher), Green was as good as gone.

But Kircher had one last move to make before delivering the blow. He called a meeting with Green and members of his staff in Stockton. Rather than tell them they were about to be fired, he told them that they had one chance to save their jobs. "The march reaches Modesto tomorrow, and I'm going to judge how goddamn important you guys are on the basis of how many AFL-CIO unions you turn out to welcome the farm workers as they come marching in." Green did his best. The next day, when the marchers reached Modesto, Kircher was delighted with himself. "They were lined up—guys with signs—and the funny part was, in the main, guys who had no understanding of what they were doing. They were sort of like paid pickets. 'Asbestos Workers Local 1215, Viva La Huelga!' 'Glaziers Union Local 79, Viva La Causa!' Bricklayers, carpenters, painters, all of them."

After the pilgrimage, Kircher closed down the Stockton AWOC office and got rid of the staff that had carried out his orders. He left Green dangling for a while, then fired him.[29]

But Cesar Chavez was reluctant to enter the house of labor. He was not fooled by Kircher's old clothes; he didn't like the ostentatious lifestyle of most labor officials. He disagreed with their ideas about organizing, and he was worried that he and his association would have less independence as part of a larger union body. Nevertheless, he could see that by the logic of the grape strike, the NFWA was at least a would-be union. The confusion during the rose strike over whether the association even wanted to sign a contract was long past. NFWA leaflets no longer declared, "We are not a union." Although Chavez still called the NFWA an "association" and occasionally corrected newsmen and supporters who called it a union, the distinction seemed largely nostalgic. Chavez, who had set out to organize Bill Kircher had himself been organized by the old pro. Before the march was over, Chavez had decided that the association's best bet would be to become an AFL-CIO affiliate. He would have to make his way through the maze of labor politics, learn to deal with other union leaders who were simultaneously scheming against one another, competing for his allegiance and trying to figure out how to snatch farm worker jurisdiction away from him. But his own maneuvering during the pilgrimage indicated that he was up to the task—as long he could mobilize a large NFWA family, and could stand at the head of a farm worker movement.

Outside Lodi, the pilgrims gathered around the green press van to listen to an announcement from Press Secretary Terry Cannon. Standing on top of the van and speaking through a bullhorn, Cannon told the marchers that the Schenley Corporation had just signed a recognition agreement with the NFWA that would raise wages to $1.75 an hour and eliminate labor contractors. The pilgrims cheered; some wept. The Schenley boycott signs were triumphantly thrown in the air. When they came down, the pilgrims ripped up some of them, and turned others over and wrote "Boycott TreeSweet," a DiGiorgio label. The NFWA was no longer a would-be union; it had a contract.

This first contract came as a complete surprise to Cesar Chavez. He was so unprepared for Schenley's capitulation that he thought the company's first offer, which came via a phone call, was a prank and hung up. But three days after that phone call, Chavez had the agreement in his pocket. And a few days after that, almost everyone involved with the NFWA had a convincing analysis of how the contract had come to be. Years later, when historians got around to telling the story, Schenley's reasons for signing would seem so compelling that this first contract would take on an air of inevitability. It is a trick of time, a reminder that history is a record of relatively free and therefore unpredictable human action, but that the post-hoc telling of the tale tends to hide, in Nietzche's words, "the original note of action, need, and terror." As they marched to Sacramento, the pilgrims had no idea what was coming. They made their sacrifice with no guarantees; they walked into an unknown future.

The Schenley Corporation's willingness to sign a contract revealed a hitherto ignored division among the table grape growers. The vast majority of the grower-shippers were exclusively in the business of farming, with most of their land and capital tied up in the grape industry. But Schenley was a large conglomerate whose principal business was liquor. Table grapes represented less than 0.5 percent of its total corporate sales. With such a small stake in the world of Delano agribusiness, the corporation was unwilling to risk bad publicity to its corporate name just to maintain a united front with the other growers. One Delano grower, Jack Pandol, publicly charged that Schenley's "Eastern" board of directors had "sold out the Delano community." Privately, some others complained about the Eastern Jews who owned and operated the renegade corporation.[30]

But the anti-Semitic growers missed the main point: the primary role of the boycott. Schenley was explicit about why it signed. James Woolsey, a Schenley vice president, explained that since the company's 1965 harvest was the largest in the history of the Delano ranch, and since the local managers had no difficulty securing workers, the company had originally concluded that "no labor dispute or strike even existed." Subsequently, however, "the entire world seemed to us to recognize the NFWA [as the representative of our employees]." The company received letters from more than forty states, mostly from "college students, members of religious organizations, and some unions, including the ILWU and the United Auto Workers." The company was sensitive to this pressure, he explained, because it "relies heavily on advertising the high quality of its products." Moreover, all other Schenley products had carried a union label since 1941, and the company had "sixty-two contracts with fifty-nine locals of sixty international unions." Woolsey explained that "even more damaging than any decline in our sales was the adverse publicity that accompanied the boycott and the NFWA organizing activities."[31]

Victory is never an orphan, and many stories of how the Schenley contract was won circulated in the NFWA family. Another hot cargo campaign seems to have helped. During the pilgrimage, Friends of SNCC and the NFWA put up a picket line at San Francisco's Julliard Alpha

Liquors, a major Northern California distributor of Schenley products. When that picket line was joined by San Francisco Teamsters, union employees of Julliard Alpha left work, and Teamster drivers refused to enter the warehouse. The left-wing journalist Sam Kushner, who had contacts inside union circles, said that it was this illegal picket line that drove Schenley to the negotiating table, and Woolsey included the San Francisco sympathy strike in his public explanation of why the company settled.[32]

Gilbert Padilla had his own explanation of the victory. Although Padilla marched for a few days, his main assignment during the pilgrimage was to continue to head up the boycott in Los Angeles. After a speaking engagement at a West LA Women's Democratic Club, a secretary gave him the phone number of her boss, whom Gilbert understood to be some official in a bartenders union. "The following day I called him. I figured, well, he's a bartender . . . maybe he will give us a drink or something." Blackie Levitt was in fact the head of Bartenders Local 284 of the Hotel and Restaurant Employees and Bartenders International Union. He invited Padilla to address a meeting and was so impressed that afterward he and the secretary concocted a plan to help the boycott. They wrote a memo instructing bartenders not to serve Schenley-owned or -distributed liquors. The secretary made sure the memo got onto the desk of a company vice president. In a few days Levitt called Padilla to report that Sidney Korshak, a seasoned "labor fixer" working for Schenley, had come to Levitt's office to complain about the illegal secondary boycott. Levitt invited Padilla over to meet Korshak. Gilbert was there when Korshak made a call to Lewis Rosenstiel, the seventy-five-year-old Schenley CEO. They reached him at the side of a pool in the Bahamas. Rosenstiel, who was unfamiliar with the whole dispute, didn't even know that Schenley owned table grape acreage. He told Korshak to sell the whole ranch. Korshak argued that they could get some good publicity by signing a contract with a farm workers union instead. Rosenstiel gave his approval. A few days later, Korshak called Chavez on the march and convinced him to come to Los Angeles to negotiate the contract.[33]

But Cesar's interpretation of the victory counted most of all. In the talks that Korshak arranged at his Beverly Hills mansion, Chavez was accompanied by Chris Hartmire, a few strikers who had at one time worked at Schenley, and Padilla. Also at the meeting were Bill Kircher, W. J. Bassett, an AFL-CIO official from LA County, Jerry Veracruz of a Los Angeles Teamsters local, and Jack Goldberger, a Teamsters attorney. Korshak was prepared to sign a contract for Schenley; at issue was who would sign for the workers. The AFL-CIO reps hoped that he would sign with AWOC, although Kircher envisioned an eventual AWOC-NFWA merger. The Teamsters, whose power in the meeting derived from their hot cargo actions, were willing to support the NFWA, as they still hoped that it would merge with them. The hostility between the Teamsters and the AFL–CIO was so great that Kircher refused to be in the same room with Veracruz and Goldberger. In the midst of the squabbling, Cesar retired to the billiards room to play pool. Korshak lost patience and told the other unionists: "You should be making love to me; I'm the company, I'm ready to sign a contract, and you guys can't get together! You get together, and when you do and make up your minds who's going to sign it, then I'll deal with you."

Chavez knew where his power lay. He came in from the billiards room and told Korshak, "There's no reason for me being here. You sign a contract with whomever you want, but the boycott stays on."

In Chavez's account, that was the turning point. Soon after, a compromise was reached. The contract would be with the NFWA, and the AFL–CIO would initial it as an "official observer." The main lesson couldn't have been more clear. A few years later, Chavez told Jacques Levy how they had won the contract: "It was the boycott."[34]

Just as the Schenley contract brought the boycott from the periphery to the center of the NFWA's strategic focus, the overall success of the *peregrinación* confirmed the compelling authority within the NFWA of the psychology and style of Catholic penance. The NFWA had always had a strong Catholic inclination, but the pilgrimage transformed an inclination into an essential. The pilgrims took a basic Catholic ritual, penance, and spun it into the thread that helped hold together their organization. The new thread still contained the basic strands of the original mystery— suffering as an exemplary, redemptive act—but now the pilgrims wove it into the fabric of their politics. Marching to Sacramento on bloodied feet, they connected contrition for their own sins to their hopes for social justice. It was a connection that would hold throughout UFW history.

In retrospect, incorporating penance into politics makes some sense. Within the Catholic tradition, penance is already a public act in the primarily private drama of redemption. The sinner confronts his or her transgressions, repents, and confesses to the priest, all in private. The priest imposes a series of external actions, penance, which express this internal repentance. When the steps are completed, the sinner is reconciled with God—until the next inevitable sin, which begins the drama again. The penance is not punishment; it is a public demonstration of the sinner's contrition. Without penance, this drama would be a private matter between the sinner, priest, and God. Public acts of penance show the rest of the believing world that the sinner is on the road to salvation.

Penance shown during the Lenten season lends itself even more easily to politics because it is not only public, it is collective, "a corporate action that involves the whole community."[35] For forty days before Easter Catholics collectively prepare themselves for the coming celebration of the Resurrection. That preparation—meant to purify souls and distance believers from sin—originally involved an imitation of Christ's journey, through fasting and a symbolic carrying of the cross. But by the mid-twentieth century in the United States, imitation had been largely replaced by meditation on the Passion, plus sorrow for one's own sins, and a self-selected, individual penance. Within popular Catholic practice, Lenten penance usually involved the performance of a distasteful deed or, more typically, the sacrifice of a legitimate pleasure—giving up something for Lent.

But how is penance connected to justice? The NFWA had a partial answer: just as Lenten penance is preparation for the Resurrection, it can also be preparation for a political struggle, a demonstration of the pilgrims' readiness for the required sacrifices. The Plan of Delano explained, "The penance we accept symbolizes the suffering we shall have in order to bring justice to these same towns, to this same valley. The Pilgrimage we make symbolizes the long historical road we have traveled in this valley alone, and the long road we have yet to travel, with much penance, in order to bring about the Revolution we need." For Chavez, the pilgrimage was more than a symbol. "This was an excellent way of training ourselves to endure the long, long struggle, which by this time had become evident," he told Levy. "So this was a penance more than anything else—and it was quite a penance, because there was an awful lot of suffering involved in the pilgrimage, a great deal of pain."[36]

On their way to Sacramento, however, the pilgrims also discovered that public penance itself can lead directly to power. Pain gave them moral authority in their fight against the growers. This last part was left mostly unsaid, neither articulated in the Plan of Delano nor explained by Chavez, but most of the pilgrims could feel it. As they suffered, their temporal authority grew, and their spirits soared. Enthusiastic farm workers welcomed them to their towns, high-level Catholic and Democratic Party officials joined them on the march, a powerful grower signed a contract. Chavez, most of all, could feel the connection between the shedding of his own blood and his growing power. His blisters were among the worst, his back hurt, he strained a muscle in his calf, he couldn't walk without a cane. "By the time we reached Richgrove, only about seven or eight miles from Delano, my right ankle was swollen like a melon, and the sole of my left foot was just one huge blister. Since this was a penitential walk, I refused to take any painkillers. By the time we got to Ducor I was running a temperature. I was so miserable, I thought I was going to die . . . [The next morning] my ankle was still swollen. But I marched all that day, about seventeen miles to Porterville. By then, my leg was swollen up to just below my knee, and my blisters were beginning to bleed."[37] A few days later, Chavez's personal authority had magnified many-fold. George

Meany's personal envoy was openly courting him; Governor Brown was scrambling to reach a mutually satisfactory accommodation; at the Schenley negotiations, Chavez, barely able to walk, held the strongest hand.

Penance turned out to be so politically effective that some—especially the conservative Catholic growers, but also a few secular NFWA activists and supporters—questioned its spiritual authenticity. Any outward demonstration of internal religious feeling is subject to doubt, and Chavez left himself open to suspicion because he had often defended the role of religious feeling and ritual in politics in terms of its political efficacy. The same argument he had used to win over the secular New Leftists inside the NFWA he used again on Bill Kircher during the pilgrimage:

> I'll never forget one night we were talking. It was toward the end of the march. He [Chavez] held his two hands in fists, like they were holding something, palms up, fingers closed. He looked at one closed hand and said, "Today we must have the Eagle and Our Lady of Guadalupe; when we get contracts we won't need Our Lady," and he opened one hand. It wasn't that he was taking advantage of the Church, it's as if he knew that to get from where the farm workers were to where they had to go, they needed help.[38]

But getting contracts was not a final victory, and there would never come a time when farm workers would no longer need divine help. Chavez maintained his hold on Our Lady, and the more he needed her, the more she strengthened her hold on him. That original need predated his politics. He had been making a Lenten penance since he was a child. The fact that it was politically useful did not make it less meaningful. Quite the opposite: its political utility only made it more genuinely felt.

Terry Cannon and Gilbert Padilla learned how serious Chavez was about Lent the first night of the march. Chavez had banned all alcohol on the pilgrimage, but after that first difficult day, Cannon and Padilla had gone to a Richgrove bar before bedding down. They figured the ban was a loose one, but after they had had a couple of beers, Chavez came into the bar looking for them. He was furious. People in leadership simply could not flout the rules. He threatened to remove Cannon as press secretary and ban Padilla from the march. "He was so anxious to keep the whole thing pure," Cannon remembered, "he really wanted a pilgrimage, a penance." At the same time Cannon could see the practicality of Chavez's concern. The march "was so fragile at the beginning, Chavez was so worried that it might not work, and if the pilgrims turned out to be a bunch of drunks we would have been sunk."[39]

Chavez's successful introduction of penance into politics is distinct from both Catholic Social Action, which preceded it, and Liberation Theology, which followed it. The pilgrims made Catholic ritual itself an instrument of political action. This attracted many devout Catholics who had a prior interest in politics—the *cursillista* movement was particularly active in the pilgrimage, and it was during the march that their song, "De Colores," became the unofficial NFWA anthem—but it went beyond what typical Catholic activists had done before. Leo XIII had argued that the exemplary behavior of the Catholic workers would win "the good will of the rich" and the "protection of the government," and something like that had happened during the pilgrimage, but what Leo meant by "exemplary behavior" was respect for private property and the practice of moderate tactics, not public penance as political art. Nor did the NFWA's penitential politics fit the mold of Liberation Theology, although the association's shift to a focus on social justice rather than redemption did foreshadow Liberation Theology's substitution of Christ the Liberator for Christ the Savior. Nevertheless, Liberation Theology does not emphasize the personal sins of the oppressed but rather sees humanity's sinfulness as embedded in unjust social structures. Penance, therefore, is not a common theme of the liberationists, who believe the poor have suffered quite enough already.

Some NFWA stalwarts held just such a view. While all could agree that farm workers were familiar with sacrifice and that the struggle ahead would require more of it, not all agreed that sacrifice in itself was a positive good, personally or politically. Epifanio Camacho and the people around him certainly did not believe in the virtue of self-inflicted pain. Rudy Reyes and other young Filipinos were trying to win as much as they could while suffering as little as possible. Even the *El Malcriado* team wavered. The first editorial about the pilgrimage declared, "The march will be a penitential march, public penance for the sins of the strikers, their own personal sins as well as their yielding perhaps to feelings of hatred and revenge in the strike itself." But soon Esher and Adair started having second thoughts. Adair was particularly concerned about the shift inside the NFWA from a spirit of mutual self-interest to the celebration of sacrifice. *El Malcriado*'s next issue described "the sufferings of the march" as "a penance for the sins of everyone—on both sides of this bitter fight."[40]

But that was a minority view. Chavez's logic was accepted by most. Angie Hernandez, Chavez's main walking companion on the pilgrimage and the daughter of one of the earliest NFWA activist couples, said later, "Some people had bloody feet, some would keep on walking and you'd see blood coming out of their shoes." Blistery, bleeding feet are not unknown to farm workers. Maria Saludado, who would soon travel the country for the boycott, often told NFWA supporters about the day that she, as a young girl, had been forced to work while her feet bled.[41] That externally imposed pain had led to nothing but her own tears and her father's humiliation. Now the pilgrims, marching to Sacramento on bleeding feet, were ennobled and toughened, and grew in moral authority.

On Easter Sunday morning, the pilgrims, camped at Our Lady of Grace School on a hill overlooking the Sacramento River, awoke to a gentle rain. The skies cleared for a while as they celebrated Easter Mass, lined up four abreast, and walked across the bridge to the state capitol. They were led by two men on horseback in full *charro* regalia, a large tapestry of Our Lady of Guadalupe, and a barefoot farm worker, Roberto Roman, carrying the large two-by-four cross that he had borne all the way from Delano. On the Sacramento side of the river, 5,000 more exultant supporters—students, trade unionists, Mexican Americans, *cursillistas*, a little boy playing a large saxophone, antidraft protesters—waited to join them for the last trek to the capitol steps.

The rain ceased, and the sun shone brightly during the benediction. Although the main metaphor was Catholic, the prayers were ecumenical. A rabbi made reference to the Israelites crossing the River Jordan. Protestant Chris Hartmire saw Camus' rebel walking among the pilgrims. Later, written commentaries on the march would go even further: John Gregory Dunne compared the last day of the pilgrimage to DeGaulle's triumphant return to Paris; veteran left writer Paul Jacobs saw in it the promise of a grand reconciliation among liberals, radicals, and ex-radicals, who, having failed to organize farm workers themselves, could now unite behind the indigenous leadership of Cesar Chavez, Dolores Huerta, and Gilbert Padilla.

In the final three-hour rally the whole unlikely coalition was given a full opportunity to display itself. The fifty-seven farm workers who had walked the entire way, *los originales*, sat in the place of honor on the stage. Gilbert Padilla was the master of ceremonies. Epifanio Camacho, Dolores Huerta, Augie Lira, and Chavez spoke for the NFWA. Unity was the word of the day. The schism among Western monotheists was put on hold as a long list of Catholic, Protestant, and Jewish leaders pledged their support. Competing union officials also temporarily put aside their differences: Bill Kircher, Louis Goldblatt of the ILWU, Jack Goldberger of the Teamsters, and Paul Schrade of the UAW all addressed the crowd, though not one another. The pilgrims and their supporters interrupted the speeches with various chants, verses of "De Colores," and excited *vivas*. They remained enthusiastic until the rain started to come down hard at the end of the day. After the rally, many walked over to Sacramento's Guadalupe Church, where there was one last candlelight service, followed by a big party featuring free beer and tequila provided by the Schenley Corporation.

The unity rally masked all manner of disagreements and some troublesome contradictions. But on Easter Sunday 1966, it did not matter that eventually the coalition would fall apart. That is not remarkable; most coalitions do. The striking truth was that Cesar Chavez, the quiet man who gave a modest speech on Sunday, was able to hold most of this coalition together for as long as he did. Long enough to force the entire California table grape industry to capitulate four years hence.

Democratic Delano

April to September '66

Old Highway 99 ran north–south, along the railroad tracks, separating farm worker Delano on the west from white Delano on the east. In the 1950s when the state expanded 99, the city fathers arranged to have the new highway run through the west side of town, scarring the farm worker neighborhoods while leaving undisturbed their own east Delano. But the dividing line between east and west remained the railroad tracks, the packing sheds that ran alongside them, and a string of farm worker restaurants and bars just off the old highway. One of the bars was People's. The farm workers who walked through its doors entered a long dark room that ran parallel to the tracks. There was a jukebox, a dance floor, a half dozen small tables and chairs, a dart board, and four pool tables, one of them for snooker. The bathrooms stank; the toilets often ran. When crowded, People's held about a hundred—dancing, drinking, talking, shooting and watching pool. In People's' prime, from 1966 to 1968, James Brown's "Papa's Got a Brand New Bag" and Marvin Gaye's "I Heard It Through the Grapevine" were frequently blasting from the jukebox. The Vicente Fernandez Rancheros were still available for a dime, but were not getting as much play as they once had. Mocha and Ann, the pro-union, lesbian proprietors had put Luis Valdez and Augie Lira's 45 "Huelga General" and "Picket Sign 45" in the box, but hardly anyone listened to them.

Mocha and Ann tended the bar and lived together in the back, but People's wasn't a gay bar. It was a farm worker bar where lesbians were welcome, as were a group of male cross-dressers who regularly came up from Bakersfield to dance with the surplus of single men. Before the strike a few prostitutes had come in, but when People's became the union's main recreational hangout, the prostitutes moved on to other bars where they could get more steady work. A few mildly antiunion regulars who stayed on as friendly foils joked that the bar girls couldn't stand all the free competition, referring to the many visiting female supporters whom the union crowd brought over to People's for dancing, drinking, and what might be called intercultural exchange. The bar was a ten-minute walk from the union hall and the Pink House, maybe five minutes from the Teatro Campesino's tortilla factory rehearsal space. Filipino Hall was even closer.

Pro-union farm workers and staffers were there every night of the week, but Friday night, after the weekly meeting at Filipino Hall, People's was packed and jumping. Farm worker and non-farm worker volunteers who had just received their weekly $5 stipend reassembled almost immediately at the bar, with the money to buy a drink or two but knowing full well that the out-of-town visitors, freshly inspired by the meeting, could always be counted on to buy the drinks. It was almost always a good party, much looser than a formal union function, but a regular, accepted part of union life. Cesar Chavez didn't come often, but when he did, he followed a routine. First, he played on the snooker table, disdaining the easier 8-ball games. His technique was solid, but what made him one of the best players in town was his strategic sense—at least according to Augie Lira, a skilled snooker player himself, who counts as one of his minor life achievements that he took a few games from Cesar Chavez. After his usual triumph at the snooker table, Chavez moved over to one of the tables next to the juke box, where he quietly joined whatever conversation was going on. He never drank at People's, and he usually left early. Chavez drank at private parties, and he and Helen were excellent dancers, but he did neither at People's.

Amid the drinking and the dancing and the pool, many people talked politics. All opinions were welcome, and the conversations were unscripted, a spirit completely different from the controlled discussions at Filipino Hall. Most of the talk was in good humor, but occasionally tempers flared, and every once in a while blows were thrown. (In one infamous incident, Epifanio Camacho beat up a scab in the toilet after the poor fellow attacked Camacho while he was peeing.) Fights were quickly broken up. Political disputes, however, were rarely stopped, even when the participants got angry at one another. People's was the place where scores of ordinary unionists argued out the issues, just as retreats were the occasions for the leadership to do the same. Sometimes, members of the executive board (or others who were in the circles close to Chavez) would come to People's to defend their own positions. The AFL-CIO's Bill Kircher, also an excellent snooker player, enjoyed himself at People's, happy to defend the prospect of an NFWA-AWOC merger against its many critics. Gilbert Padilla, Tony Orendain, and Manuel Chavez were also regulars when they were in town: Padilla, an expert storyteller, was able to do the different voices of everyone he was ridiculing, able to hold an astonishing amount of alcohol and still talk on; Orendain, a polemicist, would push his disagreements with the rest of the executive board; Manuel Chavez, a charming scoundrel, exaggerated his adventures, and sometimes embarrassed almost everyone in the cash-strapped crowd by flashing a roll.

People's was not exactly a center of opposition. A free speech zone, the folks at *El Malcriado* called it, and they, along with the Teatro crowd, helped set the tone for the free-wheeling debates. Although there was not a People's position on questions facing the union, there were certain tendencies that usually carried the night. Camacho, Rudy Reyes, and Tony Orendain were an informal triumvirate, united in their opposition to the Catholic Church, their belief in self-defense, and their displeasure at the union's emergent anti-immigrant policies. Their arguments were well received but not universally accepted. The only issue that almost everyone agreed on (at least while they were partying at People's) was that the union leadership should not go overboard in demanding too many sacrifices from the staff, strikers, and volunteers. *Los sacrificios* were routinely ridiculed at People's.

But People's was not a café debating society where detached observers made wry comments about passing events. Those arguing were part of the parade, inhabiting and improvising the parts they were talking about. A good conversation at People's could change what people did; conversations—the words people spoke—were themselves actions, human events in the improbable chains of causality that constituted the politics of the time. An evening at People's was exhilarating, not just because of the games, alcohol, music and flirtations, but because people were collectively shaping their own lives, highly conscious that they were making history.

And history was moving furiously fast. There was always too much to do, too many places to be at once, too many issues to consider, too many messes to clean up, too many fronts on which to fight. It would be an exaggeration to call it the best of times and the worst of times, even in the history of the UFW. The period that began after the pilgrimage and ended in 1968 would be followed by some terribly intense conjunctures of hope and fear, victory and defeat. But if the exhilarated and exhausted folks who lived through this period of democratic Delano ever happened to encounter Dickens's description of revolutionary Paris, they would have understood what he meant.

Across twenty tumultuous months, the virulently antiunion DiGiorgio Corporation moved for a representation election in the fields and the sheds; the Teamsters became the NFWA's rivals in the fields; farm workers across the country hurried to join the struggle; the NFWA affiliated with the AFL-CIO; troubles developed between Chavez and Teatro Campesino, and Chavez and *El Malcriado*. It all had to be talked over, argued out, immoderately debated, carefully considered. And People's was the place to do it. Mocha and Ann made good money off the flowering and pruning of democratic Delano.

★   ★   ★

Soon after the pilgrims discarded their "Boycott Schenley" signs and shifted their focus to TreeSweet and S&W Fine Foods, the DiGiorgio Corporation's CEO called a press conference and announced that the company had authorized the California State Mediation and Conciliation Service to hold elections for union representation at its Sierra Vista Ranch. All unions were welcome to participate, and he challenged the NFWA specifically to prove that it represented his workers.

DiGiorgio was one of the giants of California agribusiness, and the rise of the farm workers movement coincided with a period of profound change within the firm, as a second generation of DiGiorgios was in the process of restructuring the company that the first generation had built. Starting in 1888, at the age of fourteen, Joseph DiGiorgio had transformed his Baltimore lemon exchange into a vertically integrated agricultural corporation that by the mid-1930s was the third largest landowner in California, the biggest producer of plums and grapes in the world, and an aggressive opponent of farm workers' attempts to organize unions. Mr. Joseph, as he came to be called, was a brilliant, cheerfully ruthless son of a large Sicilian lemon grower, who organized the first wholesale fruit auctions in America; then he moved to California to, as they say in the industry, "control the source." Through a series of quick, shrewd maneuvers in the early 1920s he set up two enormous grape plantations in Kern County: the 6,000-acre Sierra Vista Farms, near Delano, and the 9,000-acre DiGiorgio Farms, near Arvin. His agricultural success on the barren lands of Kern County rested on three pillars: the electric pump, which allowed him to mine water as deep as 1,200 feet below his land; the jump in grape prices that accompanied Prohibition; and the plenitude of cheap labor—Filipinos, Mexicans, Okies—whom he separated into different crews, housed in separate quarters, and fed in separate cafeterias. It worked so well that Mr. Joseph, whose English remained primitive and consciously comical, became the acknowledged "Kubla Khan of Kern County," a man who bragged that if he had remained in a Sicilian seminary (he was kicked out for fighting), "I would be Pope or there'd be a new Church." *Fortune* magazine called him "one of the most relentlessly self-entertained egoists on the U.S. business scene."[1]

The second-generation, nephews of the childless Mr. Joseph, started to remake the corporation soon after his death in 1951. The efficiency of their uncle's electric pump forced the decision upon them. Sierra Vista and DiGiorgio Farms had pumped so much water that in some places the land itself had collapsed forty to fifty feet, a mere curiosity to the DiGiorgios until water from the wells started coming up salty.[2] That was serious. Without water, the land, valued at more than $3,000 an acre in the late 1940s, would be worth little more than the $90 an acre Mr. Joseph had originally paid for it. Water from the federally financed Central Valley Project could be used legally only on farms no larger than 160 acres.

Western agribusinessmen had been fighting that legal requirement for decades, but when the DiGiorgios entered the battle, backroom arrangements were harder to make, and in 1952 the family's significant political power could get them no more than a ten-year grace period. The nephews decided that they would use those years to diversify, and then see what happened in 1962.

The man who led the transformation was Robert DiGiorgio, a cultured San Francisco lawyer and accountant who became president and CEO. No broken-English, jolly egoist he, Robert had grown up among French servants on Riverside Drive in New York City, attended the Lawrenceville School in New Jersey, spent a pleasant four years at Yale in the midst of the Depression, and gone on to Fordham Law School before apprenticing in the Washington and New York legal department of his uncle's agricultural leviathan. Robert DiGiorgio arrived in California in 1938, at the age of twenty-six, and slipped smoothly into San Francisco high society. As he made his way to the top of what was then called DiGiorgio Fruit, he also earned a respected place in the highest levels of the California ruling class. He became the youngest member of the board of directors of Bank of America and also served on the boards of Union Oil, Pacific Telephone and Telegraph, Carter Hawley Hale Stores, and Newhall Land and Farming. He joined the exclusive Pacific Union and Bohemian clubs, and also mingled with the merely rich at the San Francisco Golf and Commonwealth clubs.

Robert DiGiorgio's place at the California corporate table helped him to remake his uncle's business. He moved quickly. In 1955, 85 percent of DiGiorgio Fruit's income came from direct sales of fruit and wine. By 1960 that had fallen to 20 percent. In 1964, two years after Robert DiGiorgio became president and CEO, but long after he had been the unofficial leader of the business, the percentage of fruit and wine sales had fallen to 13 percent. DiGiorgio was now a significant power in food and lumber processing—not too far removed from the land but far enough to make a successful exit if necessary. "Fruit" was dropped from its corporate name.

Uncle and nephew, an American tableau. Mr. Joseph was barely five and a half feet tall, with a full head of hair swept back from a prominent forehead, a hawk's nose, and thick, expressive lips. His chief critic, Ernesto Galarza, wrote that the patriarch had "a countenance creased with the scars of merciless business battles," and he described a bronze bust that Mr. Joseph commissioned for himself and then placed at the entrance to DiGiorgio Farms as having "the puckered lips of one who has just nipped a not-quite-ripe plum, and the gimlet stare of a man who knows he will not be stared back at."[3] Robert DiGiorgio, who also had a strong nose and full lips, towered over his uncle but nevertheless managed to appear meek, almost small, by comparison. His face was unmistakably soft, and his shy public smile was full of warm good wishes for the world beyond the camera.

The differences in style masked their unity on the question of labor. In 1939 Mr. Joseph became president and chief corporate fundraiser for Associated Farmers, an antilabor association that sponsored antipicketing ordinances throughout rural California, organized blacklists of union activists, fought federal relief for strikers, and directed the pick-handled vigilantes who attacked striking farm workers in the mid- and late 1930s. He also led the attack on *The Grapes of Wrath,* in which a farm called Digregorio symbolizes California corporate agriculture. The book was subjected to a public burning and was banished from schools and public libraries in Kern County. The cultured, French-speaking Robert DiGiorgio was no less vicious. During the National Farm Labor Union's 1947 strike against DiGiorgio's Arvin plantation, Robert's counterattack included mass eviction of strikers who had been living on company property, hiring goons who beat picketers with chains and pick handles, and launching a nighttime raid on the home of the strike leader, Jimmy Price. The raiders fired into the house during a union meeting, hitting Price in the head with a small-caliber bullet, a wound from which he subsequently recovered—causing Robert DiGiorgio to conjecture that Price might have shot himself in the head to get pro-strike publicity.

Having defeated the strike, Robert set out to destroy the NFLU and any union that might follow. His main weapon was the lawsuit. DiGiorgio sued the NFLU for libel over a film the union had produced about the strike. With no money to defend itself, the union settled out of court, paying $1 in damages and promising to recall and destroy all copies of the film. Ten years later, when a copy of the film turned up, shown by AWOC, DiGiorgio sued again, successfully, and had a photograph taken of the AFL-CIO's $50,000 settlement check, which he showed around for the amusement of his business friends. Next he sued several people working for a string of monthly labor newspapers in California because, among other things, they had published Galarza's view of the DiGiorgio libel campaign. That suit finally came to nothing, but the process took years.

Following the advent of the NFWA's boycott in 1966, DiGiorgio summoned *The Movement* reporter Brooks Penney to his San Francisco office and read him a prepared statement detailing those earlier lawsuits and asserting that *The Movement* had also committed libelous offenses. The CEO then earnestly admitted that, yes, many farm workers were poor, but growers were hardly responsible for that unfortunate fact: "If a steelworker takes his pay out and drinks it up and doesn't provide for his wife and family and lives in a hovel, then no one blames U.S. Steel. But if a farm worker does the same thing it is the grower's fault. We can't be our brother's keeper."[4] Just one month later, after Schenley's capitulation, DiGiorgio's historic resistance to the right of farm workers to organize a union began to melt away. Robert could see that the new, diversified DiGiorgio conglomerate was almost as vulnerable to a boycott as Schenley had been. Most of its money was made outside of Kern County, and the company had been negotiating since 1962 with the federal government about how to dispose of its land. He sought to control events through a union election.

Cesar Chavez was suspicious of DiGiorgio's invitation. As Chavez already knew, an election does not necessarily contest power; it can just as easily ratify it, especially when employees are voting on their boss's turf. Since no labor law covered farm workers and their employers, who would determine the rules governing an election? Who would be eligible to vote? Only currently employed workers, or everyone who had worked at the company since the strike began? What protection would workers have against company intimidation, discipline, harassment, firings, and eviction from company housing? Score one for the new, sophisticated generation of DiGiorgios. "Mr. Chavez," as DeGiorgio politely referred to Chavez, had been calling for elections for almost a year. Well, let him have one—an election he couldn't win.

A bad offer, but one that Chavez could not refuse. Farm workers, quite familiar with the power that foremen and supervisors wield on the job, might not have been bothered if Chavez had laughed off DiGiorgio's obviously crooked offer. But to church leaders and the union's other liberal backers, elections were a symbol of self-determination. The union leaders could not say no to elections and maintain the confidence of their coalition supporters. During another retreat, the leadership formulated its basic strategy: negotiate with DiGiorgio for election rules that would give the NFWA a reasonable chance to win, and put pressure on those negotiations by stepping up the DiGiorgio boycott and by forcing Governor Pat Brown to intervene.

Intensifying the boycott was the easier task. In Chicago, trade unionists and students physically blocked the S&W Foods distribution center. In many cities, students organized "shop-ins," filling shopping carts with S&W cans and then abandoning them at the cashier counters. Boisterous marches through grocery stores often resulted in the removal of DiGiorgio products from the shelves, at least for a while. *El Malcriado* quoted an enthusiastic boycotter: "No thinking person will eat or drink any S&W products until the DiGiorgio tradition of hate, violence, and greed is removed by a union contract." Chavez was direct about the goal of the boycott: "Unless DiGiorgio negotiates, S&W is finished." It was not mere bravado. Within a couple of weeks DiGiorgio was marketing its canned goods under a new label.[5]

Governor Brown was harder to crack. As negotiations over election rules began, he was in the midst of a surprisingly tough primary run for the Democratic nomination against Los Angeles Mayor Sam Yorty. Yorty's strength was based on the coalescing right-wing sentiments of the rapidly increasing Southern California suburban voters, who feared black rioters and student protesters. Brown eventually prevailed, but he could see that the coalition that had swept him to power in 1958 and reelected him in 1962 was coming apart. Previously he had been able to hold the allegiance (at least on Election Day) of unionists, African Americans, Mexican Americans, and Catholics without being completely deserted by affluent Protestant suburbanites and a significant minority of the business class, including agribusinessmen, for whom he had pushed through an enormous new state-funded irrigation project. But his Republican opponent, Ronald Reagan, was even more rooted in the Southern California rootlessness that had produced the Yorty votes and seemed to be much better than Yorty at expressing white dissatisfaction in an openly antiuniversity, antiobscenity, antiblack campaign. Brown could not afford to alienate any part of his old coalition. That meant he had to try to finesse the difference between his agribusiness and his Mexican American support.

Then the DiGiorgios overplayed their hand. First, they welcomed the Teamsters into their fields, severely ratcheting up the level of struggle on the ground. Next, they torpedoed the negotiations by abruptly announcing, on June 21, that in three days the company would hold privately supervised elections, using its own ground rules, at the Sierra Vista and Borrego ranches. When Bill Kircher and Dolores Huerta got advance news of the dirty deal, they busted up a DiGiorgio press conference. Kircher elbowed his way into the San Francisco Press Club, called the startled DiGiorgio a "damn liar" in front of the TV cameras, and easily convinced reporters that his charge was true. Chavez announced that the NFWA would boycott the election, and successfully sued to take its name off the ballot. The vote went ahead as scheduled, but nearly half the workers refused to participate, and when the Teamsters won overwhelmingly it hardly mattered at all.

The NFWA now had enough ammunition to make a solid hit on Brown. Kircher saw him first, and made it clear that continued AFL-CIO support depended on his help in throwing out the rigged election. Huerta went to the convention of the Mexican American Political Association (MAPA) and convinced the leadership to ask for a private meeting with the governor. When Brown showed up, both Huerta and Chavez were there. The MAPA participants—including Bert Corona, who was head of the Viva Brown clubs throughout the state—told the governor that their endorsement, previously considered automatic, now depended on what he did about the DiGiorgio mess.

If both the AFL-CIO and MAPA deserted him, Brown's other liberal support would flag, and he would have no chance against Reagan. He called Robert DiGiorgio, a personal friend, and let him know what he was going to do: ask the American Arbitration Association (AAA) to investigate the situation. Two weeks later the AAA declared the election invalid and recommended a new vote, supervised by the AAA, with precisely the ground rules that the NFWA had wanted. All workers who had been on the DiGiorgio payroll since the day before the 1965 strike would be eligible to vote; that meant 2,000 workers, only 700 of whom were currently employed. The NFWA would have to suspend its boycott, and DiGiorgio would have to negotiate a contract with the certified election winner. Chavez submitted the proposal to a mass meeting at Filipino Hall, and an enthusiastic crowd accepted it unanimously.

The NFWA had done it again. In a situation where it was protected by no labor law, in an environment ruled by what folks at People's called "the law of the jungle," its leaders had skillfully used their boycott power and political support to outmaneuver the powerful DiGiorgios. But there was little time to be smug. It was mid-July of 1966; six weeks of electioneering lay ahead.[6]

When Robert DiGiorgio invited the International Brotherhood of Teamsters (IBT) onto his ranches in 1966, he was following a tradition that went back as far as the 1930s, when large elements of the Teamsters bureaucracy increased their power by offering themselves up as an alternative to the radical rank-and-file unionism of the day. Employers responded favorably for two main reasons. First, these Teamsters were unapologetic "business unionists." Dave Beck, the union's second international president, explained the concept to the rank and file: "You men haven't anything else to sell but labor . . . We are trying to formulate a policy of operating a business organization to sell that labor . . . I have a world of admiration for the Standard Oil Company because it is efficient . . . I think we ought to run ours along the same lines."[7] Second, most of the Teamsters' members were truck drivers who have a key role in economic strife, as their willingness, or refusal, to move a product is often the difference between winning or losing a strike. For the employers, it was good to work with union officials who shared their values; it was even better that those officials had some control over the people who moved materials in and out of their factories, fields, warehouses, and stores.

The DiGiorgio campaign marked the beginning of an eleven-year contest between the farm workers'union and the Teamsters, which at the time had been banned from the AFL-CIO for alleged racketeering. During that period the Teamsters initiated and then abandoned farm worker organizing drives on five different occasions, each time either violating signed agreements or breaking secret compacts with other people in the labor movement or with various growers and their associations. The Teamsters' intermittent interventions in the battles of the fields were consistent with their earlier history. But it would be a mistake to view their record in the fields between 1966 and 1977 as primarily a list of shameful betrayals by one unified organization. Rather, their shabby record was mostly a direct consequence of various conflicts within that organization, where no one— not even the International President of the union—could control or make agreements for the rest of the IBT's multilayered, semi-autonomous, economically independent bureaucracy. This thoroughgoing bureaucratic autonomy, so complete that it might more accurately be called bureaucratic anarchy, had typified the IBT from its inception at the turn of the twenti- eth century, and neither the first International President, Dan Tobin, nor his successor, Beck, could ever do much about it. It wasn't until Jimmy Hoffa took over the presidency in 1957 that any serious attempt was made to curb the power of big-city locals and regional joint councils. But even Hoffa's limited success depended on the partial cooperation of the union "barons."[8]

"Barons" was a common name used to describe the powerful local Teamster officials, and their jurisdictions were often called baronies. The feudal language fit. By the early sixties there were four layers of organi- zation that sat upon the backs (and lived off the dues) of the working Teamster: the local, the joint council, the conference, and the International.[9] Each level owed dues to those above it but operated with a considerable amount of autonomy in its own fiefdom; local Teamster officials were like barons who could, within limits, ignore or disobey a weak king, and like the ancient aristocracy, they were often involved in internal schemes, squabbles, and alliances through which they hoped to extend their local and regional power. Those internal disputes often went back generations—like fiefdoms, the labor baronies tended to be handed down from father to son—and the changing shape of competing interests and loyalties was mostly opaque to those outside the top fami- lies. Thus, what looked like betrayal to the AFL-CIO, the farm workers, or the growers was often simply a matter of top Teamster bureaucrats making agreements that lower bureaucrats ignored, or the result of some other family intrigue way beyond the ability of anybody outside the IBT to grasp.

In the 1960s, when some Teamster locals in Los Angeles and San Francisco with significant Mexican American memberships initially helped the National Farm Workers Association and Agricultural Workers Organizing Committee by conducting quick hot cargo campaigns, it was a demonstration of that bureaucratic autonomy. Teamster tradition usually allowed local leaders to take such action, and in this case the locals received active support from the San Francisco, Los Angeles, and Central Valley joint councils, and passive support from the union's Western Conference and International leaders, as there was some hope, from President Hoffa on down, that any young farm worker union would eventually choose to affiliate with the Teamsters.

The intervention in the DiGiorgio campaign reversed this policy and was probably initiated by ambitious midlevel bureaucrats who knew that Kircher had pushed Green aside. They also had good reason to believe that Chavez would never join their union. He had already rebuffed a few Teamster overtures, one from Hoffa himself. Worse, according to a story well known in Teamster circles, Chavez had haughtily refused to accept a shoebox filled with $100,000 in bills, a supposedly no-strings-attached gift from the Teamsters.[10] A man who would do that couldn't be trusted. Those midlevel officials convinced the more careful chairman of the union's Western Conference, Einar Mohn, to go along with the planned intervention. Mohn in turn got an okay from Hoffa, who was preoccupied with his simultaneous efforts to stay out of jail and tie up a national master freight agreement.

Hoffa and Mohn were not wholehearted supporters of what amounted to a raid on territory being staked out by Kircher in the name of the AFL-CIO. They simply were not inclined to interfere with the moves of those below them, so long as the latter continued to pass along the agreed-upon share of membership dues, as well as showing formal fealty and support for the long-range goals of the higher powers. But in a prelude of reversals to come, just twenty-five days after the Teamsters first entered the DiGiorgio fields, and before the sham election, Mohn announced that the union was withdrawing from the campaign. Pressure from the Catholic clergy, mobilized by the NFWA, seems to have been the deciding factor, as Mohn made the announcement in a letter to the seven California bishops and to Archbishop John Cody of Chicago.[11] Hoffa, not wanting to offend any more people than he already had, agreed, while reiterating that the Teamsters would still continue to organize farm workers. But Hoffa's waffling and Mohn's announcement did nothing to slow down Teamster organizing at DiGiorgio, as local Teamster officials allowed their name to remain on the ballot for the first election. By the time the ground rules for the second election were announced, Hoffa was about to go to jail, and Mohn reversed himself and authorized the union to reenter the fray they had never actually deserted.

The Teamsters had three advantages in the eleven-year battle between the IBT and the various iterations of the farm workers union, which were regularly noted by contemporary reporters covering the story: wealth (they were the biggest and richest union in the U.S., and spent about $30 million trying to get a foothold in the fields); cooperation of the bosses; and power in the trucks. They also had three distinct disadvantages, one well noted, one the flipside of an advantage, and the third barely understood. Most reporters could see that Teamster strategy and tactics were determined by white men who had no understanding of farm worker life and conditions. They could also see that the growers' open preference for the IBT hurt the Teamsters among the most militant and active farm workers. What almost no one recognized, though, was that the Teamsters' internal autonomy prevented them from developing a consistent, disciplined, unified plan of action. By contrast, the organization that emerged out of the transformation of the NFWA into a union suffered from no such disability. Under whatever name, the farm workers union did not have an autonomous, nor even a semi-autonomous, staff. It had no locals. It became a disciplined, centralized organization, quite capable of developing a unified plan of action, and then making sure that the plan was carried out by its staff. Eventually, that rigid structure would become brittle and break, but for a long while the unchecked power of the UFW's center made it quite effective in the battle against the theoretically top-down Teamsters, who rarely could get anyone to unify on anything.

By the time of the DiGiorgio election, NFWA leaders were already convinced that the boycott in the cities, and not the organization of workers in the fields, was the key to ultimate victory. But for the boycott to be effective, union supporters had to be sure that the NFWA was the authentic voice and organization of California farm workers. The DiGiorgio election provided that opportunity. Years later Chavez said: "I knew that if we lost this one, we would lose the union, because the public wouldn't have supported us after that. We hadn't established credibility with the public yet."[12]

This produced a peculiar logic in the NFWA's farm worker organizing. As the boycott strategy took hold, workers understood that part of the reason their participation mattered was precisely because of the impression it made on potential supporters. People continued to maintain picket lines even though they were not stopping scabs; people came to Friday-night meetings knowing that they were putting on a show of strength for visitors; workers came from all over to vote in the DiGiorgio election to declare their union colors to their supporters, as well as to the boss and one another. No one felt used. Most everyone understood that the NFWA had to walk on two legs. Farm workers were mostly grateful for all the support they were receiving. They understood, perhaps as well as Chavez, that the union's survival depended on it.

In what he considered a do-or-die situation, Chavez called on his old mentor, Fred Ross, to get out the vote. Ross prepared a three-by-five card for every one of the 2,000 eligible voters. He assigned a specific organizer to a certain number of cards. He made the organizers responsible to a team of coordinators, and the coordinators responsible to him. Ross reported only to Chavez, although others were sometimes welcome to sit in on the meetings. His team varied from twenty-five to fifty people, many of them called back from the boycott, and included students, clergy, farm workers, and about a dozen organizers on loan from the AFL–CIO. They began their workday before six, passing out the daily leaflets that had been run off the night before. At eight there was a meeting at the Pink House, led by Ross, where organizers discussed tactics and were given afternoon assignments. At noon, the organizers returned to the Sierra Vista Ranch, where for an hour they could circulate among the workers and debate with the Teamster organizers. Then it was back to the Pink House to give reports, eat, and rest. At five, they met again to plan their nighttime visits to the company barracks and to workers who lived in town. Written reports had to be filed at the end of each day. The meetings were not idle chit-chat. Ross was a tough taskmaster who believed deeply in his craft and was intolerant of sloppy work or tardiness. For their sixteen-hour days, all but the AFL–CIO organizers were paid $5 a week.

One of the farm worker organizers was Eliseo Medina. Just twenty years old, he seemed even younger, with dimpled cheeks, a wide smile, warm brown eyes, and thick black hair falling across his forehead. As good as he looked, he sounded even better. His soft voice, said one of his many female admirers, could charm the rattles off a snake. Fred Ross paid more attention to his well-reasoned words. All his working life, Ross had been on the lookout for natural leaders; he had immediately recognized Cesar's abilities thirteen years before. It didn't take him long to spot Medina. Ross quickly assigned him to the crucial nighttime house meetings, where the organizers could talk to workers without the interference of Teamsters, supervisors, or foremen. The bilingual Medina already had done some house meetings; Dolores Huerta had found him on the early grape strike picket lines and set him to work with another early volunteer, Elaine Wender. After one meeting, Wender told him something he would continue to hear for the next fifty years, "Boy, you sure can talk."[13]

He came by it honestly. Both his mother and father enjoyed politics, and his father was once the mayor of the small town in Zacatecas where Eliseo was born in 1946. During Eliseo's early years, his father spent much of his time working in the fields of California, first as a bracero and later without papers. The family decided to migrate to the United States in 1954; his mother and the five children moved to Tijuana, while his father continued to work across the border. After two more years of separation, the whole family finally crossed the border legally.

They arrived in Delano in July of 1956, and Eliseo, ten, immediately went to work pulling leaves at Perelli-Minetti, a vineyard where his father had worked many times before. After the first year in Delano his dad took him and then his brother into the fields on alternating weekends during the school year to "teach them how to work." He learned well enough, and the day after his eighth-grade graduation, he went to work in the table grapes at Tudor & Sons. He did it all: planting, pruning, thinning, pulling leaves, picking. He was fifteen and a professional farm worker.

Medina had been working full-time in the fields for four years in 1965 when he noticed *El Malcriado* at the local grocery store. The issue featured the story of the NFWA's victory over a labor contractor who was forced to pay back wages. Nineteen-year-old Medina was impressed. "Nobody ever challenged the growers, and the labor contractors were like the princes of the church," he would say later. "And then all of a sudden, here's this report that this contractor—and a white guy no less; it wasn't just any old contractor but a white guy—who got nailed. So I got really interested and I would always look [for *El Malcriado*]. Because all of a sudden it was like Mexicans could do something and they could win."

Eliseo's mother noticed his interest in the newspaper and urged him to join the NFWA. He didn't want to. He had gone to CSO meetings with his father, and he figured this new organization wouldn't be much different from that one, not exciting enough to shake loose his money for dues. The newspaper only cost a dime though. Late that summer, following the news of the grape strikes in Coachella and Arvin, he got all excited. He wasn't alone. The whole town seemed on edge, as the harvest and presumably the strike, were headed its way. One day in September his sister and mother came home exclaiming, *"Estamos en huelga."* They were among the few Mexicans to walk out with the Filipinos. Medina, who was off work because he had broken his leg in a foolish accident, watched from the sidewalk over the next few days as the striking Filipinos marched through town. He listened to the radio and read the newspaper. He went to the September 16 NFWA meeting at the Guadalupe Church. When he returned home, he took a hammer and smashed the piggy bank that held all his savings, counted out ten dollars and fifty cents, and on September 17 went to the association's office on Albany Street and paid three months' dues.

The Friday night meetings "were like revivals," Medina later recalled. "There was all this great fun, and reports and speeches . . . It was just a sense that you were all together on the same thing. Even people I didn't know . . . It was eye-opening . . . You never knew such things existed. People would come, and ministers and priests and people from other places. And then they announced all these famous politicians and unions . . . Wow! " His mother and sister remained strikers for a long while, but didn't get involved in organizational work. His father, in a pattern not unique to their family, had gone back to Mexico a few years earlier. The family had been divided for so long that the attempt to reunite in the U.S. had failed. Eliseo's mother and father remained married and friendly, but not together. When his brother joined the Army in 1964, Eliseo became the oldest man in the household; when the strike began, he took over his father's place as the person who would represent the family in public life. His mother not only approved, she was proud.

Medina hit the picket line, and by mid-November he was a picket captain. Most of the Mexican farm workers had gone back to work by then, and his picket line was maintained almost exclusively by college students. "They talked about a world I was not familiar with. They talked about Berkeley and civil rights and stuff that I hadn't even heard about. It was extremely interesting." He accompanied Dolores Huerta and Jim Drake on trips to Los Angeles, where he watched them operate at meetings and on picket lines. He started talking at house meetings. He picked up politics quickly.

Not until the DiGiorgio campaign was Medina introduced to Cesar Chavez, and then he met Fred Ross. He was surprised by the discipline Ross demanded, but he didn't mind the work. He joined a small crew of people that included Robert Bustos, Eskiel Carranza, Ruth Trujillo, and Alice Tapia, and they became a famous, sometimes scandalous, organizing crew. They did most everything: mornings they leafleted, afternoons they were at Sierra Vista Ranch, evenings they spent in town. Once, when Bustos and Medina were driving on Sierra Vista Ranch property, which was against election rules, with a loudspeaker on top of their car, they passed a Teamster caravan. The Teamsters sped ahead of them, blocked their way, and came walking toward them. Eliseo tried to speed past the men without running anyone down, but someone reached into the car and busted him in the mouth. He had a fat lip that needed stitches, but it all felt good. "It was just tremendous. I was sold. I never even thought I wanted to do anything but what I was doing at this time. It was just so exciting."

The DiGiorgio campaign was not particularly violent—physical intimidation was not likely to win many votes. Epifanio Camacho and other picket captains toned down their rhetoric, stopped the name-calling, and recited the reasons that people should vote for the union: to gain higher wages and dignity on the job, to limit the power of foremen and contractors. The presence of the Teamsters, however, threatened to ratchet up the tension. Teamster organizers were often big men whose expertise at physical coercion was part of their organizing repertoire, which lent weight to their campaign argument that the workers would be better off with the big, powerful professional Teamsters union than with the rag-tag collection of amateurs, radicals, clergy, and communists who made up the NFWA. The Teamster attack on Eliseo Medina and Robert Bustos, unusual enough to receive a lot of publicity, was not unique. Chavez asked Bill Kircher if the AFL-CIO could provide people to protect NFWA organizers. Kircher called the head of the Seafarers Union in San Francisco and asked him to send down some "able bodies." Soon, fourteen Seafarers arrived, just as big and as experienced in picket line violence as the Teamsters. Cesar was thrilled: "When they came, word got out to the Teamsters that the Seafarers were in town. After that, the Teamsters didn't come near us. The Seafarers were great, beautiful guys who were admired by the workers."[14]

At the same time, Chavez was delighted by another tactical innovation, which he described as "a beautiful demonstration of the power of nonviolence."[15] After an early injunction barred NFWA pickets and organizers from gathering on the public road opposite DiGiorgio fields, Antonia and Maria Saludado, two of the union's most effective and dedicated organizers during the campaign, suggested that the union set up a shrine to the Virgin of Guadalupe there instead, and hold a prayer meeting. Richard Chavez built the shrine in the back of Cesar's station wagon and parked the car-cum-shrine next to the main DiGiorgio gate. The police did not have the courage to enforce the injunction against a religious ceremony, and soon the union was holding Mass every evening in front of the station wagon for non-DiGiorgio farm workers, union supporters, and DiGiorgio workers who had just come off the job. The Mass included a discussion of election issues, songs, and signing of union authorization cards. The shrine also became a place where organizers, picketers, and workers could meet at all hours of the day without being harassed by the police or Teamsters. Women in their work clothes kneeling in the dust behind the station wagon were a powerful sight, often photographed by visiting newsmen.

The shrine and the Seafarers were much discussed at People's. Folks generally approved of both tactics, but the Seafarers were not as universally applauded as Chavez later claimed. Camacho, Reyes, and a few others were a bit insulted that the leadership had decided to call in others to defend farm workers; they insisted that farm workers could defend themselves. A few people pointed out that the NFWA's use of these union enforcers demonstrated the tactical, as opposed to philosophical, nature of the leadership's commitment to nonviolence. Those who favored a self-defense strategy for the NFWA argued that calling in the Seafarers was an unofficial endorsement of their line.[16]

This issue, however, was eclipsed by another: the formal merger of the AWOC and the NFWA, under the auspices of the AFL-CIO. Merger talks had begun during the pilgrimage. At that time Kircher had told the *Los Angeles Times* that he looked forward to the day when the NFWA would join the AFL-CIO. Chavez, too, had said, "We realize that we are entering the big leagues now, and we will soon be part of the mainstream labor movement."[17] But not everyone in the NFWA thought that was a good idea, and even among those who did, the exact terms on which the association should join the AFL-CIO were a matter of some debate. In mid-July negotiations between Kircher and Chavez had already gone on for three and a half months.

The points of dispute were no mystery. Cesar Chavez wanted money and support (especially money, to counter the deep pockets of the Teamsters), but he also wanted autonomy. He was well aware that top AFL-CIO officials had the authority to appoint and dismiss AWOC organizers, and had the final word on AWOC organizing strategies and budget matters. Anything resembling that would be unacceptable to him. Kircher, who was becoming increasingly enamored of the whole NFWA operation, was willing to grant a good deal of autonomy to the new body, but whatever deal he made had to be approved by George Meany, and the AFL-CIO chief was not accustomed to giving people money without maintaining some control over it. Chavez was not unfamiliar with that basic rule of politics. He wanted a steady supply of money, but he knew he had to be careful about what kinds of strings were attached.

Chavez often brought his top lieutenants, Dolores Huerta and Jim Drake, along with him to the negotiations. He had chosen them carefully. Huerta was suspicious of the AFL-CIO, and Drake was pretty much against affiliation. Like others from the Migrant Ministry, he still cherished the idea of the NFWA as an association of farm worker families, and he was sure that organizing goal would be discarded once the NFWA became a regular union. With such negotiators at his side, Cesar Chavez figured he could get a better deal out of Kircher and Meany. As the negotiations began, opposition to the merger developed from a variety of new sources. A delegation of Mexican farm workers visited Chavez and objected to any merger with the "Filipino union." Chavez dismissed their objections as pure prejudice, but the prejudice was reinforced by the fact that many foremen and supervisors in the grape fields were Filipinos and that Filipino farm workers often had a slightly privileged position in many companies. Consequently, some Mexican workers feared that the Filipinos would somehow take advantage of their position in the fields to exert undue influence in a merged union. Filipino farm workers were even more suspicious. They simply counted noses and concluded that any joint union would be dominated by Mexicans. Most of the remaining AWOC staffers were sure they would lose their jobs in any merger, and they were right about that.

Meanwhile, outside the NFWA and the AFL-CIO, Paul Schrade of the UAW and officials of the ILWU also expressed misgivings. The ILWU was already independent of the AFL-CIO, and the UAW was about to leave it. Both Schrade and ILWU officials had built up a large amount of goodwill inside the NFWA. They had been early supporters of the association, and they were continuing to provide money and supplies even as the NFWA drew closer to Kircher. ILWU officials had been especially helpful to Huerta in her negotiations over the first Schenley contract. They went through the ILWU's Hawaii farm worker contracts with her, showed her the various ways that hiring halls worked, and instructed her in the basics of contract negotiation. Neither they nor Schrade were heavy-handed about their opposition to the merger, but they warned that although Kircher might be a good guy, standing behind him was an autocrat who had taken the AFL-CIO down a conservative path and destroyed many progressive unions a whole lot bigger and stronger than the NFWA.

The most serious opposition came from the radicals on the staff. They were mostly white, but not exclusively. For them, the NFWA and the farm worker movement it represented was a challenge to the whole system of social relations in the California fields, and thus was part of a bigger movement for fundamental change in America. They believed that affiliation with the AFL-CIO would necessarily blunt the organization's radical edge and reduce its effectiveness as a union. The association's growth, they argued, had depended on its willingness to use the techniques of the civil rights and student movements, tactics that AFL-CIO officials publicly opposed. Furthermore, those officials had not adequately supported the civil rights movement, had sold out the social vision of the best elements in the labor movement, and were among the biggest supporters of the escalation of the war in Vietnam. In the summer of 1966, as B-52s began the carpet-bombing of North Vietnam, this last objection was particularly intense.

Chavez was undaunted. Without a formal merger of the AWOC and the NFWA, the names of both unions might appear on the DiGiorgio ballot on August 30, which would split the anti-company, anti-Teamster vote. Chavez knew that the bulk of the farm workers supported both the merger and affiliation with the AFL-CIO, that no one on the executive board would oppose it, that key elements of his staff, including Marshall Ganz, understood why the merger was necessary, and that he could persuade almost everyone else that, all in all, the merger was the right thing to do. Yet he also realized that he could use opposition to the merger as a bargaining chip. He stretched out the negotiations on purpose, encouraging those opposed to affiliation to express their complaints directly to Kircher in a series of meetings set up by the executive board. Chavez enjoyed the cleverness of the tactic. The board bombarded Kircher with meetings, he recounted gleefully to Levy, and when Kircher couldn't make a meeting Chavez would complain to him about the difficulties he himself was having with his own opposition. "I would call Bill in Washington and tell him, 'We're having another meeting!'"[18]

Chavez's negotiating strategy worked just fine. The new United Farm Workers Organizing Committee (UFWOC) won an unprecedented amount of autonomy from the AFL-CIO. Its National Executive Board was the highest authority in the UFWOC, answerable to no one in the

AFL-CIO. In addition, according to Larry Itliong, the AFL-CIO set up a million-dollar revolving fund for UFWOC, to be replenished every year.[19]

As members of the new National Executive Board, Chavez chose himself, Gilbert Padilla, Dolores Huerta, and Tony Orendain; Kircher chose Itliong and Philip Vera Cruz, from AWOC, and added Andy Imutan, a Filipino businessman who was not a part of either AWOC or the farm worker community but had been an ardent supporter of the NFWA since the strike began. Itliong was made assistant director to Chavez. This board was explicitly provisional, meant to serve as long as there was an organizing committee. Once UFWOC had won enough contracts to be a self-supporting union, a new convention would elect a new board.

The attempt to retain the allegiance of large numbers of Filipinos failed, and eight Filipino organizers from AWOC went to work for the Teamsters. The full impact of that would not be felt until later, after the DiGiorgio campaign. Of more immediate concern was the disappointment of many of the young radicals. At the final mass meeting before the merger, some of them actually voted No to the overwhelmingly endorsed proposal. As that vote had taken place in the middle of the DiGiorgio campaign, all of the dissenters were loyal enough to swallow their opposition and continue working. Nevertheless, their uneasiness festered. Perhaps Chavez had been a little too clever. By encouraging dissent as a bargaining tool against Kircher, he had validated it, and after the pressure of the DiGiorgio campaign passed, Chavez would discover that he could not automatically turn it off.

Election day was high drama. Most reporters, although sympathetic to the UFWOC, felt that the Teamsters would win. They had been winning elections where they were supported by the bosses for more than thirty years. They were pros, and UFWOC, despite their new AFL-CIO affiliation, were amateurs. People were saying that the Las Vegas odds were three to one against Chavez. On the day of the election, UFWOC headquarters was a beehive of activity, with Fred Ross running a typical election mobilization, while the Teamsters organizers spent another day lolling by the motel pool. After the polls closed, the ballots were put in a Highway Patrol car and driven to San Francisco to be counted. One representative each for DiGiorgio, the Teamsters, and UFWOC rode in the same car to observe the count. Dolores Huerta was so worried that the count would be rigged that she gave the UFWOC observer some Dexedrine so he would stay alert. After the ballots were counted, the Dexedrine kicked in, and he couldn't sleep all night. Back in Delano, many UFWOC supporters couldn't sleep either. A bleary-eyed group of a couple hundred gathered at Filipino Hall the next day to hear Chavez announce the results. First, he read the results of the separate shed worker election, which the Teamsters won. Then he read the field worker results: UFWOC, 530; Teamsters, 331; No Union, 9.

What came to be called the dragnet had made the difference. Five hundred and thirteen people who were eligible to vote but not currently working at DiGiorgio had cast ballots.[20] None of them had been mobilized by the Teamsters. How they got to the polls remains one of Padilla's favorite stories, but first an interlude to consider a curiosity of the election results, those nine votes in the "No Union" column, a tiny number, significant only because Chavez organized for those votes, too, and they came at a price.

Like Saul Alinsky, Chavez believed so deeply in the righteousness of his cause that he saw little wrong with small deceptions, called *movidas* in Spanish. Alinsky was open about his enjoyment of the dirty trick, but for Chavez, Alinskyism had to coexist with the tradition of Catholic Social Action, which is hostile to the proposition of doing a little bad to achieve a greater good. Throughout his political life, Chavez was the supreme strategist, making careful calculations of how one act might lead to another, willing to dissemble in pursuit of a higher cause, but at the same time he believed in the power of moral example beyond any calculation of ends and means. He was the serpent and the dove. He both loved the *movida* and was repelled by it.

Chavez used Bill Esher to carry out a minor dirty trick in the DiGiorgio election. Because the company was throwing its support to the Teamsters, no one was campaigning for the "No Union" choice on the ballot. According to Esher, Chavez explained to him privately that an active campaign for No Union would be one way to divide the Teamster vote, and he carefully instructed Esher on how to carry it out. "It was an undercover operation. I rented a post office box in Visalia, and I sent out leaflets to all the DiGiorgio workers calling on them to vote No Union. Chavez was very concerned that we didn't get caught. Very, very careful. He gave me strict instructions. 'Don't ever go to that PO Box,' he said. The whole thing was very secret. I used a secret typewriter. I wrote up all the leaflets in secret, and got them secretly printed. I was absolutely exhausted when it was over. I was putting out *Malcriado* at the same time."[21]

After that initial discussion, Chavez kept his distance from the *movida*. The leaflets were sent out under the name of "The DiGiorgio Committee Against Unionism" and the "Tulare County Right to Work League." One leaflet listed Gary Allen, a member of the John Birch Society, who had written pamphlets against the NFWA, as a director of the No Union campaign. That proved to be a mistake, although not fatal. Someone told Allen about the leaflet, and he complained to the *Fresno Bee* and the FBI on the day before the election. When the No Union vote turned out to be insignificant, however, no one followed up with an investigation.[22]

Esher's second mistake was more damaging. After the election, he borrowed Kathy Lynch's car and went on a short vacation. Kathy was sometimes secretary to Chavez, and her car was a known union vehicle.

> I drove through Visalia, and I foolishly disobeyed Chavez's orders and I went to the PO Box and picked up the mail. And in the mail was a carton of cigarettes. The growers had the post office staked out around the clock. And they saw me walk out with the carton of cigarettes, and get in Kathy's car. Later, during the DiGiorgio [contract] negotiations, the union lawyer, Alex Hoffman, told me that at one important moment, the DiGiorgio lawyers told him that they had this information, and they used it to help negotiate down the wage settlement. So a thousand workers got 25 cents less an hour. I felt awful. Chavez had been right. He knew how to do those things, and I didn't. And I hadn't paid attention to his superior wisdom.[23]

The dragnet of ex-Digiorgio workers, however, involved neither *movidas* nor secrecy; it was a straight product of organizational know-how, cultural savvy, and AFL–CIO money. Calculating from the eligibility list that about half the potential voters no longer lived anywhere near Delano, Fred Ross put together teams to travel to Washington, Oregon, the Imperial Valley, Texas, and Mexico to track down the out-of-towners. Three and a half weeks before election day, Gilbert Padilla and four others piled into a station wagon with a black eagle painted on the sides and hit the road for El Paso–Juárez with a list of 250 names. "We went into it a little worried," says Padilla.

> So many people have multiple names, and addresses change all the time, and El Paso is a pretty big place. But within the farm worker community people know who is who, and how to find each other. Most farm workers lived in Juárez, or rather in the *colonias* on the hills above Juárez. Those are *colonias* of what the Mexicans call *paracadistas*, "parachuters," people who arrive, as if from the air, build themselves a shack, and settle in. In 1966 there were five main *colonias* of *paracadistas* outside of Juárez, with names like Zapata, Villa, Flores-Magón, whatever. They had no running water, no formal sewage, no nothing, [but] they each had their own little governing organizations. People would get together regularly and talk about the *colonia*'s problems—water, crime, garbage—and try to find ways to solve them. And the *colonias* had leaders. I remember in particular this one woman, Señora Lechuga she was called. She had a long political history, plenty of experience; she was one of the best people I have ever seen at running a meeting. She was some kind of Mexican Communist, but I never could get all them initials straight.

We got into the *colonias* through Juan Flores. I had known a Juan Flores when we were trying to organize the Anza-Borrego Ranch before the first crooked DiGiorgio election. That Juan Flores was a good guy, one of our strongest people on the ranch, well respected by the rest of the workers. And I saw a "Juan Flores" with an El Paso address on the [eligibility] list. We couldn't find him in El Paso, but after a while we found him in Juárez. Not in one of the *colonias* but in the city proper. And was he happy to see me! He invited me into his house, I met his family, we had a few drinks. It was a regular reunion. I explained to him what we were doing and I showed him the list. And he said, Let's go to the *colonias* and find these people. So we went to all these meetings. At night, with no lights, meeting around a big fire, people talked about who is going to clean up the garbage. And Juan would introduce me, and I would explain about the union and the struggle we were in, and then read people the list. And people would say, "Oh sure, we know that guy; he works in the grapes in California." And the next day we would go find him.

We got to be known. People knew what we were there for. And pretty soon we had enough people to make up a caravan with a bus and several cars. Over fifty people. We offered free food and a bus ride. The AFL–CIO was involved now and we had more money to use. A couple people who had never worked at Digiorgio told us they had and came along for the ride.[24]

About half of all the out-of-towners' ballots, 247, were thrown out by the American Arbitration Association because the voters had either not worked at DiGiorgio, or not worked there long enough. That left 266 votes that had been brought in by the dragnet teams, and UFWOC had won by 199 votes.

In some respects, the Teamsters had been right to be confident. They had won the election in the fields among those currently on the DiGiorgio payroll. Working through the supervisors and foremen, and with the open support of the company, they had been able to defeat Ross's disciplined, hard-working organizers. But they lost the election elsewhere. The Teamsters had little contact with the farm worker world beyond the DiGiorgio vineyards. Even if they had paid attention to the rest of the eligibility list, their organizers could not have made their way to places like the Juárez *colonias*. And if by some chance they had, they would not have found as many people willing to accompany them back to Delano. The few freeloaders aside, that journey would be made only by people with a serious commitment to the new union, not by people who would want to vote for the company-supported Teamsters.

After Chavez announced the results, he challenged the growers to hold secret-ballot elections on farms throughout the state or face a general strike.[25] He raised the specter of a general strike without any serious plan to call one, but farm workers, inspired by the election results, had plans of their own. Within a few weeks, wine grape workers at the Perilli-Minetti and Goldberg farms, without any prior consultation with UFWOC, went on strike, demanding higher wages and union recognition. Perilli-Minetti and Goldberg had not been struck in 1965, so some of the original union supporters who hadn't wanted to cross picket lines had gone to work there. They were among the leaders of these new walkouts. It wasn't just grape workers in Delano who responded to the DiGiorgio victory. Citrus workers in Ventura, vegetable workers in the lower Santa Clara Valley, and others in various agricultural areas of the nation walked off their jobs. Moreover, just as Chavez had predicted, the DiGiorgio victory solidified support in the cities. Effectively using the threat of a boycott, the UFWOC won recognition and contracts from seven more wineries, and for the first time it held some contracts outside of the Central Valley, in Napa and the lower Salinas Valley.

Left out of the victory celebration were hints of problems to come. The UFWOC had not been able to overcome the power of foremen and supervisors in the DiGiorgio vineyards. Many elections in the vineyards lay ahead, and never again would the eligibility lists include so many people who were not subject to company coercion. In a number of cases this would not matter, as the companies would urge their workers to vote for UFWOC to get the grape boycott off their backs. Later, however, the bosses would stand strongly against the union, and in a majority of state-supervised elections on table grape farms, the UFW would be defeated by the Teamsters.

But neither that nor the disaffection of many Filipinos—workers and former AWOC staff—proved to be the most distressing aspect of the DiGiorgio victory. Following the election, an arbitrator ruled that the new contracts would not include successor clauses. Robert DiGiorgio then began to sell off his agricultural holdings. Within two years he had sold the Sierra Vista, Arvin, and Yuba City–Marysville ranches, and converted the Anza-Borrego Ranch into a golf course and recreational center. None of the new owners was bound to re-sign with UFWOC, and none of them did.[26] Thus, to the grape workers of the lower Central Valley, the DiGiorgio victory became, in many respects, an empty triumph, a demonstration of the ultimate power of the bosses to have their own way. The shutdown in Anza-Borrego cost farm workers a few hundred jobs. People didn't blame UFWOC, but many farm workers stopped thinking of the DiGiorgio election as a victory.

Such problems hardly registered with the boycott coalition. The DiGiorgio election victory became vital proof that UFWOC truly represented California farm workers, an impressive performance often cited by UFWOC organizers and literature as the grape boycott continued. None of that literature mentioned that by 1968 the DiGiorgio contracts had been lost. Thus, "DiGiorgio" came to mean something different to a New York City boycotter and a Delano grape worker—a contradiction hardly noticed at the time, but a harbinger of the ultimate struggle between the two souls of the union.

Cutting Back and Rooting Out

October '66 to January '67

Rapid out-of-control growth often prompts a gardner to prune, weed, root out, cull. He or she hopes not to stifle growth but to control it, to encourage what is desired by suppressing what is not, thus shaping the overall scheme to the gardner's vision. Following the DiGiorgio election, UFWOC was in dangter of growing too fast, of being overwhelmed with too many plants to tend, too many rows to hoe. The new AFL-CIO organizing committee had no choice but to support the Delano strikers at Goldberg Farms and Perelli-Menetti. When the Teamsters signed a back-door contract with Perelli-Menetti, UFWOC responded with a new boycott that had to be organized and staffed. The union had to find the time to negotiate contracts and set up hiring halls at the several wine grape companies far from Delano that had buckled before the threat of a boycott. Governor Pat Brown, having delivered on his promise in the DiGiorgio election, came to the union for support in his campaign against Ronald Reagan. Excited by all the activity, more volunteers streamed into Delano.

"It was totally chaotic," Bill Esher recalled. "Too many things had to be done simultaneously, and all of a sudden these new volunteers are around. Fifty young white kids. It couldn't be the loose organization that it had been before. There had to be some kind of change, just because of the size of it."[1]

Chavez did not shy from the gardner's task. He pruned, culled, and shaped. He told some of the volunteers to move on. He gave distant assignments to others, knowing that they would quit rather than carry them out. In Friday-night meetings he talked more about discipline and unity, pointedly warning his audience about the perils of disloyalty. Not content to weed out objectionable individuals, he ultimately moved against the two most independent institutions in the union family, *El Malcriado* and El Teatro Campesino. Many people were shocked and worried about who or what was next. Some left the union on their own, arguing that the man with the pruning shears had gone too far and killed two of the most beautiful plants in the garden. The early bloom of a free-wheeling democratic Delano was gone. Whether a more mature, structured democracy would take its place was as yet unknown.

Chavez's main ally in the makeover of the union in the period between the fall of 1966 and the winter of 1967 was LeRoy Chatfield, the once Brother Gilbert. Chatfield's grandfather had been a prosperous rice grower in Colusa County, just north of Sacramento; his father was a successful Sacramento real estate developer. His mother, a devout Catholic, sent her firstborn to a Catholic elementary school and then to the closest Catholic high school, Christian Brothers High in Sacramento. In 1948, Chatfield, then fourteen, started boarding there among a population of boys heavily weighted with the "juvenile delinquents" of the day, who were subject to the physical discipline of their instructors. The young, well-behaved Chatfield quickly identified with the brothers who ran the school rather than with the disobedient boys. He considered the man in charge of the boarders a "hero of sorts," and admired him for his combination of "firmness and compassion." A year later, Chatfield, a sophomore, entered the Benedictine seminary, where eventually he took the religious name of his hero, Brother Gilbert.[2]

Chatfield remembers his fifteen years of religious life, from the age of fifteen to thirty, as "rather monastic," the most difficult part being the forced separation from his family during his years at the seminary when he was allowed but one visit a month and three weeks at home in August. The most consistently satisfying time seems to have been from the late 1950s to the early 1960s, when he was assigned to teach at Sacred Heart High School in San Francisco. His interest in Catholic Social Action deepened in a city percolating with the activity that would boil over a few years later. He found himself on the edge of early civil rights protests and met people from the Catholic Worker collective. Their day-to-day devotion to poor people impressed him, and privately he noted that although his own order had been founded to help poor children, it was currently helping "upper-middle-class and middle-class kids and their families continue their progress up the social ladder."[3] The Catholic Worker activists introduced him to the debate about the morality of nuclear war; he in turn discussed civil rights and nuclear war with his students at Sacred Heart and urged them to do what they could to put their convictions into practice.

In 1962, he was sent to Garces High School in Bakersfield as vice principal, dean of discipline, debate coach, and teacher of religion. His social views now in place, he taught peace in his classes, participated in the NAACP campaign against the repeal of California's Fair Housing Act, set up a Saturday school and then a summer "friendship school" for poor children, brought the Delano farm worker organizer Cesar Chavez to speak to his classes, and marched, in full religious vestments, in support of the Linnell rent strikers, He became a minor public figure. But Bakersfield was not San Francisco, and soon after Brother Gilbert arrived, some parents were circulating a petition to have him fired.

Brother Gilbert liked Chavez's modest style. The two spoke of Cesar's interest in farm worker co-ops as a primary vehicle for farm worker liberation. They drew close; in the summer of 1965 Brother Gilbert introduced Chavez to his religious superiors, imagining that they would grant the National Farm Workers Association a contract with the Christian Brothers Winery in the Napa Valley. The only discernible outcome of the meeting was to alert the top men in the Christian Brothers' hierarchy more thoroughly to the activities of their wayward brother in Bakersfield. In October of 1965, one month after the grape strike began, Brother Gilbert asked to be released from his vows so that he could join the NFWA. Ordinarily such requests take several months, sometimes years, to be granted; the Christian Brothers granted Brother Gilbert's request in forty-eight hours.

In his first NFWA assignment, LeRoy Chatfield was a combination roving ambassador for the association and Chavez's personal envoy, raising money for future farm worker co-ops from religious people and liberals in the Bay Area and Los Angeles. By the spring of 1967 he was well on his way to becoming a sergeant to the staff in Delano. The former dean of discipline viewed the young volunteers as something like novices in a religious order. When in Delano, he was the one person conspicuously absent from the scene at People's, the one most demanding of more sacrifice, and ever watchful for signs of who might be shirking his or her duties. The joke at People's was "So, tell me, what sacrifice did LeRoy make for the union? He sacrificed his vow of chastity."[4]

After leaving the Benedictines, Chatfield had hooked up with Bonnie Burns, an NFWA volunteer and onetime student of his, who had also been a teacher at the Garces Saturday school. They were married in less than a year and settled in Torrance, near Los Angeles, where they focused on fundraising among wealthy supporters in Beverly Hills and West LA, soliciting pledges of $100. None of the money was tax-deductible, and Chatfield deposited it all in a simple bank account. His LA contacts led him to Joan Baez, who agreed to make her first West Coast appearance in two years, in two back-to-back concerts at the Santa Monica Civic Auditorium in December 1966, with all of the proceeds going to UFWOC. The concerts were immediately sold out, and afterward Chatfield had something like $75,000 in his new bank account.[5]

Chavez was most pleased by how Chatfield combined a practical ability to get things done—especially on matters related to money—with an uncanny capacity for staking out the moral high ground. After the concert Chavez asked him to come back to Delano, and Chatfield quickly slid into the position of main aide and confidant. After the concert Cesar and LeRoy arraged a swap: Chatfield would turn over the management of the money he had been accumulating to Chavez, and Chavez would put Chatfield in charge of managing the operation and finances (and a far larger bank account) of the new Farm Worker Service Center, which had recently been set up as a tax-exempt 501(c)(3) nonprofit. Chavez would now have charge of the smaller account, whose use was unrestricted, and Chatfield would get the larger account (originally funded by the Reuther-controlled Industrial Union Division of the AFL-CIO, and later by various liberal foundations), which technically was limited to the support of social services.

This simple arrangement by two devout, practical men set the structure for the finances of the future UFW. The union would have its own account, holding farm worker dues, allowances from the AFL-CIO, and direct donations by supporters. The Farm Worker Service Center would have various accounts—including the union's medical and pension plans—loosely monitored by the federal government as charities. It was a highly successful system. When Chatfield left the union in 1972, he estimated that $6 million was in the Service Center accounts, completely separate from the union's official finances.[6]

Money was only one side of hardheaded practicality. Chatfield maintained complete control over the Service Center. With a staff of about a dozen, including his wife, Bonnie, and the cheerfully skilled Jessica Govea, the center became the prime example within the union family of a well-run, efficient operation. Chavez wished that the rest of his unruly organization could run so smoothly, and he looked to Chatfield for advice. At the same time, Fred Ross, who also ran a tight ship, was urging Chavez to demand more discipline from the volunteers. Bill Kircher, personally much looser than both Ross and Chatfield, simultaneously suggested to Chavez that he should tighten up what now had become a formal AFL-CIO organizing committee. The stage was set for what some people eventually would call "the first purge."

The pruning of democratic Delano was done primarily in the name of efficiency, discipline, and unity. But it also had an explicit political content: Cesar pruned to his left, while allowing his right to flourish. One of his most useful tools was a standard instrument of internal union repression: anti-Communism. Chavez and the three top advisers cheering on the pruning were anti-Communists of long standing. Fred Ross had promoted the Community Service Organization as an acceptable alternative to the Communist Party in the 1950s; Bill Kircher was a veteran of the purge of Communists from the Congress of Industrial Organizations; Chatfield had picked up the anti-Communism of Catholic Social Action. Chavez's anti-Communism included strands of Alinskyism and Catholic Social Action, but it was neither just an inheritance from his ideological forefathers nor a simple reflection of the popular anti-Communism of his formative political years. His interest in farm worker co-ops reflected a well-thought-out preference for voluntary co-operative association over any form of socialism—whether of the sort practiced by the existing Communist regimes or by the social democracies of Western Europe.[7]

Chavez did not introduce the issue of Communism into union politics. Agribusiness and its allies did that. From early on in the grape strike, *The Delano Record* and grower-sponsored right-wing pamphlets decried the "Cuban communist-trained Chavez lieutenant, Luis Valdez," and listed purported visits to Delano by various Communists, either actual party members or others whom the right-wing ideologues mistakenly identified as Communists, such as Saul Alinsky. The external anti-Communist attack reached its height in July of 1966, when the California State Senate held hearings in Delano on Communist influence in the union. Although those hearings concluded that there was no credible evidence of Communism in the farm workers movement, the investigation forced the union into a defensive position on the question of reds just a few months before Chavez began looking for ways to rein in the union volunteers.

Chavez's principal target was Eliazer Risco, a pro-Castro Cuban who had been invited to Delano by Luis Valdez at the beginning of 1966 and had settled in as a volunteer, working primarily with the Teatro Campesino and as a translator for *El Malcriado* and the Migrant Ministry. Risco was as unlikely a character as one might find anywhere in the 1960s, a period that offered plenty of candidates. He fled Cuba in 1958, when he was twenty-one, after Batista's police killed Frank País, a student leader who supported the July 26 Movement. País had been carrying a list of sympathetic contacts, one of whom was Eli Risco, a few years his junior and a fellow member of the same Santiago Baptist Church. Risco headed straight for Kansas, to the Ottawa Baptist College, in hopes of becoming a minister. But Kansas couldn't hold him, and he soon left for California, interested in meeting San Francisco's North Beach poets. On the way he stopped in Sacramento and enrolled at Sacramento State, where he participated in Quaker protests against nuclear war.

Next stop, Stanford, in 1964, where Risco became a graduate student in Latin American Studies and cochairman of the Stanford Committee for Peace in Vietnam. In that capacity he met Luis Valdez, who was in the process of moving to San Francisco. According to Risco, they became friends over Cuban cigars and rum. Later, after Valdez had settled in Delano, he urged Risco to come to the Central Valley and live amid a Latin American populist movement rather than just study such movements up in Palo Alto. Risco made one visit, withdrew from school, and came to Delano to stay.[8]

Eli Risco became one of the more colorful figures in the NFWA. He defended the Cuban Revolution, got along well with the Migrant Ministers because of his Baptist background, and was often accompanied by a blonde Venezuelan co-ed from UCLA who had arrived in Delano driving a gold Chevy Camaro and often paid for the drinks at People's. Risco lived in one of the two Delano houses that the union had rented for volunteers and slept under his large poster of "Carlos Marx." He was comfortably literate in both Spanish and English, and although that was also true of a number of people, it was unusual enough to make him a valuable contributor to the association. After the pilgrimage and during the DiGiorgio campaign, he became one of the more vocal opponents of the merger of the NFWA and AWOC, arguing at People's and at general meetings that the AFL-CIO would destroy the association's populist character. He was by no means a leader of the opposition, as there wasn't a formal opposition to lead, and to the extent that there was an informal one, that mantle would have been worn by others.

A party precipitated his dismissal from Delano. It was early 1967, while the union was embroiled in the Perelli-Minetti boycott. Sam Kushner, a reporter who covered the union for the Communist Party's *People's World*, invited Risco and a few others who were in Los Angeles working on the boycott to his house. Risco remembers that Dolores Huerta, Luis Valdez, Donna Haber, and Ruth Robinson were also there, "talking and singing and jiving,"

> . . . and it came out that we had copied the *corrido de la huelga* from an older *corrido de la revolución*, and we sang it with the revolutionary words, and from there we went on to songs of the Spanish Civil War, and finally the "Internationale." We then had a serious conversation with Kushner about the farm worker movement, the development of the proletariat, and the Communist Party. It was the kind of conversation you would have on campuses all the time. We weren't necessarily going to join the party, but there was a lot of talk. And Dolores didn't say much. When we got back to Delano, after a few days I was called in by Chavez, and he asked me about what happened at Sam Kushner's. Basically my reaction was, "Hey, we were just talking." And he said he was not happy with that kind of talk and that it didn't belong in Delano or in the union. It wasn't like before the sun sets in Delano, you have to be out of town. He didn't take me into the shed or on a long car ride. But when I left that meeting I knew I had to look for something else to do.[9]

Doug Adair, an editor of *El Malcriado*, heard the story at People's: "There was a party at Sam Kushner's house, Dolores was there and so were many of the people who got purged. We figured that Dolores fingered them."[10] Who was actually at the party and who was not has been impossible to reconstruct, but soon after Risco left town, he was followed by Ida Cousino, Ruth Robinson, Donna Haber, Bob Fisher, Bob Solodow, and a few others, most of whom were prominent, committed volunteers who had opposed, with various levels of intensity, the AFL–CIO merger. All of them were on the left of the volunteer staff. Like Risco's, their dismissals were not heavy-handed; according to Eddie Frankel, who decided to keep on working for the union, people were given a choice to give up their "radical politics" or leave Delano.[11] Some people, sensing the drift to the right, left on their own. One of the volunteers who privately complained to Chavez about Risco's banishment reports that Chavez responded: "Well, if you feel that way, maybe Delano and the union are not the right place for you—think about it."[12]

What shocked many people on the rest of the staff was the quality of those who were told to leave. Adair: "Hell, they might have been would-be revolutionaries, but they were very solid, very good organizers, who had been useful in the DiGiorgio campaign; they were very hard workers." Luis Valdez saw Risco's departure as the beginning of a "process of purging . . . which was ugly, it got real ugly, because specific radicals were being pinpointed within the union . . . and asked to leave. So people were paranoid, they were distressed, they were anxious, they were angry, they were whatever. And the union is joining the AFL–CIO, you know; all this is happening at once, so people are saying, What the hell is happening here?"[13]

Nevertheless, the anxiety soon passed. UFWOC was on a high. A strike victory at Goldberg Farms was followed by contracts at a handful of wineries, a pact with the Teamsters conceding organizing in the fields to UFWOC, and finally, in July 1967, a contract at Perelli-Minetti. Although the purge had had the proverbial chilling effect on a certain kind of left-wing talk in the union, it did not freeze all political conversation. Nor did the purge become well known outside the union's immediate circle, as none of the people who left broke ranks publicly with the union. Risco, for example, used his connection with the union to secure his place in the Chicano movement in Los Angeles, where he founded the seminal underground newspaper, *La Raza*.

The purge was so gentle, in fact, that some didn't see it as a purge at all. The informal position among some members of the staff and the Executive Board, which had not been advised in advance of Risco's expulsion, was that the union had a right to pick and choose among its volunteers. After all, argued Marshall Ganz in defense of Chavez's action, didn't the union have a right to define itself, to put limits on what was acceptable behavior inside the union and what was not? Or, as Gilbert Padilla put it: Did the Executive Board really have no choice but to accept Risco and his Karl Marx poster, even though both could bring some serious repression down on the union? The staff was divided on that question, and the matter was almost entirely dropped, its memory kept alive only by the self-described radicals, most of whom remained grouped around *El Malcriado* and Teatro Campesino. They were the next to go.

The life and death of *El Malcriado* present as a good an illustration as any of the trajectory of a scrappy farm worker community organization that swiftly mutated from family association to strike vehicle to independent union to big labor affiliate and movement emblem. *El Malcriado*, the "bad boy," both goaded and represented the organization that had spawned it, until finally it could do neither without betraying its own unruly spirit or violating the discipline of its increasingly demanding parent.

When the grape strike began in September of 1965, *El Malcriado*'s one-man staff, Bill Esher, was distributing 3,000 Spanish-language copies of the paper and had just started to print about 1,000 in English, which were intended for young Mexican American farm workers raised entirely in the United States, who could read English better than Spanish.[14] Soon after the new edition came out, about twenty little grocery stores stopped carrying the paper, because for the first time the store proprietors could read the thing and were a bit frightened by its antigrower message. But the loss of store outlets was more than made up for by the paper's newfound popularity in Los Angeles and the Bay Area, and soon after the pilgrimage the press run jumped to more than 8,000 in English and more than 3,000 in Spanish. Although the editors still wanted the paper to be "the voice of the farm worker," that voice was directed at new ears. Doug Adair put it succinctly. Speaking of both the Spanish and English versions of the paper, he recalled years later: "By 1967 our audience is the boycott. It isn't farm workers at all."[15]

Adair had come onto the staff in 1965 to help with the English edition. Final responsibility for the paper fell to Esher, but after the pilgrimage, and eighteen months of putting out an issue every two weeks, Esher was tired and worried about burning out. He was not satisfied with the intermittent love affairs he had had with supporters who passed through town, and he preferred the small, slow pace of the NFWA before it had been thrown into the storm of big-time media attention and politics. He often left Delano to take a break and started thinking about leaving for good.

As Esher began to pull away, Adair became the central figure at the paper, and quite a figure he was. Douglas Adair III, child of two college professors whose families had settled in Virginia before the American Revolution, was a 1964 Phi Beta Kappa graduate of Pomona College, a Woodrow Wilson Fellow in American history at UC Berkeley, and a mischievous young man who came to Delano, he said, because he wanted to be a farm worker. That intention was genuine, and he would remain with the union for almost twenty-five years, moving back and forth between the staff and the vineyards, ultimately becoming a small Coachella Valley date grower, a farm worker with a mortgage. The young Adair was also interested in politics, although not the variety common to the volunteers who streamed into Delano about a year after he did. A Democratic Party activist in high school and a picketer for Adlai Stevenson at the 1960 Los Angeles Democratic National Convention, by the time he reached Delano he was a Republican and self-described agrarian democrat, recruited to that particular political combination by his father's doctoral thesis on the politics of Thomas Jefferson and his admiration for California's liberal Republican senator, Thomas Kuchel. As a first-year graduate student at Berkeley, he threw himself into the Free Speech Movement, delighting in the supposed contradictions of being a Young Republican in the midst of his radical compatriots. He was proud to be a maverick, and even before he got to Delano and became an official bad boy, he was well on his way to developing his own manner of being both in a movement and independent of it.[16]

He had arrived in Berkeley in a 1935 canary-yellow Ford pickup, which he used to begin a little gardening business in the affluent Berkeley hills. Soon his interest in flowers and plants outstripped his commitment to his studies. When a fellow student activist, Marion Moses, told him about a summer project of the Student Committee for Agricultural Labor, where students would work in the fields near Visalia, he signed up. It was the summer of 1965, and he ended up living in the Linnell labor camp during the rent strike. He met Gilbert Padilla and was swept away by his charm. Padilla introduced him to Chavez. Adair's first job was picking peaches, and he soon found himself in the middle of a typical farm worker strike, a spontaneous walkout at the beginning of the raisin season prompted by a reduction in pay. An incident in that strike earned him immediate notice. When he went to a strike breaker's house to talk to the offending worker, the young man's father opened the door, listened to Adair explain the reason for his visit, coolly removed the black, horn-rimmed glasses from Doug's face, and knocked him down with a single blow. Adair calmly got back on his feet and said to the man who had just flattened him: "I'm sorry you hit me, but gosh, we are not here to threaten you or anything, we just wanted to explain what was going on."[17] The astounded attacker invited Adair and a few others in for coffee, where they engaged in a friendly discussion about the strike and the situation in the fields.

Bill Esher heard the story of the Phi Beta Kappa working in the fields who could talk to a man who had just hit him in the face and recruited him to the paper. Esher assured him that there was plenty of work in the grapes near Delano, and he would be able to find a job whenever he wanted. Esher was also interested in the 1935 pickup, as he needed a vehicle to distribute the paper. Adair arrived a few weeks before the grape strike and loved the activity and excitement. Farm workers gave him the nickname "Pato": for a Spanish speaker the vocalized *g* at the end of *Doug* is hard to distinguish from the *k* sound at the end of duck, and *pato* means "duck." That wasn't his only nickname; he was also called *malcriado*, not just because he worked on the paper but because of his irreverent, boyish, defiant humor. He became friends with Rudy Reyes and continued to look to Gilbert Padilla for his basic orientation on farm worker politics. He was a regular at People's. He loved the Teatro, and hung out with Augie Lira. He slept on the floor of the Pink House, or in an abandoned structure beneath a water tower, and finally in a back room at the *Malcriado* office. He admired Cesar, and although they never were close, Adair did not question Chavez's legitimate authority over the NFWA family. Once ensconced in Delano, he wrote to his parents, enthralled by what he described as the Chavez dream of a new life of dignity and purpose for farm workers, a life he had decided to share.

Adair was in the process of becoming the main person at the paper during the DiGiorgio campaign, the last time *Malcriado* would be used as a tool to organize farm workers. That campaign intensified the original contradiction inherent in Chavez's conception of the paper. *El Malcriado* was more independent than ever, and, to a certain extent, Cesar liked it that way, especially now, because the paper was coming under increasing attack from the growers and their allies. At the same time, Chavez considered the DiGiorgio vote so important that he and his head organizer, Fred Ross, began to give Esher and Adair strict orders about what should and should not be in the newspaper. When either of the young editors strayed, by intention or mistake, Ross and Chavez were upset. Ross made it clear to Adair that he didn't think it was smart to have a newspaper associated with the union but not under the union's complete control.

The paper's main audience was beginning to change from farm workers to the emerging coalition of their supporters in the cities. That coalition was wide and included some elements, such as AFL-CIO officialdom and Democratic Party functionaries, who were easily offended and accustomed to throwing their weight around. Now that they were reading *El Malcriado*, they found plenty of reasons to complain. Their objections usually reached Chavez through the AFL-CIO's Bill Kircher, and then Cesar would call in Esher and Adair and pass along the criticisms with a relatively gentle admonition to be more careful. When Chavez felt that his warnings were ignored, Dolores Huerta would characteristically deliver a more forceful reproach. Sometimes Kircher would talk directly to Adair, as the two of them got along well, and occasionally spent an evening together at People's.

The first major point of contention was Governor Pat Brown. In the period between the beginning of the strike and the agreement that provided for a second, ultimately successful DiGiorgio election, the governor was a common target of the NFWA and *El Malcriado*. Brown had continued to authorize small numbers of contracted Mexicans to labor in the California fields for two years after the Bracero Program was terminated by the federal government. He refused to intervene in the 1965 grape strike and famously declined to greet the pilgrims on Easter Sunday. So no one complained in January 1966, when *El Malcriado* put Augie Lira on the cover playing a foolish-looking Governor Brown in a Teatro skit; or in May 1966, when the NFWA was still trying to pressure him to intervene in the DiGiorgio election and *El Malcriado* called him "a liar, a traitor to the Mexican-Americans and farm workers who voted for him, and a fool who will believe any lies the growers tell him"; or after Brown and Reagan emerged victorious from the California primaries, and *El Malcriado's* headline screamed "Tweedledumb and Tweedlestupid," accompanied by a cartoon of a fat grower lifting the hands of both candidates in victory, all three standing on top of a defeated farm worker.[18]

But the NFWA's relationship to the governor changed after Brown authorized the reversal of the first, rigged, DiGiorgio vote. In exchange for his intervention, the NFWA, MAPA, and the AFL-CIO promised to support the governor against Reagan. This was not a serious departure for Chavez, who selectively supported liberal Democrats throughout his career and had supported Brown in both his 1958 and 1962 races, but it was too quick a shift for Doug Adair and many other union supporters and volunteers. Although Adair and the others understood the political trade-off, they could not accept Brown as an ally. In an issue before the second DiGiorgio election, Adair's editorial stated that *El Malcriado* didn't trust the state senators, who had come to town for hearings on Communist influences in the union, "any more than we do Governor Brown." In response, Ross and Chavez reminded Adair of the new relationship to Brown. But two issues later *El Malcriado* again criticized Brown for continuing to bring contracted Mexicans into California and featured a full-page Zermeño cartoon of a worried Brown pacing in front of a scale that tilted toward the side of the fat grower and away from the side of poor little Don Sotaco. And even in issue number 46, in which Esher and Adair reported the union's endorsement of Brown's reelection campaign under a headline "Viva Brown," they closed the article with a warning: "In the past the politicians have bought the farm workers' vote with promises and then betrayed them. It better not happen again."[19]

In issue number 48, their last issue before the election, they devoted the entire back cover to a subscriber's angry open letter to Brown, complete with an uncomplimentary photo of the governor coupled with a photo of a Delano cop. The letter, in large print, criticized Brown on a number of counts, and concluded: "I know that Reagan would be a terrible thing for California if he were to become Governor, but are you any better if you just talk nice and do nothing to protect the workers who are exploited mercilessly?"[20]

That did it. Kircher reported to Adair that people in the AFL-CIO had called Chavez directly and said, "How dare you print this. You are going to elect Reagan." Kircher himself wanted to know, "How can you possibly believe that Brown and Reagan are the same?" Adair answered that Brown had already been the governor for two terms and had done almost nothing for farm workers. Why did Kircher think he would be any better the next time around? Maybe it would be better, Adair added, to have an open enemy in office rather than a secret one. Adair's position was shared by many of the student volunteers who had come to Delano, and by a minority of people throughout the state who were fed up with both the Republicans and the Democrats and were beginning to build what would become, for a time, the most powerful third party in the country, the Peace and Freedom Party. Kircher was not convinced, but the two men remained on good terms. Chavez's patience, however, already worn thin, was now almost worn out. He was committed to a politics of putting pressure on the Democratic Party by supporting Democrats who helped him and punishing those who didn't. But even beyond the particular issue of Brown, Chavez could see that his *Malcriado* problem had intensified. The paper had become UFWOC's most prominent public face and was in the hands of some people whose judgment he did not fully trust.

A fundamental dissonance between the paper and the union leadership had become plain in the different responses each had to the disparate organizing initiatives and strikes that erupted in areas outside of the lower Central Valley immediately after the DiGiorgio election. A late September 1966 issue of *El Malcriado* featured an article about tomato strikers in San Jose, a long letter from the leader of another tomato walkout in Davis, California, a "flash" announcement of a cucumber strike of Texas migrants in Wisconsin, and an editorial declaring that the tomato strikes were the beginning "of a struggle that will soon bring justice to every tomato field from California to Florida."[21] Those reports left some large questions unanswered, even unasked. Chavez and Ross were highly suspicious of "spontaneous" strikes initiated by temporarily enthusiastic farm workers without much prior preparation. Who were the people leading these strikes, and how far could they be trusted? For example, the strike leader in San Jose, a man they had never heard of, was calling his organization the Santa Clara Valley branch of the United Farm Workers Union. What should UFWOC do about that? And if it wasn't clear how much help UFWOC could give California farm workers, what could the union possibly do to help struggles arising in places as far away as Wisconsin, New Jersey, and Florida? *El Malcriado*'s ardor was all very nice and was shared by most of the folks talking politics at People's, but Cesar Chavez and those around him were worried.

Already, in the midst of the DiGiorgio campaign, the union had been drafted into a walkout of melon workers in the lower Rio Grande Valley that, in various permutations, would engage union personnel, resources, and energy for a year and a half before sputtering to an unsatisfying conclusion. Centered in Starr County, the poorest county in Texas and the seventeenth poorest in the United States, where five major growers grossed more than $10 million a year mostly in melons and winter vegetables and paid workers just forty to eighty-five cents an hour, the Texas campaign made great copy. It involved mass meetings and mass arrests, a sit-in on the Mexican side of the border, where many of the workers lived, a 450-mile march to Austin, and the sweep of border politics from Tejano-Mexicano relations to paramilitary repression by the Texas Rangers. When melon workers struck on June 1, 1966, *El Malcriado* declared it to be the beginning of "a revolution for justice . . . the biggest revolution in Texas in one hundred years." Gilbert Padilla, however, remembers that the Executive Board was uneasy.[22]

The Texas workers had declared themselves NFWA affiliates without consulting the Executive Board. Their first strike raised wages to $1 an hour, but did little to establish the union; a second strike was lost at the beginning of the vegetable harvest that October, as was another melon strike the next year. Padilla, sent to Starr County to head the Texas project in 1967, called it "a bad scene." The towns were too small, the people too poor and desperate. "I told Cesar, 'Look, Cesar, you know how much trouble we are having in California, well California is a snap compared to Texas.' Cesar said we had made a commitment, and we had to stay. The tequila kept me going. I hit the bottle and made the best of it."[23]

At People's, Adair compared the Texas campaign to an unwanted child, who could be neither fully embraced nor abandoned—until Hurricane Beulah settled the question in August of 1967 by dumping four feet of water into the Starr County union office. After that, the Texas experience became notable mainly for how it shaped Chavez's stance regarding future farm worker organizing away from California. For the next couple of years, UFWOC's answer to out-of-state farm workers was an admonition to wait until we win in the California table grapes, then we will be in a stronger position to help you. But what may have been reasonable in 1967 became less reasonable later, as that definitive California victory always proved to be just out of reach. And so the union continued to tell farm worker activists and would-be farm worker organizers in other parts of the country to delay their own projects and to join the nearest UFW support organization. Eventually some people would ignore that advice and start organizing farm workers without UFW support or approval. That disturbed the UFW leaders, who worried that these other efforts would diminish the power of their boycotts and take away some of their funding sources. For Chavez, building a disciplined organization was indispensable to victory; movement without organization always spelled disaster, and he believed that his organization alone understood best how to organize farm workers. Thus, as the years went by, the UFW would consistently oppose would-be farm worker organizers outside of California or outside of the UFW.[24]

From early on, however, the *Malcriados* believed that rather than urge people to wait until the union won in California, UFWOC could say that it was tied down in California and could not offer much help to other areas, while at the same time encouraging other people to organize on their own. Bill Esher, writing in the December 1966 issue of *The Catholic Worker* about organizing in Washington, Oregon, and Idaho, stated: "Farm workers . . . will take it on themselves to organize those three states, using the small helps that we [UFWOC] can give them. The process is just as simple and complex as that."[25] Chavez believed that Esher's sentiments were foolish and naïve. He didn't think farm workers, on their own with just some "small helps," could successfully organize in the Pacific Northwest, or anywhere else.

The war in Vietnam was another source of conflict between Chavez and *El Malcriado*'s editors. By 1966 the broad national consensus on the war had been shattered. The AFL-CIO, however, remained LBJ's most important pro-war ally and UFWOC's single biggest financial supporter. Chavez tried to finesse the problem by arguing that since most farm workers supported the war, UFWOC would have to remain neutral. It was true that many farm workers were pro-war, but many were not, and the union never polled its members or had an open vote on the question. Chavez rightly figured that such a vote would be divisive, and his statement went unchallenged. Neutrality on the war, Chavez explained to Adair, meant that *El Malcriado* had to be silent on the subject.[26]

But the entire *Malcriado* staff opposed the war, as did most all of the farm workers and volunteers who hung out at the paper's office. Adair, who felt almost as strongly about the war as he did about justice for farm workers, fudged a little. In June 1966 he wrote a centerfold article about the unfairness of the draft but added at the end, "*El Malcriado* says: We hope they change the draft laws and make them fair. Actually, we hope that they end the draft completely. War is always bad for farm workers. This present awful mess in Vietnam is especially bad. We are not even officially 'at war.' This draft should not be necessary in peace time. And we wouldn't have the war or the draft if we didn't go meddling in other people's business so much." A few months later, he and Esher gave a full page to a reader's letter against the war with accompanying photos of Mexican American and African American GIs. The letter writer explained that he had supported "the *huelga*" for years and now was calling on his "*amigos*" for support in the struggle against the war. He reviewed his reasons for opposing the war and asked, "What do you believe?" Esher and Adair refrained from answering.[27]

The two were willing to engage in this kind of small-scale defiance of Chavez's orders because so many people in the UFWOC family, including its religious supporters, were against the war. Even on the Executive Board there was a slim antiwar majority: Dolores Huerta, Gilbert Padilla, Philip Vera Cruz, and Tony Orendain were opposed; Andy Imutan was a gung ho supporter; Larry Itliong was undecided; and Chavez was strategically neutral.[28] The Executive Board, never took a formal vote on the war, and its antiwar members accepted Chavez's argument that UFWOC leaders should not appear at antiwar protests. But as those protests became more popular that rule became harder to follow. In the fall of 1966 Chavez forbade any volunteers from carrying a UFWOC flag, sign, or banner in an upcoming San Francisco march organized by dozens of student, church, and antiwar groups. *El Malcriado* was not an official part of the UFWOC, Adair reasoned, and he and Marsha Brooks, one of LeRoy Chatfield's former students who helped out at the paper, did walk through the streets of San Francisco to Kezar Stadium, along with more than 50,000 other marchers, all the while carrying *El Malcriado's* own banner: a large red flag with the unmistakable black eagle in the center, and "El Malcriado, Voice of the Farm Worker" written across the top in white letters. It was just the kind of maneuver that delighted Adair, the authentic *malcriado*, and he never heard anything from Chavez about it.[29]

By the time of that march, however, Chavez had already decided that the paper was too much like its name: reckless and disobedient. The decisive moment, as far as Esher and Adair were concerned, had come in mid-October 1966, when Perelli-Minetti sued *El Malcriado* for an inaccurate story on the firing of some UFW activists, and the paper had to print several pages of retractions. It was in the middle of the boycott against the wine maker, and prior to publication, Adair had consulted with Chavez, who felt the story had some holes. Adair and Daniel De Los Reyes, the editor of the paper for a very short time, conscientiously tried to fix the article. When the company sued anyway, Chavez was so angry that he told Esher that Adair had purposely disobeyed him and that he should never be left in charge of the paper again.[30]

The conflict was not easily resolved. Financially independent and occupying its own building, *El Malcriado* was both part of the union family and apart from it. Not only Adair and Esher but its other volunteers occasionally challenged the union leadership at meetings, and they did not always back down in the ensuing arguments. They even broke up a meeting at Filipino Hall, where, as Adair remembered it, LeRoy Chatfield and Jim

Drake were calling for more sacrifices, harder work, more time on the job. Adair asserted that, on the contrary, the staff needed more time off, and a chorus of people agreed. Mack Lyons, an African American DiGiorgio worker who had been brought onto the staff, said he needed more time for his family. Kerry Ohta, a Japanese American from Forestville who later married Augie Lira, supported him. Marsha Brooks chimed in, defying her former teacher Chatfield. Others followed their lead. People were burned out, they said. Chatfield got angry. He reminded the volunteers that they had no right to negotiate with the union; they should either do what they were told or get out. Adair remembers answering: "What do you mean? Of course we can negotiate with the union. Life is about negotiating with everybody." Chatfield and Drake gave up. Their meeting ended in a shambles.[31]

The departure of Eli Risco had shocked the *Malcriado* staff. They knew him well; he had worked regularly on the paper. And just a short while before Chavez had politely ushered the other people out of Delano and UFWOC, *El Malcriado* had run "The Lieutenants, A New Generation of Farm Worker Leaders," which mentioned, among others, the soon-to-depart Ida Cousino. Adair had been on Chavez's side in the debate over the AWOC merger. He was the only person on the *Malcriado* staff who supported it, because he figured it was the one best way to solidify the relationship between Mexican and Filipino workers, but he couldn't understand why people had to leave over that disagreement—if, in fact, that disagreement was the reason they had left. Adair argued at People's that one of the worst things about the purge was that it was done without explanation. What were the charges and the evidence? Who decides who leaves and who stays? What did people say in their own defense? Nobody knew. All they knew was that their friends were gone.[32]

After Adair was finished being outraged, he got depressed. Delano had changed. Conversations were more guarded. People were looking over their shoulders. Who was next? It wasn't bad enough to make him quit the union, and, besides, his deep respect for Chavez led him to doubt some of his own behavior. He felt he was too much the *malcriado*, a thorn in the side of the emerging UFWOC establishment, and he wanted to get away. Texas was a convenient out. It was April 1967, and *El Malcriado* had been covering the Texas story in almost every issue for the previous nine months. Adair's mentor, Gilbert Padilla, was already in Texas, as was his Wobbly friend, Eugene Nelson. Others on the way out of the union had gone by Texas to visit. The newspaper staff agreed to send him to Starr County. Once he got there his enthusiasm returned, despite the poverty and difficulty of the situation. He put out a Texas edition of the paper, which unashamedly promoted farm worker movements all over the country. He mass-produced a large poster of Zapata, which became hugely popular in the Chicano and New Left movements, and which helped *El Malcriado*'s shaky bank account. He wrote warm accounts of the Texas battle in *Liberation*, *The Catholic Worker*, *The Nation*, and *The Texas Observer*. His Spanish improved; his commitment to farm worker life deepened.

Back in Delano, now with an increased workload, Esher was almost as unhappy as Adair had been. He deeply admired Chavez, but he shuddered at the changes he saw in him. One incident stood out. After the NFWA affiliated with the AFL-CIO and became UFWOC, Chavez distributed gasoline credit cards to much of the staff. When the first month's bills arrived, he called people together, bawled them out for how much money had been spent, would not listen to one word of explanation, and cut up their cards on the spot. Esher had never seen Chavez treat people so shabbily. He thought to himself that Chavez was treating the staff like children.[33] "I began to see well-intentioned people who came to help getting used, and used up, much as people in a war get used up. I was afraid of it happening to me . . . I was rankled by my proximity to the union, which now had at least as much authoritarian structure as any of the employers we opposed."[34]

Esher blamed the changes on the transformation of the small association into a larger union, the national media attention that accompanied it, and the influence of LeRoy Chatfield. "I always disliked LeRoy," he said.

> He was like the kind of guy a corporation brings in to fire a bunch of people and whip everybody into shape. He was very authoritarian, both in his personality and in the kind of structure that he set up in the Service Center . . . And he kept himself isolated. He and Bonnie lived somewhere else, separate. He was not one of the crew; he was the boss. And Cesar took to him. Cesar began attracting people who could work in that kind of structure. The only people who would last in Delano were the ones who would take orders. In some ways, this change was required by the new situation . . . It couldn't be the loose organization it had been before . . . But Cesar and LeRoy went overboard.[35]

Esher lasted a little less than three months after Adair left for Texas, and then he too departed. Marsha Brooks put out two issues of the paper by herself and then gave up. The last issue of the original *Malcriado* was dated August 16, 1967. Cesar Chavez was relieved.

That last issue of *El Malcriado* included a seven-paragraph story on El Teatro Campesino. After summarizing the history of the theater, naming many of the actors, listing some of the more popular *actos* and songs, and touting its current tour, the story concludes: "The Teatro has been noted for their loyalty and dedication as they unselfishly gave so much of themselves for the benefit of us, the farm workers of America. They are artists, but of a rare breed. They are artists who have dedicated their lives to a cause they believe in. They have never forgotten us in our struggles, and we can never forget them. They are leaving a void that will be impossible to fill."[36]

This last line in the last issue of *El Malcriado* was, for many years, the only public acknowledgement that the Teatro had actually left the union. And the place and timing of the announcement fit perfectly, as the purge, the closing of the original *El Malcriado*, and the banishment of El Teatro Campesino, all within six months, were of one piece.

The purge had hit the Teatro hard. Donna Haber was Luis Valdez's girl friend. Eli Risco had come to Delano because of Valdez. Some of the others who were purged were also close to the Teatro, but for Valdez the loss of his friends was not as serious as the loss of "openness" in the UFWOC and the new feeling of what he called a "witch hunt."[37] And Valdez, despite all of the Teatro's success, was himself a likely target. He had come to Delano not only as a would-be theater director but also as a committed radical, an occasional writer for Progressive Labor's *Chispa*. He and the rest of the Teatro stood to the left on most of the issues confronted by the union. They were against affiliation with the AFL-CIO, doubtful about the alliance with the Catholic Church, and strongly against the war in Vietnam.

The political differences between Chavez and the Teatro went beyond debates at union meetings or gossip at People's. After its great success on the pilgrimage and its first tour of college campuses, the Teatro returned to Delano and worked on new material, which the company performed at the tortilla factory. One of the *actos* was against the war. Augie Lira remembers the consequences: "Cesar came and watched it. He . . . never cracked a smile. And after the play he talked to me, Luis, Felipe, Roy, and a couple of other people. Cesar told us very quietly that we should leave the issue alone. That it was just going to cause problems." Later, the Teatro members decided that they would no longer do their antiwar material in Delano but would perform it on the road. Someone told Cesar about it, and he warned them again, in what Lira calls "no uncertain terms."[38]

The Teatro reluctantly dropped the antiwar material but added an *acto* critical of the Catholic Church. It did not preview this one in Delano but just did it on the road. Felipe Cantú played the Pope. The *acto* opened with farm workers on the stage underneath a big platform, holding it up. Cantú came in as the Pope, murmuring his own comic Latin. Some of his church lackeys helped him onto the platform. As his weight bore down on the farm workers below him, he blessed them. Cantú was "hilarious," reported Lira. "Cesar was furious about it." Again someone had called him and snitched. "He threatened to split us up. To send Felipe to one place to work on the boycott, me to another place, and Luis to a third." He reiterated that the Teatro had to stick to farm worker issues. "No plays, no songs, no anything that criticized the war or the church."[39]

LeRoy Chatfield was not just offended by the Teatro's radical politics; he simply didn't like the players. They stayed up so late they often missed early-morning picket line duty; they drank beer and smoked weed. Getting drunk, high, and staying out late were not introduced to Delano farm workers by the Teatro, of course, but Chatfield's criticisms resonated enough with some of the more conservative farm worker families that he was emboldened to make some small moves against the troupe. He called a meeting to complain that members of the Teatro (and *El Malcriado*) were shirking their picket line duty, and were thereby demoralizing the other folks who had to picket in order to get access to the union's food supplies and other benefits. Adair and Esher retorted that many times they had to stay up to work on the paper; the Teatro performers explained that they usually rehearsed late into the night. On this issue, Chavez intervened against Chatfield; *El Malcriado* and the Teatro were allowed to send one representative each to the early-morning picketing.[40]

Some folks in Delano whispered one other criticism of the Teatro, which reflected what was happening to the union as a whole: the Teatro had deserted Delano and abandoned the workers, they said. The charge did not gain much momentum, as the Teatro remained overwhelmingly popular in Delano, but it did presage the future, as the Teatro's absences, like the shift in *El Malcriado*'s intended audience, were among the first visible signs of UFWOC's turn toward its supporters in the cities. After its success on the pilgrimage, the Teatro was on the road to Bay Area colleges, then back home to work on the DiGiorgio campaign, then back on the road for two weeks, hitting five colleges and universities in Washington and Oregon, and labor gatherings in Spokane, Seattle, Yakima, and Portland. The Teatro brought $2,100 home to the union from that Northwest Tour, *El Malcriado* proudly announced, at the same time advertising another tour of Northern California, starting in upscale Marin County. After two more California tours, the troupe was off to Texas for three weeks. *El Malcriado* explained the value of all this travel to the struggle in the fields and started calling the Teatro "the touring theatrical company of the Huelga."[41]

Luis Valdez frankly acknowledged the change in focus, but he maintained that it originated with Chavez, who told him that the early tours were good for the boycott—as they certainly were, raising money and spreading the word. In retrospect, Valdez sees the issue somewhat differently: "Cesar had begun to emphasize the boycott a lot more, and he eventually was subject to the same accusations that they leveled against the Teatro real early, or *Malcriado*: in the sense that he was paying more attention to the boycott than he was to the strike; that he was paying more attention to the organizing in the cities than he was to organizing in the ranches. And it was real easy to, I think, criticize the Teatro for this because we were literally out of town."[42]

Although the final break came over a disagreement on whether the Teatro should go on a national tour, Valdez did not believe that the tour was the key problem. He considers Cesar's attempt to cancel the tour as a form of punishment for what Chavez called Luis's effort to "politic" among the workers. Thirty-three years later, Valdez recalled the chain of events. A number of farm workers, upset about the purge because of all the dissatisfaction that followed, asked Luis to come with them to talk it over with Chavez. Valdez, unwilling to play the role of intermediary, urged them to talk to Chavez themselves, but they were reluctant. "People didn't know what to do. They didn't want to confront him. I certainly didn't want to confront him." Finally Valdez suggested that all the folks who were unhappy about the purge should gather at People's on a Sunday afternoon to discuss what to do. When the day came, the Teatro found itself alone at People's. Luis and the others played a few games of pool, and left.[43]

The next morning Valdez was summoned to Chavez's office. "What happened at People's?" Cesar asked. Luis tried to explain, but Chavez was having none of it. He accused Valdez of trying to organize against him. He said that the Teatro had lost touch with *la causa* and threatened, once again, to break it up. Then Chavez called an Executive Board meeting and proposed that the Teatro not be allowed to go on its upcoming national tour. A shrewd move: canceling a tour could be seen as an attempt to get the Teatro back to its roots.

A split Executive Board voted four to three to cancel the tour, with Philip Vera Cruz casting the deciding vote against the trip. Before the vote, Valdez had explained that the tour was already booked and that the union would look very bad if it canceled. After the vote, he says, "I stood up and said, 'Well, if that's the way you feel about it, I have no choice, I have to pull the Teatro from the union.' And Chavez said, 'Well, what are you going to do?' And I said, 'We will just be independent. We have nothing against the strike, and really nothing against the union. But I figure that what I am doing is just as important.'"[44]

After Luis left the meeting, Cesar sent someone to the tortilla factory to take away the Teatro's green van. The Teatro had bought the van from a union supporter for $800, and Valdez's position was that it belonged to the Teatro. But Chavez argued that the money had come from donations the Teatro collected on tour for the union, and that people in the union couldn't decide on their own how to spend such money; therefore, the van belonged to the union.[45] But when Chavez's people came to take the van, there was a standoff, which lasted most of a day and threatened to become violent. Word spread through the flabbergasted union community. Finally, Chavez called Valdez in and declared peace. The Teatro could keep the van and go on tour. What would happen after the tour was left unsaid. People in Delano figured the Teatro was gone for good. They were right.

The tour was fabulously successful. In Denver, Chicago, Detroit, Washington, New York—everywhere—the performers were warmly received, and on college campuses they were a smash hit. They did their strike material and raised money for the union. Chavez played his part, too. Luis had been calling Cesar, trying to stay in touch, trying to find some basis on which they could remain part of the union. Chavez was cold and uncommunicative on the phone but publicly friendly. He sent Valdez a telegram before a New York performance to be read to the audience. The telegram praised the Teatro members for all the work they were doing for the union and congratulated them on their success.

"We all knew that the telegram was just publicity and that we wouldn't be able to go back," said Augie Lira. "And when we got back, Chavez said you can't work here anymore, you are out. We had meetings with the Executive Board and argued our case, but really there was no way we could stay any longer."[46]

A small group of people relocated with Valdez to a farm in Del Rey, about seventy miles from Delano. The Teatro had no money of its own, and faced a period of extreme poverty. Felipe Cantú with a family to support, stayed behind.[47] Life in Del Rey was hard—they tried to make some money farming and failed miserably—but politically the players thrived. They continued to tour, performing primarily for students, and they found themselves at the center of the expanding Chicano movement. "We saw the Chicano movement grow right in front of our eyes on all campuses," recalls Valdez. "They needed the Teatro Campesino to come through just as a symbol of a rising consciousness."[48] The Teatro continued to do strike material and promote the union, but it also picked up on the interests of its audiences, especially the young Chicanos. The *actos* started to emphasize cultural pride. Together with the photographer George Ballis, the Teatro members made a movie of Corky Gonzalez's "I Am Joaquin," a long poem that had been passed from hand to hand within the Chicano movement. They called themselves "cultural nationalists" and came to believe "that culture could be a focal point for community organizing." Although the Teatro did not change its name, it became a Chicano theater, not a farm worker theater.

The Fast

July '67 to June '68

In December 1967, *The Nation* identified the leader of the United Farm Workers Organizing Committee as Hector Chavez. Although the pilgrimage had moved the organization onto the edge of the national stage, and the DiGiorgio victory had alerted farm workers across the country to the possibility that the new union might actually win, Cesar Chavez was not yet a famous man. Not even to copyreaders at *The Nation*. It was Chavez's twenty-five-day fast—begun two months after the magazine called him Hector—that transformed him into a national figure on his way to the cover of *Time*, and a fit subject for Peter Matthiessen to profile in *The New Yorker*. But Chavez did not fast to become a celebrity, and his new position in the national consciousness was only one of the many surprising consequences of what he sometimes called his extended meditation on nonviolence.

The curtain rose on the fast seven months before it began, in the sweltering July days of 1967, as grape pickers in the lower Central Valley returned to work. UFWOC now had eleven contracts, nine in wine grapes, covering about 5,000 workers. The most recent one, at Almaden Winery, put the basic wage at $1.80 an hour and included the now-standard hiring hall, vacation and holiday pay, and increased piece rates. The union had just laid the cornerstone for the first building of its new headquarters on the recently purchased Forty Acres outside of Delano. Under the cornerstone were the original statement of purpose of the National Farm Workers Association and its first constitution, the Schenley contract, the AWOC charter, the black-eagle flag, strike buttons, the Plan of Delano, and the first issue of *El Malcriado*. The Teamsters had just agreed, for the second time, to leave farm worker organizing to this new AFL–CIO organizing committee. The UFWOC leadership had the initiative again and was free to decide what to do next.

In a series of executive board and leadership meetings, the basic choice was between focusing on wine or table grapes. Bill Kircher pushed for finishing up in the wine. UFWOC already had about half the wine industry signed up, he argued, and since the contracts increased the cost of labor, union wineries would have to pay more to harvest their grapes than their nonunion competitors.[1] To Kircher, the logic was inexorable: a competitive industry cannot indefinitely be half union and half nonunion, any more than a country can long endure being half slave and half free. Moreover, Kircher believed that "the winery operations . . . were the most vulnerable to boycotts; I wanted to go after everything that was in a bottle until we had 100 percent of that part of the grape industry."[2]

Most of the others in the leadership circle disagreed. Cesar was the most adamant. The wine companies were scattered all over California, while the table grape acreage was concentrated in and around the lower Central Valley. Chavez and his closest colleagues had been organizing the Mexican American grape picking families of that region since 1962. The farm workers who now served as union volunteers all came from that community, and they were the true base of the union. It wouldn't make sense to begin a new organizing drive in other parts of the state. And the wine grape pickers were different—mostly single Mexican men who spent their long off-seasons back in Mexico because wine vineyards, requiring much less pre-harvest preparation than table grapes, provided less year-round employment. Table grapes were also the bigger prize, employing thousands of workers, rather than the hundreds in wine vineyards. Kircher's position got little support on the executive board.[3]

But how to go about renewing the fight in the table grapes? The grape strike was two years old, and now was pretty much a strike in name only. The leadership decided to target Giumarra Brothers Vineyards. It was only one company, but it was the largest in table grapes, with 6,000 acres, 2,500 workers at peak season, annual sales of more than $12 million, and an estimated profit of between $5.5 million and $7.5 million a year.[4] It helped that most of its table grapes were in the Bakersfield area (a half-hour drive from Delano) near DiGiorgio's Arvin Ranch, which had a union contract and where Giumarra strikers could be dispatched to work.

UFWOC leaders did not believe that they could win a strike at Giumarra. What they hoped to do was use the strike to kick off a boycott. Nevertheless, they tried to make the strike as effective as possible. They organized house meetings, where workers complained that the foremen demanded such a high-quality pack—requiring slower, more careful work—that the pay at Giumarra, although nominally the equal of other companies, was actually lower. After those initial discussions, the organizers passed out authorization cards, and soon more than 800 workers, a clear majority of Giumarra's mid-July workforce, had agreed to have the union represent them. This early campaign was so focused on the workers and came off so well that Henry Anderson, the head of Citizens for Farm Labor, concluded an article in *Farm Labor* on the campaign with a wish, wrapped in an impression: "We are privy to no UFWOC secrets, but we have the impression that

Chavez, after two years filled with fund-raising, greeting dignitaries, testifying at legislative hearings and other distractions, is determined to get back to the root and the source: organizing agricultural workers so well that they can guide their own destinies forever afterward."[5]

What Anderson called "distractions" the union leaders saw as basic elements of a winning strategy. They didn't believe they could organize people in the fields without mobilizing their supporters in the cities; therefore, they would have considered it a serious mistake to think of one activity as opposed to the other. Thus, when Giumarra refused to meet directly with the union, Chavez announced that UFWOC would start both a strike and a boycott if the company did not agree to representation elections by July 24. When the deadline passed, the union held a fiesta at the Bakersfield fair grounds featuring a free barbecue and dance for Giumarra workers and their families. Six hundred people rose in unison, endorsing the union's call for a boycott against the company and pledging not to work during any strike. Less than a week later, on August 3, after two other mass meetings, 200 people, among them some Giumarra workers, set up the first picket lines at a few of Giumarra's vineyards. The strike had begun. The week before, boycott organizers in New York, Chicago, San Francisco, and Los Angeles had already contacted large supermarket chains and asked them not to buy Giumarra grapes.[6]

Fred Ross and Chavez had chosen Eliseo Medina to MC the Bakersfield event, and immediately afterward Ross congratulated Medina on a job well done. Medina had been one of the original thirty organizers conducting the Giumarra house meetings. Under Ross's direction he had focused on the labor camps, where he was popular enough to become a natural choice to be one of the main public faces of the union.

The fiesta turned out to be Medina's last assignment as an organizer of Giumarra workers. "The next day Chavez calls me, and he says, 'Well, we're going to have to go out and do a boycott, and we'd like to ask you to go out and do a boycott in Chicago.' . . . And I said, 'Well, sure, where's Chicago?'"[7]

At the time, no one disputed that decision, as all agreed that the Giumarra campaign would be won in the cities, not the fields. Years later, however, some would question the wisdom of sending a natural leader away from Delano on the eve of a big strike to talk to boycotters instead of using him to motivate farm workers. Later, after Chavez had sent Medina on multiple assignments far away from the fields, a few people came to believe that Chavez's 1967 decision was rooted in an early fear of Medina's growing popularity among the workers, and his desire to remove a potential rival from the farm worker community.

Union leaders were so sure that a win over Giumarra would come from boycott pressure rather than from the strike that they anticipated some of the difficulties that might follow a boycott victory. When Chavez announced the deadline for the company to agree to representation elections, he also said that the company would "not get two bites from the same apple": if Giumarra turned down his first offer of elections, the union would not agree to elections later. The boycott demand would be for a union contract, not for an election. In this way, UFWOC hoped to avoid the problem it had encountered at DiGiorgio, where the majority of the people actually working in the grapes had not voted for UFWOC. In any battle where a strike was lost but a boycott won, that might happen again. "No two bites from the same apple" was meant to prevent it.

Giumarra owned many vineyards, spread over sixty miles, from Wheeler Ridge near the foothills of the Tehachapi Mountains (the southern edge of the Central Valley) to Ducor, just north of Delano. Able to mobilize 200 pickets on the Thursday that the strike began, UFWOC concentrated its forces at the Edison Ranch, just east of Bakersfield. On Monday a company spokesman allowed that "pickets have brought some failure of workers to enter the fields."[8] In Edison, union railroad workers, citing the AFL-CIO's endorsement of the strike, refused to move their trains across UFWOC picket lines, leaving railroad cars filled with scab grapes stranded on the Giumarra spur. Eventually, supervisory personnel would couple up the stranded cars, but the point had been made: in the coming battle, farm workers would enjoy unprecedented levels of support from other union workers.

On Tuesday, just five working days after the strike began, Judge Kelley Steele of the Kern County Superior Court issued a temporary restraining order restricting the number of legal pickets at Giumarra fields. The order easily could have been written by the company's lawyers. No more than three pickets could stand at each side of the main entrances to the vineyards, and in all other areas adjacent to Giumarra fields, picketers had to stand at least fifty feet apart. The order not only guaranteed that picketers could not interfere with the free movement of scabs in and out of company property; it also made it difficult for picketers to inform workers that a strike was in process. While it was legal for UFWOC to go on strike, the restraining order made it illegal to do what was necessary to win.

But the leadership never planned to win the strike by stopping production. It declared its intention to obey the court order and occupied itself with a combination of lawful symbolic picketing, hit-and-run actions by others who harassed strikebreakers and evaded the police, and intermittent acts of vandalism against the company. Meanwhile, it initiated a new tactic. Two days after Judge Steele's order came down, 150 UFWOC pickets, led by Chavez, appeared at the Bakersfield Federal Building, charging that the Immigration and Naturalization Service was failing to arrest illegal aliens and legal resident aliens ("green-carders") who were working at Giumarra

vineyards.* U.S. Labor Secretary Willard Wirtz had issued a regulation prohibiting green carders from working at struck ranches just three weeks earlier in
response to the UFWOC campaign in Texas. Chavez told the *Bakersfield
Californian* that the AFL-CIO was "bringing pressure in Washington" for an
investigation of the charges. Jim Drake told the *Fresno Bee* that UFWOC
"contemplated" some kind of court action against the INS.[9]

The following weekend, the INS arrested a foreman transporting nine
undocumented workers from Giumarra's Edison Ranch to a Caritan ranch,
where he supervised grape picking. Chavez told the press there was a
"planned operation" to bring in both legal and illegal Mexican aliens to
harvest the Giumarra crops behind UFWOC picket lines. The INS, denying that it was responding to pressure, arrested more than 500 undocumented
workers in Kern County fields in one week, sixty-two of them at Giumarra.
Next, UFWOC organizers, who were familiar with many of the strikebreakers, drew up lists with the names of green-card scabs. When *El
Malcriado* resumed publication as an official "organ of UFWOC," in January
1968, five months after the strike began, it published those names, with an
explanation that "every day UFWOC is submitting lists of green card
strikebreakers to the Immigration Service."[10]

The presence of so many undocumented workers and green-carders in
the fields was but a small reflection of what was happening throughout
California agriculture, with or without a strike. Mexican immigrants, legal
and illegal, originally given easy access across the border so that they could
replace the departed braceros, would soon become the dominant majority
in the agricultural workforce, diminishing the role of Mexican American
farm workers. Consequently, UFWOC's decision to pressure the INS
carried some immediate (and many future) dangers. In pitting itself against
"wetbacks" and green-carders, UFWOC risked alienating a growing
percentage of the workforce that it needed to organize. It also intensified
already existing divisions within farm worker communities. Furthermore,
UFWOC was now in the strange position of trying to force the *migra* to be
more active when, generally, all farm workers wanted to see less of the
migra, not more. The *migra* were despised throughout the various farm
worker communities because they characteristically mistreated all people of
Mexican origin, documented and undocumented. UFWOC did couple its
public calls for INS raids with statements that it was not against green-
carders in general and with the charge that the *migra*'s failure to act was just
another example of the way they functioned as a tool of the bosses.

---

* Often I use the term "illegals" or "illegal aliens" because they were the formal expressions used by UFWOC at the time. To change them post-hoc would misrepresent the
union's attitude toward the underdocumented. Informally, many UFWOC staff, including
Doug Adair in *The Nation*, on December 11, 1967, used the term "wetbacks."

Disclaimers aside, the Giumarra INS campaign reinforced the impression among farm workers that UFWOC was primarily a Mexican American organization, acting in the interests of settled farm workers and against the interests of recent Mexican immigrants.

The UFWOC campaign was not some silly mistake. *El Malcriado* had complained about "wetbacks" in its earliest issues. In 1965, strikers claimed that carrying an NFWA picket sign was proof to the *migra* that you were legal.[11] Calling on the *migra* to deport scabs was a logical next step. The campaign also had deep precedents within organized labor. The AFL in California had consistently opposed immigration and focused its organizing efforts on domestic workers. The Bracero Program had reinforced traditional trade union opposition to immigration. The National Farm Labor Union in the Imperial Valley strike of 1951 had not only pressured the INS to prevent illegals from crossing the border; its own organizers had attacked undocumented workers with baseball bats. When Bill Kircher testified before a Senate hearing in September 1967 that "green card immigrants are undermining and undercutting the wages and working conditions of U.S. citizens," he was saying what union officials had been saying as long as anyone could remember.[12]

Yet Cesar Chavez and the people around him did not always follow the AFL-CIO line. And Chavez had proved to be quite capable of opposing racial, ethnic, and national divisions within the farm worker community in the past. So the question remains: Why did he embrace a policy that immediately antagonized many farm workers and made it more difficult to unite farm workers in the future? It is not a question that was directly put to him in 1967, but historical distance permits three possible answers.

The first concerns demographics: the demographic shift in the California fields, from Mexican Americans to Mexicans, was just beginning in the midsixties, and Chavez did not foresee how large that shift would be and, therefore, how disastrous it would be to take a position against undocumented workers and green-carders. The second concerns an outmoded strategy: in 1959, when Chavez first organized farm workers, his group successfully opposed the Bracero Program; seven years later, it didn't seem too different once again to be pressuring the Labor Department and the INS to restrict the use of Mexican labor. These two explanations, however, do not adequately answer the question. For a start, although Chavez may have missed the demographic shift in 1967, he couldn't have missed it in 1974 when it was in full flower, and yet Chavez and the UFW would then promote another, even larger campaign against the undocumented. The second explanation is also inadequate because Chavez, rather than being bound by earlier experience, often had showed himself to be strategically flexible, able to shift gears quickly depending on the political climate and opportunities.

A third explanation remains: Chavez could ignore the effects of the INS campaign on farm workers because he was not primarily concerned about organizing them at that time. What mattered was publicizing and organizing the boycott. Pointing the finger at "illegals," green-carders, and INS failures helped explain to boycotters why strikes weakened or collapsed. In 1967, it would have no negative impact on boycott organizing. Whatever damage was being done among farm workers could be taken care of later.

Rudy Reyes went to work at Giumarra's Edison Ranch a couple of weeks before the strike. Larry Itliong had asked him to go in as a "submarine," the UFWOC term for someone working in the fields with the specific purpose of spreading the word about the union. Reyes didn't have enough time to do much organizing, but he did bring a few young Filipino workers to the fiesta at the Kern County fairgrounds. They enjoyed the party, but on the morning of the walkout they continued working, and he found himself alone on a road next to one of Giumarra's vineyards. "I tried to burn a telephone pole so that it would fall across the road and block the bus carrying strikebreakers," he recalled. He gathered up some grape boxes, piled them around the base of the pole, and set them on fire. "It didn't work. . . . The pole didn't catch fire."[13] The next day Reyes joined the regular picket line, but away from the line he and a small crew spent the next several months planning and carrying out various acts of vandalism against the company—the kinds of things farm workers almost always do when they have a beef with their bosses. They cut the guy wires supporting the grape vines, being careful not to damage the vines. They sabotaged irrigation pumps. They burned down a couple of packing sheds.[14] They made sure not to hurt anyone. Rudy Reyes considered it neither violence nor self-defense. It was not much different from Halloween pranks. He put sugar in a company bus's gas tank. He put a strong laxative in the Giumarra labor camp breakfast milk.

"Vandalism was the same thing as boycotting," he said. "You were hurting them in the pocketbook. In some ways the boycott was just another extension of burning the sheds. And it was a blessing to some of the members who were bored with the boycott. They wanted some more action. Vandalism was one of the things that kept violence from erupting."[15]

The distinction between violence and vandalism was common currency among the UFWOC staff. News of a burned packing shed or disabled irrigation pumps brought cheers at informal parties, at the same time that UFWOC leaders were denying any knowledge of who might be perpetrating such acts. How much the leaders did know is a matter of conjecture. Rudy says that Chavez knew about some of it, but not all. Tony Orendain, who occasionally joined in on the vandalism even while he was secretary-treasurer of UFWOC, says that Chavez asked to be kept in the dark. "'I don't want to know,'" Tony remembers Chavez telling him, "'so I won't have to lie when people ask me about it' . . . but he knew in general what we were doing." Even Chris Hartmire, who was far from the vandalism himself, believes that Chavez knew all about it, but maintained a position of "plausible deniability."[16]

Grower vandalism strengthened the general support for vandalism among UFWOC staffers. Six months before the Giumarra strike began, someone firebombed the UFWOC building in downtown Delano. The same night someone started multiple fires in the Pink House and the print shop. Union cars were regularly damaged. A parked VW bus used by union staff was firebombed. Another firebomb was thrown into the union's co-op gas station. In July, less than three weeks before the Giumarra strike began, someone slashed the tires of five union cars.[17] Firebombings are always dangerous, but most of the other vandalism against the union, like the vandalism against the companies, was relatively petty stuff, fairly standard in the small towns of the Central Valley.[18] In such a climate, hardly anyone on the union staff, even those who were most adamant about nonviolence, criticized (either publicly or privately) what was generally considered to be the humorous, mostly harmless, union pranks of Rudy and his friends.

As the Giumarra picket lines dwindled and the company was able to get its grapes picked without costly delay, however, union vandalism ceased being an informal, ad hoc operation. Chavez assigned his cousin Manuel to head up the "research committee," whose ostensible purpose was to trace the routes of the refrigerated railroad cars carrying Giumarra grapes so that boycotters could picket them when they arrived at their destination. The research committee did that, but it also did what it could to damage or destroy the refrigeration units on those cars. Years later, Fred Hirsch, who had been an important part of the research committee, explained the close connection between the committee's two objectives: "It is a lot easier to boycott grapes if they are cooked or frozen."[19]

Manuel Chavez and Hirsch worked out of what they called the "war room," which they set up in a rented building within walking distance of the Pink House. They put large maps of the railroad lines out of Bakersfield on the walls and discussed their research with much of the UFWOC family. Friendly railroad workers gave them the numbers of the refrigerated freight cars carrying Giumarra grapes. As the trains passed through Delano on their way north, peaceful picketers would stand alongside the tracks at the same time as teams of drivers jumped in their cars to follow the trains. In the Fresno, Stockton, or Roseville railroad yards or on the slow ride into the Sierras those teams smashed the refrigeration units with hammers, cut lines that led from the units into the railroad cars, and shot up the refrigeration system with hand guns at close range, or with high-powered rifles at longer range. No one ever got hurt, and the adventure stories told by the research team were often entertaining. Manuel Chavez told the best stories, with Reyes coming in a close second. Hirsch had the best results. These *movidas* provided much cheer to the small number of Giumarra pickets.[20]

Between 1965 and 1970, the grape strike was relatively free of violence in the sense of physical force used against human beings. That was somewhat surprising, given the high-level stakes, the long history of violence in the California fields, the absence of a labor law providing a legal, institutional method of resolving agricultural disputes, the celebration of revolutionary violence in Mexican culture, and the contemporary violent events in the United States. People on both sides carried guns—some growers brandishing rifles and shotguns, some picketers concealing pellet guns, BB guns, and a few handguns—but rarely used them. Growers occasionally sprayed pickets with pesticides; strikers rushed the fields to chase out scabs when they got the chance, and threw rocks and dirt clods at them. In town, away from the picket lines, fist fights between strikers and strikebreakers were common, and sometimes involved knives. Growers often drove dangerously close to pickets on the side of the road. Once a sales representative for a struck grower angrily drove a truck through a picket line and hit Manuel Rivera, breaking his pelvis; in retaliation a Filipino striker ran over a grower, breaking his hip. In the worst episode of the entire five years, Teamster goons severely beat DeWitt Tannehill, an AWOC organizer who drove the coffee truck in the pilgrimage to Sacramento, forcing him to strip and then sodomizing him with a stick.[21]

There were several reasons why there wasn't more violence. Most people don't like violence much—either receiving it or dishing it out—and unless they are stampeded into it by social circumstance, they will avoid it. On the company side, growers realized that violence would boomerang, as the union would publicize it across the country and use it to strengthen the boycott. Thus, growers were restrained from orchestrating an updated version of the vigilante campaigns that they had led against strikers since World War I. In addition, Chavez's early declaration that the strike would be nonviolent, his penitential fast in 1968, and his other declarations of nonviolence restricted the amount of violence on the strikers' side of the picket line.

Chavez's call to nonviolence, however, did not ever grow into an internal union campaign to eliminate all violence from the strike. The union rarely offered nonviolent training for people who picketed, as did the early Student Nonviolent Coordinating Committee in the South. And although Chavez developed an idiosyncratic nonviolent philosophy of life, on only a few occasions did he or anyone else try to teach that philosophy to the union family. Thus, the majority of activists believed that, within the union, nonviolence was a tactic, not a way of life. And tactics can change, depending on the circumstances. Certainly, union activities were enveloped in Catholic ritual, which reinforced Chavez's pledge of nonviolence, but many union activists had long treated Catholic ritual as just that, religious exercises with little relationship to lived experience.

Chavez's own commitment to nonviolence was intermittent, sometimes even inconsistent. LeRoy Chatfield, one of the union's most aggressive proponents of nonviolence, recounted years later that before the fast, Chavez's attitude toward strikers' violence seemed "ambiguous." "Some things he winked at, some things he disapproved of, some things he didn't want to know."[22] In 1965, Cesar's authority to impose his own pledge of nonviolence on the entire union membership had been somewhat limited, but that had changed by the time of the Giumarra strike. The pilgrimage had reinforced the union's pious public profile and enhanced Chavez's authority. The purge had demonstrated that Chavez was in control institutionally and that volunteers who opposed him could easily be removed from the union. Some of the most militant exponents of self-defense, however, were not volunteers but striking farm workers. Epifanio Camacho, in particular, had considerable support from other farm workers, so removing him would not have been a realistic option for Chavez at the time, had he wanted to do so. But that didn't appear to be the case. Chavez not only did not remove him, he made him a picket captain in the Giumarra strike, just six months after Camacho had been arrested once again, this time for fighting in front of the McFarland post office.[23]

Camacho himself reports that during the strike, Chavez gave him the same instructions, almost to the word, that he had given Tony Orendain: "'I know that you do a lot of *chingaderas*.* But don't tell me what you are doing, because I don't want to know. So when people ask me about it, I won't know anything."[24] Henceforth, Camacho, already arrested six times by the local police, was more careful to hide the activities of his picketing crew. On a few occasions, Chavez called on Camacho to say the prayer opening the Friday-night meetings. Epifanio would come forward and ask God to give the strikers patience and to help them be nonviolent while elsewhere his crew "punctured tires, burned boxes, chased scabs, and destroyed irrigation pumps."[25] He felt like a hypocrite, but he consoled himself with the idea that he was just following Cesar's lead and that public declarations of nonviolence coupled with secret vandalism and aggressive self-defense was the true union policy.

In the fall of 1967 the Giumarra boycott did not go well. Table grapes, unlike wine and alcohol, are sold in retail outlets without brand identification. Because educating consumers proved difficult, the early boycotters focused on shippers, wholesalers, and retailers, who knew the origin of the grapes they shipped, bought, and sold. Giumarra countered by establishing new labels. Then, in an act of industrywide solidarity, other Delano grape growers sold their labels to Giumarra, which used them on its own boxes.

---

*   Hard to translate, probably best rendered as "I know you do a lot of stupid shit."

On a trip to New York, the largest national market for California table grapes, Fred Ross found that Giumarra's label switching had everyone confused. Neither the boycott staff nor some of the retailers could distinguish between scab and non-scab grapes, and consumers didn't have a clue. The boycott's prospects seemed bleak.

In December the boycott leaders regrouped in Delano, and at another retreat the union leadership made two major decisions. First, the boycott would be extended to all California table grapes. The grape itself would be the label, and because California supplied 85 percent of the national market, virtually no grapes would be okay to buy or eat. The growers had united against the union so that they wouldn't be defeated one by one, but united they became a single target. Second, the union would send its best farm worker organizers out on the boycott. Ross was the primary advocate of that proposal; he contended that farm workers promoting their own cause would be more effective than young white volunteers arguing for them. Since the harvest was over, and there didn't seem to be much for farm worker staff to do in Delano, the rest of the leadership agreed.

In January UFWOC sent telegrams to the other Delano growers requesting meetings to set up union recognition procedures. The growers did not respond, nor did they respond to mediation offers from the California State Mediation and Conciliation Service, nor from church and political figures. Although hardly anyone was working at the time, UFWOC declared all of the ranches on strike. Within the union, such strikes subsequently became known as "legitimacy strikes," as their sole purpose was to legitimize the boycott.[26]

That winter more than fifty people, UFWOC farm worker staffers and their families, boarded a used school bus along with Fred Ross, Dolores Huerta, and Eliseo Medina, and left for a cross-country trip to New York City. Motorists and bystanders at gas stations and roadside cafés would never confuse this bus and its passengers with Ken Kesey's psychedelic trippers traveling the roads at the same time, but in many ways the farm workers were more adventuresome. Most of them had never spent any time outside of rural California, except perhaps for some time in Mexico; all but a few were monolingual in Spanish. They had no idea how long they might be gone. They had almost no money in their pockets. They had no idea where they would be staying in New York, nor even whether they would remain in that city for very long. They were betting their individual futures and their families' destinies on the success of what was at the time a shaky proposition: that a tiny union that had just failed in a boycott of Giumarra Vineyards would be able to win an even bigger boycott of all California table grapes.

★   ★   ★

Once again, Cesar Chavez turned to religious penance to extricate himself from a bad political fix. The penitential fast, like the pilgrimage, emerged from the gloomy tule fog and an equally impenetrable political winter. It was pruning season again, and despite the strike, Giumarra had more than enough workers. Picketing was so weak that some workers didn't even know they were breaking a strike.[27] There was no Teatro to lift people's spirits; no playful *Malcriado* to poke fun at the bosses and raise hopes. Many ardent picketers were now in New York; those left behind were so demoralized that they often skipped the fog-bound picket lines altogether.

Only one picket squad remained regularly active, the one led by Epifanio Camacho. His close comrades, Jorge Zaragosa, Manuel Rosas, and a few others, as well as a small number of older Filipinos specialized in hit-and-run activities. Hidden in the fog, on back roads far from the police, they would shower surprised pruners with rocks and dirt clods. In early February, after Camacho's crew chased a car caravan of scab pruners that was leaving the vineyard, one of the strikebreakers complained to the police that a UFWOC picket had damaged her fender with a chain. The "attack" was front-page news in the *Delano Record* the next morning, along with another report that picketers had set off firecrackers on the edge of a Giumarra field. A few nights later, an empty farm labor bus was firebombed. The next night an irrigation pump was burned.[28] On Valentine's Day, less than a week later, Camacho was served with a subpoena to appear in court. He had been charged with contempt for violating Judge Steele's injunction limiting picket line activities and the conduct of the strike. Three hundred "John Does" were also listed as violators of the injunction. Also charged with contempt of court was Cesar Estrada Chavez.

Camacho appeared in court the next day and pleaded not guilty. Chavez had not yet been served a subpoena and was unsure of how he was going to respond.[29] It would not be hard to defend mass picketing in violation of the court order that required picketers to stand fifty feet apart. Even arson and rock throwing would not have been too serious in most strikes. But much of UFWOC's appeal depended on its public commitment to nonviolence, and if that commitment proved to be hollow, the union would be seriously damaged at a time when it was already wounded.

Violence, the black power leader H. Rap Brown had recently told the country, was as American as apple pie. In February of 1968, television news was serving up an extra helping. The same week that Camacho and Chavez were charged with contempt of court, U.S. troops in Vietnam, reeling from the Tet Offensive, suffered their highest level of casualties in the history of the war—543 dead and 2,547 wounded.[30] On the weekend after Valentine's Day, when Chavez was still doing all he could to avoid the subpoena-carrying sheriffs, Reies Tijerina, a Chicano leader who had led an armed raid on a rural New Mexico courthouse, spoke at a Black Panther rally in support of Huey Newton in Los Angeles. He called for unity between black and brown revolutionaries. At the same rally Stokely Carmichael praised the urban uprisings of the previous three years and urged blacks to continue their guerrilla warfare. That same month, in a contentious strike at the *Los Angeles Herald Examiner*, a scab printer was shot dead.[31]

In danger of being added to this growing list, Chavez decided to recommit himself and his union to nonviolence through a penitential fast. He began preparing himself the day after Camacho was served with the subpoena. He talked to only one person about his decision, LeRoy Chatfield. "We were close at the time and we talked often," Chatfield remembered. "In the days immediately before he announced the fast . . . he didn't believe that he could do it physically. It wasn't looking too good. He was practicing. And he got too hungry."[32]

One late morning in the course of this practice, he was working at the Pink House with Virginia Hirsch when a sheriff knocked at the door. Virginia spotted the lawman and informed Chavez, who told her to say that he was out of town. Then Cesar leaped out a back window and got into Virginia's car, which was parked behind the house. After dispatching the sheriff and waiting a short time, she walked to her car, where Cesar was crouched in the back seat. Virginia drove the car to her house. They laughed nervously.[33]

"It was close to noon. Chavez said he was hungry. I said I made spaghetti yesterday and I have lots of it. He ate three bowls. And some carrots and salad. And then someone came to pick him up." On February 19, "we were called to the meeting, and he told us he was on a fast. Oh my God, I thought. After eating my cooking, Chavez never wants to eat again."[34]

About seventy-five people were at Filipino Hall that Monday. Chavez began the meeting on the stage alone, speaking at a lectern. He gave a rambling speech, mostly quiet, but sometimes loud and angry—unusually emotional for a Chavez public appearance. His theme was violence and nonviolence. He criticized those who condemned the war in Vietnam but supported violence in the vineyards of Delano. He denounced "saboteurs," who were endangering the union with macho acts of vandalism. Violence would hurt the union, he argued, just as it had already hurt the black civil rights movement. He was fasting, he said, as penance for the union's fall into violence, and he would continue to fast until he was either ignored and forgotten or all union members renewed their commitment to nonviolence. This was a personal decision, he said. It would not be put to a vote. Nor did he want people to talk about it. He was going to walk out to Forty Acres and nobody should try to stop him. "I am doing this," he said, "because I love you."

People didn't speak until Chavez had left. Camacho angrily denied that his picket squad had been violent, arguing that most of them were elderly Filipinos who couldn't fight anyway. Others rose to express their worries. Larry Itliong said that they should try to convince Chavez to give it up. Manuel said that it would be pointless to try to talk him out of it. Chatfield was slow to respond. Eventually, in an impassioned speech that closed the meeting, he declared that instead of wasting time arguing, he was going to take every precaution to protect Chavez's health. He would make sure Chavez had blankets, a good bed, a clean place to rest. Forty Acres would now be sacred ground, he announced. No cars would be permitted there until the fast was over. After his speech, the meeting broke up. General Counsel Jerry Cohen, who was concerned that the union would miss Cesar's leadership, went up to LeRoy. Chatfield was way ahead of him. He told Jerry not to worry. "This thing is going to be on national TV."[35]

Forty Acres, the hoped-for physical and spiritual center of the union, sat a few miles out of town, near the city dump, still a brown, barren, flat piece of land. A trailer housed a clinic, which had become a major draw for local farm workers. Doctors and dentists regularly came up from Los Angeles and tended to farm workers covered by UFWOC contracts, or those who joined the union independently. A two-room adobe structure, meant to be a co-op gas station, was being used for storage. Behind it stood a small, one-room temporary wooden structure, which was to be the office of the reestablished *Malcriado*. Cesar had decided to resurrect the paper but henceforth it would be reviewed by the union legal staff before going to press. A new editor, David Fishlow, had been brought in to run it, and Doug Adair, back from Texas, was asked to stay on as business manager—after getting a serious dressing down for his past errors from Jim Drake and Chavez. As soon as the meeting at Filipino Hall ended, Adair and Fishlow started planning volume 2, no. 1, and put out the issue a few days later: "Frame-Up" jumped out in large block letters on the cover, superimposed over the first page of the subpoena.

The adobe house, built under the direction of Richard Chavez, with homemade bricks and enormous exposed wooden beams, was an architectural gem, meant to express the cultural brilliance of common Mexican folk. Twenty to thirty yards behind it, Rudy Reyes had put in a lovely kitchen garden, which extended up to the *Malcriado* shack. The adobe had two large rooms connected by an arched passageway. Near the back of one of the rooms was a small walled-off storage area, and in that room, behind a closed door, first on a cot, and then on a stiff mattress on a board on the floor, Chavez fasted.

The first night, Nick Jones and Virginia Rodriguez set up a tent outside the adobe and declared their intention to stay there for the duration of the fast. They were among the new union couples: he was one of the more competent student volunteers, and she was a farm worker daughter who worked in the legal office with Virginia Hirsch. Tony Mendez, one of the 1965 strikers, also put up a tent. Manuel Chavez, seeing the enormous potential in a tent city of Chavez's supporters, went to Tony Orendain, and asked for union money for tents and supplies. Orendain refused: Chavez had said the fast was a personal act. So Manuel went to Chatfield, who took money for the tents out of the Service Center's funds. Chatfield supervised the cleanup of the room across the passageway from where Chavez was fasting, and it became a combination chapel and center of operations. A few people built an altar and put up bright paper flowers and an oil painting of the Virgin of Guadalupe. LeRoy and his wife, Bonnie, fastened a photograph of Jack Kennedy to the large union banner that hung on a side wall. Mendez added a crucifix. In a few days the banner was filled with offerings. Father Mark Day, the UFWOC priest, announced that there would be a Mass every night while Chavez fasted.[36] About a hundred people came to the first Mass. Chavez, as would be his custom, left his cot, walked through the passageway, and joined the celebration. He took the host and sipped the wine. Sometimes he spoke briefly. As he weakened, he spoke less.

The UFWOC leaders were nothing if not organizers. In a couple of meetings run by Chavez, they sorted out assignments. Marshall Ganz was to make contact with the various ranch committees and get them to bring as many farm workers as possible to Delano. Manuel was to arrange security; he personally would often guard the door behind which Cesar was fasting. The legal department would take care of setting up a time for Chavez's court appearance, where he would answer the charge of contempt of court. Marion Moses and Peggy McGivern, volunteer nurses, would watch over Cesar's health. LeRoy Chatfield would oversee the whole operation.

Five days after Chavez walked from Filipino Hall to Forty Acres, Chatfield called the press. Chavez had said the fast was personal, but he did not object—the fast was both personal and political. Even in that first speech, he had made it clear that his fast had an audience, albeit a limited one of union members whom he hoped to convince to give up their violent ways. But he also had a wider audience in mind. One does not announce a secret to fifty people if one wants it kept. The fast was a response to the subpoena, and to be an effective response, it had to be public.

So why the early plea that no one speak of it? Yes, the fast was political, but it was still personal. Too much attention would spoil the peaceful atmosphere conducive to a religious experience. Moreover, as Chavez well knew, penance always has its doubters. Is the public act an expression of internal contrition or just an act for show? No human can know for sure. The act of contrition is between the sinner and God. A public penance, no matter how difficult, can cover up an insincere private repentance. Inviting the press in from the start would have encouraged such doubts. But UFWOC had to invite the press. As a compromise, Chavez refused to be interviewed while fasting. He didn't have to talk to newsmen; the fast, like Billy Budd's silence, spoke for itself. It was beyond words. His aides could make the political points.

The first story about the fast appeared on Sunday, February 25, in the *Los Angeles Times*, filed from Delano by Harry Bernstein, the *Times* labor reporter. After describing the nightly Masses and the scene at Forty Acres, Bernstein wrote that the fast was Chavez's response to calls for violence by other Mexican American leaders, as well as an answer to his own followers' talk of "burning the fields and arming themselves with rifles." Bernstein quoted Chavez's speech at Filipino Hall: "We cannot build a strong union and bring dignity to farm workers based on violence. . . . The deliberate taking of a life of a grower would make the cause for which we fight meaningless." Bernstein made no mention of the subpoena. In his next story two days later, about Chavez's court appearance, he reported that "Chavez insists his fast is not linked to the contempt charge but that it is intended to get a new 'commitment' to the achievement of justice through nonviolence."[37]

Was the fast nothing but another *movida*, a fraudulent use of religious penance? Some people, both inside and outside the union, thought so at the time. They couldn't have been more mistaken. The fast's political utility did not trump its religious authenticity. Did Chavez tolerate vandalism and small-scale violence before the fast? Certainly. But that made his penance even more heartfelt. He was contrite about his own actions, not just the behavior of his followers. Did he mislead people about the true origin of the fast as a countermove to the subpoena? All the more to be penitent about.

Sixteen years earlier, Father McDonnell had propelled Cesar Chavez into public life by showing him that anger at injustice and a strong sense of religious duty were compatible. But as Chavez would soon learn from Fred Ross and Saul Alinsky, politics was also a game of dirty tricks, small deceptions, staged events, where ends justified means. The organizer had to take on the burden of doing dirty tricks, although for Alinsky that was hardly a burden. His *movidas* were fun, and, as he wrote, "The mutual goal is so bright that it is not important if one must go through a few devious valleys and shadows in the struggle for a people's world."[38]

Some were shocked by Alinsky's forthrightness; others were fascinated, just as people were shocked and fascinated centuries before, when Machiavelli laid out the problem in all its naked splendor. To build a strong, united Italy, the Prince must not only be willing to engage in dirty tricks, he must master them. To be good, the Prince must first learn to be bad. Often the bad could be publicly displayed; sometimes it had to be hidden, and if it became known, the Prince must blame it on his subordinates. But Machiavelli believed in God, in Heaven and Hell, and no secrets could be kept from Him. Here was Machiavelli's true heroism, stated pithily in his declaration, "I love my native city more than my own soul." To save that city he was willing to jeopardize his relationship with God.

Cesar Chavez is closer to Machiavelli than to Alinsky. Although Chavez was a modern man and his faith was shaped by a never-ending struggle with doubt, he was a believer. Alinsky was not; for him the only problem was what other people might think of the organizer's dirty tricks, not what the organizer might think of himself. But that was a concern for Chavez because his "self" could never be hidden from his God. Chavez, however, found a softer resolution to the problem than the one Machiavelli offered: penance. Chavez made the difficult choices required by politics to build his union and help his people, and then was genuinely contrite. Thus, he had it both ways. As long as his penance was genuine, he could continue the politics. As he told Levy, without explaining the logic, during the fast he realized that "if I am going to save my soul, it's going to be through the struggle for social justice."[39]

One week after his announcement of the fast, Chavez went to the Kern County Courthouse to enter his plea. He arrived supine, in the back of a station wagon, on a makeshift bed. Jerry Cohen, his lawyer, and LeRoy Chatfield, his confidant, helped him from the car to the judge's chambers. The two white men, both over six feet tall, walked on either side of the short brown man who staggered between them. The three walked through a path that opened up through a crowd of more than 1,000 people, most of them farm workers, kneeling in two neat lines from the courthouse steps, through the outer doors and up to the entrance of a second-floor court-room. The people on their knees prayed, sang hymns, or maintained total silence. Chatfield had been right. The image was flashed on TV screens across the country, along with the news that the man in the middle, held up by his two aides, was weak because he was fasting for nonviolence.

Inside the courthouse, the three men went up the escalator. "You have the press on the left side as you go up to the second floor of the hearing," recalled Jerry Cohen, "and Chavez stumbles at the top of the escalator, and I am on one side of him. And I said, 'Are you okay?' And he turned to me, with his face away from the press and he winked."[40]

Jerry wasn't the only one who saw the wink. Fourteen-year-old Liza Hirsch, who was living in the Chavez household at the time, also was at the top of the escalator, and she figured the wink was for her. It was not a wink either would ever forget, and both would struggle to interpret it. For Cohen it was a sign that Chavez had maintained his sense of humor, that he was not taking himself too seriously, that he was conscious of how "he spent himself" for the cause. For Liza, the wink was an intimate connection in the midst of a spectacle, a way of saying we are still human beings, friends even, despite the extravagant pageant we have created around us. The wink did not negate the sincerity of the show, but it did acknowledge that it was a show, a performance, a staged event.

The judge was overwhelmed. Giumarra's lawyer asked him to clear the court, as the farm workers were potentially disruptive. The judge refused saying, "If I kick these farm workers out of the courthouse, it'll be another example of goddamned gringo justice." Instead, the judge delayed the hearing until the next day. But the next day was a repeat performance, with Cesar Chavez one day weaker. On the second day, Judge Morton Barker, sent from Los Angeles County to help the overextended Kern County Superior Court system, put the trial date off for a month and a half, saying, "To continue this trial now would do great and irreparable damage to Mr. Chavez, and this court would not tolerate such a thing." John Giumarra Jr., a graduate of Stanford Law, who had recently passed the bar, was a bitter loser. In Judge Barker's chambers he complained: "You mean a guy can get out from under a criminal charge by going on a hunger strike?" But the plea of the privileged, well-fed heir of an agribusiness giant didn't have a chance against the moral witness of all those kneeling farm workers. A few weeks later, Giumarra quietly withdrew its complaint. After that, Jerry Cohen declared, "the courthouse was our turf."[41]

Back in the storage room at Forty Acres, Chavez renewed his interest in the Mahatma, the great soul, Mohandas Gandhi. In Oxnard in 1959, when Chavez organized the burning of the Farm Service referral cards, he told big John Soria that he had modeled the action on the Gandhi-sponsored burning of registration cards in South Africa. In 1965, Chavez was still talking up Gandhi to his assistants; Bill Esher reports that Chavez read Louis Fischer's *The Life of Mahatma Gandhi* several times. In both the rose and the grape strikes, and many thereafter, Chavez asked people to take a solemn oath not to scab, just as Gandhi had done in the strikes that he had led. The current fast was partially inspired by Gandhi's first fast for a public cause, begun in the midst of a losing textile strike. Gandhi had fasted not to pressure the bosses but "to steady the strikers," as Fischer put it. "I fasted to reform those who loved me," Gandhi declared, just as Chavez was later to do.

Like Chavez, Fischer's Gandhi was a great showman who knew how to maximize the political effect of his moral experiments and exercises. After the pageant at the courthouse, Cesar studied Gandhi with renewed intensity. "I couldn't really understand Gandhi until I was actually in the fast; then the book became much more clear. Things I understood but didn't feel—well in the fast I felt them," he later told Peter Matthiessen. The fast proved the theory. Nonviolence was working, and Chavez could see how it had worked before. During the fast, Chavez came to believe that not only Gandhi but Christ and even Moses were nonviolent heroes. Before the fast, nonviolence had been both tactic and creed for Cesar Chavez. Most of those close to him believed that in the early years the tactical considerations were primary. By the end of the fast, the creed had seeped deeper into his soul.

Chavez talked about Gandhi mostly after the fast, and usually to visiting intellectuals or on the boycott circuit. During the fast, in Delano, UFWOC organizers continued to present the act as a part of Mexican Catholic tradition, as a *sacrificio* for the union. Strictly religious fasts are common in Mexico, religious-political hunger strikes only slightly less so.[*] Dolores Huerta, responding to the charge that Chavez was trying to play God during his fast, explained: "I know it is hard for people who are not Mexican to understand, but this is a part of Mexican culture—the penance, the whole idea of suffering for something, of self-inflicted punishment. It's a tradition of very long standing."

A week after the court appearance, Richard Chavez built a simple, elegant cross and planted it in the ground in the middle of the small tent city. Chavez had wanted a cross above the first union office on Albany Street; he had also flirted with the idea of placing the Stations of the Cross at Forty Acres.[42] He had been talked out of both those plans, but now no one would dare oppose his request that Richard erect a prominent cross at the union's new home. Several women, following another Mexican Catholic tradition, walked on bleeding knees from the edge of Forty Acres to the place where Chavez was fasting. A wave of religious passion washed over the union. Ganz, the rabbi's son, could see its political utility. In charge of mobilizing farm workers to come to Delano, he traveled to the areas where UFWOC had contracts and talked to the ranch committees:

> So workers in Hollister who got this contract—and they hadn't done much to get it, you know, they signed up, participated in negotiations, and got this contract—all of a sudden they were confronted with the fact that there was a price attached to all this. And it was in a language they really understood. This guy was fasting. . . . Well, why? they asked. Well, the problem of the strike and the danger of violence, but also the fact that it is going to take a whole lot to win this thing, and maybe we can convince him to start eating again if we show that we are going to do what it takes to win. Well, what's that? Well, we are going to go to

---

[*] Even an ex-president, Carlos Salinas, went on a short hunger strike after he left office as an answer to charges of corruption. Opponents went to the mansion where he was fasting and threw food at his house.

Delano. We are going to start boycott picket lines. So the whole thing got translated into what they needed to do in Hollister to build the union. To make it stronger. To participate in the movement. To be willing to go to the cities.[43]

Nothing was as effective, though, as a meeting with Chavez himself. Lying on his mattress, he received visitors one by one. At times, farm workers waited in line for their audience with the suffering leader. It was organizer heaven. "The fast turned out to be the greatest organizing tool in the history of the labor movement—at least in this country," said LeRoy Chatfield. "Workers came from every sector of California and Arizona to meet with Chavez, to talk to him about the problems of their areas. . . . Chavez had more organizing going on while he was immobilized at the Forty Acres than had ever happened before in the union."[45] Not only workers came. For the first time, bishops of the Catholic Church came to Delano, met with Chavez, and endorsed the union. Chicano activists also poured into town. Reies Tijerina, the Chicano would-be revolutionary, came to talk to Cesar Chavez, to declare his support for the union, and to chide reporters for their attempts to drive a wedge between him and Chavez. Oscar Acosta, who was working as a lawyer with radical Chicano groups in Los Angeles and was known as the Brown Buffalo, left his audience with Chavez in tears. In a passage in his autobiographical novel, *Revolt of the Cockroach People*, he gives an account of what transpired in the adobe's storage room when he met Chavez:

> The woman leads me to a door at the rear of the chapel. . . . She opens the door and whispers with her eyes how I must not disturb him too long. I enter and close the door behind me. It is very dark. There is a tiny candle burning over a bed, illuminating dimly a wooden cross and a figure of La Virgen on the wall. My ears are buzzing. There is a heavy smell of incense and kerosene. I don't move. I hear nothing. I no longer have any idea of why I have come or what I will say.
> "Is that you, Buffalo?" The voice is soft, barely audible. He coughs.
> "Yeah, Chavez."
> "Sit down."
> I approach the bed and finally make out the frail form. It leans toward me, offering a limp hand. There is so little life left in him. I hear his short breaths but can barely detect the outline of his features against his skull. He struggles to keep his eyes open, then lies back and sighs.
> "This is really something," he murmurs. "Do you know how long I've been waiting for a Chicano lawyer to come up here? But I knew the day would come."

I have no idea what to say, what he is expecting. Finally I manage to say something.

"Hey, Chavez . . . I always wanted to come down here, but . . ." Would he understand my confusion? "But . . . I dropped out for a while."

"And now you're back?"

"Well . . . that's what I've come for. I need your advice."

And then there is silence. His breathing becomes regular. Perhaps he has fainted from weakness. I sit beside the bed, gritting my teeth and balling my fists. I can hear the sputtering of the candle.

"Buffalo?"

"Yeah, Cesar. You all right? Should I leave now?"

His eyes open and he sighs again deeply. "No, I'm OK. How about you? How you doing?"

"OK . . . I'm down in LA now. I've been there for a few months, trying to write."

"I know. I've heard from Risco."

"Oh, yeah? . . . Well, I've sort of taken some cases. The guys that got busted during the Blow Out last month." He must have heard the question in my voice.[45]

"You're with Risco and Ruth [Robinson], aren't you?" he asks gently.

"Yeah . . . Well, that's what I want to talk to you about."

"Those two are great organizers," he says proudly. "They used to run our paper before going down south. I keep up."

There is silence again. In the darkness, I think again of his words. The Father of Chicanos, Cesar Chavez, has heard of me.

"Buffalo?"

"Yeah, I'm here, Cesar."

"So how are things in LA?

"All right, I guess."

"Are you guys trying to get the *viejitos* to join you, too?"

"Look," he says, a little stronger. "I know LA is a graveyard for organizers. You, personally, Brown Buffalo, a Chicano lawyer, have got to help those kids. Nobody else is going to do it. The militants are doing a terrific job. Aren't you satisfied?"

"Oh yeah." I think about his philosophy of non-violence. "I didn't know if you would approve," I say lamely. I don't know how to explain to him where I'm at.

"Listen, *viejo* . . . it doesn't matter if I approve or if anyone approves. You are doing what has to be done. "*¿Que mas vamos a hacer?*"

"It's not exactly what you do . . ."

"So what? I'm a man, just like you, no? Each of us has a different role, but we both want the same, don't we?"

Role? Want the same? "I guess . . ."

"Come on, *viejo*! Don't be so . . . They tell me you are one hell of a lawyer. Don't give up so easy, *hombre*."

"But I don't want to be a lawyer!" Finally I get out a part of it.

"So?" he says, leaning up again. "Who in his right mind would want to be a lawyer, eh?"

Again he falls back. I hold my breath until I can hear his own breathing. Now it is my turn to sigh deeply as I wipe tears from my squinting eyes. The door opens behind me. The woman puts her fingers to her mouth to indicate my time is up. I arise to leave.

"Buffalo?"

"Yeah, Cesar."

"You go back to LA and take care of business. OK, viejo?

"OK, Cesar . . . And you take care of yourself."

I'll be fine. You tell them I said hello."

"OK Cesar. Adios."[46]

Many inside the union family were put off by the religious aura that surrounded Chavez. Tony Orendain was the most vocal of the critics. When Orendain went to the storage room to talk about union business, he turned his chair around and sat with his back to the union leader. He ascribed the fast to Chavez's desire to win the support of the Catholic Church; it had nothing to do with Gandhi, he maintained, because Gandhi encouraged massive civil disobedience, while Chavez was simply making a martyr of himself. Orendain also was upset about Chatfield's use of Service Center money to promote and control the event. There was so much money around—$27,000 spent in twenty-two days, Tony maintained—that Orendain started telling people, "While one was fasting, others were feasting." Epifanio Camacho tried to ignore the fast. He felt that he was the target of Chavez's complaints, but that it would be impossible to answer them in the midst of the spectacle. He spent the three weeks fixing union cars. Fred and Virginia Hirsch had divided emotions. They appreciated the political usefulness of the show, but, as Fred saw it, the workers were being used as props, extras, in Chavez's passion play. The Hirsches did not attend the Masses and were annoyed when Chatfield and Ganz asked them to explain why. "It was like clipboard city," Virginia remembered, "everybody had a clipboard checking on everybody else. It seemed like at that point things really turned. Nick Jones had a clipboard. Marshall had a clipboard. LeRoy had a clipboard. And they were checking on what people did, when they came, and how long they stayed."[47]

Doug Adair was even more internally conflicted. He thought the fast was unfairly directed at Tony Orendain, Rudy Reyes, and Epifanio Camacho. He figured that Chavez knew what they were doing before he went on the fast and had not done much to stop them. What about Manuel, he would ask. Is the fast against Manuel's activities, too? But Manuel operated as an instrument of Chavez's policy. And Adair was also wary of all the talk of "*los sacrificios*." Why couldn't people acknowledge that they also had fun in the struggle? Why promote a circus of sacrifice, complete with women walking on bloodied knees? But what most disturbed Adair was that before the fast, Chavez, though the leader of the union, had also been a "brother," with whom one could argue and even criticize. During the fast it became impossible to disagree with him. He was now on a pedestal, no longer a brother but an unapproachable father.

At the same time, Adair was deeply moved by the fast. He believed in Chavez's vision of nonviolent struggle, could understand the profound religious feeling behind it, and admired Chavez's personal courage.

> The last time I had a deep, philosophical, one-on-one dialogue with Cesar was in the little room in the gas station. He mentioned that he hadn't seen me very often at the nightly Masses, and I admitted that I rarely went, that I had work to do, and that quite frankly I found them a circus, a show put on for the media . . . which I was dutifully recording in *Malcriado*. I told him that I understood his fast to be a deeply personal action, and that on that level I was tremendously moved, and was praying for him, with him. He expressed horror for the circus aspects. . . . He went on to discuss the moral choice of nonviolence in terms that I found totally convincing, and said that this was an issue that had to be won in the hearts and souls of the members, not an issue to be put to the vote of the executive board, or membership, where cynicism and hypocrisy would make the vote meaningless.

Adair, too, was in tears when he left his meeting with Chavez, although even as he cried he knew that the wonderfully empathetic master organizer had told him exactly what he needed to hear.[48]

The austere Chatfield, who believed that the fast was an organizing triumph, and the playful Adair, who thought that the fast transformed Chavez's relationship to the union, were both right. The fast pulled together the ranch committees, united them for the first time in a common project. Before the fast, Jerry Cohen observed, the union was just a collection of separate entities; after the fast, it became a united force. Chavez's dramatic sacrifice also brought many new farm workers into UFWOC's orbit—mostly older people, both Mexican and Mexican American, attracted to the religious ritual and symbolism. The fast also energized the boycott, as so many people in the rest of the country, exhausted by the violent times, responded to Chavez's sacrifice for nonviolent political action.

Simultaneously, as Adair understood, the fast prepared the ground for what would come next. Chavez fasted for those he loved; he suffered so others could triumph; when people visited him in the humble storage room, they felt the presence of greatness. Some could see an aura above his head.

Is such charisma essentially antidemocratic? Some thought so at the time, and given what happened in the UFW's not entirely glorious future, it is tempting in retrospect to agree with them. But charismatic leaders can open democratic paths as well as close them. Movements of the poor or powerless, which are always undertaken against great odds, need leaders who can motivate and enthuse, help people see that other worlds are possible and that despite everything, their sacrifices will not be in vain. Charisma, the gift of grace, need not be monopolized by the leader but can spread among an inspired people.

Charismatic leaders do, however, often turn out to be enemies of democracy. Many times the gift remains exclusive; the leader has it and his followers don't. People participate, but they depend on the leader to show them the way, to tell them what to do. They give themselves up to the charismatic one, rather than find themselves through him and with him. And the leader, invested by the people with the wisdom and grace to decide on the right course, may be overwhelmed by his own authority, or grow intolerant of those who do not wish to follow his path.

In Delano in 1968, folks saw it both ways. Camacho was horrified when he saw people kneeling as Chavez walked up the courthouse steps. But Dolores Huerta saw the same scene as an honest expression of Mexican Catholic culture, and was hopeful about the future of a union where so many farm workers would travel so far to show their support. Between Camacho and Huerta there were all manner of opinions, even private wars raging inside people, as they saw and felt this dramatic turn in Chavez's relationship to some (by no means all) of the farm workers and volunteers who had cast their lot with the union.

Chavez's new authority also intensified his own burden. He now had to deal with the hopes of an increasing number of followers who wanted to believe that Cesar Chavez had the magic touch, that he alone could solve the political puzzles that confronted them. With so many people believing it, how could he dare to doubt it? Wouldn't uncertainty on his part constitute a betrayal of his people's faith? And if the power of his union partially depended on the people's belief that he would unfailingly lead them to victory, what should he do when things went wrong?

But it wasn't Cesar's new charisma that put democracy in peril in the union, as much as it was the coupling of Chavez's charisma with his desire to maintain strict control over his organization. Charismatic leaders are not always so interested in controlling institutional affairs. Compare Chavez to his contemporary Martin Luther King Jr., whose charismatic leadership helped to transform a whole people. The photographer Bob Fitch saw both men at work in their own organizations. He took photos of King and his staff first and then arrived in Delano. "There was an enormous competition among [Chavez's] lieutenants for his attention, and great infighting among the brothers and sisters for the shreds of power that came with having his ear," Fitch recalled. He had seen some of that in the people around King, but it was more pronounced in UFWOC.

> In the strategy meetings, King dealt with a group of black preachers with tremendous egos, and various hangers-on, and articulate street hustlers. The meetings were very contentious. King would listen as each person spoke, and the various players argued among themselves. At the end he would summarize what each person had to say. Go around the room and sum up their arguments in a respectful way. And then he would offer an opinion on what should be done, usually, but not always, to general approval. But his decision was always an offering. Chavez was very different. Cesar was also a fine listener, but his decisions always concluded the discussion. He had the first and last word. What he had to say was not an offering. He didn't sum up other people's opinions. His opinion became the opinion of the meeting.[49]

On the last night of the fast, as he was walking to the *Malcriado* office, Doug Adair noticed Rudy Reyes on the edge of his garden, amid some big boulders, tending an outdoor fire. He walked over to talk to him, and discovered that Rudy was mixing kerosene and soap, making it into a jelly, and putting it in bottles. He was making Molotov cocktails.

"Rudy, what are you doing?"

"Don't ask me, ask Manuel. I have orders from Manuel. He told me to cook it up because we will need it later."

Adair argued with him. It was the last night of the fast, he said, and the place was filled with people, including reporters from all over. And what a spot, right next to the highway. Any moment a Highway Patrolman could come over and bust the whole operation. Reyes answered that this was the place where they had cooked up the material before. It was close to a streetlight so they could see what they were doing, and they often had a fire going by the boulders to cook up some coffee, cowboy style. It didn't have anything to do with the fast, he said; they were going to use the stuff later.

Adair did his best to convince him that he should put out the fire and throw everything away. Then he looked for help. He finally found Dolores Huerta, who rushed to the scene. She told Reyes to get rid of everything immediately. After a short protest he did so. Adair and Huerta went back to her house, where Adair had been staying and taking care of Huerta's younger kids while she was on the boycott in New York. Later a loud banging awakened Adair. Manuel Chavez was outside pounding on the door and screaming. Dolores let him in. Manuel was drunk, enraged. He had a handgun, and he said he was going to kill Adair, the snitch. Neither Adair nor Huerta took him seriously. It was Manuel putting on one of his shows. Dolores calmed him down, and they all went to bed. They needed their rest. The next day Cesar Chavez was scheduled to conclude his twenty-five-day fast by breaking bread with Bobby Kennedy.[50]

The junior senator from New York arrived in Delano in a political fix of his own. Since at least 1965, when he first started to put together the coalition of the poor and the young that he hoped would help him recapture the presidency for a Kennedy, he had not known what to do about the number one issue of the day, the war in Vietnam. Initially he supported Johnson's 1965 escalation, since it was an extension of his brother's policy. But as the conflict gradually became the dreaded "land war in Asia," and as opposition to the conflict grew, he staked out a position independent of Johnson's, calling for bombing halts and negotiations. He was still well short of the antiwar positions of senators Fulbright, Morse, and McCarthy, but he had become enough of a critic to anger the president and gain the allegiance of many of the antiwar young.

Only after the Tet Offensive demonstrated to Washington officialdom that there was no light at the end of the tunnel did Kennedy, like many others, openly oppose the war. Nevertheless, he rejected the idea of putting maximum muscle into his opposition by running against Lyndon Johnson in the 1968 Democratic primaries. He was too much a political realist and too much a regular party man to take on a sitting president of the United States of his own party in what he was sure would be only a protest campaign. He still felt that his best bet politically would be to wait until 1972. So the antiwar movement found another candidate, the quirky, ironic, nonparty man, Eugene McCarthy, who was willing to take up what promised to be a losing crusade. Kennedy, whose political appeal depended so much on his brother's martyrdom and his own youthful image (he was wearing his hair longer), found himself losing the allegiance of the actual young to the new challenger, whose first test of his "children's crusade" would be in New Hampshire, two days after Bobby helped Cesar Chavez break his fast.

Kennedy did just fine in Delano, where several thousand people came out to see him and Chavez. Kennedy was gracious and humorous, and handled himself well in the crowd. He had courage and history on his mind, and several times he called Chavez a hero, and added that some day people in the crowd would tell their children and grandchildren that they had marched with Cesar Chavez. The UFWOC leader more than held his own. He graciously agreed to receive the sacramental bread twice from the hands of the junior senator, so that a photographer would not miss a historic photo opportunity. Chavez's speech, read to the crowd by Jim Drake, was brief and elegant:

Our struggle is not easy. Those who oppose our cause are rich and powerful, and they have many allies in high places. We are poor. Our allies are few. But we have something the rich do not own. We have our own bodies and spirits and the justice of our cause as our weapons. When we are really honest with ourselves we must admit that our lives are all that really belong to us. So it is how we use our lives that determines the kind of men we are. It is my deepest belief that only by giving our lives do we find life. I am convinced that the truest act of courage, the strongest act of manliness is to sacrifice ourselves to others in a totally nonviolent struggle for justice. To be a man is to suffer for others. God help us be men![51]

That following Tuesday, Eugene McCarthy got 42 percent of the vote in New Hampshire. Four days after that, Robert Kennedy entered the race. Two weeks later, Lyndon Johnson announced his decision not to run for reelection. What had been inconceivable a short time before had actually happened. Four days after Johnson's announcement, Martin Luther King Jr. was shot dead, and African Americans rioted in most major U.S. cities. The upheavals of nineteen sixty-eight were well under way. Chavez would become a Kennedy delegate, and UFWOC volunteers would be crucial in mobilizing the votes of Mexican Americans that gave Kennedy the edge over McCarthy in the California primary. For a short while, perhaps as long as an hour, Chavez and UFWOC—with perhaps 5,000 members but several tons of goodwill in multiple U.S. constituencies—seemed to be on the road to seeing their man become president of the United States of America. Dolores Huerta was standing on the platform at the Ambassador Hotel while some 200 farm worker volunteers were at the back of the hall, having arrived at the celebration just as Kennedy was finishing his remarks. Moments later, offstage, Sirhan Sirhan fired the shots. "It was like they had blown the bottom out of the boat," said Bert Corona, the longtime Mexican American activist who was standing near Huerta. With King and Kennedy gone, Cesar Chavez had a new role to play in the country. He was not only the main representative of the Chicano people, he was also the nation's principal symbol of nonviolent political action. Neither *The Nation* nor anyone else would ever get his name wrong again.

Boycott Heroics

June '68 to July '70

Between the end of his fast in March 1968 and the signing of Delano grape contracts in July 1970, Cesar Chavez spent at least a third of his working days flat on his back in a hospital bed.[1] Lying down was supposed to ease his back pain. Sometimes the bed was in an actual hospital, O'Connor in San Jose; a few times the bed was set up in St. Anthony's Franciscan Seminary, behind the Santa Barbara Mission. Most of the time it was in a newly rented house across the street from the Pink House, in what became, for a while, his combination office and second home. In addition to the bed, the room included a standing blackboard, a small dresser, and a few chairs—one a rocking chair for Cesar. The walls were painted a bright rosy pink, as was the bed. Behind the bed hung a wooden crucifix and a photograph of a statue of St. Francis by Beniamino Bufano. On the other walls hung photos of Gandhi and Bobby Kennedy, a small piece of material with "Love" embroidered on it, and a black poster of the two dead Kennedys and Martin Luther King Jr. with the word "Why?" scrawled across it in red ink. In his biography of Chavez, Jacques Levy concluded his description of the bedroom-office with "The spirit of martyrs fills the room."[2]

Back pain is notoriously difficult to diagnose. When Chavez first went to the hospital, immediately after the fast, the official explanation was that a lack of calcium had further deteriorated a degenerative disk. When he twisted his back after a 1968 Labor Day picnic, the local doctors said only that "something was wrong with his spine." That something was severe enough to keep him in the hospital for nearly a month and on his back until February 1969, when Dr. Janet Travel, who had treated President Kennedy, came to Delano to examine him. Dr. Travel quickly concluded that Cesar's right leg was shorter than his left, and that one side of his pelvis was smaller than the other, which twisted his spine and contracted the muscles on the right side of his back. That condition caused periodic muscle spasms, which eventually became chronic. Whatever the merits of the doctor's diagnosis—she had said pretty much the same thing about Kennedy—her remedies alleviated the pain: a shoe lift, light exercise, daily back massage, a pillow to support the hip while sitting up, and a rocking chair.

Back trouble linked Chavez directly to farm workers, most of whom suffer some kind of back pain, and he did not hide his condition. Quite the reverse. He allowed himself to be photographed in bed, willingly discussed his condition with visiting reporters, and often moved from the rocking chair to the bed to receive visitors. Many suspected, according to Will Thorne in the *Riverside Press-Enterprise*, that the hospital bed might be "all flummery—simply good showmanship," and that Chavez was creating an "air of himself as the bed-ridden martyr while senators and civil-rights leaders and newspaper men make pilgrimages to his bedside." Thorne himself rejected that idea (after reporting it), and seemed to share the view of Gilbert Padilla, Jerry Cohen, and many others in the union, who maintained that the pain was real, and also that Chavez played it for all it was worth. Whatever the mixture of pain and performance, a visitor could hardly miss the dramatic contrasts: physical weakness and political power.[3]

Chavez's power was not conjured up through some magic trick from his hospital bed. It had multiple and complex origins, none more crucial than his unquestioned authority over the 300 full-time volunteers who made up the UFWOC staff in the late 1960s. The number is evocative. Cortez commanded about 400 in his conquest of Mexico. David in his cave, seeking safety from the crazed King Saul, rallied less than 500 for his victorious campaigns against the Philistines. Three hundred is the size of a large company, led by a captain, or a very small battalion, led by a major. It is a small enough number so that its leader can know everyone fairly well, and big enough to do a lot of damage against a disorganized or dispirited foe. Cesar Chavez was not a military commander; nevertheless, his suggestions became orders, his ideas became canon, his presence, thrilling. UFWOC was not an army, but it was in combat, and Chavez directed the fight. He could summon people to his bedside for consultation and instruction at all hours of the day and night. He could send members of his staff on secret missions that they knew Chavez would disavow if the deeds became public. And, most important of all, Chavez could send more than 200 of those volunteers to strange cities to live and work in dire poverty for a couple of years, carrying out a project that often seemed doomed to fail. Two years was long back then, when the future was unsure. Many people stuck it out only because they had a deep faith in their leader.

The leader did not lose faith in his project, even when fortune, so often his ally, seemed to desert him. Chavez had bet heavily on the Kennedy run, bringing boycotters back to California and throwing more than 200 volunteers into the campaign. But electoral politics were only one part of his program, and after the assassination he seemed to regain his balance more quickly than most. Five days later he was driving into the Coachella Valley with his cousin Manuel and Marshall Ganz, planning his next move.

Caught up in Kennedy's race, UFWOC's leadership had not been paying much attention to the harvest of more than 10,000 acres of Coachella Valley table grapes. About a month earlier, the union had sent pro forma telegrams to the Coachella growers offering secret ballot elections and negotiations, and threatening a boycott and strike. As expected, the growers sent no official answer, but Chavez had received an unofficial one. Lionel Steinberg, the manager of David Freedman & Co., the largest grape grower in the Coachella Valley, wanted to talk. Steinberg was a definite power in the grower community, but as a Jewish liberal Democrat, he was also an oddity. He had been Governor Pat Brown's first appointee to the California State Board of Agriculture, and cochair of Farmers for Kennedy and Johnson in 1960. In May 1968, he and Chavez met alone and in secret at Steinberg's home. They were both supporting Bobby Kennedy's presidential run at the time, which was enough to make the meeting friendly but not enough to bring them to agreement on a union contract. The meeting came to nothing, and Coachella's picking season began without incident.

If not for Sirhan Sirhan, there probably wouldn't have been any job action in Coachella at all, because a significant percentage of UFWOC volunteers would have followed the Kennedy campaign through the general election.[4] Instead, Cesar Chavez, Manuel Chavez, and Marshall Ganz—still driving the rented yellow Pontiac that the Kennedy people had put at the union's disposal, still trying to sort out their anger and pain—did their best to put the might-have-beens behind them and focus on the problem at hand. Only four weeks of harvest were left in Coachella. Any serious strike should have already begun. What should UFWOC do?

During Cesar's quick, sad trip to New York for Bobby Kennedy's funeral, he had heard one piece of good news: early indications were that the grape boycott would be surprisingly effective. When the first grapes had started arriving in New York from the Coachella Valley in late May, an unofficial hot cargo campaign had greeted them. Months of worker-to-worker contact and the official endorsement by the city's Central Labor Council had paid off in an explosion of illegal solidarity. Seafarers, who piloted the barges that brought all California grapes from the railroad cars in New Jersey to the enormous wholesale produce market at Hunt's Point in the Bronx, simply refused to allow the cargo onto their boats. Some grapes ended up in the Hudson River. Many that did get through were spilled or lost or mishandled at Hunt's Point.[5] Coupled with that, who knew what even a late strike in Coachella might do? Lionel Steinberg had been willing to talk; maybe with some pressure in the fields, he would be willing to sign.

But striking involved risks. Another large losing strike would not only discourage workers; it might broadcast UFWOC's uneven support in the vineyards, and thus serve not to legitimize the boycott but to damage it.

Nonetheless, all three men thought they should strike. It didn't hurt that when they arrived in the valley, they were greeted by a crowd of enthusiastic farm workers at a church hall meeting.[6]

Coachella farm workers had a good deal of leverage, and they knew it. Their power was rooted in the particularities of climate and geography. Extraordinarily high temperatures in the valley meant that Coachella grapes were the first to mature and hit the market, about a month before the first Central Valley grapes could be harvested in Arvin-Lamont or the first Arizona grapes in Yuma. Being first to market meant that for a short while the growers received atypically high prices—sometimes as high as $30 a box, compared with the $5 a box or less they might make when other grapes started to be picked, packed, and shipped. And the drop from $30 to $5 could happen in just a few days. High temperatures also meant that the grapes had to be picked quickly. Two days of very hot weather could make harvestable grapes too soft to ship to eastern markets and mean a difference of millions of dollars in a gross that averaged $15 million a year but fluctuated widely from season to season. Thus, Coachella farmers were often in a hurry, and when farmers are in a hurry, farm workers have power.

Their power, however, was diminished by their diversity. There was no standard Coachella grape picker. The year-round workers who pruned, girdled, thinned, tipped, and pulled leaves came from Mexican and Mexican American families who lived in the valley towns of Indio, Thermal, Mecca, and Coachella. They made up only 30 percent of the harvest workforce. Another 10 to 20 percent were skilled Filipino workers, who lived in Delano but came down to Coachella to work and live in labor camps for the six-week season before following the harvest north. They specialized in field packing, were highly prized by many growers, and had considerable leverage in on-the-ground disputes. The rest of the workers were primarily migrants from the lower Rio Grande Valley, whose main home was the Mexican border states of Tamaulipas and Nuevo León, and who followed the grapes from Coachella into Arvin, Delano, and sometimes even Fresno and Lodi, living in labor camps. Finally, a small but growing percentage of workers drove 100 miles from Mexicali on Monday mornings and spent the harvest week living in their cars, with friends, or in the camps, then returned to Mexicali Saturday night for one day at home. Some even made the round-trip from Mexicali on a daily basis (in their own cars or in grower buses) leaving their homes at about one in the morning and returning at about six at night. They carried green cards, white cards, or no cards at all. Mutual suspicion divided all of these workers from one another, with the local workers especially worried that the growing number of people coming from Mexicali could undercut their wages.[7]

Manuel stayed in Coachella to prepare for the strike. Cesar and Marshall returned to Delano. Other organizers came and went. After making an early appearance in the valley, Larry Itliong returned home to Delano, refusing to urge the Filipino workers to walk off their jobs. "I knew damn well we were not going to win that strike in that short period of time," he would later explain. "Why? They [the growers] can put in ten people for every-one we put out . . . And who is going to replace the Filipino strikers? The Mexicans will. How would I look to my countrymen? And brother Chavez is not going to be able to stop the Mexicans from getting those jobs. And I knew that. So what were we contemplating? We had the boycott going. And besides . . . they told me they sent me there [just because] we want to make our boycott, including Coachella, legal."[8]

Despite their concerns about Filipino participation, UFWOC organizers arranged for a strike vote at a large barbecue and dance. They knew they were late. The harvest of the Perlette grape variety was over; the Thompson grapes were just beginning. According to the California Department of Employment, the workforce had fallen from a high of 3,000 to a low of 1,500 to 2,000. There is some dispute as to how many workers voted to have UFWOC represent them, but the real counting would be done on the picket line. On Thursday, June 20, the first day of the strike, Steinberg's David Freedman & Co. was the main target. Freedman hired mostly local workers, who considered UFWOC their own and were most willing to follow their newly famous leader. *El Malcriado* reported that 300 people picketed, and Chavez told the *Riverside Press-Enterprise* that 850 to 1,000 workers walked off the job. The paper's own estimates were 100 picketers and 600 strikers.[9] Even the lowest estimates are impressive, representing a much higher percentage than had responded to the better-organized Giumarra strike. After that first day, Steinberg raised the wages to $1.65 an hour, and 20 cents a box, more than matching what workers were making under UFWOC wine grape contracts and setting a standard wage for the rest of the 1968 grape harvest. Some workers returned to the job immedi-ately, while others moved on to get a head start in Arvin-Lamont, believing that they had won the basic battle. But it was too late in the season to get Steinberg to meet again. The harvest was successfully, albeit expensively, completed.[10]

Some green-carders and undocumented workers had come from Mexicali to break the strike. Some locals never went on strike, and migrants from Texas, Tamaulipas, and Nuevo León also crossed the picket lines. Nevertheless, Chavez focused his public attacks on scabbing "wetbacks" and "green-carders," and blamed them and a lax Border Patrol for weaken-ing the strike. He stated publicly that UFWOC might use civil disobedience to stop the scabs at the border, but nothing came of the threat.[11] As the harvest came to an end, the union extended the strike to twelve other growers. That was mostly a formality, meant to spread the strike (and boycott) to all Coachella Valley table grapes. Then Chavez called the strike off, citing excessive violence, although there had been only a few minor incidents on the picket lines. He also announced that some Coachella workers would now join others on the boycott. Jerry Cohen put it bluntly to the *Press-Enterprise*: "What we have to do now is win on the boycott."[12]

Helen Serda was on the bus that left Delano for New York City in January of 1968. She hadn't wanted to go on the boycott. She was nineteen and in love with Jerry Hernandez, and she didn't want to leave him. Her father, the captain of the bus, and Julio Hernandez, her future father-in-law and a UFWOC Executive Board member, had arranged for her to make the trip. They wanted to separate the young couple and had convinced Chavez that it was the right thing to do. "It will only be for two weeks," Chavez had told her. Unable to ignore her parents' wishes and unwilling to disobey Chavez, Helen dutifully got on the bus. Three months later she returned to California with her father. After New York they were assigned to the LA boycott, where they worked on the Kennedy campaign. She was reunited with Jerry there, and after two more years of boycotting grapes, Helen and Jerry would be married.[13]

Helen Serda had been the first in her family to join the grape strike, back in 1965. Having been kicked out of Delano High School in her senior year over a minor disciplinary dispute, she was picking grapes at Schenley's with her mother, grandmother, and grandfather when the strike began. Intrigued by the picketers, ignoring her mother's admonition not to get involved, she went on her own to a meeting at a small black church that the farm workers called La Iglesia Negrita. "Chavez was speaking really beautiful, and it was packed. Everybody would be shouting, 'Long live the strike, long live the cause.' It was all my people and I felt really, really, really good. And so after a few days I decided to walk out on strike." Over the next several months she became an enthusiastic *huelgista*: picketing, working in the office, partying with other young people on strike and with the "visiting hippies from Berkeley." She first met Jerry on one of the picket lines.

Her parents came around to the strike slowly. Helen brought home literature and left it about the house. She talked up the union. On a few occasions she even picketed fields where her family was working. Her dad, who sometimes worked as a foreman, was impressed by his daughter's arguments and secretly started to pass information to Chavez about the vineyards and the bosses. In 1966, during the DiGiorgio campaign, he walked out of the fields and publicly joined the cause. His wife left her job to work in the strike kitchen. The younger children, already school chums of one of the Chavez girls, joined the other high school students who were wearing black eagle buttons to school—and got in trouble for it. The Serdas became a union family: strong, loyal, hard-working members of the 300.

Helen Serda was born in Delano and hadn't seen much of the world outside the Central Valley. So that first bus trip to New York was an adventure. On the second night out, the bus stopped at Reies Tijerina's Chicano nationalist compound in New Mexico, where the boycotters ate, cleaned up, swapped stories, sang songs, and slept on the floor. Tijerina and other militants spoke to them. Most of the night, Helen talked to Tijerina's daughter, Maria, who had spent several days in solitary confinement after an armed confrontation with police. There were several posters on the walls, Helen remembers. "What if somebody gave a war and nobody came?" one asked. Later, she saw that poster all over.

In New York City, Serda and about thirty-five other boycotters stayed in the big headquarters of the Seafarers International Union in Brooklyn. She loved the accommodations. They lived in several rooms of a dormitory for out-of-town seamen. There were good hot showers, clean bathrooms, and a cafeteria down the street. The union sold meal tickets to the seamen, but the boycotters got them for free, even getting extra lunches to share with people they met on the picket lines. The Seafarers lent the boycotters a small fleet of union cars. Union officials arranged sightseeing trips. They provided free medical care. Some sailors and low-level union officials joined the Delano crowd on picket lines and demonstrations. Antonia Saludado met her husband at Seafarers Hall. Helen Serda opened up to the world.

In general, however, the boycott work was hard. Most boycott organizers were not as fortunate as the group in New York and had to find places to stay, raise money to live, and learn how to operate in cities without large Mexican American communities. Boycotters typically drove to a new city with little seed money. The first six arrivals in Chicago had $85 among them. It was not unusual for boycotters to spend the first few nights sleeping in their car as Julio Hernandez, his wife, Fina, and five children did in Cleveland, before moving to cots in the basement of a church. People contended with various illnesses, accidents, dull meals, long hours, lack of sleep and privacy. Yet many boycotters had a great time. "On the one hand it was tough," Jessica Govea said. "On the other, it was an incredibly liberating and wonderful experience."[14] The boycott gave people a chance to learn new things (several farm worker women drove cars for the first time) and to be effective in a world beyond their small California farm towns. That wider world welcomed them. In Boston, Detroit, and Chicago, local civil rights coalitions declared Marcos Muñoz, Higinio Rangel, and Eliseo Medina "men of the year." Thousands of delegates to the convention of the Toronto Federation of Labor gave Jessica Govea a standing ovation as they pledged their support to the union. Private deprivation was offset by public happiness. Having experienced the joy of politics, most of the farm workers swore they would never work in the fields again—although Fred Ross, who was in charge of training the boycotters, admonished them not to say that publicly.[15]

The boycott campaigns typically began with presentations to sympathetic church and union leaders. Those meetings usually featured short speeches by farm workers in which they recounted their own histories and the overall story of the union. Many of the farm workers spoke Spanish better than English, and sometimes memorized their speeches word for word. Ross insisted that the various presentations be consistent with one another, and that the union story follow a single narrative. He took great care in helping people learn how to construct a story that would appeal to the various parts of the coalition. In New York, Ross would listen to people rehearse their speeches and make suggestions and changes. Often he critiqued the boycotters' performances after meetings. People had to get the union story right. Later, when the UFW was torn by internal struggle, Ross told Marshall Ganz that the union's basic problem was that its single story had broken up into several different, competing ones.

Under Ross's direction, Helen Serda and her compatriots learned their scripts. Serda herself frequently gave testimony to accompany the appearances of Dolores Huerta, whose vigor and passion made her the star attraction in New York. They visited unions, churches, and schools. They did a lot of picketing. Their first target was the enormous Hunts Point food distribution facility in the Bronx, covering several blocks, and where they sometimes got lost. When the picketing began, New York workers often wouldn't touch the grapes. The jobbers got mad. Cops were called but were hesitant to bust a picket line. Soon, however, the big produce distributors got an injunction limiting the number of pickets. Less than a month after she got to New York, Helen Serda was in jail, along with twenty-two other boycotters, mostly women, and one six-year-old boy. Ross had set the stage for the arrests and called the press. Serda was "furious" because Ross had not told them they were going to be arrested. After several hours in a holding cell, they were released on their own recognizance. The next day the charges were dropped, but a picture of the boy, crying in his arrested mother's arms, had already made one of the New York dailies. Support for the boycott surged.

Ever since the Massachusetts textile strike of 1912, strikers had come through New York looking for support. The farm workers were the first to come and stay, determined not to leave until they won. Most of the city's unions endorsed their cause. Some older union officials supported the strikers as a way of connecting to their own pasts, when they, too, had had to fight to establish their unions. The few active progressives within the unions supported the farm workers as a simple act of solidarity, and in hopes of reinvigorating their own locals. They also dreamed, along with Walter Reuther, that the farm workers' struggle could spark a new national alliance of progressive unionists. But help also came from many union chiefs who aided the farm workers as a cover for their own inadequacies.

Paul Hall of the New York Seafarers, second only to Reuther and the UAW in financial and material support for UFWOC, was himself a notoriously corrupt and conservative union boss, one of the union chiefs who would lead the labor stampede to Richard Nixon in 1972.

But in the winter and spring of 1968, the Delano strikers won them all over—progressive and conservative alike—with their down-home ways, their enthusiastic picket lines, their willingness to throw their whole lives into their struggle, and their impressive presentations at public meetings. One of the most impressive was a televised confrontation between Antonia Saludado and the grape grower John Giumarra Jr. Guessing wrong, Giumarra claimed that Saludado was a student supporter and had never worked in the fields. In fact, Saludado had tied vines, thinned, and tipped in Giumarra's own fields for several seasons. She answered him angrily, carefully describing his vineyards and ended with a flair: "You may not recognize me, but I recognize you. Because I am one of your workers. I have been on your farms so many times. I know the grapes that you have. I can tell you how many seeds you got in your grapes."[16]

Moved by such testimonials, New York's unionized workers brought back the old days for more than a month, using the on-the-ground (and on-the-water) techniques that had spread the union movement in the 1930s but had been outlawed by the Taft-Hartley and Landrum-Griffin acts in the 1940s and '50s. In mid-July, 100 California growers, who until then had publicly proclaimed that the grape boycott was ineffective, swallowed their pride and sued the New York City Labor Council and some individual unions for $25 million in lost income for violation of the hot-cargo, secondary-boycott provisions of the National Labor Relations Act. The hot-cargo campaign was called off, but serious damage had been done. In June and July of 1968, ninety-one car lots of grapes reached New York City, compared with 418 car lots in 1966. New York did not stand alone. By 1969 UFWOC had boycott offices in twenty-eight U.S. cities and three in Canada. In all but a handful of the offices, people who had come out of the fields were part of the staff, and in the majority, a farm worker was the formal boycott leader.[17]

With most UFWOC staffers stationed in boycott cities, a "skeleton crew," a term visiting journalists typically used, was left in Delano. Large numbers were not needed there, as UFWOC's primary interest was no longer organizing farm workers. No one doubted that the boycott was the key to victory. La huelga had become a mythic rallying cry, a call to general rebellion rather than a specific reference to workers' withdrawal of their labor power. The dogs told the story. Chavez's first German shepherd guard dog, which Jacques Levy helped him train in 1968, was named Boycott. The second dog was named Huelga.

Like the 300 as a whole, the group of volunteers who stayed behind were about half ex–farm workers and half young Anglo and Chicano volunteers, who came to Delano and stayed long enough and worked hard enough to be put on the payroll of $5 a week plus basic expenses. (Exceptions were LeRoy Chatfield, and the UFWOC legal staff who earned low regular salaries, and the "worker priests," who were paid by the Migrant Ministry but were under direct UFWOC control.) Chavez had earned his authority within the ranks through his proven political judgment, his ability to build personal relationships, his hard work, and his charismatic sacrifice for the cause. But his power over the volunteers was also embedded in the structure of the organization. Cesar personally recruited many of the volunteers, and even when other top staffers wanted to add someone to the payroll, the recruit often had a preliminary interview with Chavez. He alone could fire anyone on the spot, and sometimes he did. The pay structure meant that volunteers who did not live in boycott houses had to show their basic bills (rent, gas, electricity, food, and clothes) to union officials, and since Chavez was a master of detail and very concerned about how UFWOC money was spent, he often knew the exact financial situation of many of his staff. This gave him much more power over people's lives than would have been the case if the union had been paying regular salaries (even low ones) and left individuals to figure out how to pay their own expenses. If Cesar Chavez became a father to the union after the fast, as some claimed, then this system of payment helped institutionalize that role. Father paid the bills, and gave his children an allowance.

Chavez wielded his authority with ease. He told volunteers when they arrived, "You have come to work for the farm workers, so you do what we want you to do." The earlier debate between LeRoy Chatfield and Doug Adair was over, and Chatfield had won: there was no negotiating with the union. Chavez specifically warned the new staffers against having any "hidden agendas." He also warned them that farm workers were not saints, and volunteers should neither romanticize them nor expect gratitude. "You have to understand," he said, "that you may work very hard and the day will come when they will just boot you out, or they won't appreciate what you are doing."[18]

The staff did not cringe under Cesar's authority, as it was generally assumed that Chavez knew what was best for the organization, and nothing was more important than loyalty. Chavez demanded it. Gandhi "had all kinds of rules and insisted they be obeyed," he noted. "He wouldn't put up with anybody being half loyal or ninety percent loyal. It was one hundred percent loyal or nothing at all."[19]

After disloyalty, the worst charge against a staffer was not working hard enough. People were criticized for sleeping late or sitting around reading newspapers or gabbing among themselves. A person considered a slacker did not last. As a rule the staff worked long hours, six and often seven days

a week. Jessica Govea remembers that a sixteen-hour workday was standard, and in certain circumstances (for example in election campaigns) she
went without sleep. Being hospitalized for exhaustion was almost a badge
of honor in the union, and again Chavez stood as a model, as his periodic
hospitalizations often were attributed to overwork. The commitment to
constant work went so deep that people were given make-work rather than
be allowed to sit in a UFWOC office with apparently nothing to do.[20]

A spirit of virtuous sacrifice prevailed. Drinking was discouraged. People
were encouraged to perform acts of public penance. During demonstrations on the boycott, people often kneeled and prayed. Chris Hartmire and
Joe Serda fasted in front of a Safeway store in Los Angeles. Antonia
Saludado's sister Maria picketed in her bare feet in the snow in Indianapolis,
as did Juana Trujillo later in Philadelphia. Others stood at LA freeway
entrances all day holding boycott and electioneering signs. Pain and triumph
were partners, and the cross above Chavez's bed made perfect sense.

The staff insisted on a rough equality of condition among themselves.
Those who lived away from the collective boycott houses were regarded
with suspicion. Special privileges were sniffed out, openly discussed, and
sometimes reported to people in authority. Jerald B. Brown, in his doctoral
dissertation, reports a mini-rebellion among Los Angeles boycotters because
two picket captains were sleeping in beds while the rest were on the floor.
Staffers were expected to suffer together, equally. Some of the resentment
directed at LeRoy Chatfield had to do with the fact that he lived away from
the rest of the Delano staff in an attractive private home with his wife,
Bonnie.

Equality of condition, however, did not mean equal say in decision-
making. Top-down decisions were taken for granted, although they were
sometimes subject to formal approval in a mass meeting. Staffers who
disagreed strongly with the direction UFWOC was going, simply quit the
organization. Boycott offices had tactical independence from Delano, but
overall strategy was determined by a small group of people, many of whom
were Anglos. The Chavez family—Richard, Manuel, Helen, Cesar, and
Dolores Huerta—certainly retained ultimate power during the grape
boycott, but in practice, Anglo advisers usurped the position of the other
Executive Board members. Larry Itliong and Phillip Vera Cruz, who had
never been close to Cesar, saw their authority on the board diminish due
to the shrinking number of Filipino farm workers and staff members. Andy
Imutan, a small businessman rather than a unionist, actually became more
important to the day-to-day operations of UFWOC, as he could handle
the books. Gilbert Padilla, who had been with Cesar since 1955, was often
incapacitated by drink during the first years of the boycott, and having
"failed to organize his wife," spent a lot of time dealing with a painful
dissolution of his marriage. Julio Hernandez, always regarded more as a

loyal follower than a leader, had been sent on the boycott to Cleveland. Tony Orendain, the most consistent voice of opposition among the leadership, was kept at arm's length by Chavez, and in 1969 was sent to Texas.

The Anglo advisers thus became the second circle of leadership at the top. Jim Drake, Chavez's chief administrative assistant, declined in importance only as LeRoy Chatfield, formally the head of the Service Center, became Chavez's main confidant outside the family. Jerry Cohen headed the legal department, and as litigation (both defensive and offensive) became an important part of the union's activities, he and Chavez got close. Chatfield and Cohen were rarely given boycott assignments outside of Delano. Marshall Ganz, at times director of organizing and at times national boycott director (sometimes both), was sent to Toronto to head up the Canadian boycott, but regularly came back to Delano for consultations and remained close to the top. When he gave up the position as boycott director, it was taken by Jane Brown, whose anthropologist husband, Jerald, had come to Delano to write his Ph.D. thesis. She never got into the second circle of decision-makers, but she did get close to Cesar, who called her Juanita. She often accompanied him on trips to boycott cities and was among the handful of people trained to give him therapeutic back massages.

The white kitchen cabinet did not go unnoticed. Some farm workers and a few Chicano staffers resented the prominent position of so many whites in what was essentially a Mexican and Mexican American union, but there were few open complaints, as Chavez consistently championed the diversity of the staff and opposed any form of internal discrimination. If Chavez resented his own reliance on his white staff or the boycott's dependence on white support, he did a very good job of hiding it. Typically, when Reies Tijerina, leader of the movement to reclaim New Mexican land grants, complained privately to Cesar and Manuel because the UFWOC legal staff was headed by a man named Cohen, Chavez reported the incident back to the staff and stressed that he and Manuel had defended Cohen and opposed Tijerina's anti-Semitism.[21]

An early written criticism of the white advisers came from an Anglo on the staff, Fred Hirsch, when he and his wife, Virginia, left the organization in July of 1968. The separation was mostly friendly—Fred and Ginny's fourteen-year-old daughter, Liza, stayed behind in Delano, living with Chavez and Helen in the Chavez home—but Fred and Virginia had been uncomfortable members of the 300 before they resigned. They had both opposed the fast. They did not participate in the RFK California primary campaign. Like many committed labor leftists, Fred Hirsch was suspicious of Bobby Kennedy because of his early performances on the anti-Communist McCarthy Committee and the antilabor McClellan Committee. Neither abstention had gone unnoticed, and in late June, when vandals cut down the cross that Richard Chavez had erected at Forty Acres, rumors circulated that Fred Hirsch had done it. When Hirsch heard that Manuel was one of the main people spreading the rumors, he figured that it was time to leave.

Virginia Hirsch, a friend of Helen Chavez's whose legal work brought her closer than her husband to the top leadership, had also come to have deep doubts about the whole UFWOC project. Granddaughter of a coal miner, and a union veteran herself, she worried about the middle-class background of so many people close to Chavez. They didn't seem to be building a union, she thought; their eyes were on something else. She remembered taking a call in fall of 1967 for Marshall Ganz from the president of a wine grape ranch committee in Northern California. At the time Ganz was responsible for organizing the ranch committees and also had major responsibility for reviving the floundering Giumarra boycott. The ranch committee president

> . . . said they were having a real beef, that the company wasn't dealing with the contract well, and the problem needed to be taken care of and that we had to send somebody up there. So Marshall came in just about then, and I gave him the message. And he said okay. Then, about an hour later, this guy called again. And, he said, Look we really need to talk to somebody. And I called Marshall, and Marshall said, "Oh damn it, if it weren't for these ranch committees, we could get on with the boycott." It was the trigger to me that something was wrong.[22]

Before they left, Fred Hirsch wrote a "for your eyes only" memo that he sent to every member of the Executive Board and to LeRoy Chatfield. The long rambling complaint made four main points, mincing no words: (1) the fast had been a hypocritical misuse of religious symbolism; (2) white outsiders had been brought into the union and placed at key positions of power where they stood in the way of farm worker advancement inside UFWOC; (3) the organization was autocratic, as Chavez and his white advisers made all the important decisions; (4) inside UFWOC there was contempt for people's labor, as volunteers were given make-work and moved from job to job willy-nilly.[23]

Hisch did not want his criticisms circulated beyond a close-knit group, so he carefully marked all the copies with the names of the recipients. If any copy appeared, everyone would know who had leaked it. No one on the Executive Board ever responded to his critique, and the internal debate that he and Virginia had hoped for never took place.

Not that Fred's point of view would have found many echoes among the 300 members. Epifanio Camacho and some of the farm workers around him had similar complaints, but although they talked among themselves, they never discussed their doubts at open meetings. Chicano staff resentment was muted, but some supporters outside UFWOC agreed with the Hirsch's general critique. George Ballis, the SNCC photographer and editor of *The Valley Labor Citizen*, felt that Chavez purposefully surrounded himself with white volunteers because no matter how powerful they got, they could never challenge his leadership of the union, while top Mexican American or farm worker aides potentially could. Ballis believed that Chatfield, Cohen, Ganz, and Drake were in the positions they held precisely so that people like Eliseo Medina, Epifanio Camacho, and Pablo Espinoza would not be.[24] But Ballis's opinions counted for little, and Fred and Virginia's publicly friendly departure was barely noticed. Chavez's commitment to a diversified union and vocal opposition to discrimination was welcomed by many on a staff that was about half white and within which there were several Mexican-Anglo couples and marriages. Besides, who had time for internal dissension? In the summer of 1968 there was plenty of work to do.

After the growers' July 1968 lawsuit forced an end to the New York City hot-cargo campaign, the boycott never again enjoyed the support of this kind of sustained job action. Instead, UFWOC focused on getting major retail chain stores to stop buying and selling California grapes. It did this mostly through public moral persuasion, but there was a secret effort as well—the *chingadera*, or dirty trick. Soon after the harvest had ended in the Coachella Valley, Manuel Chavez, Richard Chavez, Rudy Reyes, and his girlfriend, Mary Bernier, drove across the country to join the New York City boycott campaign. "Manuel was in charge of the out-of-order things," Reyes explained. "He was going to New York to do that, and Mary and I went to work on his team. Manuel was doing a lot of maneuvering in New York, messing up the supermarkets. I had my arm in a sling, but I had a razor blade and I cut the sacks of rice and flour while Manuel was setting off firecrackers elsewhere in the store. On the way to New York, Manuel had brought a lot of firecrackers from Mexico, and he would put them in paper sacks and shoot them off."[25]

Reyes understood such pranks as an extension of the boycott shop-ins, carried out sporadically by the regular boycotters, which Manuel and Rudy occasionally joined. The shop-ins targeted the large stores, especially A&P, which refused to take grapes off the shelves. While picket lines marched outside, undercover boycotters would fill their shopping carts—often with grapes crushed on the bottom—and line up at the cash registers. Once there, they would express shock that the store was being picketed, would loudly declare their support for striking farm workers, leave their filled shopping carts clogging up the lines, and join the picketers outside.

The shift from shop-ins to firecrackers and razor blades was followed by further escalations. Manuel Chavez and Reyes started operating at night, using slingshots to send marbles crashing into storefront windows. "But the marbles wouldn't make any cracks, they would just go through the glass, and nobody noticed," said Reyes. "So Manuel said that wasn't any good. Nobody is noticing it, and there is no impact. So we moved on to other stuff."[26]

In September they began what would prove to be a short-lived fire-bombing campaign. On September 13 they threw flaming soft-drink bottles filled with gasoline through the window of an A&P store in the Bronx. Two days later they hit a Key Food store in Manhattan. Neither amounted to much; the damage was under $10,000. A month later they struck again, hitting A&P stores in Brooklyn, Manhattan, and the Bronx in quick succession. The material damage was again low, but in Manhattan they stumbled into disaster. Two stock clerks had been working in the store when the firebombs flew in at 3:16 am. As they scrambled to put out the fire, one of the clerks suffered first- and second-degree burns, and had to be hospitalized briefly. Two days later the story was in the *New York Times*, and although the city fire chief said he had no evidence linking the bombings to the boycott, he did point out that all the stores had refused to remove scab grapes. UFWOC denied all connection, although unidentified boycotters told Peter Matthiessen that the "bombings were probably the work of sympathizers whom they could not control."[27]

Reyes felt terrible. "I was happy to do vandalism, but I didn't want to hurt people. I think that Manuel was a bit more callous than that. He liked to do grandiose things. He didn't care if people got hurt." When Chavez heard about the bombing, he got angry and ordered Manuel back to California. He and Huerta wanted Reyes to return, too, but Rudy wrote a letter to Chavez saying he didn't want to go back. "I didn't mention what it was all about, but said that if I stayed in New York I would be a better person."[28] He and Mary Bernier remained on the boycott until the contracts were signed in July 1970. The *chingadera* campaign was never resumed.

More typically, the union applied pressure on the big supermarket chains by organizing consumers and getting endorsements from liberal politicians, union officials, and church leaders. Back in 1966 the Plan of Delano had explicitly rejected any condescending aid. "We do not want charity at the price of our dignity," it declared. Nevertheless, as the grape boycott progressed, the UFWOC message—unevenly but relentlessly—began to take on the feel of a charity campaign. Photographs of farm workers in boycott literature emphasized their poverty and hopelessness. One famous pamphlet, designed by a woman who worked in a major New York advertising firm, featured a photo of a forlorn child sitting on a bed in a labor camp and a bare light bulb hanging from an electrical wire over her head, captioned: "Every grape you buy helps keep this child hungry." Farm workers, dressed in work clothes, asked for money at fancy cocktail parties, where fashionably dressed people were asked to close their eyes and imagine a day in the life of a poor farm worker mother. On the picket line and in demonstrations, UFWOC staffers put their suffering on display. The message was unmistakable: Look at how we suffer; please help us. In the late 1960s, the spirit of the grape boycott foreshadowed what was to become a popular ethos of the seventies and eighties: victimhood as an avenue to power, symbolized by Chavez himself, flat on his back in pain, his political power on the rise.

But charity never trumped solidarity in the grape boycott. The construction of the victim–as–hero didn't become popular in the United States until the complete rout of the movements of the 1960s; it is a strategy of the defeated, a bow to noblesse oblige. Although the grape boycott grew out of the loss of the 1965 grape strike, in 1968 it was part of a movement on the rise. The black eagle flew in the air of early 1960s optimism, even though it arrived on the scene as that optimism began to wane. The boycott was playful as well as serious. In Toronto, boycotters released a huge "huelga" balloon, which flew to the ceiling of a supermarket that continued to sell grapes. When the harried store manager punctured it with a slingshot, hundreds of boycott leaflets fell on the shoppers below. *Chingaderas* were relatively innocent pranks as well as hidden attacks, tricks meant more to amuse than to intimidate: firecrackers, itching powder, a sound machine whose particular rhythm was supposed to make people defecate. Boycotters suffered, but they also had fun.

In 1969, despite all the pressures on boycotters to turn themselves into objects of charity, pressures to which some farm workers occasionally succumbed, two new battles brought them back to the path of solidarity: the fight against pesticides, and their belated entry, through a back door, into the movement against the war in Vietnam.

Jerry Cohen and the legal department took the lead in UFWOC's campaign against pesticides. Cohen had joined the union staff in May of 1967, in the middle of the Perelli-Minetti campaign. His father, a Lithuanian Jew, was a career Navy doctor, and his mother, an Irish Catholic nurse. Both parents were liberal Democrats. Jerry came of age in the early civil rights movement, and was further sensitized to prejudice because of the mild opposition in both of his parents' families to the union that created him. In 1959 he went to Amherst College, where he and his roommates led a losing fight against the fraternity system. He entered Berkeley's Boalt Law School in 1963, found most of his classes boring, but was inspired by the Berkeley Free Speech Movement. Upon graduation he was determined to use his law degree to help people in the movement and got an offer from William Kunstler and Arthur Kinoy at the Center for Constitutional Rights. He would be helping the civil rights movement in the South, but living and working in New Jersey. He didn't like that idea. He wanted to live among the people he would be representing, so he took a job with California Rural Legal Assistance in McFarland, near Delano. He wanted to work with farm workers, whose fight he had heard about while at Berkeley, but CRLA rules forbade working directly with UFWOC, and Cohen found himself stuck in federally funded divorce cases or legal disputes with the local welfare department. Less than four months later, Chavez had recruited him over a beer at People's.

Cohen: "But I don't know anything about labor law."

Chavez: "That's great. Neither do we. We'll learn together."[29]

Cesar was forty and Jerry, twenty-six; the two hit it off immediately. It turned out that Chavez knew quite a bit about labor law, and was an excellent teacher—better than most of the professors Cohen had had at Boalt, where the standard pedagogical practice was still education through humiliation. "I would go to court, get the hell beat out of me on an injunction, and Chavez would be enthusiastic, tell me I had done a great job, and show me how we could make political points even out of our losses."[30] Almost every UFWOC campaign had its legal dimension—offensive, defensive, or both—and Chavez was fully involved in formulating legal strategy. Virginia Hirsch, who had been a legal secretary, helped Cohen set up their office in the kitchen of the Pink House, down the hall from Cesar's office. The legal department grew as the lawyers Paul Driscoll, Chuck Farnsworth, David Averbuck, and Bill Carder joined, and law students helped out in the summer. Cohen, a sharp wit, was irreverent and popular.

Jessica Govea introduced him to the pesticide issue. While she was working at the Service Center, two sisters came in who had similar rashes and periodically felt nauseated and light-headed at work. They suspected pesticides, but their foreman had assured them that it was just "heat exhaustion." One of the women was pregnant. Like many farm workers, the two were not naïve about pesticides, which they called sarcastically *la medicina*. Ordinarily they were casual about exposure, not wanting to know too much, since there was little they could do about it except quit. But the risks the future mother could accept for herself she wouldn't accept for her baby, especially when she had access to people at the UFWOC Service Center who seemed both willing to help and unafraid to challenge the authority of the foremen. What pesticide was on the grape leaves, and what would it do to the baby? She brought the question to Jessica Govea, and Govea took it to Jerry Cohen.

Cohen, whose own wife was pregnant with their second child, was troubled by the story but at first did nothing. When Govea moved from the Service Center to the legal office, she brought the pesticide issue with her. The sister who had come in to complain had miscarried. Then, in Visalia, Govea met another farm worker family that had suffered a pesticide tragedy. The father had come home after a day's work of spraying a vineyard, "and his little girl, a three-year-old, ran to embrace him. You know, threw herself around his legs to hug him, and she was dead by the next morning. The pesticide he had been spraying, just the residue on his clothes, was enough to permeate her skin and kill her."[31]

That was it. In August 1968, without any particular preparation, almost casually, Jerry Cohen went to the Kern County agricultural commissioner's office and asked to look at the pesticide records; he wanted to know which ones were used, how often, and in what quantities. The commissioner, C. Seldon Morley, said it would take him awhile to get the records together. When Cohen left, Morley called a local spray duster, Packwood Aviation, and the company quickly went to a local judge who issued a temporary injunction preventing the release of pesticide records to UFWOC on the grounds that they were trade secrets. "Sorry, there is nothing I can do," Morley told Cohen a few days later. The battle was joined.

Cohen talked to farm workers, two UFWOC clinic nurses, Marion Moses and Peggy McGivern, and a few concerned biologists and doctors. While learning the issues—the differences between chlorinated hydrocarbons and organic phosphates, the exponential growth in chemical farming after World War II, the nonenforcement of scant regulatory law—Cohen began to build a new picture of the union's antagonists. UFWOC had taken on the entire food chain gang: not only the big Central Valley growers but some of the nation's largest chemical companies, a whole industry of pesticide propagandists, advisers, and applicators, large supermarkets, and researchers at the University of California. But the more extensive the enemy, the more allies UFWOC might find. Preparing the case against the injunction, Cohen met representatives of the nascent environmental movement, then riding a high tide of public sentiment against DDT. Their campaign focused entirely on DDT's threat to the environment and consumers and ignored its effect on farm workers. When UFWOC established that DDT and other powerful chlorinated hydrocarbons were used on table grapes, its battle to protect the health of farm workers became a central focus of the national anti-DDT, antipesticide campaign. Consumers could now boycott A&P and Safeway not only to help poor farm workers but also to avoid poisoning their own families.

UFWOC made Cohen's appeal of the original injunction into a political show trial, featuring testimony from both farm workers and experts. It was covered widely in the press, and the superior court judge's decision to uphold the injunction only made matters worse for the industry.*After the

___

* The judge acknowledged that organic phosphates and chlorinated hydrocarbons were a "hazard to human health and welfare," but upheld the injunction because requiring the disclosure of the pesticide information would "seriously hamper the essential cooperation existing between all segments of the pesticide industry and the farmers on the one hand and

growers refused to meet with Chavez in private to discuss the question of pesticides, UFWOC declared that the protection of farm workers and consumers would become the number one issue of the boycott.[32] In San Francisco, nursing mothers protested DDT residues on food. Supermarket picketers passed out leaflets carrying a warning in big letters, "Eating Grapes May Be Hazardous to Your Health," along with photographs of crop-dusting planes spraying vineyards. The union pointed out that given the cozy relationship between the agricultural regulatory agencies and agribusiness, a union contract with antipesticide provisions was a surer way of stopping chemical residues on food than state or federal law. Through its Democratic Party contacts, the union arranged for several congressional hearings on the pesticide menace. Farm workers appeared at the hearings not as victims but as advocates, leading the collective fight against dangerous chemical agriculture.

Just as the pesticide campaign united UFWOC with environmentalists, the union's protest of increased U.S. Department of Defense purchases of scab grapes finally brought it into the antiwar movement. In January 1969 word first came in from sympathetic jobbers at the big-city wholesale markets that growers were selling large quantities of grapes to the Department of Defense. By June the DOD, badgered by reporters' questions, offered an explanation. Yes, the brass admitted, the Pentagon had already bought almost twice as many grapes as it had the whole previous year, and shipments to soldiers in Vietnam had increased from .5 million pounds to 2.5 million pounds. Grapes were cheaper now, they said, and the increased purchases should not be interpreted as Pentagon support for the growers. Rather, not to take advantage of low prices just because a labor dispute was in process would be a form of intervening in the strike on the side of the union. *El Malcriado* featured brilliant Zermeño cartoons welcoming the fat patron to the marvelously ugly "military-industrial complex." Boycotters passed out fact sheets at antiwar rallies and refusing to eat grapes became a symbol of resistance in the GI movement. Chicano sailors threw boxes of grapes into the Gulf of Tonkin, much as Seafarers had thrown them into the Hudson River. Nixon's Defense Department, in the popular phrase of the time, had picked up a rock only to drop it on its own foot.[33]

Although the AFL-CIO's Bill Kircher continued to advise caution on the war, Chavez knew that opposing it would cost him a few friends and was unlikely to cause a significant rupture with labor officialdom. Also, the war now belonged to the Republicans and many of Chavez's fellow Democrats opposed it in various ways. The Pentagon's grape-buying spree clinched the matter. In October of 1969, Chavez added his name to a full-page ad in the *New York Times* endorsing the Moratorium to end the

---

with the commissioners on the other." See *El Malcriado*, April 1-15, 1969.

war in Vietnam, a large demonstration against the war on October 15, 1969. Relieved staffers finally were able to carry the black eagle in antiwar demonstrations across the country—even in Delano, where a proud *Malcriado* reported, "UFWOC members, undaunted by a light rain, joined over 100 other Delanoans in a [antiwar] candlelight march" through town.[34]

Four years after the grape strike began, Monthly Federal Market Service reports and yearly Department of Agriculture statistics, although not entirely reliable, sustained the boycotters' hope that the boycott was working. The numbers were piling up. In 1969, the top forty-one grape consuming cities, accounting for 75 percent of the total grape market, bought 22 percent fewer grapes than in 1966. The greatest success was in the big cities. Baltimore was down 53 percent; Boston, 42 percent; Chicago, 41 percent; New York, 34 percent; Detroit, 32 percent; Philadelphia, 23 percent. By the end of 1969 more than 20 percent of the total harvest was in cold storage back in Delano, almost a third more than in the previous year. The drop in demand also drove down prices, although prices fluctuate so much during a season that the overall economic effect of the price depression could not be easily tracked. UFWOC knew the growers were losing money—Lionel Steinberg of David Freedman & Co. had admitted that in 1968—but nobody knew how much.[35]

UFWOC had achieved those startling results by focusing on the chain stores, which by the 1960s accounted for 50 to 75 percent of all grocery store sales in the top eight table grape markets. The basic UFWOC strategy was to pick target stores (many of them in black or working-class areas) of large chains and to boycott those stores until the entire chain stopped buying table grapes. Chains, organized on the basis of high volume and low margins, were particularly vulnerable to this kind of pressure, as they were unable to absorb significant losses at even a few of their outlets. The figures from California indicated just how important the chain store strategy was to the boycott's success. Shipments to Los Angeles and San Francisco were down only 16 percent and 19 percent, respectively, reflecting the general trend that the farther away from Delano, the more popular the UFWOC's appeal, and the specific fact that the state's largest supermarket, Safeway, refused to stop buying grapes. Yet even Safeway, thoroughly integrated into California agribusiness and unwilling to break ranks, privately urged growers to sign contracts, as did the Bank of America, the growers' largest creditor. But those two private defections didn't come until the end, and in many respects they were the end.[36]

The growers did not know what to do. "There is no strike," they repeated over and over, but the truth of that assertion could hardly set them free. They had defeated the original strike, and the various little ones that followed, and they had the production figures to prove it. They had had to

raise wages and improve working conditions in the process, but even
though the increased wages had brought the vast majority of the workers
back into the vineyards, they did nothing to blunt the boycott in the cities.
The growers were befuddled: beating the strike should have been good
enough, and they were neither intellectually nor emotionally prepared to
leave their communities and fight UFWOC on a strange, urban terrain.

The California Farm Bureau and Safeway hired the public relations firm
of Whitaker & Baxter to lead the antiboycott effort. The firm had made its
name in a campaign against President Truman's national health insurance
plan, which it had labeled "socialized medicine." But it couldn't produce a
similar miracle here. Through paid advertisements, friendly op-ed pieces
and legislative speeches, the PR experts argued that the boycott was a
violation of "consumer rights," and promoted the health benefits of eating
grapes. In an attempt at humor, they distributed thousands of bumper stickers proclaiming, "Eat California Grapes, the Forbidden Fruit." The
campaign was a $2 million blunder.

The growers fell back on farm worker front groups (the Agricultural
Workers Freedom to Work Association, and Mothers Against Chavez),
whose nicely compensated representatives showed up at UFWOC press
conferences and demonstrations and went on well-financed speaking tours
of major boycott cities. The growers invited the Teamsters into the fields
through the back door, but the various local and regional Teamsters officials, still smarting from their earlier defeats, turned down the offer. A few
brave growers did try to engage the enemy on its own turf. Johnny
Giumarra Jr. flew to Toronto to debate Jerry Cohen on television. Keene
Larson, a Coachella Valley grower, outraged by the difference between the
reality he knew at home and what he heard UFWOC boycotters saying in
the cities, actually went on a "truth tour." It was too little too late. His
truth didn't have a chance against the already familiar truths of more than a
hundred boycotting farm workers.

The growers even changed their position on farm labor legislation,
finally offering to accept the constraints of the National Labor Relations
Act in exchange for its protection from secondary boycotts. They would
put up with federally supervised elections as long as UFWOC would be
prevented from boycotting grocery chain stores. But Cesar Chavez was
several jumps ahead of them: he had already shifted his own position before
the growers' change of heart. At the same time that the AFL-CIO was
testifying in Congress about how farm workers should be covered by the
NLRA, Chavez was telling West Coast reporters that inclusion in the
NLRA, as currently constituted, was unacceptable to his union. Just as
industrial unions had had an opportunity in the 1930s to establish themselves without restrictions on secondary boycotts, farm workers, too, should
have that chance, he said. This angered George Meany and infuriated the

growers. But by the time the growers got around to having California's Senator George Murphy and President Nixon promote their new farm worker legislation, Chavez had already lined up a Democratic-controlled Senate to block it, even without Meany's support.

Finally, the growers called on Governor Reagan to arrange state-supported union elections in the fields. Again, too late. No two bites from the same apple, Chavez had said, and the growers couldn't mount a powerful enough campaign to make him eat those words. Their call for elections hardly got a headline.

It may cause some wonderment that Reagan and Nixon could not be more helpful. Reagan repeatedly called the boycott illegal and immoral; he regularly ate grapes at public functions and called the strikers "barbarians." His Board of Agriculture spent public money in an antiboycott campaign. His Department of Employment refused to certify many of the legitimacy strikes, and he authorized the use of prisoners to work the fields. Nixon was just as aggressive. He ate grapes at the 1968 California announcement of his run for the presidency and was at least indirectly responsible for the increased Department of Defense purchases of boycotted grapes after he became president. Although he had been involved in California farm labor politics long enough to know that farm workers were not covered by the NLRA, and therefore not subject to its restrictions, he called the boycott illegal and said it should be opposed with the "same firmness we condemn illegal strikes, illegal lockouts, or any other form of lawbreaking."[37]

But the social movement that UFWOC was riding to victory did not disappear as Reagan took office in Sacramento in 1966 and Nixon in Washington in 1968. Their elections signaled the prospect of a long period of reaction, but it took a while for their reactionary policies to set in. UFWOC did not need to win a majority of the nation's voters. All it needed to do was mobilize a minority of consumers. The president and governor may have boosted grower morale when they cheerfully ate grapes for the cameras, but the larger effect was to publicize the boycott even more widely among the UFWOC-friendly population.

Meanwhile, smaller growers were going out of business, and the big growers were scared. Something had to be done. Before the beginning of the 1969 Coachella harvest, Lionel Steinberg had indicated to Ted Kennedy that he again was willing to start secret talks with the union. Nine other growers wanted to talk, too—four from Coachella and five from Arvin-Lamont, including a leading Arvin grower, John Kovacevich, another liberal Democrat.

Chavez didn't attend the talks, which became public but went nowhere. The growers weren't ready to concede on anything but wages, and UFWOC could afford to wait. Steinberg's and Kovacevich's willingness to negotiate with UFWOC did not change the mind of boycotting

consumers, but it did enrage the rest of the industry. Although the ten
growers represented only about 12 percent of the $140 million California
table grape harvest, their decision to talk with UFWOC broke the unanimous public rejection of the union that the table grape growers had
maintained since the first strike in 1965. Allen Grant, the president of the
California Farm Bureau Federation, was furious. The growers who were
negotiating with UFWOC, he said, "would have the boycott hanging over
their heads." He called for legislation to outlaw the "illicit" and "immoral"
secondary boycott. Jack Pandol, a large grower from the Delano area,
claimed that Steinberg and Kovacevich were negotiating behind the backs
of their workers: "It is unmoral, un-Christian, and un-American to sell the
workers against their will. If the American people buy this boycott, they are
likening themselves to those who engage in campus disorders and the
country will go to hell."[38]

The union's legitimacy strike in Coachella that season, its picket lines
and dramatic demonstrations, did not disrupt the harvest any more than in
earlier years.[39] Yet midway through the harvest Steinberg and Kovacevich
called for federal mediation, a tribute to the boycott's effectiveness and an
unmistakable sign of grower vulnerability. After the talks were called off,
the growers' negotiator said that if the union couldn't rule the table grape
industry, it was determined to ruin it.

Among many on the UFW staff, the 1969 Coachella strike was remembered more for its effect on Gilbert Padilla that for any advances in the
fields or on the boycott. During the strike, alcohol passed his lips for the
very last time. "I got back from Texas in December 1968," remembers
Padilla.

> I was helping with the ranch committees. Chavez was in bed. He wanted
> me to go to Coachella and lead the strike. I did, but I was nipping pretty
> good. One day, Manuel and I had to drive to Mexicali. It was miserable
> and hot. I was driving and Manuel was drinking beer. When we got to
> Brawley we went to visit an old friend who was passed out in front of his
> swamp cooler with a big bottle of wine in front of him. I drank the
> bottle, and that started me on a horrible drunk that ended in Mexicali
> with Manuel and a couple of women. I didn't enjoy any of it. Almost a
> week had passed, and I just felt awful sick. When I sobered up, I never
> touched liquor again.[40]

Chavez, attended in his hospital bed by Marion Moses, was back in
Delano, calling most of the shots in Coachella from more than two hundred
miles away. When he heard about Padilla's binge he was furious. He told
Gilbert that he had to quit drinking or leave the union. For Padilla, in 1969,
leaving the union was unthinkable. Marion Moses looked around for a

treatment center. She chose some people doing "aversion therapy" in the San Francisco Bay area, and Giblert went there for a couple of weeks. He doesn't think the therapy did much good, but the center was a good place to dry out. And he appreciated Moses' help, still introducing her years later as "the person who saved my life." But what really stopped his drinking was waking up in Mexicali, sick and ashamed. At that point in his life, that was all the aversion therapy he needed. Sober, he finally had the courage to go through his divorce. He became active on the Executive Board again. In early 1970, he, his oldest son, Tomás, and Doug Adair went to Philadelphia to work on the boycott.

Historical thinking—consideration of the whys and wherefores of the past—tends to mask the uncertainties and anxieties of human action. Looking back at the 1969 table grape sales and knowing what was going to happen six months later, we forget the importance of will and choice. It becomes hard to see, to remember the situation in which people found themselves and how they interpreted it at the time. In retrospect we can see that things looked good. The summer of 1969 had brought the UFWOC, and especially Cesar Chavez, unprecedented media attention: a two-part profile by Peter Matthiessen in *The New Yorker* and a July 4 cover story in *Time*. Matthiessen called the union and its idealistic, nonviolent leader standard bearers of a "New American Revolution." *Time's* story, titled "The Grapes of Wrath, 1969, Mexican-Americans on the March," focused on "the wider aspirations of the nation's Mexican-American minority," called Chavez the "personification" of the "Chicanos' bleak past, restless present, and possible future," and resoundingly supported bilingual education, a "new pluralism," and the grape boycott. And as the boycotters prepared for the 1970 season, the numbers indicated that the table grape growers were losing money.

But were they losing enough to force them to sign a contract? The great majority of growers had completely stonewalled the union. Perhaps, despite all their losses, they would continue to do so. It would not have been impossible. More small growers would have gone out of business, but the big boys might have held on, absorbed the losses, and waited for the boycott to wane. Wouldn't it fizzle out eventually? In 1970, couldn't a perceptive person feel a new political wind? How long would *New Yorker* writers call for a "New American Revolution"? Movements come and go. Maybe 1969 would turn out to be the apex of boycott power. Who knew?

That year Marshall Ganz had brought a delegation of Canadian unionists to California to witness a few days of the Coachella strike. Afterward, Cesar asked Marshall to remain in Delano for a while and see what could be done to make life uncomfortable for scabs. Ganz stayed until September, about four months, working on a campaign of minor *chingaderas*. He got some tear gas from Berkeley students who had "liberated" it from the Oakland police during a riot in People's Park, and rigged up some field toilets so that scabs tear-gassed themselves when they used them. A few months after returning to the boycott in Canada, he asked Chavez to bring him and Jessica Govea back to Delano. Marshall wanted to work with farm workers; he had some ideas about how to enliven the movement in the fields. Chavez agreed, and Ganz began to make preparations to leave.

But in late January, Cesar wrote to Marshall saying that he should stay in Toronto. There was "a lot of discussion and soul searching going on right now in Delano," Chavez wrote, and since it seemed "hopeless to expect to keep [the strike breakers] from picking grapes, then the boycott is our only hope, and we will have to give it the kind of attention that we have never given it in the past, including the top leadership of the union, and all of the energy and talent that they possess." Not only were Marshall and Jessica to continue boycotting, but the whole union had to increase the boycott efforts, because "right now I think the boycott is the only way." The letter has the tone and flavor of a discussion among equals, and Chavez closes it saying, "I would very much like to hear your thoughts on the matter."[41]

Three days later Ganz replied with three and half pages of single-spaced type:

> I have also been doing a lot of thinking about what I am doing. Twenty-six is different from twenty-one. You know I have no plans to leave the union—I believe in it and in what we are doing and, of course, my life has revolved around it for the past four or five years. I hope you know this. Perhaps I have a selfish desire to be more at the center of things, or perhaps it is a need to have some kind of greater responsibility or to do work which is more fulfilling. I have always enjoyed working with you—whenever there was the opportunity—because I felt not only that I was making a contribution, but that I was learning and growing in capability and understanding.[42]

Ganz went on to discuss some of the complications of the Canadian boycott and responded to Chavez's pessimism about stopping the strike breakers, saying that an anti-scab campaign was "something we have always flirted with, but never systematically carried out." He allowed that "there may be very good reasons for this," but argued that there is great potential for more effective action in the fields: a one-day general strike, slowdowns, sloppy work, arriving late or leaving early. He outlined a possible campaign of farm worker civil disobedience in the vineyards to reinvigorate the boycott in the cities. All of his proposals involved more farm worker participation in the union, because, he reasoned, "supporters . . . respond to what the people directly involved are doing."

Finally, Ganz expressed his worries that the boycott may have ebbed:

"The words boycott and strike suggest an event which has a simple beginning and an end, and, in most people's experience, it means less than four or five years." The solution was "to communicate that what is happening is more than just a strike—it is a farm worker movement—and the boycott is just the current expression of that movement." He closed by saying that he had "just been letting my mind wander over various possibilities," and that he "would like to hear what things are being thought about."[43]

Chavez's response is dated four days later, and it is almost as long as Ganz's. "I am sorry that you were disappointed," Chavez wrote; "it was a mistake not to have reported to you in full" the reasons for his change of mind. He was "more convinced than ever that we have not exploited all the potential power that we have in the cities," and that "the boycott is the only real alternative to bring the employers to the bargaining table." If it had been up to him, the union would have focused more attention on the boycott long ago, but "things didn't work out that way . . . mostly because I didn't push hard enough because of my dishonesty to accept the responsibility and deal with the consequences of my decisions." He attributed this partly to his problems with his back. But times had changed:

> I have now returned to my job with the same resolve that I've always felt in life. That is, that I don't get into anything because I want to lose, and that organizing farm workers and winning this strike is a must with me. So I have made some challenges. I'm cracking the whip. I'm determined that the Delano contingent of the strike is going to be turned around and that we're not going to permit ourselves to be comfortable and to work at administration from eight in the morning to six in the afternoon. Because of my determination to bring the struggle to a head, and the pressure that has been created on the people in Delano, we are now going through a period of uncertainty and some below the surface friction.[44]

The problem in Delano, Chavez wrote, originated in the union's lack of power in the fields, which "creates a lot of frustration which in turn converts by some mysterious force into an ever-expanding administration of the union." Rather than do more in Delano, the boycott must be intensified. "I am not concerned that the boycott may dwindle because I don't believe that great advances come about by accident; rather they are forced by man's will and determination and sacrifice."[45]

The Coachella growers, first to market, were the first to cave in. Following Steinberg's lead, they signed a contract with UFWOC in April of 1970, well before the May harvest. The three-year contract tied the growers to the previous year's strike-induced wage of $1.80 an hour and twenty-five cents a box, with a raise to $2.05 an hour by 1972. Wages were the easy part; the growers also had to submit to protective pesticide regulations, including a complete ban on DDT and four other pesticides (DDT was banned on UFW organized farms before it was banned by the federal government later that year). A joint worker-grower committee would oversee pesticide use. The growers also agreed to contribute ten cents an hour to the UFWOC-administered Robert F. Kennedy Health Plan and two cents an hour to the loosely defined UFWOC economic development fund. The contract made fresh drinking water, field toilets, and regular rest periods mandatory, and prohibited profiteering on labor camp rents, meals, and transportation. It spelled out a formal grievance procedure. Finally, the growers were forced to swallow what they most feared: a closed shop and a union hiring hall.

When established unions renegotiate contracts with employers, "contract language" is often tidied up in early negotiating sessions before the two parties sit down to discuss the difficult question of wages. Here, the reverse was true. Having gotten its foot in the door with the Schenley and wine grape contracts, UFWOC now smashed it to pieces and made itself at home in the living room of California agribusiness. The contract language the union had insisted upon provided for a whole new architecture of relations between farm workers and their bosses. Workers no longer would be dependent on foremen and contractors for their jobs. They would get their jobs through the union hiring hall; before they could be fired, the company would have to prove its case in a regular grievance hearing. In some ways, the union shop and the "good standing" provision theoretically made it easier for the union, rather than the employers, to discipline and fire workers. No one knew how these new contractual relations would actually work in table grapes—they had proved troublesome to the bosses but not impossible to work out in wine grapes—but the growers had been slow to accede to them for a reason: they threatened to curtail their control over the workforce.

Less than a month later, before the harvest hit their own vineyards in Arvin-Lamont, Arizona, and Delano, Bruno Dispoto and Anthony Bianco signed similar contracts. Bianco and Dispoto had been outspoken opponents of the union, but in the end they made sensible business decisions required by the new balance of forces. Bianco was already in the first stages of Chapter 11 bankruptcy, and Dispoto did not want to lose his position as a distributor for the already unionized Coachella grapes which were getting a bonus of as much as a $2 a box because they carried the black eagle into boycotted eastern cities.[46]

Word of the new contracts spread quickly throughout farm worker California. Peach workers south of Fresno went out on strike as did melon workers in the Imperial Valley and citrus workers in Ventura. Chavez threatened a "general farm labor strike [that] will shut down agriculture in California this summer or next" and referred to "impatient farm workers in other crops [who] see striking workers winning contracts." In the midst of negotiations with the table grape growers, he made quick visits to Ventura and Salinas to talk to halls overflowing with excited farm workers. He urged caution and patience, but promised that the union was coming for them, too. The walkouts led to a contract at Roberts Farms, which operated 46,000 acres of table and wine grapes, almonds, citrus, and peaches in Kern, Fresno, Tulare, and King counties. In Santa Maria, the union sent letters to the vegetable companies asking for recognition. Tenneco, the thirty-fourth largest company in the United States, which had been aggressively buying up table grape farms that were under pressure from the boycott, signed. S. A. Camp, who had bought up most of the DiGiorgio holdings and then refused to honor the UFWOC agreements, reversed himself and gave in.[47]

Giumarra held out, but not for long. By mid-July, in time to save the current season, the company was suing for peace and accepted the UFWOC contract language after a little more than a week of negotiations. The union refused to sign with Giumarra unless the company rounded up the twenty-eight other major Delano grape growers and brought them to the table to sign. The Giumarras did that in half a day. UFWOC made one final demand. The Delano growers would have to come to Reuther Hall at Forty Acres to sign in front of a room full of farm workers. The growers were not in a position to say no. Jacques Levy, who was driving Chavez around California to visit striking farm workers and sitting in on the final negotiations with the table grape growers, was there to report the scene. First he quotes Richard Chavez:

> The growers came in through the back door because the hall was full of people. The only empty seats were at the head table where there were microphones. So they filed in one by one, someone from each company, and sat down facing the people. They were very uptight. They looked pretty sick. But Giumarra was very cheerful. He made a speech that finally peace had come to the valley, that we were going to work together. It was a great thing. People were very happy, singing and cheering. The hall was so crowded, it was just solid bodies, and there were more people outside that couldn't get in. There were twenty-nine contracts signed that day.

Chavez, wearing a white barong Tagalog, a formal Filipino shirt, finally addressed the crowd:

> The strikers and the people involved in the struggle sacrificed a lot, sacrificed all of their worldly possessions. Ninety-five percent of the strikers lost their homes and their cars. But I think in losing those worldly

possessions they found themselves, and they found that only through dedication, through serving mankind, and, in this case, serving the poor and those who were struggling for justice, only in that way could they really find themselves.[48]

Six months earlier, in January 1970, at a meeting in Delano to honor a small group of organizers who were about to be sent throughout the country to open new boycott offices or reinforce others, Chavez had told the assembled farm workers and union supporters that the "organizers would go down in history as the heroes of the farm workers' struggle for liberty."[49] What, then, was the place of the farm workers in "the farm workers' struggle for liberty"? What about the workers who did not leave their jobs and risk their homes, who did not choose to become full-time staff members, who didn't want to venture out to America's cities to become hero organizers? About 10,000 of them had continued to work in the symbolically struck table grape vineyards from the Coachella Valley to Fresno. If the difference between winning and losing did not depend on these workers' willingness to withdraw their labor and stop production, then where did they fit in UFWOC's battle plans? If they weren't the heroes of their own liberation, who were they?

UFWOC leaders never posed the question in that fashion, but an answer was immanent in their practice. On various occasions they had called upon those workers to show boycotters in the cities that they wanted UFWOC to be their union. But when picket lines proved to be largely symbolic, when the unorganized workers were back in the fields picking the grapes, the UFWOC leaders had to explain them away—both to their allies and to themselves. The explanations were many: the majority of the workers supported the union, but were afraid to show it; they were too poor to strike and had to work; they were wetbacks and green-carders, who hardly understood what they were doing and could accept low wages because they lived most of the year across the border; they were committed scabs, traitors, and kiss-asses, who didn't give a damn for anybody else.

The explanations were not all wrong, but they were not calculated to organize or even to win friends among the scabbing farm workers. This is standard: union activists and scabbing workers are rarely on good terms. What was special about this strike, however, was that despite the loss in the fields, the union won in the cities. And the 10,000 people working in the vineyards, some of whom had no use at all for the union, and many of whom were, at best, indifferent to it, now would work under union contracts, and would become, for the next three years, about 90 percent of the union's membership. Chavez's accurate prediction that the organizers would be the heroes of the farm workers' struggle carried an enormous but barely noticed challenge. How was the union going to deal with the nonheroes, the ordinary farm workers who got contracts through little effort of their own and who overnight became the overwhelming majority within the union?

Don Watson, an ILWU ships clerk and UFWOC supporter, was in Delano to celebrate the contract victory. UFWOC had agreed that the contracts would not go into effect unless the workers endorsed them within thirty days of the signings, and Watson volunteered to help with the endorsement elections. The elections were mostly pro forma affairs, as it was no secret that the growers wanted the workers to endorse their decision so that the boycott would be called off. The day after the Reuther Hall celebration, Watson, Richard Chavez, and Johnny Giumarra Jr. went to sign up Giumarra workers and to talk to them about the upcoming vote. "Junior did most of the talking," Watson reported. "He was urging the workers to sign up in the union . . . The workers were timid, shy, taking orders from the patron . . . They were cringing, they didn't want to sign, they would not have signed if Junior hadn't been urging them . . . I thought, 'This is a union?' "[50]

Transforming such workers into a conscious, functional union would be hard, but not impossible. After all, the new contracts did improve wages incrementally and working conditions significantly. With the contracts in hand, couldn't the union organizers win over the 10,000? If the vast majority of grape workers were now better off, wouldn't they eventually forget the earlier slights and insults from union organizers and striking workers? What would be so difficult about a campaign to educate the workers about the benefits of the union?

The answers to those questions would have to wait. After the Forty Acres celebration, Chavez, his top lieutenants, and much of the staff rushed off to the Salinas Valley, where vegetable growers had just signed contracts with the Teamsters union in response to the grape growers' capitulation and the current farm worker upheaval. Soon, UFWOC was in the middle of a strike that, in ways no one anticipated, would determine the future of the union. A year would pass before the union leadership would again pay serious attention to grape workers.

Farm workers Win a New Deal

Salinas Before the Storm

In August 1970, when the United Farm Workers Organizing Committee staff arrived in full force, the temperature in Salinas averaged a pleasant seventy-four degrees. A cool breeze from nearby Monterey Bay hit the town between eleven-thirty and noon every morning, then swept down the Salinas Valley to San Lucas, seventy miles farther from the sea, where temperatures were about ten degrees higher, and where farm workers toiling in the fields could expect a sometimes refreshing, often howling, wind. Salinas is a narrow coastal valley, no more than twenty miles across at its widest point, framed by the Gabilan Mountains on the east and the Santa Lucia range to the west; its river runs south to north and empties into Monterey Bay at the valley's head. It is a farmer's dream, with rich alluvial soil, sufficient but not oppressive summer heat, a gentle rainy season (ten to twenty inches a year), a deep aquifer, and two man-made lakes that, back then, provided plenty of water. The Pacific Ocean keeps the valley cool in the summer and warm in the winter. Meteorologists describe the climate as Mediterranean. Braceros called it *la crema*, the cream of the farm worker circuit.

That summer of 1970 the temperature in Delano averaged over ninety degrees, and at midday one would have had a hard time locating any mountains or pointing toward the sea. But the differences in topography and climate between Delano's monotonous flats and Salinas's long picturesque valley were more than matched by their contrasting farm worker populations.

The root of that difference goes back to the Bracero Program. Only a few braceros had worked in the table grapes in the Central Valley. In the twenty-three years between 1941 and 1964, table grape production remained mostly in the hands of older Filipinos and settled Mexican American families. But the vegetable and strawberry fields of Salinas were bracero country. During World War II, contracted Mexican men began to replace the Filipinos who had dominated the Salinas agricultural workforce since the 1920s. In the last year of the program, 1964, more than 11,000 braceros were working in the valley, doing about 80 percent of the field work.[1] They could not be replaced quickly, and 1965 and 1966 were crisis years. The tumult didn't ease until the former braceros returned, as relatively free, though often undocumented, members of an agricultural working class.

In 1970 the Salinas Valley still bore the mark of the bracero. The extensive system of labor camps that the growers had been obligated to build under the old program—some right in the city of Salinas, others on the outskirts of town, still more strung down the valley, all the way to King City—remained open, and many of the returning workers moved right back in, paying rent to their bosses. According to the census for Monterey County, which covered the whole Salinas Valley, including the city of Monterey, half of the 9,798 farm workers in 1970 lived in "group quarters."[2] Most of the others lived in the south county towns of King City, Soledad, Gonzalez, Greenfield, and Chualar, which even during the Bracero Program had been home to small groups of more permanent Mexican and Mexican American families. Some of the returning braceros, along with new Mexican immigrants, moved into the Alisal section of Salinas, and what had been a small barrio in white-dominated Salinas began to flower into a full Mexican community.

The Bracero Program had established a semi-apartheid system in the city of Salinas. Forbidden to bring their families to California, the braceros had sent no children to local schools; without cars, they had been trapped in the labor camps. A seasonal and controlled population, they were legally separate from local political life and effectively excluded from local culture. Salinas, whose wealth depended on brown labor, remained a white town. After the program ended, and the braceros returned as green-carders or undocumented workers, many brought their families. They came in cars, and even if they continued to live in the camps, they moved freely about the town. Their families used the city parks. Their children went to the city's schools. Some stayed around in the off-season and used the county's welfare system. Between 1960 and 1970 the official population of Salinas more than doubled, from 28,000 to 58,000, with the greatest increase in Spanish-surnamed residents.[3] All of this was deeply disturbing to many parts of white Salinas. And when Cesar Chavez came to town and led what amounted to a brown rebellion, more than a few white Salinas farmers went berserk.

Returning from her boycott outpost in Montreal, Jessica Govea was among the first who noticed the difference between the Delano grape workers and the Salinas vegetable workers. As a daughter of first-generation Mexican immigrants, she was in an excellent position to understand the contrast:

> The Salinas workers were so much more confident than the Delano workers . . . They were clear about why they were going on strike, and what they wanted to change by going on strike, and they felt they had

every right to do that. Some of that confidence reminded me very much of my father, who had come [from Mexico] as an immigrant. He had that kind of self-confidence. You know, my dad was not a cap-in-hand guy. And the Salinas people I met—I am using a broad brush—were the same. They were not cap-in-hand guys.[4]

Govea believed that the second-generation Mexican Americans in Delano "had been beaten down in the United States on so many fronts, especially in school . . . Their identity was something to be ashamed of, rather than something to be proud of." They had been damaged by coming of age in America, whereas the first-generation immigrants in Salinas, the men like her father, "were sure of their identity . . . They were very alive. There was an electricity, a vibrancy that was different from Delano. It wasn't slow or languid. It was like, Hey, let's go. Let's do this. And to me, the difference was very noticeable."[5]

What Govea didn't pick up on so quickly was the extraordinary working abilities of many of these Mexican men. Their confidence was rooted not only in their cultural heritage but in their strategic importance in agricultural production. Many of the men who reminded Jessica of her father—the piece-rate lettuce harvesters, the locally famous *lechugueros*, who cut and packed the Salinas Valley's $50 million lettuce deal—were relatively well paid, skilled workers, successful people in their own communities. Delano had no comparable workers. The closest would be the grape girdlers, men like Epifanio Camacho. But the grape girdlers, numbering in the hundreds, were a small percentage of the Delano workforce, while the *lechugueros* numbered in the thousands, and were about a quarter of the Salinas vegetable workers. More important, the girdlers were paid on an individual piece-rate basis, each man paid just for his own work. Such a system tended to produce strong individuals. The *lechugueros*, on the other hand, were paid collectively for what they produced, and they divided that equally. They were not just strong individuals; they were strong crews.

Hermilo Mojica—or Mojica, as he was called by nearly everyone—belonged to such a crew. His first name was rarely mentioned, he was just called Mojica (mo-HEE-ka), pronounced like the name of the famous North American Indian tribe and suggesting that the small, soft-spoken man might come from a long line of warriors. Warrior he was, son and grandson of warriors, but not of the Mohican variety. Immigration officials got his name wrong, butchering Múgica, a name made famous in Mexican politics by Hermilo's father's first cousin, General Francisco Múgica, who was Lazaro Cardenas's closest *compañero* to his left, and the man most responsible for the nationalization of the Mexican petroleum industry in 1938.

Mojica's paternal grandfather, the general's uncle, gave Hermilo his first lessons in politics: the land belongs to the people who work it, but they had to fight to get it, and they will have to fight to keep it; Mexico must stay independent of the United States and remain in control of its own resources and economic policies; the Mexican Revolution, the first great social revolution of the twentieth century, still lives and is an example to revolutionaries throughout Latin America. These lessons of Mexican history as interpreted by the left wing of the Partido Revolucionario Institucional (PRI) in the late 1930s and '40s were distilled in the one great international event that made the name Múgica famous throughout Mexico: the order forcing the foreign oil companies to leave.

Mojica's political bloodlines were not just paternal. His mother, Maria Alfaro, was the most militant member of the family. Her father, Jose, was a leading revolutionary in Santa Cruz de Villa Gómez, the small town in southeastern Michoacán, where Hermilo grew up. Three rivers converge in Santa Cruz de Villa Gómez, and several battles were fought to control the town during the Mexican Revolution. Mojica's mother knew the details of those battles, and her son remembered them as revolutionary bedtime stories.[6]

Mojica's father was the longstanding president of the municipality of San Lucas of which Santa Cruz de Villa Gómez was a part. A local *ejiditario* and small-town PRI politician, he was the most conservative of Hermilo's teachers. He sometimes warned the boy to stay out of politics, as there were too many inconsequential squabbles, and instead of fighting for the people you spent your life sorting out petty feuds in boring committee meetings. Mojica now thinks that he is more like his mother than his father. "Although," he adds, with a quiet, almost under the breath laugh, "I have done my time on quite a few committees."

Political prominence did not guarantee wealth in Santa Cruz de Villa Gómez. His father, like the other *ejiditarios*, had a hard time forcing a living out of the land. Mojica's two brothers, like many other young men in town, got bracero contracts and went to the United States. Mojica did not want to leave, and his father counseled against it, not wanting to lose all his sons to his country's bad neighbor to the north. But as the only young man still at home, Mojica had to do all the field work and take care of the horses and oxen; his father, busy with political work, helped out only during the harvest. So in 1959 Hermilo Múgica, then twenty-five, borrowed some money and made his way to Empalme, the standby station for would-be braceros going to California. He paid a peso a night for a spot on the floor in a building that was part garage, part stable. Finally, after two months, his name was called. Counting the food, water, and bribes, it cost him 2,000 pesos to get to the bracero processing center in Calexico, where he was examined and fumigated. It was thoroughly humiliating, and he thought of his father, wondering if it had been a mistake to leave Santa Cruz de Villa Gómez.

On his first job, picking strawberries in Chualar, near Salinas, he worked only four or five hours a day. There was not enough work for the hundreds of braceros who were packed into the tin-roofed camp, but every extra man in the camp meant more dollars for the growers, who were overcharging them for food and other necessities, like soap. The men quickly figured out that scam but couldn't understand why they were treated so badly. It all seemed so unnecessary: the vicious foremen, the foul-talking supervisors—why couldn't they learn a person's name, instead of calling him a number? What profit did they make out of that? Mojica's first struggle on this side of the border was to try to make the foremen call him by his name, instead of Number Sixty-Seven. He lost.

His second battle he considered an *empate*, a tie. It was about Mexican Mother's Day, May 10. In the week leading up to it, Mojica had carried on a joking argument with a foreman named Martinez, saying that Mother's Day was one of the most important holidays in Mexico, that people there didn't have to work but got paid anyway, and since the braceros were all Mexicans picking berries on land stolen from Mexico, they should get the same paid holiday. Martinez said that the sun must have got to Number Sixty-Seven, and even if the gringos had stolen the land, they stole it fair and square, and who ever heard of a successful thief being forced to pay off his victims? On and on they bantered, about who was lazy and who wasn't, who were the traitors and who were the fools. On May 10, everyone had to work, and Mojica felt bad all day. And on payday the checks came up short. Not content with his little victory, Martinez had wanted a big one. With a straight face, he told Mojica and the others that he remembered distinctly that he had granted Number Sixty-Seven's request and had given the whole crew the day off.

Mojica didn't argue; the arguing had been for fun. He called the office of the Mexican consul in San Jose. The vice consul who came to investigate was known to many of the braceros. *Hierritos*, they called him, "the little iron one," because he was so soft when acting in their defense. Everyone on the crew assured him that they had worked on Mother's Day. Martinez showed him the time book and said the men were confused. The crew never did get paid, but within the week, Martinez was gone. A partial victory and they had done it themselves. Mojica figured it was a Mother's Day present for his mom.

Right after Martinez left, the other foremen marked Number Sixty-Seven as a subversive. They were going to send him back to Mexico, they said. What kind of threat was that? he answered; Mexico was home. When the foremen started talking violence, Mojica jumped the fence and became what the Border Patrol called a "skip," a runaway bracero. He walked along Highway 101 until he came to Campo Vasquez, where his older brother was living. By this time Mojica's brother was a "special," like Pablo

Camacho, and could travel freely back and forth across the border and around California. Campo Vasquez wasn't a bracero camp but belonged to Tony Vasquez, a labor contractor for Mann Packing, the biggest broccoli grower in the Salinas Valley. Vasquez liked Mojica's brother, and he put Mojica to work on one of the broccoli crews.

Mojica was now officially a fugitive, an illegal, but there were tens of thousands of them working in California agriculture at the time, and no one bothered him. He even used his real name, Hermilo Múgica. Two years later, in 1962, when the bosses and the INS vastly increased the resident alien program, Mojica and his brother were among the first fifty workers at Mann Packing who received green cards. It was in that process, on his official papers, that the name Múgica's was written as Mojica.

Like so many other Mexicans, Mojica returned to his home in Michoacán immediately after his presence in the United States was legalized. Three months later he was back in Salinas cutting broccoli. Later he hit the asparagus harvest in Stockton, the apples in Watsonville, and the olives in Lindsey. He went down to Mexicali, and just as he ran out of money, the Imperial Valley lettuce harvest beckoned. The experienced men carried him throughout the short season while he learned the work, and in the spring of 1964, he returned to Salinas as a *lechuguero*:

> Mostly I worked for Salinas Lettuce Co-Op. I liked the work. It was better than working the ladders [in the apple and olive orchards]. I am not very big, and the ladders were heavy. And you could make good money in the lettuce. At the time we were making one hundred fifty dollars a week. That was not bad in 1964. Other people were making like eighty dollars a week. They were paying us the standard twenty-five cents a box. Pretty damn good. And for the next twenty-two years I was a *lechuguero* . . . The work wasn't that hard. The political fights were more difficult than the farm work, and more dangerous, too.

The official seal of Salinas features nineteen rows of bright green lettuce sitting under a friendly sun, one of the rare cases in which the designers of a city crest got it right. In 1969, the year before UFWOC arrived, more than a third of every agricultural dollar earned in the valley was tied to lettuce, and from June through August, Salinas workers cut and packed more than 90 percent of the nation's crop. Not that other vegetables were insignificant. In 1970, Salinas grew more than half of all the celery, broccoli, and cauliflower in the United States, as well as every one of its artichokes. In midsummer it produced 80 percent of all the fresh vegetables sold commercially throughout the country. Add the valley's strawberry bonanza, and the gross receipts of Salinas agribusiness topped $150 million, making the valley's relatively few 160,000 cultivated acres among the most lucrative agricultural land in human history.[7]

Lettuce is almost as old as wine. Persians planted it 500 years before Christ. The ancient Greeks ate it. Europeans grew it in the Middle Ages. The Italians and the French both claim to have developed the head lettuce variety, with its crisp, sweet leaves and compact size. In the late eighteenth century, a French explorer brought head lettuce to the New World, leaving some seeds with the Franciscan fathers at the Carmel Mission, about thirty miles from the Salinas Valley. In the California Gold Rush, 150 years later, lettuce became a moneymaker, earning its producers fifty cents for a dozen heads.[8]

Lettuce is fragile. Once it's cut, it wilts quickly. If its temperature is carefully regulated it can stay good for about three weeks. It couldn't become a reliable national commodity until the development of the refrigerated railroad car in the early 1920s. Before that, truck farmers grew lettuce when weather permitted, and sold it in regional markets. East of the Rockies, lettuce was unavailable most of the year, and economists figured that annual national consumption was about one head per person. By 1929 that had jumped to more than seven heads, and lettuce was big business. To make it even bigger business, this unstorable commodity had to be in all of the country's markets all the time, which meant it had to be grown in volume year-round. Even Salinas's ideal weather wasn't that good; the valley could produce lettuce for only eight months, and that was stretching it. So the big growers in Salinas bought into the winter deals (as agribusinessmen universally describe harvest seasons) in the Imperial Valley and Arizona, and some of them even secured a piece of the short summer deals in the Midwest and East. By World War II, a few of the biggest companies could deliver lettuce to the nation's retailers every day of the year. They advertised their product as "Head Lettuce—Nature's Concentrated Sunshine." Among themselves they called it green gold.[9]

The "growers" didn't actually grow anything. They owned or leased the land and made the decisions. In Salinas throughout the 1920s and '30s, Filipinos did the physical work. They planted the seeds, weeded and irrigated the fields, and thinned the young plants. When it was time to harvest, they cut the lettuce and threw it into wagons, first drawn by horses and later by tractors. The wagons were offloaded into trucks waiting at the edge of the fields, and truckers delivered the produce to packing sheds along the railroad tracks, sometimes as far as twenty miles away. In the sheds, white workers, both men and women, trimmed the outer leaves, packed the green gold into wood-slated boxes, filled the boxes with ice, stacked them in the refrigerated railroad cars, and sent them on their journey.

Browns in the fields and whites in the sheds was a regular (although not universal) practice in early California agriculture, spurred by the oft-stated belief that Filipinos and Mexicans couldn't do the shed work and by a conscious strategy, less commonly expressed, of making unity difficult and unions unlikely.[10] The magnates of the Spreckels Sugar Company, which for many years controlled the West Coast sugar refining industry, had introduced this strategy into the Salinas Valley in the early twentieth century. The lettuce growers happily adopted it, recruiting from California's big supply of experienced, self-described "fruit tramps" for the work in the lettuce sheds. The strategy was largely successful: the growers and shippers first demolished the fieldworkers' unions with shed-worker support, and then destroyed the shedworkers' unions, amidst field-worker indifference. During World War II, using the protection of the National Labor Relations Board and taking advantage of the general labor shortage, the white shed workers rebuilt their union and established themselves as powerful players in the Salinas lettuce deal at exactly the time that braceros were replacing most of the Filipinos in the fields.

In the early 1950s, braceros in the fields were making eighty-eight cents an hour, while the unionized fruit tramps in the sheds were earning $1.63, with health benefits.[11] Dividing the races into different job categories now took second place to what the growers could make by replacing the higher-wage white workers with lower-wage brown ones. They did it by changing the lettuce pack. They got rid of the ice. The lettuce was cooled in a large vacuum tube after the braceros had packed it into cardboard boxes in the fields. Although this braceros' "field pack" and subsequent vacuum cooling actually took more labor time than the shed workers' "cowboy pack," the wage gap between browns and whites was so great that by 1956, just four years after maverick grower Bud Antle first introduced the technology on a large scale, 92 percent of all lettuce was packed in the fields and vacuum cooled. The shed workers were replaced by a few forklift drivers and loaders, who transferred the boxes in and out of the vacuum tubes and into truck trailers and railroad cars. The fruit tramps, who had held on since the 1920s, were gone—although even in 1970, if one wandered into the right bar in Salinas, an old tramp could still be found who was willing to argue that the "cowboy pack" was a better product than any "god-damned Mexican pack."

With labor costs down, production up, and the nation's consumers getting used to year-round lettuce and fresh vegetables, a green gold rush was on. Starting in the 1950s, Salinas Valley agricultural land was converted from mechanized field crops (sugar beets, beans, and barley) to labor-intensive lettuce and vegetables at an average rate of 3,000 acres per year.[12] The high volume of thirsty vegetables required the growers to reshape the valley: the two major tributaries of the Salinas River were dammed for irrigation, with the cost passed on to the city's water consumers.

And yet none of this could take the risk out of lettuce farming. For a small farmer, green gold is as big a gamble as the yellow variety. Growers might have a few seasons in succession where they lose money, followed by a season where they win big. A lettuce grower has to have enough money, or enough credit, to survive the periods of low prices between the short spurts of high ones. And the prices shift not only from season to season but within a season—within a couple of weeks lettuce can jump from a price so low that the growers will leave it to rot in the fields to a bonanza price that can make up for years of losses. The price volatility (and consequent gamble) is primarily due to the lettuce plant's unpredictable rate of growth, which periodically overloads or underloads a market where demand is steady. Lettuce has to be cut within a couple of days of when it matures, and since it can't be stored after it is cut, growers have no way of evening out the supply. The lettuce industry, Salinas farmers boast, is not for the faint of heart.

Nor is it for those without deep pockets. Like most agricultural producers, lettuce growers need money at the beginning of the season to buy the seeds, pay the workers to plant them, and then pay other workers to thin and weed the crop. They need money to buy the fertilizers and pesticides and to pay the workers to apply them. They need to buy boxes and staples, maintain tractors and other equipment. And they need to spend all of that money before they get one penny back from the first box of sold lettuce. Once the harvest ends and they have settled their debts, they have to go back to the waiting game again, receiving no income until the next harvest. This constant delay between expenditures and sales is a central reason that small and medium-sized farmers end up hopelessly indebted.

Small growers have another problem. A box of lettuce is not a national commodity unless it is quickly cooled after it is packed. A grower might be able to sell uncooled lettuce in Salinas but not much farther away. In the days of the lettuce sheds, a grower who didn't have enough capital to build or rent a shed and pay the ice bill had to sell his product to the growers who did.[13] Thus, even before the vacuum tube, a small group of grower-shippers dominated the lettuce industry, and with the tubes, which cost more than $100,000 each, grower-shipper power increased. By the early 1960s, the Salinas Valley lettuce and vegetable deals were controlled by fewer than three dozen grower-shippers, who dominated the economic lives of almost 300 other small farmers. The grower-shippers lent money, scheduled plantings, specified when and how to use pesticides and fertilizers, hired the harvesting crews, for which they charged a fee, and sold and shipped the final product. Through the particulars of their individual arrangements with the cash-strapped farmers, they insulated themselves from the lows in the market, and took full advantage of the highs. Grower-shippers got rich, and farmers hung on.

This is a familiar story: big fish eat little fish. But there is always the danger that even bigger fish will come along. In 1968, some did. Purex, one of the nation's largest companies, bought out a few Salinas growers-shippers and swam like a shark into the local lettuce fields. The local architect of the deal, Howard Leach, was the perfect person for the job. It would have been hard to find anyone more local: his father was past president of the California Rodeo Association, a position with even more prestige and power in Salinas than mayor, a post he also had once held. But Leach's hometown credentials were augmented by out-of-town sophistication. After graduating from Salinas High, he went to Yale and then Stanford, where he got an MBA. He returned to Salinas and co-founded Valley Packing Company, which quickly became a relatively big player in the local vegetable industry. Leach then negotiated the deal with Purex and became the president of Purex's farming operations, renamed Freshpict. To his nervous local competitors he explained that the association with Purex did not change the essential nature of the business but only gave Freshpict "access to greater amounts of capital and marketing knowledge than we had in the past."[14] Within two years, Freshpict was farming 42,000 acres in California, Arizona, Colorado, and Mexico, and selling lettuce, celery, and broccoli year-round, along with seasonal shipments of artichokes, Brussels sprouts, asparagus, cherry tomatoes, bell peppers, cabbage, carrots, green onions, and rapini.

Six months after Purex came to town, the old United Fruit Company, now called United Brands, arrived. It bought out nine local companies, renamed the conglomerate InterHarvest, and put two local agribusinessmen, Tom and Robert Nunez, in charge. United Fruit had been dubbed "the Octopus" in Latin America. Now one of its tentacles had stretched into the American West. Within two years InterHarvest was farming about 20,000 acres of lettuce in the Salinas and Imperial valleys, and a few thousand acres in Arizona.[15] When UFWOC arrived in 1970, InterHarvest was producing about 20 percent of Salinas Valley lettuce and about 50 percent of its celery. It had gotten so big that the Federal Trade Commission issued a complaint, critical of the overreaching size of the Octopus's new lettuce operation, but the complaint predictably came to nothing.

Then another whale splashed into the pond. In the first months of 1970, S.S. Pierce & Co. of Boston, one of the nation's oldest and most respected food companies, bought out several strawberry operations in Salinas, Watsonville, and Oxnard. The new company, Pic-N-Pac, leased more than 1,400 acres of strawberry fields and also picked up contracts with growers to pack apples, plums, cherries, peaches, apricots, melons, artichokes, spinach, and varieties of specialty lettuce. It bought Salinas's largest strawberry cooler and brought some new strawberry machines into town, which it said would revolutionize strawberry harvesting.

The locals couldn't figure out how scared to be. Then three months after the S.S. Pierce/Pic-N-Pac agreement, news came from Coachella that the first big table grape company had signed with UFWOC. Soon Chavez had locked up the whole Coachella Valley. Next it became clear that he would win in Delano, too. Now it was time to panic, which is exactly what the Salinas Valley grower-shippers did. And the history of lettuce as a commodity jumped into a whole new future.

In 1970, there were about 3,000 *lechugueros* in the Salinas Valley.[16] From April to September, these piece-rate workers cut and packed about 85 percent of all the iceberg lettuce sold commercially in the United States and Canada. That is a statistic that merits pause: six months, 3,000 men, 1.5 billion heads of lettuce.

How did they do it? Almost entirely by hand. Typically, even today, thirty-six men work on a piece-rate crew harvesting head lettuce. Nine trios, twenty-seven men, cut and pack. Two men on a flatbed truck stitch together the empty cartons using a pneumatic stitcher, and one of them distributes the cartons to the workers. The truck and the stitcher are the only power-driven tools used in the process. One man sprinkles water on the lettuce after it is packed. Two men staple the boxes closed. Four men load them onto the trucks. Working together, they can produce in one hour 300 to 700 cartons each containing twenty-four heads of lettuce, depending on the size of the lettuce and the condition of the field.

Iceberg lettuce is planted on long, slightly raised beds, two rows to a bed. Bent at the waist, the cutters move down the narrow furrows between the beds. They wield an unimposing wooden-handled knife with a five-inch blade, which they sharpen a few times a day. A right-handed cutter reaches out with his left hand, grabs the compacted ball of lettuce, which sits in the middle of looser leaves, tilts the plant away from him, and with a quick thrust of his knife cuts the thick tap root. He lifts the lettuce from the ground, trims his cut with a second swift stroke of the knife, shakes the head to send the outer leaves flying, and gently places it butt up on the discarded leaves, while choosing the next head to cut. The action takes longer to describe than to execute. An experienced cutter can do it in about four seconds.

He cuts from 2,000 to 5,000 heads a day. But cutting is only part of the job. A field of lettuce matures unevenly. A cutter must also decide which heads to cut and which to leave. Some heads are clearly not ready, as the leaves have not yet sufficiently turned in on themselves to form the ball. But others are problematic. To cut or not to cut? Unskilled cutters have to touch the lettuce to know. An experienced *lechuguero* decides to cut just by the "look" of the lettuce. For some, learning how to do that takes a few weeks; for others, a couple of months. Others never learn, and they don't make it as *lechugueros*.[17]

Selecting and cutting is the easy part. In a trio, a *lechuguero* must also know how to pack, for the men rotate tasks during the day. Many people have learned how to cut lettuce quickly but have not made it on a piece-rate crew because they could never learn to pack. A packer, following behind the two cutters in his trio, must squeeze twenty-four heads into the 10-by-16-by-20-inch carton: two layers with four rows of three heads each, the bottom layer with the lettuce butts up and the top layer with the lettuce butts down. When the lettuce is small, the packer picks up two heads, one in each hand, then uses those to pick up a third head. When the lettuce is big, a packer will use his knee or the side of his leg to help hold two heads while picking up the third with his free hand. A good packer throws the heads into the carton and almost never has to adjust them. He can pack all twenty-four heads in less than a minute.[18]

When one watches a lettuce crew from fifty yards away, the workers seem to move slowly. At twenty-five yards, the cutters' rhythmic action makes them appear to swing almost comfortably over the beds, even though they are bent low, with their hands near the ground. Up close, the mixture of concentration and speed is startling. Some of the men banter as they work, but no one would mistake lettuce cutting and packing for a game. It seems more like a magic trick. The lettuce flies through the workers' hands—from the first cut on the ground, to lying butt up on the bed, to being packed away in the box—too quickly to be believed. Any doubt about the skill of the men who do the job is cured forever by giving the work a try.

Lechugueros not only have extraordinarily dexterous hands; they must have the endurance to do the work hour after hour, day after day, season after season. Wrists swell, backs hurt, fingernails are damaged and even lost as packers jam lettuce into the boxes. But what most sets *lechugueros* apart from other farm workers is the internal solidarity of the crews. In 1970, before there was a union, there were united lettuce crews. The men were often relatives or close friends, just as on the piece-rate celery crews. Many lived together, ate together, and traveled up and down California (and back and forth to Mexico) in the same cars and vans. The experienced taught the inexperienced how to do the work until they could do it themselves. Within their own communities, they were the big money makers, respected for their abilities even by the growers and often deeply admired by friends and family. Some of the very best were the stuff of legend. As disputes arose at work, as crises came and went, some men could be counted on for help or wise counsel. Leaders emerged.

Mario Bustamante was one of the legends. A champion worker, fast and efficient, he was one of the few men who could not only cut and pack but also load the full boxes onto the flatbed trucks that drove through the fields. When I first saw him in 1978 in the union office, he was thirty years old.

Someone pointed him out to me, "That's Mario Bustamante, the famous *lechuguero*." He was just under six feet tall, broad-chested, with a large nose and chin, bushy black hair, and a full Mexican mustache. Even among farm workers, he seemed especially vigorous. He owed part of his fame to his extraordinary determination: after ruining his back at work, he had an operation that fused two discs, and then returned to his piece-rate lettuce crew. I have yet to hear of anyone else who managed to do that. When I first saw him in the union office, humorously holding forth about some situation on his crew, he was already a force in the fields.

Bustamente was born in Mexico City, six blocks from the famous thieves' market in Tepito.[19] On his mother's side of the family there had been wealth. At the beginning of the twentieth century his maternal grand-father owned enough land in southern Guanajuato to support a life of leisure in Mexico City. When his haciendas were overrun and abandoned during the revolution he took his family to the U.S., where they lived until order was restored in Mexico, in the 1920s. When they returned to Mexico City they were of diminished means. Mario's mother married a butcher, Salvador Bustamante, a man who worked for wages—not even the owner of a small shop. The two had seven children. Mario was the second, the first son.

As a child, Mario skipped school to go to work with his father, where he would sweep or clean or even cut up a few bones. He earned a peso or two, and learned a little from watching the men slaughter the cows and pigs and prepare the various cuts of meat. In 1954 his father left for the United States, crossing the border illegally. For a few years he traveled between the California fields and Mexico City every six months. In 1958 he left and didn't come back. Mario was ten. He remembers the waiting. Quietly, secretly, his mother sent inquiries, but they were messages into the void. No money, no word, no nothing. After a few years, Mario gave up his father for dead.

His mother did not give up hope, but to get needed cash she began sell-ing anything she had of value: her bed, other furniture, jewelry, clothes. Later she took in laundry. Mario left school without finishing the sixth grade. He and a friend got a job selling newspapers in the Plaza of Santa Domingo, two blocks from the Zócalo, Mexico City's big central square.* But he couldn't make enough money. His mother had to stand in line, starting at two in the morning, to buy government-subsidized milk and *masa* for tortillas. Mario started making women's sandals for two pesos a pair. He learned how to make more complicated shoes, with tongues and heels, and got pretty good at it.

---

* That was in 1959. When Mario visited Mexico City in the late 1980s his boyhood friend was still selling newspapers at the same spot.

But he didn't like it. He wanted to learn his father's craft. At thirteen he got a job at the biggest slaughterhouse in Mexico City. It was owned by a Russian, and the workers were mostly Arabs, Germans, and Spaniards. Mario was put to work helping the man who delivered the meat to restaurants and hotels. He saw real wealth for the first time and made more on tips than he made in wages. Times were still tough, but like most workers everywhere, Mario sampled some of the merchandise, and the Bustamante family at least ate well.

When Mario was fourteen a man came to the slaughterhouse with a message from his father: "In case you ever get to Mexicali, look me up." He didn't give an address. Mexicali is a small town, the man told Mario. "Everybody knows him. He will be able to help you out." Mario told his boss. The old Russian gave him 500 pesos, a letter of recommendation, and a kiss on the lips. Mario gave his mother 200 of the pesos and told her he was going to Mexicali for a better job. He said nothing about his father. An aunt accompanied him on the forty-eight-hour bus ride. Looking out the window he saw crops growing in the fields for the first time. In Mexicali, his aunt helped him find a cheap hotel and then went on to Los Angeles. It was the first of May 1963. Mario was fifteen.

About 500,000 souls lived in the "small town" of Mexicali at the time. Mario had forty pesos and a photograph of his father taken when his dad was eighteen. He carried no luggage. The room cost ten pesos a night. He began his search confidently, but after two days he stopped looking for his dad and started looking for work. He got a job in a butcher shop, which paid the Mexicali minimum wage, slightly higher than the Mexico City minimum.

Walking down Ocampo Street almost seven months later, a few days before Jack Kennedy was assassinated, Mario saw his father, Salvador, walking toward him. It had been five years, but there was no mistaking his dad. He stopped and waited. His father stopped, too, grabbed him by the shoulders, pulled him forward so their faces almost touched, and whispered, "Are you Mario?"

The boy couldn't speak. His father took him by the arm to a Chinese restaurant. They sat and drank tea together. His father cried. He was living with another woman. He couldn't go home, but he would do everything he could to help his son. Even after this meeting, after hearing how hard life was for his wife and children, he never did send money back to Mexico City. But he was true to his word about helping his eldest son, and it was the boy who sent money home.

Mario's father got him a pass to cross the border. It was a one-day pass, but once on the other side, people stayed as long as they wanted. Together, they took a bus to Arizona. On the way Salvador showed Mario a lettuce knife, which he said was the key to a better life. If he could learn how to hold it and use it, to love it and care for it, he could make good money. Mario knew nothing about lettuce. He didn't see his first head of lettuce until he went to work in a lettuce field.

His father worked on a piece-rate crew. He and the two others in his trio were paid the standard 25 cents for each box of lettuce they cut and packed: $2 to $3 an hour, depending on how good the lettuce was. The federal minimum wage was $1 an hour at the time, and the Mexican minimum was about one-eighth of that. Mario's first job was to put a piece of waxed paper over the top row of lettuce before the box was stapled closed. He made $1 an hour. After a while he would take short turns learning to cut and pack. He got tired quickly. He wanted to quit and go home. But the hourly pay was good. He was sending his mother $20 to $30 every week.

One evening the immigration police raided the Jefferson Hotel in Phoenix where the workers were living. They took Mario away; his father went with him. At the detention center, the elder Bustamante explained that the boy's mother was born in Kansas. That was true, and in 1963, with the Bracero Program clearly waning and an INS policy of making it easy for Mexicans to immigrate, the official was inclined to believe him. Mario was released; Salvador was never even asked for his papers. A few weeks later in court, a clerk gave Mario a letter saying that he was legally in the country and had a right to U.S. citizenship. Mario has carried that paper ever since.

A few months later, following the lettuce, the two Bustamantes arrived in Salinas. Farm workers were everywhere. It seemed to Mario that more people lived in the labor camps than in the whole town. His father worked the harvest, but Mario could make more money on a piece-rate lettuce thinning crew. He made even more money when he moved to the strawberries. Meanwhile, his dad had gone to work for a different company and had to leave the labor camp where he had bunked alongside his son. Mario was sixteen and mostly on his own.

When the strawberries were slow, Mario sometimes joined his dad in the lettuce fields, trying to learn the job of a closer. It wasn't easy. The lettuce seemed too big for the cardboard boxes, and the closer had to throw a metal frame around the corners to force the boxes shut so he could then staple them. It all had to be done in less than a minute. Several seconds more and a worker fell hopelessly behind, slowing down the loaders. Helping his dad, Mario wasn't pressured, but he wasn't good enough to work on his own. Disappointed, he again tried cutting and packing. That was even harder. The older men tried to help him. "Cut it like this, pack it like that. Be sure to pick up three at a time. Move your hands this way; don't worry about your thumbnails, you always lose them."

"You know, how they teach you to do anything," he remembered years later. "Fierce, but affectionate."

By 1966 Mario was a *lechuguero*, working at Merrill Farms and proud of it. "Merrill had the most famous *lechugueros*. A few were Chicanos but the bulk of them were Mexicans. Pablo, Jose the lefty, and my cousin Jose: that was one great trio. Paul, Charro, and el Vera Cruz: they were another. There were several great ones . . . Everybody working in the lettuce knew about the best ones. They were called *campeónes*, champions, and many of them worked at Merrill . . . because Merrill had a lot of the best fields, with the best lettuce, where you could make the most money."

Mario Bustamante saw Cesar Chavez for the first time in 1969, the year that his younger brother Chava arrived from Mexico City and joined the Merrill lettuce crew as a water boy. Bustamante had never heard of Chavez, but he went along with his brother and father to a meeting. Chavez talked about the grape strike and said he would return to Salinas after they won in Delano. He told people to get ready. After the meeting, over a few beers, Mario's father said he had been impressed. "You boys are about twenty, and it seems okay. But wait until you're forty. You are going to want to stop in the afternoons. People die young out here. If they treated us with more respect, we wouldn't have to die so young." He said that he would join Chavez immediately when he came and really started to organize.

With the help of his father and brother, Chava Bustamante became a closer on the Merrill crew. It was fast, and when the lettuce was good, each man could make $300 a week. But there were a lot of problems on the crew. It was a new one that the Merrill foremen had formed after the Bracero Program ended, meshing the trios into a single crew, bringing together bracero skips, undocumented workers, green-carders, and a few Mexican Americans. The shortage of workers drove up the rate a bit, and most crews started to get a few cents more per box than the standard twenty-five cents. But nobody was sure of the ground rules. Who was in the *bola*—who shared in the piece rate? Sometimes the water boys were in; sometimes not. Nor was there a regular agreement about the closers, loaders, and box makers. It took some battles to work things out.

Earlier that season Mario's father, Salvador, had been at the center of one such battle. The loaders, who were outside the *bola*, making their own rates, tended to fall behind; the foremen had been forcing the cutters to stop their work and help the loaders catch up, without paying the cutters extra. "It was in the beginning of the season, March or April," Mario recalled.

My father was working as a closer. And he started talking it up with people. "We have to put an end to this," he would say. "Either they pay us for loading or we stop loading." I was younger, and I would go help them load without thinking twice about it, just for the pleasure of changing jobs for a while. . . . We were making more money than any other crew in the valley, so why cause trouble? But my father was organizing it, so I had to go along. And the whole crew agreed.

We picked a day, and when they told us to go load, we refused to do it unless we were paid for it. We just stopped working, sat down in the midst of the lettuce. The American supervisor arrived and told us we were all fired; our checks would be waiting for us at the office . . . We didn't even take the company bus. We walked back to camp, just to show how defiant we were. We hadn't been back an hour when another supervisor came and said that the company agreed that we didn't have to load anymore. Not only that but they were going to pay the water boys by the hour, separate from the *bola*. That wasn't even one of our demands. But they gave us that, too. And would we please, please go back to work. They took us back to finish the field that very day.

It was the first time I saw that we could win things in the fields. No more loading for free! We were so happy. What a terrific experience.

That winter, while working in the Imperial Valley, Mario Bustamante heard on the radio that Chavez was coming to hold a mass meeting in "the hole," the place in Calexico where people waited to get work. Bustamante went to hear him, but it was a little depressing. Chavez, Fred Ross, and two or three other people from the union were there, but only a handful of farm workers. Chavez promised more union services in Calexico and asked them to join the union. Bustamante went to the UFWOC office and paid $10.50 for a three-month membership.

By July 1970 Chavez was back in Salinas. This time the hall was filled, and folks were excited. The Teamsters were about to come into the fields, Chavez said. They were going to sign a contract to represent the workers and force everybody to join their union. "There is going to be one hell of a fight," Salvador Bustamante told his two sons after the meeting. "Individuals don't matter right now. What matters is that we win for everybody."

Mojica was at that meeting, and he was also in the middle of a fight at Salinas Co-op. The labor contractor who had melded the trios into the Salinas Co-op crew had added some dead men, the infamous *muertos*, to the payroll and pocketed the extra checks. Whenever a company representative would come to the fields, workers would try to tell him what was happening, without success. Next the workers formed a committee and went to the office to show the company men the names of the *muertos*, who didn't exist. But the company wanted proof. So early in the 1970 season, Mojica contacted a Salinas lawyer, who came to the lettuce fields to make a notarized record of how many people were working on that particular day. The contractor got mad and fired five field workers.

After that the committee backed off. Mojica and the others went to the camps after work and contacted other people with *muertos* on their crews. They didn't know what they were going to do next, but they did have a network of people who wanted to do something. "We had a lot of people, but we were afraid. Who was going to lead? Who was going to explain our position to the bosses? We were still in the middle of it when Cesar arrived. And when he asked us to organize our crews, we had the whole valley organized in three days. He couldn't have done it without us, but we couldn't have done it without him. I felt that he was the man I had always been waiting for, even though I didn't know I was waiting."[20]

"Reds Lettuce Alone": Farm workers Stun Salinas

August to December '70

When the Salinas strike began in the late summer of 1970, throttling fruit and vegetable production throughout the valley, the force of it surprised almost everyone. Until then, California growers had argued that the UFWOC strikes were phony shows, staged for reporters. Salinas changed that. "This is a bona fide worker walk out," the *California Farmer* acknowledged in the midst of the strike. "True there are a few students and a priest or two with their nose stuck in, but for the most part, growers admit the strikers are workers and their families."[1] Afterward, Jack Hayes, president of the California Tomato Growers Association, warned his fellow businessmen: "Chavez moved in with such force that it is hard to imagine unless you were there. For a thirty-day period, they blocked every county and ranch road with forty to fifty pickets."[2]

The three reporters who had covered the farm workers' organization from the beginning—Ronald Taylor of the *Fresno Bee*, Dick Meister of the *San Francisco Chronicle*, and Harry Bernstein of the *Los Angeles Times*—were also swept away by the effectiveness of the strike. Bernstein called the Salinas strike of 1970 the biggest in farm worker history (ignoring the 1933 cotton strike and a few other Depression-era battles). Ed Maples, president of Local 78 of the Amalgamated Meat Cutters and Butcher Workers Union, who had been through every Salinas shed-worker or farm worker strike since World War II, called it "the biggest strike I ever saw."[3]

Even the union staff was caught off guard, Cesar Chavez most of all. Three days after it began, Chavez was still predicting that "the strike cannot be maintained for more than a few days, as some of the workers will leave the area, and others will start scabbing."[4] But after the first day the strike got stronger, not weaker. And for the next three weeks the strikers crippled Salinas Valley farm production, causing a deep split in the growers' weak united front and securing the union's first unasterisked labor victory.

The only people not surprised by the strike were the workers. With Chavez in town triumphantly riding the wave of the new grape contracts and urging Salinas workers to organize to win their own, the crew leaders quickly realized their dream of a valley-wide organization. Within a few days they had most of the workers on board. Their first battle was to convince the union staff of that.

Just as the capitulation of the grape growers excited farm workers around the state, the new contracts worried agribusiness. The Salinas Valley growers, still grappling with the reorganization of the industry after the end of the Bracero Program, decided to use the Teamsters as a shield against the newly triumphant UFWOC. Nine years earlier, Bud Antle had signed with the Teamsters to avoid the more militant AWOC and had been kicked out of the Salinas Valley Grower-Shipper Association for doing so. The people who had ostracized him then now mimicked him. But what had been a smart tactic in 1961 was a panicky mistake in 1970. If the Salinas growers had just lain low, UFWOC might have moved against the citrus industry in Oxnard, where Cesar Chavez had spent all of 1959 organizing workers and where a strike was under way. Or perhaps Chavez would have stayed home and worked on integrating the new grape workers into the union. But when the growers signed five-year contracts with Teamster locals in Salinas and Watsonville covering about 5,000 vegetable workers, UFWOC had to act. Instead of a shield, the Teamster contracts became a target.[5]

On July 29, immediately after the celebration of the grape victory at Reuther Hall in Delano, Chavez made the three-and-a-half-hour trip to Salinas, where he accused the Teamsters of a "Pearl Harbor type sneak attack." UFWOC represented 90 to 95 percent of the farm workers in the Salinas Valley, he claimed at a press conference, and he promised pickets in the fields soon.[6]

There had been small UFWOC committees in Salinas, Hollister, Gilroy, and Watsonville since 1968 and 1969, put together by Gilbert Padilla and Robert Bustos. Those vegetable and strawberry workers, about a dozen active members in each committee, had met several times a year to hear UFWOC news and to discuss local conditions.[7] They had organized that first meeting where the Bustamantes and some 200 others heard Chavez outline the coming deal between the Teamsters and growers. Two and a half days after that deal was confirmed, they managed to get 3,000 excited, festive farm workers to come to the football field of Hartnell College to hear the union's plans. Speaking at the end of the rally, Chavez told the workers not to sign the Teamster cards that foremen were circulating in the fields, but to sign UFWOC cards instead. He told them to organize committees on their crews and to send five representatives to the new UFWOC office. He held the biggest companies most at fault for the sweetheart contracts and listed InterHarvest, FreshPict, and Pic-N-Pac by name, explaining that they could be effectively boycotted. Finally, he called for a vote authorizing a strike and boycott. Many of the afternoon speeches had been interrupted with shouts of "*Huelga!*" but now the workers rose to their feet and chanted for several minutes: *"Huelga, huelga, huelga!"* Chavez rhythmically pumped both fists and joined in. Ray Tellis, who reviewed hundreds of hours of Cesar Chavez on tape for his movie *The Fight in the Fields*, said that this was Chavez's most animated moment ever captured on film. He and the crowd got so carried away that after a brief consultation with someone else on stage, Chavez had to return to the mike to explain that the workers had just voted only to authorize a strike, not to walk out the next morning. They should return to their jobs, elect their committees, and wait for further instructions.[8]

Some lettuce crews ignored Chavez's plea and went to the UFWOC office instead of to work on Monday morning. They wanted to strike. It was already August, the lettuce season was two-thirds over, they argued, and in less than two months the growers could cut lettuce in other areas, making a strike ineffective. Marshall Ganz and Fred Ross tried to calm them down. The strikes had to be company wide, they explained, and urged the men to return to the camps, sign up everybody at their companies, and go back to work. To the organizers' surprise, many of them were soon back in the office with stacks of signed cards.

Among the people who came streaming into the office that first day was Salvador Bustamante. Marshall Ganz was impressed. "Salvador Senior came through the door looking for cards and wanting someone from the union to go with him to talk to the workers in the camp where he worked, D'Arrigo. He was a big man with a big mustache and a manner not to be turned away. . . . I agreed to go with him."[9] Ganz had never seen anything like it. In Delano "the workers were hopeless and terrified . . . The people who were first attracted to our meetings were the malcontents, the ones everyone thought were jerks. We had to work to get beyond them to the natural leaders and get them on our side. In Salinas, . . . it was the community leaders, the heads of families, who were on our side from the start. We were lucky. There was no way we had the staff to go out and organize ranch committees ourselves."[10]

Chavez did not spend much time talking to the workers at the office. He was in a room in the back or in the home of a Salinas supporter, plotting boycott strategy. For all his enthusiasm at the rally, he couldn't see why Salinas would be any different from the numerous weak or failed strikes he had witnessed before, whereas the prospects for a boycott seemed good. The old United Fruit, which owned InterHarvest, still made 60 percent of its profits in bananas. It had spent millions to make its Chiquita Banana famous, paying thousands of workers to stick two and a half billion Chiquita labels on its otherwise undifferentiated product. It also owned Baskin-Robbins and A&W Root Beer, delicious boycott opportunities. Cesar had LeRoy Chatfield alert the Chiquita distributors that a boycott might be on the way. Chatfield called Jack Fox, the outgoing United Fruit president, and told him that it could get very hot for the company all over the United States. As a taste of how hot, boycotters picketed the company's world headquarters in Boston, urging consumers to shun its lettuce, bananas, ice cream, and root beer.[11]

Cesar also dispatched Anna Puharich to talk to Eli Black, the incoming CEO. An ex-rabbi relatively new to the business world, Black had just organized a hostile takeover of this venerable colossus of Central America. A liberal, he had vague ideas about reforming the company and establishing a better relationship with the so-called banana republics. He knew little about agriculture and less about lettuce, but he understood image—part of the reason he had renamed the company United Brands—and he quickly decided that he couldn't afford an extended boycott campaign. Over the objections of the company's old guard, Black sent two of United Brand's top negotiators to Salinas to settle the dispute and sign.[12]

That would not be simple. United Brands already had a contract with the Teamsters. Soon the jostling began, as many different players with conflicting interests tried to work out strategies, establish alliances, feel out enemies, and protect and extend their turf. For three weeks, as workers deluged the UFWOC office arguing for a swift strike, Teamsters, growers, and UFWOC officials met and re-met in various shifting constellations, seeking to snooker or sandbag one another. They huddled in offices, motel rooms, cafés, bars, and automobiles all over town. A long conversation might result in more confusion than clarity. Many went without sleep. Ganz later said he had felt he was living in the "fog of war."

The first major move involved the AFL-CIO. Chavez and Bill Kircher flew to Washington to get George Meany's support against the Teamster contracts. But the Teamster International President, Frank Fitzsimmons, had got there first and promised to back out of the contracts peacefully. Meany didn't want any unnecessary fights, and he refused to condemn what he believed would be a short-lived raid by the IBT. When a disappointed Chavez returned to the West Coast, he was not surprised to discover that Fitzsimmons orders had been stalled somewhere in the feudal Teamster hierarchy between Washington and Salinas.

Fitzsimmons's main interest was to avoid a nasty fight with Meany that might interfere with his effort to repel attempts by the jailed Jimmy Hoffa to unseat him. By comparison, a few farm worker contracts did not matter much. But out in Salinas, those contracts counted for a lot. Local Teamsters officials not only wanted to extend their dues base, they also were trying to protect their position in the Northern California food-processing industry (canneries, sheds, and frozen-food plants), where a growing majority of the workers were Chicanos and Mexicans, potential defectors to Cesar Chavez. And these mostly small town Teamsters, who knew the Salinas scene well, had plenty of room to maneuver.

Bill Grami, the Teamsters' Western Conference organizer, led the effort by local officials to square the circle of those following Fitzsimmons's orders while pursuing their own interests. Jerry Cohen, UFWOC's lawyer, tried to pin Grami down in negotiations and ended up admiring his skills: "He was incredibly smart and very clever with words. He honestly felt that in the long run it would be better for farm workers to be in the Teamsters. And he was awfully slick. We would leave the meetings and think, Wow, we really made some progress, but then we couldn't figure out what he actually said."[13] In retrospect it is clear that Grami was pretending to follow Fitzsimmons's orders to get out of the contracts while carrying out his own policy of staying in the fields. It might have worked—the various charades and deceptions might have gone on until the end of the season, if the growers hadn't brought the workers into the battle, gambling that they would side with their employers. But the growers had cast their dice into a turbulent wind.

The Teamster contracts were closed-shop agreements: once the contracts were signed on July 27, the workers had ten days to sign up with the union or be fired. Grami stretched that out, saying, first, that the contract provisions had to be explained to the workers. At Merrill, where Mario and Chava Bustamante worked, the explaining was done by Tom Merrill himself, who told his assembled employees that they would have to sign up with the Teamsters. Mario stood up and said that the crews didn't want to be represented by people they didn't know. Some discussion followed. "Finally we told Merrill and the other company people to leave, that we didn't want to listen to them anymore. And they did. They got nothing from us."[14] At other companies, workers simply left the fields after those explaining sessions and came to the UFWOC office. So many came that UFWOC put out a leaflet saying, "Don't sign the Teamster cards, but don't leave your job either."[15]

In the midst of this confusion, FreshPict decided to enforce the closed shop. Jose Dzib, who had first come to California as a bracero in 1955, had helped organize a bracero strike in the peaches in 1959, had gotten his green card in 1963, and was cutting celery at FreshPict. He remembers the day the foreman passed out Teamsters cards saying that whoever didn't bring the card back signed the next day would not have a job. The crew sent Dzib to the UFWOC office, and the next day he led a caravan of fired workers to meet with Chavez. "Mr. Chavez was very happy to see the group of us organizing ourselves to be a part of his union," Dzip recalled. "He asked, 'Do you know what a strike is?' We answered, 'We have already decided to strike.' Then Cesar explained that no one knew how long it would take. It could be a short time or a long time without winning. 'You are the ones affected, so think carefully before taking this step.' We voted to strike unanimously."[16]

The next day, August 8, 200 to 300 pickets shut the company down, as all FreshPict crews left the fields. "A beautiful Saturday," Dzib called it. The company had gambled and lost; now it tried to stop the strike. Grami, able to dodge Fitzsimmons's directives, faithfully followed FreshPict's. A master of delay, he could also move quickly. On the very day of the walk-out he called Jerry Cohen asking for a meeting with Chavez.

Cohen: "Like when?"

Grami: "Like right now."

Chavez was back in Delano, where his second daughter, Eloise, was getting married. Helen had anticipated just this kind of problem. She had been reminding Cesar that the wedding was August 8, and that he had to be there. And so he was, walking Eloise down the aisle, when Cohen, a guest at the wedding, caught his eye. Chavez took his daughter to the altar, and then went back to Cohen's aisle and kneeled down to hear the news. Grami wanted to talk.

"Just to talk or do they want to deal?" whispered Chavez. "Call back and ask him."

Jerry took Cesar aside as the wedding party was leaving the church. Grami wanted to deal; they were scheduled to meet in Paso Robles, about halfway between Delano and Salinas, that night. Helen pressed her husband to stay long enough to have the ceremonial dance with Eloise, which he did. Then his contingent in the wedding party—Jerry Cohen, Dolores Huerta, and Manuel and Richard Chavez—drove off.[17]

The meeting in Paso Robles went through the night. As dawn arrived on Sunday, both sides had tentatively agreed to sign a new jurisdictional pact. Grami also consented to Chavez's suggestion to call in the Ad-Hoc Bishops Committee on Farm Labor, which had helped negotiate the grape contracts. Grami thought that in exchange for the loose accord on a new Teamster-UFWOC pact, UFWOC had agreed that the bishops would call for an end to the action in the fields, and that UFWOC would abide by that request.[18] But Chavez kept the pressure on by authorizing a continued strike at FreshPict. In a series of rallies back in the Salinas Valley that same Sunday he urged other workers not to strike. Nevertheless, on Monday a worker from Pic-N-Pac, the biggest strawberry outfit in the valley, called the UFWOC office and told Marshall Ganz that some of the strawberry workers were on strike. The Pic-N-Pac workers, migrant families from the Rio Grande Valley and Mexico, lived in two large camps: a trailer park ("La Posada") in Salinas and an old bracero camp in Soledad. When the FreshPict workers had walked out the La Posada families just happened to be in the midst of their own battle, demanding cheaper rents and a higher piece rate. With the strike train already on the track, they figured, why not get on board? They were massed in front of the trailer park when Ganz and a few other union organizers arrived. Ganz was astounded by the enthusiasm of the crowd, and after some discussions, the strikers went out to the strawberry fields to make sure no one was working, and then reconvened for a mass meeting with Chavez. He appealed to them to return to work, but his pleas went unheeded, and the workers voted unanimously to continue their strike the next day.[19]

Strikers closed FreshPict and Pic-N-Pac Monday, Tuesday, and Wednesday. On Wednesday, UFWOC also endorsed a walkout at Oshita Farms, where the union was particularly strong. Chavez told Grami he would not call off any of the strikes until he had his signature on an agreement. Unlike in the grape legitimacy strikes, UFWOC refused to obey a temporary restraining order limiting the picketing; Chavez himself went to the Fresh-Pict office to be served with the order so he could officially defy it. Msgr. George Higgins from the Bishops Committee flew in from Washington to help mediate. Herb Fleming, president of the Salinas Valley Grower-Shipper Association, complained disingenuousnessly that the growers were simply caught in a jurisdictional dispute between two unions. His next remark was more honest: "We would expect them [the Teamsters] to work something out that would prevent any labor disturbance in our area."[20] By Thursday, Fleming's wish seemed to have come true. Msgr. Higgins, Grami, and Chavez were sitting together at a press conference announcing a "historic agreement."

The new pact solved nothing. It reiterated that UFWOC had jurisdiction in the fields and that the Teamsters had jurisdiction in the canneries, sheds, and frozen-food plants, but it left the only question that really mattered—the status of the three dozen Teamster contracts with field workers—to follow-up negotiations between Grami, Msgr. Higgins, and Herbert Fleming. Chalk one up for Bill Grami. He had the UFWOC just where he and Fleming wanted: waiting on the sidelines. In exchange for the "historic agreement," UFWOC had agreed to suspend its strikes for six days to give the Teamsters and the growers time to figure out what to do with their back-door contracts.

The strikers returned to their jobs, warily. The strawberry workers immediately engaged in a slowdown. Many of the *lechugueros* were uneasy. As it was now mid-August, they knew the lettuce companies would be vulnerable for just a month more, and they were sure the negotiations were just a big stall. But Chavez wasn't worried, telling Levy, "Some people feared . . . we were losing time by stopping the strike. But we always say that we have more time than money, and I wasn't really concerned if we lost a week or ten days."[21] Few shared Chavez's apparent calm. Ganz and Cohen were confused. Was Grami really going to rescind the contracts? Were the growers looking for a way out? Who was double-crossing whom? Again, the fog of war.

At just this moment, Chavez decided to go on a fast. Initially he told workers that the fast was a protest against the temporary restraining order. Next he told the writer Eric Brazil that it was a "fast of thanksgiving" for the historic agreement. Later he told Levy that he was also fasting out of concern about "hatred and violence," that he was "distressed and needed strength," and wanted to "get the proper perspective of what was happening in Salinas." When the fast began Chavez was already exhausted; he immediately went to bed and remained there, complaining of extreme pain, while conducting regular strategy sessions.[22]

It is a familiar snapshot. Chavez in bed, wracked by pain, holding court. The date could be February 1968, the time of the first fast, or May 1969, during the second Coachella strike. The same scene would be replayed again and again, until the very last hours of his life. Chavez in bed at the center of the storm. Weakness mixed with strength; power enhanced by pain; sacrifice as prelude to triumph. But this time the ordeal lasted only six days. "The fast was a flop," Chavez told Levy. "Generally when I go on a fast I develop amazing vitality. But I was worn out, and I think I was too preoccupied with what was going on."[23] He went to a Franciscan retreat near San Juan Bautista, a twenty-minute drive from Salinas, to recuperate and plan his next move.

While Chavez fasted, Grami and Fleming, watched over by Higgins, had supposedly been working out a way for the Teamsters to exit the fields. But Chavez had also been busy, directing negotiations with Purex/FreshPict and United Brands/InterHarvest. Will Lauer of United Brands and Bill Tincher, the president of Purex, had both come to Salinas. Chavez had dispatched Cohen and Chatfield to negotiate with them and arranged by telephone for more boycott picketing in Boston and Los Angeles. But now Chavez could apply pressure not only in the cities but from the fields. Cohen, Ganz, and Chatfield, sitting at his bedside, listened to Chavez's strategy for negotiating with Lauer: "[Tell him] 'We want you to move fast. There is tremendous pressure from the workers to strike.' Come in tougher than hell! 'Either you have good relations with us, or all hell breaks loose!' "[24]

By this point UFWOC had moved its Salinas headquarters to an old post office on Wood Street. Over the next fifteen years, the union would use both the parking lot and the grounds of an elementary school next door for rallies and overflow meetings. The hall, which held about 200 people when jam-packed, was long and narrow, with offices in the back and a meeting area in front. Above the offices was a walled-in loft with a peephole, which post office management had used to monitor the activities below. A few union staffers used it to watch the pivotal meetings in the tug of war between the most militant workers and union staffers over the timing of the Salinas general strike.

By August 18, Grami, Fleming, and Msgr. Higgins had been negotiating for six days. The monsignor believed that with four more days of talks they might get a settlement, and he promised the growers peace in the fields while talks continued. But the workers had just learned that the five-year Teamster contracts gave the lettuce crews only a two-and-a-half cent raise in the piece rate over the life of the contract: half a penny a year. Furious, they were in no mood for more stalling, no matter what the union leaders told them.

Back in San Juan Bautista, Chavez was still worried that the workers would not be able to sustain an effective strike for long. Afterward, when it was clear his worries had been unfounded, he blamed others: "The reports that I was getting from Marshall Ganz were that we still didn't have all the ranches put together. Some didn't have committees. They hadn't met, or if they had, the meetings were slipshod. On some of the ranches in the Watsonville area, we couldn't even identify the workers, there was such a mess-up of support. I was worried, too, that we wouldn't have enough leadership to go around, and that some of the workers wouldn't stay out long enough because they weren't well organized. They had the enthusiasm, but they weren't structured yet for the strike."[25]

Ganz insists he told Chavez that the workers were well organized and capable of striking: "I remember going to San Juan Bautista with Fred Ross when we were trying to convince him that the committees were for real, which he was skeptical about—for probably pretty good reason, given as we had never seen anything like Salinas before, any of us."[26]

Chavez never put much hope in the Grami-Fleming negotiations, but believed that the pressure of UFWOC's boycott threats might produce contracts without risking a strike. Moreover, Monsignor Higgins had said that he would leave Salinas if UFWOC rejected his four-day extension, and Chavez did not want to lose the support of the Bishops Committee. He sent Dolores Huerta to convince the workers to wait. She faced 300 to 400 workers who overflowed the union hall. When she reported that Chavez was urging them not to strike for four days, they cried, "*Huelga!*" When she scaled back, pleading for twenty-four more hours, they shouted, "No!" Finally, she got the crowd to agree to meet again the next night to resume the discussion.[27]

Five hundred workers crammed inside and outside the hall that second night. Cohen and Ganz were in the loft watching through the peephole. When Huerta, Father Duran, and Monsignor Higgins climbed onto the desk that served as the speakers' platform, the workers began to chant, "*Huelga!*" Duran waved them into silence and then introduced Higgins. Speaking in English with Duran translating, the monsignor argued his case.

Some of the things I will have to say . . . may not meet with your complete approval. . . . I'm here as a mediator. During these four or five days, I petitioned for an extension of time. I was convinced there was substantial hope . . . I am the first to admit there was some misunderstanding. I acted as a friend of the farm workers, in the hope that it will be best for all workers. I've come here to ask you to give me until Saturday. I'm speaking to you as man to man. If I'm wrong, there are no restrictions of the steps you can engage in. I'm asking you as strongly as I can to wait until Saturday.

"No, no, no," the crowd shouted.

"I'm asking you to accept my good faith. I've done the best I can," Higgins answered. "If there is a strike my good faith is destroyed; I can no longer act as a mediator. If I made a mistake, I'm sorry."

Again scattered cries of "*Huelga!*" greeted Duran's translation. Huerta jumped in to help out. She read a telegram from Chavez, which combined a call for patience with his best attempt at militant rhetoric: "My dear brothers, I recommend strongly to you that we support the Bishops Committee in their request for an extension. The only thing we have to lose by waiting is our chains."

The workers applauded the telegram, and Huerta continued that the union had never won its battles through strikes alone. A short delay would allow the union to mobilize its supporters and keep the Bishops Committee in town. "We are not engaged in this battle for just now, but this is forever," she said, "for all farm workers, not just those in Salinas."

The call for the extension was cheered for the first time, but one shout carried above the noise of the crowd: "All the growers want is more time. Either we have a strike or there is no strike." Workers who had just applauded the extension now applauded for an immediate strike.

"All of us have this feeling," Huerta countered. "But it is a matter of timing. It's not just for ourselves, but for all. If we can win by waiting, let's do it. We're not afraid of anybody."

The discussion raged for more than an hour. Huerta skillfully changed its focus to the election of negotiators to meet with any growers who might be willing to talk immediately. Eric Brazil, writing in the *Salinas Californian*, reported that a consensus developed in favor of waiting. Jacques Levy wrote that a clear majority voted for the three-day moratorium. Bill Akers in the Watsonville *Register-Pajaronian* mentioned no vote but reported that the workers agreed to delay their strike. Years later Mojica remembered the meeting but not a vote. He supported the delay. The Bustamantes were sure it was a stall and wanted to strike but were not worried about waiting a few more days.[28]

Up in the loft, Ganz and Cohen took turns at the peephole. Ganz was impressed with Higgins's performance. Cohen knew that no matter how much the workers wanted to strike, they wouldn't do it without the union's support. He thought Higgins was sharp, but by this time he agreed with the workers. So he enjoyed seeing the sweat bead up on the top of the monsignor's bald head. "We were laughing about the pressure the workers were putting on him. But, you know, we were stunned little turkeys, too. These workers were different than any other workers we had met before. Young and middle-aged men, confident, sophisticated, and determined. Higgins was having trouble with them, but we didn't know what to do with them either."[29]

Like so much in politics, the debate over the three-day extension was largely symbolic. There was not much difference between striking on Thursday or Monday. But the debate mattered, as it became the first public airing of the most active workers' understanding of the situation and an open clash between their assessment and that of the top union staff.

The shape of the debate and the positions of the players within it make an illuminating snapshot of the state of the union. The Salinas workers: sure of themselves, knowledgeable about their own turf, pushing the union officials to action, but unwilling to defy their directives. Chavez: worried about the staying power of the workers, placing his bets on the boycott, recuperating from a fast, and directing strategy from relative seclusion. Huerta: sharing the excitement, anxious for action, but willing to fight for Chavez's position. Cohen and Ganz: looking at the workers through a peephole, admiring their intelligence and strength, but not yet down in the pit.

The Watsonville *Register-Pajaronian's* front-page headline on Thursday afternoon proclaimed, "Angry Farm Workers Talked Out of Strike." But the farm workers would have to wait only one more day to see their judgment confirmed. On Friday afternoon, Fleming and Grami held separate press conferences to announce that the growers and Teamsters would honor their contracts, which now numbered about 200 and covered farm workers not only in Salinas but throughout the vegetable industry in Santa Maria, the Imperial Valley, parts of the Central Valley, and Arizona. Fleming said that Salinas farm workers "are basically loyal and have been with us for years," and that although he "anticipated some problems in the fields ... UFWOC's strength remains to be seen." Fleming was blunt about the Teamster closed-shop clause. "If they [the workers] don't choose to be Teamsters, they don't choose to work for me."[30]

Characteristically, Grami was more opaque. He insisted that he had spent the previous ten days "encouraging growers to deal with UFWOC, but that if anyone unsold growers on UFWOC it was UFWOC itself, by its picketing and general tone of militancy."[31] He said he stood behind the contracts but he still hoped to see the problems resolved at the conference table—an unlikely prospect since the point of his press conference was to announce that negotiations had failed. In case any growers might contemplate rescinding the contracts on their own, Grami also announced that the Teamsters would not grant individual releases. A strike was now inevitable.

It was to begin on Monday morning, August 23. On Sunday, 3,000 people attended a UFWOC rally, the same number that had come to the Hartnell football field three weeks earlier, but this time, Eric Brazil reported, "The crowd was conspicuously devoid of Anglo curiosity seekers; it was a farm worker rally and it meant business."[32] In addition to the black eagle flags, the workers carried banners that identified them by company and crew. Ganz introduced the presidents of twenty-seven ranch committees, who filed to the microphone one by one and announced the workers' decision to strike the next morning. One worker raised a tattered chair above his head as a symbol of the miserable conditions at the labor camps and the bosses' disregard for the workers who had made them rich. That picture dominated the front page of the Monday *Salinas Californian*.

Chavez did not come to the rally. He was too sick, Dolores said, before she read his statement to the workers. Chavez quoted Thoreau and declared a "new order" in agriculture. "We are entering a just and necessary struggle, not a struggle of our own choosing, but a struggle we have been forced into. Everything we have done, we have done in good faith. Our good faith has been received with a slap in the face of the farm workers."[33]

Chavez's absence surprised Marshall Ganz and Jerry Cohen. This was the mass rally that would kick off the strike, not an internal debate at the union hall. And he had not seemed so sick to them. In San Juan Bautista he had quit his bed for a rocking chair and had been actively directing negotiations with United Brands, Purex, and Higgins. Brazil, in the *Salinas Californian*, didn't repeat Huerta's explanation that Cesar was too sick to come. Chavez, he wrote, "was still in seclusion after a six day fast which ended last Sunday." Marshall looked on the bright side: without Chavez there, the rally put the spotlight on the rank and file. Ganz also knew that Chavez did not like the dramatic inspirational speeches that the occasion called for and that he was still worried that the strike would fail. No matter, in the excitement of the moment, Chavez's nonappearance went largely unremarked.

During the three-and-a-half-week strike that followed, the Federal-State Market News Service provided an exact measure of the success of the workers' battle to stop production. The FMNS is a government agency that counts the boxes of lettuce (and other commodities) that leave the fields, and estimates the wholesale prices they earn. In ordinary times its reports are watched carefully, as one day's figures are used by buyers, sellers, and brokers to help determine the next day's prices. The first day of the strike, FMNS reported that the volume of lettuce was "insufficient to quote." For the next two days, volume was about 20 percent of normal; the first two weeks, about 33 percent. Toward the end of the strike, "loadings increased slightly and represented about one-half of the normal movement for this time of year." Normal shipping levels did not resume until the week of September 21, after the strike had been over for five days.[34]

The wholesale price of a carton of lettuce zoomed from $2 to $5 a box on the first day of the strike and remained there until the strike was over. With the price so high (lettuce growers in 1970 reported that their break-even point was $1.85), growers stopped harvesting less lucrative vegetables and shifted the few local strikebreakers into lettuce production. They paid what they called "combat pay," as much as $5 an hour (more than $28 in 2010 dollars) to anyone who had experience cutting and packing the green gold. They hired white high school athletes and gave them a crash course in lettuce harvesting. They mobilized all supervisory personnel; they recruited a few scabs from Mexicali; they bid among themselves for the services of the few Filipino crews who refused to go on strike; and they hired armed guards to protect the people who tried to harvest the lettuce. Despite all their efforts, only in the last days of the strike, when UFWOC focused its picketing efforts against only a few vulnerable companies, did the growers manage to get half their normal production of lettuce out of the fields.

As the growers rushed to cut every possible head of lettuce, the production of other fruits and vegetables fell dramatically. From August 24 to September 19, tomato production was 57 percent of normal; celery, 48 percent. Strawberries fell from 13,000 crates the day before the strike to 2,000 crates four days later, to no crates at all shortly thereafter. The last months of the strawberry season were entirely lost, costing the growers an estimated $61 million. The numbers made a point that the growers did not dispute. Daryl Arnold, who went from FreshPict to head the Free Marketing Council, a growers' organization formed after the strike specifically to counter UFWOC, warned Imperial Valley growers of the new, uncomfortable truth: "UFWOC are experts at getting workers out of the fields."[35]

Getting workers out of the fields required no special expertise in Salinas in 1970. A picket line was usually enough. But these picket lines were not cut from the standard post–World War II, AFL-CIO pattern. The picketing was a massive, enthusiastic demonstration of power and authority. In the first week of the strike there may have been as many as 3,000 active picketers under the black eagle flag facing off against a few hundred would-be scabs. Instead of distributing food and clothes and $5 a week, the union paid conventional strike benefits: $25 a week to each striker, $15 to his or her spouse, and $5 for each child in a striking family. The arrangement was required by the large number of strikers in proportion to union staff and volunteers, who couldn't have handled payment in-kind to so many people. It also reflected, and reinforced, the relative independence of the striking workers from the union staff. The money for the benefits came from various large donations, including an interest-free loan of $125,000 from the Franciscan Fathers of California.[36]

The strike, an enormous social upheaval, was remarkably free of violence and vandalism. The strikers didn't need either, as their overwhelming numbers were intimidating enough. Picket tactics varied. Some strikers went to the labor camps, talked to would-be scabs, and then prevented company buses and vans from going to the fields. Other strikers were already out on the edges of the fields, standing around early-morning fires, regaling each other with strike stories, rumors, and jokes, and ready to mass in front of any cars that tried to enter the ranches. Still others, traveling in large car caravans with horns blasting and red flags flying, went from field to field looking for scabs, and when they found them, they either parked their cars and marched into the fields, yelling and chanting, or simply drove onto company property to confront the few people who dared to work.

If not quite a full-fledged festival of the oppressed, it was a pretty good party. Mario Bustamante, the strike captain at Merrill Farms, remembers the first day. He was in a caravan of twenty-two cars, carrying more than a hundred people. After a whole day of looking for scabs without success, reports came into the union office that a lettuce crew was working at one of Merrill's ranches. The caravan took one of the company roads into the fields until it reached a blockade of cars. The strikers parked and walked toward a crew that was working about a quarter-mile away. Tom Merrill, who spoke some Spanish, recalled, "I met them and told them they were trespassing and asked them to move. They continued to walk right past me."[37] Mario considered Merrill one of the best ranchers in Salinas. Every year he opened his camp about a week before the season so that workers had a place to stay and eat while waiting for the first day of harvesting. After Merrill told the strikers to get off his land, he called Bustamante out by name. "He said, Mario, don't be a fool. He told me to leave, that I had an opportunity to get ahead in his company and in this country. He said that in the future I could be a tractor driver or a foreman or something, and that I was ruining my chances."[38]

Bustamante considered the appeal pitiful, and he and the strikers walked past Merrill and his wife, Anne, to talk to the small crew of older Filipino men, who usually worked as irrigators and hadn't cut lettuce for years. Their work was slow and inefficient. The strikers outnumbered them by about four to one. They reasoned with the Filipinos and were largely respectful, although some insults were thrown as it became clear that the men were going to continue to work. Soon several cars of Monterey County sheriff's deputies arrived.

The strikers delayed as long as possible. Like the crew and the supervisors, the deputies were badly outnumbered. They told the workers they were trespassing and had to leave. The workers answered, playfully, that they couldn't understand English. As everyone waited for a deputy who could speak Spanish, one lawman tried to pantomime the order for the strikers to quit the field. Other deputies insisted that there must be someone who spoke English. Marshall Ganz was in the crowd. He had not played a leading role in the afternoon's events and was not identified by the Merrills or the sheriffs as either a non-Mexican or a union official. When one of the deputies told Ganz that he was trespassing, the strike co-coordinator responded in fine farm worker Spanish that he didn't speak English.

Finally the deputy-translator arrived and the men left the field. In an affidavit, Anne Merrill complained that the deputies had made no arrests and expressed irritation that "a Spanish-speaking deputy was required to advise them. But I had heard them conversing in English previously." Even if the Merrills were among the best employers in the Valley, as Bustamante believed, they were in no mood to enjoy the joke.

Throughout the strike, the county sheriff and local police departments were unable to do much more than they had done at the Merrill Ranch. There simply weren't enough of them—perhaps fifty—to control several thousand striking workers spread throughout the seventy-five-mile Salinas Valley. Nor did the scores of temporary restraining orders have much effect. UFWOC advised people that the TROs were unconstitutional because they had been granted *ex parte*, that is, without the union's being notified and allowed to argue in court against their issuance. The strikers continued picketing; in response, the police merely asked them to sign citations acknowledging that they were violating the TROs. Only those who refused to sign were arrested.

Many strikers who rushed into the fields to confront scab crews weren't as polite as Bustamante's group. But in fifteen pages of affidavits put together by a growers' committee to document the strikers' "violence," only two incidents of physical violence against strikebreakers are recorded. And those two are well short of serious beatings.[39] But there were plenty of affidavits about intimidating threats. "I was warned that I had better watch out if I was caught by myself in Soledad." "The pickets told us to stop work. I asked what would happen if I did not stop work. They told me that they would come back and if I was still working they would not talk as nice to me. They told me they would beat me up if I continued to work." "When I arrived at the Trescony Ranch, I observed fifteen to twenty pickets at the ranch. They would not let me go into the ranch but stood in front of my car so that I could not drive down the road. I told them I wanted to work and was coming to work, but they told me I could not go into the ranch because of the strike. I was afraid if I went they would hurt me, so I did not go to work and returned to my home."[40]

Strikers did intimidate scabs, but it was all done in the light of day, as an open expression of their power. Almost universally, they limited themselves to tactics they could defend to friends, family, and the farm worker community. There were no firebombs nor clandestine crews of union enforcers and few vandals. Daytime militancy made nighttime raids unnecessary. In rallies at the union hall, Chavez stressed nonviolence, as he always did in public, but he also endorsed violating the TROs and encouraged people to prevent production nonviolently. The daytime success meant that Chavez didn't need to call on his nighttime expert. Manuel Chavez stayed in Santa Maria, where he was in charge of a parallel lettuce strike that had less support than the strike in Salinas and where night action did flourish. Also in Santa Maria, a striker shot and wounded a Teamster organizer.

Fistfights occurred in Salinas at night, instigated by both scabs and strikers. One set of rules applied when the cops or bosses were watching; another when they weren't. But even when the police weren't watching, other strikers were. People still had to answer for their actions and hardly anything was done that anyone was ashamed of. One of the most celebrated strike stories was recounted by Bustamante:

> One time in Gonzales, near the end of the strike, they were bringing in three trios to do the work of two lettuce crews. But any scabs at all hurt the enthusiasm of the people. Well, it didn't hurt the enthusiasm of the strong, but it dampened the energy of the weak. You know, "Oh my God, there goes a truck." Just an empty truck passing would discourage some people. So anyway, there we were on the picket line, when the Salinas priest who was helping the strike, Father Duran, arrived.
>
> He said, "What's happening here? There are people in the field working."
>
> And we answered, "Yes, we have been here since three in the morning, but the police came and escorted them into the fields, what can we do?"
>
> He asked, "Where are the police now?"
>
> "They escorted the scabs in and then left."
>
> And while we were talking a company car with a supervisor in it drove up. "Don't let it go in," Father Duran told us.
>
> "But Chavez told us no violence," we answered, knowing full well we were talking to a priest. The father just shook his head and jumped up on the hood of the car. And from there he jumped on the roof of the car and started jumping up and down, caving in the roof. We couldn't believe it. There was this priest up on top of the company car, jumping

up and down. And nothing happened. When the cops came again, we denied everything, and nobody ever pressed charges, even though Duran must have been easy to identify. We learned from that. When the police weren't around, you had to get to it. And when the cops came, you just talked.[41]

The growers, lacking support among workers, hoped they could gain the upper hand through the authority of courts and police agencies, while Teamster officials had less confidence in the law and brought in their own professional enforcers. Shortly after the signing of the "historic agreement," Ted (Speedy) Gonsalves, secretary-treasurer of Teamsters Local 748 in Modesto, arrived in Salinas accompanied by fifty to seventy-five men, who traveled around town in a car caravan of their own to "provide protection," they said, for people willing to work. Speedy rode in a black limousine equipped with refrigerator, bar, and two AC units. Many of his men wore black pinstriped suits and dark glasses. They brandished weapons, harassed and threatened members of the Bishops Committee, and beat up a few people. They accomplished nothing, other than further discrediting the anti-UFWOC forces and providing an easy day for reporters, who could effortlessly pound out a feature story about the self-satirizing goons.

No one dared to take responsibility for Speedy and his boys. Although they usually stayed at the same Salinas motel as Grami, he claimed to have no control over them and not to know who had sent them. Four months after the strike, Speedy Gonsalves was deposed from his Modesto post and his local was put into receivership, partly because of his role in the strike. Some witnesses at his internal Teamster trial said that he had been sent to Salinas by the Teamsters International, but Grami (who was working for the Western Conference, not the International) denied that any Teamster official had authorized the goons and claimed that he had ordered Gonsalves out of Salinas many times—orders that Speedy ignored. The comic book goon operation had cost $50,000, money that had come from Local 748's treasury. The most interesting tidbit from his trial was sworn testimony by Gonsalves' personal secretary, Darlene Houch. She said she had been in a meeting in September at the Tee and Turf restaurant, a main grower watering hole, where Speedy had met with "three unidentified Salinas Valley growers" and asked them for $100,000 "to keep his men in Salinas." According to Houch, the growers answered that "they had already paid him several thousand dollars each but would discuss it with other growers that evening."[42]

The trial had as much to do with internal Teamster politics as with malfeasance. The Teamsters had lost the battle, and they needed scapegoats. Gonsalves's crime was that he had been ineffective, producing more ridicule than fear. Other goons (some of them Teamsters) did a better job.

Jerry Cohen received a professional beating that sent him to the hospital for more than a week. Mojica saw a striker hit so hard with a baseball bat that blood came out of his ears. Cleofas Guzman, the leader of an InterHarvest lettuce crew, was shot in the foot, supposedly by accident, as the grower's shotgun-toting security guard was scrambling to safety under a barrage of flying rocks. On several occasions UFWOC's Wood Street office was hit with BBs. Once someone shot it up with a 30-30. Here and there, freelancing goons, supported by the Teamsters, growers, or simply operating on their own, terrorized individual strikers. It was all in vain.

On the Sunday of the kickoff rally, despite the apparent breakdown between the growers and UFWOC, United Brands/InterHarvest had got a pledge from the union that it would not be included in the strike. In semisecret negotiations, the company's representatives, John Fox and Will Lauer, who had been ordered by their CEO, Eli Black, to settle with UFWOC, had been working on a deal for the boycott-threatened company. Fox and Lauer, members of the old guard at United Fruit, were uneasy about any settlement at all and were determined to get as good a deal as possible. Wages and the limits of the bargaining unit were at issue, as were the Teamsters, because no one knew how difficult it might be to get a recision of the Teamster contract. As a further complication, Fox and Lauer, representatives of a transnational giant, also had to make some kind of peace with local agribusiness. If they signed with UFWOC, what would they say to the Chamber of Commerce, the Salinas Valley Grower-Shipper Association, and all the local suppliers with whom they had to do business? Lauer had decided that he needed an election to prove that the UFWOC represented his workers, but negotiators Jerry Cohen and Dolores Huerta had refused his request. Lauer petitioned Monsignor Higgins to convince Chavez. Chavez, in San Juan Bautista, didn't want a vote. With a strike imminent, he saw no reason to risk an election and the inevitable cooling-off period it would require.

Back in Salinas, Huerta, Cohen, and Ganz came around to the idea of an election, under pressure from Higgins. They believed they could win a card-check election, and in an unusual act of disobedience, they approved it without telling Chavez. Higgins would check the authorization cards against the company's list of about 1,000 employees to see if the UFWOC had signed up more than half of them. Both sides insisted that he do it alone. Higgins understood that they both wanted UFWOC to win. While he was conducting the vote, an InterHarvest vice president came by just to make sure Higgins understood the ground rules.

"Well," the company man said, "for God's sake, brother, they've got to win! We've got to negotiate! I'm not asking you to sell your soul, but they've got to win."[43]

On Sunday morning Higgins informed both sides that UFWOC had won the vote. He refused to divulge the figure.*

When Monday came, however, the union staff couldn't keep its no-strike pledge at InterHarvest. Although no pickets appeared at the company's fields, many InterHarvest workers didn't want to miss the party. Lauer opened the talks on Monday with a complaint: "Before we begin the negotiations, I would like to understand what happened in the field this morning. We had promises of no economic action. No matter what the circumstance, no matter what the event!"[44] The day's negotiations ended in an impasse, and no further meetings were scheduled. On Tuesday, InterHarvest workers officially joined the strike and shut the company so completely that it didn't even try to harvest.

On Wednesday, some of the men who worked in the coolers, members of Local 78 of the Amalgamated Meat Cutters and Butcher Workers Union, refused to cross UFWOC picket lines. Local 78 had a lineage in the valley dating back to CIO organizing in the sheds in the 1930s. Its two full-time officers, Ed Maples and Jerry Breshears, had been through several battles against the Teamsters. Although the union had a no-strike clause in its contract, Local 78 called an emergency meeting of its membership. Fred Ross spoke, asking the predominately white workers for continued support. Workers spoke of the long history of Teamster cooperation with the local bosses, their own unwillingness to cross any picket line, and their interest in farm workers' having a legitimate union. They also were upset because some of their men who had refused to cross the picket line had been fired. Jerry Breshears emphasized that the union could not officially endorse a walkout, and that there could be problems for those who refused to work, but he did not hide his admiration for the wildcat. Breshears closed his speech with an emotional appeal wrapped in a warning: "It is real easy to help people when there is no retaliation. Real easy to make a sacrifice if there is no sacrifice. If you really want to help, you have to be willing to take the risk."[45] The next day, all 300 union cooler workers stayed off the job.

Local 78's wildcat did not have much material impact on the strike. Not much lettuce was being picked anyway; most of the fourteen vacuum coolers in Salinas and Watsonville were idle; and during the wildcat the companies

---

* In 1974, Higgins told Jacques Levy that the number of UFWOC authorization cards was actually less than half the number of employees at the company. Levy reminded Higgins that he had revealed that to Levy back in 1970 but that Levy had left it out of the book, *Cesar Chavez: Autobiography of La Causa*, suggesting instead that UFWOC had won the election. Higgins told Don Watson in 1979 that he had lied in 1970 in the interest of a higher good. Losing the card-check election is not too hard to understand. Getting cards signed was not a high priority, and UFWOC simply had not had enought time or enough people circulating the cards among the InterHarvest workers. Explaining Levy's and Higgins's understanding of journalistic and ecclesiastical ethics is a little more difficult. "George Higgins interviewed by Jacques Levy, April 11, 1994," Post Mortem Records, Box 37, Folder 743, transcript pp 14–17, Levy/Yale; George Higgins, interviewed by Don Watson, Washington D.C., September, 1979, in Watson Collection.

mobilized enough supervisory personnel to operate the few that were needed. But the open support of the cooler workers for the farm workers' strike changed the situation in the valley. Local 78 was a well-respected local institution, an accepted part of the social scene. It had now gone over to the out-of-town enemy, what the Salinas establishment considered a cabal of outside agitators. Even more disturbing to Salinas officialdom, the white workers' wildcat had broken the bonds of racial solidarity. As a fruit tramp who had been through the battles of the 1930s told Eric Brazil, this strike had the mark of a winner because "the Okies and the Mexicans finally got together."[47]

Dolores Huerta headed the union's negotiating team, just as she had been the formal leader of negotiations with the grape companies. Chavez had picked her for the task, and she was a good choice. Thoroughly loyal to him, she also had by far the most formal education among the four founders of the union and could quickly pick up the intricacies of contract language. She had benefited from the counsel of ILWU and AFL-CIO officials during her first negotiations with Schenley. Seemingly tireless, she was a good bet to keep her wits about her through the occasional all-night sessions.

From the beginning, the union had insisted that rank-and-file committees help negotiate the contracts. Originally, this was to show the growers that the situation in the fields had changed: no longer could they set standards and wages arbitrarily; no longer could they ignore their workers. But the presence of the rank and file had other benefits. The workers had the best understanding of the situation in the fields; without them it would have been harder to negotiate working conditions and seasonally adjusted piece rates. Also, the need to translate the proceedings into Spanish provided union negotiators with time to consider their responses and to caucus.

During the negotiations, Dolores Huerta became a star. She did not fear the bosses. She talked backed to them, interrupted them, made jokes at their expense. She never backed down. She not only articulated the workers' current grievances, she talked about the humiliations farm workers had suffered over generations. She never let a grower's racist remark or semi-racist assumption pass. She defended women and children. She attacked pesticides. She also used her position as translator to give the workers a running, confidential, often humorous analysis of what was happening. All of this was done in front of large negotiating committees—the committee of InterHarvest workers had more than twenty people—at multiple ranches. That meant that hundreds of rank and filers, influential ones, watched and listened. They were outraged along with Dolores and amused by her. They told friends and fellow workers the stories.

Dolores Huerta had long before established herself in Sacramento as a farm worker advocate and had demonstrated over the years in New York City that she could expertly represent farm workers to the boycott coalition. But she did not have the patience of a good organizer and had not been useful in the slow work among farm workers in Delano. Now, finally, during the elaborate, drawn-out Salinas negotiations, she had found an authentic place for herself among the workers: the people's champion.

United Brands/InterHarvest did not have much trouble getting a recision of its contract from the Teamsters. Grami wouldn't sign it, but his boss, Einar Mohn, who had less personal investment in the contracts, did. With the way clear, its fields and coolers closed down, and its Chiquita Bananas under the direct threat of a boycott, the old United Fruit company signed the first UFWOC contract in the Salinas Valley. Standing on a flatbed truck at a nighttime rally of about 1,000 workers outside the Wood Street office, Chavez called it the best contract in UFWOC history. It included a hiring hall, strict seniority provisions, grievance procedures, field foremen as part of the union, ten cents per hour for the Robert F. Kennedy Medical Plan, a ban on five pesticides, and a workers consultation committee on future pesticide applications. What most distinguished this contract from those that came before, though, was the wage agreement. In Delano the contract had not raised wages significantly from what was already being paid in the fields. The contract itself had been the victory. In Salinas, here workers had dramatically shut down production, wages jumped by an average of 20 percent. Hourly wages rose to $2.10 an hour (from $1.75 the year before, and $1.85 in the Teamster agreement), and piece-rate wages rose even more. For instance, celery workers went from fifty-two cents per box to sixty-one cents.

Chavez saved the best, the lettuce wages, for last: the *lechugueros* would now get forty and a half cents a box. At first when he read the figure there was only a murmur through the crowd. But then a roar swept from the ground up to the flatbed truck. People embraced, jumped in wild celebration, and chanted a long line of *vivas*— *Viva la huelga! Viva la union! Viva Cesar Chavez!* The *lechugueros*, the backbone of the strike, would get a wage 62 percent higher than the twenty-five cents a box they were paid at the end of the Bracero Program, just five years earlier. It was 29 percent higher than the thirty-one and a half cents a box that they were making before the Teamster contracts, and 13 percent higher than the Teamster rate. That meant they could earn as much as $10 an hour, placing them among the best-paid workers in the country.

Agribusiness was stunned. Spokesmen for other grower-shippers called the settlement "horribly inflationary." Small growers said they would go out of business if they had to match such a contract. The Salinas Valley Grower-Shipper Association expressed its continued determination to stick by its Teamster contracts. The gulf between the out-of-town transnational corporation and the local agricultural leaders had become too wide to bridge. Tom and Robert Nunez, the owners of one of the firms that United Fruit had acquired when it put together InterHarvest, and who had then been appointed executive vice presidents of the company, resigned rather than endorse the contract. They were replaced by Harold Bradshaw, an agribusiness executive whose main professional experience was not in the Salinas Valley vegetable industry.

Local growers declared war on the "unholy alliance" between the two sets of out-of-towners: giant corporations and union agitators. On the Monday that the InterHarvest strikers went back to work, pickets appeared at the two InterHarvest coolers. A couple dozen small farmers and their wives walked together with Teamster produce drivers carrying American flags and signs saying "Citizens Against United." The next morning, a couple hundred of them imitated striking farm workers and prevented the produce trucks from going to the fields, thereby shutting down all InterHarvest operations. By Wednesday, 300 high-spirited people were at the picket line: Teamster drivers, small growers and their wives, medium-sized grower-shipper executives, and a few strike-idled white shed workers, who were paid just to be there. A lunch wagon distributed free coffee, donuts, and sweet rolls. A Cadillac, a Jaguar, and a 1970 Chevrolet station wagon blocked the InterHarvest driveway. People waved American flags and handmade signs: "You Can't Run the Valley From Boston"; "Support Your Local Farmer"; "For Sale Cheap—Call United Fruit"; "Don't Sell Out the Community"; "Reds Lettuce Alone." The last slogan soon appeared on bumper stickers all over town.[47]

The success of that picket line—InterHarvest temporarily suspended its operations while it decided what to do—brought forth a whole new organization, the Citizens Committee for Local Justice (universally referred to as the Citizens Committee). Leaders of the committee claimed that their picket line was no different than the picket lines that had been blocking production for the last week and a half, but their attempt to play victim seemed a bit of a stretch. A full-page ad they placed in the *Salinas Californian* sounded a bit whiny: "It appears no one seems to care about the people who live in the Central Coast of California. InterHarvest is being run from Boston. They did not care anything about Salinas . . . Chavez doesn't care about Salinas." The ad concluded with an open expression of the secret desire of most folks whose world has just been transformed by a catastrophic event. "It would be nice if we could go back in time, back to July."[48]

Although the committee was unsure of its long-term strategy (publicly it called on InterHarvest either to quit its UFWOC contract or to quit the vegetable business), its picket line made perfect short-term sense. Under the pressure of the strike, lettuce prices remained at $5 a box. As long as the Citizens Committee could prevent InterHarvest from cutting and packing lettuce, the price would stay high. If InterHarvest started selling lettuce, the market price would probably fall, as the conglomerate produced about 20 percent of the Salinas crop. Knowledgeable whispers made the obvious connection. The small amounts of lettuce the strike-bound growers did manage to harvest would be more valuable so long as those same growers could stop the InterHarvest trucks. Tom Merrill continued to guard his Filipino scabs. Anne Merrill played a leading role at the InterHarvest truck yard.

Meanwhile, the farm worker strike at other companies continued to flourish, with lettuce shipments remaining between a quarter and a third of normal. In addition, two large strawberry cooperatives, Naturipe and Watsonville Berry Co-op, whose growers employed about 2,500 workers, announced that they were giving up on the rest of the strawberry season and had started talking to UFWOC. Union pickets focused on FreshPict and secret discussions between the union and top officials of its parent, Purex, continued even though FreshPict's local president, Howard Leach, was prominent in the Citizens Committee. In the southern Salinas Valley the strike intensified and crippled Monterey County's two largest tomato producers. Cesar Chavez was now openly optimistic.

The Citizens Committee had two last gasps. The first came in the early morning of Thursday, September 3, at the InterHarvest truck yard. More than 200 committee members picketed in the driveway, blocking the truck exit. Not a hundred yards away, on the same side of the street, Speedy Gonsalves and his fifty enforcers watched and waited. Directly across the street from the driveway, about a hundred striking members of Local 78 also stood by. On the same side of the street, a handful of UFWOC staffers, including Marshall Ganz and Fred Ross, observed the action. Eight Salinas policemen and three private security guards were entrusted with keeping the peace among these 350 combatants.

To the east, the tug between the night's blackness and the coming dawn produced a nearly blood-red sky. Then the lights of a single InterHarvest truck flashed on and the engine turned over. The defenders of local agri-business fell silent, as some fifty other trucks flashed their lights and revved into life. Well-dressed growers' wives linked arms with produce executives in front of the driveway and taunted the local police. The trucks, warmed to their task, suddenly shut down, and the Citizens Committee burst into ecstatic cheers. Protesting, picketing, politics—it was more fun than any of these representatives of the valley's establishment would have guessed!

Ten minutes later the sound of a truck's motor put an end to the celebrating.

"Come on, let's block this road, people," someone called out.

"Clear the driveway!" shouted Salinas Police Sergeant Roy Hanna through a bullhorn. His thin blue line of eight policemen stood in front of the truck as it stopped on the edge of company property. The crowd swarmed around the cab, angry at the Teamster driver who was prepared to betray his own community. The enemy was clear: the United Fruit Company in league with a Commie union.

"Get a good look at his face."

"It's got the hammer and sickle on it."

"Boy, you better park it. Park that damn truck."

For five minutes the police watched as the crowd blocked the truck and berated the driver. Finally the gear sounded again, and in an exquisite moment of excitement and fear, the picketers jammed their bodies against the front of the truck. As they realized that the driver had put the truck in reverse, they screamed with joy. He backed away from the driveway, turned off the motor and lights, and left.

"Reds Lettuce Alone!" the growers chanted. The sky was completely light, and they had won. The picketers were enjoying their free coffee and donuts when an InterHarvest executive walked over to tell the small group of UFWOC observers and the Local 78 picketers that the company would not work that day. The cooler workers were furious. In a meeting that night they denounced InterHarvest's capitulation to local agribusiness and voted unanimously to go back to work. If the whole thing was a game, they didn't want any part of it.[49]

It hadn't been a game. Real choices were made in that rosy light. But it was a false dawn for the Citizens Committee. That afternoon Purex/FreshPict and UFWOC officially resumed negotiations, and Purex representatives announced that they had a Teamster recision in their pocket. Moreover, embarrassed local police officials made it clear that they would control the crowd at the next showdown. InterHarvest would remain closed until after Labor Day, when the Citizens Committee would enjoy its final moment in the sun.

A rally that day fully displayed the committee's strength and its weakness. Some 2,500 people came to the Hartnell College football field, reported the *Salinas Californian*. The speakers, mostly local farmers, stood in front of an enormous American flag, and a small plane circling above towed an even bigger one. In the crowd, people waved more flags and held up signs saying "Boycott Chiquita" and "Reds Lettuce Alone." Only a handful of brown faces dotted the crowd, but the one Mexican American farm worker who spoke, Lena Garcia, received the crowd's warmest reception. Her denunciation of UFWOC stood alone, though, as the union was virtually ignored during the day's festivities. The focus of the speakers' wrath was United Fruit—as the company was usually called during the rally—with one speaker even calling it the Octopus. The main speaker, Bill Hitchcock, laid out the argument:

> Any giant conglomerate willing to sacrifice all of us . . . in this Salinas Valley for its own safety thousands of miles away is way off base. It is in the wrong ballpark and in the wrong league . . . Residents of the Salinas Valley community want assurance that our local economy isn't at the mercy of some banana boat landing 3,000 miles away. . . . InterHarvest is three percent of United Fruit's total operation. . . . They were scared because they had so

many other products, and they could sign an inflated contract . . . and spread
the risk. . . . But the Valley's other produce men can't.[50]

The growers' rage against United Brands was not demented paranoia. The
company had no long-term interest in the local economy. Its directors hadn't
even bought land in the valley; they leased it so they could make a quick
getaway whenever profit dictated. The conglomerate cared nothing for local
politics. It was not interested in who served on the city council, nor did it have
much stake in maintaining the exclusive right of whites to control the town.
It had dealt with Spanish-speaking governments, unions, and peasant associations for half a century in Latin America; it could do the same in Salinas.

But the main problem for local Salinas Valley agribusiness was neither
the distant conglomerates nor out-of-town labor agitators. Their predica-
ment was so local that they could smell it: fields of lettuce, tomatoes, and
strawberries rotting because thousands of local farm workers had shut down
the harvest. That and the Citizens Committee's speakers' refusal to discuss
Cesar Chavez and the union revealed the group's essential weakness. The
cheer that enveloped Lena Garcia was a cry of farewell to a world gone by.
Not only was the InterHarvest contract a new class bargain, giving farm
workers a larger share of the wealth they produced but it also finally shut
the door on the bracero era, when Mexican farm workers could be excluded
from the cultural and political life of the town. The strike marked the
emergence of the Mexican and Mexican American community as significant players in Salinas. Mexicans had shut down the harvest. Mexicans and
Mexican Americans had marched through town, overwhelmed the police,
massed at city council meetings, and overflowed courtrooms. No wonder
Salinas thought it had been attacked by Communists. Here the cliché made
sense: an old world had died and a new one was being born. The cheer for
Señora Garcia was a nostalgic sigh. If only we could go back in time. If only
those farm workers were all like Lena . . . if only . . .

It was terribly hard for old-time Salinas loyalists to face up to what had
happened. Eric Brazil had tried to tell them, but they never got a chance
to hear it. A week into the strike he had filed a story for the *Salinas
Californian* about the meetings outside the UFWOC office attended by
500 to 1,000 workers every night. He wrote about the live music: the
accordion player, the mariachis, the child vocalists who belted out Mexican
folk favorites. He described the couples dancing in the dust. He retold a
couple of jokes by strikers who came to the microphone to report on the
day's activities. He described the excitement of Chavez's surprise arrivals.
He was blunt. "A new public forum has developed in Salinas during the
past seven nights. Establishment Salinas does not participate in it. It is
conducted almost entirely in Spanish. But the nightly rally in the dusty
parking lot of the United Farm Workers Organizing Committee's 13

Wood Street headquarters is the only show in town." It was too much truth all at once. The editor of the *Salinas Californian* killed the story.[51]

The week after Labor Day, the third week of the strike, the local growers suffered one blow after another. On Wednesday, helmeted police marched outside InterHarvest straight into the growers' picket line and split it into two columns, forming a corridor for the trucks. The would-be streetfighters were never again able to rebuild their picket lines. That afternoon D'Arrigo, a locally owned and managed medium-sized grower-shipper, announced that it had agreed to negotiate with UFWOC. In a half-page ad in the *Salinas Californian* it told the "Citizens of Salinas": "From what we have seen in the past two weeks it is quite obvious to us that the majority of our field workers prefer UFWOC to represent them rather than the Teamsters. . . . We cannot stand the continued loss of harvested crops and compete with publicly owned corporations who are free to harvest and sell while we are bottled up in a strike."[52]

Two and a half weeks of a solid strike had ripped asunder the unity of the local growers. Henceforth, Salinas agribusiness would have difficulty portraying itself as merely the victim of outsiders. The D'Arrigo family, who had farmed in the Salinas Valley for three generations and whose commitment to local agriculture was manifest in its ownership of substantial amounts of Salinas land, had made matters worse by explaining its decision: the strike had proved that the workers wanted UFWOC to represent them. The other local growers had no answer to that.

On Friday the major local strawberry growers, ten companies employing nearly 1,000 workers, agreed to recognize UFWOC. That meant that of all the major strawberry growers, only Pic-N-Pac/S.S. Pierce, the one grower most vulnerable to a boycott, was still holding out. It, too, eventually would capitulate, but its intransigence demonstrated the other side of the conglomerate coin. Although more vulnerable to a boycott, the big corporations also had deeper pockets, which made them more capable of waiting out losses in the fields. Growers whose whole business was in Salinas did not have that luxury.

One last capitulation finished off the week. One of the area's largest artichoke growers, L.H. Delfino, recognized UFWOC. He, too, had deep roots in Salinas, but on the first day of the strike all of his workers had walked out, and after two weeks only a handful had returned. He had 1,000 acres of artichokes, and he couldn't afford to lose them all.

By the fourth week, although the union still had hundreds of active pickets, the general strike was effectively over. On September 16, Superior Court Judge Anthony Brazil (Eric Brazil's father) made it final, ruling that the strike was a jurisdictional dispute between UFWOC and the Teamsters and was therefore illegal. The ruling ignored the obvious alliance of forces, but in the absence of hard evidence that the growers had "financed, controlled, dominated, or interfered with" the Teamsters, it did make some minor sense in strictly legal terms. (The revelations from Speedy Gonsalves's Teamster trial were at that point still months away. Brazil's ruling was eventually reversed by the California Supreme Court, which ruled that the Teamsters and growers had colluded.) Although UFWOC had violated many court orders in the previous weeks, Chavez decided to honor this one. As the victim of a seemingly outrageous judicial order, the union could end the strike with dignity, just as the battle was in danger of petering out.

The judge issued his order on Mexican Independence Day. That afternoon, at least 600 workers gathered for a meeting and free barbecue at La Selva Beach, just outside Watsonville. People ate the chicken, drank the beer and soda, listened to the mariachis and the patriotic songs, and heard a report from Chavez. The strike was over, he said, and the boycott had begun. He urged the remaining strikers either to volunteer for the boycott or to find fieldwork wherever they could get it.

Mario and Salvador Bustamante were in the crowd. Salvador was back at work at D'Arrigo. He would continue to be an important part of the various walkouts and on-the-job actions that the union used to pressure the D'Arrigo negotiations. Mario, president of the Merrill strike committee, was still on strike. He was "disappointed that the union could so easily separate itself from the problems of the people who were still striking" and "felt thrown to the winds," he said later. "But I knew we had won more than we lost." When no other grower would hire him, he left Salinas earlier than usual for the harvest in the Imperial Valley.[53]

Mojica was also at the barbecue, and also still on strike, hanging out with Salvador Sembrano, the president of the Salinas Co-op strike committee. But he didn't feel abandoned. Although he and Sembrano didn't want to go on the boycott, they wanted to continue to help the union. They managed to get jobs at one of the other nonunion lettuce companies, where they had a double mission as "submarines" for the union—making note of the strong union people on the crew—and cutting and packing a lot of soft lettuce, which would make the nonunion product less desirable to the buyers than the union lettuce. Eventually, their *plan cochino* ("pig plan") would be discovered, and they would be fired. But they managed to get away with it at a few companies before the season ended.

Picket lines continued at the companies that were still negotiating. After FreshPict unilaterally declared a one-week recess in the negotiations, all of its crews walked off the job. The much-diminished Citizens Committee offered to step into the breach, announcing that it would supply all the workers that FreshPict needed as a demonstration of local solidarity with the giant conglomerate's refusal to give in to the union. It quickly had to scale back that offer to one celery crew; nevertheless, the Citizens Committee made quite a show of it. About eighty people— growers, their wives, reporters, three television crews, various supporters, and hangers-on—arrived at the FreshPict office one morning, trying to stay warm while waiting for the labor contractors, who had promised to bring some actual *apieros* to do the work. But the contractors, reluctant to get on UFWOC's bad side for just a couple of days' work, never arrived. The growers decided that they would cut the celery themselves. About two dozen, among them Tom and Anne Merrill, volunteered for the job and rode to the fields with reporters and television crews in tow. That after-noon they appeared in an action photo on the front page of the *Salinas Californian*: Anne with her hair in a bandana, celery knife in hand, in the act of trimming a badly cut piece of celery; Tom standing above a raised box, a piece of celery in his right hand, about to pack it away. What the *Salinas Californian* did not say was that the crew of growers did not manage to cut and pack a single box of celery. A couple of hours after embarrassing themselves in front of the television cameras, they left the field with a lot of unpacked, badly cut celery lying on the ground. A Citizen Committee spokesman told Eric Brazil, "We could cut it, but we couldn't put it in the box; we didn't know how."[54]

On October 9, after the fourth worker walkout, Purex/FreshPict signed a contract with UFWOC, and the local wonder-boy Howard Leach resigned from the company. The next day Pic-N-Pac signed, too. A bit earlier Brown and Hill Tomatoes had signed, the owner explaining that he simply couldn't get any workers without a UFWOC contract. Meyer Tomatoes also signed. None of the companies had much trouble getting the Teamsters to rescind their contracts. On October 16, the Teamsters' president, Fitzsimmons, announced that his union would leave the fields. Two weeks later, Grami said the Teamsters would not enforce its contracts. The local Salinas growers would have to fight UFWOC on their own—at least for a while. Finally, D'Arrigo signed in mid-November. UFWOC farm workers would now pick about a quarter of Salinas Valley lettuce and more than half of its tomatoes. And although most of the strawberry grow-ers had ultimately backed out of the negotiations, the union had the biggest grower under contract.

The day after Chavez called off the strike, he held a press conference announcing the boycott of all lettuce not harvested by workers under UFWOC contracts. He was optimistic. The uncertainty that had accompa-nied mass action had passed, and now the struggle could take a more familiar form. Cesar, who had moved from his San Juan Bautista retreat to the home of a supporter in upscale Carmel Valley, came to the press confer-ence relaxed and confident. He was direct: "The boycott is the best nonviolent weapon the poor and dispossessed have." He was coy: "It is something we didn't want to do because the boycott is a most powerful weapon."[55]

The lettuce boycott, however, was never as effective as the grape boycott had been. Lettuce is a staple, and people not only buy it directly but eat it in prepared sandwiches and salads at restaurants and fast food outlets. It is much harder to exclude from a standard American diet than grapes. Also, a few months after the boycott began, UFWOC suspended it, hoping that negotiations between themselves, the Teamsters, vegetable growers, and AFL-CIO officials would result in an agreement that would give the union the majority of the lettuce contracts. Those negotiations lasted for nine months, and the extended boycott moratorium demoralized the boycott teams and confused consumers. And then, once the boycott was up and running, it had less than a year to be effective, as the union was thrown back into a battle with the grape growers.

The *lechugueros* never participated in the lettuce boycott to the same extent as the grape strikers. The transition from militant grape striker to boycotter had been relatively smooth. The National Farm Workers Association had paid the grape strikers in kind: they received food, clothes, and rent assistance, plus five dollars a week. With little structural difference between a staffer and a striker, the NFWA easily brought some of the strikers onto the staff and then assigned them to the boycott. But the striking *lechugueros* were not paid in kind; joining the UFWOC staff would have been a much bigger change for them and few people did it. Also, when the Salinas strike ended there were more than a thousand union jobs in the fields, giving the most militant vegetable and strawberry workers another option besides going to work for the union. If they could get a dispatch from the union hiring hall, they could work at a union company and carry on the struggle there.

The scarcity of *lechugueros* on the boycott and on the union staff pointed to a peculiar inversion in the relationship between the staff and the workers. The grape workers, whose strike had been ineffective, were more heavily represented on the staff than were the lettuce workers, who had proved their strength in the fields. In 1970, this was barely discernible. I have found no reference to it at the time, nor anyone who now claims to have recognized it back then. By 1980, however, this inversion, colored by several parallel developments and coupled with multiple independent factors, would be an essential element of the UFW's internal warfare and subsequent decline.

The growers who had held out against the strike prepared themselves for the boycott. They prominently displayed the Teamsters' bug on their lettuce boxes and proclaimed themselves the innocent victims of a jurisdictional dispute. Bud Antle, who had had his Teamsters contract since 1961, took the lead in the grower offensive. Although UFWOC had not initially authorized a strike at Antle, many of his workers had walked out anyway, and Chavez was intrigued by what he was sure was a rich boycott opportunity. Dow Chemical, the manufacturer of napalm then being used in

Vietnam, supplied the wrapping for Antle's lettuce. Dow also owned more than 1,000 acres that Antle leased for lettuce production in Arizona and had a representative on Antle's board of directors. In September, even before the strike ended and the boycott had officially begun, *El Malcriado* proclaimed: "Dow Chemical Company, which brought you napalm, now brings you Bud Antle lettuce."

Characteristically, Antle sprang into action. Soon after the InterHarvest contract was announced, he bested all the UFWOC rates by a few pennies, and raised the piece rate for *lechugueros* by 10 percent, to forty-four and a half cents a box. After UFWOC officially declared the boycott, he filed a complaint in court asking for a preliminary injunction to stop it. A pro-grower Salinas Superior Court judge, Gordon Campbell, ruled in Antle's favor, and ordered Chavez to call off the boycott, issue a public statement that he had done so, and post a $2.75 million bond to protect Antle against possible damages if the union's appeals of his ruling failed.[56]

The union refused to comply. Campbell ordered Chavez to show cause why he should not be held in contempt for failure to carry out the court's directives. That order made it clear that the judge intended to jail the union leader. Chavez did not let the opportunity slip by. On the Sunday before his contempt hearing, he was in New York City talking to worshipers at Riverside Church, saying, "Probably we'll find ourselves spending some time in jail." The "ourselves" was regal; no one else in the union was under the court order.[57]

For the contempt hearing on December 4, 1970, UFWOC organizers knew exactly what form the public show of solidarity should take. A UFWOC leaflet set the religious tone, which had been absent during the strike:

> CESAR CHAVEZ—our great leader, he who gave the word to struggle, carrying as his standard his faith in God and the Virgin, who loves the Raza and those who work hard in the fields and are badly paid for it, and who have remained firm despite all setbacks—has been ordered to go to court as if he were a common criminal. We will unite and give him all the support he needs, so that he can move one step closer to winning our cause. United, always united, we will win. Long live Cesar Chavez. Chavez with his ideals will carry us forward.

The leaflet was signed: Union de Trabajadores Campesinos de Cesar Chavez, The Farm Workers Union of Cesar Chavez.[58]

Organizers rented buses and encouraged farm workers from around the state to come to Salinas; 2,000 showed up. As they gathered at the Wood Street office in the early-morning drizzle, Father Duran and Marshall Ganz, standing on a flatbed truck, admonished them to remain orderly, silent, and dignified on the one-mile walk to the courthouse. This was not a time for homemade flags and signs, enthusiastic chants, the undisciplined exuberance of mass action. Organizers distributed candles and professionally printed signs saying, "Libertad Por Chavez." Standing alongside Duran and Ganz were Dolores Huerta, Gilbert Padilla, Larry Itliong, and even Luis Valdez, who had come from Fresno for the occasion. Cesar, Helen, and several of their children joined the two-by-two procession as it moved down Alisal Street. When the throng arrived at the courthouse, they had to wait three hours for the hearing to begin. Chavez, at the front of the line, sat cross-legged on the ground among the standing crowd.

During the hearing, Chavez remained silent. As expected, the judge ordered him to jail, and he was quickly taken away. Jacques Levy distributed Chavez's statement to the press: "Boycott Bud Antle! Boycott Dow! And boycott the hell out of them! Viva!" The next day Helen Chavez read a second statement, this one directly following the spirit and example of Gandhi's letters from jail:

> I'm in good spirits, and they're being very kind to me. I was spiritually prepared for this confinement; I don't think the judge was unfair. I am prepared to pay the price for civil disobedience. I am still very committed, and I'm not bitter at all. At this point in our struggle there is more need than ever to demonstrate our love for those who oppose us. Farm workers are being damaged every day by being denied representation by the union of their choice. Jail is a small price to pay to help right that injustice.[60]

The statement, far removed from the spirit and realities of the strike, was exactly what a lot of people wanted to hear at the close of 1970. Just a few months earlier, the Los Angeles police had attacked the antiwar Chicano Moratorium demonstration and killed three Mexican Americans, including a *Los Angeles Times* columnist, Ruben Salazar, in the street fighting that followed. The police riot had enraged the Chicano movement and pushed it to the left. Chavez's pointed reference to the need for love "at this point in our struggle" was not lost on his audience in the badly damaged liberal-left coalition that he was hoping to hold together for the lettuce boycott.

The right people responded. Ethel Kennedy visited him in jail, as did Coretta Scott King, Andrew Young, and San Antonio's Patrick Flores, the first Mexican American bishop in the United States. George McGovern reiterated his support for the boycott and called for Chavez's release. A *New York Times* editorial declared that "Mr. Chavez" was as "firm in his dedication to nonviolence as Mahatma Gandhi" and called his arrest a "discredit to the law." The California Supreme Court agreed and ordered his release on Christmas Eve. Chavez walked out of jail, talked briefly to the press, and visited the shrine that the union had set up across the street from the jail-house. Four hundred people were there to greet him. "It will soon be two thousand years ago that the Prince of Peace was born and brought to the world the message that blessed are those who struggle for justice," he told them. "It seems to me that those words say if you are fighting for justice He will be with you. I'm very happy to be with you."[60]

In a mundane—rather than messianic—sense, however, Chavez had not been with the workers during the strike. Even when he was at Wood Street, he did not develop strong personal ties with many Salinas strikers. Instead he tended to seek the company of his chief aides and the people who had come to Salinas from the boycott cities. Every evening after the strike rallies Marshall Ganz chaired a meeting of the rank-and-file strike committees, and Fred Ross chaired a meeting of the ex-boycotters, who had specific duties in the strike. Chavez often stopped by Ross's meeting but he rarely attended Ganz's. Mario Bustamante, one of the most promi-nent leaders of the strike, regularly participated in those daily meetings with Ganz. He does not remember ever being in a small group meeting with Chavez in 1970. He saw Chavez at the rallies, from a distance.[61]

Chavez, ever careful about his control over the union, did not seem wary of the potential power of the rank-and-file Salinas leaders. Despite their early contentiousness over timing and their demonstrated capacity for independent action, they followed his general strategy. Nor did he worry about the prominent roles Huerta and Ganz had played. Although Huerta was the UFWOC leader most likely to challenge Chavez in private strategy sessions, she would always carry out his wishes in public. Ganz, whose willingness to endorse and even participate in militant mass actions made him popular with the most active strikers, was both loyal to Chavez and in no position to challenge his leadership in the Mexican and Mexican American union. The potential leaders who did worry Chavez were Eliseo Medina and Marcos Muñoz, veterans of the organization who had come to it straight from the fields when it was still the NFWA. They had dynamic public personas and had been highly successful on the boycott in Chicago and Boston, respectively. Both Mexican immigrants, they could relate to the Salinas strikers. Ganz remembers that Chavez was distressed "about their expectations in terms of leadership roles" when they arrived in the valley to help out in the strike: "That was the first time I sensed from Chavez anxiety about emerging leaders. It wasn't the rank-and-file lettuce workers. It was Eliseo and Marcos in particular. They both had farm worker credentials. Young, ambitious guys who had a right to expect, how to put it, some power. Power in the union. Chavez was very concerned about the consequence of that."[62]

Despite Medina's request at the end of the Salinas strike to be appointed field office director in Delano, Chavez sent him back to his boycott duties in Chicago. Muñoz was dispatched to Boston. It wasn't that Chavez feared that Medina and Muñoz would challenge his overall leadership of the union, Ganz observed. It was something else. "Chavez told me he was worried that their coming back would start internal politics, [which] he regarded as a plague on the organization."[63]

Up on the Mountain,
Out in the Fields, Back in the Cities
January '71 to November '72

LeRoy Chatfield stumbled upon the deserted tuberculosis sanatorium that was to become the new national headquarters of UFWOC soon after Chavez was released from the Salinas jail. A flyer happened across his desk announcing that Kern County was going to auction off the old sanatorium and 280 acres of surrounding land in the Tehachapi foothills. For a few years Chavez had been talking about finding a place for the union's regular retreats; recently he had expressed a need for a national office. Chatfield thought the former sanatorium might serve both functions. He and Chavez walked the property a couple of times, and then Chatfield arranged for a movie producer, Eddie Lewis, and his wife to accompany them on one of those visits. The deal was closed just as Chatfield envisioned it: Lewis bought the property, leased it to the National Farm Worker Service Center, UFWOC's 501(c)(3) nonprofit, on easy terms and with an option to buy. In the process, Lewis earned a handsome tax write-off. It was one of the things that Chatfield did well. When he left the union, about three and a half years later, his first job was selling real estate.[1]

Chavez named the complex Nuestra Señora Reina de la Paz, Our Lady Queen of Peace, and defended his decision to move there to doubters both inside and outside the organization. He led with a democratic argument: as long as he stayed in Delano, he would dominate it; only if he left would the local workers develop their own leadership and identity. Also, getting away from Delano would be good for the staff, as they no longer would be overwhelmed by the problems of one crop and one locale and could concentrate on the problems of the whole union. La Paz would also be a place where staff and union members could retreat, relax, plan strategy, and build community. Others argued that the move would be good for the leader himself and therefore good for all. At Forty Acres he was swamped by farm workers who wanted to see him. Away in La Paz, he would have time for rejuvenating walks in the foothills, where he could think over the big picture or find a few moments of quiet relaxation.

Chavez's confident defense quieted the rumors, political disagreements, and personal gripes that accompanied the decision. But the small internal ruckus over the move turned out to be prophetic, as La Paz became a primary marker in UFW history, an arena for mutual self-destruction that figuratively rivaled the cannibalism of the Donner Party, which had been trapped in the higher mountains to the north. (But it was a prophecy that no one—not even the most severe critics of the move—ever made; a future, but a mere six years away, that no one could foresee.)

The opposition to the move was inchoate, most directly expressed by some of the wives and children, who simply did not want to live in so isolated an area. Helen Chavez was among those most opposed to being uprooted. She had spent some unhappy times as a child at the old county-run sanitarium and had no wish to return. She did not decamp to La Paz until the late summer of 1971, several months after Cesar and most others had moved in. Some of the staff quietly worried that the move would disconnect them from the reality of the fields; a few even argued that the union was abandoning the farm worker struggle. One vocal critic of the move was Jerry Cohen. "I dragged my heels," Cohen said, "and I remember Le Roy and Marshall calling and saying, 'The heart of the union is here in La Paz; you have to be here, the legal department has to be here.' And I said, 'No, the heart of the union is either in Salinas or Delano.' But finally, if all the work is going to be done there, you move there."[2]

The "there" was more pleasant than the vast, flat farm factories on the valley floor. Sometimes it was even beautiful. La Paz sits in a bowl, just beyond the foothills, with semi-dramatic mountains on all sides and a sometime stream running through it. It has four distinct seasons, with a spectacular spring of poppy gold and lupine blue. It gets freezing cold and very hot, but the winters are free of the depressing valley fog, and its summer heat does not reach the oppressive highs of Delano. The nights are clear and good for stargazers; the light at daybreak is splendid. Chavez enjoyed it most mornings, after his usual four or five hours' sleep.

La Paz is just off Highway 58, ten miles below the mountain town of Tehachapi, and about the same distance above the spot where the Joads, after their epic journey from Oklahoma, stopped to view the California fields below them. To the east, on the other side of the Tehachapis, is the Mojave Desert, and to the south, the Los Angeles Basin. Bakersfield is just a half-hour drive to the northwest, and Delano is another half hour beyond that—which undermined the argument that La Paz was too far away from the fields. Physical distance was never the problem.

A dozen structures sat on the sanitarium grounds, all a short walking distance from each other. At the center was the main administration building, a white wooden structure with hardwood floors, small windows, a large meeting room, and space for several offices. Although Richard Chavez had supervised extensive clean-up and restoration, visiting journalists described the buildings as "dilapidated." The central heating system never worked efficiently. Freight trains passed so close to the administration building that people had to stop talking until the noise subsided. The deserted rooms of an old two-story hospital housed the unmarried volunteers, and some small wooden structures became home to volunteer families. People who did not cook in their own quarters took their meals in a dining room that had an adjoining kitchen; the dining room was also used for occasional movies and dances. Soon, double-wide trailers were added for additional families, and finally a "north unit" opened, where eventually staff members would take turns savaging one another in what they called "the Game."

But the Game was hidden in an unknowable future and would not have seemed a logical outcome of the social relations among the first La Paz residents. These fifty adults, with some fifteen children in tow, were united by their dedication to farm workers, their belief in their leader, and their willingness to work hard. Fourteen-hour days were common, with an hour for lunch and an hour for dinner, five days a week. On Saturdays, the staff quit work at five. A multidenominational service was held on Sunday, but attendance was not mandatory. Staffers didn't usually leave La Paz unless they had specific assignments. Vacations were generally frowned upon, and Fred Ross's edict was often quoted without irony: "Injustice never takes a vacation."

La Paz fits comfortably in the California tradition of intentional communities, but in the early years this one did not focus on its own internal life. La Paz existed to serve farm workers, not to develop new ways of collective living or to solve the personal problems of its inhabitants. What little time people had for a private life was their own. There were no regular community meetings, and those that did occur—only Cesar had the authority to call them—dealt with problems in the kitchen (vegetarians versus meat eaters, who cooked and who cleaned), room assignments, and general maintenance.

For all the early talk of La Paz as a place to relax, adult recreation was minimal: walks in the hills, a few movies, dances on holidays, basketball. The swimming pool, which had been restored soon after La Paz opened, was quickly emptied; Chavez argued that its upkeep was too expensive. The small basketball court was mostly deserted. Chavez had told Jerry Cohen and the legal department that they shouldn't shoot baskets before six or seven p.m. because such play would demoralize people who still faced several more hours of work. Cohen, who had played in a regular pickup game in Delano, was inordinately proud that he managed to defy Cesar on this one, and often shot baskets in the late afternoon.

The main beneficiaries of life at La Paz were the children. Most of them in the early days came from the Murguía, Chatfield, Drake, Cohen, and Chavez (Cesar and Helen; Richard and Dolores) families. A few of the mothers of the preschoolers set up an informal child-care center and devoted much of their time to it, with full encouragement from Chavez and without being work-baited by other adults. Older children took a bus into the town of Tehachapi to attend the local schools and had the run of the La Paz compound in the afternoons and evenings. It was a good place to grow up, and the children developed an especially tight community of interwoven lives and attachments.[3]

Security precautions were conspicuous at La Paz. Chavez, who had traveled with armed bodyguards since the shooting of Bobby Kennedy, went into hiding for most of August 1971, after the Federal Bureau of Alcohol, Tobacco, and Firearms uncovered what looked like a plot to assassinate him. Various police investigations concluded that there was no prosecutable case, but UFWOC officials took the alleged plot quite seriously. Under Chatfield's direction a chain-link fence was built around the Chavez house; guards were posted at the gates to the compound; everyone who entered or left was required to show identification and sign in and out; and people were assigned to patrol the grounds day and night.[4] The security arrangements raised the pitch of La Paz's ultraserious atmosphere; they also served as a reminder of how important the leader was.

Chavez brought all the weight of his considerable authority to running the union from its new headquarters. UFWOC now represented about 40,000 farm workers, working under 150 contracts, in many different agricultural areas. Its annual budget was over $1.5 million, and it had administrative control of a series of official nonprofit subsidiaries—the Robert F. Kennedy Medical Plan, the Martin Luther King Farm Worker Development Fund, the Farm Worker Service Center, the Farm Worker Credit Union—that together accounted for much more than the union's own financial resources. Tens of thousands of people and millions of dollars all had to be administered by a volunteer staff whose primary qualification was loyalty to the leader and the organization.

Chavez approached the challenge with his own brand of dedicated enthusiasm, and among his intimates he rarely lost a certain lighthearted style. He had one deficiency, however, noted by most everyone: when he got to La Paz, his involvement in minutiae intensified. Susan Drake, his first secretary there, said he read 95 percent of the incoming mail and personally dictated most of the responses. Marion Moses, his sometime nurse, called him a control freak. The AFL-CIO's Bill Kircher was exasperated: "He ran the credit union meetings. Now, I know that credit union meetings are important, but God almighty a couple of administrative officers could run it, but no, Chavez had to be there . . . going over every detail."[5] One of his administrative assistants put it like this: Chavez was like a chef cooking pancakes on a mile-long griddle who insisted on personally flipping every one and ended up burning them all.

Even Chavez recognized his limitations. According to Chatfield, "He told me over and over that he was not interested in spending his life administering a union. . . . On so many different occasions he would say that his strength, his calling, was to get things going. He talked about going to East LA and starting over. He even sent me to East LA to find a center for organizing." But Chatfield's explorations came to nothing, and Chavez could neither bring himself to leave nor shuck his controlling ways. Of all the arguments he had made for the move to La Paz, the silliest was that he left Delano so that the leaders there could call their own shots. They couldn't, and the only person who could was no longer among them. Chatfield put it best: "Wherever Chavez was, that is where the control was. That was a given. Some people say that was part of the problem. But that is just who he was and what the situation was. That is how the whole operation worked."[6]

The most disastrous consequence of Chavez's management style was the plan that he devised for the new hiring halls. Chavez talked the matter over with Chatfield, Jim Drake, and Marshall Ganz (especially Ganz) in the early spring of 1971, then tested his decision on the members of the Executive Board who happened to be in La Paz, and finally imposed his will on the field offices around the state. It is not surprising, given this top-down process, that his new policy was out of touch with the realities of farm worker life and served to alienate thousands of farm workers from the union. Later, even the proud Ganz would admit that the hiring hall scheme had been a colossal error: "We were taking a meat clever to all the existing social relationships." But at the time, Ganz took the plan to the field offices and defended it against those—including the board members and hiring hall heads Larry Itliong, Richard Chavez, and Gilbert Padilla—who thought it a disastrous mistake that would complicate the union's position in the fields.

Compared with the drama of strikes, heroic penance, or union intrigue, the mechanics of a hiring hall may seem mundane, but as the site of closest contact between workers and the union, the halls went a long way in shaping farm worker attitudes to UFWOC and the UFW. It was there that the workers who had continued to pick grapes in the boycott years, and who had been denounced as scabs, fools, and illegals, had their first taste of what the new union power might mean—and it mostly tasted awful, further souring them on the union.

All of the 1970 UFWOC grape contracts had clear language that required the employers to get their workers through a hiring hall and left questions of seniority and management of the hall to the union. Because so much of the union staff had rushed off to Salinas, the hiring for the 1970 grape harvest had been a haphazard affair. Richard Chavez, who had been left to head up the Delano field office, had complained vigorously at the time about being understaffed, and called the hiring procedure "a complete mess."[7] Chavez was determined not to have a repeat in 1971, and he and Ganz began devising standard rules for the field offices and hiring halls. To them, the union seemed too decentralized and unstable.[8] Some of the top leaders were in charge of most of the main field offices (Manuel Chavez in Calexico, Richard Chavez and Larry Itliong in Delano, Gilbert Padilla in Fresno), and they were running their offices independently, according to their own styles. Andy Anzaldua, an ex-cop and antipoverty worker whom Chavez had put in charge of the Salinas office, needed more direction, as did the other relatively inexperienced volunteers who headed the fourteen other new field offices scattered throughout rural California.

Chavez and Ganz understood their job to be twofold: to bring the union under central control and to make it the new, dominating power in the fields. The contracts, they believed, gave them the tools with which to do that. The grievance procedure and "good standing" clause meant that the union had a large say in who could be fired. The hiring hall provisions theoretically gave the union the first and last word on who could be hired. But whether this language could be translated into power depended on how the halls actually worked.[9]

Previously, hiring was done by contractors, foremen, and supervisors, and in some areas through a morning shape-up. At companies that had labor camps, living in company housing and working in the company fields went together. Many ranches had developed an informal policy of company seniority, with the boss as the ultimate arbitrator of disputes. Thus, large numbers of workers had developed a substantial commitment to individual growers and vice versa. Chavez and Ganz proposed to redirect the workers' commitment to the union. Henceforth, seniority would first be determined by how long the member had been in the union, not by how long he or she had worked at a particular ranch. When work orders arrived at the hiring hall, first crack at the jobs would go to the people who had been in the union the longest. Only afterward would preference be given to the people who had previously worked at the ranch, if they were at the hiring hall on the days the dispatches were distributed.

Chavez and Ganz also insisted on a strict interpretation of the rules about the payment of dues. Henceforth, all union members would have to pay full dues throughout the year, even during their months off, and unless all their dues were paid, they could not be dispatched to work. The official reasoning was that since some union benefits were paid year-round, why not dues, too? But unofficially, Chavez and Ganz thought year-round dues would teach workers that the union not only was the most powerful institution in the fields but also could be a significant force in workers' lives, off the job. Year-round dues implied year-round participation. The union would be more akin to a community organization than a simple trade union, one capable of changing power relations in the rural towns where the union was based—or so Chavez and Ganz earnestly believed.[10]

The two leaders anticipated some difficulty in imposing the rules. The vast majority of workers would owe some back dues, which ran $3.50 a month, payable quarterly for $10.50. Because most farm workers were short of cash at the start of a new season, paying back dues would be a hardship. But Ganz and Chavez reasoned that most of the workers were now enjoying the benefits of the union without having been part of the five-year fight to establish it and requiring that they pay up now was not too much to ask. As Fred Ross said, "This was the first time we'd gotten so close to many of these workers. They'd been imported as strike break-ers, and now, overnight, they were blanketed by a union . . . What had happened was that the original strikers, the boycott workers, and the college kids had handed these workers a union. So in order to make these workers conscious, they had to go through a lot of the same things the original strikers had gone through."[11] In other words, sacrifice and pain.

It was still common, among the union staff and militants, to call those who had continued to work during the five-year strike "scabs" or *esquiroles*. From those workers' point of view, however, there had been no strike after the initial harvest-time drama of 1965. What had followed was mostly symbolic, a demonstration staged for boycott supporters far away, a notional strike, without sustained pickets or organization in the fields. Can there be scabs when there are no picket lines to cross? When most workers didn't even know about the union? To those in La Paz and elsewhere who had made the union a zealous cause, such questions didn't even arise. Years later, a repentant Ganz was blunt: "Our attitude was sort of like, 'Well, fuck 'em.' We sort of said, 'Well look, they got all the goodies, and they got to take some responsibility.'"[12]

Chavez made a series of short visits to various hiring halls to explain the new rules, accompanied by David Burciaga, director of the Arvin-Lamont field office. Those visits were not nearly enough to do the job, so Chavez dispatched Ganz to talk to the field office directors. Marshall Ganz found himself in a difficult position. He held the title field office coordinator (as well as boycott coordinator), but some of the directors of the most impor-tant field offices were on the Executive Board, and he wasn't; most of them were older than he; and many had been in the union longer. His authority with them depended not on his title or experience but on his relationship to Chavez. Marshall knew that when the staff disagreed with Cesar's orders, it would be easier to blame him, Ganz, than to blame Chavez; Marshall felt that his relations with the staff would inevitably become combative. On their side, many staffers complained that Ganz was arrogant. Some lower-level people were afraid of him. The way Gilbert Padilla saw it:

Marshall was an impressive figure. He was smart—everyone knew he came from Harvard and SNCC. He worked as hard as anyone. His Spanish was excellent and he got along with many of the workers. And he supposedly carried the word from Cesar. But he pissed people off. He loved Cesar like a daddy, and he even started to talk like him. One time I had to tell him, "Hey, you are not Cesar; stop imitating him." Ganz gave orders; he questioned people's work habits; he demanded that they give an account of themselves.[13]

As always, the grape harvest began in the Coachella Valley; there, the local workers were relatively strong supporters of the union whereas the Filipinos and migrants from Texas and Mexico were either indifferent or hostile. Ganz laid out the rules to the field office director, Tony Lopez, and held a series of meetings with the ranch committees and organizing committees, all of whom were dominated by local workers. A ratification vote was thus not too difficult to secure, but it did not represent majority assent, and in Coachella paying back dues ended up being unpopular with just about everyone. People who had not traveled north with the harvest, and who neither pruned nor tipped, had not worked since the previous spring. Migrants who followed the harvest had not worked since the previous October or November. When they returned for the May harvest, they discovered that they might be anywhere from $21 to $31.50 behind in their dues. Since people often worked in large family groups, many families had to pay more than $100 to get dispatches for everyone. Few people had that kind of money.

Ganz's orders were that no one could get a dispatch until all the back dues were paid. No exceptions. Folks scrambled to raise the money. Many went to their old supervisors and foremen, who gave them advances on their wages. Thus, a policy meant to increase loyalty to the union ended up throwing workers back on the mercy of their bosses. Also, no worker was guaranteed a dispatch to the place where he or she used to work, and no rule provided for families to be dispatched together to the same ranch. Most families had only one car, so family members who were suddenly working many miles apart also had to pay for rides from fellow workers or foremen.

The scene at the hiring hall itself was chaotic. Grape season starts with a bang. In a space of a few days, growers sent thousands of work orders to the union office. That spring of 1971 four or five union staffers, unfamiliar with the local scene and administering unpopular rules, were trying to do a job that previously had been done by dozens of local contractors. Angry workers, some with borrowed money in hand, others with no money at all, lined up to try to get their old jobs back. The hall was not big enough; lines stretched out the door, and hundreds waited in a public park across the street. It could take several hours to get to the window where the precious dispatches were being distributed, for a hefty price.[14]

The bosses were as angry as the workers, perhaps more so. The earlier the grapes are picked the better the price. The grapes were ready, but the pickers were waiting in line at the union hall. Some employers went to the hall to try to expedite the process; some simply hired people without dispatches; others complained to La Paz. Ganz, who had built good relations with some of the Coachella growers during the period when they had the only table grape union contracts, fielded their frantic, disbelieving phone calls: "What are you guys doing? Don't you want to keep this thing?" But La Paz remained firm and ignored employer warnings. Years later, Ganz would lament, "They were absolutely right. They saw the feedback among their own workers. We always had a hard core of total believers who would say, 'Right on.' But that's not everybody. It's not even most people."[15]

The Mexicans and Mexican Americans who lived in Coachella year-round were harmed the least. Those locals, the original social base of the NFWA, were more likely than the migrants to have pruned in the winter, and tipped and pulled leaves in the spring. Having worked off and on throughout the year, they were not so far behind in their dues. Also, they had had time to get familiar with the local field office, often had inside information on exactly when the harvest dispatches would be distributed, and sometimes didn't have to wait in line. The few people who had joined the union before the first contracts in 1970, and who therefore had first shot at the jobs, also were almost all local workers. The new rules therefore reinforced the identification of the union with the interests of resident Mexicans and Mexican Americans. In the table grapes it was among them that the UFWOC found its relatively small group of *huesos colorados* (bloody bones) as the hard-core believers were known in Spanish.

The vast majority of Filipino farm workers traveled in crews, worked every year at the same ranches, and lived in the same company-owned camps. For them, everything had changed when they arrived in Coachella in 1971. All the time they had lived and worked together counted for nothing. Their crews could be broken up, and many of them lost their customary harvest-time homes. The hiring hall was indeed the new center of power, but to the Filipinos it was a foreign power that operated in a foreign language, Spanish, by rules they hardly understood. Already estranged from the union by the bad feelings at the end of the 1965 strike and the 1967 NFWA-AWOC merger, the Filipinos (still 15 to 20 percent of the table grape workforce) were now overwhelmingly opposed to "the Mexican union."

Chavez and Ganz got heat about their rules from the staff as well. David Burciaga told Chavez that the union seniority rule "didn't make any sense at all." Burciaga had extensive experience working with farm workers, growers, and the political machinery of the Central Valley. He had left school after the seventh grade and became a champion cotton picker, able to pick more than 500 pounds in eight hours. After World War II he worked as a cotton presser, became an official with the ILWU, and plunged into the small world of Bakersfield progressive politics. He met Chavez in early 1954 and later helped build the Bakersfield Community Service Organization chapter. Burciaga organized part-time for the NFWA, helping out in the 1965 grape strike and the DiGiorgio election. When the Delano growers signed in 1970, he joined the union staff full-time, and Chavez appointed him director of the Arvin-Lamont field office. But when Burciaga complained, Chavez was not in a mood to listen, which surprised his old friend, since listening was what Chavez had been best at. To Burciaga, it seemed that by 1971 Chavez believed that any idea he had was a good one: "If he thought it up, it would work." Burciaga insisted that the new seniority idea wouldn't. When Chavez and he traveled together to the field offices to explain the new rules, Burciaga refused to explain union seniority. He made Chavez do it.[16]

When the harvest began in Arvin-Lamont, Burciaga ignored union seniority and simply sent people out to the ranches where they had worked before. It was still hectic, but it seemed to be going well enough. In the midst of the rush, Ganz arrived. Although Burciaga admired some qualities in this man eighteen years his junior—"Marshall was a good organizer, and he treated the workers fine, real good. They loved him, too"—he also felt that Ganz's arrogance and veneration of Chavez often trumped his own good judgment.

"How come you are not doing it by union seniority?" Ganz wanted to know.

"What for, Marshall? We've got them all at once, you know. That would take a long time, going worker by worker," Burciaga replied.

"But you got to do it that way."

"Here." Burciaga gave Ganz the seniority list. "You do it."

Ganz took the list and carefully explained to the workers what he was going to do. The workers were outraged. Some threw beer cans at him. Burciaga was pleased.

"Well, it was chicken-shit. Can you imagine you work at Kuvacevich for years and years, and then here comes a guy that belongs to a union and is going to take your job next year. Nobody would accept that, right?"[17]

In Delano, Richard Chavez headed the field office. He opposed both union seniority and back dues. Years later he blamed those policies for pushing people away from the union. Workers "hit the roof" when they heard that before they could be dispatched they had to pay dues for the months they hadn't worked in the off-season. Union seniority was even worse: "A lot of these people came and worked for the same boss, same grower every year. Okay? But no, we're gonna have union seniority. It was stupid, stupid, stupid . . . I fought a lot against it, but I didn't win it. And so people were pissed off . . . that they turned to the Teamsters."[18] Padilla, who had success-fully led the Fresno hiring hall through the first, tough, 1970 season, went to Delano to watch the hiring hall in action the following year:

> It was the craziest thing I had ever seen. There was a little window inside this big hall at Forty Acres. The hall was full of people waiting to go to work: 100 to 200 people, all anxious to go to work, without any idea of what was happening. And someone was screaming from inside the window, "Anybody here from 1962?" Few could even hear what was being said. And those who could hear couldn't understand it. "Anybody here from 1963?" And all the way down the line. It was horrible. I went around talking to people, and they were pissed off. So I knew I wasn't going to implement it.[19]

Padilla's authority within the union had grown since he had given up booze, enough so that when he told Chavez he wasn't going to enforce the new rules, Chavez did not, perhaps could not, order him to comply. At the three Fresno-area field offices that Padilla oversaw, workers were dispatched first by company seniority, and then on a first come, first served basis. If workers didn't have enough money to pay their back dues at the beginning of the season, they were sent to work and instructed to pay their dues out of their first paychecks. It seemed to work well, but Padilla never tried to organize the other field office directors to follow his lead.[20]

Al Rojas, in charge of the table grape field office in Poplar, had more experience and leverage than most directors but not enough to defy the edicts from La Paz. Poplar was a small town of a few hundred, but it strad-dled one of the main roads between Delano and Fresno traveled by thousands of workers going from their homes and labor camps to the vine-yards and orchards. Most of the workers assigned to the Poplar office had not been enrolled in UFWOC the year before, because their ranches were beyond the reach of the Fresno and Delano field offices. The 1971 season was the first time they had any experience with the union. It did not go well. Large numbers of workers, put off by the long wait for a dispatch, simply went directly to their old ranches. When Rojas or his assistant, Saeed Al-Alas, eventually found them, they suspended the workers from their jobs. One time Rojas discovered some hard-core supporters working without dispatches. "We didn't have enough money to pay, and we needed to go work," they told him, "and we figured we could come back and pay you after we made some money." He suspended them, just as he had the others. Thus were friends turned into enemies.[21]

But the problem went beyond the dispatch system. At the two largest farms, Roberts and Elmco, many of the workers were strong unionists, especially at Roberts, where there had been a short strike just before the owner signed the contract. But at the other companies, the union was largely unpopular, except for a few hard-core *huesos colorados*. Most workers had scabbed, and had been uninterested in UFWOC before the 1970 settlement. Wages had risen only slightly in the first contract—without a UFWOC office in the area, conditions had not changed much in the fields. This fact was not lost on Rojas. He soon realized that the union was an outside power that was imposing itself on the workers before they experienced any of the benefits it had supposedly won for them in the contracts.[22]

Rojas complained about the problems to his friend Larry Itliong, who agreed with him but said that he had no influence with Chavez or the Executive Board. On the few occasions when the field office directors were called to La Paz to spend a weekend discussing hiring hall procedures—Rojas recalled only "two or three" such meetings in the two years that he headed the Poplar office—people were free to air their complaints, but revision of the rules was not on the agenda.

Rojas was upset at the time, but it wasn't until twenty years later that he could articulate an alternative approach: go slow; preserve company seniority; develop a good stewards program; teach the workers how to negotiate with their foreman and supervisors. But the union did pretty much the opposite. It used the contract to try to force the workers to become good unionists. And it failed miserably. The workers could see little difference between buying a job from a contractor and buying it from the union through "back dues." "We were talking about taking power away from the contractors," Rojas said. "Now the union became the super contractor."[23]

When Ganz and Chavez were formulating the hiring hall policies in La Paz, Ganz had gone on a visit to ILWU locals in the San Francisco Bay area to learn how they ran their halls. But the ILWU model did not serve UFWOC well in 1971. Union seniority on the docks did not translate well into union seniority in the fields. Unlike farm workers, dockworkers do not have any particular loyalty to a single company. They can unload a ship in a number of days, and their employers change with every ship that comes into port. But trying out union seniority in the fields was not the essence of the problem. Nor did the initial experiment with back dues in itself damage the union. The problem was that these policies were imposed on a workforce largely suspicious of the union from the beginning, and that these wary workers had no practical way to alter the leadership's decisions.

Ganz and Chavez had missed the democratic content of the ILWU example. The ILWU came to power because of a popular strike on the docks that evolved into a general strike in San Francisco. When the ILWU set up its hiring hall in 1935, the dockworkers were predisposed to support it, as most of them considered the union their own. In the table grapes, UFWOC had won because of the power of the boycott, even though most of the workers had continued picking grapes in the fields. When UFWOC set up its hiring halls in 1971, many grape workers were set to dislike it, no matter what the policies, as their previous experience with the union was, at the very best, minimal.

Furthermore, dockworkers had a way of influencing the dispatchers and the dispatch rules; UFWOC members did not. In the ILWU, dispatchers were (and are) elected officials. When workers are dissatisfied with them— suspect them of unfairness or corruption—they can run candidates against them. Also, the hiring halls operate out of locals where all the principal officers are elected, and therefore subject to some measure of popular control. Union democracy is by no means guaranteed in ILWU hiring halls, but it is not institutionally blocked. UFWOC was an entirely differ- ent kind of operation. Neither dispatchers nor the directors of the field offices were elected. They were all appointed by the staffers above them. Rank-and-file farm workers could vote only for their representatives on the ranch committees. Those committees were often pressured to ratify the rules that had been previously formulated in La Paz. But such votes meant very little; the rules remained unpopular and with few exceptions, the committees had little power within the union.

Don Watson, the ILWU clerk and labor historian, visited Delano in 1971. He had been there in August 1970, a supporter who had come to help celebrate the boycott victory. He had been recruited to go to the fields to help sign up workers after the grower capitulation and had been dismayed by the passive attitude of many of the new members. But what he found in 1971 was worse. He knew what a hiring hall was supposed to look like. This was not it. "In Delano they didn't have a union. It was a hiring hall where workers went to pay their money so they could go to work. That's all it was. From the workers' viewpoint it was a racket."[24]

In mid-October, before the harvest season ended, Larry Itliong resigned as the assistant director of UFWOC. In an interview with *Fresno Bee* reporter Ron Taylor, he explained: "I don't have any problem with Cesar; as far as I'm concerned I have the greatest admiration for him. I am not quitting to make things harder for him." But Itliong added that he was unhappy with the group of "intellectuals" who formed a "brain trust" around Chavez.

> All you can say is that the thinking of these people does not relate to the thinking of the farm workers, and brother Chavez is . . . with them day in and day out. Instead of trying to understand the problems of farm workers,

he [Chavez] is swayed by the grandiose thinking of these people . . . who have created this monster organization on the behalf of the farm workers. I don't know how I could say it any other way.[25]

Itliong also had a dispute with the union about his personal budget of $500 to $550 a month to support his wife and seven children. He later publicly criticized the use of volunteer labor to run the union (rather than a professional staff), adding that the "brain trust" was "Anglo," and that Chavez risked alienating "minority group members" by keeping Anglos in key positions. Privately, he complained to both Rudy Reyes and Al Rojas about the way Filipinos were being treated in the union, and about Chavez's unwillingness to listen to criticism. His job had become impossible, he explained, because the Filipino workers looked to him to represent them in UFWOC, but the union leadership paid no attention to what he had to say.[26]

Chavez never responded to Itliong's charges and accepted his resignation with regret. Neither Ganz nor Cohen nor Chatfield (along with Drake, the principals of the "Anglo brain trust") can remember discussing the resignation, either among themselves or with Chavez. The charge that Anglos were a danger to a "minority group" union does not appear to have stung in 1971. Later, when the charge reappeared in another form, Ganz and Cohen were taken by surprise. At the time, Ganz dismissed Itliong as an old-style unionist (which he certainly was) who could not adapt to UFWOC's unorthodox tactics and techniques; Cohen and Chatfield ascribed the resignation to Itliong's jealousy of Imutan and Vera Cruz, who were closer to Cesar, and to his concern about not being paid a union official's regular salary.

Itliong's critique that this "monster organization" was "on the behalf" of farm workers would have been difficult for almost anyone in the heady air of La Paz to understand. And perhaps Itliong did not fully understand it either. "I don't know how I could say it any other way," he had concluded. Another way would have required a full democratic world view, an understanding that "on the behalf" is only one third of Lincoln's democratic formula "of the people, by the people, and for the people." But as a veteran old-style unionist, Itliong did not have the language of democracy in his arsenal.

Where Lincoln's triple incantation was understood—not by the leadership in La Paz but by the farm workers who considered the union their own—the hiring hall rules were not so much of a problem. In Salinas those working under union contracts were not suspicious of UFWOC; they had made it a player in the region with their general strike and believed that it belonged to them. When the hiring hall rules came down from La Paz, the Salinas workers did their best to cooperate with union officials to make the regulations work. Also, union seniority was not as great a problem in Salinas because relatively few workers there had joined the union before 1970, so almost everyone started out on an equal footing. Nor did most of the Salinas workers have significant problems with back dues: most union lettuce workers traveled to the Imperial Valley during the winter, where they worked under contract for InterHarvest, FreshPict, and D'Arrigo, and paid their dues while they worked. When they returned to Salinas, they did not owe dues. Workers had some problems with the hiring halls but nothing on the scale of what happened in the Central Valley.

In Salinas the main harvest-time problem was in the fields. Still heady from their strike victory, union workers spent considerable time and energy testing its limits. Workers paid by the hour slowed down their pace; piece-rate workers sped up so as to make more money per hour, and the quality of their work sometimes suffered. Foremen had a tough time adjusting to the new balance of power, and the workers didn't make it easy on them. Until the 1970 contracts were signed, there had been no formal rules in the fields: foremen had used their powers arbitrarily, and workers used theirs when they could get away with it. As far as many of the workers were concerned, the new contracts simply made it easier to exercise their age-old harvest-time tactics. Job actions to settle disputes— slowdowns, work stoppages—increased.*

Top management complained directly to La Paz, saying that union officials had to teach the workers that their job actions were prohibited by the contract. Otherwise, production costs would rise and the few union companies would not be able to compete with their nonunion rivals. Local union staff members often tried to restrain the workers, urging them to settle their differences with the company in formal negotiations, as provided for in the contract and not on the job. Sometimes those warnings worked, sometimes not. On occasion some staffers used the crews' willingness to exercise their power in the fields to force the companies to settle ongoing contractual disagreements. La Paz also encouraged workers to leave their jobs en masse for a day's protest in Sacramento or San Francisco, a practice that enraged management, as it was impossible for them to find enough substitute workers for a one-day assignment.

Back in the Central Valley there were only a few companies and crews where the workers had made the union their own, Salinas-style. Doug Adair, the former *El Malcriado* editor, who belonged to one of them at Tenneco-Ducor, called them "liberated crews." Tenneco, an oil conglomerate out of

---

* The workers' use of slow-downs and work stoppages was partly a consequence of their special status as agricultural employees. Denied the protections of the NLRA in 1937, they were also free of its discipline, and had not been forced into a system of highly regulated, rule-bound industrial jurisprudence.

Houston that dealt in everything from Australian real estate to nuclear submarines had bought up large tracts of Central Valley agricultural land on the eve of UFWOC's 1970 victory. It had gotten the Ducor Ranch from the Bank of America, which had foreclosed on J. J. Divizich, a pioneer Yugoslav grape grower who had gone bankrupt in the late 1960s, partly as a result of the grape boycott. Tenneco-Ducor employed more than 1,000 workers at peak season, several hundred of whom lived at a half dozen labor camps. Rudy Reyes, the onetime prankster and uneasy dirty-trickster, came off the boycott and went to work at what had been a primarily Filipino camp in 1971. He became one of the driving forces in building Tenneco-Ducor into one of the most militant union companies in the Central Valley.

Reyes was an oddity—a Filipino who supported the UFW—when he arrived at the camp, dispatch in hand. Most of the Filipinos in the camp were angry at the union; as a consequence of the dispatch system, about half the Filipinos who had worked there for years were gone, and the rest had to share their hundred-bed bunkhouse with Arabs and Mexicans. The Arabs were all Yemenites, people the growers had been bringing into the California fields since the end of the Bracero Program. Reyes was elected shop steward, with support from his wary Filipino compatriots and others. He and another former union staffer, Macario Bustos, who was elected president of the ranch committee, did what they could to build solidarity in the camp, on their crew, and throughout the company.

"There was a lot of trouble with the food," Reyes remembers, "because the Arabs didn't eat pork and we love pork, so we had to have meetings about what should be served."[27] In the course of those meetings, Reyes and Bustos explained that the new UFW contract prohibited the camp manager from making money off the meals, and they united the workers around a plan that soon ended the longtime practice of gouging workers on the food bill. Bustos, one of the few workers with a car, gave free rides whenever he went into town, cutting into the camp manager's practice of charging five bucks a pop for that service. After Reyes complained loudly that the roof over his bed leaked, workers convinced the company to pay to redo the roof, work that was done by volunteer UFW carpenters. Out in the vineyards, Bustos and Reyes demanded what had been guaranteed in the contract: toilets, drinking water, regular breaks. The workers began to see the effectiveness of the union. Ultimately they forced the replacement of the old camp manager with a new man, who was given strict orders by Tenneco-Ducor to get along with the union.

Doug Adair joined his old friend Reyes at the Tenneco-Ducor camp soon after the new camp manager arrived. He had been on the boycott in Philadelphia when the grape contracts were signed in 1970, and had been sent to St. Louis to help form a committee for the lettuce boycott before returning to California to work in the fields. Adair enthusiastically embraced camp life. He got along well with the Yemenites, most of whom were strong union supporters (the hiring hall had worked well for them) and started learning Arabic and reading some Middle Eastern history. He learned to distinguish the Marxist southern Yemenites from the royalist northern ones and made allowances for their political and cultural differences. He took groups of Yemenite workers down to Arvin to get driver's licenses at a Department of Motor Vehicles office where fluency in English was not required. He encouraged attendance at union meetings and was an active, militant presence on his pruning crew.

Decades later he remembered his two years at the Tenneco-Ducor camp as among the happiest of his life. He had called it a "liberated crew," he said, because:

> . . . at most ranches, the foreman would indicate whom he preferred for steward, and that's who got elected, and the crew remained under the foreman's control. But on a few ranches, the steward was willing to take on the foreman or the company on behalf of the workers, and the workers would back him up. . . . Along with nearby Roberts Farms, Freedman in Coachella, and, of course, Schenley, Tenneco-Ducor became one of the model union grape companies. If we had had enough time, we could have spread our example throughout the industry.[28]

Taken together, a rigid leadership at the top of a top-down hierarchy enforcing an inappropriate formula on noncooperative growers and a suspicious membership go a long way to explaining the hiring hall disasters of the 1971 table grape harvest. But it is not the full explanation. La Paz failed to adjust its hiring hall rules in the face of many staff and rank-and-file complaints partially because it had its hands full with another matter: a new, well-organized, grower attack. Under siege, forced to remain on a war footing, the union leaders had neither the time nor the inclination to work out the problems down on the floor of the Central Valley. Instead, they turned their eyes away from the vineyards and back to the cities, in an effort to defend themselves from a national legislative and electoral campaign meant to cripple the surprisingly triumphant little union.

The assault was formidable: coordinated by national agribusiness, spearheaded by the Nixon administration, and funded by millions of dollars of California grower money. Waging the battle against this offensive propelled the union leaders into electoral politics and back into the arms of their liberal supporters. They did not go there reluctantly. Chavez continued to tell the world that the boycott was the union's most powerful weapon and it logically followed that the boycott coalition was one of its most important constituencies. And why wouldn't Cesar, now securely set up at La Paz, be more than willing to turn his attention back to the cities? In the vineyards he was a controversial figure, and though generally popular with farm workers, he was not universally so. Among liberals he was a hero: "one of the greatest living Americans," according to George McGovern.[29]

The nation as a whole, however, was in a different mood than it had been in 1965 when the black eagle flew for the first time as the banner of a would-be union. Richard Nixon, not Lyndon Johnson, was now in the White House. Ronald Reagan, not Pat Brown, was the California governor. The original civil rights coalition that Chavez held together long enough to win the grape boycott was gone and would be hard to rebuild. The Chicano movement was strong, but it was not an adequate substitute for the earlier broader alliance. The trend was not yet entirely clear to the actors themselves but reaction was blowing in the wind and was just about to blow down the last, feeble electoral gesture of the sixties: the McGovern campaign. The union had to defend itself in the midst of this new political climate. It did remarkably well.

In 1971, the growers decided to strip the union of its powers through legislation. Having successfully opposed farm labor laws since the New Deal, growers swallowed some pride and reversed course. California's Senator George Murphy introduced a bill in Congress that permitted secret ballot elections for agricultural workers—while also making most seasonal workers ineligible, outlawing harvest strikes, and prohibiting secondary boycotts. Murphy's bill did not go far, as UFWOC had too much power in the Democratic-controlled Congress. So the growers turned to state legislatures, hoping that the union would be stretched too thin to fight effectively state by state. The growers were successful in Kansas and Idaho, but UFWOC was able to beat them back in agricultural states that also had significant urban populations: Oregon, Washington, New York, Florida, and California.[30]

In UFWOC's backyard the growers had managed to get a Southern California Democrat, Kenneth Cory, to help them. In June 1971 Cory proposed a bill that would make both harvest strikes and secondary boycotts illegal. Chavez was furious and went straight to the head of the Democratic table, meeting with Assembly Speaker Bob Moretti in Los Angeles and Willie Brown, the chairman of the California Assembly's Ways and Means Committee, in Sacramento. Both men assured him that Cory's bill would never get out of Brown's committee. With that guarantee, the union mobilized 2,000 people for a midweek demonstration in Sacramento, dwarfing the earlier pro-grower demonstrations, which never numbered more than a couple of hundred. The Los Angeles Times described the demonstration on the capitol steps as "festive" and "carnival like." The rally began with the announcement that Cory had withdrawn his bill. Workers and their families sang, chanted, and cheered. Chavez, feeling the power of his quick victory (the bill had been introduced less than a month earlier), berated the growers and the politicians. He wasn't going to thank the Democratic leadership for killing the bill, he said, because that would be "like thanking the hangman for imposing an unjust sentence and then going on to commute the sentence."[31]

Chavez had learned through the years to cooperate with the Democratic Party, but he never gave the Democrats a blanket endorsement, and he was always willing to move against those who opposed union interests. After Alex Garcia, a Chicano assemblyman from East Los Angeles, mistakenly supported the Cory bill, Chavez convinced Art Torres, a twenty-five-year-old recent law school graduate who had been working for the union, to run against Garcia in the Democratic primary. Torres lost, but he won two years later. The message: any Chicano Democrat in California who crossed Cesar Chavez was not going to have much of a political future.

Seven months after the victory over the California bill, Chavez formally became president of the newly dubbed United Farm Workers, or UFW, now a genuine union. George Meany presented the union charter in February 1972, in a private ceremony, witnessed only by Monsignor George Higgins. No representative of the workers was present, and the legally important change from an organizing committee to independent affiliate was not matched by any restructuring of the organization. Like UFWOC, the UFW would not have locals with elected principal officers in control of their own budgets. This produced an unnoticed irony: the UFW, supposedly a radical alternative to the old-time AFL-CIO unions, actually had less structural democracy than most of its famously bureaucratic sister affiliates, whose workers could at least vote for their local officials.

Irony aside, the new UFW was not inclined to change as the 1972 grape season began. The Executive Board reaffirmed the hiring hall rules and established a schedule of specific fines for people who were behind in their dues or who worked without dispatches. With La Paz playing a hard hand, an atmosphere of compulsory participation pervaded the union. Some ranch committees voted to make union meetings mandatory; workers who didn't attend were fined. In some halls, workers not only had to be in good standing to get on the dispatch list but had to do some kind of union task—go on a day trip to Los Angeles to help with the boycott, for example, or to Sacramento to lobby the legislature.[32]

Workers complied because they had to. People adapt. The 1972 harvests were less chaotic. The field offices were better prepared, and many workers had been careful to pay their entire dues when they were laid off at the end of the 1971 season. A few ranches with strong committees arranged for seasonal workers to be recalled at the start of the harvest without having to be dispatched from the hall, allowing company seniority to trump union seniority without a formal change in policy. Moreover, by 1972 more workers did have a better understanding of the benefits of union membership, and preferred the arbitrary rulings of the union to the arbitrary rule of the contractors and foremen. Workers complained less; union staffers were optimistic that the worst problems were behind them. The top leaders paid even less attention to the messy details of the hiring halls. They were besieged by other problems.

In March 1972 the White House had opened another front against the union. Nixon's chief counsel for the National Labor Relations Board filed a suit in federal court arguing that the UFW was now under the jurisdiction of the National Labor Relations Act because the union was boycotting nine small Napa Valley wineries where some employees (in the distillery and bottling divisions) were not farm workers. He contended that if any members of the UFW were covered by the NLRA, or if the UFW was trying to organize workers covered by the NLRA, then the entire union should be subject to all the restrictions of national labor law, including the prohibition against secondary boycotts. This was serious. If the NLRB could bring the UFW under its jurisdiction, Nixon could not only make its boycotts illegal but also wreck legal havoc on all of the union's operations.

Chavez denounced the suit as an attempt by the "Republican Party at the highest level . . . to destroy our union." Shortly after, he announced a "boycott of the Republican Party." It would include massive petition and letter-writing campaigns, simultaneous picketing of Republican headquarters in 150 cities, and a threat, four years after Chicago '68, to disrupt the upcoming Republican National Convention in San Diego. This direct attack on the Republicans as Republicans threw the union into semiofficial partnership with the national Democratic Party during a presidential election year and won wide support. Ultimately the Republicans chose to back down. They moved their national convention to Florida (the UFW threat had ratcheted up the Republicans' fears about holding the convention in California) and the NLRB counsel agreed to a privately negotiated settlement in which the UFW simply pledged not to organize nonfarm workers.[33]

Provided they could repel the political assaults directed against them, UFW leaders were generally optimistic about the national situation in 1972. In early March the union won contracts in Florida orchards that supplied oranges to Minute Maid, a subsidiary of Coca-Cola. No significant mobilization of Florida farm workers had been necessary. The UFW had simply parlayed the bad publicity from an NBC documentary on semi-slavery in the Florida fields with Coca-Cola's vulnerability to a boycott.[34] With an increased share of agribusiness dominated by conglomerates that owned other boycottable products, perhaps the union could extend its power throughout the country as it had in Florida, avoiding the battles that had frustrated its earlier organizing efforts in Texas.

In the wake of the Florida victory, the UFW announced the resumption of the lettuce boycott. Negotiations that were supposed to result in a transfer of about 200 Salinas vegetable contracts from the Teamsters to the UFW had broken down the previous fall. Chavez predicted the lettuce boycott would take three years to win. Its kickoff would require pageantry as much as organization. In the spring of '72, Chavez decided to go on another fast.

He made the announcement at a rally in Phoenix: "We are going to fast so that men and women throughout the state understand we are here to build not to destroy."[35] Despite the "we," Chavez alone would fast, and this time there was no confusion and debate among his followers. His lieutenants—LeRoy Chatfield, Marshall Ganz, and Jim Drake—were, as Chatfield said, "seasoned pros . . . [who] knew what would attract support, attention, and the press."[36]

They considered Arizona a propitious place for a major campaign. The state legislature was set to pass a bill that would make harvest strikes virtually impossible, outlaw secondary boycotts, and erect major legal obstacles against primary boycotts of agricultural products. Governor Jack Williams, a conservative Republican who had publicly praised the John Birch Society, supported the bill. There was little local opposition, and no whirlwind campaign could stop Williams and the legislature. But both could be badly embarrassed in the rest of the country, and a campaign against the Arizona law could warn other governors and state legislatures not to try to pass similar legislation. Furthermore, Arizona had large numbers of poor people—especially Chicanos and Native Americans—who did not participate in the political life of the state but whom the union leaders believed they could mobilize against the governor. Finally, Arizona was a short stop on the mostly California lettuce circuit, where a few thousand union *lechugueros* working for InterHarvest, FreshPict, and D'Arrigo, might spark a drive among other farm workers in the state.

On May 11, 1972, Governor Williams signed the Arizona bill less than an hour after the legislature passed it. At the same moment, Cesar Chavez began his fast in Phoenix. Most of the union's heavy hitters were already in town, and they quickly divided up the necessary tasks. Chatfield worked with Chavez on the logistics of the fast. Ganz organized a national campaign of lettuce boycott pledges, and arranged for big-name politicians and celebrities to come to Phoenix. Dolores Huerta and Richard Chavez moved throughout the state talking to students and community groups. Manuel Chavez went to San Luis, where the cantaloupe season was about to begin, to see what he could do to launch a melon strike. Jim Drake headed up a simultaneous campaign to register voters and to collect petitions to recall the governor.[37]

In the biggest Phoenix barrio the union took over a community center, where Chavez rested in a small air-conditioned room to the side of the main hall. The nightly Masses, the supporters with their home-made crosses and banners, the comings and goings of VIPs, all were smoothly directed by the UFW's "seasoned pros."

"As Chavez is growing weaker, we are growing stronger," Chris Hartmire told the crowd one night after Mass. Coretta Scott King visited and announced: "I will go back to Atlanta and encourage black people and all people to boycott lettuce." George McGovern, who had already received the union's endorsement in his campaign for president, met with Chavez and described him afterward as "a man who, in the biblical phrase, has been anointed to bring good news to the poor."[38]

Twenty days into the fast, Cesar was moved to a nearby hospital. His doctors said he was endangering his health and publicly urged him to take some substantial nourishment. On June 4, the twenty-fourth day of the fast and the fourth anniversary of the assassination of Robert Kennedy, Chavez took food for the first time at a special memorial Mass in honor of the late senator. People gathered in the banquet room of one of Phoenix's better hotels for the Mass. Robert Kennedy's oldest son, Joe, was a featured speaker. A representative from American Federation of State, County, and Municipal Employees presented the union with a check for $46,000. Paul Schrade of the United Auto Workers, who had been wounded in LA when Robert Kennedy was assassinated, was introduced. Midway through the program, an ambulance arrived bearing Chavez. His appearance was a surprise. The crowd hushed as he made his way to the front of the room, dressed in a white Nehru jacket and flanked by his flamboyant doctor, Jerome Lackner, and Joan Baez. Baez sang several songs during the Mass and sat next to Chavez during Communion. Chavez broke the bread, gave a piece to Baez, took a piece himself, and managed a wane smile. Soon he was back in the ambulance, returning to the hospital.[39]

It was all a great success. Although Chavez was too weak to talk, a written statement was read to the crowd. The conclusion read: "So long as we are willing to sacrifice for that cause, so long as we persist in nonviolence and work to spread the message of our struggle, then millions of people around the world will respond from their hearts, will support our efforts, and in the end we will overcome. *Sí se puede.*"[40] Those last three words had recently become the union's new slogan. Most people attributed them to Dolores Huerta. While trying to get the Phoenix campaign started, she had heard so many people tell her, *No se puede, no se puede,*—it can't be done, it can't be done—that she formulated a standard answer: *Sí se puede.* The slogan quickly became popular in the Chicano community where it remains an exclamation of encouragement to people who are about to undertake a difficult task, so popular that it became part of Barack Obama's campaign for the presidency as "Yes we can."

The UFW was able to make this contribution to the national culture partly because it had a well-established mechanism, and genius, for publicity, but also because it had achieved so much in the wilds of Arizona. It publicized the new lettuce boycott; it registered more than 100,000 voters and got nearly 150,000 people to sign a recall petition, which set the stage for the subsequent emergence of a small measure of Chicano political power in the state. Although the campaign did not win any new UFW contracts, it did reach down to some Arizona farm workers. A quick cantaloupe strike organized by Manuel Chavez was strong enough to force the growers to raise their piece rates in order to get their melons picked.

The biggest payoff came at the Democratic National Convention in Miami in July. Delegates put the lettuce boycott in the party platform, and the chairman of the Illinois delegation, delivering the votes that clinched the nomination for McGovern, declared that "the great State of Illinois has just proudly joined the campaign to ban lettuce." He later told a newsman, "Frankly, I don't know a damn thing about it."[41] No matter. When Ted Kennedy opened his prime-time TV speech on the final night with the salutation "Fellow lettuce boycotters!" the conventioneers cheered, and support for the UFW had become an identifying emblem of the nation's liberal Democrats.

While the UFW was pleased by the outcome of the convention, George Meany was displeased. The AFL–CIO had been on the opposite side of the struggle for the nomination, supporting its old friend Hubert Humphrey. Meany was not only upset about the McGovern victory; he was outraged at the changes in the Democratic Party rules that guaranteed that a certain percentage of delegates to the convention would be women and minorities. He had opposed just such quotas in the construction unions; viewing them in combination with McGovern's opposition to the Vietnam War (which many labor officials still supported), Meany concluded that the Democratic Party had been taken over by the radical left.[42] For the first and only time in its history, the national governing board of the AFL–CIO refused to endorse the Democratic candidate for president. Richard Nixon, with his long antiunion record, thus got open entry to the white male union members who would eventually be called Reagan Democrats. If the liberal dream of political realignment received its first mortal blow at the 1964 convention when Walter Reuther engineered the betrayal of the Mississippi Freedom Democrats, Meany's 1972 attack on McGovern was the coup de grâce. Realignment had depended on a liberal-labor alliance that would force the conservatives out of the Democratic Party. But when the liberals took over the machinery of the Democratic Party, big labor dropped out.

The UFW was still little labor, though, and, as an independent affiliate of the AFL-CIO, it was free to endorse whomever it wanted. And the UFW was not alone in its endorsement of the doomed McGovern. Led by the UAW, about half of the AFL-CIO affiliates held to tradition in supporting the Democrat. Meany, a master of rewarding friends and punishing enemies, had one more reason to be wary of Chavez and his farm worker union. Was it a union at all, Meany asked Kircher, or was it just an extension of the troublesome radical movement that was damaging the country?

Chavez was an expert at massaging differences within his boycott coalition and managed to maintain good relations with most AFL-CIO officials, Democratic Party pros, and McGovern enthusiasts. He had earned their respect: ever since the California primary in 1968, the farm workers had demonstrated a consistent ability to deliver the goods in registration campaigns and on Election Day—and nothing except money is more important to all political party operatives and most labor officials. Also, Chavez's consistent opposition to La Raza Unida, the independent third-party effort pushed by large numbers of Chicano activists, endeared him to the Democratic professionals on both sides of the McGovern-Meany dispute. Even though his attack on La Raza Unida caused considerable friction with other Chicano leaders, Chavez remained the symbolic godfather of the overall Chicano movement. He had earned that mantle in the 1966 spring pilgrimage, and he was too good a politician to lose it.

Chavez's boycott coalition in 1972 may not have been what it once was, but in that election year he was still able to call on it to support the union in its most severe test so far: Proposition 22. Prop 22 was a statewide ballot initiative sponsored by the California Farm Bureau that would prohibit secondary boycotts, delay harvest strikes for sixty days, and effectively disenfranchise seasonal workers in all farm worker elections. When the petition earned enough signatures to qualify for the November ballot, UFW leaders decided to throw all their energy into defeating it.

AFL-CIO officials strongly supported their efforts. Even the Teamsters, who had endorsed Nixon and whose intentions in the fields were still murky, opposed the grower-sponsored proposition. Chavez assigned LeRoy Chatfield to direct the campaign and summoned hundreds of lettuce boycotters from their posts around the country to work full-time to defeat the proposition. There were forty campaign committees, each of which was responsible for a specific area of the state and reported to Chatfield daily. Chatfield demanded discipline and sacrifice. Using a technique that Marcos Muñoz had developed in Boston, he encouraged volunteers to become "human billboards." Wearing a "No on 22" sign, they lined up single file at freeway ramps, shopping centers, or busy intersections, spending the entire day in one spot so that commuters would see the same people while heading to work and returning home. At a UFW reunion thirty years later, a former boycotter proudly described how she had breathed car exhaust all day on an LA freeway ramp for the union. It was the California version of barefoot in the snow.

The campaign to defeat Proposition 22 did not depend only on the public self-sacrifices of hundreds of volunteers. As was standard Chavez practice, the union used its ties to high officials in the California Democratic Party to its own advantage. In a series of meetings with California's secretary of state, Jerry Brown, Chatfield presented affidavits from people who testified that they had been tricked into signing the Proposition 22 petitions that had put the issue on the ballot. Brown, as astute a politician as his father, Pat, decided to initiate a suit to disqualify the proposition, and in so doing not only initiated a life-long friendship with the UFW but also put himself in the center of an election campaign in which he wasn't even running and established his liberal credentials within the California Democratic Party. Although the suit did not prevail, it put the growers on the defensive, a position they were never able to overcome. On Election Day Proposition 22 got less than 42 percent of the vote, despite the Nixon landslide. What Jerry Brown had guessed had now been proven true: the UFW was well on its way to being one of the most effective electoral machines in California.

Meanwhile, back on the farm, the UFW had a mixed record. In Salinas, InterHarvest–United Brands was under orders from its CEO, Eli Black, to cooperate with the union, and had ceded an extraordinary degree of control over the work process to the crews, especially the militant piece-rate lettuce crews. The company didn't put up much of a fight either when the union struck InterHarvest in September 1972, the day after the two-year contract expired. The orderly work stoppage resembled a ritualized industrial strike, where the company accepts the shutdown of its facilities while it negotiates a new contract. The company did not try to use strikebreakers, and the three-year contract that resulted from negotiations raised hourly wages by 16 percent. The piece rates did not rise as fast, and the company did manage to win a new clause in the contract that gave it more control over "the quality of the pack."

The success at InterHarvest, the biggest vegetable company in Salinas, blunted the impact of the union's failure to hold two of its other Salinas Valley contracts. Brown & Hill Tomatoes refused to renew its contract and imported scabs to break the ensuing six-week strike. The D'Arrigo management complained that the hiring hall staff was inexperienced and difficult to work with, and Andrew D'Arrigo told *The Packer*, one of the main trade publications, "The disagreement is over whether the workers have a right to stop work any time they want to . . . It's over who controls the quality of the package, them or us."[43] D'Arrigo concluded that it was impossible for his company "to live" with a UFW contract, and also refused to renew. His complaint, although exaggerated, had validity: companies with union contracts faced stiff competition from nonunion growers, who paid less to produce a product over which they had more control and which they could sell for a higher price. The problem of nonunion competition would recur throughout UFW history and would figure large in the union's final collapse, but at this time it received little notice in La Paz.

The union suffered an even greater jolt in 1972 at Schenley. The first company to have a union contract—it had signed during the Easter pilgrimage in 1966—Schenley had been a San Joaquin Valley union stronghold. Its workers earned top wages, had successfully fought for better working conditions in the fields, and were covered by the union medical plan. Turnover was limited, and the few dispatches every season were prized possessions. The ranch committee had more independent power than any other in the valley, and large numbers of people voluntarily attended union meetings, where they debated matters of substance. No union official messed with Schenley's long-established seniority list, and because the 500 Schenley workers (at peak season) were mostly local residents, they were likely to have their dues paid up. In the Central Valley, Schenley shone as the UFW's jewel.

In February 1971, Buttes Gas & Oil took over the entire 5,000-acre Schenley operation. It changed the name to White River Farms and brought several experimental harvesting machines into the fields—awkward contraptions that damaged the vines as they moved through the vineyards but, if perfected, threatened to replace the majority of grape pickers. Conglomerates new to agriculture often were the first to try out such machinery. They had the necessary capital. S.S. Pierce, the corporate owners of Pic-N-Pac, tried to use machines to pick strawberries, a colossal failure which contributed to its decision to quit the strawberry business in 1972.[44] Mechanical wine grape harvesters ultimately were more successful, and their experimental use in the Buttes' vineyards convinced workers that the company intended to get rid of them and the union.

The UFW contract that Buttes inherited expired in June 1972, and negotiations broke down soon after the harvest began in late August. The company announced it would harvest without a contract; the workers voted to strike, and every worker at White River Farms left the fields.

In this high-stakes face-off, both sides called on their allies. The workers had the active support of union militants from nearby ranches, as well as what it considered its trump card: the ability to mobilize a campaign in the cities to boycott Schenley liquors. The company had the active support of the Nisei Farmers League, Japanese fruit tree growers near Fresno who were in the midst of defending themselves from a UFW organizing campaign and figured that helping to defeat the union elsewhere was the best way to get it off their own backs. Buttes also found a number of labor contractors who were eager to bring in strike breaking workers. In the communities, the UFW had no greater antagonists than these labor contractors, whom the union hiring halls had put out of business. The contractors, for their part, had little trouble finding willing scabs. Some were newcomers who had been recruited from the border and initially did not know what they were doing. But others knew the union well. Migrants from Texas and Mexico who had lost out to local Mexican Americans at other farms in the hiring hall chaos constituted one set of potential strikebreakers. Filipinos were another, as were undocumented workers, who had been scapegoated by the union since 1965.

The policy of keeping the undocumented out of the union was being actively enforced in the Central Valley as the strike began. A year earlier, La Paz had sent a task force through the valley to find people without papers who were working under UFW contracts and to replace them with legal union loyalists.[45] Those who had been chucked out of the union had little moral compunction about breaking a UFW strike.

Two days into the strike, a pickup truck driven by the brother-in-law of a scab-herding contractor rammed through a picket line and hit a striker, Maria Arévalo. She was not seriously injured, but the warning was clear: this would not be a polite fight. Strikers massed in front of the company fields, ignoring a temporary restraining order that had set limits on picketers. Buttes had five major ranches stretching from Delano, in Kern County, to Poplar, in Tulare County, and initially the various law enforcement agencies did not rush to enforce the TRO against hundreds of angry strikers. But sheriff's deputies and police did escort some strikebreakers into the fields, and the harvest was restarted on a reduced scale.

Within a week the Tulare County sheriffs had assigned more than eighty deputies to the strike and had begun selectively to enforce the restraining order. Richard Chavez and Dolores Huerta, working with the ranch committee and Al Rojas, director of the Poplar field office, developed a two-pronged strategy. Solidarity was the first prong. Pressuring the INS to arrest and deport undocumented workers was the second.

On several scheduled days, hundreds of workers from other union ranches took the day off and came to the picket lines. Together, they violated the TRO and subsequent court injunction and did what they could to intimidate scabs as they went to work. Chavez, preoccupied with Proposition 22, never visited the picket lines, but he did formally request the Fresno County district attorney to investigate the employment of "illegal aliens" at the struck farm.[46] Union leaders also convinced one of their strongest friends in Congress, Phil Burton of San Francisco, a Democrat, to demand that the INS arrest the strikebreaking illegals. Interviewed from jail after her arrest early in the strike, Huerta pointed her finger at the Tulare County sheriff: "The deputies are escorting illegal aliens into the fields to help break our strike." Leaving jail after one of his arrests later in the strike, Richard Chavez told a local reporter, "We have sent delegations to the U.S. Border Patrol office and called it every day. We ask over and over for them to arrest these people we know are illegal aliens. Every time we go down to the office, we get thrown out." The Tulare newspaper quoted picketers denouncing "illegals" or "wetbacks" and reported on strikers' attempts to make citizens' arrests of the undocumented.[47]

Undocumented workers helped break the strike, but the scab harvest did not depend on them—there were enough documented scabs. Two and a half weeks into the strike, an INS roadblock stopped six buses and several cars carrying scabs to a Buttes ranch, and immigration officers went through the buses checking papers. The officers arrested sixty-eight people, leaving a couple hundred more who had their papers in order to continue on into the struck fields. The percentage of undocumented scabs turned out to be no higher, and probably considerably lower, than the percentage of undocumented in the general farm worker population.

The two sides collided that day when the scab buses reached a few hundred massed pickets, and police arrested seventy-five unionists in the confrontation. At the Delano Ranch, some sixty-five more were arrested, and by the end of the week about 250 UFW strikers and supporters were in jail for violating the TRO, with bail set as high as $500 each. With so many strikers in jail, the company managed to get 350 strikebreakers into the fields.

The strikers regrouped. On Monday, October 2, about 1,000 people returned to the Poplar ranch and then traveled in car caravans from one ranch to another, stopping to harass any strikebreakers they found. The next day, 400 people massed at the Delano ranch, overwhelming and outflanking the local police. Strikers broke the windows of a couple of police cars that had been left unattended; others used grape stakes to bash in the windows of one car in which police were sitting. From an out-of-the-way road about seventy-five strikers entered the ranch, Epifanio Camacho among them:

> We went in and were confronted by two security guards, and one of them . . . shot at us. He shot right at a man who was with me. But he was shooting blanks. He just wanted to scare us . . . When the man realized the guard didn't have any bullets, he said, "You, *hijo de la chingada*, come on shoot me right in the chest." And he tore open his shirt, and exposed his chest . . . The rest of us just ran right past him . . . I wasn't even in

front. By the time I arrived where the tractors were . . . the tires were punctured, the trailers busted up, the toilets turned over, everything was all fucked up. Everywhere.[48]

The next time guns were fired, they had real bullets. It was October 7, a Saturday night. Thirty to fifty Anglo men armed with rifles, rocks, and bottles gathered in a lot across from the Poplar UFW office. Ernesto Saldívar was in the office alone. Five men, all carrying rifles, forced their way inside and told him they were giving the union only a few days to leave town. Saldívar locked the hall and hurried to the memorial auditorium, where Al Rojas, Dolores Huerta, and several ranch committees were meeting. When they returned to the hall, it had been ransacked, and they counted forty-five gunshot holes in the inside and outside walls. Some of the Anglos were still there, most quite drunk. Sheriffs dispersed the mob but refused to provide protection for the hall. "If we put a car in front of the union office, every house in the county would want one, too," Undersheriff Lawrence John explained to the *Tulare Advance Register*.[49]

The next afternoon a mob started forming again in front of the UFW office. Rojas called the sheriff's office several times. Nothing. He was inside with his wife, Elena, and a few others, and called Delano for reinforcements. As night fell, someone at the sheriff's office told Rojas that an officer was on the way. "We were thinking any minute the cops were going to come. But they didn't come," Rojas said. "So as it got darker, they started shooting at us. Bullets started coming. I didn't believe they were bullets, but they started hitting the drywall with that thud sound. And then the glass was flying all over."

When the shooting stopped, men rushed into the union office and dragged the black eagle flag and the Mexican flag across the street. Al and Elena Rojas followed the men outside. From across the street, someone threw a bottle. "I heard a really ugly thud," Rojas recalled. "I turned around, and blood was coming down Elena's head and face." The police still weren't there, but Dolores Huerta had arrived with a dozen others from Delano. More unionists came, and together they confronted the mostly drunk men across the street. Finally the sheriff's deputies came but they made no arrests.[50]

By the end of the next week the harvest was over. Buttes had lost more than $1 million in what should have been a $3 million harvest. But its spokesman declared that the company would never return to the bargaining table. What had been the union's oldest and best contract in the Central Valley was lost.

Chavez announced that a Buttes boycott would soon begin, and union activists working on the election folded the strike into their arguments against Proposition 22. But what happened at White River Farms was mostly forgotten, as the euphoria that followed Proposition 22's defeat washed out the memory of the union's earlier debacle in the fields, at least among the staff. In the vineyards, however, many workers couldn't forget that the contractors had found plenty of people willing to break the strike.

There was also a sour, more private, note in the electoral triumph. LeRoy Chatfield had spent the last several days of the campaign with Chavez. "He was really uptight," Chatfield told the reporter Ron Taylor. "He was pacing the floor, and asking if we were doing everything we could. I'd never seen him so worried. We didn't know what to do with him, how to make the best use of him. We put him on the human billboard for a while." The night before the election, Chatfield recounted twenty-four years later, Chavez's anxiety was at its height. He told Chatfield, "If we lose, you have to take the blame." Chatfield was astonished. Chavez's slogan had always been "There is no defeat . . . just another opportunity." But now Chavez had a position to defend. If the union lost, it could no longer be half laughed off as an opportunity for organizing. Blame would have to be deflected from him, the leader.[51]

The union did not lose, so no one had to take the fall. Nor did Chavez's remark destroy his relationship with his "ardent apostle," as Chatfield was characterized by a reporter who covered the Arizona fast.[52] But Chatfield did not forget the remark, and his attitude toward Chavez cooled. Cesar tried to smooth matters over, but "trying to make it up to me made it worse for me," Chatfield said, "because it was no more real than what had happened [on election eve] . . . it didn't erase [it]."[53] A little more than a year later Chatfield left the UFW. Personal reasons, he said. Chavez was still the greatest man he had ever met, a true saint for farm workers. But with one less apostle.

22

"Fighting for Our Lives"

April '72 to September '73

The 1973 table grape strike was a crushing defeat for the UFW. The union was pushed out of its dominant position in the table grape industry, never to return. Thousands of grape workers, people the union had failed to win over during the years it had them under contract, crossed its picket lines. Those who had been the victims of the hiring hall and back dues fiascos, who had been fined for not coming to meetings, who had been blamed for failed strikes, and kicked out or kept out of the union for lack of documents had their moment of revenge. As the bountiful scab harvest came in, the union reaped what it had sown.

But if a giant defeats a weaker opponent it seems wrong to attribute the defeat to the weaker party's mistakes, even its big ones. In 1973, the growers were formidable. They had the support of the Nixon administration in Washington and the Reagan administration in Sacramento. They influenced city and county governments, and the courts. They could count on the loyalty of local labor contractors, supervisors, and top foremen and their families. Isn't it, then, misleading to stress the UFW's errors? Against such power can the union's contemptuous attitudes, moral lapses, and tactical failures count for much?

But agribusiness was not omnipotent, nor the UFW powerless. The union had won the hearts of liberals throughout the country, as well as the institutional backing of the Democratic Party and AFL-CIO. In the fields, it held the allegiance of hundreds of *los huesos colorados* in the grape industry and thousands more who sided with the union but weren't hard-core. It embodied the hopes of farm workers in California and the nation, as well as many in Mexico, who were in a mood to fight for a new distribution of power between workers and their employers. Those sentiments were felt on the ground in 1973, when grape workers loyal to the UFW turned their failed strike into a small rebellion against the civilian and police powers of the Central Valley. The strike was lost, but the rebellion inspired an extended struggle that, a year and a half later, won the most labor-friendly law in U.S. history, the California Agricultural Labor Relations Act.

All things considered, the battle in the vineyards was not an unfair fight, and the UFW's mistakes were not insignificant in the overall balance of forces. Worse, the UFW leaders, unchallenged by democratic debate, rarely admitted their faults, either to themselves or their supporters. In 1973, and throughout their history, they always explained away the union's defeats. The Republicans came to power. The national climate turned against unions. We were swamped by illegal immigrants. That litany, though partly legitimate, obscured the truth that haunted the UFW throughout its history and, having been ignored, spelled its doom: that ultimately a union's power depends on the support of the workers.

Nevertheless, it is possible that the growers might not have won the table grape strike without the intervention of the Teamsters. By 1973, the workers were getting used to some of the UFW's new rules, and the worst hiring hall practices finally were being reconsidered. The UFW and the growers might have worked out an accommodation if the growers had not been able to get help from the biggest and richest union in the country— if the only option for the workers had been no union or a company union. The Teamsters, often comical and sometimes deadly, were indispensable allies. But the Teamsters could not compete with the UFW without raising wages and benefits, thereby making themselves into a passable version of a real union in the fields. Starting in the Coachella vineyards, the UFW and Teamsters signed a series of contracts that leapfrogged each other and produced a dramatic jump in wages and conditions for all California farm workers. The growers could win only by bringing in the Teamsters; the Teamsters could compete with the UFW only by signing good contracts; and, thus, until the UFW-Teamster Pact of 1977, the growers could only win by losing.

An early warning came from below. In April 1972, about a year before the Coachella table grape contracts were set to expire, a group of grape workers went to La Paz for a meeting. Epifanio Camacho was among them. It was April 7, his Saint's Day, a reason why he remembers the incident so well. After the meeting Camacho met privately with Chavez and Dolores Huerta. Camacho spoke bluntly: The growers were not going to re-sign, he said. The union had to prepare people for a fight. Huerta was silent, but Chavez told Camacho he was wrong. In a few months the InterHarvest contract was going to run out, and he would call the owner in New York and renew the contract over the phone. The new contracts in the grapes would be locked up before the old contracts expired.[1]

Strange—why would Chavez answer a warning about the grape contracts with a boast about the UFW's biggest vegetable contract? Camacho could have got the particulars wrong. But maybe not. He had caught Chavez at a moment of high confidence. Cesar had just returned from New York, where he had been an honored guest at a seder at the home of Eli Black, the United Brands/InterHarvest CEO, and had also read from the Torah at Black's upscale Upper West Side temple. Black considered the Chavez reading a public relations triumph: Cesar's friendship was further proof that Black could run the old United Fruit Company in a manner both humane and profitable.[2] Chavez knew how valuable he was to Black. And he was nearly right about the InterHarvest contract: it took more than a phone call to renew, but not much more.

Warning signs about the table grapes continued to appear. In midsummer 1972, the Bishops Committee relayed an offer from the Teamsters: if the UFW would leave the vegetables, the Teamsters would let them have the grapes. "Let us have the grapes?" wondered Jerry Cohen. The UFW already had the grapes. It must be a threat—a threat Chavez chose to ignore. Then, in September 1972, Chavez was again in New York, this time with Marshall Ganz and Anna Puharich, for discussions about the new InterHarvest deal. Afterward, Eli Black and Ganz went to Yom Kippur services. Later there was a party at Black's home; Black called Cesar into his study. He had an offer to pass along from Richard Nixon. If Chavez and the UFW would endorse Nixon for reelection, Nixon would get the Teamsters out of the fields.[3] Danton, who told his fellow French revolutionaries that what was required of them was "audacity, audacity, and more audacity," would have been one "audacity" short in describing Richard Nixon. But if a professional anti-Communist could open the door to China, as Nixon had done with his February 1972 trip, why couldn't that same longtime ally of California agribusiness make a pact with Cesar Chavez?

Chavez presented the offer to the Executive Board, where it was soundly rejected. The UFW's commitment to McGovern and liberals and Democrats was as much a matter of principle as of political necessity. Nevertheless, the unusual offer had its ominous side. In 1972 the Teamsters were barely in the fields. They had the Bud Antle contract and a few dozen other Salinas Valley vegetable contracts, which they weren't bothering to enforce. If Nixon could offer to get the Teamsters out of the fields, couldn't he also send them back in?

Nixon already had a thick relationship with Frank Fitzsimmons, the Teamsters president, who was using his Nixon connection to consolidate his position atop his nearly ungovernable union. Jimmy Hoffa had picked Fitzsimmons to take his place while he was off in jail because Hoffa felt that Fitz was too ineffectual to prevent him from running the union from his cell and then reclaiming his presidency once he got out. But Fitzsimmons, like so many marionettes before and since, began to pull some of his own strings. He did Nixon some favors. He stayed on the Pay Board and Price Commission after other labor leaders had quit in protest. His Teamsters

Mario Bustamante, Salinas, 1979.

Aristeo Zambrano with daughter
Sylvia and nephew Julio Cesar
Maravilla, Salinas, 1982.

Hermilo Mojica with daughter Ambar, Salinas, 1982.

Cesar Chavez and Cleofas Guzman, Salinas, 1979.

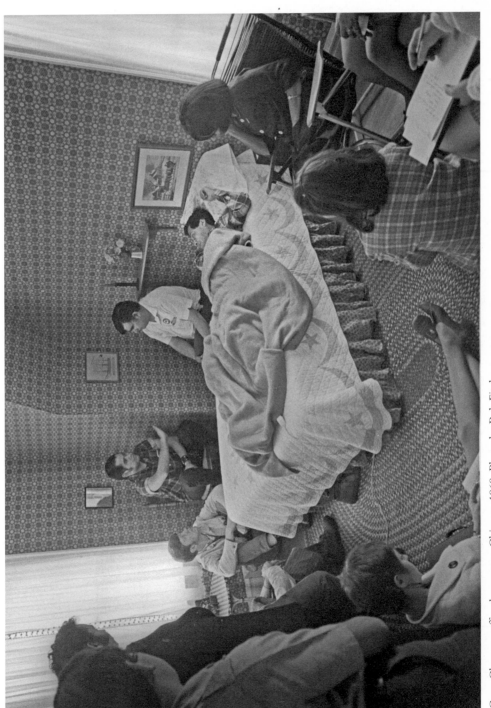

Cesar Chavez, staff and reporters, Chicago, 1969. Photo by Bob Fitch.

Jessica Govea, Salinas, 1970.
Photo by Doug Foster.

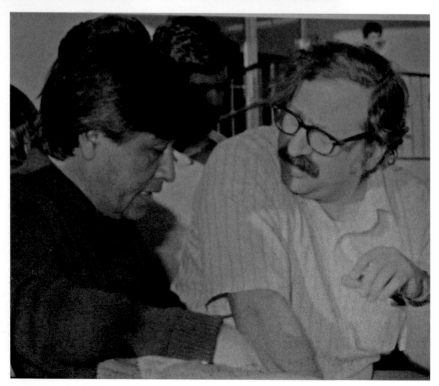

Cesar Chavez and Marshall Ganz, Imperial Valley, 1979. Photo courtesy of Imperial
County Historical Society.

Eliseo Medina, La Paz, 1976.

Gilbert Padilla, La Paz, 1976.

Manuel Chavez, Salinas, 1970. Photo by Hub Segur.

Mario Bustamante and
Gretchen Laue, Gilroy, 1981.

Richard Chavez with a box of union label grapes, Coachella, 1970. Photo by Bob Fitch.

Jerry Cohen, Salinas, 1979. Photo by Doug Foster.

Dolores Huerta, Salinas, 1970. Photo by Bob Fitch.

were the only international union to support Nixon openly in 1972. In return Nixon granted Fitz some easy courtesies. His Justice Department dropped a fraud prosecution against Fitzsimmons's son and denied a request from the FBI to put in wiretaps for an investigation of the misuse of Teamsters pension funds. Nixon invited Fitz to White House dinners, flew him around in Air Force One, and gave him small gifts bearing the presidential seal, which Fitzsimmons proudly showed to friends. Finally, the president bestowed the ultimate favor: he pardoned Hoffa but attached a rider requiring him to stay out of Teamster politics, thus barring him from taking back the presidency for ten years.[4] Nixon got a million dollars in cash for the rider.[5] Then, after the money helped Nixon get reelected in 1972, Fitzsimmons agreed to help Nixon and agribusiness destroy the UFW.

Fitzsimmons could see no downside. He would not only cement his relationship with the president but also shore up his position in his own organization. Bill Grami, the shrewd, double-talking Western Conference organizer who had been in charge of the farm worker effort in Salinas, had never given up his ambitions in the fields. He would be delighted by Fitzsimmons's decision and would move into action quickly, a serious consideration inside the Teamsters behemoth, where the president's orders were often ignored or delayed. Moreover, Hoffa had let it be known that the Teamsters never should have backed out of the fight with Chavez. Fitzsimmons would take that particular arrow out of Hoffa's quiver and, he hoped, win the loyalty of Teamsters officials who openly agreed with Hoffa.

This colossal backroom deal (engineered by Charles Colson, the Nixon hatchet man who became a born-again Christian as he was about to be convicted of his Watergate crimes) was put on public display at the American Farm Bureau Federation's annual convention in Los Angeles in December 1972. Fitzsimmons was the keynote speaker. He chided the conventioneers for their "nineteenth-century attitudes" toward labor, attacked the UFW as a "revolutionary movement that is perpetrating a fraud on the American public," and called on the Farm Bureau to join the Teamsters in "an alliance . . . an accommodation, which will work for the benefit of your organization and mine."[6] It was left to Grami to drop the other shoe, or in this case the whole rest of the wardrobe. Two days after the convention Grami announced that the Western Conference of Teamsters had formed its own Agricultural Workers Organizing Committee. Within a month the committee had renegotiated the Teamsters unexpired 1970 lettuce contracts and raised wages to $2.30 per hour, five cents more than the InterHarvest contract, with a comparable raise for the piece-rate workers.[7] The contract included unemployment insurance, health insurance, a seniority clause, and grievance procedures. It did not establish a hiring hall, leaving the growers free to hire through contractors, and provided no mechanism for enforcing the grievance and seniority clauses. Grami's intention was transparent: to fight for the allegiance of California farm workers by matching or bettering the wages and benefits won by the UFW, while maintaining friendly relations with the employers by giving them a relatively free hand in hiring, firing, and control over production.

Grami drew on his multi-million-dollar budget to buy his way out of one of his biggest problems. Reversing Teamster tradition, he hired a staff of bilingual Chicanos, recent Salinas Valley high school graduates, who earned from $225 to $350 a week, in addition to their loosely supervised expense accounts.[8] Eventually he named David Castro, a Teamster official from Hayward, as secretary-treasurer of the new Teamsters farm worker Local 73. Grami was godfather to one of Castro's children, and he predicted that Castro would become "the Teamsters' answer to Cesar Chavez."[9] Grami's attempt to hire his way into the Chicano movement never went far. Caught between their high-paying jobs and their ethnic loyalties, the new hirees frequently rebelled. Grami did not completely trust them anyway and had saved the most important organizing jobs for old-time Teamsters operatives. He appointed Ralph Cotner, a veteran organizer-enforcer, to head the effort in the Coachella vineyards. Cotner didn't give a damn about Chicano nationalism and figured he could get the grape contracts away from Chavez through a combination of collusion with the bosses, high wages, and terror.

As evidence of the Teamsters' intentions piled up, Chavez continued to believe that they would stay out of the vineyards. As late as March 1973, Chavez was incredulous when he got a phone call from the Coachella field office director, Ray Huerta, saying that the Teamsters were in the vineyards. "One of the workers came in and told me there were Teamsters out there signing up the workers," recalled Huerta.

> I said okay and went and checked it out. Of course, nobody would tell me nothing, but I found out that they were there. I immediately went and called Cesar and told him. He said it was bullshit and that I didn't know what I was talking about. I said: "I'm telling you, that's what I heard." So he sent out Barbara Macri and Frank Ortiz [to investigate] . . . And they went back and said I was chasing ghosts. And Cesar called me and told me I was chasing ghosts. Three days later I called Cesar and told him the ghosts had just opened an office in Indio. He said he didn't believe it. And then he told me to go shut it down.[10]

By the time formal negotiations between the UFW and the Coachella growers began in late March, 1973, most of them already had met secretly with Cotner and decided to throw in their lot with the Teamsters. When it became clear to UFW leaders that their talks were going nowhere, they did not panic. They had beaten the Teamsters at DiGiorgio and Schenley and fought them to a standstill in Salinas; they figured that a combination of strikes and boycotts could do it again. But could they? Their legitimacy strikes in Coachella in '68 and '69 had not significantly interrupted production. Would a 1973 strike be any different? Would it at least be strong enough to build enthusiasm for a new boycott?

A first task for the UFW was to establish that it was the choice of the workers. Chavez once again called on the reliable Monsignor George Higgins, who had made sure that the UFW won the InterHarvest card-check election in 1970. Five days before the contracts were due to expire, UFW staff took Higgins and his team of eighteen, including the California Democratic congressmen George Brown, Edward Roybal, and Phil Burton, along with Catholic, Protestant, and Jewish clergy, to the fields. They asked the workers to mark their preferences on a printed ballot, and then announced the results at a press conference: UFW, 795; Teamsters, 80; No Union, 78. Higgins presented a written statement to reporters: "It is clear to us that the vast majority of farm workers in the Coachella Valley want to be represented by Cesar Chavez and the UFW and resent the intrusion of the Teamsters."[11]

There is no evidence that workers were coerced into signing the cards or that, on this occasion, the cards were incorrectly counted. The UFW staff had, however, taken the Higgins team only to fields where the UFW was popular, and, according to Chris Hartmire, Higgins knew it:

> The Bishops Committee, that is to say the official Catholic Church, became convinced that the UFW represented righteousness in the early 1970s in Salinas. They decided to take sides when they saw in Salinas that the Teamsters were a company union for the bosses. So they went to Coachella in the early spring of 1973 so committed, with Higgins as their leader. And they participated in a phony election. An election that was just a straw vote by workers in the fields carefully chosen by the UFW. It was in no way a fair election. And the Bishops knew it. And then that election was used to show the world that the UFW had the support of the vast majority of the workers.[12]

It did not have that support, as the strike would soon demonstrate. But that brute fact never got out to the rest of the country. In the wake of the strike, the UFW helped make a movie about it, *Fighting for Our Lives*, that was far more potent than the Higgins survey. The movie, nominated for an Academy Award in 1975 and used by the UFW to raise money and promote the follow-up grape boycott, is not a fraud. It was constructed out of real events, and conveyed authentic emotions. But like Higgins's survey, it is selective. And like the survey results, it was designed to advance an unsupportable conclusion: that the UFW had the overwhelming support of grape workers.

The film could not begin to take the proper measure of the situation. The day the UFW contract expired, the Teamsters immediately signed up all but two of the growers to the kind of contract that had been secretly discussed in January. It raised wages to $2.30 an hour, added thirty cents a box as incentive pay, and dispensed with a hiring hall. When the two remaining companies, Freedman and Larsen, signed with the UFW several hours later, their contracts paid workers ten cents more than the Teamster contracts.[13] Leapfrogging was under way: wages in the vineyards were now more than twice what they had been at the end of the Bracero Program. The Freedman contract became a problem, however. Over the three previous years, many local workers who strongly supported the UFW had managed to get dispatches to work at Freedman, where the owner, Lionel Steinberg, was friendly toward the UFW. Thus, about 700 of the most committed unionists were removed from active participation on the picket lines, as they continued working under the new contract. Since the peak-season labor force was about 5,000 workers, that meant that about one-seventh of the grape pickers in the valley, self-selected UFW loyalists, would be forced to cheer from the sidelines.

This caused a quandary. When the old contract expired, the harvest, delayed by cool weather, was still a month and a half away. Yet there was still preharvest thinning to finish up, and the UFW leaders did not want to let the Teamsters contracts go into effect without a fight. With the most dedicated members in the fields thinning Freedman's vines, who would do the fighting?

Lechuguero Hermilo Mojica, the bracero skip with a Mexican revolutionary education and background, volunteered for the job. He was not alone. About 150 vegetable workers—men and women, primarily lettuce, celery, and broccoli harvesters—made the 450-mile journey from Salinas to Coachella on Sunday, April 15, the day before the strike began. Mojica and his fellow vegetable workers, most of whom had never picked a grape in their lives, came to Coachella as a straightforward act of solidarity. Their union was under attack. They knew their antagonists. The growers had different names, but they were growers. The Teamsters were the same hacks and goons who were doing the ranchers' dirty work back home in Salinas. Along with their serious conversations, these spirited young men and women joked, laughed, and flirted as their caravan made the ten-hour journey. They called themselves La Division Del Norte, after Pancho Villa's troops in the Mexican Revolution, and figured they were going to link up with the contemporary California version of Zapata's Division of the South.

Mojica and Robert Garcia, the lettuce foreman who had joined the UFW during the 1970 strike, were in one of the lead cars. They were now full-time staffers for the union on various special assignments. Mojica made $25 a week, and the union also paid the rent and utilities on his house in Salinas, where his wife and three-year-old child lived. His wife also received $50 a week for expenses, and squeaked by with the help of food stamps. Garcia was the leader of the team, and their assignments, usually emanating from Ganz, combined political persuasion (Garcia was one of the union's good story tellers and Mojica was a convincing polemicist) with a small amount of muscle. They were smart, tough guys, but by no means enforcers. (That job was left to Manuel Chavez and his crew.) When they arrived in Coachella on Sunday afternoon, they were greeted by a small contingent of grape workers—no more than a couple of dozen. Where the hell was the Division of the South?[14]

It didn't exist. On the first day's picket lines there were just a few hundred workers, many of them from Salinas. Of the couple of thousand local people supposedly on strike, only a few dozen picketed over the next few days; the rest were working, thinning grapes.[15]

That first morning the picketers traveled from field to field in a car caravan, stopping to talk to workers wherever they found them. The strikers boldly marched into growers' vineyards, their flags flying, their hearts full of fight. These forays into struck fields are always a mixture of persuasion and compulsion, but on this first day, most of the action was talk. Frank Del Olmo, a Spanish-speaking *Los Angeles Times* reporter, who accompanied the strikers into two fields, wrote that they used a combination of "shouting, pleading, and cajoling." By the end of the day, several crews of thirty to forty workers had joined the strike, while the majority continued to thin the grapes.[16]

The first night of the strike, the *huelga* vandals appeared: arsonists burned down a packing shed and some people with machetes destroyed four acres of grape vines.[17] Barn burning is an ancient weapon in all manner of agricultural disputes. This particular fire was probably partial retaliation for two recent arsons that had destroyed the UFW field office in Calexico and damaged the adobe garage in Delano. The destruction of grape vines, however, is not typical: striking farm workers don't usually destroy the perennial plants that they get paid to plant, prune, thin, and harvest. There was only one other similar attack. When the strike moved north, 600 walnut trees were cut down at a newly struck orchard near Porterville. Although these may have been the acts of enraged strikers, more likely they were carried out by bands of non-farm worker vandals, some operating on their own and at least one crew, according to Pablo Espinoza, under the direction of Manuel Chavez. Espinoza, then head of the field office in Lamont, remembers that Manuel's band amounted to no more than a handful of adolescents from Mexicali who knew nothing about the strike. One of them told Espinoza that Manuel had sent them "to help out." Espinoza wanted none of that kind of help, checked them into a motel, and ignored them until they finally left.[18]

The Teamsters, too, did not favor vandalism. They preferred open threats of violence and direct physical force. That first day in Coachella, "somebody saw a pickup coming, with two Teamsters in it," Mojica remembered.

> The one who was driving was also holding a gun, so we ran. There was sand all around, only sand, so they must have brought some rocks with them. Wham, the rocks hit. One hit me in the arm, and it hurt, and it was quite a few days before it stopped hurting. Another rock went right by me and hit Alicia Uribe in the face and knocked her to the ground. She was a young woman who had come with us from Salinas. She had a lot of energy and enthusiasm. She had been hit just below the eye, and we were worried that she might lose it.[19]

On the second day of the strike, a local judge issued a temporary restraining order, severely limiting picket line activity. Jerry Cohen had seen this kind of TRO in Salinas and explained to Chavez that it provided the union with a political opportunity. The judge had granted the TRO without giving the UFW a chance to comment, and therefore it was unconstitutional (independent of its overbroad limitations on peaceful picketing). In California state law at the time, when First Amendment rights were at issue, grieved parties had a right to challenge such an order by ignoring it, rather than by appealing to a higher court. Cohen assured Chavez that those arrested for violating the TRO would eventually have all charges dismissed. The judge had provided the union with a platform on which to stage a no-cost civil disobedience campaign.

By the end of the week there had been 311 arrests for violating the order. Initially people were arrested on the picket lines, taken to jail, booked, and released the same day or the next morning. By the end of the week, folks were being arrested and booked in the fields, and never taken to jail. Many people, assured that all the charges would be dropped, were arrested more than once. The *Riverside Press-Enterprise* reported that some were arrested four times between Tuesday and Friday.[20] Many of those arrested were part of the Division of the North: Robert Garcia and the women from the Salinas FreshPict broccoli crew were among the first to go, enthusiastically chanting and singing as they entered the paddy wagon. By Friday, Cohen had convinced the judge of his mistake, all the charges against those arrested were dropped, and another hearing was held with UFW lawyers present, which resulted in a more liberal court order that allowed unlimited numbers of strikers to picket peacefully.

Winston Churchill once remarked that there is nothing so exhilarating as being shot without effect. The same is true, in a minor key, of being arrested without effect. More than a hundred strikers (probably about half of those on the picket line) were willing to put themselves in the hands of the police and had a glorious time in what was ordinarily a scary situation. People tore up the seats and dismantled the windows of the vehicles that took them to jail. They refused to unclench their fists so they could be fingerprinted and booked. They forgot all their English when being questioned by non-Spanish-speaking policemen. They identified themselves in ridiculous ways ("My name is Guadalajara Jalisco"), to the delight of their fellow prisoners and to the confusion of the booking officers, who knew they were being made fools of but didn't understand how. Those arrested that first week were not able to stop the thinning of the grapes, but they were not depressed. Many were looking forward to what promised to be a bigger fight in the coming harvest.[21]

The short period during which picketers were able to march into the fields and outnumber scabs, security guards, and Teamsters functionaries came to an end by the third day. Thirty "Allen Rifles," white security guards who had been hired by Nisei farmers near Fresno in earlier UFW strikes and were sometimes called the "Nisei Guard," appeared on the picket line carrying guns. But the serious muscle came from the Teamsters, who were determined not to be outnumbered. They proposed to protect the strikebreakers with what they called guards. The Chavistas called them goons. Both sides called the flatbed that carried some of them from picket line to picket line "the garbage truck." Some were house movers from a Los Angeles Teamsters local who were on strike. Others were freelance enforcers. Most of them were big; a few were giants, well over 300 pounds. They were paid $67 a day for their services, and some were proud to be considered professionals of violence. Their typical weapons were clubs, chains, baseball bats, ice picks, and tire irons. A few packed guns. Eventually, more than 300 were sent to the Coachella Valley, which meant that at times there were as many goons as strikers. They remained in Coachella (with a few forays up into Lamont) for two and half months. They didn't kill anyone, as their specialty was the bad beating that stopped just this side of homicide.

The goons were perfect for the documentary film crew, and they enthusiastically played their parts. They mugged for the cameras, intensifying their threats and invectives when press microphones were near. They dramatically stomped on an effigy of Cesar Chavez with a noose around its neck several times so that newspaper photographers could get a good shot. They quickly became a public relations disaster for the Teamsters, and a convenient and effective foil for the UFW.

Chavez did not let the theatrical opportunity pass. He asked Hartmire to organize a group of clergymen who would be willing to be arrested for violating the TRO. The day after the goons arrived, the scene was all blocked out and ready to be performed. Making sure that goons, cops, and newsmen followed, a UFW caravan led all the actors to their places in front of a struck field. The goons assumed their positions on one side of the road, screaming, threatening. On the other side of the road, Hartmire led a group of kneeling picketers in prayer. Before he could finish, sheriff's deputies arrested him, and then two other Protestant ministers who took his place, as the goons jeered. It was all caught on film, and prominently featured in *Fighting for Our Lives.*[22]

Although the scene was staged, it was not unreal. The players were playing themselves, with the possible exception of a few kneeling farm workers who might not have been particularly religious but who understood the requirements of the day. The goons were in fact violent; the cops did arrest people for violating an unconstitutional TRO; Chris Hartmire did believe in the power of prayer; the farm workers were engaged in a campaign of civil disobedience. But there was another truth that never got into the movie: behind the goons, out in the fields, on this fourth day of the strike, before the growers had initiated any campaign to bring in scabs from other areas, plenty of farm workers were thinning the grapes.

Cesar Chavez understood that although this other truth could be edited out of a movie, it had been a glaring problem in the dress rehearsal. The main show, the harvest, was still a month and a half away. The UFW would have to revise the script.

Chavez did not delay in extending the battle beyond the fields. On the second day of the strike he flew to Washington and held a hurry-up press conference where, in the company of several congressmen and Monsignor Higgins, he called for a congressional investigation of Teamster-grower collusion. After the conference, with Jerry Cohen he went directly to AFL-CIO headquarters, where he hoped to win the support of George Meany. According to Cohen, Chavez expected the union chief to be a tough sell. Meany had not yet commented on the Teamsters' reentry into the fields, and had been open about his criticisms of the UFW. He didn't like the union's reversal on including farm workers in the National Labor Relations Act; he was upset about secondary boycotts of supermarkets that employed union labor. Although he distrusted the Teamsters, who had been kicked out of the AFL-CIO in 1957 when their Mob connections became an embarrassment, he still believed that the extension of the Salinas strike to Bud Antle had destroyed an imminent settlement between the UFW and the Teamsters, and he disapproved of the UFW's use of a volunteer staff.

That last complaint later became a central piece of the semiofficial trade union explanation of the UFW's eventual decline and fall. Chavez's union, labor chiefs were beginning to say, was failing to make the transition from a "movement" to a regular, viable trade union. As one unidentified AFL-CIO official told Harry Bernstein of the *Los Angeles Times* a week after Chavez's Washington trip, Chavez and his associates are "erratic people who are so wrapped up in some kind of class struggle they can't be relied on to just negotiate a labor agreement and enforce it like other unions do."[23] Sitting at the top of a union bureaucracy that discouraged the active participation of its memberships and that owed much of its power to congenial relationships with the employers, Meany and his friends wanted the UFW to settle down, jettison its wider goals, and cooperate with the growers—to be, in short, more like the Teamsters. They interpreted the administrative ineptitude of La Paz as a problem of too much democracy and were blind to the democratic deficiencies of the UFW. Meany believed that the UFW was in trouble in Coachella because it had failed to build a decent relationship with the grape growers. He was incapable of understanding that the UFW's problem was its failure to build a decent relationship with the grape workers.

Whatever may have been discussed in private between Chavez and Meany, the UFW got what it wanted from the face to face encounter. As Chavez and Cohen were returning to California, Meany issued a statement that accused the Teamsters of a "vicious and disgraceful" campaign to destroy the UFW, and pledged full support for the "small, struggling union." Meany also said that he had instructed Bill Kircher to provide "all possible assistance to the farm workers," and that additional aid for the UFW would be discussed at the next AFL-CIO executive council meeting.[24] In the meantime, Meany assigned thirteen AFL-CIO organizers to the UFW's campaign in the grapes and dispatched them to Coachella, under Kircher's leadership. By assigning so many organizers, Meany could exercise some control over how the strike would be run. AFL-CIO organizers began to restrict access to the picket line megaphones, encouraging chants of "Chavez *Sí*, Teamsters No" and discouraging longer speeches about class solidarity and the Mexican Revolution. If the UFW couldn't clean up its act, Meany would do it for them.[25]

In the interval between his meeting with Meany and the AFL-CIO executive council meeting in May, Chavez made a monumental, but unannounced, change in UFW strategy. "We came around to the position that we needed a farm labor law," Cohen explained. "Because without a law, whenever we got a contract, the Teamsters would just go in the back door and take it from us. It was the law of the jungle. We had operated well in the jungle, but we needed some way to prevent the Teamos from backdooring us every time we got a contract. And we could only get that through an overall legal settlement, a law."[26]

The idea disturbed some insiders. Operating without a law, the union had been free to leverage its support in the general population against the growers. A farm worker law might limit its ability to win contracts through boycott pressure, and would necessarily involve farm worker elections to determine rights of representation. Thus far the UFW had been wary of elections—sometimes supporting them and other times not, depending on the situation. Although the UFW staff was confident that they represented the interests of farm workers, they were uneasy about putting that to a test in an election where people who had gotten their jobs by breaking a strike would be free to vote. If the UFW were to commit itself to a farm labor law, who would get to vote in the elections, and what would be the ground rules?

Chavez and Cohen took a couple of long car rides and talked it over. Once they decided to go for as good a law as they could get, Chavez figured that he could use this change in strategy to win a major concession from Meany. Operating under the law of the jungle, Meany believed, was part of what kept the union an unreliable movement rather than a dependable trade union; legal constraints would settle it down. Now that Chavez, for different reasons, had adopted Meany's position, he decided that in their next meeting he would let Meany talk him into what he already wanted.[27]

In exchange, the UFW needed money, lots of it, to pay strike benefits so that the union could put up a better showing in the coming harvest than it had in the thinning. Cesar had come up with a rewrite of the failing script. After outfoxing the old fox when they met again in early May, Chavez listened as Meany announced at a press conference that the AFL-CIO was giving the UFW $1.6 million to help it defeat "the most vicious strikebreaking, union-busting effort I've seen in my lifetime." Chavez said that the money would be used to pay strike benefits and would enable the workers "to have a real strike for the first time."[28] Cesar's concession on the labor law went unannounced.

At a Memorial Day rally back in Coachella, Bill Kircher told the cheering strikers that the $1.6 million was just for the first three months of the strike and that the AFL-CIO constitution allowed the executive council to match it with another $1.6 million for the next three months, if needed. An animated Chavez told the crowd that the growers had been surprised by the union's strong backing from the AFL-CIO and urged all grape pickers to sign up for the strike so they could start receiving their benefits, $70 a week plus meals. He referred to unspecified worker grievances against the union, but added that the growers made a "grave error" when they concluded that because of those grievances the workers "were ready to kick us out."[29]

The harvest began in earnest on Monday, June 11. Five hundred people were on the picket lines that day; soon there were nearly 1,000, facing off against some 300 Teamster "guards," with more than 4,000 workers in the vineyards. The protagonists were relatively well paid. The Teamsters continued to make $67 a day. The UFW pickets had gotten a raise to $90 a week, plus meals at the strike kitchen and staple food to take home. The wages of the strikebreakers varied, depending on the condition of the grapes and the speed of the crews, but the fastest pickers, working in the best vineyards under the new Teamster and UFW contracts, could make as much as $400 for a five-day week.[30] Thus, pickers and goons were making about the same, while the strikers earned one-fourth as much. The UFW strike benefits, however, were more than just symbolic and were large enough to anger some UFW staffers, who continued to make $5 a week plus expenses.[31]

As the cameras rolled, the battles between the Teamster goons and the Chavista pickets followed their own dynamic and often had little to do with the harvest. The two forces, locked in a fight that seemed more gang war than class war, held center stage. The Teamsters were almost always the aggressors, focusing their attacks on the most active strikers, picket line captains, and midlevel UFW leaders. Often they would pick out a prominent union figure in the morning, tell him this was his day for a beating, and follow through by day's end. Marshall Ganz, standing on a picket line one afternoon, was knocked out with one punch after he had been told earlier that it was his turn. Patrolling the back roads, driving private cars, the goons looked for opportunities to terrorize stray strikers. At five one morning, two roaming Teamsters mistook a lone scab foreman for a Chavista. They took him out in the desert, ignored his explanations, beat him badly, stabbed him several times with an ice pick, and left him.[32]

The goon violence was well chronicled in the press and quickly became an embarrassment to top Teamster officials. Frank Fitzsimmons tried to undo the damage by hiring a Las Vegas public relations firm, an inept effort even by Fitzsimmons's standards. The PR agency was owned by men with felony criminal records, the *Wall Street Journal* reported. Worse, when the Las Vegas "investigators" arrived in Coachella, they were attacked by the goons. One of the PR men, called to a meeting with the Teamsters' Ralph Cotner at an Indio restaurant on June 18, was punched in the face by an enormous enforcer, who told his victim, lying on the restaurant floor, "to get out of town." Cotner then reinforced the warning: "There are four more guys standing over there who are madder than hell at you, who are willing to do the same thing to you, unless you get the hell out of here right away."[33]

What was Cotner up to? One of the Las Vegas victims told the *Riverside Press-Enterprise* that Cotner was trying to sabotage any coming deal between Fitzsimmons and Meany. By this time, Hoffa was out of jail but not yet dead; Nixon was in the middle of the Watergate whirlpool and unable to extend any more favors; and Fitz, scrambling to defend his presidency, had reversed course again and begun to negotiate yet another farm worker settlement with Meany. Getting readmitted to the AFL-CIO would refurbish his image, prove that his union had kicked out the Mob (it hadn't), and enable him to portray Hoffa as the vehicle through which the gangsters were trying to get back in. Meany had a list of what he wanted in exchange, including an end to the Teamsters' raid on the UFW. By ratcheting up the violence on the ground in Coachella, Cotner was hoping to so foul relations that no settlement at the top would be possible. Another disgruntled goon told the *Riverside Press-Enterprise* that the day after the attack on the Las Vegas man, Cotner told the guards, "We're gonna, from now on, not wait for them to come to us; we're gonna go at them, and we're gonna run the Chavistas out of town."[34]

Attacks on the pickets did increase, but they may not all have been driven by internal Teamster politics. The threats and counterthreats, coupled with periodic outbreaks of violence, had their own logic. On the morning of June 19 a time bomb destroyed a farm worker's car, although it was unclear whether the worker was a scab or a UFW loyalist. Later that morning 500 UFW pickets blocked the main road in Mecca, preventing workers from getting to the vineyards. They threw twisted nails onto the highway, causing blowouts on twenty scab cars and three sheriff's vehicles, including the chief's. That same day, Bill Grami was hit in the head with a rock. The next day several UFW pickets bloodied three scabs with grape stakes. The Teamsters responded with a rock attack on a car caravan in which Chavez was riding, and a nighttime arson that destroyed the trailer home of a UFW picket captain.[35]

The violence peaked the next morning, Saturday, June 24. After a ritualistic exchange of insults, one of the goons threw a firecracker, and some 200 Teamster guards charged about twice as many UFW pickets. For more than a half-hour, according to a Riverside County sheriff's deputy, there was "a mad melee of fights and beatings all over the fields." Ralph Cotner was among the goons. Another startled deputy reported that as soon as the fighting started, "weapons, including iron pipes, clubs, tire irons, machetes, and belts seemed to come out of nowhere." When the deputies finally established order, six Teamsters and five Chavistas were arrested, and five people (all UFW members) were taken to the hospital, two with major head injuries.[36]

Over the next few days, one hundred clergy and laymen from the United Church of Christ marched on UFW picket lines, and deputies from Riverside and neighboring counties stood between the Teamsters and UFW forces. The goons had one more attack in them. A couple hundred of them traveled north to Lamont, in Kern County, where UFW activity had just begun, and charged a small rally of unarmed unionists with the now familiar arsenal of baseball bats, pipes, and chains, injuring several Chavistas and sending one sixty-year-old man to the hospital with a fractured skull and cracked ribs.[37]

That was their last hurrah. Not even the Teamsters, their reputation already in the gutter, could tolerate the bad publicity, graphically reported in papers from the *Los Angeles Times* in the West to the *New York Times* in the East. Einar Mohn, president of the Western Conference of Teamsters, announced on July 4, "We have been given assurances that there are now enough law enforcement agents in Coachella Valley to protect our members from the UFW, and since that is the only reason we sent people there in the first place, we will remove the men."[38] Mohn's statement was only 90 percent ridiculous. The goons had prevented large numbers of strikers from rushing scabs in the vineyards, but their open, celebratory use of violence had made them the main story of the strike. Mohn had to get them off center stage so that people would notice the other story: there were more than enough workers picking the Coachella grapes.

When the goons left, so did the UFW pickets. There were two weeks left to the harvest, but a last-minute, all-out battle with the scabbing workers would have damaged the image of the Chavistas as nonviolent victims. They headed north with the camera crew, hoping that the lasting image from Coachella would be of vulgar, bare-chested thugs battering strikers half their size, and not the 2,910,019 lugs of grapes harvested during the season—16,923 lugs more than had been picked the year before.[39]

Despite the successful harvest in Coachella, the men at the top of California agribusiness still had plenty to worry about in the summer of 1973. As the UFW strikers went on to raise havoc in the Central Valley, workers under Teamster contracts in food processing and trucking intensified the pressure on the industry. For the first time in two decades, 65,000 cannery workers struck in the midst of the July peach, pear, and apricot harvests and as the harvest of canning tomatoes was just beginning. No one crossed the picket lines, and thousands of pounds of peaches and apricots had to be sent to California landfills. The Teamster strike shut down eighty-four separate canneries and won a 15 percent wage increase over the three-year life of the contract. The employers also agreed to pay overtime after forty hours of work, which meant a lot of money, because many people worked more than sixty hours a week during the harvest. The agreement guaranteed equal pay for men and women on the cannery line, an affirmative action fund to provide education and training for minority workers, and—quite worrisome for the rest of agribusiness—a clause permitting the workers to honor picket lines by other Teamsters in sanctioned walkouts.[40]

For the first time in a generation, the Teamster cannery officials had felt a greater need to consolidate their support among the workers than to improve their cozy relationship with the bosses. The vast majority of the workers on the cannery floor were Mexican American women who were inspired by the struggles in the fields and whose wages had stagnated while farm worker wages rose. Many of these women came from the same communities as farm workers—they had spent time in the fields themselves, and some lived with one or more people laboring in the orchards and vineyards that produced the fruit that was sent to the canneries. In 1973 they were ready for their own *huelga*. At the same time, union officials, mostly white men, were worried that the UFW might move onto their turf, and, in fact, UFW officials were openly using this possibility as a chip in the ongoing Teamster-AFL-CIO-UFW negotiations. One Teamster official told an LA Times reporter that the cannery strike proved to the workers that the Teamsters were not a "sweetheart union."[41]

A second Teamster strike caused agribusiness even more consternation. For three weeks, from mid-July to early August, more than 400 truck drivers shut down the Watsonville-Salinas vegetable deal.[42] No scabs took their places; the growers had not used scabs against the overwhelmingly Anglo drivers since the 1930s. Thus, with no one to deliver the empty boxes to the fields, to fold and stitch them, to take the produce-filled boxes back to the coolers and sheds, whence they would be trucked and railroaded across the country, there was no point in harvesting. Vegetables rotted in the fields, about 10,000 Salinas farm workers were idled, and the growers lost an estimated $20 million, about $1 million a day.[43]

Since the 1940s, the relatively small number of Teamster truck drivers, most of whom were Anglos, had used their crucial role in the production process to make themselves among the highest-paid hourly workers in agribusiness. Unlike in the canneries, strikes by truck drivers were not rare. This one, however, took a scary turn for the grower-shippers, as the Teamsters rank and file, in a meeting that featured a couple of fist fights, rejected a three-year 39 percent wage-benefit increase two weeks into the battle. That refusal threw the strike into the unknown. The Anglo truckers, who also had seen their wages fall in relationship to those of Mexican and Mexican American farm workers, were keen to maintain their position as the strongest unionists in agriculture. Three top grower-shippers flew to Washington to beg the Nixon administration to invoke the Taft-Hartley Act to force the truck drivers back to work. No president had ever done that in a produce strike, and the embattled Nixon did not do it now. The grower-shippers offered a 42 percent raise over three years, and renewed negotiations. A week later, the drivers voted 206 to 160 to accept.[44] The harvest resumed, but the grower-shippers' anxiety was unrelieved. Where and when would the upward wage spiral end?

That anxiety oozed all over the pages of *The Packer*, the produce industry's weekly newspaper. Its editorial writers maintained that the main problems were the ongoing farm worker movement and the refusal of the UFW to adopt a "business-like approach." But the tactic of using the Teamsters to get rid of the UFW also worried them. They feared a future where the Teamsters represented all the workers involved in growing, harvesting, processing, and moving produce—from the fields to the canneries to the trucks to the supermarkets. *The Packer* editorials proposed new legislation providing for secret ballot elections in the fields and outlawing secondary boycotts. Without it, the present intolerable situation would continue indefinitely.[45] Thus, at the same time that Chavez had quietly decided that the UFW needed legislation to prevent backdoor Teamster raids, growers were also calling for a new law. Meany had long argued for legislation. With different motivations, all of the players at the top, pushed by the upheaval at the bottom, began to work toward a negotiated settlement. Meanwhile, the UFW strike moved north.

"Time is God's way of preventing everything from happening at once," I once read on a bathroom wall. But God didn't have it quite worked out in the Central Valley in the summer of 1973. Everything did seem to be happening at once. Having lost in Coachella, the UFW waged three different strikes from early July to mid-August, spread out over 150 miles, from Wheeler Ridge in the south to Firebaugh in the north. While peaceful pickets cajoled scabs in Parlier, other strikebreakers were bombarded with rocks in Lamont. While some people were crowding the jails in Fresno, others were storming the fields in Mendota. While officials at the top tried to work out a stable compromise, farm workers on the ground fought for a quick win. The same day that police and demonstrators joked with each other at a peaceful demonstration, one county away cops brutally beat men and women picketers. The union's movie title was no exaggeration: some people were fighting for their lives.

   How to do justice to the complexity of the situation? How to describe it? Imagine three transparent overlays, each bearing, in a different-colored ink, the story of three separate strikes. One of the strikes is on the East Side of Fresno County, another is on the the West Side, and the third is in Kern County to the south. A patient reader who peered through the pages at the sandwich of accounts might grasp, at least on a symbolic level, the way things felt in the course of that astonishing battle. For a month and a half as many as 3,000 pickets, 10,000 strikebreakers, and hundreds of sheriff's deputies, police, and highway patrolmen clashed. Many small rural communities were shattered; several hundred UFW militants had the time of their lives. Still to come are periods of greater militancy, of larger and deeper levels of mass action, but no other moment in UFW history contains such a multiplicity of contradictory simultaneous events.

Here is the arithmetic: the Giumarra contract and twenty-eight other Delano table grape contracts were due to expire on July 29. They covered about 9,000 workers, the UFW's biggest block of members. Already, thirty Coachella table grape companies, nineteen Arvin-Lamont ranches, and two Fresno County wine grape companies, Gallo and Franzia, had left the UFW and signed with the Teamsters. About thirty orchards outside Fresno had not renewed their contracts; eight of them had signed with the Teamsters, and the rest had gone nonunion. If Giumarra and the other Delano growers also did not re-sign, the union would fall from a high of 150 contracts covering 40,000 workers to a low of twelve contracts covering 6,500 workers, in just three months.[46]

Witnessing the defeat in Coachella and assuming they had enough workers willing to scab, the growers had little incentive to sign with the UFW. So long as they could tolerate the higher wage costs, at least in the short term, they could harvest their crops. The only thing the UFW had to offer was the promise of social peace. And so its strategy was to make the Central Valley ungovernable and to lay the ground for another boycott.

The battleground terrain was varied. What Fresno locals called the East Side, an area that straddles southern Fresno and northern Tulare counties, was characterized by small family farmers who tended their grape vines and fruit orchards with a few year-round employees and then hired scores of workers for the harvest. Some of those small farmers were Nisei Japanese, who never had had contracts with the UFW and had helped to break the strike at White River Farms (Schenley) in 1972. But most were Anglos, many of them successful Dustbowl immigrants, whose small businesses were dominated by the "big eight" grower-shippers who owned the sheds and warehouses, and under whose labels the fruit was marketed. The UFW's contracts, secured in 1970 and covering a few thousand year-round and seasonal workers, had expired on April 15, 1973, and all the growers had refused to renew.

An hour's drive west lay the 30,000 acres of cantaloupe fields on Fresno County's West Side. From Huron in the southwest corner of the county up through Five Points, Mendota, and finally Firebaugh in the northwest corner, the year-round residents numbered in the low thousands, the towns on the map little more than a few stores and a gas station along a country road, a sharp contrast to the bustling communities nestled among the East Side's vineyards and orchards. Scattered throughout the monotonous landscape were rundown motels and labor camps, which in July and August housed the few thousand melon pickers and packers, whose labor produced Fresno County's $20 million cantaloupe deal. The pickers were mostly from Mexicali; the packers were Anglos, some from El Centro, others from Salinas, longtime members of Salinas's militant Local 78, led by the UFW *amigo* Jerry Breshears.

The UFW had no contracts in the melons, but short strikes at the start of a cantaloupe harvest were the rule, making the *meloneros* among the highest-paid farm workers in California, rivaling the *lechugueros*. Melons often must be picked on the very day they are ready. Standing on the side of the fields, refusing to work until grievances or wage demands are settled, is quite effective when there are only a few hours left to pick the rapidly ripening crop. Also, the work was extremely difficult: the *melonero* had to walk up a ramp moving through the fields, carrying bags of about 100 pounds, and dump the melons so they could be packed in crates. Not many people could do the work for long, which limited the scab pool. And, like the *lechugueros*, the *meloneros* had an extraordinary level of internal solidarity. The crews were paid collectively and split the money among themselves; often the fifteen to eighteen men on a crew came from the same town in rural Mexico, and cousins, brothers-in-law, brothers, even fathers and sons, worked together. In a strike, growers typically conceded quickly on the wage demands, and over the years some had agreed to negotiate with the UFW. But after the work resumed, the growers had stonewalled. In 1973, some began signing with the Teamsters.

To the south, stretching from the foot of Tejon Pass to Delano, lay the 8,000 square miles of Kern County, known in the industry as the Arvin-Lamont-Delano district, where the bulk of California's table grapes are grown. As important as Kern County was to agribusiness, it was even more important to the UFW. In 1973, more of its members lived in Kern County than anywhere else. La Paz sat in the foothills above the county seat of Bakersfield. In downtown Delano, on the valley floor, the union had rented its first building and put up its first sign. On the outskirts of town, Forty Acres remained the union's biggest, most ambitious field office, where the Delano growers had capitulated just three years earlier.

After the defeat in Coachella, Kern County farm workers loyal to the UFW were in no mood to concede. At the Tenneco-Ducor Ranch, Rudy Reyes reported that activists were determined to win, for a defeat would mean that they would have to leave their homes in the camps. At the Arvin-Lamont field office, Pablo Espinoza noted that the Teamsters' baseball bat attack on a peaceful rally in a public park had steeled the resolve of many workers. Epifanio Camacho, at Roberts Farms in McFarland, said that the Delano-area militants had organized themselves into small groups and were prepared to fight hard.[47]

These people did not want to wait years for another boycott to take effect. What would they do in the meantime? After striking and losing, would they be able to return to their jobs? No one knew. Also, many of them knew people who would likely scab. This Kern County strike, so central to the UFW's future, was also a small-town rivalry between extended families. The strikers were especially bitter about the local farm workers who had scabbed in 1965, enjoyed union wages and benefits under the contracts, and now would scab again. Furthermore, most of the Mexican American and Mexican loyalists did not look kindly on the Filipinos. Perhaps the strike could be won on boycott picket lines in distant cities; the strikers couldn't know. They wanted to win it on their local turf, against their local enemies.

The battle in the Central Valley would rage across the East Side, the West Side, and Kern County (Arvin-Lamont-Delano). It began on July 4, with a general strike in the orchards of the East Side. That was audacious. The union could have waited for the grape harvest in early August, and marshaled all its forces in the south at Arvin-Lamont and Delano. Instead, it opened a second, northern front, just as the nectarine, plum, and early peach harvests began. Almost 500 picketers massed before dawn at the exits of the Fresno County Housing Authority migrant labor camp; when several small growers arrived to plead with the 600 residents to come to work, everybody refused. Later that morning, the strikers enthusiastically drove to the orchards to call on other workers to join them. Word spread and nearly 800 signed up for strike benefits. By the end of the first week, more than 1,000 people surrounded the labor camp, which by then was useless as a source of scab labor because people who wanted to work had moved out. The strikers did not stop the harvest that first week, but they damaged it.[48]

On the East Side, many farm workers supported the strike from the start. Some of the credit goes to Gilbert Padilla, whose Fresno-area field offices had been less heavy-handed than those in Coachella, Arvin-Lamont, and Delano. Gilbert regularly allowed people to go to work without paying back dues, he did not apply the union seniority rules, and he refused to cooperate with the La Paz–mandated search for illegals. But the union's popularity had other sources as well. A strike in 1970 had helped produce the first contracts, so workers felt that the union was partly their own. Because Arabs and Filipinos did not work in the trees, there was less ethnic division within the workforce. Since Fresno is farther from the border than the southern vineyards, the strike was less vulnerable to scabs imported from Mexico.

That last detail makes the tactical shift that occurred five days into the strike all the more suspect. On July 9, instead of driving to the trees to thwart the harvest, some 800 picketers converged on the INS office in Fresno, protesting the Border Patrol's failure to deport undocumented workers picking fruit in the orchards. That same day, 350 miles away, almost as many people picketed the *migra* in Indio for its failure to deport "illegal aliens" during the Coachella strike. From the Mexican border to Fresno, the UFW demonstrated that it could mobilize 1,500 people on the same day. But to what end?[49]

Almost from the moment the fight opened in 1973, Chavez had sought to create a plausible explanation for its possible defeat. Back in June in Coachella, when a reporter from the *Riverside Press-Enterprise* asked him, "Will the UFW win its strike this year?" he paused and replied, "This year? A lot depends on how much cooperation we get from the Border Patrol. They're between us and victory at this point.'" Chavez did not give interviews casually, and that one, granted on the eve of a strike, would have been carefully considered. He also told the reporter, "There are at least ten locations I know of where wetbacks are staying." Although the union had often blamed its defeats on "illegals," by 1973 it no longer used the term "wetbacks" in public statements. Chavez used it twice in the interview and argued that some 300 of them were scabbing in the grapes. The agent in charge of the INS regional office, Henry Felchin, had expressed doubt regarding Chavez's figures and told the reporter, "I personally met with his [Chavez's] attorneys as late as last week to set up procedures where they would advise us of any locations where they had information where illegal aliens might be found. They gave us information, and from it, we located five illegals."[50]

The numbers, liberally thrown around, were always less important than the perception they were meant to create. But undocumented workers were not the key to the union defeat in Coachella. The people who crossed the picket lines were the usual pickers: Filipinos, daily and weekly migrants from Mexicali (many of them green-carders), veteran migrants from Texas and Mexico (some legal, some not), and many local workers, too. Five years later, during a debate on the Executive Board, Marshall Ganz had to remind his colleagues that scabbing "wetbacks" had not been the problem in Coachella:

> Let's not kid ourselves. We all know that in Coachella in 1973 we didn't have the workers. We didn't have the members. We shouldn't kid ourselves about that. Those who were there, we know. A lot of them we couldn't even buy for ninety bucks a week. You know, let's be honest about it. I got a lot of those contracts ratified in 1970, and I know how we got them ratified. We never really organized the people. We never really got them. We never really had them."[51]

On the East Side though, the UFW did "have" a significant portion of the orchard workers, and the strike was off to a strong start. In the trees the workers were exclusively Mexican Americans and Mexican immigrants, many of the latter undocumented. Demonstrating against illegals at the beginning of the strike labeled some of them the enemy and ruined any chance of uniting orchard workers on the basis of their common Mexican culture and origin.

On the West Side, no UFW-sponsored melon strike had ever focused its wrath on undocumented workers, nor would it in 1973. The *meloneros*, Mexicans rather than Mexican Americans, were staunchly loyal to the UFW, despite its reputation in the grape fields as a *"pocho"* (Mexican American) union. Ever since 1965 the union had been a great asset in a series of strikes that had driven up wages. Manuel Chavez had negotiated the increases; UFW lawyers had protected workers from reprisals and represented those who were arrested. Although the strikers had not won contracts, that also meant they didn't have to pay union dues or endure the UFW's petty rules. In the second week of July, as they prepared for yet another strike, the *meloneros* were united.

Meanwhile, in Arvin-Lamont, attention was more focused on dissuading the small number of preharvest scabs from preparing the vines for picking. About 800 people picketed some of the growers who had deserted the UFW for the Teamsters. The goons had been retired, and only local law enforcement, ranch foremen, and supervisors stood between strikers and strikebreakers. Without the Teamster "guards" standing between them, there were more fights between cops and strikers and strikers and scabs. The news from Gallo—California's biggest wine producer, with 500 workers at peak season—heightened the sense of crisis, as it raised the entry wage immediately upon signing with the Teamsters to an all-time high of $2.76 an hour, plus piece-work incentives. Would UFW loyalists ever get to enjoy such gains under UFW contracts?[52]

A week later the Arvin-Lamont harvest began. Within days it was clear that there were enough scabs to bring in the harvest, and the union turned to civil disobedience to disrupt it. Once again a judge had issued temporary restraining orders without hearing UFW testimony opposing them. More than a hundred miles away on the East Side, a Fresno County judge had done the same. On July 19, 439 people at Lamont and 435 strikers on the East Side peacefully submitted to arrest.[53]

That would be the only such mass arrest in Kern County that summer, as officials, perhaps aware that they were handing the union a publicity opportunity, abruptly reversed policy. But Fresno County did not, and the continuing arrests would make Fresno the UFW's enduring emblem of 1973 and a marker in Chicano history, shorthand for a liberating act of rebellion against years of exploitation and humiliation. On July 20, 400 more East Side picketers were arrested, 80 percent of them repeats from the day before. This time, rather than sign citations, the protesters decided to clog the jails. Fresno County officials, who had already spent more than $100,000 policing the East Side orchard strike, were furious. But they wouldn't admit defeat, and continued to enforce the illegal TROs.[54]

As the East Side action turned to civil disobedience, union leaders no longer tried to win the orchard strike; rather, they wanted to demonstrate to the world that the TROs made the strike unwinnable. To provoke mass arrests, they restricted picketing to ranches covered by the TROs. Scabs in the trees increased; periodically, strikers rushed the fields to try to get them out but with diminishing success. About fifty small growers, armed with clubs and sometimes a shotgun or two, took to gathering near the UFW's mass protests. Their purpose, they said, was to defend the people who wanted to work. The result: a clear photographic contrast of peaceful pickets and armed growers.[55]

Full production was being resumed, but the defeated East Side strike receded in the light of the victorious rebellion. A few hundred local Mexican American farm workers were willing to get arrested again and again, and to spend days, nights, ultimately weeks, in jail. They sang, fasted, gave the police false names, played havoc with the Fresno County court system, and openly, joyfully, defied their jailers. Unlike the 1966 Easter pilgrimage, where quiet, humble penance was transformed into power, the farm workers who submitted to arrest in Fresno in 1973 would not submit to much else.

Across the valley, the West Side *meloneros* were winning their strike the traditional way. They walked out after the East Side civil disobedience began, and their mass participation in the first days cut production in the melon fields by an estimated 75 percent. That forced the grower-shippers to raise wages and to make a historic concession by changing the basis on which the piece rate was calculated. As far back as anyone could remember, growers had paid the *meloneros* by the number of cantaloupes that were packed in the sheds, not by the number of melons that had left the fields. Since the 1920s, workers had complained that they were being cheated, either because the boxes were miscounted or because melons were being culled by the packers. For the first time, after nearly fifty years of debate and struggle, the growers, including those who had signed with the Teamsters, agreed to pay on the basis of how many linear feet of melons were picked in the fields. Wages jumped to a high of $7 an hour, with one grower claiming he was paying $9.[56]

Strikers would ordinarily return to work after such a victory, but this time, in the midst of its losses in the vineyards and orchards, the UFW was more interested in winning new contracts, especially if it could pry some companies away from the Teamsters. Manuel Chavez urged the workers to continue the strike, and in a resounding endorsement of the union, a majority (in some companies, the vast majority) agreed. But a crucial minority of the regular crews did not. At the biggest company, Tri-Produce, which had signed with the Teamsters, eight of thirty-five crews returned to the fields, setting the stage for an unusual, bitter battle among the *meloneros*.[57]

July was nearly over and decisions had to be made about the expiring Delano grape contracts. The UFW and the growers had been negotiating since the middle of the month: John Giumarra Jr. headed the growers' committee and Chavez, atypically, led the UFW's team. The Delano growers seemed willing to make some kind of accommodation. The main problem was the hiring hall. Giumarra, content to reform the hall rather than gut it, proposed a hiring hall jointly run by the growers and the UFW. As the July 29 deadline approached, the union's top staff overwhelmingly supported this compromise, but the Executive Board agreed with Chavez that a contract with the Delano growers would confuse the approaching boycott, and the union should give up nothing to get it.[58]

The semiopen internal disagreement was highly unusual but came to nothing except for the firing of Susan Drake, Chavez's personal secretary, who wrote to him saying that many staffers favored a settlement but were afraid to tell him. At the negotiating table, Chavez stalled. He put up one obstacle after another, asserting, for instance, that the union reserved the right to prohibit a Teamster grape picker in Coachella or Arvin-Lamont from working on a UFW ranch in Delano. As Chavez filibustered, Cohen feigned close attention while exchanging competing lists of baseball all-star teams with the UFW lawyer Tom Dalzell.[59]

Those who favored a compromise thought that Chavez was getting bad advice from Frank Ortiz, the new field office director in Delano, who was optimistic about a Delano-area strike. Cohen and Padilla also thought that Chavez couldn't admit that the union was unpopular at the place of its birth and therefore was predisposed to agreed with Ortiz that they could win in Kern County. But Chavez was playing a hand that had many more cards in it than stopping the scabs in Delano. While he was stalling in Kern County, the first union supporters from the cities, priests and clergy, were being arrested on Fresno's East Side; they were sure to be dedicated boycott leaders once they returned home with their stories of sacrifice and civil disobedience. In Washington, George Meany's talks with Frank Fitzsimmons were continuing, and Chavez knew from Bill Kircher that they were going well. Perhaps, as Cohen believed, Chavez was overly optimistic about stopping the Delano scabs, but to Chavez, whether the scabs were stopped or not wouldn't make the difference.

Chavez continued to stall and the Delano contracts expired. Thirty minutes later, just past midnight on July 30, someone set fire to a Giumarra truck, thereby announcing the start of the last big push of the Central Valley strikes. As many as 2,500 workers appeared on the Kern County picket lines, most of them massed in Arvin-Lamont, where the harvest was fully under way. Giumarra, the picketers' main target, had 2,000 scabs in its vineyards. A couple thousand more were at other ranches, fewer than half the number that would be needed at peak season. Thus were the forces arrayed: 2,500 strikers, 4,000 scabs, and just 150 lawmen to stand between them.[60]

From the first morning it was clear that the sheriff's deputies and local cops couldn't do the job. Strikers were running into the vineyards all over the county. Frustrated deputies, not used to such open defiance, went berserk. They beat the people they managed to arrest, whacking them with their batons after they already had been subdued. When other strikers tried to free people from the deputies, the cops' rage flared, and the beatings got worse. To the outnumbered, isolated, often frightened rank-and-file guardians of the law, it didn't matter whose head got bloodied. Safely removed from the scene, Chief Criminal Deputy Loren Fote said, "We are not going to deny that some picketers were probably beaten, but if any were it was while they were entering fields illegally or attempting to free prisoners from deputies. If that is the treatment they got, it is what they asked for."[61]

But brutality was no substitute for small numbers. Nor did the sheriff's new helicopter, which flew just six feet off the ground as it herded strikers into the arms of waiting deputies, dampen the spirits on the picket line. The outnumbered deputies simply could not prevent the strikers from confronting the scabs, who worked in small crews scattered over thousands of acres. In response, the scabs and the growers escalated the weaponry. To the strikers' massed numbers and occasional rocks and sticks, they would answer with guns.

On July 31, Chief Deputy Fote told the press that "it appeared that workers in the fields were arming themselves," and that "there was nothing illegal about it."[62] He also reported, without comment, that one grower in Kern County confronted UFW picketers with a shotgun. Chavez turned away. On that second day of the strike he went to Chicago for a one-day meeting with Meany.[63] When he returned to California he focused his attention on the civil disobedience campaign in Fresno.

The public face of the UFW's Central Valley strategy remained the image of peaceful mass arrests on the East Side. Most reporters were more interested in civil disobedience than in the battle that was ominously taking shape in the vineyards or in the open warfare among the *meloneros*. Out in the vast emptiness of the West Side, unsoftened by any nearby farm worker community life, away from the media's gaze, striking melon workers physically intimidated those who dared to work. They rushed the fields, sometimes more than 150-strong, to stop the scabs, some of whom they knew well. One night in Firebaugh, about thirty people attacked the El Rancho Motel, where seventy scabs were staying, breaking twenty-four windows with rocks and bottles, and damaging two farm labor buses parked in back.[64] During one rush into the fields, a ranch manager, Jack Harris, was hit over the eye by a flying rock, and, he said, trampled to the ground. His picture, blood dripping from his eyebrow, appeared on page six of the

Fresno Bee, across from the picture of a priest wearing his clerical collar submitting to arrest on the East Side. The next day, Harris was arrested for trying to run down strikers with his pickup truck.[65]

In Kern County, the day after Chavez left for his meeting with Meany, the first gun was fired. From the open window of a passing truck, someone shot about a dozen bullets at a group of UFW pickets. An eighteen-year-old was hit in the shoulder.[66] Word of a shooting travels fast. Some strikers started bringing guns to the picket lines, hidden in their lunch bags.[67] Chief Deputy Fote, who had made no attempt to disarm anyone, observed that Kern County was becoming an "armed camp" and the situation was "to the point where we could very well have a shooting here unless tensions ease."[68] Of course, someone had already been shot, but he and his superior, Sheriff Charles Dodge, unwilling to confiscate weapons, continued to make dire predictions about coming violence, which encouraged more people to take up arms, if only in self-defense.

The strikers rushed into the vineyards less frequently—once inside they might come upon armed growers, foremen, scabs, and an occasional anti-union, anti-Mexican freelance adventurer. Instead, they took to showering the strikebreakers' cars with rocks as they drove to and from the struck vineyards. Before dawn on August 3, 300 to 400 strikers blocked roads on the fringes of Delano, attacking the stopped cars with rocks and bricks. Later that morning a few carloads of strikers forced a bus filled with scabs to stop on the side of the road and then broke fourteen of its windows as the passengers cowered inside.[69]

That same day, in a Fresno city park, Chavez appeared at a rally promoting nonviolence. The UFW, he said, would "make Fresno another Selma, Alabama," and urged "friends across the United States to come to Fresno and take part in mass arrests."[70] Protestant and Catholic clergy responded by the scores, in what Father Eugene Boyle of San Francisco called "the largest group of religious persons ever arrested and jailed in this country." Seventy-five-year-old Dorothy Day joined the parade to jail and remained there for two weeks, along with more than 300 others. It would be mid-August before Fresno County finally abandoned the restraining orders, and all of the protesters were released.[71]

Chavez was not ignorant of what was transpiring in the grapes and the cantaloupe fields when he urged nonviolence on those in Fresno who were already peacefully submitting to arrest. As Pablo Espinoza put it, "Cesar was aware of vandalism and violence. He couldn't stop it, and he didn't try to stop it. He was never around it, of course. And the official policy of the union was always peaceful arrests."[72] But Chavez's own cousin was directing arsonists in Kern County and openly endorsing the intimidation of scabs on the West Side. Other high-level UFW officials may have quietly approved of rushing the fields and going after scabs, but none of them bragged about it, as Manuel Chavez did.

Manuel's no-holds-barred attitude did not hurt Chavez's reputation with some farm workers who doubted the efficacy of the UFW's espoused pacifism, but Manuel was not universally admired by farm worker radicals. Camacho didn't like him, nor did the Bustamantes. Mojica, who was not above some vandalism of his own, had a particular distaste for Cesar Chavez's *primo hermano*. The West Side strike happened to hit full stride at the same time that the InterHarvest *lechugueros* in Salinas were idled by the Teamster truckers' strike. Fresno's West Side is about an hour and a half's drive over Pacheco Pass from the Salinas Valley, and many of the most militant Salinas workers—the decommissioned Division of the North—regularly participated in the cantaloupe strike. Mojica went once and decided he didn't want to be part of an operation headed by Manuel, especially when Manuel's henchmen were around. Mojica said he had:

> . . . never agreed with what they did. In the first place, they always spoke badly of farm workers. They didn't like farm workers. I never got along with Manuel. He called farm workers stupid. *Una bola de memes, bola de pendejos* [a bunch of fools, a bunch of pubic hairs—very strong Mexican epithets]. He was a Chicano who really thought a lot of himself. He was there because he could make money. I never thought he was with us because he believed in our cause. We always had some higher criteria for what we were doing, some ideal we were trying to go by—but not this guy.[73]

As it turned out, violence did not win any contracts in the melons. Eventually the high wages and the concession on the method of calculating the melons won the day. Production resumed, none of the Teamster contracts were repudiated, and the strike dribbled away. Likewise in Kern County: hit-and-run raids, rock throwing, and surprise attacks could not overcome the numerical superiority of experienced grape pickers determined to stay in the vineyards. Even in the strike's dramatic first week, the Federal Market News Service reported, more than 110,000 lug boxes of grapes were picked and packed every day, slightly more than the year before.[74]

In the second week, small arsons—some flaming empty grape boxes here, a shed there—produced a few brief, hopeless lights in the dark valley nights, but Cesar Chavez knew it was a losing proposition. As the week began, he flew out of town once again, this time to appear before a special session of the Massachusetts State Legislature, which endorsed the grape and lettuce boycotts after hearing him speak. He was in Fresno the next day, traveling to various strike scenes with Congressman Ed Roybal, telling him that "forty to sixty percent of the strikebreakers were illegal aliens," the highest estimate the union had yet made.[75] While futile battles raged around him, Chavez was preparing the ground for the campaign to come.

Then, within days, Chavez and the UFW almost got a reprieve. Earlier, George Meany had surprised many when, in the midst of negotiations with Frank Fitzsimmons, he had publicly criticized the UFW, denouncing its dues policy as unpopular among the grape workers and unprecedented in U.S. labor.[76] He had also announced that Chavez finally had agreed to support the inclusion of farm workers in the National Labor Relations Act, either a flat-out mistake by Meany or an attempt to puff up what Chavez had told him a few months before. The AFL-CIO boss had inflated some other minor UFW concessions, providing Fitzsimmons with cover for a staggering reversal, which the Teamster boss duly delivered. Giving away at the negotiating table what the table grape growers and local Teamsters were winning on the ground, Fitzsimmons agreed in principle to cancel all the grape contracts that the Teamsters had signed since April.[77]

Negotiations between Western Conference Teamsters officials and the UFW to work out the details of what the two bosses had agreed on in Washington began on Thursday, August 9. An unidentified UFW official told the *Fresno Bee* that a settlement could be reached by the weekend. But by midmorning on Friday the talks were over. Fitzsimmons could not give away what he didn't own. While he and Meany were negotiating at the top, local Teamster officials and Delano table grape growers were doing their own negotiating. John Giumarra Jr., consistent with the editorial advice of *The Packer* and *The California Farmer*, had not been eager to sign with the Teamsters after the UFW contract expired. He had the workers he needed to break the strike without the Teamsters, so why should he give them a foothold? But when the *Fresno Bee* proclaimed that Einar Mohn of the Western Conference of Teamsters was going to give the other grape contracts back to the UFW, Giumarra's position changed. As the talks between Mohn and Chavez began, Giumarra and most of the other Delano growers hurriedly signed essentially the same contracts with the Teamsters that the growers had agreed to in Coachella and Arvin-Lamont.[78]

Jerry Cohen called it a sneak attack, "like Pearl Harbor." Chavez said, "We've been stabbed in the back," a metaphor he repeated several times over the next few days. Mohn and Fitzsimmons insisted that Jim Smith, the head of the Teamsters' farm worker office in Delano, had acted on his own, defying their orders. Fitzsimmons repudiated the contracts, transferred Smith out of Delano, shut down the office there, and consulted with Meany. Mohn called for a renewal of the negotiations with Chavez. The internal Teamster politics were nearly unfathomable: insiders speculated that Smith was working with Grami, who was now working with Hoffa. But the Teamsters were only part of the equation. Giumarra laughed when he heard that Fitzsimmons had thrown out his contract. He had negotiated it in good faith, he said, had the signature of a certified Teamsters official on it, and was not about to give it up. Nor was the UFW going to let the Teamster hierarchy off the hook, although AFL-CIO officials assured Chavez that Mohn was not the backstabber but instead had been stabbed himself.[79]

On the ground, the grape workers' hope for a settlement dissolved into desperate rage. Chavez visited the picket lines in the company of several clergymen and called for the sheriffs to disarm the strikebreakers, but he was powerless to alter the deadly trajectory of events. Soon after the talks collapsed, two UFW pickets who were overturning grape boxes on the side of a field were shot by someone working in the vineyards. One man got a .22 bullet in his hip; the other was grazed in the forehead. The next day two shots were fired into the Teamsters' office in Arvin, and three UFW members were arrested for firebombing an electric pump.[80] That same afternoon a car with a UFW decal was rammed by a Giumarra truck. The three Anglos in the truck and the three Mexicans in the car had all been drinking. The Mexicans shouted "*Huelga!*," one of the Anglos flipped them the bird, and then a passenger in the truck hit the car's window with a beer bottle. A man in the car retaliated with a shot from a .22, hitting one of the Giumarra workers in the back and just missing his kidney.[81]

Bottles and rocks continued to fly; guns appeared more frequently. In the midst of a rock and dirt clod fight near Earlimart, a scab stepped forward and brandished another .22 rifle. The picketers, among them Chavez's son Fernando, ran and ducked behind their cars. The strikebreaker, Luis Rivera, fired six or seven shots at the cars shielding the strikers, but sheriffs, who observed the scene, didn't arrest Rivera until the next day. By that time, the first UFW striker, Naji Daifullah, was dead. He had been drinking at a bar in Lamont when Kern County sheriff's deputies arrived, responding to a report of a fight. Someone threw a bottle at one of the deputies, and Daifullah ran outside. Deputy Gilbert Cooper easily caught up with the inebriated Daifullah, and hit him with his oversized flashlight. Daifullah died either from the blow or from the impact when his head hit the ground. The deputies dragged him sixty feet and threw him in their car. The coroner ruled his death an accident.[82]

Chavez called for a three-day fast, and the UFW planned a funeral march through Lamont, but before the funeral took place, another striker had been martyred. This one, Juan De La Cruz, was killed on the picket line. De La Cruz, born sixty years before in Aguas Caliente, Mexico, had come to Delano in 1960 after working many years in the fields of Texas and Arizona. He had joined the union in 1966 during the DiGiorgio election. He was standing near his wife, Maxima, a little apart from their fellow picketers, watching over the cars that had brought 100 to 150 strikers to a four-way stop on Wheeler Ridge Road, south of Arvin. At about three p.m. on

August 16, according to testimony at the subsequent trial, two Filipino farm workers, Ernest Baclig and Bayani Advincula, who had completed their days' work at Dalton Anderson Ranch, were driving to Arvin so that Bayani could send a telegram home to the Philippines. When they stopped at the intersection, they exchanged insults with the assembled UFW pickets. Sheriff's deputies had left about twenty minutes earlier, called away to another strike scene. When Baclig, the driver, turned right onto Wheeler Ridge Road, strikers threw rocks at his 1965 Chevrolet, hitting it several times. The twenty-year-old Advincula picked up a rifle that was lying on the floor of the car and fired six shots out the window. He hit four parked cars and Juan De La Cruz, who fell dead to the ground beside his wife.*[83]

Ten thousand people walked behind Daifullah's coffin; 6,000 followed De La Cruz's. After Daifullah's burial, Chavez told the assembled strikers that the Executive Board had unanimously voted to suspend the strike. Later that night at a rally of 2,000 farm workers in Delano, he said that the strikers would win back their contracts through the boycott and the ballot box. The Delano harvest still had three or four months to go, and many in the crowd, not just the *huesos colorados* but others who had been transformed by this failed strike but successful rebellion, did not cheer the decision. They wanted to fight some more.[84]

Chavez was probably right to halt the strike. Few strikes are won when there are more scabs than pickets. Better to accept the results on the ground and try to use the enthusiasm of the strikers to fight elsewhere. That had been part of the plan from the beginning. But the prudent decision to call off the strike could not make up for the failure the strike had revealed. The UFW had been born in the vineyards in 1965, when Filipinos and Mexicans reached out to one another in solidarity. Eight years later it appeared to be dying in the grapes, as a Filipino finger pulled a trigger that sent a bullet through a Mexican heart.

---

* In July, 1976, a jury acquitted Advincula of murder, believing he had acted in self-defense. (*Fresno Bee*, July 22, 1976)

Forcing the Great Concession

August '73 to June '75

It was easier for outsiders to know La Paz than to know the fields. The people in La Paz were literate and interested in communicating with a larger world. They held press conferences, cultivated reporters, issued press releases, and operated in a culture where few things were more important than the difference between good and bad publicity. The farm worker world was hidden, as obscure as pruners in the tule fog, made up of people who either lived outside the law or were uncounted and unaccounted for by government agencies and academics. Farm workers didn't issue press releases. They lived in an oral, sometimes outlaw, culture, and often hid themselves from public view. Nor could one learn their full story through the UFW staff; when the staff showed farm workers to the world, it displayed its own construct of them, designed to elicit sympathy, even pity. This even when the staffers were former farm workers. Schooled by Fred Ross and others, they learned to exhibit a version of themselves useful to the boycott.

In the fall of 1973, the union's top staff retreated to La Paz to plan their next moves. They had lost the table grape contracts. They now had so few members they could actually count them: 5,723. Dues had fallen from more than 57 percent of the union's revenue to less than 15 percent.[1] The union would have to rely on outside supporters—liberals, labor, churches—to pay its bills. Press releases continued to be upbeat, but the outlook was bleak.

A report from the fields (if there had been any) would have read differently. Only the mood of those grape workers loyal to the UFW would have matched the dark uncertainty at La Paz. They had fought, and now they had to return to the vineyards defeated, once again subject to the whims of triumphant bosses. Elsewhere, however, in the vast, nearly invisible farm worker world, people were not feeling so bad. Wages were higher than ever before, and rising. A good number of farm workers, untouched by the troubles in the UFW, looked to the union for help in their own battles. The valiant fight in the orchards, melon fields, and vineyards of the Central Valley had inspired farm workers around the country, and even in parts of rural Mexico. The union, nearly destroyed, still danced in the imagination of those workers who were looking for a fight. While La Paz fretted, farm workers were gathering off stage, practicing their lines, about to push their way into history once again, not on the defeated Central Valley plain, but in many of the other farm worker communities of California.

As La Paz regrouped, a small, barely noticed strike—a little eddy that seemed to flow against the current—proved to be a better clue of what was to come in the Californian fields than the plummeting numbers of UFW members. In late August of 1973, not long after Juan De La Cruz had been buried, dozens of farm workers outside Stockton stopped picking tomatoes. Although influenced by the militancy of the just concluded grape strike, they were neither formally connected to the UFW nor informally in contact with UFW organizers. They had gotten together and walked out, as farm workers often do, in response to a change in operations. Throughout the bracero years the men had put the fruit in wooden boxes, which they carried to the edge of the fields. They were paid by the hour. Starting in 1973, the growers had the workers put the tomatoes in buckets and then dump the buckets into bins. They offered twenty cents a bucket. About a month into the four-month season, the workers, many of them ex-brace-ros, demanded twenty-five cents. When the growers refused, they refused to work. The growers, worried about the harvest, quickly gave in, but two days later dropped the pay back to twenty cents, assuming that the loosely organized workers couldn't enforce the informal agreement. It was all stan-dard tactics in a typical farm worker dispute.[2]

But times had changed. A delegation of tomato workers went to the UFW field office in Stockton and asked the director, Maria Elena Serna, to help them put together a new walkout. When they resumed their strike, waving the black eagle flag, they were joined by union militants from a nearby Franzia vineyard. The *tomateros* streamed out of the fields, and the growers resumed negotiations. This time, at the suggestion of Serna, the talks were observed by the San Joaquin Valley labor commissioner, and the newly organized "Tomato Workers Committee" demanded thirty cents a bucket. The growers conceded, and although no contract was signed, the new rate was broadcast on the local Spanish radio stations, and the bosses couldn't reverse their concession.[3]

Bill Duarte, manager of the San Joaquin Farm Production Association, had dismissed the resumed strike in an interview with *The Packer*. "This thing is not connected to the UFW at all," he said. "I think it is just local people. I think they have stolen a few flags and tried to make as much noise as possible." But what comforted Duarte—that the strike was initiated by "just" local people—would soon prove a great discom-fort to the rest of California agribusiness.[4] The *tomateros* were among the huge numbers of legalized ex-braceros working in the fields who now, several years after the program ended, were confident enough to use more fully the power they had. And they knew that by calling in the UFW, or threatening to, they could put more pressure on their bosses. Alone, those two factors would have been dangerous enough to the growers. Mix in the UFW's desire to raise as much trouble in the fields as it could to pressure the California legislature to pass a worker-friendly farm labor law, and the result would blow up in the face of California agribusiness.

In the third week of September 1973, after the *tomateros* had won their pay raise, the UFW held its First Constitutional Convention. Three hundred and fifty delegates, most of them farm workers, gathered in Fresno. They came from the few companies that still had contracts—a large contingent came from InterHarvest—and from the ranches where they had had contracts and lost them. Others came from the recently reconstituted boycott committees and from various organizing committees around the country. A large press corps, perhaps surprised by the absence of hospitality rooms where they could get free drinks and food, filed reports on the differences between this gathering and a regular AFL-CIO convention. The delegates ate bag lunches, not fancy meals; they stayed at supporters' homes, not at expensive hotels. They showed up for the plenary sessions, and were attentive.

Despite these differences, this gathering did not depart radically from the pattern of most union conventions, which are designed to be demonstrations of strength and unity, with all big decisions made in advance and presented to the delegates for ratification. True to form, the delegates heard from various important supporters: Senator Ted Kennedy, Leonard Woodcock, the president of the United Automobile Workers; Paul Hall of the Seafarers; Bishop Hugh Donahue, chair of the National Conference of Catholic Bishops; Jack Henning, of the California AFL-CIO; and a representative from Los Angeles' mayor, Tom Bradley, who announced that he had formally urged Secretary of State Henry Kissinger to nominate Cesar Chavez for the Nobel Peace Prize. In their own presentations, Chavez and other UFW leaders stressed the three main political concerns of the convention: farm labor legislation, settlement of the ongoing war with the Teamsters, and renewal of the grape and lettuce boycotts, which Chavez called "the only weapon we have left."[5]

Some necessary business got done. The UFW finally solved the back dues crisis by converting to a check-off system, with workers paying 2 percent of their income to the union. Chavez reshuffled the Executive Board, without significant opposition. Gilbert Padilla became secretary-treasurer, replacing the long out-of-favor Tony Orendain. To the four original members of the UFWOC Executive Board—Dolores Huerta,

Richard Chavez, Mack Lyons, and Phillip Vera Cruz—were added Pete Velasco, Marshall Ganz, and Eliseo Medina. Velasco's selection preserved two seats (out of nine) for Filipinos, a representation much larger than their proportion of the membership, and perhaps an attempt to reverse the poisonous ethnic relations that had hurt the union in 1973. Velasco, a devoted follower of Chavez, was also a safe vote for him on the board. Ganz and Medina were fresh blood, along with Mack Lyons, a generation younger than the others. Appointing Ganz was a recognition of reality: if the board was to reflect the people who were actually running the UFW, he had to be on it. His presence also signaled that people from outside the farm worker community could have a substantial role in the union. Medina, although not as important as Ganz in day-to-day decisions, was admired by the staff for his political skills and his work in building the boycott. Leaving him off a board that included a yes-man like Velasco would have alarmed some, and intensified the rumors that Chavez was worried that Medina might eventually challenge him for leadership. But the problem was not solved when Chavez put him on the board: once there, Medina became Chavez's acknowledged heir-apparent.

Chavez and other board members took the delegates through the hundred-plus pages of the new constitution line by line; when questions arose, the leaders responded, and each section was ratified by voice vote. No one challenged the absence of a provision for union locals. Field offices, the closest thing to locals, would continue to be run by people appointed by the Executive Board. Union members would be able to elect only the ranch committees and, every two years, delegates to the convention, who would elect the Executive Board. The ranch committees, however, had little independent power, except in a few special cases. And, as this first convention demonstrated, voting for the Executive Board meant endorsing candidates preselected by Chavez.

No one questioned, either, the constitutional provision granting boycott volunteers who had served six consecutive months full union membership, the same as farm workers covered by union contracts.[6] The provision did not alter the distinction between volunteers and farm workers. Volunteers, serving at Chavez's pleasure, did not last long if they openly promoted positions contrary to the leadership; farm workers, who were in the union because they worked under contracts, could not be dismissed for disagreeing with Chavez or anybody else. Symbolically, however, the change enshrined an oddity observed seven years earlier by SNCC's Mike Miller, who wrote to Chavez noting that the NFWA would be a volatile hybrid, simultaneously a staff organization and a farm worker organization. That was now built into the UFW's constitution, reinforced by the stark truth that 85 percent of the UFW's budget came from non-farm worker sources and by Chavez's claim that the boycott was the only weapon left. The

UFW now was officially a two-souled body: a farm workers' union and a volunteer boycott organization rolled into one.

Not everyone at the convention was blind to the troubles ahead. Among the boycotters, some were worried about the lack of democratic structure and culture within the union. Many of them were leftists, and while most refrained from open criticism of the union leadership, they did discuss their misgivings among themselves. A small group, the International Socialists (IS), was forthright enough to publish their criticisms in a "Special Convention Edition" of *Workers Power*, in which they offered what is called on the left "critical support." While championing the gains of the UFW and praising the commitment of the leadership, the paper criticized specific union policies and practices, including problems in the hiring halls, allocation of too many resources to the boycott, and the attack on undocumented workers. These problems, the authors argued could be addressed by making the union more democratic.

The UFW must build a democratic structure which permits and encourages open criticism and even opposition to the policies of the leadership. It should have area committees and conventions with decision-making power. Decisions should represent the field workers, not the union staff or boycott committees.

The first UFW convention is not likely to make all these important changes in the union. Delegate apportionment under-represents the field workers in relation to boycott houses and staff. But more importantly, many of the field workers and staff who oppose some of Chavez's policies are afraid to speak out.

The problem of growing bureaucracy in the UFW will not be solved in one convention, but the struggle to make the union more democratic will go on as the field workers recognize that a democratic union is necessary to win against the growers.[7]

No one at the convention spoke out on these matters, although fear was a smaller factor than the fact that few people agreed with what the newspaper said. Those, like Epifanio Camacho and some of the staff, who had doubts about particular UFW policies, knew better than to raise a fuss at a big public event. The IS may have had the "correct line," but in 1973 there were only a handful who would line up with them. The "Special Edition" is best understood as part of the clutter on the convention floor, picked up by a UFW staffer and filed in some box back at La Paz, only to become a flash in the pan of a historian mining the UFW archives.

After the convention Chavez returned to La Paz and again immersed himself in bureaucratic business. "I felt I had to straighten out La Paz," he told Jacques Levy. "I couldn't allow sloppiness and independence as it

existed. I was ready to fire everyone if necessary and start from scratch."
For months he was up and working by two or two-thirty a.m. and didn't
quit until 10 at night. He signed every check, reviewed every detail. He
ordered the heads of the departments to write down every action they took
and to send a record to his office. He studied those reports, went over the
expenditures in the various boycott offices, and intervened where he saw
problems. As Bill Esher had observed ten years before, Chavez approached
the administration of the union with the mentality of a small businessman.
But the UFW was no small business; it had hundreds on staff and was
spending about $225,000 a month. Exhausted, Chavez had difficulty
accepting that some matters in the union would be beyond his control. Nor
did it help that this large organization was still run mostly by volunteers,
and that many things did go wrong. Chavez tried to assert his command
through memos on every conceivable matter.[8]

One morning workers at La Paz found a memo on their desks saying,
"From now on you will be referred to by number, rather than name." The
staff member's telephone extension would serve as the number; furthermore, "Nonworking wives will be known by their husband's number,
followed by a lower case 'a.' Sí se Puede 4."[9] Four was Chavez's extension.
The memo was a prank by Jerry Cohen and his wife, Madeleine, but for a
couple of hours, Cohen said, La Paz was in "real turmoil." One woman
had two telephones and didn't know what to do. She asked her supervisor,
who pondered the question and came up with an answer. Chavez was mad,
amused, and shocked all at once, said Cohen—but he didn't stop getting up
in the dead of night, trying to oversee every move and plug every hole.

Chavez reported to the Executive Board that things at La Paz were
"bad" and that he had to "confront" the people responsible. The first on
the block was the UFW's business manager. A paraplegic who had been
injured in a diving accident in 1964, Jack Quigley had worked as financial
officer for several nonprofits before coming to the union in 1971. When
LeRoy Chatfield left the UFW in 1973, Quigley was promoted and was
generally credited within the staff with putting the UFW's complicated
financial matters in good order.

The 1973 strike had been hard on Quigley and his staff, though. Their
office processed more than 100,000 checks that summer, using adding
machines, pencils and paper, and a few electronic calculators. They faced
the complications of duplicate names and changing Social Security numbers,
while trying to meet the accounting requirements of the federal government and the AFL-CIO. They worked eighteen- to twenty-hour days, for
$5 a week.[10]

On top of disbursing the strike fund, the office had to deal with cash
reimbursements for the organizers' expenses. Before the strike started,
Chavez once again had taken away the staff's gasoline credit cards. Over

Quigley's objections, he ordered the staff to pay for the gas and send the receipts to La Paz. The system was cumbersome, slow, and required the business office to keep large amounts of cash on hand. When Chavez returned to La Paz after the strike, Quigley recalled, "he was horrified" that there was more than $600 in the safe. Quigley explained about the gasoline payments and offered to show Chavez the documentation, but Chavez declined. "Nor did he own up to having made the decision that caused the cash to be there in the first place."[11]

Quigley wasn't exactly fired. A few days after the confrontation over the $600, he went to the hospital for a serious ulcer that had developed on his backside during the long workdays. When he returned after two months in the hospital, Chavez told him that he was being transferred. It was a demotion, and Quigley resigned.

After the failed 1965 strike, the NFWA had been saved by its liberal, church, and union supporters, many of whom had been upset by the turn to Black Power in the civil rights movement, and estranged from the militant opposition to the war in Vietnam. In 1974, however, when the UFW again turned to its urban friends for life-sustaining help, it was a different historical moment, and their reasons for supporting the union had changed. This was especially true of organized labor, which at the time of the second national grape boycott was suffering through an emblematic turning point in its own, often sorrowful history. It was bad timing for the UFW leaders. Just as they were prepared to settle into the AFL-CIO as a more or less regular union, the AFL-CIO entered a period of calamitous decline.

The UFW's attempt to find a firmer place for itself inside official labor was not just a matter of making backroom deals. Politically, the union was looking for a place in what it hoped would become a rebuilt house of labor. In 1974, *El Malcriado*, the UFW's on-again, off-again publication, included a special labor section that enthusiastically reported on encouraging developments in the rest of the union movement: the Miners for Democracy victory in the UMW; the rapidly expanding and militant Local 1199 (then an independent part of the Retail, Wholesale, and Department Store Union); textile workers' campaigns in the South; the Farah boycott in 1973. Citing the rising number of strikes in 1972 and 1973, the paper predicted that worker discontent would "explode in 1974" in a broadly based insurgency among U.S. workers, a rebellion that would include farm workers and the UFW.

But U.S. labor struggles failed to "explode" in 1974, and the insurgencies of the two previous years turned out to be the end of a brief era of rank-and-file militancy rather than the dawn of a new day. The rebellion among the organized working class had begun in the late 1960s, and, as with so much else in American culture, black people had led the way. The Black

Power movement, propelled by the ghetto conflagrations, had been taken up by African American workers in the industrial heartland, who challenged the long tradition of discrimination by management and their unions, and brought the spirit of the urban uprisings onto the factory floor. Many young white workers joined, fighting for more control over production and more say in their unions. Caught between a steep rise in the cost of living, a productivity push by employers, and the refusal of top labor officials to join the fight against discrimination and work speedups, workers responded with wildcat strikes and nascent reform movements. In the late 1960s, workers struck more often than they had in the 1930s and '40s, excepting the extraordinary year of 1946. But instead of uniting with the rank-and-file upsurge, and using it to strengthen their unions, top AFL-CIO officials joined management in opposing most of the new insurgencies. When the employers began a new attack on union power in the wake of the 1974–75 recession, the labor movement was never able to mount a successful counterattack. Real wages and working conditions for the entire U.S. working class have been declining ever since.[12]

As that decline began, the UFW entered into negotiations with the AFL-CIO, hoping to get George Meany's continued help in its struggle against the Teamsters, its push for labor legislation, and its renewed boycotts. Meany and Chavez held a series of parlays between the fall of 1973 and the spring of 1974, but they had to make their deals without the help of Bill Kircher. Meany and Chavez had never much liked each other, and Kircher had served as a buffer, absorbing the heat. But Meany held Kircher partly responsible for the failed 1973 strikes, and Kircher resigned and took a less taxing job within the AFL-CIO. Their mediator gone, Meany and Chavez had to deal with each other directly, at a high point of mutual need.

Chavez provided Meany with progressive cover for his steadfast opposition to most rank-and-file organizing and his long-term betrayal of American liberals. Chavez came relatively cheap when compared with all that had to be ignored or forgotten: Meany's failure to support an organizing drive in the South following the civil rights movement; his opposition to affirmative action in his federated unions; his support for the war in Vietnam; and his tacit support of Nixon against McGovern. Chavez's need was more direct. Having lost about 80 percent of his membership to the Teamsters, he needed political and financial support to rebuild, and he had to win that help from a man who disagreed with the way Chavez did business. They negotiated intermittently. Chavez's need was more profound, so Meany could extract favors: La Paz would be on the itinerary of various Latin American labor leaders who were being wooed by the AFL-CIO's CIA-aided operation, the American Institute for Free Labor Development (AIFLD); Chavez would refrain from criticizing Meany to West Coast reporters; the UFW would contribute to the AFL-CIO fund for Israel and issue a statement of support for Israel in the aftermath of the 1973 war.

Such favors were sometimes solicited directly, sometimes indirectly. The support for Israel, for instance, came in response to a November 12, 1973, letter in which Meany asked Chavez to contribute to the fund or directly to the Israeli Histadrut, and to "call upon" other unions to do the same. "Please advise us of such contributions," Meany added.[13] Two weeks later, in the midst of discussing the AFL-CIO's latest approach to the Teamsters on the UFW's behalf, Meany sent word to Chavez through Jerry Cohen that "the statement on Israel was helpful."[14]

Meany also took the liberty of criticizing Chavez publicly: he implied that the $1.6 million strike fund had been wasted, saying that "it was Chavez's own people who went to work behind the picket lines in Coachella, and that didn't indicate much support from the workers for Chavez." He told reporters that he admired Chavez but that he was "an idealist," "a dreamer," who had failed "to develop a real viable union."[15] Chavez was in no position to fight back. After someone in Meany's office leaked to a labor reporter that Chavez had privately complained that he couldn't control his own "crazies," Chavez composed a letter of mild rebuke to Meany but had second thoughts and never sent it.[16]

Chavez's restraint didn't completely pay off. In exchange for the AFL-CIO's full support for the renewed grape and lettuce boycotts, and its tolerance for the Gallo boycott (it had angered the International Union of United Brewery, Flour, Cereal, Soft Drink and Distillery Workers, which had contracts with Gallo), the UFW gave up its secondary boycott of stores with union employees, most notably the big grocery chains Safeway and A&P. The compromise weakened the boycott, but didn't prevent the union from leafleting outside stores that handled the boycotted goods. With the Teamsters, Meany negotiated yet another truce agreement with Fitzsimmons, which again quickly succumbed to internal Teamsters intrigue, legal threats from growers, and pressure from the Nixon administration.[17] Most troubling, Meany refused any additional contributions to the UFW strike fund.

Strapped, the UFW turned to Walter Reuther's successor at the United Automobile Workers, Leonard Woodcock. The UAW had reduced its contributions to the UFW after the 1970 boycott victory, but it still had pretenses as the standard bearer of "social unionism," as opposed to Meany's "business unionism." In 1974, Woodcock announced that the UAW would give the UFW $10,000 a week[18]. That spurred donations from other unions, and by the end of 1974 the UFW had collected more than $1 million in union donations, accounting for more than a third of its overall income.[19]

The UAW's reasons for supporting the UFW were not too different from those of its old rival, Meany. In a series of Detroit wildcat strikes in 1973, UAW officials had led the opposition to the strikers, hoping to secure their own position as junior partners of the Big Three auto manufacturers. In the last wildcat strike at Chrysler, endorsed by leaders of the UAW local at the struck plant, more than 1,000 UAW officials, many wielding baseball bats, attacked the picket line and broke the strike. That finished off the rebellion within the UAW, and brought a symbolic end to the short era of U.S. rank-and-file militancy. At a UAW convention nine months later, however, in an attempt to assure others (and themselves) that they were still progressive unionists, many of these same bat-swinging officials endorsed Woodcock's decision to fund the UFW and gave their guest speaker, Chavez, a series of standing ovations.[20]

Thus, as Chavez moved firmly into the company of progressive union officials, those officials were beating back the kind of movement that might have given the industrial unions some protection against corporate America's coming offensive. While Chavez and the UFW were hoping for a different outcome—the growth of the worker rebellion of the late sixties and early seventies—Chavez eventually found himself following the UAW's reactionary lead. In the early 1980s, he would destroy the nascent movement of his own rank-and-file militants, thereby setting up his union for the slightly delayed but even more sweeping counteroffensive of California agribusiness. What the events of the mid-seventies make clear is that Cesar Chavez's attack on his own membership fits easily into the ripe tradition of U.S. labor.

In late January 1974, a contractor's bus taking people to work at the aptly named High and Mighty Farms skidded into a drainage ditch near Blythe, on the edge of the Imperial Valley. The seats were not properly fastened to the floor. They broke loose on impact and careened to the front, crushing the driver to death and preventing many of the workers from scrambling out of the overturned vehicle. Seventeen workers drowned in the putrid waters of the ditch.[21]

Bus accidents are common in the farm worker world. Two months after the Blythe disaster, twelve more farm workers died when another contractor's bus crashed near the border. But the High and Mighty crash was spectacularly morbid, and Mexicali newspapers featured close-ups of the victims, trapped in what the papers called the "wheeled coffin." The farm workers were nominally Teamsters, but the UFW rushed to aid the survivors. It organized a memorial service where Chavez spoke; it collected money from supporters and farm workers throughout California, and amplified the grief and rage of the Imperial Valley farm worker community. UFW organizers and legal staff investigated the accident, throwing a spotlight on the little-known movement of workers to the fields and back, and pressured the legislature and the Highway Patrol, which regularly avoided inspecting farm-labor buses, to enforce safety standards.

The labor contractor who owned the bus, Jesus Ayala, was a well-known scab herder and strikebreaker. The driver, fifty-five-year-old Pablo Navarro Arellano, was in the midst of an eighteen-hour workday when the accident occurred. Typically, his job began at two a.m., when he went to the enormous shape-up at *el hoyo*, the hole, in Calexico, picked up the workers, and then drove about 130 miles to the farm. There he supervised the lettuce thinning for ten hours, drove back to *el hoyo*, dropped off the workers, cleaned out the bus, and finally left for home and a few hours' sleep. The lettuce thinners were paid nothing for the four hours' travel time between the hole and High and Mighty Farms.[22]

The accident spurred union *huesos colorados* into action. For weeks they gathered at the union field office before the sun came up, climbed onto a UFW bus, and went to *el hoyo* to talk to workers. Most of them cheered when they heard that seventeen of Ayala's buses—one for each dead farm worker—had been firebombed while stationed in the contractor's parking lot. Chayo Pelayo was one of these hard-core loyalists, and her workday rivaled that of the doomed bus driver. Mornings her alarm went off at one a.m. She got up and made lunch for herself, her husband, and their children; walked fourteen blocks to get the UFW bus; talked and leafleted at *el hoyo* for a while; sat down and ate breakfast with her friends; and then thinned lettuce at InterHarvest for eight hours. After work she went to the Calexico field office to talk over the next day's plan. Then she went home, helped her sister-in-law with dinner, put the children to bed, and went to her own bed for her standard four hours' sleep.[23]

Chayo Pelayo is one of those remarkable people who have had what statisticians might call a miserable life but who has no sense of misery or defeat about her. She was born in 1938 on a dry subsistence farm near Santa Rosalia, Jalisco. The oldest of fifteen children, she started planting corn when she was four, and soon thereafter was helping take care of her brothers and sisters. At fifteen she married, and her first five pregnancies ended either in stillbirths or babies who didn't make it past day four. Her sixth child lived, and with that daughter she decided to follow her husband, Jorge, to Mexicali, where he lived while working across the border in the melons. It was 1961; she was twenty-three.

Her husband had been a bracero, then a "special"; eventually he got a green card. They crossed the border together and settled in El Centro, where she had five more children. Relatives joined them, and often she, Jorge, and their children lived in the same small house with another sister, her husband, and their children. They all worked in the fields.

By 1971, Jorge was a strong unionist, active in many melon strikes, and Chayo Pelayo took up the union banner. She got a dispatch to InterHarvest during the Imperial Valley lettuce season, worked at union companies in Coachella during the table grape harvest, moved on to Arvin-Lamont and sometimes Delano before returning to the Imperial Valley in the early fall, where she would have time off until the winter lettuce thinning began. One of her sisters and a brother-in-law worked the same circuit. Jorge sometimes accompanied them, and sometimes he followed the melons. At every stop, Chayo and her sister volunteered for extra work at the local UFW field office. They leafleted before going to work; they helped people on their crews get assistance from the UFW service centers; sometimes they worked as submarines at nonunion ranches.

Pelayo respected Chavez, but her basic loyalty was to the union, and to the activists among her fellow workers. She did not care for the people who ran the union office in Calexico—Manuel Chavez, Oscar Mondragon, Gilbert Rodriguez—because they seemed unaware of the problems faced by workers in the fields. When it came to her day-to-day union work, she trusted the advice of her sister, her husband, Marshall Ganz and Jessica Govea—especially Jessica—and Mario Bustamante, who was usually around the Calexico office during the winter lettuce season.

Chayo had been a heroine of the 1973 grape strike. She had been arrested several times, and was so uncooperative that four police officers once angrily threw her several feet into a paddy wagon. During one stay in jail, she spent twenty-four hours in solitary confinement. She was a tireless picketer and captained a small group of strikers. Neither she nor Jorge were interested in going on the boycott, and in the winter of 1973–74 they were back in Calexico—Chayo in the lettuce, her husband in the melons. Years later she had "beautiful memories" of the *el hoyo* effort. At times she was the person who was lifted to the top of a bus, took the megaphone, and spoke to scores of people below. She told the story of the death bus; she denounced the Teamsters and the bosses; she urged the workers to join the UFW. She was cheered and embraced, delighted by her ability to hold the workers' attention. "It was easy," she said. "We believed in the cause."

Encouraged by the response to Pelayo and the others, the UFW organizers called a one-day work stoppage, or *paro*, throughout the Imperial Valley on February 22, 1974, as a demand for higher wages and a protest against Teamster contracts that covered almost all of the Imperial Valley's 8,000 workers. As many as 500 workers actively picketed. They did not completely shut down the day's harvest, but so many workers stayed off the job that the bosses claimed that Washington's Birthday had been a paid holiday all along. That got some laughs at the rally afterward, as Manuel Chavez pointed out that not even Jesus Christ's birthday was a paid holiday.[24]

Jesus Garcia, a Bud Antle *lechuguero* who joined the *paro*, explained his decision to a UFW organizer: "Now that the growers see that Chavez's movement is helping and supporting us, they show some interest in what we need and what we want . . . and if the union falls then the growers will [again] do whatever they want to us."[25] This was more than just one opinion among many. People who had little direct experience with the UFW understood that the growers had improved wages and working conditions because they were afraid of the union. Now, knowing that the union had suffered a stunning loss in the vineyards—but unsure as to why—thousands of workers elsewhere came to the UFW's defense.

The Imperial Valley *paro* and the semi-autonomous strike wave that followed fit a familiar pattern. California farm workers had always been more willing to take risks in the fields when people were around to support them. The strikes of the early 1930s and the late 1950s to early '60s were prompted not so much by the rather limited direct organizing of the Communist Party in the thirties and the AWOC in the sixties, but rather by self-organized walkouts of farm workers emboldened by the presence of those outside forces. In 1974, before the *paro* had even ended, Imperial Valley asparagus workers had realized that this was a moment not just to defend the UFW but to fight for their own demands. They figured right.

The asparagus season had just begun. The delicate spears grow from clumps of stem tissue called crowns, which farm workers bury four to six inches below the surface. After a dormant period, the spears shoot out of the crowns overnight, and that is no exaggeration: when the temperature is in the eighties, spears can grow seven to ten inches in twenty-four hours. At the beginning of the season, the spears must be cut off every other day; later, every day—otherwise they will flower, the crown will throw up no more shoots, and the cutting season will end. Bent at the waist, the workers thrust an eighteen-inch knife into the ground, cutting off the asparagus spears close to the crown but without damaging either the spear (which must be in good enough shape to sell) or the crown (which is unusually sensitive and may, if injured, stop producing spears). The growers' almost daily need for skilled harvesters was the basis for the relatively high wages of California asparagus workers. A few steps behind lettuce and melon workers, they averaged $4 an hour in 1974, or about $18 an hour in 2010 dollars.[26]

The grievance of the 1,500 asparagus workers was not unlike that of the West Side *meloneros*. Traditionally, the asparagus crews were paid for the number of boxes they packed in the fields. Those boxes were then trucked to sheds, where other workers unpacked them, discarding spears that were too short or too long, and repacked the acceptable spears. This season, without informing the Teamsters, who held the somewhat fictive contracts, the six major growers unilaterally decided to pay the field workers for the number of repacked boxes. The asparagus workers were discussing what to do when the UFW called the *paro*.[27]

On the morning of the one-day shut down, some asparagus workers told the UFW organizers that they intended to stretch the *paro* into a strike.[28] At a hastily arranged meeting the organizers explained to the workers that the UFW could not pay strike benefits but that it would endorse the strike and represent the workers in any negotiations. At five the next morning, 500 asparagus workers showed up outside the Calexico field office and voted to strike. Most others stayed at home; according to *The Packer*, production was off by a half to two-thirds.[29]

The growers faced the prospect of losing their entire three-month, multi-million-dollar season. By the second day they returned to the old system of payment. Then, they sued the UFW for damages and secured a court order to limit picketing. They also threatened to bring in cutting machines—an empty threat, as the only available machine damaged the spears and could be used only for asparagus that would go to canneries, commanding a significantly lower price. As one worker told *El Malcriado*, if they had a machine that could do the work, they wouldn't have waited for a strike to use it.[30]

The workers stayed out for a week, trying to get the best piece rate they could, and stormed the buses of the one contractor who dared to bring in scabs. Then they called off their strike and proudly returned to work. The Teamsters contracts were still in force, but the UFW had publicized their phony character. Moreover, the UFW had won many friends, not only among asparagus workers but throughout the Imperial Valley. The growers tried to grasp what had happened to them. One grower complained, "The workers are using Chavez to make more money." As the 1974 season moved north, other workers would do the same.[31]

In keeping with his role as the architect of a two-souled organization, Chavez had proclaimed after the UFW's convention, "In our present struggle, we must organize not only among farm workers but also among consumers. So we are pulled by two constituencies, and we must remain in contact with both."[32] But those two constituencies hardly commanded equal attention. In January 1974, 449 of the 544 full-time volunteers working for the union were assigned to the boycott. Sixty-two worked at La Paz, and only thirty-three worked in the field offices or as roving organizers.[33] Most of the Executive Board members were dispatched to the cities, leaving only Chavez and Philip Vera Cruz based at La Paz—and Chavez was often on the road. The distribution of the staff roughly reflected the source of the union's income, although worker dues accounted for 15 percent of the UFW's revenues, more than double the percentage of staff dealing with farm workers. The union may have had two souls, but its head, heart, and most of its belly were living in the cities.

Soon after the murder of Juan De La Cruz, the UFW had sent a caravan of hundreds of farm workers from Delano out to the boycott offices across the country. It had been a hurry-up job. The union wanted to get the most active strikers to the cities while they were still in the mood to fight, and it wanted to get the boycott rolling before the shock of De La Cruz's martyrdom wore off. Prospective boycotters were given a quick orientation about city life, received assurances that their California bills would be paid by the union, and got their assignments.

Within a few months, many of the farm workers had quit the boycott. Large families had problems with everything from baby-sitting to housing. To keep costs low, most people lived collectively in convents, seminaries, union offices, or large boycott houses. The people from religious orders and the single, middle-class volunteers brought a spirit of voluntary poverty to these collectives that the people who had spent their lives in involuntary poverty could not understand. Often the differences couldn't be worked out. Some workers got sick; others didn't like the boycott routine; some simply lost the faith and gave up.[34]

The biggest crises for the worker volunteers, however, was uncertainty about their bills back home. Some had mortgages, and others owed finance companies for furniture, cars, and appliances. People knew that some boycotters between 1967 and 1970 had lost their homes and many had lost their cars. None had the union's promise to cover the bills in writing. When La Paz was slow to make the first month's payments (some bills were purposely not paid, as the staff waited to see who would stick to the boycott), many felt betrayed.[35] Eliseo Medina, directing the Ohio boycott, wrote to La Paz sternly recommending that in the future, "new boycotters be given in writing what the union can and cannot pay and other pertinent information." Medina also complained about being told, when he called La Paz to straighten out a bill, that "only Cesar could make the decision and he was out of town." That prompted his final suggestion: "When it is necessary for Cesar to be away, someone should be authorized to make decisions and deal with our problems."[36]

As the farm workers left the boycott, religious people came on. The UFW now had full support from the National Conference of Catholic Bishops and the National Council of Churches. Priests, nuns, seminarians, and ministers easily got leave to work full-time for the UFW. They did not have bills back home to worry about, nor did they challenge union policies as did some of the student, union, and left volunteers. Their support added to the moral legitimacy of the UFW's cause among liberal consumers in a way that the others' could not. For many of these religious staffers, the highlight of the 1974 boycott was their leader's private audience with Pope Paul VI that year. Chavez gave the Pope a red and black UFW flag, and Paul VI praised Chavez for his "sustained effort to apply the principles of Christian social teaching."[37] Back in 1964, the National Farm Workers Association had use a quote from Pope John XXIII about Christian service as if it were an endorsement of the association. Ten years later, the UFW got the real thing.

In 1974, in the 118 days between the June and October Executive Board meetings, at the height of the strike wave in the fields, Chavez was at La Paz for thirty days and on the road for eighty-eight. He spent fifty-seven days on the boycott circuit, nine days at labor meetings, seven days visiting farm worker strikes, five days meeting church leaders, and seven days meeting various other groups.[38] His two major responsibilities had become administering the union, which he did badly, and shoring up boycott support, which he did magnificently. His boycott work removed him from close contact with farm workers, and so did his position at the apex of his organization, for information in the UFW typically flowed from top to bottom, isolating its president from the farm worker world. Thus, as he became the living symbol of the U.S. farm worker movement around the world, he moved farther away from the fight in the fields.

The thorns on the eight- to sixteen-foot lemon trees along the Southern California coast are so nasty that the lemon pickers, already burdened by weighty bags slung over one shoulder, wear heavy gloves, padded sleeves, and helmets as they reach from their tripod ladders for the small yellow fruit that sustains their lives. The manager of a harvest association once said that watching the piece-rate workers quickly cut the lemons from the trees, toss them in their bags, go up and down their ladders, and empty their sacks into the bins is like watching a ballet. A ballet choreographed by the dancers who have, over the years, figured out how to do the work as easily and efficiently as possible. A bracero, Merced Raya, invented the curved clipper that allows the workers to separate the fruit from the tree with a single cut. Another, unknown, worker invented the tie that allows the pickers to hold onto the ladder and reach far into the trees to cut the lemons loose with one hand. The job is so hard and requires so much skill that one would expect lemon pickers to be the best-paid workers in agriculture. They are well paid, but not the best, partly because *limoneros* are paid individually and don't have the internal solidarity of lettuce and melon crews, but mostly because ripe lemons can stay on the trees for about a month before they are too big for the fresh market, so a lemon strike has to last for several weeks before it begins to hurt the bosses.[39]

Since 1965, no one in the industry has underestimated the skill of the *limoneros*. "It was the worst year of my life," said Jack Lloyd, manager of the Coastal Growers Association. When the Bracero Program ended, the growers were deprived of more than 90 percent of their workforce. The harvest associations tried to use domestic workers: Native Americans from Arizona, New Mexico, and South Dakota; African Americans from Louisiana and Mississippi; Anglo day-haul workers from Los Angeles; and local Mexican Americans who had been shut out of the orchards since 1941. "People wouldn't last till noon," Lloyd remembers. Once we got two busloads from Texas, seventy-two people, and after one day sixteen were left; and after two days, two were left."[40] That year 24,000 workers were employed to fill a peak of 3,000 harvesting jobs. Lloyd's CGA employed 8,517 harvesters, who averaged just seventeen days of work each.[41]

Lloyd had coordinated the Bracero Program in Ventura County for three years before he became the manager of the CGA. "In 1965, the Department of Labor had all these figures that said there were available domestic workers. They told us: Look, try it out, and if it doesn't work, we will be sure you get Mexicans again. We thought it would be another Bracero Program, but what they did was open the floodgates and let the Mexicans return." But the lemon growers didn't need just any Mexicans; they need the *limoneros*. Between 1966 and 1968, the Ventura County Citrus Growers Committee, which had been the primary contractor of braceros, simply eliminated the INS middleman and sent their own bilingual representatives to Michoacán, Jalisco, and Guanajuato, where they tracked down the experienced lemon pickers and gave them formal letters saying that they would be employed when they arrived in the U.S. The ex-braceros then went to the U.S. consulate in Mexico City, where they could exchange those letters for green cards. By 1970 the *limoneros* were back in the orchards performing their ballet for wages that were 45 percent higher than they had been in the last bracero year. Some of the harvest associations, anxious never to suffer another 1965, provided health and pension plans, subsidized housing, paid vacations, and even private unemployment benefits.[42]

But workers seldom stand pat when they have a strong hand. The citrus industry in Ventura County was grossing more than $50 million a year by the early 1970s, and the fastest workers were still averaging just over $4 an hour. Through slowdowns, negotiations in the fields, and periodic refusals to work, they pushed their wage and benefit package higher. On January 24, 1974, just before the lemon harvest hit its peak, a couple of hundred lemon pickers walked off the job.[43]

Again, the dispute began after a grower initiated change in the conditions of operation. For years the *limoneros* had dumped their sacks into wooden field boxes, but in 1974 the Santa Paul Growers, one of the medium-sized grower associations, substituted larger metal bins. Over several days, the workers calculated how many more sacks it took to fill the bins and concluded that the company's new piece rates had been reduced. On the edge of an orchard, in the early-morning light, an elected workers' committee tried to negotiate new rates. This was not unusual. There is no fixed piece rate in the lemons. As one monograph explains it, "In most areas, these piece rates are determined in an ad hoc fashion: a foreman examines the height of the trees, the probable yield and size of the fruit, and orchard conditions, and announces a piece rate for picking. If the announced piece rate is too low, workers refuse to pick or do not appear the next day."[44]

When the Santa Paula supervisors declined to change the rates, the workers refused en masse to work. Meeting at the local Mexican Catholic church and assisted by two legal aid lawyers, they wrote up a list of thirteen demands, including a guaranteed minimum wage (no matter what the orchard yield), a better vacation package, a pledge against reprisals, and arrangements for communication in Spanish as well as English. They called their action a stay-at-home. They did not picket other companies, and not one of them returned to the orchards. An attempt by the growers to bring in scabs failed.

One week into the strike, at another mass meeting, the workers threatened to call in the UFW, which merited a front-page mention in the only local newspaper covering the stay-at-home. In fact, the workers had already made contact with a UFW organizer, who had told them the union could do no more than help with a food drive and the mobilization of outside support. Negotiations continued, and by the end of the next week the workers had won a signed agreement that accepted most of their demands, including a new minimum piece rate for the bins.[45]

When the UFW Executive Board convened a few weeks later for its March meeting, no one mentioned the lemon pickers' victory. It was probably unknown to most of the board members. No one mentioned the surprising asparagus strike either, or even the union's relatively successful Imperial Valley *paro*. The discussions centered on administrative matters, and on the grape, lettuce, and Gallo boycotts. When they did talk about strike strategy, they focused yet again on the table grapes. What to do about the upcoming harvests in Coachella and the San Joaquin? Ganz interjected that the union was stronger in the vegetables, that the Executive Board should put some energy and resources into organizing a strike in the Salinas Valley. His objections were ignored. The union "had more support in the grapes than we had in the lettuce," Chavez said in passing, while making another point.[46] For Chavez, closer to the Mexican American grape pickers than the Mexican lettuce cutters, this view would die hard.

Much of the talk at the March meeting was frank, an attempt to be realistic about the union's prospects in any upcoming strikes. About scabs in the vineyards, Chavez said, "If we didn't get them out last year, we are probably never going to get them out." And yet, he argued, some kind of strike was necessary: "What happens on the boycott is the important thing, because if you don't have a fight here while you are boycotting grapes over there, your boycott is going to be harder because, see, there is nothing to fight about over there; you see, your fight is not meaningful, it is hard to interpret it."[46]

That left only two difficult options, Chavez argued. A minimal, symbolic picket line (what Cesar at one point called "a fake strike") might rebound against the union "as it gives the image that the union is dying, because here there were thousands of people last year, and now there are a few." But a big strike would be expensive and draining and would almost certainly lose. Chavez recommended an all-out strike. It would hurt the quality of the grapes (with less-experienced scabs working), harass the growers, and demonstrate that the UFW was still around.

Huerta argued for concentrating on Delano; Chavez favored Coachella, and everyone else on the board agreed with Cesar. In the course of their six-day meeting, they took a bus from La Paz to Coachella for a one-day stop to talk to the local field office directors and farm workers before resuming discussions in their mountain retreat. Many questions occupied them. What was the actual relationship between the strikes and the boycott? Without AFL-CIO money, how much could the union afford for strike benefits, and how would smaller benefits affect people's willingness to strike? Was it more important to picket the thinning or to interfere with the picking and packing? And what had actually happened in the disastrous strike the year before?

Richard Chavez, the truest realist among them, voiced his concern: "Before we decide to go on strike, we have to go out there and talk to the people and see what is happening. I myself couldn't make a decision like this before I went to the area and saw, and got reports." Richard didn't call for the customary mass meetings where people would vote a strike up or down; he simply observed that all the strategy in the world could not substitute for solid knowledge about what the potential strikers thought. The union leaders didn't have it, and they weren't going to get it on a one-day stop in Coachella, he said. He also warned about the dangers of getting it wrong. "If we do strike in Coachella then it could work against us. Cause the people [on the boycott] are asking more and more who is doing the picking, who is doing this and why can't you get the scabs out? Who is picking? Where are your members, where are they?"

He finished with an observation about the 1973 strike: "Let's face it, last year I think as many people as you got out, the big troops that you got out, the thing is that we bought it, we bought that goddamn strike. I had a hell of a time explaining that $90 a week [to union supporters] you know, a really, really bad time explaining it."[47]

Although paying strike benefits hardly invalidates a strike, Richard Chavez's implication that the 1973 strike had been unpopular angered his brother, who rushed to its defense, exaggerating its effectiveness, reminding them that the "5,000 people" who got arrested were "turned on . . . and are not going to forget that." The UFW had maintained that a little more than 3,000 people had been arrested. Even that figure was inflated by about two thirds, as many were arrested multiple times. Chavez's exaggeration is in some respects a small matter; all people, especially those in politics, exaggerate to their advantage. But when, as here in this meeting, their listeners have some independent knowledge of what's under discussion, it limits the tendency to exaggerate. This corrective mechanism, however, usually did not work with the UFW, as union leaders spent so much of their time "interpreting" (as Chavez put it) what was happening in the fields to potential boycotters, who had no knowledge of farm worker life or activities. And as they were believed so completely by their supporters, the union leaders often got carried away by their own interpretations.

Earlier in this eight-day meeting, the Executive Board had viewed the rough cut of *Fighting for Our Lives*. At some level, most of the board members knew that the film was a distorted account of the 1973 strike. At the same time, absent an independent assessment of the strike, nothing stopped them from eventually believing it. Blinded by their distortion of 1973, how could they intelligently decide what to do in 1974? Back in 1969, Peter Matthiessen had observed that Chavez "was optimistic about the past." But once he fixed up the past, how could he make any reasonable calculation about the future? Ultimately, as Jerry Cohen later observed, reality has its way of working itself back into the picture, and then "It bites you in the ass."[48]

The executive board made two conflicting decisions that March: It would have an all-out strike in Coachella, and Manuel Chavez would be in charge. But during the board meeting, Manuel had argued against an all-out strike. The best approach, he had said, was to force the contractors not to bring workers to a struck ranch. That could be done by physically confronting contractors at the places they picked up workers (as had been done in *el hoyo*), or threatening to break them, one by one, by telling employers that the union would leave them alone if they would stop using a particular contractor. Strikers, he said, should visit contractors, talk to people in their homes, find different ways to put economic pressure on the growers. The point was to harass the growers and contractors ceaselessly with what he called a "ministrike," which would be handled by crews of specialists, who would be paid a higher level of strike benefits than others. He would need "four good groups (at least ten in a group)," he said, "to picket, roam, generally bother the growers."[49]

In the late sixties, the NFWA and the UFWOC had already introduced what they called legitimacy strikes and publicity strikes, neither of which involved the mass withholding of labor. Now, in 1974, in the vineyards from Coachella to Fresno, the UFW developed what might be called the harassment strike. In Coachella it consisted of intermittent and ineffective picket lines; rallies and protests at the courthouse after people were arrested; reports to local INS officials about illegals in the fields; and some sabotage. Manuel Chavez claimed that the harassment hurt the quality of the thinning, but privately he agreed with the growers that it didn't significantly interfere with the harvest. By the end of the strike he concluded that if the union wanted to mount a more successful fight in the future it would have to organize year-round rather than cobble up an intensive effort for a brief period during the thinning and harvest.[50]

The strikes in Arvin-Lamont, Delano, and Fresno were similarly unsuccessful. The *huelgistas*, never more than sixty and often as few as twenty, were not typically farm workers who came from the vineyards they were targeting, but instead were *los huesos colorados* from all over the San Joaquin. Their work was routine and they became increasingly isolated from the bulk of the grape workers, who continued to work. Many of those who had struck in 1973 were now working in the vineyards and were now being denounced as scabs. Pablo Espinoza, director of the Arvin-Lamont field office, felt sympathy for them and reported to the executive board that they were "ashamed and hide from us."[51]

Some union stalwarts were also disillusioned. Epifanio Camacho foundered without a mass movement. He had no taste for symbolic picketing or anything that smacked of a "fake strike." He got a dispatch to Perelli-Minetti, the wine grape company where the UFW still had a contract, and continued to agitate, fighting for the rights of workers to carry transistor radios, organizing against the company's attempt to get rid of older grape pickers, and protesting the union's failure to provide written contracts for all union members. He annoyed the Delano field office, and few of his fellow workers were in a mood to listen. Finally, he met some people who not only listened but told him he was right, a couple of members of the Progressive Labor Party, a small communist oranization. They began to court him, and sent him their newspaper, *Challenge*, which Camacho passed along to other workers, as he couldn't understand it. Since Camacho was a committed anti-Communist, the PLers had a major educational task before them, but they persevered. When they provided him with a lawyer who got some picket line charges against him dropped, they had their man.

It did not take long for his relationship with the UFW to unravel. Chavez personally banned him from distributing *Challenge* at any UFW-sponsored activity and told him not to accept help from a PL lawyer. Local field office staff began telling people that Camacho was a Communist and they should stay away from him. Within a year of his first contact with PL, he wrote an open letter to Chavez saying that the rumors were true, he was a Communist. He criticized the union for its anti-Communism, pacifism, and collaboration with the bosses. Camacho was laid off from

Perelli-Minetti at the time, and being low on the seniority list he was not recalled when the company started to rehire, nor could he get a dispatch for any other job at the hiring hall. He complained to the UFW field office but did not persist. He would spend the next several years attending conferences and appearing at forums as PL's expert on the farm labor question, a people's champion disarmed, pushed into the shadowy, off-stage debates of sectarian politics, and one more casualty of the passing of a mass movement among San Joaquin Valley farm workers.[52]

Just as Chavez and the executive board had feared, the table grape strikes became badges of weakness, not of strength. But in a surprising twist, the UFW's failure in the table grapes did no harm to its main political project of 1974: getting a favorable farm labor law passed in the California legislature. Emboldened by the puny harassment strikes, the San Joaquin growers figured they had a good chance to win any state-regulated farm worker elections. The rest of agribusiness, anxious about continued boycotts and the mass activity of farm workers in other parts of the state, longed for greater control. Out of that mixture of strength and fear, California growers increasingly came to endorse in principle an Agricultural Labor Relations Act.

A sober consideration of the California map had to dampen any excess bravado among the growers. Through the center of the state, from Coachella to Fresno, a few hundred farm workers were a petty annoyance to the table grape companies. Meanwhile, in a string of cities along the coast—Oxnard, Santa Paula, Morgan Hill, Watsonville—and throughout the great Sacramento Delta from Stockton to Sacramento, as many as 10,000 farm workers, starting on their own but quickly looking to the UFW for help, were on strike in the spring and summer of 1974.

The union leadership had neither expected nor planned for the strikes, but once they got rolling, they did not let the opportunity pass. A crew of UFW organizers, led by Manuel Chavez, rushed from strike to strike, helping people organize, increasing the sense of crisis in the local communities by publicizing the battles and threatening to enlarge them, and making sure the strikers focused their attack not just on the bosses but on the Teamsters and the need for a farm labor law.

The first strike started in mid-May in a strawberry field at American Foods in Watsonville. Braceros had once worked most of the strawberries, and now the pickers were primarily green-card ex-braceros and the undocumented. Many lived in a labor camp on the edge of town, between a slaughterhouse and a wrecking yard. The camp had once housed braceros rent-free, but now the workers had to pay rent for housing that had fallen into disrepair. As the strawberry season began, a company supervisor, who also owned the camp and collected the rents, announced that the fastest workers would be paid by the hour, and the slowest workers by a piece rate: the inverse of what the pickers wanted and a departure from past practice. When a delegation of workers couldn't talk him out it, the whole crew of forty left the fields.

Three days earlier, Cesar Chavez had spoken before a packed crowd at a local junior high school. He introduced a hometown organizing committee and promised to open a UFW office in Watsonville. One of the American Foods workers had been there, and he convinced the other strikers to go for help to the UFW office, twenty miles away in Salinas. The field office director, Robert Garcia, immediately endorsed their strike, and organized a regular picket line at the company's three strawberry fields around Watsonville. Three days later only a handful of the 150 workers remained in the fields. Two days after that, the strike was won. American Foods sold its crop (the land was leased) to Pic'd Rite, the one strawberry company in the area with a UFW contract. Wages in that contract were about 20 percent higher than what the strikers had been paid, and the workers themselves could choose to work by the hour or by the box. It made for quite a victory party. As usual, the word spread—this time 250 miles south, to Oxnard.[53]

Wind, *huelga*, fire, each in turn, swept across the Oxnard plain. While the start of the northern strawberry harvest was launched with a strike victory, the end of the southern harvest was being plagued by a hot Santa Ana wind. Picking strawberries in a Santa Ana is especially brutal. The wind throws dust in the eyes of the pickers and damages the tender berries. Foremen had to be especially harsh to ensure that the workers didn't put bruised berries in their baskets. But the workers were being paid by the basket, and the extra sorting cost them time and lost pay. Often at the end of a season, when the berries thin out and it takes longer to fill a basket, workers demand an adjustment in the piece rate, and occasionally growers comply. A late-season raise was built into the UFW contract and was common in the Watsonville area, but it was observed only intermittently in Oxnard. This time, harsh conditions plus the news from the north stiffened the workers' determination. Raise the piece rate, many of them said, or we end the Oxnard season about three weeks early.[54]

On May 25, workers at the Oxnard division of American Foods were the first to go out. The company had sold the harvest only on its three Watsonville fields; in Oxnard there wasn't much harvest left to sell. The workers, however, knew that pickers throughout the area were angry about the uncompensated wind-induced extra work, and, together with UFW organizers, they decided to spread the strike.

At Pleasant Valley Farms, a worker took off his shirt, made it into a flag, and walked through the fields with five friends urging people to strike. Three-quarters of the workers joined them. At Driscoll, the biggest producer, eighty workers left one field, held a meeting, and decided to drive to other Driscoll ranches, calling people out. At Martinez Farms, the entire crew left their jobs, but only after they disabled a tractor and trailer. Three days into the strike, about 2,000 people, nearly half the workforce, had stopped working, and *The Packer* estimated that production had been halved.

The growers responded quickly. Only a few raised the piece rate. As it was the end of the season, some just shut down operations early, while others sought court and police protection to complete the harvest. The most conservative judge in town and a police chief eager to try out some new toys were happy to oblige. The judge issued an order limiting the number of pickets to five at each ranch, at a time when as many as 500 strikers were caravaning from field to field. The chief called out the tactical squad, armed with new stun guns as well as the usual assortment of batons, plastic shields, shotguns, and pistols. The chief also brought out his new helicopter. It flew low and herded strikers into the clutches of the tactical squad. Fights broke out between strikers and police. A barrage of rocks hit the helicopter. The cops arrested an entire caravan of cars. All in the first week.

Cesar Chavez had rushed into town and, speaking at the Oxnard Community Center, urged several hundred workers to resist the illegal TRO nonviolently. He also warned that any wage gain could be easily lost unless they also won a contract. He then left the strike in the hands of his cousin, Manuel, who quickly raised the stakes. He bluffed, saying the union was ready to spend $500,000 to win the strike. He told reporters that if any contractor broke the strike, every labor contractor in Oxnard "would pay." He threatened mass civil disobedience.

But Manuel Chavez did more than talk big. Together with small groups of workers, he carefully measured the scene. As in Watsonville, many strikers were undocumented, and some were not new to politics. Jesus Madrigal, the man who had hoisted his shirt on a staff, explained in Spanish to a local journalist that the strikers were acting in the tradition of the Mexican Revolution, and, as in that revolution, sacrifices made by one generation would lead to victories in the next. It was not a remark typical of a UFW spokesman, but Manuel had no trouble adapting to it. Also, he was smart enough to distance this strike from the UFW's anti-illegal line.

At the end of the first week, Cesar Chavez returned and marched with a couple of thousand workers through La Colonia, where he had led one of his earliest marches in 1959. He promised to fill the jails with strikers, and said he would be the first one arrested (although privately the union had decided against a civil disobedience campaign). By Monday morning of the second week UFW organizers were urging the strikers to comply with a new, somewhat less restrictive restraining order. That position met with some resistance, but it was consistent with the way most of the workers felt. They had struck in fury for more than a week, but with the season's end so near they had little leverage. They had cost the growers several hundred thousand dollars; they had defended themselves honorably against grotesquely overarmed police. For most, it was time to move on to the next crop.

Manuel Chavez stayed and led a rear-guard action of about a hundred strikers. They picketed some fields; they complained about police tactics to the Ventura County Board of Supervisors and the Oxnard City Council. A few vandals did their thing. Seven minor fires caused about $20,000 damage to sheds, bunkhouses, and equipment. The strike had come in on a hot wind. It went out with a barn burning.[55]

The Stockton fresh tomato pickers were next. On Monday, July 22, at the beginning of the harvest, a supervisor fired a crew of workers because they refused to work for $2.45 an hour. The *tomateros* preferred the thirty-cents-a-bucket piece rate they had won the year before, because experienced pickers could earn two to three times more than at the hourly rate, and they could earn their money in a shorter workday, sparing themselves the oppressive midafternoon delta heat. The fired workers marched to neighboring fields, and by the next day, 500 people were in the strike caravans, sometimes driving straight into the fields to stop the harvest. Nearly thirty sheriff's deputies and more than twice as many private security guards arrested a few strikers but couldn't deter the rest. A contractor fired a pistol in the air; the *tomateros* moved right past him.[56]

One hundred miles to the south, Manuel Chavez was running a small harassment strike in the melons on Fresno's West Side when he heard about the rampaging tomato pickers. He arrived in Stockton on Wednesday, met with some of the strikers, and conferred with Cesar Chavez on the phone.[57] At a rally of several hundred workers the next day he said the UFW would set up a strike kitchen and begin paying strike benefits. He added that the strike would extend to the cucumbers, the only other crop being harvested in Stockton at that time, and would thus become a "general strike." This was the beginning of a major effort to unionize the tomato workers, he told the *Stockton Record*, and the UFW also intended to begin organizing among the 50,000 Teamster cannery workers in the area, most of whom were Mexican Americans.[58]

These were just threats, but coupled with the walkout, they did the trick: some tomato growers immediately restored the thirty-cent piece rate, and others raised the rate to thirty-five cents a bucket. Most pickers returned to work, but the UFW did not call off the strike. For the next week a few hundred strikers picketed and clashed with managers, private security guards, and sheriff's deputies. Meanwhile, Manuel Chavez was fifty miles away, holding a news conference in Sacramento on the UFW-sponsored farm labor bill, which was being debated in the state assembly. He claimed that 85 percent of Stockton's tomato workers were on strike, and advocated immediate elections. His claim was a considerable exaggeration, but few noticed as the continuing fights in the fields kept the strike in the headlines. Manuel blamed the violence on grower-hired vigilantes who were "disguised as armed guards," and called for federal intervention. If the legislature did not pass the proposed law, he warned, there would be a general strike of farm workers throughout California. The threat seemed credible. The *Stockton Record*, a supporter of agribusiness, called the legislature "gutless" for its longtime failure to pass a farm worker law.[59]

Some strikers were initially enthusiastic about picketing but now uneasy about continuing the strike. Jose Magaña had been picking tomatoes in Stockton as a bracero since 1943; his son Luis arrived in 1970 at the age of fifteen and started working beside his father after just a few months of school. The strike was partly a fiction, they believed, and antagonisms were developing between *tomateros* who had won their wage demands and the people who remained on strike. But the strike had ceased to be their own. It was in the hands of the UFW, which had its own agenda. The strike was not declared over until late September, long after it had any meaning in the fields, after which the UFW closed down the local office, which it had promised to keep open. Many of the local tomato pickers came to agree with Luis, who concluded that they "had been used by the union."[60]

In the heat of the battle, however, most workers had been thankful for the UFW's help. And on August 7, two and a half weeks after the strike had begun, many *tomateros* who had returned to work left the fields again and joined a UFW caravan from Stockton to Sacramento. There, union staff ushered them into the biggest legislative chamber available, where the Assembly Labor Relations Committee had rescheduled its hearing to accommodate the more than 500 visitors. The crowd overflowed into the halls, and the *Stockton Record* called the demonstration the "biggest and loudest in recent Capital history." Farm workers sang, chanted, and screamed their approval when the committee backed the UFW-favored bill by a vote of 5 to 3.[61] One week later, a smaller crowd would cheer the bill through the Assembly Ways and Means Committee, guaranteeing that it would get to the assembly floor, where it was sure to pass later that fall. The bill, which included the basic UFW package of demands, would not get through the Republican-controlled state senate, but it became the starting point of negotiations for the final bill the next spring.

As Epifanio Camacho had said almost a decade before, strikes are contagious. The quick success of the fresh pick *tomateros* (whose tomatoes go directly to grocery stores and supermarkets), with their spirited rallies and mass demonstrations, inspired the people who worked in the tomatoes that were trucked to the canneries for processing. Those workers, too, picked up the UFW flag and used it to win a small increase in pay. They didn't win much else, however.

Their fight was unique because their work was quite different from that of other fruit and vegetable farm workers. The picking of processing tomatoes was the one job in all of California agriculture where growers had succeeded in replacing "the cunning of the hand" with machines. Through years of cross-breeding, a scientist at UC Davis had developed a tomato that ripened uniformly and had a thick enough skin to be picked, undamaged, by a machine that had been developed in tandem with the fruit. The machine rolled through the fields, ripping the vines from the ground, separating the fruit from the vines, and depositing the tomatoes on a conveyer belt, where about twenty human sorters picked out the dirt clods and the damaged or unacceptable tomatoes. In 1962, 1 percent of California processing tomatoes were picked by this machine. In 1964, the last year that braceros were available, the machines still picked less than 4 percent. In 1965, the machines picked 25 percent of the crop; two years later, 95 percent. By 1974, the machines picked every processing tomato in California.[62]

In the aggregate, tomatoes for processing bring bigger money than the ones destined for the fresh market. In 1974, processing tomatoes passed lettuce as the number one moneymaker in all California vegetable and fruit production, grossing about $375 million. The processing machine, which cost about $65,000, had changed the nature of the deal. During the bracero period, more than 4,000 growers had produced processing tomatoes; by 1974 less than 600 remained, although acreage and production had steadily increased. While 50,000 workers had picked the tomatoes in 1964, fewer than 20,000 sorters stood over the conveyer belts in 1974. The pickers had been Mexican men, but now, between 65 and 80 percent of the sorters were Mexican American women. The rest were a combination of green-card migrants, some African American and Anglo men, and a few undocumented Mexicans. The area of production shifted, too: the Sacramento Delta remained important, but new production centered on Fresno's West Side, whose scant population allowed for the large holdings on which the picking machine could be most effective. Finally, in an affront to traditional agricultural practices, the machines, ablaze in flood lights, often ran around the clock, forcing their human operators and sorters into two twelve-hour shifts or three eight-hour ones. Here alone the title of Carey McWilliams' book made complete sense: the tomato machine was a rolling factory in the fields.[63]

As the fresh-tomato season came to an end, the UFW refrained from calling a strike in the processing fields. But the sorters riding through the fields, knowing the union was around, pulled off a series of short *paros* of their own. Typically, Al Rojas, by then a Sacramento-area UFW orga-nizer, would receive a phone call from a supervisor of one of the machines, saying that the workers had requested that he come immediately. When Rojas arrived, the machine was often idle, the workers standing around, sometimes arguing with the supervisor or the owner. The disputes were many: the company wasn't rotating positions on the conveyer belts; or an eight-hour shift had been extended to twelve hours; or people had heard that workers on another farm were making more; or the head sorter was playing favorites. Rojas often could arrange some type of settlement, which occasionally involved a small raise, and the jubilant sorters climbed back on the machine. No contracts came out of this, but the workers were grateful for the union's help.[63]

As the processing-tomato harvest hit its peak in early September, the Teamsters intervened. David Castro, head of Teamsters farm-worker Local 1973, announced that his union was going to win contracts for the machine sorters by "breaking the link between the agricultural fields and the canner-ies."[64] Small groups of Teamsters picketed farm entrances, urging Teamster truckers not to take the sorted tomatoes out of the fields. They also picketed early in the morning at the truck yards, urging the truckers not to go to work. These were the tactics that had spread Teamster power in the West from the 1930s until the late '40s, when the Taft-Hartley Act made such actions illegal and therefore less common. In 1974, although many rank-and-file Teamsters honored the picket lines, the officials who had planned the action didn't have the will to see it through, and after a spurt of violence the effort collapsed.

The Teamsters action prompted a UFW reaction, but that fared only slightly better. Early in the morning on the day after the Teamsters appeared in the fields, Rojas spoke to scores of quickly assembled people at the edge of a field of one of the biggest companies. After taking a strike vote, people marched into the fields and stopped the machines. By the end of the day several hundred people were on strike. Despite this enthusiastic beginning, the strike did not last. Mechanization had done its job. Over the previous decade, 30,000 people who had picked processing tomatoes had been thrown out of work. Many of them were available to scab, and people who did have jobs were reluctant to risk them by striking for more than a day or two. After the growers raised the hourly wage from $2.40 to $2.70, and imported a contingent of black workers from Sacramento and Mexican men (many undocumented) to sort the tomatoes, most people returned to work. The strike degenerated into yet another harassment campaign, greatly increasing antagonisms among the diverse workforce. The workers had won a little, and lost a lot.[65]

★   ★   ★

Three more small strikes concluded the season. On August 21. the *limoneros* whose stay-at-home in February had initiated the 1974 strike season helped bring it to a successful end with a follow-up strike. The *limoneros* were angry because the SP Growers, in Santa Paula, in violation of the terms of their earlier agreement, had refused to tell them in a timely fashion what the piece rates would be and had fired some workers for participating in the earlier action. The strikers demanded reinstatement of the fired workers, an extension of the piece-rate increase to orange picking, and the firing of a particularly obnoxious foreman. For twenty-three days no scab crossed the picket line. On the second day, the strike leader, Juan Gonzalez, knew exactly how to worry his boss: "We want a twenty-five percent increase in wages if we pick oranges. We want one contract for all. If we don't get it, we want to join the UFW."[66]

The strikers called La Paz, and the UFW sent the organizer Ben Maddock to Santa Paula. He remained behind the scenes as the company refused to negotiate. The workers asked Maddock if Cesar Chavez could come to town. Two weeks into the strike, Chavez did, speaking to some 300 people in Santa Paula. Two days later, about the same number marched to Santa Paula from Oxnard, many carrying UFW flags. SP Growers hired a new manager, resumed negotiations, and capitulated. In addition to raises and a compromise on the February agreement, they replaced the offending foreman. They had temporarily saved themselves from the UFW.[67]

At the same time, a hundred mushroom pickers in Morgan Hill, north of Salinas, left the dark mushroom sheds when they heard that an over-bearing foreman had fired a popular worker. An elected committee went to the manager to protest; he refused to reverse the foreman's decision and asked each worker one by one whether he was going to return to work, and fired them one by one when each refused. Hearing this, the other workers went to the UFW office in Salinas for help. They had other griev-ances: the mushroom buttons mature unevenly but the mushrooms must be picked when they are ready, so pickers had to report to work seven days a week, sometimes working as few as two hours, sometimes as many as twelve, with no daily minimum or provision for overtime pay. Recently the pickers had been required to clean and sort the mushrooms as well, without a raise in the piece rate of seventy-six cents for a ten-pound basket. Although they had paid vacations (one week per year of service), the company paid no health benefits, and working year after year in the dark led to various ailments, including failing eyesight. The next day, September 6, the workers struck. They were strong enough the first week to get the foreman fired. The strike petered out after that, as about half the work-force, a combination of regulars and scabs imported from San Francisco and Oakland, were in the sheds.

Officially called off after seven weeks, the rebellion in the mushrooms belongs in a history—even one as detailed as this—only because it was a small squall in a larger storm, and because of its prototypical character: it was started by workers angry at an arbitrary foreman, a change in operations, and an indefinite work schedule required by the uneven maturing process of nature; once they walked out, the workers sought the UFW's help; the union endorsed the strike, and paid benefits to those who were willing to stay on and harass the company after the strike was clearly lost; and, finally, the union transferred the paid *huelgistas* to other battle grounds. Throughout the strike, the *huelgistas* spent one day a week in San Francisco, walking on picket lines for the Gallo boycott.[68]

The strike storm climaxed in the orchards of Watsonville. Pajaro Valley apple growers had made themselves a UFW target by signing with the Teamsters before the season began, but there was no shortage of local issues. The Teamster contracts, negotiated without consulting the workers, neglected to raise wages but extracted union dues; workers were charged exorbitant rents to live in company camps or old bracero quarters; and some growers even charged the workers a fee for getting a "safe" Social Security number. That last outrage pointed to one of the main questions the workers and UFW organizers talked over at the Salinas office. About 90 percent of the apple pickers were undocumented; would they support a strike?

At the time, regular dispatches from La Paz declared not only that illegals were the majority of the strikebreakers but also that they couldn't be organized because they were vulnerable to deportation. Although the Salinas field office, under the direction of Robert Garcia and Jerry Kay, had kept the volume on the union's anti-illegal position down low, union activists were familiar with the argument and were influenced by its logic. Perhaps the undocumented would be afraid to fight, some said, and even if they fought and won, they couldn't become union members because of their legal status. But Kay and Garcia had rarely enforced that UFW rule, and Garcia, one of the more militant and independent field office directors, decided to give a strike a try.

The morning of September 23, after a small UFW caravan arrived at an orchard of the Buak Fruit Company, the entire crew, thirty-five to forty people, got down from their ladders and, to a chorus of shouts and screams, joined the strike. As had become standard in the 1974 strikes, the workers demanded higher wages and the Teamsters' departure from the fields. The scene was repeated at the next Buak orchard, and soon Buak canceled the day's work. At the Watsonville union hall, ninety-seven people signed UFW authorization cards. Most of them, Garcia reported, showed Social Security cards rather than green cards as identification, an almost sure sign that they were undocumented.

The next morning, union cars ferried more than a hundred strikers to the main Buak orchard, on an isolated back road. No one was working in the trees. The Buaks, father son, stood some twenty yards inside the property line, talking to a few idled forklift drivers. Two dozen Santa Cruz County deputies arrived, outfitted in full riot gear. But the deputies remained in their cars and the strikers began to jeer them. About two hours later, a green and white bus and two smaller vans, escorted by another sheriff's cruiser, stopped in front of the picket line. The *migra* had arrived. The picket line fell silent, but no one ran. The door of the bus opened and the man in charge, Officer Sill, stepped out, and looked around. Silence, broken by the shout of one lone worker: "*Abajo con la migra.*" Down with the *migra*.

"Hell, they didn't tell me it was going to be like this," Sill said. He got back in the bus and drove a hundred yards to a private road, where he met with the Buaks.

The strikers were now chanting, "*Abajo con la migra. Abajo con la migra.*"

The UFW's Alfredo Santos left the picket line to find out what was going on. Sill said that the sheriff's office had called and said they had "eighty wets in hand, waiting to be picked up." But now that he was here, he said, he could see that no one had been arrested, and since he didn't have the manpower to do it, he was going home. The green and white vehicles made one more pass by the picket line, which serenaded their departure. For hours, the strikers replayed what had happened, marching buoyantly up and down the road and telling each other stories of earlier encounters with the *migra*. Using a stick as a mock microphone, the men mimicked a radio program, with the workers taking turns belting out popular tunes, couples dancing in the street, and a baritone voice reporting to the imagined radio audience how the *migra* had turned tail and run.

Buak was one of the biggest apple growers in the Pajaro Valley, and its workers usually picked 3,000 to 3,500 bins a week at this point in the harvest; the few scabs produced less than 200. In the second week, Buak raised the rate from $5 a bin to $8.50, explaining to the Watsonville *Register-Pajaronian* that when he had signed the Teamster contract, he personally had wanted to pay a higher wage, but the smaller growers had objected and the Teamsters had not pressed the issue. The raise pulled thirty to forty strikers back to work, but even with outside scabs, the workforce was at half strength. The UFW paid the strikers $27 each the first week, and $56 each thereafter. Some Teamster organizers were reduced to picking apples themselves. They also jumped a couple of UFW organizers, breaking one man's arms with a pipe. Manuel Chavez arrived from Sacramento with a couple of young men that second week. One of them, a teenager, carried a chain and knew how to use it. A few more fights—this time more evenly matched—followed. A contractor's bus burned.

After three weeks, with the harvest almost concluded, the UFW's Garcia declared victory: the strike had raised wages (many other growers had followed Buak's lead), and had exposed the fraudulent Teamster contracts. Privately, he explained that nobody was foolish enough to believe that these kinds of strikes could win the UFW contracts. Rather, this one was valuable to the UFW as a "publicity strike," adding pressure on the Teamsters, the legislature, and the growers.[69]

Finally the growers sued for peace. Two years of strikes, disruptions, boycotts, and harassment had clinched the case. Others besides the growers were anxious to bring the conflict to an end. Law enforcement officials throughout the state had had their budgets wrecked fighting the UFW. Supermarkets large and small had been harassed for the past eight years. The editorial pages of every major newspaper in the state, including the agribusiness trade journals, were calling for peace. The politicians had to deliver it. Some kind of accommodation with the UFW was their best hope. The UFW was ready to be accommodated. What it needed was the right kind of law. That is what it got.

Most concessions are meant to tame an adversary, and the California Agricultural Labor Relations Act was no different. Although it conceded to the UFW a legal framework within which the union could potentially thrive, it was also meant to diminish the unruly power of the farm worker movement by bringing it under the formal structure of law. But this concession smelled more of victory than co-optation. The two state actions that framed the bill's passage make the point. In April 1975, just before the last negotiations over the final shape of the ALRA began, the California Industrial Safety Board banned the use of the short-handled hoe, an implement that had ruined the backs of generations of farm workers. Four months after the ALRA passed, the California legislature and Governor Jerry Brown granted California farm workers the right to unemployment benefits. Thus, by the summer of 1975, California farm workers were covered by a comprehensive labor law, minimum-wage guarantees, unemployment insurance, and industrial safety requirements, and were the focus of new interest by government statisticians and academics, all achieved in the fourteen years since that dawn in the Imperial Valley when the first bracero climbed over the fence to join a strike at the Dannenberg Ranch. California farm workers, sometimes on their own and often led by the UFW, had torn down the wall that agribusiness had built in the 1930s to keep the New Deal out of their fields and orchards. Despite all the losses and setbacks that the UFW suffered later, that wall has never been rebuilt.

The California Agricultural Labor Relations Act was not a neutral law. Like the Wagner Act, the ALRA was meant to help workers organize themselves into unions. Subsequently this grand concession would be doubted by some farm worker organizers, who argued that the UFW had done better when agricultural relations were governed by the law of the jungle. But the fact that in the long run the UFW was defeated in the California fields cannot be blamed on the new labor law; although the law on its own did not guarantee success, it provided the framework within which a healthy union, leading a farm-worker movement, could have thrived.

The pressure from the fields did not automatically result in a union-friendly law. The UFW had to translate the widespread desire for peace into a campaign for specific legal language that would protect farm worker elections from being swamped by the overwhelming power of the employers. That was no mean trick, but the UFW was in an excellent position to pull it off. It had troops to deploy and a willingness to use them; it was familiar with Democratic Party politics and Sacramento lobbying; its legal department was smart, skilled, and dedicated.

The union was especially good at using its farm worker loyalists and boycott volunteers to compel politicians both friendly and unfriendly to vote right. Alinsky had always insisted, and in the CSO years Chavez had learned, that if a community organization were strong enough, it need not be pushed around by politicians but could hold these perpetual office-seekers to account. In the struggle for the ALRA, there is little doubt about who was doing the pushing. Farm workers and their supporters overflowed the chambers in most every important legislative hearing; Los Angeles boycotters canvassed the districts of recalcitrant legislators, urging voters to call their representatives and demand that they support the UFW's position; the union called rallies and demonstrations in Sacramento in the midst of touchy negotiations.

The UFW was almost as hard on its friends as on its enemies. When the gubernatorial candidate Jerry Brown was slow in calling Democratic Assembly leader Leo McCarthy about getting the early version of the UFW's bill out of committee, farm workers and UFW lawyers entered Brown's Los Angeles office, sat down, and waited until LeRoy Chatfield, then Brown's campaign manager, came to find out what they wanted. Oh, nothing, they answered, they were just measuring the office to see how many farm workers it could hold. Brown called McCarthy the next day. And once Brown was elected, and was again slow to take up the matter, the UFW organized an immense march to Modesto, where, in one of Chavez's favorite tactical expressions, they killed two birds with one stone, and kept the stone. They promoted their already highly effective Gallo boycott, and they threatened to go to Sacramento and have it out with Brown. "We like Governor Brown," Chavez said in his speech, "but we like farm workers more." A few weeks later, Ganz, Brown, Chatfield, Cohen, and a few others were meeting through the night in the Governor's office, framing the deal that would become the law.[70]

In the negotiations that followed, Teamsters were in one room, growers in another, and the UFW legal team in a third, with Brown shuttling among them. The UFW benefited from two additional particulars. The first was the presence of LeRoy Chatfield. After leaving the UFW, Chatfield had gone into real estate, which only proved to him that his true vocation was politics. He then went to work for Richard Alatorre, a state legislator close to the UFW. Brown, who had dealt with Chatfield in the 1972 campaign against Proposition 22, hired him away from Alatorre. Eventually, Chatfield became Brown's chief of staff. Brown did much of the negotiating over the labor law himself, but Chatfield was perfectly positioned to promote the UFW's views.[71]

Even more important for the union's purposes were Brown's national ambitions: he wanted to be president, and he knew that Chavez could help. The nationwide boycott organization, with more than 500 paid staff and thousands of volunteers, would be useful in a national campaign—crucial for a freshman governor with few contacts outside California. Cesar Chavez himself, with his connection to the Kennedys and his popularity among liberals, had become a factor in the calculations of Democratic Party insiders. If Brown wanted Cesar's support in a run for the presidency, he would have to get Chavez a law that he liked.

The final wording of the ALRA was a triumph for the UFW legal department. Chief Counsel Jerry Cohen and UFW lawyers Tony Gaenslen, Sandy Nathan, and Tom Dalzell negotiated the details with Brown. In preparation, they had spent a couple of weeks with AFL-CIO experts on the National Labor Relations Board, and they understood the intricacies of labor law better than any of the government or grower negotiators. They got almost everything they wanted: ranch rather than craft units, the agricultural equivalent of industrial organization; elections only during peak production times and within seven days of an election petition, or forty-eight hours if a strike was in process; specified unfair labor practices with a "make whole" agreement if the employer was found guilty of such practices; language preventing procedural maneuvers from delaying a vote; the right of strikers to vote in the elections if they had walked out within three years of the law going into effect; and the union's continuing right to boycott, with only limited restrictions. The final wording was endorsed by the California Farm Bureau and every other important agricultural organization in the state. What the growers got was the prospect of stability in the fields and relief from union recognition via boycott. At least some of them were convinced that, even under rules essentially written by UFW attorneys, they could win elections in the fields.[72]

Soon after the ALRA became law in 1975, Governor Brown appointed its first five-person board. The chair was Bishop Roger Mahoney, an open advocate of unionization in the fields, and a semiopen supporter of the

UFW. He was joined by Joseph Grodin, a liberal law school professor; Joseph Ortega, a Chicano attorney and quiet friend of the union; Richard Johnson, a grower attorney who headed one of the more liberal grower organizations; and LeRoy Chatfield, current chief of staff to Governor Brown and onetime chief of staff to Cesar Chavez. The union's legislative victory had its exclamation point. Farm workers and the UFW had won one of the best labor laws in the world, and the board that would enforce it represented a four to one vote in their favor. A UFW leaflet showed a runner breaking the tape at a finish line under the big, bold words, "The Race Is Won!"[73]

The Wet Line

May '74 to March '75

Nothing in California's Agricultural Labor Relations Act prevented undocumented workers from voting in secret-ballot elections for union representation. Amid the celebrations of the new law no one remarked on that publicly, and years later Jerry Cohen did not recall the question ever arising during the months of negotiations. That is odd, because while the law was being crafted, while farm workers were demonstrating for their own New Deal in Sacramento and striking over wages, conditions, and respect in the fields of California, the UFW was vigorously—as it turned out, disastrously—engaged in what it called the Campaign Against Illegals.

In May 1974 a memorandum from Cesar Chavez to all UFW "entities in California, Arizona, and Florida" announced "the beginning of a MASSIVE CAMPAIGN to get the recent flood of illegals out of California" (emphasis in original). The memorandum was clear: "We consider this campaign to be even more important than the strike, second only to the boycott. If we can get the illegals out of California, we will win the strike overnight. This campaign, therefore, is our number one priority here in California, and we expect all Union entities to cooperate to make it successful."[1]

Chavez introduced the campaign on May 20 in a staff meeting at La Paz. Extensive notes of the meeting record not one word of dissent. On June 13 he unveiled the full plan to the Executive Board. Again, no objections were voiced. In the six months that followed, until December, when the campaign was officially ended, there is no record that any member of the Executive Board registered any reservations about what became an organized, systematic attack on undocumented workers, nor did any Executive Board member subsequently interviewed remember criticizing it.

Scapegoating illegals had been part of the tool kit of the union in all of its incarnations—National Farm Workers Association, United Farm Workers Organizing Committee, and United Farm Workers of America—since 1965, but the scale of this new campaign was unprecedented. Between June and October, Chavez did what he could to throw the weight of his whole organization into the effort. Prodded by twice-a-week directives from La Paz, a few volunteers in the San Joaquin Valley field offices tracked down illegals where they worked and lived, informed local INS officials, and, on forms provided by La Paz, documented the Border Patrol's typical refusal to take any action. In mid-July the union reported to the INS the addresses of more than 300 illegals in Arvin-Lamont, more than 500 in Delano, and more than 1,200 in Porterville. By mid-September, the Selma field office had reported 2,641 illegal aliens to the Fresno Border Patrol office, which, the union volunteers complained, resulted in the arrest and removal of only 195 people.[2]

The illegal invasion of the fields became a main subject of Chavez's speeches, the primary focus of most UFW press releases, a favorite topic to discuss with visiting reporters. UFW literature accused illegals not only of taking jobs and dooming strikes but of bringing disease into California.[3] When the campaign was criticized by some on the boycott staff, and by many union supporters, the UFW carried on, polishing its arguments, banishing a few of its internal critics and denouncing those who opposed it as "pro-grower" and "antiunion."

For the first time the boycott offices were also involved. They collected more than 40,000 signatures on a petition calling on the Justice Department and Immigration and Naturalization Service to enforce the immigration laws and to remove the "hundreds of thousands of illegal aliens now working in the fields." The petition explained that "these illegals are breaking farm worker strikes, displacing farm workers from their jobs in the U.S. and depressing agricultural wages."[4] A letter-writing campaign to Congress made the same demands. In an executive session of the House Subcommittee on Labor and Monetary Affairs, Chavez testified about the Border Patrol's disregard for the UFW's documentation and called on Congress to increase funding so that the INS could deport those living and working in the United States illegally.[5] When the government wouldn't, or couldn't, sufficiently execute deportations, the union took action itself, fielding an extralegal gang of a couple of hundred people who policed about ten miles of the Arizona-Mexico border, intercepted people attempting to cross it, and brutalized the captives.

Some things are understood only in retrospect, but that cannot be said about the UFW's Campaign Against Illegals. Plenty of people recognized its risks. They argued that the campaign reinforced the differences among farm workers rather than trying to unite them; they complained that the call for increased Border Patrol raids seemed to ally the UFW with the *migra*, one of the government agencies most hated in the fields, even among legal workers. The campaign was politically and ethically reprehensible, the critics said, and it would hurt the union's support among farm workers.

Cesar Chavez dismissed these criticisms as empty moral arguments, removed from the actual situation in the fields. If undocumented Mexicans had been only a small percentage of California farm workers, used exclusively as strike breakers, his claim would have made some sense, and the practical repercussions of his policy might have been minimal. But the percentage was spectacularly high, and not just where there were strikes. The union leaders, particularly Chavez, seemed blind to the consequences of this demographic shift that was happening before their eyes.

That shift was well under way by the mid-1970s. When the NFWA was founded, in 1962, California farm workers had been a diverse bunch: braceros, Filipinos, whites, blacks, Tejano migrants, Mexican migrants (documented and not), Mexican American migrants, and settled Mexican Americans. Although the braceros did much of the stoop labor, dominated vegetable harvesting, and worked in several tree crops, domestic farm workers still played a significant role in the table grapes and many other crops.[6] By the mid-1980s, when the UFW was defeated in the fields, less than 10 percent of California farm workers would be native-born, and more than 80 percent would be born and raised in Mexico.[7] At the time of the union's attack on the undocumented, this trend was already making headlines in the mainstream press. In 1974, the *Fresno Bee* estimated that in 1973 there were between 40,000 and 50,000 illegals in the San Joaquin Valley. The California Rural Manpower Report estimated that about 120,000 undocumented workers did some farm labor in California in 1974. If that figure is correct, then in the year that the Campaign Against Illegals became the UFW's number one priority, more than half of the people working in the California fields were undocumented.[8]

That should have been plain to any union official involved in that year's semi-autonomous strike wave. For good reason Manuel Chavez told the press during the Oxnard strawberry strike, "We are not going to go out looking for illegals."[9] Cesar Chavez liked to say, as he did to the Greater Washington DC Central Labor Council, that "if the illegals were to be taken out of the places where we are now striking, the strike would be over tomorrow."[10] But if the illegals in Watsonville had been snatched by the Border Patrol that September morning in front of the Buaks' apple orchard, the strike would have been over for lack of strikers, not for lack of scabs. When the UFW's Robert Garcia calculated that about 90 percent of the apple strikers were illegals, he was seeing the future.

With its Campaign Against Illegals, the union set itself against most of the people working in the California fields. Cesar Chavez had made himself the boy with his finger in the dike, trying to hold back the mighty wave of immigrants.

He would fail, and his union would never completely recover. Given the criticisms of the campaign by a few on his own staff and by many of its most committed individual and institutional supporters, and given that the demographic shift in the fields was obvious to so many independent observers, why did Chavez persist in this disastrous policy?

The most direct answer is the primacy of the boycott in his strategic vision. At the June 24, 1974, meeting where he lined up the Executive Board behind his policy, he called the anti-illegals campaign "an iron-clad argument for the boycott."[11] He initiated the campaign just as it was becoming clear that Manuel Chavez's "ministrike" in the Coachella grapes was an abysmal failure. Having lost in Coachella, he knew that the union would have little chance of success in the minimally funded harassment strikes in Arvin-Lamont, Delano, Porterville, and Fresno. Focusing on illegals once again would provide a ready answer for those questions that, as Richard Chavez had noted in March, were often raised on the boycott: Why aren't more people on the picket lines? Why are there scabs in the vineyards? Now he could say: the illegals are scabbing. Having a response to the questions of his urban supporters was more important to Chavez than the consequence of his policy among farm workers.

But that is not the full story. The anti-illegals campaign was not just a strategic mistake, nor just another example of the boycott soul of the union trumping the farm worker soul. In some respects, the UFW's antipathy toward illegals was not about the boycott at all. An exchange of memos between Liza Hirsch and Chavez points to something deeper.

To Cesar
From Liza
Date June 10, 1974

Attached are two leaflets from the Delano people who are working on the illegals campaign. The first has gone out without any prior notice to anyone here, but only about 100 copies were distributed. The second is awaiting word from us. I want to know what you think of them, particularly the stuff in the first leaflet about "la unión no esta contra los ilegales si no trabajan donde hay huelga" [the union isn't against illegals if they don't work where there is a strike] when we are in fact stating our opposition to illegals in general in the boycott campaign. These seem all right to me, though badly written.

Also: should I or should I not check with you on matters like this? This is one of the kinds of things I'm unsure about.

Thank you again.
Liza

To Liza
From Chavez
Date 25 June, 1974
    This first leaflet from Delano is a bunch of shit. We're against illegals no matter where they work because if they're not breaking the strike they're taking our jobs. They can't be farting around like this in Delano just because they're afraid of being criticized.
Get on them about it.[12]

Liza Hirsch, the daughter of Fred and Ginny Hirsch, had stayed behind in Delano when her parents departed in 1969, quietly making a series of criticisms of UFWOC on their way out. Liza, then fourteen, lived in the Chavez household, where she became a favorite project of Cesar's. To improve her Spanish he spoke to her only in that language, although he spoke to his wife and children mostly in English. Already politically sophisticated for her age, she was more interested in the union than were Chavez's own kids, and he enjoyed talking politics with her. She was one of the handful of people who were trained to massage his back, and one of the special few who spent long stretches of time with him during the 1968 fast. With Chavez's encouragement, she decided that she would one day go to law school and return to Delano as a union lawyer. By 1974, that plan was in its middle stages. Liza had gone to Reed College and had graduated in just three years, although she had spent much of her time running the Portland boycott campaign. Just nineteen and poised to enter Berkeley's Boalt Law School in the fall, she was Chavez's personal assistant and the head of the Campaign Against Illegals.[13]

Chavez appointed her to the position primarily because she was so precociously competent. But Liza was also one of the open leftists in the union hierarchy; if she not only endorsed the campaign but actually ran it, others in the union who shared her views might hesitate before attacking it. Convincing her to take the job had not been easy. She later recalled the meeting she had with Cesar when he gave her the illegals assignment.

> He went and stood on his head while he talked to me. He had done that four or five times before. Sometimes when he was angry with me; sometimes in a jovial mood. It was disconcerting, talking to a man who was standing on his head. He gave me an assignment that was a punishment to me. He knew I would hate it. He counted on my obedience. The reasoning that resonated with me, the way he got me to agree was by saying that if you really believe Jack London's definition of a strikebreaker, and breaking a strike is a consequential thing, then it is not wrong to call the Border Patrol to get the scabs out. A lot of us did believe that, and that is the way he brought us along. He knew we would do it, despite

our reservations . . . I knew it was wrong then. I was talked into it, but I knew it was wrong. I have been doing penance for my role in the illegals campaign ever since.[14]

What makes the exchange of memos between Chavez and his 19-year-old assistant historically significant is not Chavez's blunt language or imperious tone. What matters is the question at the heart of the memos: Was the campaign just against illegal strikebreakers or against illegals in general? Chavez delivered the definitive answer. Although on a few occasions when defending itself against left criticism the UFW insisted that it opposed illegals only when they acted as scabs, the argument that illegals were "taking our jobs" everywhere in the fields was used from the start of the campaign to its end.

And who was "we"? The implicit "we" was not just Delano-area grape pickers but the entire Mexican American farm worker community, the first people Chavez had organized. These people, Cesar's true base, whose families had come to the U.S. in the 1920s and settled in the Central Valley, were on the losing end of the demographic shift. They did not force the anti-illegals campaign upon the union leadership, as Chavez sometimes defensively claimed, although a fair number of them did support it.

In 1974 the UFW was still, conceptually, a union of legal, domestic farm workers. That is how the union defined itself. Most of its leadership had come from that group; so had most of the farm workers recruited onto the staff. That self-definition had been clinched in the first two table grape contract years when the union kicked out some members who could not produce papers proving they were legally in the U.S.[15] It was underscored in the Buak strike when some union officials worried that even if the strike was won, the strikers would not be able to join the UFW because they were illegal.

Chavez's phrase "taking our jobs" could slip easily into the memo to Liza because he automatically thought of the jobs in the fields as belonging to legal Mexican American farm workers, people who came from the same background as he. He thought this even though, since the loss of the table grape contracts, most of the unionized jobs in the fields were not held by Chicanos, and the majority of UFW members were Mexicans, either green-carders or undocumented workers. That fact had not changed the UFW leaders' image of their union. If anything, the stripping away of the grape contracts only heightened the leaders' identification with the losing side, their original constituency. Consequently, the 1974 Campaign Against Illegals was less a policy mistake—like the back dues, hiring hall debacle—than a reflection of the essential nature of the UFW.

★   ★   ★

In the mid-1970s, farm workers considered the Border Patrol more a bad joke than a serious threat. Now, more than thirty years later in the midst of a very different U.S. attitude toward the Mexican border, understanding the joke requires a measure of historical imagination. Back then, near some Baja California towns like Tecate and San Luis, and even in areas not far from Tijuana, the border was completely open. Furthermore, the number of Border Patrol agents in rural California was laughably low. In Salinas, three agents were responsible for four counties. In Fresno ten agents patrolled six counties. From Bakersfield to the Oregon border the INS employed no more than seventy-four people, who were supposed to find and deport several hundred thousand undocumented workers.[16]

Few people who were picked up by the *migra* went through official deportation hearings. Most signed voluntary waivers (using whatever name was convenient) and were bused back across the border. Commonly, people paid about $30 for a white card—a three-day pass that enabled migrants to travel on the U.S. side and stay within twenty-five miles of the border—then crossed back to the U.S. unimpeded and were at their jobs within a day or two. Some simply waited for the INS to leave, and then recrossed at the exact spot where they had been dropped off.

The migra's lackadaisical attitude was not some kind of bureaucratic snafu. Since the end of the Bracero Program the INS had been purposefully underfunded so that undocumented Mexicans would have easy access to the United States, where their labor was still needed. In 1980 *The New York Times* reported that by the 1970s the INS had become an agency "almost programmed to fail."[17] With its chief mission a fraud and a farce, corruption flourished. A 1972 federal Investigation of the INS, Operation Clean Sweep, exposed widespread selling of legal papers by Border Patrol officers, as well as narcotics trafficking, perjury, smuggling, bribery, and fraud—all of which remained unprosecuted two years after the investigation was completed.

By 1975, Los Angeles INS officials were so overwhelmed that they contracted Arrow Charter Lines to transport undocumented people across the border. Two enterprising Arrow bus drivers figured out how to make a little extra money on their round trip. Frank Del Olmo of the *Los Angeles Times* reported one woman's description of how it worked: "When the bus arrived at the San Ysidro border crossing, she said, the women who were to return with the driver hid under seats at the rear of the bus or in its lavatory while the other illegal immigrants got off and crossed into Mexico on foot. . . . She said the driver then turned the bus around and headed back to Los Angeles . . . and dropped her off at her home in the El Monte area, where she paid him $75."[18]

At about the same time, the INS began to put aliens who had accepted voluntary departures on the cheapest available Mexican flights from border towns to their home towns deep inside Mexico. An INS official explained the genesis of the program to the *Fresno Bee*: "Many times it's just so much easier" [for the deported workers] to come back across the border rather than go through the costs of trying to make it back to their interior homes." So the INS began to pay their airfares. But, as Howard Frank, then a private lawyer specializing in immigration cases, noted, "Once on the plane, they had the opportunity of not being flown home but of getting off at the same airport . . . after the plane had flown around in a circle." Presumably, people then recrossed the border and returned to their old jobs.[19]

Such stories have a double edge. Although the *migra* often treated the people they captured cruelly, and sometimes acted as political police by moving against immigrants who engaged in left politics, and although they stood as a potential annoyance to everyone without papers, they did not actually prevent people from crossing the border. But because the charade was so naked and the INS so corrupt, many on the UFW staff believed that U.S. immigration policy could be changed. Perhaps the border could be closed and the movement of new immigrants reversed. After all, not so long before, Cesar and Helen Chavez, Gilbert Padilla, and Dolores Huerta had won what seemed like a similar campaign against the Bracero Program. If a broad coalition in the late 1950s and early '60s could pressure the federal government to end the extensive importation of contracted Mexican workers, why couldn't the better organized boycott coalition in the 1970s pressure the feds to get the INS to enforce already existing laws? And if the border were closed, the bad joke exposed and annulled, top UFW officials were sure that the union would have a better chance in the California fields.

While Chavez and others in the union inventoried the corruptions of the official Border Patrol for reporters and government officials, many miles away men wearing armbands saying "UFW Border Patrol" hunted illegals. For about three months, from late September to early 1975, anywhere from 35 to 300 people were employed on what the union called the "wet line." They lived in a string of twelve to seventeen large army surplus tents, set up within fifty yards of the border in a line stretching east of the small town of San Luis, Arizona. They were paid $10 a day plus expenses. They operated mostly at night, using dune buggies, cars, vans, and small trucks to chase people down. During the day, they also had a small plane to track people from the air.[20]

County, state, and federal officials gave the UFW a free hand in this wilderness. No judge's order put any limit on what the union's night patrol might do to the people it caught, nor did Mexican authorities in the cities of San Luis, Sonora, or Mexicali provide any protection to those who tried to cross illegally. If you got picked up by the UFW, you were on your own.

The union's official line was that none of its enforcers treated anyone badly. Unofficially, most UFW staffers have said that they knew that the wet line sometimes got rough. How rough is hard to know. Only two cases of violence made it into the Yuma County court system. In one, a jury convicted two men from the UFW Border Patrol of aggravated battery after five of their number intercepted three undocumented workers. According to the victims' testimony, the five took them to the UFW field office in San Luis and questioned them, then drove them back near the border, beat them with sticks and a battery cable, robbed them of their money, stripped one of his clothes, and left them in the desert. This case was prosecuted only because the men had dared to return to the official San Luis port of entry and reported the assault to some Yuma County sheriffs, who took them to the UFW office, where they identified two of their attackers. In the second case, a UFW patrolman pleaded guilty to misdemeanor assault. The seventeen-year-old victim had gone straight to the U.S. Border Patrol to complain; the agents turned him over to some sheriff's deputies who helped him find and identify his assailant.[21]

The Baja California newspapers, as is their custom, painted a particularly lurid picture of what happened in the Yuma County nights, including accounts of wet-line beatings, rapes, knifings, and even murder. The paper's frequent accounts of UFW violence played a large part in making the wet line infamous among farm workers, although it is impossible to know how many of the reported incidents really happened. Six years after the fact, when some of the UFW's internal problems had become public, Robert Lindsey of the *New York Times* went to San Luis and reported: "Interviews in the last week on both sides of the border confirmed that many Mexican aliens were beaten while attempting to approach the border." Without comment, Lindsey relayed Yuma County Sheriff Travis Yancey's assertion that the UFW sentinels beat people with "clubs, chains, and five-foot-long flogging whips comprised of intertwined strands of barbed wire." But Lindsey got many of the details wrong; he also failed to mention that the sheriff who was outraged in 1979 was the same sheriff who had done almost nothing to stop the UFW's open use of violence in 1974.[22]

The wet line was born in a badly timed lemon strike and fathered by Manuel Chavez, who had little interest in lobbying or letter writing. Since the 1960s, Manuel had been given a free hand to run any union operations that dipped into Baja California. He was the head of the Calexico field office; he led many of the border area strikes; and he knew many Baja California politicians, police, and union officials personally and seemed to have enough money to influence them. Where the money came from was not always clear. Sometimes, Cesar gave him off-the-books funds; other times Manuel simply signed Cesar's name on UFW checks, or appropriated money intended for others. He always seemed to have enough.[23]

For a while, Manuel supervised all the field offices along the border, including the one in San Luis, whose first director, Alfredo Avila, had occasion to learn how Manuel got some of his money. Avila had grown up in Chicago. His father was a steel worker who had come from Juarez, and his mother was a Mexican American whose mother had been a farm worker in California in the 1920s. In 1966, Alfredo, just graduated from high school, was inspired to work on the grape boycott after hearing Cesar speak to his youth church group. Determined to become a community organizer, he went to Texas to work with Gilbert Padilla. From there he went back to the boycott in Chicago and a couple of other cities. He helped out in the 1970 Salinas strike, after which Chavez assigned him to work with Manuel in Calexico; from there he went to Arizona to run the San Luis field office.

> I didn't have enough money to run the office, so I called La Paz to complain. I don't remember who I talked to. The guy in La Paz told me that they were sending me twice the amount that I was receiving. "What?" I said, "I am not getting but half." The money was going through Manuel. One week after that conversation, Cesar personally came to San Luis. It was late at night, and he knocked on the office door where my pregnant wife and I were living. Part of what I needed the money for was to rent a house. Cesar ordered us to go to Houston for the lettuce boycott. It was suspended a couple of weeks later. I had agreed to go to Houston because I knew I could take better care of myself and my wife on the boycott than in San Luis. But even at the time I was suspicious of Cesar's motives for sending us away.[24]

Not a particularly shocking story but typical of the way Manuel operated and a good example of how he was protected by his cousin. But shuffling off a volunteer who stumbled upon Manuel's petty graft was not nearly as serious as shielding Manuel from criticism of the wet line. And as it happened, the UFW's "border patrol" was directed out of the very office from which Chavez had expelled Alfredo Avila and his pregnant wife.

The 18,000 acres of lemon orchards sat on a mesa that ran for twenty-six miles from San Luis Rio Colorado north to Yuma, where California, Mexico, and Arizona come together. Mexico threw its shadow on two sides of the orchards, with Baja California on their western edge and Sonora to their south. It is all borderland, more connected to the history and culture of Mexicali, which is only a forty-minute drive from San Luis along Baja's Highway 2, than it is to Arizona proper, whose capital, Phoenix, is 200 miles northeast of the Yuma County lemons.

Manuel worked both sides of the border, although the U.S. side didn't amount to much. San Luis, Sonora, had about 20,000 souls; San Luis,

Arizona, no more than a few hundred, and Gadsen and Somerton together, small towns on the road north to Yuma, only a couple of thousand more. Many of the field workers in Yuma County lived in San Luis, Sonora, and crossed the border every day with white cards or green cards. Some crossed at the beginning of the harvest season and lived in labor camps strung between Yuma and the border. Others lived in makeshift camps in the orchards. Those without papers stepped through a hole in the chain link fence near downtown San Luis, Sonora, or walked a few hundred yards east into the desert, where the fence became two strands of wire strung between posts. They ducked under the wire and walked onto the U.S. side, where harvest association buses and vans waited to take them to their jobs.

Those jobs were at the center of just about everything in Yuma County. Its fertile soil was created by eons of Colorado River flooding and the irrigation projects that channeled the river into canals following World War II. In 1973 the county grossed over $165 million from agriculture, more than from every other enterprise (military bases, manufacturing, and services) combined. Forty percent of Yuma County's workforce, 12,000 people, were agricultural laborers, working some 47,000 acres of land, which produced the big-risk moneymakers, lettuce and melons, as well as the safer, more reliable lemons.

About 2,500 of those workers picked the lemons, a crop then valued at about $30 million. The season lasted from August to March, and at its height in November–December, the Yuma *limoneros* picked about 90 percent of the entire U.S. crop—a statistic that should make one stop and take notice. These *limoneros* were incredibly productive: for two months of the year, 2,500 of them, performing the same ballet as the *limoneros* in Ventura, picked nearly nine out of ten lemons sold in every single store in America—from the littlest mom and pop to the biggest supermarket.

For eight months of work they earned about $5,000 a year, without any of the benefits *limoneros* received in Ventura. The same outfits controlled the industry in both places: Ventura-based Sunkist owned eight out of nine Yuma County packing sheds and controlled 85 percent of its lemons. Technically, Sunkist was a kind of cooperative, a joint venture of the people who owned the land, the packing sheds, and the shipping infrastructure, and then contracted out the care of the orchards and the picking of the fruit to a growers' association and various harvesting associations. Actually, however, Sunkist worked like most other corporations. The people who owned the land and sheds were investors, and the top employees of Sunkist ran the show. About 80 percent of the landowners were absentee, including some big agribusiness corporations, East Coast financial families, and a group of dentists and doctors from Los Angeles. Most local power resided in the hands of four growers who controlled the thirty-five-member growers association and who supervised the care and harvesting of

70 percent of the fruit. The small growers, as usual, were bit players in the industry but fought hardest against the union. They were the men who carried shotguns in their trucks. The strike would bankrupt two of them.[25]

In August, at the beginning of the 1974 season, the harvesting association lowered the piece rate. The workers tried to renegotiate, but supervisors refused, saying a bonanza harvest was expected and workers would make a lot more money later in the year. The workers did not want to wait. It was early in the season and most of the fruit was too small to pick, so it took a long time to fill the bins. In the 100-plus degree weather, some workers were filling no more than half a bin and thus making $6 or $7 a day, less than the national minimum wage. They wanted to strike, and they were pressuring the UFW's Catarino Torres at the San Luis office for help.[26]

Manuel Chavez initially discouraged the idea, but after meeting with a large, enthusiastic crowd that clamored for a strike, and consulting with Cesar, Manuel agreed. On August 27, 200 workers walked out of the orchards, and within a couple of weeks about 1,500 were on strike, with no more than 300 pickers still in the trees. Manuel started the strike benefits at $50 a week and raised them to $60 in the second week. As long as the lemons remained small and the piece rate low, the *limoneros* could make about as much money picketing as working, and they took up the UFW banner. The growers tried to recruit scabs, but without much luck. Some apple pickers came down from Washington but lasted less than a week. Hardly anyone but an experienced desert *limonero* can put up with a day's work in the trees in the August heat of the Yuma Valley.[27]

Spirits were high, but, as Manuel would later admit, the strike had started too soon. The peak season was still two months away. The numbers on the early picket lines were exciting but not decisive. No grower answered Manuel's request for negotiations. Production was greatly reduced, but the growers had a lot of time to get their act together before they would face a serious crisis—probably a month.[28]

If lemons are not picked within a month of when they are ready, they can get too big for the fresh market. Those that are too large can be sold for processing, but at about a quarter of the fresh price. Also, if the lemons go unpicked for too long, the trees' branches can break, requiring the growers to spend more money on pruning, hurting the next season's crop, and sometimes ruining the trees. Finally, even if the growers eventually defeated the strike, they could find themselves in a marketing order bind. The secret to Sunkist's success was the "pro-rate," the government-approved market-ing order that limited how many fresh lemons each grower could sell, month by month, and therefore protected investors from the dangers of overproduction. Thus, even if the strike were to ebb, and a increasing number of scabs were able to pick the lemons that had been left on the trees, the struck growers would not be able to sell all of them on the fresh market. Everything over their pro-rate would have to go to processing, where there were no limits on how much they could sell, but where earnings would be lower.[29]

A few weeks into the strike, the growers raised the piece rate from between $12 and $14 a bin to $18 a bin, $2 more than it had been at a comparable time the year before. But most of the lemons were still too small to pick and the strike held. The harvesting associations and contractors started recruiting scabs from the interior of Mexico, announcing high wages in the Arizona lemon groves on the radio and in newspaper ads as far away as Michoacán. By mid-September, when there were more lemons to pick and the workers could fill their bins faster, some strikers started going back to work. By October, six weeks into the strike, with the trees so heavy with lemons that experienced workers could make up to $7 an hour, about half the strikers had returned to their jobs. They were joined by an increasing number of Mexicans who had come a long way for the good money. Production increased. In September, the growers had shipped out less than a third of the pro-rated marketing order. In October, they managed to get nearly 60 percent.[30]

The strike was not yet beat, but it was crippled. Many strikers, too proud and loyal to scab but unwilling to stay on for $60 a week in what looked like a losing cause, moved onto the migrant trail. At least 300 active strikers remained, however, and the union was still able to mobilize nearly 1,000 people for demonstrations. Those people fought hard to save their strike. Typically, they massed in large groups from Yuma to the border to challenge the scabs as they got onto the harvesting buses in the early morning. There were many fights. Strikers threw rocks; some used slingshots.

The established forces of the law came down hard on the picketers. Nothing much happens between Yuma and San Luis except work, so anyone who interferes with it is committing a serious offense. Judges don't look favorably on strikes, the police even less so, and there is no liberal civil society to restrain them. Police used tear gas and smoke bombs against the strikers; they beat people while arresting them; they sometimes Mace'd those already in custody; they brandished pistols and shotguns. Judges set bail at outrageous levels, even on misdemeanors, and gave any convicted strikers maximum sentences. It was all very open. The county attorney told the board of supervisors that he "was looking for a way to break the strike."[31]

On September 25, after a reported exchange of gunfire between a sheriff and a striker, a judge banned all picketing. It was a violation of his order for any person to go to an orchard and picket or to show up in places where strikebreakers got on buses. But the judge's order said nothing about waiting near the border to stop undocumented people who were coming to work in the lemons.[32] Now that the border was the one place where it was still legal to confront scabs, Manuel decided to make the workers' informal border challenges into a formal, publicized patrol, and the wet line was born.

The fullest account of the wet line comes from a 1978 article by Tom Barry. A highly regarded reporter, Barry spent several months talking to politicians, police, labor leaders from Baja California, farm workers and UFW organizers. Seeking an outlet for his manuscript, Barry sent it to the Center for Investigative Reporting (CIR) where it ignited a spirited debate, much of it centered on the possible damage it might do to the farm worker movement. The article was never published, but fifteen months later, after the internal disputes in the UFW had become national news, Robert Lindsey drew on Barry's research for his piece about the wet line in the *New York Times*.

Salvador Sandoval Yala, the city attorney of Ciudad Morales, who headed a Mexican federal investigation into the San Luis strike, told Barry that "wet line patrollers had beaten, stripped and robbed undocumented workers." An unnamed Mexican labor official said, "There were many, many beatings during the strike, especially right along the border. The men were stripped, beaten, and sent back across. I saw two men who had been beaten with chains, and I know of one worker who had his fingers crushed with a brick." A reporter for *El Malcriado* who asked not to be identified said, "There were many cases of atrocities, including one man who had a knife stuck up his nose and ripped out just like in the movie Chinatown."[33]

That is not the worst of what Barry was told. Mexican workers and Baja labor chiefs spoke of murders and castrations on the wet line. But three years after the events, Barry was unable to uncover any bodies or any other physical evidence except for a few scars that some of the people he interviewed said came from a beating on the wet line. The power of his account comes from the repetition of similar charges made by twelve different people, some named and others not.[34]

The details of the two Yuma County felony convictions, which Barry seems not to have known about, are remarkably similar to the testimony of Barry's informants. Also, many in the California fields during this period were aware that Manuel kept people around him—the young man with a chain sent to the Buak apple strike, for instance—who were capable of seriously hurting people. And the wet line was made up of a combination of lemon strikers and people whom Manuel brought from California.[35] Thirty years later Lupe Sanchez, a UFW organizer from Phoenix in 1974, described what he witnessed during the Campaign Against Illegals and while serving on the wet line:

The wet line left a really ugly impression in my mind. Why the hell are we trying to organize against them [the undocumented] when we have to be organizing them and making them part of the union? And the national campaign was another ugly scene . . . The UFW, we, actually went out and organized committees of people within the state of Arizona to go onto farms where there were no strikes and identify undocumented workers working for a company . . . [On the wet line] I went out a couple of nights, and we had campfires and so forth . . . [One morning] I went over to the place where we all had breakfast, a group of them were hosing out the trunk of their car. It had a hell of a lot of blood in it.. I said, "Fuck, I'm not going to be part of this bullshit." And I told Manuel and said, "I am sick of it," and I got in my car and drove back to Phoenix.[36]

When Lindsey, the *New York Times* reporter, asked Chavez about the UFW border patrol, he replied: "We had a wet line, it cost us a lot of money, and we stopped a lot of illegals. If it [violence against border-crossers] happened, I know nothing about it. I tried to look into it. I talked to all of the Mexican officials I could get hold of; I checked everybody to get a feeling of what had happened, but I didn't find anything that made me feel that anything wrong had happened."[37] Chavez took another tack when he was not talking to the press. After the lemon strike was defeated, a delegation of San Luis workers went to La Paz to complain about misspent strike funds, excessive violence, and Manuel's drinking. Alfredo Osuna, one of the people in the delegation, told Barry that Chavez flatly replied, "Whatever Manuel does is all right by me."[38]

Here Chavez may have been playing to his audience, defending his *primo hermano* in accordance with a code of family loyalty. Earlier, in mid-October, a few weeks after the wet line was up, Manuel had gone to La Paz to give a report on the strike to the Executive Board. After the meeting the board decided to travel to San Luis. The union was spending more money there than anywhere else that year—eventually the strike cost the union $1,235,580.87—and often board members would travel to an important farm worker site after concluding their meetings.[39] There was to be a rally in San Luis, where Chavez would make his first appearance since returning from a trip to Europe. According to the *Yuma Daily Sun*, 700 people attended the rally, but Chavez did not speak, remaining in his room at the Americano Motel because of what the paper called "his recurring back injury." The newspaper ran a picture of him holding a news conference from his bed. He told the reporters round his bedside that if the lemon growers wouldn't agree to talk, the union might have to boycott, and explained that he was in bed because "I'm one of those 10 percent of people who have one side of their body shorter than the other. It's the same problem President Kennedy had."[40]

Gilbert Padilla recalled the events somewhat differently:

We drove from La Paz after the Executive Board meeting, and when we passed an immigration checkpoint outside of Coachella, some cop eyeballed us as we went past. And he ran to his car . . . and caught up with us and followed us all the way to San Luis. So we were a little spooked already. And then Manuel told us that there had been a threat on Cesar's life. Manuel and Dolores got all upset about it and decided that Cesar shouldn't leave the motel and that guards should watch the place. So to save face he faked his back hurting. His back was fine. He hadn't complained in La Paz; he had ridden the whole way from La Paz without saying anything about it, and all the way back, too. He faked it. We all talked about it. Dolores and Manuel and Cesar were the people who thought it was the best thing to do. I was pissed. I told him, "Nobody is going to shoot you, man."

Manuel staffed the wet line. It was his people running the show. Calacas, Oscar Mondragon, Gilbert Rodriguez, the whole crew . . . I heard it was very brutal. People got badly beat up. We stayed at the motel that Manuel had taken over. He had his booze and women there. On the way back, Richard and I were really pissed. Here we were out on the boycott, begging people for donations, turning summersaults to get them, and there was Manuel, spending it like water.[41]

Chavez sent Jerry Cohen to San Luis a few months after the visit to investigate the death threat, but Jerry found nothing. Marshall Ganz, who was also on the trip, would not comment on Padilla's account. After returning to La Paz, most of the Executive Board members, including Padilla, flew back to their boycott assignments. Chavez immediately checked into a San Jose hospital, where he remained for a week. A hospital spokesman said, "He was placed in intermittent pelvic traction, underwent physical therapy, and got lots of rest."[42] Was this part of the act? I doubt it. More likely, after faking a back incident, Chavez had a real one. It would be entirely consistent with his history. While his *primo hermano*, a Mr. Hyde to his Dr. Jekyll, was beating people up at the border, Cesar's own pain put him in traction doing penance for Manuel's sins.

Nothing Chavez did, though, could stop stories of the wet line from becoming common coin in the farm worker world, a collective memory that still counts in the California fields. Alberto Escalante, a longtime UFW organizer, loyal to the union, remarked in 2004, "Unfortunately, I still run into people whose first experience with the UFW was a beating they received out in the Arizona desert."[43]

The Campaign Against Illegals did meet with some resistance from farm worker communities, field offices, and boycott volunteers. Chavez was unwilling to go to the mat with farm workers over this question. In the San Joaquin field offices, typically a single loyalist did all the reporting to the INS. Lupe Murguía in Delano explained that farm workers "did not want to report illegals, their brothers." The Oxnard and Salinas field offices barely participated in the campaign. People in Salinas filed three formal complaints; Oxnard filed five. La Paz continued to send them packets and instructions on how to carry out the campaign, but Chavez did not put any extra pressure on the field office directors to comply. He was willing to carry out the campaign with a coalition of the willing, and avert his eyes from those in the field offices who disobeyed.[44]

With the boycotters, however, Chavez was not so liberal. Three paid staffers in Florida were fired after they presented their objections to the campaign at a Florida boycott staff meeting.* Chavez had already dismissed their argument that dividing the workers would ultimately hurt the union. "We have a choice to be for the illegals and against our own workers, or be for our workers and against the illegals," he had written to one of the protesters. Even as reports came into La Paz that farm workers, some of them paid *huelgistas*, refused to participate, Chavez claimed that UFW members and strikers "are pressuring us to take adequate action to get them [illegals] out of the fields because their jobs are being taken away and their wages reduced." When a boycott staffer in Atlanta refused to participate in the campaign, she too was fired.[45]

The three from Florida sent out an open letter addressed to "Friends of the UFW" nationwide, describing what had happened to them, arguing that undocumented workers were being fingered to the Border Patrol in areas where there were no strikes, and suggesting that "regional meetings have been called in the past to unify the union and may be appropriate now." Letters of complaint poured into La Paz. The all-volunteer New Orleans Farm Workers Support Committee wrote that they would not support "this splitting policy of deportation," and asked Chavez to "reconsider the policy." Similar letters from individual boycott staffers and entire volunteer support committees came in from San Antonio, Tucson, Phoenix, Erie, Kalamazoo, Salt Lake City, and Orange, New Jersey. Chavez didn't answer the letters and never called a meeting to discuss the issue. The mini-rebellion within the boycott staff died quietly.[46]

Much more fuss was raised by forces outside the union. In September, in

---

* Mack Lyons, an Executive Board member and head of the Florida boycott, received a letter of congratulations from Chavez after reporting that he had fired the three: Paul Pomphrey, Paul Murphy, and Mary Martin. According to Liza Hirsch, Lyons would not have fired them on his own and at least would have checked with Chavez in advance.

the midst of the dwindling Stockton tomato strike, at a UFW barbecue in the university town of Davis, Chavez pointedly criticized those "pseudo revolutionaries in the cities . . . [who] don't have to deal with the daily reality of having workers thrown out of their jobs in favor of illegals."[47] Cesar repeated the charge that the union's critics were naïve and unrealistic in several speeches and in an editorial in *El Malcriado*, prompting an answer from, among others, Miguel Pendás of the Socialist Workers Party. Pendás argued that since "undocumented workers are and will remain a large, significant component of the agricultural workforce" the only "realistic" course was for the union to try to organize them by becoming a "champion of their rights."[48] That view was held beyond the left and gained fairly wide currency in barrios of major U.S. cities and throughout southwestern Spanish-speaking communities. The extent to which the criticism became common opinion can be measured by Chavez's need to answer it publicly.

The most damaging opposition came from the Centro de Acción Social Autónoma (CASA), the "most salient progressive organization functioning in the Mexican community" in the 1970s, according to the Chicano historian Juan Gomez Quiñones.[49] Founded in the 1950s by Mexican workers in the U.S., CASA combined left politics with the self-help programs of an old-style *mutualista*. Its substantial, active membership always argued for the rights of immigrants and stressed the basic unity of all people of Mexican descent. Despite the UFW's previous sporadic blasts against illegals, CASA's leader, Bert Corona, had remained on good terms with Chavez. But friendly personal relations only went so far. In 1974, as the UFW was pressuring Congress to act to deport more Mexicans, CASA organized several large demonstrations against deportations and the INS.

In Los Angeles, CASA and the UFW's boycott committee were the two strongest groups in the Mexican American and Mexican community. CASA's opposition to the Campaign Against Illegals, regularly articulated in its newspaper, *Sin Fronteras*, damaged the LA boycott coalition. Mexican American students, hitherto strong boycott supporters, began dropping out. Increasingly, people in East Los Angeles crossed boycott picket lines. Jim Drake, head of the UFW in LA, formally forbade UFW staffers from attending CASA mobilizations, although a few staffers and many volunteers left behind their UFW insignias and signs and went to the CASA rallies and marches anyway.

CASA's opposition to UFW policy made criticism of the UFW by left and Chicano organizations more acceptable. In February 1975, the National Lawyers Guild delivered a sharp rebuke to the union. Back in the summer of 1974, some student members of the guild working with the UFW had refused to report on undocumented workers in Fresno County. Those students, supported by others who worked with CASA, took the dispute to the guild's National Executive Board, which passed four motions: (1) in general support of the UFW; (2) in support of CASA and the rights of the undocumented; (3) in support of another National Lawyers Guild summer project with the UFW, on the condition that guild members would not report the undocumented to the INS; (4) for formal disapproval of the UFW policy of reporting undocumented workers, including strikebreakers, to the INS.[50]

The arrow hit its mark. "They're rats, they're strikebreakers," Chavez told his board. Publicly he and other top UFW leaders refrained from answering, and refused the guild's offer to talk over differences.[51]

The March 1975 Executive Board meeting, where CASA and the Guild were discussed, had a mean-spirited tone. Not only were CASA members "rats," Chavez said; they were potential saboteurs who could be part of a "CIA attack on the union." Dolores Huerta called the guild resolutions a "very vicious attack," similar to the actions of the Teamsters and the growers. Padilla agreed: the guild was on the side of the growers. Three members of the UFW legal staff who had not resigned from the guild were called on the carpet: "How can you fight for us when you belong to such a chicken-shit outfit?" Chavez asked. The three reiterated their pledges of loyalty, but the Executive Board, almost as one, badgered them, threatening to fire them if they didn't resign from the guild. They were not fired or completely humiliated, only dressed down.[52] But it was a taste, a promise of things to come.

Victory in Hand, Confusion at Heart

Living with the Law

July '75 to January '77

The first elections for union representation under the direction of the Agricultural Labor Relations Board were held in early September, 1975. Cesar Chavez spent most of the two months prior to the elections walking around the state of California. He began his 1,000-mile *caminata* in the company of a small group of supporters on July 1, symbolically touching the border fence at San Ysidro, walking up the coast to Salinas, driving to Sacramento, and then continuing his walk down the Central Valley, ending at La Paz. Cesar was forty-eight years old; the march lasted fifty-eight days. Along the way he stopped in farm worker communities, spoke most nights at rallies big and small, and met with individual farm workers and UFW organizers. Many of his stops were in areas previously untouched by the UFW.

The walk annoyed Marshall Ganz. He thought Chavez was abdicating his leadership responsibilities and had lost interest in the practical details of how to organize the election campaigns. Walking around the state in the pre–cell phone era, he was difficult to contact, unavailable for staff conferences, and unhelpful in forming a union position on the opportunities and limits of the election law. Chavez countered that he was bringing the good news of the law to farm workers across the state, explaining its provisions, and helping to build momentum for the elections.

He was news in every town he passed through. Farm workers lined up to see him, carrying Instamatic cameras so they could record their moment standing beside the famous man. Stories are still told of his miraculous physical endurance, his ability to set the pace on the march and outlast men more than twenty years his junior. Marc Grossman, the union's representative to the press, who became a sort of personal publicist for Chavez, paid homage. At night, after each day's marching was done, he helped wash his leader's feet.[1]

At the evening rallies, Chavez's speech was preceded by a showing of *Fighting for Our Lives*. Chavez sat through every showing, Grossman explained, because "he thought it would be disrespectful [to the farm worker audience] to leave."[2] The movie includes an extended shot of Chavez, dignified and unafraid, walking in front of a line of threatening Teamster goons. It is a fine visual representation of Cesar's courage and determination, and watching it night after night probably did not diminish his conception of himself. But more was at stake than Chavez getting too caught up in his own greatness. The film truthfully shows the heroism of the 1973 grape strikers, but it hides the other truth that there were more than enough workers willing to break the strike and harvest the grapes. Chavez watched the film perhaps as many as fifty times. Was it likely that by the end of the march he would still remember what it left out?

The most important stop on the march was Fresno, where the UFW held its second biannual Constitutional Convention just ten days before the elections were to begin. Seven hundred delegates held what was essentially a pep rally, with a couple of thousand sympathizers looking on. "Today we stand on the threshold of total victory in the fields of California," Chavez said in his opening speech. "Our time has come." Utterly confident, he warned that some growers might not sign contracts even after the UFW won. Then the union would return to the boycott, "our most potent nonviolent weapon and the surest means of achieving total victory for our union and restoring peace to the fields."[3]

The convention's only important business was to ratify a change in the UFW's stance on undocumented workers. In a meeting back in June, Jerry Cohen had explained to the union's Executive Board and its field office directors that because the law was silent on the question of illegals, they would be able to vote in the upcoming elections. That news provoked dismay. The union had just campaigned against illegals and had refused to dispatch them to jobs at many hiring halls, so now workers without papers were afraid that they would lose their jobs if the UFW won the elections. Tanis Ybarra, the Fresno field office director, put it bluntly: "We were told to do a job on the illegals, and in West Fresno we did that. No one wants them, and everyone has let them know it . . . We don't have anything to offer them. Because of this, they can't vote for us."[4]

To general consternation Ybarra also pointed out that a recent government report had put the number of illegals in the San Joaquin Valley at 110,000. Initially the board members looked for ways to exclude illegals from voting, but Cohen explained that such challenges would be tied up in the courts for years. Next, the board considered delaying the elections, and focusing on the boycott, but Eliseo Medina argued that without election victories it would be difficult to build a strong boycott. Chavez, who was among those most concerned about illegals having the vote, said that the union could not stop the Teamsters from filing for elections, so any delaying tactic probably would not work.

Richard Chavez drew the realistic conclusion: "We should just go in and organize the workers no matter who they are." Both Manuel Chavez and Robert Garcia reported that the anti-UFW feeling among illegals was uneven, and that in many areas undocumented workers were strong UFW supporters. Manuel Chavez ultimately advocated trying to delay the elections, but Garcia agreed with Richard Chavez that the only option was to try to win the illegals over to the union. No vote was taken, but that position held.[5]

In early July, while Chavez was on the *caminata*, the UFW distributed a leaflet, entitled, "Open Letter to Farm Workers from Cesar Chavez," which tried to rectify what Chavez now called a "mistake." Although he didn't make it exactly clear that the mistake was the union's own, there was little doubt what he was talking about:

> The farm worker law necessitates unity among all farm workers, strikers and nonstrikers, Blacks, Mexicans, Filipinos, Whites, workers, whether they be citizens or immigrants . . .
>
> For the last three years we have, at times, fallen into the trap of allowing the exploiters to divide us—some of us on one side and the rest of us on the other. Now, with the help of the law, we have the opportunity and power to unite . . .
>
> We have all committed errors, since to err is human. But we have to recognize that mistakes are not the consequence of any difference between us but are the result of misunderstanding. Now, under the light of the new law, we must see one another anew.[6]

The convention made this change explicit. The delegates passed resolutions that welcomed all workers into the union, including "*los visitantes*," and called "for amnesty for all illegal workers in the country." Chavez mentioned those resolutions in his welcoming speech and defiantly declared, "If the growers can import illegal workers to exploit them, then we can organize illegal workers to liberate them."[7] Now it would be up to the organizers to minimize the damage that had been done since the UFW first started scapegoating illegals more than a decade before.

After the convention, the workers and organizers returned to the final preelection push, most of the boycotters returned to the cities, and Cesar resumed his *caminata*. He hit the towns south of Fresno and then walked the last fifteen miles up into the Tehachapis from Arvin, accompanied by a hundred supporters. The marchers were enthusiastically welcomed by the La Paz staff, and the *Los Angeles Times* reported that Chavez looked "tan and fit."

The basic election rules were straightforward. When a union submitted authorization cards or a petition signed by fifty percent of the field workers at a company, an election would be held within seven days, or forty-eight hours if the workers were on strike. Another union could add its name to the ballot by filing cards or a petition signed by twenty percent of the workers. If only one union filed the election would be between that union and no union, for example the UFW versus No Union. If two or more unions filed the workers would chose between them. In the subsequent election, if a union won over fifty percent of the votes, it was authorized to represent the workers, and the company was obligated to bargain, in good faith, with the winning union.

The first farm worker election was held on September 5, 1975, only a week after the first official meeting of the Agricultural Labor Relations Board. Not all of the regulatory personnel had been hired, few had been trained, and some field offices had neither desks nor telephones. Nevertheless, in its first month the board conducted 178 elections, in which more than 25,000 farm workers voted. It was a ludicrous pace.[8]

The board's inadequate staffing and preparation were not as serious as its split personality. The ALRA had been both a concession to the farm worker movement and an attempt to tame it. Through the power of appointment, Governor Brown had built that dual purpose into the agency that would administer the law. At the top, four of the five board appointees supported the UFW and did what they could to carry out the law's mandate to promote farm worker organization and collective bargaining. But Brown also appointed as the board's general counsel Walter Kintz, who had learned his craft working seventeen years for the National Labor Relations Board, which was famous for its bureaucratic delays and weak enforcement policies. Kintz tried to stay neutral among the contending parties. The lawyers, hearing officers, and field examiners he hired, also mostly NLRB veterans, tried to establish long-term procedures and precedents at the expense of direct intervention in the battle at hand. Few spoke Spanish. Kintz and his staff moved slowly, a pace they had mastered in adjudicating industrial disputes. A slow pace in a fast world worked to the advantage of the growers and the Teamsters.

The growers fought to win. Some of the bigger ones hired prominent antiunion law firms, such as Littler, Mendelson & Fastiff, based in San Francisco, and Seyfarth, Shaw, Fairweather & Geraldson, of Chicago, to help them devise anti-UFW strategies. Following their advice, the growers challenged certain provisions of the law procedurally and simply ignored others. They would play the ALRB as industry played the NLRB, where employers violated the law with relative impunity. This was no secret. Less than a month into the elections, Alan Grant, the president of the California Farm Bureau, publicly encouraged growers to violate the ALRB's access regulations, which allowed union organizers to come into the fields to talk to workers at specified times during the day. Grant assured growers that even though barring organizers from the fields would result in an unfair

labor practice charge, this was a mere "slap on the wrist."[9] Kintz did nothing to prevent this open defiance of the law, which intensified the split
between the governing board and the general counsel.

Like the growers, the Teamsters had their strategy, tactics, and
personnel in sync. The various levels of the bureaucracy were finally
working in harmony. Jimmy Hoffa had disappeared, on July 30, 1975,
and Frank Fitzsimmons no longer needed to swing back and forth
between the different parties who might help him secure his job. Bill
Grami, the ambitious Western Conference of Teamsters organizer, was
gone. The new Western Conference director, Andy Anderson, had
placed a loyal soldier, Ralph Cotner, at the head of the farm worker
operation. They had a straightforward plan: negotiate a wage and benefit package better than the UFW's; attack the UFW for its 2 percent
dues and its abysmal administration of the 1970–73 table grape contracts;
fight the growers enough to persuade the workers that they were not a
company union, while maintaining good enough relations with the
growers to use them as allies.

The Teamsters struck their first blow in July, while Chavez was on his
1,000-mile walk. They renegotiated 135 vegetable contracts, extending them
for the next three years, with a 25 percent increase in wages and benefits. The
entry wage went up 41.5 percent, to $2.95 an hour ($11.94 in 2010 dollars).
Bud Antle, as was his custom, went a step higher, putting the hourly minimum at $3. Some in the industry continued to worry, as the *Packer* put it, that
"our worst fears—that the Teamsters will eventually control the fresh fruit
and vegetable industry from field to supermarket—are beginning to be realized."[10] But most were still more concerned about the UFW.

Then, in balloting at the Delano table grape ranches, the UFW was
badly beaten. The results were startling: the Teamsters had wins at nineteen
ranches and the UFW, just eight. At the twelve ranches too close to call
because of challenged ballots, the UFW eventually picked up only one
additional victory. At the twenty ranches where both the Teamsters and
the UFW were on the ballot, the Teamsters won fifteen and the UFW, five
elections.[11] Years later the UFW's Delano field office director, Ben
Maddock, observed concisely: "We told the world we were going to win
the elections, but we forgot to tell the workers."[12]

Sixty percent of the workers voted either for the Teamsters or for No
Union. Forty percent voted for the UFW.[13] Filipinos, who made up as
much as 20 percent of the workforce, voted as a bloc against the UFW.
Mexican migrants, who had been particularly hurt by UFW policies
concerning back dues and union seniority, tended to vote Teamsters or No
Union. Even some Mexican American and Yemenite workers, put off by
the UFW's imperious attitude toward its members, voted for Teamster
representation.[14]

"We ran against their history," said Pete Maturino, one of the twenty-five Teamster organizers working on the Delano elections," and we had the help of the growers."[15] The growers blocked UFW organizers from entering the fields. They manipulated employee lists, making it difficult to determine who was eligible to vote. Some foremen physically threatened pro-UFW workers, fired others, and openly campaigned for the Teamsters. General Counsel Kintz didn't issue a formal complaint against a Delano grower until September 25, when thirty of the thirty-nine elections had already been held, too late to alter the atmosphere of fear in which many of the elections took place. In the legal battle between concession and containment, the growers won the first round.

The growers also told undocumented workers that if the UFW won, they would lose their jobs.[16] Despite the UFW's attempt to explain its policy reversal, the growers' claim was credible. When the Border Patrol made a series of raids during the campaign, it added to the general anxiety.

Bad as the interference of the growers and the *migra* was, those closest to the ground were under no illusions that it had made the decisive difference. Chayo Pelayo, the dedicated UFW volunteer, was working at the time with her sister at Giumarra, the largest table grape grower in the state. They campaigned openly on their crew for a couple of weeks. They were fired, but not before they got a feel for the mood of the workers. "A lot of the people were on the side of the foremen," Pelayo said. "We really didn't have much support. They were afraid, but they also didn't like the union. And the people who didn't like the union were waging their own campaign on the inside, about the dues, all the meetings, all the reasons they had to be against us."[17] The UFW lost at Giumarra.

Ben Maddock, in charge of the election team in Delano, admitted, "A hell of a lot of workers didn't like us." And Chavez, he said, had been overconfident. "Cesar Chavez thought every Mexican in Delano was going to vote for us, and he didn't put the resources in."[18] For the politically important Gallo campaign, Maddock noted, Chavez had assigned Richard Chavez and Dolores Huerta; Gallo had only a few hundred workers, and those top people still couldn't win. Maddock had to deal with some 8,000 workers, and the only staff organizer he had was Frank Ortiz. The rest of his campaign staff was made up of Service Center and hiring hall volunteers.

After the first few Delano ranches had voted against the UFW, Fred Ross was rushed in to help, but the results did not improve. After his complaint about inadequate staffing, Maddock came to a sadder conclusion: "When we got the law, we had not won over the workers. We won the contracts on the boycott. And then when we had the people under contract, we didn't win them over either."[19]

Chavez was surprised by the Delano results, but he remained publicly upbeat, arguing that the elections were tainted by the ALRB's sloth and lack of action. Privately, he told Maddock that the Executive Board had erred in not giving him enough help, but he also transferred Maddock out of Delano, demoting him to his private security staff. What Chavez did not do was revise his assessment of the UFW's strength or popularity in the Delano vineyards.

The UFW did much better in the Salinas Valley, winning forty-one elections. At the forty-seven ranches where the Teamsters and the UFW were on the same ballot, the Teamsters won at twenty-five and the UFW at twenty-two. But the UFW still won the overall vote by 52 percent to 42 percent, with No Union picking up just 6 percent.[20]

Why the difference between Salinas and Delano? The ALRB was no more agile on the Central Coast than it had been in the San Joaquin Valley. The Teamsters were no less formidable an adversary. The Salinas growers, however, were not as united against the UFW as the table grape growers had been.* And because the number of Filipino workers in the Salinas Valley was insignificant, there was no bloc voting against the UFW by ethnic minorities.

What mattered most, though, was the history of the UFW in Salinas. Because the union had arrived there in 1970 as the vehicle for a successful strike, because it hadn't had the same problems at the hiring halls and hadn't made the undocumented a target, the UFW was more popular among the workers in Salinas than it was in the Central Valley. The 1975 elections confirmed it, and so did the campaign that secured the victories.

Two and a half months before the elections began, forty full-time worker volunteers, most of them *lechugueros*, started organizing. At five in the morning they went to the camps with leaflets. At seven they regrouped for a meeting with Marshall Ganz, who directed the Salinas campaign. Then they went into the fields—if they weren't blocked by foremen or police— to talk with workers at breaks and at lunch, as well as immediately before and after work. At night there were house meetings, and finally there was a late-night review with Ganz, which often did not break up until after midnight. "It was hard, but beautiful," Hermilo Mojica recalled.

Ganz had called for worker volunteers at a large Salinas rally in June. Jose Renteria was one of those who jumped onto the stage. It was not a spur-of-the-moment decision. His father, a legalized ex-bracero, had brought his family to California in 1967, when Jose was fourteen. The boy had a

---

*   InterHarvest, the biggest company, did not campaign against the union, and much of the UFW's margin of victory in the overall vote was due to its 1,167–28 win there. But those results were partially offset by the Bud Antle results, where the tally was Teamsters 880, UFW 267, No Union, 45.

brief stay in high school—he could speak but a word or two of English—
and then went to work with his father. They worked in the strawberries,
"It was very hard . . . After work I took a shower. I was fifteen years old,
and the tired would wash away, but my father was tired all the time." Then
he and his father got a job on an hourly broccoli crew at the Crosetti
Ranch in Watsonville. In 1969 Jose's father joined the UFWOC there,
some twenty people who paid dues and met once a month to talk about the
union. In 1970 father and son struck together, and the excitement of the
mass struggle overwhelmed the sixteen-year-old. In 1974 he worked his
way onto a contract lettuce crew, not so much for the money as for the politics.
"I had the union in my mind all the time. I had noticed in the '70 strike that
the lettuce workers were more militant, more radical. And that is why I moved
to the lettuce. I wanted to be with the more radical group."[21]

In the election campaign Ganz made Renteria responsible for his own
employer, Crosetti, where the UFW won. Renteria also helped at other
lettuce companies, and after the lettuce season was over, he became an
organizer at the small Watsonville apple ranches, where the union won
twelve out of thirteen elections. Ganz asked him to stay on as field office
director in Watsonville. Renteria agreed. He was twenty-one. Six years
later he would be a candidate for the UFW Executive Board, running
against the official slate endorsed by Cesar Chavez.

The main job of the worker-volunteers was to build UFW committees
on the crews. These committees of on-the-job advocates would then
become the center of an election campaign. The Bustamante brothers,
Mario and Chava, were committee members at their ranches, Chava at Cal
Coastal and Mario at InterHarvest. Ganz also sent Mario to meet with
workers at other companies where the elections were in doubt. Mario
Bustamante, the popular, fast, and accurate *lechuguero*, was also a good
talker, and he enjoyed it:

> We went to talk to them, just regular talk. And if people didn't want to
> talk we left them alone. And I liked listening to Marshall Ganz whenever
> I happened to hear him . . . so I kept on coming to the union hall after
> work to do what I could to help . . . And if Marshall would send me out
> to a particular place to talk to people, I would always do it with pleasure,
> even if I lost a day of work . . . I wasn't one of the workers who
> volunteered to leave my job and work full time during the elections . . . I
> was a part-time unionist."[22]

The combination of victory in Salinas and defeat in Delano produced
friction within the UFW staff. Ganz was proud of his worker-intensive
approach and was upset that Chavez did not schedule a staff meeting to
analyze what had worked and what had not. Instead, there were

recriminations and hurt feelings, criticisms that were unanswered and unheeded. But the internal squabbling missed the point, which the Teamsters' Pete Maturino made best: "In Delano the UFW had mishandled the contracts; in Salinas they had the Mario Bustamantes of the world, the skilled *lechugueros*, on their side."[23]

Throughout the state, the UFW's local record turned out to be the strongest predictor of how it would fare in elections held that first month. In Stockton, where the UFW had supported the 1974 strikes but had no contracts to administer, the union did well, sweeping the two fresh-tomato elections 165 to 9 and winning six of eight contests in the canning tomatoes. The UFW lost at Franzia Winery, where it had once had a contract, along with the familiar problems of back dues and seniority. At the large table grape ranches near Fresno, the union could not even get enough signatures to force elections. In the San Diego County tomato fields, where the union had no contracts but was a symbol of farm worker power and achievement, the UFW overwhelmingly won seven of eight elections against No Union.

In the row crops of Santa Maria, where a relatively large percentage of the vegetable workers were Filipinos, the Teamsters put up a strong campaign and won seventeen contests, to the UFW's five. But the UFW wins included Bruce Church, the third-largest lettuce company in the state. In the Oxnard row crops and nurseries, the UFW benefited from its support of the '74 strike wave, and the final tally was eleven wins for the UFW, three for the Teamsters, and one for No Union.[24]

Growers at White River Farms, scene of the brutal 1972 strike, prevented the ballots from being counted on the grounds that the union did not have enough qualifying signatures. No second election was held. At Gallo the Teamsters won the election by less than 100 votes—but 129 former UFW strikers who were eligible to vote had their votes thrown out. Gallo also openly violated the ALRB access rules, and its foremen regularly intimidated workers sympathetic to the UFW. Eventually the ALRB charged Gallo with fifty violations of the new state law, but the company's lawlessness distracted from the reality that the Teamsters also had solid support from the large number of Portuguese workers and some of the Mexicans.

Yet even with the ALRB's early lax performance and its failure to enforce many of its own rules and regulations, the UFW made a strong showing wherever workers knew little about the troubles with the grape contracts and the union's offensive against undocumented workers. Overall, in the first thirty days of ALRB elections the UFW scored eighty-seven victories with 52 percent of the vote; the Teamsters had seventy-three victories with 31 percent of the vote; and No Union got nineteen victories and 16 percent of the vote.[25]

★   ★   ★

On September 15, after losing most of the Delano elections, Chavez held a press conference calling for the resignation of General Counsel Kintz. He accused Kintz of siding with the growers, not enforcing the access rule, accepting inflated employee lists from employers, and not issuing unfair labor practice (ULP) charges.[26] Chavez's charges were not fanciful, although he didn't mention the pressure put on the board by the high number of early elections. Also, Kintz didn't so much side with the growers as try to remain neutral, rather than carry out the law's mandate to promote farm worker unionization. But Chavez did not soften his attack. Standing in front of the Sacramento ALRB office amid a crowd of farm workers and supporters, he said he was "totally disgusted" with the way the elections were being run.

The ensuing UFW campaign, meant to explain away the early defeats in the table grape elections and change the way the ALRB was being administered, was a model of political mobilization and a powerful demonstration of UFW support, both in the fields and across the country. Less than a week after Chavez's initial complaint, sixty-five church leaders from seventeen states were on their way to California to tour the fields and check on how the law was working. As soon as the clergy returned to their congregations, the AFL-CIO sent its own emergency team to investigate the elections. At the end of the second week, hundreds of workers rallied in Sacramento and Fresno to demand Kintz's resignation, and a group of thirty held an impromptu sit-in at the ALRB's office in Sacramento.[27]

The UFW had created a major crisis for its chief political ally, Governor Jerry Brown. If Kintz wouldn't resign, Chavez demanded, Brown should fire him. But Kintz defiantly refused to resign and argued that no one could fire him, as the ALRB was an independent state agency. Brown was stuck. His most important achievement, the ALRA, was being attacked by his most important supporters. The UFW boycott coalition, which Chavez had now set against him, was exactly the national organization that Brown needed to extend his political career beyond California. But Brown could not afford a public battle with the growers, either. The fight in the fields had exposed his over-clever contradictory appointments to the board, his attempt to finesse the difference between the growers and the UFW, between concession and constraint.

Brown initially responded to the UFW's demands by urging all parties to give the law and the board time to work. But as the pressure increased, Brown forced Kintz to accept the creation of a new task force that would speed up ALRB procedures. Soon, with Brown's blessing, the task force took over the administration of the agency, and its dynamic head, Sam Cohen, pushed Kintz aside.[28]

Cohen, who told a suspicious state senator that he was "no relation to

Jerry Cohen except by cultural heritage," pranced only briefly on the stage of farm worker history, five months, but prance he did. Testifying before the State Senate Labor Relations Committee he said, "You know, there is some reluctance for any stranger to tell somebody what to do especially when they have been doing it for a while, but I'm personally not bothered by that sort of thing."[29]

The son of a traveling shoe salesman, he had graduated in three years from Vanderbilt, got bored studying political theory at Berkeley, transferred to Boalt Law School, and became a highly successful trial attorney specializing in criminal cases. At tall, good-looking, aggressive man who favored expensive suits, at thirty-eight he was a senior partner of a large San Jose law firm when Brown recruited him to the task force, at the suggestion of Secretary of Agriculture Rose Bird. He knew almost nothing about labor law, he disarmingly told anyone who asked, but he knew how to make things work.

Cohen hired a half dozen young trial attorneys ("they were all tough, mean, and reasonable"), convinced the chief investigator from a large Los Angeles law firm to join him on the task force, and brought on a small group of young bilingual field examiners. He either replaced or ignored the middle managers whom Kintz had brought from the NLRB, and co-opted the few ALRB lawyers and investigators who were sympathetic to his plans. Cohen explained to his team that the ALRA stipulated that the board would follow NLRB procedures "where applicable," but as far as he was concerned, in most cases the NLRB was not applicable. The task force, he said, would enforce the law. That didn't mean it would favor the UFW, but neither would it mistake the law's intent: to help farm workers organize and vote in free elections.[30]

Initially, the new team worked in relative obscurity. Kintz was still the nominal general counsel, and along with the board chairman, Bishop Roger Mahoney, he took the public heat. The UFW continued its call for Kintz's resignation. Agribusiness waited to see what would happen. The Teamsters were quicker to figure it out, but typically unsubtle in their reaction. After a board hearing, they roughed up Bishop Mahoney and board member LeRoy Chatfield, and slashed the tires of the bishop's official car.[31]

Sam Cohen's first move was to streamline the unfair labor practice investigations. "I said to the growers we are sending an investigator down to get a statement. If you don't give him a statement I am going to assume that you don't want to give a statement and I will file a complaint." Under the NLRB procedure followed by Kintz and his team, an employer had had ninety days to give a statement in response to a charge of an unfair labor practice. Cohen simplified the ULP forms, empowered the field examiners to make recommendations on remedies, ordered the lawyers to make a quick judgment on whether to file a complaint, and immediately scheduled hearings. Within a month, decisions on unfair labor practices started to come. Fired workers were reinstated with back pay. One Oxnard employer had to rehire thirty-five workers. Growers had to issue public apologies for violating the law, as well as pay back wages.

In early November 1975, after Cohen had been on the job for a month, agribusiness began its counterattack. Two Central Valley legislators announced that they would oppose any new funding for the board, which had outspent its initial budget and was now operating on a $1.25 million loan from the California State Finance Department. "There's no way they're going to get another five million out of the legislature to run this fiasco," said one senator who had opposed the original bill. But the showdown was almost two months away, as the governor couldn't request a vote on emergency funding of the board until the legislature reconvened in January 1976. Until then, Cohen had the $1.25 million.

The UFW countered the growers' complaints by intensifying the pressure on Brown. In late November, the union organized a sit-in of about sixty workers at Brown's office, demanding faster action on ULP charges and the removal of the now-irrelevant Kintz. Brown met secretly with Jerry Cohen, trying to arrange a settlement. Cohen, with the wind at his back, urged Brown to aggressively enforce the law. Brown then agreed to meet with a delegation from the continuing sit-in, on the condition that the others who were occupying the ALRB office would leave. Five people made up the UFW delegation: Marshall Ganz and four farm workers, including Hermilo Mojica. They met late into the night. It is an unlikely snapshot in California history. Mojica—farm-worker warrior, bracero skip, great nephew of Francisco Mújiga, the man in Cárdenas's cabinet most responsible for nationalizing gringo oil, explaining to Brown, the earnest, ambitious ex-seminarian governor, how he had been arrested four times in Salinas while urging farm workers to vote for the UFW. All translated by a rabbi's son, Harvard dropout, former SNCC Mississippi volunteer, and the lead organizer of the UFW, Marshall Ganz. Brown, his presidential ambitions about to be smothered in the cradle, assured them that he would enforce the law.[32]

Fully confident and with Brown's continuing support, Sam Cohen led the ALRB into the Imperial Valley, where elections were impending. He got the El Centro city attorney ("a friend of a friend") to agree to instruct the police not to arrest union organizers for going on company buses to talk to farm workers. This reversed the previous policy, which prohibited the UFW from "trespassing" on company-owned vehicles. Sam Cohen and his team of trial attorneys preferred the fields to their desks, just as they had preferred courtrooms to their law books. When they could, they responded to calls of distress, rushed to the fields to inform everyone of the ALRB regulations, and enforced the law before it could be violated. They went into fields, restaurants, and day-haul pickup spots to pass out leaflets explaining the law and to talk to farm workers, assuring them of their rights and the protection of the state of California. They produced radio ads for Spanish-language stations that gave the local phone number of the agency where farm workers who thought their rights were being violated could call. The two bilingual, bicultural members of the task force—Shirley Trevino, a community organizer from San Jose, and Carlos Bowker, who had arrived in the Imperial Valley from Mexico at the age of twelve and had worked its fields as a young man—worked sixteen-hour days and had the time of their lives.[33]

Much of that time, at least the early-morning hours, was spent in *el hoyo*, working alongside nearly forty UFW organizers, pretty much the entire union organizing staff. Cohen authorized Trevino and Bowker to go on the company buses and require the foreman–bus driver to leave so that the workers would be free to ask questions about their rights.

Sam Cohen liked *el hoyo*. He often went there early in the morning, with his state badge prominently pinned on his chest, to stand amidst the thousands of chatting workers waiting to depart for the fields, and to help Bowker and Trevino if necessary. One morning, well into the election season, he was accompanied by Secretary of Agriculture Rose Bird, confidante of Jerry Brown's, who came to see the action. Harry Bernstein, who had been covering the UFW for the *Los Angeles Times* for ten years, was with her. Bowker was standing next to them reading one of the board's leaflets over a loudspeaker: "Campesinos, these are your rights. You have a right to vote for the union of your choice. You have a right to vote for no union. Your ballot is secret. Nobody will know how you voted. You have a right to vote without being intimidated. If a union or boss or anyone intimidates you, they are breaking the law. If you need our help, call us, the State of California Agricultural Relations Board."[34]

Just then, the crowd of farm workers parted as a dozen blue-jacketed men approached the loudspeaker. At the lead was Roy Mendoza, whom Ralph Cotner had made head of the Teamsters' Imperial Valley organizing. Mendoza had come to do what he did best, intimidate his adversaries—in this case, whoever was working the mike. Cohen introduced himself, and just to make sure that Mendoza understood what he had walked into, introduced him to Bird and Bernstein. Mendoza nodded to Bird and then, with that deft public relations touch for which the Teamsters were famous, said of the *Los Angeles Times* reporter: "You couldn't pay me enough to shake the hand of that sonofabitch."

Mendoza then turned his tongue on Cohen, attacking him for the way he was running the board. The workers crowded in to get a better look. Bowker, assuming the Teamsters were armed and knowing that most of the workers carried their work knives, tried to calm things down. Bird ran into the state-run employment office and called the highest Teamster official she could find, warning that if Sam Cohen got hurt the state would come down hard on the Teamserts. Mendoza left, but he was back an hour later, enraged. Whoever Bird had called had called him. This time, Cohen answered his verbal fusillade—the two men, jaw to jaw like umpire and manager, shouting in each other's faces, while hundreds of workers watched and thousands stood nearby. The next day Ganz told Cohen that it was the talk of the valley, how he had stood up to the Teamsters, and that it had changed everything.[35]

The UFW probably would have done well in the Imperial Valley even without Sam Cohen. Organizing among vegetable workers was easier than it had been in Salinas. People felt more at home in the Imperial Valley; most workers lived on Mexican soil, across the border in Mexicali. The Imperial Valley season was short, and if a worker got fired the consequences weren't as serious as being blackballed in Salinas, where the season lasted six months. Also, Hermilo Mojica remembers that the winter of 1975–76 was the first season that farm workers collected unemployment insurance, and some of them quickly figured out that they could collect unemployment from their Salinas jobs under one name and Social Security number while working for another company in Imperial Valley under another name. So even if they were fired for union activity, they would not jeopardize their Salinas jobs. No one was afraid to talk for the union.[36]

The UFW swept the elections, outpolling the Teamsters 2,095 to 929. The UFW was now sitting in the front room of the vegetable industry. Not only had it won big in Imperial but it had signed fifteen contracts with Salinas vegetable companies soon after their election victories were certified. More Salinas certifications were on the way, and there was no reason these Imperial victories wouldn't also be converted into contracts. Given the Imperial sweep, the statewide numbers also looked better. By February 1976, the ALRB had conducted 429 elections, with conclusive results in 331of them. The UFW won 198; the Teamsters, 115; No Union or small shed and dairy unions, 18. The UFW had garnered 55 percent of the farm worker vote, and the Teamsters 32 percent.[37]

Agribusiness did what it could to stop the UFW from setting up housekeeping in its midst. Some in the legislature tried to weaken the ALRA through amendments, but the Democratic leadership of both houses and the governor said that it was too soon to monkey with the law, which had worked fairly well. Among the legislators petitioning for the amendments, however, were a few rural Democrats who had voted for the original bill. Their defection meant that the board would not get the supplementary funding that it needed, and on February 6, 1976, a little more than five months after it was established, the board shut down. His short, flamboyant contribution to the history of state power complete, Sam Cohen returned to private practice.

Away from the headlines that the shutdown provoked were a couple of back-page stories. The South Central Farmers Association, representing table grape growers, had not joined the rest of organized agribusiness in attacking the ALRA.[38] The law had been good for them. Also, the UFW did not send farm workers to Sacramento to pressure the legislature to keep the board open, as it had threatened. Privately, the union's leaders were not dismayed by a board shutdown. Toward the end of the Imperial elections, voting had begun in the Coachella Valley. The UFW had lost all five table grape elections at small companies where it had held union contracts from 1970 to 1973. Big losses in the Coachella vineyards were expected if the board stayed open, and the union welcomed the postponement. The Teamsters wanted more than a postponement. In April, Governor Brown told Jerry Cohen that he had received a call from the Teamsters saying they wanted out of the fields.[39]

The election campaigns of 1975 tested the organizational efficiency of the UFW. Occurring simultaneously but hundreds of miles apart, they required legal, political, and financial expertise and specific knowledge of local crops, demographics, and farm businesses. Not only did the union have to operate at a new furious pace but there was now an independent measure of its success or failure, an electoral win or a defeat. Although there were victories for the staff to celebrate, the union hadn't done as well overall as most people expected. Chavez decided that something had to be fixed.

"I'm going to learn management systems and how to manage, and then I will teach the Executive Board," he announced at a January 15, 1976, meeting of the board. The UFW now had more than 500 full-time volunteers, and was spending about $200,000 a month. Separate from that budget, the staff also administered fourteen nonprofit agencies, some of them funded by contractually fixed grower contributions, and others by private donations. By March 1975, these 501(c)(3) agencies had accumulated more than $7 million, and Chavez half jokingly complained to the Executive Board that the administration of so much money had become a problem for him. With more contracts being signed in the wake of the election victories that problem was sure to grow.[40]

Most of the nonprofits were without functioning governing boards, rules, or regulations. The volunteers who directed them had been recruited to the UFW because of their loyalty to the cause or the leader, and few had the necessary skills. Although Chavez was suspicious of experts and believed that with hard work and dedication the volunteers could become competent, he was realistic enough to know that the union needed more expertise and coherence.

Much within the UFW was now beyond Chavez's control. During the elections he had focused on the campaign against Kintz, and let others handle the rest. He remained ultimately responsible for the fate of the organization, but he shared that responsibility with many others. He did not shirk his own uncomfortable conclusion. If he wanted to maintain control over the UFW, he would have to learn how to manage it. Always a troubled administrator—Lionel Steinberg, his biggest booster among the growers, had called him the worst in the world—he decided that he had no choice but to learn the job. Undamaged by school, endlessly curious, with the confidence of a classic autodidact, he knew he could do it.

Crosby Milne and his "Management by Objectives" became the latest of Chavez's enthusiasms. Milne was a retired Navy systems management expert who had been introduced to the union by his son, who worked on the Oakland boycott. Milne came into the UFW to help and was shocked by what he found. There seemed to be no organizational system at all; he stopped counting when he got to fifty or sixty people reporting directly to Chavez. He convinced the swamped union president that he needed a system, a plan, a way of making people in the organization accountable. Chavez introduced him to the Executive Board in January. On February 16, 1976 the board began a five-day retreat at the isolated San Antonio Mission in the southern Salinas Valley, where Crosby Milne taught them his stuff.

Milne drew up an organizational chart, calling it a "directive system with instructions and notices." He explained the difference between a target budget and an operating budget. He spent a lot of time teaching the idea of Specific, Attainable, Measurable objectives (the SAM strategy) and how to shape realistic goals and strategies. He led the union leadership through a discussion of the 501(c)(3)s and helped the board members define their explicit purposes and place in the union. He led the inevitable brainstorming session, in which everyone shouted out answers to the core questions: Where are we going? Where did we come from? What are we going to do? Can we manage it?[41]

The Executive Board was generally enthusiastic, and unanimously passed a series of motions that endorsed the ideas that Milne had presented. They said that they expected him to be around for a few years to help put the system into place. Marshall Ganz and Jessica Govea were particularly relieved that some form of accountability was being introduced into the union. Gilbert Padilla was a little more skeptical, but he didn't see anything wrong with getting the union staff better organized.

Many of the Milne reforms helped get important jobs done. Organizational charts are useful; budgeting is a bit of an art, or at least, a complex skill. But as a system, Milne's military approach to management questions served to reinforce the antidemocratic structure and culture of the union.[42] Throughout the retreat Milne argued, and the participants agreed that the union needed more power at its center. Characteristically, he urged the Executive Board members, who had been scattered around California working in the field offices and on the election campaigns, to move back to La Paz, where they could make policy and issue directives.

What power and authority, then, remained on the periphery? The Executive Board had pondered an alternative to this top-down system: union locals with officials democratically elected by the workers. In 1976, locals were not an abstract question. The union could have immediately begun to set up locals in Salinas, Calexico, Oxnard–Ventura, Fresno, and Florida, with others added later. Officials from the UAW and the AFL-CIO who had given the union substantial help during the election campaigns were privately and publicly urging Chavez to set up locals. A month and a half before the Milne retreat, *The Packer* reported that a UAW staffer, Russell Leach, had assured a Grand Rapids, Michigan, audience that "official UFW locals will be set up in geographic areas, like any other union."[43] Locals, and the democratic structure they promised, were a real possibility. Board members briefly considered the matter, and rejected it, unanimously. Not one of them argued for locals.

The retreat summary cites three "factors" against locals: they will use up money; they are parochial, that is, the local officials will be concerned about themselves rather than the whole union; and they are hard to establish among migrants. The last reason was ridiculous, and the Executive Board probably knew it. Salinas had a nine- to ten-month season; by the mid-1970s farm workers were only slightly more migrant than many construction trade workers. But the first two reasons mattered. Money is a form of power, and the Executive Board wanted that power at La Paz. The fear that parochial local leaders with power would prove to be a self-interested, divisive force went together with Chavez's distaste for politics in the union. Despite his own considerable political skills, "politics" was a dirty word for Chavez. In his vocabulary it meant manipulation, deceit, and the pursuit of personal interest. Long after the UFW's collapse Marshall Ganz recalled, "Chavez always said that he hated politics. That politics destroyed organizations. And so there wasn't going to be any politics in the UFW. And that's why we didn't have local unions, that's why we didn't have local elections, local treasuries, because if we had those things there would be politics."[44]

As far as Chavez and the board were concerned, it was easier to maintain unity through orders given to an appointed staff rather than to persuade a group of local officials to act in the interest of the whole union. But politics cannot be wished or ordered away. Instead of democratic politics, the union was left with a palace politics of the most intense variety, complete with alleged conspiracies and periodic purges.

The people at the retreat were not insensible to what they were doing. Where, they wondered, would workers fit in their new organizational chart? They looked for ways to strengthen the ranch committees, the one place where workers could directly vote for people to represent them. But the only suggestions that the Executive Board came up with were empty rituals. Fred Ross said that a grand celebration should be held when the ranch committee members were sworn into office, with Chavez attending when possible. The two resolutions on ranch committees were characteristically paternalistic: "That the Executive Board sets policy and recognizes the importance of having ranch committees take credit for the work that the service entities do for the members"; "That the ranch committee be given some kind of identity if not autonomy as a group."

Crosby Milne did stay around for a few years, teaching the various union departments how to use SAMS, but within a year he had lost Chavez's ear. The Milne system didn't give Chavez the kind of control he sought. Chavez never did want to be the CEO of a big corporate union, or the admiral in a military hierarchy. As Bill Esher had noted more than a decade earlier, Chavez was both the dreamer of big dreams and a small businessman. The dreamer wanted to lead a movement. The small businessman, despite Milne's chart, could not free himself from an obsessive concern with petty financial details. In the next couple of years, to the dismay of many, Chavez spent a lot of time trying to reduce the union's telephone and travel expenses.

One story tells much: Chavez's mania for central control, his small-business concern over tiny amounts of money, his disregard for the autonomy of the field offices and the independent action of farm workers. After the election defeats in Delano, Maddock and the Delano volunteers started having weekly potlucks. Workers and staff would make food, then sell it to themselves and anyone else who came by the office. Folks ate, talked, and made a little money for the field office. When Chavez heard about it, he demanded that the money be sent to La Paz.[45]

The election organizing of 1975 had had its downside. The organizers came onto a ranch for a short period, promised a lot, and then, having been highly available to the workers before the vote, rushed on to the next election once the votes were counted. Putting all of its attention on winning as many elections as possible, the union was sloppy about postelection follow-up. It had no set method for maintaining contact with the workers, and no particular person or groups formally responsible for engaging them afterward. Often the road from winning an election to getting a contract was long and arduous. It became longer and more arduous when union officials were not actively organizing the workers to keep the pressure on. The promised benefits were slow in coming. Many workers felt abandoned; some felt betrayed.[46]

At the Crosby Milne retreat the Executive Board acknowledged that in most places postelection organizing simply had not been done. But the board was largely dismissive of the problem, almost blaming the workers for their high expectations. The retreat summary notes: "For the limbo period, it is important to explain [to the workers] the whole process of certification; the whole process of how organizers are not going to be around to kiss them all the time." As part of its general reorganization plan, the board made Eliseo Medina the head of Contract Administration, and gave him ultimate responsibility for postelection follow-through, but over the next ten months the board did not give him the people or resources necessary to do the job.[47]

Almost a year after the first elections began, an unnamed UFW official told The Packer that the union had converted 113 certified elections into only thirty-five new contracts. In November of 1976, Chavez told a special organizing meeting that the union had picked up fewer than 6,000 new members in the aftermath of the 1975 elections. After an internal investigation, Ganz concluded in May of 1977 that in the vegetables, where the union was strongest, the UFW had contracts with fewer than half the companies where it had achieved certified victories. Some of this failure can be attributed to company stonewalling. But as the union demonstrated in a few cases, employer delays could be overcome by organized action of the rank and file. Gilbert Padilla was one of the few people assigned to negotiate contracts in 1976. "We didn't get more contracts out of the elections because there wasn't enough follow-up," he said. "We were too busy doing other things."[48]

Chief among those other things was extending the union's political influence. Political power, the ability to shape the policy of the state, became the locus of the union's hopes and fears and resources in 1976, the place where it believed its future would be won or lost. It tried to mobilize its allies in the cities to make the farm labor law permanent and to vault its man, Jerry Brown, from the governor's office to the presidency. Cesar Chavez, Dolores Huerta, Jerry Cohen, and Marshall Ganz became major players in California politics and minor figures in national political circles.

Chavez's commitment to conventional politics sat comfortably beside his distaste for political discussion within his own organization. Chavez, a man of wide interests who had something authentic to say to most of the people in his diverse coalition, can be allowed some internal contradictions. But there is more. He was good at playing the electoral and legislative game partly because he disdainfully held it at arm's length, and wielded his power without mercy. It was a dirty business, he thought, and if politicians needed not only his endorsement but also money, he would pay. And if they didn't deliver, he would punish. What he was willing to do in Sacramento he did not want anyone to do inside his union. Sacramento was already corrupt; he wanted to keep the UFW pure.

This concern with electoral and legislative politics is a constant in UFW history, but the union's interest in politicians and state power intensified after the passage of the ALRA, as the administration, interpretation, and funding of the farm labor law became a central battleground in the fight among the growers, the Teamsters, and the UFW. The outcome of that struggle depended to a certain extent on the California legislature. Its members could not be ignored. After the passage of the law, giving financial support and lending election-time personnel to favored Democratic Party politicians became a central item on the UFW's agenda. Within a couple of years, the UFW would also become the second largest financial contributor in California statewide elections, and would regularly reward or punish legislators on matters far removed from farm worker issues. Eventually, the union's passion for giving cash to politicians became so great that the UFW jeopardized its standing among farm workers, continuing to impose a mandatory levy on its members despite widespread worker protest.

The initial ratcheting up of the union's political action began after the ALRB closed down, and the UFW, quite reasonably, did what it could to get it refunded. The chosen weapon was a ballot initiative, Proposition 14, which would make the law, the board, its funding and access rules permanent, amendable only by another proposition passed by the state's electorate.

Getting the initiative to qualify for the ballot required a monumental staff effort. In only twenty-nine days of April canvassing, UFW volunteers got over 700,000 signatures, more than double the number necessary. Many people worked around the clock; a few were so exhausted when the campaign was over that they left the union. In retrospect, many volunteers felt that the petition drive was the most effective collective project of their lives. It was also the last great accomplishment of the union's boycott infrastructure.[49]

For months growers had been demanding eight new agribusiness-friendly provisions to the ALRA. They dropped seven of those demands even before the petition signatures were turned in; soon after the proposition had qualified, they dropped all efforts to change the law. In June 1976, the speaker of the assembly, Leo McCarthy, assured the UFW that the ALRB would be reinstated without changes as part of the overall budget settlement in July. The growers' allies in Sacramento were upfront about what had happened. State Senator George Zenovich of Fresno said, "The best offense against the initiative [Prop 14] would be an operating, functioning, fully-funded ALRB."[50]

At about the same time as the union decided to launch Proposition 14, Jerry Brown announced he was running for president. From its inception, his bid for the Democratic nomination was tied to the UFW and the fate of the labor law. In a meeting back in October 1975 when George Meany urged Brown to do something about the ALRB, Brown discussed the possibility of a run for president with the AFL-CIO chief.[51] Then Brown did what Meany wanted, and turned the farm labor board over to Sam Cohen. The ALRB task force had been, among other things, a chit in presidential politics. Brown had no national campaign organization when he declared his candidacy, in March 1976, and asked LeRoy Chatfield to become his national campaign coordinator. Chatfield resigned from the ALRB, pleasing the growers, and used the UFW boycott network to build a nationwide volunteer group, Citizens for Brown. Political observers agreed that apart from Brown's reputation as a refreshing nonpolitician, his only significant accomplishment had been bringing a kind of peace to the California fields.

The Democratic Party bosses hoped to use Brown, late getting into the race, to stop Jimmy Carter, and then give the nomination at a brokered convention to Hubert Humphrey, who was sitting out the primaries. Brown entered his first primary in Maryland and beat Carter by twelve percentage points. The two people most responsible for that victory were Nancy Pelosi, a young California politician with strong family ties to Maryland's corrupt Democratic bosses, and Gilbert Padilla, who mobilized the boycott coalition that he and his wife, Esther, had built in Washington in the late 1960s and early '70s. After that success, Marshall Ganz and a dozen UFW organizers went to Oregon to help run a write-in campaign for Brown. Also working with Ganz were a dozen former ALRB staffers and Sam Cohen cohorts, including Carlos Bowker, Shirley Trevino, and Maurice Jourdane.[52] Brown got a startling 23 percent of the vote, finishing third, even though his name was not on the ballot. Ganz went on to Rhode Island and New Jersey, bringing some forty organizers and mobilizing several hundred volunteers. Brown won those two primaries and the one in California, probably the only victory that would have been his without the UFW organizers.

Brown won every primary where he was on the ballot, but he hadn't entered enough primaries, and Carter's victory in Ohio gave him enough delegates for the nomination. The Democratic Party pros gave way, but the UFW leaders were not discouraged. They had established the union's reputation as an effective national political force and recruited more people to the cause. A large part of the leadership (Chavez, Huerta, Ganz, Govea, the Padillas, Artie Rodriguez, Jerry Cohen) went off in mid-July to New York City to polish the union's national reputation at the Democratic Party Convention. Cohen, Ganz, and Govea were Brown delegates. Chavez nominated Jerry Brown for president in a prime-time speech. Four years earlier, the lettuce boycott had been the iconic fight that united the delegates. This time, the UFW fundraiser, held after Carter was formally nominated, became one of the places where all the contending factions made peace.[53]

When the principals returned to California, Brown, Assembly Speaker McCarthy, and other Democratic officials tried to persuade the UFW Executive Board to drop Proposition 14. It was only late July, and the UFW still had time to do so gracefully. The ALRB had been fully funded without any changes, just as McCarthy had promised. The initiative had served its purpose, he argued, and it was not sound public policy to prohibit the legislature from amending a law. Governor Brown talked to Chavez on the phone and traveled to La Paz to talk to the board. As long as he was governor, he vowed, there would be no substantive changes to the law. The growers would have the active support of the bankers and cannery bosses in defeating the proposition, he argued, and the union might lose. Politicians who supported the proposition would be vulnerable. The campaign would cost a lot, emotionally and financially. The union, he said, didn't understand how the proposition was "sensitizing the opposition," and convincing people who were otherwise neutral to line up with the growers.[54]

Chavez and the board ignored the advice of the political pros. Marshall Ganz, who fully supported proceeding with the initiative, later called it an act of hubris: full of themselves from their series of small political triumphs, the union leaders thought they understood the electorate better than Brown and the regular Democratic Party operatives. They didn't. California voters thrashed Proposition 14, 63 percent to 37 percent. The growers had managed to turn the election into a referendum on property rights and race, their TV ads suggesting that access rights for union organizers would allow dark-skinned men to invade the homes of small growers and endanger their white wives and daughters. Some of the UFW's liberal and moderate supporters also had defected once the ALRB was refunded and as concerns arose about legislation that, in the words of a *Los Angeles Times* editorial, would be "frozen into law by initiative."[55]

Wrongheaded as it was, the decision to go ahead with the Proposition 14 campaign was in line with almost everything the UFW did in 1976: it was embedded in conventional politics, focused, above all, on securing the union's claim on state power, and was only marginally involved with farm workers. The few assigned to farm worker organizing tried to warn Chavez about the consequences of such priorities. Larry Tramutt, a stop staffer at La Paz, warned that the field offices were underfunded and neglected.[56] Eliseo Medina estimated that although the union was the chosen representative of tens of thousands of workers, it had only fifty ranch committee members. Trying to negotiate contracts with just a handful of negotiators, Medina had not had time to organize the ranch elections. He registered a polite complaint in September when Chavez canceled a statewide ranch committee conference in order to put most of the union's resources into a union nominating convention to endorse politicians in the November elections. In his year as contract administrator, Medina later complained, he was unable to "establish the institutional life of the union."[57]

Meanwhile, although the Teamsters International had signaled a desire to leave the fields, its local organizers aggressively stepped up their activities. They established ten field offices. They signed new table grape contracts and raised wages at some ranches, and encouraged wildcats and vandalism at others.[58] In Salinas, they ignored several court injunctions and led the workers in a lettuce strike that forced a substantial wage increase. Soon nearly forty companies were paying the new Teamster standard lettuce rate, $3.40 an hour and 54 cents a box. By contrast, fifteen new UFW contracts paid $3.15 an hour and 51 cents a box. Most frightening to the growers was how the Teamsters had won the gains. When the field workers struck, the Teamster drivers and box stitchers honored their picket lines. When the drivers and stitchers struck a few days later, the field workers returned the favor. An August 1976 editorial in the *Salinas Californian* titled "Role Switch in Farm Labor Fuss" captured the shifted balance of union activity:

> Whereas in the years since 1970 the UFW has been the moving party in the court battles, walkouts, strikes and other disputes that stipple the farm labor record, we now witness Teamsters Farm Local 946 in the UFW role . . . But even though the shoe is on the other foot . . . the effective defiance of the court order by the Teamsters illustrates what most observers of the farm labor scene have known all along. If the rank and file members of a union feel strongly enough about what they're doing, there is, as a practical matter, no way to force them to go to work.[59]

It was the Teamsters who took advantage of that lovely, mostly forgotten, proletarian truth. With only a few exceptions, the UFW did not.

Yet workers at the thirty-some vegetable companies that had signed UFW contracts were still doing well. They weren't being paid quite as much as the Teamster farm workers, but working conditions were better wherever there was a UFW contract. At InterHarvest the workers virtually controlled production. They set the pace of work; they imposed their own quality standards; by strategic use of the hiring hall they determined who was hired, and they had a lot to say about who could be fired. This, despite the fact that Eli Black, Cesar Chavez's friend, was no longer around to ensure that InterHarvest kept Chavez happy. Trapped in a financial scandal, his

plan to put a pretty face on the company's Latin American empire a shambles, he had committed suicide in 1975, leaving a two-word suicide note:
"Early retirement."

Although Black's policy of accommodation with the UFW continued,
the union had its own problems at Interharvest and at the other union
companies. The union's RFK Medical Plan was badly administered. Checks
to doctors came late, or never. Piece-rate workers, who typically work less
hours than hourly workers, didn't qualify for many of the benefits. Dolores
Huerta told the Executive Board in September that many of the piece-rate
workers felt "betrayed," as they had pointed out the problem before the
1975 negotiations and had been told that it would be taken care of.[60]

Companies were concerned about the extra expense of signing with the
union. For every UFW worker under contract growers paid sixteen and a
half cents an hour into the RFK Medical Plan; 10 cents an hour into the
Juan De La Cruz Pension Plan; 5 cents an hour into the MLK Service
Center account. This made their production costs higher than at the
Teamster companies, even though the companies with Teamster contracts
paid a higher wage. The workers' control of the fields also raised production costs. Hourly workers worked more slowly than the hourly workers at
Teamster companies. UFW piece rate workers worked faster than those at
the Teamster ranches, and in their hurry they sometimes produced an infe-
rior pack. The companies with UFW contracts explained to union leaders
that over the long term they could afford to pay more only if other companies paid the same. Either the UFW had to convince workers to increase
production and improve "the quality of the pack," or it had to organize the
rest of the vegetable industry into the UFW.

These problems required the active interest of the union leadership and
an extended dialogue between the leaders and the rank and file. Neither
happened. At the top, Cesar Chavez had little interest in such matters. In
the fall of 1976 he was caught up with electoral campaigns. Ben Maddock
accompanied Chavez to most of the dinners, rallies, and fundraisers as his
driver and chief security man. What became clear to Maddock then would
become common opinion among most top UFW staffers in the next year:
"Organizing farm workers was not his main goal . . . We went to Georgia
and Denver to campaign for Carter among Chicanos. He enjoyed that a lot
more than farm worker elections and running a union."[61]

Chavez took the defeat of Proposition 14 hard. Polls had predicted the
initiative losing by a wide margin, but Chavez had believed that his 300
experienced boycott organizers and thousands of Election Day volunteers
would engineer an upset. According to Maddock, he and Chavez had been
fasting for sixteen days when the final results came in. They broke their fast
and drove from LA back to La Paz:

I broke the fast with two steak sandwiches, and I almost died . . . Well, coming back over the grapevine we both got sicker than dogs . . . I told Chavez I have to pull over . . . He said it is snowing. I said I don't give a shit; I am getting sick. So we both got out. I can't remember how he broke his fast, but he didn't break it right. Generally, he would eat a very little bit and then just drink until his stomach was ready. I was a novice. We went out there and my stomach was dying . . . We both vomited . . . And I can remember him coming up all of a sudden. He said, "We lost Ben, how could we have lost?" After the defeat he was a changed man . . . that night he was as sick as I was, and he was different . . . He never really came alive again.[62]

Maddock's story made the rounds, told, exaggerated, and retold within the union for years, as many insiders came to believe that the defeat forever altered Cesar Chavez. Proposition 14 was the first time that Chavez had petitioned the general public and lost, and this loss was his town, for he had pushed the Executive Board to go through with the campaign, despite the advice of almost every political friend the UFW had. Years later Marshall Ganz said that the loss undermined Chavez's self-confidence, robbed him of his sense of humor, and pushed him over the edge into severe paranoia.[63]

Maddock's story lives on because of the substantial purge that followed the defeat, and the subsequent purges and turmoil that bedeviled La Paz and the union over the next several years. But not everyone agrees with his assessment. Chavez loyalists dismiss it as an exaggeration. Many other staffers, even victims of the purges, believe that the periodic firings and dismissals were calculated political maneuvers rather than the result of some sudden plunge into paranoia. In fact, in 1976 the timing isn't even right because Chavez began gearing up for a purge two months before the Proposition 14 defeat and his infamous breakdown on the grapevine.

In early September Chavez had warned a meeting of the National Farm Workers Health Group, the 501(c)(3) that ran the clinics, that "some people working in the clinics are purposely trying to foul us up." He named a registered nurse, Kathleen McCarthey, as "having done a very professional job of screwing us up," and told Jessica Govea, who was involved with the clinics, to "keep her eyes open for people with hidden agendas." "It may be necessary to fire some people," Chavez said.[64]

Several days earlier Chavez had confided to Ganz that his cousin Manuel had told him that McCarthey had used her position at the Calexico clinic to turn farm workers against Manuel and the union. Chavez had also heard that she had visited Cuba, and was a committed leftist. After the 1967 purge Chavez had continued to allow some leftists onto the boycott and Service

Center staffs, as long as, in his judgment, they did not put their own politics ahead of union policies. But the charge against McCarthey was different. Chavez told Ganz that McCarthey was a "spy," a "paid agent," part of a conspiracy bent on wrecking the union.[65]

Chavez jumped from Kathleen McCarthey to her friend Joe Smith, the new editor of *El Malcriado*, who had recruited McCarthey to the union. The September 15, 1976, edition of *El Malcriado*, the first issue in a year and a half, became an object of his suspicion. The "bad boy" had become trouble again. The paper had been shut down as part of the 1967 mini-purge. It repeatedly fell out of favor after starting back up in 1968, and was closed down again in 1975 because the Executive Board considered it too left and regretted hiring an ex-member of the Maoist October League as editor. Smith, a four-year boycott volunteer with progressive politics and a conservative personal style, who had edited his college newspaper, had looked like a safe replacement

But four days after the paper came out, the Executive Board was debating whether Smith had disobeyed orders and put information in the paper that he knew would hurt the union.[66] Chavez accused Smith of "playing games with the board" and threatened to close the newspaper and fire the staff. All at the meeting agreed that mistakes had been made, and some agreed with Chavez that they had been deliberate. Ganz remarked, "Either they [the *Malcriado* staff] are deliberately flaunting policy or they had the attitude they don't care about policy." Only Richard Chavez suggested, "Maybe it is not possible to please us."[67]

Publication was again suspended, and Smith was sent out on the Prop 14 campaign. But Richard Chavez had come closest to identifying the real problem with *El Malcriado*, which was not the editors but the claustrophobic internal life of the UFW. Although the Executive Board and a few others debated the big issues facing the union, the volunteer staff was never included. Once Chavez and the board set policy, the staff was only supposed to discuss the best ways to carry it out. Debating the decision itself was bad form at best and evidence of "another agenda" or "disruption" at worst. Such debates—like the supposed parochial interests of local leaders—exemplified the kind of internal politics that Chavez believed would destroy the union's unity, and make it ineffectual in the world.

Farm workers were not invited to participate in policy debates. The board's discussions are full of arguments about what farm workers think and want, but the UFW never brought an issue of any importance to farm workers to decide. It was always a matter of convincing workers of one union policy or another, bringing them on board. During strikes, and on a few projects in which farm worker participation was indispensable, Ganz, Govea, and Medina encouraged open debate among rank-and-file leaders, although often it was the workers who forced their way into the discussion.

In general, however, the union leaders were not interested in educating the workers about the choices the UFW faced.

Such disregard for political education and debate limited the scope of any UFW newspaper. The original *Malcriado*, "the voice of the farm worker," had tried to present a diversity of farm worker opinions, which was one reason it was shut down. Its successor, "the official voice of the UFW," could not possibly give that voice its proper tone and timbre, because the paper's editor and staff were kept ignorant of the whys and wherefores of the official line. As it turned out, no one could do that except Cesar Chavez. He alone was the official voice of the UFW, and the new *Malcriado*'s first issue was also its last, replaced six months later by "The President's Personal Newsletter."

At some point during the *Malcriado* crisis, Chavez decided that the UFW's national boycott director, Nick Jones, was at the center of a conspiracy to disrupt the union. The first hint of Chavez's suspicions came during the September meeting, which Jones attended. Jones had doubted that Smith was deliberately undermining the union, but he agreed with much of the critique of *El Malcriado*, and he reminded Smith that the union needed "absolute controls" of its public communications. Chavez immediately responded, "Nick, you should remember that it was on your recommendation that Brother Joe was hired to be in charge of the paper."[68]

Jones had been with the union for ten years by then, not part of the inner circle but close to it, and was generally considered an absolute Chavez loyalist. He grew up in Fargo, North Dakota, where his father was a union carpenter, proud that he had never crossed a picket line. At North Dakota State University, in the early 1960s, Nick hung out at the Catholic center and soon took a position against the war in Vietnam, which proved troublesome, as he had a four-year ROTC scholarship. He left college and went to Chicago, where he worked with Students for a Democratic Society. He was drafted and eventually got conscientious objector status. In 1966, at the age of twenty-three he showed up in Delano, was recruited onto the staff and sent to Seattle to work on the boycott. A year later he married Virginia Rodriguez, a member of one of the original 1965 strike families and a former secretary to Chavez. Chris Hartmire put him on the payroll as a "migrant priest," and he built a career on the boycott.[69]

Jones had fully supported the minipurge in 1967. During Chavez's 1968 fast Nick and Virginia were the first people to put up a tent outside Forty Acres and played a major role in the religious celebrations there. Jones was one of Chavez's first bodyguards; he protected the Chavez house in Delano with a shotgun and taught many other guards how to use their weapons. He and Cesar traveled together during the grape boycott years, and they lived in close quarters on the road. His appointment as national boycott director, just six months before he was purged, was a measure of Chavez's trust.

As he rose in the organization there had been some problems, however. He did not like life at La Paz and chafed under close scrutiny. Years earlier he had had a major dispute with Dolores Huerta, and the two of them did not get along. He had a series of disagreements with Ganz, and Jones was open about his intention to run against him for a seat on the Executive Board at the 1977 convention. That threat carried some weight, since it wasn't entirely clear how much power the 300 boycotters, outnumbering the rest of the staff by about three to two, might have in union elections. Although they could not get their man elected to the board over a Chavez veto, these full-time boycott volunteers, many of whom Jones had recruited and whom he now led, represented a potential semi-independent voice, and thus a separate center of power, in the union.

Jones had expressed doubts about going ahead with the Proposition 14 campaign, and Ganz and Chavez had criticized him for being slow in mobilizing boycotters to California to work on it. He was also close to the Communist Party, but initially that wasn't an issue. Jones explained: "Not that he [Chavez] thought I was a card-carrying Communist. But we had good support from Communists in the boycott activities. And I spoke openly about that because I didn't see any reason to hide who was out there supporting us . . . They came and didn't ask for rewards of any sort, or try to play their agenda on us, they came and supported us."[70]

But what was tolerated in good times became intolerable in bad. As the prospects for Proposition 14 dimmed, Chavez began to add it all up: maybe Nick was plotting against the union; maybe he was hoping the proposition would lose so that he could advance his own career in the UFW; maybe he was putting CP sympathizers and other leftists into key positions so that they could sabotage the Prop 14 effort; maybe the union was the victim of a conspiracy.

Gilbert Padilla first heard the theory just before the big defeat:

> We lived in these two houses close together. And it was real late at night. And Cesar comes knocking on the door and gets me up. And we go outside and are walking between the houses and Cesar says, "I got to talk to you because they are trying to destroy the union."
>
> And I said, "Who in the hell is trying to destroy the union?"
>
> "The Communists. I think it is the Communists, and I know who they are. And I know who is harboring them . . . Nick Jones and all those guys from Denver and Chicago. They are here and they are trying to fuck us."[71]

Five years earlier, in another moment of high anxiety over a statewide ballot initiative, Chavez had told his then chief of staff, LeRoy Chatfield, that Chatfield would have to take the blame if it lost. When this latest initiative lost, the distraught Chavez knew where to look for people to blame. All the full-time volunteers who had been working on Proposition 14 were summoned to La Paz for a supposed debriefing. When some of them started criticizing the strategy, Chavez came into the room through a window and shut off the discussion, angrily telling the surprised staff that they were servants of the farm workers and didn't have a right to criticize the leadership.[72]

Following the meeting, Marshall Ganz and Fred Ross directed individual interviews of each volunteer. "We were quizzing them, How did they get on the boycott, and did they have links with Nick Jones? And, I mean, it was like a little star chamber," Ganz later said. "It was like a little interrogation we were doing to determine the loyalty of the people, and then we were making judgments about them. . . . And then we'd say, 'That one is okay. That one is not okay.'"[73]

Ganz and Ross cast a wide net. Nearly half the boycott staff was fired or given demeaning assignments that the leadership knew they would not accept. The boycott machinery was dismantled, and three of the four regional directors resigned. Joe Smith and the staff of El Malcriado were fired. The boycott soul of the union was strangled; later it would be partially revived, but in a completely different form.

In the midst of the interrogations, Nick and Virginia Jones resigned. In their letter of resignation, Nick described a private meeting with Chavez in which Chavez said that the UFW had been "infiltrated" by leftists, and that Jones was either leading them or was naïve, or was "using them to gain some political advantage inside the UFW." He accused Jones of bringing "spies" to La Paz and said that "time would tell if he were guilty."

According to the Joneses' letter, Chavez was upfront about the question of Communists: "He told me how I had kept him informed about 'splinter groups' but never about 'mainliners.' He was referring to Communists, and I told him I had never been given any reason to since I had never had any problem from Communists. I told him that had I become aware of anything detrimental to the UFW stemming from Communists, I would have informed him."

The Joneses' letter of resignation also urged the leaders of the union to set "guidelines for fairly and responsibly weighing each staff member's work instead of basing decisions on chismes [rumors] and cheap accusations." It called on their "brothers and sisters to continue their dedicated service to the United Farm Workers as the only union for U.S. farm workers."[74]

When parts of the letter were published in the Los Angeles Times under the headline "UFW Aide Quits, Alleges Chavez Antileftist Bias," Chavez's publicist, Marc Grossman, claimed that the staff turnover had nothing to do with "ideology" but rather was a question of "competence"—just as in 1967 Chavez had said that the minipurge was about staff laziness, not politics.[75] Nick and Virginia quickly denied having anything to do with the *Times* story and sent another letter to the staff, urging everyone to "get behind the leadership and expect the best from them in terms of decisions and trust," as "the union is under severe pressure because it is a decent union and it deserves the trust and respect of all of us."[*] Nevertheless, scores of protest letters descended on La Paz, and Chavez sent the new boycott director, Larry Tramutt, on a tour of what remained of the boycott offices to deliver the union's explanation of what had happened.

"There was no purge of leftists," Tramutt insisted. "A number of people left the union. One was fired. It was a question of competence. Other people analyzed it differently and chose to make a political statement. Some had political ambitions in the union and were trying to create a platform to promote themselves politically." But Tramutt added a warning: "Any organization worth its salt will be infiltrated by the left or the right. It happened to the Panthers in Chicago. They were infiltrated by the FBI. And the left infiltrates organizations, too. It is silly and asinine to think that the farm workers have not been infiltrated. You can't be uptight and always looking over your shoulder. But we would be stupid and idiotic to think that it [the UFW] hasn't been."[76]

In California, Tramutt was accompanied by Fred Ross, who warned the boycotters about "disrupters" and "losers" in their midst. "Chavez is the only one who can hire anyone or fire anyone in this union," Ross declared.[77]

No one on the Executive Board objected to the political cleansing. Ganz and Ross were the lead inquisitors, but Gilbert Padilla and Dolores Huerta also interrogated the boycott staff. When Joe Smith and a top staffer, Steve Rivers, requested formal hearings to answer the charges against them, the board unanimously rejected the request, falsely claiming that the UFW constitution forbade it.[78] Thus, the entire board assented to what was most frightening about the purge: those who were punished either were given no reason or were presented with unsubstantiated charges, and were not allowed to face their accusers or defend themselves.

In retrospect, Padilla, Govea, Medina, Ganz, and Philip Vera Cruz wished that they had stood up to Chavez. Although some of them said that there was incompetence on the staff and that some of the firings were justified, none of them believed that there was a general conspiracy to damage the union. Many years later Ganz said:

---

[*]   The Joneses' refusal to publicly discuss their resignations became the standard practice of people who left the UFW staff. Believing that any open criticism of the union would only help the growers and that the union was still good for farm workers, the vast majority of ex-staffers remained quiet about their own difficulties in the UFW.

I came to believe that my failure to challenge Cesar about Joe Smith, not to mention Nick and Virginia, was a moment of failure in a moral crisis. I apologized to Nick when I saw him in Chicago many, many years ago, but I know I owe him a "public apology." As he recognized, those of us on the board all had ways to rationalize why it didn't matter that much, that you had to break eggs to make omelets, and other forms of sophistry, mostly to avoid getting into a fight with Cesar, [and] isolate ourselves, or just get on with the illusion that this would all go away so we could just get on with our work.[79]

A moral failure it was. And those who failed would pay. Having collectively participated in a major bloodletting, they were not equipped to stop the bleeding that was to come.

Nick Jones himself never believed that the defeat of Proposition 14 radically changed Cesar Chavez. Jones has always thought that the purge that followed was essentially political, driven by Chavez's fear of the growing independence of the boycott staff and his need to blame someone for the election disaster. Jones, who went on to work with other unions for twenty-five years, now sees the purge as but an intensified version of the antidemocratic politics common within U.S. labor. It would be hard to disagree. There is no need to root Chavez's actions in any supposed personal breakdown in the snow. The purge's mix of anti-Communism, scapegoating, and peremptory firing of staff was neither exotic nor deranged. It put Chavez squarely in league with the "union bosses" he so commonly scorned.

As it happened, around the time that Chavez's lieutenants were rooting out disrupters, loyalists of the Teamsters' hierarchy were enforcing their superiors' will upon rebellious underlings in California. The circumstances were quite different from those roiling the UFW, but the decision-making process and policy execution were equally high-handed.

The Teamsters International had indeed decided to quit the fields for good. The reason was money. Back in April of 1975 when Jerry Brown told Jerry Cohen that the Teamsters wanted out, *The Packer* reported that the union was spending $100,000 a week on its farm worker adventure. After the Teamsters losses in the 1975–76 Imperial Valley elections, the per capita dues that the Western Conference Teamsters and the International Teamsters could expect from earlier victories weren't going to cover the expenses. The International was especially worried about the UFW antitrust suit against the Teamsters and growers that was bound to involve thousands of hours of legal work, for which the Teamsters were paying top dollar while the UFW was paying a subsistence wage. A series of stop-and-start negotiations between the two unions finally culminated in an agreement in January 1977.

The agreement gave the UFW almost everything it wanted. It divided jurisdiction so that the UFW got all workers covered by the ALRA, and the Teamsters got those covered by the NLRA—that is, non–field workers. The Teamsters would turn over their contracts to the UFW, on the condition that the workers ratified UFW representation. There was explicit language committing the unions to cooperate, and an explicit method of enforcement. The Teamsters could keep the Bud Antle contract, which they had negotiated in 1961, and the UFW would drop all legal actions it had initiated against the Teamsters.[80]

This pact did not please the farm worker organizers of Teamsters Local 946. They were collecting dues from more than 10,000 members, and they anticipated dues from many thousands more, as they expected to win the next round of table grape elections. Their overhead was low; Local 946 had not been named in the various antitrust and civil rights suits that were burdening the Teamsters hierarchy. Many of the local's organizers had been fighting the UFW for years, and they believed they were the best union for farm workers.

Bridging the gap between the low-level Teamster organizers and the top officials of the Western Conference and the International was the obedient head of the farm workers division, Ralph Cotner. Cotner was a professional of violence but also a servile instrument of his superiors. He would not sabotage an agreement that they had signed. Thus, any rebels at the bottom of the hierarchy would have to fight for their jobs not only without their leader but against him.

They had but a slim chance. In January, Cotner fired most of them. When the organizers refused to leave their jobs, he and a gang of large men personally shut down or vandalized the local offices. Sometimes they did it during the day, sometimes at night. They hit Indio, Fresno, Lamont. The biggest and most important office, Bakersfield, was next. The organizers there had been fond of Cotner, respected his toughness, and admired his ability to drink and tell stories through the night and be ready for work the next morning. They had believed him when he told them months earlier not to worry about all the rumors of UFW-Teamster talks, because Local 946 was there to stay, and the Teamsters would never leave the fields. When Cotner and his enforcers arrived in Bakersfield, Pete Maturino, the head of the office, and his men were waiting for them. Instead of putting up a fight, the Bakersfield contingent made a great show of presenting Cotner with a gift. He unwrapped the present in front of the two groups of men. It was framed and inscribed: his one-time friends had given him a golden hatchet.[81]

"The Game"

February to June '77

Eliseo Medina was as surprised as anyone on the Executive Board when Chavez scheduled its February 1977 meeting at Badger, California, the home base of Synanon in the Sierra foothills. Relieved to have the Nick Jones mess behind them, he and Marshall Ganz especially had been looking forward to capitalizing on the Teamsters' exit from the fields. They both had prepared organizing plans: Medina for the citrus, Ganz for the vegetables. Once they got to Badger, such plans appeared to be folly, and Medina had the first presentiment that maybe "I'm in the wrong outfit."

> We sat in this room that has all these seats, like in the colleges, that are steep and look down on a stage-like area. So Chuck Dederich [Synanon's leader] and a bunch of people are playing the Game. And we are watching it. What the hell is this about? And then Chuck invited Cesar to come down and participate. So Cesar went into the middle of that. In the course of the Game, I remember distinctly, Cesar said that he was trying to build this movement and keep moving forward but that he felt hampered by the people around him who didn't want to follow him. He felt like they didn't share his vision. So Chuck Dederich said, Well, you know what you ought to do, Cesar, you ought to get rid of all these old guys with these outmoded ideas, get yourself some new, young people who aren't spoiled by bad experiences.[1]

The Synanon Game was an early form of attack group therapy. Chavez had had his first go at it in 1975, while on his 1,000-mile *caminata*. Among those accompanying him then had been a half dozen people from Delancey Street, a San Francisco self-help group of reformed ex-convicts, alcoholics, and drug addicts who were active UFW supporters and had been influenced by Synanon. About halfway through the march, the Delancey Streeters had suggested that the marchers play the Game. Twelve to fifteen people sat in a circle and took turns ganging up on one another. They played in the evenings as they walked into the lower Salinas Valley, and then gave it up. On those occasions the Game had good-naturedly focused on problems of the march—who was acting self-important, who was doing the work, the various ways that people were, in the parlance of the Game, "assholes." Despite the mutual accusations, the Game had been fun and the people who played it remained friends.

Chavez was not in good humor when he sprang the Game on the Executive Board at Badger. "We spent four days there," Gilbert Padilla recalled. "It was an immaculate place. Everything was very neat and cordial. Everybody was wearing the same thing: bald-headed and overalls. Dederich was the founder. In the mess hall, he sat about two or three feet above the ground, and whoever sat with him was privileged to be sitting with the founder . . . About the fourth day, Dederich came and talked to us. 'Cesar,' he said, 'you are a very important national leader. And if these old cronies here don't follow you, drop 'em.' "[2]

From the arena stage Chavez goaded Dolores Huerta and Jerry Cohen into playing the Game. The Synanon people, clearly prepped, began to attack Cohen for taking the legal department out of La Paz and back to Salinas, deserting Chavez. "I couldn't stand it," Cohen said later. "I had to get away from them all. I went into a bathroom stall to take a dump and read *Sports Illustrated*. And then, there on the pot, coming piped into the stall I hear a recording of some Synanon person talking rapturously about the first time she shaved her head."[3]

Chavez and Dederich went way back. They first met in the mid-sixties, when Synanon was universally acclaimed as a successful therapeutic community for recovering heroin addicts. A few years later union volunteers started traveling from Delano to Santa Monica to get their teeth fixed in the free dental clinic that Dederich had put together as a service to the poor and as a way of maintaining good relations with city authorities. During the Proposition 14 campaign UFW volunteers regularly took their meals at the revamped six-story beach club that Synanon owned in Santa Monica.

By then, Dederich had moved Synanon's main headquarters to Badger, an isolated spot about a hundred miles of country roads northeast of La Paz. It was a startling geographic coincidence for the two old friends, and Dederich recultivated the relationship, sending a driver and car to La Paz to bring Chavez to Badger on periodic visits. Dederich, thirteen years older than Chavez and an imposing three hundred pounds, had become Cesar's newest teacher. Chavez returned from those Badger sojourns enthusiastic. "He talked to us about it all the time," Gilbert Padilla remembers. "He told us how effective they were, how much money they were making, that they had an Air Jet and their own airstrip, and that they were doing good things with delinquent kids and ex-addicts."[4]

Badger was home to two different communities: A few dozen of Synanon's elite lived at the "home place," and a couple of hundred

Synanon newcomers, mostly troubled kids or people trying to recover from addiction, lived a short drive away. The home place had saunas, hot tubs, riding stables, an excellent kitchen, and a large dining room. The newcomers lived in barracks, under strict discipline and supervision. They did all the physical work at their own place and at the home place. Those who overcame their problems and demonstrated the cheerful competency that was the Synanon norm would receive privileges, perhaps even working their way up to the home place, where the Synanon leaders were engaged in "experiments with the business of living."

The experiments were well capitalized. Back in the sixties Dederich had turned his flair for small business and his grasp of nonprofit fundraising into millions of dollars—nearly $9 million a year by 1976. Some of the money came from people who were recruited from Synanon clubs in Los Angeles, San Francisco, Berkeley, Detroit, and New York City. Dederich invested the money wisely, mostly in California real estate, and when he settled in at Badger he had at least $20 million in assets, and perhaps $10 million more.[5]

No longer restricted to recovering addicts, Synanon became an intentional community, part of the bourgeoning human potential movement, open to all who would pay a monthly membership fee and participate in its alternative program for living. Its membership became increasingly middle class and professional—primarily young and middle-aged adults dissatisfied with their bourgeois lives and looking for meaning in community. Synanon's first move, from Los Angeles to Marin County, was symbolically perfect: Marin was one of the wealthiest counties in the country, and since the early seventies Northern California had been home to all manner of utopian and dystopian adventures in collective life. The next move, to Badger, also fit nicely with the spirit of the times, as many of the disaffected fled further into the countryside to live in isolated communes.

Dederich's family profited handsomely from all this. Not one to dress matters up in prettified language, Dederich declared to the *Los Angeles Times*: "I like to be paid for what I do, like any other American. I'm not a nun or a monk. I'm an American businessman."[6] In 1975, partly to protect its money from government investigators, Synanon officially registered as a religion. That wasn't entirely fraudulent. It had a sloppy New Age ideology of "conscious participation in the evolution of the species" and the "reconciliation of the dichotomies of life," along with a set of compulsory rules of behavior. Members had to abstain from sugar, alcohol, and drugs; engage in a ritualized set of physical exercises four times a week; clip their hair to no more than one-quarter inch in length; and wear a uniform of bright orange overalls. In 1976, at the time that Cesar Chavez was making his periodic trips from La Paz, another requirement was added. All men over eighteen who had been with Synanon for more than five years had to have vasectomies, because instead of begetting their own babies, Synanon members were going to take care of the abused and abandoned children of the world. The rule was firm—have a vasectomy or leave—with only one exception: Chuck Dederich, the religion's high priest and lawgiver, the ultimate judge in all Synanon disputes, he alone didn't have to get cut.[7]

The one constant throughout all these changes was the Game. It worked equally well with heroin addicts, troubled teens, and bored professionals. Several people would "Game" a targeted individual, exposing faults, criticizing behavior, breaking the person down. The charges, sometimes spoken quietly, often screamed, occasionally funny, didn't have to be factually true; the point was to confront and humiliate people for their debilitating life patterns so that they could overcome them. The Game could be a powerful, effective, and entertaining experience: powerful enough to keep people off heroin, as long as they continued both to play the Game and live in the Synanon community; effective enough to transform sullen adolescents into cheerful workers; entertaining enough to attract and hold some members of the distraught middle class. But it was often vicious. Most people who joined a Synanon club or community soon left, either pretty much as they were before or only slightly damaged. A few stayed on and prospered. Some withered under the attacks and were badly hurt.

But the Game was not so much about helping individual Gamers as it was about creating a Synanon cadre. It didn't matter that most people came and left; they were "assholes" who couldn't be redeemed. What mattered was that enough people stayed around, emotionally dependent on the people who had simultaneously humiliated and befriended them, willing to work for little pay and do what they were told as long as they were allowed to continue to live in the Synanon community.

It was just this combination of an obedient cadre and a feeling of community that Cesar Chavez liked. He didn't go for the whole program, but he invidiously compared the efficiency at the Badger home place with the inefficiency of La Paz, and the comradeship of the Synanon members with what he considered the constant carping within his own organization. Most of all, he admired Dederich's ability to get other people to take up his vision of the way things should work, and then willingly, happily, do what they could to make that vision a reality.

The Game was the key, Dederich insisted. And as it turned out, Cesar Chavez was good at it. He could withstand almost any attack, and he knew how to home in on other people's weaknesses. He figured that if he could bring the Game to La Paz, he could create a better, happier, more productive union.

Elsewhere within the UFW staff, some people had been developing different ideas about efficiency, camaraderie, and reorganization. In response to a memorandum from Crosby Milne soliciting staff ideas on personnel policies, nine paralegals in Salinas decided to take Milne at his word and write up a proposal that he would have a hard time folding into some rationalization of the current administrative system. They had checked it with their supervisor, Jerry Cohen, and sent it to La Paz. It was waiting on Cesar's desk when he returned from Badger.

The plan—a detailed proposal to end the volunteer system and pay UFW staffers meager but regular wages—had its genesis in a toothache. The bad tooth belonged to one of the paralegals who needed root canal work but couldn't afford it. The union was paying the paralegals $10 a week, plus the cost of the rent and the food they ate at the White House, one of the UFW staff houses in Salinas. Most of them also collected Food Stamps and were enrolled in Medi-Cal, the state poverty health plan, which would not pay for the dental work. Bob Thompson, a paralegal who had worked directly for Chavez in La Paz from 1972 to '74, remembers that the guy with the sore jaw was advised to ask Chavez or Dolores Huerta for the money. "That's like a poor farm worker going to the grower and asking for a favor," Thompson thought. "Here we were fighting to get farm workers basic benefits, and we didn't have the rights to any benefits ourselves."[8]

The paralegals talked about it, and began considering problems other than their own. During the ALRB election campaigns they had met a lot of workers who, Thompson said, "knew the fields and the issues in the fields a lot better than we did." Some would be obvious candidates to join the UFW staff, but most workers, especially those with families, could not afford to come onto the staff. The ones who did, and were successfully trained, often moved on to salaried positions at California Rural Legal Assistance or other government and quasi-government agencies.[9] There were a few ex–farm workers on the staff (some of them paid as migrant priests), but the majority of the staffers were still young people without financial responsibilities, or middle-class people with money from home, or religious people who had taken vows of poverty. Overwhelmingly, they were Anglos. The only way to change that, the paralegals reasoned, was to start paying the staff a regular wage.

Their proposal was short, straightforward, and egalitarian. To reduce staff turnover, make the union more effective, hold the staff more accountable, and hire more farm workers as staff, the union should pay a regular wage. The wage would start out at $450 per month, plus $50 for each dependent. That was about a $100 less than the monthly minimum wage that farm workers earned under union contracts. Over a five-year period, the wage would be raised until it was equivalent to minimum union farm worker wages, but it would go no higher.[10]

The proposal provided for the union to pay into the staffers' Social Security, unemployment insurance, and workers' compensation funds, which the union was not doing at the time. The paralegals also requested that staff be included in the union's RFK Medical Plan and the Juan De La Cruz pension plan, or equivalent programs. It requested written policies on vacations, holidays, time off, leaves of absence, sick days, and per diem payments. Finally, in the wake of the purge, it requested that hiring, firing, and transfer policies be specified in writing, and that personnel review boards be established in every region to "hear all grievances, disputes or differences between staff members and their immediate supervisors at the request of any party."[11]

On the last page of the proposal, the paralegals did allow that although the recommendations of personnel review boards "would be given great weight," the final decisions on personnel disputes would be made by the UFW Executive Board. That was hardly enough to soften the impact of the document. The paralegals would be quickly rebuked, but the issue they raised would not be decided until sixteen months later, by a count of five to four on the Executive Board, in the single most contentious vote in UFW history.

Three weeks after their introduction to Synanon, members of the Executive Board met again, this time at La Paz. "We are coming apart at the seams," Chavez told the board, He bemoaned the union's inefficiencies: "The buildings in La Paz are pretty much in a shambles. We can't take care of our cars. Our whole fleet of buses is just a bunch of junk." His conclusion: "We need to deal very directly and concretely with the whole idea of building a true community if possible in La Paz."[12]

Chavez dominated the three-day discussion more than usual, and he insisted on his central themes: La Paz is inefficient and not bringing in new recruits; we need to build a caring community at La Paz that will attract more volunteers and be an example for farm workers; the union needs to rediscover its movement identity and roots, and not become just a job for the staffers, or just a vehicle for higher pay and better benefits for a small group of unionized workers. The main way to rekindle the UFW's move-ment energies, Chavez forcefully argued, would be to play the Game. He and eleven people he had chosen from the La Paz staff would leave for Badger to learn how to do it. He chose mostly "younger people who have been in the union all their lives." Among them were his son Paul (Babo) Chavez; one of his sons-in-law, David Villarino; two of Dolores Huerta's children, Laurie Head and Emilio Huerta; Richard Chavez's daughter, Suzie; and Cesar's devoted young publicist, Marc Grossman. They would go once a week for six weeks, and then bring the Game to La Paz, becom-ing the seed from which the new community would grow.

Simultaneously, Chavez would make a thorough review of other inten-tional communities in order to formulate a plan to transform La Paz. Chris Hartmire had already been investigating such communities at Cesar's request and had sent him a confidential progress report just before the Executive Board meeting.[13] Now Hartmire would visit communities in Europe, while Chavez would visit Sunburst, a farming commune near Santa Barbara. He didn't have all the answers, he told the board, so he needed to learn more.

Although he constantly praised Synanon, Chavez said he understood the difference between it and the UFW. The members of Synanon were focused "entirely within themselves," he said, while the UFW was focused on the work it was doing in the world. He allowed that that difference might make it impossible to import the Synanon model to La Paz, and even if it was imported, it would have to be reshaped to meet the UFW's needs. This was an experiment, he said, but one he was determined to carry out.

Central to the experiment was a shift in the UFW's understanding of democracy. Synanon was not a democracy. Chavez had no trouble acknowledging that. Hartmire's "tentative thoughts and conclusions" on intentional communities began: "Communities that last usually have an ideological or religious base and an authoritarian structure reinforced by group pressure and discipline."[14] But democracy was, at the very least, an important ideal within the union. Chavez told the board they would have to think more carefully about that: "We've never been very clear about democracy in the union, and I think we mislead people. There is no question that the voice of the workers at the convention sets the policy of the board. But when we say that, we don't make it clear to the staff that they don't have the same rights. But they don't, and there is no structure for it and there shouldn't be."[15] Chavez added that the board, too, was a problem. Contending points of view in the leadership of the union confused the staff, he said. The board spoke in many voices; it needed to speak in one.

Chavez championed the formulation of democracy he had learned from Dederich, an idea that eventually became popular at La Paz. Synanon had both a triangle and a circle. The triangle was the way the organization was structured outside the Synanon Game: Dederich at the top and others below him, following his orders. It was hierarchical and authoritarian and meant to be so. The circle was Synanon's life inside the Game: here there was no hierarchy, no authority. Supposedly, Dederich was no better than anyone else in the Game room. Dederich called it "pure" democracy. People could say whatever they believed in the Game, let out all the things they were hiding, and then return, refreshed, to their assigned work. The circle and the triangle were reconciled. Democracy and unassailable hierarchical power, said Dederich and then Chavez, could live comfortably inside the same organization.

At that March meeting the paralegals' proposal became Exhibit A of what was wrong with the union. They want wages, Chavez explained, because our mission isn't clear and we have lost that movement feeling.

People want to write down policies because there is a breakdown of trust, an absence of community. We can't afford to pay people, Chavez added. But cost was not paramount. Chavez called the proposal "a challenge to our philosophy," tantamount to a demand from the staff for union recognition from the Executive Board. Paying salaries would inevitably produce a staff of union bureaucrats, just going through the motions, without the dedication of those who work for love and not for money, he argued, saying that the proposal had to be rejected in order to have a chance to preserve and rebuild the UFW as a movement.[16]

Chavez had a similar response to an attempt by the personnel relations department to set down in writing formal holiday policies for the staff. Chavez rejected the idea outright, reprimanded the staffer who presented it to the board without first showing it to him, and then laid out the choices he saw for the union: "We only really have two places to go. We are actually management, but this is not a company. We can move toward a wage structure with benefits, days off, etc., based on money. Or the other way is to make a real movement out of this. We are not either now. We were, but we are not now."[17]

The board soundly rejected the paralegals' proposal and made only minor objections to Chavez's plan for community building a la Synanon. Marshall Ganz felt that the community-building should not focus on La Paz but should begin in the field offices, where the most important work was being done. Richard Chavez agreed that he personally had lost the movement spirit, but thought that it might be just a question of age, of being tired and feeling the weight of all the years of struggle. Eliseo Medina was quiet, except to say that if they were serious about playing the Game they should stop making jokes about it and give it a try. Gilbert Padilla admitted to being confused.

Dolores Huerta was especially enthusiastic. "We've lost the feeling," she said. We have a "jungle of human relationships," and we leave ourselves open to criticism because "we don't care about people." She thought that the Synanon Game would go a long way toward helping the union clean itself up. She wanted to be part of a movement, to increase the feeling of community in the union, and was annoyed with those who wanted to turn away from the movement and work for money. Pete Velasco and Mack Lyons concurred. Like Chavez, Marshall Ganz saw the paralegals' proposal as a symptom of a larger malaise. The paralegals had lost the spirit of sacrifice, he said, and he agreed that they wanted wages because the union's purpose was no longer clear.[18]

After the meeting was over, Chavez dispatched Ganz, Huerta, and Lyons to Salinas to explain to the paralegals why their proposal had been rejected. The meeting lasted six hours. Huerta took point. "You guys are from middle-class backgrounds," she told the paralegals. "Who are you to ask?

This is money from the union, the blood of the workers, and you want it for yourselves."[19] They were pinkos, Huerta charged, tainted by some of the legal staff's earlier opposition to the Campaign Against Illegals; they were rich reds, and their proposal was silly, radical posturing.

The issue did not die. Robert Garcia, a foreman in the fields before he joined the UFW, said he needed more money. From Oxnard, Bobby De La Cruz, an ex–farm worker, let it be known that he wanted more money. In Delano, Glorio Soto, another ex–farm worker, started a little campaign for a paid staff.[20] Those people and others never put together a proposal, and the question wouldn't come to a head until later when the union lawyers made a formal request for a raise. But the lawyers never did consider including the paralegals' key democratic demand: that the entire staff be paid a wage no higher than what was earned by the lowest-paid unionized farm worker. That, like so much else that is beautiful in this world, was thrown into history's capacious trash can.

Cesar Chavez's interest in intentional communities was not all that unusual amid the alternative-living New Age spirit of California in the 1970s. Nor was his focus on loyalty, discipline, and a near-religious unity of purpose much of a leap for a man whose earliest experience of intense group solidarity was religious, from the *cursillo*. The Game's objectives were similar to the *cursillo* exercise in rejection and renewal, which had so intrigued Chavez nearly twenty years before. Even his preoccupation with reforming La Paz and his disregard for what most people would have called the heart of the union—the life and labor of farm workers—is not surprising.

The volunteers constantly surrounded Chavez in his daily life and work, and like any manager, he demanded efficiency and loyalty from them. But there was more. Chavez believed that the volunteers, not the workers, were fundamental to the union's success. That idea was rooted in Alinsky's celebration of the organizer as the agent of history and his portrayal of the neighborhood as an immobilized object that needs an outside organizer to activate it. The idea was reinforced by Chavez's ten years in CSO, where he, the traveling organizer, arrived in what seemed to be a quiet town and put together one community organization after another. Now, the UFW volunteers were the potential organizers, while the workers stood in place of the passive neighborhood.

The union's formative period, between 1965 and 1970, supported this ideological predisposition. The grape strike, after a brief spasm of enthusiasm, had quickly petered out. The volunteer staff had organized the boycott and won the table grape contracts, without the workers, almost despite them. In the midst of the boycott Chavez declared that the volunteers were "the heroes of the farm worker movement." Now in 1977, burdened by the belief that the staff had lost that movement feeling, Chavez decided to concentrate his energies on the staff so that, once again, they would be capable of heroic efforts, of making history. Then he and they could turn their attention back to the sporadically enthusiastic, but generally immobile, workers.

Chavez was not demanding an outrageously large change. La Paz in 1977 was already not far from the community he had in mind. People lived together in a remote area, shared a commitment to service and sacrifice, believed in the righteousness of their cause and the dark power of their enemies, often celebrated and worshiped together, and had immense respect for their unrivaled leader. Although the staff members living outside of La Paz were less tied to the leader and more free to go their own ways, many lived even more collectively than the people at La Paz, sleeping and eating together at the group homes that the UFW rented for boycotters and field office workers. Although many had come from well-off families, they had chosen to live poor, and had a deep sense of their own moral rectitude. Moreover, the purges had taken a toll: especially at La Paz, but also out on the periphery, the UFW staff was becoming hostile to dissent or independent thought of any kind.

Was this not already a kind of semireligious, intentional community? Couldn't it be made tighter, more efficient, more harmonious through a judicious use of the Synanon Game? Didn't the Teamsters' exit from the fields give the union an opportunity to focus on its administrative problems? Cesar Chavez had not gotten where he was without taking considerable risks, nor had he timidly followed a conventional path. He believed this experiment was worth the chance.

Chavez's attempt to remake La Paz could not be checked by the union's farm worker membership. La Paz was, to a startling degree, financially, structurally, and culturally independent of the farm worker world. Perhaps the mountain didn't even need the valleys. Unlike in other unions, the UFW administrative staff did not depend primarily on membership dues. Historically, contributions from unions, liberal supporters, progressive churches, and foundations were a bigger source of the union's income.* Structurally, there was no guaranteed place for farm workers on the UFW staff. Culturally, the language of the staff was overwhelmingly English, and the dominant ethos was the selfless sacrifice of the privileged for the downtrodden.

The independence of the mountain from the valleys was essential to the Synanon experiment, and Chavez knew it. The Game was to be played

---

* Before 1969, dues were no more than 16 percent of the UFW's income. After 1970, during the peak years of the table grape contracts, dues reached 60 percent of revenues, but fell back down to 15–21 percent in the years between the loss in the table grapes and the beginning of ALRB elections and the contracts that followed. In those years, contributions made up the difference between dues and expenses. In 1977 dues revenue was on its way back up to the 60 percent range.

first at La Paz, and then in the field offices. Maybe in the long run, he said, farm workers would play it, too. But he surely knew that farm workers, particularly those from Mexico who tended to be social traditionalists, would be shocked to sit in a circle of men and women calling one another "assholes" and "bitches," the Synanon expletive for female assholes. So, in the meantime, he insisted, no one should say anything about the Game to farm workers.[21]

Chavez's lifelong fascination with Gandhi also influenced his thinking on La Paz, although in this case he seriously misread Gandhi's legacy. "La Paz is going to be like a little ashram," he told the Executive Board meeting in March.[22] Nobody pointed out the inherent conflict in La Paz being both an ashram and the administrative center of the UFW. Gandhi never made such a mistake. His ashram was the administrative center of nothing. It was the retreat where he sometimes lived, and where he was the spiritual leader. He did not try to make it the administrative body of the Indian National Congress. Within the Indian National Congress different points of view were expressed, tolerated, and debated. The Congress sometimes rejected Gandhi's policies and defeated his designated candidates. Gandhi did not aspire to have the same kind of influence and control over the Congress that he had at the ashram.

But Chavez wanted to combine his ashram with his union. He wanted to bring the unity of will and purpose characteristic of a religious, intentional community into the union, starting with La Paz, then moving down to the field offices, and perhaps finally, into the farm worker community itself. That was a catastrophic wish. Within a California farm workers union of any meaningful size there would necessarily be differences of interest, opinion, politics, ethnicity, political, and religious orientation that needed space to be discussed, debated, shared, argued out, and compromised. The culture and structures within which such interchanges can take place are contrary to the culture and structure of an ashram or any other intentional community. Perhaps Cesar could have had his ashram and his union if, like Gandhi, he had kept them separate. Combining the two meant death to both.

In the year and half from the spring of 1977 to the fall of 1978, while most people stationed at La Paz played the Game at least once a week and many of the outlying staff drove to the Tehachapi foothills to play it on Saturdays, the only real debate that took place at the highest level was whether the UFW would choose to be a movement or settle into being what Chavez dismissed as "just a union." This was not one idea among many that concerned the leadership; it was the central idea. It helped people interpret what was happening to them, influenced their actions, and shaped their opinions. This idea, this false choice and the actions that flowed from it and were justified by it, do not fully explain what happened to the UFW.

They are best understood as a reflection and intensification of two larger problems: the antidemocratic structure and culture of the union, and the enormous gulf between the membership and the staff. Nevertheless, the thinking that justified the savaging of La Paz is not insignificant to the story.

Chavez posed this choice between movement and union to combat the proposals for a paid staff and written policies, but he did not invent the choice just to maintain his authority over his staff. Chavez's doubts about unions were there at the founding of the National Farm Workers Association, in the leaflets that were stamped, "The Farm Workers Association is not a union." Once the UFW began to operate as a union in the early 1970s, much of Chavez's opposition to unionism was transformed into opposition to conservative business unionism. Together with other progressive unionists, committed church organizations, and sympathetic consumers, he had imagined that the UFW would help build an overall movement that would help workers and poor people everywhere. But even within this new orientation, Chavez remained pessimistic about the power of workers on the job, and as the national rank-and-file upsurge of the 1970s waned, Chavez dropped his short-lived enthusiasm for a new progressive alliance or some kind of Poor Peoples Union.

After the UFW fought to win and then enforce the Agricultural Labor Relations Act, Chavez again became uneasy about the strict trade-union focus of his organization. Uneasy and a little bored. Moreover, his early prediction that union success would produce an elite group of workers seemed to be coming true. During the March board meeting he cited the high wage of vegetable piece-rate workers several times as a reason to worry that these privileged few would be unconcerned about others still trapped in poverty. Winning higher wages for some workers wasn't a bad thing, he said, but he was interested in something more.[23]

Chavez still called that "something more" a movement, but the authoritarian community that he was building at La Paz had little to do with any actual historical social or labor movements. The civil rights movement, for example, was decentralized, heterogeneous, with no commanding center. People acted through a vast variety of organizations, many of them ad hoc and ephemeral. SNCC, SCLC, and CORE were loosely aligned with differing ideologies, structures, and strategies; none of them ordered people into action. The same is true of the anti–Vietnam War movement, the union movement of the 1930s, and the populists before the turn of the nineteenth century. They are all characterized by local initiatives worked out in face-to-face discussion, not top-down mobilization.

Cesar Chavez took two characteristics of historical movements—that they are made up of volunteers rather than salaried employees and that they engender feelings of community in their participants—and made them the defining characteristics, all the while ignoring the democratic nature of most mass movements. Nor did he intend to build a cadre organization that would operate alongside other groups and initiatives within a movement. His organization was meant to be in command, "*una sola unión*," with no competitors in the fields, and with the power to order the mobilization of both loyal farm workers and those not so loyal, who would have to participate to keep their jobs. Perhaps the most striking difference between what Chavez was trying to build and a democratic mass movement such as late nineteenth century populism was that at the height of their power the Populists argued out their politics in more than a thousand independent local newspapers. For the UFW, even one newspaper was too many.

A farm worker movement, however, was just what the UFW needed in order to become an established union in the fields. Movement and union were not antithetical; they went together. Although certain sectors of agribusiness were trying to make peace with the UFW, most of the growers would not accept the full establishment of institutionalized workers' power, even mediated through union officials, unless they were forced to do so. The best way to force them, to make the farm workers union an incontrovertible fact in the fields, was through the power and creativity of a farm workers movement.

There were the makings of such a movement in 1977, but they were not at La Paz. They were on the crews, on some of the ranch committees, and among workers who energetically, even joyfully, participated in union activities. In the fields, union workers had taken unprecedented control over their jobs. During the strike wave that forced the ALRA through the legislature and the subsequent campaigns that won representation elections, many workers had gained invaluable political savvy and experience, and were now confident about their futures. Farm workers were already in motion, and it was their movement that had to be nurtured and built. But that wasn't the movement that Cesar Chavez had in mind.

One afternoon while Aristeo Zambrano was cutting broccoli at Associated Produce in Salinas, Mario Bustamante walked into the field and introduced himself. Bustamante was then the ranch committee president at another Salinas vegetable company, Green Valley. After he finished his day's work cutting lettuce he liked to go to other union fields and talk to people who were still working. He knew approximately which fields were ready to be cut, and when he saw a crew of harvesters he'd park his car and walk right up to them. At Associated Produce, the workers directed Bustamante to the shop steward, Zambrano, who knew Mario's brother, Chava, and had also heard of Mario. Union business quickly came up, and Zambrano explained a problem the crew was having with the foreman. After talking to a few workers and then the foreman, whose reply Mario found unsatisfying, he went back to Zambrano and suggested that he stop the crew and resolve the issue immediately. It took less than fifteen minutes. From this fine beginning a friendship grew, and not long after, Bustamante asked Zambrano, an anticlerical agnostic, to be the godfather of his next child. They became compadres.[24]

Down in the valleys union workers were getting together in this way, formally and informally. They elected ranch committees and stewards. They learned about seniority, about which grievances were valid and which were worthless, and about how to file them. A few ranch committees established themselves as powerful forces in their own companies and helped set policy in the field offices. In the Salinas and Watsonville offices, workers argued about what the union should be doing, and about Mexican and U.S. politics. But what most concerned them was the situation in the industry. At this point the UFW had 22 percent of the vegetable industry organized, with contracts at twenty-one of the ninety-six principal companies, covering about 7,000 workers. It had been certified or was awaiting certification at thirty more. If all of those eventually signed contracts, about half the California-Arizona vegetable industry would be in union hands, the UFW would more than double its vegetable worker membership, and would earn nearly $2 million yearly in dues just from the vegetables. But the situation was volatile. The industry would not long remain part union and part nonunion. And these UFW workers were becoming better organized at the same time that the union leadership was distracting itself, allowing nonunion companies to go unchallenged. In the long run, the union workers' development of their own power exacerbated the contradiction of a vegetable industry only partly unionized, but in the short run it was good times on the union ranches.[25]

Aristeo Zambrano was one of the new, younger militants and in 1977 he had been elected ranch committee president at Associated Produce. Like Hermilo Mojica, he came from a family of *agraristas*, Mexican agrarian militants who had supported and been supported by President Lázaro Cárdenas in the 1930s. Many workers in the union in the Imperial and Salinas valleys came from this same political and geographical background, from the small towns of Michoacán, Guanajuato, and Jalisco, where *Cardenismo* had been so popular. In Zambrano's family, however, left politics was not just a memory, a cherished tradition, but rather a concern of current daily life.

Zambrano was a third-generation political militant. His maternal grandfather, Manuel Martinez, had led a delegation of peasants on a nearly 300-mile walk from Chavinda, Michoacán, to Mexico City to petition the government to divide up the old, local haciendas into *ejidos*, community owned plots of land worked by individual families. Martinez had returned from the capital with the *ejido* deeds and a rifle, one that supposedly had belonged to Lázaro Cárdenas. Aristeo's father used to take that rifle down off the wall and ceremoniously place it between the horns of his ox every day he went to work in the fields. The story told in the Zambrano household was that after Cárdenas gave the delegation the formal deeds to the *ejido*, he called Aristeo's grandfather into his private study, took the rifle out of a locked cabinet, and presented it to him, uttering words that had been repeated so often to the young Aristeo that he sometimes believed he had heard them himself: "Señor Martinez, in the other room I gave you some papers that say that the land of the old hacienda belongs to the people of Chavinda; now here in this room I give you the rifle you will need to make sure the land remains yours."[26]

Manuel Martinez was elected first president of the *ejido* and remained in the post until he died. Jose Zambrano, Martinez's son-in-law and Aristeo's father, succeeded Martinez as president of the *ejido*, a post he held even after he began working as a bracero several months a year in the Salinas Valley. Eventually he bought a green card and brought his family to Hayward, California, to live on the grounds of the carnation nursery where he worked. Jose Zambrano remained active in *Chavindeño* politics, especially after he retired and moved back to his hometown. He was part of a community vigil that protected the city's leftist mayor from a possible physical assault by Partido Revolucionario Institucional goons after the PRI-directed election fraud in 1990. During the vigil, Aristeo's father died of a heart attack, just as he would have wished: behind the barricades.

Aristeo Zambrano already had a political resume when he came to Hayward at fourteen. Two years earlier, in 1968, he had walked through the streets of Chavinda with some older leftists collecting funds for striking students in Mexico City. In Hayward he dropped out of school to work in the nursery but honed his reading skills on the newspapers and magazines that his father had around the house, *Siempre*, the leftist weekly from Mexico City, and *Granma*, the newspaper of the Cuban Communist Party. He read Castro's speeches and went on to sample Guevera, Lenin, and Mao. What he understood best, though, were *Los Agachados* and *Los Supermachos*, the political comic books of Mexico's popular left-wing cartoonist, Rius. From the comic books he went on to Rius's more substantial pedagogical efforts: *Marx for Beginners*, *Mao for Beginners*, *Darwin for Beginners*, and others. "I received my first taste of politics from my grandfather and father, but it was Rius who educated me, it was Rius who oriented me in the world, and then, later, I had my own political experiences in the UFW, plenty of them."[27]

Zambrano's wife, Esperanza, came from a California farm worker family. Her father had died of a heart attack picking grapes in Madera, at forty-four, as Esperanza worked beside him. Esperanza told Aristeo that they could make more money in the fields of Salinas than they could in the small factories or nurseries around Hayward. They moved in 1974, and Esperanza went to work bunching onions at D'Arrigo, where she worked for the eleven years they lived in the Salinas Valley. She eventually became the shop steward on her crew. Aristeo worked briefly in the strawberries and then cut lettuce by the hour. It was a lot harder than the nursery, without much more money. But in 1976 he made his way onto a piece-rate broc-coli crew at Associated Produce, where the UFW had won an election in 1975. Affable and an entertaining talker, he was elected to the three-person negotiating team that helped secure the first UFW contract. Next he was elected ranch committee president.

Zambrano regularly went to the union hall after work. In addition to becoming Mario Bustamante's compadre and getting closer to Chava Bustamante, Aristeo got to know Mojica, Cleofas Guzman, and several others who in a few years would become the most pivotal rank-and-file activists in UFW history. "We had lots of meetings. Our group came together in '77 and '78. We were all working in the fields, but we would go to the union hall after work to see each other and talk."[28]

He met broccoli workers from Mann Packing; together they helped broccoli workers at Arrow Lettuce Company win an election and negotiate a contract. There he met Berta Batres, who would become part of that vital activist group. Workers from the three companies formed a small informal committee and started to talk to workers at nonunion broccoli companies. They confronted firsthand, on the ground, the problem of an industry that was part union, part nonunion.

In the 1970s, most broccoli workers walked behind a conveyer belt that was hooked up to a tractor that moved through the fields. They cut the broccoli and threw it on the belt. The belt carried the broccoli to twelve large bins, carried by a flatbed truck that drove alongside the tractor. A worker on the flatbed truck jumped in and out of the bins and moved the end of the conveyer belt from one bin to another as they filled with broc-coli. When they were all filled, the truck took the bins to a packing shed, whereupon another truck, with empty bins, moved into place beside the conveyer belt. The crew was paid on the basis of how many bins it filled a day, and the UFW contract specified that the bins must be filled to the top.

But where was the top? At nonunion companies, foremen demanded that the workers pile the broccoli a foot or two higher than the rim of the bin in what was called a *copete*, or crest. By the time the bins arrived at the packing shed, the broccoli had settled close to the top of the rim. Union crews filled the bins level, and when they arrived at the shed, the broccoli was a foot or more below the rim. In a single day a crew produces hundreds of bins, and in a ten-month season, tens of thousands; multiply the one-foot difference by the number of bins in a season, and the union companies were getting significantly less broccoli for their money.

That difference mattered. In addition, the nonunion companies' labor costs were lower because, although they'd been forced to pay the same wages, they were not paying into the UFW's various benefit plans. The union companies sought the union's help in getting the workers to put the *copete* on, but what was bad for the company was good for the workers. They were paid by the bin, so the higher they filled them the less money they made. Zambrano and his friends concluded that the only way to solve the problem was to organize the other broccoli companies so that no workers in the valley would put on the *copete*. They did what they could to promote such a drive, but because the union had put organizing in the Salinas Valley on hold while they built their new community in La Paz, little was done about the difference between union and nonunion labor costs.

Zambrano got along well with Ganz and with the Salinas field office director, Robert Garcia. He enjoyed arguing with Ganz about Middle East politics, Aristeo taking the side of the Palestinians. Marshall was a good, friendly debater, and they had no trouble cooperating on union matters and disagreeing about Israel. Zambrano also got close to Gilbert Padilla, who recruited him to be part of a workers committee to help settle union grievances in Salinas. Zambrano considered it a good lesson in trade unionism. In the winter of 1977–78, Padilla tried to convince Zambrano to join the union staff as a volunteer. Aristeo might have agreed if he were single, but he had a wife and a child and couldn't afford it. Besides, Esperanza didn't want to leave the Salinas farm worker community and live in La Paz. So Zambrano stayed down in the valley, continued to cut broccoli, and became one of the most active ranch committee presidents in the UFW. Nobody told him about the Synanon Game, the purges at La Paz, or the debate about a paid staff.[29]

One of the few workers who knew anything about La Paz was Chava Bustamante, the younger, smaller, quieter brother of the dynamic Mario. Chava had cut himself loose from Mario soon after he mastered the job of cutting and packing lettuce. No dispute was involved; they remained close, but Chava didn't want to work every day in his big brother's shadow. In the early 1970s Chava worked for nonunion or Teamsters companies and traveled the entire lettuce circuit. He was loyal to the UFW, went to an occasional rally, but was not much interested in union affairs. He got married and had a couple of kids. During the 1975 election campaign he was working at Cal Coastal, a medium-size lettuce company, where the hours were long, sometimes ten a day. Chava hated the long days and signed up for the election committee, working with Garcia and Ganz. After the UFW beat the Teamsters in the balloting, Chava was elected to the negotiating team, and after the contract was signed in '76, to ranch committee president.

Gilbert Padilla recruited him onto the valleywide grievance committee, where he worked with Zambrano and others. In the fall of 1977, top Salinas staffers were so taken by Chava's union work that they recruited him onto the staff and arranged to have him paid a regular salary of $150 a week. That was highly unusual. Only lawyers, doctors, Fred Ross, LeRoy Chatfield, and a few others had been paid salaries. For Chava the pay was still less than half of what he averaged as a *lechuguero*, but he was willing to take it in order to work full-time for the union.

In the Imperial Valley, Chava Bustamante helped negotiate some contracts, administered others, set up steward elections, trained people on how to file grievances, and helped organize ALRB elections at a couple of small companies. Thoughtful and soft-spoken, he was popular with the workers and got along with most of the growers.

As a member of the staff he visited La Paz a few times. He was intrigued by it all: the elaborate security, the religious icons, the assumption of Chavez's infallibility, the dedication of the mostly Anglo volunteers.

> It was so white, but I had a lot of respect for those people because of their commitment. Here was a man or a woman from Harvard or from some other very prestigious school, educated, and so on. And here they are wearing rag tag clothes and without a decent place to work or sleep . . . I tried to understand where that commitment came from. The other thing that was noticeable was the level of discipline they had. And the power the leaders had over them. They could be sent anywhere without having a say about it. And there was this feeling that this group of Chicanos, like Frank Ortiz, Cesar, Dolores, Gilberto [Padilla]—but Gilberto I never really saw like this, he never took on this kind of self importance—but this group of Chicanos had this army of white people, to be their servants. That's the way they treated them.[30]

Chava never saw the Game, but he heard a lot about it. He was curious and asked Garcia for details. Garcia invited him to come to La Paz with the rest of the Imperial Valley staff on a Saturday to play. At the last minute, Garcia had to tell Bustamante he wasn't permitted to come, as farm workers were not supposed to know about the Game. Shortly after, Garcia informed him that the union would no longer pay his salary; word about it was getting out. So Chava returned to cutting and packing lettuce at Cal Coastal in the Salinas Valley.

Up in the mountains, the staff was now playing the Game routinely, and in the process the La Paz community developed stricter limits, tighter edges. What had been tolerated as acceptable opinion, criticism, or complaint was redefined as bitching, bad-mouthing, or active organizing against the union.

When a few people complained about a new policy of opening all staff mail not specifically labeled "personal," Chavez decided the time had come to act. He chose the community committee as the venue for the spectacle. The community committee was a relatively long-standing group that was responsible for handling some inevitable problems of group living: Whose dogs were barking at night? Who left the kitchen a mess? Whose turn was it to sweep the common rooms? The committee was chaired by Esther Padilla; a sympathetic listener, she was good at the job. Gilbert Padilla sometimes gave her a hand. Together with Chavez, they planned what would come to be called the Monday Night Massacre.

It was all carefully orchestrated.[31] First, a few people circulated a petition calling on Chavez "to act immediately to remove from La Paz those who spread discord and unhappiness." In response, Esther convened a meeting of the entire community. Although he had helped plan the meeting, Chavez behaved as if he were hearing the charges for the first time. Esther regretted to inform him of the troublemakers in their midst. Chavez sat in the back with his head down, sad and shocked. The charges were vague, but the consequences were not. Department heads read off the names of the people who had to go. They had to leave right then, in front of the crowd.

The meeting did not come off exactly as scripted. Some of those who'd been singled out protested or tried to defend themselves. One young woman apologized for her bad attitude, promised to change, and tearfully pleaded to be allowed to stay. She was ejected with the rest. One young man, David McClure, a plumber and handyman who had asked to be assigned to fix up the UFW field offices around the state, demanded to hear the charges against him—not general accusations but specific charges.

Chavez broke from the script and joined the attack. McClure, he said, was plotting against the union; he knew it, and he shouldn't act dumb. Chavez ordered him to shut up and get out. McClure refused to leave. With a hundred people looking on, two union security men removed him from the meeting. They deposited him in his room and called the Tehachapi Police, who came to La Paz and arrested him for trespassing.

About thirty people were fired or quit that night and in the days that followed. The rest of the community got the message: no complaints allowed. Gilbert and Esther Padilla came to regret their role. "I was half a Moonie," Gilbert half explained. "Besides, there were some people who I thought should be fired." Unlike other memorable or historic events, where many more people claim to have been present than actually were, in the case of the Monday Night Massacre some who were probably there claim not to have been, and others who admit to having been there can't remember a thing.

Less than two weeks after the public shaming, Chavez sent a memo to members of the Executive Board, suggesting they, too, had better improve themselves.

I am convinced that:

1. Most of my orders to you must be negotiated, a frustrating process for me. (A faint glimmer of realization was evident on some of your faces when I was making this point.)
2. Although there is a counter element at work in the movement that we should all recognize, we are so desperate for staff that we ignore this danger even when it strikes us in the face.
3. We exhibit an unbelievably total disregard for policies among ourselves which passes bad habits to our staff, members and supporters.
4. We don't carry out our teachings so that we say the same thing in the same way. This causes confusion.[32]

To keep people on track, Chavez had begun issuing the "President's Newsletter," which he wrote in conjunction with Marc Grossman. Chavez explained in the first edition that the newsletter was not a newspaper. "It is not a gossip sheet or a form of pleasure reading," he admonished. "It is a vehicle by which we can notice you with official instructions and information, and is the only official publication of the United Farm Workers." It was distributed only to the staff and "a small number of close outside friends." Ranch committee presidents were the sole farm workers to receive a copy.[33]

The newsletter was published twice a month from March 1977 to November 1978, with a five-month break in the last half of 1977. Its tone is royal. Chavez refers to himself as "we," gives detailed reports of his own activities, as well as general news about what is happening in the union, especially at La Paz. In the first edition he announced that March 31 would henceforth be honored throughout the union as Founder's Day, reminding staff that it was only two weeks away and that "it should be a day of reflection and celebration for everyone in the farm workers movement." March 31 was Chavez's birthday; the union's founding convention was in September.

In Coachella, Doug Adair didn't much like the newsletter, nor was he happy with the rumors he had heard about the Game and the Monday Night Massacre. Working under a union contract in the Freedman vineyards, he didn't have to worry that Chavez could summarily fire him, as Chavez had done to troublesome people on the UFW staff. He decided to write Chavez a letter.

Dear Cesar,

I read with sadness, if not surprise, your Notice of 3-77-1 on the "President's Newsletter." As editor of the *Malcriado* in 1965, you managed to be both the Director of the Union and an editor who could put out a vigorous, free-wheeling, wide-ranging paper, not afraid to step on toes or kick shins, a true *malcriado*. The paper has never had a better editor.

But as the Union has grown, I sense that you and the Board have become less and less willing to allow a newspaper going to farm workers under union sponsorship, which will deal with controversy, news (bad and good), rank and file issues, and input from the fields. The trend has been steadily towards a carefully controlled house organ of the "official" position of the union, or of one individual within the Union. If the Union has no "official position," the issue is not discussed. If the news is bad, don't mention it . . .

But my years of working at Tenneco opened to me the vast reservoir of experience, knowledge, and wisdom which exists within the membership. At Tenneco there was a "union" position on some issues, but on others there was a constant dialogue, a variety of positions, dreams and desires, a constant ferment of views . . . If there is a forum for debate within the union, the ideas and energy unleashed are bound to aid the union. This is our strength. And in addition to offering the membership ideas and attitudes from peoples, from crops, from cultures foreign to their own, such a debate might well help us to avoid mistakes that have come back to haunt us.

The "President's Newsletter" is a fawning, sycophantic, self-serving sheet of narrow views and sanitized news, printed at union expense. We can, and should, do better.

Viva la Causa
Doug Adair [34]

Less than two months later, on May 6, 1977, Cesar Chavez began the fourth issue of his newsletter by assuring his readership about his mental health: "The current agribusiness line, as growers are busy building company unions, is, 'Cesar Chavez is tired; he has been seen talking to himself, he is going crazy. He should resign for the good of the union.' "[35] He denied that he was going crazy, and said that this propaganda was no different from the growers' earlier assaults on the union's leadership.

But it wasn't agribusiness that Chavez was warning the staff about. It was Gilbert Padilla. During the Nick Jones purge, Gilbert had been troubled by Cesar's suspicions. "He thought the most innocent people inside the union were trying to destroy it. They were doing things like messing up the cars, not putting oil in them on purpose. That was crazy."[36] After the purge, Cesar continued to talk to Gilbert about saboteurs in their midst, coming by Padilla's house late at night, calling him outside to go for a walk and then speaking in a hushed voice about conspiracies. Chavez's infatuation with Dederich worried Padilla even more, and he decided to talk to some others on the Executive Board. In the early months of 1977, Padilla toured around California warning his compatriots. He talked to Dolores Huerta, Richard Chavez, Chris Hartmire, Marshall Ganz, Eliseo Medina, Crosby Milne, and Jerry Cohen: "I told them that he was acting strange, seeing things that weren't there, seeing insurgents, communists taking over the union. I told them that he needed a rest. That we had to make sure he got a rest. Richard and Crosby agreed. All the others said some version of 'Well, I talked to him the other day and he seemed okay to me.' And somebody told him what I was doing."[37]

Chavez confronted Padilla, and when Gilbert replied that he thought Cesar did need a rest, Chavez let the matter drop—except for the peculiar denial in the newsletter. But Padilla continued to worry, and thirty years later he was still contending that Chavez went crazy. Several other insiders belatedly concurred. Marshall Ganz, who disregarded Padilla's 1977 warning, later said:

> Something happened in the course of those years that just really shattered something within him. I don't know exactly what. It was an accumulation of many things. But he sort of lost his soul there. And became a very different person. The Cesar of 1979 was a very different guy from the Cesar of 1969. It was like he went through a serious personality change. And I don't know what the definition of madness is, and I think some of it is related to questions of charisma and power and so forth, and that makes it understandable. But I think that is what happened to him: he went mad.[38]

The case for Cesar's madness does not rest solely on his proclivity to see malignant forces and conspiracy, nor on the various purges of the union staff. In the summer of 1977 he also got interested in Silva Mind Control, a form of meditation and self-healing, and promoted it strongly among the staff. Using its techniques, he claimed he could alter his brain waves so that he stayed alert even after he had got very little sleep. He made mind control a central part of the curriculum when he established a school for union negotiators in the winter of 1977.

Chavez used Silva Mind Control in his venture into *curanderismo*, Mexican folk medicine. In the mid-1970s, Chavez had started treating people within the union who had physical ailments. Many on the staff believed in Cesar's healing powers. He cured their headaches, earaches, back pain, allergies and hives. Richard Chavez, though often doubtful about Cesar's enthusiasms, believed in his power to heal. "Any minor headache was no problem. To him, it was no problem. He'd get you and use mind control and lay hands on you, and the headache was gone." But others were bewildered or shocked. An outraged Jose Renteria reported that Chavez, with Ganz and Padilla looking on, claimed to have cured

Renteria's ulcer simply by waving his arms over him in a dark room. Pablo Espinoza said that Chavez offered to do "bloodless surgery" on the failing kidney of Espinoza's wife and the congenitally defective knee of his son.[39]

But does this amount to madness? The loyalists in the leadership and staff did not think so. Many of them tried Silva Mind Control, went to Chavez with their ailments, and believed that people inside the union were conspiring against it. Nor did everyone who eventually clashed with Chavez believe that he went crazy. Jessica Govea thought that Chavez was simply acting "oddly." Jerry Cohen believed that Chavez was a master of internal power struggles, and was willing to use all the weapons at his command (including bizarre accusations) to outmaneuver his antagonists. Eliseo Medina was stunned by Padilla's visit in 1977 and thought Gilbert was doing the union no good with such talk. Thirty years later Medina still rejected any suggestion of madness: "Chavez was a genius, and genius has its quirks."[40]

Silva Mind Control, one such a quirk, came and went just like so many of his other intellectual obsessions, which he dove into and then abandoned. Like Gandhi, he was an inveterate faddist. It was part of his being an autodidact, uninfluenced by school learning, open to all manner of new ideas. More alarming was his claim to have healing powers, for such claims are often the flip side of paranoia. But the laying on of hands, like *curanderismo*, doesn't necessarily indicate madness. Healers are common in Mexican culture, part of a rich tradition of folk medicine, and Chavez came by it honestly: his mother was a sometime *curandera*.

People had been calling Chavez crazy ever since he declared his intention to defeat the Bracero Program and organize all of California's farm workers. In the early sixties, "crazy" had described his unrealistic belief in his own ability to mount a serious challenge to California agribusiness. The audacity of his vision, the power of his will, and the single-mindedness of his pursuit helped him prevail when lesser, more reasonable, "saner" men got discouraged and gave up. But what was helpful in winning power was harmful once he got it. His willfulness, his supreme belief in his own way, his personal combativeness played havoc once he was securely in command of a large, complex, powerful organization. He didn't change; his situation changed.

Marion Moses—a nurse who came to Delano in 1966, left for medical school in 1971, and came back as a union doctor in 1983—was in a unique position to assess what had happened to Chavez while she was away. "I told my friends that the good news was that Cesar hadn't changed, and the bad news was that Cesar hadn't changed. He was a control freak when I first met him, and a control freak when I came back . . . Only one thing had changed. Cesar had always been a great listener, but in 1984 he wasn't listening anymore."[41]

There is a certain convenience to the notion of an extraordinary break in the trajectory of an extraordinary man, the dramatic event that changed everything and catapulted the story of the UFW and Cesar Chavez from out of the tangled web of human action, political power plays, and ordinary calamity into something both simpler and more mysterious, more terrible and hence more grand. But while the idea that Chavez went mad may make for a more dramatic story, it also trumps all other explanations of what went wrong in the UFW. If the leader went nuts, nothing else matters—not the lack of locals, nor the antidemocratic ethos, nor the power of agribusiness, nor the compliance of the inner circle, nor the financial, physical, cultural, linguistic, and political separation between the membership and the staff, nor the plain old mistakes. These fade into the background as Chavez's supposed madness—his cruel purges, his paranoia, and his wild claims of being able to perform bloodless surgery—come to center stage. Absent any evidence that he was certifiably ill or clinically mad, the charge mainly serves to block a serious reckoning of what actually happened to the UFW.

There is plenty of evidence that Cesar Chavez was paranoid. But his paranoia was primarily a political phenomenon, not a psychological one. He was most paranoid about Communists; it wasn't just plots he saw around him, but Communist plots. Chavez learned politics during the Red Scare, from anti-Communist Catholic priests and the anti-Communist Fred Ross. Such paranoia is an ideological fault, not a character disorder.

Chavez was surely more paranoid in the late 1970s, when he was the unassailable head of a powerful organization, than he was in the mid- and late 1960s, when his organization was relatively weak and his position not so commanding. But isn't that essentially a political matter? Doesn't unchecked power breed paranoia? That idea is as old as the Old Testament. When the Jews send Samuel to ask God to give them a king, God warns the Jews that a king will oppress and exploit them. What God doesn't say, but what comes to pass, is that the first king of the Jews, Saul, becomes so suspicious of David, who loves and supports him, that he attempts to assassinate David in his sleep, and then slaughters his other loyal supporters, believing that they are his enemies. The message is clear: the sparkling jewel in the back of every king's crown radiates suspicion, shines with paranoia.

At the time Padilla concluded that Chavez was "acting crazy," Cesar Chavez was immune from criticism within his union, not subject to the give and take of ordinary politics. In the discussions on the Executive Board, only Dolores Huerta, who never deserted him in public, felt free enough to criticize Chavez regularly. Others swallowed their doubts and followed the leader. A good measure of how deranged political life had become at the top of the UFW was the reaction of Marshall Ganz and Jerry

Cohen to Gilbert Padilla's warnings about Chavez's mental health. Ganz thought that perhaps Chavez had sent Padilla on a mission to test who was loyal and who was not. Cohen thought that perhaps Cesar was pretending to be crazy in order to fool Padilla into destroying his own credibility. Such palace politics would make the courtiers of Louis XVI blush.

Nick Jones, a victim of Chavez's political paranoia, later said: " Cesar Chavez never would have been as crazy as he was had there been a good democratic structure in the UFW."[42]

Cesar Chavez did not go crazy and destroy the union. The reverse is closer to the truth: the UFW was crazy, and it destroyed Cesar Chavez.

"That Wall Is Black": The La Paz Makeover

April '77 to December '78

If the membership had been consulted about what the union's organizing priorities should be in the spring of 1977, the UFW might have avoided the calamity that awaited it in the vineyards of Coachella and Delano. But the members, now overwhelmingly vegetable workers, were not consulted. And so, defying the evidence on the ground and the logic of the recent past, the Executive Board once again followed its historical and emotional attachments and decided to concentrate its efforts not in the vegetables, where workers were in motion, but in the table grapes, where it would learn, yet again, in the words of the veteran organizer Alberto Escalante, that "some of those grape workers really hated the union."[1]

Marshall Ganz argued against it. Not only did the union have more support in the vegetables, he reasoned, but since the vegetable industry operates year-round—moving back and forth between the Salinas and Imperial valleys—it could potentially provide the union with an uninterrupted flow of dues income. The vegetables should be the UFW's base, he maintained, and once that base was consolidated it could be the platform for expansion into other areas.[2] But Chavez and most of the board and staff, all firm in the belief that grape workers were the authentic core of the UFW, had a point to prove after having lost the first round of ALRB elections in the vineyards. They had made up their minds back in the fall of 1976 that the grapes were their priority, and they simply reiterated that commitment in the spring of '77.

In the "President's Newsletter" of May 20, 1977, Chavez optimistically announced that "most of the union's top organizers are in Coachella and are moving ahead with energy and enthusiasm."[3] Ganz was sent to work with the other heavy hitters Jim Drake, Artie Rodriguez, Ben Maddock, and Eliseo Medina, who was in charge. Tom Dalzell and Ellen Greenstone, from the legal department, were assigned to the campaign full-time. Even Chavez tore himself away from reforming La Paz to make three separate visits.

Doug Adair, who worked on the campaign, was impressed with the leadership of Medina and the work of most of the organizers. The growers' strategy was to treat the workers well, organize through the foremen, and mobilize the Filipinos against the UFW. Some growers did harass and intimidate, but it was mostly against the organizers rather than the workers, and it was not widespread. "All in all," Adair concluded, "[in Coachella] they were relatively free elections."[4]

As expected, the UFW had a smashing victory at Freedman, the first table grape grower to sign with the UFW and still the best place to work in the Coachella Valley. Local UFW loyalists, who lived in town year-round and were always available when Freedman dispatches came up at the hiring hall, flocked to the polling station and voted UFW 750 to No Union 19. The UFW picked up victories at two small companies where the work-force was also made up almost entirely of local residents. It won a close contest at Tenneco, where Medina timed the election so that Tenneco's citrus workers, who were pro-UFW, would vote alongside the grape workers, who by and large were not. That victory was tied up in appeals, and the UFW never got a contract. At Mel Pack, a medium-size grape grower, there was a similar result.

Everywhere else, though, the UFW lost or was rebuffed without the formality of a vote.[5] About 40 percent of Coachella's 5,000 workers had not shown enough interest in the UFW to sign petitions forcing an ALRB election. The UFW had made a large mistake. It could have easily won at Freedman, left Coachella, and concentrated its organizing in the vegetables. Instead, it wasted energy and resources in a doomed campaign. Alberto Escalante, the election campaign cartoonist who had been on organizing drives all over the state, was upset, noting:

> We should have stayed in the row crops after we regrouped again. I learned within a couple of hours after starting organizing in the vineyards again in Coachella that some of those grape workers . . . had more than enough reason to be pissed off at the union and union leadership. It was then that the skeletons started to rattle and fall out of the closets of every grape growing area we'd ever been in. And it got pretty ugly, too! Not the way we were treated by the *lechugueros*. Now they really wanted us to organize everywhere they went.[6]

Confronted with defeat, the UFW's answer to the world was to attack the ALRB's new general counsel, Harry Delizonna, saying he had "lost the confidence of the farm workers in the law's ability to protect their rights."[7] But the union didn't seem to have an answer to itself. The organizers were not called to La Paz for a debriefing, and no systematic effort was made to figure out what had gone wrong. Instead, the union turned on its own.

It is a sad story. In the midst of the failing campaign, a UFW organizer was raped by a grape worker. After consulting with Medina, she decided not to go to the police, concerned that the publicity would detract from the campaign. Some UFW women heard about the incident and started to meet to discuss how to defend themselves from a similar attack. Hearing of this, the top organizers called a meeting of the entire organizing staff, where they denounced the women's group, explained that there would be no caucus of any kind inside the UFW, and fired Phyllis Hasbrouck, the woman whom they identified as the lead organizer. Ganz, Drake, Maddock, and Rodriguez sat as informal judges at the meeting.[8] Many years later Ganz said, "Yes, we were all part of it, caught up in the management- by-purging approach rather than simply meeting with Phyllis, one on one, talking about what her concerns were, seeing if they could be addressed or not . . . we were already caught up in the paranoia."[9]

After the thumping in Coachella, the UFW could have reversed course and sat out the Delano table grape season. It would have meant admitting to itself and to others that the 1975 elections had been an accurate measure of the UFW's weakness in the vineyards. Cesar Chavez would have had to take the lead; he would have had to argue strongly to his troops that it was prudent to skip Delano, and he would have had to explain that decision to the UFW's outside allies, who had heard him say for over a decade that the union was overwhelmingly supported by Delano grape pickers. He had said it so often, to audiences for whom the farm worker world was invisible and who therefore offered no restraint on his exaggerations, that he probably believed it himself. For whatever combination of reasons, Chavez pressed on to Delano.

He also thought that he could change the balance of forces with Filipino workers if he visited their homeland. Thus it was that Cesar Chavez decided to tour the Philippines as a guest of Ferdinand Marcos. He was encouraged in this by Andy Imutan, the San Joaquin Valley businessman and entrepreneur who had served briefly on the UFWOC Executive Board and who now headed up a Stockton-based Filipino community organization. Imutan, a strong supporter of Marcos, made all the arrangements with the government and accompanied Cesar and Richard Chavez, and David Martinez, an ex-boycotter who had risen quickly on the La Paz staff, on the two-week trip.

When Chavez mentioned the tour to the Executive Board and a few others, Phillip Vera Cruz, the veteran Filipino leader, and Chris Hartmire of the Migrant Ministry were the only people who opposed the idea. According to Vera Cruz, he told Chavez, "I don't approve of it. I don't like the form of government Marcos has created . . . It's a dictatorship. There are thousands of political prisoners, people are arrested without charges or benefit of trial."[10]

Vera Cruz's opposition did not stop the Chavez excursion, but it did mean the end of Vera Cruz in the UFW. A symbol of the Mexican-Filipino alliance at the heart of the 1965 grape strike, his position on the Executive Board had become less tenable since the ALRB elections, as neither he nor his fellow board member Pete Velasco could deliver Filipino votes. Unlike Velasco, who was an enthusiastic team player, Vera Cruz was somewhat aloof. He lived in Delano, not La Paz, and he hardly spoke during meetings. Privately, Chavez dismissed him as "the little philosopher."[11]

Sometime in late June of 1977, Chavez decided that Vera Cruz was not just opposed to the Philippines trip; he was another traitor. Although Vera Cruz did not talk much, he did take extensive notes at board meetings, and Chavez suspected that Phillip was passing inside information to his leftist friends. Chavez had also been told by an aide that Vera Cruz was going to resign from the union and write a book attacking him. Much of Chavez's suspicion, however, focused on Vera Cruz's wife, Debbie Volmer. Chavez told Jerry Cohen that Volmer was manipulating her husband and was part of a Communist conspiracy against the union. Cohen answered that Volmer couldn't manipulate anyone, that there was no Communist conspiracy, and that whatever Vera Cruz was doing, he was doing on his own.

But Chavez persisted. It was not an easy time. Someone had given Helen Chavez a love letter intended for her husband that had been opened in the mail room, and Helen had left La Paz. Chavez mistakenly thought the person who passed the letter along was a politically motivated Debbie Volmer. Distraught, he decided to call a meeting of the board and other union leaders to discuss the attacks on him, personal and political, and expose Philip Vera Cruz. He told Cohen to draw up a pledge of silence, which he would ask the participants to sign at the meeting's conclusion. Chavez assured Cohen that Vera Cruz would refuse to sign it, thus revealing to everyone his intention to betray the union.[12]

According to Cohen, Chavez's primary interest was to have the discussion and only secondarily to trap Vera Cruz. "There was a lot of frustration" throughout the leadership, Cohen said. "How are you going to have a discussion of all this if someone is going to blow the whistle? I don't think the essence of this was to set Philip up."[13]

According to Ganz and Padilla, it was. The pledge committed the signers "not to discuss the matters discussed at today's meeting in any manner whether by written publication or orally." Only Vera Cruz and Manuel Chavez, who left the meeting early, did not sign. When Vera Cruz refused, Padilla, alerted by Chavez beforehand, became suspicious of his intentions. "I had gone into that meeting saying I was going to resign," said Padilla. "This is not long after I told people that Cesar was acting crazy, and nobody had paid any attention to me. I really thought I wanted out. But when

Philip wouldn't sign the pledge of silence, it put some doubts in my mind. I had second thoughts and decided to stay."[14]

Fifteen years later Vera Cruz did collaborate on a book about the union, an oral history told to a couple of scholars at UCLA. In it he said that the dispute was about his right to keep a copy of his papers when he left the union, and to say and write anything he wanted to about the union and about Chavez. He described the intense pressure that Chavez and Cohen, in particular, put on him to sign the pledge of silence. He said he refused on the basis of his First Amendment rights, and then Marshall Ganz and Pete Velasco maneuvered him out of the meeting, which continued on without him. It was the last board meeting he ever attended.[15]

In his oral history, Vera Cruz criticized himself for being too "passive" as a union official and "not fighting like hell for what I knew was right." He was very careful to distinguish between his support for the union and his criticisms of Chavez. He praised Chavez, but argued that the main problem in the union was the lack of internal democracy, for which he blamed Chavez and the people around him:

> " . . . Cesar was seen as so important, so indispensable, that he became idolized and even viewed by some of his followers as omnipotent. I have been invited to speak at many different universities and often Chicano students who heard so much about Cesar ask me if Cesar was really a democratic leader. As an officer in the union, . . . I always had to temper my personal opinions . . . But one thing the union would never allow was for people to criticize Cesar. If a union leader is built up as a symbol and he talks like he was God, then there is no way that you can have true democracy in the union because the members are just generally deprived of their right to reason for themselves.[16]

Four days after the meeting where Vera Cruz refused to sign the pledge, Chavez talked about the incident to a group of people who were about to play the Game at La Paz. Like so many other discussions there, this one was taped. The recording reveals a side of Cesar Chavez which he successfully hid from the public.

> The board is here to play the game, everybody except Pete and Philip. Pete agreed to play with the Executive Board only, which is a kind of change. Philip didn't because we got in a big fight with him at the board meeting for taking materials to write a book and refusing a legal commitment like all of us did that he will not take anything from the board to write a book. It came from when he told Kent [Winterrowd] about six or seven months ago that he was going to resign and he was

going to write a book blasting me and saying about how corrupt the union was, and he was about ready to do that.

Anyway, we got into a big fight. He is married to Debbie Volmer, who is a fucking asshole, you know. She is part of the goddamned—we give her credit for all kinds of shit. Anyway, we gave it pretty hard, really hard, but he was well programmed. We really gave it to him. It was a game. Everybody, for more than three hours . . .

Because of what happened with Philip, I have been having a running fight with the board, except Dolores. Everybody else has been kind of taking me on because, in their own way, like back-biting and going around my back and all those things that happen in a group because also, remember, we have been infiltrated by leftists and by Commies, and that's what they know. But, ah, how bad it was what Philip proposed, that we had to get on him.

Well, I had been trying during the board meetings to set up an environment where we could get Philip. But just before we started, Chris [Hartmire] made just an amazing kind of attack on me, you know, about he was pissed off because we got rid of Joe Smith . . . He [Hartmire] doesn't know because he wasn't involved here, you see. He doesn't know. It is kind of a churchman's kind of thing. What they are saying is they want to be nice to everybody because, like, that's their mission in life, and they can't be sonsofbitches or bastards when they have to. So he was very torn about that when he came to the board meeting. But he said, seriously, he said that I was surrounded by a group of mechanistic bureaucrats who kiss my ass and we were feeding one another, and really I was kind of fucked up because I was getting after people and accusing them of being, you know, assholes. And sure enough about two hours later we got in a big argument with Philip, and then I laid out some of the shit that I have on Debbie and all that stuff. So after we got through with Philip we took a break and outside he [Hartmire] said, "Oh shit, I never realized that." And I said, "Well, you know, you shouldn't. The only ones who should know are Dolores and me, because we are the ones being attacked. And you guys don't get attacked, so why is that, you know?"

Well we found out that the big leftists went out to fuck up a family, they are fucking up two or three families, like a mechanic in Delano, they fucked him up pretty bad. They are fucking up another family in Oxnard . . . so we have a few problems.[17]

In the Philippines the Chavez party got an official nineteen-day tour. Chavez was feted. He spoke to government officials, labor leaders (those not in jail), and Filipino newsmen tolerated by the martial law regime. On accepting an honorary doctorate from Far Eastern University, he said, "The

Filipino people, through the leadership of President Marcos, are committed to the cause of human dignity and social justice, particularly to farm workers." He received another award directly from Marcos and told a Manila reporter: "President Marcos is a wonderful man; his sincerity comes through for the workers. The Martial Law administration here is unique. It's different in terms of the American concept of martial law. I didn't believe it from Filipino friends who told me until I got here." At a farewell press conference he said farm workers were treated better in the Philippines than in the U.S., and he extolled "the welfare-oriented programs of the government to improve the lot of the people."[18]

The coverage in the Manila press did no damage. What hurt was when Chavez said the same kinds of things into the tape recorder of a *Washington Post* reporter, adding that Filipino union leaders had all told him they were better off than they were before martial law was introduced.[19]

Letters of protest rained on La Paz. Especially outraged were Protestant and Catholic activists who had been doing political work in the Philippines. Some had been jailed by Marcos, others had been expelled from the country. The Church and Society division of the National Council of Churches expressed its "dismay" and demanded that Chavez condemn Marcos and the Philippine government for human rights violations. The largest U.S. anti-Marcos Filipino group sent Chavez a letter detailing martial law arrests, torture, and repression, and requested a private meeting with him so that they might change his mind before engaging in a public fight. Jerome Berrigan, brother of the popular radical priests Daniel and Philip, wrote that Marcos is a "documented torturer, murder, and violator of human rights," and said that Chavez "owed his supporters and admirers, as well as the American peace community, an explanation." A former Peace Corps volunteer on the island of Negros, Elizabeth Freeman, whose sister Nan was a UFW martyr killed on a picket line in Florida in 1972, wrote that Marcos's land reform was a fraud, that strikes and mass demonstrations were illegal in the Philippines.[20]

Chavez would not back down. He accused the *Post* of misquoting him, while simultaneously defending his trip and continuing to praise the Marcos regime. Instead of meeting with activists, he went on the attack, beginning with critics on his staff. He called a meeting of La Paz and field office volunteers. That meeting, in August of 1977, after the grueling Coachella campaign and before the union's September convention, is as good an example as any of what it now meant to serve in the UFW. Debbie Adair recalled:

> People were exhausted, people were discouraged, there was a lot of weirdness with the Game at La Paz, and the whole thing with Phyllis in Coachella. And then he [Cesar] goes to the Philippines and embraces the

dictator . . . Nobody liked it. It was such a blatant ploy for votes that we were all disgusted. It was disgusting. We didn't agree with it, and there was a lot of talk about it. I remember a couple of people just left. One person said that's it, I can't take it anymore and left . . . So they [the UFW leadership] called a meeting in La Paz. It was a meeting about us criticizing. "It has come to our attention that there is unhappiness about this." There was quite a discussion about it. Warnings about criticizing Cesar. Cesar is making decisions for the good of everyone, they said. And I remember Ellen Starbird stood up and said something about embracing the dictator, and she was going to be gone. And other people stood up and said, I cannot accept this. This is something I cannot live with. And then Max Avalos stood up and said, "If Cesar tells me that wall is black, then that wall is black." He was pointing at a white wall. And then there was silence. Everyone knew right then. Kaboom. It was the last brick to fall into place. Everybody who was going to stay, stayed. And everybody who was leaving, left.[21]

Debbie stayed. Her reasoning was much like that of many other volunteers out on the periphery. She was in Coachella, and she didn't have to play the Game. She told herself that she was doing good work at the clinic, and that the union was not in La Paz. It was down in the valley. To hell with La Paz, she thought, I am going to keep on building the union.

The protests did not deter Chavez from highlighting his Philippine adventure at the UFW's third constitutional convention, in Fresno in August, 1977. He invited Marcos's secretary of labor, Blas Ople, and the Philippine consul general, Roman Arguelles, to address the delegates. They were escorted onto the stage with great fanfare by residents of Agbayani Village, a Filipino retirement home in Delano built by the UFW a few years before. Doing everything he could to mobilize Filipino support for the union despite the scant number of Filipino delegates to the convention, Chavez also arranged for Fred Abad, one of the Filipino leaders of the 1965 strike, to be the only person to nominate him for reelection as president.

The embrace of the Marcos regime provoked a spat at the convention amid the leadership's engineered display of unity. In the gallery, Debbie Volmer shouted, "*Abajo con martial law!*" as Chavez introduced Ople. Security staff escorted her out of the building. Rudy Reyes got to the microphone, asked Ople to tell Marcos to lift martial law, and received loud applause. Philip Vera Cruz, while announcing his resignation from the union, denounced the presence of Marcos's representatives as honored guests, reminded people that the UFW had passed a resolution against Marcos at the previous convention, and said, simply, that martial law and democracy were antithetical: "You know, brothers and sisters, it can't be hot and cold at the same time."[22]

At the convention, Chavez filled Vera Cruz's seat on the board with one of the most popular people among the staffers, Jessica Govea. The older originals—Cesar and Richard Chavez, Dolores Huerta, Gilbert Padilla, and Pete Velasco—still held the majority, but the addition of thirty-year-old Govea meant that if any board dispute broke down along generational lines, Ganz, Medina, Lyons, and Govea would need only one crossover vote to win. Since close votes were rare, that didn't seem as significant as Govea's relationship with Marshall Ganz. Her appointment indicated that Chavez still had enough confidence in Ganz to put his partner and closest ally on the board.

The only significant constitutional change at the Fresno convention made farm workers' contributions to the union's political fund mandatory. Under the Labor Management Reporting and Disclosure Act of 1959 (also called the Landrum-Griffin Act), lobbying, direct contributions to political candidates or parties, and political campaigns aimed at the general public cannot be funded with compulsory union dues. Rather than set up a separate political action committee, as do most unions, the UFW had established an extra holiday, Citizens Participation Day, and companies under contract would send the equivalent of one day's pay into the UFW's Citizens Participation Fund. UFW members had to sign a form authorizing the company to send the money to La Paz. Most workers agreed, but enough people weren't signing in 1977 that the Executive Board decided that political contributions should be mandatory.[23] If members refused to turn the holiday pay over, they could be kicked out of the union and lose their jobs. Word of the proposed change filtered down from La Paz to the field offices, to the ranch committees, and to the membership. It provoked an uproar at Cal Coastal, Green Valley, and Admiral, where workers voted to instruct their delegates to oppose a mandatory Citizens Participation Day payment at the convention, which they did. Chava Bustamante was one of the leaders of a No vote on the measure. The No vote was small and easily defeated.

After the vote, Chava Bustamante was called to a private meeting, where Dolores Huerta, surrounded by workers who supported the board, accused him of being disloyal. He was not intimidated. He personally understood the need for the political funds, but he would not defy the wishes of the people he represented. In fact, he told me, "It was one of the first signs of people coming of age in the union . . . They were acting as if the union belonged to them, as if they had a say in what union policy should be."[24]

The small No vote and the flare of dissent over Marcos were not the only off notes amid the unity chorus. There had been enough talk about the La Paz purges that Chavez felt he had to make some reference to them in his opening speech. He was restrained: "Many volunteers have worked, sacrificed, and suffered with us on the picket lines and in the jails. But instead of helping the farm workers to build their own union, some volunteers have come with the notion that they would do the work for the farm workers.

Some came with the idea of saving the farm workers from their own union. Some have come with their own political and social values and have attempted to convince the workers to adopt them."[25]

Or, as Marc Grossman put it to Harry Bernstein of the *Los Angeles Times*, "If any s.o.b. comes in with his own political or social agenda and tries to impose that agenda on this union, then we will kick him out." When a reporter from *Workers' Vanguard* asked about a rival union headed by the former UFW organizer member Tony Orendain, the Texas Farm Workers Union, Grossman had security throw the reporter out, explaining to the others that "this is our convention" and "Commie freaks" aren't welcome.[26]

The main business of the August convention had been mobilizing for the upcoming election at the union's old Delano nemesis, the biggest and most influential table grape grower in the world, Giumarra. Chavez called the election the union's "top priority." The election was the theme of the conventioneers' march through Fresno, was constantly championed from the podium, and aroused the most enthusiastic cheers from the floor. Perhaps people cheered so loudly to mask their doubts, perhaps not, but given the UFW's recent record in the grapes, the Giumarra election was a gamble. And on September 26, 1977, after a three-week campaign blitz, the UFW lost: No Union 900, UFW 673.[27]

The UFW challenged some of the ballots, but even if all the challenged ballots had been UFW votes, No Union would still have been the victor. The Giumarra workers had many of the typical complaints, but the question of undocumented workers dominated the contest. Giumarra, which had been preparing for the election while UFW organizers were busy in Coachella, had loaded its crews with recent Mexican immigrants, many undocumented. By way of explaining the UFW defeat, Marc Grossman estimated that 65 percent of the workers were "illegals."[28] Estimates in the field were somewhat lower—perhaps 50 percent. Once people without papers were on the crews, and thus eligible to vote in the election, the foremen made sure that they knew the UFW's old history regarding illegals. In a sworn affidavit submitted by the UFW to the ALRB, two Giumarra workers, Damasio Tirado and Jose Ramirez, said that their supervisor told them that under the old union contract people without papers couldn't get dispatches to jobs, that "Chavez never gave illegals a chance and didn't get them any work."[29]

Early in the campaign the Immigration and Naturalization Service was active in and around the Giumarra fields and conducted several raids. The union had not called the INS; it suspected the company had, and it did everything it could to overcome its past. On September 7, in the first week of the campaign, Jim Drake, the head organizer, and Maurice Jordane, an ALRB agent, called Chavez to alert him to the dangerous situation. *Migra* agents had stationed themselves at the entrance to two Giumarra ranches and had just taken away two people. "The company has been saying that if the UFW wins, the Border Patrol will come in and pick up the people," Jordane said. Drake's message was even more disturbing: the *migra* had picked up people from seven crews over two days, and "the foremen are telling people we [the UFW] are opposed to illegals." Chavez immediately complained to the INS director, Leonel J. Castillo, and gave him a list of Giumarra workers being held by the INS. UFW supporters around the country sent hundreds of mailgrams to Castillo and President Jimmy Carter. Castillo announced that the INS would not raid Giumarra during the election campaign—a promise he did not keep—and the INS released eight undocumented workers, who returned to their crews with written legal permission to remain in the United States for thirty days. The UFW widely publicized this victory, which, Drake later concluded, "picked up more votes for us than any other thing."[30]

But it wasn't enough. Rarely has the coop been more crowded with chickens coming home to roost. Ten years of opposition to the undocumented and a couple of years of badly administered contracts are not easily overcome in a three-week blitz. Guadalupe Cordova, an organizer, said, "The company knew how to use rumors about the *migra*, dispatches, dues, etc. All of it influenced the undocumented to vote against the union." She added, "The union ought to support and help in a more forceful and open manner the undocumented worker, we ought to talk to them, so that in the future we can count on their support."[31]

The defeat intensified Chavez's retreat into internal union politics. At the October 10, 1977, Executive Board meeting he was outlandishly defensive, saying that he knew beforehand that the election would be lost but he hadn't stopped it or said anything before "because he didn't want to hurt people's feelings."[32] The meeting notes do not record how people responded. Everyone knew that hurt feelings had become a regular part of Chavez's reform of La Paz, and rarely stopped him from doing what he thought was right.

Five days later Chavez dressed down critics of his trip to the Philippines in front of about 400 people. So many of the union's important allies, especially its religious ones, had complained to La Paz that Chavez decided to invite some of them to Delano for a public "discussion." It was a set-up. A busload of staffers from La Paz, pro-Marcos Filipinos mobilized by Imutan and union loyalists from Delano far outnumbered the thirty to forty religious activists who had been invited and the couple of dozen others who had come on their own. Chavez opened with a short statement, saying that he did not support martial law and that although he had found much to like on his trip, he was not defending the Marcos regime. He then turned the floor over to five representatives of the Marcos government, who spent most of the next five hours aggressively defending the dictatorship. When Leon Howell, a reporter for the liberal journal *Christianity and Crisis*, commented that despite Chavez's disclaimer the meeting seemed to be another union endorsement of martial law, someone from the crowd shouted, "Do you support marital law, yes or no?" A few in the crowd then started chanting, "Yes or no! Yes or no!" Chavez jumped to his feet, and, pointing at Howell, screamed: "I answered that in my speech, and he knows it."[33]

The meeting ended in disarray, and the clergy left more distraught than before. A few publicly renounced their support for the UFW; most quietly became less active in the coalition. Howell wrote that soon after screaming at him, Chavez knelt before him, politely asking if Howell had heard him say that he did not support martial law. Yes, he had, Howell, answered, but what about all the evidence to the contrary? Chavez's attempt at reconciliation dissolved into anger, and he glared at Howell, saying, "If you misquote me I'll sue you, I'll haul your ass to court."[34] The flabbergasted Howell concluded his article on the event with the hope that someone whom Chavez trusts would "reach him" on the issue. No one ever did. Four months later, when a Protestant churchman from Norway wrote to complain about Chavez's continuing support of Marcos, Chris Hartmire wrote back: "I believe a strong supporter should assume that Chavez knows what he is doing and keep his mouth shut about things he doesn't understand."[35]

Nineteen seventy-seven ended in pessimism at La Paz. Always doubtful about the power of farm worker strikes, Chavez now worried that the UFW couldn't count on winning contracts through elections, either. As 1978 began, the leadership looked ahead to the vegetable contracts scheduled to expire at the end of the year, and many at La Paz thought the union might lose those, too. Would farm workers alone ever be able to sustain the union? Chavez thought not.

In the spring of 1978 he urged the Executive Board to endorse a three-part program: intensify efforts to sign contracts at certified companies to increase the union's dues income; cut back most other UFW trade union activities; do what it could to find money other than dues to fund the burgeoning enterprises at La Paz. As it turned out, this program dovetailed quite nicely with Chavez's longstanding call for the UFW to become a "movement" organization rather than just a union. How it all fit together makes a surprising story.

Dues revenue as a percentage of total UFW income was actually increasing at this point; it hit new highs of 61 percent in 1977–78 and 66 percent in 1978–79. But those increases, primarily the result of new vegetable contracts, did not lift the gloom in La Paz. Up in the foothills of the

Tehachapis, the dramatic defeats in the vineyards overshadowed the eleven election victories in the Salinas Valley in 1977 and the signing of new contracts there and in the Imperial Valley.[36] Dues income totaled nearly $1.5 million in 1977–78, but dues alone, Chavez fretted, would not support the UFW staff.[37]

Nevertheless, Chavez had some other, excellent financial news. The interrelated union-allied organizations centered at La Paz were collecting significant amounts of new money. The National Farm Worker Service Center (NFWSC), set up by LeRoy Chatfield in 1969 as a charitable trust, had assets of just under $900,000 in 1977 (the assets' worth would climb to $6 million by 1985).[38] Its directors were Cesar and Richard Chavez, Chris Hartmire, Gilbert Padilla, Fred Ross, and Frank Denison, one of the union's lawyers.

The Robert F. Kennedy Medical Plan, funded by grower contributions, had $6.8 million in assets in 1978.[39] That money was supposedly overseen by a ten-member board of trustees, five each from the contributing companies and the union, but the grower representatives were indifferent overseers of the funds. The Juan De La Cruz Pension Plan, also capitalized by grower contributions and administered in La Paz, had accumulated as much as 2.5 million dollars but by 1978 had distributed no money to farm workers.[40]

The Martin Luther King Jr. Educational Fund, a 501(c)(3) nonprofit, also nourished by grower contributions, was governed by a board made up of two grower representatives, Chavez, Padilla, and, as the supposedly neutral party, Monsignor George Higgins. Figures for its 1977–78 assets are unavailable, but by 1985 it had more than $8 million in assets.[41] It ran the farm worker Service Centers, usually operated out of the UFW field offices, in which volunteers helped UFW members secure benefits from various government agencies. The Citizenship Participation Fund was completely under the control of the UFW, administered by the UFW board member Mack Lyons.

Those five entities controlled the overwhelming majority of the money, but there was also the Farm Worker Credit Union, the National Farm Worker Health Group, which operated the clinics, and seven other bodies all theoretically independent of the UFW but centered at La Paz, operated by UFW volunteers, and controlled by the UFW leadership. Chavez dubbed the entire group of union-allied organizations "movement entities." Taken together they constituted what he and the rest of the La Paz staff called the Farm Worker Movement. In 1978 the Farm Worker Movement had at least $10 million in assets.

With Jimmy Carter in the White House, Chavez and the Executive Board aimed to capitalize the movement entities further by seeking federal grants. In 1977 and '78 they won nearly $1.8 million in five separate grants from the Department of Labor and the U.S. Community Service Agency for the Farm Workers Credit Union and the NFWSC.[42] The grant funds were used to help pay off bad credit union loans, help build a microwave telephone system, buy office equipment and supplies, and provide $683,000 to teach farm workers English, mechanics, printing, communication, building maintenance, and landscaping.

Back in the days of the National Farm Workers Association, during the Johnson administration, Chavez had received a grant from the Office of Economic Opportunity, but he had been forced to turn it down when the NFWA joined the grape strike and started its journey toward becoming a union. Now, as Chavez became nervous about the future of his union, he once again applied for government money, not for the UFW but for the movement entities.

The Farm Bureau and various right-wing journalists charged that the federal grants illegally aided the UFW. Certainly, the supposedly independent organizations were all actually controlled by the UFW leadership and staffed by UFW volunteers, and they shared facilities, equipment, and other resources with the union. The mechanics, printers, and maintenance folks who were being trained with federal money spent their time working on National Farm Workers Service Center cars that were used by UFW organizers, printing UFW materials, and maintaining the grounds and buildings at La Paz. The microwave telephone system was supposed to be used just by the service centers, but in the short time that it ran efficiently it was used by UFW staff as well. Many of the people who earned salaries from the grants donated them to the UFW and took the now-standard $10 a week plus expenses instead. All of this was either against the law or highly suspect, because a condition of the grant money was that it not to be used to aid the union.

But it was also small potatoes. Nobody was getting rich off the money. People worked hard and lived simply at La Paz. Manuel Chavez was the only staff member who had money to burn, and he was mostly burning it and not sequestering it away in secret bank accounts. Nor is it of great significance that some money and resources were mingled that should have been separate. That was easily handled by a little creative bookkeeping, and negotiations with the UFW-friendly Carter administration.

What did matter was that the La Paz staff had a separate income stream independent not only of membership dues but to a large extent of the UFW itself. The medical plan, the pension plan, Citizens Participation Day funds, and the Martin Luther King Jr. Educational Fund could not be sustained forever without ongoing contributions from contractual growers, but the plans were already highly capitalized, and some money would still be there to manage and administer even if the union lost most of its contracts. In addition, the money in the NFWSC and the other, smaller, movement entities was not structurally tied to the UFW in any way. Put simply: the La Paz staff could potentially survive without the UFW.

Cesar Chavez understood that. According to Padilla, in 1977 and '78 one of Chavez's favorite conceits was that the union was like mistletoe on an oak tree, dependent on the growers for its existence. "We need a life of our own," he insisted. "We have to be the tree, not the mistletoe."[43] Not that Chavez was planning to abandon the union; rather, he shifted his attention to the other projects he controlled, to grow them into that tree that would stand by itself. Typically, to a group of visitors to La Paz in June 1978, he proudly described the UFW as but one of the fourteen entities that made up the Farm Worker Movement.[44]

This was mostly a word game: Chavez called the string of interrelated farm-worker organizations that he controlled the Farm Worker Movement and then concluded that because the UFW was a part of it, it was not just a union, but a movement. But to the extent that this was a mere linguistic trick, Chavez was the one most tricked by it. He could deceive himself because he was blind to the democratic content of actual movements. The fact that no active farm workers were central figures in the Farm Worker Movement did not bother him. He believed he could run the farm worker movement from his ashram in the Tehachapis. He believed the farm worker movement's organizational form could be all of those nonprofit programs and services administered by the loyal, dedicated volunteers who were being tempered in the Synanon Game. The Farm Worker Movement was so named because it accurately reflected his ideas about a farm worker movement.

Thus, cutting back the UFW and seeking outside funds for the La Paz agencies were part of a consistent policy. As the one movement entity that could not receive government funds or tax-exempt donations, the UFW had to be able to pay its own bills. The Giumarra defeat indicated that the union might never get enough contracts to do so: hence the cuts and consolidation. More money for the other movement entities would build the farm worker movement and protect the La Paz leadership and staff. If the union could not earn enough dues to support the staff, the most disloyal staff members could be laid off, and the most loyal could be put to work managing the other agencies at La Paz, where even in 1978 a full third of the staff was already assigned.[45] The Farm Worker Movement would survive even if the UFW languished. In some ways Chavez had done what he set out to do: he had learned to be a good administrator. Here he is at his most far-seeing, conceptual, administrative best. Long after the UFW was finally defeated in the fields, the Farm Worker Movement, in the form of a nonprofit family business, would continue to flourish.

Within this new plan, the antileft, anti-Communist, antidisloyalty purges made sense. Leftists did not fit well in the Farm Worker Movement. Even the most cooperative among them would insist that farm workers have some role in the farm worker movement besides being recipients of benefits delivered by 501(c)(3) charities or objects to be mobilized by volunteer organizers. Sooner or later, these volunteers would prove to be disruptive and disloyal. Liza Hirsch, the child of Communists and protégé of Chavez since her early teens, was the next to go.

Hirsch was going to spend one more summer as a volunteer in the legal department before getting her law degree and going to work for the UFW. But in the spring of 1978, Cohen informed her that Chavez had crossed her name off the list of law school students who were scheduled to work with the union. Liza was devastated. Chavez refused to talk to her, Cohen gave no explanation, and Padilla could tell her only that Chavez was crazy and she had to accept his decision. She refused to do so. She attended the May wedding at La Paz of Jenny Padilla, one of Gilbert's daughters, even though Gilbert had warned her not to come. After the ceremony, she approached the head table, where Chavez was seated among the wedding party and honored guests. When Cesar saw her coming, he yelled out, "Get that Communist bitch out of here," and his bodyguards escorted the sobbing Hirsch to the gate.[46]

Witnessed by so many people, the purge of Liza Hirsch was considered one of Cesar's cruelest, most irrational expulsions. But why not take Chavez's choice of words—"Communist bitch"—seriously? Communist: Hirsch was no Communist, having rejected her parents' politics partly due to Cesar's influence. But despite her role in the Campaign Against Illegals, she remained an open leftist. Bitch: Unlike many others of her generation who enthusiastically embraced the Game, Hirsch had managed to avoid playing it without exactly refusing to do so. For Chavez, a non-game play-ing leftist was a dangerous combination. He could easily conflate Liza's leftism with Communism—he did that all the time—and her rejection of the Game made her an asshole, or, as female assholes were often called in the Game, a "bitch."

The expulsion of Liza Hirsch capped the anti-leftist, anti-Communist purge of the UFW staff. It came on the heels of the March-April Executive Board meeting where the union and its main support operations were cut back. The cuts were all proposed by Chavez, and together they constitute quite a list. The entire boycott operation was dismantled, and the twenty-five volunteers who still served in the major cities were either dismissed or reassigned. The hiring hall was eliminated from new contracts, eliciting some dissenting remarks from Marshall Ganz and Eliseo Medina. The legal department was to discard all "cases not directly beneficial to the union and/or its members," mainly a lingering antitrust suit against the growers. Health clinics and field offices were to be closed or consolidated, the chief effect of which was that by the end of 1978 only two health clinics remained. Initiatives in Florida, Texas, Arizona, Oregon, and Washington, where local farm worker organizers had been petitioning the UFW for help, were put on hold, as once again the union adopted a no-growth policy outside of California.[47]

Perhaps most troubling for the long-term future of the UFW, the Executive Board decided to conduct new organizing campaigns only among workers who came to the union seeking representation. This meant that the union would not only stay away from the vineyards but would not initiate a large-scale organizing campaign in the vegetables either, leaving the vegetable industry only partly unionized.[48]

In discussing this plan for downsizing, the Executive Board once again considered establishing union locals, and rejected the idea. This time the main argument against them was that locals would have their own treasuries, they would send only part of the dues along to La Paz, and they would add a costly amount of paperwork. Dolores Huerta jokingly introduced a new reason to be concerned about locals. After Chavez had given his standard warning about the "politics" that locals would bring to the union, Huerta shouted: "You can watch your seat on the board, brothers. If you want to come back here, you won't be having a staff." This suggestion that they might be voted out of office and replaced by leaders of union locals elicited some nervous laughter.[49]

Only Marshall Ganz expressed doubts about what was happening. He was still upset about the earlier choice to organize in the table grapes instead of the vegetables. He expressed his reservations about the role of Synanon in the union. Again he warned about the danger of leaving the vegetable industry semi-unionized. He still opposed locals, but he voiced a new concern about the relationship between La Paz and the rank and file. As director of organizing, he was mostly out in the field, and perhaps his uneasiness owed to his spending more time talking to farm workers than to the rest of the board. Perhaps it was simply a resurfacing of the democratic leftism that he had brought from SNCC twelve years before. Perhaps it was his realization that monumental decisions about the union's future were being made without consulting any farm workers. Whatever their origin, his remarks to the Executive Board in the spring of 1978, captured by the union's taping system, reveal his distaste for autocratic procedures. Although informal and incomplete, they are, unhappily, the clearest defense of union democracy in the entire archival record of the internal debates of the UFW leadership:

> I think there is probably some question about whether I have some different view of the membership or something like that. You see, I do have a feeling that we don't take into consideration enough the realities of building responsibility out there in ranch committees and in the membership when we make decisions. If we make a decision here [in La Paz] because it is the best decision but we don't assess what the impact is

over there [among farm workers] but just assume that whatever decision we make we can sell to the membership—see, I don't think that is exactly where it is at, and in reality, it isn't where it is at.

See, you have to give them real responsibility, or we shouldn't bullshit about it. Either we have to give them some real responsibility and real power to make a decision, like in contract negotiations, or we shouldn't bullshit about giving them real responsibility and authority to make their own decisions. I am talking about within the scope of the policy of the union. Because it has to be real; it can't be phony. Because if it is phony it doesn't work, because everybody knows it's phony. You can't pretend that people are going to make decisions and then not really do it.

We have a real constituency out there that has its own politics, its own demands, its own problems, its own weaknesses, its own hassles, and we have to take all that into consideration whenever we do things. And I am not sure we always do that. It is not not caring about the membership, but it is not recognizing the dynamics that are at work among the membership. Particularly in the industry that I have been working with that has some particular problems because of the Teamster history, because of the fact that the lettuce workers are an elite, which is a problem, but also very militant and so forth. Most national unions when they make decisions have to weigh the impact on the locals, how to deal with the locals, and how to play it. We just seem to assume that whatever we decide and whatever way we go is automatically okay. It is not automatically okay.[50]

Rank-and-file workers did have their own politics. At the very moment when Cesar Chavez was cutting back and consolidating the UFW, thousands of *limoneros* in Oxnard were expressing those politics by pushing at the union's door and trying to force their way in. "*Viva la unión!*" they yelled, as the UFW Executive Board was doing what it could to make the union independent of its farm worker base. "*Viva Cesar Chavez!*" they chanted, as Chavez prepared the way for his possible retreat into a string of federally designated charity organizations that he called the Farm Worker Movement.

During a recess in the March-April meeting, Eliseo Medina was back at the Oxnard field office when a delegation of lemon workers from Coastal Growers Association showed up and announced that they were on strike, and they wanted the UFW to represent them. The whole company was out, massed at the CGA camp, trying to decide what to do next. The strikers urged Medina to come with them and lend them a hand.

Coastal Growers was the largest lemon harvest association in Ventura County, employing more than 1,000 lemon pickers, about 20 percent of all the *limoneros* in Ventura County—"the lemon capital of the world." Almost half of them lived in the camp. When the *limonero* delegation arrived with

Medina in tow, he learned that the strike had started when a foreman had refused to raise the piece rates even in orchards with tall, difficult-to-pick trees. The strike had spread as the workers went from orchard to orchard where all of the foremen, without any good explanation, were refusing to adjust the piece rates. Amid a chorus of *vivas*, Medina was hoisted onto the roof of a car as hundreds of workers crowded around. He explained the ALRB election rules, and as soon as he climbed down off the car, people divided up into crews, elected representatives to serve on a strike committee, and signed union authorization cards.

By the next day, the cards had been signed and submitted, and ALRB officials held a preelection conference right there at the camp with 400 workers trying to listen in. That evening, Chavez came to the camp to speak at a rally of more than 1,000 people. It was March 31, his birthday, and in pouring rain the strikers serenaded him with "Las Mañanitas," the Mexican birthday song. The election was held the next day; the result: UFW 897, No Union 42.[51]

Chavez immediately returned to La Paz for the resumption of the Executive Board meeting, but the workers decided to stay on strike. Just because they had voted to have the UFW represent them was no reason to go back to work. Union representation was not their final goal. They wanted a contract guaranteeing higher wages and better working conditions. The election results had given them some leverage. But they also knew that the farm labor law had not changed the basic truth in the orchards: if they could maintain their unity, they would be a hell of a lot more powerful striking than working.

The Coastal Growers Association battle had not been a typical UFW election campaign. UFW organizers had not initiated it and were in no position to call it off. The strike belonged to the workers' committee, and while Medina could influence the people on the committee, he could not order them around. And what they were doing made sense. Over the past two and a half years Medina had argued at board meetings that no one seemed to be responsible for the period between an election victory and its certification. All too often the workers had been abandoned, the enthusiasm of the election campaign had dissipated, and by the time contract negotiations had finally begun, the workers were not in a mood for action in the fields to influence them. The continued CGA strike might solve all those problems at once.

On the third day of the renewed Executive Board meeting, Medina reported that Coastal Growers was still on strike and had been joined by lemon pickers at Casitas, a small ranch. He asked the board to formulate a policy on the Ventura citrus industry and decide "how strong of an effort we want to make." According to the board notes: "Brother Cesar Chavez stated that it was too early to make a decision right now. There are other things that need discussing and will influence any decisions needed for the Oxnard area."[52]

This was the moment the board turned to the issue of cutbacks. Hours later, after those had been approved, Medina again brought up the question of the *limoneros*. What about strike benefits? The workers were asking if the union would be willing to pay them. Chavez said no, and according to the board notes suggested "that Brother Eliseo go back to Oxnard and lead the workers into going back to work as soon as possible. We could then try to get the state to certify us right away and start negotiations."[53]

The very next day, before Medina had a chance to go back to Oxnard and try to call off the strike, he was summoned out of the board meeting for an urgent phone call. He returned to tell the board that the Coastal Growers' attorney had just made an offer. If the workers would return to work, the company was willing to telegram the ALRB chairman and request immediate certification of the election. The strikers' strategy had worked. The offer was accepted, although the *limoneros* didn't return to their ladders until after the telegram was sent and the election was certified.

In the face of such success, Chavez did not try to stand in the way as the workers kept up the pressure. After five weeks of strike, on-the-job action, lockout, mass marches, and sit-ins in the city, contract negotiations between the company and the union intensified. Finally, thirty-eight days after the first walkout, Coastal Growers signed a contract providing for a 22 percent raise over three years.[54]

Eliseo Medina was thrilled. At that Executive Board meeting Chavez had made him the UFW's new organizing director, replacing Marshall Ganz. Just as Medina was taking the job, the *limoneros* had opened up a whole new path, developed a new approach to the opportunities presented by the ALRB. The workers could lead the process from beginning to end. "It was the first time in the history of the union that we had gone from strike to election to certification to bargaining a contract in a very compact, concentrated time. And that made me think that that was a model that we needed to adopt in the union to try to take it away from the lawyers and make it into a workers' movement."[55]

In the citrus organizing campaign that followed under Medina's direction, about 2,000 *limoneros* at six different companies voted for the union and then successfully pressured the growers to support quick certifications. By the end of the campaign, the UFW represented some 70 percent of the lemon pickers in Ventura County and had contracts at the largest harvesting association and at the two largest ranches.[56]

Medina's excitement did not last long. After the citrus campaign was over, he started drawing up plans to organize the rest of the state. But although Chavez had jumped on board the runaway train in Oxnard, he wouldn't endorse a comparable campaign anywhere else. Organizing had been put on hold. "I moved to Fresno to be organizing director," says Medina. "But there was no staff and no resources allocated to organizing. And it became clear to me that that was not going to be the direction of the union. And it solidified in my mind that perhaps I had overstayed the time that I could be useful to the union."[57]

The remaking of La Paz and the transformation of the UFW staff did not go unchallenged. Individually, people fought all along the way. The clearest example of resistance was David McClure, the volunteer who refused to leave the meeting the night of the Monday Night Massacre and had to be removed from La Paz by the Tehachapi police. Others demanded hearings when they were dismissed, or sent letters of protest to Chavez, or even registered their complaints in the alternative press. Individual board members dissented from certain policies but made no joint effort to block Chavez's overall plans. The only organized collective attempts within the staff to deter Chavez from his La Paz makeover came from the legal department. The first initiative had come from the paralegals; the next came from the lawyers themselves, led by one of Chavez's closest allies on the staff, Jerry Cohen.

Cohen didn't like Synanon, but he was not, like Liza Hirsch, a consistent opponent of the Game. He was good at it, didn't take it too seriously, and defended it as relatively harmless. He fully supported Chavez's right to hire and fire at will, and was a Chavez ally in the purge of the *Malcriado* editor Joe Smith. Nevertheless, trouble had been brewing between Chavez and Cohen ever since in 1974, when Cohen moved the legal department to Salinas. Although Chavez respected Jerry's abilities and was proud of the legal department, he was uneasy about its growing independence and authority. The entire Salinas operation, Chavez believed, was becoming too loose and was not sufficiently loyal. "We have three unions in Salinas," he told a group of staffers at La Paz in the fall of 1977. "The field office is one union, the legal department is one union, and the clinic is another union." They "don't talk to each other," and some staffers weren't "friendly" to him. "People like that have to be thrown out," he added, "and that is what we are doing."[58]

Cohen felt the pressure against him increase when Chavez began to ask him in front of others how many of his lawyers were Chicanos, although Chavez knew full well that there was only one, Marcos Lopez. What had been a point of pride in 1967, when Chavez defended the almost exclusively white legal department to Reies Tijerina, had become in 1977 a way of chiding Cohen and a possible avenue of attack against the lawyers. As Chavez was suspicious of Salinas, so the lawyers were wary of La Paz. Tom Dalzell, one of the earliest recruits to the legal department, said there was a feeling that much of what went on at La Paz was "ridiculous" and "crazy." Sandy Nathan recalled that he and his fellow lawyers thought "the people up there were the Moonies of the union" and that the "whole Synanon influence was appalling."[59] The lawyers depended on Cohen to protect them from Chavez, and Nathan said that he and others were disappointed because Cohen couldn't shield them enough.

At the March–April Executive Board meeting Cohen had not objected to pruning the department. He was as eager as Chavez to wrap up the anti-trust case against the growers, and he was not entirely happy with the complications that came with such a sizable staff. In 1978 there were seventeen lawyers and about two dozen paralegals, the standard office jealousies, and some political differences. The more left-leaning lawyers had started their own internal study group, and some felt that Cohen was reluctant to give them the more challenging and interesting assignments. Cohen was tired of the office politics, and he agreed that perhaps the legal department would be better off if it were smaller.[60]

After the board meeting, Chavez increased his pressure on Cohen to get the legal department to come to La Paz to play the Game. The Game was at its apex at La Paz in the spring of 1978, with some on the staff playing twice a week, and the field office staff coming to play on Saturdays. For people from Salinas, it meant leaving home at about five in the morning, driving the four and a half hours to La Paz, playing the Game, eating, and then driving back at night. So far, the legal department had avoided making the trip.

Besides the hardship involved, the legal staff was deeply hostile to the Game and the whole Synanon influence. By this time Dederich and his experiment in living had fallen into one problem after another. He was sued by parents who said that Synanon had physically abused their children. Newspapers and other media reported that Synanon had purchased large amounts of weapons and ammunition. Tapes of meetings revealed the existence of a Synanon enforcement team that beat up the organization's enemies. In late 1977, *Time* magazine described them as a weirdo cult of compulsory wife-swappers. Chavez stayed loyal to his friend Chuck Dederich, even convincing his mostly reluctant Executive Board to promote Synanon's boycott of *Time*. The low point for Synanon would come a few months later, in the fall of 1978, when a rattlesnake bit the hand of a Los Angeles attorney who had successfully sued Synanon. The snake, its warning rattlers cut off, had been put in the unsuspecting lawyer's mail-box. Dederich was accused of masterminding the bizarre assault, and Chavez spoke in his defense at a news conference organized by Synanon. When Dederich pleaded no contest to conspiracy to commit murder, Chavez finally dropped his public support for what was considered a criminal religious cult, a minor version of the People's Temple, whose mass suicide in Jonestown, British Guyana, shocked the nation just one month after the rattlesnake attack. Nevertheless, within the UFW Chavez would continue to distinguish between Synanon's unfortunate trajectory and the usefulness of the Game.[61]

Now, in April 1978, Cohen thought the Game might actually be helpful in bringing matters to a head between La Paz and the legal staff. He was tired of playing the middleman. Sandy Nathan, worried that the Game would cause a permanent rupture between the attorneys and Chavez, urged him to reconsider. But Cohen said that if something wasn't done to change the dynamic between La Paz and the lawyers, the legal department eventually would be cut to pieces.

The lawyers went to La Paz to play the Game on six consecutive Saturdays between April 15 and May 20, 1978. They arrived at one of the Games dressed in short-sleeved white shirts and thin ties, mimicking Mormon missionaries or airport LaRouchites. They marched into the Game room in mock military formation, chanting and singing. They ridiculed the Game while playing it, and put unrelenting heat on what they considered the excessive hero worship of Chavez at La Paz. The lawyers had heard that some people were saying that they could see a nimbus over Cesar's head, so they claimed that Cohen had ascended to heaven and that they couldn't see him at all. They were gamed on their elitism, the salaries they received, and the supposedly easy life they were leading in Salinas while everybody else was working so hard at La Paz. As a spoof on an old story that Chavez had turned down a volunteer's request for more expense money because he needed underwear, one lawyer dropped his pants and showed his backside so that Chavez could verify that his underwear was hopelessly tattered.[62]

Generally, the Game was a rough affair, filled with yelling, swearing, and personal attacks, some quite venomous. But despite the theory of the triangle and the circle, Chavez, like Dederich, was somewhat off limits. He was occasionally gamed, but, on the evidence of the tape recordings, he was mostly treated with deference. Few people swore at him, and people who otherwise screamed at one another quieted down to hear what he had to say. The lawyers' attacks were unusual, and some of Chavez's most loyal staffers believe that the "mocking" of Chavez played a large part in the eventual shutdown of the legal department. When the lawyers danced in, one staffer wrote to Tom Dalzell, they danced themselves out of a job.

Cohen's idea had backfired. Chavez "now knew what our thinking was on 'building community' at La Paz." he later said. "That is what he wanted to know. The Game blew it up. Afterwards, he was biding his time and figuring out what to do next."[63]

For their part, the lawyers believed that after the drama of the Games a debate had been joined, and it was now time to bring the question of money out into the open. The attorneys received a stipend of $600 a month, out of which they paid their own expenses. The stipend was both symbol and substance of their relative independence from La Paz—they did not have to bring in their bills to get them approved—but it was still low, and many of them argued that it was not enough to support a lifelong commitment to the union.

Typically the lawyers' stipends had been negotiated between the lawyers and Chavez, but Chavez had already let Cohen know that this year such matters would have to go to the board. The lawyers decided the time had come to face the issue head-on. Encouraged by Cohen, some of them even played the Game among themselves to make sure that all their opinions and feelings about wages and money would be taken into account. In the course of one Game, Cohen revealed that he was being paid substantially more than the rest of them, in fact about four times as much: $28,500, still low for a lawyer but a respectable wage. That piece of information, coupled with the overall desire for stability, convinced the attorneys that they should collectively petition for a raise. Most asked for $400 more a month; two asked for a raise of $860. Collectively, the raises would double the UFW's costs for the legal department, to $20,000 a month. Brushing aside his fear that he might be overplaying his hand, Cohen included the entire list of proposed raises in his official report to the June 1978 Executive Board meeting.[64]

It was the opening that Chavez had been waiting for. The request had neither the egalitarian spirit nor elegant simplicity of the paralegals' earlier plan. It was a request by the highest-paid staff workers to make even more money. It came from the one department completely dominated by white professionals, most from relatively well-off families. Chavez had not broadcast the paralegals' proposal to the rest of the staff, as it would have appealed to too many people. But he knew he would have little trouble mobilizing against this one, and he called for a one-week review period so the entire staff could "discuss" the plan.

It became jump-on-the-lawyers week. Gilbert Padilla, who had been sympathetic to the paralegals, sided with Chavez. The lawyers were trashed at a La Paz community meeting he chaired, and people were encouraged to write to Cesar to explain their views. Chavez received at least a dozen letters, most of them critical of the legal department. Padilla also discussed the proposal with the Delano staff, while Chavez went to Salinas to tell the lawyers that rather than get raises they should relocate to La Paz and work for $10 a week like everybody else.[65]

When the actual proposal came before the board on June 25, Chavez had combined the lawyers' request with a plan for a paid staff.[66] Now, a vote against the lawyers also meant a vote to retain the union's system of volunteerism, and to reject requests from any of the volunteer staff for regular pay checks. It was a clever inside move, more evidence in support of Jerry Cohen's contention that Chavez was especially skillful at protecting and augmenting his power on the board. To anchor the point, just before the deciding vote Chavez threatened to resign if the lawyers won, making his leadership an issue in the debate,. After the week-long Chavez-directed campaign against the lawyers and the open hostility of the La Paz vs. legal department Games, a decision to grant the lawyers a raise would have given Jerry Cohen a large victory in what had become a nasty confrontation between the union's president and its general counsel.[67]

Marshall Ganz was appalled that instead of quietly accommodating the lawyers' request, as he had in the past, Chavez had escalated the issue. Although previously a strong supporter of volunteerism, Ganz believed this vote would determine the future of the legal department. The resolution did not specify that the department would either move to La Paz or be shut down, but according to Ganz, everyone understood that would be the outcome if they voted against the raises and to retain the volunteer staff. Ganz did not consider the lawyers expendable. ALRB elections involved multiple complex legal procedures, and therefore the lawyers had become a crucial element in UFW organizing. Moreover, the Western Growers Association had recently lawyered up, hiring an eleven-attorney staff to serve grower-shippers who wanted to continue to fight the UFW.

Eliseo Medina was on the same side of the issue as Ganz, for different reasons. He was not primarily concerned about the legal department. One reason the *limonero* struggle had been so exciting was that the workers had not needed lawyers to appear for them in a series of energy-sapping ALRB hearings. But Medina did care deeply about the question of paid staff:

> I felt that if the workers were ever going to actually have it be their union, they needed to take power. And all the power in the union was basically in the staff. And all the staff were volunteers who were able to work, at the time, for $10 a week and room and board. But . . . we had some lettuce workers who were making $25,000 a year, which was real money in those days. They could not afford to leave those jobs—because they had families and all that—and come to work for $10 a week for the union. And so we had this really serious contradiction: the more successful we were in driving up wages the less likely we were that the rank and file indigenous leadership within the union would rise up and take charge of the organization. So I thought the volunteer system had outlived its usefulness. Because now we didn't need volunteers. Now we needed the workers themselves to do it.[68]

Gilbert Padilla did not regard the vote as a referendum on the legal department's future, and the documentary record suggests that the general understanding was that the department would be rebuked and trimmed, not fired.[69] Nevertheless, just before the vote, Chavez warned that although he wanted to keep Jerry Cohen, if the board adopted his proposal against the raises and for volunteerism, there was a chance that Jerry and the legal department might leave the union. Despite the warning, the board voted five to four for Chavez's proposal. The younger members were all on the losing side.

"It took my breath away," Ganz recalled. "I couldn't understand what in the world he [Chavez] was thinking. We seemed to be scuttling our capacity to fight. Cesar also seemed to be either getting rid of Jerry, or else determined to publicly emasculate him."[70]

Kings emasculating princes is as old as politics, even older than the Old Testament. Chronus, the Greeks' first lord of the universe, didn't stop at emasculation. He devoured his children to remove them as potential threats. Although Cohen was no competitor for the throne, he was a former much-beloved protégé now openly challenging his onetime mentor. Cesar, uneasy on his throne, struck Jerry down. It was all too reminiscent, Chavez told Chris Hartmire, of what had happened to him in CSO, when he was pushed out of his own organization.[71]

After the vote, Cesar summoned Jerry to La Paz. They took a long walk. According to Cohen, Chavez insisted that the legal department either come to La Paz and work as volunteers or leave the UFW. It was exactly as Ganz had feared. But Chavez's demand was not a direct consequence of the vote by the board, which had affirmed its desire to "keep costs as they are" and to "do everything possible to keep Jerry from leaving." Chavez had added the demand that Cohen come to La Paz. He offered to continue to pay Cohen a salary to train a new group of lawyers, but only if he moved back to union headquarters. Cohen refused, and convinced Chavez to close down the department in sections over the period of a year, so that the union would not be left defenseless. It was a sad, frank, wide-ranging discussion, with Chavez at one point saying: "I'm building an army of true believers, Jerry. What's wrong with that?"

"It depends on what you use them for," Cohen answered.[72]

Cohen cried on the way back to Salinas. At a meeting that night that he had called to tell people the news, the other lawyers were astounded. They had suspected that their request would be rejected, or that the department would be trimmed, but they were not prepared for this. Layoffs proceeded according to a schedule. Marco Lopez accepted Chavez's offer and moved to La Paz, where he became, for a short while, the new general counsel. A department of five people, making the same money they had been making before or a little bit more, remained in Salinas, chagrined and demoralized but not completely defeated. After the immediate crisis subsided, they had some hope that perhaps this lean legal department would be allowed to continue intact. That hope was dashed in a series of meetings between Sandy Nathan, Jerry Cohen, and Chavez, and the remaining lawyers either left immediately or stayed on until June of 1979. Tom Dalzell lasted until January 1980. Jerry Cohen continued as a negotiator, making the same salary he had before, until he resigned in June of 1981. His fears had been well founded. In this game of palace politics, he had overplayed his hand.

After the formal vote to retain the volunteer system, Eliseo Medina took a leave of absence. For some time he had felt out of place in the UFW, a minority voice whose vision for the union was consistently different from that of most of the other leaders, especially Cesar Chavez. After the 1975 ALRB elections, he had argued that the union was not putting enough resources into the field offices and the ranch committees. Later he had maintained that the union didn't have enough qualified staff to administer their new contracts adequately. It was all to no avail. On the question of whether the UFW should be a movement or a union, Medina was unequivocally on the side of union. He felt that the UFW was not doing nearly enough "to institutionalize its gains," that is, solidify and regularize its power on unionized ranches.

The experience with the *limoneros* in Oxnard and its aftermath had been exhilarating, but Chavez's response had been disappointing. In a meeting shortly after the Oxnard victories, Chavez ridiculed Medina's new statewide organizing plan. It was much too expensive, Cesar said, and irresponsible. According to Jessica Govea and Jerry Cohen, Medina was visibly shaken by the virulence of Chavez's response, and left the room before the meeting was over.

Medina submitted his formal resignation in August 1978, a month after asking Chavez for the leave. Chavez didn't try to dissuade him. He wished him luck and let him go. Medina did not languish. He went on to a successful career in organized labor, becoming an international vice president of the Service Employees International Union (SEIU) and one of the highest Chicano union officials in the United States.[73] He maintained an official silence about what had happened in the union for the next twenty-seven years.

Medina's resignation was another devastating blow for Ganz and Govea. The staff had considered Medina Chavez's heir apparent. He had come out of the fields, his family had been among the original grape strikers, he had served the union admirably in various capacities. He was smart, charming, dedicated, persuasive, and good-looking. Medina never believed that Chavez was wary of him, fearful that he might pose a threat, but now that Chavez had accepted his resignation—apparently without regret—it was a moot point. Those who might challenge

Chavez for leadership of the union no longer had the most obvious candidate to rally around.

In the fields, Medina's resignation hardly registered. "We didn't even notice it," Mario Bustamante recalled—"not that anybody bothered to tell us."

28

Imperial Strike

August '78 to March '79

In retrospect, Marshall Ganz believed that the union and the companies "stumbled into the strike" of 1979. The way Ganz saw it, the California vegetable growers believed that the union's tardiness in submitting its contract proposal, and its wide publication of its initial demands, were not mistakes but rather signs that the UFW was not much interested in compromise. The growers, in Ganz's view, didn't help matters by insisting, inaccurately, that President Carter's wage guidelines legally prohibited them from offering any more than a 7 percent raise per year. Thus, each side read intransigence in the other, and the lateness of the hour didn't give them time to feel each other out, maneuver at the table, and discover a set of acceptable trade-offs.[1]

Perhaps. But compromise would have required the negotiators to bridge the gulf between the growers' desire to keep costs down and to take back control of production, and the workers' hope that they had the power both to change their place in society and to maintain their control of the fields. The negotiators also would have had to figure out how to defuse the contending parties' explosive mix of skepticism, anger, anxiety, hope, and disappointment. The union officials and the growers were chronically suspicious of each other's motives. The workers combined the righteous anger of the long-exploited with the fervent hope that their situation in the world was about to change. The growers were not only anxious about their survival, but resentful of the workers' increased autonomy on the job. Maybe it all could have been worked out, but it is not surprising that it ended in war.

War is what many of the principals called it from the time it began, in January of 1979, until the end, in September. The examples are many. Andy Church, the companies' chief negotiator: "If we are pushed on it, we will have a war." Marshall Ganz: "It looks like it is going to be a war." Ronald Kemp, the new labor relations man at Sun Harvest (formerly InterHarvest): "I feel like I am running a war and a business." Chava Bustamante: "It was, like—well, I have never been in a war, but it was like a war." Louis Curiel, an Imperial Valley supervisor: "There's people who are getting armed. This thing is going to be mounting to a war." And Hermilo Mojica: "We had three different groups to take scabs out of the fields. It was like three different companies in a war."[2]

What they meant was a shooting war, not a metaphorical or class war. For in the midst of the strike, certain kinds of violence became legitimate for many of the protagonists, and people who had the guns and were willing to use them had a tactical advantage.

Back on December 31, 1978, before the war began, as the union and twenty-eight vegetable companies were awaiting the expiration of their contracts, it is true that none of the forces involved were anticipating what would unfold. In 1978 the growers knew more or less what had been happening in La Paz. Word had filtered through to them about the vote against a professional staff, the Synanon Game, and the resignations of most of the UFW lawyers. They also were aware of (and some were promoting) the workers' displeasure over the mandatory political contribution and their issues with the RFK Medical Plan. The growers concluded that the UFW was not only in disarray and inept at the top but also losing strength at the bottom and couldn't sustain a long strike. They didn't hope to break the UFW, but they wanted to reform it, force it to become more malleable, conventional, cooperative. They believed they could win a strike and thereby eliminate the hiring hall, get their crews under control, narrow the labor cost differential between themselves and the nonunion companies, discipline the union, shake up its leadership, and shape its future direction. At Sun Harvest, the latest incarnation of United Fruit's operation in California, Ronald Kemp, a veteran of half a dozen Central American strikes, put the last point diplomatically: "Sometimes a protracted strike resolidifies and strengthens both the company and the union, reestablishing more appropriate relationships by better identifying the meaningful leadership in the union."[3]

For their part, the active vegetable workers were fairly optimistic about the union's, and their, prospects. By the summer of 1978 the UFW's increased emphasis on signing contracts was paying off. More negotiating teams had made good on previous election victories, and although no new organizing was going on, there were more contracts. One internal union document listed forty-seven in Salinas and Watsonville by the end of 1978, as well as twenty-four in the Imperial Valley, covering altogether slightly more than 19,000 vegetable workers, almost two-thirds of the union's total membership. This was more than twice the number of members that Ganz estimated the union had in the vegetables just a year and a half earlier. The union's annual report to the Labor Department confirmed the spike in membership, listing dues revenues of almost $2 million in the last half of 1978 and the first half of 1979.[4]

Workers may have been in the dark about what was happening up on the mountain, in La Paz, but they saw the increased union presence down in the valley in the clear light of day. Although still less than 50 percent of the vegetable industry was unionized, the union had contracts at two of the three biggest companies, and confronted no apparent obstacle to organizing many of the remaining nonunion ranches. The workers were not the only ones to notice. In June 1978, Tim Linden, *The Packer*'s main reporter covering the vegetable industry, wrote in an opinion piece, "The union is here to stay and must be dealt with as such." He argued that "most people [growers] in California would agree that they would be much better off if they would have accepted unionization ten years ago," and concluded that it would be cheaper for growers to settle with the UFW now rather than later.[5]

In La Paz, Chavez looked ahead to the looming contract expirations by convening a one-day meeting in late August of 143 ranch committee members from the companies facing contract expiration. The union had an opportunity to negotiate a master contract for the vegetable industry, Chavez told the delegates. Always willing to have worker participation in contract negotiations, Chavez had the workers break into small groups and discuss problems with their current contracts, report back to the general session, and elect a ten-member industrywide negotiating committee, and five alternates. Chava Bustamante was one the ten negotiators; his friend Aristeo Zambrano was an alternate. Following the conference, Chava told his brother Mario that there might be a strike in the vegetables, starting in the Imperial Valley.[6]

Chava's guess reflected the enthusiasm of the delegates, not the wishes of the union leadership. Chavez hoped that a master contract could be negotiated without a strike. On September 10, two weeks after the formation of the workers' negotiating team, Chavez told his brother Richard, Dolores Huerta, Oscar Mondragon, Frank Ortiz, Larry Tramutt, and a few others that the UFW's negotiating plan could be called "*el plan de flote,*" because the union wouldn't swim forward; it would float in place, content to win "more money, more benefits, more dues." The group set a formal goal: "Negotiate the vegetable contract by January 1, 1979."[7]

But it was late—mid-November—by the time Chavez asked Ganz to handle the vegetable negotiations. The two had had a rough patch over the previous few months, during which Ganz and Govea had first tendered their resignations, then withdrawn them once Chavez agreed that they could live outside La Paz. Ganz refused to head up the negotiating team, but he agreed to help develop the union's demands by doing an economic study of the vegetable industry.

What he discovered surprised him. Although the growers' gross receipts and profits were at all-time highs, much of the UFW wage gains had been eaten up by the runaway inflation of the mid-1970s. Vegetable workers who were making $3.70 an hour had gained only 13 percent in real purchasing power since the first InterHarvest contract in 1970. Even the raises of the elite piece-rate *lechugueros*, who averaged about $11.60 an hour in 1978, had failed to match the Labor Department's estimate of a 71 percent rise in the cost of living between 1970 and 1978.[8]

When Ganz compared the UFW contract with others in the vegetable industry, the results were more startling. Hourly workers in the coolers earned a minimum of $8 an hour; piece-rate workers in the coolers made from $15 to $40 an hour, depending on classification. Teamster trucker-stitchers, who made the boxes in the fields and drove the produce from the sheds to the coolers, had a minimum base rate of $7.10 an hour, plus incentive pay that could raise their wages to $12 to $15 an hour. These workers also got large contributions to their medical and pension plans. The UFW had fought its way into the industry, but farm workers still made significantly less than other, mostly white, unionized workers who handled the food after it left the fields.[9]

Ganz presented the numbers to Chavez, who was also surprised, and authorized Ganz to take them out to the workers to use in formulating the negotiating demands. The two men made no decision on what to do after that. Without realizing it, Ganz and Chavez were taking the first steps toward a strike.

Time was tight. The contract was due to expire in a little more than a month. Ganz, working with the rank-and-file negotiating committee, held a series of meetings. When they saw the figures, the workers were not so surprised. "Oh," Ganz recalled one worker saying, "I wondered why I was making more money and feeling all the poorer."[10]

Out of these meetings came the UFW's contract proposal: $5.25 an hour as the basic wage, with comparable or even higher raises throughout all job classifications, including piece work; a one-year contract; a quarterly cost-of-living adjustment; expanded overtime and travel pay; bonuses for working in bad conditions; and substantial raises in grower contributions to medical, pension, and service center funds. Ganz estimated that the total package represented a jump of about 70 percent in grower labor costs; when the growers saw it, they calculated that it would raise the price of their labor nearly 200 percent.

The proposal did not give ground on the hiring hall, as the union had already done in some of its grape contracts. When the subject came up in Ganz's meetings, the vegetable workers adamantly refused to make that concession. They argued that if the right to hire was returned to the foremen, the crews would slowly lose much of their power over the pace and conditions of work.

The proposed contract contained one particularly remarkable demand. The employers would pay one or two workers at each company to work full-time to administer the union contract in the fields. This idea, modeled on UAW committeemen, had been promoted in the Executive Board by Ganz and originally had been opposed by Chavez, but he changed his position and endorsed it after he won the vote on the volunteer system.[11] Ganz believed that Chavez, having won the main fight, had meant to give the opposition a consolation prize. Jerry Cohen believed that Chavez supported the idea of what came to be called "the paid reps" only because he thought the growers would never grant it. The workers enthusiastically embraced the proposal, and with Chavez's blessing it was included in the union's opening package.

Ostensibly the union's proposal was about money, well within the tradition of U.S. labor relations. But Ganz's comparison of the UFW contract with other grower contracts, covering workers with some of the highest wages in the U.S. working class, gave another dimension to the farm workers' demands. If the UFW could win what it was asking, farm workers would no longer be the poor cousins of other unionized U.S. workers. They would be poised to take their place at the top of the labor pyramid among auto, steel, transportation, and skilled construction workers.

The farm workers understood it exactly that way: if they could get these wages and benefits, their social and economic position in the United States and Mexico would fundamentally change. They could afford to work seasonally and collect unemployment, rather than follow the crops. Many could buy homes in the United States, and rebuild their homes in Mexico. Their children wouldn't have to leave school to go to work to help with the bills. They could retire without going hungry or being a burden on their children. One unnamed striker told Doug Foster of the *Salinas Californian*, "We want the kind of economic wages and benefits so that our children aren't ashamed to say, 'My papa, my mama, are farm workers.' "[12]

While Ganz and Chavez prepared for the negotiations they were getting along better than they had for a long time. They spoke almost every day. They still did not have a worked-out strike plan, but they now understood that a strike might well be on the way. At each company Ganz organized strike authorization votes that were either unanimous or nearly so. The workers also authorized their ranch committee to name a strike coordinator. Ganz had carefully constructed the strike organization:

> We came up with a kind of military structure. The ranch committee remained the civil government. But the ranch committee would appoint [the coordinators]. . . . [Then] people would adopt the *reglas de huelga*, the strike rules. Once the strike coordinator was named, then everybody would follow orders. So we had a military organization made legitimate by civilian rule. And the strike coordinator would name his crew coordinators and so we had this cadre organization ready to operate.[13]

Strike preparations were going full bore among the workers by late December. Every ranch committee also appointed a representative to a welfare committee, which was organized and led by Jessica Govea; once the strike started she would also be responsible for distributing the $25 weekly strike benefits to regular picketers, as well as gas reimbursements and other money that came from La Paz. The committee members, mostly women, were veterans of earlier strikes. They made up a list of food items and sent it to the Migrant Ministry and other groups. Chris Hartmire raised most of the money to buy the tons of beans, rice, flour, bread, canned vegetables, and evaporated milk that would be distributed each week to as many as 3,000 striking families. Small teams from the welfare committee went to landlords, furniture stores, car dealers, and phone and utility services to inform them that a strike was imminent and that people would have trouble paying their bills. In a surprisingly large number or cases, they were able to negotiate a delay in payments. The workers would not be starved into submission.[14]

Chava Bustamante was certain that there would be a strike and that Cal Coastal, which had fields in the Imperial, San Joaquin, and Salinas valleys, would be one of the first companies to go out. Figuring that he would be spending considerable time in negotiations, Chava had convinced his brother Mario to come work at Coastal to keep the strikers well organized. Mario made his way onto a crew during the short fall season in Huron, where lettuce dispatches were relatively easy to get. He convinced some other militant *lechugueros* to join him: "I told people Cal Coastal was going to be on strike, and it was going to be hard, and it would require a lot of sacrifice. The people who didn't want to commit to that went other places, and the people who wanted to fight came on."[15] Hermilo Mojica was one of the people Mario recruited. When the Cal Coastal workers voted unanimously to authorize the strike, Mario was named strike coordinator. He appointed Mojica picket captain.

Meanwhile the growers were also organizing. Fierce competitors in ordinary times, they quickly agreed to negotiate as a team, hoping that a master contract would reflect their collective strength rather than the vulnerability of any particular company. But unity would be hard to maintain for long. The twenty-eight vegetable firms under UFW contract were a collection of grower-shippers of various sizes; there were growers who owned their own land, those who leased it, harvesting companies, harvesting co-ops, giant conglomerates, companies that operated only in Salinas, only in the Imperial Valley, and many in both places. Some were only in lettuce; some only in tomatoes. Some harvested lettuce in the Imperial Valley and broccoli and cauliflower in Salinas. It was a heterogeneous coalition in a highly differentiated, complex industry.

The biggest difference was between Sun Harvest, the second largest lettuce grower in the United States, and everybody else. In 1978 the company contributed only 2 percent to the $2.5 billion gross of its transnational parent, United Brands. That brute fact meant that its corporate masters might sacrifice sensible business practices at Sun Harvest in order to protect their bigger stakes elsewhere—namely, Chiquita bananas, which made up 20 to 30 percent of their income.[16] And if Sun Harvest were to repeat the performance of InterHarvest in 1970 and accept what the rest of the industry considered a bad deal, the workers would put great pressure on every other company to match it.

The top officials of Sun Harvest assured their uneasy fellow growers that 1979 would not be a redo of 1970. When Eli Black killed himself in 1975, he also killed his dream of a liberal, publicly popular United Fruit Company, where the man at the top could worship alongside Cesar Chavez. The new executive leadership had changed the company's name and brought in Carl Sam Maggio, a veteran California agribusinessman, to put the farming operation in order. They hired Ronald Kemp, who had spent most of his working life on Central American and Hawaiian banana and sugar plantations, to represent Sun Harvest in the negotiations. He would take command once the strike started. This was his seventh strike, but his first on mainland U.S. soil. He didn't intend to settle for anything but a sound, livable union contract. "We are a different company now," he told the reporter Doug Foster. "We are pragmatic businessmen."[17]

Ganz's figures were right. The vegetable industry was thriving, but nonunion companies generally were making more than the ones with union contracts. Going into negotiations, the growers were determined to close the gap by taking back control of production. Paul Fleming, the president of Admiral Packing, a midsize grower-shipper, expressed the sentiments of most of his fellow growers: "We are going to get a contract that is going to allow us to run our businesses the way we feel they should be run. Our company has experienced a complete collapse of quality control. In order to survive we are going to have to be able to determine how our crops are packed."[18]

On January 19, 1979, one day after the growers submitted their three-year, 7-percent-a-year contract proposal, about 1,700 workers went on strike, shutting down four companies: Sun Harvest, Cal Coastal, Vessey & Co., and Mario Saikhon. The twenty-eight growers would do what they could to stay united; the UFW meant to disunite them by forcing one company to capitulate, and then pressuring the others to follow.

The Imperial Valley lettuce harvest, involving some 8,000 *lechugueros*, was about half over before the strike began. It had been a good season so far. In mid-January a box of lettuce, which cost about $3.50 to produce, was selling for around $7. Collectively, the growers were making more than $1 million on the 350,000-plus cartons of lettuce they shipped out of the valley every day.

In the first week of the strike, no lettuce was cut at any of the struck fields. No union members worked, and despite job advertisements in Mexicali newspapers and the recruiting efforts of labor contractors and foremen, the growers were unable to get any strikebreakers. Jon Vessey, the smallest of the struck growers, whose operation was exclusively in Imperial, told the press that he had $300,000 worth of lettuce rotting in the fields.[19]

More than 1,000 strikers were on the picket lines, most of them spread out over the thirty-two mile-long, twenty-six-mile-wide Imperial Valley, while three separate caravans of about twenty cars each—guerrilla pickets, as they were known in the California strikes of the 1930s—drove the rural roads of the vast battleground looking for scabs.

Mario Bustamante was the leader of the caravan operation, and Hermilo Mojica was the captain of one of the three convoys. They and about twenty other strike leaders met with Marshall Ganz every afternoon to give reports on what had happened during the day, discuss strategy and tactics, and plan for the next day. During the first three weeks, the union promoted one-day walkouts at some of the ranches that weren't being struck but where UFW members were working without a contract. Ganz would pick the companies the day before; the car caravans would converge on the ranches the next morning and Bustamante and Mojica, leaving their compatriots at the side of the fields, would walk up to the crews and ask them to join the strike for the day. It worked every time, with no need for long explanations or coercion. The *lechugueros* sheathed their knives and walked out of the fields, to cheers from the waiting strikers.[20]

In the first week, workers at five more companies officially walked out, pushing up the number of strikers to more than 3,000. The struck growers decided to put together small harvesting crews made up of foremen, company supervisors, relatives, friends, and high school students, almost all Anglos. Ron Hull, general manager of the Imperial Valley Growers Association, acknowledged that such people couldn't cut much lettuce, but he hoped their example would encourage some skilled *lechugueros* to return to work: "These past few days were very encouraging. You know they [the strike breakers] didn't get rushed or chased out of the fields. Hopefully if that occurs, word will get around to the workers, and some of them will come back."[21]

Not chasing out these makeshift crews was a matter of strike policy. Best to leave them alone, the strike leaders thought, or ridicule them from the edge of the fields as they ineptly tried to wield harvest knives. The strikers called them circus performers, clowns.

On Monday, January 29, ten days into the strike, official policy broke down. The circus clowns were working in a Vessey field near Holtville, and some 700 strikers were at the edge of the fields exchanging taunts with the pickers and security guards. Many of the insults were nasty and racial. The guards carried shotguns, and some held leashed Dobermans, but they were badly outnumbered by the strikers—scores versus hundreds. One group of strikers entered the field, turned over an unguarded stitcher, and set it on fire. When the sheriffs arrested one of the intruders, a dozen strikers freed him from his captors. That touched off a general melee. The sheriffs called in a helicopter, which flew so low that it knocked one of the strikers over, breaking his leg. Two more men were arrested and freed, one running off among his comrades with his wrists still handcuffed behind his back. Retreating to a hillside, Mojica saw clumps of sheriffs, guards, and strikers in hand-to-hand combat.

The guards and sheriffs tried to lead the frightened harvesters and the small amount of lettuce they had cut out of the fields through a side road, but about 500 strikers blocked the way. The sheriffs decided to form a convoy and force their way through. A lead car crashed through the line, knocking over one of the strikers, but the buses and other cars did not follow. The guards, also scared, formed a phalanx in front of the convoy and slowly advanced.

The strikers threw rocks. Some of the guards fired their shotguns while others used their dogs to clear the way. The sheriffs wielded their batons. More strikers were knocked down. The grower caravan of some thirty buses, trucks, and cars fought its way through. The strikers broke windows as the vehicles passed. The caravan made its way to Mario Saikhon's ranch office, where paramedics dealt with what an ambulance attendant dismissed as "goose eggs and lacerations." The strikers took two of their comrades to a hospital, the one hit by the helicopter, the other beaten as the caravan broke through the human barricade.[22]

Ganz, who arrived at the end of the battle, was angry and disappointed. He felt that only the growers benefited from the confrontation. The sheriff, Oren Fox, a liberal by Imperial Valley standards who had recently been elected with some Mexican American support, was alarmed. This was the first serious violence in the strike, and he was worried that it would get worse. He blamed the incident on the strikers, but he was not happy with the behavior of the security guards, either. One of his sergeants told a *Los Angeles Times* reporter that the guards "were thugs and criminals, who had somehow gotten licenses to carry guns." A Saikhon guard told the reporter he regretted not having been at the fight: "I sure wish I had been. I would have liked to have shot me one."[23] With help from neighboring counties, Sheriff Fox upped his strike force from thirty-five to eighty men.

Jon Vessey had been in the midst of the battle and he was outraged. Later that same day he went to a court hearing where Marshall Ganz was testifying about a contested strike injunction. While Ganz was answering questions on the stand, Vessey shouted from the audience, "Did you orchestrate the violence today?"[24] The judge expelled him from the court-room, but he couldn't expel the anger. Small growers like Vessey were losing hundreds of thousands of dollars they couldn't afford to lose. Men accustomed to command confronted a world beyond their control. Upset with their inability to manage their crews before the strike and now unable to save their spoiling crops, their anger turned to rage. After the fight in the Vessey field, one unidentified grower told the *Salinas Californian*, "We are packing guns. It looks like some people are going to get blown away. I just hope if it happens it's Mexicans that get it."*

Two days after the fight, the growers once again put their make-shift strikebreaking crew to work in what they called Volunteer Harvest Day. At a preparatory rally, Alice Colace, the wife of the struck grower Joe Colace, had declared that it was important to "spread the word" to potential harvesters: "We'll have to tell the friends we play bridge with, the friends we play tennis with."[25] About 300 of the growers' friends and family members, supervisors and foremen, made a show of cutting lettuce for fifteen camera crews and several reporters. The UFW sent only seventy-five pickets to stand quietly and watch the performance, but called eight more companies out on a one-day strike. The contrast was not lost on the protagonists. The volunteer harvesters could barely manage to cut and pack the lettuce. One, standing in the wrong place at the wrong time, was bombarded by heads of lettuce that spilled off a conveyor belt. Meanwhile, away from the cameras, the one-day walkout idled more than half the valley's fields and cost a new group of growers several hundred thousand dollars.[26]

Cesar Chavez made his first strike appearance immediately after Volunteer Harvest Day. In daily contact with Ganz, buoyed by the progress of the strike, he gave one of the more spirited speeches of his career to 3,000 enthusiastic farm workers. This was a dream strike, he said, because "there are no scabs and the people are totally organized." He praised the workers for conducting the strike themselves with minimal help from the staff. He defended the UFW's contract proposal and said that with enough sacrifice and struggle they would win. "You have three jobs," he told the cheering crowd, "strike, strike, strike." His job was different, he explained. "My job is in the cities . . . among large churches, labor unions, and student groups . . . to bring food and money in here, medical aid, all the things

---

* This is the quote as it appeared in reporter Doug Foster's notes and in the Gannett-owned *Nevada State Journal* on February 2, 1979. Foster's editors at the *Salinas Californian*, also owned by Gannett, cut the last line about hoping Mexicans would be the ones killed. As the UFW asserted at the time and as the local newspapers were keen to hide, the confrontations between the circus and the strikers inflamed the racial antagonisms already inherent in the overall battle between mostly Anglo bosses and the predominately Mexican farm workers.

people need." Not usually fond of speechifying, he got caught up in the excitement of the moment and provoked a great roar from the crowd by saying, "I feel the way I never felt before. We have thirty years of struggle behind us, but I am spirited and encouraged. I feel I can fight for another hundred years."[27]

The price of lettuce spiked. Nine companies were now on strike. Very soon that number would rise to eleven. Coupled with the one-day walkouts at un-struck companies, on any given day more than half the 8,000 *lechugueros* in the Imperial Valley were on strike. The consequent fall in production, the highly publicized battle in the Vessey field, and a light rain, which sped up the deterioration of the uncut lettuce, pushed the price the growers received to $12 a box on Volunteer Harvest Day. By Friday, February 2, the day after Chavez's speech, lettuce was selling for $14 a box.[28]

A lot of green gold was going to waste. According to a grower spokesman, Fred Karger, $2 million worth of lettuce had already rotted in the fields. With the price at $14, growers could make a clear profit of more than $10 a box if they could get their lettuce cut and packed. That was no problem for the companies (both union and nonunion) not being struck; they could still turn out more than 200,000 boxes a day. But the multi-million-dollar harvest of the nonstruck growers made it all the worse for the struck ones. Not only were they losing the opportunity of bonanza profits; they also had to watch as their competitors had the harvest of a lifetime.

Mario Saikhon was not willing to sit back and watch. He was one of the largest growers exclusively in the Imperial Valley. In his twenty-five years of farming he had become a rich man. Not that he had started out poor. His father, one of the approximately 5,000 Punjabis who came to California in the early twentieth century, had begun farming in the Imperial Valley in 1910. Unable to buy land because of the California Alien Land Law, he and a Punjabi partner leased it. Unable to bring a bride from India because of the U.S. immigration laws, he married a Mexican farm hand. Mario was one of their three children. After his father died of a heart attack in 1942, his mother remarried, to another Punjabi. Mario's stepfather got his big break when he used an Armenian American front man to buy up some Fresno vineyards at a bargain price in what the official family history describes as a "distress sale by a Japanese family leaving for [the Japanese internment camp at] Manzanar."[29] With the money they made from those vineyards, the Saikhons returned to the Imperial Valley in 1949 and prospered, benefiting greatly over the next sixteen years from the low wages paid for bracero labor.[30]

But it was not easy for Mario Saikhon. A Punjabi–Mexican, he had been treated roughly in high school, and then had become a bit of an outcast among the Anglo farmers, whom he enjoyed beating in business. Although he spoke fluent Spanish, he was known among farm workers as a particularly tough and aloof employer. He was determined to win the strike, and put up most of the $500,000 that the growers spent to hire a PR firm, the Dolphin Group, which published a series of anti-UFW, anti-Chavez ads in major California newspapers during the strike. The other struck growers, Saikhon told Doug Foster, "were afraid to do what was necessary to win the strike."[31]

He wasn't. On Sunday, February 3, Saikhon put the first skilled scabs to work: a hundred mostly Filipino farm workers whom he had brought in from the San Joaquin Valley. The alert strikers rushed into the fields to confront them, but just as quickly turned back, as the strike breakers were guarded by a large number of sheriff deputies and Saikhon guards. Others followed Saikhon's lead. Sun Harvest's Kemp brought in strikebreakers from Arizona, Texas, and the San Joaquin. Although negotiations between the UFW and the growers resumed on February 6, the talks were without substance, as the negotiators waited to see what would happen in the fields.

In the excitement of the fight, more workers left their jobs, sometimes at the urging of the union and sometimes without. Even a few Bud Antle crews left the fields, although their Teamster contract had not expired. At Bruce Church, the third-biggest lettuce grower in California, which was not yet being struck, the union called a series of off-and-on walkouts that severely limited production. A sheriff's spokesman said that the strike is "running us crazy," and the next day Sheriff Fox said that it was approaching the point of an "industry general strike," in fact if not in name.[32]

The more than 1,500 active regular picketers badly outnumbered the 300 strikebreakers, 80 sheriffs, 35 policemen, and about 100 private guards. Increasingly around the valley where strikebreakers were poorly protected and the picketers had overwhelming numbers, the strikers would rush into the fields to coerce the scabs into stopping work. The strikers rarely attacked the scabs; their numbers were intimidation enough. Mario Saikhon, who witnessed one of these charges into his fields, told Foster, "They went in there to storm the field to get people out. They didn't hurt anybody. My opinion is that they weren't trying to hurt anybody, they just wanted to get people out of the fields."[33]

The strike coordinators and Ganz also initiated what they called "*la huelga tecolote*," the owl strike, in which picketers massed on the road next to the Saikhon camp at night and made as much noise as they could to prevent the strikebreakers from sleeping. Judging from the shouts from inside the barracks, this seriously annoyed the scabs, and early Friday morning, February 9, someone inside the camp fired several shots into the air.

Later that day the strike escalated. At Bruce Church the workers declared themselves officially on strike. At Admiral the workers voted to strike but went into the fields the next morning and started cutting lettuce. When hundreds of picketers entered the fields, as planned, the crews announced they were on strike and walked off in celebration. Rows of cut lettuce were left unpacked, never to reach market. The growers were overwhelmed; the strikers had the initiative.

Early the next morning, Saturday, February 10, the sheriffs detained several strike captains, then massed in front of a Sun Harvest field to protect 125 strikebreakers from the 500 strikers who had followed the large, heavily guarded Sun Harvest convoy. At midmorning the strikers rushed the fields, broke some windows, and flattened some tires. The sheriffs repelled them with tear gas, the first time gas was used in the strike.

Fifteen miles away, three predominantly Filipino crews—two working for Saikhon, one for Vessey—were harvesting a struck lettuce field, while about a hundred strikers watched. Neither private guards nor sheriffs protected the scabs. Forty to sixty men ran into the fields, some of them carrying sticks, shouting, *"Huelga, huelga, huelga!"* In the front, unarmed, was twenty-eight-year-old Rufino Contreras; trotting behind him was his brother Fortunato; back on the picket line was their father, Lorenzo. Between the three of them, they had worked together for more than twenty years in the lettuce fields of Mario Saikhon. When the shouting, running men were within thirty yards of the scab crews, shooting came from three different directions. Rufino was hit below the right eye with a .38 caliber bullet; he gave a quick cry, and fell facedown into the lettuce. The other men hit the ground as the firing continued. Some tried to reach Rufino. Others ran away. The blood of Rufino Contreras, father of two, spilled red onto an uncut head of green gold.

The sheriffs arrived about a half hour later. After talking to several witnesses, they arrested three men: Froilan Perez Mendoza, a Saikhon truck driver who had been trying to recruit scabs in Mexicali and whose Mexicali home had been slightly damaged by a fire bomb eight days earlier; Alfredo Barriga, a longtime Saikhon foreman; and Anthony Andreas San Diego, the Filipino contractor who had brought the strikebreakers to the Imperial Valley and who two days before had come into the fields with a pistol tucked in his waistband. The deputies took the three men to jail, where they were booked on suspicion of murder. Less than two hours later Mario Saikhon bailed them out at a cost of $7,000 each for Barriga and Perez and $8,100 for San Diego, who was on probation for a previous conviction of assault with a deadly weapon. A week later, a striker charged with throwing a rock at a bus had his bail set at $10,000.[34]

As the news of Rufino Contreras's death spread, workers congregated in front of the union office in Calexico and at *el hoyo*. Hundreds had gathered by late afternoon, and a couple of thousand by nightfall. Some stood in front of a homemade shrine to the new martyr. It was an impressive sight, with a picture of Rufino surrounded by candles and thousands of flowers. Above the makeshift altar was a large banner, perhaps five feet long, whose careful lettering situated Contreras's assassination in the long sweep of Mexican and California farm worker history: "*Rufino Contreras murió por los ideales de Flores Magón*"—Rufino Contreras died for the ideals of Flores Magón.[35]

Angry, shocked, the assembled workers exchanged rumors, asked questions. Why had the sheriffs started the day by rounding up the picket captains? Why weren't there any cops or guards at the Saikhon field? Was it true that the assassins had already been bailed out of jail? Chava Bustamante recalled that he "felt a combination of the most incredible rage and impotence. . . . I didn't mind the fights, and some of us getting hurt by the dogs or the cops. I figured that was part of the deal. But Rufino was murdered in cold blood in front of eyewitnesses, and the killers were already back on the street. Oh, how the odds were stacked against us."[36]

Most workers immediately concluded that the pickets had been lured into the fields where men with guns were waiting for them. The evidence that emerged over the next several days cemented their belief that the killing had been a plot, a premeditated murder.

There was no lack of motive. The struck growers were losing money; shooting a striker as he ran into the fields was a way to regain the initiative.

The shots had come from three directions simultaneously, suggesting prior planning. During their investigation, the sheriffs confiscated three guns that they believed were used in the shooting. One of them was found in Mario Saikhon's office safe.[37]

No one was protecting the scabs that morning. Saikhon explained that ever since a court order had forbidden his guards from carrying arms, they weren't doing him any good, so he didn't have them there.[38]

The sheriff's deputies weren't on guard because he didn't know strike-breakers would be working there that day, Sheriff Fox told the *Imperial Valley Press*. Every afternoon since the strike had begun the growers met to plan what they were going to do the next day; then they called Fox and let him know where the work was going to be done so that he could provide protection. According to Fox, the day before Contreras was killed, Saikhon had not told him that any scab work would be done at that site.[39] Saikhon, who died in 1993, never denied the sheriff's story.

Mario Bustamante, Mojica, and others believed that the sheriffs were part of the plot. According to Bustamante, the deputies knew that the strike captains were careful before they allowed people to rush the fields. Some strikers always wanted to do it, but the captains wouldn't always let them. By removing the captains from the picket lines, supposedly so that they could join lawmen in a "conference" on the strike, the deputies made it more likely that the strikers would fall into the trap.[40]

The bullet that killed Contreras was never found, and defense attorneys argued there was no way to know which of the accused, if any, had killed the striker. They added that the shooters had fired in self-defense. In the preliminary hearing, they moved to dismiss the charges. The prosecutor, District Attorney Fielding Kimball, declined to counter the defense motion. Superior Court Judge William E. Lehnhardt later told the *Washington Post*, "He [Kimball] didn't care. He didn't actually say, publicly, in front of the defense lawyers that he wanted the charges dismissed, but he let it be known. He wasn't ready to take that stance publicly. It had to be me." Two and a half months after the killing, when the strike action had moved on to Salinas, Judge Lehnhardt dismissed the murder charges. No lesser chargers were ever brought, no trial ever held, no responsibility ever determined, no one brought to justice.[41]

On the day of the murder, Cesar Chavez and Marshall Ganz had been in Los Angeles for secret discussions with a high corporate official of United Brands who had flown in from Boston. When they got the news, they drove back to Calexico. Chavez did what he could to get the complete story, and then, late that night, talked to a couple of thousand gathered farm workers. He urged them not to seek revenge but to leave justice to the courts, as more violence would just make it harder to win the strike. Responding to the workers' desire for some kind of action, he called for a one-day general strike.

The next morning thousands of farm workers attended a Mass at *el hoyo*. Chavez again urged restraint, and pleaded with people not to drink alcohol during the mourning period. He invited people to join him in a fast until the Wednesday funeral. After Mass, he held a press conference. He called the shooting "cowardly, dastardly," and said that some growers were "beasts who would stop at nothing to make money." He called for a legislative investigation of the murder and for a state law to make strikebreaking illegal. He announced that the union would stop all picketing from Monday through Wednesday, and he called on the growers to cancel work for those three days.[42]

The growers held their own press conference, where a spokesman called Contreras's death "tragic and senseless," but also said, "Cesar Chavez must be held accountable, because the tactics of orchestrated terrorism and rioting are his." The growers would suspend work on the day of the funeral, but not until then: "We call on Mr. Chavez to end the illegal mob actions and call upon him to end this strike." He urged Governor Brown to send in the National Guard. A few hours later 3,000 farm workers holding candles marched silently through the streets of Calexico.[43]

Monday morning the pickets did not return to the fields and instead went to *el hoyo* for the start of their general strike. Chavez's speech was upbeat, militant. He asked who among them was willing to make the same sacrifice that Contreras had made. Thousands said they were ready. After the rally, strikers surrounded the growers' busses and massed in the streets of Calexico, urging people not to go to work. Nearly everyone agreed. *The Packer* reported that so little lettuce was shipped that day that no price for a box of lettuce was listed, a nearly unprecedented occurrence. The *Los Angeles Times* reported that the prevailing spirit in the street that morning "bordered on joy."[44]

At an afternoon press conference, Chavez, encouraged by the complete shutdown of the valley, made a startling announcement: The strikers had a right to go into the fields nonviolently to talk to the people taking their jobs, and they would continue to do so. Not only that, he would lead them: "I swear to God, I will go into the fields peacefully, and if I have to rot in jail, I will. If the growers want to shoot at me, let them shoot at me."[45]

The next day he repeated the pledge. Chavez's promise matched the mood of the strikers. Since Contreras's slaying there had been one mass gathering after another, all attended by thousands of determined people. Murdering a striker does not necessarily stop a strike. It didn't seem to be stopping this one. Chava Bustamante was hopeful, and even Lorenzo Contreras, Rufino's father, had moved beyond despair, telling a reporter, "If he is the last one, and it brings a settlement, it may be worth it."[46]

On Wednesday, ten thousand people marched from the funeral in *el hoyo* to the cemetery three miles away, where ten priests conducted the Mass. Governor Brown was there, and he asked the mourners to "rededicate ourselves to the struggle Rufino died for and in." Chavez gave the eulogy: "The company sent hired guns to quiet Rufino Contreras, but wherever farm workers organize, wherever they stand up for their rights and strike for justice, Rufino Contreras is with them."[47]

The very next day, he said, he would march into the fields of the struck growers and talk to the strikers. "I will be out there tomorrow," he told United Press International. "We'll be in there together, expect the worst."[48] Governor Brown declined to send the National Guard, but Sheriff Owen Fox, with a force that now numbered about a hundred deputies, arranged for a hundred more to be on standby. He didn't know what to expect. Would Chavez go into the fields alone? Would he lead others? Would there be a campaign of mass civil disobedience?

None of the above. Instead, after the funeral, Cesar Chavez did what he could to cool off the strike. He returned to Los Angeles and the United Brand negotiations, announcing that a major firm had broken away from the collective talks and wanted to negotiate a separate peace. The UFW spokesman, Marc Grossman, issued a series of upbeat reports on what were revealed to be Sun Harvest negotiations. But the talks never went anywhere, and after three days they were over. Ronald Kemp explained their origin and purpose. "We had a meeting with Mr. Chavez at his request. At that meeting our sole objective was to get the conflict out of the press and the fields and back to the bargaining table. Period. That has now been accomplished."[49]

Chavez abruptly removed Marshall Ganz from leadership of the organizing effort and replaced him with Frank Ortiz, an old friend and loyalist who had been brought on to the Executive Board in the wake of the Medina and Lyons resignations.[50] The day after the funeral, Ortiz told the strike coordinators that Chavez wanted them to stop aggressive picketing. No more strike caravans, no more rushing the fields or one-day walkouts. Mario Bustamante told him to go to hell; the strike had to be intensified, not weakened.[51] Others agreed. The meeting broke up. From then on the coordinators and Ortiz met only sporadically, and when they did, they fumed at each other. The number of people on the picket lines diminished. Two days after the funeral, the growers shipped more than 300,000 boxes of lettuce out of the valley, about 100,000 more than they expected, one grower told the *Imperial Valley Press*. Within the week as many as 500 farm workers would be scabbing unmolested in the fields.

The strike coordinators were confused, angry, desperate. They didn't know why Ganz had been replaced. They didn't want to defy Chavez, and they weren't well organized enough to counter Ortiz's orders. Mario Bustamante came to a sad conclusion. "Before there had been a true fight against the bosses, but the day Ortiz arrived, that was the end of the fight. So the assassination of Rufino Contreras had achieved exactly what the growers wanted it to achieve. It had stopped the strike."[52]

What to make of this missed Gandhian moment? Why did Chavez fail to lead farm workers into the fields to talk to the strikebreakers, as he pledged to do? Why didn't he mount a massive campaign of civil disobedience, as his hero Gandhi had done so many times? The massive demonstrations leading up to the funeral had put people in a determined, hopeful frame of mind. They wanted more action, not less. Why did Chavez back down?

There are several possible answers. Chavez had always been dubious about the power of strikes. What was unusual in this strike was not Chavez's decision to shut down mass activity, but his enthusiasm for the strike before Rufino was killed. He originally endorsed the 1979 strike because the union had already won a place in the fresh vegetable industry, and he did not anticipate an all-out union-busting attempt by the growers. Perhaps it would be like the 1973 InterHarvest strike, where the company didn't even try to bring strikebreakers into the fields. Chavez had, in a sense, "stumbled" into the strike as Ganz and others claimed. But once the animated workers and the worried growers confronted each other, the logic of events took over. The strike was so successful in its early stages, the organization so solid, that Chavez departed from what he thought about the weakness of strikes, and passionately endorsed this one. Once Contreras was murdered, he reverted to form.

Nor would it have been easy to convert the Imperial Valley strike into a nonviolent campaign. This was quite different from the 1968 strike, the occasion for Chavez's first fast for nonviolence. That strike was mostly symbolic, with fewer strikers than scabs, and with violence limited to a few incidents of rock throwing and some nighttime vandalism. Here the strikers greatly outnumbered the scabs. They and their rank-and-file leaders believed they had a right to rush the fields, and although they didn't as a rule take up weapons, hundreds were willing, even eager, to physically fight the people who were taking their jobs. As Chava Bustamante put it, the fights, the dogs, and the cops were "part of the deal."

Chavez could not easily have changed that dynamic. The UFW did not train picketers in nonviolence, unlike the early civil rights organizations. Chavez was sincerely committed to nonviolence, but had not attempted to educate the farm worker membership in its techniques. Such training would have been hard to begin in the midst of a strike.

Finally, there was Contreras's murder. Chavez was shocked, hurt, overpowered by the anguish of Rufino's widow. During his 1968 fast he had said that a union victory was not worth a single death. Under different circumstances, he had shut down the 1973 strike after the deaths of Juan De La Cruz and Naji Daifullah. In the wake of this assassination, accompanying people into the fields in open trespass would have been a dangerous business—even nonviolently, even with Cesar Chavez in the lead. Did Chavez have enough authority to keep the angry strikers in line? They would probably remain nonviolent when Chavez was with them, but what about when he wasn't? Even if the workers had remained nonviolent, the growers had demonstrated that their long history of using deadly force against striking workers was not over. They weren't likely to shoot into a crowd that Chavez was leading, but Chavez couldn't be everywhere. Could the growers be restrained? The County Board of Supervisors and the county judicial system weren't going to stop them. The $7,000 bail was clear evidence that the growers might indeed get away with murder. On both sides people were enraged. Maybe the Gandhian option would force one of the growers to sign, maybe not. Chavez didn't want to gamble on it.

Most likely, Chavez's pledge to lead people into the fields was primarily rhetorical flourish. There is no evidence that there was any preparation for such a campaign. Few people even remember that Chavez made that promise. Probably, leading people into the fields nonviolently is something Chavez wished he could have done. But he didn't, and the Gandhian moment passed.

Cesar Chavez not only walked away from the Gandhian moment, he walked away from the strike itself. He removed Marshall Ganz and replaced him with Frank Ortiz, who ran the strike into the ground. Ganz was aghast. He hated to see the strike go downhill so fast. He was also dismayed when he heard, indirectly, that Ortiz and others were blaming him for Contreras's murder. David Martinez, the other new member of the Executive Board, quietly spread the word, telling people that Ganz had convinced the workers to go into the fields against their better judgment, despite Chavez's explicit orders to the contrary. Jessica Govea and Gilbert Padilla said that they heard Chavez himself suggest that Ganz was partly responsible for Contreras's death.[53]

The rumors had little basis in fact, and less moral validity. The people responsible for Contreras's death were the ones who pulled the triggers, and those who encouraged them to do so. Nor can anyone on the union staff be blamed for putting the strikers in harm's way. The workers needed no one to tell them to chase scabs from the fields. The practice, in use since at least the 1920s, belonged to the rank and file. "We knew it was dangerous," said Mario Bustamante. "But our attitude was clear. These fields were the places we worked. This is where we spent most of our lives. This is where our sweat irrigated the ground, where we ruined our backs. And we had every right to be there, preventing people from taking our jobs."[54]

Ganz never told them to rush the fields, says Bustamante. But he didn't tell them not to either, and he always stressed that they should be careful on the picket lines.

> I never heard Marshall tell people to go into the fields. But he knew we were doing it. Ganz gave us a certain amount of liberty to decide these tactics on our own. He knew if we led people into the fields we would do our best to avoid problems, to do it without sticks and rocks, to try to talk people out of scabbing, not beat them up. He knew that we were going to do the best we could to limit the out-and-out violence. He knew us. He had confidence in us.[55]

Chavez, too, was aware that people were running into the fields, and he probably condoned it, at least indirectly. Chavez and Ganz spoke every day on the phone in the early days of the strike. What they said was known only to the two of them. Chavez is now dead; Ganz, speaking carefully, told me, "The first couple of weeks of the strike he was right with the program. We were all on the same wave length and trying to do the best we could, we would describe what was happening in the strike, and he would say, 'Oh that's great, that's terrific,' but when Rufino was killed, Chavez pulled me out. . . . I kept Cesar fully informed on everything that was going on, and so far as I know, never encouraged anyone to do anything that was contrary to his expectations."[56]

Ganz chooses to leave it like that and not say exactly, as best he can remember, what Chavez said to him about strikers going into the fields. Perhaps the two of them talked in a coded language and Chavez avoided either explicitly endorsing or condemning the practice. That's how Ganz had talked to the strike coordinators, always adding that they should be careful. Chavez may have done the same with Ganz.

Once Contreras was killed, Chavez likely bombarded himself with second thoughts and regrets, clamping down hard on all mass activity and blaming a subordinate for winking at a rank-and-file action that he probably winked at too. Ganz was devastated: "That was the time I felt most like I was being set up to take a fall of some kind. I hadn't ever felt like that in the union before. I really felt bad. I felt like I was being used, really used."[57]

With Ganz gone, the coordinators met and talked things over among themselves. About three weeks were left in the harvest. More and more scabs were working. The negotiations were going nowhere. The organizers didn't believe they could do anything to force any company to capitulate in the short time left in the Imperial Valley season, but they wanted to do something to reanimate the strikers, and to rebuild their own internal organization. They wanted to end the season on an up beat, so that people could renew the strike in Salinas with enthusiasm, believing they could win.

They decided on another one-day general strike and convinced Ortiz to permit it, although Ortiz would have little to do with organizing the event, and he kept them and their strike at arm's length. On the morning of February 21—eleven days after Contreras was shot and one week after his funeral—Mario Bustamante began speaking over the sound equipment mounted on the roof of a truck being driven through the streets of Calexico by a fellow Cal Coastal striker, Alvaro Sanchez. It was 3 a.m., but people were already waiting in the parking lots around town for buses that would take them to the fields. "Nobody is going to work today," Bustamante announced. "We are going to shut down the valley in honor of our comrade, Rufino Contreras. We are going to show the bosses that we are still on strike."[58]

An hour later a caravan of cars was lined up behind the sound truck, which was making its way to *el hoyo*, where the bulk of the workforce was boarding other buses bound for the harvest. Several people spoke into the microphone: "We are going to show the growers that they cannot

intimidate us. *Viva Rufino Contreras, viva la huelga, viva Cesar Chavez.*"
Groups of strikers went onto the buses and convinced people to get off.
People who didn't have cars of their own piled into others', and the cara-
van set out to shut down the valley. A spokesman for Sheriff Cox, Richard
Wilson, guessed that 2,000 people were riding in those cars, but Bustamante
thinks there were more.

They hit an Abatti lettuce field first, on Highway 111 between Calexico
and El Centro. Abatti was not one of the struck companies, although its
UFW contract had expired. Fewer than 150 people were working there. A
company supervisor parked his truck in the road leading into the fields.
Strikers got out of their cars and ran right pass the supervisor, whose truck
had sunk to the ground with four flattened tires. Five hundred strikers
approached the crews, who immediately left the fields. No blows were
thrown. The strikers moved on. The scene was replayed elsewhere, as
workers were either sympathetic to the cause or afraid of challenging so
many angry strikers.

The trouble began when one group of strikers ran into the circus, now
a mixture of high school students, the relatives of small growers, and a few
regular scabs. The strike coordinators didn't want to bother with them, but
battle discipline had broken down over the previous week and a half. The
strikers were no longer divided into distinct crews under the leadership of
picket captains. With no intermediate leaders, the coordinators stood alone,
unable to direct the thousands of angry strikers, most of whom wanted one
more chance to hit back at the people who had exploited them for years
and shot down their comrade. By the time Mario Bustamante arrived at the
field, a fight was well under way. He had never seen the people so angry,
and would never see them that angry again.

"It was like Vietnam," one of the sheriff's deputies, a Vietnam
veteran, told a reporter from the *Imperial Valley Press*. That was a wild
exaggeration in all but one respect: after two police helicopters swooped
down to herd the strikers out of the fields, people pulled up the metal
stakes of a nearby fence and threw them at the helicopter blades, as the
Vietnamese had done when they used fields of stakes to prevent helicopters from landing in the jungle. The strikers turned over a stitcher,
broke the windows and flattened the tires of every vehicle they could
find. They broke down an irrigation gate and flooded the fields. They
damaged at least eight patrol cars. The badly outnumbered sheriffs,
cops, and guards had superior weapons—batons, tear gas, guns—all of
which they used. Eventually they drove the strikers, who were armed
with rocks, sticks, and the metal stakes, back out of the fields. Both
Sheriff Wilson and Mario Bustamante said afterward that they were
surprised no one was killed. The *Imperial Valley Press* reporter summed
it up with another martial reference: "The series of clashes between the

police and striking farm workers had all the earmarks of a war zone. The only thing missing was death."[59]

It had been a day of rage, proving little beyond the obvious: people were still willing to fight and the coordinators were not capable of carrying on the strike without the support of the union staff. Negotiations ground on. The growers offered a new proposal, barely different from the first. Chavez countered by announcing to a rally of about 1,000 workers in *el hoyo* that the union would boycott Chiquita bananas. A Sun Harvest spokesman shrugged off the threat. "You need machinery for an effective boycott," he said, "We don't think Cesar has that machinery anymore."[60]

The union offered a few serious concessions at the bargaining table, but the growers declared an impasse. In the fields the companies cut as much lettuce as they could until the season ran out two weeks later. By the end of the harvest the price of lettuce had dropped down to $6 per box. The struck growers never could make up what they had lost. The Federal Market News Service estimated that 6,500 acres of lettuce (about 16 percent of the total planted) had gone unharvested because of the strike. The *Salinas Californian* estimated that the struck growers had lost about $24 million.[61]

Meanwhile, their competitors, including those allied with them in negotiations, enjoyed a banner year. The strike had cut down supply so much—up to 35 percent in February, according to one set of agricultural economists—that the price had been driven up. It peaked at $14, and didn't fall below $8 to $10 for several weeks in a row, prompting the *Imperial Valley Press* to state, "Never has the price of lettuce been as high for as long a period as it has been this year." Gross sales topped $76 million, a record. Agricultural economists estimated that receipts would have been no higher than $35 million if there had been no strike.[62]

The growers who were hurt were badly hurt, but not enough to get them to accede to the UFW demands, or even to adjust their bargaining posture substantively. It may have taken a shooting to do it, but they had survived the first three months of the war. The rank-and-file strike leaders had already moved on, worried about the future but hoping for a fresh start in the next campaign. The growers seemed to agree with them. The strike would be decided in Salinas.

The UFW Executive Board met at La Paz in the waning days of the Imperial Valley harvest. Chavez set out the agenda, then said:

> But before we get to [the agenda], we have to get to something even more crucial. . . . And that is that we have a very bad situation between some people on the Executive Board. They are not talking to each other. They are not working together. And it is having a tremendous impact on

the strike. It is shortchanging the workers and driving me up a wall. We need to talk about that. Frank and Marshall don't get along, and Jessica and Frank don't get along. And I don't know, they all seem to have their own group of people working around them, and I think it is just fucking chicken shit. And I want to end that. We are not going to tolerate that. Frank has his gang, and Marshall has his gang, and I have gone there and it just looks like shit, you know. I hope this Executive Board will do something, and if not, I will do something.[63]

What followed were several hours of intense dispute. It was March 11. The harvest wasn't yet finished, but the strike was, at least in the Imperial Valley. No one doubted that. It was the basic premise of the discussion. Marshall Ganz delivered even more bad news. A few union crews at Bruce Church, Admiral, and Growers Exchange had deserted the strike and gone back to work. Some Saikhon workers had formed a new crew and gone to work for another company. The board's mood was dark. What people had hoped would be a short, winning strike was now going to be a long one.

Chavez got the meeting off to a bad start by encouraging people to think that the main problems were the personal differences between Frank Ortiz and Ganz and Govea. He maintained that position throughout the meeting, often insisting that the only way to solve the problems was to play the Game. The Game would enable people to get all their petty differences out in the open, he said; it would "clean us all up," and enable the board to work together harmoniously.

There were personal differences and competing cliques, even, perhaps, people trying to sabotage one another's work. These were human beings, not saints, and there is some of that in all organizations, even when times are good. Although they never played the Game that day, the Executive Board did scream and shout at one another for a quite a while, and maybe it did them some good, as the collapse of the strike had produced a considerable amount of back-biting and rumor-mongering. Nonetheless, the emphasis on personal antagonisms covered up the political disagreements. And the great questions of the strike—what had happened, and what should happen next?—were left unexplored.

The personal disputes were clearly linked to opposing positions on strike strategy. Ortiz complained that Govea had balked when he asked her to write a check for Manuel Chavez. This was a challenge to his leadership. Govea said that she had wanted to be sure that Cesar had authorized the expenditure. The two argued a while about this incident in their personal feud, and then they went on to argue about the next one. But this wasn't just any check. It was money for Manuel to pay the bail of people who had been arrested in Mexicali in a nighttime attack on a man suspected of herding scabs to the Imperial Valley. As such, it went to the heart of an important strategic issue in the strike: How to deal with scabs? Govea disapproved of Manuel's tactics. Before he took over the strike, Ortiz had been working with Manuel, and he, too, was associated with covert Mexicali attacks on scabs and scab herders. The conflict over the check was essentially political, not personal.

Perhaps a meeting of the Executive Board was not the place to talk about nighttime vandalism, especially since the discussion was being taped.* Even those on the board who favored Manuel Chavez's tactics did not believe that what he was doing was good in itself—which was part of the reason he operated under the cover of darkness. Manuel's defenders believed that his tactics were a necessary, distasteful means to a possibly good end. Perhaps this was debated by the board; there is no record of it.

Other political matters were suggested, touched upon, and dropped. Much of the meeting consisted of attacks on Marshall Ganz, mainly by Chavez and Ortiz: people said he was hard to work with; he didn't sufficiently involve the staff; he didn't enforce discipline on the picket lines; he bad-mouthed Manuel and interfered in Manuel's work; he was so concerned about his own assignment that he gobbled up the union's resources and made it hard for other staffers and board members to get their jobs done.

At one point the topic became the different styles of work of Ortiz and Ganz.

GANZ: We work really different. Because I work really hard to involve people and give them ownership of the damn thing, and you don't take that approach.

ORTIZ: Absolutely. I do it with different tactics and in different ways. Democracy is great, but democracy is not worth a damn when you are in a war.

GANZ: I am not talking about democracy. I am talking about spending the time and the attention you have to spend with the leadership to make the thing go, so it doesn't become all unglued. There is no way you could run that strike with the staff, no way. The staff I was given were helpful, but they were messengers basically.

ORTIZ: That's all they were.

End of discussion. But a significant matter was at stake here: Who did the strike belong to—the workers and their rank-and-file leadership, or the

---

* Often, however, people at the taped meetings talked as if they didn't know or didn't care that the meetings were being taped. They had been assured that the tapes were going to be recorded over, once they had been used to write up the meeting notes. Sometimes the recorder was in sight and sometimes not.

staff? What was the proper role of the strike coordinators? Where did the staff and national officers fit in? What would everyone's role be in Salinas?

The conversation simply moved on to more gripes about Ganz. It became mean. Chavez polled everyone except Govea, asking if they could work with Ganz. Richard Chavez didn't answer directly, and Gilbert Padilla answered humorously, but for the others it became an opportunity to bash Ganz further. Chavez closed saying, "I can work with Marshall. I can. I fight with him. I think he is an asshole, but I work with him." It was meant as a joke, and Chavez got a laugh. And to a certain extent it was a backhanded endorsement of Ganz, a plea to the board to make the effort to work with him. It may in fact have helped, for by the end of the meeting much of the personal antagonisms seemed to have been overcome, and Ganz and the others laughed and joked together.

Richard Chavez had once again been a voice of reason. His refusal to join in the shouting and carping, his calm tone coupled with Padilla's all-around good humor, kept the meeting from getting completely mean-spirited. Richard also tried to nudge people away from personal pettiness: "Marshall said the strike went to hell because Frank wasn't showing proper leadership. That is what Marshall said. And Frank is saying something else. He is saying he didn't get cooperation from inside; that is why the strike went to hell." But, Richard reminded the board, the strike was purposefully "deescalated." Closing down the strike was the fault of neither Ortiz nor Ganz. It was a conscious decision at the top: a decision made on the basis of advice he gave Cesar, advice that turned out to be wrong. After Contreras's funeral he had made inquiries at Cesar's behest about how much of the lettuce season remained. No more than a week or a week and half, several people (including Ganz and Ortiz) told him. But it turned out that almost a month was left. What's the point of blaming the people who carried out the policy? Richard said. The question was "Did we deescalate too soon?"

A general discussion followed about the Imperial Valley lettuce season. Padilla said that it usually lasts to the middle of March, and if people had bothered to ask him, he would have been happy to tell them. Ganz admitted that there had been more lettuce left than he'd realized.

"We should call the strike off," Richard suggested. But what that meant exactly, or on what basis the strike should be continued, was not discussed. The board broke for lunch. When the meeting resumed, such questions were left hanging. Instead, the group mostly argued about the efficacy of playing the Game. Whom had it served? Who had supported it? Who had undermined it? Why had it been abandoned by the union? Would it be helpful to play it now? Again, there were shouting matches, one between Dolores Huerta and Gilbert Padilla, another between Dolores and Jessica Govea, in which Dolores called Jessica *loca*, crazy. Chavez answered her:

CHAVEZ: *Jessica no está loca. Todos estamos locos.* [Jessica isn't crazy. We are all crazy.] This is a fucking loony Executive Board. I am going to bring the growers here, and sell fucking tickets to raise money for the strike. Five dollars a ticket for every grower to come observe an Executive Board meeting.

GANZ: I'll bet they would have a lot of fun, too.

CHAVEZ: Because they are winning.

GOVEA: They sure are.

PADILLA: And that is the way it is.

Nervous laughter and small talk followed. A few minutes later the meeting ended.

"Esta Huelga Está Ganada"

March to September '79

The rhythms of sowing, thinning, weeding, and reaping presented two main opportunities for the UFW to revive its strike in Salinas. The first chance would come in late April or early May (depending mostly on the whimsy of the weather), when the spring lettuce harvest began. That would be the start of a large two-month harvest, the first opportunity for the growers, handlers, and shippers to make money in the Salinas Valley. After that the fields would be sown again, thinned and weeded, and harvested for a second time from late July or early August until mid-September. This second harvest was called the summer lettuce. The plantings were staggered so the transition was relatively smooth, but between the two harvests, from late June to late July, there was less lettuce ready to cut. The *lechugueros* called this period *el invernito*, the little winter, because for four or five weeks they didn't have as much work. The "spring harvest," "little winter," and "summer harvest" formed the cadence of their lives, understood in their muscles and bones as well as in their minds, a natural pace that also shaped the debates inside the UFW.

Salinas workers didn't just cut and pack lettuce. Between April and September they produced about 75 percent of all the fresh vegetables sold commercially in the United States, an amazing accomplishment for the some 15,000 workers who did it in the 1970s. The Salinas strike would hit the broccoli, celery, cauliflower, and tomato fields, too. And all those crops had their own rhythms of sowing and reaping, cycles that would also help shape the contours of the strike. For instance, Salinas broccoli was harvested eleven months a year. Three of the companies on strike in the Imperial Valley also cut, packed, and shipped broccoli in Salinas. That meant that almost two hundred broccoli cutters (as well as scores of lettuce thinners and weeders) had been on strike for four months by the time the spring lettuce harvest arrived.[1]

The lettuce harvest didn't move directly from the Imperial Valley to Salinas. From early March to mid-April it followed what farm workers call *la corrida*, hitting in order Yuma, Blythe (a desolate desert town on the Arizona-California border), and Huron-Firebaugh, hamlets on the west side of the San Joaquin Valley accessible only on two-lane country roads. No settlement between the growers and the UFW would be made on the basis of anything that happened on this migrant trail, but the growers, especially the big boys, Sun Harvest and Bruce Church, used the *corrida* to recruit and train a growing number of strikebreakers. They got off to a good start in Yuma, where the union was hampered by strict court injunctions and by Native American tribal leaders, who denied the UFW the right to enter reservations where Sun Harvest had leased land. It was safe to scab in Yuma, and the company foremen and some independent contractors rounded up a fair number of anti-UFW Filipinos as well as Mexican farm workers who were willing to break the strike. Many of the Mexicans were hourly workers who were looking for a chance to get on piece-rate lettuce crews. Some of them got discouraged and left once they had to face UFW harassment, especially in Huron. Even for those who lasted, two months is not enough time to become an accomplished *lechuguero*. Nonetheless, as the harvest approached the Salinas Valley, the growers had a fair number of scabs who could do a halfway decent job.

The problem was how to protect them once they got to Salinas. The answer: camps, guards, sheriffs, cops, and guns. Sun Harvest enclosed four camps with eight-foot Cyclone fences topped with three strands of barbed wire, watched over round the clock by armed guards. So many Cyclone chain-link fences were thrown up around company camps that the Salinas fence-building businesses were swamped with work, and growers had to hire fence contractors from the nearby Santa Clara Valley.[2]

To augment the eighty Monterey County deputy sheriffs, the growers hired 350 private security guards, some of them off-duty policemen, others from local security firms or from San Francisco and Los Angeles businesses that specialized in strike protection. The guards were armed, and at some of the struck companies they carried their guns into the fields. As early as mid-March a guard at Admiral had stuck his revolver in a picketer's chest and convinced him to back out of a struck field.[3]

The most dangerous guns, however, were the ones carried by some foremen, scab herders, and strikebreakers. They served as the last line of defense and were fired to ward off strikers who were advancing into the fields, or were used to threaten peaceful picketers when sheriff deputies and policemen weren't around. These guns made their appearance even before the lettuce harvest began and received a semi-endorsement from a Salinas police official. In a scuffle in front of a Sun Harvest cauliflower shed, a group of strikers freed one of their comrades from the grasp of a Salinas policeman. Someone inside the shed fired a .45 over the head of the strikers, encouraging them to back away from the officer, who had been pummeled to the ground. Captain Hanna of the Salinas Police refused to arrest the Sun Harvest mechanic who had fired the gun or to confiscate his pistol, declaring that he should be commended for saving the policeman's life.[4] Once the lettuce harvest got under way, the gunfire would increase, and strikers would know that anytime they went into the fields they risked being shot.

While the growers put together a defense, the union, too, was preparing for renewed war. In March, soon after the board meeting, Chavez put Ganz back in charge of the strike. Despite the internal attacks on Marshall Ganz, Chavez knew that no one else on the board had sufficient authority among the active workers to revive the battle. Ganz pulled the coordinators together and resumed regular meetings. Mario Bustamante was relieved; they could fight again, he thought. The primary job of the committee was to keep the picket lines going and do what they could to discourage strike-breakers who were working in the broccoli fields and doing the final weeding before the spring lettuce harvest. They also renewed the *huelga tecolote*, where strikers stood outside the scab camps at night and made a lot of noise.

But there was something that Ganz didn't tell the rank-and-file coordina-tors. When he reappointed Ganz, Chavez had put a strict limit on the strike. Six of the companies that had been struck in the Imperial Valley also operated in Salinas. The workers at those companies would continue their strike, but no new companies would be added. That limit would dramatically change the character of the fight. In the Imperial, at the height of the strike, more than 2,000 active picketers confronted no more than a couple of hundred strikebreakers. In Salinas, once the harvest got well under way, the six struck companies could put nearly 2,000 scabs in the fields. Because not all of the strikers would picket—some took jobs at nonstruck union companies—the UFW would regularly have no more than 750 people on the picket line.[5] This meant that for the most part the strikers could not intimidate the scabs with their numbers, which deemphasized the role of mass action.

Ganz didn't tell the coordinators about Chavez's order because he didn't want a battle between the rank-and-file leadership and La Paz. Moreover, while Chavez was traveling around promoting the Chiquita boycott, he sometimes threatened and often hinted that a bigger strike was coming. Ganz decided to go with what Chavez was saying in public, and he told the strike coordinators that the strike was limited to start but they would extend it when the time was right. He didn't think he was hiding too much. Who knew what Cesar might decide to do as the strike wore on? Ganz had consistently refrained from discussing the disputes at La Paz with anyone but the Executive Board and Jerry Cohen. He saw no reason to change.

The strike committee's most prominent leaders, Mario and Chava Bustamante, Cleofas Guzman, Aristeo Zambrano, and Sergio Reyes, were not happy about the limits. In a general strike, they argued, it would be difficult for the companies to find enough scabs to do the work. Extend the strike and the thousands of new strikers would once again, as in the Imperial Valley, be able to keep the scabs out of the fields. The people on strike agreed. They wanted their fellow union workers to join them on the picket lines. They asked the coordinators again and again, "When are we going to pull out of the other companies?"

In the Imperial Valley there had been very little vandalism on the U.S. side of the border. The strikers controlled the fields during the day, and they didn't have to operate at night. Strikers damaged some grower property during a few of the daytime battles, but that was part of an open fight with the sheriffs, guards, and the few scabs. Manuel Chavez's crew had been active at night on the other side of the border, but Ganz and the strike coordinators considered the Mexicali attacks extraneous to the strike. That was Manuel's style of fighting, and many found it distasteful.

In Salinas, however, nighttime vandalism became a regular tactic. Small groups of people, or sometimes just a single man, destroyed irrigation pumps, firebombed farm equipment, broke company windows, disabled company buses, and attacked the parked vehicles of the most well-known scab herders. The violence, directed almost exclusively against property, was meant to damage the struck companies financially in a situation where the strikers were having trouble stopping production. Vandalism flourished because mass action stuttered. It all fit together. According to Chava Bustamante and Hermilo Mojica, the person who clandestinely promoted much of the vandalism, provided some of the tools to do it and the ideological justification for it, was also the man who had shut down mass action in the Imperial Valley: Frank Ortiz.[6]

The Salinas strike committee had no official or operational connection to the nighttime vandalism that peppered the early days of the strike in Salinas. Ortiz moved in and out of town, recruiting people and supplying them with the tools of the trade. Ganz and others knew what he was up to, but it wasn't anything people talked about much, nor was it particularly frowned on. An early April firebomb attack on a scab herder's home in King City was an exception, not universally popular, and produced several debates among the active strikers.

The strikers' willingness to challenge the strikebreakers and the police during the day plus the incidents of nighttime vandalism put into public question the UFW's commitment to nonviolence. Two journalists who had been sympathetic to the union, Harry Bernstein and Ronald Taylor, wrote an article in the Los Angeles Times in mid-March saying, "Chavez today insists that he still abhors violence, but he has made few public statements on the issue. There have been no fasts and no marches to protest violence."[7]

Two weeks later Chavez responded in a letter to the LA Times in which he recited the injuries suffered by strikers in the Imperial Valley: the shotgun wounds, the broken legs, the fractured skull, the bodies smashed by helicopter attacks. He wrote movingly of the murder of Rufino Contreras. How many growers had been hurt or killed? he asked. He concluded by reminding the two reporters of his own history: "Did it ever occur to you that perhaps this time the ones who must raise their voices against violence, along with ours, the ones who must march in our footsteps on the long road to Sacramento and fast in our cubicle against murder, this time, must be those who are responsible for it?"[8]

In the face of UFW vandalism the growers could count on the institutionalized violence of the state. They had the loyal assistance of the Highway Patrol, sheriffs, and police, who did what they usually do in strikes: protect those who are breaking them. The Monterey Country sheriff's deputies were particularly bad. Only six of the eighty deputies spoke Spanish. The deputies often treated those they arrested roughly. Once they got people in the county jail they held them for up to three days without bringing charges and did what they could to humiliate them. Strikers commonly reported that the jailers put cockroaches in their food.

But the growers did not get the help they wanted from Governor Brown. As the strike began he was just starting his second run for president, and he would need UFW support. He refused to pressure the union to accept arbitration or mediation. He appeared at UFW rallies. The rules set by his Agricultural Labor Relations Board were favorable to the strikers, and the bosses never could get an injunction that severely damaged the union's ability to strike.[*] Although he didn't support the Chiquita boycott and couldn't control the armed representatives of the state, the fact that Brown was governor and that ALRB rules regulated the strike was a distinct advantage for the UFW. To a large extent it vindicated the union's longtime support for Brown and the close attention it had paid to Sacramento. Better for the UFW to have a state divided and ambivalent than uniformly antiunion. The strike injunctions in Yuma in the state of Arizona had proved that.

The ALRB also got a court order that allowed delegated union representatives to go into the Salinas fields at regularly assigned times to talk to the strikebreakers. These orchestrated meetings, intended by Judge Richard Silver to substitute for unsupervised rushing of the fields, were often successful, and some strikebreakers left the fields as a result. Chava Bustamante was one of the people delegated to talk to the strikebreakers. "It really changed my mind about the scabs," he said.

---

*   The growers's lawyers could not go directly to a judge and seek a court order. They had to file an unfair labor complaint with the ALRB, and the labor board would decide whether to seek an injunction, and if so, what kind. Thus, the early court orders allowed 150 people on single picket lines, many more than the growers wanted.

I saw them as victims, not enemies like the bosses and the scab herders. And most of the times we went in, some people who had been breaking the strike walked out with us. That was one of the most powerful experiences I ever had. I realized that everyone has a conscience, that everyone lives by some sort of moral standards, and that you can appeal to what is the best in people, and if the situation is right they will respond. And think of what that meant to the people who remained behind and continued to break the strike. What was on their minds? "Oh my God, are we the only assholes out here?" Nobody wants to think like that.[9]

The spring harvest began on April 17. Prohibited from extending the strike and unenthusiastic about the vandalism, Ganz developed a plan that involved large numbers of workers and maintained pressure on companies that were not being struck. It was playfully called the *pre-huelga*, and it became a semi-legend among veterans of 1979. An open-ended plan of action, it was a jewel of many facets, cut and polished by the tools the *pre-huelgistas* had at hand. It brought collective action back into the strike, and it was fun.

"We had meetings every day, and we decided what we were going to do, where we were going to hit, and how we were going to hit it," recalled Aristeo Zambrano, who helped organize the *pre-huelga* at three different broccoli companies. "We had a contact in every crew. And we would tell that one representative what we were going to do. And we would tell him in the morning, just before his crew went to work. It was a surprise for everyone . . . Some days some crews would do it, other days other crews . . . We were strong, well organized, disciplined, and powerful."[10]

The basic plan of the *pre-huelga* was simple. On any given day, UFW workers at a company with an expired contract might work for a couple of hours and then inform the foremen that they were done for the day, but would be back tomorrow. Less often, they might work too slowly to cut all the lettuce or broccoli or celery that the company had sold that day. Occasionally they might skip over lettuce or broccoli or cauliflower that was ready to cut, causing the grower to lose part of the harvest. Or they might put in a regular day's work as if nothing were happening. On the days of *pre-huelga* action, when foremen and supervisors asked if they were on strike, the workers would explain, "No, we are not on strike, we are on pre-strike." "*No estamos en huelga, estamos en pre-huelga*" became a famous line at the Salinas union hall, a symbol of the workers' control of the fields.

The *pre-huelga* worked. Crucial to its success was the unity and discipline of the piece-rate crews. These were the men (and some women, in the broccoli), who had worked together in close cooperation for years and were not likely to split apart under pressure. When the crew leaders explained the tactics for the day, people followed their direction. If disagreements developed, people argued matters out. They did not go their own way. Although Ganz introduced the idea, it was within the rich farm worker tradition of slow downs, sit-downs, and collective no-shows on scheduled days of work. The *pre-huelga* only required that the workers act in a more organized way, in coordination with other union crews throughout the valley.

Also decisive was the growers' unwillingness to fire their regular crews. If they fired them, they would have to go through the difficulty and expense of finding scabs. And so the bosses put up with these periodic disruptions, hoping to get as much product out of the fields as they could without being added to the list of the companies officially on strike.

The *pre-huelga* had some other advantages. Since the workers spent many days doing their jobs as usual, they still made a few hundred dollars most weeks, substantially more than if they had been on strike, and the union was spared the expense of paying the $25 weekly strike benefits. The *pre-huelga* also kept the crews together as collective actors. When people went on strike full-time, crew unity often relaxed, and some folks drifted away, moving on to other areas or taking temporary jobs.

The *pre-huelga* was exciting. "*Poder*" and "*sorpresa*"—"power" and "surprise"—are the words most commonly used to describe it. When Mario Bustamante returned to Salinas, he went back to his regular company, Green Valley Produce, which was not on the strike list. The ranch committee president and strike coordinator, he called the *pre-huelga*:

> . . . a genius plan. It helped the strikers, it helped the union, it helped the *pre-huelgistas* . . . Every day we could feel our power on the job, as the foremen and supervisors nervously waited to learn what we had decided to do. It also raised the hopes of the people who were on strike. Because when we would leave our job at eight-thirty in the morning, we would go to a nearby company that was on strike, with just a few people on the picket line, watching some scabs work. And we would arrive as a surprise. Sixty, ninety, one hundred twenty people honking our horns in a caravan, waving our flags, full of enthusiasm, coming to join their little picket line. And of course it was a surprise to the police, too. So sometimes it was an opportunity for us to enter the fields and chase out the scabs.[11]

The growers didn't talk much about the *pre-huelga*, as it often shamed them, but the *Salinas Californian* reported that "sporadic, unscheduled work stoppages were wreaking havoc with company operations." Don Nucci of Mann Packing told the paper, "First they stop for part of the day, work less a few days a week, and then go out together. Nobody knows for how long." George Mursante of Arrow Lettuce said, "It is a new deal every day . . . You never know what to expect."[12]

There have been many on-the-job campaigns in the history of the U.S. working class. Often they have been more myth than substance, as labor unity disintegrated under the pressure of working under the boss's roof. But this was the real thing, made possible by the unique internal solidarity of the crews and the special characteristics of agricultural production. It was widespread. It tried the patience of the growers; there were many stories of foremen and supervisors going slightly berserk under the pressure. But it couldn't be overused or go on forever. The strike coordinators knew that. Eventually the growers would fire or suspend the *pre-huelgistas*, which was all right. It would be a perfect transition into the extended strike they were expecting.

In the midst of the spring harvest, Ganz organized strike authorization votes at the union companies that were not on strike. Chavez had not relented on spreading the strike, but he did not oppose the votes. The meetings were spirited. At Mann's, the biggest broccoli harvester in the valley, the vote to authorize a strike was 220–0; at Associated Produce, 42–0; at Harden Farms, 400–1; at Arrow Lettuce, 105–0; at Oshita, 110–0. Throughout the valley, only a handful of people voted No. The news heartened those who had been on strike for five months.[13]

Following the votes—in the procedure that Ganz was so proud of—the ranch committees chose people to serve on the strike committee and the welfare committee, which now combined *huelgistas* with *pre-huelgistas*. Those committees were invigorated by the fresh blood. The welfare committee became especially creative in finding ways for strikers to make some money. Working with the strike coordinators, it arranged for strikers to rotate into the nonstriking and *pre-huelgista* union crews for a couple days of work. This was another mark of internal solidarity, as it required the people on the crews to give up their jobs for a few days to support their brothers and sisters on strike. It also was well organized, with rotation schedules both among the strikers and the crews. External solidarity also helped, as Bay Area and Los Angeles unions and churches sent tons of food to Salinas. The ILWU arranged for strikers to work a week on the docks in San Pedro and San Francisco, where they picked up checks many times bigger than $25.[14]

On the first day of the spring lettuce harvest, Cesar Chavez was in Washington, D.C., speaking at the National Press Club. He had two themes: the boycott of Chiquita bananas; and the federal government's failure to enforce immigration laws. He put particular emphasis on "illegals." He distributed a six-page UFW press release that identified the camps of struck growers where undocumented scabs were living. It also detailed times and places that the growers had moved illegals around California. Finally, it chronicled the union's unsuccessful attempts to get the INS to enforce the laws against importing, housing, and transporting undocumented workers, as well as the agency's failure to remove scabbing illegals from the fields. "Illegal aliens threaten the union's life," Chavez said. "Strike breaking, condoned by the White House, is breaking the union."[15]

He was particularly hard on Jimmy Carter. Playing his own, not insignificant card in the coming contest for the Democratic presidential nomination, Chavez charged that Carter had refused to order INS Commissioner Leonel Castillo to enforce the immigration laws. In the 1976 elections, the UFW had registered 400,000 voters and had assigned 300 staffers to work for Carter, Chavez said, but "we have not heard from him since." Chavez added that the UFW was "cool" to Carter, and looked favorably on the candidacies of Edward Kennedy and Jerry Brown.[16] Democratic politicians were still sorting out their own loyalties in the possible challenge to a sitting president, but some rushed to embrace Chavez. Senator Harrison Williams of New Jersey announced that the Committee on Human Resources, which he chaired, would soon hold a hearing in Salinas.

Chavez was the first witness when the Williams Committee convened ten days later. Five hundred Salinas workers shouted, clapped, and chanted for fifteen minutes before he spoke. Cesar began by denouncing the dismissal of murder charges in the Rufino Contreras case. He called for a federal investigation and introduced three witnesses to the murder who told the committee what they had seen. Chavez then attacked the actions of law enforcement agencies in the strike, putting emphasis on the INS. He again cited incidents where the Border Patrol had refused to act on UFW information of unlawful actions.[17]

Chavez and the UFW had enough cachet in Washington and the Democratic Party to make the gambit work. The next day an INS assistant commissioner announced that the agency had just established a twenty-five-man task force "in answer to requests from the public and parties involved in a farm labor dispute and to handle the influx of undocumented aliens into the area." Ordinarily the agency had only five officers in Salinas, which limited it to deporting no more than thirty undocumented workers a day. In its first day of operation the new task force reported apprehending 335 undocumented aliens, the majority from scab camps.[18]

In an unprecedented intervention by a U.S. government body in support of a farm worker strike, the INS dramatically went into struck fields and pulled out undocumented workers. On the Monday after the Senate week-end hearings, the Border Patrol checked the papers of fifty-five strikebreakers at Cal Coastal and found that twelve were undocumented. On Tuesday they hit an Admiral field, but found only five undocumented scabs. That same week they raided a Sun Harvest crew and got a few more. The raids confirmed what most people on the ground already knew. Undocumented

workers were not the bulk of the strikebreakers, and the percentage working as scabs was no greater than the percentage in the general farm worker
population. The task force stayed around for a month more, rounding up
and deporting about a hundred workers a day, mostly at ranches that had
nothing to do with the strike. Marshall Ganz called that "unfortunate," but
observed that at least the INS activity would reduce the overall labor supply
in the area, and thereby help the strike.[19]

Generally the strikers both cheered the arrival of the *migra* and made
nervous jokes about it. When the INS pulled strikebreakers out of one
field, I heard one striker laughingly say, "I sure as hell hope they don't
come here and check our picket line." The strike committee was ambivalent. Chava Bustamante supported the raids, although years later he decided
they were wrong. Back then he figured it was a simple question of ends and
means. Winning the strike was more important than anything else. Sabino
Lopez, a strike coordinator from Sun Harvest, was a strong supporter of the
raids, and even testified about illegal scabs at the Williams hearings.[20]

Mario Bustamante opposed the intervention of the *migra*. If the union
could get the sheriffs and police to intervene on the side of the strikers, or
at least to stop escorting the scabs in and out of the fields, that would
matter, he told his *compañeros*. But the Border Patrol's help was bound to be
insignificant and would only make the undocumented mad at the union.

Mario Bustamante's biggest complaint, however, was about how the
decision had been made. "Why weren't we involved?" he asked at the time.
Already in April, he was thinking that the strike belonged to the coordinators, or at least belonged to them enough so that they should have a say
about all major decisions. That was a minority opinion at the time. Four
months later most would agree.[21]

After the formation of the INS task force, Chavez continued to talk
about undocumented strikebreakers while on the boycott trail, but he
didn't make it into a major campaign, as he seemed to be doing at the
National Press Club. On the road, Chavez began talking about a boycott of
lettuce, as well as bananas. In Salinas, the issue of the scabs' legal status came
and went.

In early May, as the UFW was taking strike votes and rumors of an extended
strike rippled through the valley, formal negotiations between the union
and the growers resumed. Chavez had made Jerry Cohen the new head of
the negotiating team, even though he was no longer the UFW's general
counsel and the legal department was in the process of being shut down.
The negotiating team included several staffers and rank-and-file negotiators. Cohen talked frequently to Andy Church, the main industry
representative, while others had informal discussions with representatives of
individual companies.

The union's chief target remained Sun Harvest. Less than a week after Sun Harvest began to cut its lettuce with inefficient scabs, a vice president of United Brands came to Salinas to negotiate. The UFW made a serious offer, the first major negotiating concession from either side. It accepted a three-year contract, and nearly split the difference on most wage issues. In the highly symbolic basic wage, the union proposed $4.70 an hour in the first year, $5.25 in the second year, and $5.62 in the third year, along with a modest cost-of-living clause in the last year of the contract. The union negotiators were willing to withdraw many of their proposed language changes but would not give away the hiring hall or the "good standing" clause.*[22]

Simultaneously Cohen made a similar offer to Andy Church. Both Sun Harvest and Church rejected the proposal without making any counteroffer. Cohen told the *Salinas Californian* that the growers' negotiating position was "backwards, obstructionist, and recalcitrant." Ganz told the *Watsonville Pajaronian* that their refusal to bargain was "a form of cowardice," and that he didn't think anyone on the growers' side "had the balls to settle." Both Cohen and Ganz predicted an expanded strike, Cohen stating, "The funds are available for what we believe will be the largest and perhaps the longest agricultural strike in U.S. history," and Ganz predicting, "There's going to be a [wider] strike. It's going to be costly."[23]

The price of lettuce, which had been low, jumped to $6 a box as the big buyers hastened to secure a few days' advance supply before the strike spread. And then—nothing. *The Packer* headline read, "Strike Activity in California Again Calmer Than Rumors." The price of lettuce fell to the break-even point of $3.50 a box. As the spring harvest wore on and the big non-UFW growers like Bud Antle, Hansen, and Merrill stepped up production, the price fell even lower, down to $2.[24]

Those rock-bottom prices became the union's public excuse for not extending the strike. In early June Chavez said, "We're better off not striking while the price is like this. If the price goes up, we will strike the other growers, though. We'll strike all the other growers in the Salinas Valley."[25] It was a spurious explanation, as everyone in the agricultural industry knew. The price had been high when the May negotiations broke down. If the union successfully extended the strike, the price would shoot up again.

The growers became more confident as it became clear that the strike wouldn't be spread. Some told local reporters that the union had neither the strength among the workers nor the money to finance an extended strike. Mirroring the growers' confidence was the disappointment of many

---

*   The clause allowed the union to expel a member from the UFW for a wide range of reasons. The growers maintained that the clause gave the union too much power over the workers, a power they felt undermined their own authority.

of the active strikers. As despair mixed with anger, vandalism increased. In early June, the Monterey County Sheriff's Department made an interim report: since the strike began there had been 223 windows smashed; 108 vehicles dented or damaged; 131 tires slashed; 98 irrigation pumps destroyed; 1,281 other attacks on various types of farm equipment; 31 acres of lettuce slashed; and 22 strike-related arsons.[26]

On the early morning of May 20, Chava Bustamante and Hermilo Mojica were arrested for possession of an incendiary device. According to Chava:

> Frank Ortiz would come to the strike committee meetings and then after the meetings he would invite us out to coffee for a talk. He always had Lupe Bautista and Gilbert Rodriguez with him. They were his *pistoleros*. He said, look, there are some other things we have to do to give them a message that this is going to be a costly strike. He gave us the *cacahuates*, the twisted steel spurs that punctured tires. Lupe Bautista gave me the detonation caps. Not just to me but to others, too. Since Ortiz was Cesar's dog, I figured this was checked off by Cesar, although we will never know exactly what Cesar officially approved of . . . I assume that Marshall knew what he [Ortiz] was up to, but I don't know if it was coordinated or not. I figure that Marshall and Cesar had plausible deniability. Ortiz never told us exactly what to do. He gave us the materials and encouraged us in the vandalism . . .
>
> [The detonation cap] was a combustible powder inside a small canister usually used for film. It had a makeshift top that dissolved in gasoline. So what you were supposed to do was fill a plastic bottle with gasoline, then wait for the right moment and drop the canister into the bottle and leave. When the gasoline dissolved the top, the powder dropped into the gasoline causing it to explode. That was the idea. I suppose that it worked, but I never actually tried it . . .
>
> The night Mojica and I were arrested, first we went with about twenty-five Cal Coastal strikers and did some nighttime harvesting. We had machetes that Ortiz had given us. We went and destroyed about eighty acres of lettuce in three different fields . . . After we were done, I called Mojica aside. I had kept the firebomb materials in my house, in my closet, for about a month. I showed them to Mojica and said let's go to [the town of] Gonzalez and send a message to Morena, the Cal Coastal scab herder. We drove down together. We were going to break his car window and throw the bomb in the car. But Mojica couldn't break the window, and he was making too much noise trying. So I was afraid we were going to wake up the whole neighborhood, and I said let's get out of here. So we left. But on Highway 101 we passed a Highway Patrolman coming in the other direction. The guy circled

around and stopped us . . . He said we had a broken light, but I don't think we did. He questioned Mojica, and everything seemed okay. But then he came around and asked for my identification. Once he saw my name, that was it. The entire Gonzalez police force was there in a matter of minutes.

The story I told the judge was that the fire bombs were given to me by a guy on the picket line. But that wasn't true. Lupe gave them to me, and Ortiz encouraged me to use them. Vandalism was a policy of the strike, and Ortiz was in charge of it.

But nobody made me try to firebomb the scab herder's car. It wasn't anybody else's decision but my own. I take responsibility for it. It was one of the stupidest things I have ever done in my life. But for me it was what I needed to change my life around. The three months I was in jail I read a lot. I read Flores Magón in jail. I wrote some poetry. And right then and there, sitting in jail regretting what I had done, I decided to stop kidding myself about things, about some of my visions of myself. I decided I didn't want to be a leader who gives his whole life to some cause. I had a more modest goal. I would be an organizer, more in the background, but an organizer in the movement for justice.[27]

In early June, six months into the strike and with about three weeks left in the spring harvest, the growers moved off their original wage position of 7 percent for the first time and made a new offer that averaged out to 10 percent a year. The union had lowered its first-year wage demand by 50 cents; the growers now responded by coming up 13 cents. The union also had dropped many of its nonwage demands, but the growers were intransigent, still demanding the end of the hiring hall and significant changes in the work rules and grievance procedure. Cohen answered by putting the UFW's last offer back on the table, but kicking the first-year wage up 15 cents just to indicate the union's displeasure.[28]

The strike committee had its own response. The growers made their offer on Wednesday, June 6. The UFW negotiating committee countered on Friday. The workers answered on Monday, June 11, 1979. Black Monday, it came to be called.

With Ganz's full cooperation, the coordinators worked out the plan in his office, complete with detailed maps of the Salinas and Pajaro valleys tacked up on walls. Workers at the ten UFW companies not on strike would leave their jobs for the day and join the picket lines at the six struck firms. The workers would be divided up into several car caravans of 150 to 200 people, each led by a strike coordinator. (Mojica and Chava Bustamante, then out on bail, would remain at the command center, Ganz's office, as they were already in enough trouble.) The first caravans would go to the camps to try to stop the scab buses as they left for the fields. The next would be decoys, leading the sheriff's deputies away from the day's main targets. The next caravans would confront unprotected scabs in designated areas of the Salinas and Pajaro valleys. After the lawmen rushed to cover those fields, the first caravans would hit secondary targets. It worked exactly as planned.[29]

There had been no detailed discussion of what exactly people would do when they arrived at the fields. Zambrano remembered that the coordinators had agreed "we would go in harder," but nothing more explicit than that had been said. As many as 2,000 workers participated, with several hundred rushing into fields more than a hundred miles apart. Often they confronted only security guards and strikebreakers. Usually the scabs and guards retreated without putting up a fight. In some fields, however, they stood their ground. The strikers' weapons were mostly picket sign sticks and rocks; the strikebreakers used whatever was at hand: pieces of metal they took off the lettuce wrapping machines, and on a couple of occasions, their knives.[30]

Twelve people were taken to the hospital. The one serious injury was to a Sun Harvest striker, Joaquin Perez, who, after stumbling to the ground, was stabbed repeatedly in the buttocks by a scab. It took surgeons five hours to sew up his punctured rectum. The Salinas Californian editorialized, "Only a merciful God and skilled surgeons kept him from becoming a martyr alongside the man killed earlier this year in the Imperial Valley."[31]

The late-arriving deputies, aided by Highway Patrolmen and police from Salinas, Marina, Gonzalez, and King City, arrested 134 strikers. Only one strikebreaker was arrested, the man who had knifed Perez, and he was taken in only after the strikers demanded it.[32]

Police authorities, newspapers, and growers spoke of "UFW goon squad terror." The workers' mood, however, was buoyant, and lechugueros who were temporarily suspended from Green Valley Produce for their participation reinforced the UFW picket lines. For the first time, the newly enthusiastic strikers went to nonunion fields—Hansen, Merrill, Norton, Crown, and D'Arrigo—and peacefully urged workers to walk out for a day, and many complied. The supply of lettuce fell, and the price shot up.[33]

At the next scheduled negotiating session the growers acted tough and dramatically exited, complaining about UFW-sponsored violence. But just four days later, in secret talks with Chavez and Jerry Cohen ninety miles away in Paso Robles, the top industry negotiators conceded on the hiring hall and several other important matters. In addition, the four men talked for some time about ways to change the grievance procedure that would be acceptable to both parties. It was the first time since the beginning of the strike that the growers had made any serious modification of their demands. Nevertheless, the growers were still adamant about management rights, and there was nothing close to an agreement on the final shape of the economic package. At the end of the meeting, Dick Thornton, grower attorney and a lead negotiator, said that the union "terrorism" had to stop. If it didn't, the growers would fight back.[34]

With Chavez and Cohen he was pushing on an open door. Cohen had always maintained that running into the fields hurt negotiations. Chavez may have wavered for a while in the Imperial Valley, but he was generally against any open intimidation of scabs. He didn't need Dick Thornton to tell him it had to stop. He had arrived in town unannounced the day after Black Monday. According to Ganz, Chavez was furious about the mass charges into the fields and warned Ganz not to do it again. And he reiterated his opposition to any extension of the strike.[35]

The customary midsummer slowdown of the lettuce harvest was especially dramatic in 1979 because of a strike, but not the UFW strike. From mid-June to mid-July, many independent truckers parked their rigs in protest against the high price of fuel, the fifty-five-mile-an-hour speed limit, and the lack of uniform truck size and weight regulations throughout the country. It was a weak copy of the 1974 truckers strike, not nearly as powerful or widespread. Less able to mount massive convoys to block highways, the truckers discouraged others from breaking their strike with sniper fire and arson. It didn't disturb the economy much, except the fresh fruit and vegetable business, especially lettuce.

By 1979, 90 percent of the lettuce was being shipped out of Salinas in trucks and only 10 percent in railroad cars. With independent truckers in short supply, the price to carry a load of lettuce across the country doubled, which led to a lowering of demand for lettuce in the East and the price of lettuce in Salinas. On some days in July, the price of lettuce fell below $2 a box, less than the cost of harvesting it. Some growers suspended their lettuce crews for a few days. Others disced their fields.[36]

As the harvest slowed down, so did enthusiasm for the strike. "Morale was low," Ganz said. "I remember going around and meeting with every picket line. And having hour-long meetings with them, and talking with them, and asking them to decide whether they really wanted to stay with it or not. And trying to recommit everybody to this thing because it was a very, very hard time."[37]

In this not so little winter, Marshall Ganz and the strike committee got even closer. Ganz had some staff help, mainly from Jose Renteria, Art Mendoza, Bill Granfield, David Valles, and Jessica Govea. Marshall and the coordinators spent hours together, trying to figure out how to keep the strike alive. Mario Bustamante compared Ganz to a boxer, looking for an opening wherever he could find it, and then throwing jab after jab, while he waited for an opportunity to land a bigger blow. Mojica called him a master organizer, equally concerned with the big picture and the tiniest detail. Aristeo Zambrano, who loved tactical discussions, would spend as much time as he could listening to Ganz.

During these talks Chava Bustamante began to suspect—without being told anything by Marshall—that there was a split between Chavez and Ganz. "After Black Monday, I got the idea that Chavez wanted to end the strike." But Chava thought the difference went deeper than that:

> Chavez preached to us. You got the feeling he was doing charity work, helping us out, showing us the way things were, enlightening us about the way the world worked. He was very paternalistic. Marshall never patronized us. He pushed us to the max. He never treated us like *pobrecitos* [poor little folks]. He was merciless in how much he demanded from us. He believed that if we could get together and work hard we had the power and the ability to achieve a lot. And because he believed it, we believed it.[38]

Most of the other strike coordinators still saw Cesar as the leader of the union and Marshall as his faithful lieutenant. They did not know that Ganz and Chavez were feuding while they were struggling to keep the strike alive. Ganz wanted to extend the strike; Chavez wanted to keep it small, and begin to send workers out to promote the boycott. The two argued mostly over the phone. Chavez even threatened to end the strike benefits and keep the strike going symbolically, as had been done in the grapes fifteen years before.[39]

Ganz did not mention the dispute to anyone on the strike committee. But he did talk to Jessica Govea and to Jerry Cohen, who recalled the conversations he and Ganz had had while meeting twice a week for breakfast:

> Cesar was telling Marshall that he was not going to win there in the fields. Cesar wanted Marshall to set the stage slowly and surely for the boycott . . . The sense that Marshall was giving me at those breakfast meetings was Cesar's lack of commitment to the strike, and that we were going to have to win this on our own. I started to feel that we—me, Marshall, and Jessica—were being squeezed between Cesar and the growers. That our problems internally were as serious as our problem with the growers.[40]

As the "little winter" came to a close, the strike coordinators, in conjunction with Ganz, Govea, and Cohen, came up with a plan. They would greet the summer harvest with a sixty-five-mile march from San Ardo in the southern extreme of the Salinas Valley to Salinas itself, proclaiming as they walked a coming general strike, and pointing toward a grand rally in

Salinas, which would kick off the last, great battle of the war. Marshall called Cesar and told him about the plan, emphasizing the march rather than the war. Chavez thought a march was a good idea, but he wanted it to be a mix of farm workers and their supporters; he wanted it to focus on the boycott; and he wanted it to start in San Francisco.

Ganz and Chavez argued it out, right up to the last moment. They finally decided on two marches. On July 21, Ganz told a Salinas rally of 500 farm workers that Cesar Chavez would lead a ten-day march from San Ardo to Salinas, stopping along the way for daily meetings with farm workers. Meanwhile, the UFW's urban supporters would march from San Francisco, publicizing the strike and the boycott. They would meet for a mass rally in Salinas. "If an agreement with vegetable growers has not been nailed down by then," reported Doug Foster of the *Salinas Californian*, "Chavez will announce a general agricultural strike to begin the day after the mass rally."[41]

Two days later, in La Paz, Chavez announced that he would lead a march of farm workers and their supporters from San Francisco to Salinas, which would culminate in a rally on August 11, and a one-day UFW convention on August 12. He said nothing about the march from San Ardo or about a general strike. Foster called La Paz for clarification, but Marc Grossman refused to comment beyond saying that "marches have been a traditional tactic when farm workers escalate the struggle."[42]

On July 31 Chavez spoke to a rally of about 1,000 people in San Francisco, telling them that the UFW would now "begin in earnest" the boycotts of lettuce and Chiquita bananas, which he had announced three months before. They would also target two United Brand subsidiaries, Morrell Meats and A&W root beer. Chavez compared the San Francisco–Salinas march to the 1966 Easter pilgrimage from Delano to Sacramento. Father Bill O'Donnell's passionate invocation was right on message: "Almighty God, let the boycott be the great equalizer to bring justice to farm workers."[43]

The next day, the marchers began their trek south to Salinas. Less than a hundred people joined, and except in San Jose, the numbers continued to fall. Outside of Gilroy there were no more than forty people marching. Some reporters commented that Chavez wouldn't be able to mount the same kind of boycott in 1979 that the union had led in the excitement of the 1960s. But Chavez stayed optimistic. He told the press that he would urge the upcoming farm-worker convention to go "all out" for an international boycott, and that he would propose sending 600 boycotters across the country as soon as the convention broke up. Up at La Paz it was full speed ahead; Fred Ross was put in charge of rebuilding the boycott.

Then, on Saturday, August 4, some explosive news hit. Bud Antle signed a new contract with the Teamsters, paying $5 an hour as the basic wage and

85 cents a box to *lechugueros*. The wage settlement was not much different from what the UFW had asked for back in January, and included a re-opener—Antle management had agreed to readjust its wages after a UFW settlement, so that Antle always paid twenty-five cents more an hour than UFW-contracted companies.[44]

That $5 an hour lit up the sky. Grossman, Chavez, and Ganz crowed: See, the growers could have paid these wages all along. Church, Thornton, and Kemp scrambled. Bud Antle always pays more than the rest of the industry, they explained. Sun Harvest's Kemp went further; he would gladly pay the same wages as Antle if his foremen could control the crews the way Antle's foremen did. But no one felt the news as dramatically as farm workers, especially those active in the strike. Antle workers had won what the UFW was demanding; with a further push, they could win it, too.

The Antle victory was not a stroke of luck, not an independent event, separate from the UFW's seven-month struggle. Nor was it a back-door agreement between the Teamsters and the boss. The Antle contract was won through a fight, a battle that was closely linked (in both personnel and tactics) to the UFW's war in the fields. Back in January, Froilan Medina, a Bud Antle *lechuguero* and friend of Mario Bustamante's, had met with Ganz and Chava and Mario Bustamante and had offered to work in league with the UFW inside Antle. The offer was accepted, and Medina continued to meet informally with some people on the strike committee.[45]

Medina had led a few Antle walkouts at the height of the strike in the Imperial Valley. In mid-July he and others organized protests in the fields against a sweetheart contract offer being pushed by an old anti-UFW Teamster hack. On July 30, just as the UFW strike committee was working hard to build the march, Medina and other rank-and-file workers led a walkout of Antle *lechugueros*. Two hundred and fifty came to a rally at Sherwood School, right next to the Salinas field office, and mixed with the excited UFW strikers. The walkout helped to get rid of the union hack, put pressure on Antle management, and won the $5 an hour, eighty-five cents a box deal four days later.[46]

The day after the Antle announcement, 1,000 farm workers began their march in the tiny town of San Ardo, and Chavez flew in to join them. Over the next few days he flew back and forth between the two marches, talking at rallies in both places. In San Ardo he announced that he was going on a water-only fast for "love and patience." "The fast is not a protest," he explained to Doug Foster.

> It is not a means of pressuring the growers or of winning the strike. Or a way to compel the farm workers to continue the strike. It is not a fast for nonviolence. It is a fast for patience and love. For patience within ourselves and with one another, patience to deal with all the obstacles

that are in the way and the great odds we face. It is a fast for love, love of God, love of ourselves, love of our families, of our friends, of our enemies. Love for our cause."[47]

The farm workers' march exploded as it moved north through the small towns of the valley: more than 1,000 in Greenfield; 1,500 in Soledad; larger than that in Castroville. Outside of Soledad, 400 Meyers Tomato workers left their jobs to join the cavalcade of chanting workers. The walkout just as the tomato season was getting under way accelerated the talks between Meyers and UFW negotiators. Outside Soledad, the *pre-huelgistas* at Oshita, Salinas Marketing, and Green Valley joined in, leaving their jobs with no intention of returning until they had won the contract they wanted. In Castroville 1,000 more workers left the fields and joined the march. When the small northern march hit the farm worker town of Watsonville, 3,000 people attended the rally.

Chava Bustamante said that the march felt like a scene in the Marlon Brando movie *Viva Zapata*, where the campesinos come out of the corn-fields to join the Zapatista advance on Mexico City. Ganz, speaking to the crowd of Watsonville farm workers, compared the San Francisco and San Ardo processions to Villa's Division of the North and Zapata's Division of the South. Chava had learned his history in the movies. Ganz had learned his in books. Both knew that they were in the midst of a great event, comprehensible only through comparison with other grand achievements.

The mood of the marchers was captured by Cleofas Guzman, the strike coordinator from Sun Harvest. He heard a little voice in his head, he told the exhilarated workers at the march rallies; it kept telling him over and over, "*Esta huelga está ganada, esta huelga está ganada*"—"This strike is won." It became the unofficial slogan of the march. People started using it as a salutation. "*Nos vemos. Esta huelga está ganada*"—"See you later. This strike is won."

As the march approached Salinas, many on the strike committee had figured out that Chavez was more interested in the boycott than he was in extending the strike, but they weren't too concerned. They had their mission, and Ganz seemed to be on board. Also, as the final rally approached, Chavez had begun to mention an expanded strike as well as a bigger boycott. And since Ganz continued to introduce Cesar effusively at the rallies, the strike coordinators assumed that any differences between the two regarding strategy was not great and could be worked out. In any event, as far as Mario Bustamante was concerned, the general strike was now too big to call off.

The police said that 15,000 to 20,000 people marched into Salinas on August 11. The great majority were farm workers. Six horsemen and twenty-two mariachis led the parade. Behind them walked Cesar Chavez arm-in-arm with Governor Brown. Beside them were John Henning, secretary-treasurer of the California AFL-CIO, and Mario Obledo, California's secretary of health, education, and welfare. They all spoke at the rally, along with various priests, rabbis, ministers, and an extraordinary farm worker child who belted out a series of Mexican ballads. Brown was made to wait so long before he spoke that he missed his plane to Los Angeles, a reminder of the UFW's displeasure over his failure to endorse the boycott. But he did not disappoint when he finally took the stage. Farm workers should be paid as well as factory workers, he said. He urged the growers to settle. He concluded with some vivas. "*Viva la raza. Viva Cesar Chavez.* Go out and win. The victory is yours."[48]

Finally Chavez spoke. He promised an extended strike and a full-on boycott. He told the workers that their demands were just, and they would win. He said that 400 people would soon be sent out to the boycott cities, and 200 more would follow. Foster wrote that he looked tired, somewhat shaky on his legs. He had been fasting for a week, walking ten miles a day for ten days, flying between the two marches. He had two more meetings scheduled for that evening. Neither would be particularly easy. One would be especially hard.

"With reference to the speeches in this history," Thucydides explained in the first book of *The Peloponnesian War*, "some were delivered before the war began, others while it was going on; some I heard myself, others I got from various quarters; it was in all cases difficult to carry them word for word in one's memory, so my habit has been to make the speakers say what was in my opinion demanded of them by the various occasions, of course adhering as closely as possible to the general sense of what they really said."

I presume that I am not the only historian who has sifted and resifted through old newspapers, reread (just one more time!) my notes on what people told me they could remember, made one more trip to the archives, all the while wishing I might use Thucydides' method instead. But educated guesses and artful reconstructions are not necessary to relay what happened next at Salinas' Hartnell Community College in what would become an extraordinary moment in UFW history. For months the workers had been locked in a blind conflict with the union leadership that was, in its own way, as serious as their conflict with the growers. This night they would confront each other, face to face, and it would all be captured on tape.[49]

At that hurry-up meeting the board's first order of business was preparations for the convention the next day. Scores of details had to be worked out. Some people would be up most of the night getting ready. As the board settled those issues, the workers' strike committee waited in the next room. Finally, Chavez brought up the political matter at hand.

CHAVEZ: Okay. Now let's get to the more serious stuff . . . The big problem right now is, ahh Marshall, you want to put it in your own words?
GANZ: What do you mean?
CHAVEZ: About the—

Ganz was in a tough spot. The opportunity for a finesse had passed. Ganz still tried for a possible compromise.

GANZ: Well, I don't know. My perception is that we need to go all out on the boycott. And the strikers are all for going all out on the boycott, but the nonstrikers want to and believe that they can be effective striking. And that's one question.
CHAVEZ: Let's deal with that one.
GANZ: . . . See everybody thought we were going to call for a general strike on Monday, right? If we announce to all the world that we are not going to strike, period, then we close off all our options, and it seems to me that we need to keep options open, rather than close them . . . That's one. The other is that the [workers at the] pre-strike companies themselves are really antsy about striking. They want to strike. [Ganz explained what the *pre-huelga* was.] The other problem that we have to deal with, see, I haven't been able to explain why we haven't struck, because a lot of them [the workers] thought we should have struck in May. It was really hot then, and it was ready to go, and a lot of them thought we should have. But we didn't, and we put the brakes on when the industry began bargaining. Then we saw that the industry bargaining was just shit, and so now people say, Well, let's strike. And the one reason I haven't been able to give is that there isn't money. And I haven't given that reason because I question the wisdom of giving that reason.[50] Maybe we have to give that reason. But if you don't give that reason then you have to deal with it in another way . . . But is that, Cesar, what you—
CHAVEZ: Are the strikers going to be here?

Ganz answered, yes, both the strike coordinators and the rank-and-file negotiating team, "the whole group that is involved."

CHAVEZ: What point do they want to make?
GANZ: They want to make a resolution tomorrow to call for a general strike. I mean I haven't. That is just what's out there.

Chavez outlined how the Executive Board should talk to the strike committee. Start with the good news: Meyers Tomatoes was close to signing a contract:

CHAVEZ: And then we should maybe hear from the board that . . . we know that the [workers at the] companies want to strike now, and we want to strike, too. But there are some considerations we have to make. We do not want to say it openly at the convention . . . [but] . . . we don't have the money. And if we spend that money on the strike, then we can't do a boycott. And then say that we don't want to close the door to a strike, but we don't think that a strike right now would be as valuable as the boycott, and then once the boycott is functioning then the strike becomes like the final shot in the head . . .

DAVID MARTINEZ: That sounds reasonable. Once we get a boycott—

GANZ: The response they are going to give is that by that time all the work will be over and we will be back in the Imperial Valley . . . There is another consideration. There has sort of been a general thing going around since the Imperial Valley: Well, gee, we should have struck everybody, and we shouldn't have struck one at a time. Because their feeling is that it is a lot harder for people to recruit scabs if everybody has to recruit scabs than if one company has to recruit scabs.

By the end of the discussion, Chavez had adopted Ganz's position that at the convention the union should keep its options open. Ganz was relieved, but Chavez quickly warned him that voting for a general strike was far different from actually intending to go on strike.

The workers, waiting in the next room, had guessed what was coming. They weren't interested in a boycott. They talked the matter over as they waited. Chava Bustamante urged anyone who might speak in favor of the boycott to speak up there, while they were among themselves. No one did.

As the workers walked into the Executive Board meeting, the language changed from English to Spanish. After some joking around, Chavez called the meeting to order; about forty workers introduced themselves. Chavez said he had already been to many meetings that day: "I am tired, and let's take care of this quickly because we have to come back early tomorrow."

Ganz outlined the possible Meyers Tomato contract. It looked like they were going to get $5 an hour, a steep rise in the contribution to the medical plan, and some provision for paid reps. Chavez told the workers that Meyers wanted to sign by the next day, before the convention was over. He said the contract would have some impact on the lettuce negotiations, but he didn't know exactly what. The news was no surprise. The rank-and-file negotiators had already told the strike committee all the details. There was a relatively easy conversation, not too contentious. Then Chavez opened the larger question, and what followed was unlike any discussion that he had ever had at La Paz.

CHAVEZ: We have a problem that we cannot say in public: we are broke. We have spent $2.8 million on this strike. We don't have money and we don't know if we are going to win quickly. This affects the whole union. We don't want the growers to know about it. It would be difficult to have a general strike. Not difficult, impossible . . . We are not saying we are not going to strike, but we already have a month preparing for the boycott. If the opportunity arises we can have a strike as the coup de grâce, because we have the boycott. But to have a strike now won't protect us from the scabs they have brought to mess us up . . . Sun Harvest is the easiest to boycott. It never takes us more than three months to win a boycott. In the wines it took us less than ninety days.[51]

CHAVA BUSTAMANTE: And Gallo?

CHAVEZ: That was an exception. We didn't have a strong boycott. We didn't have everybody on the boycott . . .

CHAVA BUSTAMANTE: . . . I am going to speak the truth. We are in a dead end. You say we don't have money. I see the necessity to have a general strike in all the companies that are in the union. And if we don't do it, we are going to lose all the energy and good morale that we have built up, and all the strikers are going to be very disappointed. Those of us in Coastal have to make a decision that we are going to live with forever.

Dolores Huerta talked about the mechanics of boycotting lettuce, and how successful it could be on the East Coast. She reminded the committee that if they beat Sun Harvest, or another big company, the other, smaller companies would have to follow. Aristeo Zambrano spoke next, and then the dam broke.

ZAMBRANO: When we declared the strike, the people were hungry to go on strike. But the growers saw it as a bluff because nothing happened. We came to negotiate, and nothing happened. And the people went cold, like ice. And it was a lot of work to get this march going. And it was a lot of work to renew the people's faith in the union. And now we will lose that faith because we are not going to do anything. And everything is going to be more difficult, and the growers are going to figure out what is happening. We have to announce that the general strike is going to start on Monday. If the people know that we are not going on strike because we don't have any money they are going to be disillusioned.

JAVIER AYALA (Veg Pack strike co-coordinator): There is another thing . . . The *pre-huelga* was like a feint, as if we were going to do something, but we didn't follow through. So the growers know that we are afraid to follow the example of the strikers who have been on strike for seven months . . .

GANZ: But what is the alternative?

WORKER: *Huelga.*

MARIO BUSTAMANTE: *Huelga General.*

WORKER: *Huelga.*

WORKER CHORUS: *Huelga, huelga, huelga.*

Rigoberto Perez, one of the strike coordinators, tried to make peace. He had come to the meeting ready to go on strike, but now that he heard there was no money, he was ready to follow the orders of the Executive Board. "Make a good plan," he pleaded.

Huerta didn't try to paper over the differences. She jumped to Chavez's defense, asking, "What force does a strike have when there are scabs?"

AYALA: We shouldn't be afraid of scabs. We have faith in God that this general strike that we have planned for the thirteenth will work. None of us have died of hunger. We shouldn't be afraid of anything. There are always resources. People on strike receiving strike benefits can lower their benefits and give some of the money to others. [Applause] We need a general strike in Salinas. In the whole country.

CHAVEZ: It is very difficult, very dangerous to go on strike now. The way I see it, we are not going to win. And if we don't win for a long time, we are going to spend the resources of the union. And that is going to damage the other members of the union who are really many more than the people here. I can't do this in good conscience. Look, we have to go on the boycott. We haven't been able to beat Sun Harvest, and we have the most power at Sun Harvest. So how can we beat the others? It is clear. It is clear.

People began talking over one another and among themselves. "We have to go in turns," Ganz shouted. Jose Morales of Sun Harvest, usually a strong supporter of Chavez and the Executive Board, argued that a general strike would make it easier to boycott. When Huerta answered, Morales pointedly said, "I want Cesar to answer me."

MORALES: If we go on the boycott, where are we going to get funds for our families? If we don't have the money to strike, why do we have the money to boycott?

CHAVEZ: With the boycott, we have won strikes that were lost in the fields. With a boycott, we are certain to win. With a general strike, it's a risk, a throw of the dice. And we cannot risk breaking the union.

We can't do it. And there are a lot of members of the union who are not here right now.

Mario Bustamante, sitting next to Ganz, finally entered the fray.

MARIO BUSTAMANTE: I want to say something about the strike. If we don't go on strike, the company is going to come down on the leaders. And not only the company, but the workers will come down on the leaders, too . . . We had a meeting with the ranch committee and told them that every ranch was going to organize itself and be ready to go on strike. In the last discussion we had with Jim Work [a Green Valley Produce executive] he said he was ready for the strike. And I said we are ready, too. So they suspended us for the week that is coming. If we go back to work now, what are they going to think? And they fired two people. And what is going to happen to them if we go back to work? Are we just going to let them be fired? This is my opinion: if we don't go on strike we are going to have to abandon everything, abandon all our fellow strikers. The faith that everybody had in us will turn into dust.

ARMANDO RUIZ (strike coordinator at Sun Harvest): There is no lack of money. We are members of the AFL-CIO with seven million members. We can go to the locals and ask for one dollar a week.

CHAVEZ: They are not going to give it. They never have given it. It is not realistic.

WORKER: If we don't go on a general strike, what is going to happen to us who have been on strike for seven months? We have gone week to week hoping that the rest of the people were going to go out on strike. And in every meeting we say they are going out on strike. A month and a half ago, the morale fell. But it came back with the marches. And what is going to happen if we tell the people that we are not going to do anything now? What are the growers going to say about us?

Worker after worker spoke up for a general strike. A few sided with Chavez. "When the Executive Board tells us something, they know what they are talking about, and we are just acting like hot-heads when we say no," one declared, adding, "Cesar has said that it is not the right time to do it. He has told us." Mario Bustamante replied, "But we have the right to say what our opinions are."

Finally, a strike coordinator made an attempt at compromise.

STRIKE COORDINATOR: If the workers want a strike and there are no funds, we can do it for two weeks, and then we can go on the boycott if it doesn't work. We have to give the people the satisfaction of going on strike. Now the best thing would be to give us two weeks to fuck up the growers. In 1970 we were on strike for three weeks without money. And I think we can last longer now because we are better organized. Yes, we can last three weeks. And I think that is long enough for the thing to be decided.

WORKER: How can we keep both the devil and God happy? Cesar says we are going on the boycott. We have told the people that we are going on strike. What are we going to do? Well, I think the *compañero* has said it well. We go on strike for a couple of weeks, and if it doesn't work then we go on the boycott.

GANZ: But if the companies know we don't have any money and we are only going to strike for two weeks, they will just wait us out.

MARIO BUSTAMANTE: I want to tell a story about a burro and a coyote. The coyote is walking behind the burro, and he sees that a piece of meat is hanging from the burro, and he wants it, but he waits for it to fall by itself, and it never does. We are like that coyote. What the hell are we waiting for? Let's grab it.

People laughed and applauded. When they quieted down, Dolores Huerta tried to go back to basics.

HUERTA: In order to win a contract, we have to put economic pressure on the company. But when we go on strike and the company gets scabs, what pressure is there? That's the problem . . . There are plenty of scabs in the valley. And we all know it. And if we ignore it, that is a mistake . . . [People shout to interrupt, but she continues on] What I am saying is if we go on strike and the companies put in scabs, we won't be putting any pressure on the companies. So we go on a boycott to keep up the economic pressure. And the people aren't going to lose their jobs. Because the people are not going on the boycott. Only the leaders are. The people are going to keep working. And the majority are not going to strike without money. And we all know it. We all know it. We are in a difficult position with the people because we have told them that we are going on strike, and we have to figure out how to get out of this. But we are fooling ourselves if we think we are going to win in just a few weeks.

MARIO BUSTAMANTE: I am going to talk about my father, may he rest in peace. He was one of the original strikers at D'Arrigo And when they called off the strike and went on the boycott he wasn't able to get a job for more than a year. After all that time that he had worked at D'Arrigo. If the compañeros who are now on strike go on the boycott they are going to lose their seniority. Because this isn't going to be resolved in a month or two. They are going to lose their seniority and their jobs. If there is no money for the strike, and we know that people who go on the boycott are going to lose their jobs, then we are a bunch fools to end it like this. Better to sign a bad contract now, whatever we can get, and then when we have more funds in three years we can go on strike. People won't lose their work or their jobs, and with a signed contract we can put these fucking people who are scabbing against us out of work. [Applause]

ZAMBRANO: There is something else. People are saying that they are going to replace us with scabs, and that some of us have already been replaced. But the scabs who are inside are there only because the union hasn't let us get them out. One day that we went in, in just one day, we put them in a very bad situation. Just half a day, in the morning . . . So let's not remain with our hands tied. The scabs are working. But we can get rid of them. As long as we are allowed to. [Applause]

The argument was mostly over. Mario Bustamante made one more point: "Scabs will never be able to do the quality of work we do. And so the companies have lost. They have lost. And we should never be afraid of scabs, because they will never be able to work like us." Then he said that the meeting had gone on too long.

It was twelve-thirty in the morning, and Ganz suggested suspending the discussion. Tomorrow at the convention they would pass a motion that endorsed everything: "Strike, boycott, legal attack, everything." Then they could meet again later and decide what they were actually going to do.

What time? someone wanted to know. Ganz turned to Chavez. Cesar hadn't said anything for a long time. He answered in a quiet, flat voice: "I don't know. For me, I don't know. Before the convention it would be too early. I don't think we can meet before." Mario Bustamante wanted to make a final point.

MARIO BUSTAMANTE: If in the convention the resolution says we are to go on the boycott, I'm telling you right now I am not going to support it. I agree let's continue the discussion, but if the resolution is for the boycott, I won't vote for it.

GANZ: Tomorrow we have to say boycott, strike, everything, so as not to close off any roads.

MARIO BUSTAMANTE: I am telling you, I won't support a motion just for a boycott.

MANY VOICES (including Huerta's): No, no, no, it's not going to be anything like that.

CHAVEZ: Like I said before, there are three things we are going to ask for—

GANZ (interrupting Chavez): Expand the strike, put the boycott in place, and start a legal attack.

The meeting had been polite but unambiguous. Cesar Chavez had had an argument with the rank-and-file leadership, and lost. They had consistently applauded people who spoke against his position. They had chanted "*Huelga*" in the face of his opposition.

Chavez was not used to losing a debate within his union. He blamed it on Ganz. He didn't believe the workers had opposed him on their own. Ganz must have manipulated them, he complained later. Well, losing one argument was hard to take, but not the end of the story. Cesar Chavez knew how to fight.

Mario Bustamante was late getting back to Hartnell College the next morning. He had been assigned to work on the convention's resolutions committee. Only one resolution, the tenth, concerned the union's strategy in its current battle with the vegetable industry. Bustamante fumed as he read it. It called for "a total mobilization of all the union's resources . . . to engage the growers in all-out economic warfare until victory is won." But then it specified only one action: "that both struck and nonstruck growers who have refused to renew their UFW contracts or accept the farm workers just contract demands be boycotted in earnest." Mario's suspicion the night before had been entirely justified. The Executive Board had proposed a boycott resolution, and ignored the strike.

Mario was furious. He shouted at Gilbert Padilla that the strike committee was being double-crossed. Padilla was the resolutions committee chairman, the gatekeeper, whose job was to keep anything discomfiting to the organization's leadership from reaching the convention floor. But the gatekeeper opened the gate. Just back from Washington, D.C, Gilbert was doubtful about the success of the boycott, and he had been impressed by the strike committee's arguments. He told Mario to write up an amendment to the resolution, and he would see that it got to the floor.[52]

Bustamante retired to another classroom and wrote up the amendment. He took it to Marian Steeg, a UFW staffer then heading up one of the negotiating teams, who helped put what he had written into formal language and translate it into English. It endorsed the boycott and a "massive legal offensive," but closed with these words:

WHEREAS, the strike must be extended because we feel that by doing so, we can arrive at a quicker victory,

THEREFORE BE IT RESOLVED by the membership of the United Farm Workers of America, AFL-CIO, that the strike be extended, so we can fulfill our obligations as men and women and leave an example to our children.[53]

Bustamante and the strike coordinators were not new to politics. Many had been in the union for at least nine years—Mario, for eleven. They had attended conventions, knew about resolutions and votes, understood rules of order. What the strike committee had won the night before would not be taken away from them through convention maneuvering. And Padilla was as good as his word. The amendment made it to the floor through the regular channels. Bustamante read it to the 248 delegates sitting on the Hartnell basketball court and the 500 observers in the bleachers. Cesar shot angry looks at Padilla and Bustamante but was in no position to oppose it. It passed unanimously amid chants of "*Viva la huelga!*"[54]

As the Sunday convention was coming to a close and people were starting to leave, Chavez asked them to wait. He introduced Benjamin Perez of the Meyers Tomato negotiating committee. With the full committee standing behind him, Perez described the contract they had just signed. They got the $5 an hour, a cost-of-living clause, a 300 percent increase in the medical plan, no displacement by machines. There was the thunder of stamping feet. The bleachers started to shake. People got up and snaked-danced through the aisles. The chant was overwhelming. "*Huelga, huelga, huelga.*" On the podium, Cesar Chavez, some members of the Executive Board, and a few invited guests tried a chant of their own. "Boycott, boycott, boycott." It could barely be heard.[55]

Back in February, when Chavez had put Frank Ortiz in charge of the strike in the Imperial Valley with orders to reduce mass activity, the strike committee had been unable to act. Its members had been working together as a committee for less than two months, and had neither the internal cohesion nor the authority to battle Ortiz for control of the strike. Now, six months later in Salinas, Bustamante, Chavez, Ganz, and all the other protagonists woke up on the morning after the UFW convention in a different world.

Chavez knew it. He had been defied in a face-to-face confrontation and on the floor of his own convention. He had no pry-bar with which to dislodge Ganz and the strike committee from power. They would do what they would do; he wouldn't finance them, but he couldn't stop them. He believed they couldn't win the strike, and he hoped they wouldn't do too much damage. He returned to La Paz, kept himself busy with boycott plans, and waited to see what would happen.

On Monday morning every one of the 350 workers at West Coast Farms in Watsonville joined the strike. Augustín Herrera, the strike coordinator, simply stopped holding them back. He had told the Executive Board at the Sunday night meeting that he had promised the workers that they would join the strike if there were no settlement by Monday. He kept his promise. He didn't check with anyone. As far as he was concerned, Resolution 10 as amended by Mario Bustamante and unanimously approved by the convention gave him all the authority he needed.

West Coast Farms, a medium-size locally owned lettuce and celery grower-shipper, was a bit of a special case. As part of an arbitration in 1977, the UFW had agreed that when its contract expired the new negotiations would concern only wages and benefits. The company had hoped that by getting the union to keep all other language off the table, contract talks would go more easily.

Separate negotiations between West Coast and the UFW had begun in March, and had made some progress during the spring harvest. West Coast workers had walked off the job three times to pressure the company, and twice they had rallied in the parking lot outside the room where the talks were being held, their chants audible at the negotiating table. Marian Steeg, who had once directed the Watsonville field office and who now led the negotiating team, worked closely with Herrera and the ranch committee. She had approved those earlier walkouts, but she had also urged the workers not to join the strike fully until they had UFW authorization. After the convention she had a pretty good idea of what the West Coast workers would do. That Monday morning she went to the beach so she wouldn't be around to tell them not to do it.[56]

In Salinas, Marshall Ganz went to work as usual. He hadn't spoken to Chavez after the convention; the Executive Board and the strike committee had not decided when to meet again. Ganz knew about the West Coast workers, but he didn't know what he was going to do. He was talking matters over with some people in the field office when Mario Bustamante walked in. It was mid-morning. Everything was quiet, low-key.

"What's happening?" Mario asked.

"Nothing much," Marshall said.

"What do you mean, nothing much?" Bustamante wanted to know. "Why aren't we organizing the general strike?" Ganz told him that there was no money for it. Chavez certainly wouldn't authorize the money and might even stop the current strike benefits. Bustamante started to yell, accusing Marshall and Cesar of betraying the strike. He damned a few more people and then stormed out of the office. Ganz hesitated for only a few moments, and then followed Bustamante out the door. He saw him a little ways off, walking down the street. Ganz got in his car. When he pulled up alongside, Mario believed that Marshall had come to fight him, to defend his honor after being insulted. No, it wasn't that, Ganz said; he wanted to talk. Bustamante got into the car.

They drove to the quarry east of Salinas. Ganz did his best to explain Chavez's position and that of the various other actors in the union. Even at this point, with all that had happened, Ganz didn't criticize Chavez. He told Bustamante about the West Coast strike. There was proof, Bustamante argued, that they could carry on the strike without Chavez, without La Paz, without strike benefits. It was a long talk. By the time they got back to the union office, the discussion was over. The result was no surprise, no departure from what had been happening over the last several months. When the choice had to be made between the Executive Board and the strike committee, Marshall Ganz took the side of the workers.[57]

But did it have to be a choice? Wasn't it possible for Ganz to please both God and the devil? Chavez was not trying to intervene, after all. He wasn't on the phone giving orders. He wasn't on the phone at all. And the convention had spoken, unanimously. If the strike committee carried out the policy that had just been affirmed, why should it be considered an act of rebellion?

But that argument wouldn't do, and Ganz knew it. The convention may have passed the Bustamante amendment, but Ganz and the strike committee knew that it was against Chavez 's wishes. Cesar had not intervened only because he could not. He had been pushed aside by the workers on the strike committee. It was now their strike to win or lose, and Ganz had cast his lot with them. There was no way out of it.

Ganz and Bustamante called the strike committee together. They acted judiciously. They supported the West Coast workers; on Tuesday, when the tomato workers at Gonzalez Packing walked out in south Monterey County demanding a contract like the Meyers contract, the strike committee endorsed this second extension of the strike. On Wednesday, the committee filed petitions with the ALRB for access at the nonunion companies, as both threat of and preparation for a bigger strike. On Thursday, Marc Grossman told the press that Chavez was "closeted with aides" and would remain in La Paz planning strategy until the end of the week. "We plan to expand the strike, but are holding off on a day-to-day basis."[58] The West Coast and Gonzalez workers had already expanded the strike. What La Paz had to say was worse than irrelevant.

That same week it rained in Colorado. The strike committee joked that God was on its side. The rain slowed down the Colorado lettuce harvest. That, combined with the strike activity in California, pushed the price of lettuce to $12 a box. With the exception of a few rumor-induced spikes, the price of lettuce had been low all season. Now with a little more than a month to go in the season, the growers were hoping for a summer bonanza to counter their losses in the lousy spring harvest. West Coast, without deep pockets, needed the windfall profits as much as anyone.

The other growers were worried. Perhaps trying to convince themselves, they told the *Salinas Californian* that the new Meyers contract added no pressure on the lettuce companies, because the two-and-a-half-month tomato season was completely separate from the lettuce deal. *The Packer* claimed that the only significance of the Meyer agreement was "the publicity it gave the union."⁵⁹ But it was more like momentum than publicity. The next day, the Friday after the convention, Sun Harvest reopened separate negotiations with the union. Carl Sam Maggio, who ran Sun Harvest, took over the talks. He was worried that West Coast would sign an agreement that he would then be forced to accept. On Saturday, Gonzalez Packing signed on to the basic Meyers contract. The UFW had now signed the two biggest tomato companies in the valley—at $5 an hour, with paid reps and no giveaways in the contract language.

Jerry Cohen led the Sun Harvest negotiations. He was in constant communication with Marian Steeg, at the head of the West Coast talks. West Coast was the more vulnerable of the two companies. Steeg felt she was close to a deal, and told Cohen to back off a bit, and wait for her to reel in West Coast. On Saturday night, two weeks after the West Coast workers had walked out, the company signed. Its owner, Mitch Resetar, explained that he had "suffered severe financial losses during the work stoppage." Brad Bennet, also of West Coast, offered a partial apology to the rest of the industry: "The outlook is bleak. We just did what we had to do for ourselves right now, but we probably created a lot of hard feelings."⁶⁰

The contract was a stunner: $5 an hour immediately, with retroactive pay to the contract's expiration date—meaning an average $700 cash bonus to every West Coast worker; a cost-of-living adjustment, which would enable hourly workers to make $6.20 in July 1981, a 67 percent hike over their present wages. The labor price for a box of lettuce jumped from fifty-eight cents under the old contract to seventy-five cents a box in the new one, with an increase to eighty-two cents in the final year of the three-year deal. A union representative, paid by the company, would help administer the contract.⁶¹

Sunday morning, about eight hours after West Coast had signed, Sun Harvest's Maggio was having breakfast with Cohen at a hotel in Monterey. Maggio was ready to settle, but he needed some guarantee that the union would improve the quality of the pack. Without that, he said, it would be hard to sign. Cohen called the paid reps the solution to the problem; they would work with the crews and the foreman and guarantee a better pack. Improving quality would be part of their job of administering the contract. Maggio knew the members of the Sun Harvest ranch committee. He respected them, he told Cohen. By the time breakfast was over he had accepted Cohen's assurances that the union was committed to a quality pack.

As they were leaving, Maggio made a parting remark. It had been a minor theme since March, always in the background. "Tell me Jerry, when are you guys going to get around to organizing the rest of the industry?"⁶²

Other growers, ignorant of Sun Harvest's moves, were not yet ready to settle. The industry negotiator Andrew Church and the spokesman Mike Storm did their best to control the fallout from the West Coast contract. Church said that West Coast had signed only because the main issue of the strike—company control of the crews—was not on the negotiating table. Storm told the *Salinas Californian* that the company had settled because of the two-week strike, and "if Cesar wants a contract with the fifteen other growers, it's going to have to be on different terms than those."[63]

The rank-and-file leaders agreed with Storm: the two-week strike had forced West Coast to sign. As it turned out, the strike committee hadn't needed more money to win the strike. Nor had scabs blunted the walkout. The West Coast workers had gambled and won. So had the Gonzales Packing workers. It was going to be easier now for other workers to make the same bet.

The strike committee began to broadcast the newly won wages on radio spots and in thousands of leaflets that they distributed in the camps and the fields. On Monday morning, August 28, the first working day after West Coast signed, farm workers throughout the Salinas Valley began to enforce that deal as the new standard wage. They sat down in the fields or refused to leave the company buses. Supervisors and foremen held impromptu negotiations with balking workers. Most companies soon agreed to pay $5 an hour and 75 cents a box. The highly committed nonunion companies even paid a few cents more: Merrill went up to $5.10 and Hansen up to 76.5 cents a box. The sit-down was widespread. At Cal Coastal, even scabs refused to work, demanding that their wages be raised to the new industry standard.[64]

By the end of the week the fields were a bit calmer. The UFW leaflets had urged people to demand a UFW contract and not settle for just higher pay. "Don't let them substitute cat meat for rabbit" the leaflet's headline enjoined.[65] Tomato workers at Fruden Produce took the directive to heart. They left the fields, filed for a forty-eight-hour election, and voted 201–4 for UFW representation. A UFW legal worker, Steve Matchett, told the press, "It was like a locomotive that couldn't be stopped." Nonetheless, by Friday many of the workers were back in the fields, satisfied with just the wage concessions. That day the bigger news hit: Sun Harvest settled, and on UFW terms. The contract language, which Andy Church had said would impede further agreements, differed little from the old contract. The union kept the hiring hall and the grievance procedure was changed only slightly, and not to the union's disadvantage. "Good standing" remained, and the company agreed to the paid reps and got no new work rules giving them more control over the crews.

Some said it was all over but the shouting. That was only half true. They shouted most of the night at the UFW field office. But some of the biggest fun was yet to come.

★ ★ ★

On Tuesday, September 4, 1979, after Sun Harvest workers had ratified the contract and gone back to the job, workers at all the other companies negotiating with the UFW went on strike. It was a mini–general strike: it did not hit the nonunion companies that still made up more than half of the vegetable industry in the Salinas and Pajaro valleys, but it was big and impressive enough. Although the scabs at Sun Harvest had been fired, the other companies didn't try to bring them in. This was no longer a strike that could be stopped by scabs.

Nor would the union settle for anything less than it had already won. One ranch committee president said, "They are going to give us a new proposal, but there is nothing to negotiate about. Sun Harvest and West Coast: that is what we want." Marshall Ganz was more blunt. "The workers have walked out because they don't want any bullshit negotiations. Time for that kind of negotiation is over. They want the language of the Sun Harvest contract and retroactive pay back to January 1 or January 15, depending on when the contract expired."[66]

Many of the struck growers couldn't even put up a brave front. One small grower told Doug Foster, "It's a scary situation. You have the feeling emanating out of the workers that 'What's mine is mine. What's yours in mine too.' You should be able to dictate how you want your work done. Under the Sun Harvest contract you can't. But what are you going to do? If they put enough pressure on you, especially when you're my size, you're going to crack."[67]

As the mini–general strike entered its second week, the weather turned hot, over 100 degrees. It seemed to be another gift from heaven. In that heat, if mature lettuce isn't harvested in a day or two, it will bolt and be worthless. If the growers were going to have to sign eventually anyhow, it would be best to sign now while there was still something to harvest.

Mann Packing was the next to fall. It was the biggest broccoli company, and broccoli is even more susceptible to the heat than lettuce. Three days later, ten days into the general strike, with 500 acres of lettuce rotting in the fields, representatives of nine more firms lined up in the halls of the Towne House Motel, waiting for their turn to walk into the room where Jerry Cohen, Marshall Ganz, and Anne Smith had contracts ready for them. Eventually, all but one of the UFW companies in Salinas signed. Nine months after receiving the union's first contract proposal, the growers were surrendering to terms not much different from those that they once dismissed as "staggering" and "outrageous."

As they waited to sign in the halls of the Towne House, Jerry Cohen reached Cesar on the phone. Jerry excitedly described the scene, and suggested that Cesar come see it for himself. Chavez declined, saying he didn't feel comfortable in Salinas. He sent his brother Richard, who celebrated with the workers in his stead.[68]

It had been four and a half weeks since the convention and the meeting at Hartnell Community College, not a happy time for Chavez. He planned for the boycott, issued occasional statements about the strike, and thought over what had happened in Salinas. The problem was Marshall Ganz. He said as much to Padilla, Ortiz, David Martinez, and Richard in a morose evening discussion over pizza and beer in Tehachapi. "What are we going to do about Marshall?" Padilla remembered Chavez asking the group. "He has his own union in Salinas."[69]

Down in the Pajaro and Salinas valleys there had been an almost continuous celebration ever since West Coast Farms had signed. The picket lines were festive, the meetings raucous, spirits high. The workers were playful, some delirious with joy. They talked and talked, stayed up most of the night, played soccer, ran races. The foot races became a favorite activity, something to do with their excess energy as they waited for the victory that was sure to come. They knew who the fastest runners were, and they matched them against each other, betting on the outcome. One of the champions was Cleofas Guzman, the diminutive, highly respected strike coordinator. One evening, Cleofas was matched against the six-foot-one Jerry Cohen, whose judgment had been impaired by a few beers and who had let it be known that he had run the 440 in college.

Dusk was turning to dark as they lined up on the Sherwood School grass, next to the UFW field office. Aristeo Zambrano insisted afterward that it was a clear win for Cleofas, and that Jerry fell down after he had been beaten. Cohen swears that he was in the lead until he stepped in a hole and tore his Achilles tendon. After the race, the workers picked Jerry up, and then they all went out and drank some more.

The Good, the Bad, the Unlikely

September '79 to December '80

Perhaps the most judicious course of action, not uncommon in the annals of political history, would have been for Cesar Chavez to go to Salinas, make peace with those who had defied him, and claim credit for what had been won. But Cesar Chavez didn't know how to do that. He had built an organization that did not tolerate dissent, and he had no experience of continuing to work with people who had disobeyed him. He had not spoken to Marshall Ganz, either in person or by phone, since the August convention, and he wouldn't do so until early November. For Chavez the Alinskyite, the hero-organizer had become the organizer-villain.

During this period when the two weren't speaking, Ganz had gotten caught up in the exploding strike, the contract signings, and the question of how to put more pressure on the few stubborn union companies—Bruce Church, Admiral, Growers Exchange, and Cal Coastal—that had not yet signed. Chavez had gone ahead trying to build the boycott. The day after the August convention he had called a two-day conference at which the Executive Board, minus Ganz and Govea, decided to send most of its members and the top union staffers to major U.S. cities to set up and administer the boycott offices. Gilbert and Esther Padilla were to return to Washington, DC; Richard Chavez and Dolores Huerta to New York, David Martinez to Toronto, and Frank Ortiz to Chicago. Ganz and Govea were assigned to Los Angeles in absentia. Ganz was uninterested in the boycott plans and had seen no need to go to La Paz for the conference, and though he had heard, indirectly, that he and Govea had been assigned to Los Angeles, neither made any plans to relocate.

In response to the defiance from Salinas, Chavez began a quiet offensive against Ganz. Initially the whispered complaints included the accusations that Marshall had masterminded the walkout at West Coast Farms and had manipulated Mario Butstamante at the convention. But those were soon dropped because Bustamante's resolution and the West Coast walkout had become heroic deeds, minor legends in the fields. Continuing to attribute them to Ganz would only add to his prestige. But other darts remained in Chavez's kit: Ganz had promoted strike violence that had resulted in Rufino Contreras's death; Ganz and Govea had defied a clear order of the

Executive Board; Marshall had told the organizers Jose Renteria and Artie Mendoza that they didn't have to bother with the boycott either. Frank Ortiz and Oscar Mondragon went to Salinas and spread the word in a few private discussions: Ganz was out of control, doing whatever he wanted. He and his associates were defying Cesar Chavez.[1]

Ganz heard some of the rumors. He did not call Chavez and try to explain himself. He didn't think he needed to. He had made the right choice and had the contracts in his pocket to prove it.

On September 26, Ganz did send a five-page memo to Chavez. "The following are some thoughts I hope you find useful," it began. It included a list of the companies that hadn't yet signed, a plan for continuing the strike, a proposal to "organize the competition," some notes on the lettuce markets that might be useful for boycotters, a proposal to begin work on revising the RFK Medical Plan, and a suggestion that the paid reps be quickly elected and trained. At the end of the memo Ganz made a gesture acknowledging the silence and the rumors: "The current situation is ridiculous and untenable. If you want my resignation—although I believe I can continue to make a valuable contribution to organizing the UFW into a real national union and want to do so—just tell me."[2]

Chavez never answered. He was too smart to part ways with the coordinator of the most successful farm worker strike in U.S. history in the immediate aftermath of its triumph. He was willing to attack Marshall at board meetings, and he allowed his loyalists to whisper charges against him to the staff. But although Chavez was afraid of Ganz's growing power, he could not confront it head-on. Not yet.

A few days after Ganz's symbolic baring of his throat, negotiations began over the process by which the paid reps would be selected, and their job descriptions. The new contract language was incomplete: the union would "designate a full-time representative" who would be responsible for enforcing the contract, and would be paid by the company at the same rate as other people in his or her job classification.

Discussions to refine the job description took place at a distance, each side bunkered in its own territory, unwilling to travel to the other side's turf. In La Paz, the Executive Board proposed that the paid reps be appointed by Chavez and be considered part of the regular union staff, subject to the president's direction. In Salinas, Ganz held some small meetings of the rank-and-file leaders. "Marshall didn't tell us what to do, but he agreed when we decided we would argue for elected positions and independence from the field office director and La Paz," Aristeo Zambrano recalled. "We weren't thinking of the battles yet to come; we had no idea they were coming . . . But we knew that to do their jobs of helping to enforce the contract, in order to maintain the respect and support of the people who worked under those contracts, the paid reps had to be elected and independent."[3]

The Executive Board chose Ruth Shy, one of the most competent, well-respected staffers, and Richard Chavez to present its proposal to Salinas. Ganz organized a large group of people to receive the mission from the mountain. At least forty people—members of the strike committee, the rank-and-file negotiating committee, and representatives from ranch committees throughout the valley—gathered in a large room at Sherwood School. Shy and Richard Chavez presented their proposal and opened discussion from the floor. After a polite but pointed debate, the question was put to a vote. The decision was not unanimous, but it was overwhelming. The paid reps should be elected and have specific job descriptions that distinguished them from the rest of the staff.

Shy passed this news to La Paz. Chavez and Ganz, still not talking to each other, reached a compromise through her: the members at each company would elect their ranch committee and its president, as they always had, and then Chavez would confirm that the president would be the paid rep. In that way, Ganz explained in a memo, the paid rep "would be accountable to his ranch community and to the overall union." After the negotiations were over, Marshall and Cesar talked on the phone for the first time in almost three months.[4]

Those negotiations, even done at arm's length, were a unique episode of democratic dialogue and decision-making inside the UFW, never to be repeated. An Executive Board proposal on an important matter was presented to a large group of rank-and-file leaders who rejected it and substituted one of their own, which was then slightly modified and accepted by the people at the top. The only comparable give-and-take between the UFW center and the periphery occurred during the formulation of contract demands. But generally those proposals amounted to a long, indiscriminate list, and except for the workers' determination not to give up the hiring hall in 1979, they didn't have the same weight as this structural innovation in the union.

Not only was the procedure unique, so was the result. Hammered into the union staff by farm worker power, the paid reps were a small democratic wedge that potentially could shift the weight of the entire edifice from the mountain to the valley. For the first time in UFW history, people who worked for the union would be elected by their fellow workers rather than appointed by La Paz. Not entirely dependent on Cesar Chavez for their jobs, accountable primarily to the people who elected them, the paid reps threw the union's organizational chart into chaos.

Chavez conceded only because he had to. A month after the workers had taken the strike into their own hands and won it, Chavez and the Executive Board were in no position to issue a decree on how the reps should be selected. They had to negotiate. And once the workers had voted on their own proposal, it became difficult for Chavez and the board to reject it.

But there is more. Chavez was willing to accept elected paid reps because he didn't believe that rank-and-file workers, even the leaders of the 1979 strike, would, on their own, oppose his policies.[5] He did not see the paid reps as a threat—he thought he could handle them even if he didn't control their jobs or their income. The danger was what he had called "malignant forces" during the Nick Jones purge, the people who might organize the workers against him.

The negotiations ended in mid-November, and the first ranch committee election was held at Sun Harvest a month later. Cleofas Guzman won as president of the committee and paid rep, defeating Armando Ruiz. Sabino Lopez, another strike leader, was elected vice president and, because of the company's size, became the second paid rep. There was no doubt about the meaning of the results. Ruiz was the incumbent ranch committee president and a fierce supporter of La Paz. During the Hartnell College meeting he had got caught up in the enthusiasm of the moment and uncharacteristically opposed Chavez, but in the latest negotiations he had reverted to form and had spoken in favor of the La Paz recommendations. His defeat by a vote of 523 to 127 signaled a shift away from the more moderate local leaders in favor of the militants who had led the strike.[6]

At forty-one, Cleofas Guzman was a little bit older than most of the other strike leaders. A native of the small town of La Palma, Michoacán, he had snuck across the border in 1956 and gone to work in the fields. A year-round Sun Harvest *lechuguero*, he had been active in the union since the first Salinas strike in 1970, when he was shot in the foot by a foreman during a picket line scuffle. Thrown into the leadership of the 1979 strike, this small and often quiet man had flourished. He was the one who told the strike rallies "*Esta huelga está ganada*," his public confidence setting the tone for the triumphant closing weeks of the strike. Now he was the paid rep at the most important union company, and in the elections that eventually followed, he would be joined by many of the other leaders of the strike, paid reps all: Aristeo Zambrano, Augustín Herrera, Javier Ayala, Simon Reyes, Rigoberto Perez, Hermilo Mojica, Juan Flores, Mario Bustamante, and Berta Batres.*

Berta Batres was the only woman among the paid reps. She had come to the United States in 1970, at the age of seventeen, sitting in the back seat of a car driven across the border by an Anglo couple that had gone to Mexico to find someone to take care of their baby son. But Berta did not last long

---

* The only major strike leader missing was Chava Bustamante, whose company, Cal Coastal, had not yet signed a contract. By the time Coastal did sign, more than two years after the strike began, Chava was working for California Rural Legal Assistance, and was doubtful as to the prospects of rank and file power in the UFW. He decided not to return to the fields.

as a nanny, and soon she was cutting broccoli in the Salinas Valley. By the late 1970s she was making $16,000 to $20,000 in an eleven-month season, wages comparable to those of other skilled U.S. workers, and a fortune compared to what she had made in Mexico.

For Batres the fields were a step up in the world. As a child in the tiny farm town of La Escondida, Durango, her life had swung between poverty and prosperity, a rise and fall that left her precociously sensitive to rural class distinctions. Her father, who taught her to plant beans when she was five, went to the U.S. as a bracero, and she was raised by her mother and paternal grandparents. From her grandmother, a fan of Pancho Villa, she learned of the dire days before the revolution, when her grandfather had been paid in corn rather than money and her grandmother would take her children out to the fields to teach them the names of the flowers and birds to help them forget how hungry they were. The stories did not match Batres's own early childhood, however, for the money her father sent from the U.S. enabled her grandfather to buy some cows and a bull, which he husbanded into a small, rural slaughterhouse, and relative affluence. In primary school Berta was one of the better-off students and was treated as such by teachers and classmates. But the good times didn't last. Something happened; Batres was not sure what. Did Grandpa gamble or drink the money away? Did he fail to bribe someone who had to be bribed? Did the cows get sick? Whatever the answer, her grandfather's business disappeared, and the stories of prerevolutionary hunger became more vivid. The eight-year-old, now without extra money, was no longer so popular at school.

She retreated into books, did well as a student, and at sixteen was attending a rural teacher's college in 1969, when her schooling was interrupted by politics. The student movement, which had reached its dramatic apogee in Mexico City in 1968, had finally arrived in the provinces. Excited by the political ferment, she went on strike with her fellow students. She never returned to class. The strike lasted so long that she took a job at the Mexican Social Security office. It soon became distasteful. The office staffers looked down on their poor clients. Those without money they shamed. Those who paid a little bribe got quick service. Batres thought about her own life. At one point, her mother would have been among those able to pay the bribe; after the cows were gone, she would have been among the humiliated. Batres complained to her boss, but he barely understood what she was talking about.

When the Anglo couple came through town looking for a nanny, she jumped on board, willing to test her luck in El Norte, like her father. She had no idea that her grandmother's stories, the ideas that had swept through her teacher's college, the politics that had made her an object of suspicion in the Social Security office would all serve her well on the other side of the border. Popular on her piece-rate crew, instrumental in bringing the

UFW to her company, Arrow Lettuce, she became an articulate local leader, sensitive to social rank and with an experienced political eye. She mixed easily among the all-male paid reps, and took the measure of their strengths. Mario Bustamante may have been the most audacious, Mojica the most strategically minded, and Zambrano the most politically educated, but Cleofas Guzman, she said, "stood rooted in the ground, a small man whose integrity made him a thousand feet tall." From the summer of 1979 to January 23, 1981, for Berta Batres, and for all the rest, it was the voice of Cleofas Guzman that carried the most authority.[7]

The 1979 strike, though powerful and successful, had left the union in a perilous position. Of the UFW companies with operations in both the Salinas and Imperial valleys, three were still in difficult negotiations, and Bruce Church had defiantly refused to sign, as had all of the grower-shippers based exclusively in Imperial. Union membership in fresh vegetables had fallen from about 40 to less than 33 percent. The strike had intensified the problem that Ganz had first called attention to in 1977. The UFW could not last in a highly competitive industry that was part union, part nonunion. It had to grow or die. Although most of the nonunion growers matched union wages to keep the UFW out, they still had a comparative advantage. Moreover, many of the grower-shippers who signed in the heat of August and September did so only out of desperation, and despite the fact that the eight-month strike had turned them decisively against the union.

Mike Payne, the general manager of Bruce Church and a committed right-winger, had publicly pledged that the company would never sign a UFW contract that included the hiring hall and a good-standing clause. During the strike Church had induced a significant number of its workers to cross the picket lines, and afterward had raised wages above the Sun Harvest standard. The company had actually expanded during the strike, becoming the number two lettuce grower in the state, behind Bud Antle. Sun Harvest, meanwhile, fell from second to fifth because of its strike losses and a subsequent decision to reduce its acreage in the Imperial Valley by half.[8] All this was proof, some growers openly argued, that the UFW did not have a firm hold on the future.

The 1979–80 winter lettuce season did nothing to damage the Imperial Valley's reputation as the graveyard of farm worker unions. The Imperial companies had followed the events in Salinas with mixed emotions. They hated to see any UFW success, but as long as they themselves remained nonunion, that success also gave them a boost over their union competitors. Bruce Church's open defiance of the union gave the desert growers hope that they, too, could resist the UFW as the harvest hit the Imperial Valley in December.

They didn't just hope. In the off-season, the eight Imperial Valley companies that were still being struck had formed solid scab crews, enclosed a few of their smaller fields with Cyclone fences, and expanded their lettuce plantings into grower-friendly Arizona. They paid more than the wage they had offered ten months earlier, when they had declared an impasse in negotiations. The ALRB objected, asserting that this meant that they had bargained in bad faith, but a judge ruled in the companies' favor. If he had ruled the other way, the eight growers would have been prevented from raising their wages, and would have had a hard time keeping their scabs.[9]

On the union side, the enthusiasm of the summer had fallen victim to the exhausted emotional, political, and economic resources of the rank and file. The hot weather, torrid passions, and high lettuce prices that had forced so many Salinas companies to capitulate did not automatically migrate 450 miles south to Imperial, and the remarkable rank-and-file democracy that had characterized the last month and a half of the Salinas strike could not last indefinitely. Momentum would have to be rebuilt in the desert, among workers who were tired and in dire need of the high wages that they could get by returning to work.

This was true even among the strike leaders. Zambrano, Batres, and Ayala went back to their jobs at union broccoli companies in Salinas. Mario Bustamante also stayed in town, working at a few off-season jobs in the fields. Cleofas Guzman, Sabino Lopez, Armando Ruiz, and several other members of the old strike and negotiating committees returned to work at Sun Harvest's Imperial Valley fields. As paid reps, Guzman and Lopez had their hands full getting the ranch committee together and dealing with the problems involved in resuming work after an eight-month strike. Mojica moved to Mexicali and was actively trying to renew the Imperial Valley campaign, but he, too, spent much of his time cutting lettuce at a nonstruck company.

Nor were the union officials united in an effort to rebuild a big, powerful strike. Chavez's faith in the boycott had not been shaken by the Salinas victory in the fields. All he wanted from the Imperial Valley season was discernible evidence that the strike was still alive, especially at Church, so that the top union leadership could use some news from the fields to help rebuild the boycott organization. Marshall Ganz, however, had just seen mobilized workers turn what looked like defeat into victory, and believed that if the workers could renew the pressure on the growers, if they kept on shaking the tree, more fruit might fall.

As Ganz and Chavez started talking again, their mutual need overshadowed their differences, and Cesar agreed that Marshall would follow the harvest to Imperial to see what he could do with Church and the other struck companies. Not much, as it turned out. It is one thing to continue a movement that is already in motion against the wishes of the popular leader supposedly at the head of the parade, and quite another to get something started from scratch without much help from the top. And for most of the workers, the strike was over. Only 200 to 400 active strikers were left to carry on the battle against several crews of committed scabs in the midst of some 7,000 satisfied farm workers earning the biggest money of their lives.

Early in the season the union caught a break. When the state employment department vacated its office in the middle of *el hoyo*, the union quickly rented the building from the city of Calexico and converted it into its new Imperial Valley office. "The Hole," the two-acre, blacktopped shape-up site, is sacred ground in farm worker history, the place where twenty-six years later a handful of aging paid reps would scatter the ashes of Jessica Govea. In 1980 it was not just a historical marker; *el hoyo* remained the main transit point for the majority of people who worked in the Imperial fields, the forum for hundreds of daily conversations among workers, and the best possible spot to initiate organizing drives. When the Western Growers Association found out about the new union hall, its representatives offered to pay the City Council 50 percent more than the UFW was paying to rent the place. They were too late.[10]

Raising the black eagle over *el hoyo* deserved some sort of celebration. Ganz and others urged Chavez to help make the ceremonial opening of the union hall a powerful new beginning for the Imperial Valley strike. Chavez, out on the boycott trail, declined. Nevertheless, 1,500 workers attended the party. Rufino Contreras's father raised the union banner on the pole that had once held the American flag. Farm worker children sang songs, some workers spoke about the renewed strike, Cleofas Guzman encouraged the crowd, and a Los Angeles priest presented the host and delivered a sermon. He called Cesar Chavez the new Moses, and the Imperial Valley a modern-day Promised Land. The new Moses, however, was in Washington, DC, talking up the boycott at an AFL-CIO testimonial dinner for George Meany.[11]

Ganz and a new strike committee tried to resurrect the *pre-huelga*, but the job action was not effective against companies that didn't fear being drawn into a powerful strike. After the first *pre-huelgistas* were fired, others backed off, and the tactic was dropped. Admiral and Growers Exchange finally signed contracts in mid-December, but not because of anything that happened in Imperial. Ganz, the Executive Board, and the strike committee decided that strikers at other companies should voluntarily return to work while the union continued to negotiate, but the companies refused to take back the workers, and two judges turned down ALRB petitions that would have forced them to do so.[12] Some strikers held on for the $25 a week and food donations; a few got dispatches to scarce union jobs; most did what they could to find work at nonunion companies.

Chavez made his first public appearance in Imperial late in the season, on February 10, at a memorial service for Rufino Contreras. The rally was slightly smaller than for the christening of the union hall, and was more subdued. In a news conference before speaking to the crowd of workers and supporters, Chavez told newsmen that the boycott campaign against Bruce Church's Red Coach lettuce was the "key to the success of the strike." The battle could last five years, as long as it had taken the union to win the grape boycott.[13]

But 1980 was not 1966. The social movements that had sustained the table grape boycott were long gone. The student movement did not survive the end of the Vietnam War. The civil rights movement had been hopelessly fractured by government repression, its inability to change conditions in the North, and the limits of its partial victory in the South. The brief rank-and-file labor upsurge of the late sixties and seventies had been assaulted by union bureaucrats and finished off by unemployment and a corporate offensive. A conservative backlash threatened the progressive tradition within organized religion. Ronald Reagan was about to ascend to the presidency over the prostrate remnant of FDR's grand coalition. The left had suffered a profound historical defeat, and the inability of the Red Coach boycott to get off the ground was just one tiny part of it.

The UFW had changed, too. No longer a band of embattled enthusiasts, it had become an institution with a long history—long enough to have squandered some of its political capital and alienated some of its supporters. Chavez's flirtation with Ferdinand Marcos had damaged the UFW's link to the remaining progressive elements within the Protestant church. The targets of the Nick Jones purge and the Synanon Game, although not public tattletales, had told their stories privately to friends and comrades, the very people who had been among the most faithful boycott picketers. The "wet line" and the Campaign Against Illegals had alienated not only what was left of the left but also some Chicano groups for whom the original boycott had been their baptism into politics.

And the UFW had already taken its first hit in the mass media. In 1979 the *New York Times* had published Robert Lindsey's investigation of what had happened five years earlier on the "wet line" in the Sonora Desert. Although mostly concerned with charges of violence on the wet line, the article also detailed one of Manuel Chavez's failed scams: After the 1974 lemon strike, Manuel, using the name Manuel Camacho, had convinced a San Joaquin Valley agribusinessman, William Hamilton, to invest $140,000 in a Baja California melon deal. Manuel had leased more than 1,000 acres in the Mexicali Valley and supervised the construction of a packing shed. The melons turned out not to be good enough for the U.S. market, and Manuel sold what he could to Mexican distributors, stiffing Hamilton for his entire investment. Manuel tried to put together another Baja deal in 1976, to import onions into the U.S., which also didn't work out. In 1977 and 1978 he went looking for money to start a tomato deal in Sinaloa and Sonora, but couldn't find any takers.[14]

The Hamilton-Manuel Chavez partnership was more than just a simple conflict of interest. Manuel Chavez had been the UFW's main organizer among melon workers in Arizona and California, leading strikes that had effectively limited melon production and raised wages. Operating a Baja melon deal that was financed by a California grower and was designed to import melons into the U.S. at the same time that he was promoting U.S. melon strikes threw into question the whole reason for the melon walk-outs. Perhaps they were just part of Manuel Chavez's business plan.

A similar scam had sent him to jail in 1964, when he was simultaneously organizing for the National Farm Workers Association and working for a produce company, and was convicted of forging the company's checks. That had involved a few hundred dollars, and the NFWA was tiny. Now he was dealing with hundreds of thousands of dollars, and the UFW was the most important agricultural union in U.S. history. Hamilton consulted Mexican and U.S. attorneys but then dropped the matter. He told Tom Barry, the reporter who first investigated Manuel and the wet line, that he was "ashamed," and "didn't want to go around bragging about what a fool I had been."

A thousand acres of melons in Baja California could not be slipped by Mexican farm workers. In the mid-1970s Manuel's would-be Mexican empire was well known in the California fields and had been used by Teamsters organizers to try to discredit the UFW. But when Lindsey's story appeared in the *Times*, it was largely unknown to the union's liberal supporters. Chavez told Lindsey that he didn't believe that Manuel had been doing business in Mexico "for his own personal profit," and said that Manuel hadn't been "a paid official of the UFW for some time." Both answers were carefully constructed. Manuel had justified his Mexican adventures by saying that he would use the profits to finance farm worker organizing in the U.S. He did go on and off the UFW payroll across the years, but at the time of the Hamilton deal he was participating in discussions at La Paz about the upcoming ALRB elections.

A year later, just as the Bruce Church boycott was getting under way, the UFW took two additional hits in the mass media. NBC's *Prime Time* charged that the union was using millions of dollars in U.S. government grants illegally and wastefully. The then-influential liberal columnist Jack Anderson heard some of the reports from ex-staffers and wrote that the UFW had become "a violence-prone, tyrannical empire under the iron-fisted rule of Cesar Chavez."[15] The UFW produced witnesses who contradicted Anderson, and he wrote a retraction. After failing to stop the airing of the *Prime Time* segment, Chavez called on the Carter administration to investigate the La Paz charities and prove the allegations. The charities were ultimately exonerated, but some damage had been done.

None of this helped rebuild the boycott coalition. Having dismantled the boycott infrastructure, Chavez could not put it back together again. It was a painful loss. Although the boycott had misshaped the union in many ways, it had also been crucial to the union's early success. Now, in 1980, despite the setback in the Imperial Valley, farm worker power was more pronounced than it had ever been in the 1960s. The farm worker movement was not yet dead. It had just scored its greatest victory, and its power was semi-institutionalized in more than a hundred contracts and in the new system of paid reps. Nevertheless, the UFW still faced an awesome task: organizing the majority nonunion sector of the vegetable industry. In that fight farm workers could have used the support of their old allies. But the alliance was finished. Ganz and Govea were not the only Executive Board members who failed to go on their boycott assignments. Dolores Huerta and Richard Chavez didn't go either—with Cesar's approval. Most of the union leaders who did go were back in La Paz within several months. By 1981 there would be only three people in the Chicago boycott office, and hardly anyone on what had once been large, spirited boycott picket lines. The days of mass participation in UFW boycotts were over.[16]

Without a strong boycott, and not believing in the power of the workers, what was Chavez to do? He turned, again, to Democratic Party politics. In February 1980, Chavez briefly explained his strategy to the *Salinas Californian* reporter Doug Foster: The growers needed more than just good labor relations—they were also concerned about increased pesticide regulation, cheap irrigation water, zoning regulations that protected agricultural land, and the rapid increase of imported produce. Those issues would be decided primarily in Sacramento. "The industry will have to ask for our help," he told Foster. "Sooner or later they're going to have to come to us and make a deal."[17]

To deliver on such large issues, though, the union needed more than just friends in Sacramento. It needed a substantial piece of legislative clout. To get it, Chavez thought he had to do more than just mobilize workers to pressure legislators, or develop alliances with well-placed liberal politicians, or provide volunteers and money at election time. In addition, Cesar Chavez would try to capture the second most powerful political job in California, speaker of the California Assembly, not for himself but for a man who would owe the position to him.

This was a morally dangerous move. Chavez did not have a generous view of politics. Just as he didn't see political discourse as a way of democratically deciding the issues that confronted his union, he didn't view politics in the larger society as a legitimate debate on matters of public interest. "Our involvement in politics is not because of a love of politics," he would tell a reporter in 1985.[18] Politics was an unfortunate necessity, a sacrificial immersion in a world of lies and deception in order to extend the power of the union. But could Chavez operate in this polluted arena and retain his saintly reputation? More important, could he immerse himself in what he considered sleazy intrigues and still maintain his own sometimes shaky hold on ethical standards of political maneuver?

In December 1979, as the Imperial Valley lettuce harvest was getting under way and as Governor Brown was preparing for his second presidential run, Chavez decided to get in the middle of a duel for the speakership. Sacramento politics is not short of colorful stories about brutal fights between erstwhile friends. This is one of the gaudier ones.

The prize was control of the flow of all legislation originating in the state of California. Since Jesse Unruh's reforms of the 1960s, the speaker of the Assembly had become the second most powerful office holder in the state. By appointing the members and chairs of assembly committees, controlling the money for their staffs, and assigning legislation to one committee or another, the speaker could bury legislation he opposed and sunshine bills he supported. The speaker also controlled a large pool of money provided by wealthy donors, which he dispensed at his discretion to Democratic candidates for their election campaigns.[19]

In 1974, Leo McCarthy, an Irish Catholic, had won the speakership in a contest against his fellow San Franciscan Willie Brown, the flamboyant black legislator who had supported the UFW since 1966. Both liberals, they hardly had any principled differences, but after the vote McCarthy had exiled Brown's supporters to unimportant committees and shorted them on campaign funds. McCarthy's closest aide was Howard Berman, a Jewish liberal from Los Angeles. Berman served as majority leader in the Assembly for five and a half years, a position he owed to McCarthy, whom he called his mentor.

The drama began in mid-December 1979, when Berman told McCarthy in a closed-door meeting that he would run against him as speaker, and that he had the votes to beat him. Sacramento was alive with explanations for this remarkable betrayal. Berman offered the rather weak defense that McCarthy was planning to run for higher office and was neglecting his job. Others complained that McCarthy was not putting all the money he was raising into the fund for Democratic Party candidates for the Assembly but instead was stashing some away for his own future race for the U.S. Senate. Pundits argued that since McCarthy favored Ted Kennedy in the battle for the 1980 Democratic nomination against President Carter, the other candidate, Governor Brown, wanted McCarthy out as speaker and had asked Cesar Chavez to urge Berman to act. It was all routinely denied. Probably the best explanation was that Berman was looking to advance his own career, and he thought he had a chance to win. Betraying his friend and mentor didn't count for much by comparison.

No one but Howard Berman knows for certain whether Chavez urged him to run. But Chavez did support Berman as soon as he declared. Cesar liked the younger Berman, and didn't like the more seasoned McCarthy, who had opposed Proposition 14 as unnecessary and politically stupid, as it proved to be. Otherwise, the two candidates were virtually indistinguishable on UFW matters, voting with the union most of the time. But Chavez had had nothing to do with McCarthy's becoming speaker. Even with Brown in the governor's office, Chavez didn't have the juice in Sacramento to deliver enough to the growers on pesticides, land, and water to get contracts in exchange. If he could play a large role in making Berman the speaker, Chavez's power in Sacramento would multiply several-fold, and he just might be able to win there what he was sure he couldn't win in the fields.

Such logic was by then common fare within union circles, as many AFL–CIO leaders tried to win in electoral politics what they had lost on the picket line or across the negotiating table. But generally union officials stayed out of debilitating internal Democratic skirmishes and supported whoever came out on top. The head of the state AFL–CIO and the chief of the LA County Federation of Labor tried to broker peace between McCarthy and Berman. When they failed, they declared themselves neutral. That was the position of most California labor chiefs, although Jerry Whipple of the UAW and Jimmy Herman of the ILWU stood by McCarthy. Herman said he gave McCarthy his endorsement so that no one might think that Chavez spoke for the ILWU or all of labor.

By tradition, the party that controls the Assembly selects the speaker. First the Democrats would hold a caucus vote. Then the Democrats would vote as a bloc to elect as speaker whoever had won the caucus. Inside the Democratic caucus, Chavez had two powerful allies: Assemblymen Art Torres and Richard Alatorre. Torres had once been a young UFW staffer, and Alatorre, an assemblyman from LA's East Side, was called the "UFW's best friend in the legislature." At first Torres had called Berman's move a "stab in the back," and Alatorre had insisted that he would stand by McCarthy, who was "fair and compassionate." But after meeting with Chavez on Christmas Day, 1979, in San Jose, both men switched sides, changing a 26–24 line-up in McCarthy's favor into a 26–24 vote for Berman.

The caucus fight had been particularly nasty. People were promised jobs, threatened with retaliation, guaranteed or denied money. Moreover, when Berman first deserted him, McCarthy had appointed his old nemesis, Willie Brown, as the new majority leader. Brown was in charge of securing the black assemblymen for McCarthy; with many of the Jews in Berman's camp, racial and ethnic tensions were added to the caucus fight over money and influence.[20]

When the vote came to the floor of the Assembly in early January 1980, tradition and custom were cast aside. Instead of voting for Berman, McCarthy's supporters abstained. The Republicans, delighted by the Democrats' troubles, also abstained. Berman had just twenty-six Democratic votes. He needed forty-one, half the Assembly, to win. McCarthy remained speaker. Eric Brazil of the *Salinas Californian* wrote, "The Assembly corridors were figuratively slick with blood." He could have added money.

Berman did not give up. Strongly encouraged by Chavez, he decided he would support candidates in the June and November elections who would pledge to help him when the vote on the speakership came up again in 1981. But what could Berman's support mean when he had no access to the kind of funds that McCarthy controlled? That is where Chavez, the UFW, and almost $300,000 of the farm workers' Citizens Participation Day contributions would come in. Before it was settled, a few more knives would be stuck in a few more backs.[21]

Meanwhile Jerry Brown was flailing about in the waters of presidential primary politics. A couple dozen UFW staffers and Marshall Ganz did all they could to revive the spirit of Brown's '76 campaign, but Brown got lost in the battle between a sitting president and the last surviving Kennedy brother, finishing a distant third in three straight primary contests. He withdrew from the race on April Fool's Day. The only person appearing with him when he made the announcement to the press was Cesar Chavez. Afterward Brown offered Ganz a job as a special assistant, responsible for building a new political organization in California. Ganz was tempted. He had been in the UFW for fifteen years. He had been feuding with Chavez for a while, and was concerned about where Cesar was taking the union. Ganz told Brown he would think about it, and then went to Salinas to visit some of the leaders of the 1979 strike. He found a bunch of distressed people. At that point no other ranch committee elections had been held since Cleofas Guzman and Sabino Lopez had become paid reps back in November. The RFK Medical Plan was a mess. The workers had heard nothing about a new organizing drive. "Isn't the union going to follow through on what we won in 1979?" they asked.[22]

Ganz and Govea went to La Paz to negotiate with Chavez. They were trying to decide whether to leave the union, they told him, but they would be willing to stay if Govea was put in charge of the RFK Medical Plan and if Ganz was sent to Salinas to put together the paid rep elections and plan for an organizing drive that summer. In the midst of their negotiations the *LA Times* reported that Brown had already hired Ganz and quoted one administration insider as saying, "Marshall is very loyal to Cesar, but . . . I think he is ready to try something new."[23]

Chavez was not pleased, with either the announcement or the ultimatum implied in the negotiations. Doug Foster of the *Salinas Californian*, who in an earlier article on the Brown campaign had noted Ganz's "legendary" organizational skills, now wrote that the news that Ganz might leave had upset local union members, who feared that the employers would "take Ganz's departure as a sign that the UFW had given up on gaining any leverage on the picket line."[24]

Chavez was still not ready to let Ganz and Govea leave his organization, but he did not intend to give them a free hand: Govea would do much of her work in La Paz, and Ganz would be on a limited, supervised budget and would be given only four organizers.[25]

By late April, 1980, Marshall Ganz and Jessica Govea were back at work. Jessica had the harder task. The union was paying a heavy price for incorporating the RFK Medical Plan into its own operation. Union medical plans are almost always set up independent of both the employer and the union; thus, when workers have problems—and there are always problems with insurance—typically the union rep intervenes with the medical plan administrators, and the workers' complaints are not focused on the union. In the UFW the plan belonged to the union, and therefore so did the problems and the workers' discontent. At one point in 1978 Chavez had told the Executive Board, "Maybe we should give the growers the plan and let them administer it. And we can handle the grievances. Fuck them. Let them have the plan."[26] Chavez was joking; he wasn't about to give up an account then worth almost $7 million, but what he facetiously suggested is precisely what most unions do.

The plan had been manageable as long as UFW membership was low. Ralph and Maria Magaña had administered it, with no more than one or two rotating volunteers, beginning in 1971. They had no experience in medical plan procedures, but with few claims the office functioned well enough. After the union lost the grape contracts, in 1973, the membership plunged, but the undisbursed grape grower contributions to the plan, conventionally invested, continued to grow. In that period the ratio of reserves to claim payments was so high that the IRS warned that the plan could lose its tax-exempt status. The picture changed after passage of the ALRA and the winning of new contracts. The Magañas had handled 380 claims in February of 1975, but three years later they were handling 2,500 claims a month. Nothing was computerized, so the Magañas had to check through hundreds of pages just to verify one claim. They consistently asked Chavez for more personnel. Instead, Chavez ordered most of the La Paz staff to help out with the paperwork one day a month. In July of 1978, Bobby De La Cruz, director of the Oxnard field office, reported that claim settlements were so slow that "no doctors accept the medical plan in Ventura County." A few months later Larry Tramutt told the Executive Board, "The depth of the problem is outstanding." He had found mail in the RFK department "several months old that had not been opened." Ralph Magaña said it could take "three months or more" to process a claim.[27]

In 1978 Chavez often blamed worker complaints about the medical plan on troublemakers, assholes, and Communists. As it happened there were three Maoists from the Revolutionary Communist Party (RCP) in the Salinas fields at the time, working among 15,000 farm workers. Despite their quite limited influence, the La Paz tapes are peppered with warnings from Chavez about these Communists, whose numbers he greatly exaggerated. Although Chavez generally restricted his denunciations to his La Paz intimates, in August 1978 he warned the members of the rank-and-file negotiating committee who were visiting the union headquarters about these "theoretical Marxists" who had come from the universities to destroy the UFW. They were like "snakes in the grass" and they had to be "kicked out" of the union. When Aristeo Zambrano heard the charge he was insulted: "What Chavez couldn't understand is that farm workers were upset about the medical plan. We didn't need anybody to agitate us. We could figure it out and be angry on our own."[28]

Problems with the medical plan had worsened by 1979 and 1980, when the union represented some 30,000 workers. Govea took over but had no authority to bring on a significant number of new volunteers to deal with the casework and paperwork. The problems of duplicate names, false Social Security numbers, and late grower payments persisted. When she first arrived, it took several months for a standard medical claim to be paid. She had to devise new benefit schedules to fit the substantial jump in payments that the growers put into the plan as a result of the 1979 strike. Her energy and organizational skills made a difference, as did her authority with the workers who were trying to get their bills paid, but it remained a slow operation.

After Ganz organized elections at the other ranch committees and twenty more people had been elected paid reps, the medical plan became one of their chief concerns. It was now mid-May of 1980, and the paid reps wasted no time going about their business. They met together formally once a week, gave work reports, discussed union policies, and talked over problems at their companies. They met regularly with their ranch committees and with the membership. Hardly a meeting went by when there wouldn't be some complaint about unpaid medical bills and the consequences: doctors unwilling to take patients, credit ratings ruined because the doctors who did take patients had turned the unpaid bills over to collection agencies. Workers were especially annoyed because the grower contribution to the plan in the new contract had increased sharply, and yet the problems continued. The paid reps in turn complained to Govea and Jose Renteria, the new director of the Salinas field office. They worked with volunteers to try to solve individual problems. They filled out forms; they called La Paz to find out why bills weren't paid. With Jessica in charge, they were optimistic that things might change, but the workers' complaints continued and the paid reps were swamped with the paperwork necessary to track down exactly why it was taking so long to pay peoples' medical bills.

Unable to get much help from La Paz, they did what they could to resolve matters on their own. They formed a committee of five, headed by Mojica, and visited doctors, dentists, and clinics in search of some solutions. They couldn't do anything about making the checks come faster from La Paz, but they did make other small improvements. In cases where the plan paid only a portion of the bill, they made agreements with some doctors for the workers to pay off the rest in small monthly payments. They arranged for a dental clinic to stay open at night so that people could go after work. They successfully pressured La Paz to provide ID cards for those covered by the plan. Much to Chavez's displeasure, they showed up at meetings of the plan's trustees to try to find out how the plan worked and how much money was actually in it.[29]

Despite the problems, in the spring of 1980 the paid reps were optimistic, and they were having a good time. Many of them went to the fields first thing in the morning and talked to the workers before going to the office. Mario Bustamante and Hermilo Mojica always carried their knives and often worked for a while, giving people a hand. At the office, the paid reps stood out—a farm worker presence in a field office where hitherto most of the volunteers had not come from the fields. The reps were already the fabled doers of heroic acts during the strike; many of them were entertaining, compelling storytellers as well as good listeners. Compared with the union volunteers, all of the reps were well paid, some of them extremely well paid by U.S. working-class standards. The reps who had worked on piece-rate crews were making as much as $500 a week; some of the volunteer staff, struggling on $10 a week plus expenses, were bothered by the pay differential, but that wouldn't become an open issue for another year.

In a sense, the power of the 1979 strike had created a UFW local in Salinas through the back door. Here were twenty-two local officials, elected by the rank and file, whose main job was to enforce the union contracts. Nonetheless, they were less than a local: although they were personally well paid, they did not control their own budget, since members' dues went directly to La Paz. Yet in many ways they were stronger than the vast majority of U.S. union locals in 1980. They had been born of a recent struggle; membership meetings were well attended; wages were rising rather than falling; the field office was a favored place to hang out for much of the rank and file. After the sunburst of 1979, a smaller but steady demo-cratic light continued to shine in Salinas.

The paid reps enjoyed their authority. They didn't see it as opposed to the union's power, but rather as part of it. They acknowledged, some more than others, that their relationship to Chavez had been changed by the Hartnell College meeting—the strike had proved them right and him wrong. But so many months later they were not in rebellion against Chavez or the union; they were enthusiastic unionists. They were prepared to fight within the union for what they thought was right. They were willing to take their leader on if necessary, but he was still their leader.

Their new role gave the reps a new perspective. "Now that I didn't have to cut lettuce five or six hours a day," said Mario Bustamante, "I could look around more calmly, more intelligently, and see what was happening." And they didn't like everything they saw and learned about the union.

> I would visit the fields in the morning, talk to the workers, see that everything was okay, and then I would go to the office around nine or ten in the morning. I started to see who did what. I started to talk to people in La Paz about the medical plan. I started to talk to people who were working on the services. And I started to see the areas in which the union was not doing a good job. I didn't complain. But I began to wonder, Where the hell is the money going? The services we were getting for the money that we were paying were not good enough. We were paying dues like carpenters, 2 percent of our checks, and yet our offices were poor, a mess. Why? . . . So I started to think, There is something wrong here.[30]

As the Salinas spring turned to summer, the paid reps continued to focus on the medical plan and on two other issues—the quality of the pack and organizing the competition. These two were connected. "The union companies couldn't control their workers. So what other boss is going to want to sign with the union if it meant turning his operation over to his employees?" Bustamante rhetorically asked the crews. The paid reps got the foremen and the workers together, away from the job, to talk things over. As a group, the reps understood both the origin of the problem and the legitimacy of the employers' complaints. "The workers had spent their lives being pushed around by one foreman or another," Mojica said, "and now that they had some control over their jobs, plus seniority and a grievance procedure, many of them just told the foremen to go to hell."[31] While the reps were not willing to negoti-ate away the crews' control over the pace and quality of the work, which they had won through ten years of struggle, they did agree that the bosses could insist on some basic standards of workmanship. It was

a difficult, often contradictory, position, and Bustamante took the lead
in making that argument to the crews:

> The workers had to learn that they had the responsibility to do a decent
> piece of work. That was the first job of the paid reps. . . . We had to
> teach it to everyone. So one of the first things we did was to have a series
> of meetings with the people. We told them straight out, if you want to
> get the contracts quicker next time, without so much struggle, then we
> have to improve the quality of the pack . . . I had five or six meetings
> with the workers at Green Valley just about this. I was so insistent on it
> that some people said I was a traitor, that I had gone over to the side of
> the bosses . . . But we made headway. The work improved, even at Sun
> Harvest. We just ran out of time.[32]

Organizing the competition was the largest problem, and the chief topic
of conversation at the paid reps' weekly meetings. Eventually they voted to
devote half of their time to organizing, although the vote was not binding
and many of the reps continued to focus entirely on their own companies.
This kind of organizing was not part of their formal job description, but the
reps did not consider the vote an act of rebellion. "We didn't think of it as
a defiance of anyone," Zambrano said. "It didn't interfere with us doing
our jobs, and it was for the cause. We thought it was necessary for the
survival of the union."[33] Mojica, Bustamante, Zambrano, Batres, Guzman,
and others started getting up even earlier in the morning and going to the
cafés in downtown Salinas where workers had breakfast before the day's
work began. They met over morning coffee with workers at the nonunion
companies, talking about the union, listening to their complaints, and met
again after work with those who were willing. They formed little committees of UFW enthusiasts at some of the nonunion companies; some of the
committees operated openly on their jobs, but most were semisecret.

Marshall Ganz helped the paid reps develop an organizing plan, and
although they all knew there would be some trouble ahead, Ganz gave
them no reason not to be hopeful about the union's prospects. He appeared
to be in good humor. He met regularly with Jerry Cohen at the International
House of Pancakes, where, Cohen said, "we plotted how we were going
to win this next battle with Cesar, how we were we going to get him to
commit the union's resources to organize the rest of the Salinas vegetable
industry." They thought they could win because they had won the dispute
with Chavez at the end of the strike, because the paid reps were such good
unionists, and because the reps had been willing to stand up to Chavez
when they had to. Ganz and Cohen talked it over, morning after morning.
But they never invited Cleofas Guzman or Mario Bustamante or Hermilo
Mojica or any of the others to join them.[34]

The growers, meanwhile, were coalescing. Nonunion wages remained slightly higher than the union standard; some of the bigger companies introduced medical plans and the foremen were on their best behavior. Unionization elsewhere had thus become highly beneficial to nonunion workers. At several companies, knots of antiunion workers who had been UFW antagonists on picket lines actively opposed the union. Other workers would have to be organized despite them.

Some employers with union contracts began to plan ways to rid themselves of the UFW. Their methods were as varied as the industry, where grower-shippers, large and small growers, cooperative harvesting associations, and custom harvesters,[35] made a series of yearly deals among themselves, which distributed the work, risks, profits, and losses of agricultural production. Conceptually it was not terribly complicated: some grower-shippers who held UFW contracts renegotiated their deals with smaller growers and shifted their field work to nonunion growers, custom harvesters, and contractors. In practice it was extremely difficult to follow, as private companies appeared and disappeared—"ghost companies," the farm workers called them—and the intricacies of their shifting relationships were not public knowledge. Union workers knew they were being replaced, but they didn't know if a lease had been allowed to lapse, if the company had subcontracted the work, or if the old union companies had financial ties to the new nonunion ones.

Sun Harvest led the way. Having lost $17.5 million during the strike and having slashed its acreage in the Imperial Valley, the company began to shed some of its Salinas operations. It ended its small strawberry deal, reduced its broccoli and cauliflower acreage, and notified the union that it might replace one of its two celery crews with a celery machine that harvested for soup. It renegotiated some of its year-to-year contracts with carrot, leaf lettuce, and tomato growers, so that some of the work that had been done by Sun Harvest union employees now became the responsibility of growers who brought in nonunion contractors or custom harvesters.[36]

In 1980 this reorganization did not affect the company's lettuce deal, which was the main source of union employment, but nevertheless, workers pressured the union to do something about it. The much-diminished UFW legal department did what it could to investigate Sun Harvest's machinations, to pin down the actual relationships between the company and the new nonunion operators, and it prepared to file a charge with the ALRB. Meanwhile, the number of union jobs at Sun Harvest continued to fall.

Similar moves were being made at other companies. Mann Packing, the Salinas Valley's biggest broccoli grower-shipper, had taken the first steps out of the union during the 1979 strike. The company grew about 20 percent of its broccoli on land it either owned or leased. The rest of

Mann's broccoli was grown by independents, then harvested by the Mann broccoli crews, and shipped out under Mann's labels. When the 1979 *pre-huelga* at Mann delayed the harvest and threatened to ruin the crop of some of Mann's affiliated growers, a few of those growers brought in contractors to try to harvest the broccoli before it went to seed. During the mobilization of 1979 the strikers had managed to stop most of that scab work, but in 1980 some of the affiliated growers renegotiated their contracts with Mann so that they no longer used Mann's harvesting crews. Instead, the broccoli was harvested by some of the same contractors the growers had used in the strike, although it was still packed and shipped by Mann.[37]

Ganz and the paid reps did not ignore the ghost companies taking away UFW broccoli work. In the broccoli, unlike in the lettuce, the UFW had a good chunk of the Salinas Valley industry under contract, about 75 percent, and the reps were easily able to track down these new nonunion operations. They visited the contractors' camps, talked to the nonunion workers, had them sign union cards, and talked some into walking out of the fields. It was effective, but not enough to scare off the growers. The next year more of them would arrange to do their own harvesting with nonunion contractors, and Mann would start to lay off some of its union crews.[38]

The story was only slightly different at Green Valley Produce. Green Valley was an independent harvesting association that harvested its member-growers' lettuce. Duing the strike, according to Mario Bustamante, one of the growers, Tom Borchard, had brought in a scab contractor to cut the lettuce that Green Valley's crews couldn't get to, as the company was crippled by the *pre-huelga*. Borchard hadn't been too successful during the strike, but in 1980 he formed a new company, and began to harvest his own lettuce as well as the lettuce of some of his fellow growers in Green Valley Produce. As far as Bustamante and the Green Valley *lechugueros* were concerned, Borchard's new workers were simply scabs, taking away their work. They picketed and harassed the workers in the fields, but couldn't get many to stop. Bustamante tried to get help from Green Valley's management, because Borchard's company was taking away Green Valley's work, too. But Green Valley never gave the ranch committee its records of who had dropped out of the association and what land they owned or leased, so it was impossible to detail exactly what was going on, and the union never even filed unfair labor practice charges with the ALRB.

All of these grower maneuvers were only a start, a hint of what was to become the entire reorganization of the California vegetable industry. The small stream in 1980 would become a substantial river in 1981, and a wild flood in the mid-1980s. If Cesar Chavez, Dolores Huerta, Gilbert Padilla, Marshall Ganz, Jessica Govea, Jerry Cohen, the paid reps, and an engaged rank and file had stood together arm-in-arm, they might have been able to dam it. Initially divided, then at war with each other, and finally shattered from within, they didn't stand a chance.

In the summer of 1980 the divisions among the union protagonists did not seem fatal, although the major players were imagining different futures, and had different assessments of where their power lay. Chavez was banking on his and the union's political leverage in Sacramento. Marshall Ganz was counting on the workers' ability to remake the union. The paid reps were taking the temperature on the ground and finding reasons to believe they could still counter the growers by organizing the masses of California's unorganized workers. The piece-rate vegetable crews were back at work, for the most part enjoying their recent triumph, and poised to go back into action when called upon to do so.

Chavez still held a tight rein on new organizing. In July of 1980, as the *invernito*, the little winter, was coming on in Salinas, the UFW had forced new ALRB elections at only two companies, neither of them important lettuce grower-shippers. Chavez came to town for the first time late in the month to meet with the ranch committees to talk about Govea's proposed changes in the medical plan and to support a belated, and still limited, organizing drive. As people at the field office were preparing to meet him, a few carloads of garlic workers made a surprise entrance, declaring that they were on strike and had come to the UFW to get some help.

The garlic fields were hard, hot, and badly paid, and Salinas Valley farm workers did what they could to avoid them. The season began in Gilroy and Hollister, both about a half hour's drive from downtown Salinas, but the workers were Tejanos from the Rio Grande Valley and Mexicans from Texas border states. Jammed into cars and pickup trucks with campers, they arrived in California in mid-July. They worked the first batch of garlic for six weeks and then moved down to King City at the southern end of the valley, where the work lasted until October. Whole families often traveled together, with some going home early so that the kids could get to school, and others finishing up in Central Valley, where the fields were even hotter and the pay even worse.

Adults and teenagers typically spent most of the day bent over or on their knees. A machine had preceded them through the fields, loosening the earth to make it easier to pull up the garlic bulbs. Skilled, quick hands pulled the bulbs from the ground, cleaned and clipped the roots, trimmed the tops, and threw the bulbs in a bucket. Women who were topping garlic and also watching small children would sometimes leave the cropped bulbs on the ground, and then try to get the kids to put them in the bucket. That usually didn't last long, and often girls of eleven or twelve were put in charge of their younger siblings at the side of the fields.

Except in an especially bad field or in surprisingly bad weather, people were paid by the bucket. Families that worked together were paid under one or two Social Security cards, and by the end of the four-month season, if all had gone well, a family could clear a few thousand dollars for their labor. Two to three thousand people made this run, and together they pulled, trimmed, and topped about 90 percent of the fresh garlic grown in the United States.[39]

As with lemons, the piece rate for garlic was negotiated in the fields between the foremen and the workers, depending on the size of the bulbs, the quality of the field, and the time left in the harvest. Overall, however, wages were low, and garlic strikes were ineffective because the bulbs can remain in the earth for a relatively long time before they go bad—although eventually they do discolor, which lowers their value.

In 1980, however, the workers figured their position had changed. They had heard about the UFW victory the year before, and they knew that the majority of workers in the Salinas Valley were now making at least $5.65 an hour, with piece-rate workers making considerably more. With the center of the union but a short drive away, they reasoned that they might be able to put up a fight of their own. When foremen refused to adjust the piece rate for the early crop, some workers walked out and drove down to the Salinas field office.

This is what unionists call a "hot shop," a place where the workers are already on the move and call in the union to help. Chavez, Ganz, and the paid reps all championed the cause. Chavez agreed that Ganz, Steve Matchett, John Brown, and Artie Mendoza should shift their efforts from lettuce to garlic, and sent one of his La Paz loyalists, Larry Tramutt, to help them. Marc Grossman came down from the mountain and spent some time in the small Hollister office talking to the press. Chavez also allowed Ganz to spend money on the campaign, starting with an initial $2,000. The paid reps were especially enthused; some of them spent most of the next month in Gilroy, talking up the union among the garlic workers. Their efforts in the lettuce, absent the concerted backing of La Paz, had not gone well, and the garlic campaign muted their disappointment. The garlic workers were a better indicator of the future, they hoped. When the time was right, when each set of workers was willing to fight, the union would sweep up one crop after another.

Chavez spoke at a garlic workers' rally in the mission town of San Juan Bautista on July 24, a few days after he had arrived in Salinas. By then at least 1,200 workers were on strike, and every garlic field in the area was deserted. A garlic strike committee, working in close collaboration with UFW organizers, issued a demand for an hourly wage of $5, up from $3.10, and a piece rate of $3 a bucket, up from $1.80. The UFW immediately filed for forty-eight-hour elections at several ranches; it won the first one

128 to 4, and then the next eighteen straight, outpolling the growers 1,130 to 255.[40]

Ganz, the organizers, and the garlic strike committee decided to copy the tactic that the citrus workers and Eliseo Medina had used in Ventura in 1978. After winning the early elections, the workers remained on strike, hoping that the employers would not fight ALRB certification and would quickly sign contracts. But the growers did challenge the election results, despite their indisputable outcome. By fighting certification at every turn, the growers could delay the beginning of negotiations until the harvest was mostly over, taking whatever losses a continuing strike might mean. Anxious about losing much of their season and being forced to return to Texas or Mexico with empty pockets, the strike committee negotiated a return to work without a contract but with a new wage of $4 an hour and $2.50 a bucket, nearly a 30 percent raise.

On August 8, 1980, twenty days after the walkout began, 500 striking workers greeted the strike committee's announcement of the settlement with spirited "*vivas.*"[41] With the workers back in the fields, the UFW continued to hold seven-day elections, winning thirty-one of them. Eventually the ALRB certified all of them, giving the UFW representation rights for about 2,000 garlic workers, as well as a few hundred mushroom, pepper, pear, onion, and tomato workers, who had joined in the fun. The union promised that the following season they would negotiate the contracts that had eluded them.

It had been more like a fire than a hot shop. Sometimes wild, often contained, the campaign had quickly spread through most of Santa Clara and San Benito counties. Chavez was excited by the garlic battle, but worried, too. It had gotten bigger than he expected, and toward the end of the campaign, he turned against it. Chavez skipped the victory march and celebration even after the local organizers had announced that he would come. He then summoned Tramutt back to La Paz. Tramutt, a ten-year UFW veteran and one of Chavez's most devoted followers, had toured the country's boycott offices in 1976 with Fred Ross, explaining away the purge of Nick Jones. Now the wheel was about to turn. What he had seen in the garlic fields astonished him, and he was effusive in telling Chavez about the energy, militancy, and leadership of the paid reps, and the self-organizing of the garlic workers.

"In a second I realized my time had come," Tramutt later said. "Cesar had a way of pursing his lips when he was angry. He looked at me and said, 'Who are you working for? Are you taking orders from Moscow?' "[42]

Tramutt soon resigned. Chavez's Moscow baiting was probably just a matter of habit, something to be said against anyone who he thought was organizing farm workers without him or against him. He could offer no specifics. His usual targets, the three Revolutionary Communist Party members in Salinas, were no longer active in the fields and he couldn't blame them. No other leftist parties or organizations were involved in the campaign. Aristeo Zambrano was an avowed leftist but without party affiliations. Some UFW loyalists had already red-baited him, unsuccessfully, when he ran for the position of paid rep, but Chavez hardly believed that Zambrano was running the show in Gilroy and Hollister. Much later, Zambrano concluded, "The garlic elections were a feather in Marshall's cap, and as far as Cesar was concerned he had enough feathers already."[43] Ganz himself was stumped by Chavez's change of heart toward the mostly flourishing garlic venture. He guessed that someone must have said something to Chavez that unsettled him. He didn't know what, but it must have been significant, because at the end of this largely successful strike, Cesar Chavez once again turned against Marshall Ganz, and this time he never let up.

Ganz, partly disarmed, remained on the stage for a while longer. Others would exit before him. The next to go was Gilbert Padilla, one of Chavez's closet friends, his partner in CSO, and an original founder of the National Farm Workers Association/UFW. Back in June, Chavez had recalled Padilla from his Washington, DC, boycott duties and assigned him to negotiate the grape contract at the Freedman Ranch in the Coachella Valley. Freedman's 1,200 workers made it the single biggest company under UFW contract in 1981, topping even Sun Harvest. It had been the first table grape company to sign with the union, in 1970, and was the largest employer in the Coachella Valley.

For months the Freedman ranch committee had been trying to get help from La Paz in preparing proposals for renegotiating the contract. Letters from the ranch committee president, Armando Sanchez, and the secretary, Doug Adair, had been ignored. Only two inexperienced people staffed the Coachella field office, and they didn't have the authority, time, or information to be of much use. Starting in February, on their own, the Freedman ranch committee members studied the contract, met with workers in large and small groups, and formulated their proposals. From reading the newspaper they knew that their real wages had been falling since their last contract in 1977 and that the union had recently won $5 an hour in the vegetables. Under their old contract, they were still making $3.76 an hour, plus a bonus for each box at harvest time. The Freedman workers, many of whom lived in Mexicali and were quite aware that five bucks had become the minimum wage in the vegetable fields of Imperial, wanted $5 an hour too.[44]

By the time Padilla was called in, the harvest had begun, and the workers were nervous and angry. He made a brief exploratory visit to Coachella and reported that the situation was a mess, the field officers were incompetent, and the negotiations were already very late. Chavez disagreed. There was still plenty of time, he said. The only problem at Freedman was that people were agitating the workers. Chavez pointed the finger at Doug Adair, Rudy Reyes, and a radical Arab grape picker, Ahmed Shoibi. "The Commie, the huk, and the PLO," he called them. They were roiling the waters, he said, attacking La Paz and making it difficult to reach a settlement.[45]

Padilla told Chavez that was crazy; Adair and Reyes were longtime union loyalists, and an Arab grape picker could hardly be held responsible for unrest among Mexican workers. Padilla and Chavez argued. Chavez insisted that the workers were being organized against La Paz. Padilla, with renewed concerns about Chavez's sanity, went back to Coachella to start negotiations. Although Lionel Steinberg, Freedman's manager, was not ideologically opposed to the union, he was a businessman who knew that time was on his side. He delayed, and told the local press, "Union officials were always too busy with Governor Jerry Brown and U.S. Senator Teddy Kennedy to meet with us."[46]

On June 10, the day the contract expired, the company made an informal first offer: a 2-cent raise per hour. That afternoon, standing on a flatbed truck, Padilla told some 300 workers of Steinberg's proposal. The temperature was over 100 degrees, and the workers were hot. They had just finished a day's labor, and some had already started on their first beers. Many started to shout "*huelga!*" Padilla tried to explain that it was too soon to walk out. People came onto the flatbed, including Reyes and Shoibi, complained about all the delays, and urged an immediate strike. When Padilla tried to answer, the crowd shouted, "Go back to La Paz! Go back to La Paz!" Some workers threw empty beer cans at the flatbed.[47]

Padilla left. Adair took the microphone and tried to make peace. He said that the offer was an insult, and that they had to do something in the fields, but he warned that only a third of the company was even at the meeting, and it was too soon for a walkout. He did not carry the day; people voted to strike immediately.

When Adair finally found Padilla after the meeting, Gilbert was mad. "Let them have it," he told Adair. Let Reyes and Shoibi run the negotiations and the strike; he was going back to La Paz. Adair talked him out of it, and they both braced for the next day. The strike was too hasty, a very partial walkout that Reyes tried to call off at the last moment. The low turnout was a mark of weakness, and convinced the most militant workers that they did need Padilla and the ranch committee. Padilla suggested that the workers carry out a *pre-huelga*. He called Ganz, who came and described what had been done in Salinas. The workers enthusiastically took up the tactic, now and then collectively walking off the job before the day's work was completed. They also planned two all-day *paros*, when nobody would work at all.

It was a persistent, low-intensity battle, and throughout it little was right between Chavez and Padilla. Chavez criticized Padilla's handling of the negotiations and continued to complain about Adair, Reyes, and Shoibi. Padilla reiterated that Chavez's fear of them was ridiculous, and said the main problem in Coachella was not the radicals but La Paz's neglect of the field office. He also complained about the old Valiant that he had to drive back and forth to Coachella, one of the fleet of cars that Chavez had insisted would be the standard UFW automobile because of its sturdy slant six engine. The engine in Gilbert's Valiant ran fine, but the rest of the car was falling apart. The radiator leaked badly, and nursing it through the blazing heat from Coachella to La Paz could add an hour to the four-hour journey. Insisting on the Valiants was nuts, Padilla argued at La Paz, another example of the twisted priorities of the union, which was giving away big money to politicians but refused to provide its officers and organizers with reliable cars. Cesar, unused to sustained complaint, was growing tired of his old comrade.[48]

After the second *paro*, on July 2, as the season was nearing the end, the company offered a 28 percent raise over the two years of the contract: $4.50 in the first year and $4.80 in the next. Under Steinberg's piece-rate proposal, on a good harvest day fast workers would make up to $6 an hour. The company's contribution to the medical plan went up by 75 percent. Chavez came in for the last two days of the negotiations, tied up some loose ends, and the workers overwhelmingly accepted the contract.[49]

Although some workers grumbled about the missed chance to get the $5 basic wage, the settlement set a new standard in the table grape industry, and most workers considered it a victory. The triumph belonged to Padilla, the ranch committee, and the rank and file, and was won despite the negligence of La Paz. Once again, Chavez shunned the victory dance and barbecue.

For Gilbert Padilla, the cord snapped a few months later, in October, when Maria Rifo, a dedicated Chavez loyalist who had been with the union since 1968, was charged with counterorganizing at La Paz, and deposited in tears outside the union gate. Gilbert was outraged. Rifo wasn't counterorganizing against anybody. She was being made to take the fall for some program of Chavez's that hadn't worked out. "And besides, how could anybody organize against Cesar at La Paz?" Gilbert asked. "Who was she going to organize, Helen?"[50]

Padilla couldn't let it go. Not with so much else going wrong: the nonsense about Adair, Reyes, and Shoibi; the penny-pinching toward the field offices and Chavez's general lack of interest in the fields; the Valiant's goddamn radiator. Padilla and Chavez argued again, bitterly. A week after

Rifo was expelled, at a meeting in which the Executive Board decided to give nearly $300,000 to California politicians, Padilla got into a shouting match with Dolores Huerta and David Martinez. Huerta was working on a voter registration drive and she found herself in competition with Fred Ross's son, who had left the UFW and was the head of another get-out-the-vote campaign. When Huerta called Fred Ross junior a traitor to the farm worker movement, Padilla blew up. Ross was born and brought up in the union, Padilla said. Why does he have to be a traitor, why can't he just be somebody else looking for money to do voter registration? Huerta and Padilla had been shouting at each other for years, and they went at it again.[51]

The next day at a Credit Union meeting that Padilla chaired, Huerta was first to speak. She called on Gilbert to resign from the UFW because he had been badmouthing Chavez, telling people that he was crazy. Padilla started to answer, and then David Martinez, Frank Ortiz, and others joined the attack. Chavez said nothing. Padilla recognized the pattern. He had seen it many times. People called it the haircut, a bit of the Synanon Game that had crept into regular life at La Paz. The target was attacked from all sides, charged with crimes he may have committed alongside others that were complete fabrications. At the end he either submitted or left the union. Gilbert showered the group with colorful curses and walked out of the room.[52]

He wrestled with the problem through the night. He had met Cesar at a house meeting in 1955, where Chavez had told him his plan to win power for farm workers in their communities and on their jobs. It was what Gilbert had been looking for since he had come back from the war. Chavez had been fun to work with then, walking the neighborhoods, doing his surveys, talking, joking, eating, scheming. And Chavez had helped him beat alcohol in the late sixties, insisting that he go to a clinic where he put the bottle behind him once and for all. Then there was DC and the boycott, the grape contracts, the great strikes, the negotiations with the employers, the exploding wages, the friends in the union he had made over the last twenty-five years. Could he leave it all behind?

Padilla called Chavez the next morning. "I said, 'Cesar, I am going to honor your wish and resign.' He said, 'Okay' and hung up. That was the last time I ever talked to him."[53]

Less than two weeks after Padilla resigned, Jerry Cohen sent Cesar Chavez a letter of resignation. The proximate cause was Cohen's belief that Chavez was sabotaging a settlement with Sam Andrews, a large, diverse company—melons, lettuce, cotton—that employed hundreds of workers in both the Imperial and the Central valleys. Cohen was conducting the talks, but during negotiations Chavez withdrew two separate union proposals after the company had accepted them. Chavez was so determined to restrict

Marshall Ganz's power in the union, Cohen concluded, that he didn't want another contract to be signed with a major lettuce company on Marshall's turf[54]

Cohen's letter made no accusations. He offered to stay on for three months so that he could finish up the work he was immediately involved in. He didn't think that Chavez had gone crazy. He believed that he, Marshall, and others had lost a power struggle, that they had been outmaneuvered by a very smart man. He continued to talk to Chavez on the phone over the next few years. Often they argued; sometimes they joked and laughed. By the mid-1980s that, too, would end. In 1986, Cohen wrote an op-ed piece for the *LA Times* in which he held Cesar Chavez responsible for the "UFW's failure . . . to fulfill its promise."[55]

Cohen's departure as a negotiator did not have much effect on the union. The main damage had been done earlier, when the legal department was dismantled. From the mid-sixties to the late seventies, the UFW had had the whip hand. More than a dozen skilled lawyers, backed up by dedicated paralegals, worked for the UFW at very low wages while the union's foes, the growers and the Teamsters, had to hire their own attorneys for hundreds of dollars an hour. The UFW's legal advantage only increased with the passage of the ALRA. Jerry Cohen and Sandy Nathan had helped write the law, and the entire UFW legal department understood it better than even the best lawyers on the other side. After the early influence of the NLRB veterans on the ALRB waned, the Labor Board's lawyers and investigators relied on the UFW legal department for research, expertise, and direction.

All of that was over. By November 1980, the legal department consisted of five inexperienced lawyers and a handful of even less-experienced paralegals, just as the growers' legal resources were steadily increasing. Large farms, such as Pik'd Rite, brought in union-busting law firms. The Western Growers Association, lacking a full-time staff attorney until 1972, had by 1981 a legal department of fifteen attorneys who worked at nominal cost for WGA members.[56] The growers' attorneys had become experts on the ALRB. They developed their own *plan tortuga*, their "tortoise plan." WGA lawyers, representing individual growers, began to challenge every decision that went against them in ALRB hearings, successfully gumming up the works. By 1981 there were more than 1,000 unfair labor practice charges pending before the ALRB, and it took an average of thirty months for the board to make a final decision on a complaint. Pro-union workers were fired without immediate redress, and by the time a union election victory had been certified, it was hard to mobilize the demoralized workers to put pressure on negotiations.[57]

The Labor Board and ALRB officials, still largely sympathetic to the UFW, had a hard time streamlining the procedures. As long as the growers' lawyers were willing to appeal every decision, they slowed down the process so successfully that the agency lost much of its ability to protect the UFW's right to organize. Board members, all Brown appointees, couldn't do much about it. The staff was even more frustrated. By December 1981, the ALRB director in Salinas, Lupe Martinez, explained: "Once you get the appellate process going, it just prolongs the final decision . . . That's the problem with the entire legal system, not just the ALRB."[58]

Cohen had pointed out years before that as good as the ALRA and the board were, they were no substitute for a farm worker movement. "The law is a tool, not a crutch," Cohen had warned in the midst of the first ALRB elections. By that he meant that when organized workers were pressuring the growers and the board, UFW lawyers could make the law work for the union. Absent farm worker pressure, the board would be of little help. By the time Jerry Cohen completed his work, in March 1981, the union would be gripped in a civil war, incapable of pressuring anybody. By then the law would be neither tool nor crutch. The ALRA, on paper the best labor law in U.S. history, and the board, all liberal Jerry Brown appointees, would be but a legal spider web, snaring the UFW in its procedures, so that the growers could come in for the kill.

By itself, Chavez's interference in the Andrews negotiations might not have counted for much with Jerry Cohen. But like Maria Rifo's expulsion for Padilla, it was one affront, one act of disrespect, one mistake too many. Ever since that first fight over the legal department, Cohen's biggest fear had been that La Paz would strangle what he and the others were trying to accomplish in Salinas. All those mornings he and Ganz had spent alone at IHOP talking over the future of the union had recently crystallized in a document that Ganz had presented to the Executive Board in mid-October. After the board turned it down, Cohen felt that "the noose got a little bit tighter."[59]

What was dubbed "Marshall's Plan" was a response to Chavez's latest managerial enthusiasm, known as the Top Management Plan. This was Chavez's third proposal, or, more accurately, his second and a half, in four years: Crosby Milne and Management by Objectives; Chuck Dederich and Synanon; and Peter Drucker's refinement on the Milne scheme. The new plan came from the Mayo Clinic via Sister Florence Zweber, a Franciscan nun who had done an excellent job straightening out the finances of the union and the La Paz movement entities.[60] The Top Management Plan separated those who "set the vision" and directed the organization from those who carried out the policies. It promised yet another new understanding of objectives, tasks, structures, and strategies. It began with the questions: "What is our business? Where are we going?" As antidemocratic as any of the earlier plans, it emphasized strict unity of purpose and action. The management team was to communicate with the people who carried out the tasks in "the same voice" and with the "same mind." Chavez said that it would take five years to put the plan completely in place, but he insisted on its importance to the UFW. The absence of a management team was "the single biggest block to the growth and forward thrust of the union," he told the Executive Board.[61]

Chavez had sent the Executive Board reading materials on the plan back in July of 1980 and discussed it at numerous La Paz meetings throughout the summer and fall. Before he fully adopted it, however, he wanted the Executive Board's approval. He scheduled a November 10 meeting to vote on it, and asked people to be prepared for a full discussion of its merits and implementation.

Ganz, Govea, Padilla, and Cohen had disliked the plan from the start; they considered it a colossal waste of time, another diversion from the main job at hand: organizing the rest of the vegetable industry. As the final vote on the plan approached, and after Chavez had surprised Ganz by turning against the garlic campaign, Marshall decided to offer an alternative. He had authored many internal documents in his fifteen years in the UFW, nearly all of them intelligent and interesting. This last one was the most interesting of all. In twenty single-spaced pages he argued against Chavez's newest managerial reform and laid out a whole different structure and direction for the union.

The document is courteous but direct. The trouble with the Top Management Plan was that the main challenge of the hour was not administrative; the problem was not how to manage a successful organization, as the UFW was not yet successful. Instead, "our practical choice is grow or die." Moreover, "our best leadership need to be in a position where it can most effectively lead . . . not at headquarters reflecting on what must be done . . . but out in the field doing it." Ganz invoked the example of St. Paul, one of Chavez's New Testament favorites: "St. Paul did not spend his time figuring out how to administer the Vatican—he went out and organized, recruited, built. The problem of building a world-wide church was dealt with when there was a church. First things first."[62]

Marshall's answer to the question "What is our business?" was straightforward. "Our goal should be to build a strong, democratic national farm workers' union." He rejected Chavez's recurring talk that the UFW should be more than a union, arguing that although unions have weaknesses they are still the "most effective way for working people to improve their lives." Trying to build something more, something wider, he wrote, will divert energies and "interfere with our effectiveness."

The union is in great danger, he warned. "The small part of California agriculture we have organized cannot long exist as an island. The growers have the hope left to keep fighting. The island must either become the continent or the sea will swallow it up." And public support will wane, especially if people are called on to back the same fight over and over. The ALRA, a powerful asset, most likely has only two more years of life in its present form. It all adds up to an emergency in the fields, a time for action. "*Dale gas,*" he concluded. Step on the gas.

Ganz recommended that the UFW be reorganized into regions, with regional directors—some could be Executive Board members—exercising real power, with budgets and the authority to hire and fire. The headquarters of the union should be moved out of La Paz, with the old mountain buildings converted into an educational center. Working in a place like Fresno would give union staff a "balanced and realistic perspective," and "free us from all the problems of running a community like La Paz and enable us to put that energy into building a union." The volunteer policy must be "drastically revised," with long-term staff being paid "moderate but reasonable salaries" and covered by union medical and pension plans. The legal department must be rebuilt, with the union paying sufficient salaries to do so.

Marshall's Plan allowed for the "possibility" of locals, under the direction of the regional managers, but it did not recommend them. And although Ganz argued for the legitimacy and utility of differing points of view, conflicting opinions, disputes over resources, and sharp disagreements within the union, he stopped short of proposing a bottom-up, democratic structure. The regional directors were still going to be appointed by Chavez, and their budgets would not come directly from membership dues but would be allocated by the Executive Board.

Ganz submitted the plan in October, just as Gilbert Padilla was resigning. He made no attempt to broaden the discussion beyond the Executive Board. He did not show the document to the paid reps or tell them anything about the plan. Marshall's Plan was not a call to action, not even an invitation to a general debate. For him, it was essentially a last testament, a specific alternative laid before the Executive Board by the losing party, one last chance to clarify his views before he, Govea, and Cohen were gone for good.

Marshall's Plan, however, meant something entirely different to Cesar Chavez, and it did not please him. It called on the union to reverse the course that he had set over the past several years: professionalize the staff; bring back the legal department; move out of La Paz; disperse authority; tolerate diversity and dissent. Ganz was not calling him crazy. This was more serious: a reasoned, direct, open rejection of his policies. It might even be a quasi-manifesto, a call to action by others in the union who opposed him. It didn't matter that after the Executive Board voted down Marshall's Plan, Ganz and Govea, in a gesture of unity, voted for the Top Management Plan, giving it unanimous board approval at the November 10, 1980, meeting. Ganz had written an opposition tract, and Chavez knew that an opposition leader would need soldiers.

After the vote, Chavez started to move. Within four days, Oscar Mondragon visited Cleofas Guzman. Mondragon, recently appointed to the Executive Board, had been one of Manuel Chavez's chief lieutenants on the wet line. He had gone to jail for the fire bombing of the nineteen buses in Calexico after the 1974 High and Mighty Farms bus accident. Any message that he delivered carried weight. He told Guzman that there were two groups in the union, one led by Cesar Chavez and the other by Marshall Ganz. Cleofas and all the other paid reps would have to choose between them.[63]

Civil War

November '80 to October '81

A cupped hand that hides a mouth, delivering a dirty secret is one of the dominant images of palace politics, and so of the UFW in the desperate, cataclysmic period of 1980–81. Gossip was more than a behind-the-scenes, semisalacious commentary on the main action; it was part of the action. Well-sown rumors blighted reputations, sprouted lies, threatened lives. Gossip's cousin, the secret deal, became a controlling force from Sacramento to the Mexican borderlands. Disagreements were interpreted as disloyalty and differences meant betrayal, while betrayal, or fear of it, prepared the ground for a terrible conclusion.

It was a mark of the perverse culture of La Paz that the brisk betrayals and backroom deals of the state capital appeared if not quite wholesome, then at least more like comic opera by comparison. In the state elections of November 1980 Chavez seemed to have won his gamble on Sacramento politics. Tallying the results, the pundits reported that Howard Berman had a commanding margin in the Democratic caucus and was poised to become the new speaker of the Assembly. Chavez had made his man, and the UFW leader was now more powerful than ever, declared Eric Brazil in the *Salinas Californian*.[1]

Neither Brazil nor Chavez counted on Willie Brown. Having been named second-in-command a year earlier in the midst of the McCarthy-Berman feud, Brown had no intention of conceding power to the upstart Berman. He went to the Republican leader of the Assembly, Carol Hallet, and offered her various inducements for the Republicans to join with the Democratic caucus minority and support him as the new speaker. The capitol press corps trilled. Because all the bartering was private and only the principals knew what was being promised to whom, or what the promises were worth, the month-long intrigue was a deep well from which bucket upon bucket of speculation could be drawn, providing delightful draft for political columnists and Sacramento insiders. For them, the question of which liberal Democrat was going to be speaker had little to do with anything besides a fight for personal power. For Chavez, though, it was a deadly serious contest between a man who would be beholden to him and one who would not.

After pocketing the Republican votes, Willie Brown went to work on the Democrats who supported Berman. They should leave the loser, he said; once he was speaker, he wouldn't forget his friends. The two Chicano assemblymen, Art Torres and Richard Alatorre, accepted Brown's offer. Chavez, stung, couldn't dissuade them. At a press conference with six other Mexican Americans—politicians, a priest, and some businessmen— he blasted the lawmakers' "flip-flop" and warned that Brown's alliance with the Republicans was dangerous to farm workers and the Hispanic community. A couple hundred farm workers and La Paz volunteers went door to door in Torres's and Alatorre's East LA districts, denouncing the two as traitors and pressing people to sign petitions to get them to reverse their vote.[2]

As the decisive caucus meeting approached, farm workers lined the halls to the meeting room. Their signs urged the two Chicano legislators not to desert their communities. Alatorre and Torres walked through the gauntlet shoulder to shoulder with Brown, who became speaker that day and reigned for the next fourteen years. As the reward for his victory, some Republicans got committee chairs; the power to assign bills to committees shifted from the speaker to the Democratic-controlled Rules Committee; a number of other people were given profitable posts; and, of special concern to the UFW, Brown promised the Republican leader that he would keep further pesticide regulation bottled up in committee, which he did for two years.[3]

Chavez rejected a Torres-Alatorre peace offer and waged a debilitating fight against them and their proxies within various Mexican American organizations. The feud diminished UFW support among some Chicanos and limited the UFW's power in Sacramento, but Chavez continued undaunted.[4] Much of his political support came from white liberals, and he still had plenty of money. He made his own peace with Willie Brown, a pact that was facilitated by $750,000 in UFW contributions, which Brown would use to lock up his position in the Assembly in future elections. UFW contributions lagged those of the California branch of the American Medical Association by only $667. The farm workers' Citizens Participation Day pay, which bypassed the workers and went straight to La Paz, had enabled the union to become the second-biggest political contributor in the state.[5]

Yet Chavez was in a box. All the money at his disposal had not made him a kingmaker and would not solve the union's problems in the fields. He had kneecapped Ganz at the November Executive Board meeting, and taken organizing off the table as an official union priority. His long-favored alternative, the boycott, was now no alternative at all. In the valleys, the questions of work, power, who had it, who didn't, and how to get it were as stark as ever. Cleofas Guzman and the other paid reps had taken it upon themselves to confront those questions, but Chavez didn't know those reps in any real sense, and he felt less and less sure that he could trust them. In November 1980, as the Imperial Valley lettuce harvest was beginning, he had exiled Ganz to off-season Salinas, leaving him with little to do. He made Oscar Mondragon director of the Calexico field office. Mondragon was a Mexican, a *lechuguero* who joined the UFW staff after the 1970 strike. He was one of the few staff people who came from the paid reps' world, but Mondragon had no answer for the strategic problem that Cleofas and the others were wrestling with.

The six Imperial Valley companies still had not signed contracts and were not being picketed. Most of the former strikers were scrambling for jobs with other employers. But the number of jobs had decreased as Imperial lettuce acreage fell to a new low of less than 30,000 compared with 42,000 in 1979.[6] Bruce Church, the largest of the struck companies, looked as if it would never sign. The union had offered a major concession in negotiations, agreeing to amend the "good standing" clause in the direction the company had suggested. Instead of responding with a concession of its own, Church made new demands.[7]

The mood in the Calexico office was bleak. Mondragon tried to assure workers that there were still two remaining paths to victory—the lettuce boycott and a possible ALRB ruling that the growers had been bargaining in bad faith. The latter seemed more promising. An ALRB hearing officer had issued a complaint against the growers for "surface bargaining," going through the motions, but not bargaining in good faith. If the full board upheld the complaint, the growers would have to compensate the workers for lost wages since the beginning of the strike. This "make whole" remedy could amount to as much as $5 million at each company, and the union hoped that after such a ruling the employers would sign quickly so as to minimize their liability.[8]

Neither the boycott nor the pending ALRB case required much from the workers. They were expected to wait and put their confidence in the union leadership. That did not sit well with many of the paid reps, who were worried about the shrinking number of union jobs and wanted to continue organizing at the nonunion companies. From Mondragon they learned for the first time, straight out and in no uncertain terms, that the union planned no new organizing in the vegetables.[9]

Cleofas Guzman did not accept that. He and other paid reps argued it out with Mondragon, sometimes in private, sometimes in open meetings. And, quietly, Mondragon pulled other workers aside, repeating what he had first told Guzman: there were two opposed groups in the union, and they had to choose sides.

Mario Bustamante arrived in Imperial toward the end of November.

Soon after he got there he went to a meeting at the union office. "Cleofas was arguing with Oscar Mondragon," Bustamante recalled. "Cleofas was saying we have to continue organizing . . . I said, 'Cleofas is right.' After the meeting, I was called to another one. Mondragon wanted to talk to me alone. 'Look, Mario, here in the union there are two groups. One is made up of enemies of Cesar Chavez. That is Marshall Ganz's group. I was a friend of your father's, and your father was with Manuel Chavez. I want you to join with us, to come over to our side.'"

"I don't see two groups," Mario said. "And as far as I am concerned, Marshall Ganz is not an enemy of Chavez. He has never said anything bad to me about Chavez. And what Cleofas was telling you tonight is the truth. We have to organize the people. Not sit on our hands. I am in the group that organizes. And if you are in a group that doesn't organize, then I guess there might be two groups: one that doesn't do anything, and one that is trying to do something."

"Okay," Mondragon replied, "I now consider you an enemy."[10]

One night not long after, Bustamante was at the union hall filling out medical forms. Problems with the medical plan persisted, and the paid reps were still trying to solve them. He could hear the voices of Oscar Mondragon, Gilberto Rodriguez, Lupe Bautista, and two former strikers in an adjoining office. The strikers were lettuce workers who had been at Lu-Ette, one of the Imperial Valley companies that hadn't signed. Bustamante knew them, and didn't like them. They traveled with Manuel Chavez; people called them *changos*—literally monkeys—but in this case it meant goons. The five men didn't know that Mario was listening. They were hatching a plot. The Lu-Ette strikers would go into the field the next morning and ask Bustamante for a dispatch, the document that enabled a worker to get a job at a union company. They knew that he would refuse, because he didn't have the right to give dispatches, which were not supposed to leave the office. In response, they would start a fight and beat him up.

"Why wait until tomorrow?" Mario said, walking into the room, surprising the five men. "Here I am."

One of the Lu-Ette strikers kicked Mario on the backside, and when he turned around, the other hit him in the face with a chair. The fight was over. Bustamante was down, his blood on the floor. Mondragon escorted the Lu-Ette strikers out the door. Mario got up and went to find a doctor to fix his broken nose.[11]

This was not the first time in U.S. labor history that men originally recruited to protect strikers from company goons or to take rough action against scabs later attacked union members opposed to official policies. It was the first time in the UFW, though, and because Bustamante was not shy about telling his story, word got around. Enough so that Chavez came to the Imperial Valley to talk to him, one on one.

Chavez didn't say much; he listened and took notes. Bustamante told him about Mondragon's formulation that there were two groups in the union and that the paid reps had to choose one or the other. Mario assumed that Cesar would agree that this was nonsense, and he reiterated his own position in favor of increased attention to organizing. He laid out a few other concerns and gripes. Some Mexicali policemen had come to the field office and had trucked away Christmas toys that had been donated to the union. Bustamante suspected that Manuel Chavez, intimate with the police, was behind it. It was wrong to slight farm worker children to curry favor with the Mexicali police, Mario said. Finally, he told Chavez the story of the overheard plot and the fight and his broken nose. Chavez made sure that he got all the information right and promised to investigate.[12]

Cesar Chavez firmly believed there were two groups in the union. He had been wary of Marshall Ganz for some time, uneasy about Ganz's power base in Salinas, which accounted for about 80 percent of the union's dues income. But the source of Chavez's disquiet now was not just the vague jealousy of a king toward his prince; it was a story that became gossip and then, for Chavez, became fact.

Ganz's guess had been right. Someone had said something to alter Chavez's attitude during the summer garlic campaign. In fact, there were two someones: Dolores Huerta and David Arizmendi. During the garlic elections, Arizmendi, an ALRB field officer friendly to the UFW, had bumped into Huerta in Sacramento. He casually asked her whatever happened to the plan that Ganz had told him about during the 1979 strike. What plan? Huerta asked. The plan to kick Chavez upstairs into a ceremonial position and take over the UFW by getting farm workers loyal to Ganz elected to the Executive Board, he is said to have explained. Hearing this, Huerta took Arizmendi to La Paz to tell the story to Chavez.

No one confronted Marshall Ganz, but the story was retold behind his back. Word passed from some Executive Board members to staffers—Ganz was plotting to take over the union—as a justification for Chavez's subsequent effort to push Ganz out. Not until years later did anyone ask Ganz for an explanation. Untested by contradictory views or open debate, this was gossip and nothing else.

Decades later it still bore the odor of the rumor mill.[13] For Huerta, the story buttressed her claim that two men destroyed the UFW: George Deukmejian, the Republican Governor who succeeded Jerry Brown, and Marshall Ganz. For Ganz, who first heard it twenty years later, the charge was preposterous. He insisted he had never discussed running a slate of candidates for the Executive Board, not with farm workers or anyone else. Jerry Cohen and Jessica Govea never heard him talk of such a plan.

He never encouraged his closest allies among the rank-and-file to oppose Chavez or to run for the board. They never heard Ganz criticize Chavez, not in the midst of his fight with La Paz nor the few times they talked to him after he left the union. In fact, his silence made them a little angry. With them he was a Chavez man to the end. "Marshall Ganz never betrayed Cesar Chavez," Mario Bustamante said, "Chavez betrayed Ganz."

But didn't Ganz hope for something very like what he was accused of plotting: that farm workers would assume more power within the union and that Chavez's policies would be overturned? He did, as did Jerry Cohen and Jessica Govea. Cohen said as much in June 1979 to a friendly newspaperman, Doug Foster, whose notes of that off-the-record conversation record reveal, in clipped phrases, a hope—though not a plan—that Cesar Chavez would become less prominent in the UFW, and that workers would take over the union. In Foster's notes, which follow, CC is Cesar Chavez:

> [Cohen said] CC may go off to Texas, fast and then march around a lot. That's what he should do.
> [Foster:] When are these guys [local workers] going to get it together to take over their own union?
> [Cohen:] When Cesar changes his role.
> [Foster:] When is he going to do that? Why can't he drop his attempt to administer?
> [Cohen:] Because he is too proud. He is an amazing man. He's stubborn. That's mainly what he is. Stubborn.[14]

Ganz was more careful than Cohen, more circumspect. But it is certainly possible that, in the tumult of the strike, Ganz made some remark to Arizmendi about workers getting more power in the union and Chavez becoming primarily the union's public face. Then Arizmendi passed it on to Huerta, and, like a wheel rolling down the road, it became a full-fledged conspiracy in the ears of Huerta and Chavez.

After all, Ganz, Govea, and Cohen had disagreed with Huerta and Chavez in a number of serious political disputes over the previous few years. Huerta and Chavez reasonably could envision something once unthinkable in the union: a fixed opposition, a permanent counter-caucus, with The Marshall Plan providing strategic orientation. They were wrong to think that Ganz and the others were out to topple Chavez, but they were not wrong to think that there was an oppositional plan in the works. That is what Cohen and Ganz had been talking about all those mornings at the IHOP: how could they maneuver within the organization to get the Executive Board to do what Chavez opposed: commit more of the UFW's resources to organize the vegetable industry? To Huerta and Chavez, this alternative position implied betrayal, a plot to bring down Chavez.

The disagreements probably could not have been resolved without either the removal of those three antagonists or a change in the structure and culture of the union. The union had long run on Chavez's power to command and everyone else's inclination to obey, and this had once given the organization a certain strength. But what had been strong became brittle with time, unable to bend in the face of internal differences inevitable in a union of thousands of workers in different crops and regions, with conflicting interests and political views. Under the pressure of serious disagreement, the union cracked. The wild accusations of conspiracy were the pathetic sounds of an organization breaking apart.

History loves ironies, and here we have one of the UFW's saddest. Huerta and Chavez accused Ganz of violating one of the most solemn codes of palace politics: one doesn't mobilize the peasants against the king. But Ganz, as much a creature of the UFW as were his antagonists, never did breach that code. Although he enthusiastically organized workers in strikes and election campaigns, he never appealed for their help in his internal disputes with Chavez. In his defense it is easy to argue that it would have been a wasted effort. But here's the irony. He never did what he was accused of doing, but it was the very thing he should have done. By keeping the active farm workers out of the internal politics of the union, he cut himself off from his natural allies. Perhaps they couldn't have saved him, but he would have left them better prepared for what would follow after he walked away.

A telephone call from Mario Bustamante to Ganz in late December 1980 foreshadowed what was to come. Mario told Ganz that two goons who were with Mondragon had jumped him at the Calexico field office and broken his nose. Marshall expressed his sympathies—there was nothing more he could do.

When he took the call, Ganz had been meeting with Cohen, Tom Dalzell, and Ann Marie Smith, at Dalzell's home in Salinas every day for about a week. They filled four large sheets of butcher paper with a detailed history of the UFW. They arranged several hundred events chronologically under various headings: including "Boycott," "La Paz," "Political," "Jedi Warriors," and "Other." The Jedi Warriors were the four of them and their allies on the union staff.

"The idea was that we were going to look at a detailed history of the union in order to figure out whether there was any way that the workers had a chance to take it over," Dalzell explained twenty-six years later. "We were looking at the history to try to make a judgment about whether a worker fight to take over the union (with or without Chavez) would have a chance for success. We also were trying to figure out what our role might be in such a fight. But in the process we decided that the workers didn't have a chance, and we never got around to discussing what our role might be."[15]

Cohen and Ganz had somewhat different interpretations of the butcher paper exercise.[16] Cohen said they were "reviewing events to see if there were any openings to continue to negotiate for what we wanted inside the union, which was essentially the rejected Marshall Plan."[17] Ganz said they were trying to figure out what had happened and what they might do next.

They were unsure of where they stood. Dalzell had continued to do legal work and some negotiating after the old legal department broke up, but he hadn't done anything for the union in months. Cohen had resigned in November, but he was still tying up loose ends and felt that Chavez had left the door open for his possible return. Smith, one of the most effective union negotiators, was still bargaining contracts. Ganz, cognizant that he was in disfavor, was wondering how much longer he could last on the Executive Board.

A major problem for this gang of four was that they were so white. That matter had come up before, but in a different form. Early in union history, Ganz and especially Cohen were advertisements for the union's commitment to diversity, which was particularly pleasing to the boycott coalition. But their high positions next to Chavez were not for show. They were skilled people, valuable to the union, and Cesar's early affection for them was rooted in his genuine curiosity and respect for disparate cultures, experiences, and abilities and for their genuine talent. Moreover, Ganz and Cohen—Ganz more than Cohen— were not just white they were Jewish, and Chavez's fascination with Judaism was acute. He appreciated both the culture and the religious texts, on a few occasions questioning Ganz about why Jewish organizers didn't use their religious and cultural heritage more in their work, as it was so rich in political meaning and inspiration.

But the diversity at the top had always engendered some resentment in the ranks. Why were there so many whites around telling us what to do, some farm workers wondered back in the 1965 grape strike. Some Chicanos on the UFW staff also quietly simmered, especially angry at Ganz for monopolizing so much of Chavez's time and the union's resources. As the New Left broke down into competing oppressed identities, complaints from Chicano nationalists increased. For a long time, Chavez had remained steadfast in his public and private defense of the union's diversity, but as Ganz, Dalzell, Cohen, and Smith were getting together in the winter of 1980 in Salinas, and as the Chicano vote promised to become more important in California politics, he began to shift his emphasis, promoting the union and its leadership as Mexican, and he insisted, rightfully so.[18]

That shift was not essentially opportunistic. Chavez and his union lived amid the race prejudice and privilege of America. Cesar had set out to build an organization of brotherhood under the skin, but he could not forget the "No Mexicans" sign that had greeted him in California as a child. However much he was embraced by white liberals, flattered by the attentions of Robert Kennedy, celebrated in the hagiographic articles of white journalists, he was a brown man in a white racist country, an exotic to the throngs of young white volunteers who came to Delano and then to La Paz to do good and endure a state of deprivation for the privilege. Brilliant, thin-skinned, and a student of history and human behavior, Chavez surely felt some disdain, and perhaps even resentment, for the array of white man's options, the ease with which those volunteers could move in and out of poverty.

Ganz had arrived as one of those young volunteers, relieved after his experience in SNCC to be part of an organization where color supposedly wasn't an issue. To the extent that Ganz believed that, he deluded himself. Here his cultural flexibility both did and did not serve him well. His ability quickly to master farm worker Spanish, to be mistaken for a Mexican on picket lines and rally platforms, to feel at home among farm workers, to fit smoothly in the farm worker world, may have prompted him to take insufficient measure of the extent to which, ultimately, he did not fit in.

That was not a problem for an organizer. The organizer could be an outsider; it was even an advantage. But Marshall Ganz had become more than just an organizer. He was on the Executive Board; he was a leader of the union. He had, on one remarkable occasion, joined forces with rank-and-filers who had openly and successfully defied Cesar Chavez. Without intending to, he had slipped into an untenable position in the UFW.

Chavez and his white protégés both understood one of the limitations that color and ethnicity placed on their relationship: the younger whites whom Cesar Chavez could, in a sense, father could also never be his heirs, never challenge him for control of the Mexican American and Mexican organization. This must have given Chavez a measure of confidence, yet ultimately it had to chafe at Ganz and the others, and Chavez, knowing a thing or two about frustrated ambition, could not rest easy. Nor could Ganz. Rapturous about multicultural leadership in the UFW, he had trouble facing up to one of its consequences: his whiteness made him an easy target once Chavez withdrew his support, and prevented him from fighting back effectively

The paid reps were his only hope. But the "Jedi Warriors" also failed the farm worker soul of the union. They all genuinely admired the rank-and-file leadership—Ganz had been instrumental in building it—but in choosing to fight the inside battle exclusively among insiders, they accepted the division between the mountain and the valley, the people who ran the union and those who were just members. Ganz trusted the workers more than Chavez did, but not enough to tell them all he knew. By keeping them out of the internal struggle to reform the UFW he hoped to protect them—and himself. In the end he could protect nobody.

After the telephone call from Mario Bustamante, Ganz passed on the information about the fight to his fellow Jedi. The last item on their butcher paper is "Mario's Nose." They rolled up the paper, put it in the closet, and went their separate ways. Nothing could be done, they concluded.

The paid reps were now on their own. Frustrated by back-room maneuvering, unable to gain ground on the issues that mattered to them, they brought their fight onto the open stage in a direct, public confrontation with Cesar Chavez. It was such a departure from the past that Chavez and Dolores Huerta could hardly recognize it for what it was. They dismissed it, to themselves as well as to others, as a rear-guard maneuver by Marshall Ganz to work himself back into power.

They couldn't have been more wrong. The battle between La Paz and the paid reps was different from the UFW's periodic internal disputes, not something that could be solved by one more staff purge. It was the final attempt by the paid reps to make themselves heard; it was an open challenge from the valley to the mountain; it was a claim by farm workers that the union was theirs.

The confrontation went beyond the specific issues at hand, as important as some of them were. Here were two worlds in collision, divided by nationality, experiences in the fields, disagreements about the way farm workers should be represented to the world, and, finally, by basic ideas about politics. In contrast to Chavez and many of the other Chicanos on the UFW staff, the Mexican paid reps did not regard work in the fields as a calamity. The work was hard, but the fields had been good to them. Many considered themselves craftsmen, like electricians or carpenters. Cesar Chavez never understood that. Nor did that view of farm work play well in Sacramento or in the cities among the UFW's middle-class supporters. But it was the living truth for most of the paid reps. Before they had come onto the staff they had not liked the way they had been used to promote the boycott, to evoke sympathy in people who knew nothing about the fields. They did not feel like victims, and they did not like to pretend that they were. They drove good cars; they ate well. They had not wanted to be obliged to wear old work clothes when they went to press conferences—as was standard UFW practice—or to appeal for support as downtrodden victims. They were workers, not beggars. They sought justice, not charity.

Once on the staff they realized that the priorities in the union were twisted by its charitable appeals. Mario Bustamante had continued to ask questions, to complain about the poor infrastructure of the union. Why did people have to wait all day in the service centers when the union had money to hire skilled professionals? Why did the union continue to use the deteriorating fleet of Valiants when it could afford reliable cars? Why was the food so bad at La Paz? Why was the union staff shopping at thrift stores for their clothes? He finally decided on an answer, and didn't like it: It was all part of the union's badge of poverty, its appeal to the public for help for poor farm workers and their impoverished union. It wouldn't have been so bad if it had been a one-day show, he thought. But the union had to live it, and the performance took precedence over the actual needs of the members.

La Paz patronized the workers. "When they took you to La Paz it was like giving an award to a child," Bustamante told me.

> They took the good children there. They gave you special food, better than the regular La Paz diet. They sat you down with different people who worked there, they showed you the little house where Cesar lived. It was almost something religious. And Cesar would greet you. 'Oh, how good of you to come.' But if you went to La Paz with something serious to talk about, they weren't interested in that; you couldn't sit down and argue something out with them. That's what frustrated me . . . They never gave you the chance to say what you had to say. Chavez could do that to people who worked in La Paz because they idolized him. I don't know what it is about lettuce workers, maybe it is because we work so hard, but it is not easy to push us around. If we have differences, we like to argue them out. Chavez didn't want to do that.[19]

Chavez had never wanted to do that. Neither back in the late fifties in Oxnard when he was talking to farm workers every day nor in the early sixties when he was founding the union. He didn't argue politics; he told exemplary stories, and looked for followers. For him, farm workers were Don Sotaco, the slumped-over cartoon figure of the early *Malcriado*, humiliated in the fields as Chavez's father had been. Don Sotaco needed to be enlightened, shown the way, encouraged to fight. But the paid reps were not Don Sotacos. They didn't need the veil pulled from their eyes. They could see well enough. They would follow a leader, but not one who was unwilling to argue things out. Chavez, Mario Bustamante concluded, didn't want comrades. He wanted disciples.

> Cesar was very good at talking to people who were new to the struggle, who were at their first meetings . . . He could enlighten them. But with

people who were already experienced in the union and had problems, Cesar didn't know what to do with them . . . The people he was best with were the boycotters, people who were above all faithful, and wouldn't demand anything from him. If he calls you a *baboso* ["fool"], then you take it. If he sends you to Canada, you go. And you stay there for a year or two. He wanted to be our new boss . . . We didn't want another boss, we wanted a leader.[20]

In one respect, this final battle was unavoidable. People like Mario Bustamante could not be integrated into the union staff without changing the nature of the whole enterprise.

During the Imperial harvest season, Cleofas Guzman, like many farm workers, lived in Mexicali, and crossed the border every workday to Calexico and the fields. On January 22, 1981, the Mexicali police stopped him and relayed a threat: Manuel Chavez had said that Guzman and Mario Bustamante were messing up the UFW, and if they didn't stop they were going to be killed. That night over dinner at the Ace Restaurant in Calexico, Guzman told this to Bustamante and Juan Flores, the paid rep at Growers' Exchange. They agreed that Cleiofas should return home to Mexicali that night, retrieve some belongings, and move to a hotel with Mario in Calexico, where they could look out for each other.[21]

The next day Bustamante learned from Oscar Mondragon that Guzman had been arrested in Mexicali. Mondragon said not to worry: the union had influence with the Mexicali police and would secure his release. It did, and afterward, according to Guzman, Mondragon instructed him to drive to San Luis, Arizona, for a meeting that night of Sun Harvest workers. He was to leave immediately. Mondragon would be waiting for him in San Luis.[22]

There is one main road between Mexicali and San Luis, Baja California Highway 2. At 6:15 p.m. on January 23, Guzman was heading east on Highway 2 in his late-model Thunderbird. Suddenly a cotton truck pulled out from a side road right in front of him. The car smashed into the side of the truck. Guzman took much of the impact to his head. He was forty-four years old. He lost an eye, and a severe brain injury left him partially paralyzed and hindered his speech forever after.[23]

Jessica Govea and Marshall Ganz were in La Paz when the news of the accident arrived. Cesar sent them to investigate. Their report back to Chavez contained only two more details about the crash: "The driver of the truck was injured because the steering wheel was seriously bent, but he fled the scene." Ganz and Govea also noted that "Oscar [Mondragon] ran the meeting in San Luis and apparently thought nothing of Cleofas' failure to show . . ."[24]

In a separate memorandum, dated April 5, 1981, two and a half months after the accident, Juan Guicho, director of the UFW field office in Calexico, reported that the cotton truck was still in the custody of the Mexicali police, the driver was never found, and the owner of the truck denied all responsibility.[25]

A few days after the crash, Guzman's daughter Maria Aguilar had done her own investigation. She had gone to the scene and talked to a woman who lived near the intersection. The woman told her that the truck had been standing at the intersection for a while before pulling out in front of the Thunderbird. After the crash, a man with an injured arm left the truck and got into the passenger seat of a nearby car, which drove away. Later Maria returned to the scene with a workmen's compensation investigator, and the woman gave the two the same account. None of these details are in the UFW reports, although they are consistent with them. Aguilar never talked to Ganz or Govea, and didn't read the results of their investigation.[26]

Guzman couldn't speak at all for many months, and when some speech returned he couldn't remember many of the circumstances of the crash. The Ganz and Govea investigation left many questions unanswered. It's not known why Guzman had been arrested in Mexicali, what the charges were, or who bailed him out. It's not known what was so important in San Luis that it couldn't wait. Or why four hours elapsed before between Guzman's arrival at *Hospital General* in Mexicali and his admission. Or why no one was notified. Perhaps his identification was on him when he arrived at the hospital, perhaps not. Accounts differ, records are incomplete. Guzman's name was not on the hospital's log. No one knew anything at the Calexico field office the next morning, not even that Guzman had never made it to the meeting in San Luis. When Cleofas failed to return home, his daughter started searching for him. She visited the jails and hospitals in Mexicali and finally found him after noticing his boots outside the door of a hospital room. In their report, Ganz and Govea concluded that "an investigation must be pursued by the '*judiciales*,'" but none was. Officially, the crash was labeled an accident.[27]

Most of the paid reps were convinced that the accident was an attempt on Guzman's life. The question was "Who's next?" They all knew the Mexican tradition of political assassination by automobile "accident." They figured that Manuel Chavez had been behind it. There had been an open threat and a motive. Guzman was their leader, and Manuel had wanted to stop him and his oppositional activities. Manuel had a well-deserved reputation for violence, and close ties to the police and others in Mexicali. Manuel, the reps believed, had got Guzman arrested, released, and then sent on the road to the waiting cotton truck. Soon, many of the reps dropped out of the disputes over organizing and union resources, focusing instead on less controversial problems within their companies. About ten remained who were still willing to struggle within the union.

None of them thought Cesar Chavez ordered the hit, but Ganz and Govea believed that Cesar was afraid that he would be blamed for it, and had sent them to investigate hoping their report would absolve him. Instead, they delivered a plain, business agent-style account, focusing on medical issues, arrangements for hospital care, bills, and support for the Guzman family. Only many years later would Ganz write:

> We never found any evidence it was intentional, but . . . Manuel was very well connected with all the local pols down there (two of them were on our payroll for a long number of years), so we'll never know.[28]

Govea was more suspicious, particularly when Chavez called her and Ganz back from Mexicali to La Paz prematurely, thus cutting short their investigation. "Cleofas was an extraordinary leader," she said. "And in a very important way Cleofas was not afraid of Cesar, nor was he intimidated by him. He was not an in-your-face guy, but he was very clear about who he was and what role he wanted to play in representing workers at Sun Harvest. And he was very principled. And it [nearly] cost him his life."[29]

Two and a half weeks after the crash, Cesar and two of his closest allies on the Executive Board, David Martinez and Frank Ortiz, went to Calexico to meet with the paid reps and field office staff to combat the many rumors surrounding the event. Chavez then sent all ranch committee presidents, field office directors, and strike coordinators a written summary of the questions raised at the meeting and his answers. What was now called the Top Management Team also produced an internal paper about the meeting that listed "Questions and Points Raised—Suggested Responses."

Point one in the Top Management document and point two in Chavez's letter concerned the role of Manuel Chavez in the union:

> Manuel Chavez is one of the founders of the union. Although he is not now a member of the Executive Board, he was the first Secretary Treasurer of the union.
>
> Like many other people, Manuel assists the President on special problems and projects. Currently he is helping the President, other union officials, and the membership in relations with the Mexican government, both on the border and in Mexico City. Part of his work includes dealing with problems of the membership with Mexican authorities and the Mexican labor movement. In his work in Mexicali, he deals with the authorities on problems of accidents, jailings, etc.[30]

The implication of the last sentence was that if Manuel arranged for Guzman to be freed from jail, that was part of his regular job, not part of a setup to assassinate him. Most of the other talking points aimed to sort out the responsibilities of the paid reps and field office staff. Some indirectly responded to people's concerns about the fight that had led to Bustamante's broken nose. Another, on new organizing, was the first direct statement on the matter that Chavez had made to the leadership of the rank and file. He was unequivocal:

> It is correct not to continue organizing. The union is certified at a large number of companies which have not signed contracts. The strike and negotiations are not over. The union will focus and concentrate on the negotiations.[31]

Rumors about Guzman's accident and Bustamante's injury persisted. The civil war had escalated. The dispute was no longer an argument on the Executive Board. It was down in the valley, and blood had been spilled.

Jessica Govea and Marshall Ganz had been in La Paz at the time of Guzman's crash because they had wanted to have just one more talk with Cesar Chavez. Ganz later recalled that they wanted to resign, that Chavez agreed, but asked them to stay for a while to work on a few planning issues, and then go to South Africa for a conference (later changed to Israel for a month-long study of agricultural practices of the kibbutzim). Govea didn't remember an offer to resign; she said they went to La Paz to figure out "how to stay in the union and stay sane . . . I really loved the union, and I really loved what we had done, and a part of me continued to have this strong respect for Cesar. You know, that held pretty firmly. I kept on hoping that things could change. I kept on wanting to believe that maybe they weren't as bad as they appeared to be."[32]

Ganz wasn't so optimistic. He considered the trip to Israel a parting gift, a gracious good-bye from Chavez. He and Jessica wouldn't formally resign until June, but in his last six months with the union, Ganz dropped out of most UFW work. He also cut his ties to the paid reps. In February and March of 1981, he rebuffed several overtures from them to get together and talk. Mojica said Marshall was deeply depressed and wouldn't answer phone calls. Berta Batres said Jessica Govea had to hold Ganz together, keep his spirits up. Bustamante recalled that he "was in hiding, licking his wounds."

Finally a meeting was arranged. Ganz did his best to explain to Bustamante. "I said, 'Look, I'm leaving the union. I can't help you. I'm gone and I can't help you anymore. And whatever you do is going to have to be on your own, and what you work out with Cesar and with the rest of the organization. I can't leave and still be involved.' "[33]

It wasn't until after they returned from Israel, in late April, that Govea knew they were through.[34] Chavez had asked them to write up their findings and present them at La Paz. Ganz wrote a detailed, enthusiastic eighty-page report. They arrived at La Paz for the presentation and were walking down a hallway toward a meeting room. Jessica was a little bit ahead of Marshall, and saw Artie Rodriguez, Cesar's son-in-law, by then a member of the Executive Board and a person she considered a friend. He was standing by the door. "Here was someone who when I had seen him last we had greeted each other affectionately, hugs and whatever, and I said, 'Hi Artie.' And I got a big fat zero, a big fat flat face, a zero. And I said to myself, well, that was it. And I got the same kind of reaction from other people, but the one from Artie is the one that stuck . . . So I knew then."

They gave their report to a room of cold faces. No one asked a question. "They didn't care a thing about what we were saying. That is not what they were there for."[35]

It is not clear exactly when Chavez decided to rid himself of Ganz and Govea. Gossip had started the process in the summer of 1980, and more gossip, at the start of 1981, may have hastened the end. It came in the form of a February 6, 1981, memo from Jose Rubio, a member of the UFW staff. Rubio and Oscar Mondragon had met with Roy Mendoza, a Teamster organizer and longtime foe of the UFW. They were discussing the soon-to-expire UFW-Teamster pact when, according to Rubio, Mendoza casually mentioned that Tom Dalzell had asked him if he would join a new union being formed by Jerry Cohen and Marshall Ganz, who were "breaking away" from the UFW. "I pretended to know what he was talking about, since I had only heard rumors to that effect," Rubio wrote.[36]

Rubio was not a person prone to stir up trouble, but Mendoza was notoriously unreliable, and this was false information. Dalzell denied ever saying such a thing. At this time Cohen had been sidelined, and Ganz was doing everything he could to stay out of the battles. There was no attempt to form another union. Years later, when some former paid reps asked Cohen and Ganz if they would join their efforts to do so, both declined and urged the workers not to try. Perhaps Mendoza had heard the rumors of internal fighting at La Paz and wanted to intensify it.

The information, though far-fetched, played into Chavez's belief that Ganz was behind his problems with the paid reps. Whether or not the memo clinched anything in Chavez's mind, there it was, on his desk, one more damning piece of evidence against Ganz.

With Padilla, Cohen, Ganz, and Govea gone or marginalized, and Guzman in a San Jose hospital barely able to speak, the remaining militant paid reps had to take on La Paz on their own. They had no map, no equivalent of the Marshall Plan, no theory of how they were going to influence the Executive Board. Instead of Ganz, they worked with twenty-seven-year-old Jose Renteria, who headed the Salinas field office. They immersed themselves in the problems of the people they represented, and tried to get the companies and the union to resolve them. Much of this was standard union work: seniority disputes, unresolved grievances, hassles between workers and union staffers. But in the spring and summer of 1981, the RFK Medical Plan again claimed most of their attention.

The RFK office at La Paz still did not have enough experienced people to do the job. Those in charge lost forms, couldn't keep information straight, often didn't know who was eligible and who was not (eligibility changed month by month, depending on how many hours people worked). They also had to deal with employers who sent their contributions only under pressure. Workers had to call La Paz to activate their claims; in some field offices the union staff, conscious of saving pennies and using every opportunity to flash their badge of poverty, asked the members to pay for the calls. Some did, and then were enraged when they were put on hold.[37]

In late March, La Paz asked the paid reps to come to the mountain to help straighten out the RFK records. The reps refused, saying it wasn't their job. They added that the union had enough money to hire competent people to run RFK, and they weren't those people. Besides, they had been to La Paz many times, and had always gotten the runaround. Among themselves, they feared that the offer was merely a maneuver to make them jointly responsible for the disaster. Their refusal fueled Chavez's suspicions that the reps were politicizing the RFK plan, using it to advance their own union careers. He could play that game, too.

On May 23, 1981, David Martinez, Oscar Mondragon, Gilberto Rodriguez, and Lupe Bautista walked into the Salinas field office while Renteria was holding a meeting with the paid reps. Martinez was the spokesman. He had come up fast in the organization. Recruited to the Chicago boycott in 1973, he was another new member of the Executive Board. An ex-seminarian, he was adept in the rhetoric of high moral purpose and equally skilled as a political hatchet man. He had helped spread the rumors that blamed Ganz for Rufino Contreras's death. Though not physically dangerous himself, he had brought muscle with him.

Martinez introduced his three companions, though that was a formality. The reps all knew Mondragon. They knew Rodriguez and Bautista too, as errand runners for Manuel Chavez and Frank Ortiz. Chavez had sent them to help with the medical plan, Martinez explained. Mondragon then said that they had come "to see if there really were problems . . . or only a lot of fuss." Bustamante took offense, and he and Mondragon argued. Renteria took Bustamante's side, said that it was his field office, that he was chairing the meeting, and Mondragon should be quiet and listen. The meeting degenerated into a shouting match and broke up.[38]

The next day Mondragon met with Hermilo Mojica separately. Mondragon had confidence in Mojica, he said, because he had once worked with Manuel Chavez. The trouble with the medical plan, Mondragon claimed, was that Bustamante and Zambrano were purposefully messing it up. He showed Mojica a medical form on which Zambrano had written an incorrect Social Security number. Mojica laughed. "That's a little mistake," he said, "I know of hundreds of other legitimate complaints where the forms were filled out correctly." Mondragon answered with a general attack on Bustamante, Zambrano, and Renteria: Bustamante had been responsible for the violence in 1979; Renteria was mismanaging the paid reps; Zambrano was a Communist.[39]

Mojica didn't budge. Mondragon, Martinez, and the others remained in town, spreading slander about Bustamante, Zambrano, and Renteria. They did not get a welcome reception; the membership knew the RFK plan problems were real, and few believed that the paid reps were either responsible for those problems or exploiting them for their own advantage. Mondragon tried to organize a recall election of Zambrano but failed.[40]

In the midst of their rumor and harassment campaign, David Martinez put an exclamation mark on the Executive Board's decision not to organize any new companies. While the Martinez team was in Salinas, a few workers from a small nursery sought out Bustamante, told him they wanted to join the union, and were ready to strike. Bustamante urged them to organize a meeting of as many of their fellow workers as they could, and then he and Zambrano went to talk to them. If they wanted union representation, Bustamante told the assembled crowd, they should strike and file for a forty-eight-hour election.

"And so they went out on strike," Bustamante recalled. "Everybody, it was one hundred percent. And David Martinez told me that the people had to go back to work. He said we were not going to represent them. That we had too much to do already. He said that the fifty [garlic] elections we had won in Gilroy were just a big drag on the union. That we didn't have anybody to negotiate the contracts. That our hands were full already. That the union would have nothing to do with these people."[41]

Martinez had spoken to Bustamante in confidence, but this was not meant to be a secret. He said much the same to a meeting of the paid reps at the field office, adding that the union was not interested in Salinas anymore; it would expand to other areas. Later, in mid-June, he told the *Salinas Californian*, "Organizing is not top priority right now."[42]

Bustamante tried to salvage what he could for the strikers. He quietly told them what had happened and recommended they go to the boss and offer to return to work without an election in exchange for a raise. The workers, disappointed, asked him to do it instead. He did, the employer agreed, and the last paid rep organizing drive was over.[43]

Jose Renteria, the young man who had become a *lechuguero* because he wanted to be at the heart of the struggle, was the next to fall. Chavez did not have to fire him. By 1981 Chavez had mastered the technique of publicly pressuring people to leave in a fashion that would warn other staffers to stay in line. In early June Renteria was summoned to a meeting at La Paz. In a room full of field office directors and their staffs, plus some members of the Executive Board, Chavez complained about Salinas. He wouldn't use names, he said, but some of the staff were creating problems for the union. Those who were doing so knew who they were and should resign. After the meeting, Renteria asked David Martinez if Chavez had meant him. Martinez replied, "No, we are not accusing you of anything. But I don't see the point of you continuing in the union." Renteria asked for a leave of absence. Chavez named Mondragon to replace him.[44]

A few days later, on June 6, Cesar Chavez convened all of La Paz for what he called a Serious Meeting, a *Junta Grave*. He had prepared five pages of typewritten notes, a systematic outline of his view of the threat looming over him and the union. The notes telegraph the gathering storm. The UFW is in danger. He has heard "persistent rumors" that that there was a "conspiracy against the union" meant to take it over or destroy it. He lists those who have told him as much: "the Governor's office, the ALRB, AFL-CIO, Teamsters, Tom Hayden, Chicano organizations and leaders, and workers."[45]

This was not the first such threat, Chavez noted. Between 1965 and 1970 there had been "infiltration . . . drugs . . . women . . . filthy money," and attacks on the leadership for affiliating with the AFL-CIO. There had been other conspiracies over the years. Now the attack was focused on La Paz, on "the head." He listed more rumors: "Cesar doesn't care about the workers"; he is "Isolated . . . Meditating—In the Garden." And the union? "Organizing—No more . . . Strength—No more."

The notes continue: the staff needed to know that the union found itself face to face with "The Big Lie." Who was behind it? The conspirators would be named "at the appropriate time." For now, it was enough to know they were ex-volunteers; standing behind them were other unions, "extremist groups," the growers and all their money. Their objective was either "dual unionism" or forming another union. "Why Do They Do It?" Because the UFW is the first farm worker union in history, the "only farm worker union," the one with "Mexican leadership," an obstacle not only to growers but political interests, because "the Mexican people are developing strength even greater than the Blacks."

The union confronted an "Emergency." The Executive Board would form a team to go out and "destroy . . . the big lie . . . end the rumors." Those assembled in La Paz were to continue on with the mission of the union and await further instructions.

Chavez himself was part of the team. No longer the leader flat on his back, converting suffering into strength while directing the battle from a sick bed, Cesar Chavez was an active combatant. For the next few months he would spend much of his time in the Hollister field office, a short drive from the alleged conspirators in Salinas.

Ganz was now formally divorced from the union but still attuned to what was going on. Some of the paid reps had helped him and Jessica move to Pacific Grove, a small coastal city a half hour's drive from Salinas. The reps carried on. They had little contact with Ganz as the summer advanced and the situation spiraled toward all-out civil war. Once, some of them came to Govea and Ganz's house for dinner. Marshall, already depressed, was distraught.

> Watching what happened . . . was just a horror, 'cause we were working close enough that we could see. We could watch Cesar. I mean, they just destroyed the whole Salinas operation, and it was just a horror to watch. One of the most painful things I've ever—I've ever seen. And it was really hard because I felt a whole lot of responsibility. On the other hand, I just didn't see how I could really challenge Cesar and the union. There was no solution to the fucking thing.[46]

Chavez's sojourn in Hollister in the summer of 1981 provides one last look at Cesar Chavez as an organizer of farm workers. Employing some of the same skills he had used twenty years earlier, he answered the critics who charged that he was isolated in La Paz, uninterested in the company of farm workers, remote from the concerns of his membership. Perhaps the Hollister adventure was also meant to assure himself that he still had the touch, that he was still popular in the fields. Now fifty-four, he returned for one last campesino campaign before he made the moves that would finally doom the UFW as a farm worker organization.

He wanted to show his son, Paul, how it was done. Before taking charge of the Hollister operation, he had made Paul, whom he still called Babo, the director of the field office there. The Hollister staff couldn't help noticing how much Chavez loved being with Babo. According to one of the staffers, John Brown, Chavez especially enjoyed the role of proud papa teaching his son the secrets of the trade, in preparation for the day when he would inherit the organization.[47]

Hollister was a good choice. A small town on the periphery of the multi-billion-dollar agriculture industry, it was something of a refuge from the union's internal battles. Yet it was close enough to Salinas for David Martinez and company to keep Chavez abreast of what those he'd branded enemies were up to. The union was popular in Hollister and throughout sparsely populated San Benito County. Four hundred Almaden workers had had a wine grape contract there since 1967. Many were now older men whose seniority rights had kept them on the job, and who enjoyed wages and benefits higher than most other Hollister workers. Chavez had made a great difference in their lives, and they were true Chavistas.

But the union's popularity went beyond Almaden. The fired-up garlic workers hoped to sign contracts consolidating their gains from 1980, and many were willing to serve on negotiating committees. In nearby Gilroy about 200 mushroom workers at Steak-Mate, inspired by the garlic strike, had also voted in the UFW, expecting to get a contract. Finally, at Bertuccio Farms, a diverse operation that included several row crops and a few apricot orchards, 400 workers who had voted for the union back in 1977 were still striving to get a contract. They were delighted that the Chavezes, father and son, had arrived to renew the battle.

In that spring of 1981, Chavez started with the basics. He and Paul spent a lot of time meeting with farm workers from the local companies. Chavez listened attentively, promoted the union with stories about victories in other areas, and looked for farm workers who would follow his lead. He scheduled rallies and marches, and arranged for the election of rank-and-file negotiating committees. Then he led the negotiations himself.

These did not go well. Many of the garlic growers, especially in Santa Clara County around Gilroy, were ready to leave farming. San Jose was immediately to the north and creeping south. The growers could make more money selling their land to developers for housing and malls than they could growing garlic. Even growers who wanted to continue found it hard, because garlic cannot be planted in the same ground year after year without risking nematode infestation, and the expanding development left less agricultural land for rotating crops. None of them wanted to sign with the UFW. For the 1981 season, in Santa Clara Valley the growers cut their garlic acreage by almost two-thirds and in San Benito by about half.[48] Then they stonewalled the union during negotiations.

The Steak-Mate talks went better, as the mushroom firm wanted to stay in business. Nevertheless, it enjoyed the advantage it had over its unionized competitors. Steak-Mate negotiated in good faith, but it was in no hurry to agree to UFW terms.

The Bertuccios, husband and wife, were the face of local agriculture in San Benito County. They lived in a spacious house on a hilltop overlooking the valley, where their families had farmed for generations. They did

not believe in unions, and although they argued that they had their workers' best interests at heart, they had a reputation among farm workers of
being particularly hard to work for. Paul Bertuccio barely went through the
motions in negotiations, and did not hide his disdain for the Chavezes.

Chavez was deeply insulted.[49] He didn't much like growers to begin
with, and the Bertuccios were especially easy to dislike. They didn't seem
to take him seriously, a slight he was not prone to overlook, especially as he
had suffered it in front of his son.

The Bertuccio workers were well organized and eager to strike. The
Steak-Mate workers were skilled mushroom harvesters, difficult to replace.
Although Chavez was not encouraging workers in most other areas to
strike, here in Hollister in his last farm worker organizing campaign, he
decided to go all the way. In mid-July, with Chavez's encouragement,
Bertuccio and Steak-Mate workers walked out of the fields, chanting
"*Huelga!*"

The strikes were popular and strong. Most of Bertuccio's 2,500 acres
were empty; in the first weeks only 60 people out of a workforce of about
400 dared cross the picket lines. Several weeks later, even fewer scabbed.
But the Bertuccios held firm. Tina Bertuccio came down from her house
and posed for a photograph beside a tractor that was discing the family's
lettuce. They were going to lose millions of dollars, she declared, but they
would not meet the union's demands. In a few months they simply stopped
farming. The next spring they began again on a reduced scale. The ALRB
charged them with bad-faith bargaining, but to little effect. Bertuccio never
signed, and eventually most strikers returned to work.[50]

Cesar Chavez did get one victory out of the strike. A local judge, citing
a decision by a higher court, had denied the UFW access to the Bertuccio
fields to talk to the few strikebreakers, because the ALRB had not yet
issued an explicit directive allowing the union in. To put pressure on the
farm labor board and to publicize the strike and the union's ongoing
boycotts, Cesar and Paul, along with forty other people, broke the local
judge's order and peacefully submitted to arrest. Once Chavez was released
from jail, he reentered the fields and was arrested again. The next day, the
ALRB granted access at Bruce Church, and under controlled conditions, at
all struck companies. All charges were dropped, but not before stories
sympathetic to the UFW and pictures of the Chavezes appeared in the San
Francisco papers. Cesar had given Paul a lesson in basic UFW strategy: a
setback on the farm could make for good publicity in the cities and force
action from the liberal friends of farm labor.[51]

At Steak-Mate it was a different story. Ralston-Purina, the corporate
owners of the mushroom farm, did not want to shut down production.
The local farm manager tried to bring in scabs, and made a deal with a
nearby San Jose immigration lawyer who provided immigrant Sikhs to

cross the picket lines. But mushroom harvesting is highly specialized work, done by athletic young men working on piece rates. The Sikhs had never harvested mushrooms before, and they made a mess of the work. Also, early on in the strike the union announced a boycott of some easily identified Ralston-Purina products: Chicken of the Sea Tuna and Chex cereals. After ninety-six days of a solid strike and some bad publicity for its brand, the company signed. Given the overall momentum against the union at the time, the Hollister campaign counted as a considerable success.

The paid reps tried in vain to meet with Chavez while he was in Hollister. Some of them still believed that Chavez was unaware of all that Martinez and Mondragon were doing. Others thought that he was being misled and if they could just get enough time to talk to him, they could straighten him out. Mojica was one of those who believed the most in Cesar Chavez. In August of 1981 he lost his faith.

Mojica had run into Cesar, Paul, and a few other staff members at the Hollister field office. Chavez said he wanted to spend some time alone with Mojica, and the two men retired to an inner office.[52] According to Mojica, Chavez began by accusing him and the other paid reps of exploiting the problems with the medical plan for political purposes. Mojica denied it, insisting that the plan was not working well. They argued but without rancor. Chavez complained that the agreement the reps had cut with the dental clinic for late hours was costing the union money. Mojica replied that he had gone to the trustee meetings, and he knew that the RFK plan could afford it. They talked like this for a while. Then Chavez said that it didn't matter if the workers had to wait a little while for their benefit checks; they would get the money eventually, and meanwhile the union was earning interest.

"The union is a business," Chavez said, "you have to understand that."

Chavez had previously pointed out at Executive Board meetings that the union earned interest on delayed benefit checks, but he had never said it to farm workers. Mojica had often heard workers complain that Cesar and Manuel Chavez were interested only in making money, but he had always refuted it. Now the word was coming from the man himself. Mojica was furious.

"Why don't you go out in the fields and tell the workers that? See if you can organize them saying that."

Chavez said he wasn't going to stand there and be blamed for the RFK plan's troubles, and he wasn't going to put up with Mojica anymore. "*Por lo bueno, soy bueno; por lo malo, soy cabrón. Te voy a chingar,*" he warned. A model of linguistic efficiency, nearly impossible to translate with full force, essentially it means, "For doing good, I'm good. For doing bad, I am a bastard, and I'm going to fuck you up."

"You know what, I have to leave now, because if I don't I might slap you in the face," Mojica answered.

He walked away, devastated. Chavez had always said that the union was a cause, and now he had told him it was a business. "That is when my world fell down on top of me. How could I have been blind for so long? Why didn't I open my eyes earlier? So I left. I bought a six-pack of beer. I never drink. And on the way home I drank a beer and a half. And when I walked in the door of my house, I vomited. I vomited all over the place. I didn't have much in my stomach, but it all came up. I was sick to the bottom of my soul."[53]

That same summer of 1981, Ronald Reagan fired the nation's striking air traffic controllers and hired scabs as permanent replacements, setting an example of union busting for the entire U.S. industrial class. The message was not lost on either local California agriculturalists or big corporate farmers such as United Brands/Sun Harvest. Their move away from the UFW had begun a year earlier, but Reagan's assault on organized labor provided ideological sustenance, and meant that the growers didn't have to hide what they were doing.

Oshita, a mid-size vegetable company with a UFW contract, subcontracted some of its thinning and hoeing work to nonunion Royal Packing. Growers Exchange, once among the state's biggest shipper-growers, sent its employees a letter saying it was planning to end all of its operations in the Imperial Valley. Starting in September 1981, the company went further, giving up all of its leases, selling its equipment and land, and eventually going out of business. Pik'd Rite, the Salinas strawberry company that had signed in the heat of the 1979 strike, announced that it would give up its main lease in Chualar and end its southern Salinas Valley deal. More growers who did business with Mann Packing brought in nonunion harvesters to cut the broccoli, and Mann laid off one of its union crews. Arrow Lettuce replaced two union crews with nonunion contractors.[54]

At Sun Harvest the workforce fell by 40 percent in 1981, and 700 UFW members lost their jobs. Nothing could have been more blatant than the way Sun Harvest turned over its cauliflower deal to two nonunion companies. It sold its trucks, cauliflower equipment, and the buses that carried workers back and forth from the fields to Big Valley Leasing and Fanciful. The new operators simply repainted them with their own colors and logos. The truck drivers and foremen were the same; they quit their jobs at Sun Harvest and went to work for the nonunion firms. The new companies, after harvesting the cauliflower with nonunion workers, transported it to a shed where it was packed and marketed by Sun Harvest, just as before. Worst of all, the cauliflower workers believed that Big Valley Leasing and Fanciful were Sun Harvest affiliates.[55] But the UFW's legal department, barely staffed and overburdened, never fully investigated United Brand's financial connections to Big Valley Leasing and Fanciful. The UFW's only response to the butchering of its most important contract was to file unfair labor practice charges with the already gummed-up ALRB. La Paz had neither the inclination nor staff to organize at the new nonunion compa-nies, nor even to rally the members against their runaway employers. Chavez was in Hollister organizing a different group of workers. Martinez and Mondragon were occupied attacking the paid reps in Salinas. And the paid reps were busy defending themselves and organizing what turned out to be their final stand in the union.

After Mojica's confrontation with Chavez in Hollister, the paid reps decided to run three of their own candidates for the Executive Board in September. They did not want to take on Chavez directly by running against his entire slate of nine incumbents. He was too popular to oppose; the reps' constituency was concentrated in Salinas; besides, they still half hoped that if their candidates could get on the board they might be able to turn Chavez around, refocus his attention on the problems in the fields.

"Farm workers on the board" was their slogan. They argued that most of the Executive Board members either had never been farm workers or hadn't worked in the fields recently enough to understand the current conditions of the membership. Their thirteen-point program included reform of the medical plan, launching a new organizing drive in Salinas, and hiring competent personnel in union offices, as well as new lawyers and negotiators.[56] They targeted the seats of Frank Ortiz, David Martinez, and Oscar Mondragon. They chose Jose Renteria, who was still on leave from his job as head of the Salinas field office as one of their candidates. Renteria was highly respected by the workers, bilingual, and knew the internal procedures of the union. They hoped to make the campaign more than a Salinas event, so their next candidate was Chayo Pelayo. She was dedicated, popular, and strong, and had worked most of her life in the table grapes in Coachella and the Central Valley, and only a few seasons in Salinas. The third candidate was a farm worker from the San Joaquin, but, reflecting the reps' inability to extend their political influ-ence beyond their own turf, he dropped out at the last moment, and even his name has been lost to memory.

The election strategy was partly defensive. The rank-and-file leaders wanted to get Ortiz, Martinez, and Mondragon off their backs and out of their positions of influence with Chavez. But the campaign was also a logi-cal extension of their victory in the 1979 strike. As a result of that battle they had been elected to represent the workers who were the main dues base of the UFW. Frustrated by their inability to shape union policy in the valley, they wanted to extend their power to the mountain. Over the previous two years they had learned that they needed a voice on the Executive Board to protect what they had won in 1979. Although the boycott was largely dead as a useful tactic and dues had outpaced donations as the union's largest source of income, the board still overrepresented the boycott soul of the organization, the part of the union whose prime function was to advocate for farm workers among supporters in the cities, which now was accomplished mainly through the UFW's string of charity organizations and Democratic Party politics. "Farm workers on the board" was meant to change that. The actual candidates, if victorious, would give the farm worker soul of the union some power at the top.

La Paz didn't see it like that. The union had no experience of open, serious competition for Executive Board posts. Tony Orendain had protested his removal from the official slate at the first UFW convention, and Al Rojas had temporarily stood for office without Chavez's approval in 1975, but neither had campaigned among the workers or put up much of a fight. Despite their slim chances and the fact that they proposed only three new people for a nine-member board, the paid reps offered an alternative program, which they promoted in a series of leaflets, meetings, and small and large conversations. In a union without a tradition of political debate, La Paz considered that treason. Unable to acknowledge the farm workers' ability to organize themselves, La Paz fell back on conspiracy, blaming the campaign on evil, behind-the-scenes manipulators who had once been in the union's inner circle.

La Paz answered the paid reps' challenge with a political sledgehammer. David Martinez, Frank Ortiz, and Dolores Huerta led the counterattack. They accused the candidates and the reps of being the dupes of Marshall Ganz, who wanted to take over or destroy the UFW. It hadn't been a big jump to remake Ganz from a hero-organizer into an evil one. In Chavez's view, organizers "got ordinary people to do extraordinary things," and evil organizers could make them do bad things. Neither was it a big leap to remake the villain-organizer into the villain Jew. A set of talking points, circulated during the campaign against the paid reps, included the observation that "some Jews with a superiority complex who think we Mexicans are *pendejos* ['fools'] . . . have used our people . . . Their goal is to take power on the Executive Board." The talking points claimed the Jews were led by Marshall Ganz but also included Jerry Cohen and members of the old legal department.[57] Within the Mexican Catholic farm worker community, where Jews were an exotic rarity, the ill-intentioned manipulator working behind the scenes easily became the evil Jew exercising power from the shadows.

Later, Huerta consistently denied that she had attacked Ganz as a Jew. She said she had told workers that Ganz was master-minding the campaign, and reminded them "that Marshall Ganz was in charge of the strikes where all the deaths had occurred, and that in all the other strikes there had been no deaths." She blamed Jessica Govea for the RFK plan mess, saying, "Jessica had been in charge of the medical plan during the period of very bad administrative problems."[58] But Jew-baiting continued, and in the midst of the campaign, Mojica attended a meeting at the UFW office where Huerta and Mondragon sketched out a Jewish conspiracy against the union:

> Dolores Huerta and Oscar Mondragon told the farm workers that we, the paid representatives, wanted to destroy Cesar, and that Marshall Ganz was our leader. They also said that Marshall Ganz was being pressured by the 'Jews' and that the UFW Board of Directors had proof. And that the proof was in letters that a priest had sent to Marshall Ganz. They said these letters would prove that the Jews were behind all this and that the people backing Marshall Ganz were the paid representatives, Jessica Govea, Gilbert Padilla, and everyone else who had left the Union. They said that we were all Marshall's people.[59]

Anti-Semitism may have had some effect on the farm worker campaign trail, but it became an embarrassment when it was reported later in the *New York Times*.[60] The paper quoted a former UFW organizer, Scott Washburn, who said he had heard Frank Ortiz tell farm workers that "the Jews were trying to take over the union—the two Jews, Jerry and Marshall." Chavez asked Ortiz for an explanation, and Ortiz wrote him a letter admitting that he had talked against Cohen and Ganz:

> I did mention Jews, but not in the context they have put it. I said "too bad these guys had to be Jews because our best support all across the country comes from the Jewish people and organizations," also, that the Jewish people through all of history have been the most discriminated in the world and now we had Marshall and Jerry working against us; that this was sad that they were Jews and were saying racist things about you and Mexicans.[61]

Ortiz said he had told the workers that Ganz had refused to obey orders and had spread lies about Chavez and La Paz; and that Cohen had led the lawyers out of the UFW and had said of Chavez, "That short fat little Mexican was going to come crawling on his knees to beg him to come back and save the Union."[62]

Chavez told the *New York Times* that he was satisfied that the "really disgusting" allegation of anti-Semitism had no foundation. He reminded the *LA Times* reporter Harry Bernstein that "we supported the State of Israel and gave money away to Jewish people like Howard Berman." The Anti-Defamation League, whose officers had written La Paz letters of complaint, was appeased, and the flap among the union's liberal supporters didn't last long.

Ganz and Cohen weren't the La Paz team's only targets. They also attacked the paid reps directly. Among the talking points was the claim that the paid reps were not qualified for high office in the UFW because they couldn't speak English; that Renteria was a puppet; that Pelayo had a good heart but was not very smart; that Zambrano wanted the union to fail so that there would be a revolution; that Mario Bustamante was earning $20,000 a year but was unable to do the job of a paid rep; and that Mojica was but an instrument of Bustamante.[63]

The reps struck back. They had studied the UFW constitution and knew of its provision prohibiting union members from libeling one another. In the summer of 1981 they filed internal charges against Mondragon. The Executive Board, with Chavez chairing, dismissed all the charges. The hearings had been little more than a restatement of the leadership's gripes against the paid reps, this time to their faces: they were playing politics with the medical plan, had failed to obey orders, had pursued organizing although that wasn't in their job description, and were generally insubordinate.[64]

Later the reps filed more internal charges, claiming that the Executive Board candidates were bad-mouthing them and using union funds to run for office. Again there were trials, and again the Executive Board ruled that its own had done no wrong. Some of the reps also went to the union hall and signed cards withdrawing their authorization to have their Citizens Participation Day pay sent to La Paz. They didn't want to give money to the people who had come to Salinas to attack them, they explained. This infuriated the Executive Board. At the time, the *Salinas Californian* reported that about 30 percent of the UFW membership was refusing to give the union their CPD pay.[65] Once the paid reps did the same, that figure was sure to grow.

La Paz's attack game had some effect, and to a certain extent pushed the paid reps' campaign off track. "Farm workers on the board," the reps continued to say, but the crucial issues facing the union were often lost in the midst of charges and countercharges. From La Paz Chavez made a series of telephone calls to the paid reps to build his case against their supposed exaggerations. On August 25, 1981, he called the Sun Harvest rep, Sabino Lopez. Listening in on a speakerphone were Dolores Huerta, Richard Chavez, David Martinez, and Oscar Mondragon. Sabino was upset. He told Chavez, "Yesterday morning Sun Harvest brought in three ground crews from Royal Packing to cut the lettuce in the Sun Harvest fields." Also the company had sent letters to the workers living on company property asking them to vacate their housing by September 30. The UFW's most important contract was being hollowed out from the inside, but Cesar Chavez couldn't be distracted from his purpose. The La Paz memorandum of the conversation reports that Chavez's only question to Sabino was "if in his judgment there were still a lot of RFK problems."[66]

Despite the distractions, in Salinas the paid reps' campaign was well received and La Paz's attacks sputtered. At the ranch committee meetings where delegates were elected to go to the UFW convention, Huerta tried to convince people to vote against the paid reps. She failed. The paid reps would lead the Salinas and Watsonville convention delegations. The reps understood that they lacked support in other areas. They had traveled around the state and knew that workers had similar problems, especially with the medical plan. But workers outside Salinas had not gone through the same struggles, had not had the same kind of political relationship with La Paz, were less well informed, and were less convinced that a change would do any good. Once people learned that Cesar Chavez opposed their candidates, few were willing to campaign against him. Still, Salinas stood firm. The UFW had more members from Salinas than anywhere else. The reps believed their position would get a good hearing at the convention.

On the first weekend of September, the UFW's fifth national convention opened in Fresno. Chavez and the Executive Board used various tricks to prevent the dissenting workers from getting a public hearing. They sat the Salinas and Watsonville delegations as far away from the two floor mikes as possible. They underweighted the votes of farm workers under union contracts: 185 UFW staff members were represented by ten delegates at the convention, or about one delegate for every ten staffers, whereas 25,000 farm workers with contracts were represented by 229 delegates, less than one delegate for every 100 workers. Organizing committees were granted delegate representation equal to the number of workers they could theoretically bring into the union. Thus, Texas, with little more than five staff members and some notional organizing committees, was granted five delegates. The Bertuccio workers, not yet under contract, were allowed four delegates, the same number as West Coast Farms, where workers had been under contract since 1977. Inactive organizing committees were given representation on the basis of the number of people they might, someday, bring into the union.[67]

Those were small tricks commonly used by unions to silence opponents. But just before the convention, Chavez engineered a more audacious ploy, which deserves to be enshrined in the Dirty Tricks Hall of Fame. The official delegate elections of the summer had been well organized, well attended open contests. The paid reps and their candidates had won almost all of these in Salinas. That was unacceptable, so the Executive Board, meeting just before the convention, declared an "Emergency to Exist" and passed a complicated resolution that bound delegates to vote for the candidates subsequently supported, either on a petition signed by a 7.5 percent of ranch members, or by a majority vote at any meeting attended by 15 percent of the ranch members. Executive Board members and staff then circulated petitions to secure the necessary "emergency" votes. Signatures on the petitions were then evaluated by the Executive Board–controlled Credentials Committee.[68]

This meant, as the paid reps tried to explain to the convention delegates, that at a ranch with 100 workers, the democratic choice of a majority of workers in an open contest could be trumped by only 8 ranch members who had been willing to sign a petition or come to a rump meeting. Thus, the Executive Board prevented the opposition from voting for its own candidates. Fourteen years later, David Martinez laughed when he told an interviewer about it: "So they couldn't vote, they couldn't vote for anybody but Cesar's slate."[69]

On Saturday, September 5, Chavez opened the convention warning the delegates that there were "malignant forces organized clandestinely that are jointly struggling to destroy our union." He had used the phrase "malignant forces" back in 1976 in the Nick Jones purge and in various internal disputes since. This was the first time he had said it in public, and newspapers across the country took note. He identified some of the bad guys: "the growers, the Teamsters." But as had become his custom he was vague about others: "people in and out of the union."[70]

After this ominous welcome and some opening business, Mario Bustamante approached the microphone and moved to void the Executive Board emergency resolution. Chavez called for an immediate vote. Bustamante and many of his compatriots believed that they had won the show of hands. Chavez ruled the vote too close to call, and declared that the convention would vote again after lunch.

The lunch break exploded in turmoil. Outside the hall groups of people shouted threats at one another. Several paid reps heard Executive Board loyalists, among them Helen Chavez, chant, "Death to Bustamante." A couple of Chavez militants drew back their coats to reveal handguns. Some from the Salinas delegation were also armed. Before returning to the convention floor, Jose Renteria suggested that if things got too dangerous or too outlandish, Salinas should walk out of the convention and go home.[71]

Back in the hall, delegates were given an anonymous typewritten leaflet. It said that the opposition at the convention was controlled by outside forces acting through Jose Renteria, that these forces were trying to put people on the Executive Board who would force Cesar Chavez to resign. It said that Renteria had earlier admitted that he followed Marshall Ganz's instructions to disobey orders from La Paz.[72]

Before the proceedings got under way, Mario Bustamante grabbed one of the men who had flashed a gun at him and brought him to the front of the hall. "The man is armed," he said. Chavez ordered security to take the man from the convention floor and search him. Bustamante shouted that they should search him in front of everyone. The guards took him away; they returned saying they had found no gun.

Chavez entertained a short discussion on the Executive Board emergency resolution. The *Fresno Bee* reported that forty people were lined up at the two microphones to speak when the question was called. This time the show of hands was clearly against the Bustamante motion, and Chavez ruled that it had been defeated. Jose Renteria announced that since the Salinas and Watsonville delegates weren't being allowed to vote for their own candidates, they would leave the convention. About fifty people, more than half of those two delegations, did so, while others in the hall chanted, "*Traidores, traidores.*"[73]

The next day after the incumbent slate was nominated, Doug Adair went to the microphone. He hardly knew the people from Salinas, and as they had been seated in the very back, he didn't realize that they had not returned. But he was sympathetic to their cause and he did know Chayo Pelayo well, as she and her sisters had worked at the Freedman ranch. Adair considered Pelayo a model UFW member, and if no one else was going to nominate her, he would. The nomination was ruled out of order because she was not present.

Meanwhile the Salinas delegates were talking to the press. The Executive Board's maneuver got just the kind of bad publicity that Cesar Chavez feared. On Sunday, the closing day of the convention, he did his best to limit the damage. The walkout was so bad, he said, because "the growers would interpret [it] as us having a weak union and as a time to hit us." He added: "It makes us seem like we're undemocratic. That's wrong. People read it in the newspaper. It hurts us when we go ask for the boycott."[74]

On Monday, September 7, the entire Executive Board, except for Chavez, converged on Salinas. Led by Dolores Huerta, they had come to get the rank and file to recall the "traitorous" paid reps. But they couldn't get enough signatures to force a single recall election, even though they needed only 20 percent of the members at any company. Thwarted in their open campaign, they launched a clandestine one. Agents aligned with the board tried to intimidate the reps into stepping down. According to Berta Batres, her husband received a series of phone calls saying that she was at a motel with another man. Her children told her that when they were walking home from school, they were stopped by men who said if their mother didn't stop fighting Cesar Chavez the whole family would be killed. The *Salinas Californian* reported that "Bustamante's son was allegedly taken on a ride by six people who threatened to kill him if Bustamante kept complaining about union leadership."[75]

None of it worked. The reps could not be recalled, and they would not resign. On September 17, the Executive Board put its next plan into action. Huerta, Mondragon, Gilberto Rodriguez, and David Martinez showed up at a general membership meeting of Green Valley Produce and accused Mario Bustamante of not doing his job, supporting Jose Renteria for Executive Board, and being a traitor to the union. "*Prueba, prueba, prueba*"— proof, proof, proof—the assembled workers chanted. Instead, Huerta handed Bustamante a letter from Cesar Chavez saying that he was dismissed from his position as paid rep.[76]

People were angry. Bustamante tried to calm them down. He would fight to get his job back, he told them. Chavez hadn't appointed him, so he couldn't fire him. They had elected him, and only they could get rid of him. Meanwhile, starting the next morning, he would be back on his crew cutting lettuce.

A week later, Huerta and Rodriguez went to a general membership meeting at Mann Packing and accused Juan Gutierrez of "having had private meetings with Marshall Ganz and Jose Renteria in order to form another union." Amid protests from the crowd, Huerta handed Gutierrez the same letter she had given to Bustamante. At Harden Farms, Huerta and Martinez came to a ranch committee meeting to attack Mojica, and give him notice that he had been fired. At Arrow, Huerta tried to organize a company meeting without inviting Berta Batres. Some workers let Batres know about it, and Berta, a tough, wiry woman, showed up to defend herself. When Dolores called Batres a traitor, people rushed the front of the union hall and challenged Dolores face to face. Huerta and her bodyguards made a quick exit. Batres didn't get her dismissal letter until a couple of weeks later.[77]

The Arrow Lettuce meeting was the last. Huerta would make no more attempts to mobilize the membership against the paid reps. The four other reps whom Chavez fired—Aristeo Zambrano of Associated Produce, Simon Rios of Salinas Marketing, Augustín Herrera of West Coast Farms, and Sabino Lopez of Sun Harvest—were all notified by hand-delivered letters in late October and early November. The letters were identical; only the names were different. Chavez wrote that the paid reps were "no longer my representatives." They hadn't done their jobs, and they had made "false accusations" to the membership about the union. He also explained that the reps could continue as ranch committee presidents and to work on their crews. In separate letters to the companies, he instructed the employers to stop paying the reps if they didn't return to work in the fields.

All eight of them did go back to the fields. They also sent letters to Chavez saying that they had never been "his representatives," that they had been the representatives of the people who elected them. Since he hadn't appointed them, he couldn't fire them. In preparation for a future court case, they demanded the right to a quick appeal. About a year later U.S. District Judge William Ingram would agree with them, ruling that they had been elected not appointed. But the judge refused to order them reinstated, pending further hearings. The legal maneuvering dragged on for seven years, got mixed-up with another issue, and the former reps, by then without a lawyer and without a movement, backed out of the case.[78]

The enthusiastic support that the reps had received in the face of Huerta's attacks was diluted by the solid fact of their dismissal. There wasn't much anyone could do to keep the reps in their jobs once they were fired. As it became clear that La Paz was going to make the firings stick, people's anger wore off, and they retreated into their everyday lives and struggles. The Salinas field office staff, under Mondragon, made things difficult for the people who openly supported the fired reps. Mojica was told that when his supporters went to the union hall with a grievance, the staff said, "Oh, you got a problem? Go get your friend Mojica to fix it."[79]

Within a few weeks, by Bustamante's count, about a quarter of the workers at Green Valley had sided with Mondragon's field office and Chavez. The unity of the lettuce crews was destroyed. People sat in different sections of the bus that took them to work. They insulted one another during the day. It was a catastrophe. Worried that someone might use a lettuce knife to resolve an argument, Bustamante left the company before the season ended and went to work in a nursery. A blacklist blocked him from returning to the lettuce fields for the next three years.

Throughout the valley the story was similar. At Sun Harvest, Chavez loyalists challenged the seniority of people who continued to support the old reps, and a nasty battle between the workers followed, amid continuing layoffs. Associated fired Aristeo Zambrano, who couldn't get enough support from his compatriots to fight back effectively. Berta Batres worked on at Arrow Lettuce and watched impotently as the company continued to replace union workers with nonunion crews. She broke up with her second husband, Javier Ayala, the paid rep from Veg-Pack, who dropped out of the fight after the convention and whom Chavez did not fire. Batres fell into a deep depression, and eventually hurt her back at work. "I was one of those who believed in Cesar Chavez . . . He was almost a god for me," Batres said many years later. "I thought that Ortiz and Mondragon were acting on their own, and that if we could only get through to Cesar he would support us. . . . It was so sad. He was afraid of our power. But the power we had was for the union. It was for Cesar and the union. It wasn't for anybody or anything else."[80]

Mojica kept on cutting lettuce. He, Zambrano, Bustamante, Batres, and a few others tried to keep things going for the next few years, with almost no success. Mojica managed to leaven his disappointment with irony:

> Way back before the election campaign, even before Cleofas's accident, we were telling people not to call the union "*la unión del Chavez*," to call it "*la unión de los campesinos*." I wasn't against Cesar at the time. I still

believed in him. We thought we were educating the workers, teaching them that the union belonged to them, and depended on what they did. But it never took hold. Farm workers kept on calling the UFW "*la unión del Chavez*." And you know what? It turned out that they understood the union better than we did.[81]

Nineteen years earlier Cesar Chavez had lost control of the first organization he had built, the Community Services Organization. He made sure that would not happen again. But in keeping control of the UFW, he crippled it. He politically enfeebled its local leaders and divided its ranks. The union still had the contracts, but it didn't have a united membership and a movement to protect them. La Paz had smothered the farm worker soul of the union. The body would wither and die. Only the head would live on.

Exeunt Omnes

'81 to '88

As easy as it was for the California vegetable industry to push the UFW aside, the job could not be done quickly. It took several years and was accompanied by the entire reorganization of agricultural enterprise in the Salinas and Imperial Valleys. California agribusiness, as it turned out, was as wily as the Greek god Proteus, who proved nearly impossible to capture and subdue because whenever his persuers thought they had him, he changed shape and slipped away.

Sun Harvest announced that it was going out of business in August 1983. Closing the company was quite different from the many plant shutdowns of the period, where production moved to another part of the world and the factories rusted away. What had been Sun Harvest ground did not lie fallow. It was leased by a host of nonunion companies that grew many of the same crops and had hired some of Sun Harvest's old personnel, from top executives to office secretaries to field foremen. The only people who could not continue at their old jobs were the Sun Harvest farm workers, and many of them were blackballed throughout the industry.

For the union, a fight in the fields to protect the jobs was out of the question. Instead, they turned to a renewed boycott of Chiquita Bananas and a legal challenge. The boycott never amounted to much, but the legal challenge might have gone somewhere. The union asserted that Sun Harvest had begun downsizing after the 1979 strike, entering into a series of joint ventures as a way "to subvert the union," a violation of Article 38 of the UFW–Sun Harvest contract. The union had mounted a similar challenge earlier against Oshita Inc. and lost in arbitration. But the legality of this type of industry flight from the union would not be firmly established until the Sun Harvest arbitration decision in August 1984. Going into the hearing, the union potentially had one persuasive new point to add to the argument: rumors throughout the industry had it that some of the nonunion companies in joint venture with Sun Harvest were partially owned by Sun World Management Corporation, which, together with United Brands, owned Sun Harvest. In other words, Sun Harvest was passing union work to nonunion companies that it owned. If that could be proved, it would be sufficient evidence that, in the words of a previous arbitrator, Sun Harvest had become a "game playing . . . unethical employer," in clear violation of Article 38. But the weak, disorganized UFW legal department never fully investigated the rumors and were shockingly incompetent at the hearing. Its sole witness testified to facts the company was not contesting, and even after being permitted four extensions, it submitted no written brief stating the union's case. In his final decision, the exasperated arbitrator said that he "could not be expected to speculate on what the Union believes the record establishes." He sided with the company, and Article 38 was fully entrenched as permitting union companies to pass their work to nonunion partners.[1]

Afterward, the other grower-shippers with union contracts increased their joint ventures with nonunion harvesting companies. Still, they continued to lose to the grower-shippers that were completely free of union contracts, wages, benefits, grievance procedures, the hiring hall, and what was left of the union workers' control over the pace and quality of production. Individual growers continued to leave union harvesting associations, such as Green Valley Produce. Soon, the union companies started to fall: Cal Coastal, Let-Us-Pak, Harden, Veg-Pack, and West Coast Farms were all out of business by 1986. Those were just the big boys in the vegetables; the UFW estimated that by mid-1985, more than fifty union companies had shut down.Some of those bankruptcies were legitimate, but many others were only on-paper reorganizations. A few UFW-contracted grower-shippers held out for a while, but before the end of the decade they were gone, too, and in 1987, only 1,299 union members were working in the vegetables, and only 8,681 farm workers were members of the union.[2]

It wasn't just the UFW and the grower-shippers with union contracts that went under. What had begun as a way to escape the union became a complete reorganization of the produce business as grower-shippers were replaced by shipper-retailers, whose expertise was in marketing and who were big enough to deal with the demands of the large supermarket chains. Eventually, even nonunion grower-shippers were replaced by a handful of shipper-retailers—Fresh Express, Nunez Brothers, Dole, Growers Express, and Tanimura and Antle. These new giants contracted with hundreds of growers (some of whom had been grower-shippers but were now reduced to mere growers) to plant and tend the crops. The shipper-retailers then hired nonunion custom harvesters or contractors who in turn hired the farm workers to pick the crops. This new structure purposefully left out the UFW, and the union, lacking the support of enough farm workers, had no reasonable hope of fighting its way back in. It was an escape worthy of Proteus. Seven years earlier the UFW had had the grower-shippers by the throat; now the grower-shippers had disappeared.

The disappearing act corresponded to a dramatic change in what Americans wanted to eat. Beginning in the 1970s, supermarkets stocked a wider selection of produce, with a heavier concentration of mixed greens, herbs, chard, spinach, and different varieties of tomatoes, peppers, and lettuce. The big food chains wished to sell these products year-round but did not want to deal with scores of different grower-shippers or take on the enormous job of scheduling production. The handful of new shipper-retailers took command. They decided what would be grown and when, and then signed contracts with the growers that ensured that they, the shipper-retailers, would get the bulk of the profits and avoid most of the risk. This business model is still in place in the second decade of the twenty-first century, as the produce industry continues its almost uninterrupted and unprecedented fifty-year expansion.

California agribusiness did not trample the UFW in a period of contraction. On the contrary, business was booming. Between 1970 and 1990 gross farm income in California grew from $4.7 billion to $20.2 billion, and net farm income went from $1 billion to $5.7 billion. Most of the gain was in fruit and vegetables, where over the same period acreage increased almost 200 percent. The major vegetable crops became more popular: broccoli production increased fourfold, while lettuce, cauliflower, and celery made less spectacular but nonetheless solid gains. Acreage in once-exotic but newly popular vegetable crops such as endive expanded.[3]

Everything went up but wages. Farm workers still had to cut the lettuce and the celery, wrap the leaves around the cauliflower heads, and do every other job in the fields. But the steep rise in farm worker income that began with the end of the Bracero Program was reversed as the UFW was forced out of the fields, sometimes overnight. At one artichoke company in Castroville where a contractor was brought in to replace the union, wages fell from nearly $7 an hour to less than $5 from one day to the next. Usually it took longer, but the result was the same. On union vegetable crews in 1983, hoers and thinners made $7.15 an hour plus benefits; eight years later, people hired by labor contractors to do the same work were paid $4.25 with no benefits.[4] Estimates of exactly how much real wages had fallen between 1980 and 1990 varied greatly, from 20 percent to nearly double that—and the loss on the ground in Salinas was catastrophic. Farm workers lost homes they had bought in the good years. Families doubled and tripled up in single-family houses. Some migrant farm workers lived in caves. Children left school to add one more meager paycheck to the family income. Some people didn't have enough to eat, and many filled up on bad food.

Much of what the union had won was lost. Farm workers could still get unemployment insurance if they had their papers in order, and people continued to be protected (at least theoretically) by state and federal labor laws that had officially excluded them before the UFW arrived. On paper, the California Agricultural Relations Act was still the best labor law in the nation. But everything else was gone. Breaks got shorter, people working by the hour were forced to speed up, and workers were fired without cause. In some fields, the short-handled hoe, banned in 1976, now reappeared. In other fields, slightly less brazen contractors replaced the long-handled hoes with short-handled weeding knives, which required the workers to stoop as much as they had in the old days, when the short-handled hoe was legal.

Among the losers in this reconfiguration of the vegetable industry were the piece-rate iceberg lettuce crews. In part, they fell victim to the change in consumer tastes. Beginning in the mid-1980s, health-conscious Americans began to favor Romaine and other kinds of leaf lettuce over Iceberg. Later people turned to bagged lettuce and pre-mixed salads, which saved them a few minutes when preparing dinner. These shifts allowed the growers to demobilize and nearly eliminate the *lechuguero* crews. Leaf lettuce requires less skill to cut than iceberg, because it does not ball up, so the picker does not have to choose which head to cut and which to leave for the next pass. There is no next pass; an entire field is cut at once. Lettuce that goes into bags does not have to be packed into cartons. Workers cut it and throw it directly into bins that tractors drag through the fields. There is no need for the co-operation required of the old trios, who rotated packing and cutting throughout the day

Currently, most lettuce pickers work by the hour and make from $8 to $10. For a while, piece-rate leaf lettuce crews were popular in the industry, but they are in decline now, replaced by hourly workers. Once leaf lettuce is ready to harvest, it can last longer in the fields than iceberg, and the growers do not need the faster piece-rate workers who were once necessary to pick the lettuce in the three days before it went bad. In the Salinas Valley only a handful of the old *lechuguero* crews survive. On good days they can still make over $15 an hour, but they are marginal to the industry, their years of glory long past.[5]

Although the UFW seemed to be firmly settled in the Ventura County lemon trees, it fell a long way in a short time. In 1980 UFW contracts covered about 70 percent of Ventura's lemon pickers. Five years later the UFW had no active contracts, and by 1987, the union didn't represent a single *limonero*. As in the vegetables, lemon growers left the union harvesting associations and turned to nonunion contractors to get their trees picked. But in the case of the *limoneros*, the UFW's inability to save its contracts had little to do with the internal battle between Chavez and the paid reps. The *limoneros* had sat out that struggle. In the lemons the union failed primarily because, once again, it did not organize among a new group of undocumented immigrants.

The nonunion contractors' triumph depended on the familiar, flexible business relationships of agriculture. The most powerful people in the lemon industry are the men who own the packing sheds, have access to the market, and control the distribution of the lemons. In the mid-1950s, worried about union organizers in the sheds and willing to have others take the responsibility for bracero labor, the packing house owners stopped hiring lemon pickers. Instead, a few harvesting associations contracted for, housed, fed, and paid the braceros who picked the lemons. Growers signed up with the associations from year to year, and paid them to harvest their orchards. When the bracero program ended, the harvesting associations continued to hire and contract out the harvest labor. It was mostly these harvesting associations that signed three-year contracts with the UFW in 1978, in the midst of the successful strike.

But Proteus changed his shape again. The harvesting associations, established in the 1950s to avoid labor problems, were discarded once new labor troubles began. Even before the 1978 contracts were signed, the growers and orchard owners had begun to leave the harvesting associations, instead using *limoneros* provided by labor contractors. This trend intensified once the UFW won the contracts, and growers deserted the associations in large numbers between 1978 and 1982. The nonunion contractors paid the workers the same piece rate for picking as the union associations had but provided no benefits and skimped on other expenses in so many ways that they could do the same job at a 20 percent discount.[6]

Some of the *limoneros* who went to work for the contractors were union workers who had been picking lemons for a long time. They had various reasons for leaving, including complaints about the RFK Medical Plan and the fact that some contractors controlled the best orchards, where the pickers could make the most money. The union's seniority system was also key. Many of the *limoneros* also worked in the nonunion orchards of Arizona, where the peak harvest overlapped with the beginning of picking in Ventura. But to maintain their union seniority, members had to report for work at the beginning of the Ventura season, which meant they had to leave the full trees of Arizona, where they could make more money, for the relatively empty trees of Ventura. Some workers chose to give up their union seniority and catch on later with the Ventura contractors, who paid the same piece rate.[7]

Vegetable workers had experienced similar problems with seniority in Salinas, where union members were required to work in the Imperial Valley in order to maintain their seniority with the firms that operated in both places. But the piece-rate lettuce crews pressured the union to change the rules, establishing separate seniority lists in Imperial and Salinas. The *limoneros* might have done something similar, but they worked by individual piece rate and were more prone to seek individual solutions to their problems. Instead of putting up a united fight to change the rules, some of them went to work for the contractors.

The bulk of the nonunion *limoneros*, however, were not ex-unionists. They were a new wave of immigrants, indigenous Mixtecs and Zapotecs from Oaxaca, people who often spoke Indian languages rather than Spanish; they were just beginning to appear in the California fields in the late 1970s and early '80s. Typically, these men learned to pick lemons in the Central Valley or the California and Arizona deserts, where there was less of a union presence and they could more easily get jobs. Although they were not as skilled as the longtime *limoneros*, by the time they reached Ventura they were good enough to get the work done. By 1982, working for nonunion contractors, they were a fast-growing presence in the Ventura County orchards.

The UFW ignored them. According to the agricultural economist Richard Mines, no one on the local Oxnard staff—or anywhere else in the union—spoke their languages; nor did the union try to recruit anyone who did. Not only did the union have no plan to organize among the Mixtecs and Zapatecs, union staffers didn't even make a concerted effort to get to know them. They were written off as people who couldn't be organized, a new batch of undocumented workers, sojourners in California, interested only in high wages.[8]

The UFW tried to protect union jobs through a legal maneuver. In 1978 and '79, the union filed complaints with the ALRB, claiming that the growers could not leave the Coastal Growers Association (which had a three year contract with the UFW) and give their work to nonunion contractors. But even a union-friendly ALRB ruled that since the growers had only signed one-year deals with the CGA and were not party to the three-year agreement between the UFW and the CGA, they could not be legally restrained from leaving the association once their one-year contracts expired. The great escape was legal.[9]

When its contracts with the harvest associations expired in 1981, the UFW could not reach a new agreement, and in March 1982, about 1,300 *limoneros* went on strike. That was still more than half of the lemon pickers in Ventura County and most of the people who had been covered by the UFW agreements. The growers did not try to break the strike for the first three weeks, and none of the strikers returned to work. Finally, just before the lemons got too big to sell on the fresh market, the growers started to bring in crews of mostly Oaxacan scabs. The strikers did what they could to stop them: they blockaded contractor busses; they ran into the orchards to pull out the strike breakers; they went on a four-day march through Ventura County, led by Cesar Chavez. All to no avail. After two and half

months on strike, in June 1982, the UFW signed new contracts on the
same terms that the harvesting associations had offered at the beginning of
the strike. Worse, the competence of the scab crews encouraged more
growers to leave the associations after the strike. By the time the new UFW
contracts expired in 1985, most of the associations were out of business.[10]

The UFW's response to the Oaxacans in the lemon orchards is more
than a reminder of the UFW's occasional hostility and general indifference
to the recent immigrants from Mexico. The Mixtecs and the Zapotecs
were just a small part of what Mexicans call *la reconquista*, the Mexican
"reconquest" of the American Southwest through the might of overwhelming numbers. Although the trend had started much earlier, in 1982
la reconquista intensified, as the Mexican government allowed the peso to
float against the dollar and it floated like a rock, losing 65 percent of its
value in a few months and even more over the next several years. The
ensuing economic crisis brought millions of Mexicans into the United
States, as did the amnesty provisions of immigration reform four years later.
By the end of the twentieth century, approximately 12 million native-born
Mexicans lived in the United States. There had been fewer than 2 million
in 1960. [11]

Many of the new immigrants went to the fields looking for jobs, and the
glut of new workers made it easier for agribusiness to rid itself of the UFW.
The union had been born in a period of labor scarcity; it died during a labor
surplus. But Cesar Chavez had already trampled the rank-and-file leaders of
his union before this new surge of immigrants arrived, and the disarmed
UFW would have been hard-pressed to defend itself against the growers,
new workers or not.

The bigger mystery is how Chavez, so adept at seeing the opportunities
that history provided in 1965, could have been so blind to one of the most
significant historical trends of his time: the massive migration of people
from Mexico and Central America to the United States. Chavez had tried
to put his finger in the dike early on with his Campaign Against Illegals.
Then he tried to make a limited peace with the newcomers. But he never
spoke for them or sought to represent them, never even welcomed them.
That, along with his commanding role in the destruction of his own union's
farm worker leadership, was his greatest historical failing.

In January 1983, during agribusiness's escape from the UFW, George
Deukmejian, a Republican, became the governor of California. Buttressed
by the conservative reaction and the corporate contributions bloating his
election funds (including more than $700,000 from agricultural interests),
"Duke" had made a campaign promise to "do away with government agencies that strangle business," repeatedly attacking Cesar Chavez, the UFW,
and the Agricultural Labor Relations Act. Once in office he slashed the funds

of several state regulatory agencies and fully met his obligations to the large California growers. He cut the Agricultural Labor Relations Board budget by 27 percent in his first year in office and appointed David Sterling, a longtime Republican state legislator, as the board's new general counsel.[12]

Over his seven-year run in the job, Sterling cut ALRB staff, further clogging up the agency's work; systematically rejected UFW charges against the growers; threw out previous ALRB complaints unfavorable to agribusiness; and unilaterally reduced "make whole" awards to the union by as much as 90 percent. Despite being the head of a regulatory agency whose legal charge was to protect the rights of farm workers, he carried on a public debate with Cesar Chavez, openly attacked the UFW, and served as a shill for California agribusiness.

In his first few years as general counsel, his attacks on his own agency were often blocked by its governing board, which continued to have a majority of Jerry Brown appointees until 1986. But his inability to get everything he wanted from the ALRB was secondary to his public role as a aggressive, high-profile critic of the union. In 1985, after the UFW renewed its table grape boycott, Sterling went on a national speaking tour during which he denounced the boycott and called Chavez's tactics "utterly contemptible." He also pressured Protestant church leaders not to endorse the boycott, and on one occasion told some of them that support for the UFW threatened their nonprofit status.[13] In 1990, at the end of his term he boasted to two academic researchers, "The Board is no longer responsive to the needs of farm workers."[14]

Deukmejian's cuts—the ALRB budget fell by 50 percent in the eight years that Duke was in office—coupled with his periodic rhetorical attacks on Chavez and Sterling's unabashed hostility, made Deukmejian and Sterling the public figures most associated with the UFW's defeat in the fields in the 1980s. The two men were proud of that, and helped popularize the view that they, personally, had beaten back the Cesar Chavez union. The UFW aggressively promoted the same idea, which masked the other reasons for its losses, and pointed the finger of blame at Republicans. The union had put too much faith in the law, Chavez explained to UFW supporters, and now that the law and the agency meant to carry it out had been destroyed, the union could no longer win elections in the fields, and had to renew its boycott appeals.

That explanation has stuck. Thirty years later, Deukmejian, Sterling, and the Republicans remain among the most prominent villains in semi-official UFW history; they are the people (along with Marshall Ganz, some insiders will add) who destroyed the UFW. But just as this argument obscured what was happening in the fields at the time, it has since become more an excuse than an explanation, as a simple consideration of the sequence of events demonstrates.

Let's begin with Sterling. He might never have been general counsel of the ALRB had it not been for a dispute within the California Democratic Party—a nasty ruckus that Cesar Chavez was largely responsible for keeping alive long after it had any coherent political meaning. In December 1982, after Deukmejian had won the election but before he took office, Jerry Brown had a chance to appoint a new general counsel of the ALRB. That counsel could have served a five-year term before the new Republican governor had a legal opportunity to name his own candidate. Brown nominated Nancy Kirk, a liberal attorney who was fully supported by the UFW. With Cesar Chavez sitting in the gallery taking notes, the state Senate was deadlocked on her confirmation. Surprisingly, the new Democratic state senator Art Torres was voting against her. If he had changed his vote she would have been confirmed, but he refused, thereby denying Kirk the nomination and giving Deukmejian the opportunity to appoint Sterling two months later.[15]

Torres's refusal to change his vote was the final blow in the fight with Chavez that had begun three years before when, as an assemblyman, Torres had deserted Chavez's candidate for speaker, Howard Berman, and supported Willie Brown. Chavez made peace with the more powerful Brown but refused to do the same with the former UFW staffer, Torres. When the liberal Torres decided to run for the state Senate in 1982, Chavez put considerable funds and UFW campaign workers behind his opponent in the Democratic primary, Alex Garcia, even though the reactionary Garcia was the same man whom Torres had run against, with massive UFW support, in Torres's first campaign for office. The 1982 primary campaign was considered one of the dirtiest in California's colorful political history, with much of the dirt kicked up by the UFW and Garcia, who accused Torres of adultery. After Garcia lost, Chavez refused to support Torres in the general election. Although Torres officially denied that his vote against Kirk was in retribution for the UFW's attacks, he also told reporters: "I paid very dearly for my independence. My wife and my children paid for it as well. And we are not going to let anyone tell us how to vote."[16]

Even though Chavez's relentless and unnecessary attempt to punish Torres helped put Sterling in office, it did not have a decisive impact on the subsequent course of events. Deukmejian could have cut the board's funding no matter who was its general counsel. And the board already was hopelessly inundated by grower appeals long before Duke and Sterling arrived, when Brown was still governor and the labor board was still in the hands of his appointees, as Chavez himself had claimed many times. According to ALRB records, in 1982 the board had a backlog of thirty cases before administrative law judges, forty-five appeals to the board, fifty-four complaints awaiting hearings, and 548 charges of unfair labor practices that still hadn't been investigated.[17] Agribusiness attorneys did not need the cooperation of the governor or the general consul or the Republican Party to gum up the works with their legal maneuvers.

These delays were not trivial. If a grower fired a union activist during an election campaign and the union could not get the ALRA to reinstate him or her quickly, it was much easier for the grower to silence union talk among his workers and win elections. The delays certainly worsened under Sterling, but he had not ushered them in. Nor did the union step back from elections in the fields only after the Duke and Sterling arrived. After the 1977 Giumarra defeat, the union initiated few elections and was pulled into general campaigns only by striking workers, such as the *limoneros* in 1978 and the garlic workers in 1980. In 1981–82, the fiscal year before Sterling arrived, there were only twenty-five elections in the California fields, and ten of them were attempts to decertify the UFW.[18]

Nor was it the Deukmejian-Sterling board that passed the crucial legal decisions favoring the growers. The ruling that allowed for the dissolution of the lemon-harvesting associations occurred in 1982 when the board was stocked with Brown appointees and UFW-friendly Boren Chertov was general counsel. The decisions on Article 38 in the standard UFW vegetable contract that allowed grower-shippers to replace union workers by subcontracting to nonunion companies were not made by the board at all, but by independent arbitrators.

The ALRA, no matter who its general counsel and who the governor of California, had little legal basis on which to block the general restructuring of the vegetable industry. That could have been halted only in the fields, by a farm-worker movement willing and able to stop harvesting crops until either the shipper-retailers, the custom harvesters, or the growers signed UFW contracts. But a movement capable of doing that had been undermined by Cesar Chavez well before Deukmejian became governor. The rout had already begun when he took office. He and Sterling certainly helped it along, but they mostly functioned as public cheerleaders while agribusiness swept the already debilitated union out of its fields.

Defeated as a union, the UFW transformed itself into a successful cross between a farm worker advocacy group and a family business. That wasn't an extreme makeover, as the organization had always had two souls. But as farm worker dues dwindled, the union soul died, while the boycott-advocacy soul, sustained spiritually by memories of past glory, found material sustenance in the string of nonprofit organizations that Chavez had earlier dubbed the Farm Worker Movement.

Dues dropped by more than a third between 1983 and 1984, to less than $2 million, and no one in the UFW leadership doubted that further losses lay ahead.[19] Meanwhile, by 1983, three of the nonprofits controlled by La

Paz—the Martin Luther King Farm Worker Fund, the National Farm Worker Health Group, and the National Farm Worker Service Center— had nearly $10 million in assets.[20] By 1986 that had grown to more than $15 million, earning more than $1 million in annual interest.[21] The balance sheet pointed the way forward. A financially secure future lay in the "movement entities," whose purpose was to advocate for farm workers and provide them some basic services. Just managing and spending the yearly revenues of the nonprofits was more than enough work to occupy the 150 or so organizational leaders and staffers who lived at La Paz. In time that money would also pay fifteen members of Cesar and Helen Chavez's extended family, who had majority control of the boards of directors of most of the nonprofits.[22]

Unlike the growth of the movement entities at La Paz in the mid-1970s, this was not a haphazard process. It was consciously planned and carefully executed, and some of its main features were put into place at the UFW's 1983 convention. As its first matter of business, the Executive Board proposed, and the 300 delegates endorsed, a constitutional amendment that allowed the union to transfer 25 percent of its strike fund into the boycott budget.[23] Chavez said that the UFW would use the money to initiate a "hi-tech boycott." Next, Chavez proposed that the union build a "Chicano lobby," a coalition of Chicano organizations that would promote the interests of farm workers and Mexican Americans in the California legislature. Finally, the Executive Board ensured that any rank-and-file leadership that might potentially emerge from its quickly disappearing farm worker constituency would be unlikely to challenge La Paz. Closing the chapter on the internal battle that had erupted at the 1981 convention, the delegates approved an Executive Board–sponsored constitutional amendment that required paid representatives to be appointed, not elected.[24]

The Chicano lobby never took hold—turf battles among Latino organizations blocked a united effort. But the UFW carried on in Sacramento without it. That was not easy, as the union's falling membership and consequent diminished Citizens Participation Day funds meant that the union had less money to hand out to politicians. Nonetheless, the UFW maximized its political impact, carefully choosing which Democratic politicians to support and supplying them with dedicated, skilled volunteers at election time. Until quite recently, UFW campaign workers were so important that Democratic Party candidates were willing to pay the union for them, reversing the usual flow of money in electoral politics.

But the sturdiest bridge from an impoverished workers' union to a prosperous farm worker advocacy group was the renewed boycott. At the 1983 convention—just eight months after Deukmejian took office and while the ALRB governing board and staff were still battling with David Sterling to preserve the effectiveness of their agency—Chavez told the convention delegates, "The law is dead." Since strikes had never been successful, he argued, the union had to return "to the most effective weapon which [has] served us so well—the consumer boycott." But times had changed, he told the convention, and the new boycott wouldn't rely on old tactics such as picketing supermarkets. Rather, its core tactic would be a direct-mail campaign explaining to targeted audiences why they should support the UFW. Two years later, Chavez quipped, "In the early days we would say, 'Could you come with us to the picket line?' Now we say, 'Could we get your mailing list' "[25]

The high-tech boycott was partly driven by necessity. The union no longer had enough farm worker loyalists to send to the cities to lead the picket lines, and its supply of middle-class volunteers was diminishing. The new boycott didn't need farm workers, only pictures of them, and the whole operation could be run by a few people. But the high-tech boycott was also another in a long line of Chavez enthusiasms. It was first suggested to him by an ex-UFW volunteer, Richie Ross, who had gone on to become a Sacramento consultant, reputed to have a rather loose hold on political ethics. Ross gave Chavez the fundraising strategy conceived in the George McGovern campaign, and then perfected by the successful right-wing ideologue Richard Viguerie.

Following the Viguerie model, the union sent out appeals to highly refined mailing lists, asking not only for support of its most recent boycotts but also for direct donations to the union or one of its tax-deductible movement entities. It worked fabulously. The first target of the campaign, Lucky supermarkets, quickly gave in and stopped buying and selling the Bruce Church brand of Red Coach lettuce. Once the direct-mail operation was in full gear it started to bring in a lot of money. In 1985 the union received more than $860,000 in donations, up from $184,000 in 1982. By 1987 donations topped $1.4 million.[26] After the Lucky success, however, few of the boycotts had much impact. No matter. It was just a small step to dropping the boycotts completely, expanding on the descriptions of farm worker misery in the mailers, and pegging the appeal to a less specific organizing campaign. Such appeals remain to this day a basic feature of the UFW's business model.

A commercial ethos swept through La Paz. The internal language of the union changed. The boycott became a "social marketing program." The departments of the union, now universally called "cost centers," were instructed to make up budgets that showed their "profits and losses." "Group Executives and Division Heads" were instructed in things called "back end performance analysis" and "promotion investment analysis." Executive Board meetings featured long discussions about the differing "profit potentials" of commercial and residential real estate. Potential supporters of the union became "target publics" or "markets."[27]

Some of this language had snuck into the Executive Board long before the death of the farm worker soul of the union—field offices had been referred to as "cost centers" as early as 1977. But the union didn't fully become a cross between an advocacy group and a family business until it was forced to, as a response to the grower offensive of the early 1980s that drove the UFW out of the fields. By then Cesar Chavez was fully in control of what he was doing, and he quickly guided the union through its transformation. In 1985, he told a reporter from the *Monterey Peninsula Herald*, "We are an institution now. Economic institutions have the darndest time dying off."[28]

As a substitute for an actual fight in the fields, the UFW staged one-day appearances by Chavez in California farm towns, coupled with farm worker marches and occasional walkouts. Previously such marches had kicked off organizing efforts, and had often won immediate wage gains from growers trying to protect themselves from the UFW. But in 1984 and 1985, although the union was still capable of mobilizing hundreds of people in small towns and thousands in larger places like Salinas, Calexico, and Delano, the demonstrations had little to do with trying to rebuild a movement, and they forced few concessions from the growers. Rather, they served as publicity for the new boycotts and demonstrations to the public that the UFW was still alive. Chris Schneider, a UFW legal worker assigned to the Imperial Valley, complained in an internal memo after one of these demonstrations: "Although there was a lot of interest from workers to use the stoppage as a springboard for more organizing, that didn't happen." He added that the enthusiasm generated from the demonstrations dissipated quickly, leading to even more disillusionment.[29]

In its scramble to maintain some presence in the fields and to prove that it still represented farm workers, the UFW began to sign substandard contracts that guaranteed little more than the prevailing—and dramatically falling—wages and working conditions. In 1985 the union "astonished" the negotiator at Sam Andrews by accepting his contract proposal that included no raise in wages, no good-standing clause, no hiring hall, and no medical plan.[30] In 1986 the union signed an agreement with Abatti that secured a raise from $4.65 to $4.80 an hour and, in the words of the Abatti negotiator, allowed the company "to continue operating as it has for the past eight years."[31] UFW officials explained that these new contracts were "foot-in-the-door" agreements, and that they hoped to win further gains in subsequent years. But the improvements never came, and the contracts proved unpopular with workers, as the union continued to take 2 percent of its members' earnings for dues. People working under contract sometimes received smaller paychecks than before the union signed.

But the provisions of these contracts were less important to La Paz than its continuing boycott enterprise, and the UFW was even willing to sacrifice one of its oldest, most cherished contracts in hopes of bolstering the boycott. In 1984, when the union announced its new grape boycott, UFW literature had footnoted the word "grapes" with: "except for the three percent of grapes produced under contract." That was more than inelegant, as grapes in supermarkets do not carry labels and consumers could not distinguish between union and nonunion grapes. By 1987, the Freedman contract, which had been the first one the UFW secured in 1970, was now their last remaining contract in the table grapes and the only reason for the footnote. When the contract expired the union did not negotiate a new one, although the company continued to pay into the pension plan, the health plan, and the Martin Luther King, Jr. Educational Fund, and the workers continued to pay dues. In exchange the company promised not to violate the rules or spirit of the old contract. Just a few months later, the company instituted a one-hour unpaid training program for new hires in the pruning, and a minimum number or vines that had to be pruned. Older, slower workers, high on the seniority list, were forced off the job. Neither La Paz nor the dispirited Freedman grape pickers could get those jobs back, and the UFW was completely finished in the table grapes.[32]

Meanwhile, the union did what it could to keep other organizers out of the fields and to maintain its exclusive farm worker franchise with foundations and prospective donors. Neither the Teamsters nor the Independent Union of Agricultural Workers a small group founded in 1977, run by some disreputable ex-Teamsters who had picked up a few contracts after the Teamsters left the fields in 1978, proved to be much of a threat. In 1984 the Teamsters opened up a new organizing drive in Salinas. Without the help of the growers, who no longer needed them, they couldn't do much, and they backed out a year later. The IUAW fell apart when its president, Martha Cano, went to jail for shooting and killing her husband, who happened to be the tiny union's other copresident.[33]

Some competition came from isolated groups of workers who tried to continue to organize, even as the UFW went down. Typically, the UFW dealt with them in the same manner that they treated Luis Magaña, the Stockton *tomatero*. Magaña and his father had been involved in the 1974 Stockton tomato strikes, where the workers had quickly won back their piece rates and then, under the direction of Manuel Chavez, had traveled to Sacramento to pressure the legislature to pass a farm labor law. Following that victory, and absent any sustained UFW organizing in the tomato fields, Magaña and a few of his friends started a local community and worker organization, La Asociación Lázaro Cárdenas, named for the political hero of their home state of Michoacán. Later, Magaña helped put together a farm worker organization called La Alianza Campesina. La Alianza was not a union but rather an alliance of small groups of farm workers, many of them Mixtecs and Zapotecs, that held a few conferences at which workers exchanged ideas and information. Not opposed to the UFW, they were trying to fill a gap created by the UFW's retreat from the fields.

Chavez and the UFW moved to stop them. Dolores Huerta called the California Institute of Rural Studies and tried, without success, to get Magaña fired from his job as an outreach worker on a farm worker research project. Magaña says that Chavez blocked La Alianza's efforts to raise money from liberal foundations. Once, during a 1983 tomato strike initiated by La Asociación Lázaro Cárdenas, the UFW rushed to the scene, seized control of the strike, and tried to freeze Magaña out of the new strike leadership. Magaña, who is still trying to organize *tomateros* out of an unheated office lent to him by a Stockton church, savors a memory of that particular attack. Luciano Crespo, head of the UFW organizing effort, explained to the *Stockton Record* that Magaña could not lead the strike because "Magaña is just a worker."[34]

In 1988, as wages and conditions in the fields continued to deteriorate and UFW membership continued to decline, Cesar Chavez decided to go on another public fast. This time he fasted in support of the union's grape boycott and antipesticide campaign. As it had in the 1960s, the pesticide issue directly united the interests of farm workers and consumers, but in the late 1980s it was an even better fit. The environmental movement, unlike the labor movement, had survived the spirit of reaction in the country, with consumers increasingly conscious of food and its relationship to their health. And public hearings in the state legislature in 1985 had revealed a statistically high incidence of cancer among farm worker children in McFarland, California, just down Highway 99 from Delano.

This was no publicity stunt. In McFarland, a hamlet of 6,000 people plunked in the middle of cotton fields and vineyards, twelve children were stricken with cancer between 1983 and 1988, five of them on the same block of seventeen houses.[35] Two other cancer clusters were uncovered in Earlimart and Fowler, even smaller towns farther north on 99. Various studies were undertaken but never succeeded in pinpointing which particular pesticides, biocides, fumigants, or artificial fertilizers were to blame, yet few people doubted that some agricultural chemical or combination of chemicals had produced the cancers. Agribusiness dumped 68,565,683 pounds of pesticides on the Central Valley in 1988, about one-third of all pesticides produced in the United States.[36] "Chemical farming," some people call it, and in the mid-eighties, when organic agriculture was still a fringe enthusiasm, most of agribusiness sprayed without restraint. "What they [the UFW and environmentalists] are trying to do is generate a new fear of the word 'carcinogen,'" complained the corporate counsel of the J.

G. Boswell Company, whose cotton kingdom extends up and down the Central Valley.[37]

Prior to the discovery of the cancer clusters, union boycott appeals had increased their emphasis on pesticides as part of a policy to unhinge the UFW from an exclusive concern with union contracts and remake it into what Chavez called a "food organization," which would take up the issues of consumers as well as farm workers. At the same time, boycott literature, which had always combined calls for solidarity with pleas for charity, began to feature more pictures of poor abused workers. In 1984, finally giving up on trying to put out anything like a farm worker newspaper, the UFW settled on a new national publication, *Food and Justice*, whose first objective was "to evoke compassion regarding the conditions of farm workers."[38]

Here were true victims. With help from Hollywood film-industry professionals, the UFW made a video, *The Wrath of Grapes*, which was dominated by frightful footage showing the children of McFarland: a boy without arms and legs; a girl with an ugly scar down her back where a piece of her spine had been taken out; a girl with a tumor in her eye; a boy who was dying of lymphatic cancer; interviews with the tearful, suffering parents. But the video is not just about "invoking compassion." Dr. Marion Moses warned in the video. "Workers are the canaries for the consumers . . . Workers are being harmed by the same pesticides that end up as residues in the supermarket." The message was clear. If the grapes were contaminated that was another reason not to buy them. Cesar Chavez made the call: "We need to stop this madness at the marketplace. If enough people join us, the growers will have to do something." The union mailed about 50,000 copies of the video to its list of supporters.

But the table grape industry, helped by its new export markets, did not suffer. Sales and prices remained high. Chavez was not deterred. He toured the country with his message, and then he fasted. "A fast for life," he called it. He refused to talk to reporters, but he issued a statement as the fast began. "Do we carry in our hearts the sufferings of farm workers and their children? Do we feel their pain deeply enough? I know I don't—and I am ashamed."[39]

Cesar was sixty-one years old. He fasted for thirty-six days, eleven days longer than in 1968. He lost thirty-three pounds. He was visited by politicians, celebrities, artists, including Jesse Jackson, Martin Sheen, Eddie Albert, Edward James Olmos, Robert Blake, and Luis Valdéz. He stayed in a sparse room and walked to Mass every night, helped along by his family. He was determined, relentless, as always willing to spend himself for his cause. He got old before everyone's eyes, like a veteran boxer who suddenly ages in a single round. He had built a comfortable life at La Paz for his family and those who had stayed loyal to him through all the years. But comfort wasn't for him. He wanted to fight on, even after his union was lost. In that fight he would find some redemption. In less than five years he would be dead.

Epilogue

Cesar Chavez died on April 23, 1993. After his death the UFW, led by his son-in-law Artie Rodriguez, made a genuine effort to return to the fields and regain its identity as a union. So far that attempt has been blunted. The union lost two highly publicized elections, one in the table grapes, at their old antagonist, Giumarra, and another in the strawberries in Watsonville, although subsequently they signed contracts covering more than 1,000 strawberry workers. The union has about 5,000 other members who work under contracts with wages and benefits not much different from the current low standards in the California fields. Meanwhile, La Paz's movement entities continue to thrive: they own radio stations, develop low- and middle-income housing projects, work in coalition with other groups on immigration issues, propose farm worker legislation, endorse politicians, advocate for farm workers, and burnish the memory of Cesar Chavez.

Chavez is now an official hero. California made his birthday, March 31, a state holiday. President Clinton awarded him, posthumously, the Medal of Freedom in 1994; schools, streets, parks, and stamps bear his name and image.

Gilbert Padilla picked grapes for a season after he left the union. He then worked as an organizer for the United Food and Commercial Workers Union and as a greeter in a funeral home. He is now retired and lives with his wife, Esther, in Fresno.

Dolores Huerta is president of the Dolores Huerta Foundation. She is a farm worker advocate and was an active campaigner for Hillary Clinton.

Richard Chavez died in 2011.

Manuel Chavez died in 1999.

Eliseo Medina is the international secretary-treasurer of the Service Employees Internatioal Union. He lives with his wife, Liza Hirsch Medina, in Oxnard, California.

Jessica Govea, who became a labor educator and consultant, died in 2005, after a long battle with cancer.

Marshall Ganz is a lecturer at Harvard's Kennedy School of Government and a nationally acclaimed authority on organizing.

Jerry Cohen is a semiretired lawyer. He recently cofounded the Labor Justice Project, which is fighting to have domestics and farm workers included in the National Labor Relations Act.

LeRoy Chatfield is the other cofounder of the Labor Justice Project. He is also the coeditor of a new online literary journal, *Dialogue*. He was the founder of the UFW documentation project (www.farm workermovement.org), and worked as its director for several years.

Doug Adair owns a small date farm in Thermal, California.

Rudy Reyes died in 2006.

Chayo Pelayo is retired and lives with her husband in El Centro.

Aristeo Zambrano owns a used alternator shop in Oakland.

Hemilo Mojica lives in Santa Cruz de Villa Gómez, Michoacán and coordinates public projects that are funded by money sent home from people working in the United States.

Chava Bustamante organized for the Service Employees International Union for fifteen years. He is now a staff member of Sol, a nonprofit organization that works with recent immigrants.

Mario Bustamante is a cab driver in El Centro; he and the other drivers are joint owners of the taxicab company. He lives with his wife, Gretchen Lau, a former member of the UFW staff, on fifteen acres in El Centro in a house that was once California's reception center for braceros.

Berta Batres works in a lettuce-packing shed in Salinas, where she lives down the street from Cesar Chavez Elementary School.

Cleofas Guzman lives in Huntington Park, Los Angeles, with his daughter, her children, and some of their children—four generations. He has no left eye and his right side is almost completely paralyzed, the result of the crash on the highway to San Luis and a series of small strokes since. He won't let anyone help him get dressed and insists on folding his clothes and putting them away. It takes him hours. He has got to have some work, he says. He is stubborn. Too stubborn to die, his daughter says.

Acknowledgments

My debts are legion and the few words I say here will not discharge them. I owe too much to too many. JoAnn Wypijewski took a bloated manuscript almost twice as long as this book and with a surgeon's skill saved its life. For two years, she cut, rearranged, and suggested rewrites, never losing her good humor, always confident in the face of my doubts that if we stayed at it we could get the job done. Doug Lummis read the book as it was being written, chapter by chapter, and then read it again during the final edit. He helped shape the arguments at the beginning, and made my language more responsible and economical at the end. Alexander Cockburn picked me up when I was down, his faith in the project more constant than my own. David Sweet listened carefully for fifteen years as I told him the story of the making of the book. Audrea Lim at Verso and Katherine Scott worked hard to clarify my prose.

I took my first class in political theory with Jack Schaar in 1961 and my first class with Hanna Pitkin in 1962. Until 1970, they were my teachers at Berkeley, and they have given a careful, generous reading to almost everything I have done since. When I wrote this book, I had many a "dear reader" sprinkled through the prose. Wypijewski wisely cut them all out. The dear readers I had in mind were Pitkin and Schaar.

When I started this project I had never visited an archive or conducted a formal interview. Dana Frank helped me learn how to do both, introducing me to the customs, procedures, disciplines, pleasures and displeasures of a professional historian. We all owe her some thanks, as it turns out that the standard procedures of historical research, much to my surprise, are directly connected to getting the story right.

The manuscript went through many hands before it became a book. Dana Frank, Bill Friedland, Alan and Sigrid Lönnberg, Jeff Lustig, Mike Miller, Amy Newell, Hanna Pitkin, Jack Schaar, and David Sweet all read drafts and saved me from much error and considerable foolishness. No doubt some of both remain.

William Lefevre at the Reuther Library, Sharon Massie at the Agricultural Labor Relations Board, Kent Kirkton at California State University,

Northridge, and James Fisher at the Beinecke Rare Books and Manuscript Library guided me through their archives. Doug Foster, Don Watson, and Henry Anderson gave me access to their invaluable files. Bruce Perry sent me the documents he had gathered while he was preparing a book on the UFW. Miriam Pawel and I talked to many of the same people and shared considerable information and research. Todd Chretien and Dana Frank helped with the end notes.

I started writing this book on a typewriter. I finished on a computer. I got through many technical difficulties only with the help of my daughter, Maggie Bardacke.

A grant from the Handleman Foundation allowed me to take time off from teaching at Watsonville Adult School to work on the book. Aid from Robert Pollin and the Political Economy Research Institute helped me complete the job. At the front of this book I thanked my wife, Julie Miller. I thank her again here at the end, along with my children, Ted, Jaime, Seth, and Maggie. Without my family's love, patience, encouragement, and support not only would this book never have been written, but for me, all would be lost.

Notes

Introduction

1. Spelled in Spanish, "Cesar Chavez" carries accents, like this "César Chávez." But Chavez, himself, did not write his name that way, nor was his name written that way in UFW documents, and so I have not written it that way in this book.

2. These membership numbers are high-end, peak harvest time estimates. See UFW Collection Unprocessed Files: National Executive Board, Folder "Crops," Archives of Labor and Urban Affairs, Walter P. Reuther Library, Wayne State; Marshall Ganz, *Why David Sometimes Wins* (New York: Oxford University Press, 2009); Philip L. Martin, *Promised Unfulfilled* (Ithaca: Cornell University Press, 2003), p. 76; Miriam Pawel, "For UFW, Contracts Are Give and Take," *Los Angeles Times*, March 20, 2006.

3. Pablo Camacho, author interview, Watsonville, January 20, 1995; all following quotes are from this interview.

4. Raúl Medina, author interview, Watsonville, February 1, 1995; all following quotes are from this interview.

Chapter 1

1. Anna-Stina Ericson, "The Impact of Commuters on the Mexican Border Area," *Monthly Labor Review*, August 1970, reprinted in George C. Kiser and Martha Wood, *Mexican Workers in the United States* (Albuquerque: University of New Mexico Press, 1979) p. 24; Julian Samora, *Los Mojados* (Notre Dame: University of Notre Dame Press, 1971), p. 10; U.S. Bureau of the Census, 1970, Part 6, "California."

2. An extraordinary account of this history can be found in Alan Rudy, "Environmental Conditions, Negotiations, and Crises: The Political Economy of Agriculture in the Imperial Valley of California, 1850–1993," Ph.D. thesis, University of California–Santa Cruz, June 1995, p. 204. The standard works on irrigating the desert are Donald Worster, *Rivers of Empire: Water, Aridity, and the Growth of the American West,* New York: Pantheon Books, 1985; Marc Reisner, *Cadillac Desert*, New York: Penguin Books, 1986. Two useful local histories are Mildred de Stanley, *The Salton Sea:*

Yesterday and Today (Los Angeles: Triumph Press, 1966), and Alton Duke, *When the Colorado Quit the Ocean* (Yuma, Ariz.: Southwest Printers, 1974).

3. Rudy, "Environmental Conditions, Negotiations, and Crises," p. 284.

4. Ibid., p. 12.

5. Samora, *Mojados*, p. 35.

6. U.S. Department of Agriculture, National Agricultural Statistics Service, California Field Office, "Principal Crops: Production in California, 1950–Present," Sacramento: 2008; Giannini Foundation, "Whither California Agriculture: Up, Down, or Out," Special Report 04-1, San Francisco: 2004, 3, tables 2 and 3; Agricultural Commissioner, Imperial County, "Agricultural Crop Report," 1982.

7. Giannini Foundation, "Whither California Agriculture," 3, tables 2, 3, and 12.

8. The best account of this transformation is William L. Preston, *Vanishing Landscapes: Land and Life in the Tulare Lake Basin* (Berkeley: University of California Press, 1981).

9. Steven Johnson, Gerald Haslam, and Robert Dawson, *The Great Central Valley: California's Heartland* (Berkeley: University of California Press and California Academy of Sciences, 1992), p. 210.

10. Anne B. Fisher and Walter K. Fisher, *The Salinas: The Upside Down River,* Fitzgerald Rivers of America Collection (New York: Farrar & Rinehart, 1945), pp. xv–xvii; Sandy Lydon, *The Chinese in the Monterey Bay Region* (Capitola, Calif.: Capitola Book Company, 1985), 286–9.

Chapter 2

1. Aristotle, *Politics*, New York: Cosimo Books, 2008, p. 47; Karl Marx, *Capital*, New York: Appleton, 1889, "Machinery and Modern Industry," p. 378.

2. See the work of William H. Friedland, Amy Barton, and Robert J. Thomas, especially, *Social Sleepwalkers: Scientific and Technological Research in California Agriculture*, Research Monograph No. 1, University of California, Department of Applied Behavioral Sciences, 1974.

3. P. A. Adrian et al., "A Comparative Study of Selectors for Maturity of Crisphead Lettuce," Paper #70-674, St. Joseph, Michigan: American Society of Cultural Engineers, 1970; U.S. Department of Agriculture, *Agricultural Research*, Washington: January, 1974, p. 9; Paul Kessinger, "Mechanical Harvester Research Nearly Complete," *Salinas Californian*, September 7, 1974, p. 1.

4. William H. Friedland and Amy Barton, "Destalking the Wily Tomato," Research Monograph No. 15, University of California at Santa Cruz; David Runsten and Phillip LeVeen, *Mechanization and Mexican Labor in California Agriculture*, Monographs in U.S.-Mexican Studies, No. 6, University of California at San Diego, 1981; Juan-Vincente Palerm, *Farm Labor Needs and Farm Workers in California, 1970–1979*, Sacramento: Employment Development Department, 1991, p. 42.

5. Raúl Medina, author's interview, Watsonville, California, February 1, 1995.

6. Stephen R. Sutter, "Farm Worker Injury and Illness: Statistical Guides to Prevention," *California Agriculture*, November–December, 1991; Patricia Allen, "The Human Face

of Sustainable Agriculture: Adding People to the Environmental Agenda," Issue Paper No. 4, University of California at Santa Cruz, Center for Agroecology and Sustainable Food Systems, 1994.

Chapter 3

1. Jacques Levy, *Cesar Chavez: Autobiography of La Causa*, (New York: Norton, 1975), p58. Chavez had the final edit of Levy's book.

2. Alton Duke, *When the Colorado Quit the Ocean*, (Yuma, Ariz.:, Southwest Printers, 1974), p. 57.

3. Levy, *Cesar Chavez*, p. 38.

4. Susan Ferriss and Ricardo Sandoval, *The Fight in the Fields: Cesar Chavez and the Farm Worker Movement* (New York: Harcourt Brace, 1997), p. 18.

5. Stuart Jamieson, *Labor Unionism in American Agriculture* (Washington: U.S. Department of Labor, 1945), p. 176; Devra Weber, *Dark Sweat, White Gold: California Farm Workers, Cotton, and the New Deal* (Berkeley: University of California Press, 1996), p. 211.

6. Rothstein quoted in Lawrence W. Levine, "Photography and the History of the American People in the 1930s and 1940s," in Carl Fleischhauer and Beverly W. Brannan, eds., *Documenting America, 1935–1943* (Berkeley: University of California Press, 1988), p. 38.

7. Jackson J. Benson and Anne Loftis, "John Steinbeck and Farm Labor Unionization: The Background of 'In Dubious Battle,' " *American Literature* 52, no. 2, May 1980.

8. U.S. Congress, Senate Subcommittee of the Committee on Education and Labor [La Follette Committee], Part 54, U.S. Government, Washington, 1940, pp. 19987, 19901; Cletus E. Daniel, *Bitter Harvest: A History of California Farm Workers, 1870–1941* (Berkeley, University of California Press, 1981), p. 203.

9. U.S. Bureau of the Census, *Historical Statistics of the U.S. From Colonial Times to 1970* (Washington: 1975), p. 179; Jamieson, *Labor Unionism in American Agriculture*, pp. 87, 427.

10. See David Runsten and Phillip LeVeen, *Mechanization and Mexican Labor in California Agriculture*, Monographs in U.S.-Mexican Studies, No. #6 (San Diego: University of California at San Diego, 1981), p. 24, for an invaluable chart showing the ratio of California agricultural wages to nonagricultural wages between 1880 and 1978. The ratio of farm worker wages to industrial wages began to fall during the Depression (which hit U.S. agriculture before it crippled industry) but shot up briefly after World War II, topping out at nearly 80 percent of the average industrial wage. It was the bracero program of contracted Mexican workers between 1942 and 1964 that institutionalized low farm worker wages, essentially freezing them at 1940 levels for more than twenty years at the same time that other U.S. working class incomes were on the rise.

11. Hyman Weintraub, "The IWW in California: 1905–1931," master's thesis, University of California, Los Angeles, 1947, p. 290.

12. Salvatore Salerno, *Red November Black November: Culture and Community in the Industrial Workers of the World* (New York: State University of New York Press, 1989), pp. 87, 174; Douglas Monroy, "Anarquismo y Comunismo: Mexican Radicalism and the Communist Party in Los Angeles During the 1930s," *Labor History* 24, no 1 (Winter 1983): 37; Juan Gomez-Quiñones, *Sembradores: Ricardo Flores Magón y el Partido Liberal Mexicano: A Eulogy and Critique*, Monograph No. 5 (Los Angeles: University of California at Los Angeles, Chicano Studies Publications, 1973).

13. Monroy, "Anarquismo y Comunismo," p. 39.

14. See Ralph Chaplin, *Wobbly* (Chicago: University of Chicago Press, 1948); Colin M. MacLachlan, *Anarchism and the Mexican Revolution" The Political Trials of Ricardo Flores Magón in the United States* (Berkeley: University of California Press, 1991), pp. 101–3.

15. Unless otherwise noted, all details of Padilla's biography are drawn from Padilla's interview with Doug Adair, Fresno, August 22–25, 1995, California State University, Northridge, UFWOHP, and with the author, Fresno, December 20, 1997, and August 4, 2001.

16. Camille Guerin-Gonzales, *Mexican Workers and American Dreams: Immigration, Repatriation, and California Farm Labor, 1900–1939* (New Brunswick, N.J.: Rutgers University Press, 1994), p. 26; Weber, *Dark Sweat, White Gold*, pp. 34–68.

17. By 1937, Mexican authorities reported that 450,000 people who had been living in the United States had resettled south of the border and become *repatriados*.

18. George Sánchez, *Becoming Mexican-American: Ethnicity, Culture and Identity in Chicano Los Angeles, 1900–1945* (New York: Oxford University Press, 1993), pp. 220–21.

Chapter 4

1. Jacques Levy, *Cesar Chavez: Autobiography of La Causa* (New York: Norton, 1975), p. 27.

2. Chavez quoted in Ronald B. Taylor, *Chavez and the Farm Workers* (Boston: Beacon Press, 1975), p. 66 (elisions are Taylor's).

3. Susan Ferriss and Ricardo Sandoval, *The Fight in the Fields: Cesar Chavez and the Farm Worker Movement* (New York: Harcourt Brace, 1997), p 34.

4. Joan London and Henry Anderson, *So Shall Ye Reap* (New York: Thomas Y. Crowell, 1970) p.143; Levy, *Cesar Chavez*, pp. 89–91.

5. Father Donald McDonnell, author's interview (telephone), July 26, 1997; Ann Veronica Coyle, author's interview, Watsonville, April 12, 1995; Leo Grebler, Joan W. Moore, and Ralph C. Guzman, *The Mexican American People* (New York: Free Press, 1970), pp. 461–3.

6. Eugene Nelson, *Huelga* (Delano, Calif.: Farm Worker Press, 1966), p. 49.

7. Eric O. Hansen, *The Catholic Church in World Politics* (Princeton: Princeton University Press, 1987), p. 33.

8. See Pope Leo XIII, *Rerum Novarum*, 1891, text available at papalencyclicals.net/Leo13/l13gr.

9. Douglas P. Seaton, *Catholics and Radicals: The Association of Catholic Trade Unionists and the American Labor Movement from Depression to Cold War* (Lewisburg, Pa.: Bucknell University Press, 1981), p. 20; Charles J. Tull, *Father Coughlin and the New Deal* (Syracuse, N.Y.: Syracuse University Press, 1965), pp. 4, 20.

10. Marcene Marcoux, *Cursillo: Anatomy of a Movement* (New York: Lambeth Press, 1982), 1; Edmundo Rodriguez, S.J., "The Hispanic Community and Church Movements: Schools of Leadership," in Jay P. Dolan and Allan Figueroa Deck, S.J., eds., *Hispanic Catholic Culture in the U.S.: Issues and Concerns*, volume 3 (Notre Dame, Ind.: University of Notre Dame, 1994).

11. Marcoux, *Cursillo*, p. 46; Virgilio Elizondo and Antonio M. Stevens Arroyo, "The Spanish Speaking in the United States," in Antonio M. Stevens Arroyo, ed., *Prophets Denied Honor: An Anthology on the Hispanic Church in the United States* (Maryknoll, N.Y.: Orbis Books, 1980), 12.

12. Theresa Herrera, "Influence of Faith: Cesar Chavez and the Delano Movement," senior thesis, University of California at Santa Cruz, 1995, p. 33; Douglas Warner, interview with Finian McGinn and Ed Dunn, November 2002, 7–9, in author's collection, courtesy of Douglas Warner.

13. Marcoux, *Cursillo*, pp. 41–4.

14. Ibid., p. 42

15. Douglas Warner interview, p. 9.

16. Leo XIII, *On Christian Democracy*, 1901, text available at papalencyclicals.net/Leo13/l13gr.

17. In a telephone interview on November 8, 2003, LeRoy Chatfield, the former Brother Gilbert and a close confidant of Cesar Chavez, explained, "Cesar wasn't interested in liberation theology because of his conservative Catholicism. He was a very conservative Catholic."

Chapter 5

1. John Soria, author's interview, Oxnard, January 25, 1996.

2. Two biographies of Saul Alinsky are P. David Finks, *The Radical Vision of Saul Alinsky* (New York: Paulist Press, 1984), and Sanford D. Horwitt, *Let Them Call Me Rebel: Saul Alinsky, His Life and Legacy* (New York: Knopf 1989).

3. Carl Tjerandsen, *Education for Citizenship: A Foundation's Experience* (Santa Cruz, Calif.: Emil Schwarzhaupt Foundation, 1980), pp. 688–9.

4. Saul D. Alinsky, *Reveille for Radicals* (New York: Random House, 1946; paperback, New York: Vintage, 1969); all quotes are from the 1969 edition.

5. Ibid., p. 27.

6. Horwitt, *Let Them Call Me Rebel*, p. 121.

7. Nelson Lichtenstein, *Labor's War at Home: The CIO and World War I* (Philadelphia: Temple University Press, 2003), pp. 201–2, 217–18, 243.

8. Alinsky, *Reveille for Radicals*, p. 33.

9. Alinsky, *Reveille for Radicals*, p. 90.

10. Quoted in Horwitt, *Let Them Call Me Rebel*, p. 397.

11. Alinsky, *Reveille for Radicals*, p. 135.

12. Ibid., p. 130.

13. Peter Matthiessen, *Sal Si Puedes: Cesar Chavez and the New American Revolution* (New York: Dell, 1971), p. 331; Bill Esher, telephone interview with author, July 10, 1998; John Soria, author's interview, Oxnard, California, January 25, 1996.

14. Cesar Chavez, "Conversation with SNCC," mimeographed paper, 1965, in author's collection, courtesy of Mike Miller.

Chapter 6

1. This and other details of John Soria's life are from John Soria, author's interview, Oxnard, January 25, 1996.

2. Sanford D. Horwitt, *Let Them Call Me Rebel: Saul Alinsky, His Life and Legacy* (New York: Knopf 1989), pp. 223–5.

3. P. David Finks, *The Radical Vision of Saul Alinsky* (New York: Paulist Press, 1984), p. 38; "Fred Ross," obituary, *San Francisco Chronicle*, October 1, 1992, p. D8.

4. For the letter to Ross from the bishop, see Finks, *Radical Vision*, p. 113.

5. Bill Chandler, interviewed by Robert G. Marshall, Los Angeles, March 11, 1995, transcript at California State University, Northridge, UFWOHP.

6. Corona quoted in Mario T. Garcia, *Memories of Chicano History: The Life and Narrative of Bert Corona* (Berkeley: University of California Press, 1995), p. 164.

7. Ralph C. Guzman, *The Mexican American People* (New York: Free Press, 1970), p. 40.

8. Leo Grebler et al., *Mexican American People: The Nation's Second Largest Minority* (New York: Free Press, 1970) , p. 40; on 400,000 new voters see Carl Tjerandsen, *Education for Citizenship: A Foundation's Experience* (Santa Cruz, Calif.: Emil Schwarzhaupt Foundation, 1980), p. 87.

9. Tjerandsen, *Education for Citizenship*, pp. 78–85.

10. Fred Ross, *Conquering Goliath* (Keene, Calif.: El Taller Grafico Press/United Farm Workers, 1989), p. 18.

11. Editorial, *Oxnard Press Courier*, February 3, 1959.

12. James J. Rawls and Walton Bean, *California: An Interpretive History* (New York: McGraw Hill, 1997), 379–80.

13. Cesar Chavez, Activity Report, November 11, 1958, Archives of Labor and Urban Affairs Walter P. Reuther Library, Fred Ross Sr, Papers (hereafter Ross) Box 2, Wayne State

14. Cesar Chavez, Activity Report, October 24, 1958, Ross, Box 2, Wayne State.

15. Ernesto Galarza, *Merchants of Labor* (Santa Barbara: McNally & Loftin, 1964), p. 95.

16. Jack Lloyd, Philip L. Martin, and John Mamer, "The Ventura Citrus Labor Market," Giannini Information Series No. 88-1 (Oakland, Calif.: Giannini Foundation, April, 1988); *Oxnard Press Courier*, March 27, 1959.

17. Richard Mines and Ricardo Anzaldúa, *New Migrants vs. Old Migrants: Alternative Labor Market Structures in the California Citrus Industry*, Monograph in U.S.-Mexican Studies No. 9 (San Diego: University of California,1982), p. 33.

18. Martha Menchaca, *The Mexican Outsiders* (Austin: University of Texas Press, 1995), pp. 99–101.

19. Soria interview; Ross, *Conquering Goliath*; Chavez, Activity Reports.

20. Joan London and Henry Anderson, *So Shall Ye Reap* (New York: Thomas Y. Crowell, 1970), pp. 131–2.

21. Soria interview.

22. Ross, in *Conquering Goliath,* tells the story from Chavez's point of view. Chavez believed that Guajardo and Perez were limited by their exclusively labor union orientation, and were out of touch with the workers.

23. Soria (author's interview) gave Guajardo's view of Chavez.

24. Guajardo wrote a letter to Joe Ollman, with a copy to Helstein, with her own plans to organize braceros. They were quite different from what Chavez was doing. Clive Knowles wrote to Helstein about his plans for organizing farm workers. They included quick strikes where braceros were working. "Rachel Guajardo to Joe Ollman," letter, April 7, 1959; "Clive Knowles to Ralph Helstein," letter, January 30, 1959 (author's collection, courtesy of Don Watson).

25. Cesar Chavez, Activity Report, May 23, 1959 Ross, Box 2, Wayne State.

26. *Oxnard Press Courier*, June 9, 1959.

Chapter 7

1. For descriptions of the Dannenberg Ranch sit-in see "Sheriff Jails Top Union Agents As Lawmen Buck Huge Demonstration," *Imperial Valley News*, February 2, 1961; *Los Angeles Mirror*, February 2, 1961; "Mass Sit-Down Staged By Lettuce Workers," *Los Angeles Times*, February 3, 1961; United Packing House Workers, "Imperial Valley (California—Lettuce Campaign)," memorandum, March 23, 1961 (collection of Don Watson); John Soria, author's interview, January 25, 1966; Sam Kushner, *The Long Road to Delano* (New York: International Publishers, 1975), 109–11. There are a few discrepancies in these accounts. For example, the pro-grower *Imperial Valley News* reported that there were three hundred strikers at the camp; John Soria remembers a thousand; Clive Knowles, a UPWA leader of the strike, told the writer Sam Kushner that there were fifteen hundred at the sit-in.

2. United States Department of Labor, Bureau of Labor Statistics, *Employment and Earnings*, Vol 12, No. 6, December 1965, p. 35

3. *Imperial Valley News* (February 2, 1961)acknowledged that "some braceros climbed the fence to join the demonstration."

4. Alan Rudy, "Environmental Conditions, Negotiations, and Crises: The Political Economy of Agriculture in the Imperial Valley of California, 1850–1993," Ph.D. thesis, University of California at Santa Cruz, June 1995; Henry Anderson,

"Imperialism in Our Fields," AWOC Research Paper 31, February 20, 1961, p. 3 (Anderson's collection); "Output on Par with 1960 Deal," *Imperial Valley News*, February 7, 1961.

5. Mario Bustamante, author's interview, El Centro, California, March 12, 1995; Hermilo Mojica, telephone interview with author, July 26, 2002; Hermilo Mojica, interviewed by Don Watson, Gilroy, California, August 10, 1983.

6. Mario Bustamante interview.

7. Jerry Breshears, interviewed by Don Watson, Salinas, January 8, 1980; Kushner, *Long Road*, p. 110; Soria interview.

8. Breshears interview; United Packing House Workers, "Imperial Valley (California—Lettuce Campaign)," (collection of Don Watson)

9. California, Department of Employment, Farm Placement Service, "Annual Farm Labor Report" (Sacramento: 1960), p. 49.

10. Mark Thompson, "The Agricultural Workers Organizing Committee, 1959–1962," 1963, master's thesis, Cornell University, pp. 90–134; Bob Pepper, author's interview, Las Lomas, California, May 13, 1996.

11. Edward R. Murrow, "Harvest of Shame," *CBS Reports*, broadcast November 25, 1960, transcript, pp. 27–28 (author's collection, courtesy of Bruce Perry).

12. California Legislature, "California's Farm Labor Problems: Report of the Senate Fact Finding Committee on Labor and Welfare," parts 1 and 2 (Sacramento: Senate of the State of California, 1961).

13. Linda C. Majka and Theo J. Majka, *Farm Workers, Agribusiness, and the State* (Philadelphia: Temple University Press, 1982), p. 161; Breshears interview.

14. "Organizers Say Walkout Success" January 13, 1961, "Braceros Taken From Struck Field," January 13, 1961, "600 Braceros Withdrawn in Lettuce Strike," January 17, 1961, *Imperial Valley News*; United Packing House Workers, "Imperial Valley (California—Lettuce Campaign)."

15. "Demonstration at Dannenberg Camp," *Imperial Valley News*, February 8, 1961.

16. United Packing House Workers, "Imperial Valley (California—Lettuce Campaign)," p. 4.

17. "18 Growers Lose 2,000 Braceros," *Imperial Valley News*, March 5, 1961.

18. Kushner, *Long Road*, p. 113. This strike and Meany's decision to close down AWOC is not mentioned in any of the Kennedy, Meany, or Goldberg biographies. Nor was Don Watson able to find any record of these events in the National Archives or the AFL-CIO archives in Washington, D.C. Watson thinks that the absence of these records may be part of an attempt to hide the beginning of the connection between the CIA and the AFL-CIO, in which, he believes, Arthur Goldberg played a prominent role. (Watson, September 11, 1996 interview).

19. "A union plan to ease 'cold war' between management and labor," *U.S. News and World Report*, December 19, 1960.

20. U.S. Government Printing Office, "Public Papers of the Presidents of the United States" (Washington: Office of the Federal Register, 1962), p. 639.

21. Bud Simonson, *The Packing House Worker*, United Packinghouse Workers Association newsletter, May 1963 (collection of Don Watson).

22. California Legislature, "Special Report . . . on Farm Labor Disputes: Report of the Senate Fact Finding Committee on Agriculture," parts 1 and 2 (Sacramento: 1967), pp. 63, 67.

23. Students for a Democratic Society, "The Winds of Change in the California Fields," mimeographed paper, 1966, p. 9 (in possession of author, coutesy of Ken Blum; also available at farm workermovement.org).

24. See Majka and Majka, *Agribusiness*; David Runsten and Phillip LeVeen, *Mechanization and Mexican Labor in California Agriculture*, Monographs in U.S.-Mexican Studies, No. 6 (San Diego: University of California at San Diego, 1981); Kitty Calavita, *Inside the State: The Bracero Program, Immigration, and the I.N.S.* (New York: Routledge, 1992).

25. California Legislature, "California Farm Labor Problems"; Max J. Pfeffer, "The Labor Process and Corporate Agriculture: Mexican Workers in California," *Insurgent Sociologist*, Fall 1980, p. 38; Ernesto Galarza, *Merchants of Labor: The Mexican Bracero Story* (Santa Barbara: McNally & Loftin, 1964), Chapter 17.

26. "Engle Sees Bracero End, Wetback Comeback," *Imperial Valley News*, February 17, 1961.

27. Majka and Majka, *Agribusiness*, p. 158; "California: Violence in the Oasis," *Time*, February 17, 1961.

Chapter 8

1. The epigraph is from Jacques Levy, *Cesar Chavez: Autobiography of La Causa* (New York: Norton, 1975), p. 158. Chavez calls the area from Arvin to Stockton "the San Joaquin," as do many others, although it includes both the San Joaquin River Valley and the old Tulare Basin, as discussed in Chapter One. I use the equally common term "Central Valley," as the remade landscape between Arvin and Stockton now constitutes a single geographical area.

2. Jim Drake, telephone interview, December 15, 1997.

3. Levy, *Cesar Chavez*, p. 162.

4. UPWA, "Aftermath of 1961 Strike in the Imperial Valley and Outlook for Organizing Field Workers in California, as Viewed by Several Close Observers," internal memorandum, May 4, 1961 (collection of Don Watson).

5. Jim Drake interview.

6. Gilbert Padilla, telephone interview with author, March 10, 1998.

7. "Official Ballot, September 30, 1962," National Farm Worker Association Records (hereafter NFWA), Box 5, Folder 14, Wayne State.

8. Padilla interview.

9. Gilbert Padilla, telephone interview with author, June 2, 1998.

10. Henry Anderson, "To Build a Union: Comments on the Organization of Farm Workers," mimeographed paper, November 14, 1961, 31 (in author's collection, courtesy of Henry Anderson).

11. Joan London and Henry Anderson, *So Shall Ye Reap* (New York: Thomas Y. Crowell, 1970), p. 179.

12. Ibid., p. 186.

13. "Un Movimiento," FWA leaflet, Jacques E. Levy Research Collection on Cesar Chavez, Series IV Research Collection, Box 18, Folder 389, File 28, Beinecke Rare Book and Manuscript Library (hereafter Levy/Yale).

14. Letter from Cesar Chavez to Dolores Huerta, September 17, 1962, Series IV Research Collection, Box 18, Folder 378, File 18, Levy/Yale.

15. "Farm Worker Association Statement of Purpose," Office of the President: Cesar Chavez Records (hereafter UFWOP), Box 13, Unnamed Folder, Wayne State.

16. Jessie de la Cruz, interviewed by Jorge Garcia, R. Kent Kirkton, and Claudia Cuevas, Los Angeles, September 27, 1996, United Farm Workers Oral History Project, California State University at Northridge, (hereafter UFWHOP) transcript, p 26.

17. Unless otherwise cited, this account of Helen Chavez and Dolores Huerta draws on the substantial work of Margaret Rose, especially "Women in the United Farm Workers: A Study of Chicana and Mexicana Participation in a Labor Union," Ph.D. thesis, University of California, Los Angeles, 1988.

18. Susan Ferriss and Ricardo Sandoval, *The Fight in the Fields: Cesar Chavez and the Farm Worker Movement* (New York: Harcourt Brace, 1997), p. 62.

19. Virginia Hirsch, author's interview, Santa Cruz, California, October 6, 1997.

20. Glenna Mathews, "'You Find a Way': The Women of the Boycott," *The Nation*, February 23, 1974.

21. Levy, *Cesar Chavez*, p. 161.

22. Huerta to Ronald Taylor, quoted in Margaret Rose, "Traditional and Nontraditional Patterns of Female Activism in the United Farm Workers of American, 1962–1980," *Frontiers* 11, no. 1 (1990).

23. Chris Hartmire, author's interview, Sacramento, December 6, 1997.

24. Pat Hoffman, *Ministry of the Dispossessed* (Los Angeles: Wallace Press, 1987).

25. Hartmire interview.

26. Chris Hartmire, "Report to the Rosenberg Foundation on Citizenship Education and Action in Tulare County," mimeographed paper, November 12, 1965, p. 1 (in author's collection, courtesy of Chris Hartmire).

27. Hartmire interview.

28. John Gregory Dunne, *Delano* (New York: Farrar, Straus & Giroux, 1967), p. 81.

29. Marshall Ganz, interviewed by Jacques Levy, Cambridge, Mass. April 8, 1984, transcript, pp. 42–43, Jacques E.Levy Research Collection on Cesar Chavez, Post Mortem Research (henceforth LPMR), Box 32, Folder 685, Levy/Yale).

30. Kern County Probation Report, No. 11151, June 10, 1964, (author's collection).

31. Ibid.

32. Ibid.

33. Marshall Ganz interview.

34. Bill Esher, telephone interview with author, July 11, 1998.

35. Ferriss and Sandoval, *Fight in the Fields*, p. 81.

36. Quoted in Yolanda Broyles-Gonzáles, *El Teatro Campesino: Theater in the Chicano Movement* (Austin: University of Texas Press, 1994), p. 13.

37. Unless otherwise noted, this account of Bill Esher draws on his "Campesino," a mimeographed memoir of his time in the UFW that he wrote in 1994 (author's collection) and on four telephone interviews (July 10, 1998; July 11, 1998; July 21, 1998; December 2, 1999).

38. Esher, "Campesino," 1994, p. 3.

39. Esher interview, July 11, 1998.

Chapter 9

1. The epigraph is from Pablo Espinoza, interviewed by Jorge Garcia, Visalia, April 21, 1995, United Farm Workers Oral History Project, California State University, Northridge, (hereafter UFWOHP)transcript, p. 37; Eugene Nelson, *Huelga* (Delano, Calif.: Farm Worker Press, 1966), p. 68; Bill Esher, "Campesino," mimeograph, 1994 (in author's collection), p. 8; Gilbert Padilla, interviewed by Doug Adair, Fresno, August 22 to August 25, 1995, California State University, Northridge, UFWOHP, p. 154.

2. Unless otherwise cited, the details of Epifanio Camacho's life come from his untitled mimeographed memoir, April 1993 (in author's possession) and Epifanio Camacho, author's interview, McFarland, California, June 1, 1995.

3. Nelson, *Huelga*, p. 68

4. Ernesto Galarza, *Farm Workers and Agribusiness in California, 1947-1960* (Notre Dame: University of Notre Dame Press, 1977), p. 138.

5. Gilbert Padilla, author's interview, August 25, 1995, p. 155; Epifanio Camacho, telephone interview with author, July 13, 1998. Padilla says that Huerta was not at the meeting.

6. Padilla interview.

7. Jim Drake, telephone interview, December 15, 1997.

8. California Department of Employment, "Annual Farm Labor Report, 1965" (Sacramento: September 1966), p. 56.

9. The INS allowed California growers to distribute many of the green cards. That was not just corruption, nor simple INS complicity with the growers. Rather, the agency's primary institutional charge was to police the border, and INS officials knew that with end of the Bracero Program more people would try to cross the border illegally. The more farm workers the INS could legalize, the less trouble they would have with illegals. For a detailed discussion of this subject, see Kitty Calavita, *Inside the State: The Bracero Program, Immigration, and the I.N.S.* (New York: Routledge, 1992).

10. Jack Lloyd, author's interview, Oxnard California, December 4, 1996.

11. Ronald B. Taylor, *Chavez and the Farm Workers* (Boston: Beacon Press, 1975), p. 122; Padilla interview; *El Malcriado*, no. 18, n.d.; Pablo Espinoza, Garcia interview, pp. 16–18; Strikers leaflet, reproduced in *Farm Labor* 3, no. 4, September 1965.

12. Pablo Espinoza, Garcia interview; Pablo Espinoza, author's interview, Woodville, California, February 6, 2004.

13. *El Malcriado*, no. 18, n.d; farm workermovement.org ("archives")

14. Bill Esher, telephone interview with author, July 21, 1988.

15. Ibid.

Chapter 10

1. Wine grape grower, quoted in Bill Friedland, *Trampling Out Advantage: The Political Economy of California Wine and Grapes*, forthcoming, Chapter 6. Doug Adair told me that table grape pruning is equally difficult to learn and do, and that it took him more than a year to become an average pruner. Doug Adair, telephone interview with author, January 6, 2010.

2. Jerald B. Brown, "The United Farm Workers Grape Strike and Boycott, 1965-1970," Ph.D. thesis, Cornell University, Latin American Studies Program, 1972.

3. Ibid., p. 112.

4. Friedland, *Trampling Out Advantage*, Chapter 3.

5. U.S. Department of Agriculture, "U.S. Census of Agriculture" (Washington, D.C.: 1935), vol. 3, p. 304.

6. Ken Blum, "The Other Delano Grape Growers," *Farm Labor* 5, no. 1 (December 1966); Marshall Ganz, "Five Smooth Stones: Strategic Capacity in the Unionization of California Agriculture," Ph.D. thesis, Harvard University, 2000.

7. John Gregory Dunne, *Delano: The Story of the California Grape Strike* (Los Angeles: University of California Press, 1971), p. 107.

8. Ibid., p. 106.

9. The median annual earnings of Filipino farm workers in 1965 was $2,377, for Mexicans it was $1,474, and for Anglos, $1,293. See State of California, Advisory Committee on Farm Labor Research, *The California Farm Labor Force: A Profile* (Sacramento: California State Press, 1969).

10. Rudy Reyes, telephone interview by the author, September 4, 1998; Fred Abad and Jerry Cohen, interviewed by Jacques Levy, October 15, 1993, Jacques E. Levy Research Collection on Cesar Chavez, Beinecke Rare Book and Manuscript Library, Post Mortem Research (hereafter PMR) AV, Box 671.

11. Manuel Buaken, *I Have Lived with the American People* (Caldwell, Idaho: Claxton Printers, 1948), p. 196.

12. Carey McWilliams, *Factories in the Fields: The Story of Migratory Farm Labor in California* (Berkeley: University of California Press, 1939), p. 133; Stuart Jamieson, *Labor Unionism in American Agriculture* (Washington: U.S. Department of Labor, 1945), p. 130

13. Jamieson, *Labor Unionism in American Agriculture*, pp. 129 , 180–6.

14. McWilliams, *Factories in the Fields*, p. 133.

15. "Hukbalahap" is a contraction of the Filipino term Hukbong Bayan Laban sa mga Hapon, which means "People's Army Against the Japanese." The group was commonly known as "Huks."

16. This and the following quotes are from Rudy Reyes, telephone interview, September 2, 1998.

17. Susan Ferriss and Sandoval, *The Fight in the Fields: Cesar Chavez and the Farm Worker Movement* (New York: Harcourt Brace, 1997), 1997, p. 86; Bill Esher, "Campesino," mimeograph, 1994 (in author's collection), p. 12.

18. Gilbert Padilla, United Farm Workers Oral History Project, Los Angeles, California State University Northridge (hereafter UFWOHP), August 25, 1995, pp. 183, and August 22, 1995, p. 64.

19. *El Malcriado*, no. 17, n.d; farm workermovement.org ("archives")

20. Eugene Nelson, *Huelga* (Delano, Calif.: Farm Worker Press, 1966), p. 24.

21. Bert Corona quoted in Sam Kushner, *The Long Road to Delano* (New York: International Publishers, 1975), p. 122.

22. Doug Adair, telephone interview, August 30, 1998.

23. *El Macriado*, no. 21, n.d.; Brown, "United Farm Workers Grape Strike and Boycott, 1965-1970," pp. 1–26.

24. *El Malcriado*, no. 21, n.d; Brown, "United Farm Workers' Grape Strike and Boycott," pp. 1–26.

25. Padilla, UFWOHP, August 25, 1995, p. 184.

26. Reyes, September 2, 1998, interview.

Chapter 11

1. Porter Chaffee, "A history of the Cannery and Agricultural Workers Industrial Union," Federal Writers Project, Oakland, California, MS.

2. Jim Drake, personal communication (email) to Susan Drake, August 30, 2000, (in author's collection, courtesy of Susan Drake).

3. J. Craig Jenkins, *The Politics of Insurgency: The Farm Worker Movement in the 1960s* (New York: Columbia University Press, 1985), p. 150; Ronald B. Taylor, *Chavez and the Farm Workers* (Boston: Beacon Press, 1975), p. 142.

4. Eugene Nelson, *Huelga* (Delano, Calif.: Farm Worker Press, 1966), p. 101.

5. Taylor, *Chavez and the Farm Workers* , pp. 143–4.

6. Jacques Levy, *Cesar Chavez: Autobiography of La Causa* New York: Norton, 1975), p. 193; Nelson, *Huelga,* p. 103.

7. Nelson, *Huelga,* p. 104.

8. Herb Mills, author's interview, Albuquerque, New Mexico, September 1998.

9. Ganz, *Why David Sometimes Wins, 140;* Gilbert Padilla, author's interview, August 22, pp. 78–80.

10. Padilla interview, August 22, p. 79.

11. Marshall Ganz, *Why David Sometimes Wins* (New York: Oxford University Press, 2009), p. 141; *El Malcriado*, no. 24, n.d.

12. "National Boycott Survey," *The Movement*, February 1965, farm workermovement. org ("archives").

13. Rudy Reyes, telephone interview, September 2,1998.

14. Rudy Reyes, telephone interview, August 31, 2000.

15. "Strike in the Grapes!," *The Movement*, October 1965.

16. What the memo didn't say was that although the contract allowed these acts of solidarity, the grape growers could appeal to the NLRB, arguing that such actions constituted a hot cargo campaign. If the NLRB agreed, they could overrule the contract language, and the union—although not the individual members—would be subject to fines.

17. Reyes telephone interview, August 31, 2000.

18. "Schenley (Roma) Wine Offices Picketed in SF," *The Movement*, November 1965.

19. Mike Miller, author's interviews, San Francisco, March 28 and April 8, 1999, and August 30, 2000; Mike Miller, "The Farm Workers and Their Allies in the Early to Mid-1960s," manuscript, farm workermovement.org ("archives").

20. "Boycott Supplement," *The Movement*, January 1966.

21. *El Malcriado*, no. 28, January 26, 1966, farm workermovement.org ("archives")

22. Jim Drake, telephone interview, September 10, 2000.

Chapter 12

1. Unless otherwise cited, this and the following biographical material on Marshall Ganz comes from my first interviews with him in Cambridge, Massachusetts, April 12 and April 13, 1996.

2. Taylor Branch, *Pillar of Fire: America in the King Years, 1963–65* (New York, Simon & Schuster, 1998), p. 471.

3. James Forman, *The Making of Black Revolutionaries* (Seattle: University of Washington Press, 1997), p. 429; John Lewis and Michael D'Orso, *Walking with the Wind* (New York: Houghton Mifflin Harcourt, 1999), p. 357; Robert Coles, quoted in Clayborne Carson, *In Struggle: SNCC and the Black Awakening of the 1960s* (Cambridge, Mass.: Harvard University Press, 1995), p. 138; For more on SNCC see Charles M. Payne, *I've Got the Light of Freedom: The Organizing Tradition and the Mississippi Freedom Struggle* (Berkeley: University of California Press, 1997).

4. Marshall Ganz, interviewed by Jacques Levy, April 8, 1994, Jacques E. Levy Research Collection on Cesar Chavez, Beinecke Rare Book and Manusript Library, Post Mortem Research (hereafter PMR) Box 32, Folder 685, transcript p. 59, Levy/Yale.

5. On Walter Reuther see Nelson Lichtenstein, *Walter Reuther: The Most Dangerous Man in Detroit* (New York: Basic Books, 1995); Kim Moody, *An Injury to All* (London and New York: Verso, 1988); and Branch, *Pillar of Fire*.

6. Ronald B. Taylor, *Chavez and the Farm Workers* (Boston: Beacon Press, 1975), pp. 154–5; Ganz interview, April 12, 1996.

7. Marshall Ganz, *Why David Sometimes Wins* (New York: Oxford University Press, 2009), pp. 143–4.

8. Mike Miller, author's interview, August 8, 2000; Mike Miller, "The Farm Workers and Their Allies in the mid-1960s," 2006, www.farm workermovement.org ("archives").

9. Mike Miller to Cesar Chavez, March 2, 1966 (in author's collection, courtesy of Mike Miller).

10. Marshall Ganz, "NFWA Chronology, August 6, 1965 to Dec 20 1969," unpublished paper, n.d., p. 17 (in author's collection, courtesy of Marshall Ganz).

11. Jim Drake, telephone interview, September 10, 2000.

12. Ibid.

13. Ibid.

Chapter 13

1. *El Malcriado*, no. 28, January 26, 1966; farm workermovement.org ("archives"); Doug Adair, telephone interview, November 15, 2000.

2. Fred Hirsch, author's interview, Santa Cruz, October 3, 1997; Epifanio Camacho, telephone interview, July 15, 1998.

3. Nelson, *Huelga*, 68; *El Malcriado*, no. 30, February 28, 1966.

4. Agustín Lira, telephone interview, March 28, 2001.

5. Cantú told this story to Lira. Agustín Lira, March 28, 2001.

6. Yolanda Broyles-Gonzales, *El Teatro Campesino: Theater in the Chicano Movement* (Austin: University of Texas Press, 1994), pp. 13–14.

7. Agustín Lira, telephone interview, March 28, 2001.

8. Ibid.

9. Unless otherwise cited, this and the other biographical information about Luis Valdez, including the quotations, comes from Luis Valdez, interviewed by Jorge Garcia and Kent Kirkton Monterey, California, June 5, 2001, for the United Farm Workers Oral History Project, California State University, Northridge, (hereafter UFWOHP).

10. Jeff Lustig, telephone interview, January 19, 2001. "*El respecto al derecho ajero es la paz*" is a famous quote of Benito Juarez, the first indigenous President of Mexico.

11. This was before cutting cane became a standard activity for the Venceremos Brigades, young people who went to Cuba to protest the embargo and express solidarity with the Cuban Revolution.

12. "Venceremos!: Mexican-American Statement on Travel to Cuba," in Luis Valdez and Stan Steiner, eds., *Aztlan: An Anthology of Mexican American Literature* (New York: Vintage Books, 1972), p. 217.

13. R. G. Davis, author's interview, Watsonville, January 2001.

Chapter 14

1. Marshall Ganz, *Why David Sometimes Wins* (New York: Oxford University Press, 2009), pp. 147, 148.

2. George Ballis, author's interview, Santa Cruz, February 19, 2001.

3. Luis Valdez, interviewed by Jorge Garcia and Kent Kirkton, Monterey, California, June 5, 2001, for the United Farm Workers Oral History Project, California State University, Northridge (hereafter UFWOHP), transcript p37.

4. As told to Peter Matthiessen, *Sal Si Puedes: Cesar Chavez and the New American Revolution* (New York: Dell, 1971), p. 128

5. Epifanio Camacho, telephone interview, July 13, 1998; Terry Cannon, telephone interview, September 2, 1998.

6. Arthur Schlesinger, *Robert Kennedy and His Times* (New York: Houghton Mifflin, 1978), p. 791; Evan Thomas, *Robert Kennedy: His Life* (New York: Simon & Schuster, 2002), p. 320.

7. Evan Thomas, *Robert Kennedy: His Life*, p. 320.

8. Robert F. Kennedy, Edwin O. Guthman, Jeffrey Shulman, *Robert Kennedy In His Own Words* (New York: Bantam, 1988) pp. 204-5.

9. Dunne, *Delano* (New York,: Farrar, Straus & Giroux, 1967), p. 240.

10. Quoted in Jerald B. Brown, "The United Farm Workers Grape Strike and Boycott, 1965–1970," Ph.D. thesis, Cornell University, Latin American Studies Program, 1972, p. 168.

11. Ibid., p. 160.

12. Doug Adair, telephone interview, January 13, 2001; Fred Hirsch, author's interview, October 3, 1997; Brown, "United Farm Workers Grape Strike and Boycott," p. 159.

13. Although Ganz does not remember the dispute over the route of the *peregrinación*, his notes from the February planning meeting in Santa Barbara record that there was an early discussion of marching through the small towns between Delano and Sacramento. See Ganz, *Why David Sometimes Wins*, p. 48.

14. Terry Cannon, telephone interview, September 2, 1998. Doug Adair confirms Cannon's account. No one else I talked to could remember how the route was designed.

15. Ibid.

16. "Plan of Hunger March Route," *Western Worker*, January 1, 1932; "Gigantic Demonstration Greets Hunger Marchers to San Francisco; Prepare for February Fourth!," *Western Worker*, February 1, 1932; "Demonstrate Feb. 4 Against War: Fight for Immediate Cash Relief and Unemployment Insurance, Demonstrations in All West Coast Cities to Press Demands Against Forced Labor Camps and for Adequate Relief," *Western Worker*, February 15, 1932: "Hunger March Men Convene," *San Francisco Chronicle*, January 11, 1933; "Hunger Marchers Parade Past Rolph, Refuse to Hear Him," *San Francisco Chronicle*, January 12, 1932.

17. Valdez, UFWOHP interview, p. 33.

18. "Plan of Delano," *El Malcriado*, no. 33, April 10, 1966, farm workermovement.org ("archives")

19. Bill Esher, telephone interview, January 14, 2001.

20. Valdez, UFWOHP interview, p. 33.

21. Jorge Garcia, telephone interview, December 11, 2000.

22. Luis Valdez, "The Tale of the Raza," *Ramparts*, July 1966, pp. 40-43.

23. Ibid.

24. Quoted in Ganz, *Why David Sometimes Wins*, p. 154.

25. Marshall Ganz, "Five Smooth Stones: Strategic Capacity in the Unionization of California Agriculture," Ph.D. Thesis, Harvard University, 2000, p. 491.

26. "Religion Inspires Grape Marchers," *New York Times*, March 25, 1966, p. 28; Marshall Ganz, "NFWA Chronology, August 6, 1965 to December 20 1969," unpublished paper, n.d., p. 21 (in author's collection, courtesy of Marshall Ganz).

27. Ronald B. Taylor, *Chavez and the Farm Workers* (Boston: Beacon Press, 1975), pp. 168–9.

28. Herb Mills, author's interview, Tuscon, Arizona, September 1998: Blackie Levitt, interviewed by Marshall Ganz, Los Angeles, August 8, 1996 (in author's collection, courtesy of Marshall Ganz).

29. Taylor, *Chavez and the Farm Workers*, pp. 170–73; Jacques Levy, *Cesar Chavez: Autobiography of La Causa* (New York: Norton, 1975), 214; Ganz, *Why David Sometimes Wins*, pp. 156–7.

30. Ganz, "NFWA Chronology," p. 26.

31. California State Senate Fact Finding Committee on Agriculture, Public Hearings in Delano California, July 19,20,21, 1966, "Testimony of James Woolsey, July 20," pp. 323–36, (in author's collection).

32. Ibid., p. 326; "Farm Pickets' Sortie in S.F.," *San Francisco Chronicle*, April 5, 1966.

33. Padilla UFWOHP interview, pp. 198–9.

34. Korshak and Chavez quoted in Levy, *Cesar Chavez*, pp. 216–17.

35. Catholic University of America, *New Catholic Encyclopedia*, New York: McGraw-Hill, 1967, p. 636.

36. Levy, *Cesar Chavez*, p. 207.

37. Ibid,. p. 211

38. Taylor, *Chavez and the Farm Workers*, p. 169.

39. Cannon interview.

40. *El Malcriado*, no. 31, March 17, 1966; *El Malcriado*, No. 32, April 4, 1966.

41. Susan Ferriss and Ricardo Sandoval, *The Fight in the Fields: Cesar Chavez and the Farm Worker Movement* (New York: Harcourt Brace, 1997), p. 119; Antonia Saludado, interviewed by Kent Kirkton, Pixley, California, June 11, 1995, UFWOHP, p. 3.

Chapter 15

1. Unless otherwise cited, the information on the DiGiorgios and their company comes from Ernesto Galarza, *Spiders in the House and Workers in the Field* (London: University of Notre Dame Press, 1970); "Joseph DiGiorgio," *Fortune*, Vol. XXXIV, No. 2, August 1946; Robert DiGiorgio and Joseph A DiGiorgio: From Fruit Merchants to Corporate Innovaors," an oral history conducted in 1983 by Ruth Teiser, Regional Oral History Office, Bancroft Library, University of California, Berkeley, 1986; Fred Glass, "Changing the Imagery of Postwar Labor: The Story of Poverty in the Valley of Plenty," unpublished manuscript, (in author's collection, courtesy of Fred Glass).

2. Steven Johnson, Gerald Haslam, and Robert Dawson, *The Great Central Valley: California's Heartland* (Berkeley: University of California Press and California Academy of Sciences, 1992), p. 184.

3. Galarza, *Spiders in the House*, p. 17.

4. *The Movement*, February 1966, UFW Documentation Project, farm workermovement.org ("archives").

5. On the S&W Chicago picketing, see FBI reports at http://foia.fbi.gov/foiaindex/chavez.htm, Part 1a, pp. 31–5; *El Malcriado*, no. 35, May 5, 1966; farm workermovement.org ("archives").

6. National Farm Workers Association, "History of the Delano Grape Strike and DiGiorgio Elections," unpublished report, n.d. (in author's collection, courtesy of Marshall Ganz); Taylor, *Chavez and the Farm Workers*, 190–95.

7. Quoted in Walter Galenson, *The CIO Challenge to the AFL* (Cambridge, Mass.: Harvard University Press, 1960), p. 478.

8. Samuel Friedman, *Teamster Rank and File: Power, Bureaucracy, and Rebellion at Work and in a Union* (New York: Columbia University Press, 1981).

9. The division was another layer, more or less on the level of the joint council, but not in the direct system of reciprocal obligation and loyalty.

10. Blackie Levitt, interviewed by Marshall Ganz, August 8, 1996.

11. Marshall Ganz, *Why David Sometimes Wins* (New York: Oxford University Press, 2009), p. 180.

12. Jacques Levy, *Cesar Chavez: Autobiography of La Causa* (New York: Norton, 1975), p. 234.

13. Unless otherwise cited, the details of Medina's biography and his quotes in this chapter come from an interview conducted by Marshall Ganz on August 14, 1998. (Courtesy of Marshall Ganz.).

14. Levy, *Cesar Chavez*, p. 236.

15. Ibid.

16. Epifanio Camacho, telephone interview, July 21, 2001.

17. "Grape Grower to Recognize Union," *Los Angeles Times*, April 7, 1966.

18. Levy, *Cesar Chavez*, p. 239.

19. Sam Kushner, *The Long Road to Delano* (New York: International Publishers, 1975), p. 157; Marshall Ganz, "Five Smooth Stones: Strategic Capacity in the Unionization of California Agriculture," Ph.D. thesis, Harvard University, 2000," Ph.d. thesis, pp. 409–11.

20. "AFL-CIO Apparent Farm Vote Victor Over Teamsters," *Los Angeles Times*, September 1, 1966; John Gregory Dunne, *Delano* (New York,: Farrar, Straus & Giroux, 1967), p. 166.

21. Bill Esher, telephone interview, July 10, 1998.

22. "Unions Battle to Wire in Delano Vote," *Fresno Bee*, August 29, 1966.

23. Esher interview, July 10, 1998.

24. Gilbert Padilla, author's interview, Fresno, California, August 14, 2001.

25. Ganz, "Five Smooth Stones," p. 408.

26. DiGiorgio, oral history; Public Research Institute, "California's Number One Industry Under Attack," Quarterly Report, September 1, 1968.

Chapter 16

1. Bill Esher, telephone interview, July 10, 1998.

2. The Chatfield quote and details of his biography come from his interview by Marshall Ganz, August 27, 1996, unless otherwise cited,.

3. Ibid p. 5.

4. Doug Adair, personal communication (email), June 28, 1998.

5. LeRoy Chatfield, personal communication (email), October 5, 2003.

6. What became of the Baez concert money is unclear. Chatfield told Marshall Ganz in 1996 that "the money went into an account for some future struggle." In 2003, Chatfield told me that money was used to set up a strike fund overseen by three trustees appointed by the union, and that until he left the union in 1973, "the fund was only used to accumulate interest." I have not been able to find a record of this account. According to all reports, in Salinas in 1970 the union had to borrow money to set up a strike fund. According to Ganz, Padilla, and Medina, Chavez had some off-the-books money that he could spend on union business as he wished. That would hardly be unusual in an operation of this size. But Chatfield adamantly insists that the Baez money did not become the slush fund.

7. Jacques Levy, telephone interview with author, February 6, 1998.

8. Eliazer Risco, telephone interview, November 30, 2001. According to Valdez, however, Risco arrived in Delano without a direct invitation. See Luis Valdez, interviewed by Jorge Garcia and Kent Kirkton Monterey, California, June 5, 2001, for the United Farm Workers Oral History Project, California State University, San Fernando, June 5, 2000 (hereafter, UFWOHP).

9. Risco interview.

10. Doug Adair, telephone interview, December 3, 1999; Dolores Huerta refused requests to be interviewed about this or any other topic for this book.

11. Ed Frankel, "In the Lap of the Angel of History," unpublished essay, n.d., farm workermovement.org ("essays") and http://edfrankel.com/essays/Frankel_Ed.pdf.

12. Volunteer who wishes to remain unnamed.

13. Doug Adair, telephone interview, July 16, 1998; Valdez, UFWOHP interview, p. 55.

14. Adair, Northridge interview, p. 83.

15. Doug Adair, interviewed by Greg Truex, March 10, 1995, UFWHOP, pp. 83, 93.

16. Unless otherwise cited, the Adair biography comes from Adair, UFWHOP interview, and Doug Adair, author's interview, Thermal, California, May 11, 1995.

17. Adair, Northridge interview, p. 6.

18. El Malcriado, no. 28, January 26, 1966, and no. 36, May 9, 1966, farm workermovement.org ("archives")

19. Ibid., no. 40, July 14, 1966; no. 42, August 12, 1966; no. 46, n.d.

20. Ibid., no. 49, November, 1966 (misdated in the original as April 18, 1966).

21. Ibid., no. 45, September 23, 1966.

22. Ibid., no. 37, June 2, 1966; no. 38, June 16, 1966; Gilbert Padilla, author's interview, Fresno, August 14, 2001, p. 6.

23. Padilla interview, August 14, 2001, p. 8.

24. The one exception was the Farm Labor Organizing Committee. Originally based among highly skilled cucumber workers, FLOC got the UFW's full endorsement after it established its own staying power in Midwestern fields. See Maralyn Edid, *Farm Labor Organizing: Trends and Prospects* (Ithaca, New York: ILR Press), p. 58.

25 *Catholic Worker*, December 1966.

26. Doug Adair, telephone interviews, October 2, 2001, and January 28, 2002; Doug Adair, copy of email to Latinavision, July 31, 2002.

27. *El Malcriado*, no. 41, July 28, 1966 (misdated in original as June 2, 1966); no. 49, November 1966 (misdated in original as April 18, 1966).

28. Gilbert Padilla, author's interview, Fresno, December 20, 1997.

29. Adair interview, October 2, 2001.

30. *El Malcriado*, no. 47, October 21, 1966, and no. 50, December 2, 1966; Doug Adair and Bill Esher, telephone interviews, December 14, 2001.

31. Doug Adair, telephone interview, July 30, 2001.

32. Ibid.

33. Esher interview, July 10, 1998.

34. Bill Esher, "Campesino," unpublished memoir, 1994, p. 14 (in author's collection, courtesy of Bill Esher).

35. Esher interview, July 10, 1998.

36. *El Malcriado*, no. 66, August 16, 1967.

37. Valdez, UFWOHP interview, p. 54.

38. Augie Lira, telephone interview, March 28, 2001.

39. Ibid.

40. Doug Adair, telephone interview, November 7, 1999.

41. *El Malcriado*, no. 51, December 2, 1966; no. 54, January 13, 1967; no. 60, May 10, 1967.

42. Valdéz, UFWOHP interview, p. 50.

43. Ibid., p. 54.

44. Ibid., p. 5.

45. Tony Orendain, telephone interview, August 28, 2001.

46. Lira interview, p. 6; At different times in his life, Valdez has offered alternative explanations of the split. Soon after the Teatro left UFWOC, he told the *Berkeley Barb* that they were just protecting the union from anti-Communist attacks. Later, Valdez told the historian Marcos Muñoz that the Teatro left Delano and the union because "Chavez did not agree with Valdez's efforts to locate the union in the framework of a Chicano nationalist ideology." Marcos Muñoz, Jr., *Youth, Identity, Power* (London, New York: Verso, 1989) p. 7.

47. Valdez brought Cantú back for a cameo appearance in Luis's hit movie, *La Bamba*, about the Chicano pop star Richie Valens.

48. Valdez, UFWOHP interview, p. 56.

Chapter 17

1. The union later learned that it actually had only about 20 percent of the industry. The error, shared by the entire Executive Board, is a measure of how little UFWOC yet understood about the overall shape of California agribusiness.

2. Ronald B. Taylor, *Cesar Chavez and the Farm Workers* (Boston: Beacon Press, 1975), p. 214.

3.   Ibid., p. 216; Marshall Ganz, personal communication (email), January 31, 2002.

4.   Linda C. Majka and Theo J. Majka, *Farm Workers, Agribusiness, and the State* (Philadelphia: Temple University Press, 1982), p. 186.

5.   Henry Anderson, "The Giumarra Strike and Boycott," *Farm Labor* 5, no. 3 (Summer 1967).

6.   "Vineyard Official Says Firm Unaware of Boycott," *Bakersfield Californian*, July 25, 1967; *El Malcriado*, no. 67, August 16, 1967, farm workermovement.org ("archives"); Anderson, "Giumarra Strike and Boycott."

7.   Eliseo Medina, United Farm Workers Oral History Project, Los Angeles, California State University, Northridge, August 14, 1998, (hereafter UFWOHP) transcript, p. 32.

8.   "Strike Area Sees New Workmen," *Bakersfield Californian*, August 7, 1967.

9.   "Strikers Picket U.S. Office on Truxton," *Bakersfield Californian*, August 10, 1967; "Farm Union Charges Illegal Hiring," *Fresno Bee*, August 10, 1967.

10. "Chavez Charges Growers 'Import' Illegal Aliens," *Fresno Bee*, August 15, 1967; Adair, "Cesar Chavez's Biggest Battle"; *El Malcriado*, 2, no. 6, May 15, 1968.

11. Cited in Jerald B. Brown, "The United Farm Workers Grape Strike and Boycott, 1965–1970," Ph.D. thesis, Cornell University, Latin American Studies Program, 1972, p. 264.

12. "Wirtz: Bracero Use Undercuts U.S. Farm Workers' Position," *Fresno Bee*, September 23, 1967; Bill Becker, NFW organizer, speaking at the February 22, 1996 Southwest Labor Studies Conference, San Francisco, California.

13. Rudy Reyes, telephone interview, July 20, 2001; "Giumarra Picket Lines Stay," *Bakersfield Californian*, August 4, 1967.

14. Rudy Reyes, telephone interviews, September 2, 1998, and January 29, 2002; *Delano Record*, September 29, 1967, and January 16 and February 13, 1968.

15. Reyes interview, January 29, 2002.

16. Tony Orendain, telephone interview, January 30, 2002; Chris Hartmire, author's interview, Sacramento, December 6, 1997.

17. *El Malcriado*, no. 53, January 13, 1967, and no. 65, July 19, 1967.

18. For example, on August 4, 1967, the second day of the strike, the *Bakersfield Californian* ran a story (unrelated to the strike) about local teenagers vandalizing a melon cooler and doing $300 worth of damage.

19. Fred Hirsch, author's interview, Santa Cruz, October 3, 1997.

20. Tony Orendain, telephone interview, January 30, 2002; Reyes interview, January 29, 2002; Hirsch interview; Fred and Virginia Hirsch, author's interview, Santa Cruz, February 19, 2001,

21. *El Malcriado*, no. 47, October 21, 1966; no. 50, December 2, 1966; Susan Ferriss and Ricardo Sandoval, *The Fight in the Fields: Cesar Chavez and the Farm Worker Movement* (New York: Harcourt Brace, 1997), p. 140.

22. LeRoy Chatfield, interviewed by Marshall Ganz, August 27, 1966, p. 40.

23. Epifanio Camacho, telephone interview, July 20, 2001; *El Malcriado*, no. 48, November 4, 1966.

24. Camacho interview.

25. Ibid.

26. Marshall Ganz, author's interview, April 12, 1966.

27. Doug Adair, telephone interview, January 28, 2002; Hirsch interview.

28. *Delano Record*, February 6, 1968; "Fires Damage Farm Labor Bus, Giumarra Pump, Arson Blamed," *Delano Record*, February 13, 1968; Camacho interview.

29. Virginia Hirsch, author's interview, Santa Cruz, January 27, 2002; Ferriss and Sandoval, *Fight in the Fields*, p. 141.

30. "All Time High of 543 Americans Killed Last Week," *Los Angeles Times*, February 23, 1968.

31. "Militants Call for Unity," *Los Angeles Times*, February 19, 1968; "1st Herald Strike Death, Printer Dies of Gun Wound," *Los Angeles Times,* February 22, 1968.

32. LeRoy Chatfield, telephone interview, January 29, 2002; Jerry Cohen, diary entry, February 15, 1967 (courtesy of Jerry Cohen).

33. Virginia Hirsch interview.

34. Ibid.

35. This account of the meeting comes from Peter Matthiessen, *Sal Si Puedes: Cesar Chavez and the New American Revolution* (New York: Dell, 1971), pp. 178-182, and my interviews with LeRoy Chatfield, Doug Adair, Epifanio Camacho, Tony Orendain, Jerry Cohen, Fred and Virginia Hirsch, and Jessica Govea, all of whom were at the meeting.

36. Day was authorized to minister to the union flock by Bishop Timothy Manning, of the Diocese of Fresno, after an impromptu UFWOC sit-in in his office in 1967.

37. "Farm Union Leader Chavez Fasts to Support Nonviolence," *Los Angeles Times*, February 25, 1968.

38. Saul Alinsky, *Reveille for Radicals* (paperback, New York: Vintage, 1969), p. 131.

39. Jacques Levy, *Cesar Chavez: Autobiography of La Causa* (New York: Norton, 1975), p. 276.

40. Jerry Cohen, author's interview, Carmel Valley, June 5, 1955, p. 15; Liza Hirsch Medina, author's interview, Los Angeles, California, March 4, 2002.

41. *El Malcriado* 2, no. 2, March 15, 1968; Ferriss and Sandoval, *Fight in the Fields*, p. 144.

42. Fred Hirsch, author's interview, October 3, 1997; Epifanio Camacho, telephone interview, July 13, 1998.

43. Marshall Ganz, author's interview, April 12, 1996.

44. Ferriss and Sandoval, *Fight in the Fields*, p. 143.

45. The Blow Out, a student strike in the Los Angeles public schools, was the next big event for California's Chicano movement after the pilgrimage. Eli Risco, the first person to be purged from UFWOC, was one of thirteen people indicted for conspiracy for planning the strike.

46. Oscar Acosta, *The Revolt of the Cockroach People* (San Francisco: Straight Arrow Press, 1973), 44–6.

47. Tony Orendain, telephone interview, January 30, 2002; Virginia Hirsch, author's interview, October 1997, p. 9.

48. Doug Adair, personal communication (email), June 28, 1998; Doug Adair, telephone interview, June 29, 1998.

49. Bob Fitch, telephone interview, January 27, 2002.

50. Reyes interview, January 29, 2002; Adair interview, January 28, 2002.

51. Levy, *Cesar Chavez*, p. 286.

Chapter 18

1. In a letter to Marshall Ganz in February 1970, Chavez wrote that since the fast he had spent a year in bed and another three months in too much pain to "think straight." Checking all other accounts, Chavez's own assessment seems to be only a slight exaggeration. "Cesar Chavez to Marshall Ganz," letter, February 4, 1970, Office of the President: Cesar Chavez Records (hereafter UFWOP), Box 33, Folder 6, Wayne State.

2. Jacques Levy, *Cesar Chavez: Autobiography of La Causa* (New York: Norton, 1975), p. 293.

3. Will Thorne, "Cesar Chavez Didn't Start the Strike; It Started Him," *Riverside Press-Enterprise*, May 27, 1969.

4. Marshall Ganz, personal communication (email), May 2, 2002.

5. J. Craig Jenkins, *The Politics of Insurgency* (New York: Columbia University Press, 1985), p. 169.

6. Marshall Ganz, personal communication (email), April 20, 2002; Doug Adair, personal communication (email), April 24, 2002.

7. Adair email, April 24, 2002.

8. Larry Itliong, interviewed by Jacques Levy, Delano, April 4, 1969,Jacques E. Levy Research Collection on Cesar Chavez, Principal Cesar Chavez Tape Collection, Box 5, Folder 185, transcript p. 32, Levy/Yale.

9. "Chavez Threatens Civil Disobedience," *Riverside Press-Enterprise*, June 23, 1968; *El Malcriado* 2, no. 9, July 1, 1968.

10. "Court Orders Vineyard Pickets Not to Harass Workers," *Riverside Press-Enterprise*, July 3, 1968.

11. "Chavez Threatens Civil Disobedience"; "Strikers to Stop Mexican Workers," *Riverside Press-Enterprise*, June 25, 1968.

12. "Union Ends Picket, Plans U.S. Boycott," *Riverside Press-Enterprise*, July 6,1968.

13. Unless otherwise noted, for Helen Hernandez Serda's memories of her life on the boycott see Helen Hernandez Serda, interview, September 17, 1995, for the United Farm Workers Oral History Project, California State University, Northridge (hereafter UFWOHP).

14. Susan Ferriss and Ricardo Sandoval, *The Fight in the Field: Cesar Chavez and the Farm Worker Movement* (New York: Harcourt Brace, 1997), p. 149.

15. Hernandez Serda, UFWOHP interview, p. 67.

16. Antonia Saludado, interviewed by R. Kent Kirkton, June 11, 1995, Pixley, California, UFWOHP, p. 24.

17. Jerald B. Brown, "The United Farm Workers Grape Strike and Boycott, 1965–1970," Ph.D. thesis, Cornell University, Latin American Studies Program, 1972, pp. 192, 205.

18. Levy, *Cesar Chavez*, p. 197.

19. Ibid., p. 92.

20. Chavez used make-work as a form of discipline and was proud of it. Jerald B. Brown reports that Chavez ordered Delano office idlers to cut up newspapers and put them in two plastic bags. Then at the end of the day he dumped all the paper on the floor and told the volunteers to leave the union until they were ready to work. See Brown,"The United Farm Workers Grape Strike," p. 172; Fred Ross told a very similar story about how Chavez handled slackers in 1958 in Oxnard. See Fred Ross, *Conquering Goliath* (Keen, California: El Taller Grafico, 1989) pp. 25-6.

21. Peter Matthiessen*, Sal Si Puedes: Cesar Chavez and the New American Revolution* (New York: Dell, 1971)*,* p. 145; Doug Adair and Bill Esher, telephone interview, January 13, 2001; Brown, "United Farm Workers Grape Strike," p. 176.

22. Virginia Hirsch, author's interview, Santa Cruz, October, 1997.

23. Fred Hirsch, "Some Personal Notes on Delano," unpublished memoir, June 2, 1968 (in author's collection, courtesy of Fred Hirsch).

24. George Ballis, telephone interview, January 9, 2001.

25. Rudy Reyes, telephone interview, July 20, 2001.

26. Rudy Reyes, telephone interview, January 29, 2002.

27. "3 A.&P. Stores Firebombed; Link to Grape Strike Studied," *New York Times*, October 24, 1968; Matthiessen, *Sal Si Puedes*, p. 308; Reyes interview, January 29, 2002.

28. Reyes interview, January 29, 2002.

29. Jerry Cohen, author's interview, Carmel Valley, June 5, 1995.

30. Ibid.

31. Jessica Govea, telephone interview, November 27, 2001.

32. *El Malcriado* 2, no.3, April 1-15, 1969, farm workermovement.org ("archives").

33. *El Malcriado* 2, no.7, July 1–15, 1969; Ferriss and Sandoval, *Fight in the Fields*, p. 148.

34. *El Malcriado* 2, no. 14, October 15–31, 1969.

35. Linda C. Majka and Theo J. Majka, *Farm Workers, Agribusiness, and the State* (Philadelphia: Temple University Press, 1982), pp. 194–5; Brown, "United Farm Workers Grape Strike," p. 138.

36. Brown, "United Farm Workers Grape Strike," p. 197; Majka and Majka, *Farm Workers, Agribusiness, and the State*, p. 195; Jenkins, *Politics of Insurgency*, p. 171.

37. Quoted in Majka and Majka, *Farm Workers, Agribusiness and the State*, p. 192.

38. "Farm Bureau Chief Says—Breakaway Growers 'Made Mistake,'" *Riverside Press-Democrat*, June 18, 1969; "Grower Admits Boycott Hurts—Farm Union Okays Talks," *Riverside Press Democrat*, June 15, 1968; Jerry Cohen, telephone interview, April 19, 2002.

39. At the beginning of the 1969 Coachella strike, the UFWOC, in a departure from its previous stance, made a friendly appeal to undocumented workers and green-carders

for support. Attempts to negotiate a no-scabbing agreement with Mexican labor officials were rebuffed, however, and by the end of the season UFWOC was again
blaming its defeat on wetbacks and illegals. "Kennedy Greets Grape Strike March at
Calexico Finish Line," *Los Angeles Times*, May, 19, 1969.

40. Gilbert Padilla, telephone interview, September 10, 2000.

41. Chavez to Ganz, January 27, 1970. This and the following exchange of letters can be
found in the UFW Office of the President (hereafter UFWOP), Box 33, Folder 6,
Wayne State.

42. Ganz to Chavez, January 30, 1970.

43. Ibid.

44. Chavez to Ganz, February 4, 1970.

45. Ibid.

46. "Chavez Signs Two More Grape Growers," *California Farmer*, June 20, 1970.

47. Sam Kushner, *The Long Road to Delano* (New York: International Publishers, 1975),
p. 195.

48. Levy, *Cesar Chavez*, pp. 324–5.

49. Brown, "United Farm Workers Grape Strike," p. 185.

50. Don Watson, author's interview, Oakland, California, September 11, 1996.

Chapter 19

1. Eric Brazil, "The Salad Bowl Strike," unpublished ms., 1971, p. 71 (courtesy of Eric
Brazil).

2. *1970 Census of Population and Housing, Census Tracts, Salinas-Monterey, Calif., Standard
Metropolitan Statistical Area*, Washington, D.C.: U.S. Department of Commerce, Social
and Economic Statistics Administration, Bureau of the Census, April 1972, p. 31.

3. *Statistical Profile of Salinas and its metropolitan area based on data from the 1970 federal census*,
Salinas: Salinas Chanber of Commerce, n.d., available as a folder at the Salinas Public
Library, introductory page.

4. Jessica Govea, telephone interview, March 1, 2002, pp. 36–37.

5. Ibid.

6. Unless otherwise cited, this and other biographical information about Hermilo Mojica,
including the quotations, come from my two interviews in Fresno, October 3 and 10.

7. Brazil, "Salad Bowl Strike," p. 65; Monterey County Annual Crop Reports, 1969, 1970.

8. Hub Segur, "From Seed To Supermarket," research paper, United Farm Workers
Organizing Committee, n.d., p. 2 (in author's collection)

9. Ibid.

10. Don Watson, "The Rise and Fall of Fruit Tramp Unionism in the Western Lettuce
Industry," unpublished paper read at the Southwest Labor Studies Conference,
Tempe, Arizona, March 4, 1977 (in author's collection courtesy Don Watson).

11. These figures come from Segur, "From Seed to Supermarket," p. 3. Watson, "Rise
and Fall of Fruit Tramp Unionism," has slightly different numbers, with shed workers
earning slightly more than double what braceros made. Judith Glass, "Conditions

Which Facilitate Unionization of Agricultural Workers: A Case Study of the Salinas Valley Lettuce Industry," Ph.D. thesis, University of California at Los Angeles, 1966, has a full discussion of the economics of vacuum packing and shed packing, but does not cite the wage figures.

12. Margaret FitzSimmons, "The New Industrial Agriculture: The Regional Integration of Specialty Crop Production," *Economic Geography* 62, no .4 (October 1988): 339.

13. The costs for ice could mount. The cowboy pack required three layers of ice, separated from the rows of lettuce by wax paper. Then crushed ice, delivered through a high-pressure hose, was thrown into the railroad cars. A common local claim is that before the arrival of the vacuum tube, the Salinas and Watsonville lettuce sheds used more ice than New York City.

14. "Giant Corporations Buy into Valley Produce Industry," *Salinas Californian*, February 19, 1970.

15. "Big Firms Enter Valley's Produce Industry Picture," *Salinas Californian*, July 6, 1970.

16. Three thousand *lechugueros* in the Salinas Valley in 1970 is a rough estimate made by Eric Brazil, a Salinas native and lead reporter on the *Salinas Californian* from 1960 to 1977. His impression matches the calculations of the best scholarly literature. See William H. Friedland, Ann E. Barton, and Robert J. Thomas, *Manufacturing Green Gold:* Capital, Labor, and Technology in the Lettuce Industry, Rose Monograph (New York: Cambridge University Press, 1981); Robert J. Thomas, *Citizenship, Gender, and Work* (Berkeley: University of California Press, 1985); Federal Marketing News Service, *Marketing Lettuce 1970;*. In addition to the piece-work *lechugueros*, crews of men and women cut and packed lettuce for an hourly wage. The women rode along on a movable conveyor, wrapping the lettuce in plastic film immediately after it was cut. In 1970, however, such crews produced less than 10 percent of Salinas lettuce. (Segur, "From Seed to Supermarket").

17. In the two months that I worked as an inexperienced cutter on an hourly crew, I never learned to distinguish the mature heads by sight. I was a slow cutter, and never even tried to make it on a piece-rate crew.

18. Don Razee, "Here Comes the Lettuce Harvester," *California Farmer*, October 4, 1976.

19. Mario Bustamante's recollections come from my first interview with him in El Centro, March 19, 1995.

20. Hermilo Mojica, author's interview, Fresno, October 10, 1994.

Chapter 20

1. "Salinas Strike Battle Continues in Fields, Courts," *California Farmer*, September 19, 1970, p. 7.

2. Eric Brazil, "The Salad Bowl Strike," manuscript, 1971, p. 46. Brazil, a veteran reporter for the *Salinas Californian,* covered the strike and wrote a fine book about it, which has never been published. This chapter owes much to his work.

3. Ibid.

4. Jacques Levy, *Cesar Chavez: Autobiography of La Causa* (New York: Norton, 1975), p. 388.

5. Subsequently there was a debate about whether the growers or the Teamsters initiated the discussions about the new contracts. An InterHarvest representative swore in a signed affidavit that the growers had suggested that the Teamsters move into the fields. Representatives from companies that held on to their Teamster contracts swore that the Teamsters made the first overtures. Either way, it was a back-room deal, since no one had consulted the workers.

6. "Farmers to Study Pact; Chavez Schedules Rally," *Salinas Californian*, July 30, 1970.

7. Gilbert Padilla, telephone interview, July 2, 2002.

8. "Up to 3,000 Hear Chavez, Farm Workers Union Backs Strike, Boycott," *Salinas Californian*, August 3, 1970.

9. Marshall Ganz, personal communication (email), June 27, 2002.

10. Quoted in Miriam Wells, *Strawberry Fields: Politics, Class and Work in California Agriculture* (Ithaca: Cornell University Press, 1996), p. 81.

11. Thomas P. McCann and Henry Scammell, *An American Company: The Tragedy of United Fruit* (New York: Crown, 1976), pp. 75, 155; Levy, *Cesar Chavez*, p. 332.

12. McCann and Scammell, *An American Company*, p. 156.

13. Jerry Cohen, telephone interview, June 28, 2002.

14. Mario Bustamante, author's interview, El Centro, March 1995, p. 19.

15. UFWOC, "Don't Sign Teamster Cards," leaflet, n.d. (courtesy of Eric Brazil).

16. Jose N. Dzib, interviewed by Don Watson, Salinas, October 30, 1981, p. 8 (courtesy of Don Watson).

17. Levy, *Cesar Chavez*, p. 336.

18. Notes written by a unidentified Teamster of the August 8, 1970, meeting in Paso Robles, attended by "Pete Andrade, Bill Grami, Cesar Chavez, Dolores Huerta, Jerry Cohen, Manual Chavez, Dog named Boycott" (in author's collection courtesy of Don Watson).

19. Wells, *Strawberry Fields*, 83; "Farm Labor Peace Efforts Growing," *Watsonville Register-Pajaronian*, August 10, 1970; "Farm Pickets Cited for Violating Order," *Salinas Californian*, August 11, 1970.

20. "Joint Talks Proposed by Bishops' Committee," *Salinas Californian*, August 10, 1970.

21. Levy, *Cesar Chavez*, p. 342.

22. "Workers Return to Work, Farm Dispute Shifts to Conference Table," *Salinas Californian*, August 13, 1970; Levy, *Cesar Chavez*, pp. 344–51.

23. Levy, *Cesar Chavez*, p. 350.

24. Ibid., 345; Jerry Cohen, telephone interview, June 27, 2002.

25. Levy, *Cesar Chavez*, p. 368.

26. Marshall Ganz, personal communication (email), July 1, 2002.

27. "Farm Negotiations Get Tangled," Watsonville *Register Pajaronian*, August 19, 1970.

28. To reconstruct this meeting I drew on Levy, *Cesar Chavez*, 366–67, the accounts in the *Salinas Californian* and Watsonville *Register-Pajaronian* on August 20, 1970, and interviews with Hermilo Mojica, Chava Bustamante, Mario Bustamante, and Jerry Cohen.

29. Jerry Cohen, telephone interview, August 21, 2002.

30. "UFWOC Plans Rally, Teamsters Affirm Growers Contract," *Salinas Californian*, August 22, 1970.

31. Ibid.

32. Brazil, "Salad Bowl Strike," p. 82.

33. "Ranches Picketed, Salinas Valley Hit by Produce Strike," *Salinas Californian*, August 24, 1970.

34. U.S. Department of Commerce, Federal State Market News Service Reports, "Fresh Fruit and Vegetetable Shipments, 1970," pp. 6–7, Science Library, University of California, Berkeley.

35. "Law Warns It's Prepared for Any Ag Strike Tactic," *Imperial Valley Press*, November 6, 1970; Wells, *Strawberry Fields*.

36. U.S. Department of Labor, LM-2, Union Annual Financial Reports," 1971, p. 2; Brazil, "Salad Bowl Strike," p. 127.

37. Citizens Committee for Agriculture, "Report on Violence," September 13, 1970 (courtesy of Eric Brazil).

38. Mario Bustamante, telephone interview, September 16, 2002.

39. After extensive investigation, Eric Brazil concluded that "the absence of violence was the salient characteristic of the strike." In the course of four weeks there was only one felony charge, against a grower, and he was acquitted. Of thirty-eight misdemeanor cases, nineteen were for blocking public roadways, three for trespassing, and the rest for malicious mischief, disturbing the peace, interference with a policeman in the performance of his duties, and battery. A total of 160 UFWOC members were arrested and jailed for violating TROs, but charges against them were subsequently dropped. (Brazil, *Salad Bowl Strike*, 1971)

40. Citizens Committee for Agriculture, "Report on Violence."

41. Mario Bustamante, author's interview, El Centro, March 1995, p. 20.

42. "Modesto Teamster Boss Under Fire for Salinas Valley Moves," *Salinas Californian*, January 12, 1971; "Secretary's Activities Linked to Salinas Valley, International Ousts Modesto Teamster Official," *Salinas Californian,* January 15, 1970. In a later trial, Gonsalves pleaded no contest to charges that he took money from growers. Levy, *Cesar Chavez*, p. 519.

43. Levy, *Cesar Chavez*, p. 374.

44. Ibid., pp. 378–79.

45. Fred Ross, interviewed by Don Watson, Salinas, October 13, 1983, pp. 5–6 (in author's collection, courtesy of Don Watson).

46. Brazil, "Salad Bowl Strike," p. 94.

47. Ibid.

48. "Fellow Citizens!!!" *Salinas Californian*, September 2, 1970.

49. Brazil, "Salad Bowl Strike," pp. 114–18

50. Hitchcock quoted in "Huge Rally Backs Growers," *Salinas Californian*, September 8, 1970 (elisions as in newspaper report).

51. Eric Brazil, unpublished news story, n.d. (courtesy of Eric Brazil).

52. "To the Citizens of Salinas," *Salinas Californian*, September 9, 1970.

53. Mario Bustamante, telephone interview, September 3, 2002.

54. Brazil, "Salad Bowl Strike," p. 158.

55. "Lettuce Boycott Called, Growers Stay Confident," *Salinas Californian*, September 17, 1970.

56. Antle's case was based primarily on his 1961 contract, and on a settlement of a 1968 lawsuit against *El Malcriado* in which the NFWA pledged not to "engage in organizational activities" with his employees as long as they were covered by a Teamster contract. But the union soon learned that Antle's *lechugueros* were not covered by his Teamster contract, having been excluded in 1965 when the Bracero Program ended. Antle had been having a hard time recruiting *lechugueros* to work for him because union dues were being taken out of their checks, so the Teamsters generously offered to exclude them, leaving only the wrap machine workers covered by the contract. The UFWOC argued that all of this was further proof that the Antle-Teamster relationship was another sweetheart deal, and differed from the other Teamster contracts only in being older.

57. "Chavez Asks Lettuce-Boycott Support," *New York Times*, November 30, 1970.

58. UFWOC, "CESAR CHAVEZ—our great leader," leaflet, n.d. (courtesy of Don Watson).

59. "Chavez Supporters Keep Vigil," *Salinas Californian*, December 5, 1970.

60. Brazil, "Salad Bowl Strike," p. 242

61. Don Watson, author's interview, Oakland, September 11, 1996; Mario Bustamante, telephone interview, September 3, 2002.

62. Marshall Ganz, author's interview, Cambridge, Massachusetts, April 12, 1996, p. 89.

63. Marshall Ganz, personal communication (email), July 14, 2002.

Chapter 21

1. LeRoy Chatfield, telephone interview, November 8, 2002, p. 2.

2. Jerry Cohen, author's interview, Carmel Valley, June 5, 1995, p. 32.

3. Susan Drake, author's interview, Santa Cruz, November 3, 2002; Madeleine Cohen, telephone interview, December 11, 2002.

4. In an attempt to appear consistently nonviolent, Chavez denied that his bodyguards were armed. Nick Jones, who was one of Chavez's first guards and who trained others, confirmed that they carried guns. Nick Jones, author's interview, Oakland, March 21, 2002, p, 8.

5. Ronald B. Taylor, *Chavez and the Farm Workers* (Boston: Beacon Press, 1975), p. 267.

6. The two Chatfield quotes are from Chatfield interview, November 8, 2002.

7. Levy, *Cesar Chavez*, p. 360.

8. Marshall Ganz, author's interview, April 12, 1996, p. 92.

9. Ibid., p. 94.

10. Marshall Ganz, personal communication with the author (email), April 20, 2002.

11. Taylor, *Chavez and the Farm Workers*, p. 265.

12. Marshall Ganz, author's interview, April 12, 1996, p. 95.

13. Gilbert Padilla, author's interview, Fresno, December 20, 1997.

14. Ray Huerta (Coachella's new field office director in 1971), author's interview, Thermal, California, February 17, 2003, pp. 2–3; Doug Adair, telephone interview, December 2, 2002.

15. Marshall Ganz, interviewed by Jacques Levy, April 8, 1994, Jacques E. Levy Research Collection on Cesar Chavez Post Mortem Records (hereafter PMR), Box 32, Folder 685, Levy/Yale, p. 72

16. David Burciaga, telephone interview, February 27, 2003.

17. David Burciaga, interviewed by Kent Kirkton and Jorge Garcia, n.d., for the United Farm Workers Oral History Project, California State University, Northridge, p. 43.

18. Richard Chavez, interviewed by Jacques Levy, June 14, 1994, PMR, Box 31, Folder 677, Levy/Yale, p. 100.

19. Gilbert Padilla, telephone interview, November 18, 2002.

20. Gilbert Padilla, author's interview, Watsonville, February 23, 2003.

21. Al Rojas, telephone interview, December 17, 2002, p. 2.

22. Ibid.

23. Ibid., pp. 8–10.

24. Don Watson, telephone interviews, August 14 and November 7, 2002.

25. "Chavez Aide Quits, Raps 'Brain Trust,'" *Fresno Bee*, October 15, 1971.

26. Al Rojas, telephone interview, December 17, 2002, p. 7.

27. Reyes, telephone interview, November 11,2002, p. 2.

28. Doug Adair, personal communication (email), December 12, 2002.

29. "McGovern Poses as Peace Candidate, Humphrey Charges," *Los Angeles Times*, May 21, 1972.

30. Ronald B. Taylor, *Chavez and the Farm Workers* (Boston: Beacon Press, 1975), p. 278; Linda C. Majka and Theo J. Majka, *Farm Workers, Agribusiness, and the State* (Philadelphia: Temple University Press, 1982), p. 208.

31. "Democratic Chiefs Warned by Chavez on Labor 'Harassment,'" *Los Angeles Times*, July 8, 1971.

32. "New Revised Membership Policies," August 26, 1972, UFW Information and Research Department Records (hereafter I&R), Box 47, Folder 26, Wayne State; "Aviso Importante," n.d., I&R, Box 34, Folder 34; Doug Adair, personal communication (email), December 17, 2002.

33. "Chavez Hits U.S. Move to Curb Union Boycott," *Los Angeles Times*, March 11, 1972; "U.S. Drops Bar to Chavez Lettuce Boycott," *Los Angeles Times*, May 3, 1972.

34. Dick Meister and Anne Loftis, *A Long Time Coming* (New York: Macmillan, 1977), p. 175.

35. UFW, *Sí se Puede, The Documentary*, video, 1972.

36. LeRoy Chatfield, telephone interview, November 11, 2003.

37. Taylor, *Chavez and the Farm Workers*, p. 280.

38. UFW, *Sí se Puede*.

39. Ibid.

40. *El Malcriado* 5, no. 4, June 23, 1972, farm workermovement.org ("archives")

41. "Lettuce Leaves Delegate Happy," *Los Angeles Times*, July 14, 1972.

42. Paul Buhle, *Taking Care of Business:Samuel Gompers, George Meany, Lance Kirkland, and the Tragedy of American Labor* (New York: Monthly Review Press, 1999), p. 187.

43. "D'Arrigo Goes It Alone," *The Packer*, February 3, 1973.

44. S.S. Pierce sold the company to Dave Walsh, who had headed up the company's operations in Salinas; he honored the union contract then in effect.

45. Padilla interview, December 20, 1997, pp. 8–9; "Memo from Frank Ortiz to Joe Rubio, September 6, 1972," I&R, Box 47, Folder 27.

46. "Chronology of the White River Farms Dispute," n.d., Office of the President: Cesar Chavez Records (hereafter UFWOP), Box 27, Folder 15, Wayne State.

47. "Delores [sic] Huerta: 'Deputies Violent,'" *Tulare Advance-Register*, September 26, 1972; "Strikers Jailed Trying to Arrest Aliens," *Tulare Advance-Register*, October 5, 1972; "Strikers File $650,000 Suit," *Tulare Advance-Register*, October 7, 1972.

48. Epifanio Camacho, telephone interview, November 15, 2002, pp. 1–2.

49. Al Rojas, telephone interview, January 28, 2003, p. 12; "Farm Union Seeks Weekend Protection," *Tulare Advance-Register*, October 13, 1972

50. Rojas interview, January 28, 2003, pp. 12–14; "Farm Union Hall Attacked," *Tulare Advance-Register*, October 9, 1972.

51. Taylor, *Cesar Chavez and the Farm Workers*, p. 284; LeRoy Chatfield, interviewed by Marshall Ganz, August 27, 1996, p. 57 (in author's collection, courtesy of Marshall Ganz).

52. "Ardent Apostles of Chavez," *St. Louis Post Dispatch*, June 7, 1972.

53. Chatfield, Ganz interview.

Chapter 22

1. Epifanio Camacho, telephone interview with author. November 15, 2002.

2. Thomas McCann and Henry Scammell, *An American Company: The Tragedy of United Fruit* (New York: Crown, 1976), 201.

3. Marshall Ganz, personal communication (email), July 12, 2002.

4. Hoffa's open refusal to abide by that restriction contributed to his demise. As a union lawyer, Marvin Miller, so delicately put it at the time, "There may well be a conspiracy to try to forget Hoffa between Fitzsimmons, happy with his new job; Nixon, happy with his new labor boss; and the Mob, happy with less publicity." See Edward Walsh and Charles Craypo, "Union Oligarchy and the Grass Roots: The Case of the Teamsters' Defeat in Farm worker Organizing," *Sociology and Social Research* 63, no. 2 (January, 1979): 279]

5. Ibid., citing *Time*, July 31, 1977.

6. Dick Meister and Anne Loftis, *A Long Time Coming* (New York: Macmillan, 1977), p. 184.

7. "Teamsters Gaining in Bid to Organize Lettuce Workers," *New York Times*, January 17, 1973; "The New Teamster Deal Costs a Bundle of Dough," *California Farmer*, February 3, 1973.

8. Walsh and Craypo, "Union Oligarchy and the Grass Roots," 280.

9. Ibid., 284.

10. Ray Huerta, telephone interview, February 17, 2003.

11. *Riverside Press-Enterprise*, April 11, 1973.

12. Chris Hartmire, telephone interview, December 8, 1997.

13. "Teamsters Gain California Farms," *New York Times*, April 16, 1973; "Report from the Coachella Valley," *California Farmer*, May 5, 1973.

14. Hermilo Mojica, interviewed by Don Watson, August 10, 1983; Hermilo Mojica, telephone interview with the author, July 8, 2003.

15. "Strike Launched Against Coachella grape growers" *Riverside Press-Enterprise*, April 16, 1973; Mojica, Watson interview.

16. Frank Del Olmo, "Chavez Announces Walkout, Boycott," *Los Angeles Times*, April 17, 1973.

17. "Fire Hits Grower's Shed; 33 Arrested in Farm Strike," *Riverside Press-Enterprise*, April 17, 1963.

18. Pablo Espinoza, telephone interview, July 25, 2003; Pablo Espinoza, author's interview, Woodville, California, February 6, 2004, 26.

19. "Strike Launched Against Coachella Grape Growers"; Mojica, July 8, 2003 interview; *El Malcriado* 6, no. 11, June 1, farm workermovement.org ("archives")

20. "UFW Arrests Now Total 311; Judge Eases Picketing Restraints," *Riverside Press-Enterprise*, April 20, 1973. The paper's claim is reasonable. Chayo Pelayo, one of the local grape workers, told me she was arrested several times the first week. Chavez told Jacques Levy that in the various civil disobedience campaigns against the unconstitutional TROs in Coachella and the San Joaquin Valley, people went "to jail three, four, five, and six times" (Jacques Levy, *Cesar Chavez: Autobiography of La Causa* [New York: Norton, 1975], p. 512). Rudy Reyes said he was arrested three times in one day. (Rudy Reyes, telephone interview with author, July 5, 2003); Miguel Contreras, who went on to become head of the Los Angeles Labor Council, said he was arrested eighteen times in the 1973 strike (see Philip L. Martin, *Promised Unfulfilled: Unions, Immigration, and the Farm Workers* [Ithaca: Cornell University Press, 2003], p. 174). During the summer of 1973 there were about 3,000 arrests. Given that there were multiple arrests of the same person, the number of those arrested was probably about 1,000.

21. Chayo Pelayo, author's interview, El Centro, May 20, 2004; Bruce Neuburger, "A Decade at Hard Labor: An Activist in the Lettuce Fields of the 1970s," unpublished ms., pp. 212–14 (in author's collecton, courtesy of Bruce Neuburger).

22. "135 Pickets Arrested in UFWU Confrontation" *Los Angeles Times*, April 20, 1973.

23. "Growers, Teamsters, Chavez—Three Parts of Farm Dilemma," *Los Angeles Times*, April 24, 1973.

24. "Meany Criticizes Teamsters' Drive," *New York Times*, April 19, 1973.

25. Neuburger, "Decade at Hard Labor," pp. 223–24

26. Jerry Cohen, telephone interview, August 26, 2003.

27. Ibid.

28. "AFL-CIO Will Give Chavez $1.6 Million to Fight Teamsters," *Los Angeles Times*, May 10, 2003.

29. *El Malcriado*, No. 12, June 15, 1973.

30. "Chavez Union Unable to Provide Enough Workers for Grape Grower," *Riverside Press-Enterprise*, June 11, 1973; *El Malcriado*, No 12, June 15, 1973.

31. Rudy Reyes interview, July 5, 2003.

32. "2 Teamsters charged in murder attempt," *Riverside Press-Enterprise*, June 21, 1973.

33. "Teamster PR Man Punched in Face, Ordered Out of Town by Teamster," *Riverside Press-Enterprise*, June 20, 1973.

34. "Teamster Official Blamed for Ordering Violence," *Riverside Press-Enterprise*, June 28, 1973.

35. "Worker Stabbed, Kidnapped, 2 Teamsters Charged in Murder Attempt," *Riverside Press-Enterprise*, June 21, 1973; "Grape Strike Continues, Chavez Car Object of Rock-Throwing," *Riverside Press-Enterprise*, June 22, 1973; "Six Held in Attack on Chavez Caravan," *Riverside Press-Enterprise,* June 23, 1973.

36. Ronald B. Taylor, Chavez *and the Farm Workers* (Boston: Beacon Press, 1975), p. 302. Both Taylor and the *Riverside Press-Enterprise* (June 21, 22, 23, 1973. June 24, 1973) reported that there were 400 UFW pickets in the fight. *El Malcriado* (vol. 4, no. 14, July 13, 1973) reported that there were 180 Teamsters and 100 to 150 UFW picketers and supporters.

37. "Teamsters Accused of Attacking UFW Men," *Riverside Press-Enterprise*, June 21, 22, 23, and 29, 1973; see also *El Malcriado*, July 13, 1973,

38. "Teamster 'Guards' to Leave Coachella," *Los Angeles Times*, July 4, 1973.

39. Federal Market News Service, Fresh Grape Daily Reports, July 27, 1973, Science Library, University of California Berkeley.

40. "65,000 Cannery Workers Begin Statewide Strike," *Los Angeles Times*, July 20, 1973; "Cannery Workers End 3-Day Harvest Strike," *Los Angeles Times*, July 23, 1973.

41. "65,000 State Cannery Workers Begin Statewide Strike."

42. Only the Bud Antle Company continued to work; with typical acumen, Antle had, early on, made a separate deal with the Teamster drivers.

43. "Fields Rot as Strike Nears End," *The Packer*, August 4, 1973; "Drivers Back to Work in Salinas," *The Packer*, August 11, 1973.

44. "Fields Rot as Strike Nears End"; "Drivers Back to Work in Salinas"

45. "Farm Worker Elections: Let's Face the Issue," *The Packer*, June 16, 1973; "Law Needed to End Labor Chaos," *The Packer*, August 4, 1973.

46. "Deadline Nears at Delano," *Fresno Bee*, July 29, 1973.

47. Rudy Reyes, telephone interview, July 5, 2003; Pablo Espinoza, author's interview,

Woodville, California, February 6, 2004; Epifanio Camacho, telephone interview, July 2, 2003.

48. "UFW Calls Strike As Fresno Harvest of Tree Fruit Begins," *Fresno Bee*, July 4, 1973; "1000 UFW Pickets Gather, Slow Valley's Fruit Harvest," *Fresno Bee*, July 7, 1973; *El Malcriado* 4, no. 15, July 27, 1973.

49. "UFW Pickets Abandon Vineyards to Protest Against Border Patrol," *Daily Enterprise* (Riverside County), July 11, 1973; "Farm Workers Picket Border Patrol to Protest Alleged Illegal Alien Use," *Riverside Press-Enterprise* , July 10, 1973; "UFW Pickets Patrol, *Fresno Bee*, July 9, 1973.

50. "Waiting Game Being Played in Grape Strike," *Riverside Press-Enterprise*, June 10, 1973.

51. National Executive Board Meeting, March 24, 1978, Office of the President: Cesar Chavev Records (UFWOP), AV materials, Wayne State.

52. "Chavez Sets Talks Today as Pickets March in County," *Bakersfield Californian*, July 13, 1973; "Teamsters, Gallo Wineries Sign 4-year Agreement," *Fresno Bee*, July 10, 1973.

53. "UFW Keeps Up Mass Picketing Drive; Arrests Total Tops 1,450 in 3 Counties," *Fresno Bee*, July 20, 1973; "Pickets Crowd Jail over Normal Capacity," *Bakersfield Californian*, July 19, 1973; *El Malcriado* 4, no. 16, August 10, 1973.

54. "UFW Picketing Enters 4th Day; 600 Still Jailed," *Fresno Bee*, July 21, 1973.

55. "Growers Guard Fields As Picketing Brings Arrest of More Farm workers," *Fresno Bee*, July 25, 1973.

56. "UFW Strike Slashes into County's Melon Harvest," *Fresno Bee*, July 23, 1973; "Strike of Melon Growers Goes On, 67 Jailed," *Fresno Bee*, July 24, 1973; "Violence Invades Melon Fields," *The Packer*, July 28, 1973.

57. Ibid.

58. Gilbert Padilla, telephone interview, July 8, 2003.

59. Letter from Susan Drake to Cesar Chavez, July 28, 1973 (courtesy of Susan Drake); Jerry Cohen, telephone interview, December 2, 2002.

60. "Farm Union Opens Massive Picketing Drive at Vineyards," *Los Angeles Times*, July 31, 1973; "Violence Flares as Grape Harvest in the County Continues," *Bakersfield Californian*, July 31, 1973.

61. "Violence Flares as Grape Harvest in the County Continues."

62. "Farm workers Marshal 3,000 Pickets as Bitterness Grows in Labor Strife," *Fresno Bee*, August 1973.

63. "Arrests, Trouble Mark Second Day of Escalated Grape Strike" *Los Angeles Times*, August 1, 1973.

64. "Picketing Priests, Nuns Are Arrested," *Fresno Bee*, July 31, 1973.

65. "UFW Keeps Up Mass Picketing Drive; Arrests Total Tops 1,450 in 3 Counties," *Fresno Bee*, July 20, 1973; "UFW Picketing Enters 4th day; 600 Still Jailed," *Fresno Bee*, July 21, 1973.

66. "Chavez Tours Lines, Pledges Court Orders Will Not 'Break' UFW," *Fresno Bee*, August 2, 1973.

67. Espinoza interview, p. 29.

68. "Grape Areas Now Labeled 'Armed Camp,' " *Bakersfield Californian*, August 2, 1973.

69. "Rock, Bottle Throwing Pickets Face Deputies," *Bakersfield Californian*, August 3, 1973; "Judge Eases Ban on UFW Pickets at 4 Fresno Farms," *Fresno Bee*, August 4, 1973.

70. "Chavez: 'Make Fresno Another Selma, Ala.,' " *Fresno Bee*, August 3, 1973.

71. "400 Chavez Pickets Freed from Fresno Jail by Court Order," *Los Angeles Times*, August 15, 1973.

72. Pablo Espinoza, telephone interview, December 4, 2003.

73. Hermilo Mojica, author's interview, October 3, 1994, p. 19.

74. "Vineyards Labeled as 'Relatively Calm,' " *Bakersfield Californian*, August 7, 1973.

75. Ibid.

76. "Meany Offers to Help Chavez, Teamsters Gain Peace Treaty," *Los Angeles Times*, August 2, 1973.

77. Taylor, *Chavez and the Farm Workers*, p. 308.

78. "Chavez Quits Teamster Talks amid Reports of Delano Pacts," *Fresno Bee*, August 10, 1973; "Peace Talks Collapse in Grape Strike Dispute," *Los Angeles Times*, August 11, 1973.

79. "Teamsters Shun Delano Pacts," *Fresno Bee*, August 11, 1973; "Will Resume Peace Talks Under 'Certain Conditions'—Chavez," *Los Angeles Times*, August 12, 1973; "Teamsters Shut Down Their Office in Delano," *Los Angeles Times*, August 14, 1973.

80. "2 Chavez Pickets Shot in Clash with Nonunion Workers," *Los Angeles Times*, August 11, 1973; "Shot Wounds Worker in Farm Labor Strike," *Fresno Bee*, August 13, 1973.

81. Kern County Superior Court, Probation Report, Action #16425; Kern County Sheriff's Department, Case #47-5902, Felony Crime Report, including sworn statements of Macky Joe Galvan and Albert Guerra.

82. "FBI Probe into Grape Striker's Death Requested," *Los Angeles Times*, August 16, 1973; "Death of Unionist After Scuffle in Kern County Ruled Accident," *Los Angeles Times*, August 31, 1973.

83. Kern County Superior Court, *People* vs. *Bayani Bautista Advincul*, Trial Minutes, July 6–21, 1976; Kern County Sheriff's Department, Case #L-57202, Crime Report, August 16, 1973.

84. "UFW Will Halt Picketing, Demands Protection," *Fresno Bee*, August 18, 1973; Camacho, July 2, 2003 interview.

Chapter 23

1. Executive Board Minutes, June 14, 1974, Office of the President: Cesar Chavez Records (hereafter UFWOP), Box 37, Folder 18, Wayne State; U.S. Department of Labor, LM-2, Union Annual Financial Reports, 1972–1974.

2. Luis Magaña, author's interview, Stockton, February 5, 2008.

3. Ibid.; *El Malcriado* 4, no. 20, October 19, 1973, farm workermovement.org ("archives")

4. "Pickets Strike Tomato Fields" *The Packer*, September 22. 1973.

5. Taylor, *Chavez and the Farm Workers* (Boston: Beacon Press, 1975), p. 321; "Doubt, Uncertainty Shroud Future of Chavez Farm Union" *Los Angeles Times*, September 22, 1973.

6. Linda C. Majka and Theo J. Majka, *Farm Workers, Agribusiness, and the State* (Philadelphia: Temple University Press, 1982), p. 226; UFW constitution, adopted at the first constitutional convention, Part Three, Article VIII.

7. "For a Strong Democratic Union," in "Workers' Power, A Special Supplement for the UFW Convention" (in author's collection).

8. Jacques Levy, *Cesar Chavez: Autobiography of La Causa* (New York: Norton, 1975), 515; Taylor, *Chavez and the Farm Workers*, p. 321.

9. Ibid., p. 324. Taylor, *Chavez and the Farm Workers*, p. 324.

10. Letter from John L. Quigley, Jr. to author, August 23, 2003.

11. Ibid.; see also Taylor, *Chavez and the Farm Workers*, pp. 321-3

12. Kim Moody, *An Injury to All: The Decline of American Unionism* (London and New York, Verso, 1988), pp. 86-8; See also Bennett Harrison and Barry Bluestone, *The Great American U-Turn: Corporate Restructuring and the Polarizing of America* (New York, Basic Books, 1990).

13. "George Meany to Cesar Chavez," letter, November 12, 1973, UFW Work Department Records (hereafter UFWWD) Box 1, Folder 8, Wayne State. Visits to Chavez from Latin American labor leaders, sponsored by the U.S. Labor Department, the AFL-CIO, and AIFLD started in the late 1960s and continued into the 1980s. For correspondence with AIFLD officials, see, UFWOP, Box 6, Folder "AIFLD;" UFWOP, Box 59, Folder 8; UFWOP, Box 17, Loose Documents; UFWOP, part 2, Box 26, Folder 2, all at Wayne State. For a report on the visits of Latin American labor leaders to Chavez, sponsored by AIFLD, see *El Siglo*, September 7, 1971 (courtesy of Fred Hirsch).

14. "Jerry to Cessar" memo, November 27, 1973, UFWWD, Box 1, Folder 8, Wayne State.

15. Taylor, *Chavez and the Farm Workers*, p. 317.

16. At the bottom of the letter, in Chavez's handwriting, are the words "second thoughts"; see UFWWD, Box 1, Folder 8, Wayne State.

17. Charles Colson, no longer in the administration and not yet in jail, sent word to Fitzsimmons in 1973 that Nixon didn't want the Teamsters to make any deal with Meany, who was then trying to salvage what progressive reputation he had left by leading a middle-of-the-road effort to impeach Nixon. See Edward Walsh and Charles Craypo, "Union Oligarchy and the Grass Roots: The Case of the Teamsters' Defeat in Farm worker Organizing," *Sociology and Social Research* 63, no. 2 (January, 1979).

18. Majka and Majka, *Farm workers, Agribusiness and the State*, p. 227.

19. U.S. Department of Labor, LM-2, 1974.

20. Dan Georgakas and Marvin Surkin, *Detroit: I Do Mind Dying: A Study in Urban Revolution* (Boston: South End Press, 1999), pp. 189–93; "Chavez and the State of His Union," *Los Angeles Times*, June 23, 1974.

21. *El Malcriado* 7, no. 2, February 22, 1974.

22. Ibid.

23. Unless otherwise cited, this and the following details of Chayo Pelayo's biography come from Chayo Pelayo, author's interview, El Centro, May 20, 2004.

24. *El Malcriado* 7, no. 3, March 29, 1974.

25. UFWOP, Box 16, Folder "Calexico Strike Feb 1974 Interviews" (in Spanish, author's translation), Wayne State.

26. "Results of February Asparagus Strike," UFW Information and Research Department Records (hereafter I&R), Box 28, Folder 16, Wayne State; "Conversations with Asparagus Growers," UFWPO, Box 16, Folder "Calexico Strike, February 1974," Wayne State.

27. "Results of February Asparagus Strike."

28. Ibid.

29. "Chronology of Calexico Work Stoppage and Strike," I&R, Box 28, Folder 16, Wayne State; "California Asparagus 'Inherits' Labor Woes," *The Packer*, February 23, 1974.

30. *El Malcriado*, March 29, 1974.

31. "Conversations with the Growers and Contractors," UFWOP, Box 16, Folder "Calexico Strike February 1974," Wayne State.

32. Levy, *Chavez*, 521.

33. "Report of President, March 27, 1954," UFWOP part 2, Box 37, Folder 12, Wayne State.

34. Ibid. Chavez reported to the Executive Board that one-third of the boycott staff dropped out between January and March of 1974.

35. Eliseo Medina, "Report on Strikers," UFWOP, part 2, Box 37, Folder 3, Wayne State.

36. Ibid.

37. Levy, *Chavez*, pp. 522-24

38. "Chavez Report to NEB, October 12–15, 1974," UFWOP, part 2, Box 37, Folder 23, Wayne State.

39. Jack Lloyd, author's interview, Oxnard, December 4, 1996.

40. Ibid.

41. Jack Lloyd, Philip L. Martin, and John Mamer, "The Ventura Citrus Labor Market," Giannini Foundation Information Series No.88-1 (Berkeley: University of California, Division of Agriculture and Natural Resources, April 1988).

42. Ibid., Lloyd interview.

43. "200 Citrus Pickers Stay off Jobs in Pay Dispute," *Santa Paula Chronicle*, January 28, 1974.

44. Lloyd, Martin, and Mamer, "Ventura County Citrus Labor Market," p. 4.

45. For reports on the strike published in the *Santa Paula Chronicle* see I&R, Box 28, Folder 31, Wayne State.

46. This was the first Executive Board meeting recorded on tape. Chavez explained that the recording would be used to compile the notes of the meeting, and then would be erased or recorded over. But that never happened, and tapes of this meeting, as well as many others at La Paz are now in the UFW archives(UFWOP, part 2, Box AV) at Wayne State University.

47. This and the following quotes are from "Tape of the March 28–April 2 National Executive Board meeting," UFWOP, part 2, Box AV, Wayne State.

48. Jerry Cohen, author's interview, June 5, 1995.

49. "Minutes of NEB meeting, March 31, 1974," UFWOP part 2, Box 37, Folder 12, Wayne State.

50. "Minutes of NEB meeting, June 13, 1974," p. 12, UFWOP, part 2, Box 37, folder 18, Wayne State.

51. "Minutes of the NEB meeting, October 14, 1974," UFWOP, Box 60, Folder "October 1974 Board Meeting," Wayne State.

52. Epifanio Camacho, telephone interview, July 3, 2003.

53. *El Malcriado* 7, no. 5, May 29, 1974; "Struck Firm Sells Berry Holdings," Watsonville *Register-Pajaronian*, May 17, 1974; "Pickets Pick on Salinas Berries," *The Packer*, May 25, 1974.

54. "Court Orders Follow Berry Field Violence," *The Packer*, June 1, 1974.

55. I reconstructed this strike from reports in the *Ventura County Star Press*, May 25 to June 16, 1974; *El Malcriado* 7, no. 6, June 24, 1974; and I&R, Box 29, Folder 3, Wayne State, which includes additional clippings from the *Santa Barbara News and Review*, the *Oxnard Press Courier*, and the *Ventura College Pirate Press*.

56. "Growers, UFW Confrontation," *Stockton Record*, July 25, 1974; *El Malcriado* 7, no. 8, July 25, 1974.

57. "Minutes of NEB meeting, October 14, 1974," UFWOP, part 2, Box 60, Folder "October 1974 Board Meeting," Wayne State, p. 38.

58. "UFW: Local Farm Strife Start of Major Campaign," *Stockton Record*, July 25, 1974.

59. Editorial, *Stockton Record*, July 28, 1974; "Five Arrested as Tomato Field Turmoil Continues," *Stockton Record*, July 30, 1974.

60. Luis Magaña, author's interview, February 5, 2008.

61. "UFW-Backed Secret Ballot Bill Advances," *Stockton Record*, August 7, 1974.

62. William H. Friedland and Amy Barton, "Destalking the Wily Tomato," Research Monograph No. 15 (Santa Cruz: University of California at Santa Cruz, June 1975).

63. Ibid.

64. "Harvest Pickets Increase," Yolo County *Daily Democrat*, September 7, 1974.

65. "Tomato Fields Struck," Yolo County *Daily Democrat*, September 4, 1974; Al Rojas, telephone interview, June 24, 2004.

66. "Pickers: Growers Violated February Pact in 5 Areas," *Ventura County Star-Free Press*,

August 27, 1974; "S.P. Growers, Citrus Pickers in Pay Impasse," *Ventura County Star-Free Pres*, August 22, 1974.

67. "Santa Paula Lemon Strike, from Ben Maddock to Cesar," August 26, 1974, I&R, Box 28, Folder 31, Wayne State; "Accord Reached in Citrus Strike; Pickers to Vote," *Ventura County Star-Free Press,* September 11, 1974.

68. "Mushroom Strike," n.d., I&R Collection, Box 28, Folder 37, Wayne State; "Minutes of NEB, October 14, 1974," p. 28, Wayne State, part 2, Box 60, Folder "October", Wayne State.

69. I have reconstructed this strike from stories in the Watsonville *Register-Pajaronian*, September 4, 1974, to October 14, 1974; Alfredo Santos, "UFW Strike Report on the William Buak Fruit Co. Inc.," October 19, 1974, I&R, Box 28, Folder 10, Wayne State; "Minutes of the NEB, October 14, 1974," UFWOP, Box 60, Folder "October 1974 Board Meeting," Wayne State, p. 36; and my own memory, as I was a member of the UFW at the time and an active supporter of the strike, present on the unforgettable morning when the INS arrived and left, empty-handed.

70. Levy, *Cesar Chavez*, p. 528; Jerry Cohen, telephone interview, July 2, 2004.

71. "Chatfield Hung Tough During Decade of Trouble," *Bakersfield Californian*, September 24, 1985.

72. Cohen interview, p. 72.

73. "The Race Is Won," May 31, 1975, CC, Box 35, Folder "Leaflet Series."

Chapter 24

1. "Campaign Against Illegals," May 24, 1974, Office of the President: Cesar Chavez Records (hereafter UFWOP), Box 37, Folder 20, Wayne State.

2. "Illegals Campaign—Important" July 6, 1974, UFW Information and Research Department (hereafter I&R), Box 38, Folder "Illegals 1974 (2)," Wayne State; "Fresno County Illegal Alien Documentation" n.d., UFWOP part 2, Box 17, Folder 19, "Illegal Alien Farm Labor," Wayne State.

3. "Illegals Press Statement of Cesar E. Chavez, July 1, 1974," I&R, Box 38, Folder "Illegals 1974 (2)," Wayne State.

4. Halfway into the campaign, in August 1974, the UFW changed the wording of the petition to read "undocumented workers" rather than "illegals," although they continued to use "illegals," and "illegal aliens" in other literature and public statements. See "Illegals Campaign" August 17, 1974, I&R, Box 38, Folder "Illegals '73–'74," Wayne State.

5. "Illegals Campaign" October 15, 1974, I&R, Box 38, Folder "Illegal Aliens 1974," Wayne State.

6. California Assembly Committee on Agriculture, *The California Farm Work Force: A Profile* (Sacramento: April 1969).

7. Richard Mines and Philip L. Martin, "A Profile of California Farm Workers," Giannini Information Series No. 86-2 (Berkeley: University of California, Giannini Foundation of Agricultural Economics, July 1986).

8. "Illegal Aliens: A Growing Labor Force," *Fresno Bee*, September 9, 1973; Stephen Sosnick, *Hired Hands: Seasonal Farm Workers in the U.S.* (Santa Barbara: McNally & Loftin, 1978), p. 432.

9. "UFW Vows $500,000 to Win Strike," *Ventura County Star-Free Press*, May 31, 1974.

10. "AFL-CIO News," n.d., I&R, Box 39, Folder "Illegal Project 1974," Wayne State.

11. "Minutes of NEB Meeting," June 13, 1974, 13–14, UFWOP, part 2, Box 37, Folder 18, Wayne State.

12. "To Chavez, from Liza," June 10, 1974; "To Liza, from Chavez," June 25, 1974, I&R, Box 41, Folder "Illegals," Wayne State.

13. Liza Hirsch, author's interviews, Los Angeles, March 4, 2002, and August 2, 2005.

14. Liza Hirsch, telephone interview, January 23, 2004.

15. Gilbert Padilla, author's interview, Fresno, December 20, 1997, pp. 8–9; "Memo from Frank Ortiz to Joe Rubio, September 6, 1972," I&R, Box 47, Folder 27, Wayne State.

16. "Illegal Aliens: A Growing Labor Force."

17. "Immigration Bureaucracy is Overwhelmed by Its Work," *New York Times*, January 17, 1980.

18. "INS to Investigate 'Round-Trip' Deportations," *Los Angeles Times*, January 17, 1976.

19. "Illegal Aliens Flown Inside Mexico," *Fresno Bee*, July 22, 1976; Howard Frank, interviewed by unidentified UFW staff member, I&R, Box 39, Folder 11, Wayne State.

20. "The Chavez Border Patrol," *San Francisco Examiner*, December 22, 1974.

21. "UFW Striker Arrested In Beating of Illegals," *Yuma Daily Sun*, October 1, 1974; "Motel Picketed by UFW Strikers," *Yuma Daily Sun*, November 29, 1974.

22. Robert Lindsey, "Criticism of Chavez Takes Root in Farm Labor Struggle," *New York Times*, February 7, 1979. Lindsey's article contained the most serious charges made in a U.S. newspaper. All of the other evidence here comes from interviews by journalist Tom Barry, his reports of stories in Mexican newspapers, scattered reports in the U.S. press, and interviews I did thirty years later.

23. For an example of Manual Chavez's signing Cesar's name on a series of checks, see "Eliseo Medina to Cesar Chavez," August 31, 1976, UFWOP, Box 27, Folder 17, Wayne State.

24. Alfredo Avila, telephone interview, January 26, 2004.

25. The information on the Arizona lemon industry comes from "Lemon Industry, Summary Report" November 25, 1974, I&R, Box 46, Folder 62, Wayne State; "Long, Bitter Lemon Strike Splits Yuma," *Yuma County Sun*, n.d., I&R, Box 28, Folder 31, Wayne State; "Yuma County Backbone," *Yuma County Sun*, n.d., I&R, Box 46, Folder 63, Wayne State; Foreign Agricultural Service, Horticultural and Tropical Products Division, "The U.S. Citrus Industry Situation," September 2001, www.unctad.org/infocomm/francais/orange/Doc/citrus.pdf.

26. "Court Restricts Picket Numbers," *Yuma Daily Sun*, October 3, 1974; "Minutes of

the National Executive Board Meeting," October 14, 1974, 41–2, UFWOP, part 2, Box 60, Folder "October 1974 Board Meeting," Wayne State.

27. "Minutes of National Executive Board Meeting," October 14, 1974, pp. 41–2; Lupe Sanchez, telephone interview, April 3, 2004.

28. "Minutes of National Executive Board Meeting," 93–4, UFWOP, part 2, Box 18, Folder 1, Wayne State.

29. "Lemon Industry, Summary Report," November 25,1974, Wayne State.

30. "Union Digs In For Long Fight In Citrus Groves," *Arizona Daily Star*, February 16, 1975; "Citrus Picking Wages Here Reported Topping $7 an Hour for Some Pickers," *Yuma Daily Sun*, October 8, 1974; Abelardo Perez, affidavit, March 15, 1975, I&R, Box 28, Folder 32, Wayne State; "Lemon Industry, Summary Report," November 25, 1974, Wayne State.

31. Statement of Steve Burton, UFW attorney, November 13, 1974, I&R, Box 28, Folder 31, Wayne State; "Harassment by the Sheriffs and the Courts," n.d., I&R, Box 28, Folder 32,Wayne State.

32. "Court Restricts Picket Numbers"; "Ban Is Lifted on Pickets at Citrus Grove," *Arizona Republic*, October 3, 1974.

33. Tom Barry, "The Manuel Chavez Story," unpublished manuscript, November 20, 1978, pp. 7,9,10 (in author's collection, courtesy of Doug Foster).

34. Ibid.

35. Lupe Sanchez, telephone interview, September 8, 2004; Gus Gutierrez, telephone interview, September 2, 2004.

36. Lupe Sanchez, telephone interview, April 3, 2004.

37. "Criticism of Chavez Takes Root in Farm Worker Struggle."

38. Barry, "Manuel Chavez Story," p. 9.

39. "Minutes of National Executive Board Meeting," March 29, 1975, Wayne State.

40. "Chavez Offers 'Olive Branch,' Vows to Sustain Citrus Strike," *Yuma Daily Sun*, October 17, 1974.

41. Gilbert Padilla, telephone interview, September 7, 2004.

42. "Chavez Out of Hospital," *Yuma Daily Sun*, October 31, 1973.

43. Alberto Escalante, August 31, 2004. Escalante was part of an online listserve discussion of UFW history from May, 2004 to January, 2005. I quote him with his permission.

44. "From Liza Hirsch to Boycott Cities . . . ," July 6, 1974, I&R, Box 38, Folder "Illegals 1974 (2)"; "Minutes of the National Executive Board Meeting," June 13, 1974, UFWOP, part 2, Box 37, Folder 18, Wayne State; Liza Hirsch Medina, telephone interview, September 22, 2004.

45. See "Cesar Chavez to Paul Pumphrey," June 27, 1974, I&R, Box 39, Folder "Illegals—Staff Protest," Wayne State.

46. The collection of letters and Chavez's responses can be found in I&R, Box 39, Folder "Illegals—Staff Protest," Wayne State.

47. "Chavez Says Strike Is Not Planned Now," Yolo County *Daily Democrat*, August 12, 1974.

48. "The UFW and 'Illegal Aliens,'" *The Militant*, October 11, 1974.

49. Juan Gómez Quiñones, *Chicano Politics: Reality and Promise, 1940–1990* (Albuquerque: University of New Mexico Press, 1990), p. 150.

50. "From Liza to Chavez, Re: National Lawyers Guild and UFW Illegals Policy, " March 15, 1975, UFWOP, part 2, Box 28, Folder 1, Wayne State.

51. "Minutes of National Executive Board Meeting," March 26, 1975, pp. 16–20; UFWOP, part 2, Box 18, Folder 1.

52. Ibid.

Chapter 25

1. Marc Grossman, "The 1,000 Mile March" Cesar E. Chavez Foundation, n.d. (author's collection).

2. Ibid.

3. "UFWA Opens Parley to Set Policy, Build Support," *Los Angeles Times*, August 16, 1975; Cesar Chavez, "Report to the Second Constitutional Convention," August 15, 1975 (courtesy of Marshall Ganz).

4. "Minutes of Special National Executive Board Meeting," June 13, 1975, UFW Office of the President: Cesar Chavez Records (hereafter UFWOP), part 2, Box 21, Folder 2, Wayne State, p. 11.

5. Ibid, pp. 10–16.

6. "An Open Letter to Farm Workers from Cesar Chavez," July 7, 1975, UFWOP, Box 35, Folder "Leaflet Series," Wayne State.

7. "Chavez Threatens Sit-in if Denied Access to Workers," *Los Angeles Times*, August 18, 1975.

8. Agricultural Labor Relations Board, "First Annual Report, Fiscal Years 1976 and 1977." By comparison, in the first ten months of its existence the National Labor Relations Board conducted thirty-one representation elections, involving 7,734 workers.

9. "Access to Fields," *Fresno Bee*, September 20, 1975.

10. "Teamster Power: A Bad Omen," *The Packer*, April 19, 1975.

11. The ALRB Annual Reports do not list the voting results by small enough geographical areas, so I have relied on UFW records for the results from Delano and, later, from the Salinas Valley. See "Delano Election Results, Updated September 30, 1975," UFW Central Administration Records (hereafter UFWCAR), Box 4, Folder 5, Wayne State

12. Ben Maddock, author's interview, Stockton, California, May 1, 2005.

13. "Delano Election Results, Updated September 30, 1975."

14. Maddock interview.

15. Pete Maturino, author's interview, Salinas, July 15, 2005.

16. Maddock interview.

17. Chayo Pelayo, author's interview, El Centro, April 30, 2005, p. 3.

18. Maddock interview.

19. Ibid.

20. "Salinas Election Results, as of October 2, 1975," UFWCAR, Box 4, Folder 5, Wayne State. These figures are for the Salinas Valley as an economic unit, not a geographical one. It extends from the Pajaro Valley to King City.

21. Jose Renteria, author's interview, Salinas, May 30, 1995.

22. Mario Bustamante, author's interview, El Centro, April 30, 2005, pp. 5–6.

23. Maturino interview.

24. "Election Statistical Tally, November 28, 1975," UFW Information and Research Department Records (hereafter I&R), Box 10, Folder 15, Wayne State.

25. "2 Members Roughed Up, Farm Board Says," *Los Angeles Times*, October 8, 1975.

26. At several companies growers submitted bloated lists of employees to the ALRB as proof that the union had not signed up enough workers to force an election. In a perfect Catch-22, the local ALRB staff would not allow the union to check the employee lists because, they explained, the lists proved that the union didn't have enough signatures to qualify, and without qualifying it had no right to review the lists.

27. "AFL-CIO Panel to Probe State Farm Labor Votes," *San Diego Evening Tribune*, October 2, 1975; "Agricultural Board Hit from All Sides," *Valley News and Green Sheet*, October 2, 1975.

28. "Brown, High Officials Meet on Farm Labor Complaints" *Los Angeles Times*, October 2, 1975.

29. Transcript of Hearings, California State Senate Industrial Relations Committee and Assembly Relations Committee, November 25, 1975, (courtesy of Sam Cohen).

30. Sam Cohen, telephone interview, August 1, 2005.

31. "2 Members Roughed Up, Farm Board Says."

32. Marshall Ganz, personal communication (email), August 2, 2005.

33. Carlos Bowker, telephone interview, July 25, 2005.

34. ALRB, "Campesinos, These Are Your Rights," leaflet, n.d. (courtesy of Sam Cohen).

35. Sam Cohen, interview, August 1, 2005; Carlos Bowker, telephone interview, August 3, 1975; Ganz, August 2, 2005, email.

36. Hermilo Mojica, telephone interview, August 1, 2005.

37. W. H. Segur and Varden Fuller, "California's Farm Labor Elections: An Analysis of the Initial Results," *Monthly Labor Review*, December 1976.

38. "Farmers Unit Credits New ALRB Act for Drop In Table Grape Boycotts," *Fresno Bee*, December 4, 1975.

39. Jerry Cohen, telephone interview, December 8, 2004.

40. "Notes from Executive Board Meeting" January 1, 1976, I&R, Box 21, Folder 5, Wayne State; "Minutes of National Executive Board," March 28, 1975, UFWOP, part 2, Box 18, Folder 1.

41. See "Minutes of the National Executive Board," February 16–21, 1976, I&R, Box 21, Folder 5, Wayne State.

42. In the thirty-eight-page account of the retreat discussion, the work "democratize" is used twice, both times in the description of the initial brainstorming session. Elsewhere in the document neither the word "democracy" nor any of its derivatives appear. See Minutes of National Executive Board, February 16–21, 1976.

43. "Former United Auto Workers Leader Predicts Change in UFW Emphasis," *The Packer*, January 10, 1976.

44. Marshall Ganz, interviewed by Jacques Levy, Cambridge, Mass., April 4, 1994, transcript, p. 140, Jacques E. Levy research collection on Cesar Chavez (hereafter Levy/ Yale), Box 36, Folder 685.

45. "Meeting With Legal Staff and Election Directors—November 1, 1975," 10, UFWOP, part 2, Box 40, Folder 27, Wayne State.

46. "Opening Statement for Organizing Conference," n.d., UFWOP, Box 23, Folder "Organizing," Wayne State.

47. Eliseo Medina, author's interview, Los Angeles, May 20, 2005.

48. "California Labor Still Negotiating," *The Packer*, August 7, 1976: Marshall Ganz, "Plan for the Vegetable Industry," unpublished report, May 1977 (in author's collection, courtesy of Marshall Ganz); Gilbert Padilla, author's interview, Salinas, April 10, 2005.

49. Chris Hartmire, "Argument in Support of Proposition 14: The Farm Worker Initiative," unpublished manuscript, n.d. (in author's collection, courtesy of Chris Hartmire).

50. "UFWA Ballot Proposal May Kill Opposition to Funding," *Sacramento Bee*, April 21, 1976.

51. Robert Pack, *Jerry Brown, The Philosopher-Prince* (New York, Stein & Day, 1978), pp. 80, 253.

52. Maurice Jourdane, telephone interview, July 21, 2005.

53. "Marshall Ganz, personal communication (email), August 23, 2005.

54. Cesar Chavez and Governor Jerry Brown, telephone conversation, July 27, 1976, transcript, UFWOP, part 2, Box 54, Folder "Confidential," Wayne State.

55. Los Angeles, editorial, "Farm Labor Initiative: No on 14," October 29, 1976.

56. Tramutt's family name was Tramutola, a name he took back after he left the union.

57. "Endorsing Convention," 1976, UFWOP, part 2, Box 1, Folder 17, Wayne State; Medina interview.

58. "Loss in Fire at Freedman's Hits $1 Million," *The Packer*, April 24, 1976; "Field Contract Signed by Salinas Teamsters," *The Packer*, August 28, 1976.

59. "Role Switch in Farm Labor Fuss," *Salinas Californian*, August 25, 1976.

60. "Minutes of the National Executive Board Meeting," September 19–20, 1976, p. 4, UFW Vice President's Files, Peter Velasco (hereafter VP Velasco), Box 4, Folder 43, Wayne State.

61. Maddock interview.

62. Ibid.

63. Marshall Ganz, author's interview, April 12, 1996.

64. "Minutes of National Farm Workers' Health Group—9/15/76," UFWOP, part 2, Box 18, Folder 3, Wayne State.

65. Ganz, September 14, 2005, email.

66. The specific criticisms cited in the minutes of the September 19 meeting are innocuous. Chavez had to remove an article that included some financial information about the union; he opposed another article, about an ILWU boycott that the union had not

endorsed; Chavez had not been listed as editor on the masthead. Probably there were other charges. Thirty years later Richard Ibarra claimed that instead of publishing photographs of Chavez with the Pope, the *Malcriado* staff had destroyed them.

67. "Minutes of the National Executive Board Meeting," September 19–20, 1976, VP Velasco, Box 4, Folder 43.

68. Ibid.

69. Nick Jones, author's interview, Oakland, March 21, 2002.

70. Ibid, p. 4

71. Gilbert Padilla, author's interview, Fresno, December 12, 1997, p. 18.

72. Nancy Grimley Carleton, "Working for La Causa," Farm Worker Documentation Project, www.farm workermovement.org.

73. Marshall Ganz, interviewed by Jacques Levy, April 8, 1994, transcript, p. 132, Box 36, Folder 685, Levy/Yale.

74. "To: National Executive Board, From: Nick Jones, Virginia Jones—November 14, 1976," UFWOP, Box 3, Folder 22.

75. "UFW Aide Quits, Alleges Chavez Antileftist Bias," *Los Angeles Times*, December 12, 1976.

76. Stanford University, Department of Special Collections, Fred Ross Papers 1910–1992, II, Box 39 (05), Folder 207.

77. Ibid.

78. Jerry Cohen and Chavez cited Article 49, Section 8, of the union constitution, which read: "The President shall have the duty to discharge personnel who are not performing adequately in their assigned responsibilities." But the president's duty did not cancel Rivers's and Smith's rights to a hearing. Article 8 stated that full-time volunteers who had served for six months were union members. Article 8, Section 5, required that any charges against members had to be written, and that the accused must be given a "full and fair hearing." Article 18 specified, "If the accused works full time for the union," charges against the accused "shall be in writing and sworn to by the accuser" and filed with the secretary-treasurer of the union.

79. Marshall Ganz, "personal communication (email), September 14, 2005.

80. Teamster-UFW Agreement, Addendum, and Letter of Intent, March 10, 1977 (courtesy of Jerry Cohen); Jerry Cohen, telephone interview, April 26, 2005.

81. Maturino interview.

Chapter 26

1. Eliseo Medina, author's interview, May 20, 2005, pp. 23–24.

2. Gilbert Padilla, author's interview, December 20, 1997, pp. 21–22.

3. Jerry Cohen, telephone interview, July 12, 2005.

4. Gilbert Padilla, telephone interview, July 25, 2005.

5. Richard Ofshe, "The Social Development of the Synanon Cult: The Managerial Strategy of Organizational Formation," *Sociological Analysis* 41, no. 2 (1980).

6. "What Is Happening Inside Synanon?" *Los Angeles Times*, January 31, 1978.

7. Dave Mitchell, Cathy Mitchell, and Richard Ofshe, *The Light on Synanon* (New York: Seaview Books, 1980), p. 221.

8. Bob Thompson, telephone interview, December 27, 2005.

9. Carol Schoenbrunn Lambiase, telephone interview, December 21, 2005.

10. "Memorandum to Jerry Cohen from Volunteer Staff, Legal Department," February 5, 1977, UFW Office of the President: Cesar Chavez Records (hereafter UFWOP), Part 2, Box 3, Folder 22, Wayne State.

11. Ibid.

12. "Minutes of the National Executive Board Meeting, March 14–16," 1977, pp. 21–23, 27, UFW Vice President's Files, Peter Velasco (hereafter VP Velasco), Box 4, Folder 43, Wayne State.

13. "(Confidential) Progress Report, NFWA Land Project, 3–1–77," UFW Information and Research Department Records (hereafter I&R), Box 21, Folder 25, Wayne State.

14. Ibid, 6.

15. "Minutes of the National Executive Board Meeting, March 14–16, 1977," p. 36.

16. Ibid, p. 46.

17. Ibid, p. 31.

18. Ibid, p. 48.

19. Bob Thompson, author's interview, December 27, 2005.

20. Padilla, September 12, 2005, interview.

21. Jessica Govea, telephone interview, November 18, 2002.

22. "Minutes of the National Executive Board Meeting, March 14–16," pp. 21, 57A.

23. National Executive Board Meeting, March 14–16, audiotape, author's transcript p. 21, UFWOP, part 2, Box AV, Wayne State.

24. Aristeo Zambrano, author's interview, Oakland, June 8, 1993.

25. Marshall Ganz, "Plan for the Vegetable Industry," unpublished manuscript, May 1977 (in author's collection, courtesy of Marshall Ganz). See also Chapter 27, note 2.

26. Aristeo Zambrano, author's interview, Oakland, August 23, 1994.

27. Ibid.

28. Aristeo Zambrano, author's interview, Oakland, July 11, 2005.

29. Ibid.

30. Chava Bustamante, author's interview, San Jose, November 15, 1996.

31. I have reconstructed the Monday Night Massacre from the following: "To Executive Board, Jerry Cohen, Jim Drake, From David McClure," letter, April 10, 1977, "Monday Night Massacre," La Paz memo, n.d., both in UFWOP, part 2, Box 2, Folder 22, Wayne State; "Petition to President Cesar Chavez," La Paz document, n.d., and letter from Roger Brooks to Cesar Chavez, October 20, 1978, both in UFWOP, part 2, Box 3, Folder 22, Wayne State; Nancy Grimley Carleton, "Working for La Causa," n.d., Farm worker Movement Documentation Project, www.farm workermovement.org ("essays"); Gilbert Padilla and Esther Padilla, author's interview, Fresno, December 20, 1997.

32. "Personal and Confidential To: UFWNEB Members, From Cesar E. Chavez, President, April 15, 1977," UFWOP, part 2, Box 3, Folder 23, Wayne State.

33. "President's Newsletter, vol. 1, no. 1, March 11, 1977," UFWOP, part 2, Box 2, Folder 2, Wayne State.

34. Doug Adair to Cesar Chavez, memo, May 1, 1977, UFWOP, part 2, Box 3, Folder 23, Wayne State.

35. President's Newsletter, vol. 1, no 4," UFWOP, part 2, Box 21, Folder 2, Wayne State.

36. Padilla, December 20, 1997, interview.

37. Gilbert Padilla, author's interview, April 10, 2005.

38. Marshall Ganz, author's interview, April 12, 1996, p. 123.

39. Richard Chavez, interviewed by Jacques Levy, "Family at La Paz," n.d., Vol 2, Jaques E. Levy Research Collection on Cesar Chavez,Post Mortem Research (hereafter PMR) Box 31, Folder 674, Levy/Yale, p. 60; Jose Renteria, author's interview, May 30, 1995, p. 50; Pablo Espinoza, author's interview, February 6, 2004, p. 17.

40. Eliseo Medina, author's interview, May 20, 2005, p. 6.

41. Marion Moses, telephone interview, May 2, 2002.

42. Nick Jones, author's interview, March 21, 2002, p. 18.

Chapter 27

1. Alberto Escalante, "Was Prop 14 the End of the Line?" December 26, 2004. Escalante was part of an online listserve discussion of UFW history from May, 2004 to January, 2005. I quote him with his permission.

2. Ganz's arguments were ignored by the board. Ganz then set out the argument and organizing strategy in detail in a forty-three-page document, "Plan for the Vegetable Industry," which he gave to Chavez in May 1977. He explained the dangers of leaving the vegetables only partly unionized and warned that company unions might emerge if the UFW did not fill the vacuum left by the Teamsters. A small, corrupt outfit led by ex-Teamster organizers did appear on the scene, and won four elections in the Salinas Valley in the summer of 1977, one fewer than the UFW in the same period. Marshall Ganz, "Plan for the Vegetable Industry," mimeographed paper, May 1977 (in author's collection, courtesy of Marshall Ganz).

3. President's Newsletter, May 20, 1977, p. 3, UFW Office of the President: Cesar Chavez Records (hereafter UFWOP), part 2, Box 21, Folder 2, Wayne State.

4. Doug Adair, author's interview, Watsonville, April 8, 2005.

5. State of California, Agricultural Labor Relations Board, First and Second Annual Reports, for years 1977, 1978, in author's collection.

6. The reasons for being pissed off were the same as they had been in 1973 and '75. Plus, the growers immediately matched the 25 percent raise that the union had just won at Freedman, while foremen reminded workers that, on top of all their other old gripes, the UFW's 2 percent dues would mean that union workers would make less than nonunion ones. (Alberto Escalante, "Was Prop 14 the End of the Line?," December 26, 2004.)

7. Chavez cited only a few relatively minor examples of Delizonna's failings in calling for his resignation, and mounted no protest campaign against him.

8. Debbie Adair, author's interview, Thermal, April 29, 2005.

9. Marshall Ganz, personal communication (email), September 14, 2005.

10. Craig Scharlin and Lilia Villanueva, *Philip Vera Cruz: A Personal History of Filipino Immigrants and the Farm workers Movement* (Los Angeles: UCLA Labor Center, Institute of Public Relations, and UCLA Asian American Studies Center, 1992), p. 116.

11. Jerry Cohen, telephone interview, January 26, 2006.

12. National Executive Board Meeting, June 30–July 2, 1977, audiotape, UFWOP, part 2, Box AV, Wayne State. Rumors, confessions, and accusations about Chavez 's extramarital affairs are rampant among many ex-UFW staffers. Chavez referred to this particular incident at the June–July 1977 board meeting. Apart from this one case, however, I do not believe that the rumored affairs, even if true, had a serious impact on the history of the UFW. I leave them to some future biographer of Cesar Chavez.

13. Jerry Cohen, telephone interview, January 26, 2006.

14. Gilbert Padilla, telephone interview, November 21, 2005.

15. Scharlin and Villanueva, *Philip Vera Cruz,* pp. 109–15; for another account of this meeting see Miriam Pawel, *The Union of Their Dreams,* (New York; Bloomsbury, 2009), pp. 218–19.

16. Scharlin and Villanueva, *Philip Vera Cruz,* p. 100.

17. "The Game, 7/7/77, La Paz #1," audiotape, UFWOP, part, Box AV, Wayne State.

18. "Chavez Lauds FM for Social Reforms in RP," Philippines *Bulletin Today,* August 8, 1977, UFW Information and Research Records (hereafter I&R), Box 25, Folder 11; "The Labor Leader Most Unlikely," Philippines *People,* August 2, 1997, and "Reactions of the Anti-Martial Law Movement to the Visit of Cesar Chavez to the Philippines," both in I&R, Box 25, Folder 4, Wayne State.

19. "Cesar Chavez Hails Philippines' Rule," *Washington Post,* July 29, 1997.

20. Letters of protest in I&R, Box 25, Folders 3 and 4.

21. Debbie Adair, interview, April 4, 2005. Many people tell a version of this story. The accounts of Meta Mendel Reyes (once married to Rudy Reyes) "Remembering Cesar" *Radical History Review* 58: 142, 1994, and Meta Mendel-Reyes, *Reclaiming Democracy: The Sixties in Politics in Memory* (New York; Routledge, 1996), are somewhat different but nearly identical on Max Avalos's dramatic assertion of Cesar's right to define the world.

22. Scharlin and Villanueva, *Phillip Vera Cruz,* p. 118.

23. For this to be legal, workers had to have an option of giving their holiday pay to a charity instead. They could choose one of three: The Martin Luther King Farm Workers Fund, the National Farm Workers Health Group, or The National Farm Workers Service Center--all charities controlled by the union and run from La Paz.

24. Chava Bustamante, telephone interview, January 17, 2006.

25. "Farm worker Convention Marked by Controversy," *In These Times,* September 7–13, 1977.

26. 'Chavez to Seek Nationwide Farm Union," *Los Angeles Times*, August 27, 1977; "Chavez: Farm Workers' George Meany," *Workers Vanguard*, September 1977.

27. "'No Union' Beats UFW in Vineyards,'" *Salinas Californian*, September 27, 1977.

28. Ibid.

29. Declaration of Damaso Tirado and Jose Ramirez, UFWOP, Box 33, Folder 6, Wayne State.

30. "Telephone Conversation with Mo Jourdaine [*sic*] 9/7/77" and "Telephone Conversation with Jim Drake, 9/7/77," UFWOP, part 2, Box 33, Folder 2, Wayne State; "Dirty Tricks in the Fields," *People's World*, October 1, 1977; "Jim Drake to Cesar Chavez 10-6-77," UFWOP, part 2, Box 31, Folder "Planning Organizing," Wayne State.

31. "RE: Giumarra Campaign, from Guadalupe Cordova R" (in Spanish; author's translation), UFWOP, part2, Box 31, Folder "Planning Organizing," Wayne State.

32. "Minutes of National Executive Board meeting, October 10, 1977," p. 5, VP Velasco, Box 4, Folder 43, Wayne State.

33. Leon Howell, "Chavez for the Defense," *Christianity and Crisis*, November 14, 1977.

34. Ibid.

35. "Wayne C. Hartmire to Helge Christophersen, January 10, 1978," I&R, Box 25, Folder 3, Wayne State.

36. Though notable, those eleven farm-worker elections in 1977 in the Salinas Valley stacked up poorly against the 175 ALRB elections in the same region, from King City to Watsonville, in 1975. *The Packer* took notice, remarking in both August and September of 1977 that the UFW was not organizing in the Salinas Valley ("Unionization Slows in California," *The Packer*, August 6, 1977; "Dissident Union Leads Labor Vote," *The Packer*, September 17, 1977).

37. U.S. Labor Department, LM-2, Union Annual Financial Reports, 1978 and 1979.

38. "To National Executive Board from Terry Caruthers, NFWSC Acting Executive Director," March 13, 1977, UFWOP, part 2, Box 18 Folder 5, Wayne State; U.S. Department of the Treasury, "Form 990 Return of Organization Exempt from Income Tax," National Farm Workers Service Center, 1985. (in author's collection, courtesy of Bruce Perry).

39. Robert F. Kennedy Farm Workers Medical Plan Statistical Summary," VP Velasco, Box 7, Folder 84, Wayne State.

40. Frank Denison to Eliseo Medina, July 12, 1976, UFWOP, part 2, Box 15, Folder "RFK Medical Plan," Wayne State; "Minutes of National Executive Board, Meeting April 3, 1978," p. 9, VP Velasco, Box 4, Folder "38," Wayne State; National Executive Board Meeting, June 15, 1978, audiotape, UFWOP, part 2, Box AV, Wayne State.

41. U.S. Department of Treasury, "Form 990 Return of Organization Exempt from Income Tax," Martin Luther King Jr. Educational Fund, 1985, (in author's collection, courtesy of Bruce Perry).

42. President's Newsletters, June 23, August 21, and October 9, 1978, UFWOP, part 2, Box 21, Folders 4, 7, 8, respectively, Wayne State.

43. Gilbert Padilla, author's interview, Fresno, December 5, 2005.

44. National Executive Board meeting, June 15, 1978.

45. Staff List, UFWOP, part 2, Box 24, Folder 2, Wayne State; "La Paz Community, September 1, 1978," UFWOP, Box 23, Folder "loose," Wayne State.

46. Liza Hirsch, author's interview, Los Angeles, March 4, 2002; Gilbert Padilla, author's interview, December 20, 1997.

47. "Report on Actions Taken at National Executive Board Meeting," n.d., UFWOP, part 2, Box 18, Folder 16, Wayne State.

48. The number of ALRB elections declined. In 1978–79, the ALRB held sixty-seven elections in California, seven of which ended in decertifications of union representation. In 1979–80 it held only thirty-five, resulting in three decertifications. From 1980 to 1986, the total number of ALRB elections never again topped forty, and the percentage of decerts rose. After '86, the UFW stopped filing for ALRB elections entirely, and didn't resume until after Chavez's death, in 1993. (Annual Reports of the Agricultural Labor Relations Board, 1978 to 1986) (author's collection).

49. National Executive Board Meeting, April 4, 1978, audiotape, UFWOP, part 2, Box AV, Wayne State.

50. National Executive Board Meeting, March 24, 1978, audiotape, UFWOP, part 2, Box AV, Wayne State.

51. This account of the strike comes from the following: Eliseo Medina's reports to the National Executive Board, April and June, 1978, VP Velasco, Box 4, Folder 38, Wayne State; Eliseo Medina, author's interview, May 20, 2005.

52. Minutes of National Executive Board Meeting, April 3, 1978, p. 19, VP Velasco, Box 4, Folder 38, Wayne State.

53. Ibid., 26.

54. *Ventura Star Press*, articles from March 30 to May 16, 1978.

55. Medina interview.

56. Eliseo Medina, Report to the National Executive Board, June, 1978, VP Velasco, Box 4, Folder 38, Wayne State.

57. Medina interview.

58. "Game Group 1" September 26, 1977, audiotape, UFWOP, part 2, Box AV, Wayne State.

59. Sandy Nathan, personal communication (email), December 31, 2005.

60. Bill Monning, author's interview, Moss Landing, California, November 4, 2005; Tom Dalzell, author's interview, Berkeley, November 3, 2005; Jerry Cohen, telephone interviews, December 6 and February 27, 2005.

61. Mitchell, Mitchell, and Ofshe, *Light on Synanon*; "Friends of Charles E. Dederich, Human Rights and Justice Hold a Press Conference," Los Angeles, January 13, 1979," Synanon Pamphlet, n.d., VP Velasco, Box 7, Folder 43, Wayne State; UFW National Executive Board Meeting, March 11, 1979, audiotape, UFWOP, part 2, Box AV, Wayne State.

62. Jerry Cohen, telephone interview, October 26, 2005; Dalzell interview.

63. Cohen interview.

64. "Legal Department to National Executive Board, June 12, 1978," VP Velasco, Box

4, Folder 38, Wayne State; "Lawyers Proposed Salary Raises," n.d., UFWOP, part 2, Box 54, Folder "Personal" Wayne State; Cohen interview.

65. Gilbert Padilla, telephone interview, October 20, 2005; Letters to Cesar Chavez opposing legal department raises, June 21 to June 24, 1978 (in author's collection courtesy of Miriam Pawel).

66. "Plan I and Plan II," Notes From National Executive Board Meeting, June 25, 1978 (in author's collection, courtesy of Miriam Pawel).

67. "Minutes of National Executive Board meeting, June 25, 1978," VP Velasco, Box 2, Folder "NEB 1978"; Marshall Ganz, personal communication (email), November 1, 2005.

68. Medina interview, p. 4.

69. The meeting was not taped, but there is an official typewritten eight-page summary of the arguments. ("Minutes of National Executive Board meeting, June 25, 1978") The plan that Chavez championed stated that the volunteer system would be retained, personnel benefits would be "liberalized," and "for the time being [the union would] continue to buy professional services with the intention of building up the services internally."

70. Marshall Ganz, "UFW (1978–81)," unpublished ms. (in author's collection, courtesy of Marshall Ganz).

71. Chris Hartmire to Jerry Cohen, July 7, 1978, in author's collection.

72. Jerry Cohen, telephone interview, May 4, 2000.

73. In SEIU, Medina has found himself again in a staff-intensive union that has little regard for rank-and-file power. Without being privy to the internal debates in SEIU, it would seem that Medina has finally made his peace with some of the policies he opposed in the UFW.

Chapter 28

1. Marshall Ganz, author's interview, April 12, 1996, pp. 129–30.

2. Church: UFW-Employer Negotiations, January 11, 1979, transcript, p. 2 (courtesy of Doug Foster); Ganz: "3rd Round Breakdown Reported in Ag Talks," *Salinas Californian*, May 10, 1979; Kemp: "An Investment to See It Through—Grower," *Salinas Californian*, March 23, 1979; Chava Bustamante, author's interview, November 15, 1996; Hermilo Mojica, author's interview, October 3, 1994.

3. "Strung Out Farm Strike—a Huge Test of Will," *Salinas Californian*, March 24, 1979.

4. "New Contracts 1978," UFW Vice President's Files, Peter Velasco Collection (hereafter VP Velasco), Box 4, Folder 32, Wayne State; U.S. Dept of Labor, LM-2, Union Annual Financial Reports, October 16, 1979.

5. "View from the West," *The Packer*, June 23, 1978. In the paper's next issue, July 1, 1978, Daryl Arnold of the Western Growers Association offered a rebuttal, lauding the successful de-unionization of the grape industry thanks to "stubborn resistance by the growers, not co-operation with the union."

6. "Conferencia Preparatoria para Negociaciones de la industria de verdures, 26 de Agosto, 1978" [Conference in preparation for negotiations concerning the

agricultural industry, August 26, 1978] (in author's collection, courtesy of Chava Bustamante).

7. "Community Meeting 4/4/77" (tape is misnamed), September 10, 1978, audiotape, UFW Office of the President: Cesar Chavez Records (hereafter UFWOP, Box AV, Wayne State.

8. UFW-Employer Negotiations, January 3, 1979, transcript of audiotape, p. 5, (in author's collection, courtesy of Doug Foster).

9. Ibid., p. 7.

10. Ganz interview, p. 129.

11. Minutes of the National Executive Board meeting, September 15 and 18, 1978, p. 17, VP Velasco, Box 4, Folder 32, Wayne State.

12. "Strung Out Farm Strike—a Huge Test of Will."

13. Ganz interview, p. 131.

14. Jessica Govea, telephone interview, December 6, 2002; "Contributors Giving Aid to I.V. strikers," *Imperial Valley Press*, February 23, 1979.

15. Mario Bustamante, author's interview, El Centro, May 29, 2006.

16. "Growers Dig In to Bust the Union," Watsonville *Register-Pajaronian*, March 31, 1979.

17. Ronald Kemp, notes from interview by Doug Foster, February 29, 1979, Folder 13, Foster Files. Doug Foster was a reporter for the *Salinas Californian* in 1979. He covered the strike in both its Imperial Valley and Salinas periods. He kept extensive interview notes, which he filed in weekly folders, arranged chronologically. He generously gave those files to me.

18. Paul Fleming, interviewed by Doug Foster, July 16, 1979, Folder 54, Foster Files.

19. "Salad Fans Needn't Worry—Yet," *Los Angeles Times*, January 26, 1979; "UFW 'Empties' 16 Labor Buses," *Imperial Valley News*, February 22, 1979; "Union Ignores Court Order," *Sacramento Union*, January 26, 1979.

20. M. Bustamante interview.

21. "Chavez Threatens Renewal of Lettuce Boycott," *Salinas Californian*, January 29, 1979.

22. Growers Ask Volunteers to Pick Lettuce," *Los Angeles Times*, January 31, 1979; "Volunteers Enter Fields to Pick Lettuce," *Los Angeles Times*, February 1, 1979; "Court Acts to Cool Off Farm Strike," *Salinas Californian*, January 31, 1979; "Labor Violence Leaves 20 Hurt," *Imperial Valley Press*, January 30, 1979; Mojica interview; M. Bustamante interview.

23. "Lettuce Strike Growing Bitter." *Los Angeles Times*, February 4, 1979.

24. "Court tries untangling union feud" *Imperial Valley Press*, January 30, 1979.

25. Ibid.

26. "Uneasy Truce Reached in Lettuce Fields," *Nevada State Journal*, February 2, 1979: "Sheriff Puts Staff on Alert As Lettuce Strike Spreads," *San Francisco Chronicle*, February 1, 1979.

27. "Chavez Seeks 'City Support' for Ag Strike," *Salinas Californian*, February 2, 1979; "Bitter Strike May Escalate as Chavez Taunts Growers on Boycott," *Los Angeles Times*, February 2, 1979.

28. "Lettuce Price Hikes Due to Hit Stores," Long Beach *Press- Telegram*, February 3, 1979.

29. Like the Huertas (see page 114), and the Valdézes (see page 201), the Saikhon family was an example of how California growers, a few farm workers, and some independent entrepreneurs profited from the opportunities created by the internment of Japanese Americans during World War II. See Christina Morales Guzman, Ph.D. thesis in process, University of California at Santa Cruz.

30. For more on the Saikhon family, see Jayasri Majumdar Hart, director, *Roots in the Sand*, documentary film, www.pbs.org/rootsinthesand, "Saikhon Family" link.

31. Mario Saikhon, notes from interview by Doug Foster, February 3, 1979, Folder 10, Foster Files.

32. "Farm Strike Tension Escalates in Imperial," *Salinas Californian*, February 9, 1979.

33. Mario Saikhon, notes from interview by Doug Foster, February 12,1979 Folder 12, Foster Files.

34. I have reconstructed the murder of Rufino Contreras from the reports in the *Los Angeles Times*, the *Salinas Californian*, and the *Imperial Valley Press* from February 10 to February 14; "Doubt Raised by Transcript of Dismissed Case," *Washington Post*, September 16, 1979; Mario and Chava Bustamante, author's interviews, May 29, 2006 and May 3, 2006, respectively, and Hermilo Mojica, author's interviews, October 3, 1994.

35. Bruce Neuburger, "A Decade of Hard Labor: An Activist in the Lettuce Fields of the 1970s," unpublished ms. (in author's collection, courtesy of Bruce Neuburger).

36. Chava Bustamante, author's interview, May 3, 2006.

37. "Doubts Raised by Transcript of Dismissed Case." *Washington Post*, September 16, 1979.

38. Mario Saikhon, notes from interview by Doug Foster, February 12, 1979, Folder 12, Foster Files.

39. "Farm Labor Foreman Out on $7,000 Bail," *Imperial Valley Press*, February 12, 1979; "Fox Denies he Called for Meeting," *Imperial Valley Press*, February 13, 1979; "Eight Shippers Pool Efforts to Offset UFW," *The Packer*, March 4, 1979.

40. Mario Bustamante, author's interview, March 14, 1995.

41. 'Doubts Raised by Transcript of Dismissed Case."

42. "Striker's Killing Brings Mourning, Picket Halt," *Imperial Valley Press*, February 12, 1979.

43. Ibid.

44. "Imperial Valley Vegetable Harvest Virtually Halted," *Los Angeles Times*, February 13, 1979.

45. "Non-strikers in Fields After Lull," *Imperial Valley Press*, February 13, 1979.

46. "Lettuce Fields Quiet in Wake of Violence," *San Jose Mercury*, February 12, 1979.

47. "Gov. Brown Joins 5,000 in Mourning Farm worker," *Salinas Californian*, February 14, 1979.

48. Steve Capps, "Lettuce," UPI, February 15, 1979.

49. "Produce Strife Moves into New Arenas," *Salinas Californian*, February 20, 1979.

50. Mack Lyons, victim of gambling and alcohol addictions, had been caught taking money from CPD funds. He agreed to return it, and quietly resigned from the union in 1978.

51. Mario Bustamante, author's interview, May 29, 2006.

52. Ibid.

53. David Martinez, interviewed by Davy Figaro, Palo Alto California, March 3, 1994, Jacques E. Levy Research Collection on Cesar Chavez, Post Morten Research (hereafter PMR) Box 33, Folder 694, Levy/Yale; Jessica Govea, author's interview, December 6, 2002; Gilbert Padilla, author's interview, April 11, 2006. Martinez refused my request for an interview.

54. Mario Bustamante, author's interview, May 29, 2006.

55. Ibid.

56. Ganz interview and personal communication (email), July 5, 2006.

57. Ganz interview p. 133.

58. M. Bustamante, May 29, 2006, interview.

59. "The series of clashes": "Ag Violence Stirs Memories of Viet," *Imperial Valley Press*, February 22, 1979. My reconstruction of the events of February 21, 1979, is based on reports in the *Imperial Valley Press* of February 21, 22, and 23, and M. Bustamante, May 29, 2006, interview.

60. "UFW Organizes 'International Banana Boycott," *Salinas Californian*, February 28, 1979.

61. "UFW Boycott Aims to Squeeze Grower," *Salinas Californian*, March 22, 1979.

62. Colin A. Carter et al., "Labor Strikes and the Price of Lettuce," *Western Journal of Agricultural Economics* 6, no. 1 (July 1981).

63. National Executive Board meeting, March 11, 1979, audiotape, UFWOP, part 2, Box AV, Wayne State. The rest of the chapter draws on this tape.

Chapter 29

1. Watsonville broccoli harvesters inadvertently brought the J. J. Crosetti company into the strike. Originally there had been no plan to strike Crosetti, either in Imperial or Salinas. But a UFW official mistakenly told the Crosetti ranch committee that the company was on strike in the Imperial Valley, and the Crosetti broccoli crew walked out in solidarity. When the Crosetti workers in Imperial heard the news, they also walked out, in solidarity with Watsonville. But J. J. Crosetti couldn't see the humor in it. Despite being a major power in the city of Watsonville, he did not have the deep pockets of United Brands/Sun Harvest. Once out, the Crosetti workers never went back to work. Before the strike was over, Crosetti had gone out of business. (Jose Renteria, author's interview, Salinas, May 30, 1995).

2. "Farm Strike Is Good for Fence Business," *Salinas Californian*, April 10, 1979.

3. "Farm Guards Add Guns to Strike Duty," *Contra Costa Times*, April 13, 1979; "Guards: They Play a Strike Role," *Salinas Californian*, May 30, 1979; "Pulled Pistol Triggers Concern," *Salinas Californian*, March 20, 1979.

4. "Violent Incident in Salinas," Watsonville *Register-Pajaronian*, April 7, 1979.

5. "Strike Projection, July 18, 1979," UFW Office of the President: Cesar Chavez Records (hereafter WFWOP), part 2, Box 23, Folder 1, Wayne State.

6. Chava Bustamante, author's interview, May 3, 2006; Hermilo Mojica, author's interview, El Centro, May 30, 2006. Frank Ortiz refused my requests for an interview.

7. "Farm Union's Goals Survive Internal Strike," *Los Angeles Times*, March 19, 1979.

8. Cesar Chavez, "Farm Workers and Violence," letter to the editor, *Los Angeles Times*, March 28, 1979.

9. Chava Bustamante, author's interview, San Jose, May 18, 2006.

10. Aristeo Zambrano, author's interview, Oakland, July 11, 2005.

11. Mario Bustamante, author's interview, May 29, 2006.

12. "Strike Tune-up Hits Fields of Harden, Green Valley," *Salinas Californian*, May 24, 1979.

13. Marshall Ganz, notes from interview by Doug Foster, May 15 and May 24, 1979, Folders 37 and 39, Foster Files. See Chapter 28, endnote #17.

14. M. Bustamante interview; Jessica Govea, author's interview, December 6, 2002.

15. "News from the UFW, April 18, 1979," Folder 30, Foster Files; "Chavez 'Locates' the Strikebreakers," *San Francisco Examiner*, April 19, 1979.

16. "Carter Allowing 'Illegals' to Block Strike—Chavez," *The Packer*, April 21, 1979.

17. "Senator Opens Hearing with Angry Blast," *Salinas Californian*, April 26, 1979.

18. "Williams Says U.S. Ag Labor Law Needed," *Salinas Californian*, April 28, 1979.

19. "Walkout and Patrol Raid Cut into Harvesting Force," *Salinas Californian*, May 1, 1979; "Border Patrol Raiders Applauded by Pickets," *Salinas Californian*, May 2, 1979.

20. C. Bustamante May 3, 2006, interview,; "Senator Opens Hearing with Angry Blast," *Salinas Californian*, April 26, 1979.

21. M. Bustamante interview.

22. "Growers Rebuff UFW Offer," *Salinas Californian*, May, 17, 1979.

23. "Contract Offer Rebuff Angers UFW," *Salinas Californian*, May 18, 1979; "Farm Strike in Week 17; Both Sides Refuse to Budge," Watsonville *Register-Pajaronian*, May 18, 1979.

24. *The Packer*, May 19, 1979; "Is Agriculture Strike Pooping Out in Salinas?," *Imperial Valley Press*, May 24, 1979.

25. "Rosy Report on Accord Discounted by Chavez," *Salinas Californian*, June 7, 1979.

26. "Blackout Imposed on Ag Strike Talks," *Salinas Californian*, June 5, 1979.

27. C. Bustamante May 3, 1979, interview and author's interview, San Jose, May 18, 1979. When I called Frank Ortiz for his account of these events, he declined to talk to me. Gilbert Rodriguez also turned down my request for an interview. Despite an extensive search, I could not find Lupe Bautista.

28. "UFW Weighing New Offer," Watsonville *Register-Pajaronian*, June 7, 1979.

29. Aristeo Zambrano, author's interview, Oakland, July 11, 2005.

30. "All Hell Breaks Loose in Farm Strike," *Salinas Californian*, June 11, 1979.

31. "Where's UFW Leadership?" *Salinas Californian*, June 12, 1979.

32. "The Lettuce Strike's 'Day of Rage'," Watsonville *Register- Pajaronian*, June 12, 1979; "All Hell Breaks Loose in Farm Strike."

33. "Strikers Hit Non-union Operations," *Salinas Californian*, June 13, 1979.

34. "Cesar Chavez Notes on Negotiating Meeting, 6/18/79," UFWOP, part 2, Box 23, Folder 7, Wayne State.

35. Marshall Ganz, author's interview, April 12, 1996.

36. "Transport Talk: Shutdown in '74 Revisited" and "Effectiveness of Shutdown Varies," *The Packer*, June 30, 1979; "Lettuce Moves Despite Hexes " and "Valley Escapes Massive Losses from Truck Strike," *Salinas Californian*, June 26 and June 28, 1979.

37. Ganz interview.

38. C. Bustamante May 18, 2006, interview.

39. Marshall Ganz, personal communication (email), August 2, 2006.

40. Jerry Cohen, telephone interview, August 10, 2006.

41. "Chavez Plans March to Open Intensified Strike in August," *Salinas Californian*, July 23, 1979.

42. "Cesar Calls for Two-Front March on Salinas Valley," *Salinas Californian*, July 25, 1979.

43. "100 Join in Chavez March," *Salinas Californian*, August 1, 1979.

44. "Antle Agrees to Pay $5 an Hour, Workers Say," *Salinas Californian*, August 4, 1979.

45. M. Bustamante May 29, 2006, interview.

46. "Teamster Strike Looms on Agricultural Horizon," July 26, 1979, *Salinas Californian*.

47. Cesar Chavez, notes of interview by Doug Foster, August 6, 1979, Folder 60, Foster Files.

48. Details of the two marches come from articles in the *Salinas Californian*, Watsonville *Register-Pajaronian*, *San Francisco Examiner*, and *Monterey Herald* between July 31 and August 14, 1979.

49. "Special National Executive Board Meeting, August 11, 1979," audiotape, UFWOP, part 2, Box AV, Wayne State. (translation by author and Aristeo Zambrano).

50. Members of the Executive Board generally assumed that the union could borrow money to carry on a strike, as it had done in 1970. In 1973 the union received a large strike subsidy from the AFL-CIO. In March 1978, Chavez had told the board, "Some unions are saying we can borrow money [for a strike fund] from them at zero percent interest." See National Executive Board Meeting, March 24, 1978, audiotape 2, UFWOP, part 2, Box AV, Wayne State.

51. I have edited out a few inconsequential interruptions, and some of the repetitious phrases from this opening statement.

52. Gilbert Padilla, author's interview, December 20, 1997; Mario Bustamante, author's interview, March 19, 1995.

53. "Amendment to Resolution 10, Submitted by Mario Bustamante, August 12, 1979," Folder "Take Out," Foster Files.

54. Padilla interview.

55. Jerry Cohen, telephone interview, August 8, 2006.

56. Marian Steeg, telephone interview, April 4, 2006.

57. M. Bustamante March 19, 1995, interview; Ganz interview.

58. "New Talks Hold Off 'General Strike,'" *Salinas Californian*, August 16, 1979.

59. "Strikers Rally, Await Chavez Call," *The Packer*, August 18, 1979.

60. "UFW Wins a Lettuce Pact," *San Francisco Chronicle*, August 27, 1979

61. "West Coast Farms Signs Pact with UFW," Watsonville *Register-Pajaronian*, August 27, 1979.

62. Jerry Cohen, telephone interview, August 10, 2006.

63. "UFW Wrests First Pact in Long Lettuce Strike," *Salinas Californian*, August 27, 1979.

64. "Non-union Crews—'Me Too,'" *Salinas Californian*, August 28, 1979.

65. "No dejés que te vendan gato por liebre" ("Don't let them sell you cat meat for rabbit") UFW leaflet, Folder "Take Out," Foster Files.

66. "UFW Strikes 8 More Growers," *Salinas Californian*, September 5, 1979,

67. Ibid.

68. Cohen interview.

69. Gilbert Padilla, author's interview, Monterey, California, April 11, 2006.

Chapter 30

1. Pete Velasco's notes of NEB meeting, August 20, 1979, UFW Vice President's Files, Pete Velasco Records (hereafer VP Velasco), Box 2, Folder "NEB, 1979," Wayne State; Jose Renteria, author's interview, May 30, 1995.

2. "To Cesar, From Marshall, 9/26/79," Office of the President: Cesar Chavez Records (UFWOP), part 2, Box 23, Folder 1, Wayne State.

3. Aristeo Zambrano, telephone interview, December 8, 2006.

4. "Paid Rep Plans," (UFWOP), part 2, Box 23, Folder 1, Wayne State; Marshal Ganz, "1978–81," Zambrano interview; Hermilo Mojica telephone interview.

5. Gilbert Padilla, interview, December 20, 1997.

6. "A: Presidentes, DE; Marshall Ganz, 29 de diciembre de 1979," UFW Central Administration Records (hereafter UFWCAR), Box 22, Folder "SunHarvest Marshall," Wayne State.

7. Berta Batres, author's interview, Salinas, March 24, 2007.

8. "Expiration of Sun Harvest Land Leases," UFW Officie of the President Cesar Chavez Unprocessed (hereafter UFWOP Un), Box 73, Folder "SH Research," Wayne State; "Imperial Valley Feeling Wage Impact," *Salinas Californian*, December 6, 1979.

9. "Imperial Growers Win Key Ruling on Pay Rates," *Salinas Californian*, December 21, 1979.

10. "1,500 Join in UFW Site Inauguration," *Imperial Valley Press*, November 19, 1979.

11. Ibid.

12. "Ag Strikers Denied Work Return," *Imperial Valley Press*, December 7, 1979.

13. "Chavez Joins 1,200 for Contreras Memorial," *Imperial Valley Press*, February 11, 1980.

14. "Criticism of Chavez Takes Root in Farm Labor Struggle," *New York Times*, February 7, 1979; Tom Barry, "Manuel Chavez Story," unpublished manuscript, October 31, 1978, (in author's collection, courtesy of Doug Foster). Manuel's misuse of union funds was an open secret among many union staffers. In just one example, in 1976,

Eliseo Medina discovered fifty-five unaccounted for checks in a series of checks written to finance the 1974 lemon strike, and later found one on which Cesar's signature appeared to have been forged by Manuel. He showed them to Cesar, who acknowledged that "the way my name was forged does resemble the way Manuel writes his last name." Cesar later told Medina that Manuel denied having anything to do with the missing checks, and that was the end of the matter. See UFWOP, Box 27, Folder 17; Eliseo Medina, author's interview, May 20, 2005, pp. 17–18.

15. Jack Anderson, "Chavez: From Savior to Tyrant," Ventura County *Star Free Press*, March 11, 1980.

16. "Farm Workers' Chicago Office Keeps the Faith," *Wall Street Journal*, July 27, 1981.

17. "Chavez Offers Olive Branch with a Warning," *Salinas Californian*, February 6, 1980.

18. *Bay Guardian*, June 25, 1985.

19. For an entertaining account of the way the system worked, see James Mills, *A Disorderly House: The Brown-Unruh Years in Sacramento* (Berkeley: Heyday Books, 1987).

20. The longstanding alliance between liberal Los Angeles Jews and black Democrats had recently been damaged by Berman's and Henry Waxman's support for Bakke in *Regents of the University of California* v. *Bakke*, which challenged the use of affirmative action in admissions decisions at the UC Davis Law School.

21. I have reconstructed this Sacramento spat from articles in the *Sacramento Bee*, the *Salinas Californian*, and the *Los Angeles Times* between December 1979 and February 1980. Especially valuable was the reporting of Eric Brazil for the Gannett News Service.

22. Marshall Ganz, "UFW (1978–81)," unpublished manuscript, n.d.; Mojica telephone interview.

23. "Ex-political Assistants Join Brown's staff," *Los Angeles Times*, April 19, 1980.

24. "Ganz Isn't Leaving, UFW Says," *Salinas Californian*, April 21, 1980.

25. UFW butcher paper chronology, courtesy of Tom Dalzell; Jessica Govea, interview, December 6, 2002; Marshall Ganz, "Re: Next Question," (e-mail) December 30, 2006.

26. "Community Meeting 4/4/77," mistitled tape is actually National Executive Board meeting, mid-September, 1978, audiotape, UFWOP, part 2, Box AV, Wayne State.

27. "Minutes of the Board of Trustees of RFK," 7, VP Velasco, Box 7, Folder 84; "RFK Farm Workers Medical Plan, October 31, 1979," UFWOP, part 2, Box 41, Folder "RFK '79 Board"; Bobby De La Cruz letter, July 22, 1978, UFWOP, part 2, Box 41, Folder "RFK Medical"; "Minutes of NEB, September 15 and 18, 1978," VP Velasco, Box 4, Folder 32; "RFK Report to UFW NEB, 13/16/78" VP Velasco, Box 4, Folder 32; all at Wayne State.

28. "El Problema de Infiltración," Cesar Chavez's remarks on August 26, 1978, transcript (in author's collection, courtesy of Aristeo Zambrano); Aristeo Zambrano, author's interview, August 23, 1994.

29. Hermilo Mojica, author's interview, October 3, 1994.

30. Mario Bustamante, author's interview, May 29, 2006.

31. Hermilo Mojica, author's interview, May 30, 2006.

32. M. Bustamante interview.

33. Aristeo Zambrano, author's interview, March 13, 2006.

34. Jerry Cohen, telephone interview, May 4, 2000

35. A custom harvester is an employer who does not own or lease land, but hires workers, owns harvesting equipment, and makes some independent managerial decisions about the harvest. Unlike a contractor, who just hires workers, the custom harvester is considered an employer by the ALRB.

36. "ALRB Accuses Firm of Trying to Knock UFW," *Salinas Californian*, October 14, 1981.

37. Bill Ramsey (owner of Mann Packing), author's interview, Salinas, September 17, 2006.

38. Ibid; Aristeo Zambrano, author's interview, July 11, 2005.

39. "Garlic Workers' Wildcat Walkout Spreads Rapidly," *San Francisco Examiner*, July 30, 1980; "Real Garlic Capital is Valley," *Salinas Californian*, August 2, 1980; Aristeo Zambrano, author's interview, January 6, 2007.

40. "UFW Claims One Victory in Garlic Organizing," *Salinas Californian*, July 28, 1980; "Garlic Strike Simmers," Hollister *Free Lance*, July 29, 1980; "New UFW Office in Hollister Opens with Fiesta, Services," *Salinas Californian*, August 30, 1980.

41. "Garlic Strike Settled," *Salinas Californian*, August 9, 1980.

42. Miriam Pawel, "Decisions of Long Ago Shape the Union Today," *Los Angeles Times*, January 10, 2006.

43. Aristeo Zambrano, telephone interview, January 8, 2007.

44. Letter from Doug Adair to David Burciaga, May 11, 1980 (courtesy Doug Adair); "Junta Hoy," leaflet calling workers to a meeting about the contract (courtesy of Doug Adair); Doug Adair, author's interview, Coachella, April 9, 2005.

45. Gilbert Padilla, author's interview, December 20, 1997. Chavez didn't pull the nicknames out of a hat. Rudy Reyes had been affectionately called "the huk" (a reference to the Philippine guerrilla group) since the early days of the grape strike, when he was one of the union's most creative vandals. Doug Adair remembers that both Freedman's Lionel Steinberg and Chavez jokingly referred to Shoibi as "the PLO," even though he was a Yemenite. As for Adair's being a Communist, that was a new charge and pure fantasy. But he was an original *malcriado* and did not hide his views on the union or anything else.

46. "Wildcat UFW Strikers Return," *Indio Daily News*, June 19, 1980.

47. Doug Adair, author's interview, April 9, 2005; Gilbert Padilla interview.

48. Padilla interview.

49. "UFW Workers Ratify Contract," *Indio Daily News*, July 15, 1980.

50. Padilla interview.

51. Notes of the NEB Special Session, October 8, 1980, VP Velasco, Box 2, Folder "NEB 1980, Wayne State; Gilbert Padilla, telephone interview, January 11, 2007.

52. Padilla December 20, 1997 interview.

53. Gilbert Padilla, telephone interview, November 13, 2006.

54. Archival evidence supports Cohen's memory about his conversation with Chavez.

According to La Paz notes of the telephone call, Cesar Chavez and Cohen argued about some changes in the hiring hall that Chavez had earlier agreed to, and now was opposing. But it is hard to determine whether Cesar's opposition was meant to sabotage the negotiations. Maybe not: La Paz was still working hard to get contracts at all the companies that had been involved in the 1979 strike. Five months after Cohen's resignation, the union signed a contract with Cal Coastal, a mid-sized Salinas lettuce company, right in the heart of Ganz's (and the paid rep's) turf. Eventually the UFW did sign a Sam Andrews contract, though by that time both Ganz and the paid reps had no turf—they were out of the union. See "Steno Book Notes," September 5, 1980 to November 13, 1980," UFWOP, Box 11, Folder "Paid Reps," Wayne State.

55. Jerome Cohen, "UGW Must Get Back to Organizing," *Los Angeles Times*, Op-ed, January 15, 1986.

56. "Labor Conflict Moves Indoors," *Western Grower and Shipper*, May, 1981.

57. Report to the 1981 Convention, UFWOP, part 2, Box 9, Folder 9, Wayne State; "Growers, UFW Unhappy with Farm Labor Board," *Delano Record*, September 2, 1982.

58. "Farm workers Stage Demonstration at ALRB," *Salinas Californian*, December 17, 1981.

59. Jerry Cohen, telephone interview, February 5, 2007.

60. Sister Florence, whose financial acumen had so impressed Chavez, became another committed anti-Communist in the top echelon of the union. In 1980 she told an interviewer, "If they [Communists] can get into taking this [the UFW] over, it could be a tremendous boost for them in our country . . . so that is one of the things we watch. It has happened twice since I've been here." See UFWOP, Box 33, Folder "Zweber," Wayne State.

61. Tape of Planning Meeting, December 8, 1980, Wayne State.

62. This and all quotes are from "M's Report, 10/7/80," unpublished manuscript known as "The Marshall Plan" (in author's collection, courtesy of Marshall Ganz).

63. Dalzell's butcher paper chronology; Mario Bustamante, telephone interview, April 2, 2009.

Chapter 31

1. "UFW Big Gainer in 1980 Election," *Salinas Californian*, November 8, 1980.

2. "Chavez Attacks Switch on Speaker," *Los Angeles Times*, November 29, 1980.

3. "Brown Elected Assembly Speaker over Berman with Republican Help," *San Diego Union*, December 2, 1980.

4. "For Chicanos, a Political Bloodletting," *Los Angeles Times*, December 11, 1980. Latinos represented less than 20 percent of the California population in 1980 and only 9 percent of the electorate, not enough horse to ride to serious statewide power. The great jump in Latino voter registration didn't come until 1994, in reaction to the anti-immigrant Proposition 187.

5. "State Candidates Got $8.5 million for Race," *San Francisco Examiner*, November 10, 1982.

6. "Lettuce Prices Zoom to 99 Cents a Head," *Salinas Californian*, January 5, 1982.

7. "No Letup in Lettuce Strike," *Orange County Labor News*, January 1981.

8. "UFW Strike Swaps Fields for Hearing Rooms," *Salinas Californian*, January 24, 1981.

9. Mario Bustamante, author's interview, March 14, 1985.

10. Ibid.

11. Ibid; Mario Bustamante, telephone interview, November 26, 2006; In an affidavit on May 17, 1982, Bustamante gave a slightly different version of this incident, placing Lupe Bautista, Jesus Silva, and "two other men" at the fight. On several occasions since, the last time on March 1, 2011, Bustamante told me that Oscar Mondragon and Gilbert Rodrgiguez were also there.

12. M. Bustamante, March 14, 1985, interview.

13. Dolores Huerta recounted the story to a reporter from the *LA Times* in 2005. On May 5, 2009, I requested an interview with David Arizmendi. He refused, but confirmed the general outline of the story. He said that he had explained the whole thing to the reporter from the *Los Angeles Times* and since she didn't use any of it, he did not want to waste his time explaining it again. Dolores Huerta refused to be interviewed by me on this topic or anything else. Miriam Pawel of the *Los Angeles Times* was kind enough to share with me the notes of her interviews with both. Marshall Ganz also confirmed that this is the story as he eventually heard it.

14. Jerry Cohen, notes from an interview by Doug Foster, June 29, 1979, Folder 48, Foster Files. On the Foster Files see endnote #17, Chapter 28, p. 792.

15. Tom Dalzell, author's interview, September 6, 2006.

16. Ann Marie Smith declined to be interviewed (she is reputed to have a photographic memory).

17. Jerry Cohen, telephone interview, December 28, 2006.

18. "Serious Meeting/Junta Grave, June 6, 1981," UFW Collection Unprocessed: North Hospital Unit (hereafter UFWNHU), Box 40, Folder "Dissidents," Wayne State.

19. Mario Bustamante, author's interview, April 30, 2005.

20. Ibid.

21. M. Bustamante, March 14, 1995, interview; Juan Flores, author's interview, Mexicali, Baja California, November 3, 2007.

22. Cleofas Guzman, author's interview, Los Angeles, January 24, 2009.

23. "To Cesar, From Marshall and Jessica, Re Cleofas Guzman, January 31, 1981," UFWNHU, Box 2, Folder "Cleofas Guzman," Wayne State.

24. Ibid.

25. "Memorandum to Oscar Mondragon and David Martinez, Apendice F, from Juan Guicho, April 5,1981, UFWHNU, Box 40, Folder "Administrative Letter," Wayne State.

26. Maria Aguilar, author's interview, Los Angeles, January 24, 2009.

27. Ganz-Govea report.

28. Marshall Ganz, "UFW (1978–81)," unpublished manuscript, n.d.

29. Jessica Govea, telephone interview, December 6, 2002, p. 23.

30. Cesar Chavez, "Carta Administrativa, 3 de Abril, 1981" (author's translation), UFWNHU., Box 40, Folder "Administrative Letter," Wayne State.

31. Ibid.

32. Govea, interview, p. 23.

33. Marshall Ganz, interviewed by Jacques Levy, Jacques E. Levy Research Collection on Cesar Chavez Post Mortem Research (hereafter PMR), Box 32, Folder 685, 203, Levy/Yale.

34. Ganz and Govea separated after they left the union, their personal relationship shattered along with their political partnership.

35. Govea, interview, p. 24.

36. "To Cesar Chavez, from Jose Rubio, Feb. 6, 1981," UFWHNU, Box 40, Folder "Teamsters," Wayne State.

37. To Cesar Chavez, Kent Winterrowd from Roberto De La Cruz, 2-20-81," UFWHNU. Box 40, Folder "RFK Problems," Wayne State.

38. On August 22, the National Executive Board sat to hear charges by Mario Bustamante and Aristeo Zambrano that Oscar Mondragon had slandered them. The transcript of that trial includes sworn statements by Bustamante, Zambrano, Mojica, Renteria, Mondragon and others, including an account of this May 23, 1981, meeting. The charges were dismissed. See "Mondragon Trial," UFW Office of the President: Cesar Chavez Records (hereafter UFWOP) part 2, Box 54, unlabeled folder, Wayne State.

39. Ibid; Hermilo Mojica, author's interview, October 24, 1994.

40. Jose Renteria, author's interview, May 30, 1995.

41. M. Bustamante, March 14, 1995, interview.

42. "Simmering Ag Dispute Put on Front Burner," *Salinas Californian*, June 13, 1981.

43. Bustamante's account was confirmed by Aristeo Zambrano and Berta Batres. David Martinez refused my request for an interview.

44. Renteria, interview.

45. This and the following quotes are from Cesar's notes. "Serious Meeting/*Junta Grave*," June 6, 1981, UFWHNU, Box 40, Folder "Dissidents," Wayne State.

46. Ganz, Levy interview.

47. John Brown, telephone interview, February 12, 2007.

48. "Garlic Acreage Drops, Gilroy Fete Planned," *The Packer*, May 23, 1981.

49. John Brown, telephone interview, February 12, 2007.

50. The Hollister *Free Lance* covered the strike closely from July 9 to mid-August, 1981. There were also several articles in the *Salinas Californian* and the Watsonville *Register-Patagonian*. A photo of proud Tina standing in front of her disced field was in several papers, including the *Salinas Californian*, July 24, 1981.

51. "Chavez, Son and 8 Others Jailed," *San Jose Mercury News*, August 7, 1981; "Cesar Chavez Agrees to Be Let Out of Jail," *San Francisco Chronicle*, August 8, 1981; "Chavez Arrested Again," *Salinas Californian*, August 11, 1981; "ALRB Ruling Gives Strikers Access to Growers' Fields," *Fresno Bee*, August 12, 1981.

52. John Brown, a UFW staffer, remembers Chavez and Mojica going off for their meeting, but he was not privy to their conversation. This account is Mojica's.

53. Mojica, interview.

54. Arbitration Proceedings, Oshita vs. UFW, July 1, 1982, UFWHNU, Box 73, Folder "SH Kessler Case"; "Dressler to Chavez, November 4, 1981," UFWNHU, Box 2, Folder "Growers Exchange Closure," Wayne State; "Chualar Grower Faces UFW Cutback Charge," *Gonzales Tribune*, September 23, 1981; Bill Ramsey, author's interview, September 17, 2006; Berta Batres, author's interview, Salinas, November 28, 2006.

55. ALRB Hearing, January 22, 1982 and Joint Ventures Arbitration Award, August 22, 1984, both in UFWNHU, Box 73, Folder "Sun Harvest Correspondence," Wayne State.

56. "Porque Queremos Cambios en la Mesa Directiva" ("Why we want changes on the Executive Board"),leaflet, UFWOP, part 2, Box 54, unlabeled folder, Wayne State.

57. "Inform people so they can act," UFWOP, part 2, Box 54, unlabeled folder, Wayne State.

58. Huerta is quoted in "Decision of the National Executive Board, February 2, 1982," VP Velasco, Box 2, Folder "NEB Jan. 1982," Wayne State.

59. Hermilo Mojica, notarized statement on February 4, 2009 (in author's collection, courtesy of Hermilo Mojica).

60. "Chavez Faces Internal and External Struggles," *New York Times*, December 6, 1981.

61. Letter from Ortiz to Chavez, September 11, 1981, UFWOP, part 2, Box 54, Wayne State.

62. Ibid.

63. "Inform People So They Can Act."

64. Mondragon Trial.

65. "UFW Political Fund Draws Legal Fire from Workers," *Salinas Californian*, June 15, 1981.

66. "Phone Conversation with Sabino Lopez, August 25, 1981," UFWOP, part 2, Box 54, unlabeled folder, Wayne State.

67. These figures come from official UFW documents, not from newspaper reports, which exaggerated the number of delegates. See "Delegate Body Voting Order," UFWOP, part 2, Box 9, Folder 9-10; "UFW Staff List, 7/13/81," UFWOP, part 2, Box 9, Folder "UFW Con. Conv. 1981," Wayne State.

68. "NEB Resolution, August 29, 1981," UFWOP, part 2, Box 7, Folder "Jose Renteria," Wayne State.

69. David Martinez, interviewed by Davy Figaro, March 3, 1994, Yale.

70. "Opposition to Leadership of Chavez Arises," *Los Angeles Times*, September 6, 1981.

71. Renteria, interview; M. Bustamante, March 14, 1995, interview; Aristeo Zambrano, author's interview, July 11, 2005; Batres, interview.

72. "Opposition to Leadership of Chavez Arises," *Los Angeles Times*, September 6, 1981.

73. "Dissidents Upset UFW Convention Unity," *Fresno Bee*, September 6, 1981.

74. "Chavez Attacks," *Fresno Bee*, September 7, 1981.

75. Berta Batres, author's interview, September 17, 1994; "UFW Fires Six Salinas Valley Reps," *Salinas Californian*, October 2, 1981.

76. Bustamante Dismissal, UFWNHU, Box 40, Folder "Dismissal" Wayne State; M. Bustamante, March 14, 1995, interview.

77. Dismissal letters, UFWNHU, Box 40, Folder 'Dismissal"; Batres, November 28, 2006, interview.

78. The other issue concerned the paid reps' charge that Mondragon, Martinez, and Ortiz had used union funds in their re-election campaigns for UFW Executive Board. In response to that charge, Cesar Chavez sued the paid reps for libel and slander, seeking $25 million in damages. That case had nothing to do with Judge Ingram's ruling that the reps had been elected, not appointed. But seven years after Ingram's decision, when the reps backed out of the second phase of the Ingram case, they also signed a declaration saying they had been wrong about the election funds. "We had no lawyer and no money," Zambrano said, "and the fight was over." They had to sign the declaration in order to have the slander suit dropped. For an account of the re-election funds debate, see Miriam Pawell, *The Union of Their Dreams*, p314.

79. Mojica, October 24, 1994, interview.

80. Batres, November 28, 2006, interview.

81. Hermilo Mojica, telephone interview, February 16, 2007.

Chapter 32

1. UFW and Sun Harvest, Arbitration Award, August 22, 1984, UFW Collection Unprocessed: North Hospital Unit (hereafter UFWNHU) Box 73, Folder "Sun Harvest Correspondence," Wayne State. There was also a successor clause in the standard UFW contract, but it only covered a situation where the company was sold intact to a new outfit. That didn't happen at Sun Harvest or at any of the other union companies that went out of business.

2. For the UFW's estimate of fifty company shutdowns, see California Institute for Rural Studies, Working Group on Farm Labor and Rural Poverty, "Farm Restructuring and Employment in California Agriculture," Working Paper No. 1 (Davis: February 1989), p. 26. The union continued to claim publicly that it had as many as 40,000 members in the late 1980s. I got the number 8,681 by going through internal UFW records of company-by-company membership lists. Philip L. Martin, a respected UC Davis agribusiness economist, puts union membership at a low of 6,000 as early as 1985. See "Dues Income," UFW Collection Unprocessed Files: National Executive Board (hereafter UFWNEB) Folder "Crops;" "UFW Crop Operations, 1982-1983," UFWNHU, Box 12, Folder "Company Stats and Members;" "List of Ranches" UFWNHU, Box 40, Folder "RFK Misc." all at Wayne State. Philip L. Martin, *Promise Unfulfilled: Unions, Immigration, and the Farm Workers* (Ithaca: Cornell University Press, 2003), p. 76.

3. Warren E. Johnston and Alex F. McCalla, "Whither California Agriculture: Up, Down, or Out," Giannini Foundation Special Report 04-1, Giannini Foundation of Agricultural Economics, University of California, 2004; Juan-Vicente Palerm, "Farm Labor Needs and Farm Workers in California, 1970–1989," report prepared for the California State Employment Development Department, 1991.

4. "Lean Days for Salinas Valley Laborers," *San Francisco Examiner*, June 30, 1991.

5. My description of the current state of the industry depends to a large extent on a series of interviews with Mike Dobler, one of the owners of Dobler and Sons, a Pajaro Valley–based produce company. Those interviews were in Moss Landing, California on January 31, 1995, March 20, 1997, and December 4, 2006. I also interviewed him on the telephone on December 20, 2005, and January 12 and June 14, 2006.

6. Richard Mines and Ricardo Anzaldúa, "New Migrants vs. Old Migrants: Alternative Labor Market Structures in the California Citrus Industry," Monograph in U.S.–Mexican Studies No. 9 (San Diego: University of California, San Diego, 1982), p. 108.

7. Ibid, pp. 69–70.

8. Richard Mines, author's interview, Watsonville, February 28, 2008.

9. Agricultural Labor Relations Board, "Annual Report to the Legislature," 1982–83, p. 9.

10. See the *Ventura County Star*, March to June, 1982, especially "Farm Workers Go on Strike in Oxnard," March 8, 1982; "Limoneira Workers Join Citrus Walkout," March 10, 1982; "200 Strikers Try to Block Route of Limoneira Bus," March 25, 1982; "Chavez Leads Protest March of Local Strikers, March 26, 1982; "Striker Wounded, Vandals Damage Citrus Orchards," April 22, 1982; "Citrus Strike Concession by UFW," June 3, 1982.

11. Arthur F. Corwin, *Immigrants and Immigrants:* Perspectives on Mexican Labor Migration to the United States (Westport, Conn.: Greenwood Press, 1978), pp.116–24

12. Diane Wagner, "Seeds of Change at the ALRB," *California Lawyer*, March 1987, p. 24.

13. "Church Leaders Want ALRB Official Fired," *San Francisco Chronicle*, October 22, 1985.

14. Theo J. Majka and Linda C. Majka, "Decline of the Farm Labor Movement in California: Organizational Crisis and Political Change," *Critical Sociology* 19, no. 3, 1992, p. 25.

15. Tony Castro, "The Chavez Cloud on Senator Torres' Political Horizon," *California Journal*, February 1983.

16. "Torres vs. Chavez—War of Independence," *Fresno Bee*, January 9, 1983; "Torres Ousts Incumbent Sen; Garcia; Hayden Wins Race for Assembly Seat," *Los Angeles Times*, June 9, 1982.

17. *San Jose Mercury*, January 24, 1982.

18. Agricultural Labor Relations Board, "Annual Report to the Legislature, 1981–82," p. 5.

19. U.S. Labor Department, LM-2 reports for 1983 and 1984.

20. Notes from NEB meeting, August 29, 1983, p. 3, UFW Vice President's Files Peter Velasco Records (hereafter VP Velasco), Box 2, Folder "NEB Aug 83–Dec 83," Wayne State.

21. U.S. Department of the Treasury, "Form 990 Return of Organization Exempt from Income Tax," for National Farm Workers Health Group, Martin Luther King Farm

Workers Fund, and National Farm Workers Service Center, Inc, 1986. (in author's collection, courtesy of Bruce Perry).

22. Matt Weiser, "A Union of Nonprofits," part two in a four-part series, *Bakersfield Californian*, May 10, 2004.

23. "UFW Returns to Boycott," *People's World*, September 10, 1983. A NEB resolution passed before the convention on November 13, 1982, authorized the use of the entire strike fund for the boycott. VP Velasco, Box 2, Folder "NEB January 1982," Wayne State.

24. "UFW Ends Its Fresno Convention on Upbeat Note," *Fresno Bee*, September 6, 1983; "UFW Returns to Boycott."

25. "'No-Grapes Tour' Returns Boycott and Chavez to Forefront," *Fresno Bee*, August 11, 1985.

26. U. S. Labor Department, LM-2, Union Annual Financial Reports, 1982, 1985, 1987.

27. "Strategic Planning Model, 5/23/85," UFWNHU, Box 18, Folder "Social Marketing Program," Wayne State; "To Group Executives and Division Heads from Cesar E. Chavez," UFWNHU, Box 18, Folder "Public Relations Budget," Wayne State; "To Cost Centers in California," UFWNHU, Box 40, Folder "EDD."

28. "Chavez Hopes to Rekindle the Spirit," *Peninsula Herald* (Monterey), April 7, 1985.

29. "To Oscar Mondragon from Chris Schneider, August 6, 1985," pp. 7–8, UFWNHU, Box 14, Folder "Legal-Veg," Wayne State

30. "Settlements with 2 Growers Mark Policy Shift by UFW," *Los Angeles Times*, July 30, 1986.

31. "Abatti and UFW Agree to New Labor Contract," *California Farmer*, September 20, 1986.

32. Doug Adair, author's interview, Thermal, May 30, 2005, pp. 7–10; in 1987 list of contracts, the David Freedman Company is listed as "paying dues, no contract" (see UFWNEB, Folder "Crops," Wayne State).

33. "Teamsters' Farm Organizing Drive Suffers Vote Drought," *San Francisco Chronicle*, June 30, 1985.

34. "UFW Leading Tomato Strike; Magana [*sic*] Loses Leadership Role as Union Moves in," *Record* (Stockton), July 23, 1983; Don Villarejo, CIRS cofounder, personal communication (email), February 19, 2008; Don Villarejo, author's interview, Davis, February 15, 2008; Luis Magaña, author's interview, Stockton, February 5, 2008.

35. "Why Are Town's Kids Dying of Cancer?" *San Jose Mercury News*, January 5, 1908.

36. Steven Johnson, Gerald Haslam, and Robert Dawson, *The Great Central Valley: California's Heartland* (Berkeley: University of California Press and California Academy of Sciences, 1993), p. 216.

37. Ibid, 14.

38. Notes on NEB meeting, May 3, 1984, VP Velasco, Box 2, NEB Folder, "Jan–May '84," Wayne State.

39. "Fast by Chavez over Pesticides Passes 29th Day," *New York Times*, August 16, 1988.

Sources

The documents, interviews, newspaper clips, papers, and notes that I used for this book will be available at the San Francisco State Labor Archives and the Watsonville Public Library.

Archives And Collections

Archives of Labor and Urban Affairs, Walter P. Reuther Library, Wayne State University, Detroit (Wayne State)

United Farm Workers Collection (UFW):

United Farm Workers Organizing Committee Records (UFWOC)

Office of the President: Cesar Chavez Records (UFWOP)

UFW Central Administration Records (UFWCAR)

UFW Information and Research Department Records Collection (I &R)

National Farm Workers Association Records (NFWA)

UFW Vice President's Files Peter Velasco Records (VP Velasco)

National Farm Worker Association Records (NFWA)

UFW Work Department Records (UFWWD)

UFW Collection Unprocessed Files: North Hospital Unit (UFWNHU)

UFW Collection Unprocessed Files: National Executive Board (UFWNEB)

Beinecke Rare Book and Manuscript Library, Yale Univesity, Jacques E. Levy Research Collection on Cesar Chavez (Levy/Yale)

Series IV Research Collection

Series VII Post Mortem Research (PMR)

United Farm Workers Oral History Project, California State University, Northridge (UFWOHP)

Farm worker Movement Documentation Project www.farm workermovement.org

Regional Oral History Project, Bancroft Library, University of California, Berkeley

Stanford Special Collections and University Archives, Fred Ross Collection, Stanford University

Don Watson Collection, Personal Files

Doug Foster Collection, Personal Files

Author's Interviews

I tape recorded and transcribed these interviews. Those originally in Spanish I translated into English, and note here with "Sp." I also conducted telephone interviews, most of which I transcribed. Here I list only the face to face interviews. All of them took place in California, unless otherwise cited.

Debbie Adair, Thermal, May 12, 1995, April 29, 2005, May 30, 2005.

Doug Adair, Thermal, May 11, 1995, May 29, 2005; Watsonville, April 8, 9, 10.

Maria Aguilar, Los Angeles, January 25, 2009, Sp.

Jose Alvarado, Watsonville, March 6, 1995, Sp.

George Ballis, Santa Cruz, March 3, 2000.

Berta Batres, Salinas, September 17, 1994, October 3, 1994, November 28, 2006, March 24, 2007, Sp.

Mario Bustamante, El Centro, March 14, 1995, April 30, 2005, September 2, 2005, May 29, 2006, Sp.

Salvador (Chava) Bustamante, San Jose, November, 15, 1996, May 3, 2006, May 18, 2006.

Pablo Camacho, Watsonville, January 20, 1995, Sp.

Epifanio Camacho, McFarland, June 1, 1995, Sp.

Lenin Chavarría, Watsonville, October 19, 2007.

Jerry Cohen, Carmel Valley, June 5, 1995, April 25, 2005.

Sam Cohen, Santa Cruz, August 1, 2005.

Ann Veronica Coyle, Watsonville, April 12 1995.

Tom Dalzell, Berkeley, November 3, 2005, September 6, 2006.

R.G. Davis, Watsonville, January 17, 2001.

Mike Dobler, Moss Landing, January 31, 1995, March 20, 1997, December 20, 2005, December 4, 2006.

Susan Drake, Santa Cruz, November 23, 2002.

Pablo Espinoza, Woodville, February 6, 2004.

David Fishlow, Santa Cruz, February 2003.

Juan Flores, Mexicali, B.C., Mexico, November 3, 2007. Sp.

Marshall Ganz, Cambridge, Massachusetts, April 12, 13, 1996; New Haven, Connecticut, June 15, 1999.

Cleofas Guzman, Los Angeles, January 24, 2009, Sp.

Fred Hirsch, Santa Cruz, October 3, 1997.

Fred and Virginia Hirsch, Santa Cruz, February 19, 2001.

Virginia Hirsch, Santa Cruz, October 6, 1997.

Liza Hirsch Medina, Los Angeles, March 4, 2002; September 22, 2004.

Nick Jones, Oakland, March 21, 2002.

Gretchen Lau, El Centro, April 30, 2005.

Jack Lloyd, Oxnard, December 4, 1996.

Sabino Lopez, Salinas, May 28, 1993.

Ben Maddock, Stockton, May 1, 2005.

Luis Magaña, Stockton, February 5, 2008, Sp.

Pete Maturino, Salinas, July 15, 2005.

Eliseo Medina, Los Angeles, May 20, 2005.

Raul Medina (Maniz), Watsonville, February 1, 1995.

Richard Mines, Watsonville, February 28, 2008.

Hermilo Mojica, Fresno, October 3, 1994, October 24, 1994, November 25, 2002, Sp.

Hermilo Mojica, Aristeo Zambrano, and Mario Bustamante, El Centro, September 2, 2005, Sp.

Bill Monning, Moss Landing, November 4, 2005.

Tirso Moreno, Washington, D.C., June 30, 2001, Sp.

Gilbert Padilla, Fresno, August 14, 2001, November 18, 2002, December 5, 2005; Watsonville, February 23, 2003; Salinas, April 10, 2005.

Gilbert Padilla, Esther Padilla, Hermilo Mojica, Fresno, December 20, 1997.

Chayo Pelayo, El Centro, April 30, 2005, Sp.

Bob Pepper, Las Lomas, May 13, 1996.

Rigoberto Perez, Salinas, July 27, 2001. Sp.

Bill Ramsey, Salinas, September 17, 2006.

Jose Renteria, Salinas, May 30, 1995.

John Soria, Oxnard, January 25, 1996.

Don Watson, Oakland, September 11, 1996, February 2, 2000.

Aristeo Zambrano, Oakland, June, 1993, August 23, 1994, July 11, 2005, September 7, 2006, Sp.

Additional Interviews

Doug Adair, interviewed by Greg Truex, Northridge, March 10, 1995, UFWOHP

Jerry Breshears, interviewed by Don Watson, Salinas, January 8, 1980, Don Watson Collection

Salvador (Chava) Bustamante, interviewed by Don Watson, Berkeley, July 14, 1983, Don Watson Collection

David Burciaga, interviewed by Jorge Garcia and Kent Kirkton, Northridge, n.d., UFWOHP

Bill Chandler, interviewed by Robert G. Marshall, Northridge, March 11, 1995, UFWOHP

LeRoy Chatfield, interviewed by Don Watson, Sacramento, June 29, 1981, Don Watson Collection

LeRoy Chatfield, interviewed by Marshall Ganz, Sacramento, August 27, 1996, Sacramento, in author's collection.

Richard Chavez, interviewed by Jacques Levy, La Paz, June 14, 1994, Levy/Yale

Richard Chavez, interviewed with other members of Chavez family by Jacques Levy, La Paz, November 27-28, Levy/Yale

Jerry Cohen, interviewed by Jacques Levy, September 20, 1993, Levy/Yale

Jesse López de la Cruz, interviewed by Jorge Garcia, Kent Kirkton, Claudia
  Cuevas, September 27, 1996, UFWOHP

Jose Dzib, interviewed by Don Watson, Salinas, October 30, 1981, Don Watson
  Collection

Pablo Espinoza, interviewed by Jorge Garcia, Visalia, April 21, 1995, UFWOHP

Marshall Ganz, interviewed by Jacques Levy, Cambridge, April 8, 1994, Levy/Yale

Robert Garcia, interviewed by Don Watson, Salinas, March 25, 1980, Don Watson
  Collection

Chris Hartmire, interviewed by Jacques Levy, March 17, 1994, Levy/Yale

Julio Hernandez, interviewed by Jorge Garcia, Northridge, March 9, 1995,
  Northridge, UFWOHP

Helen Hernandez Serda, interviewed by Claudia Cuevas, September 17, 1995,
  UFWOHP

Monsignor George Higgins, interviewed by Don Watson, Washington D.C.,
  September, 1979, Don Watson Collection

Juan Huerta, interviewed by Don Watson, Salinas, October 30, 1979, Don Watson
  Collection

Nick Jones, interviewed by Jorge Garcia, San Francisco, July 26, 1995, UFWOHP

Bill Kircher, interviewed by Don Watson, Cincinatti, Ohio, May 20, 1980, Don
  Watson Collection

Herman (Blackie) Levitt, interviewed by Marshall Ganz, August 8, 1996, Los
  Angeles, in author's collection

David Martinez, interviewed by Davy Figaro, March 3, 1994, Levy/Yale

Eliseo Medina, interviewed by Marshall Ganz, Los Angeles, August 14, 1998, in
  author's collection

Hermilo Mojica, interviewed by Don Watson, August 10, 1983, Gilroy, Don
  Watson Collection

Gilbert Padilla, interviewed by Doug Adair, Fresno, August 22, 1995, UFWOHP

Fred Ross Sr., interviewed by Margo McBane, Los Angeles, June 26, 1974, Los
  Angeles, in author's collection

Fred Ross Sr., interviewed by Don Watson, October 13, 1983, Don Watson
  Collection

Luis Valdez, interviewed by Jorge Garcia and Kent Kirkton, Monterey, June 5,
  2001, UFWOHP

Ricardo Villapando, interviwed by Don Watson, Salinas, October 27, 1983, Don
  Watson Collection

Books, Theses, Manuscripts Cited

Oscar Acosta , *The Revolt of the Cockroach People* (San Francisco: Straight Arrow
  Press, 1973)

Aristotle, *Politics*, (New York: Cosimo Books, 2008)

Arroyo, Antonio M. Stevens, editor, *Prophets Denied Honor: An Anthology on the
  Hispanic Church in the United States* (Maryknoll, NY: Orbis Books, 1980)

Taylor Branch, *Pillar of Fire: America in the King Years, 1963-1965* (New York: Simon and Schuster, 1988)

Eric Brazil, *The Salad Bowl Strike*, unpublished manuscript, 1971

Jerald B. Brown, "The United Farm Workers Grape Strike and Boycott, 1965-1970," Ph.D. thesis, Cornell University, Latin American Studies Program, 1972

Yolanda Broyles-Gonzáles, *El Teatro Campesino: Theater in the Chicano Movement* (Austin: University of Texas Press, 1994)

Manuel Buaken, *I Have Lived with the American People* (Caldwell, Idaho: Claxton Printers, 1948)

Paul Buhle, *Taking Care of Business* (New York: Monthly Review Press, 1999)

Clayborne Carson, *In Struggle: SNCC and the Black Awakening in the 1960s* (Cambridge: Harvard University Press, 1995)

Catholic University of America, *New Catholic Encyclopedia* (New York: McGraw-Hill, 1967)

Porter Chaffee, "A history of the Cannery and Agricultural Workers Industrial Union," Federal Writers Project, Oakland, California; manuscript at Bancroft Library, University of California, Berkeley.

Ralph Chaplin, *Wobbly* (Chicago: University of Chicago Press, 1948)

Cletus Daniel, *Bitter Harvest: A History of California Farm Workers, 1870-1941* (Berkeley: University of California Press, 1981)

Jay P. Dolan. and Allan Figueroa Deck, editors, *Hispanic Catholic Culture in the U.S.* (Notre Dame : University of Notre Dame Press, 1997)

John Gregory Dunne, *Delano* (New York: Farrar, Straus & Giroux, 1967)

Alan Duke, *When the Colorado Quit the Ocean* (Arizona: Southwest Publishers, 1974)

Bill Esher, Bill, *Campesino*, unpublished manuscript, 1994

Susan Ferris and Ricardo Sandoval, *The Fight in the Fields: Cesar Chavez and the Farm Worker Movement* (New York: Harcourt Brace & Company, 1997)

David Finks, *The Radical Vision of Saul Alinsky* (New York: Paulist Press, 1984)

Anne B. Fisher, *The Upside Down River* (New York: Farrar and Rinehart, Inc., 1945)

Carl Fleischhauer, and Beverly Bannan, editors, *Documenting America, 1935-1943* Berkeley: University of California Press, 1981)

James Foreman, *The Making of Black Revolutionaries* (Seattle: University of Washington Press, 1997)

Bill Friedland, *Trampling Out Advantage: The Political Economy of California Wine and Grapes*, forthcoming.

Samuel Friedman, *Teamster Rank and File: Power, Bureacracy, and Rebellion at Work and in the Union* (New York: Columbia University Press, 1981)

Ernesto Galarza, *Farm Workers and Agribusiness in California, 1947-1960* (Notre Dame: University of Notre Dame, 1977)

Ernesto Galarza, *Spiders in the House and Workers in the Field* (London: University of Notre Dame Press, 1970)

Ernesto Galarza, *Merchants of Labor* (Santa Barbara: McNally and Loftin, 1964)

Walter Galenson, *The CIO Challenge to the AFL* (Cambridge: Harvard University Press, 1960)

Marshall Ganz, "Five Smooth Stones: Strategic Capacity in the Unionization of California Agriculture," Ph.D. thesis, Harvard University, 2000

Marshall Ganz, *Why David Sometimes Wins* (New York: Oxford University Press, 2009)

Mario T. Garcia, *Memories of Chicano History: The Life and Narrative of Bert Corona* (Berkeley: University of California Press, 1995)

Dan Georgakas, and Marvin Sarkin, *Detroit, I Do Mind Dying* (Boston: South End Press, 1998)

Juan Gomez Quiñones, *Chicano Politics: Reality and Promise, 1940-1990* (Albuquerque: University of New Mexico Press, 1990)

Leo Grebler, Joan W. Moore, and Ralph C. Guzman, *The Mexican-American People* (New York: The Free Press, 1970)

Camille Guerin-Gonzales, *Mexican Workers and American Dreams: Immigration, Repatriation, and California Farm Labor, 1900-1939* (New Brunswick: N.J. Rutgers University Press, 1994)

Eric O. Hansen, *The Catholic Church in World Politics* (Princeton, N.J: Princeton University Press, 1987)

Bennett Harrison and Barry Bluestone, *The Great American U-Turn: Corporate Restructuring and the Polarizing of America* (New York: Basic Books, 1990)

Pat Hoffman, *Ministry of the Dispossessed* (Los Angeles: Wallace Press, 1987)

Sanford D, Horwitt, *Let Them Call Me Rebel: Saul Alinsky, His Life and Legacy* (New York: Alfred A. Knopf, Inc., 1989)

Stuart Jamieson, *Labor Unionism in American Agriculture*, Washington, D.C: (United States Department of Labor, 1945)

J. Craig Jenkins, *The Politics of Insurgency: The Farm Worker Movement in the 1960s* (New York: Columbia University Press, 1985)

Steven Johnson, Gerald Haslam and Dawson, Robert, *The Great Central Valley: California's Heartland* (Berkeley: University of California Press in Association with the California Academy of Sciences, 1992)

George C. Kiser and Martha Woody Kiser, *Mexican Workers in the United States* (Albuquerque: University of New Mexico, 1979)

Sam Kushner, *The Long Road to Delano* (New York: International Publishers, 1975)

Jacques Levy, *Cesar Chavez: Autobiography of La Causa* (New York: W.W. Norton Company, 1975)

John Lewis, and Michael D'Orso, *Walking With the Wind* (New York: Houghton Mifflin Harcourt, 1999)

Nelson Lichtenstein, *Labor's War at Home: The CIO and World War II* (Philadelphia: Temple University Press, 2003)

Nelson Lichtenstein, *Walter Reuther: The Most Dangerous Man in Detroit* (New York: Basic Books, 1995)

Joan London and Henry Anderson, *So Shall Ye Reap* (New York: Thomas Y. Corowell Company, 1970)

Sandy Lydon, *The Chinese in the Monterey Bay Region* (Capitola, California: Capitola, Book Company, 1985)

Colin M. MacLachlan, *Anarchism and the Mexican Revolution, The Political Trials of Ricardo Flores Magón in the United State* (Berkeley: Universtity of California Press, 1991)

Linda C. Majka, and Theo J. Majka, *Farm Workers, Agribusiness, and the State* (Philadelphia: Temple University Press, 1982)

Marcoux, Marcene, *Cursillo: Anatomy of a Movement* (New York: Lambeth Press, 1982)

Phillip L. Martin, *Promise Unfulfilled* (Ithica: Cornell University Press, 2003)

Karl Marx, *Capital* (New York: Appleton & Co., 1889)

Peter Matthiessen, *Sal Si Puedes: Cesar Chavez and the New American Revolution* (New York: Dell Paperback, 1971)

Thomas McCann and Henry Scammell, *An American Company: The Tragedy of United Fruit* (New York: Crown Publishers, Inc., 1976)

Carey McWilliams, *Factories in the Fields: The Story of Migratory Farm Labor in California* (Berkeley: University of California Press, 1939)

Dick Meister, and Anne Loftis, *A Long Time Coming* (New York: Macmillan Publishing, 1977)

Martha Menchaca, *The Mexican Outsiders* (Austin: University of Texas Press, 1995)

James Mills, *A Disorderly House: The Brown-Unruh Years in Sacramento* (Berkeley: Heyday Books, 1987)

David Mitchell, Cathy Mitchell, and Richard Ofshe, *The Light on Synanon* (New York: Seaview Books, 1980)

Kim Moody, *An Injury to All* (London/New York: Verso, 1988)

Eugene Nelson, *Huelga* (Delano, California, Farm Worker Press, 1969)

Bruce Neuburger, *A Decade At Hard Labor: An Activist in the Lettuce Fields of the 1970s*, unpublished manuscript, 2010)

Robert Pack, *Jerry Brown, The Philospher-Prince* (New York: Stein and Day, 1978)

Juan-Vincente Palerm, *Farm Labor Needs and Farm Workers in California, 1970-1989* (Sacramento: California Employment Development Department, Sacramento, California, 1991)

Miriam Pawel, *The Union of Their Dreams* (New York: Bloomsbury Press, 2009)

William Preston, *Vanishing Landscapes: Land and Life in the Tulare Lake Basin* (Berkeley: University of California Press, 1981)

James Rawls, and Walter Bean, *California: An Interpretive History* (New York: McGraw Hill Companies, 1997)

Marc Reisner, *Cadillac Desert* (New York: Penguin Books, 1986)

Margaret Eleanor Rose, *Women in the United Farm Workers: A Study of Chicana and Mexican Paricipation in a Labor Union* (Los Angeles: University of California, 1988)

Fred Ross, *Conquering Goliath* (Keene, California: El Taller Grafico Press, 1989)

Alan Rudy, "Envioronmental Conditions, Negotiations, and Crises: The Political Economy of Agriculture in the Imperial Valley of California, 1850-1993," PhD thesis, University of California at Santa Cruz, June, 1995

Salvatore Salerno, *Red November, Black November: Culture and Community in the Industrial Workers of the World* (New York: State University of New York Press, 1989)

Julian Samora, *Los Mojados* (Notre Dame: University of Notre Dame Press, 1971)

George Sanchez, *Becoming Mexican-American: Ethnicity, Culture and Identity in Chicano Los Angeles, 1900-1945* (New York: Oxford University Press, 1993)

Moises Sandoval, *On the Move: The Hispanic Church in the United States* (Maryknoll, NY: Orbis Books, 1990)

Craig Scharlin, and Lilia V. Villanueva, *Phillip Vera Cruz: A Personal History of Filipino Immigrants and the Farm workers Movement* (Los Angeles: UCLA Labor Center, Institute of Industrial Relations & UCLA Asian American Studies Center, 1992)

Arthur Schlesinger, Jr., *Robert Kennedy and His Times* (New York: Houghton Mifflin, 1978)

Douglas Seaton, *Catholics and Radicals: The Association of Catholic Trade Unionists and the American Labor Movement from Depression to Cold War* (Lewisburg: Bucknell University Press, 1981)

Stephen Sosnick, *Hired Hands: Seasonal Farm Workers in the U.S* (Santa Barbara: McNally and Loftin, 1978)

Mildred de Stanley, *The Salton Sea, Yesterday and Today*, (Los Angeles: Triumph Press, 1966)

Ronald B. Taylor, *Chavez and the Farm Workers* (Boston: Beacon Press, 1975)

Evan Thomas, *Robert Kennedy: His Life* (New York: Simon and Schuster, 2002)

Mark Thompson, "The Agricultural Workers Organizing Committee, 1959-62," Masters thesis, Cornell University, 1963

Carl Tjerandsen, *Education for Citizenship: A Foundation's Experience* (Santa Cruz, California: Emil Schwarzhaupt Foundation, 1980)

Charles J. Tull, *Father Coughlin and the New Deal* (Syracuse, New York: Syracuse University Press, 1965)

Luis Valdez, and Stan Steiner, editors, *Aztlan, An Anthology of Mexican American Literature* (New York: Vintage Books, 1972)

Devra Weber, *Dark Sweat, White Gold: California Farm Workers, Cotton, and the New Deal* (Berkeley: University of California Press, 1996)

Hyman Weintraub, "The IWW in California: 1905-1931," Masters thesis, University of California, Los Angeles, 1947

Miriam Wells, *Strawberry Fields: politics, class and work in California Agriculture* (Ithaca: Cornell University Press, 1996)

Donald Worster, *Rivers of Empire: Water, Aridity, and the Growth of the American West* (New York: Pantheon Books, 1985)

Index

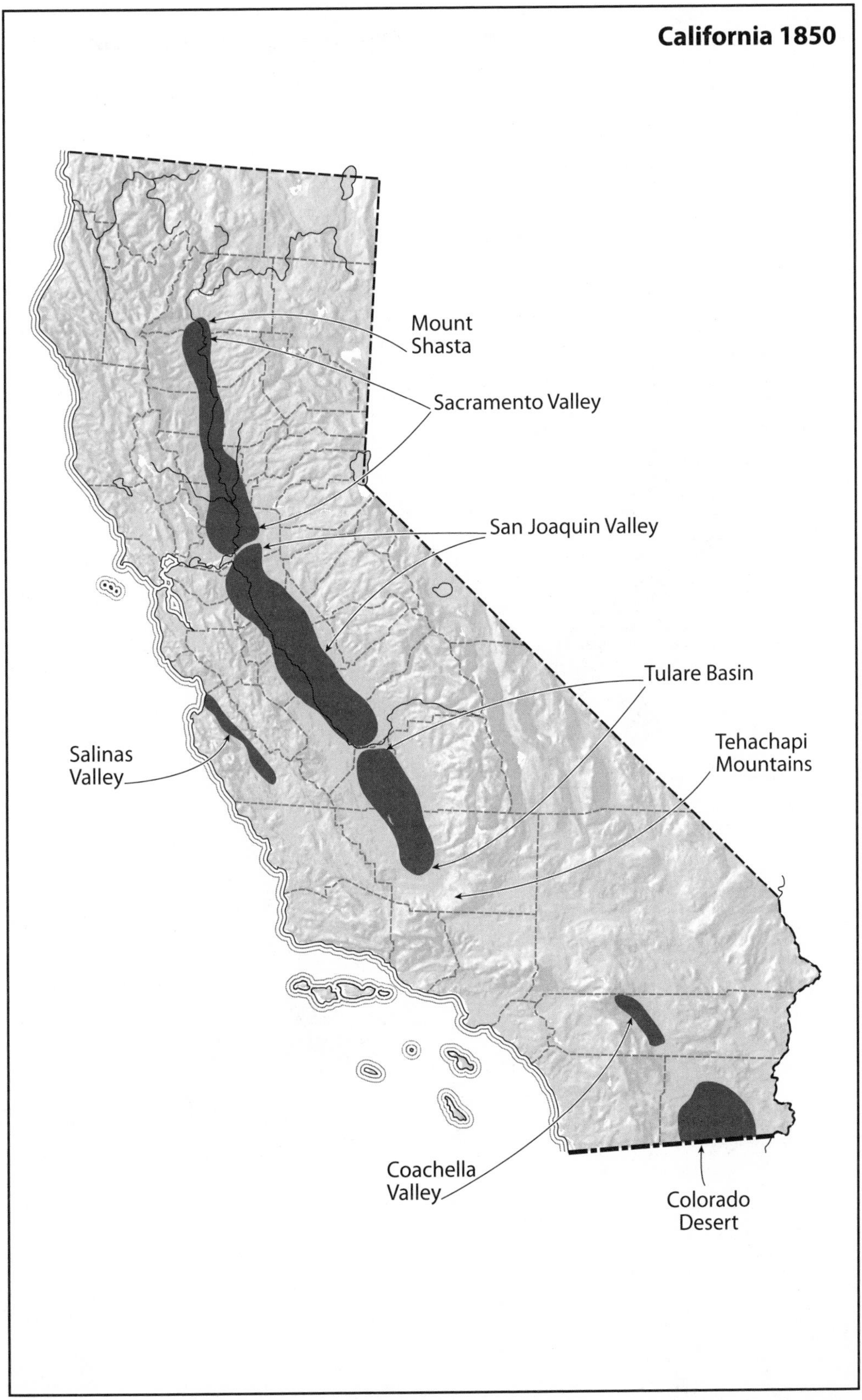

California 1850

Mount Shasta

Sacramento Valley

San Joaquin Valley

Tulare Basin

Tehachapi Mountains

Salinas Valley

Coachella Valley

Colorado Desert

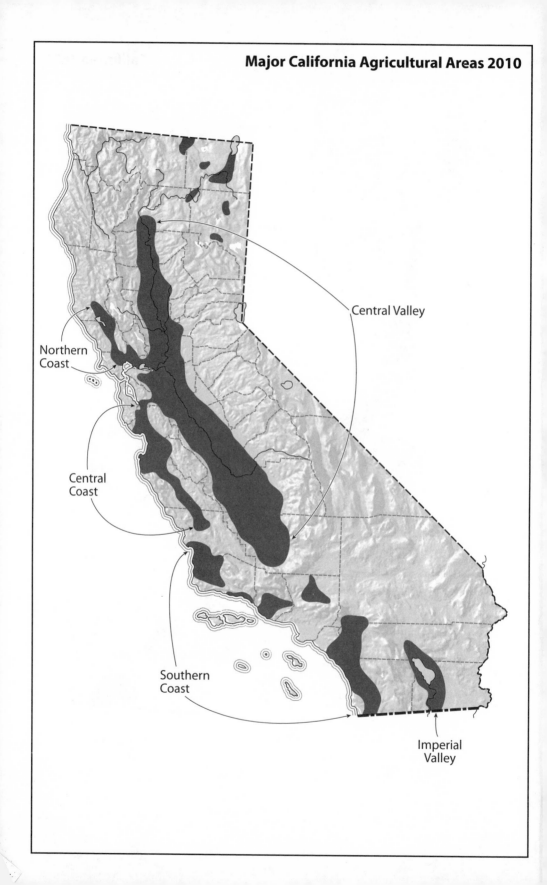

Major California Agricultural Areas 2010

Central Valley

Northern
Coast

Central
Coast

Southern
Coast

Imperial
Valley

Lettuce, Grape and Lemon Growing Areas 1975

Lemons
Lettuce
Grapes

Driving Times Between Major Cities and Towns in UFW History

Sacramento

San Francisco

1hr 15mins

3hrs

2hrs

Salinas

2hrs 15mins

Fresno

2hrs

5hrs

30mins

Bakersfield

La Paz

Mojave

30mins

3hr 30mins

1hr 45mins

Oxnard

Los Angeles

1hr

2hrs

Coachella

1hr 45mins

San Diego

El Centro

1hr

Yuma

1hr 45mins

30mins

Mexicali

San Luis

1hr